Less managing. More teaching. Greater learning.

 ## INSTRUCTORS...

Would you like your **students** to show up for class **more prepared**?
(Let's face it, class is much more fun if everyone is engaged and prepared...)

Want an **easy way to assign** homework online and track student **progress**?
(Less time grading means more time teaching...)

Want an **instant view** of student or class performance relative to learning objectives? *(No more wondering if students understand...)*

Need to **collect data and generate reports** required for administration or accreditation? *(Say goodbye to manually tracking student learning outcomes...)*

Want to **record and post your lectures** for students to view online?

 ## With **McGraw-Hill's *Connect™* Plus Accounting,**

INSTRUCTORS GET:

- Simple **assignment management**, allowing you to spend more time teaching.

- **Auto-graded** assignments, quizzes, and tests.

- **Detailed Visual Reporting** where student and section results can be viewed and analyzed.

- Sophisticated **online testing** capability.

- A **filtering and reporting** function that allows you to easily assign and report on materials that are correlated to accreditation standards, learning outcomes, and Bloom's taxonomy.

- An easy-to-use **lecture capture** tool.

- The option to **upload course documents** for student access.

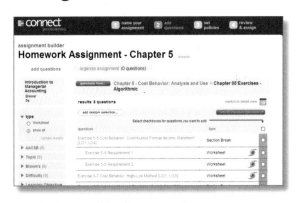

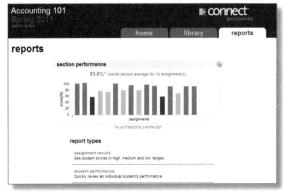

Want an online, **searchable version** of your textbook?

Wish your textbook could be **available online** while you're doing your assignments?

 ## Connect™ Plus Accounting eBook

If you choose to use *Connect™ Plus Accounting*, you have an affordable and searchable online version of your book integrated with your other online tools.

Connect™ Plus Accounting eBook offers features like:

- Topic search
- Direct links from assignments
- Adjustable text size
- Jump to page number
- Print by section

 Want to get more **value** from your textbook purchase?

Think learning accounting should be a bit more **interesting**?

 ## Check out the STUDENT RESOURCES section under the *Connect™* Library tab.

Here you'll find a wealth of resources designed to help you achieve your goals in the course. You'll find things like **quizzes, PowerPoints, and Internet activities** to help you study. Every student has different needs, so explore the STUDENT RESOURCES to find the materials best suited to you.

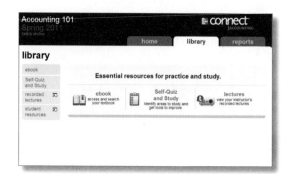

Financial Accounting

FINANCIAL ACCOUNTING

Published by McGraw-Hill/Irwin, a business unit of The McGraw-Hill Companies, Inc., 1221 Avenue of the Americas, New York, NY, 10020. Copyright © 2011, 2009 by The McGraw-Hill Companies, Inc. All rights reserved. No part of this publication may be reproduced or distributed in any form or by any means, or stored in a database or retrieval system, without the prior written consent of The McGraw-Hill Companies, Inc., including, but not limited to, in any network or other electronic storage or transmission, or broadcast for distance learning.

Some ancillaries, including electronic and print components, may not be available to customers outside the United States.

This book is printed on acid-free paper.

1 2 3 4 5 6 7 8 9 0 WDQ/WDQ 1 0 9 8 7 6 5 4 3 2 1 0

ISBN-13: 978-0-07-811082-5
ISBN-10: 0-07-811082-3

Vice president and editor-in-chief: *Brent Gordon*
Editorial director: *Stewart Mattson*
Publisher: *Tim Vertovec*
Senior sponsoring editor: *Dana L. Woo*
Director of development: *Ann Torbert*
Senior development editor: *Daryl Horrocks*
Vice president and director of marketing: *Robin J. Zwettler*
Senior marketing manager: *Kathleen Klehr*
Vice president of editing, design, and production: *Sesha Bolisetty*
Lead project manager: *Pat Frederickson*
Buyer II: *Debra R. Sylvester*
Cover and interior designer: *Laurie Entringer*
Senior photo research coordinator: *Jeremy Cheshareck*
Photo researcher: *Ira C. Roberts*
Lead media project manager: *Kerry Bowler and Ron Nelms*
Cover design: tbd
Interior design: tbd
Typeface: *10/12.5 New Aster Lt Std*
Compositor: *Laserwords Private Limited*
Printer: *Worldcolor*

Library of Congress Cataloging-in-Publication Data

Spiceland, J. David, 1949–
    Financial accounting/J. David Spiceland, Wayne Thomas, Don Herrmann.—2nd ed.
      p. cm.
    Includes index.
    ISBN-13: 978-0-07-811082-5 (alk. paper)
    ISBN-10: 0-07-811082-3 (alk. paper)
    1. Accounting. I. Thomas, Wayne, 1969– II. Herrmann, Don. III. Title.
HF5636.S77 2011
657—dc22
                                                        2010030759

Financial Accounting

SECOND EDITION

J. DAVID SPICELAND
University of Memphis

WAYNE THOMAS
University of Oklahoma

DON HERRMANN
Oklahoma State University

Dedicated to:

David's wife Charlene, daughters Denise and Jessica, and three sons Michael David, Michael, and David

Wayne's wife Julee, daughter Olivia, and three sons Jake, Eli, and Luke

Don's wife Mary, daughter Rachel, and three sons David, Nathan, and Micah

Key to *Financial Accounting's* remarkable first edition success are the five core precepts around which the textbook is built

1 **Conversational Writing Style** The authors took special care to write a textbook that fosters a friendly dialogue between the text and each individual student. The tone of the presentation is intentionally conversational—creating the impression of *speaking with* the student, as opposed to *teaching to* the student.

> The authors **successfully employ humor and a conversational writing style** in developing scenarios, examples and explanations which remain in the reader's mind and make these oftentimes complicated subjects understandable.—Dennis L. Kovach, *Community College of Allegheny County*

> It offers a very readable presentation, with easy to follow pedagogy. The writing is clear and crisp—**it is not boring.**—Al Hartgraves, *Emory University*

2 **Innovative Pedagogy** Reviewers enthusiastically embraced the innovative pedagogy used throughout the book, including **Common Mistake** boxes that help students avoid common pitfalls of beginning students and **Flip Side** problems and scenarios that show students the two sides of various accounting transactions.

3 **Real-World Focus** Students learn best when they see how concepts are applied in the real world. For that reason, real-world examples from companies, such as **Dell** and **Apple**, are used extensively and routinely to enhance the presentation. The real-world focus adds realism to discussions and serves as the foundation for exercises, problems, and cases.

> **This text has a logical layout and incorporates tools** to keep the student's attention. It makes the student think about the impact on the financials based upon the different principles and estimates selected.
> —Victor Stanton, *University of California–Berkeley*

4 **Decision Maker's Perspective** Each chapter includes one or more distinctive **Decision Maker's Perspective** sections, which offer insights into how the information discussed in the chapters affects decisions made by investors, creditors, managers, and others. Each chapter also contains **Decision Points** highlighting specific decisions in the chapter that can be made using financial accounting information.

5 **A Strong Supplements Package** The **authors write all of the major supplements** for *Financial Accounting*, including the Testbank, Solutions Manual, and the Instructor's Manual. With **iPod** material, narrated PowerPoints, online quizzing, Excel templates, and QuickBooks templates integrated into the end-of-chapter material, Spiceland's *Financial Accounting* provides the cutting-edge technology demanded by today's accounting instructors and students.

A LOGICAL ORGANIZATION

The **sequence of topics is inspired,** and I wonder why it hasn't been done before.—Laurel Bond Mitchell, *University of Redlands*

1 Accounting Information and Decision Making

Spiceland's Chapter 1 has **beautifully set the stage for the finest presentation of financial accounting pedagogy I have read to date** in a textbook format.—Sherry Gordon, *Palomar College*

2 The Accounting Information System

I like the overall layout of the chapter. Specifically, I like how the authors first cover how a transaction affects the accounting equation, and then cover the details of journal entries.——Martha Lou Fowler, *Missouri Western State University*

3 The Financial Reporting Process

STH goes **beyond the "textbook" mode** and discusses/ presents in pictures, diagrams, etc., and I think it makes the whole adjusting process much easier to understand.—Peter Theuri, *Northern Kentucky University*

4 Cash and Internal Controls

The authors provide an excellent chapter on Receivables and Sales. They provide a **comprehensive discussion, along with effective illustrations.** I prefer the STH sequence of topics.—Al Nagy, *John Carroll University*

5 Receivables and Sales

The inventory chapter in Spiceland is the **best I've ever seen!**—James Aitken, *Central Michigan University*

6 Inventory and Cost of Goods Sold

Good, comprehensive but readable walk through the many types of property transactions. Chapter 7 does an **especially good job in talking about intangible assets.**—Laura Ilcisin, *University of Nebraska–Omaha*

7 Long-Term Assets

The Spiceland chapter is excellent; it provides **comprehensive, yet easy to understand** discussions, and effective development of concepts and coverage of the topics related to current liabilities.—Marianne James, *California State University– Los Angeles*

8 Current Liabilities

THAT MAKES LEARNING MORE EFFICIENT

> Overall, the chapter **covers a complex topic in a clear way** and in the right amount of detail.—Frank Hodge, *University of Washington*

> **I REALLY** enjoyed this chapter. Spiceland has presented this chapter in a very interesting manner. I like the simplicity of the presentation. I especially like the "Decision Maker's Perspectives" throughout the chapter. Not only is this chapter well-written, it is interesting!—Steve Teeter, *Utah Valley State College*

> STH does a **great job of summarizing and illustrating** the steps in preparing both the indirect and direct methods. In addition, STH is more current than other texts in its references to IFRS.—Nancy Lynch, *West Virginia University*

> Wow! I was really impressed with this chapter! The conservative and aggressive accounting example was **really a great way to teach** students about quality of earnings. The rest of the chapter was also put together very well. Great ratio illustration with Under Armour and Nike, two companies that students are interested in.—Christa Morgan, *Georgia Perimeter College*

> The text contains **realistic examples, excellent explanations, and illustrated example problems** within the text. The EOC material is also well done. It is **definitely worth looking at for adoption.**—Kreag Danvers, *Clarion University of Pennsylvania*

> I generally like to cover selected topics in this area, so **I would definitely use [this appendix].** I think this would be very beneficial.—Stephen Benner, *Eastern Illinois University*

We received an incredible amount of feedback from over 330 reviews and focus group participants. The following list of changes and improvements is a testament to the many hours that reviewers spent analyzing our first edition, helping us to make *Financial Accounting* the **best book of its kind.** We made the following changes throughout the second edition:

- Added a concise chart of accounts in Chapter 2 and on the inside back cover of the book, and revised the account titles used in text and homework materials to match.
- Changed two different in-chapter reviews ("Stop and Go" and "Quick Quizzes") to "Let's Review" exercises. Added notation about related suggested homework next to the Let's Review exercises.
- Added marginal accounting-equation analyses wherever we do not show the mini-financial statement displays. Thus, students will have one or the other to accompany journal entries in the text of the chapter. The marginal accounting-equation analyses clearly demonstrate the equality of the accounting equation, as well as the effects of transactions on stockholders' equity accounts.
- Created a separate analysis section at the end of each chapter, beginning in Chapter 4 and continuing through Chapter 11. Each analysis section includes a comparison of financial information for two well-known publicly traded companies. Chapter 12 provides a comprehensive financial analysis of Under Armour and Nike based on the ratios developed throughout the book.
- Updated amounts for real-company data used in each chapter.
- Included an Earnings Management Case in Chapters 5 through 12.

CHAPTER 1

- In Chapter 1's simple financial statements, omitted depreciation expense—included amounts as "Other expenses," for simplicity's sake. Also, showed single-column income statement in this chapter. (Chapter 3 expands to multicolumn format.)
- In the statement of cash flows section, added sentences to explain the

idea of cash inflows and outflows shown in the SCF, use of parentheses to indicate outflows, and ad hoc definition of *net cash flows*.
- Revised and expanded the ethics discussion in the chapter. (Added new ethics subhead.)
- In appendix, replaced the qualitative characteristics framework (Illus. 1–17) with a revised version, and revised the text discussion to reflect the new framework.
- Revised end-of-chapter (EOC) materials that called for prepayments (e.g., prepaid rent, insurance) and accumulated depreciation.

CHAPTER 2

- Improved the learning experience by having the three Let's Review exercises involve the same transactions in an incremental way.
- Changed the format for transactions analyses to show the related account title *next to* (rather than *below*) the transaction amount.
- Separated discussions of transactions (6) and (7), with a separate drawing for each, so that the chapter discusses separately, and more clearly, the effects of services provided for cash and on account (accounts receivable).
- Added a preliminary chart of accounts for the accounts used in the chapter for Eagle Golf Academy.
- In the summary illustration showing the posting of external transactions to the general ledger accounts: (1) added an A = L + SE heading and lined up the relevant T-accounts below each component of the equation; (2) added transaction numbers to each entry in the T-accounts; (3) added "Bal." to each T-account.

CHAPTER 3

- Added a new Career Corner about the employment value of those who combine strong IT skills with accounting knowledge.
- In the summary Illus. 3–9, which shows the posting of adjusting entries to the general ledger accounts: (1) added an A = L + SE heading and lined up the relevant T-accounts below each component of the equation; (2) added transaction numbers to each entry in the T-accounts; (3) added "Bal." to each T-account.

- In the summary Illus. 3–17, which shows the posting of closing entries to the general ledger accounts: (1) added an A = L + SE heading and lined up the relevant T-accounts below each component of the equation; (2) added transaction numbers to each entry in the T-accounts; (3) added "Bal." to each T-account.

CHAPTER 4

- Expanded early discussion of fraud and the need for internal controls, including data from ACFE.
- Added new discussion of Section 404 of SOX.
- Replaced components of internal control illustration with new pyramid showing five components of internal control.
- Added discussion of preventive and detective internal controls.
- Revised (and shortened) the "Components of Internal Control" discussion (p. 170) and related movie theatre example.
- In "Cash and Cash Equivalents" section, added text and a journal entry for cash sale.
- Added new discussion of use of debit cards (in a section separate from discussion of use of credit cards) as a form of cash controls.
- Revised discussion of petty cash to separately account for the expenditures from the fund and the replenishment of the fund.
- Beginning in Chapter 4, added marginal accounting-equation analyses next to journal entries wherever mini-financial statements do not appear.

CHAPTER 5

- Added new "Net Revenues" heading and brief discussion, including *net revenues* as a key term.
- Expanded discussion of allowance method, to provide fuller conceptual foundation for why companies use it and its effects on the financial statements.
- Revised Illus. 5–5 covering the percentage-of-receivables method (the balance sheet approach) to focus on the balance sheet.
- Added text example to show transaction for services provided in exchange for a note receivable.

CHAPTER 6

- Heavily revised Part B, "Recording Inventory Transactions," to focus only on the perpetual system. (In the body of the chapter, entries for periodic no longer appear side-by-side with those for perpetual.) Entries for perpetual now show the effects on the components of the balance sheet and income statement.
- In the section on recording inventory transactions for perpetual, joined discussions of inventory purchases and inventory sales.
- Added new section about simple adjustment from FIFO to LIFO to reflect inventory accounting used in actual practice.
- Revised discussion of freight-out to reflect actual practice that these shipping charges are included by some companies in cost of goods sold. Provided a real-world example from Amazon.com.
- In Part B, moved purchase discounts to precede purchase returns.
- Expanded coverage of multiple-step income statement and added *multiple-step income statement* as a key term.
- Added new Appendix A, "Recording Inventory Transactions Using a Periodic Inventory System." In the new appendix, journal entries for periodic and perpetual appear side-by-side, as they did in the body of the chapter in 1e.

CHAPTER 7

- Added new section on *basket purchases,* including illustration showing allocation of cost in a basket purchase.
- Added a new Common Mistake warning related to the calculation of depreciation.
- Added a new Career Corner about the importance of accounting for those interested in law as a career.
- Added general "word formulas" for depreciation methods before showing the formula used for a specific example.
- Added an Ethical Dilemma box relating to depreciation.
- In the appendix, per reviewers' suggestions, moved the illustration about the relationship among future cash flows, fair value, and book value *before* the illustration that shows the two-step impairment process.

CHAPTER 8

- Added discussion of deferred taxes under "Other Current Liabilities."
- Expanded discussion of unearned revenues with gift cards.
- Changed "Loss Contingencies and Analysis" heading to two headings: "Contingencies" and "Liquidity Analysis."
- Revised discussion of contingencies, including contingent liabilities, warranty liabilities, and contingent gains.
- Added new IFRS box on treatment of contingent liabilities.
- Added working capital as a liquidity measure.
- Expanded the discussion of liquidity analysis.

CHAPTER 9

- Added illustrations to show how to determine bond prices using Excel.
- Added IFRS box on discount or premium as part of the carrying value of bonds payable (net method).
- Added new illustration showing convergence of bond carrying value for discount and premium as a bond approaches maturity.
- Changed discussion of "Long-Term Notes Payable" to "Installment Notes."
- Increased the coverage of leases.
- Moved appendix on bond investments to a separate end-of-book Appendix D.
- Added EOC exercises involving *annual* interest payments.

CHAPTER 10

- Added discussion of issuance of shares of stock in exchange for non-cash goods or services.
- Added example of payment of cumulative preferred stock, with dividends in arrears.
- Changed treatment of accounting for dividends by using separate accounts for cash dividends and stock dividends. This change will make the presentation of cash dividends in Chapters 2 and 10 consistent.
- Shortened the discussion on stock dividends and stock splits.
- Expanded general discussion of EPS, including a numeric example.
- For the measures in the "Equity Analysis" section, added more discussion of what the measures mean and how to use them to interpret company results.

- Moved appendix on equity investments to a new, separate end-of-book Appendix D.

CHAPTER 11

- Under "Adjustments for Noncash Components of Net Income" (indirect method), explained amortization expense as treated similar to depreciation expense.
- Added a new Career Corner.
- Revised Illus. 11–17 and 11–18 to focus solely on investing activities and financing activities, respectively.
- Added a new Illus. 11–19 that provides the complete statement of cash flows.

CHAPTER 12

- Added a new Decision Maker's Perspective, "How Warren Buffett Interprets Financial Statements," in the section on profitability analysis.
- Updated risk and profitability analysis for Under Armour in the main text and Nike in the Let's Review exercises.
- Included two new Ethical Dilemmas in the chapter.

APPENDIXES A, B, C, and E

- In Appendixes A and B, updated the annual reports for American Eagle and The Buckle for their fiscal 2010 years.
- In Appendix C, the Quick Quiz from 1e was separated into two expanded Let's Review exercises—one for time value of a single amount and the second for time value of annuities.
- In Appendix E, marginal notes were added to better highlight the topical differences between GAAP and IFRS discussed alongside in the text.

APPENDIX D

This entirely new end-of-book appendix:
- Discusses why companies invest in other companies.
- Addresses equity investments with insignificant influence including available-for-sale and trading securities.
- Contrasts the fair value method, equity method, and consolidation method for equity investments.
- Explains debt investments including held-to-maturity, available-for-sale, and trading securities.

UNIQUE PEDAGOGICAL ELEMENTS

Common Mistakes made by financial accounting students are highlighted throughout each of the chapters. With greater awareness of the pitfalls the average student will find in a first accounting class, students can avoid making the same mistakes and gain a deeper understanding of the chapter material.

Easy to read, love the Key Points and Common Mistakes—**these sound like me talking to my students** and are exactly the points I make in class! Really!—Christa Morgan, *Georgia Perimeter College*

Most of the Common Mistakes are warnings that I have in my lectures.—Lisa N. Bostick, *The University of Tampa*

Accounting is not a number-crunching desk job. Many business professionals call accounting the "language of business;" a solid understanding of accounting can lead to a wide variety of job opportunities. The **Career Corner** boxes highlight the exciting career opportunities in accounting and the important role that accountants play. These also discuss how nonaccountants use accounting information in their business functions.

Most importantly, it **offers opportunities for students to have insights into accounting careers** via Career Corners.— Chuo-Hsuan Lee, *SUNY–Plattsburgh*

Because of the widespread adoption of international financial reporting standards issued by the **International Accounting Standards Board (IASB)**, differences between international standards and U.S. GAAP are highlighted throughout the text in **International Financial Reporting Standards** boxes.

International accounting standards are very relevant today. Students need to be aware of them since we will all probably be using them soon. I enjoyed reading the discussion.—Richard Moellenberndt, *Washburn University*

The **Key Points** provide quick synopses of the critical pieces of information presented throughout each chapter.

Very easy to read!!! I like the Key Points and Common Mistakes segments in each chapter. These features would really help my students as they read the textbook and study for exams. I also like the **simplicity of each chapter.**—David Juriga, *St. Louis Community College*

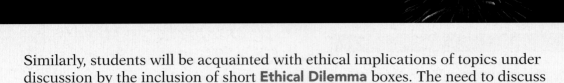

HELP IGNITE THE LEARNING PROCESS

Similarly, students will be acquainted with ethical implications of topics under discussion by the inclusion of short **Ethical Dilemma** boxes. The need to discuss ethics in accounting has become evident in light of recent accounting scandals.

> This is a good approach because it will give students an opportunity to **develop their critical thinking ability** by comparing situations that they have not experienced before.—Seleshi Sisaye, *Duquesne University*

> The "Flip Side" and "Common Mistakes" sections are outstanding and are **likely to be among the favorite parts of the book** for students.—Christian Wurst, *Temple University*

A financial transaction always involves two parties—the **Flip Side** feature demonstrates how various transactions are viewed by each participant. Including the "flip side" of a transaction—in context—enhances the student's understanding of both the initial and the related transaction. Selected homework in the end-of-chapter materials also includes the Flip Side transactions for students to reinforce their understanding of this concept.

Each chapter contains one or more **Let's Review** sections that test students' comprehension of key concepts. These short review exercises, with solutions, are intended to reinforce the students' understanding of specific chapter material and allow them to apply concepts and procedures learned in the chapter prior to attempting their homework assignment.

Let's Review

Let's Review   Bogey Incorporated has the following transactions during May:

> May   1 Purchase a storage building by obtaining a loan of $5,000.
> May   6 Provide services on account to customers, $1,800.
> May 12 Pay $1,200 cash for advertising in May.
> May 17 Repay $1,000 of the amount borrowed on May 1.
> May 25 Purchase office supplies for $800 cash.

Required:
Indicate how each transaction affects the accounting equation.

Solution:

	Assets	=	Liabilities	+	Stockholders' Equity
May 1	+$5,000		+$5,000		
May 6	+$1,800				+$1,800
May 12	−$1,200				−$1,200
May 17	−$1,000		−$1,000		
May 25	+$ 800				
	−$ 800				
	+$4,600	=	+$4,000	+	+$ 600

Suggested Homework:
BE2-2, BE2-3;
E2-2, E2-3, E2-4;
P2-1A&B, P2-2A&B

PRACTICE MAKES PERFECT WITH

Self-Study Questions consist of 10 multiple-choice questions in each chapter. Answers appear at the end of the respective chapters. Students also are directed to the course website, where these same questions are available in the form of self-grading online quizzes with a more detailed analysis of correct and incorrect answers.

> In making an adoption decision, recognizing the topical coverage is most critical, I would not hesitate to adopt this text from the perspective of the assignments.
>
> —Ron Burrows, *University of Dayton*

Review Questions are provided for each of the major concepts in each chapter, providing students with an opportunity to review key parts of the chapter and answer evocative questions about what they have learned.

> Well-written book with **excellent features** throughout each chapter. **Plenty of material** at the end of the chapter to give students extra practice.—Chris McNamara, *Finger Lakes Community College*

Brief Exercises address single concepts from a single perspective. These exercises are ideal for quick demonstrations of simple topics in class or short take-home assignments.

> Brief exercises are an **important part of student learning** (particularly given the learning style of today's student).—Dawn Massey, *Fairfield University*

A WIDE VARIETY OF ASSIGNMENT MATERIAL

Exercises typically add one or more additional dimensions to the same topics covered with Brief Exercises. An additional set of Exercises can be found on the book's website.

> This text is very complete, readable, with **several exercise and problem possibilities.** It has some new and innovative features, including the "Key Point, Common Mistake, and Career Corner" boxes. This text also introduces the Cash Flow Statement fundamentals early in the text, to enhance learning the difference between cash and accrual basis.—Mary Hollars, *Vincennes University*

EXERGISES

connect | ACCOUNTING

E8–1 Match (by letter) the correct reporting method for each of the items listed below.

Reporting Method

C = Current liability
L = Long-term liability
D = Disclosure note only

_____ nts payable.
_____ nt portion of long-term debt.
_____ tax collected from customers.
_____ payable due next year.
_____ payable due in two years.
_____ mer advances.
_____ ercial paper.

Determine proper classification of liabilities (LO1)

Problems typically address multiple concepts from the chapter or multiple levels of analytical perspective within the given scenarios. Where feasible, problems are built around real companies and business situations.

Each chapter provides twin sets of problems to offer instructors flexibility in presentation and assignment. The material in **Problem Set A** is similar in format to the material in **Problem Set B**, and each set reinforces the other. **New to the second edition, Problem Set B will now appear in McGraw-Hill Connect.** An additional set of Problems can be found on the book's website.

PROBLEMS: SET A

connect | ACCOUNTING

P8–1A Listed below are several terms and phrases associated with current liabilities. Pair each item from List A (by letter) with the item from List B that is most appropriately associated with it.

Review current liability terms and concepts (LO1)

List A	List B
_____ 1. An IOU promising to repay the amount borrowed plus interest.	a. Recording of a contingent liability.
_____ 2. Payment amount is reasonably possible and can be reasonably estimated.	b. Unearned revenues.
_____ 3. Mixture of liabilities and equity a business uses.	c. The riskiness of a business's obligations.
_____ 4. Payment amount is probable and can be reasonably estimated.	d. Disclosure of a contingent liability.
_____ 5. A liability that requires the sacrifice of	e. Interest on debt.
	f. Payroll taxes.

PROBLEMS: SET B

connect | ACCOUNTING

Review current liability terms and concepts (LO1)

P8–1B Listed below are several terms and phrases associated with current liabilities. Pair each item from List A (by letter) with the item from List B that is most appropriately associated with it.

List A	List B
_____ 1. Interest expense is recorded in the period interest is incurred rather than in the period interest is paid.	a. The riskiness of a business's obligations.
_____ 2. Payment is reasonably possible and can be reasonably estimated.	b. Current portion of long-term debt.
_____ 3. Cash, current investments, and accounts receivable all divided by current liabilities.	c. Recording a contingent liability.
_____ 4. Payment is probable and can be reasonably estimated.	d. Disclosure of a contingent liability.
_____ 5. Gift certificates.	e. Interest expense.
_____ 6. Long-term debt maturing within one year.	f. FICA

> This text is very well written and offers a set of end-of-chapter problems that **progressively challenges students** and directs them to **build problem-solving skills.**—Gregg S. Woodruff, *Western Illinois University*

CHALLENGE YOUR STUDENTS TO SEE AN **ADDITIONAL PERSPECTIVE**

The Additional Perspectives section of each chapter offers the most distinctive variety of case material available in financial accounting textbooks. Cases and activities are designed to allow students to apply the knowledge and skills they've learned in provocative, real, or realistic situations. Students are placed in the role of decision maker, presented with a set of information, and asked to draw conclusions that test their understanding of the issues discussed in the chapters. Each chapter offers an engaging mix of activities and opportunities to perform real-world financial accounting analysis:

ADDITIONAL PERSPECTIVES

Great Adventures

(This is a continuation of the Great Adventures problem from earlier chapters.)

AP8–1 Great Adventures is a defendant in litigation involving a biking accident during one of its adventure races. The front tire on one of the bikes came off during the race, resulting in serious injury to the rider. However, Great Adventures can document that each bike was carefully inspected prior to the race. It may have been that the rider loosened the wheel during the race and then forgot to tighten the quick-release mechanism.

Continuing Problem

QB

Required:
For each of the following scenarios, determine the appropriate way to report the situation. Explain your reasoning and record any necessary entry.
1. The likelihood of a payment occurring is probable, and the estimated amount is $120,000.
2. The likelihood of a payment occurring is probable, and the amount is estimated to be in the range of $100,000 to $150,000.
3. The likelihood of a payment occurring is reasonably possible, and the estimated amount is $120,000.

Continuing Problem—The story of Great Adventures progresses from chapter to chapter, encompassing the accounting issues of each new chapter as the story unfolds. This problem allows students to see how each chapter's topics can be integrated into the operations of a single company; this problem is also available in McGraw-Hill Connect.

> The book is very detailed, but **not overly technical.** The book is written at a level and in a way that is highly user friendly.—Peter Woodlock, *Youngstown State University*

American Eagle Outfitters, Inc.

AP5–2 Financial information for **American Eagle** is presented in Appendix A at the end of the book.

Financial Analysis

Required:
1. Determine whether the trend in net sales has been increasing or decreasing for the past three years.
2. Where is accounts receivable reported? Explain why using net sales to calculate the receivables turnover ratio might not be a good indicator of a company's ability to efficiently manage receivables for a retail company like American Eagle, which typically
3. Does An sheet? If

Financial Analysis: American Eagle Outfitters, Inc.—Students are asked to gather information from the annual report of American Eagle, located in Appendix A.

The Buckle, Inc.

AP5–3 Financial information for **The Buckle** is presented in Appendix B at the end of the book.

Financial Analysis

Buckle

Required:
1. Determine whether the trend in net sales has been increasing or decreasing for the past three years.
2. Where is accounts receivable reported? Explain why using net sales to calculate the receivables turnover ratio might not be a good indicator of a company's ability to efficiently manage receivables for a retail company like The Buckle, which typically sells clothing for cash.
3. Does The Buckle report an allowance for uncollectible accounts in the balance sheet? If so, how much is reported for the most recent year?

Financial Analysis: The Buckle, Inc.—Students are asked to gather information from the annual report of The Buckle, located in Appendix B.

> **A new, promising text in financial accounting is emerging.**—Ahmed Ebrahim, *State University of New York–New Paltz*

American Eagle Outfitters, Inc., vs. The Buckle, Inc.

AP5–4 Financial information for **American Eagle** is presented in Appendix A at the end of the book, and financial information for **The Buckle** is presented in Appendix B at the end of the book.

Comparative Analysis

Buckle

Required:
Try to estimate each company's ratio of total current receivables to total current assets. Do you see problems with either company's management of receivables?

Comparative Analysis—In addition to separately analyzing the financial information of American Eagle and The Buckle, students are asked to compare financial information between the two companies.

> Difficult topics are handled in a manner to **facilitate the students' learning.** Overall the book is very good and worth considering.—Tommy Moores, *University of Nevada–Las Vegas*

WITH THESE UNIQUE END-OF-CHAPTER CASES

Ethics—Encourage consideration of ethical issues as they pertain to accounting decisions including the outcome of those decisions on various stakeholders.

> Students are given opportunities for feedback of their understanding of concepts and procedures by taking quizzes and working review problems at break points within the chapter. The text has a **large quantity and variety of quality end-of-chapter assignment material.**—Tommy Moores, *University of Nevada–Las Vegas*

Ethics

AP4–5 Between his freshman and sophomore years of college, Jack takes a job as ticket collector at a local movie theatre. Moviegoers purchase a ticket from a separate employee outside the theatre and then enter through a single set of doors. Jack takes half their ticket, and they proceed to the movie of their choice.

Besides trying to earn enough money for college the next year, Jack loves to watch movies. One of the perks of working for the movie theatre is that all employees are allowed to watch one free movie per day. However, in the employee handbook it states that friends and family of employees are not allowed to watch free movies. In addition, employees must pay full price for all concession items.

Soon after starting work at the theatre, Jack notices that most other employees regularly bring their friends and family to the movie without purchasing a ticket. When Jack stops them at the door to ask for their ticket, they say, "Jack, no one really follows that policy. Just be cool and let us in. You can do the same." Jack even notices that upper management does not follow the policy of no family and friends watching free movies. Furthermore, employees commonly bring their own cups to get free soft drinks and their own containers to eat free popcorn.

Jack considers whether he should also start bringing friends and family and enjoying the free popcorn and beverages. He reasons, "Why should I be the only one following

Internet Research—Allow students to develop and practice research skills by requiring them to locate and extract relevant information from available resource material such as financial reports or official standards on the Internet, perhaps identifying the appropriate resources to support a decision.

> With the **wide range of EOC materials,** the book can be adapted to many different levels.—Joshua Herbold, *University of Montana*

Internet Research

AP4–6 Financial accounting information can often be found at financial websites. These websites are useful for collecting information about a company's stock price, analysts' forecasts, dividend history, historical financial accounting information, and much more. One such site is Yahoo! Finance (*finance.yahoo.com*).

Required:

1. Visit Yahoo! Finance and get a stock quote for **Google**. To do this, type "GOOG" in the "Get Quotes" box. Under "Financials" click on the "Cash Flow" link. Calculate Google's free cash flows for the three most recent years.
2. Calculate **IBM**'s free cash flows in the same way by typing "IBM" in the "Get Quotes" box.

Written Communication—Provide the opportunity to not only apply analysis and judgment skills but also to express information or persuade by means of a writing assignment.

Written Communication

AP4–7 Consider the following independent situations:

1. John Smith is the petty-cash custodian. John approves all requests for payment out of the $200 fund, which is replenished at the end of each month. At the end of each month, John submits a list of all accounts and amounts to be charged, and a check is written to him for the total amount. John is the only person ever to tally the fund.
2. All of the company's cash disbursements are made by check. Each check must be

Earnings Management—Provide challenging earnings management situations where students analyze the implications of their accounting decisions on a company's earnings.

Earnings Management

AP7–8 Edward L. Vincent is CFO of Energy Resources, Inc. The company specializes in the exploration and development of natural gas. It's near year-end, and Edward is feeling terrific. Natural gas prices have risen throughout the year, and Energy Resources is set to report record-breaking performance that will greatly exceed analysts' expectations. However, during an executive meeting this morning, management agreed to "tone down" profits due to concerns that reporting excess profits could encourage additional government regulations in the industry, hindering future profitability.

Edward decides to adjust the estimated service life of development equipment from

> This book has the **largest quantity of exercises and problems of any text that I've reviewed.** I think it is very important for students to work incrementally on some of the more difficult concepts. I usually don't have such an impressive quantity from which to select.—Kathleen M. Metcalf, *Muscatine Community College*

McGraw-Hill Connect™ Accounting

LESS MANAGING. MORE TEACHING. GREATER LEARNING.

McGraw-Hill *Connect Accounting* is an online assignment and assessment solution that connects students with the tools and resources they'll need to achieve success.

McGraw-Hill *Connect Accounting* helps prepare students for their future by enabling faster learning, more efficient studying, and higher retention of knowledge.

MCGRAW-HILL *CONNECT ACCOUNTING* FEATURES

Connect Accounting offers a number of powerful tools and features to make managing assignments easier, so faculty can spend more time teaching. With *Connect Accounting*, students can engage with their coursework anytime and anywhere, making the learning process more accessible and efficient. *Connect Accounting* offers you the features described below.

SIMPLE ASSIGNMENT MANAGEMENT

With *Connect Accounting*, creating assignments is easier than ever, so you can spend more time teaching and less time managing. The assignment management function enables you to:

- Create and deliver assignments easily with selectable end-of-chapter questions and test bank items.
- Streamline lesson planning, student progress reporting, and assignment grading to make classroom management more efficient than ever.
- Assign algorithmic brief exercises, exercises, or problems so each student has a different problem to work on.

SMART GRADING

When it comes to studying, time is precious. *Connect Accounting* helps students learn more efficiently by providing feedback and practice material when they need it, where they need it. When it comes to teaching, your time also is precious. The grading function enables you to:

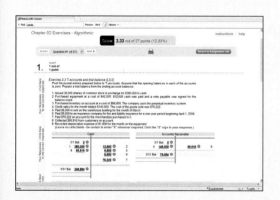

- Have assignments scored automatically, giving students immediate feedback on their work and side-by-side comparisons with correct answers.
- Access and review each response; manually change grades or leave comments for students to review.
- Reinforce classroom concepts with practice tests and instant quizzes.

ACCOMMODATE A VARIETY OF LEARNING STYLES

INSTRUCTOR LIBRARY

The *Connect Accounting* Instructor Library is your repository for additional resources to improve student engagement in and out of class. You can select and use any asset that enhances your lecture. The *Connect Accounting* Instructor Library includes:

- *eBook*
- *PowerPoint© slides*
- *Online quizzes*

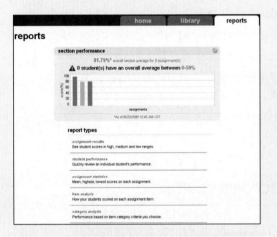

STUDENT STUDY CENTER

The *Connect Accounting* Student Study Center is the place for students to access additional resources. The Student Study Center:

- Offers students quick access to lectures, practice materials, eBooks, and more.
- Provides instant practice material and study questions, easily accessible on the go.

STUDENT PROGRESS TRACKING

Connect Accounting keeps instructors informed about how each student, section, and class is performing, allowing for more productive use of lecture and office hours. The progress-tracking function enables you to:

- View scored work immediately and track individual or group performance with assignment and grade reports.
- Access an instant view of student or class performance relative to learning objectives.
- Collect data and generate reports required by many accreditation organizations, such as AACSB and AICPA.

MCGRAW-HILL *CONNECT PLUS*

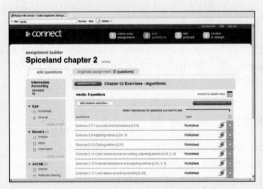

McGraw-Hill reinvents the textbook learning experience for the modern student with *Connect Plus*. A seamless integration of an eBook and *Connect Accounting, Connect Plus* provides all of the *Connect Accounting* features plus the following:

- An integrated eBook, allowing for anytime, anywhere access to the textbook.
- Dynamic links between the problems or questions you assign to your students and the location in the eBook where that problem or question is covered.
- A powerful search function to pinpoint and connect key concepts in a snap.

In short, *Connect Accounting* offers you and your students powerful tools and features that optimize your time and energies, enabling you to focus on course content, teaching, and student learning. *Connect Accounting* also offers a wealth of content resources for both instructors and students. This state-of-the-art, thoroughly tested system supports you in preparing students for the world that awaits.

For more information about Connect, go to **connect.mcgraw-hill.com,** or contact your local McGraw-Hill sales representative.

AUTHOR-WRITTEN SUPPLEMENTS

> The textbook is well organized and **noticeably written by individuals who have an excellent understanding of accounting,** the accounting profession, and the issues confronting the accounting profession. A large number of supplements for students and instructors are available, including high-tech supplements.—Richard A. Moellenberndt, *Washburn University*

> Excellent introductory textbook. It covers the essential material in an interesting and engaging manner. **It fits well with Spiceland et al.'s intermediate text.**—Rodney Smith, *California State University– Long Beach*

INSTRUCTOR'S RESOURCE MANUAL

This manual provides for each chapter: (a) a chapter overview; (b) a comprehensive lecture outline; (c) a variety of suggested class activities (real world, ethics, annual report, professional development activities including research, analysis, communication and judgment, and others); and (d) an assignment chart indicating topic, learning objective, and estimated completion time for every question, exercise, problem, and case.

SOLUTIONS MANUAL

The Solutions Manual includes detailed solutions for every question, exercise, problem, and case in the text.

INSTRUCTOR'S CD-ROM

ISBN-13: 9780077328207
(ISBN-10: 0077328205)

This all-in-one resource contains the Instructor's Resource Manual, Solutions Manual, Testbank Word files, Computerized Testbank, and PowerPoint® slides.

TESTBANK

Written by the authors, this comprehensive Testbank contains over 1,800 problems and true/false, matching, multiple-choice, problems, and essay questions.

> There's a surprise (extra or expanded coverage not often found in other texts) in virtually every chapter. If you've been teaching this course for years and long for something new and fresh, you owe it to yourself to take a look at this text.— Lowell Mooney, *Georgia Southern University*

> This is an **excellent text for the beginning accounting faculty instructor,** intermediate or advanced.—Linda Bressler, *University of Houston*

AUDIO-NARRATED SLIDES

The Audio-Narrated Slides include an accompanying audio lecture with notes and are available on the Online Learning Center (OLC). Separate sets of PowerPoints® are available for instructors and students.

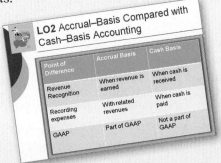

ONLINE LEARNING CENTER (OLC)

Our OLC requires no building or maintenance on your part, and is ready to go the moment you and your students type in the URL. As your students study, they can access the OLC website for such benefits as:

- Self-grading quizzes
- Apple iPod® content, including PowerPoints
- Student PowerPoint® Tutorials
- Alternate exercises and problems
- Check figures
- Excel templates
- QuickBooks templates

Additional Resources for Your Students

ALTERNATE EXERCISES AND PROBLEMS

This online manual includes additional exercises and problems for each chapter in the text. Available on the OLC.

WORKING PAPERS

ISBN-13: 9780077328252
(ISBN-10: 0077328252)

Working Papers provide students with formatted templates to aid them in doing homework assignments.

EXCEL TEMPLATES

Selected end-of-chapter exercises and problems, marked in the text with an icon, can be solved using these Microsoft Excel templates, located on the OLC.

LECTURE PRESENTATIONS

Lecture presentations are available for download to your **iPod, Zune, or MP3 device** (audio and visual depending on your device).

QUICKBOOKS TEMPLATES

QuickBooks Templates are available for selected problems in the end-of-chapter material for *Financial Accounting.* As the premier accounting software in use today, students will get a head start on learning how accounting is done in the real world!

This is a **wonderful and innovative book** that covers the basics and really makes a serious effort to bring accounting alive.—S. A. Marino, *SUNY/Westchester Community College*

ONLINE COURSE MANAGEMENT

No matter what online course management system you use (WebCT, BlackBoard, or eCollege), we have a course content ePack available for *Financial Accounting*. Our new ePacks are specifically designed to make it easy for students to navigate and access content online. They are easier than ever to install on the latest version of the course management system available today.

Don't forget that you can count on the highest level of service from McGraw-Hill. Our online course management specialists are ready to assist you with your online course needs. They provide training and will answer any questions you have throughout the life of your adoption. So try our new ePack for *Financial Accounting* and make online course content delivery easy and fun.

ALEKS®

Available online in partnership with McGraw-Hill/Irwin, ALEKS is a unique program that uses artificial intelligence and adaptive questioning to precisely assess a student's knowledge in accounting, and provide personalized instruction on the exact topics the student is most ready to learn. ALEKS targets gaps in student skills and enables students to master course content quickly

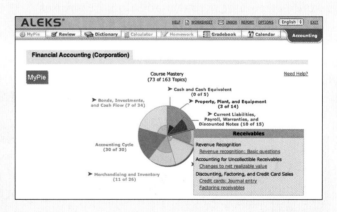

and easily within an environment tailored to each student's level of preparedness. By providing comprehensive explanations, practice, and feedback, ALEKS dramatically improves student performance and retention.

The ALEKS Instructor Module offers powerful, assignment-driven features and extensive content flexibility to simplify course management so instructors can spend less time with administrative tasks and more time directing student learning. The complimentary Instructor Module provides a course calendar, customizable gradebook, automatically-graded assignments, textbook integration, and dynamic reports to monitor student and class progress.

To learn more about ALEKS, visit **www.aleks.com/highered/business**.

ALEKS is a registered trademark of ALEKS Corporation.

ASSURANCE OF LEARNING READY

Many educational institutions today are focused on the notion of *assurance of learning,* an important element of some accreditation standards. *Financial Accounting* is designed specifically to support your assurance of learning initiatives with a simple, yet powerful solution.

Each Testbank question for *Financial Accounting* maps to a specific chapter learning objective listed in the text. You can use our Testbank software, EZ Test and EZ Test Online, or *Connect Accounting* to easily query for learning objectives that directly relate to the learning objectives for your course. You can then use the reporting features of EZ Test to aggregate student results in similar fashion, making the collection and presentation of assurance of learning data simple and easy.

AACSB STATEMENT

The McGraw-Hill Companies is a proud corporate member of AACSB International. Understanding the importance and value of AACSB accreditation, *Financial Accounting* recognizes the curricula guidelines detailed in the AACSB standards for business accreditation by connecting selected questions in the text and the Testbank to the six general knowledge and skill guidelines in the AACSB standards.

The statements contained in *Financial Accounting* are provided only as a guide for the users of this textbook. The AACSB leaves content coverage and assessment within the purview of individual schools, the mission of the school, and the faculty. While *Financial Accounting* and the teaching package make no claim of any specific AACSB qualification or evaluation, we have within *Financial Accounting* labeled selected questions according to the six general knowledge and skills areas.

Try a New e-Book Option!

COURSESMART

CourseSmart is a new way to find and buy eTextbooks. At CourseSmart you can save up to 50 percent off the cost of a printed textbook, reduce your impact on the environment, and gain access to powerful Web tools for learning. CourseSmart has the largest selection of eTextbooks available anywhere, offering thousands of the most commonly adopted textbooks from a wide variety of higher education publishers. CourseSmart eTextbooks are available in one standard online reader with full text search, notes and highlighting, and e-mail tools for sharing notes between classmates.

MCGRAW-HILL/IRWIN CUSTOMER CARE CONTACT INFORMATION

At McGraw-Hill/Irwin, we understand that getting the most from new technology can be challenging. That's why our services don't stop after you purchase our product. You can e-mail our Product Specialists 24 hours a day, get product training online, or search our knowledge bank of Frequently Asked Questions on our support website. For all Customer Support call **(800) 331-5094,** e-mail **hmsupport@mcgraw-hill.com,** or visit **www.mhhe.com/support**. One of our Technical Support Analysts will be able to assist you in a timely fashion.

A HEARTFELT THANKS TO THE MANY VOICES

The version of *Financial Accounting* you are reading would not be the same book without the valuable suggestions, keen insights, and constructive criticisms of the list of reviewers below. Each professor listed here contributed in substantive ways to the organization of chapters, coverage of topics, and selective use of pedagogy. We are grateful to them for taking the time to read each chapter and offer their insights:

Dawn Addington, *Central New Mexico Community College*
Peter Aghimien, *Indiana University –South Bend*
James J. Aitken, *Central Michigan University*
Fouad Alnajjar, *Baker College*
Janice Ammons, *Quinnipiac University*
Craig Bain, *Northern Arizona University*
Kashi Balachandran, *New York University*
Patricia C. Bancroft, *Bridgewater State College*
Randall P. Bandura, *Frostburg State University*
Lisa Banks, *Mott Community College*
Joyce Barden, *DeVry University*
Cheryl Bartlett, *Central New Mexico Community College*
Mohammad S. Bazaz, *Oakland University*
Stephen Benner, *Eastern Illinois University*
Amy Bentley, *Tallahassee Community College*
Larry Bergin, *Winona State University*
Brenda Bindschatel, *Green River Community College–Auburn*
Cynthia Birk, *University of Nevada–Reno*
Eddy Birrer, *Gonzaga University*
Sandra Bitenc, *University of Texas at Arlington*
Claude Black, *Seattle Central Community College*
David Bojarsky, *California State University –Long Beach*
Charlie Bokemeier, *Michigan State University*
Jack Borke, *University of Wisconsin –Platteville*
Lisa N. Bostick, *The University of Tampa*
Amy Bourne, *Oregon State University*
Benoit Boyer, *Sacred Heart University*
Jerold K. Braun, *Daytona State College*
Linnae Bryant, *Chicago State University*
R. Eugene Bryson, *University of Alabama –Huntsville*
Georgia Buckles, *Manchester Community College*
Charles I. Bunn, *Wake Tech Community College*
Sandra Byrd, *Missouri State University*
Scott Cairns, *Shippensburg University of PA*
Ernest Carraway, *North Carolina State University*
Bruce Cassel, *Dutchess Community College*
Valrie Chambers, *Texas A&M University*
Betty Chavis, *California State University –Fullerton*

Al Chen, *North Carolina State University –Raleigh*
Alan Cherry, *Loyola Marymount University*
Bea Chiang, *The College of New Jersey*
Cal Christian, *East Carolina University*
Leslie Cohen, *University of Arizona*
Jackie Conrecode, *Florida Gulf Coast University*
Debora Constable, *Georgia Perimeter College*
Pat Cook, *Manchester Community College*
Betty Cossitt, *University of Nevada–Reno*
Meg Costello Lambert, *Oakland Community College*
Samantha Cox, *Wake Tech Community College*
Leonard Cronin, *Rochester Community & Technical College*
Jim Crowther, *Kirkwood Community College*
Karl Dahlberg, *Rutgers University*
Dori Danko, *Grand Valley State University*
Kreag Danvers, *Clarion University of PA*
Alan Davis, *Community College of Philadelphia*
Harold Davis, *Southeastern Louisiana University*
Mark DeFond, *University of Southern California*
Guenther DerManelian, *Johnson & Wales University*
Patricia Derrick, *Salisbury University*
Rosemond Desir, *Colorado State University*
Carlton Donchess, *Bridgewater State College*
Alex Dontoh, *New York University*
Jamie Doran, *Muhlenberg College*
Lisa Dutchik, *Kirkwood Community College*
Carol Dutton, *South Florida Community College*
Cynthia Eakin, *University of the Pacific*
Susan Eldridge, *University of Nebraska –Omaha*
Sheri Erickson, *Minnesota State University –Moorhead*
Harlan Etheridge, *University of Louisiana –Lafayette*
Janice Fergusson, *University of South Carolina*
Linda Flaming, *Monmouth University*
Amy Ford, *Western Illinois University*
Brenda Fowler, *Alamance Community College*
Martha Lou Fowler, *Missouri Western State University*
Tom Fuhrmann, *Missouri Western State University*
Harlan Fuller, *Illinois State University*
Ed Furticella, *Purdue University*
Mohamed Gaber, *SUNY Plattsburgh*
John Gardner, *University of Wisconsin –Lacrosse*
Daniel Gibbons, *Waubonsee Community College*
Lisa Gillespie, *Loyola University*
Ruth Goran, *Northeastern Illinois University*
Sherry Gordon, *Palomar College*

Janet Grange, *Chicago State University*
Tony Greig, *Purdue University*
Sanjay Gupta, *Valdosta State University*
Geoffrey Gurka, *Mesa State College*
Jeffry Haber, *Iona College*
Ronald Halsac, *Community College of Allegheny County*
Heidi Hansel, *Kirkwood Community College*
Sheldon Hanson, *Chippewa Valley Technical College*
Coby Harmon, *University of California–Santa Barbara*
Erskine Hawkins, *Georgia Perimeter College*
Daniel He, *Monmouth University*
Haihong He, *California State University –Los Angeles*
Kevin Hee, *San Diego State University*
Joshua Herbold, *University of Montana*
Joyce Hicks, *Saint Mary's College*
Dan Hinchliffe, *University of North Carolina –Asheville*
Frank Hodge, *University of Washington*
Anthony Holder, *Case Western Reserve University*
Mary Hollars, *Vincennes University*
Linda Holmes, *University of Wisconsin –Whitewater*
Sharon Hoover-Dice, *Clinton Community College*
Steven Hornik, *University of Central Florida*
Kathy Hsiao Yu Hsu, *University of Louisiana –Lafayette*
Marsha Huber, *Otterbein College*
Peggy Ann Hughes, *Montclair State University*
Laura Ilcisin, *University of Nebraska at Omaha*
Paula Irwin, *Muhlenberg College*
Norma Jacobs, *Austin Community College*
Marianne James, *California State University –Los Angeles*
Raymond Johnson, *Guilford College*
Shondra Johnson, *Bradley University*
Rita Jones, *Columbus State University*
Mark Judd, *University of San Diego*
David Juriga, *Saint Louis Community College–Forest Park*
Robert Kachur, *Richard Stockton College of New Jersey*
Elliot Kamlet, *Binghamton University*
Lara Kessler, *Grand Valley State University*
Tim Kizirian, *California State University –Chico*
Janice Klimek, *University of Central Missouri*
Christine Kloezeman, *Glendale Community College*
Stephen A. Kolenda, *Hartwick College*
Emil Koren, *Saint Leo University*
Dennis Kovach, *Community College of Allegheny County*
Joan Lacher, *Nassau Community College*

Steven J. LaFave, *Augsburg College*

Sheldon Langsam, *Western Michigan University*

Cathy Larson, *Middlesex Community College*

Douglas A. Larson, *Salem State College*

Laurie Larson-Gardner, *Valencia Community College*

Michael D. Lawrence, *Portland Community College*

Suzanne Lay, *Mesa State College*

Chuo-Hsuan Lee, *SUNY Plattsburgh*

Deborah Lee, *Northeastern State University*

Christy Lefevers-Land, *Catawba Valley Community College*

Pamela Legner, *College of DuPage*

Stacy LeJeune, *Nicholls State University*

Elliott Levy, *Bentley College*

Xu Li, *University of Texas at Dallas*

Beixin Lin, *Montclair State University*

Joseph Lipari, *Montclair State University*

Joseph Lupino, *Saint Mary's College of California*

Anna Lusher, *Slippery Rock University of PA*

Kirk Lynch, *Sandhills Community College*

Nancy Lynch, *West Virginia University*

Mostafa Maksy, *Northeastern Illinois University*

Sal Marino, *Westchester Community College*

Angie Martin, *Tarrant County College*

James Martin, *Washburn University*

Peter Martino, *Johnson & Wales University*

Christian Mastilak, *Xavier University*

Josephine Mathias, *Mercer County Community College*

Betsy Mayes, *University of North Carolina –Asheville*

Lynn Mazzola, *Nassau Community College*

Maureen McBeth, *College of DuPage*

Florence McGovern, *Bergen Community College*

Chris McNamara, *Finger Lakes Community College*

Sara Melendy, *Gonzaga University*

Terri Meta, *Seminole Community College*

Kathleen M. Metcalf, *Muscatine Community College*

Jean Meyer, *Loyola University*

Pam Meyer, *University of Louisiana–Lafayette*

James Miller, *Gannon University*

Julie Miller, *Chippewa Valley Technical College*

Claudette Milligan, *Trident Technical College*

Tim Mills, *Eastern Illinois University*

Laurel Bond Mitchell, *University of Redlands*

Laura Mizaur, *Creighton University*

Richard A. Moellenberndt, *Washburn University*

Kathy Moffeit, *West Georgia University*

J. Lowell Mooney, *Georgia Southern University*

Tommy Moores, *University of Nevada–Las Vegas*

Michelle Moshier, *University at Albany*

Gerald Motl, *Xavier University*

Lisa Murawa, *Mott Community College*

Volkan Muslu, *University of Texas at Dallas*

Al Nagy, *John Carroll University*

Presha Neidermeyer, *West Virginia University*

Micki Nickla, *Ivy Tech Community College of Indiana*

Tracie Nobles, *Austin Community College*

Hossein Noorian, *Wentworth Institute of Technology*

Ron O'Brien, *Fayetteville Tech Community College*

Dan O'Brien, *North Central Technical College*

Kanalis Ockree, *Washburn University*

Karen Osterheld, *Bentley College*

Don Pagach, *North Carolina State University –Raleigh*

Janet Papiernik, *Indiana University/Purdue University–Ft Wayne*

Glenn Pate, *Palm Beach Community College*

Keith F. Patterson, *Brigham Young University*

Richard J. Pettit, *Mountain View College*

Jan Pitera, *Broome Community College*

John Plouffe, *California State University –Los Angeles*

Linda Poulson, *Elon University*

Matthew Probst, *Ivy Tech Community College of Indiana*

Atul Rai, *Wichita State University*

Richard Rand, *Tennessee Tech University*

David Randolph, *Xavier University*

July Ratley, *Shasta College*

Donald J. Raux, *Siena College*

Aaron Reeves, *Saint Louis Community College–Forest Park*

Patrick Reihing, *Nassau Community College*

Raymond Reisig, *Pace University*

Gayle Richardson, *Bakersfield College*

Laura Rickett, *Kent State University*

Sharon Robinson, *Frostburg State University*

Joanne Rockness, *University of North Carolina–Wilmington*

Carol Rogers, *Central New Mexico Community College*

Richard Roscher, *University of North Carolina–Wilmington*

Mark Ross, *Western Kentucky University*

John A. Rude, *Bloomsburg University of PA*

Robert Russ, *Northern Kentucky University*

Huldah A. Ryan, *Iona College*

Angela Sandberg, *Jacksonville State University*

Amy Santos, *State College of Florida*

Gary Schader, *Kean University*

Linda Schain, *Hofstra University*

Megan Schaupp, *West Virginia University*

Arnold Schneider, *Georgia Institute of Technology*

Steve Sefcik, *University of Washington*

Joann Segovia, *Minnesota State University –Moorhead*

Ann E. Selk, *University of Wisconsin–Green Bay*

Michael Serif, *Dowling College*

Randall Serrett, *University of Houston –Downtown*

Suzanne Sevalstad, *University of Nevada*

Kathy Sevigny, *Bridgewater State College*

Geeta Shankar, *University of Dayton*

Robbie Sheffy, *Tarrant County College*

Lori Simonsen, *University of Nebraska at Omaha*

Mike Slaubaugh, *Indiana University/Purdue University–Ft Wayne*

Erik Slayter, *California Polytechnic University*

G. Phillip Smilanick, *Truckee Meadows Community College*

Becky L. Smith, *York College of PA*

Sondra Smith, *West Georgia University*

Warren Smock, *Ivy Tech Community College of Indiana*

Mary Speth, *Sandhills Community College*

Barbara Squires, *Corning Community College*

Victor Stanton, *University of California, Berkeley*

Maureen Stefanini, *Worcester State College*

Ron Stone, *California State University –Northridge*

Arlene Strawn, *Tallahassee Community College*

Edith Strickland, *Tallahassee Community College*

Ron Strittmater, *North Hennepin Community College*

John Surdick, *Xavier University*

Jan Sweeney, *Bernard M. Baruch College*

Paulette Tandy, *University of Nevada–Las Vegas*

Linda Tarrago, *Hillsborough Community College*

Peter Theuri, *Northern Kentucky University*

Amanda Thompson, *Marshall University*

Lisa Thornton Buehler, *Truckee Meadows Community College*

Paula Tigerman, *Black Hawk College*

Theresa Tiggeman, *University of the Incarnate Word*

Melanie Torborg, *Minnesota School of Business*

Yvette Travis, *Bishop State Community College*

Nancy Uddin, *Monmouth University*

Karen Varnell, *Tarleton State University*

Stacy R. Wade, *Western Kentucky University*

Elisabeth Peltier Wagner, *Bernard M. Baruch College*

Mary Jeanne Walsh, *La Salle University*

Li Wang, *University of Akron*

Larry Watkins, *Northern Arizona University*

Olga Dupuis Watts, *McNeese State University*

Andrea Weickgenannt, *Northern Kentucky University*

Kristin Wentzel, *La Salle University*

Cathy West, *University of Massachusetts –Amherst*

Cheryl Westen, *Western Illinois University*

Allen Wright, *Hillsborough Community College*
Lorraine Wright, *North Carolina State University–Raleigh*
Christian Wurst, *Temple University*
Kathryn Yarbrough, *Appalachian State University*
Gregory C. Yost, *University of West Florida*
Thomas M. Young, *Lone Star College*
Marjorie Yuschak, *Sacred Heart University*
Emmanuel Zur, *Bernard M. Baruch College*
Robert Zwicker, *Pace University*

FIRST EDITION REVIEWERS:

James J. Aitken, *Central Michigan University*
Christie P. Anderson, *Whitworth University*
Marjorie Ashton, *Truckee Meadows Community College*
Steven Ault, *Montana State University –Bozeman*
Tim Baker, *California State University–Fresno*
Joyce Barden, *Devry University–Phoenix*
Deborah F. Beard, *Southeast Missouri State University*
Judy Benish, *Fox Valley Tech College*
Joseph Berlinski, *Prairie State College*
Eddy Birrer, *Gonzaga University*
Jack Borke, *University of Wisconsin –Platteville*
Lisa N. Bostick, *The University of Tampa*
Bruce Bradford, *Fairfield University*
Thomas Brady, *University of Dayton*
Linda Bressler, *University of Houston –Downtown*
Madeline Brogan, *North Harris College*
Carol Brown, *Oregon State University*
Helen Brubeck, *San Jose State University*
R. Eugene Bryson, *University of Alabama –Huntsville*
Charles I. Bunn, *Wake Tech Community College*
Ron Burrows, *University of Dayton*
Thane Butt, *Champlain College*
Sandra Byrd, *Missouri State University*
Kay C. Carnes, *Gonzaga University*
Bea Bih-Horng Chiang, *The College of New Jersey*
Cal Christian, *East Carolina University*
John Coulter, *Western New England College*
Sue Cullers, *Tarleton State University*
Kreag Danvers, *Clarion University of PA*
Peggy Dejong, *Kirkwood Community College*
Laura Delaune, *Louisiana State University –Baton Rouge*
Shannon Donovan, *Bridgewater State College*
Allan Drebin, *Northwestern University*
Ahmed Ebrahim, *State University of NY–New Paltz*
Thomas Finnegan, *University of Illinois –Champaign*

Linda Flaming, *Monmouth University*
Martha Lou Fowler, *Missouri Western State University*
Tom Fuhrmann, *Missouri Western State University*
Mohamed Gaber, *State University of New York –Plattsburgh*
Rena Galloway, *State Fair Community College*
Margaret Garnsey, *Siena College*
David L. Gilbertson, *Western Washington University*
Lisa Gillespie, *Loyola University–Chicago*
Ruth Goran, *Northeastern Illinois University*
Jeffry Haber, *Iona College–New Rochelle*
Heidi Hansel, *Kirkwood Community College*
Sheldon Hanson, *Chippewa Valley Tech College*
Al Hartgraves, *Emory University*
Bob Hartman, *University of Iowa–Iowa City*
K.D. Hatheway-Dial, *University of Idaho*
John Hathorn, *Metro State College of Denver*
Byron K. Henry, *Howard University*
Joshua Herbold, *University of Montana*
Margaret Hicks, *Howard University*
Mary Hollars, *Vincennes University*
Sharon Hoover-Dice, *Clinton Community College*
Steven Hornik, *University of Central Florida*
Marsha Huber, *Otterbein College*
David Hurtt, *Baylor University*
Laura Ilcisin, *University of Nebraska–Omaha*
Paula Irwin, *Muhlenberg College*
Marianne James, *California State University –Los Angeles*
Raymond Johnson, *Guilford College*
Melissa Jordan, *College of DuPage*
David Juriga, *St. Louis Community College –Forest Park*
Dennis L. Kovach, *Community College of Allegheny County*
Steven J. LaFave, *Augsburg College*
Phillip D. Landers, *Pennsylvania College of Technology*
Douglas A. Larson, *Salem State College*
Laurie Larson-Gardner, *Valencia Community College East*
Daniel Law, *Gonzaga University*
Suzanne Lay, *Mesa State College*
Christy Lefevers-Land, *Catawba Valley Community College*
Joseph Lipari, *Montclair State University*
Chao-Shin Liu, *University of Notre Dame*
Mostafa Maksy, *Northeastern Illinois University*
S. A. Marino, *SUNY/Westchester Community College*
Dawn Massey, *Fairfield University*
Joyce Matthews, *Central New Mexico Community College*
Mark McCarthy, *East Carolina University*
Robert W. McGee, *Barry University*

Chris McNamara, *Finger Lakes Community College*
Kathleen M. Metcalf, *Muscatine Community College*
Herbert L. Meyer, *Scott Community College –Davenport*
Jean Meyer, *Loyola University*
Pam Meyer, *University of Louisiana–Lafayette*
Laurel Bond Mitchell, *University of Redlands*
Richard A. Moellenberndt, *Washburn University*
Dennis P. Moore, *Worcester State College*
Tommy Moores, *University of Nevada –Las Vegas*
Ron O'Brien, *Fayetteville Tech Community College*
George Pate, *Robeson Community College*
Keith Patterson, *Brigham Young University –Idaho*
Susanna Pendergast, *Western Illinois University*
Jan Pitera, *Broome Community College*
John Plouffe, *California State University –Los Angeles*
Alan Ransom, *Cypress College*
Laura Rickett, *Kent State University*
John A. Rude, *Bloomsburg University of PA*
Amy Santos, *Manatee Community College –Bradenton*
Dick Schroeder, *University of North Carolina –Charlotte*
Ann E. Selk, *University of Wisconsin –Green Bay*
Seleshi Sisaye, *Duquesne University*
Rodney Smith, *California State University –Long Beach*
Nancy L. Snow, *University of Toledo*
Victor Stanton, *University of California –Berkeley*
Gracelyn Stuart, *Palm Beach Community College*
John J. Surdick, *Xavier University*
G. A. Swanson, *Tennessee Tech University*
Aida Sy, *University of Bridgeport*
Christine Tan, *Baruch College*
Steve Teeter, *Utah Valley State College*
Peter Theuri, *Northern Kentucky University*
Ada Till, *Prairie View A&M University*
Michael Tyler, *Barry University*
Joan Van Hise, *Fairfield University*
Marcia R. Veit, *University of Central Florida*
Stacy R. Wade, *Western Kentucky University*
Susan Wessels, *Meredith College*
Peter Woodlock, *Youngstown State University*
Gregg S. Woodruff, *Western Illinois University*
Christian Wurst, *Temple University –Philadelphia*
Thomas M. Young, *Tomball College*
Benny Zachry, *Nicholls State University*
Lin Zheng, *Georgia College and State University*
Robert Zwicker, *Pace University*

ACKNOWLEDGMENTS

Many talented people contributed to the creation of this second edition, and we would like to thank them for their valuable contributions. Ilene Persoff of Long Island University/C. W. Post Campus did a wonderful job accuracy checking our second edition manuscript. Mark McCarthy of East Carolina University contributed a helpful accuracy check of the page proofs; we thank him for his speedy and insightful comments. Carol Yacht and Jack Terry contributed the QuickBooks templates and Excel templates (respectively) that accompany the end-of-chapter material. We appreciate the very helpful Lori Cody from The Buckle, Inc., and Elizabeth Rush from American Eagle Outfitters, Inc., for helping us get permission to use their companies' annual reports in the appendices.

We appreciate the excellent Connect accuracy checking work completed by Mark McCarthy, East Carolina University; Angela Sandberg, Jacksonville State University; Janice Fergusson, University of South Carolina; and all of the staff at ANSR Source. Janice Fergusson at the University of South Carolina did an excellent job accuracy checking our Testbank. The authors also wish to thank David Bojarsky for his contributions to the Self-Quiz and Study feature in Connect.

We also appreciate the expert attention given to this project by the staff at McGraw-Hill/Irwin, especially Stewart Mattson, Editorial Director; Tim Vertovec, Publisher; Dana Woo, Senior Sponsoring Editor; Ann Torbert, Director of Development; Kathleen Klehr, Senior Marketing Manager; Daryl Horrocks, Senior Developmental Editor; Pat Frederickson, Lead Project Manager; Kerry Bowler and Ron Nelms, Media Product Managers; Laurie Entringer, Designer; and Debra Sylvester, Buyer.

ASSURANCE OF ACCURACY

Dear Colleague,

As textbook authors, and more importantly, as instructors of financial accounting, we recognize the great importance placed on accuracy—not only in the book you are now holding, but in the supplements as well. With this in mind, we have taken the following steps to ensure that *Financial Accounting* is error-free:

1. We received detailed feedback from over 330 instructor reviews, starting with first draft manuscript through the final draft submitted to the publisher. Each review contributed in significant ways to the accuracy of the content.
2. We personally class-tested the manuscript with our students before it was published.
3. Each of us wrote, reviewed, and carefully checked all of the end-of-chapter material.
4. A developmental writer went through each sentence to ensure that our language was as clear as possible.
5. Multiple accuracy checkers reviewed each chapter and its accompanying end-of-chapter material—once when the final manuscript was submitted to the publisher, and again when our final formatted pages were completed.
6. A copyeditor checked the grammar of the final manuscript.
7. A proofreader reviewed each page to ensure no errors remained.
8. Our Solutions Manual and Testbank were created by the authors and reviewed by multiple independent accuracy checkers.

Given the steps taken above, we have the utmost confidence that you and your students will have a great experience using *Financial Accounting*.

Sincerely,

David Spiceland   **Wayne Thomas**   **Don Herrmann**

Contents in Brief

Contents

CHAPTER 1

Accounting Information and Decision Making

Learning Objectives

AFTER STUDYING THIS CHAPTER, YOU SHOULD BE ABLE TO:

- **LO1** Describe the two primary functions of financial accounting.
- **LO2** Identify the three fundamental business activities that financial accounting measures.
- **LO3** Discuss how financial accounting information is communicated through financial statements.
- **LO4** Describe the role that financial accounting plays in the efficient distribution of society's resources.
- **LO5** Explain the term generally accepted accounting principles (GAAP) and describe the role of GAAP in financial accounting.
- **LO6** Identify career opportunities in accounting.

Appendix

- **LO7** Explain the nature of the conceptual framework used to develop generally accepted accounting principles.

DELL INCORPORATED: COMPUTING THE SUCCESS OF AN ENTREPRENEUR

Michael was not your average college student. Since age 12, when he started his first business venture selling stamps, he realized that if you have a good idea, work hard, and treat customers with special care, you can make money—and sometimes, a lot of money. After a series of small, successful business ventures through high school, at age 19 Michael came up with his next business idea. In 1984, with an initial investment of only $1,000, he started a company that custom-built personal computers for sale directly to customers. The company enjoyed immediate success. In 1988, the company offered for sale to the public 3,500,000 shares of stock for $8.50 per share and changed its name to **Dell Incorporated**.

By the age of 26, Michael Dell had become the youngest CEO of a company ever included on the prestigious **Fortune** 500 list. Better yet, Dell's stock enjoyed greater growth than any other stock during the 1990s. By December 31, 1999, each share had increased in value nearly 60,000%. If you had invested just $1,000 in Dell at its initial public offering in 1988, your investment would have increased to nearly $600,000 by the end of 1999!

What if instead of investing $1,000 in Dell in 1988, you had invested $1,000 in **Polaroid Corporation**, most famous for its instant-film cameras? You would have watched your $1,000 shrink to $0 by 2001, when the company declared bankruptcy.

How do investors decide where to invest their money? Thousands of stocks are available in the United States, and thousands more on stock exchanges around the world. How do investors separate the successful companies from the unsuccessful companies?

The key source of information investors use to identify successful and unsuccessful companies is financial accounting—the subject of this book. As you read through the chapters, you'll begin to understand the information that financial accounting provides to investors making business decisions. And as the contrast between Dell and Polaroid demonstrates, the payoffs for understanding (or failing to understand) the financial position of a company can be quite large.

PART A

ACCOUNTING AS A MEASUREMENT/ COMMUNICATION PROCESS

Welcome to accounting. A common misconception about this course is that it is a math class, much like college algebra, calculus, or business statistics. You will soon see that this is *not* a math class. Don't say to yourself, "I'm not good at math so I probably won't be good at accounting." Though it's true that we use numbers heavily throughout each chapter, accounting is far more than adding, subtracting, and solving for unknown variables. So, what exactly is accounting? We'll take a close look at this next.

Defining Accounting

■ **LO1**
Describe the two primary functions of financial accounting.

Accounting is "the language of business." More precisely, accounting is a system of maintaining records of a company's operations and communicating that information to decision makers. Perhaps the earliest use of such systematic recordkeeping dates back thousands of years to ancient Mesopotamia (present-day Iraq), where records were kept of delivered agricultural products. Using accounting to maintain a record of multiple transactions allowed for better exchange among individuals and aided in the development of more complex societies.[1] In this class, you'll learn how to read, interpret, and communicate using the language of business.

Today, many millions of people every day must make informed decisions about companies. While investors and creditors (lenders) are the primary users of financial accounting information, there are many others. Illustration 1–1 identifies some of those people and examples of decisions they make about the companies.

ILLUSTRATION 1–1

Decisions People Make About Companies

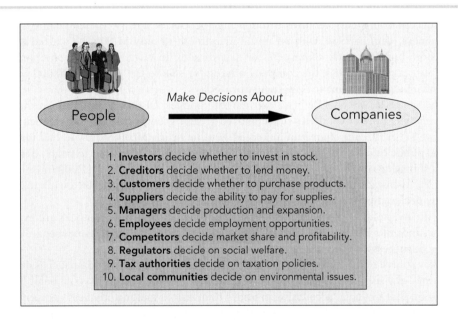

Make Decisions About

People → Companies

1. **Investors** decide whether to invest in stock.
2. **Creditors** decide whether to lend money.
3. **Customers** decide whether to purchase products.
4. **Suppliers** decide the ability to pay for supplies.
5. **Managers** decide production and expansion.
6. **Employees** decide employment opportunities.
7. **Competitors** decide market share and profitability.
8. **Regulators** decide on social welfare.
9. **Tax authorities** decide on taxation policies.
10. **Local communities** decide on environmental issues.

People and organizations need useful information in order to make good decisions. This is where accounting plays a key role. As Illustration 1–2 shows, **the functions of accounting are to *measure* the activities of the company and *communicate* those measurements to people.**

We classify accounting into two broad categories: managerial accounting and financial accounting. **Managerial accounting** deals with the methods accountants use to provide information to an organization's *internal* users—that is, its own managers. These are the subjects of another course.

---

[1]S. Basu and G. Waymire. 2006. Recordkeeping and Human Evolution. *Accounting Horizons* 20(3): 201–229.

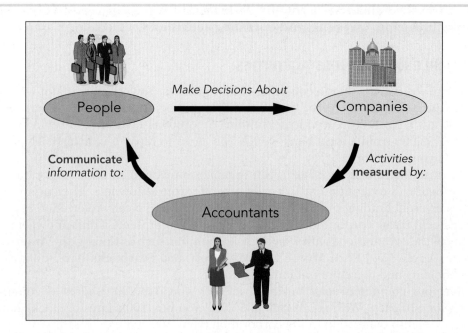

ILLUSTRATION 1–2
Functions of
Accounting

In this class, we focus on financial accounting. The two primary functions of **financial accounting** are to measure business activities of a company and to communicate those measurements to *external* parties for decision-making purposes. The two primary external users of financial accounting information (users outside the firm) are investors and creditors. **Investors** make decisions related to buying and selling the company's stock (shares of ownership): Is the company profitable? Will the company's stock increase in value? **Creditors** make decisions related to lending money to the company: Will the company be able to repay its debt when it comes due? Will it be able to pay interest in the meantime?

 KEY POINT

> The functions of financial accounting are to measure business activities of a company and to communicate information about those activities to investors and creditors and other outside users for decision-making purposes.

User's Guide For learning objectives throughout the book, you will see boxed sections, like this one, titled *Key Point*. These boxed items will highlight the central focus of the learning objectives.

Business Activities to Measure

The first of financial accounting's functions is to measure business activities. A business engages in three fundamental activities—financing, investing, and operating.

- **Financing activities** are transactions involving external sources of funding. There are two basic sources of this external funding—the owners of the company who invest their own funds in the business, and creditors who lend money to the company. With this financing, the company engages in investing activities.
- **Investing activities** include the purchase and sale of (1) long-term resources such as land, buildings, equipment, and machinery and (2) any resources not directly related to a company's normal operations. Once these investments are in place, the company has the resources needed to run the business and can perform operating activities.
- **Operating activities** include transactions that relate to the primary operations of the company, such as providing products and services to customers and the associated costs of doing so, like utilities, taxes, advertising, wages, rent, and maintenance.

■ **LO2**
Identify the three fundamental business activities that financial accounting measures.

The first role of financial accounting is to measure (or keep a record of) a company's financing, investing, and operating activities. Let's look at an example.

EXAMPLE OF BUSINESS ACTIVITIES

Suppose you want to start a computer-repair business. You estimate that it will cost approximately $10,000 to get the business up and going. However, you have only $1,000 available, so you need to get funding of $9,000 elsewhere. You begin by borrowing $2,000 from a local bank, which you agree to repay a year later. Thus, the bank is your creditor.

To raise the remaining $7,000, you organize your business as a corporation. A corporation is an entity that is legally separate from its owners. The corporation raises external funding by selling shares of ownership (typically referred to as common stock) in the corporation. Each share of stock represents a unit of ownership. Many of the corporations with which you are familiar, such as **Coca-Cola**, **American Eagle**, **Apple Inc.**, **Ford Motor Co.**, **Microsoft**, and **Starbucks** have millions of stockholders and therefore millions of owners.

For your computer-repair business, let's say you issue 800 shares of common stock for $10 each. With your original $1,000, you buy 100 shares of stock, giving you one-eighth ownership in the corporation (your 100 shares ÷ 800 shares total). Other investors purchase the remaining 700 shares, giving them seven-eighths ownership in the company.

In this example, the *financing* activities of the company are cash inflows of $2,000 from creditors and $8,000 from investors.

Creditors (local bank)	$ 2,000	} Financing
Investors (you and others)	8,000	
	$10,000	

With this financing of $10,000, your company purchases a truck costing $6,000 and equipment costing $3,000. With these resources in place, you are ready to begin operations. You start by purchasing advertising in the local newspaper for $200 and paying for the first month's office rent of $800.

You've now engaged in the second and third types of business activities: Your *investing* activities include the purchase of the truck and equipment; they involve the purchase of long-term resources. Advertising and office rent are examples of *operating* activities; they are more directly related to normal operations.

Truck	$ 6,000	} Investing
Equipment	3,000	
Advertising	200	} Operating
Office rent	800	
	$10,000	

HOW TO MEASURE BUSINESS ACTIVITIES

How should accountants measure these business activities? In other words, what information would a company's investors and creditors be interested in knowing to make informed decisions about your computer-repair business? **Ultimately, investors and creditors want to know about the company's resources and their claims to those resources.** Accounting uses some conventional categories to describe such resources and claims.

Assets, liabilities, and stockholders' equity. We measure resources owned by a company as **assets**. Recall that with the start-up funds of $10,000, your computer-repair business bought a truck ($6,000) and equipment ($3,000). You will measure the $9,000 as assets. Other assets typical of most businesses include such items as cash, inventories, supplies, and buildings. Cash is a resource used to make purchases; inventories represent resources used to make product sales to customers; supplies include resources used to perform basic business functions; and buildings are resources used by employees as a location from which to operate a company.

As discussed earlier, two parties claim the resources of the company—creditors and investors. Amounts owed to creditors are **liabilities**. The computer-repair business has a liability of $2,000 to a local bank. Other examples of liabilities are amounts owed to suppliers, workers, utility companies, and governments (in the form of taxes). Liabilities must be paid by a specified date.

Investors, or owners, claim any resources of the company not owed to creditors. You can see this relationship in home ownership: Your house (an asset) is worth $300,000. The bank that helped finance its purchase holds a $200,000 mortgage (a liability). Your *equity* in the house is $100,000. For a corporation, we refer to owners' claims to resources as **stockholders' equity**, since stockholders are the owners of the corporation.

We express the relationship among the three measurement categories in what is called the basic **accounting equation**, depicted in Illustration 1–3. It shows that a company's resources equal creditors' and owners' claims to those resources.

User's Guide Pay close attention to the accounting categories we define here. These may be new terms for you. We promise that very soon they will be second nature to you.

$$\underbrace{Assets}_{(resources)} = \underbrace{\underset{(creditors'\ claims)}{Liabilities} + \underset{(owners'\ claims)}{Stockholders'\ Equity}}_{(claims\ to\ resources)}$$

ILLUSTRATION 1–3
The Basic Accounting Equation

Another way to think about this relationship is to replace the parenthetical descriptions under each of the three parts of the equation:

$$\underset{(company\ owns)}{Assets} = \underset{(company\ owes)}{Liabilities} + \underset{(difference)}{Stockholders'\ Equity}$$

Also, as with any equation, we can move the components (by following mathematical rules you learned in high school). For example, to isolate stockholders' equity, we can subtract liabilities from both sides of the equal sign.

$$\underset{(company\ owns)}{Assets} - \underset{(company\ owes)}{Liabilities} = \underset{(difference)}{Stockholders'\ Equity}$$

Thus, the computer-repair business has assets of $9,000 but liabilities of $2,000. How much equity do stockholders have? They have $9,000 − $2,000, or $7,000.

The accounting equation illustrates a fundamental model of business valuation. The value of a company to its owners equals total resources of the company minus amounts owed to creditors. Creditors expect to receive only resources equal to the amount owed them. Stockholders, on the other hand, can claim all resources in excess of the amount owed to creditors.

Revenues, expenses, and dividends.   Of course, all businesses intend to increase the amount of their resources through their operations and eventually to own more than they owe. We broadly define such increases as profits. (Later, we'll define profits a bit more narrowly.) Because stockholders claim all resources in excess of amounts owed to creditors, profits of the company, which add to total resources, are claimed solely by stockholders, the owners of the company.

We calculate a company's profits by comparing its revenues and expenses. Revenues are the amounts earned from selling products or services to customers. For example, when your computer-repair business provides services to a customer, it earns revenues. When **McDonald's** sells you a burger, fries, and drink, McDonald's earns revenue.

However, as you've probably heard, "It takes money to make money." To operate your computer-repair business, for example, you purchased advertising ($200) and paid the first month's rent ($800). We record these amounts as expenses. Expenses are the costs of providing products and services. You'll record expenses of $1,000 for your computer-repair business.

When McDonald's sells you a Big Mac, it incurs expenses for two all-beef patties, special sauce, lettuce, cheese, pickles, onions, and a sesame-seed bun. McDonald's also pays the person who took your order, the cook behind the partition, and the person who cleans up after you're gone. Then there's the cost of having and maintaining the building, TV ads, expenses of the corporate headquarters, utilities, equipment maintenance, income taxes, interest on debt, and many, many more.

We measure the difference between revenues and expenses as net income. All businesses want revenues to be greater than expenses, producing a positive net income. However, if expenses exceed revenues, as happens from time to time, the difference between them is a negative amount—a **net loss**. You'll notice the use of the term *net* to describe a company's profitability. In business, the term *net* is used often to describe the difference between two amounts. Here, we measure revenues *net* of (or minus) expenses to calculate the net income or net loss.

Common Terms Other common names for net income include *earnings* and *profit*.

Illustration 1–4 reports McDonald's revenues, expenses, and net income from its operations around the world.

ILLUSTRATION 1–4

Revenue and Expenses for McDonald's Corporation, as of 2009

($ in millions)	Revenues	−	Expenses	=	Net Income
United States	$7,943.8	−	$4,712.1	=	$3,231.7
Europe	9,273.8	−	6,685.7	=	2,588.1
Asia/Pacific, Middle East, Africa	4,337.0	−	3,347.5	=	989.5

Notice that McDonald's generates only about one-third of its revenues in the United States, but almost half its net income comes from the United States. This means that McDonald's is able to make more profit per dollar of revenue in the United States than anywhere else in the world.

If the corporation has positive net income, it typically will distribute to its owners, the stockholders, some of those profits. It does so by making cash payments to its stockholders (usually every three months), in payments called dividends. McDonald's, for example, has paid a dividend to stockholders every three months for over 30 years. In 2009, McDonald's paid dividends of $2.05 per share. If you owned 100 shares of McDonald's stock, you would have received $205.00 from McDonald's in cash. Unlike creditors, who lend money to the company in expectation of being repaid, stockholders are not guaranteed regular cash payments from the firm.

Match the term with the appropriate definition.

1. __F__ Assets
2. __C__ Liabilities
3. __E__ Stockholders' equity
4. __D__ Dividends
5. __B__ Revenues
6. __A__ Expenses

A. Costs of selling products or services.
B. Amounts earned from sales of products or services.
C. Amounts owed.
D. Distributions to stockholders.
E. Owners' claims to resources.
F. Resources owned.

Solution:

1. F; 2. C; 3. E; 4. D; 5. B; 6. A

Let's Review

User's Guide Let's Review exercises break each chapter into manageable review modules to enhance your learning.

Suggested Homework:
BE1-4;
E1-2, E1-3;
P1-2A&B

In summary, the measurement role of accounting is to create a record of the financing, investing, and operating activities of the company. To make this possible, the firm must maintain an accurate record of its assets, liabilities, stockholders' equity, revenues, expenses, and dividends. Be sure you understand the meaning of these items. We will refer to them throughout this book. Illustration 1–5 summarizes the business activities and the categories that measure them.

	Activities Related to:	Measurement Category
Financing Activities	• Borrowing • Stockholders' investment • Distributions to stockholders	• Liabilities • Stockholders' equity • Dividends
Investing Activities	• Resources owned by the company	• Assets
Operating Activities	• Sales to customers • Costs of selling to customers	• Revenues • Expenses

ILLUSTRATION 1–5

Business Activities and Their Measurement

KEY POINT

Financing activities include transactions with creditors and owners. Investing activities generally include the purchase or disposal of productive assets. Operating activities relate to earning revenues and incurring expenses.

As you learn to measure business activities, you will often find it helpful to consider both sides of the transaction: When someone pays cash, someone else receives cash; when someone borrows money, another lends money. Likewise, an expense for one company can be a revenue for another company; one company's asset can be another company's liability. Throughout this book, you will find discussions of the "flip side" of certain transactions, indicated by the icon you see here in the margin. In addition, certain homework problems, also marked by the icon, will ask you specifically to address the "flip side" in your computations. (See page 39 for the first such example.)

Flip Side

FORMS OF BUSINESS ORGANIZATION

The computer-repair business introduced earlier was organized as a corporation. Other common business forms include sole proprietorships and partnerships. A **sole proprietorship** is a business owned by one person, whereas a **partnership** is a business owned by two or more persons. If you had decided to start the

computer-repair business without outside investors, you could have formed a sole proprietorship. Or, you and a friend could have formed a partnership.

To decide on a form of business organization, you need to understand their advantages and disadvantages. The major *advantage* of the corporate form of business is the limited liability of the corporation's stockholders. **Limited liability** means the stockholders are not held personally responsible for the financial obligations of the corporation. If the business fails, stockholders can lose no more than the investment they already made by purchasing stock. In other words, stockholders are not obligated to pay the corporation's remaining debts out of their own pockets. In contrast, if a sole proprietorship or partnership is unable to pay its legal obligations to creditors, the owner(s) may be forced to surrender personal assets, such as homes, cars, computers, and furniture to satisfy those debts.

The *disadvantage* of the corporate form of business is the higher tax burden on the owners. Generally, the corporate income tax rate is greater than the individual income tax rate. Moreover, a corporation's income is taxed twice—first when the company earns it and pays corporate income taxes on it, and then again when stockholders pay personal income taxes on amounts the firm distributes to them as dividends. This is called *double taxation*. Any income of a sole proprietorship or a partnership is taxed only once, and at the personal income tax rate.

Because most of the largest companies in the United States are corporations, in this book we will primarily focus on accounting from a corporation's perspective. Focusing on corporations also highlights the importance of financial accounting—to measure and communicate activities of a company when owners (shareholders) are typically separated from management of the company. (A more detailed discussion of the advantages and disadvantages of a corporation can be found in Chapter 10.)

Communicating through Financial Statements

■ LO3
Discuss how financial accounting information is communicated through financial statements.

We've discussed that different business activities produce assets, liabilities, stockholders' equity, dividends, revenues, and expenses, and that the first important role of financial accounting is to record the relevant transactions of a company. Its second vital role is to communicate these business activities to those outside the company. The primary means of communicating business activities is through financial statements. Financial statements are periodic reports published by the company for the purpose of providing information to external users. We have four primary financial statements:

1. Income statement
2. Statement of stockholders' equity
3. Balance sheet
4. Statement of cash flows

These financial statements give investors and creditors the key information they need when making decisions about a company: Should I buy the company's stock? Should I lend money to the company? Is management efficiently operating the company? Without these financial statements, it would be difficult for those outside the company to see what's going on inside.

Let's go through a simple set of financial statements to see what they look like. We'll start with the income statement of a simple, fictitious company. Actual companies' financial statements often report items you haven't yet encountered. However, because actual companies' financial information will be useful in helping you understand certain accounting topics, we'll sample them often throughout the book.

THE INCOME STATEMENT

The income statement is a financial statement that reports the company's revenues and expenses over an interval of time. It shows whether the company was able to generate enough revenue to cover the expenses of running the business. If revenues exceed expenses, then the company reports *net income:*

Revenues − Expenses = Net income

If expenses exceed revenues, then the company reports a *net loss.*

Now, let's look at our fictitious company. On January 1 Eagle Golf Academy begins operations by offering lessons to junior golfers. The lessons include a variety of skills intended to develop players for a top university golf program and perhaps even one day playing on the PGA Tour. For the first month of operations, Eagle Golf Academy reports its income statement as shown in Illustration 1–6.

Common Terms Other common names for the income statement include *statement of operations* and *statement of income.*

EAGLE GOLF ACADEMY Income Statement For the month ended January 31	
Revenues:	
Service revenue	$6,360
Expenses:	
Salaries expense	3,100
Rent expense	500
Supplies expense	800
Interest expense	100
Utilities expense	960
Other expenses	400
Total expenses	5,860
Net income	$ 500

ILLUSTRATION 1–6

Income Statement for Eagle Golf Academy

Notice the heading of the income statement: It includes the company's name, the title of the financial statement, and the time period covered by the financial statement. The three major captions in the income statement include **revenues** and **expenses,** discussed earlier, and the difference between them—**net income.**

We can determine from the income statement that for the month of January Eagle Golf Academy earns revenues of **$6,360.** This means that Eagle provides golf training and bills customers for a total of $6,360. Total expenses associated with generating those revenues, including salaries, rent, supplies, and other items listed here, are **$5,860.** These are typical costs that we might expect of any company. The income statement shows that revenues *exceed* expenses ($6,360 is greater than $5,860), and thus the academy is able to report net income of **$500.**

The fact that Eagle reports a positive net income is, in some sense, a signal of the company's success. The company is able to charge its customers a price higher than the costs of running the business. Do you assume most companies sell their products and services for a profit? It's not as easy as you might think. In recent years, **American Airlines, OfficeMax, Eastman Kodak, Ford Motor Co., Goodyear Tire and Rubber, ConocoPhillips, CBS, U.S. Cellular, Gateway, Sirius Satellite Radio, Sprint PCS, Blockbuster**, and hundreds of others have reported net losses.

KEY POINT

The income statement compares revenues and expenses for the current period to assess the company's ability to earn a profit from running its operations.

Decision Point

User's Guide Decision Points in each chapter highlight specific decisions related to chapter topics that can be made using financial accounting information.

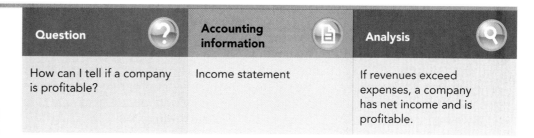

Question	Accounting information	Analysis
How can I tell if a company is profitable?	Income statement	If revenues exceed expenses, a company has net income and is profitable.

THE STATEMENT OF STOCKHOLDERS' EQUITY

The statement of stockholders' equity is a financial statement that summarizes the changes in stockholders' equity over an interval of time. The reporting period coincides with the time period covered by the income statement.

Stockholders' equity has two primary components—common stock and retained earnings. Recall that common stock represents amounts invested by stockholders (the owners of the corporation) when they purchase shares of stock. Common stock is an *external* source of stockholders' equity.

Retained earnings, on the other hand, is an *internal* source of stockholders' equity. **Retained earnings** represents the cumulative amount of net income, earned over the life of the company, that has *not* been distributed to stockholders as dividends. Since all profits of the company are owned by stockholders, any net income in excess of dividends paid to stockholders represents stockholders' equity retained in the business. Thus, both common stock and retained earnings make up total stockholders' equity. This concept is shown in Illustration 1–7.

Common Terms Another common name for retained earnings is *profits reinvested in the business.*

ILLUSTRATION 1–7

Components of Stockholders' Equity

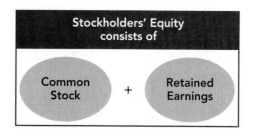

Suppose Eagle obtains financing in January by issuing common stock for $25,000. This transaction will distribute shares of common stock to investors in return for the company's receiving cash of $25,000. Let's say that at the end of January, Eagle pays dividends of $200 to stockholders. Illustration 1–8 (next page) shows the statement of stockholders' equity for Eagle Golf Academy.

When the company begins operations on January 1, the balances of common stock and retained earnings are **$0**. Once the company issues common stock, its balance increases to **$25,000**. The balance of retained earnings always increases by the amount of net income less any dividends paid to stockholders—here, $500 − $200 = $300. **The name *retained earnings* is descriptive. The balance of retained earnings represents the amount of "earnings retained" (not paid out in the form of dividends) over the life of the company.**

You will notice that some financial statements have parentheses around some amounts. As you will learn as you study this book, accounting convention uses parentheses to highlight negative amounts (such as the subtraction of dividends here) or to show cash outflows (which we will point out later).

EAGLE GOLF ACADEMY Statement of Stockholders' Equity For the month ended January 31			
	Common Stock	Retained Earnings	Total Stockholders' Equity
Beginning balance (Jan. 1)	$ -0-	$ -0-	$ -0-
Issuance of common stock	25,000		25,000
Add: Net income for January		500	500
Less: Dividends		(200)	(200)
Ending balance (Jan. 31)	$25,000	$ 300	$25,300

ILLUSTRATION 1–8

Statement of Stockholders' Equity for Eagle Golf Academy

Retained earnings includes net income less dividends. Note that the items shown here in blue come from the income statement.

COMMON MISTAKE

Dividends represent the payment of cash but are not considered an expense in running the business. Students sometimes mistakenly include the amount of dividends as an expense in the income statement, rather than as a distribution of net income in the statement of stockholders' equity.

User's Guide Throughout each chapter, you will see sections titled *Common Mistake*. Information in these boxes will help you avoid common mistakes on exams, quizzes, and homework.

By adding common stock and the retained earnings of $300, we calculate the balance of total stockholders' equity at January 31 to be **$25,300**. In accounting terms, this amount represents the value of the firm to its owners, the stockholders. The company creates value *externally* through investment by owners (common stock) and *internally* by generating and retaining profits (retained earnings).

KEY POINT

The statement of stockholders' equity reports information related to changes in common stock and retained earnings each period. The change in retained earnings equals net income less dividends for the period.

Decision Point

Question		Accounting information		Analysis	
Was the change in company value (stockholders' equity) the result of external or internal sources?		Statement of stockholders' equity		When a company sells common stock, company value increases due to external sources (stockholders). When a company has profits during the year in excess of dividends paid, company value increases due to internal sources (company operations).	

THE BALANCE SHEET

The balance sheet is a financial statement that presents the financial position of the company on a particular date. The financial position of a company is summarized by the basic accounting equation (see Illustration 1–3): **Assets = Liabilities + Stockholders' Equity.** As discussed earlier, this equation provides a fundamental

model of business valuation. Assets are the resources owned by the company, and liabilities are amounts owed to creditors. Stockholders have equity in the company to the extent that assets exceed liabilities. Creditors also need to understand the balance sheet; it's the company's assets that will be used to pay liabilities (the amounts due creditors) as they become due.

Illustration 1–9 shows the balance sheet of Eagle Golf Academy. The first thing to notice is the time period included in the heading. Recall that the income statement and statement of stockholders' equity both show activity over an *interval of time*. The balance sheet, in contrast, reports assets, liabilities, and stockholders' equity at a *point in time*. For example, Eagle's income statement shows revenue and expense activity occurring *from* January 1 to January 31; its balance sheet shows assets, liabilities, and stockholders' equity of the company *on* January 31.

The income statement is like a video (shows events over time), whereas a balance sheet is like a photograph (shows events at a point in time).

ILLUSTRATION 1–9

Balance Sheet for Eagle Golf Academy

Total assets must equal total liabilities and stockholders' equity.

We show the stockholders' equity items in purple here, to indicate they came from the statement of stockholders' equity (Illustration 1–8).

EAGLE GOLF ACADEMY
Balance Sheet
January 31

Assets		Liabilities	
Cash	$ 6,200	Accounts payable	$ 2,300
Accounts receivable	2,700	Salaries payable	300
Supplies	1,500	Interest payable	100
Equipment, net	23,600	Utilities payable	960
Other assets	5,500	Notes payable	10,000
		Other liabilities	540
		Total liabilities	14,200
		Stockholders' Equity	
		Common stock	25,000
		Retained earnings	300
		Total stockholders' equity	25,300
Total assets	$39,500	Total liabilities and stockholders' equity	$39,500

Common Terms
Another common name for the balance sheet is *statement of financial position*.

For Eagle Golf Academy on January 31, total assets equal $39,500 and include some of the typical resources owned by most businesses, such as cash, supplies, and equipment. You'll learn about many other assets as you go through this book. Total liabilities equal $14,200 and include amounts owed to regular vendors (accounts payable), as well as amounts owed for other items such as employee salaries, interest, and utilities. As you'll begin to learn, many liabilities are referred to as "payables" to signify amounts that must be paid.

The difference between assets and liabilities of **$25,300** represents stockholders' equity. Total stockholders' equity includes the amount of common stock plus the amount of retained earnings from the statement of stockholders' equity. Notice that the amounts listed in the balance sheet show that the accounting equation balances:

Assets	=	Liabilities	+	Stockholders' Equity
(resources)		(creditors' claims)		(owners' claims)
$39,500	=	$14,200	+	$25,300

KEY POINT

The balance sheet demonstrates that the company's resources (assets) equal creditors' claims (liabilities) plus owners' claims (stockholders' equity) to those resources.

Decision Point

Question ❓	Accounting information 📄	Analysis 🔍
What are creditors' claims and owners' claims to the company's resources?	Balance sheet	The amount of total liabilities equals creditors' claims to the company's resources. The extent to which total assets exceed total liabilities represents owners' claims.

THE STATEMENT OF CASH FLOWS

The **statement of cash flows** is a financial statement that measures activities involving cash receipts and cash payments over an interval of time. We can classify all cash transactions into three categories that correspond to the three fundamental business activities—operating, investing, and financing—we discussed earlier in the chapter:

- **Operating cash flows** include cash receipts and cash payments for transactions involving revenues and expenses.
- **Investing cash flows** generally include cash transactions for the purchase and sale of investments and productive long-term assets. Long-term assets are resources owned by a company that are thought to provide benefits for more than one year.
- **Financing cash flows** include cash transactions with lenders, such as borrowing money and repaying debt, and with stockholders, such as issuing stock and paying dividends.

Decision Maker's Perspective

User's Guide Decision Maker's Perspective sections discuss the usefulness of accounting information to decision makers such as investors, creditors, and company managers.

The statement of cash flows can be an important source of information to investors and creditors. For example, investors use the relationship between net income (revenues minus expenses) and operating cash flows (cash flows from revenue and expense activities) to forecast a company's future profitability. Creditors compare operating cash flows and investing cash flows to assess a company's ability to repay debt. Financing activities provide information to investors and creditors about the mix of external financing of the company. ●

Illustration 1–10 (next page) provides the statement of cash flows for Eagle Golf Academy. Notice that the three sections in the statement of cash flows show the types of inflows and outflows of cash during the period. Inflows are shown as positive amounts; outflows are shown in parentheses to indicate negative cash flows. The final line in each section shows, in the right-most column, the difference between inflows and outflows as *net cash flow* for that type of activity.

KEY POINT

The statement of cash flows reports cash transactions from operating, investing, and financing activities.

ILLUSTRATION 1–10

Statement of Cash Flows for Eagle Golf Academy

Remember, amounts in parentheses indicate outflows of cash, consistent with accounting convention.

EAGLE GOLF ACADEMY Statement of Cash Flows For the month ended January 31		
Cash Flows from Operating Activities		
Cash inflows:		
From customers	$ 4,200	
Cash outflows:		
For salaries	(2,800)	
For rent	(6,000)	
Net cash flows from operating activities		($4,600)
Cash Flows from Investing Activities		
Purchase equipment	(24,000)	
Net cash flows from investing activities		(24,000)
Cash Flows from Financing Activities		
Issue common stock	25,000	
Borrow from bank	10,000	
Pay dividends	(200)	
Net cash flows from financing activities		34,800
Net increase in cash		6,200
Cash at the beginning of the month		-0-
Cash at the end of the month		$6,200

The total of the net cash flows from operating, investing, and financing activities equals the *net change in cash* during the period. For Eagle, that net change in cash for January was an increase of **$6,200**. To this change, we add the beginning balance of cash. Because this is the first month of operations for Eagle, cash at the beginning of the month is zero. Thus, the ending balance of cash is the same as that reported in the balance sheet in Illustration 1–9. This reconciliation of the beginning and ending cash balances emphasizes that the statement of cash flows explains *why* the cash reported in the balance sheet changed.

THE LINKS AMONG FINANCIAL STATEMENTS

The four financial statements are linked, because events that are reported in one financial statement often affect amounts reported in another. Many times, a single business transaction, such as receiving cash from a customer when providing services, will affect more than one of the financial statements. Providing services to a customer, for example, results in revenues recorded in the income statement, which are used to calculate net income. Net income, in turn, is reported in the calculation of retained earnings in the statement of stockholders' equity. Then, the ending balance of retained earnings is reported in the balance sheet. **Thus, any transaction that affects the income statement ultimately affects the balance sheet through the balance of retained earnings.** The cash received from customers will be reported as part of the ending cash balance in the balance sheet and as part of operating cash flows in the statement of cash flows.

Illustration 1–11 shows the links among the financial statements of Eagle Golf Academy in Illustrations 1–6, 1–8, 1–9, and 1–10. Link (1) shows that net income from the income statement is reported in the statement of stockholders' equity as part of the calculation of retained earnings. Link (2) shows that after we calculate the balance of retained earnings, the amount of total stockholders' equity can be reported in the balance sheet. Finally, link (3) demonstrates that the balance of cash in the balance sheet equals the amount of cash reported in the statement of cash flows.

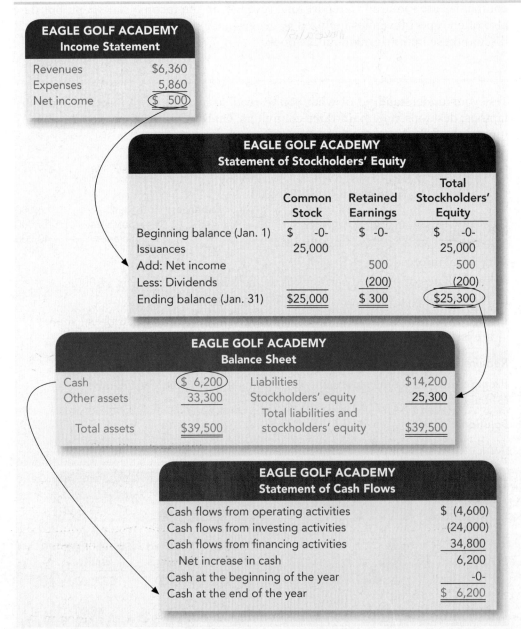

ILLUSTRATION 1–11

Relationship between Financial Statements

[1] Notice that the amount of net income on the income statement reappears in the statement of stockholders' equity.

[2] Notice that the ending balance in the statement of stockholders' equity reappears in the balance sheet.

[3] Notice that the amount of cash in the balance sheet reappears as the ending cash balance in the statement of cash flows.

KEY POINT

All transactions that affect revenues or expenses reported in the income statement ultimately affect the balance sheet through the balance in retained earnings.

OTHER INFORMATION REPORTED TO OUTSIDERS

Financial statements provide a summary of the most important financial accounting information. Two other sources of information provide important detail: (1) management's discussion and analysis and (2) note disclosures to the financial statements. Publicly traded firms are required to report both of these items in their annual reports, along with the financial statements we've discussed.

The **management discussion and analysis** (MD&A) section typically includes management's views on significant events, trends, and uncertainties pertaining to the company's operations and resources. **Note disclosures** offer additional information either to explain the information presented in the financial statements or to provide information not included in the financial statements. For example,

companies are required to report total revenues in the income statement, but they also often report revenues itemized by geographic region in a note disclosure. We'll discuss these items throughout the book.

Let's Review

Test your understanding of what you've read so far. The Computer Shop repairs laptops, desktops, and mainframe computers. On December 31, 2012, the company reports the following year-end amounts:

Assets:	Cash	$10,000	Revenues:	Service	$65,000
	Supplies	8,000			
	Equipment, net	26,000			
			Expenses:	Rent	6,000
Liabilities:	Accounts payable	4,000		Supplies	14,000
	Notes payable	10,000		Salaries	40,000

Additional information:

a. The balance of retained earnings at the beginning of the year is $7,000.

b. The company pays dividends of $1,000 on December 31, 2012.

c. Common stock is $15,000 at the beginning of the year, and additional shares are issued for $4,000 during 2012.

Suggested Homework:
BE1-5, BE1-6;
E1-6, E1-7, E1-8;
P1-3A&B, P1-5A&B

Required:

Prepare the (1) income statement, (2) statement of stockholders' equity, and (3) balance sheet.

Solution:

1. Income statement:

THE COMPUTER SHOP
Income Statement
For the year ended Dec. 31, 2012

Revenues:	
Service revenue	$65,000
Expenses:	
Rent expense	6,000
Supplies expense	14,000
Salaries expense	40,000
Net income	$ 5,000

2. Statement of stockholders' equity:

THE COMPUTER SHOP
Statement of Stockholders' Equity
For the year ended Dec. 31, 2012

	Common Stock	Retained Earnings	Total Stockholders' Equity
Beginning balance (Jan. 1)	$15,000	$ 7,000	$22,000
Issuance of common stock	4,000		4,000
Add: Net income		5,000	5,000
Less: Dividends		(1,000)	(1,000)
Ending balance (Dec. 31)	$19,000	$11,000	$30,000

3. Balance sheet:

THE COMPUTER SHOP
Balance Sheet
December 31, 2012

Assets		Liabilities	
Cash	$10,000	Accounts payable	$ 4,000
Supplies	8,000	Notes payable	10,000
Equipment	26,000	**Stockholders' Equity**	
		Common stock	19,000
		Retained earnings	11,000
Total assets	$44,000	Total liabilities and stockholders' equity	$44,000

FINANCIAL ACCOUNTING INFORMATION

To this point, you've had a simple, first look at how companies measure and communicate financial information to external users. Subsequent chapters will provide an even more detailed view of this measurement/communication process. However, before proceeding, it's important to first consider why we are studying financial accounting. Does it matter? In other words, does the use of financial accounting information result in better business decisions?

Is Financial Accounting Important?

One of the rewarding things about studying financial accounting is that it does matter! The concepts in this course have an impact on everyday business decisions as well as wide-ranging economic consequences. We'll see an example of this next and then more examples throughout the rest of this book.

■ **LO4**
Describe the role that financial accounting plays in the efficient distribution of society's resources.

Most prospering economies in the world today are structured around free markets. In free markets, firms are allowed to compete and customers are free to choose from a variety of products and services. From which company do you prefer to buy a notebook computer—**Dell**, **Hewlett-Packard**, or **Apple**? Competition among these companies helps determine the prices they charge customers and the amounts they spend on computer components, salaries, manufacturing and distribution facilities, warranties, research and development, and other business-related activities. Can these companies offer you the notebook computer you want for a price above their costs? If they can, they'll earn a profit and stay in business. If they cannot, they'll eventually go out of business. Because companies know they are directly competing with each other, they work harder and more efficiently to please you, the customer.

Successful companies use their resources efficiently to sell products and services for a profit. When a company is able to make a profit, investors and creditors are willing to transfer their resources to it, and the company will expand its profitable operations even further.

Unsuccessful companies either offer lower-quality products and services or do not efficiently keep their costs low. In either case, they are not profitable. When a company is unprofitable, investors will neither invest in nor lend to the firm. Without these sources of financing, eventually the company will fail. Clearly, you don't want to invest in an unsuccessful company and then watch your investment shrink as the company loses your money. But how do investors and creditors know the successful companies from the unsuccessful companies? Here's where financial accounting enters the picture. Investors and creditors rely heavily on financial accounting information in making investment and lending decisions.

As Illustration 1–12 demonstrates, investors and creditors have cash they are willing to invest. How do they decide which investment option provides the better opportunity? Most often, they analyze companies' financial accounting information in making their decision. In fact, **financial accounting information is essential to making good business decisions.**

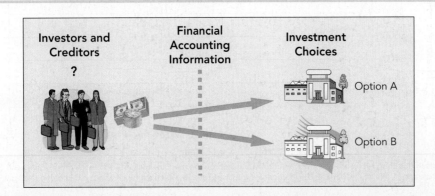

ILLUSTRATION 1–12

Use of Financial Accounting Information in Investing and Lending Decisions

KEY POINT

Financial accounting serves an important role by providing information useful in investment and lending decisions.

To demonstrate the importance of financial accounting information to investment decisions, we can look at the relationship between changes in stock prices and changes in net income over 20 years. As an investor, you will make money from an increase in the stock price of a company in which you invest (you can sell the stock for more than you bought it). So as an investor, you are looking for companies whose stock price is likely to increase. Is there a way to find such companies? Interestingly, there is: **No other single piece of company information better explains companies' stock price performance than does financial accounting net income,** the bottom line in the income statement.

What if you were able to accurately predict the direction of companies' changes in net income over the next year—that is, whether it would increase or decrease—and then you invested $1,000 in companies that were going to have an *increase?* In contrast, what if instead you invested in companies that would have a *decrease* in net income? Illustration 1–13 shows what would happen to your $1,000 investment over 20 years for each scenario.

ILLUSTRATION 1–13

Relationship between Changes in Stock Prices and Changes in Net Income over a 20-Year Period

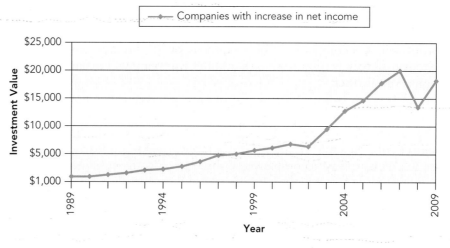

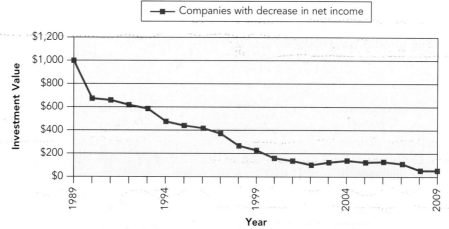

*Amounts in this chart represent the investment growth based on the median stock return of each group each year. Companies included in this analysis are all U.S. companies with listed stocks, which averages about 6,000 companies per year.

You can see that if you had invested $1,000 in companies with an increase in net income, your investment would have increased to $18,225 over the 20-year period. (The amount would have been much higher without the extraordinary events surrounding the financial crisis in 2008.) If instead you had invested $1,000 in companies with a decrease in net income, your $1,000 investment would have shrunk to $49 over this same period. This dramatic difference in the value of the investment demonstrates the importance of financial accounting information to investors. This book will provide you a thorough understanding of how net income is calculated and presented in financial statements. As you can see from the charts above, if you are able to predict the change in financial accounting's measure of profitability—net income—then you can predict the change in stock prices as well.

Investors and creditors also use information reported in the balance sheet. Consider a company's total liabilities, often referred to as *total debt*. Expanding debt levels limit management's ability to respond quickly and effectively to business situations. The "overhanging" debt, which involves legal obligation of repayment, restricts management's ability to engage in new profit-generating activities. Increased debt levels also increase interest payment burdens on the company. Failure to pay interest or to repay debt can result in creditors forcing the company to declare bankruptcy and go out of business. Understandably, then, investors and creditors keep a close eye on the company's debt level and its ability to repay.

 net income to better explains companies! stock price performance

KEY POINT

No single piece of company information better explains companies' stock price performance than does financial accounting net income. A company's debt level is an important indicator of management's ability to respond to business situations and the possibility of bankruptcy.

Rules of Financial Accounting

Recall that accounting serves two main functions in our society: It (1) measures business activities and (2) communicates those measurements to investors and creditors. Although this process might seem straightforward, it's not always. How do we measure assets? When do we record revenues? What do we classify as an expense? How should we present financial statements? These are all important issues, and the answers are not always simple.

Because financial accounting information is so vital to investors and creditors, formal reporting standards have been established. All companies that sell their stock to the public must follow these rules and must publish financial statements in accordance with those rules. The rules of financial accounting are called **generally accepted accounting principles**, often abbreviated as **GAAP** (pronounced *gap*). The fact that all companies use these same rules is critical to financial statement users. It allows them to accurately *compare* financial information among companies when they are making decisions about where to lend or invest their resources.

> ■ **LO5**
> Explain the term generally accepted accounting principles (GAAP) and describe the role of GAAP in financial accounting.

CURRENT STANDARD SETTING

Today, financial accounting and reporting standards in the United States are established primarily by the **Financial Accounting Standards Board** (**FASB**) (pronounced either by the letters themselves or as *faz-be*). The FASB is an independent, private-sector body with full-time voting members and a very large support staff. Members include representatives from the accounting profession, large corporations, financial analysts, accounting educators, and government agencies.

Not all countries follow the same accounting and reporting standards. For example, accounting practices in the United Kingdom differ from those in the United States, and those in the United States differ from those in Japan. In recent years,

> For information about the activities of the Financial Accounting Standards Board, see its website, *www.fasb.org*.

the accounting profession has undertaken a project whose goal is to eliminate differences in accounting standards around the world. The standard-setting body responsible for this convergence effort is the International Accounting Standards Board (IASB), as detailed in the following box.

INTERNATIONAL FINANCIAL REPORTING STANDARDS (IFRS)

The global counterpart to the FASB is the International Accounting Standards Board (IASB). In many ways, this organization functions like the FASB. The IASB's objectives are (1) to develop a single set of high-quality, understandable global accounting standards, (2) to promote the use of those standards, and (3) to bring about the convergence of national accounting standards and international accounting standards around the world. In 2002, the FASB and IASB signed the Norwalk Agreement, formalizing their commitment to convergence of U.S. and international accounting standards. The standards being developed and promoted by the IASB are called **International Financial Reporting Standards** (IFRS) (pronounced either by the letters or as *eye-furs*).

For more discussion, see Appendix E.

User's Guide Boxed sections on *International Financial Reporting Standards* (IFRS) are included throughout the text to emphasize the growing importance of international accounting standards throughout the world. They discuss specific instances in which U.S. GAAP and international standards differ. Appendix E at the back of the book provides more detail about differences between IFRS and U.S. GAAP.

For information about the activities of the International Accounting Standards Board, see its website, *www.iasb.org*.

More than 100 countries have chosen to forgo their own country-specific standards and either require or allow International Financial Reporting Standards as their national standards. That movement, coupled with the convergence of U.S. GAAP and IFRS, has caused many to predict that soon both sets of rules, or perhaps only IFRS, will be acceptable for financial reporting in the United States.

KEY POINT

The rules of financial accounting are called generally accepted accounting principles (GAAP). The Financial Accounting Standards Board (FASB) is an independent, private body that has primary responsibility for the establishment of GAAP in the United States.

HISTORICAL PERSPECTIVE ON STANDARD SETTING

Pressures on the accounting profession to establish uniform accounting standards began to surface after the stock market crash of 1929. The Dow Jones Industrial Average, a major stock market index in the United States, fell 40% over the period September 3 to October 29 that year. The Dow bottomed out in July 1932, after losing 89% of its value.

Many blamed financial accounting for the stock market crash and the ensuing Great Depression of the 1930s. At the time of the crash, accounting practices and reporting procedures were not well established, providing the opportunity for companies to engage in inaccurate financial reporting to enhance their reported performance. This led to many stocks being valued too highly. As investors began to recognize this, their confidence in the stock market fell. They panicked and sold stocks in a frenzy. The Dow did not reach precrash levels again until 1954.

The 1933 Securities Act and the 1934 Securities Exchange Act were designed to restore investor confidence in financial accounting. The 1933 act sets forth accounting and disclosure requirements for initial offerings of securities (stocks and bonds). The 1934 act created a government agency, the **Securities and Exchange Commission (SEC).** The 1934 act gives the SEC the power to require companies that publicly trade their stock to prepare periodic financial statements for distribution to investors and creditors.

While Congress has given the SEC both the power and the responsibility for setting accounting and reporting standards for publicly traded companies, the SEC has delegated the primary responsibility for setting accounting standards to the private sector, currently the FASB. Note that the SEC delegated only the responsibility, not the authority, to set these standards. The power still lies with the SEC. If the SEC does not agree with a particular standard issued by the FASB, it can force a change in the standard. In fact, it has done so in the past.

THE ROLE OF THE AUDITOR

It is the responsibility of management to apply GAAP when communicating with investors and creditors through financial statements. Unfortunately, however, sometimes those in charge of preparing financial statements do not always follow the rules. Instead, some purposely provide misleading financial accounting information, commonly referred to as "cooking the books." The phrase implies that the accounting records ("books") have been presented in an altered form ("cooked"). Managers may cook the books for several reasons, such as to hide the poor operating performance of the company or to increase their personal wealth at stockholders' expense.

To help ensure that management has in fact appropriately applied GAAP, the SEC requires independent outside verification of the financial statements of publicly traded companies. Such independent examination is done by auditors, who are hired by a company as an independent party to express a professional opinion of the accuracy of that company's financial statements. They are not employees of the company they are auditing. Auditors provide an independent opinion of the extent to which financial statements are prepared in compliance with GAAP. If they find mistakes or fraudulent reporting behavior, auditors require the company to correct all significant information before issuing financial statements.

Illustration 1–14 presents an excerpt from the report of the independent auditors for **Dell**'s financial statements. The auditor's report indicates that Dell's financial statements for the period mentioned have been prepared in conformity with GAAP.

DELL INCORPORATED
Report of Independent Registered Public Accounting Firm

To the Board of Directors and
Shareholders of Dell Inc.:

In our opinion, the consolidated financial statements listed in the accompanying index present fairly, in all material respects, the financial position of Dell Inc. and its subsidiaries at January 29, 2010, and January 30, 2009, and the results of their operations and their cash flows for each of the three years in the period ended January 29, 2010, in conformity with accounting principles generally accepted in the United States of America.

   Our audits of financial statements included examining, on a test basis, evidence supporting the amounts and disclosures in the financial statements, assessing the accounting principles used and significant estimates made by management, and evaluating the overall financial statement presentation. We believe that our audits provide a reasonable basis for our opinion.

ILLUSTRATION 1–14

Excerpts from the 2009 Independent Auditor's Report of Dell Incorporated

User's Guide In this book, information from actual companies is illustrated using a flipped page in the lower-right corner.

Auditors play a major role in investors' and creditors' decisions by adding credibility to a company's financial statements.

OBJECTIVES OF FINANCIAL ACCOUNTING

After measuring business activities and communicating those measurements to investors and creditors, what do financial accountants hope to have achieved? What

benefit will their services have brought to users of financial statements? The FASB has explicitly stated the specific objectives of financial accounting. These objectives are presented in Illustration 1–15.

ILLUSTRATION 1–15 Objectives of Financial Accounting	**Financial accounting should provide information that:** 1. Is useful to investors and creditors in making decisions. 2. Helps to predict cash flows. 3. Tells about economic resources, claims to resources, and changes in resources and claims.

The first objective is specific to investors and creditors. In addition to those users, though, financial accounting information is likely to have general usefulness to other groups of external users, who are interested in essentially the same financial aspects of a business as are investors and creditors. Some of these other groups were discussed in Illustration 1–1.

The second objective refers to the specific cash flow information needs of investors and creditors. The third objective emphasizes the need for information about economic resources (assets) and claims to those resources (liabilities and stockholders' equity) and their changes over time.

 KEY POINT

The primary objective of financial accounting is to provide useful information to investors and creditors in making decisions.

Underlying these three key objectives is a conceptual framework that is the foundation upon which financial accounting is built. We discuss the FASB's conceptual framework in detail in the appendix to this chapter.

An Ethical Foundation

Like all structures, accounting requires a strong foundation. For accounting, part of that foundation is the ethical behavior of those who practice its rules. You have probably encountered the topic of ethics in other business courses. Ethics refers to a code or moral system that provides criteria for evaluating right and wrong behavior. Investors, creditors, government, and the general public rely on general ethical behavior among those who record and report the financial activities of businesses. A lack of public trust in financial reporting can undermine business and the economy. Indeed, the dramatic collapse of **Enron** in 2001 and the dismantling of the international public accounting firm of **Arthur Andersen** in 2002 severely shook investors' confidence in the stock market. Some questioned the credibility of corporate America as well as the accounting profession itself.

Public outrage over accounting scandals at high-profile companies increased the pressure on lawmakers to pass measures that would restore credibility and investor confidence in the financial reporting process. These pressures resulted in the issuance of the Public Company Accounting Reform and Investor Protection Act of 2002, commonly referred to as the Sarbanes-Oxley Act (SOX), named for the two congressmen who sponsored the bill. The Sarbanes-Oxley Act provides for the regulation of auditors and the types of services they furnish to clients, increases accountability of corporate executives, addresses conflicts of interest for securities analysts, and provides for stiff criminal penalties for violators. These increased requirements have dramatically increased the need for good accounting and, at the

same time, highlighted the value of accounting information to investors and creditors. We discuss the specific provisions of SOX in more detail in Chapter 4.

Important as such legislation is in supporting the ethical foundation of accounting, it is equally important that accountants themselves have their own personal standards for ethical conduct. You cannot, though, just go out and suddenly obtain ethics when you need them. ("I'd like a pound of ethics, please.") Rather, accountants need to *develop* their ability to identify ethical situations and know the difference between right and wrong in the context of the accounting topics you will learn in this course. One of the keys to ethical decision making is having an appreciation for how your actions affect others.

When you face ethical dilemmas in your professional life (and indeed in your personal life), you can apply the following simple framework as you think through what to do:

1. Identify the ethical situation and the people who will be affected (the stakeholders).
2. Specify the options for alternative courses of action.
3. Understand the impact of each option on the stakeholders.
4. Make a decision.

Throughout the book, we will discuss some ethical decisions relating to accounting and will make clear their financial impact. These discussions will give you opportunities to practice some ethical decision making in a classroom setting.

 ETHICAL DILEMMA

You have been the manager of a local restaurant for the past five years. Because of increased competition, you notice you're getting fewer customers. Despite all your attempts to attract new customers and cut costs, the restaurant's profitability continues to decline. The restaurant owner tells you that if this year's profit is lower than last year's, you'll lose your job.

When preparing financial statements at the end of the year, you notice that this year's profit *is* lower. You know that by purposely understating certain expenses, you can falsely report higher profits to the owner for this year. That will allow you to keep your job for at least one more year and look for a new job in the meantime.

What should you do? What if you really believe the lower profitability is caused by factors outside your control? Would this make the false reporting acceptable?

User's Guide
Throughout the book, you will see boxed discussions of *Ethical Dilemmas.* These dilemmas are designed to raise your awareness of accounting issues that have ethical ramifications.

CAREERS IN ACCOUNTING

PART C

At this point in your college career, you may be uncertain of your major. Here are three important questions to consider when you make your choice: (1) Will you enjoy your major as a career? (2) Will you be good at your chosen field? (3) Will you be well paid?

After completing the first course in accounting, you will have some idea of the answers to the first two questions. You will find out whether you might enjoy accounting. You will also find out through exams, quizzes, and homework whether you have the aptitude to be good at it. Realize, however, that besides being good at

CAREER CORNER

Over 20,000 employees join public accounting firms in entry-level jobs each year, and thousands more go into other areas of accounting. While financial accountants learn how to measure business transactions and prepare financial reports, they also learn a great deal about the business itself. Because of this widespread business knowledge, accountants often play a key role on the management team. In fact, it should come as no surprise to learn that most chief financial officers (CFOs) started their careers as accountants.

Accounting, because of its dynamic and professional nature, offers an attractive career option. You can learn more about a career in accounting by visiting the website of the American Institute of Certified Public Accountants (*www.aicpa.org*). There, you can look under the *Career Development and Workplace Issues* link to find current information about job opportunities, salaries, work life for women, how to write a resume, how to interview, and other general career advice. For salary and other job-related information, consult the website of the U.S. Bureau of Labor Statistics (*www.bls.gov/oco/ocos001.htm*) or go to *careers-in-accounting.com*. In 2009, entry-level jobs ranged between $50,000 and $70,000, with $55,000 as the norm for Big-4 firms.

Is an accounting degree right for you?

the technical side of accounting, you will need interpersonal skills such as working well in teams, making presentations to clients, and leading co-workers in complex projects. As for the third question, someone definitely will pay you to be an accountant, as we discuss in the following section.

Demand for Accounting

One of the greatest benefits of an accounting degree is the wide variety of job opportunities it opens to you. With an accounting degree you can apply for almost any position available to finance majors. However, it doesn't work the other way: Finance majors often lack the accounting background necessary to apply for accounting positions.

For the past several years, accounting has ranked as one of the top majors on university campuses. Accounting firms are anticipating a 20% increase in new hires over the next several years. Because of their importance in our society, accountants are in high demand. And because of this high demand, accounting salaries are on the rise. Starting salaries are among the highest of all majors across the university.

Career Options in Accounting

User's Guide
Throughout the book, you will see sections titled *Career Corner*. These sections highlight a link between a particular topic and a career.

■ **LO6**
Identify career opportunities in accounting.

The first big decision a student makes as an accounting graduate is the choice between a career in public accounting and a career in private accounting.

PUBLIC ACCOUNTING

Public accounting firms are professional service firms that traditionally have focused on three areas: auditing, tax preparation/planning, and business consulting. We already have discussed the role of *auditors* in attesting to the accuracy of companies' financial statements. *Tax preparation/planning* is an increasingly important activity in the United States, as the complexity of tax laws related to personal and corporate taxes continues to increase. *Business consulting* is perhaps the most lucrative activity of accountants. Managers who want to better understand their companies' financial strengths and weaknesses often turn to public accountants for guidance. Who knows the business activities better than the one measuring and communicating them?

If you choose a career in public accounting, the next big decision is whether to work for one of the "Big 4" public accounting firms (**Deloitte**, **Ernst & Young**, **PricewaterhouseCoopers**, and **KPMG**) or one of the thousands of medium or smaller-sized firms. The Big 4 firms are huge, each having annual revenues in the billions. They audit almost all the Fortune 500 companies in the United States and most of the largest companies around the world, and they hire thousands of

accounting majors each year. The thousands of smaller international, regional, and local accounting firms also hire thousands of accounting majors right out of college.

Most public accountants become *Certified Public Accountants (CPAs)*. You become a CPA by passing the four parts of the CPA exam and meeting minimum work experience requirements (in some states). Most states require that you have 150 semester hours (225 quarter hours) of college credit to take the exam. Becoming a CPA can provide a big boost in salary and long-term job opportunities.

PRIVATE ACCOUNTING

A career in **private accounting** means providing accounting services to the company that employs you. Every major company in the world hires accountants. Just think of all the accounting issues at **Dell**, for example. Dell, and all other large companies, need accountants with training and experience in financial accounting, management accounting, taxation, internal auditing, and accounting information systems. Whereas working as a public accountant provides the advantage of experience working with a number of different clients, private accountants sometimes earn higher starting salaries. In fact, many accounting students begin their careers in public accounting, gaining experience across a wide array of companies and industries, and then eventually switch over to one of their favorite clients as private accountants. Other students take positions directly in private accounting right out of college.

Because of their special training and valuable knowledge base, both public and private accountants are expanding their roles to include the following: financial planning, information technology development, financial analysis, forensic accounting, information risk management, investment banking, environmental accounting, tax law, FBI work, management consulting, and much, much more. Illustration 1–16 outlines just a few of the many career options in accounting.

	Public Accounting (Big 4 and Non-Big 4)	Private Accounting
Clients	Corporations Governments Nonprofit organizations Individuals	Your particular employer
Traditional roles	Auditors Tax preparers/planners Business consultants	Financial accountants Managerial accountants Budget analysts Internal auditors Tax preparers Payroll managers
Expanding roles	Financial planners Information technology developers Financial analysts Forensic accountants Information risk managers Investment bankers Environmental accountants Financial advisors Tax lawyers	Information managers Management advisors Tax planners Acquisition specialists FBI agents Sports agents
Other career options	Governmental accounting, sole proprietorships, and education.	

ILLUSTRATION 1–16

Some of the Career Options in Accounting

A recent survey by *BusinessWeek* on ideal employers for undergraduate business majors listed the Big 4 public accounting firms in the top 12 of all companies in the United States. Three of the Big 4 were in the top five. All of the firms in the list hire accountants. This is a great time to be an accounting major.

 KEY POINT

Because of the high demand for accounting graduates, wide range of job opportunities, and increasing salaries, this is a great time to obtain a degree in accounting.

APPENDIX

■ **LO7**
Explain the nature of the conceptual framework used to develop generally accepted accounting principles.

CONCEPTUAL FRAMEWORK

The FASB establishes financial accounting standards based on a **conceptual framework,** which you can think of as the "theory" of accounting. In much the same way that our nation's Constitution provides the underlying principles that guide the "correctness" of all laws, the FASB's conceptual framework prescribes the correctness of financial accounting rules. Having a conceptual framework provides standard setters with a benchmark for creating a consistent set of financial reporting rules now and in the future. It also provides others with a *written* framework so that everyone understands the underlying concepts that accountants are to consider in preparing and interpreting financial accounting information.

 KEY POINT

The conceptual framework provides an underlying foundation for the development of accounting standards and interpretation of accounting information.

In the chapter, we discussed the three objectives of financial accounting as outlined in the FASB's conceptual framework. To satisfy these stated objectives, accounting information should possess certain characteristics. What are the desired characteristics? Illustration 1–17 provides a graphical depiction of the qualitative characteristics of accounting information.

ILLUSTRATION 1–17   Qualitative Characteristics of Accounting Information

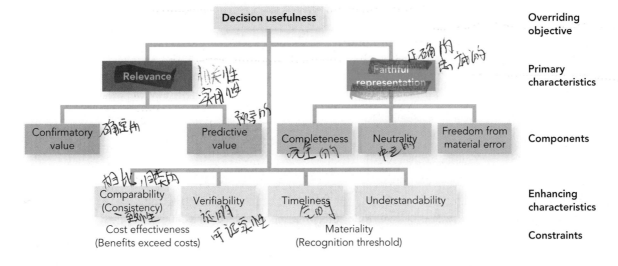

Notice that at the top of the figure is **decision usefulness**—the ability of the information to be useful in decision making. Accounting information should help investors, lenders, and other creditors make important decisions about providing funds to a company.

PRIMARY QUALITATIVE CHARACTERISTICS

The two primary decision-specific qualitative characteristics that make accounting information useful are *relevance* and *faithful representation*. Both are critical. No matter how representative, if information is not relevant to the decision at hand, it is useless. Conversely, relevant information is of little value if it does not accurately represent the underlying activity.

Relevance. To have **relevance**, accounting information should possess *confirmatory value* and/or *predictive value*. Generally, useful information will possess both of these components. For example, the ability of **Dell** to report a positive net income confirms that its management is effectively and efficiently using the company's resources to sell quality products. In this case, net income has *confirmatory value*. At the same time, reporting a positive and growing net income for several consecutive years should provide information that has *predictive value* for the company's future cash-generating ability.

Faithful representation. To be a **faithful representation** of business activities, accounting information should be complete, neutral, and free from material error. *Completeness* means including all information necessary for faithful representation of the business activity the firm is reporting. For example, when Dell reports inventory in its balance sheet, investors understand it to represent *all* items (and only those items) that are intended for sale to customers in the ordinary course of business. If the amount reported for inventory includes only some of the items to be sold, then it lacks completeness. Adequate note disclosure is another important component of completeness. Dell must disclose in the notes to the financial statements the method it used to calculate inventory reported on its balance sheet. (We discuss alternative inventory methods in Chapter 6.)

Neutrality means to be unbiased, and this characteristic is highly related to the establishment of accounting standards. Sometimes a new accounting standard may favor one group of companies over others. In such cases, the FASB must convince the financial community that this was a *consequence* of the standard, and not an *objective* used to set the standard. For example, the FASB requires that all research and development (R&D) costs be reported as an expense in the income statement, reducing the current year's net income. The FASB's objective in adopting this approach was not to weaken the financial appearance of those companies in R&D-intensive industries, such as telecommunications, pharmaceuticals, and software, even though that may have been the effect.

Freedom from material error indicates that reported amounts reflect the best available information. As you'll come to find out in this course, some amounts reported in the financial statements are based on estimates, and the accuracy of those estimates is subject to uncertainty. Because of this, financial statements are not expected to be completely free of error, but they are expected to reflect management's unbiased judgments.

 KEY POINT

To be useful for decision making, accounting information should have relevance and faithful representation.

ENHANCING QUALITATIVE CHARACTERISTICS

Four enhancing qualitative characteristics are comparability, verifiability, timeliness, and understandability. Comparability refers to the ability of users to see similarities and differences between two different business activities. For example, how does Dell's net income compare with net income for other computer manufacturers such as Hewlett-Packard or Gateway? Comparability also refers to the ability of users to see similarities and differences in the same company over time. How does Dell's net income this year compare to last year's? Closely related to the notion of comparability is consistency. Consistency refers to the use of similar accounting procedures either over time for the same company, or across companies at the same point in time. Comparability of financial information is the overriding goal, while consistency of accounting procedures is a means of achieving that goal.

Verifiability implies a consensus among different measurers. For instance, different graders will arrive at the same exam score for multiple-choice tests, but they are more likely to differ in scoring essay exams. Multiple-choice tests are highly verifiable. The same idea holds in the business world. For example, the price Dell paid to purchase a patent from another company is usually highly verifiable because there is an exchange at a certain point in time. In contrast, the fair value of a patent for a product Dell developed internally over an extended period is more subjective and less verifiable.

Firms must also disclose information related to net income that is *timely*. Timeliness refers to information being available to users early enough to allow them to use it in the decision process. Large companies like Dell are required to report information related to net income within 40 days after the end of the quarter and within 60 days after the end of the year.

Understandability means that users must be able to understand the information within the context of the decision they are making. This is a user-specific quality because users will differ in their ability to comprehend any set of information.

PRACTICAL CONSTRAINTS ON ACHIEVING DESIRED QUALITATIVE CHARACTERISTICS

Sometimes, certain information involves more time and effort than the information is worth. For example, if a friend asks what you did today, she probably wants to know the general outline of your day, but does not want to hear a recital of every move you made. Similarly, there may be practical constraints (limits) on each of the qualitative characteristics of accounting information.

One such constraint is cost effectiveness, which suggests that financial accounting information is provided only when the benefits of doing so exceed the costs. For example, knowing the profit margin earned by Dell in each country provides decision-useful information to investors and creditors. However, this information is also helpful to the company's current and potential competitors such as Hewlett-Packard and Apple as they make their own expansion plans. The competitive costs of providing this information may outweigh the benefits.

A related constraint on the type of information we provide is the concept of materiality. Materiality reflects the impact of financial accounting information on investors' and creditors' decisions. Unless an item is *material* in amount or nature—that is, sufficient in amount or nature to affect a decision—it need not be reported in accordance with GAAP. Based on the concept of materiality, Dell probably does not record all its assets as assets. Most companies record assets such as wastebaskets and staplers as *expenses*, even though these items will benefit the company for a long period. Recording a $6 wastebasket as a current expense instead of a long-term asset for a multi-billion dollar company like Dell has no impact on investors' decisions.

UNDERLYING ASSUMPTIONS

Four basic assumptions underlie GAAP. As pictured in Illustration 1–18, they are (1) the economic entity assumption, (2) the monetary unit assumption, (3) the periodicity assumption, and (4) the going concern assumption.

GAAP

UNDERLYING ASSUMPTIONS			
Economic Entity	Monetary Unit	Periodicity	Going Concern

ILLUSTRATION 1-18

Assumptions That Underlie GAAP

Economic Entity Assumption. The economic entity assumption states that we can identify all economic events with a particular economic entity. In other words, only business transactions involving Dell should be reported as part of Dell's financial accounting information. Another key aspect of this assumption is the distinction between the economic activities of owners and those of the company. For example, Michael Dell's personal residence is not an asset of Dell Incorporated.

Monetary Unit Assumption. Information would be difficult to use if, for example, we listed assets as "three machines, two trucks, and a building." According to the monetary unit assumption, in order to *measure* financial statement elements, we need a unit or scale of measurement. The dollar in the United States is the most appropriate common denominator to express information about financial statement elements and changes in those elements. In Europe, the common denominator is the euro. Dell has operations throughout the world, so it must translate all its financial information to U.S. dollars under the monetary unit assumption.

Periodicity Assumption. The periodicity assumption relates to the qualitative characteristic of *timeliness*. External users need *periodic* information to make decisions. The periodicity assumption divides the economic life of an enterprise (presumed to be indefinite) into artificial time periods for periodic financial reporting. Corporations, like Dell, whose securities are publicly traded are required to provide financial information to the SEC on a quarterly *and* an annual basis.

Going Concern Assumption. The going concern assumption states that in the absence of information to the contrary, a business entity will continue to operate indefinitely. This assumption is critical to many broad and specific accounting principles. It provides justification for measuring many assets based on their original costs (a practice known as the *historical cost principle*). If we knew an enterprise was going to cease operations in the near future, we would measure assets and liabilities not at their original costs but at their current liquidation values.

In addition to the four basic assumptions that underlie GAAP are four principles (historical cost, full disclosure, realization, and matching) that guide the application of GAAP. We will explain each of these in an appropriate context in later chapters.

KEY POINTS BY LEARNING OBJECTIVE

LO1 Describe the two primary functions of financial accounting.

The functions of financial accounting are to measure business activities of a company and to communicate information about those activities to investors and creditors and other outside users for decision-making purposes.

LO2 Identify the three fundamental business activities that financial accounting measures.

Financing activities include transactions with lenders and owners. Investing activities generally include the purchase or disposal of productive assets. Operating activities relate to earning revenues and incurring expenses.

LO3 Discuss how financial accounting information is communicated through financial statements.

The income statement compares revenues and expenses for the current period to assess the company's ability to earn a profit from running its operations.

The statement of stockholders' equity reports information related to changes in common stock and retained earnings each period. The change in retained earnings equals net income less dividends for the period.

The balance sheet demonstrates that the company's resources (assets) equal creditors' claims (liabilities) plus owners' claims (stockholders' equity) to those resources.

The statement of cash flows reports cash transactions from operating, investing, and financing activities.

All transactions that affect revenues or expenses reported in the income statement ultimately affect the balance sheet through the balance in retained earnings.

LO4 Describe the role that financial accounting plays in the efficient distribution of society's resources.

Financial accounting serves an important role by providing information useful in investment and lending decisions.

No single piece of company information better explains companies' stock price performance than does financial accounting net income. A company's debt level is an important indicator of management's ability to respond to business situations and the possibility of bankruptcy.

LO5 Explain the term generally accepted accounting principles (GAAP) and describe the role of GAAP in financial accounting.

The rules of financial accounting are called generally accepted accounting principles (GAAP). The Financial Accounting Standards Board (FASB) is an independent, private body that has primary responsibility for the establishment of GAAP in the United States.

The primary objective of financial accounting is to provide useful information to investors and creditors in making decisions.

LO6 Identify career opportunities in accounting.

Because of the high demand for accounting graduates, the wide range of job opportunities, and increasing salaries, this is a great time to obtain a degree in accounting.

Appendix

LO7 Explain the nature of the conceptual framework used to develop generally accepted accounting principles.

The conceptual framework provides an underlying foundation for the development of accounting standards and interpretation of accounting information.

To be useful for decision making, accounting information should have relevance and faithful representation.

GLOSSARY

Accounting: A system of maintaining records of a company's operations and communicating that information to decision makers. **p. 4**

Accounting equation: Equation that shows a company's resources (assets) equal creditors' and owners' claims to those resources (liabilities and stockholders' equity). **p. 7**

Assets: Resources owned by a company. **p. 7**

Auditors: Trained individuals hired by a company as an independent party to express a professional opinion of the accuracy of that company's financial statements. **p. 23**

Balance sheet: A financial statement that presents the financial position of the company on a particular date. **p. 13**

Comparability: The ability of users to see similarities and differences between two different business activities. **p. 30**

Consistency: The use of similar accounting procedures either over time for the same company, or across companies at the same point in time. **p. 30**

Corporation: An entity that is legally separate from its owners. **p. 6**

Cost effectiveness: Financial accounting information is provided only when the benefits of doing so exceed the costs. **p. 30**

Decision usefulness: The ability of the information to be useful in decision making. **p. 29**

Dividends: Cash payments to stockholders. **p. 8**

Economic entity assumption: All economic events with a particular economic entity can be identified. **p. 31**

Ethics: A code or moral system that provides criteria for evaluating right and wrong behavior. **p. 24**

Expenses: Costs of providing products and services. **p. 8**

Faithful representation: Accounting information that is complete, neutral, and free from material error. **p. 29**

Financial accounting: Measurement of business activities of a company and communication of those measurements to external parties for decision-making purposes. **p. 5**

Financial Accounting Standards Board (FASB): An independent, private body that has primary responsibility for the establishment of GAAP in the United States. **p. 21**

Financial statements: Periodic reports published by the company for the purpose of providing information to external users. **p. 10**

Financing activities: Transactions involving external sources of funding. **p. 5**

Generally accepted accounting principles (GAAP): The rules of financial accounting. **p. 21**

Going concern assumption: In the absence of information to the contrary, a business entity will continue to operate indefinitely. **p. 31**

Income statement: A financial statement that reports the company's revenues and expenses over an interval of time. **p. 11**

International Accounting Standards Board (IASB): An international accounting standard-setting body responsible for the convergence of accounting standards worldwide. **p. 22**

International Financial Reporting Standards (IFRS): The standards being developed and promoted by the International Accounting Standards Board. **p. 22**

Investing activities: Transactions involving the purchase and sale of (1) long-term resources such as land, buildings, equipment, and machinery and (2) any resources not directly related to a company's normal operations. **p. 5**

Liabilities: Amounts owed to creditors. **p. 7**

Materiality: The impact of financial accounting information on investors' and creditors' decisions. **p. 30**

Monetary unit assumption: A unit or scale of measurement can be used to measure financial statement elements. **p. 31**

Net income: Difference between revenues and expenses. **p. 8**

Operating activities: Transactions involving the primary operations of the company, such as providing products and services to customers and the associated costs of doing so, like utilities, taxes, advertising, wages, rent, and maintenance. **p. 5**

Partnership: Business owned by two or more persons. **p. 9**

Periodicity assumption: The economic life of an enterprise (presumed to be indefinite) can be divided into artificial time periods for financial reporting. **p. 31**

Relevance: Accounting information that possesses confirmatory value and/or predictive value. **p. 29**

Retained earnings: Cumulative amount of net income earned over the life of the company that has not been distributed to stockholders as dividends. **p. 12**

Revenues: Amounts earned from selling products or services to customers. **p. 8**

Sarbanes-Oxley Act (SOX): Formally titled the Public Company Accounting Reform and Investor Protection Act of 2002, this act provides regulation of auditors and the types of services they furnish to clients, increases accountability of corporate executives, addresses conflicts of interest for securities analysts, and provides for stiff criminal penalties for violators. **p. 24**

Sole proprietorship: A business owned by one person. **p. 9**

Statement of cash flows: A financial statement that measures activities involving cash receipts and cash payments over an interval of time. **p. 15**

Statement of stockholders' equity: A financial statement that summarizes the changes in stockholders' equity over an interval of time. **p. 12**

Stockholder's equity: Stockholders', or owners', claims to resources, which equal the difference between total assets and total liabilities. **p. 7**

Timeliness: Information being available to users early enough to allow them to use it in the decision process. **p. 30**

Understandability: Users must understand the information within the context of the decision they are making. **p. 30**

Verifiability: A consensus among different measurers. **p. 30**

SELF-STUDY QUESTIONS

■ **LO1**

1. Based on the introductory section of this chapter, which course is most like financial accounting?
   a. College algebra.
   b. Foreign language.
   c. Molecular biology.
   d. Physical education.

■ **LO2**

2. Financial accounting serves which primary function(s)?
   a. Measures business activities.
   b. Communicates business activities to interested parties.
   c. Makes business decisions on behalf of interested parties.
   d. Both a. and b. are functions of financial accounting.

■ **LO2**

3. Financing activities of a company include which of the following?
   a. Selling products or services to customers.
   b. Using cash to purchase long-term assets such as machinery.
   c. Borrowing money from the bank.
   d. Paying salaries to employees.

■ **LO2**

4. Investing activities of a company include which of the following?
   a. Paying salaries to workers.
   b. Using cash to purchase long-term assets such as equipment.
   c. Issuing common stock to investors.
   d. Borrowing money from the bank.

■ **LO3**

5. Which financial statement conveys a company's ability to generate profits in the current period?
   a. Income statement.
   b. Statement of cash flows.
   c. Balance sheet.
   d. Statement of stockholders' equity.

■ **LO3**

6. Which financial statement shows that a company's resources equal claims to those resources?
   a. Income statement.
   b. Statement of stockholders' equity.
   c. Balance sheet.
   d. Statement of cash flows.

■ **LO4**

7. Why does financial accounting have a positive impact on our society?
   a. It entails a detailed transaction record necessary for filing taxes with the Internal Revenue Service (IRS).
   b. It allows investors and creditors to redirect their resources to successful companies and away from unsuccessful companies.
   c. It prevents competitors from being able to steal the company's customers.
   d. It provides a system of useful internal reports for management decision making.

■ **LO5**

8. The body of rules and procedures that guide the measurement and communication of financial accounting information is known as:
   a. Standards of Professional Compliance (SPC).
   b. Code of Ethical Decisions (COED).
   c. Rules of Financial Reporting (RFP).
   d. Generally Accepted Accounting Principles (GAAP).

9. What is a benefit to a career in accounting?   ■ LO6
   a. High salaries.
   b. Wide range of job opportunities.
   c. High demand for accounting graduates.
   d. All of the above.

10. What are the two primary qualitative characteristics identified by the Financial   ■ LO7
    Accounting Standards Board's (FASB) conceptual framework?
    a. Relevance and faithful representation.
    b. Materiality and efficiency.
    c. Comparability and consistency.
    d. Costs and benefits.

Check out
www.mhhe.com/succeed
for more multiple-choice
questions.

Note: For answers, see the last page of the chapter.

REVIEW QUESTIONS

1. Explain what it means to say that an accounting class is not the same as a math class.   ■ LO1

2. Identify some of the people interested in making decisions about a company.   ■ LO1

3. What is the basic difference between financial accounting and managerial accounting?   ■ LO1

4. What are the two primary functions of financial accounting?   ■ LO1

5. What are the three basic business activities that financial accounting seeks to   ■ LO2
   measure and communicate to external parties? Define each.

6. What are a few of the typical financing activities for a company like **United Parcel**   ■ LO2
   Service, Inc. (UPS), the world's largest package delivery company and a leading
   global provider of specialized transportation and logistics services?

7. What are a few of the typical investing activities for a company like **Trump**   ■ LO2
   Entertainment Resorts, Inc., a leading gaming company that owns and operates
   casinos, resorts, and hotels?

8. What are a few of the typical operating activities for a company like **Oracle**   ■ LO2
   Corporation, one of the world's leading suppliers of software for information
   management?

9. What are the three major legal forms of business organizations? Which one is   ■ LO2
   chosen by most of the largest companies in the United States?

10. Provide the basic definition for each of the account types: assets, liabilities,   ■ LO2
    stockholders' equity, dividends, revenues, and expenses.

11. What are the major advantages and disadvantages of each of the legal forms of   ■ LO2
    business organizations?

12. What are the four primary financial statements? What basic information is shown   ■ LO3
    on each?

13. What does it mean to say that the income statement, statement of stockholders'   ■ LO3
    equity, and statement of cash flows measure activity over an *interval of time,* but
    the balance sheet measures activity at a *point in time?*

14. Give some examples of the basic revenues and expenses for a company like   ■ LO3
    The Walt Disney Company.

15. What is the accounting equation? Which financial statement reports the accounting   ■ LO3
    equation?

■ **LO3**   16. Give some examples of the basic assets and liabilities of a company like **Walmart Stores, Inc.**

■ **LO3**   17. "The retained earnings account is a link between the income statement and the balance sheet." Explain what this means.

■ **LO3**   18. What are the three types of cash flows reported in the statement of cash flows? Give an example of each type of activity for a company like **Oakley, Inc.**, a designer, manufacturer, and distributor of high-performance eyewear, footwear, watches, and athletic equipment.

■ **LO3**   19. In addition to financial statements, what are some other ways to disclose financial information to external users?

■ **LO4**   20. How does financial accounting have an impact on society?

■ **LO5**   21. What is meant by GAAP? Why should companies follow GAAP in reporting to external users?

■ **LO5**   22. Which body is primarily responsible for the establishment of GAAP in the United States? What body serves this function on an international basis?

■ **LO5**   23. In general terms, explain the terms U.S. GAAP and IFRS.

■ **LO5**   24. What was the primary reason for the establishment of the 1933 Securities Act and the 1934 Securities Exchange Act? What power does the Securities and Exchange Commission (SEC) have?

■ **LO5**   25. What is the role of the auditor in the financial reporting process?

■ **LO5**   26. What are the three primary objectives of financial reporting?

■ **LO6**   27. What are some of the benefits to obtaining a degree in accounting? What is the difference between a career in public accounting and private accounting? What are some of the traditional careers of accounting graduates? What new areas are accountants expanding into?

■ **LO7**   28. Discuss the terms *relevance* and *faithful representation* as they relate to financial accounting information.

■ **LO7**   29. What are the two components of relevance? What are the three components of faithful representation?

■ **LO7**   30. What is meant by the terms *cost effectiveness* and *materiality* in financial reporting?

■ **LO7**   31. Define the four basic assumptions underlying GAAP.

BRIEF EXERCISES

Define accounting **(LO1)**

BE1–1 Indicate whether the definition provided is true or false.

(True/False)   Accounting can be defined as:

1. _____ The language of business.
2. _____ A measurement/communication process.
3. _____ A mathematics course.

Identify the different types of business activities **(LO2)**

BE1–2 Match each business activity with its description.

Business Activities	Descriptions
1. _____ Financing	a. Transactions related to revenues and expenses.
2. _____ Investing	b. Transactions with lenders and owners.
3. _____ Operating	c. Transactions involving the purchase and sale of productive assets.

BE1–3 Match each form of business organization with its description.

Identify the different forms of business organizations (LO2)

Business Organizations	Descriptions
1. _____ Sole proprietorship	a. Business owned by two or more persons.
2. _____ Partnership	b. Entity legally separate from its owners.
3. _____ Corporation	c. Business owned by a single person.

BE1–4 Match each account type with its description.

Recognize the different account classifications (LO2)

Account Classifications	Descriptions
1. __e__ Assets	a. Amounts earned from sales of products or services.
2. __f__ Liabilities	b. Owners' claims to resources.
3. __b__ Stockholders' equity	c. Distributions to stockholders.
4. __c__ Dividends	d. Costs of selling products or services.
5. __a__ Revenues	e. Resources owned.
6. __d__ Expenses	f. Amounts owed.

BE1–5 Match each financial statement with its description.

Describe each financial statement (LO3)

Financial Statements	Descriptions
1. _____ Income statement	a. Change in owners' claims to resources.
2. _____ Statement of stockholders' equity	b. Profitability of the company.
3. _____ Balance sheet	c. Change in cash as a result of operating, investing, and financing activities.
4. _____ Statement of cash flows	d. Resources equal creditors' and owners' claims to those resources.

BE1–6 Determine on which financial statement you find the following items.

Determine the location of items in financial statements (LO3)

Financial Statements	Items
1. _____ Income statement	a. The change in retained earnings due to net income and dividends.
2. _____ Statement of stockholders' equity	b. Amount of cash received from borrowing money from a local bank.
3. _____ Balance sheet	c. Revenue earned from sales to customers during the year.
4. _____ Statement of cash flows	d. Total amounts owed to workers at the end of the year.

BE1–7 Each of these parties plays a role in the quality of financial reporting. Match each group with its function.

Identify different groups engaged in providing high-quality financial reporting (LO5)

Groups	Functions
1. _____ Financial Accounting Standards Board	a. Group that has been given power by Congress to enforce the proper application of financial reporting rules for companies whose securities are publicly traded.
2. _____ International Accounting Standards Board	b. Independent, private-sector group that is primarily responsible for setting financial reporting standards in the United States.
3. _____ Securities and Exchange Commission	c. Independent intermediaries that help to ensure that management appropriately applies financial reporting rules in preparing the company's financial statements.
4. _____ Auditors	d. Body that is attempting to develop a single set of high-quality, understandable global accounting standards.

Identify the objectives of financial accounting **(LO5)**

BE1–8 Indicate which of the following are objectives of financial accounting.

(Yes/No)	Objectives
1. _____	Provide information that is useful to investors and creditors.
2. _____	Guarantee that businesses will not go bankrupt.
3. _____	Provide information about resources and claims to resources.
4. _____	Prevent competitors from offering lower-priced products.
5. _____	Provide information to help users in predicting future cash flows.
6. _____	Maximize tax revenue to the federal government.

Identify careers for accounting majors **(LO6)**

BE1–9 Below are possible career opportunities for those earning a degree in accounting. Indicate whether the statement related to each career is true or false.

(True/False) Someone earning a degree in accounting could pursue the following career:

1. _____	Auditor
2. _____	Tax preparer
3. _____	Business consultant
4. _____	Financial planner
5. _____	Forensic investigator
6. _____	Tax planner
7. _____	Financial analyst
8. _____	Information technology developer
9. _____	Investment banker
10. _____	Tax lawyer
11. _____	FBI agent
12. _____	Information risk manager

Identify the components of relevance **(LO7)**

BE1–10 Match each of the components of relevance with its definition.

Relevance	Definitions
1. _____ Confirmatory value	a. Information is useful in helping to forecast future outcomes.
2. _____ Predictive value	b. Information provides feedback on past activities.

Identify the components of faithful representation **(LO7)**

BE1–11 Match each of the components of faithful representation with its definition.

Faithful Representation	Definition
1. _____ Freedom from material error	a. All information necessary to describe an item is reported.
2. _____ Neutrality	b. Information that does not bias the decision maker.
3. _____ Completeness	c. Reported amounts reflect the best available information.

EXERCISES

Identify the different types of business activities **(LO2)**

E1–1 The following provides a list of transactions and a list of business activities.

Transactions	Business Activities
1. _____ Borrow from the bank.	a. Financing
2. _____ Provide services to customers.	b. Investing
3. _____ Issue common stock to investors.	c. Operating
4. _____ Purchase land.	
5. _____ Pay rent for the current period.	
6. _____ Pay dividends to stockholders.	
7. _____ Purchase building.	

Required:

Match the transaction with the business activity by indicating the letter that corresponds to the appropriate business activity.

E1–2 Falcon Incorporated has the following transactions with Wildcat Corporation.

Identify account classifications and business activities (LO2)

Flip Side of E1–3

Transactions	Falcon's Related Account
1. Falcon purchases common stock of Wildcat.	Investment
2. Falcon borrows from Wildcat by signing a note.	Notes payable
3. Wildcat pays dividends to Falcon.	Dividend revenue
4. Falcon provides services to Wildcat.	Service revenue
5. Falcon pays interest to Wildcat on borrowing.	Interest expense

Required:
1. For each transaction, indicate whether Falcon would classify the related account as an (a) asset, (b) liability, or (c) stockholders' equity to be reported in the balance sheet; a (d) revenue or (e) expense to be reported in the income statement; or an (f) dividend to be reported in the statement of stockholders' equity.
2. Classify the type of activity as financing, investing, or operating.

E1–3 The transactions in this problem are identical to those in E1–2, but now with a focus on Wildcat.

Identify account classifications and business activities (LO2)

Flip Side of E1–2

Transactions	Wildcat's Related Account
1. Falcon purchases common stock of Wildcat.	Common stock
2. Falcon borrows from Wildcat by signing a note.	Notes receivable
3. Wildcat pays dividends to Falcon.	Dividend
4. Falcon provides services to Wildcat.	Service fee expense
5. Falcon pays interest to Wildcat on borrowing.	Interest revenue

Required:
1. For each transaction, indicate whether Wildcat would classify the related account as an (a) asset, (b) liability, or (c) stockholders' equity to be reported in the balance sheet; a (d) revenue or (e) expense to be reported in the income statement; or an (f) dividend to be reported in the statement of stockholders' equity.
2. Classify the type of activity as financing, investing, or operating.

E1–4 Eagle Corp. operates Magnetic Resonance Imaging (MRI) clinics throughout the Northeast. At the end of the current period, the company reports the following amounts: Assets = $40,000; Liabilities = $22,000; Dividends = $2,000; Revenues = $12,000; Expenses = $8,000.

Calculate net income and stockholders' equity (LO2)

Required:
1. Calculate net income.
2. Calculate stockholders' equity at the end of the period.

E1–5 Cougar's Accounting Services provides low-cost tax advice and preparation to those with financial need. At the end of the current period, the company reports the following amounts: Assets = $17,000; Liabilities = $14,000; Revenues = $26,000; Expenses = $32,000.

Calculate net loss and stockholders' equity (LO2)

Required:
1. Calculate net loss.
2. Calculate stockholders' equity at the end of the period.

E1–6 Below are the account balances for Cowboy Law Firm at the end of December.

Prepare an income statement (LO3)

Accounts	Balances
Cash	$ 4,400
Salaries expense	1,700
Accounts payable	2,400
Retained earnings	4,300
Utilities expense	1,100
Supplies	12,800
Service revenue	8,300
Common stock	5,000

Required:

Use only the appropriate accounts to prepare an income statement.

Prepare a statement of stockholders' equity (LO3)

E1–7 At the beginning of the year (January 1), Buffalo Drilling has $10,000 of common stock outstanding and retained earnings of $7,200. During the year, Buffalo reports net income of $7,500 and pays dividends of $2,200. In addition, Buffalo issues additional common stock for $7,000.

Required:

Prepare the statement of stockholders' equity at the end of the year (December 31).

Prepare a balance sheet (LO3)

E1–8 Wolfpack Construction has the following account balances at the end of the year.

Accounts	Balances
Equipment	$21,000
Accounts payable	2,000
Salaries expense	28,000
Common stock	10,000
Land	13,000
Notes payable	15,000
Service revenue	34,000
Cash	5,000
Retained earnings	?

Required:

Use only the appropriate accounts to prepare a balance sheet.

Prepare a statement of cash flows (LO3)

E1–9 Tiger Trade has the following cash transactions for the period.

Accounts	Amounts
Cash received from sale of products to customers	$ 35,000
Cash received from the bank for long-term loan	40,000
Cash paid to purchase factory equipment	(45,000)
Cash paid to merchandise suppliers	(11,000)
Cash received from the sale of an unused warehouse	12,000
Cash paid to workers	(23,000)
Cash paid for advertisement	(3,000)
Cash received for sale of services to customers	25,000
Cash paid for dividends to stockholders	(5,000)

Required:

1. Calculate the ending balance of cash, assuming the balance of cash at the beginning of the period is $4,000.
2. Prepare a statement of cash flows.

Compute missing amounts from financial statements (LO3)

E1–10 Each of the following independent situations represents amounts shown on the four basic financial statements.

1. Revenues = $25,000; Expenses = $17,000; Net income = _____.
2. Increase in stockholders' equity = $16,000; Issuance of common stock = $10,000; Net income = $11,000; Dividends = _____.
3. Assets = $23,000; Stockholders' equity = $17,000; Liabilities = _____.
4. Total change in cash = $24,000; Net operating cash flows = $32,000; Net investing cash flows = ($15,000); Net financing cash flows = _____.

Required:

Fill in the missing blanks using your knowledge of amounts that appear on the financial statements.

E1-11 During its first five years of operations, Red Raider Consulting reports net income and pays dividends as follows.

Calculate the balance of retained earnings **(LO3)**

Year	Net Income	Dividends	Retained Earnings
1	$1,200	$ 500	*700*
2	1,700	500	*1200* *1900.*
3	2,100	1,000	*1100*
4	3,200	1,000	*2200*
5	4,400	1,000	*3400*

Required:

Calculate the balance of retained earnings at the end of each year. Note that retained earnings will always equal $0 at the beginning of year 1.

E1-12 Below is information related to retained earnings for five companies.

Calculate amounts related to the balance of retained earnings **(LO3)**

1. **Coca-Cola** reports an increase in retained earnings of $2.2 billion and net income of $4.9 billion. What is the amount of dividends?   *2·7 billion*
2. **Pepsico** reports an increase in retained earnings of $2.4 billion and dividends of $1.6 billion. What is the amount of net income?   *4 billion*
3. **Google** reports an increase in retained earnings of $1.5 billion and net income of $1.5 billion. What is the amount of dividends?   *0*
4. **Sirius Satellite Radio** reports beginning retained earnings of −$1.8 billion, net loss of $0.9 billion, and $0 dividends. What is the amount of ending retained earnings?   *−0.9 billion*
5. **Abercrombie & Fitch** reports ending retained earnings of $1.36 billion, net income of $0.33 billion, and dividends of $0.05 billion. What is the amount of beginning retained earnings?   *1.08 billion.*

A+B−C=D
A 0.33   A=D+C−B
(0.05) A=
1.36.

Required:

Calculate the answer to each.

E1-13 Below is balance sheet information for five companies.

Use the accounting equation to calculate amounts related to the balance sheet **(LO3)**

1. **ExxonMobil** reports total assets of $208 billion and total liabilities of $97 billion. What is the amount of stockholders' equity?   *111 billion.*
2. **Citigroup** reports total liabilities of $1,400 billion and stockholders' equity of $100 billion. What is the amount of total assets?   *1500 billion*
3. **Amazon.com** reports total assets of $3.7 billion and total stockholders' equity of $0.2 billion. What is the amount of total liabilities?   *3.68 billion*
4. **Nike** reports an increase in assets of $1.1 billion and an increase in liabilities of $0.4 billion. What is the amount of the change in stockholders' equity?   *0.7 billion*
5. **Kellogg** reports a decrease in liabilities of $0.24 billion and an increase in stockholders' equity of $0.03 billion. What is the amount of the change in total assets?   *0.21 billion.*

Required:

Calculate the answer to each.

E1-14 Below is cash flow information for five companies.

Calculate missing amounts related to the statement of cash flows **(LO3)**

1. **Kraft Foods** reports operating cash flows of $3.5 billion, investing cash flows of $0.5 billion, and financing cash flows of −$4.0 billion. What is the amount of the change in total cash?
2. **Sara Lee** reports operating cash flows of $1.3 billion, investing cash flows of −$0.2 billion, and financing cash flows of −$1.2 billion. If the beginning cash amount is $0.6 billion, what is the ending cash amount?
3. **Performance Food Group** reports operating cash flows of $0.08 billion, investing cash flows of $0.53 billion, and a change in total cash of $0.05 billion. What is the amount of cash flows from financing activities?
4. **Smithfield Foods** reports operating cash flows of $0.50 billion, financing cash flows of $0.32 billion, and a change in total cash of $0.01 billion. What is the amount of cash flows from investing activities?

5. **Tyson Foods** reports investing cash flows of −$1.22 billion, financing cash flows of $0.93 billion, and a change in total cash of $0.01 billion. What is the amount of cash flows from operating activities?

Required:
Calculate the answer to each.

Identify the purpose of qualitative characteristics (LO7)

E1–15 The qualitative characteristics outlined in the FASB's conceptual framework include:

Primary Characteristics		Enhancing Characteristics
Relevance	**Faithful Representation**	f. Comparability
a. Confirmatory value	c. Completeness	g. Verifiability
b. Predictive value	d. Neutrality	h. Timeliness
	e. Freedom from material error	i. Understandability

Consider the following independent situations.

1. In deciding whether to invest in **Southwest Airlines** or **American Airlines**, investors evaluate the companies' income statements. _____
2. To provide the most reliable information about future sales, **Walmart**'s management provides unbiased estimates of the decline in inventory value each year. _____
3. In deciding whether to loan money, **Wells Fargo** uses balance sheet information to forecast the probability of bankruptcy. _____
4. **IBM** is required to issue public financial statements within 60 days of its year-end. _____
5. Employees of **Starbucks** can use the company's financial statements to understand the efficiency with which management has conducted operations over the past year. _____
6. When first requiring firms to prepare a statement of cash flows, the FASB's intent was not to discourage or promote investment in the automobile industry. _____
7. When **Harley–Davidson** reports revenue for the year, the amount includes sales not only in the United States but also those outside the United States. _____
8. The amount of total assets reported by **General Mills** can be substantiated by its auditors. _____
9. The **Cheesecake Factory** prepares its balance sheet in a clear format using basic accounting terminology to allow users to easily comprehend the company's assets, liabilities, and stockholders' equity. _____

Required:
Determine which qualitative characteristic best applies to each situation. Note: Each of the nine characteristics is used once and only once.

Identify business assumptions underlying GAAP (LO7)

E1–16 Below are the four underlying assumptions of generally accepted accounting principles.

Assumptions	Descriptions
1. _____ Economic entity	a. A common denominator is needed to measure all business activities.
2. _____ Going concern	b. Economic events can be identified with a particular economic body.
3. _____ Periodicity	c. In the absence of information to the contrary, it is anticipated that a business entity will continue to operate indefinitely.
4. _____ Monetary unit	d. The economic life of a company can be divided into artificial time intervals for financial reporting.

Required:
Match each business assumption with its description.

For additional exercises, visit **www.mhhe.com/succeed** *for Exercises: Set B.*

PROBLEMS: SET A

P1–1A Below are typical transactions for **Hewlett-Packard**.

Classify business activities (LO2)

Type of Business Activity	Transactions
1. _Financing_	Pay amount owed to the bank for previous borrowing. C
2. _Operating_	Pay utility costs.
3. _Investing_	Purchase equipment to be used in operations.
4. _Operating_	Provide services to customers.
5. _Operating_	Purchase office supplies. (not long-term)
6. _Investing_	Purchase a building.
7. _Operating_	Pay workers' salaries.
8. _Operating_	Pay for research and development costs. (not long-term)
9. _Operating_	Pay taxes to the IRS.
10. _Financing_	Sell common stock to investors.

Required:

Indicate whether each transaction is classified as a financing, investing, or operating activity.

P1–2A Account classifications include assets, liabilities, stockholders' equity, dividends, revenues, and expenses.

Assign account classifications (LO2)

Account Classifications	Accounts	Related Transactions
1. _Stockholders' equity_	Common stock	Sale of common stock to investors.
2. _Assets_	Equipment	Equipment used for operations.
3. _Liabilities_	Salaries payable	Amounts owed to employees.
4. _Revenues_	Service revenue	Sales of services to customers.
5. _Expenses_	Utilities expense	Cost of utilities.
6. _Assets_	Supplies	Purchase of office supplies.
7. _~~Assets~~ Expense_	Research and development expense	Cost of research and development.
8. _Assets_	Land ~~Liabilities~~	Property used for operations. Amounts owed to the IRS for federal
9. _~~Expenses~~_	Income tax payable	income taxes. (Liabilities) ?
10. _Liabilities_	Interest payable	Amount of interest owed on borrowing.

Required:

For each transaction, indicate whether the related account would be classified as an (a) asset, (b) liability, or (c) stockholders' equity to be reported in the balance sheet; a (d) revenue or (e) expense to be reported in the income statement; or an (f) dividend to be reported in the statement of stockholders' equity.

P1–3A Longhorn Corporation provides low-cost food delivery services to senior citizens. At the end of the year, the company reports the following amounts:

Prepare financial statements (LO3)

Cash	$ 1,300	Service revenue	$ 62,700
Equipment	24,000	Cost of goods sold	52,400
Accounts payable Debt	3,400	(food expense)	
Delivery expense	1,600	Buildings	30,000
Salaries expense	4,500	Supplies	2,400
		Salaries payable	900

User's Guide Problems marked with this icon can be solved using Microsoft Excel templates.

In addition, the company had common stock of $30,000 at the beginning of the year and issued an additional $3,000 during the year. The company also had retained earnings of $16,200 at the beginning of the year.

Required:

Prepare the income statement, statement of stockholders' equity, and balance sheet for Longhorn Corporation.

Understand the format of financial statements and the links among them (LO3)

P1–4A Below are incomplete financial statements for Bulldog, Inc.

BULLDOG, INC. Income Statement	
Revenues	$34,000
Expenses:	
Salaries	(a)
Advertising	5,000
Utilities	3,000
Net income	(b)

BULLDOG, INC. Statement of Stockholders' Equity	Common Stock	Retained Earnings	Total S. Equity
Beginning balance	$ 9,000	$6,000	$15,000
Issuances	1,000		1,000
Add: Net income		(c)	(c)
Less: Dividends		(2,000)	(2,000)
Ending balance	$10,000	$9,000	$19,000

BULLDOG, INC. Balance Sheet			
Assets		**Liabilities**	
Cash	$ 3,000	Accounts payable	(d)
Accounts receivable	2,000	**Stockholders' Equity**	
Supplies	8,000	Common stock	(e)
Equipment	9,000	Retained earnings	(f)
		Total liabilities and	
Total assets	$22,000	stockholders' equity	(g)

Required:

Calculate the missing amounts.

Prepare financial statements (LO3)

P1–5A Cornhusker Company provides the following information at the end of 2012.

Cash remaining	$ 3,800
Rent expense for the year	6,000
Land that has been purchased	20,000
Retained earnings	?
Utility expense for the year	3,900
Accounts receivable from customers	6,200
Service revenue earned during the year	32,000
Salary expense for the year	12,300
Accounts payable to suppliers	1,700
Dividends paid to shareholders during the year	2,200
Common stock that has been issued prior to 2012	15,000
Salaries owed at the end of the year	1,900
Insurance expense for the year	2,500

Required:

Prepare the income statement, statement of stockholders' equity, and balance sheet for Cornhusker Company on December 31, 2012. No common stock is issued during 2012, and the balance of retained earnings at the beginning of 2012 equals $6,300.

Identify underlying assumptions of GAAP (LO7)

P1–6A The four underlying assumptions of generally accepted accounting principles are economic entity, monetary unit, periodicity, and going concern. Consider the four independent situations below.

1. McAdam's is a local restaurant. Due to a bad shipment of potatoes, several of the company's customers become ill, and the company receives considerable bad publicity. Revenues are way down, several of its bills are past due, and the company

is making plans to close the restaurant at the end of the month. The company continues to report its assets in the balance sheet at historical (original) cost.

2. Uncle Sam's Tax Services is owned and operated by Sam Martin. The company has the usual business assets: land, building, cash, equipment, and supplies. In addition, Sam decides to buy a boat for him and his family to enjoy on the weekends. Sam includes the boat as an asset on the balance sheet of Uncle Sam's Tax Services.

3. Tison International, a U.S.-based company, has operations in the United States and in Europe. For the current year, the company purchased two trucks in the United States for $10,000 and three trucks in Europe for €20,000 (euros). Because of the differences in currencies, the company reported "Five Trucks" with no corresponding amount in the balance sheet.

4. Trumpets Etc. sells specialty music equipment ranging from African bongo drums to grand pianos. Because of the fluctuating nature of the business, management decides to publish financial statements only when a substantial amount of activity has taken place. Its last set of financial statements covered a period of 14 months, and the set of financial statements before that covered a period of 18 months.

[handwritten: monetary unit; Economic Entity; periodicity]

Required:

For each situation, indicate which of the underlying assumptions of GAAP is violated.

P1–7A Listed below are nine terms and definitions associated with the FASB's conceptual framework.

Understand the components of the FASB's conceptual framework (LO7)

Terms	Definitions
1. _____ Completeness	a. Requires the consideration of the costs and value of information.
2. _____ Comparability	b. Ability to make comparisons between firms.
3. _____ Neutrality	c. Comprehending the meaning of accounting information.
4. _____ Understandability	d. Including all information necessary to report the business activity.
5. _____ Cost effectiveness	e. The business will last indefinitely unless there is evidence otherwise.
6. _____ Verifiability	f. Recording transactions only for the company.
7. _____ Decision usefulness	g. Implies consensus among different measures.
8. _____ Economic entity assumption	h. Accounting should be useful in making decisions.
9. _____ Going concern assumption	i. Accounting information should not favor a particular group.

Required:

Pair each term with its related definition.

PROBLEMS: SET B

connect |ACCOUNTING

P1–1B Below are typical transactions for **Caterpillar Inc.**

Classify accounts (LO2)

Type of Business Activity	Transactions
1. Operating	Pay for advertising.
2. Financing	Pay dividends to stockholders.
3. Operating	Collect cash from customer for previous sale.
4. Investing	Purchase a building to be used for operations.
5. Operating	Purchase equipment.
6. Investing	Sell land.
7. Financing	Receive a loan from the bank by signing a note.
8. Operating	Pay suppliers for purchase of supplies.
9. Operating	Provide services to customers.
10. Investing	Invest in securities of another company.

Required:

Indicate whether each transaction is classified as a financing, investing, or operating activity.

Assign business transactions to account classifications (LO2)

P1–2B Account classifications include assets, liabilities, stockholders' equity, dividends, revenues, and expenses.

Account Classifications	Accounts	Related Transactions
1. _assets_	Cash	Receive cash from customers.
2. _revenues_	Service revenue	Provide services to customers.
3. _assets_	Supplies	Purchase supplies.
4. _assets_	Buildings	Purchase factory for operations.
5. _expenses_	Advertising expense	Pay for cost of advertising.
6. _expenses_	Equipment	Pay for cost of advertising.
7. _expenses_	Interest expense	Purchase equipment for operations.
8. _liabilities_	Accounts payable	Pay for cost of interest.
9. _stockholders' equity_ Dividends	Dividends	Purchase supplies on credit.
10. _liabilities_	Notes payable	Distribute cash to stockholders.
		Borrow from the bank.

Dividends

Required:

For each transaction, indicate whether the related account would be classified as an (a) asset, (b) liability, or (c) stockholders' equity to be reported in the balance sheet; a (d) revenue or (e) expense to be reported in the income statement; or an (f) dividend to be reported in the statement of stockholders' equity.

Prepare financial statements (LO3)

P1–3B Gator Investments provides financial services related to investment selections, retirement planning, and general insurance needs. For the current year, the company reports the following amounts:

Advertising expense	$ 32,500	Service revenue	$122,600
Buildings	140,000	Interest expense	2,500
Salaries expense	64,100	Utilities expense	14,500
Accounts payable	5,400	Equipment	22,000
Cash	4,500	Notes payable	25,000

In addition, the company had common stock of $100,000 at the beginning of the year and issued an additional $10,000 during the year. The company also had retained earnings of $21,300 at the beginning of the year and paid dividends of $4,200.

Required:

Prepare the income statement, statement of stockholders' equity, and balance sheet for Gator Investments.

Understand the format of financial statements and the link among them (LO3)

P1–4B Below are incomplete financial statements for Cyclone, Inc.

CYCLONE, INC. Income Statement	
Revenues	(a)
Expenses:	
Salaries	$12,000
Rent	6,000
Advertising	4,000
Net income	(b)

CYCLONE, INC. Statement of Stockholders' Equity			
	Common Stock	Retained Earnings	Total S. Equity
Beginning balance	$13,000	$6,000	$19,000
Issuances of stock	(c)		(c)
Add: Net income		4,000	4,000
Less: Dividends		(d)	(d)
Ending balance	$15,000	$7,000	$22,000

CYCLONE, INC.
Balance Sheet

Assets		Liabilities	
Cash	$ 1,000	Accounts payable	$3,000
Supplies	(e)	**Stockholders' Equity**	
Land	5,000	Common stock	(g)
Building	15,000	Retained earnings	(h)
		Total liabilities and	
Total assets	(f)	stockholders' equity	(i)

Required:
Calculate the missing amounts.

12-31

P1–5B Tar Heel Corporation provides the following information at the end of 2012.

Prepare financial statements **(LO3)**

23300
36000

Salaries payable to workers at the end of the year *Debt (L)*	$ 2,300
Advertising expense for the year *(SE)*	9,400
Building that has been purchased	70,000
Supplies at the end of the year	3,600
Retained earnings	36,000
Utility expense for the year	5,000
Note payable to the bank	20,000
Service revenue earned during the year	64,400
Salary expense for the year	25,700
Accounts payable to suppliers *(L)*	6,700
Dividends paid to shareholders during the year	(?)
Common stock that has been issued, including $5,000 that was issued this year	25,000
Cash remaining	4,200
Interest expense for the year	1,600
Accounts receivable from customers	12,200

Current Asset, on an balance sheet

Required:
Prepare the income statement, statement of stockholders' equity, and balance sheet for Tar Heel Corporation on December 31, 2012. The balance of retained earnings at the beginning of the year equals $23,300.

P1–6B The four underlying assumptions of generally accepted accounting principles are economic entity, monetary unit, periodicity, and going concern. Consider the following four independent situations.

Identify underlying assumptions of GAAP **(LO7)**

1. Fine Groceries has over 1,000 grocery stores throughout the Northwest. Approximately 200,000 customers visit its stores each day. Because of the continual nature of grocery sales, the company does not publish an income statement. The company feels that it has an indefinite life and a periodic report would mislead investors.
2. Pacific Shipping provides delivery of packages between the United States and Japan. During the current year, the company delivered 3,000 packages for its U.S. customers totaling $25,000 in revenue. For its Japanese customers, the company delivered 1,000 packages totaling ¥1,000,000 (yen). The company's income statement indicates that total revenue equals 4,000 packages delivered with no corresponding amount in the income statement.
3. Schuster Typewriter has provided some of the finest typewriters in town for the past 50 years. Because of the advance of electronic word processors and computers, customer demand has dwindled over the years to almost nothing in the current year and the company can no longer pay its debts. For the most recent year, the company reports its assets in the balance sheet at historical (original) cost.

4. John Brewer Carpet specializes in the installation of carpet and wood flooring. The company has the usual business expenses: salaries, supplies, utilities, advertising, and taxes. John took his wife and two daughters to Disney World. John reported the airfare and hotel expenses in the income statement of John Brewer Carpet.

Required:

For each situation, indicate which of the underlying assumptions of GAAP is violated.

Understand the components of the FASB's conceptual framework (**LO7**)

P1–7B Listed below are several terms and definitions associated with the FASB's conceptual framework.

Terms	**Definitions**
1. _____ Predictive value	a. Decreases in equity resulting from transfers to owners.
2. _____ Relevance	b. Business transactions are measured using a common denominator.
3. _____ Timeliness	c. The indefinite life of a company can be broken into definite periods.
4. _____ Dividends	d. Information helps in understanding prior activities.
5. _____ Confirmatory value	e. Agreement between a measure and the phenomenon it represents.
6. _____ Faithful representation	f. Information arrives prior to the decision.
7. _____ Materiality	g. Information is related to the decision at hand.
8. _____ Monetary unit assumption	h. Information is useful in predicting the future.
9. _____ Periodicity assumption	i. Concerns the relative size of an item and its effect on decisions.

Required:

Pair each term with its related definition.

*For additional problems, visit **www.mhhe.com/succeed** for Problems: Set C.*

ADDITIONAL PERSPECTIVES

Continuing Problem

Great Adventures

(The Great Adventures problem continues in each chapter.)

AP1–1 Tony Matheson plans to graduate from college in May 2012 after spending four years earning a degree in sports and recreation management. Since beginning T-ball at age five, he's been actively involved in sports and enjoys the outdoors. Each summer growing up, he and his father would spend two weeks at a father/son outdoor camp. These fond memories are part of the reason he chose his major. He wants to remain involved in these outdoor activities and provide others with the same adventures he was able to share with his dad. He decides to start an outdoor adventure company. However, he's not sure he has the business background necessary to do this.

This is where Suzie Ramos can help. Suzie also plans to graduate in May 2012 with a major in business. Suzie and Tony first met their sophomore year and have been friends ever since as they share a strong interest in sports and outdoor activities.

They decide to name their company Great Adventures. They will provide clinics for a variety of outdoor activities such as kayaking, mountain biking, rock climbing, wilderness survival techniques, orienteering, backpacking, and other adventure sports.

Required:

1. What are the three primary forms of business organizations Tony and Suzie might choose for Great Adventures? Explain the advantages and disadvantages of each. Which form do you recommend for Great Adventures?

2. Discuss some of the typical financing, investing, and operating activities that a company like Great Adventures is likely to have.
3. What specific account names for assets, liabilities, stockholders' equity, revenues, and expenses would the company likely use to record its business transactions?
4. To report company performance, Suzie plans to prepare the four primary financial statements. Explain the type of information provided by each statement.

American Eagle Outfitters, Inc.

Financial Analysis

AP1–2 Financial information for **American Eagle** is presented in Appendix A at the end of the book.

Required:

1. Determine the amounts American Eagle reports for total assets, total liabilities, and total stockholders' equity in the balance sheet for the most recent year. Verify that the basic accounting equation balances.
2. American Eagle refers to its income statement using another name. What is it?
3. Determine the amounts American Eagle reports for net sales and net income in its income statement for the most recent year.
4. For investing activities, what are the largest inflows and largest outflows for the most recent year reported in the statement of cash flows? For financing activities, what are the largest inflows and largest outflows?
5. Who is the company's auditor? (See the Report of Independent Registered Public Accounting Firm.) What does the report indicate about the amounts reported in the company's financial statements?

The Buckle, Inc.

Financial Analysis

Buckle ⊟

AP1–3 Financial information for **The Buckle** is presented in Appendix B at the end of the book.

Required:

1. Determine the amounts The Buckle reports for total assets, total liabilities, and total stockholders' equity in the balance sheet for the most recent year. Verify that the basic accounting equation balances.
2. The Buckle refers to its income statement using another name. What is it?
3. Determine the amounts The Buckle reports for net sales and net income in its income statement for the most recent year.
4. For investing activities, what are the largest inflows and largest outflows for the most recent year reported in the statement of cash flows? For financing activities, what are the largest inflows and largest outflows?
5. Who is the company's auditor? (See the Report of Independent Registered Public Accounting Firm.) What does the report indicate about the amounts reported in the company's financial statements?

American Eagle Outfitters, Inc. vs. The Buckle, Inc.

Comparative Analysis

Buckle ⊟

AP1–4 Financial information for **American Eagle** is presented in Appendix A at the end of the book, and financial information for **The Buckle** is presented in Appendix B at the end of the book.

Required:

1. Which company reports higher total assets?
2. Which company reports higher total liabilities? Does this always mean this company has a higher chance of not being able to repay its debt and declare bankruptcy? Explain.
3. What relevant information do total assets and total liabilities provide to creditors deciding whether to lend money to American Eagle versus The Buckle?

4. Which company reports higher net income? Does this always mean this company's operations are more profitable? Explain.
5. What relevant information does net income provide to investors who are deciding whether to invest in American Eagle versus The Buckle?

Ethics

AP1–5 Management has the responsibility of accurately preparing financial statements when communicating with investors and creditors. Another group, auditors, serves an independent role by helping to ensure that management has in fact appropriately applied GAAP in preparing the company's financial statements. Auditors examine (audit) financial statements to express a professional, independent opinion. The opinion reflects the auditors' assessment of the statements' fairness, which is determined by the extent to which they are prepared in compliance with GAAP.

Suppose an auditor is being paid $1,000,000 by the company to perform the audit. In addition, the company plans to pay the auditor $500,000 over the next year for business consulting advice and another $200,000 for preparing its tax returns. The auditor and management of the company have always shared a friendly relationship, which partly explains the company's willingness to give the auditor additional work for $700,000.

Required:
How might an auditor's ethics be challenged while performing an audit?

Internet Research

AP1–6 The purpose of this research case is to introduce you to the Internet home pages of the Securities and Exchange Commission (SEC) and the Financial Accounting Standards Board (FASB).

Required:
1. Access the SEC home page on the Internet (***www.sec.gov***). Under "About the SEC," choose "What We Do." What is the mission of the SEC? Why was the SEC created? What are the two objectives of the 1933 Securities Act? The 1934 Securities Exchange Act established the SEC. What does the 1934 Act empower the SEC to require?
2. Access ***www.sec.gov/investor/pubs/begfinstmtguide.htm***. What are the four main financial statements discussed by the SEC? What does each report? What information is disclosed in the notes and management discussion and analysis (MD&A)?
3. Access the FASB home page on the Internet (***www.fasb.org***). Select "Facts About FASB." Describe the mission of the FASB. What is the relation between the SEC and the FASB?
4. Obtain a copy of the annual report of **ConocoPhillips** for the most recent year. You can find the annual report at the company's website (***www.conocophillips.com***) in the investor information section or at the SEC's website (***www.sec.gov***) using EDGAR (Electronic Data Gathering, Analysis, and Retrieval). The SEC requires that Form 10-K, which includes the annual report, be filed on EDGAR. Answer the following questions:
   (a) Did ConocoPhillips prepare the four financial statements discussed by the SEC?
   (b) In the MD&A section, how does the company describe its business environment?
   (c) Find the note disclosures to the financial statements. What does the disclosure on segment information discuss?

Written Communication

AP1–7 Maria comes to you for investment advice. She asks, "Which company's stock should I buy? There are so many companies to choose from and I don't know anything about any of them."

Required:

Respond to Maria by explaining the two functions of financial accounting. Specifically address the four financial statements reported by companies and the information contained in each. Also explain the role of the auditor in the preparation of financial statements. What advice can you give her about finding a company's stock to buy?

Answers to the Self-Study Questions

1. b   2. d   3. c   4. b   5. a   6. c   7. b   8. d   9. d   10. a

The Accounting Information System

Learning Objectives

AFTER STUDYING THIS CHAPTER, YOU SHOULD BE ABLE TO:

- ■ **LO1** Identify the basic steps in measuring external transactions.
- ■ **LO2** Analyze the impact of external transactions on the accounting equation.
- ■ **LO3** Assess whether the impact of external transactions results in a debit or credit to an account balance.
- ■ **LO4** Record transactions using debits and credits.
- ■ **LO5** Post transactions to T-accounts in the general ledger.
- ■ **LO6** Prepare a trial balance.

WALMART: SHELVES OF BUSINESS TRANSACTIONS

Walmart opened its first store in Rogers, Arkansas, in 1962. By 1967, the company had increased to 24 stores totaling $12,600,000 in sales, and the following year it expanded operations to Missouri and Oklahoma. Today, Wal-Mart Stores, Inc. (the parent company) is the world's largest retailer with over $400,000,000,000 in sales. (That's $400 billion!) With nearly 2 million employees worldwide, it's the largest private employer in the United States and Mexico and one of the largest in Canada. Each year Walmart purchases from over 60,000 vendors merchandise totaling $300 billion. More than 175 million customers visit Walmart stores each week.

With its huge numbers of financial transactions and relationships with customers, suppliers, employees, and government agencies, Walmart poses a challenge to potential investors and lenders who need to understand its financial position today. Obviously, its past performance represents a success story. Sam Walton, Walmart's founder, started his career at **J. C. Penney** in 1940, earning just $75 per month. In 2009, the Walton family's net worth totaled nearly $90 billion (*www.forbes.com*). If you had invested $1,000 in Walmart in 1970 when it first issued stock, your investment would have grown to more than $1 million by the end of 2009.

But is Walmart still a good investment? Would you want to invest $1,000 today? While the past provides useful information, what is the current financial position of Walmart? What is its potential for the future? For investors to fully understand the financial position and profitability of any company, a system must be in place that can summarize and communicate thousands (or even billions) of economic events.

As you may realize by now, summarizing and communicating economic events is the role of financial accounting. In this chapter, we review the process accountants use to identify, analyze, record, and summarize economic events affecting a company's financial position. Having a firm grasp of this process is key to your understanding of financial accounting.

MEASURING BUSINESS ACTIVITIES

In this chapter, we examine the accounting information process using a manual accounting system. Most business enterprises use a computerized accounting system due to the sheer volume of data they must process. Computerized data processing is fast, accurate, and affordable. Our focus on a manual accounting information system, though, will provide you an essential understanding of the basic model that underlies the computerized programs.

This chapter provides a foundation for the remaining chapters. We'll consider the *measurement role* of financial accounting and examine the process firms use to identify, analyze, record, and summarize the external economic events affecting their financial position.

Measurement of External Transactions

■ **LO1**
Identify the basic steps in measuring external transactions.

Recall from Chapter 1 that the two roles of financial accounting are to (1) measure business activities of the company and (2) communicate those measurements to external parties for decision-making purposes. The business activities, or transactions, we want to measure and communicate are classified as either external or internal. **External transactions** are transactions the firm conducts with a separate economic entity. Examples are selling products to a customer, purchasing supplies from a vendor, paying salaries to an employee, and borrowing money from a bank. **Internal transactions** are events that affect the financial position of the company but do not include an exchange with a separate economic entity. Examples are using supplies on hand and earning revenues after having received cash in advance from a customer. In this chapter, we focus on the measurement of external transactions. We save internal transactions for Chapter 3.

 KEY POINT

External transactions are transactions between the company and separate economic entities. Internal transactions do not include an exchange with a separate economic entity.

Measuring external transactions is a six-step process, as outlined in Illustration 2–1. These steps are the foundation for the remaining chapters in this book. Make sure you understand them before you proceed.

The first step in the measurement process involves gathering information about a transaction. Source documents such as sales invoices, bills from suppliers, and signed contracts provide information related to external transactions. These source documents usually identify the date and nature of each transaction, the participating parties, and the monetary terms. For example, a sales invoice might identify the date of sale, the customer, the specific items sold, the dollar amount of the sale, and the payment terms.

Companies record the effects of transactions in accounts. An **account** provides a summary of the effects of all transactions related to a particular item over a period of time. For instance, *asset accounts* include Cash, Supplies, and Equipment. All transactions affecting cash are summarized in the Cash account; all transactions affecting supplies are summarized in the Supplies account; and so on. Examples of *liability accounts* include Accounts Payable, Salaries Payable, Utilities Payable, and Taxes Payable. *Stockholders' equity accounts* include Common Stock and Retained Earnings. A list of all account names used to record transactions of a company is referred to as the chart of accounts. (Later in the chapter, we'll see a preliminary chart of accounts. A comprehensive chart of accounts provided at the back of the

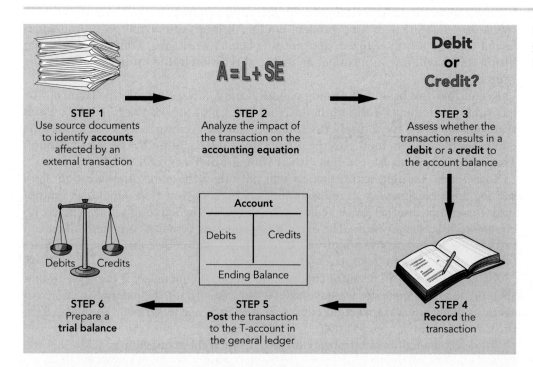

ILLUSTRATION 2–1
Six Steps in Measuring External Transactions

book includes all accounts used in the book. Keep this handy for reference throughout the course.)

In this chapter and throughout the remainder of the book, you'll learn how to compute the balance of each account and eventually use these account balances to prepare the financial statements introduced in Chapter 1. But first, let's work through steps 2–6 of the measurement process to see how external business transactions are summarized in account balances.

 KEY POINT

The six-step measurement process (Illustration 2–1) is the foundation of financial accounting.

Effects of Transactions on the Basic Accounting Equation

The activities we want to record are those that affect the financial position of the company. That means they affect the accounting equation you learned about in Chapter 1. Remember, the basic accounting equation shows that resources of the company (asset accounts) are equal to claims to those resources by creditors (liability accounts) and owners (stockholders' equity accounts).

■ **LO2**
Analyze the impact of external transactions on the accounting equation.

$$\underbrace{\textbf{Assets}}_{\text{(resources)}} = \underbrace{\textbf{Liabilities} + \textbf{Stockholders' Equity}}_{\text{(claims to resources)}}$$

The basic accounting equation

When **Walmart** borrows cash from a bank, its financial position is affected because assets (cash) increase and liabilities (the loan payable to the bank) increase. So, Walmart records that event in its accounting records. On the other hand, when

Walmart hires Ralph as a front-door greeter, that action doesn't change the company's assets, liabilities, or stockholders' equity; Walmart's financial position is unaffected the day Ralph is hired, and until he begins work. Yes, Walmart hopes that hiring Ralph will favorably affect its financial position in the future, but the hiring itself does not.

Recall that the basic accounting equation must always remain in balance: The left side (assets) equals the right side (liabilities plus stockholders' equity). **Each transaction will have a dual effect.** If an economic event increases one side of the equation, then it also increases the other side of the equation by the same amount. That's what happens, for example, when Walmart borrows cash.

Sometimes, though, a transaction will not affect the *total* of either side. Let's say **Wendy's** buys new cash registers for its stores, paying cash. One asset (equipment) goes up; another asset (cash) goes down by the same amount. There's no change to assets *as a whole*. The accounting equation remains in balance. You can tell whether a transaction affects the accounting equation by considering its impact on the company's total resources—its total assets.

As the balance in an account changes, we record the increase or decrease in that specific account. Let's say we have $50,000 in cash. That's the *balance* in the Cash account. Now say a transaction causes cash to increase by $1,000. The balance in the Cash account is now $51,000.

To see the effect of each transaction, ask yourself these questions:

1. **"What is one account in the accounting equation affected by the transaction? Does that account increase or decrease?"**

2. **"What is a second account in the accounting equation affected by the transaction? Does that account increase or decrease?"**

After noting the effects of the transaction on the accounting equation, ask yourself this:

3. **"Do assets equal liabilities plus stockholders' equity?"**

The answer to the third question must be "yes." **At least two accounts will be affected by every transaction or economic event.** While some economic events will affect *more* than two accounts, most events we record affect only two accounts.

The best way to understand the impact of a transaction on the accounting equation is to see it demonstrated by a few examples. Let's return to the Eagle Golf Academy from Chapter 1. Illustration 2–2 (next page) summarizes the external transactions for Eagle in January, the first month of operations. (You may also want to refer back to the financial statements in Illustrations 1–6, 1–8, and 1–9 to remind yourself how the transactions will eventually be reported.) Note that business activities usually occur in this same order for a new company—obtain external *financing*, use those funds to *invest* in long-term productive assets, and then begin normal *operations*. We discussed these business activities in Chapter 1.

On the following pages, we discuss the impact of these 10 transactions on the accounting equation.

TRANSACTION (1): ISSUE COMMON STOCK

To begin operations, Eagle Golf Academy needs cash. To generate cash from external sources, Eagle sells shares of common stock for $25,000. Let's reflect on this for a moment. Imagine being the sole owner of Eagle Golf Academy. To get your business going, you take $25,000 from your personal funds and invest it in your business. Although your personal cash decreased, the cash of your company *increased*, and so did your equity or ownership interest in the company's assets. Now, imagine instead

Transaction	Date	External Transactions in January	Type of Activity
(1)	Jan. 1	Sell shares of common stock for $25,000 to obtain the funds necessary to start the business.	Financing
(2)	Jan. 1	Borrow $10,000 from the local bank and sign a note promising to repay the full amount of the debt in three years.	Financing
(3)	Jan. 1	Purchase equipment necessary for giving golf training, $24,000 cash.	Investing
(4)	Jan. 1	Pay one year of rent in advance, $6,000 ($500 per month).	Operating
(5)	Jan. 6	Purchase supplies on account, $2,300.	Operating
(6)	Jan. 12	Provide golf training to customers for cash, $3,600.	Operating
(7)	Jan. 17	Provide golf training to customers on account, $2,500.	Operating
(8)	Jan. 23	Receive cash in advance for 10 golf training sessions to be given in the future, $600.	Operating
(9)	Jan. 28	Pay salaries to employees, $2,800.	Operating
(10)	Jan. 30	Pay cash dividends of $200 to shareholders.	Financing

ILLUSTRATION 2–2

External Transactions of Eagle Golf Academy

that the company is organized as a corporation and that by investing $25,000 in it you are becoming one of its many stockholders or owners.

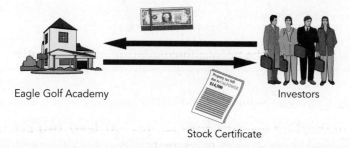

Eagle Golf Academy

Stock Certificate

Investors

(1) Issue common stock

It's time to ask the three questions we asked earlier:

1. **"What is one account in the accounting equation affected by the transaction? Does that account increase or decrease?"**

Answer: **Cash.** Cash is a resource owned by the company, which makes it an asset. The company receives cash from you, so cash and total assets **increase** by $25,000.

2. **"What is a second account in the accounting equation affected by the transaction? Does that account increase or decrease?"**

Answer: **Common Stock.** Common Stock is a stockholders' equity account. Issuing common stock to you in exchange for your $25,000 increases the amount of common stock owned by stockholders, so common stock and total stockholders' equity both **increase.**

Issuing common stock for cash increases both sides of the accounting equation:

Assets	=	Liabilities	+	Stockholders' Equity
Cash ↑ +$25,000	=			Common Stock ↑ +$25,000

TRANSACTION (1)

Initial investment of $25,000 by stockholders

3. "Do assets equal liabilities plus stockholders' equity?"

Answer: **Yes.**

Note that the accounting equation balances. If one side of the equation increases, so does the other side. We can use this same series of questions to understand the effect of *any* business transaction. Let's try another one.

 COMMON MISTAKE

It's sometimes tempting to *decrease* cash as a way of recording an investor's initial investment. However, we account for transactions *from the company's perspective*, and the company *received* cash from the stockholder—an increase in cash.

TRANSACTION (2): BORROW FROM THE BANK

Seeking cash from another external source, Eagle Academy borrows $10,000 from the bank and signs a note promising to repay it in the future.

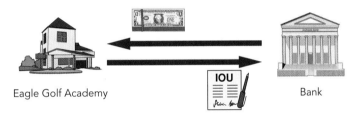

(2) Borrow from bank

Eagle Golf Academy   Bank

1. "What is one account in the accounting equation affected by the transaction? Does that account increase or decrease?"

Answer: **Cash.** Cash is a resource owned by the company, which makes it an asset. The company receives cash, so cash and total assets **increase.**

2. "What is a second account in the accounting equation affected by the transaction? Does that account increase or decrease?"

Answer: **Notes Payable.** Notes payable represent amounts owed to creditors (the bank in this case), which makes them a liability. The company incurs debt when signing the note, so notes payable and total liabilities **increase.**

Borrowing by signing a note causes both assets and liabilities to increase:

TRANSACTION (2)

Borrow $10,000 from the bank and sign a long-term note

Assets	=	Liabilities	+	Stockholders' Equity
Cash ↑ +$10,000	=	Notes Payable ↑ +$10,000		

3. "Do assets equal liabilities plus stockholders' equity?"

Answer: **Yes.**

After these two transactions, the accounting equation remains in balance. The total resources of the company equal $35,000. Creditors' claims to those resources total $10,000, and the remaining resources of $25,000 were provided by stockholders. Illustration 2–3 summarizes the effects of the two financing activities we've analyzed so far.

Assets	=	Liabilities	+	Stockholders' Equity	
Financing Activities:					
(1) Cash ↑ +$ 25,000				Common Stock ↑ +$ 25,000	
(2) Cash ↑ +$ 10,000		Notes Payable ↑ +$ 10,000			
Total $35,000	=	$10,000	+	$25,000	

ILLUSTRATION 2–3

Summary of Initial Financing Transactions of Eagle Golf Academy

Regardless of the number of transactions occurring during the period, the accounting equation always must remain in balance. For brevity, we do not address the three-question process for Eagle's remaining eight transactions, but you should ask yourself those questions until you feel comfortable with the process.

 KEY POINT

After each transaction, the accounting equation must always remain in balance. In other words, assets must always equal liabilities plus stockholders' equity.

TRANSACTION (3): PURCHASE EQUIPMENT

Once Eagle obtains financing by issuing common stock and borrowing from the bank, the company can invest in long-term assets necessary to operate the business.

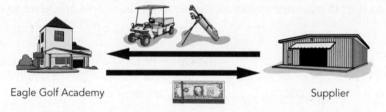

Eagle Golf Academy   Supplier

(3) Purchase equipment

Buying equipment from a supplier causes one asset to increase and another asset to decrease:

Assets	=	Liabilities	+	Stockholders' Equity
Equipment ↑ +$24,000				
Cash ↓ −$24,000				

TRANSACTION (3)

Purchase equipment with cash, $24,000

Notice that purchasing one asset (equipment) with another asset (cash) has no effect on the category totals in the accounting equation. One asset increases, while another asset decreases. Once we add transaction (3) to the accounting equation, we see in Illustration 2–4 (next page) that the accounting equation remains in balance.

TRANSACTIONS (4) AND (5): INCUR COSTS FOR RENT AND SUPPLIES

Eagle Academy now engages in some operating transactions: It pays one year of rent in advance, $6,000, and purchases supplies on account, $2,300. Because the rent paid is for occupying space in the future, we don't want to record it as an expense immediately. Instead, we record it as an asset representing the right to occupy the space in the future. We call the asset *prepaid rent* and, as we discuss later in the course, we'll report this amount as expense over the next 12 months, as the time we've prepaid

ILLUSTRATION 2–4

Summary of Initial Financing and Investing Transactions of Eagle Golf Academy

Assets		=	Liabilities		+	Stockholders' Equity	
Financing Activities:							
(1) Cash ↑	+$25,000					Common Stock ↑	+$25,000
(2) Cash ↑	+$10,000		Notes Payable ↑	+$10,000			
Subtotal	**$35,000**	=		**$10,000**	+		**$25,000**
Investing Activities:							
(3) Equipment ↑	+$24,000						
Cash ↓	−$24,000						
Total	**$35,000**	=		**$10,000**	+		**$25,000**

expires. Other common examples of prepaid assets include prepaid insurance and prepaid advertising. These items often are purchased prior to their use.

(4) Incur costs for rent

Purchasing rent in advance causes one asset to increase and one asset to decrease:

TRANSACTION (4)

Pay one year of rent in advance, $6,000

Assets		=	Liabilities	+	Stockholders' Equity
Prepaid Rent ↑	+$6,000				
Cash ↓	−$6,000				

Next, Eagle purchases supplies with the promise to pay cash in the future. This promise creates a liability. We refer to a liability of this type, in which we purchase something on account, as an *account payable*.

(5) Incur costs for supplies

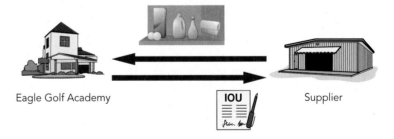

Purchasing supplies with the promise to pay cash in the future causes an asset (supplies) to increase and also causes a liability (accounts payable) to increase:

TRANSACTION (5)

Purchase supplies on account, $2,300

Assets		=	Liabilities		+	Stockholders' Equity
Supplies ↑	+$2,300	=	Accounts Payable ↑	+$2,300		

Effects of Transactions on the Expanded Accounting Equation

To better understand how revenues increase stockholders' equity, let's expand the accounting equation. As discussed in Chapter 1, we can divide stockholders' equity into its two components—common stock and retained earnings. Common stock represents investments by stockholders. Retained earnings represents net income earned over the life of the company that has *not* been distributed to stockholders as dividends. Both of these amounts represent stockholders' claims to the company's resources. Next, we can split retained earnings into its three components—revenues, expenses, and dividends. Illustration 2–5 presents the expanded accounting equation, which shows these components.

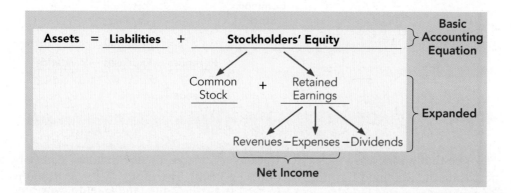

ILLUSTRATION 2–5

Expanded Accounting Equation

Be sure to notice the effects of revenues, expenses, and dividends on retained earnings (and therefore on total stockholders' equity) in the expanded accounting equation:

1. We *add* revenues to calculate retained earnings. That's because revenues increase net income, and net income increases stockholders' claims to resources. **Therefore, an *increase* in revenues has the effect of *increasing* stockholders' equity in the basic accounting equation.**
2. We *subtract* expenses and dividends to calculate retained earnings. Expenses reduce net income, and dividends represent a distribution of net income to stockholders. Both expenses and dividends reduce stockholders' claims to the company's resources. **Therefore, an *increase* in expenses or dividends has the effect of *decreasing* stockholders' equity in the basic accounting equation.**

 KEY POINT

The expanded accounting equation demonstrates that revenues increase retained earnings while expenses and dividends decrease retained earnings. Retained earnings is a component of stockholders' equity.

TRANSACTIONS (6) AND (7): PROVIDE SERVICES TO CUSTOMERS

To see an example of how revenue affects the expanded accounting equation, let's look at the two revenue transactions for Eagle Golf Academy. In transaction (6), Eagle provides golf training to customers who pay cash at the time of the service, $3,600.

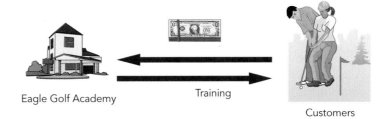

(6) Provide golf training for cash

Eagle Golf Academy   Training   Customers

Providing training to customers for cash causes both assets and stockholders' equity to increase:

TRANSACTION (6)

Provide golf training to customers for cash, $3,600

Assets	=	Liabilities	+	Stockholders' Equity		
				Common Stock	+	**Retained Earnings**
Cash ↑ +$3,600 =						+$3,600
				Revenues − Expenses − Dividends		
				Service Revenue ↑		

Notice that an increase in Service Revenue (↑) increases stockholders' equity by increasing the Retained Earnings account (+$3,600). Therefore, the basic accounting equation remains in balance (Assets = Liabilities + Stockholders' Equity).

As shown in Illustration 2–5, revenues are a component of retained earnings. When a company earns revenue, the amount of retained earnings (or net income) in the business increases. We can increase retained earnings by increasing its revenue component. Stated another way, an increase in revenues increases net income, which increases retained earnings, which increases total stockholders' equity:

Revenues → **Net Income** → **Retained Earnings** → **Stockholders' Equity**

In transaction (7), other customers receive golf training but promise to pay $2,500 cash at some time in the future. The fact that some customers do not pay cash at the time of the service doesn't prevent Eagle from recording revenue. Eagle has *earned* the revenue by providing services. In addition, the *right* to receive cash from a customer is something of value the company owns, and therefore is an asset. When a customer does not immediately pay for services with cash, we traditionally say the services are performed "on account," and we record an *account receivable*.

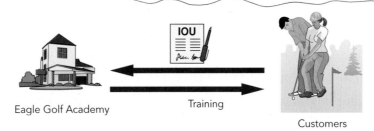

(7) Provide golf training on account

Eagle Golf Academy   Training   Customers

Providing services to customers on account causes both assets and stockholders' equity to increase:

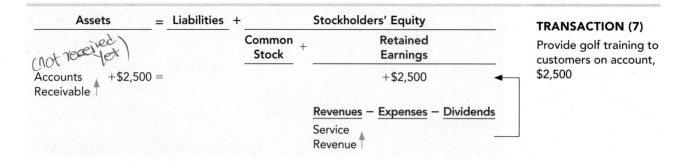

(not received yet)

Assets	=	Liabilities	+	Stockholders' Equity

			Common Stock	+	Retained Earnings

Accounts Receivable ↑ +$2,500 = | | | | +$2,500

Revenues − Expenses − Dividends
Service Revenue ↑

TRANSACTION (7)
Provide golf training to customers on account, $2,500

TRANSACTION (8): RECEIVE CASH IN ADVANCE FROM CUSTOMERS

Companies sometimes receive cash in advance from customers. Let's assume that Eagle receives $600 from customers for golf training to be provided later. In this case, Eagle cannot now report revenue from training because it has yet to provide the training to *earn* those revenues. Instead, the advance payment from customers creates an obligation for the company to perform services in the future. This future obligation is a liability (or debt), most commonly referred to as *unearned revenue*.

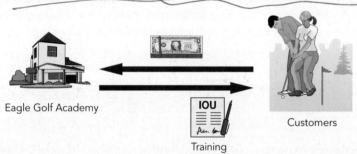

Eagle Golf Academy   IOU   Customers
Training

(8) Receive cash in advance

Receiving cash in advance causes both assets and liabilities to increase:

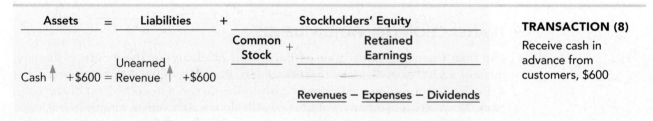

Assets	=	Liabilities	+	Stockholders' Equity

			Common Stock	+	Retained Earnings

Cash ↑ +$600 = Unearned Revenue ↑ +$600

Revenues − Expenses − Dividends

TRANSACTION (8)
Receive cash in advance from customers, $600

COMMON MISTAKE

Don't let the account name fool you. Even though the term *revenue* appears in the account title for *unearned revenue*, this is not a revenue account. *Unearned* indicates that the company has yet to earn this revenue and therefore is still obligated to provide the service in the future. This current obligation creates a liability.

TRANSACTION (9): INCUR COSTS FOR SALARIES

Companies incur a variety of expenses in generating revenues. Eagle Academy incurs salaries expense of $2,800.

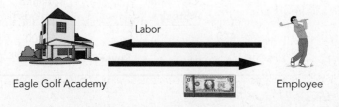

Labor

Eagle Golf Academy   Employee

(9) Incur salary costs

Paying salaries for the current period causes assets and stockholders' equity to decrease:

TRANSACTION (9)

Pay salaries to workers, $2,800

Notice that an *increase* in Salaries Expense (↑) results in a *decrease* in Retained Earnings (−$2,800). As a result, the accounting equation remains in balance, with both sides decreasing by $2,800. The concept of expenses flowing into retained earnings is the same concept that we see in transactions (6) and (7) where revenues also flow into retained earnings, but in the opposite direction. **Expenses *reduce* net income and therefore *reduce* the amount of retained earnings,** a stockholders' equity account. Stated another way, an increase in expenses decreases net income, which decreases retained earnings, which decreases total stockholders' equity:

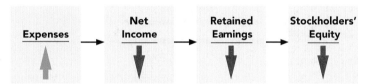

Beyond salaries expense, companies have a number of other expenses. Most expense accounts are labeled with the *expense* title. For instance, common expense accounts include Supplies Expense, Utilities Expense, Rent Expense, Advertising Expense, Interest Expense, and Insurance Expense.

TRANSACTION (10): PAY DIVIDENDS

The final financing transaction of Eagle Golf Academy for the month is the payment of a $200 cash dividend to stockholders. Recall from the previous chapter that a dividend represents a payment of cash to the owners (stockholders) of the company. Normally a company wouldn't pay dividends after only a month in business, but we make this assumption here for purposes of illustration.

(10) Pay dividends

Paying dividends causes assets and stockholders' equity to decrease:

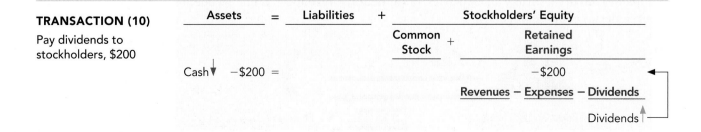

TRANSACTION (10)

Pay dividends to stockholders, $200

Like expenses, dividends *reduce* retained earnings, but dividends are *not* expenses. Instead, dividends are distributions of part of the company's net income to the owners, reducing the amount of earnings that have been retained in the business. Therefore, an *increase* in Dividends (↑) results in a *decrease* in Retained Earnings (−$200). The accounting equation remains in balance, with both sides decreasing by $200. Because retained earnings is a stockholders' equity account, when retained earnings decreases, so does stockholders' equity.

 COMMON MISTAKE

Students often believe a payment of dividends to owners increases stockholders' equity. Remember, you are accounting for the resources *of the company*. While stockholders have more personal cash after dividends have been paid, the company in which they own stock has *fewer* resources (less cash).

Illustration 2–6 summarizes all 10 of the month's transactions we just analyzed for Eagle Golf Academy.

Assets		=	Liabilities		+	Stockholders' Equity	
Financing Activities:							
						Common Stock ↑	+$ 25,000
(1) Cash ↑	+$ 25,000						
(2) Cash ↑	+$ 10,000		Notes Payable ↑	+$ 10,000			
Subtotal	**$35,000**	=		**$10,000**	+		**$25,000**
Investing Activities:							
(3) Equipment ↑	+$ 24,000						
Cash ↓	−$ 24,000						
Subtotal	**$35,000**	=		**$10,000**	+		**$25,000**
Operating Activities:							
(4) Prepaid Rent ↑	+$ 6,000						
Cash ↓	−$ 6,000						
(5) Supplies ↑	+$ 2,300		Accounts Payable ↑	+$ 2,300			
(6) Cash ↑	+$ 3,600					Service Revenue ↑	+$ 3,600
(7) Accounts Receivable ↑	+$ 2,500					Service Revenue ↑	+$ 2,500
(8) Cash ↑	+$ 600		Unearned Revenue ↑	+$ 600			
(9) Cash ↓	−$ 2,800					Salaries Expense ↑	−$ 2,800
Subtotal	**$41,200**	=		**$12,900**	+		**$28,300**
Financing Activity:							
(10) Cash ↓	−$ 200					Dividends ↑	−$ 200
Total	**$41,000**	=		**$12,900**	+		**$28,100**

ILLUSTRATION 2–6

Summary of All 10 External Transactions of Eagle Golf Academy

Let's Review

Bogey Incorporated has the following transactions during May:

May 1 Purchase a storage building by obtaining a loan of $5,000.
May 6 Provide services on account to customers, $1,800.
May 12 Pay $1,200 cash for advertising in May.
May 17 Repay $1,000 of the amount borrowed on May 1.
May 25 Purchase office supplies for $800 cash.

Required:

Indicate how each transaction affects the accounting equation.

Solution:

	Assets	=	Liabilities	+	Stockholders' Equity
May 1	+$5,000		+$5,000		
May 6	+$1,800				+$1,800
May 12	−$1,200				−$1,200
May 17	−$1,000		−$1,000		
May 25	+$ 800				
	−$ 800				
	+$4,600	=	+$4,000	+	+$ 600

Suggested Homework:
BE2-2, BE2-3;
E2-2, E2-3, E2-4;
P2-1A&B, P2-2A&B

PART B

DEBITS AND CREDITS

As we saw in the previous section, external transactions have the effect of increasing or decreasing account balances. While the terms *increase* and *decrease* are well understood, accountants more often use the terms *debit* and *credit* to indicate whether an account balance has increased or decreased. Here, we introduce those terms, discuss their effect on account balances, and show how we record transactions using debits and credits.

Effects on Account Balances in the Basic Accounting Equation

■ LO3
Assess whether the impact of external transactions results in a debit or credit to an account balance.

You will need to learn how to increase and decrease account balances using the terms debit and credit because that's the language of accounting. Although debit and credit are derived from Latin terms, today *debit* simply means "left" and *credit* means "right." Their use dates back to 1494 and a Franciscan monk by the name of Luca Pacioli. It is easy to visualize the use of these directional signals by means of an accounting convention called a "T-account."

A **T-account** is a simplified presentation of an account, in the shape of the letter T. Across the top, we show the account title. On the two sides created by the vertical rule, we record debits and credits, as Illustration 2–7 shows. The left side of the T-account is the debit column. The right side is the credit column.

ILLUSTRATION 2–7
T-Account Format

Account Title	
Debit	Credit

The effect that debits and credits have on various accounts depends on the nature of the specific account. Illustration 2–8 summarizes the effects that debits and credits have on the accounts in the basic accounting equation.

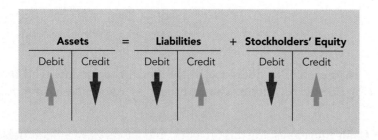

ILLUSTRATION 2–8
Debit and Credit Effects on Accounts in the Basic Accounting Equation

We refer to *increases* in accounts on the left side of the accounting equation—assets—as debits. Just the opposite is true for accounts on the right-hand side of the accounting equation: **We refer to *increases* in liabilities and stockholders' equity as credits.**

The rules reverse for *decreases* in accounts: Assets decrease with a credit. Liabilities and stockholders' equity decrease with a debit.

 COMMON MISTAKE

Students sometimes hear the phrase "assets are the debit accounts" and believe it indicates that assets can only be debited. This is incorrect! Assets, or any account, can be *either* debited or credited. Rather, this phrase indicates that debiting the asset account will increase the balance, and that an asset account normally will have a debit balance. Similarly, the phrase "liabilities and stockholders' equity are the credit accounts" does *not* mean that these accounts cannot be debited. They will be debited when their balances decrease. Rather, the phrase means that crediting the liabilities and stockholders' equity accounts increases their balances, and they normally will have a credit balance.

 KEY POINT

For the basic accounting equation (Assets = Liabilities + Stockholders' Equity), accounts on the left side are increased with *debits*. Accounts on the right side are increased with *credits*. The opposite is true to decrease any of these accounts.

Now, let's look again at the transactions of Eagle Golf Academy, but this time using debits and credits rather than increases and decreases to record the account changes. As we do, ask yourself these three questions for each transaction:

1. "Is there an increase or decrease in the *first* account involved in the transaction? Should I record that increase or decrease with a debit or a credit?"
2. "Is there an increase or decrease in the *second* account involved in the transaction? Should I record that increase or decrease with a debit or a credit?"
3. "Do total debits equal total credits?"

The answer to this last question must be "yes."

Recall our first example: Eagle issues common stock for cash of $25,000 in transaction (1).

TRANSACTION (1)

Initial investment of $25,000 by stockholders

Assets	=	Liabilities	+	Stockholders' Equity
Cash ↑ +$25,000	=			Common Stock ↑ +$25,000

Cash	
Debit	Credit
25,000	

Common Stock	
Debit	Credit
	25,000

1. "Is there an increase or decrease in the *first* account involved in the transaction? Should I record that increase or decrease with a debit or a credit?"

Answer: **Cash increases.** Cash is an asset, and assets have a debit balance. We record an increase in cash with a **debit** to the Cash account.

2. "Is there an increase or decrease in the *second* account involved in the transaction? Is that increase or decrease recorded with a debit or a credit?"

Answer: **Common Stock increases.** Common Stock is a stockholders' equity account, and stockholders' equity has a credit balance. We record an increase in common stock with a **credit** to the Common Stock account.

3. Do total debits equal total credits?

Answer: **Yes.**

The bank borrowing of $10,000 in transaction (2) has the following effects:

TRANSACTION (2)

Borrow $10,000 from the bank and sign a long-term note

Assets	=	Liabilities	+	Stockholders' Equity
Cash ↑ +$10,000	=	Notes Payable ↑ +$10,000		

Cash	
Debit	Credit
10,000	

Notes Payable	
Debit	Credit
	10,000

1. "Is there an increase or decrease in the *first* account involved in the transaction? Should I record that increase or decrease with a debit or a credit?"

Answer: **Cash increases.** Cash is an asset, and assets have a debit balance. We record an increase in cash with a **debit** to the Cash account.

2. "Is there an increase or decrease in the *second* account involved in the transaction? Should I record that increase or decrease with a debit or a credit?"

Answer: **Notes Payable increases.** Notes payable are liabilities, and liabilities have a credit balance. We record an increase to notes payable with a **credit** to the Notes Payable account.

3. Do total debits equal total credits?

Answer: **Yes.**

To record a decrease in an account, see transaction (3), in which Eagle pays cash to purchase equipment. Recall that this transaction results in an increase in equipment and a decrease in cash, both asset accounts.

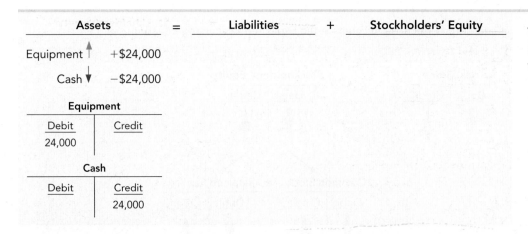

1. **"Is there an increase or decrease in the *first* account involved in the transaction? Should I record that increase or decrease with a debit or a credit?"**

   Answer: **Equipment increases.** Equipment is an asset, and assets have a debit balance. We record an increase in equipment with a **debit** to the Equipment account.

2. **"Is there an increase or decrease in the *second* account involved in the transaction? Should I record that increase or decrease with a debit or a credit?"**

   Answer: **Cash decreases.** Cash is an asset, and assets have a debit balance. We record a decrease in cash with a **credit** to the Cash account.

3. **Do total debits equal total credits?**

   Answer: **Yes.**

Effects on Account Balances in the Expanded Accounting Equation

Remember that accounts on the *left* side of the accounting equation (assets) increase with debits or the *left* side of an account. Accounts on the *right* side of the accounting equation (liabilities and stockholders' equity) increase with credits or the *right* side of an account. This was demonstrated in Illustration 2–8.

As we discussed previously in Illustration 2–5, we can expand the basic accounting equation to include the components of stockholders' equity (common stock and retained earnings) and the components of retained earnings (revenues, expenses, and dividends). Because common stock and retained earnings are part of stockholders' equity, it follows directly that we increase both with a credit. We saw this demonstrated for transaction (1) in the section above: Common stock increased, so we credited that account.

Revenues *increase* retained earnings ("there's more to keep"). Retained Earnings is a credit account, so we increase revenues with a credit. Expenses, on the other hand, *decrease* retained earnings ("there's less to keep"). Thus, we do the opposite of what we do with revenues: We increase expenses with a debit. **A debit to an expense is essentially a debit to Retained Earnings, decreasing the account.** Similarly, dividends *decrease* retained earnings, so we also record an increase in dividends with a debit. In Illustration 2–9 (next page) we show the effects of debits and credits on the components of stockholders' equity in the expanded accounting equation.

ILLUSTRATION 2–9 Debit and Credit Effects on Accounts in the Expanded Accounting Equation

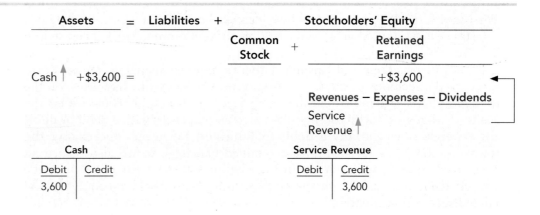

 KEY POINT

The Retained Earnings account is a stockholders' equity account that normally has a credit balance. The Retained Earnings account has three components—revenues, expenses, and dividends. Revenues increase the balance of retained earnings. Expenses and dividends decrease the balance of retained earnings. Therefore, we increase revenues with a credit (similar to retained earnings) and increase expenses and dividends with a debit (opposite of retained earnings).

To see an example of the revenue, expense, and dividend components of retained earnings, let's refer back to transactions (6), (9), and (10) for Eagle Golf Academy: When providing services to customers for cash, in transaction (6), the company earns revenue. The impact of this revenue transaction on the related accounts is shown below.

TRANSACTION (6)

Provide training to customers for cash, $3,600

Assets	=	Liabilities	+	Stockholders' Equity		
				Common Stock	+	Retained Earnings
Cash ↑ +$3,600 =						+$3,600
						Revenues − Expenses − Dividends
						Service Revenue ↑

Cash				Service Revenue	
Debit	Credit			Debit	Credit
3,600					3,600

Paying workers' salaries for the current period in transaction (9) represents an expense and looks like this:

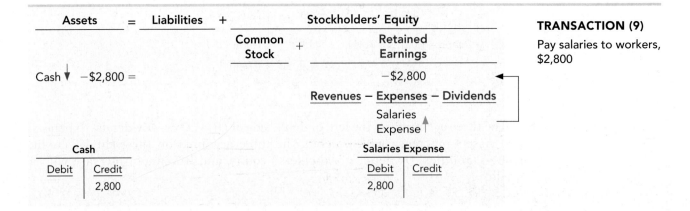

TRANSACTION (9)

Pay salaries to workers, $2,800

Eagle will record the payment of dividends in transaction (10) as:

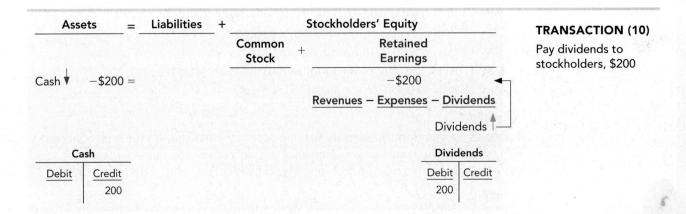

TRANSACTION (10)

Pay dividends to stockholders, $200

In the last two transactions, both expenses and dividends are increasing. These accounts have debit balances, so we increase their account balances with *debits*. However, retained earnings (a component of stockholders' equity) has a *credit* balance. A debit to an expense or a debit to Dividends is the same as a debit to Retained Earnings, reducing the balance of stockholders' equity.

Decision Point

Question ?	Accounting information 📄	Analysis 🔍
How much profit has a company earned over its lifetime for its owners and retained for use in the business?	Retained earnings	The balance of retained earnings provides a record of all revenues and expenses (which combine to make net income) less dividends over the life of the company.

Illustration 2–10 (next page) provides a simple memory aid that can help you remember debits and credits. Remember the acronym **DEALOR** and you'll be able to recall the effect that debits and credits have on account balances.

ILLUSTRATION 2–10
Effects of Debit and Credit on Each Account Type

	DEALOR	
	Dividends	**Liabilities**
	Expenses	**Owners' equity**
	Assets	**Revenues**
Debit and Credit Rules:	Debit ↑	Debit ↓
	Credit ↓	Credit ↑

Common Terms Another common name for stockholders' equity is *owners' equity,* since stockholders are the owners of a corporation.

The three accounts on the left, or debit, side of **DEALOR**—**D**ividends, **E**xpenses, and **A**ssets—increase with a debit. The three accounts on the right, or credit, side—**L**iabilities, **O**wners' (stockholders') equity, and **R**evenues—increase with a credit.

Let's Review

Bogey Incorporated has the following transactions during May:

May   1 Purchase a storage building by obtaining a loan of $5,000.
May   6 Provide services on account to customers, $1,800.
May 12 Pay $1,200 cash for advertising in May.
May 17 Repay $1,000 of the amount borrowed on May 1.
May 25 Purchase office supplies for $800 cash.

Required:

For each transaction, (1) identify the two accounts involved, (2) the type of account, (3) whether the transaction increases or decreases the account balance, and (4) whether the increase or decrease would be recorded with a debit or credit.

Solution:

Date	(1) Accounts Involved	(2) Account Type	(3) Increase or Decrease	(4) Debit or Credit
May 1	Buildings	Asset	Increase	Debit
	Notes Payable	Liability	Increase	Credit
May 6	Accounts Receivable	Asset	Increase	Debit
	Service Revenue	Revenue	Increase	Credit
May 12	Advertising Expense	Expense	Increase	Debit
	Cash	Asset	Decrease	Credit
May 17	Notes Payable	Liability	Decrease	Debit
	Cash	Asset	Decrease	Credit
May 25	Supplies	Asset	Increase	Debit
	Cash	Asset	Decrease	Credit

Suggested Homework:
BE2-5, BE2-6;
E2-6, E2-7;
P2-3A&B

Recording Transactions

■ **LO4**
Record transactions using debits and credits.

We have just seen how to assess whether the impact of an external transaction results in a debit or credit to an account balance. Next, we'll learn how to formally record transactions using those same debits and credits in a journal. A **journal** provides a chronological record of all transactions affecting a firm. Prior to the

widespread use of computers, companies recorded their transactions in paper-based journals. Thus, the term *journal entry* was used to describe the format for recording a transaction. Today, nearly all companies have easy access to computers, and paper-based journals have become obsolete, but the term *journal entry* continues to be commonly used. Illustration 2–11 shows the format we'll use throughout the book to record a company's transactions.

Date	Debit	Credit
Account Name	Amount	
Account Name		Amount
(Description of transaction)		

ILLUSTRATION 2–11

Format for a Recorded Transaction, or Journal Entry

The entry that records a transaction has a place for the date of the transaction, the relevant account names, debit amounts, credit amounts, and a description of the transaction. We first list the account to be debited; below that, and indented to the right, we list the account to be credited. The entry has two amount columns—one for debits, one for credits. Because the amounts always represent dollar amounts (not number of units, for example), the dollar sign ($) is not used. As you might expect, the left-hand column is for debits, the right-hand column is for credits. **The amount of the debit must always equal the amount of the credit.** It is acceptable to include a description of the transaction at the bottom. (For learning purposes, we include descriptions.)

 COMMON MISTAKE

Many students forget to indent the credit account names. For the account credited, be sure to indent both the account name and the amount.

Think of recording a transaction as if you're writing a sentence form of the "accounting language." For example, "On January 1, Eagle Golf Academy issues shares of common stock for cash of $25,000." Here is this same sentence about transaction (1) written in the language of accounting:

January 1	Debit	Credit
Cash (+A)	25,000	
Common Stock (+SE)		25,000
(Issue common stock for cash)		

TRANSACTION (1)

Initial investment of $25,000 by stockholders

Just as every English sentence uses at least one noun and one verb, every accounting sentence includes at least one debit and one credit. While not a formal part of recording transactions, we'll use a notation in parentheses beside the account name in the first few chapters of this book to help you get more familiar with the effect of debits and credits on the account balance. Thus, the entry shows that transaction (1) causes total assets to increase (+A) and total stockholders' equity to increase (+SE). You will need to learn to read and write in the language of accounting as this is the language used throughout the business world.

Accounting is the language of business.

Let's try a few more transactions. In transaction (2), Eagle Academy borrows $10,000 from the bank. Eagle records the transaction as:

TRANSACTION (2)

Borrow $10,000 from the bank and sign a long-term note

January 1	Debit	Credit
Cash (+A)	10,000	
Notes Payable (+L)		10,000
(Borrow by signing long-term note)		

Both total assets and total liabilities increase by $10,000.

In transaction (3), Eagle Academy purchases equipment for $24,000 cash. Eagle records the transaction as:

TRANSACTION (3)

Purchase equipment with cash, $24,000

January 1	Debit	Credit
Equipment (+A)	24,000	
Cash (−A)		24,000
(Purchase equipment for cash)		

Here, one asset increases, while another asset decreases. We record the remaining transactions of Eagle Academy later in the chapter.

 KEY POINT

For each transaction, total debits must equal total credits.

Let's Review

Bogey Incorporated has the following transactions during May:

May 1 Purchase a storage building by obtaining a loan of $5,000.

May 6 Provide services on account to customers, $1,800.

May 12 Pay $1,200 cash for advertising in May.

May 17 Repay $1,000 of the amount borrowed on May 1.

May 25 Purchase office supplies for $800 cash.

Required:

Record each transaction.

Solution:

May 1	Debit	Credit
Buildings (+A)	5,000	
Notes Payable (+L)		5,000
(Purchase building with note payable)		

May 6	Debit	Credit
Accounts Receivable (+A)	1,800	
Service Revenue (+R, +SE)		1,800
(Provide services on account)		

May 12	Debit	Credit
Advertising Expense (+E, −SE)	1,200	
Cash (−A)...		1,200
(Pay advertising)		

May 17	Debit	Credit
Notes Payable (−L)	1,000	
Cash (−A)...		1,000
(Repay portion of note)		

May 25	Debit	Credit
Supplies (+A)	800	
Cash (−A)...		800
(Purchase supplies for cash)		

Suggested Homework:
BE2-7, BE2-8;
E2-8, E2-10, E2-11;
P2-5A&B, P2-6A&B

Posting

The journal provides in a single location a chronological listing of every transaction affecting a company. As such, it serves as a handy way to review specific transactions and to locate any accounting errors at their original source. But it's not a convenient format for calculating account balances to use in preparing financial statements. You don't need to stretch your imagination too far to see that even for a very small company with few transactions, calculating account balances from a journal would very soon become unmanageable. Just imagine how lengthy the journal would be for **Walmart**. If each sales transaction with a customer took about one inch of space, the journal would be over 150,000 miles long by the end of the year.

To make the process more efficient, we transfer information about transactions recorded in the journal to the specific accounts in the general ledger. The <u>general ledger</u> includes all accounts used to record the company's transactions. The names of these accounts are listed in the *chart of accounts*. Illustration 2–12 provides the chart of accounts for Eagle Golf Academy based on the 10 transactions we've covered to this point. Later, we'll introduce other transactions and accounts for Eagle. In addition, at the back of the book, you'll see a comprehensive chart of accounts that includes *all accounts* used throughout the book.

■ **LO5**
Post transactions to T-accounts in the general ledger.

EAGLE GOLF ACADEMY
Chart of Accounts (preliminary)

Assets	Liabilities	Stockholders' Equity
Cash	Accounts Payable	Common Stock
Accounts Receivable	Unearned Revenue	
Supplies	Notes Payable	**Dividends:**
Prepaid Rent		Dividends
Equipment		
		Revenues:
		Service Revenue
		Expenses:
		Salaries Expense

ILLUSTRATION 2–12

Preliminary Chart of Accounts for Eagle Golf Academy

The process of transferring the debit and credit information from the journal to individual accounts in the general ledger is called posting. **Since we post all transactions to the general ledger, each account provides in one location a collection of all transactions that affect that account.** Computerized systems automatically and instantly post information from the journal to the general ledger accounts.

A formal general ledger account includes an account title, account number, date, and columns for increases, decreases, and the cumulative balance. As described earlier, accounts are easier to visualize if we use the T-account format. With the additional information learned since we first discussed T-accounts, we can now more formally define a T-account as a simplified form of a general ledger account with space at the top for the account title and two sides for recording debits and credits. Consistent with our previous discussion of debits and credits, the left side of the T-account is the debit column. The right side is the credit column.

Let's see how debits and credits are posted to a T-account by looking at Illustration 2–13, where we have posted the cash transactions of Eagle Golf Academy. (The corresponding transaction numbers are included in parentheses, simply for teaching purposes.) For each transaction that involves cash, we post the debit in the journal as a debit to the T-account. Similarly, we post every credit in the journal as a credit to the T-account. Note that we do not have to put "+" signs or "−" signs beside the numbers in the T-account. With all transactions collected in one place, we can now easily calculate the *ending balance* of cash. We calculate the ending balance of $6,200 by totaling all debits and subtracting the total of all credits.

ILLUSTRATION 2–13

Cash T-Account for Transactions of Eagle Golf Academy

Cash					
Debits			**Credits**		
(1)	25,000				
(2)	10,000				
			(3)	24,000	
			(4)	6,000	
(6)	3,600				
(8)	600				
			(9)	2,800	
			(10)	200	
Bal. 6,200					

Total Debits (Increases) = $39,200

Ending Balance → Bal. 6,200

Total Credits (Decreases) = $33,000

To review:

- For assets (such as cash), an amount in the debit or left column *always* means an increase in the balance. An amount in the credit or right column *always* means a decrease in the balance.
- Just the opposite is true for liabilities and stockholders' equity: A debit to a liability or stockholders' equity T-account *always* means a decrease, and a credit *always* means an increase.

Also, notice that transactions (5) and (7) are not posted to Eagle's Cash T-account. These transactions did not include the receipt or payment of cash, and therefore they do not affect the balance of cash. Only transactions that involve cash affect the balance of cash and are posted to the Cash T-account.

COMMON MISTAKE

Some students think the term "debit" *always* means increase and "credit" *always* means decrease. While this is true for assets, it is *not* true for liabilities and stockholders' equity. Liabilities and stockholders' equity are increased by credits and decreased by debits.

KEY POINT

Posting is the process of transferring the debit and credit information from transactions recorded in the journal to the T-accounts in the general ledger.

Summary of the Measurement Process

To better understand the measurement of external transactions, let's apply the first five steps outlined in Illustration 2–1 to each of the 10 transactions of Eagle Golf Academy. These steps are detailed in Illustrations 2–14 through 2–23.

Step 1: Use source documents to analyze **accounts** affected.	**Cash** (asset) and **common stock** (stockholders' equity) both increase by $25,000.	**ILLUSTRATION 2–14** Transaction (1): Issue Shares of Common Stock for $25,000

Step 2: Determine impact on **accounting equation.**	Assets = Liabilities + Stockholders' Equity
	+$25,000 = +$25,000
	(Cash ↑) (Common Stock ↑)

Step 3: Determine **debits** and **credits** for accounts.
1. Assets increase with a debit, so **debit** Cash, $25,000.
2. Stockholders' equity increases with a credit, so **credit** Common Stock, $25,000.

Step 4: Record transaction.	January 1	Debit	Credit
	Cash	25,000	
	Common Stock		25,000

Step 5: Post to T-accounts.

Cash		Common Stock	
(1) **25,000**			(1) **25,000**
Bal. 25,000			Bal. 25,000

Step 1: Use source documents to analyze **accounts.**	**Cash** (asset) and **notes payable** (liability) increase by $10,000.	**ILLUSTRATION 2–15** Transaction (2): Borrow $10,000 from the Bank and Sign a Long-Term Note

Step 2: Determine impact on **accounting equation.**	Assets = Liabilities + Stockholders' Equity
	+$10,000 = +$10,000
	(Cash ↑) (Notes Payable ↑)

Step 3: Determine **debits** and **credits** for accounts.
1. Assets increase with a debit, so **debit** Cash for $10,000.
2. Liabilities increase with a credit, so **credit** Notes Payable for $10,000.

Step 4: Record transaction.	January 1	Debit	Credit
	Cash	10,000	
	Notes Payable		10,000

Step 5: Post to T-accounts.

Cash		Notes Payable	
(1) 25,000			(2) **10,000**
(2) **10,000**			
Bal. 35,000			Bal. 10,000

ILLUSTRATION 2–16

Transaction (3): Purchase Equipment with Cash, $24,000

Step 1: Use source documents to analyze **accounts**.	**Equipment** (asset) increases and **cash** (asset) decreases by $24,000.	

Step 2: Determine impact on **accounting equation**.

Assets	=	Liabilities	+	Stockholders' Equity
+$24,000 −$24,000 =				
(Equipment ↑) (Cash ↓)				

Step 3: Determine **debits** and **credits** for accounts.

1. Assets increase with a debit, so **debit** Equipment, $24,000.
2. Assets decrease with a credit, so **credit** Cash, $24,000.

Step 4: **Record** transaction.

January 1	Debit	Credit
Equipment	24,000	
Cash		24,000

Step 5: **Post** to T-accounts.

Equipment		Cash		
(3) **24,000**		(1) 25,000	(3) **24,000**	
		(2) 10,000		
Bal. 24,000		Bal. 11,000		

ILLUSTRATION 2–17

Transaction (4): Pay One Year of Rent in Advance, $6,000

Step 1: Use source documents to analyze **accounts**.

Prepaid rent (asset) increases and **cash** (asset) decreases by $6,000.

Step 2: Determine impact on **accounting equation**.

Assets	=	Liabilities	+	Stockholders' Equity
+$6,000 −$6,000 =				
(Prepaid Rent ↑) (Cash ↓)				

Step 3: Determine **debits** and **credits** for accounts.

1. Assets increase with a debit, so **debit** Prepaid Rent for $6,000.
2. Assets decrease with a credit, so **credit** Cash for $6,000.

Step 4: **Record** transaction.

January 1	Debit	Credit
Prepaid Rent	6,000	
Cash		6,000

Step 5: **Post** to T-accounts.

Prepaid Rent		Cash		
(4) **6,000**		(1) 25,000	(3) 24,000	
		(2) 10,000	(4) **6,000**	
Bal. 6,000		Bal. 5,000		

ILLUSTRATION 2–18

Transaction (5): Purchase Supplies on Account, $2,300

Step 1: Use source documents to analyze **accounts**.

Supplies (asset) increases and **accounts payable** (liability) increases by $2,300.

Step 2: Determine impact on **accounting equation**.

Assets	=	Liabilities	+	Stockholders' Equity
+$2,300 =	+$2,300			
(Supplies ↑)	(Accounts Payable ↑)			

Step 3: Determine **debits** and **credits** for accounts.

1. Assets increase with a debit, so **debit** Supplies for $2,300.
2. Liabilities increase with a credit, so **credit** Accounts Payable for $2,300.

(continued)

| Step 4:
Record transaction. | January 6
Supplies
   Accounts Payable | Debit
2,300 | Credit

2,300 | **ILLUSTRATION 2–18**
(concluded) |

Step 5: Post to T-accounts.

Supplies	Accounts Payable
(5) **2,300**	(5) **2,300**
Bal. 2,300	Bal. 2,300

| Step 1:
Use source documents
to analyze **accounts.** | **Cash** (asset) and **service revenue** (revenue) increase by
$3,600. | **ILLUSTRATION 2–19**
Transaction (6): Provide
Golf Training to
Customers for Cash,
$3,600 |

Step 2: Determine impact on accounting equation.

Assets	=	Liabilities	+	Stockholders' Equity
+$3,600	=			+$3,600
(Cash ↑)				(Service Revenue ↑)

Step 3: Determine debits and credits for accounts.

1. Assets increase with a debit, so **debit** Cash for $3,600.
2. Revenues increase with a credit, so **credit** Service Revenue for $3,600. The increase in revenues increases stockholders' equity.

Step 4: Record transaction.

January 12	Debit	Credit
Cash	3,600	
Service Revenue		3,600

Step 5: Post to T-accounts.

Cash		Service Revenue
(1) 25,000	(3) 24,000	(6) **3,600**
(2) 10,000	(4) 6,000	
(6) **3,600**		
Bal. 8,600		Bal. 3,600

| Step 1:
Use source documents
to analyze **accounts.** | **Accounts receivable** (asset) and **service revenue** (revenue)
increase by $2,500. | **ILLUSTRATION 2–20**
Transaction (7): Provide
Golf Training to
Customers on Account,
$2,500 |

Step 2: Determine impact on accounting equation.

Assets	=	Liabilities	+	Stockholders' Equity
+$2,500	=			+$2,500
(Accounts Receivable ↑)				(Service Revenue ↑)

Step 3: Determine debits and credits for accounts.

1. Assets increase with a debit, so **debit** Accounts Receivable for $2,500.
2. Revenues increase with a credit, so **credit** Service Revenue for $2,500. The increase in revenues increases stockholders' equity.

Step 4: Record transaction.

January 17	Debit	Credit
Accounts Receivable	2,500	
Service Revenue		2,500

Step 5: Post to T-accounts.

Accounts Receivable	Service Revenue
(7) **2,500**	(6) 3,600
	(7) **2,500**
Bal. 2,500	Bal. 6,100

ILLUSTRATION 2–21

Transaction (8): Receive Cash in Advance for Golf Training to Be Given Next Month, $600

Step 1: Use source documents to analyze **accounts**.	**Cash** (asset) and **unearned revenue** (liability) increase by $600.

Step 2: Determine impact on **accounting equation**.

$$\underline{\text{Assets}} = \underline{\text{Liabilities}} + \underline{\text{Stockholders' Equity}}$$
$$+\$600 = +\$600$$
$$(\text{Cash} \uparrow) \qquad (\text{Unearned Revenue} \uparrow)$$

Step 3: Determine **debits** and **credits** for accounts.

1. Assets increase with a debit, so **debit** Cash for $600.
2. Liabilities increase with a credit, so **credit** Unearned Revenue for $600.

Step 4: **Record** transaction.

January 23	Debit	Credit
Cash	600	
Unearned Revenue		600

Step 5: **Post** to T-accounts.

Cash				Unearned Revenue	
(1) 25,000	(3) 24,000				(8) **600**
(2) 10,000	(4) 6,000				
(6) 3,600					
(8) **600**					
Bal. 9,200					Bal. 600

ILLUSTRATION 2–22

Transaction (9): Pay Salaries to Employees for Work during the Month, $2,800

Step 1: Use source documents to analyze **accounts**.	**Cash** (asset) decreases and **salaries expense** (expense) increases by $2,800.

Step 2: Determine impact on **accounting equation**.

$$\underline{\text{Assets}} = \underline{\text{Liabilities}} + \underline{\text{Stockholders' Equity}}$$
$$-\$2,800 = -\$2,800$$
$$(\text{Cash} \downarrow) \qquad (\text{Salaries Expense} \uparrow)$$

Step 3: Determine **debits** and **credits** for accounts.

1. Assets decrease with a credit, so **credit** Cash for $2,800.
2. Expenses increase with a debit, so **debit** Salaries Expense for $2,800. The increase in expenses decreases stockholders' equity.

Step 4: **Record** transaction.

January 28	Debit	Credit
Salaries Expense	2,800	
Cash		2,800

Step 5: **Post** to T-accounts.

Cash				Salaries Expense	
(1) 25,000	(3) 24,000			(9) **2,800**	
(2) 10,000	(4) 6,000				
(6) 3,600	(9) **2,800**				
(8) 600					
Bal. 6,400				Bal. 2,800	

ILLUSTRATION 2–23

Transaction (10): Pay Cash Dividends of $200 to Shareholders

Step 1: Use source documents to analyze **accounts**.	**Cash** (asset) decreases and **dividends** (dividends) increase by $200.

Step 2: Determine impact on **accounting equation**.

$$\underline{\text{Assets}} = \underline{\text{Liabilities}} + \underline{\text{Stockholders' Equity}}$$
$$-\$200 = -\$200$$
$$(\text{Cash} \downarrow) \qquad (\text{Dividends} \uparrow)$$

Step 3: Determine **debits** and **credits** for accounts.

1. Assets decrease with a credit, so **credit** Cash for $200.
2. Dividends increase with a debit, so **debit** Dividends for $200. The increase in dividends decreases stockholders' equity.

(continued)

Step 4: **Record** transaction.	January 30	Debit	Credit	**ILLUSTRATION 2–23**
	Dividends	200		*(concluded)*
	Cash		200	

Step 5: **Post** to T-accounts.				

Dividends		Cash	
(10) **200**		(1) 25,000	(3) 24,000
		(2) 10,000	(4) 6,000
		(6) 3,600	(9) 2,800
		(8) 600	(10) **200**
Bal. 200		Bal. 6,200	

A summary of the external transactions recorded for Eagle Golf Academy is provided in Illustration 2–24.

January 1	Debit	Credit
Cash (+A)	25,000	
Common Stock (+SE)		25,000
(Issue common stock for cash)		
January 1		
Cash (+A)	10,000	
Notes Payable (+L)		10,000
(Borrow by signing long-term note)		
January 1		
Equipment (+A)	24,000	
Cash (−A)		24,000
(Purchase equipment for cash)		
January 1		
Prepaid Rent (+A)	6,000	
Cash (−A)		6,000
(Prepay rent with cash)		
January 6		
Supplies (+A)	2,300	
Accounts Payable (+L)		2,300
(Purchase supplies on account)		
January 12		
Cash (+A)	3,600	
Service Revenue (+R, +SE)		3,600
(Provide training to customers for cash)		
January 17		
Accounts Receivable (+A)	2,500	
Service Revenue (+R, +SE)		2,500
(Provide training to customers on account)		
January 23		
Cash (+A)	600	
Unearned Revenue (+L)		600
(Receive cash in advance from customers)		
January 28		
Salaries Expense (+E, −SE)	2,800	
Cash (−A)		2,800
(Pay workers' salaries)		
January 30		
Dividends (+D, −SE)	200	
Cash (−A)		200
(Pay cash dividends)		

ILLUSTRATION 2–24

Summary of External Transactions Recorded for Eagle Golf Academy

Illustration 2–25 provides the general ledger accounts after posting the external transactions summarized in Illustration 2–24. Account balances are in bold, and transaction numbers are shown in parentheses.

ILLUSTRATION 2–25   Posting of External Transactions of Eagle Golf Academy to General Ledger Accounts

Assets	=	Liabilities	+	Stockholders' Equity

Cash

(1)	25,000	(3)	24,000
(2)	10,000	(4)	6,000
(6)	3,600	(9)	2,800
(8)	600	(10)	200
Bal. 6,200			

Accounts Receivable

(7)	2,500	
Bal. 2,500		

Accounts Payable

	(5)	2,300
	Bal. 2,300	

Common Stock

	(1)	25,000
	Bal. 25,000	

Retained Earnings

	0
	0

Supplies

(5)	2,300	
Bal. 2,300		

Prepaid Rent

(4)	6,000	
Bal. 6,000		

Unearned Revenue

	(8)	600
	Bal.	**600**

Service Revenue

	(6)	3,600
	(7)	2,500
	Bal.	**6,100**

Salaries Expense

(9)	2,800	
Bal. 2,800		

Equipment

(3)	24,000	
Bal. 24,000		

Notes Payable

	(2)	10,000
	Bal. 10,000	

Dividends

(10) 200	
Bal. 200	

Transaction numbers are shown in parentheses. Account balances are in bold.

■ LO6
Prepare a trial balance.

Trial Balance

After we've posted transactions to the general ledger accounts, **the sum of the accounts with debit balances should equal the sum of the accounts with credit balances.** This is expected because debits were equal to credits for every transaction posted to those ledger accounts. To prove this to be the case and to check for completeness, we prepare a trial balance. A trial balance is a list of all accounts and their balances at a particular date, showing that total debits equal total credits. Another purpose of the trial balance is to assist us in preparing adjusting entries (for *internal* transactions). We discuss adjusting entries in Chapter 3.

Using the account balances calculated in Illustration 2–25, we can now prepare the trial balance of Eagle Golf Academy. The trial balance appears in Illustration 2–26 (next page). Notice that accounts are listed with the debit balances in one column and the credit balances in another column. Asset, expense, and dividend accounts normally have debit balances. Liability, stockholders' equity, and revenue accounts normally have credit balances.

 COMMON MISTAKE

Be careful. Just because the debits and credits are equal in a trial balance does not necessarily mean that all balances are correct. A trial balance could contain offsetting errors. For example, if we overstate cash and revenue each by $1,000, both accounts will be in error, but the trial balance will still balance, since the overstatement to cash increases debits by $1,000 and the overstatement to revenue increases credits by $1,000.

ILLUSTRATION 2–26

Trial Balance of Eagle Golf Academy

EAGLE GOLF ACADEMY
Trial Balance
January 31

Accounts	Debit	Credit
Cash	$ 6,200	
Accounts Receivable	2,500	
Supplies	2,300	
Prepaid Rent	6,000	
Equipment	24,000	
Accounts Payable		$ 2,300
Unearned Revenue		600
Notes Payable		10,000
Common Stock		25,000
Retained Earnings		0
Dividends	200	
Service Revenue		6,100
Salaries Expense	2,800	
Totals	$44,000	$44,000

Total debits equal total credits.

It may seem unusual that the Retained Earnings account has a balance of $0. As we explained earlier, retained earnings is a composite of three other types of accounts—revenues, expenses, and dividends. Those three accounts have balances at this point, but those balances haven't yet been transferred to retained earnings. This transfer is known as the *closing process,* and we will discuss it in Chapter 3. Since this is the first period of the company's operations, retained earnings will start at $0. As time goes by, the retained earnings balance will be the accumulated net amount of revenues minus expenses and dividends.

Decision Point

Question	Accounting information	Analysis
How does the accounting system capture the effects of a company's external transactions?	Account balances	The effects of external transactions are summarized by recording increases and decreases to account balances during the year.

ORDER OF ACCOUNTS

The trial balance is used *for internal purposes only* and provides a check on the equality of the debits and credits. Since the trial balance is not a published financial statement to be used by external parties, there is no required order for listing accounts in the trial balance. However, most companies list accounts in the following order: assets, liabilities, stockholders' equity, dividends, revenues, and expenses. As we'll see in Chapter 3, the trial balance simplifies preparation of the published financial statements. Asset, liability, and stockholders' equity accounts are reported in the balance sheet. Dividends are reported in the statement of stockholders'

CAREER CORNER

The accuracy of account balances is essential for providing useful information to decision makers, such as investors and creditors. That's why the Securities and Exchange Commission (SEC) requires all companies with publicly traded stock to have their reported account balances verified by an independent auditor. Independent auditors use their understanding of accounting principles and business practices to provide reasonable assurance that account balances are free from material misstatements resulting from errors and fraud. Tens of thousands of audits are conducted each year. Because of the huge demand for auditors, many accounting majors choose auditing, also referred to as public accounting, as their first career. For an auditor to legally certify a company's account balances, the auditor must be designated as a Certified Public Accountant (CPA).

equity. Revenue and expense accounts are reported in the income statement. Having the accounts listed in order of those classifications in the trial balance makes it easier to prepare the financial statements.

KEY POINT

A trial balance is a list of all accounts and their balances at a particular date. Debits must equal credits, but that doesn't necessarily mean that all account balances are correct.

KEY POINTS BY LEARNING OBJECTIVE

LO1 Identify the basic steps in measuring external transactions.

External transactions are transactions between the company and separate economic entities. Internal transactions do not include an exchange with a separate economic entity.

The six-step measurement process (Illustration 2–1) is the foundation of financial accounting.

LO2 Analyze the impact of external transactions on the accounting equation.

After each transaction, the accounting equation must always remain in balance. In other words, assets always must equal liabilities plus stockholders' equity.

The expanded accounting equation demonstrates that revenues increase retained earnings while expenses and dividends decrease retained earnings. Retained earnings is a component of stockholders' equity.

LO3 Assess whether the impact of external transactions results in a debit or credit to an account balance.

For the basic accounting equation (Assets = Liabilities + Stockholders' Equity), accounts on the left side are increased with *debits*. Accounts on the right side are increased with *credits*. The opposite is true to decrease any of these accounts.

The Retained Earnings account is a stockholders' equity account that normally has a credit balance. The Retained Earnings account has three components—revenues, expenses, and dividends. Revenues increase the balance of Retained Earnings, while expenses and dividends decrease the balance of Retained Earnings. Therefore, we increase revenues with a credit (similar to retained earnings) and increase expenses and dividends with a debit (opposite of retained earnings).

LO4 Record transactions using debits and credits.

For each transaction, total debits must equal total credits.

LO5 Post transactions to T-accounts in the general ledger.

Posting is the process of transferring the debit and credit information from transactions recorded in the journal to the T-accounts in the general ledger.

LO6 Prepare a trial balance.

A trial balance is a list of all accounts and their balances at a particular date. Debits must equal credits, but that doesn't necessarily mean that all account balances are correct.

GLOSSARY

Account: A summary of the effects of all transactions related to a particular item over a period of time. **p. 54**

Chart of accounts: A list of all account names used to record transactions of a company. **p. 54**

External transactions: Transactions the firm conducts with a separate economic entity. **p. 54**

General ledger: All accounts used to record the company's transactions. **p. 75**

Internal transactions: Events that affect the financial position of the company but do not include an exchange with a separate economic entity. **p. 54**

Journal: A chronological record of all transactions affecting a firm. **p. 72**

Posting: The process of transferring the debit and credit information from the journal to individual accounts in the general ledger. **p. 76**

T-account: A simplified form of a general ledger account with space at the top for the account title and two sides for recording debits and credits. **pp. 66 and 76**

Trial balance: A list of all accounts and their balances at a particular date, showing that total debits equal total credits. **p. 82**

SELF-STUDY QUESTIONS

1. Which of the following represents an external transaction?　　　　■ LO1
   a. Lapse of insurance due to passage of time.
   b. Use of office supplies by workers over time.
   c. Payment of utility bill.
   d. Depreciation of equipment.

2. Which of the following is *not* a step in the process of measuring external transactions?　　　　■ LO1
   a. Analyze the impact of the transaction on the accounting equation.
   b. Record the transaction using debits and credits.
   c. Post the transaction to the T-account in the general ledger.
   d. All of the above are steps in the measurement process of external transactions.

3. Which of the following transactions causes an increase in total assets?　　　　■ LO2
   a. Pay workers' salaries for the current month.
   b. Receive cash payment from a customer billed in the previous period.
   c. Issue common stock in exchange for cash.
   d. Purchase office equipment for cash.

4. Which of the following transactions causes an increase in stockholders' equity?　　　　■ LO2
   a. Pay dividends to stockholders.
   b. Obtain cash by borrowing from a local bank.
   c. Provide services to customers on account.
   d. Purchase advertising on a local radio station.

5. Which of the following causes the accounting equation *not* to balance?　　　　■ LO2
   a. Increase assets; increase liabilities.
   b. Decrease assets; increase expenses.
   c. Increase assets; increase dividends.
   d. Decrease liabilities; increase revenues.

6. A debit is used to increase which of the following accounts?　　　　■ LO3
   a. Utilities Expense.
   b. Accounts Payable.
   c. Service Revenue.
   d. Common Stock.

■ LO3

7. A credit is used to increase which of the following accounts?
   a. Dividends.   c. Cash.
   b. Insurance Expense.   d. Service Revenue.

■ LO4

8. Providing services to customers on account for $100 is recorded as:

a. Accounts Receivable	100	
Service Revenue.....................................		100
b. Cash...	100	
Accounts Receivable.............................		100
c. Service Revenue	100	
Accounts Receivable.............................		100
d. Service Expense	100	
Accounts Payable..................................		100

■ LO5

9. Posting is the process of:
   a. Analyzing the impact of the transaction on the accounting equation.
   b. Obtaining information about external transactions from source documents.
   c. Transferring the debit and credit information from the journal to individual accounts in the general ledger.
   d. Listing all accounts and their balances at a particular date and showing the equality of total debits and total credits.

■ LO6

Check out
www.mhhe.com/succeed
for more multiple-choice
questions.

10. A trial balance can best be explained as a list of:
    a. The income statement accounts used to calculate net income.
    b. Revenue, expense, and dividend accounts used to show the balances of the components of retained earnings.
    c. The balance sheet accounts used to show the equality of the accounting equation.
    d. All accounts and their balances at a particular date.

Note: For answers, see the last page of the chapter.

REVIEW QUESTIONS

■ LO1

1. Explain the difference between external transactions and internal transactions. If a company purchases supplies from a local vendor, would this be classified as an external or internal transaction?

■ LO1

2. List the steps we use to measure external transactions.

■ LO2

3. Each external transaction will have a dual effect on the company's financial position. Explain what this means.

■ LO2

4. Describe the impact of each of these external transactions on the accounting equation.
   a. Receive a loan from the bank.
   b. Pay employee salaries for the current period.
   c. Receive cash from customers for services provided in the current period.
   d. Purchase equipment by paying cash.

■ LO2

5. Jerry believes that "dual effect" indicates that, for all transactions, one account will increase and one account will decrease. Is Jerry correct? Explain.

■ LO3

6. What is the normal balance (debit or credit) of assets, liabilities, stockholders' equity, revenues, and expenses?

■ LO3

7. Jenny has learned that assets have debit balances, while liabilities have credit balances. Based on this, she believes that asset accounts can only be debited and liabilities can only be credited. Is Jenny correct? When would we credit an asset and when would we debit a liability?

8. For each of the following accounts, indicate whether we use a debit or a credit to *increase* the balance of the account.   ■ **LO3**
    a. Cash.   c. Utilities Expense.
    b. Salaries Payable.   d. Service Revenue.

9. For each of the following accounts, indicate whether we use a debit or a credit to *decrease* the balance of the account. (Compare your answers to those for Question 8.)   ■ **LO3**
    a. Cash.   c. Utilities Expense.
    b. Salaries Payable.   d. Service Revenue.

10. Suzanne knows that an increase to an expense reduces retained earnings (a stockholders' equity account). However, she also knows that expense accounts have a *debit* balance, while retained earnings normally has a *credit* balance. Are these two pieces of information consistent? Explain.   ■ **LO3**

11. What is a journal? What is a journal entry?   ■ **LO4**

12. Provide the proper format for recording a transaction.   ■ **LO4**

13. Explain the phrase "debits equal credits."   ■ **LO4**

14. Record each of the following external transactions using debits and credits.   ■ **LO4**
    a. Receive cash of $1,200 for providing services to a customer.
    b. Pay rent of $500 for the current month.
    c. Purchase a building for $10,000 by signing a note with the bank.

15. Describe the events that correspond to the following transactions.   ■ **LO4**

	Debit	Credit
a. Supplies	20,000	
Cash		20,000
b. Accounts Receivable	30,000	
Service Revenue		30,000
c. Accounts Payable	10,000	
Cash		10,000

16. What does a T-account represent? What is the left side of the T-account called? What is the right side called?   ■ **LO5**

17. Describe what we mean by posting. Post the transactions in Question 15 to appropriate T-accounts.   ■ **LO5**

18. What is a general ledger? How does it relate to the chart of accounts?   ■ **LO6**

19. What is a trial balance? To what does the term "balance" refer?   ■ **LO6**

20. If total debits equal total credits in the trial balance, does this indicate that all transactions have been properly accounted for? Explain.   ■ **LO6**

BRIEF EXERCISES

BE2–1 Below are the steps in the measurement process of external transactions. Arrange them from first (1) to last (6).

List steps in the measurement process (**LO1**)

_____ a. Post the transaction to the T-accounts in the general ledger.

_____ b. Assess whether the impact of the transaction results in a debit or credit to the account balance.

_____ c. Use source documents to identify accounts affected by external transactions.

_____ d. Analyze the impact of the transaction on the accounting equation.

_____ e. Prepare a trial balance.

_____ f. Record transactions using debits and credits.

Balance the accounting equation (LO2)

BE2–2 Using the notion that the accounting equation (Assets = Liabilities + Stockholders' Equity) must remain in balance, indicate whether each of the following transactions is possible.

a. Cash increases; Accounts Payable decreases.

b. Service Revenue increases; Salaries Payable increases.

c. Advertising Expense increases; Cash decreases.

Balance the accounting equation (LO2)

BE2–3 Suppose a local company has the following balance sheet accounts:

Accounts	Balances
Land	$ 8,000
Equipment	?
Salaries Payable	3,300
Notes Payable	?
Supplies	1,600
Cash	6,200
Stockholders' Equity	12,500
Accounts Payable	1,200
Prepaid Rent	2,200

Calculate the missing amounts assuming the business has total assets of $30,000.

Analyze the impact of transactions on the accounting equation (LO2)

BE2–4 The following transactions occur for Badger Biking Company during the month of June:

a. Provide services to customers on account for $40,000.

b. Receive cash of $32,000 from customers in (a) above.

c. Purchase bike equipment by signing a note with the bank for $25,000.

d. Pay utilities of $4,000 for the current month.

Analyze each transaction and indicate the amount of increases and decreases in the accounting equation.

	Assets	=	Liabilities	+	Stockholders' Equity
(a)					
(b)					
(c)					
(d)					

Understand the effect of debits and credits on accounts (LO3)

BE2–5 For each of the following accounts, indicate whether a debit or credit is used to increase (+) or decrease (−) the balance of the account. The solution for the first one is provided as an example.

Account	Debit	Credit
Asset	+	−
Liability		
Common Stock		
Retained Earnings		
Dividend		
Revenue		
Expense		

BE2–6 Fill in the blanks below with the word "debit" or "credit."

Understand the effect of debits and credits on accounts (LO3)

a. The balance of an *asset* account increases with a _____ and decreases with a _____.

b. The balance of a *liability* account increases with a _____ and decreases with a _____.

c. The balance of a *stockholders' equity* account increases with a _____ and decreases with a _____.

d. The balance of a *revenue* account increases with a _____ and decreases with a _____.

e. The balance of an *expense* account increases with a _____ and decreases with a _____.

BE2–7 The following transactions occur for the Panther Detective Agency during the month of July:

Record transactions (LO4)

a. Purchase a truck and sign a note payable, $14,000.

b. Purchase office supplies for cash, $500.

c. Pay $700 in rent for the current month.

Record the transactions. The company uses the following accounts: Cash, Supplies, Equipment (for the truck), Notes Payable, and Rent Expense.

BE2–8 The following transactions occur for Cardinal Music Academy during the month of October:

Record transactions (LO4)

a. Provide music lessons to students for $12,000 cash.

b. Purchase prepaid insurance to protect musical equipment over the next year for $3,600 cash.

c. Purchase musical equipment for $15,000 cash.

d. Obtain a loan from a bank by signing a note for $20,000.

Record the transactions. The company uses the following accounts: Cash, Prepaid Insurance, Equipment, Notes Payable, and Service Revenue.

BE2–9 Consider the following T-account for cash.

Analyze T-accounts (LO5)

Cash	
12,000	7,200
3,400	1,400
2,500	4,500

1. Compute the balance of the Cash account.

2. Give some examples of transactions that would have resulted in the $3,400 posting to the account.

3. Give some examples of transactions that would have resulted in the $1,400 posting to the account.

BE2–10 The following transactions occur for the Wolfpack Shoe Company during the month of June:

Analyze the impact of transactions on the accounting equation, record transactions, and post (LO2, 3, 4, 5)

a. Provide services to customers for $25,000 and receive cash.

b. Purchase office supplies on account for $15,000.

c. Pay $6,000 in salaries to employees for work performed during the month.

1. Analyze each transaction. For each transaction, indicate by how much each category in the accounting equation increases or decreases.

	Assets	=	Liabilities	+	Stockholders' Equity
(a)					
(b)					
(c)					

2. Record the transactions. The company uses the following accounts: Cash, Supplies, Accounts Payable, Salaries Expense, and Service Revenue.

3. Post the transactions to T-accounts. Assume the opening balance in each of the accounts is zero.

Prepare a trial
balance (LO6)

BE2–11 Using the following information, prepare a trial balance. Assume all asset, dividend, and expense accounts have debit balances and all liability, stockholders' equity, and revenue accounts have credit balances. List the accounts in the following order: assets, liabilities, stockholders' equity, dividends, revenues, and expenses.

Cash	$5,600	Dividends	$ 400
Salaries Payable	600	Rent Expense	1,500
Prepaid Rent	800	Accounts Receivable	3,400
Accounts Payable	1,500	Common Stock	5,200
Retained Earnings	1,300	Service Revenue	6,100
Salaries Expense	2,000	Advertising Expense	1,000

Correct a trial
balance (LO6)

BE2–12 Your study partner is having trouble getting total debits to equal total credits in the trial balance. Prepare a corrected trial balance by placing each account balance in the correct debit or credit column.

Trial Balance

Accounts	Debit	Credit
Cash	$ 6,300	
Accounts Receivable		$ 1,600
Equipment	9,400	
Accounts Payable	2,900	
Unearned Revenue		1,200
Common Stock	10,000	
Retained Earnings		3,200
Dividends	700	
Service Revenue		3,500
Salaries Expense	2,200	
Utilities Expense		600
Total	$31,500	$10,100

EXERCISES

Identify terms associated
with the measurement
process (LO1)

E2–1 Listed below are several terms and phrases associated with the measurement process for external transactions.

List A	List B
_____ 1. Account	a. Record of all transactions affecting a firm.
_____ 2. Analyze transactions	b. Determine the dual effect of economic events on the accounting equation.
_____ 3. Journal	c. List of accounts and their balances.
_____ 4. Post	d. Summary of the effects of all transactions related to a particular item over a period of time.
_____ 5. Trial balance	e. Transfer balances from the journal to the ledger.

Required:
Pair each item from List A with the item from List B to which it is most appropriately associated.

Analyze the impact
of transactions on
the accounting
equation (LO2)

E2–2 Below are the external transactions for Shockers Incorporated.
1. Issue common stock in exchange for cash.
2. Purchase equipment by signing a note payable.
3. Provide services to customers on account.

4. Pay rent for the current month.
5. Pay insurance for the current month.
6. Collect cash from customers on account.

Assets	=	Liabilities	+	Stockholders' Equity
1. Increase	=	No effect	+	Increase
2. increase		increase		Not effect
3. increase		Not effect		increase
4. Decrease		Not effect		Decrease
5. Decrease		Not effect		decrease
6. Increase		Increase		Not effect

Required:

Analyze each transaction. Under each category in the accounting equation, indicate whether the transaction increases, decreases, or has no effect. The first item is provided as an example.

HW **E2-3** Green Wave Company plans to own and operate a storage rental facility. For the first month of operations, the company had the following transactions.

1. Issue 10,000 shares of common stock in exchange for $32,000 in cash. A↑, SE↑
2. Purchase land for $19,000. A note payable is signed for the full amount. A↑, L↑
3. Purchase storage container equipment for $8,000. A↑, A↓
4. Hire three employees for $2,000 per month. (No effect on the accounting Equation)
5. Receive cash of $12,000 in rental fees for the current month. A↑, SE↑
6. Purchase office supplies for $2,000 on account. A↑, L↑
7. Pay employees $6,000 for the first month's salaries. A↓, SE↓

Analyze the impact of transactions on the accounting equation (LO2)

Required:

For each transaction, describe the dual effect on the accounting equation. For example, in the first transaction, (1) assets increase and (2) stockholders' equity increases.

E2-4 Boilermaker House Painting Company incurs the following transactions for September.

1. Paint houses in the current month for $15,000 on account. *Pay it latter* (A↑, SE↑)
2. Purchase painting equipment for $16,000 cash. (A↓, A↑)
3. Purchase office supplies on account for $2,500. A↑, L↑
4. Pay workers' salaries of $3,200 for the current month. (A↓, SE↓)
5. Purchase advertising to appear in the current month, $1,200. (A↓, SE↓)
6. Pay office rent of $4,400 for the current month. (A↓, SE↓)
7. Receive $10,000 from customers in (1) above. on account (Account Receivable) (A↑, A↓)
8. Receive cash of $5,000 in advance from a customer who plans to have his house painted in the following month. (A↑, L↑)

Analyze the impact of transactions on the accounting equation (LO2)

Required:

For each transaction, describe the dual effect on the accounting equation. For example, for the first transaction, (1) assets increase and (2) stockholders' equity increases.

E2-5 At the beginning of April, Owl Corporation has a balance of $12,000 in the Retained Earnings account. During the month of April, Owl had the following external transactions.

1. Issue common stock for cash, $10,000.
2. Provide services to customers on account, $7,500.
3. Provide services to customers in exchange for cash, $2,200.
4. Purchase equipment and pay cash, $6,600.
5. Pay rent for April, $1,200.
6. Pay workers' salaries for April, $2,500.
7. Pay dividends to stockholders, $1,500.

Understand the components of retained earnings (LO2)

Required:

Using the external transactions above, compute the balance of Retained Earnings at April 30.

Indicate the debit or credit balance of accounts (LO3)

E2–6 Below is a list of common accounts.

Accounts	Debit or Credit
Cash	1. _D_
Service Revenue	2. _C_
Salaries Expense	3. _D_
Accounts Payable	4. _C_
Equipment	5. _D_
Retained Earnings	6. _C_
Utilities Expense	7. _D_
Accounts Receivable	8. _D_
Dividends	9. _D_
Common Stock	10. _C_

Required:

Indicate whether the normal balance of each account is a debit or a credit.

Associate debits and credits with external transactions (LO3)

E2–7 Below are several external transactions for Hokies Company.

	Account Debited	Account Credited
Example: Purchase equipment in exchange for cash.	Equipment	Cash
1. Pay a cash dividend.	Dividends	Cash
2. Pay rent in advance for the next three months.	Prepaid Rent	Cash
3. Provide services to customers on account.	Accounts Receivable	Service Revenue
4. Purchase office supplies on account.	Supplies	Accounts P
5. Pay salaries for the current month.	Salaries E	Cash
6. Issue common stock in exchange for cash.	Cash	Common Stock
7. Collect cash from customers for services provided in (3) above.	Cash	Accounts Receivable
8. Borrow cash from the bank and sign a note.	Cash	Accounts Payable
9. Pay for the current month's utilities.	Utilities Expense	Cash
10. Pay for office supplies purchased in (4) above.	Account Payable	Cash

Hokies uses the following accounts:

Accounts Payable	Equipment	Accounts Receivable
Cash	Supplies	Utilities Expense
Prepaid Rent	Rent Expense	Service Revenue
Common Stock	Notes Payable	Retained Earnings
Salaries Payable	Salaries Expense	Dividends

Required:

Indicate which accounts should be debited and which should be credited.

Record transactions (LO4)

E2–8 Terapin Company engages in the following external transactions for November.

1. Purchase equipment in exchange for cash of $22,400.
2. Provide services to customers and receive cash of $5,800.
3. Pay the current month's rent of $1,100.
4. Purchase office supplies on account for $900.
5. Pay employees' salaries of $1,600 for the current month.

Required:

Record the transactions. Terapin uses the following accounts: Cash, Supplies, Equipment, Accounts Payable, Service Revenue, Rent Expense, and Salaries Expense.

E2–9 Below are recorded transactions of Yellow Jacket Corporation for August.   *Identify transactions* **(LO4)**

	Debit	Credit
1. Equipment	8,800	
Cash		8,800
2. Accounts Receivable	3,200	
Service Revenue		3,200
3. Salaries Expense	1,900	
Cash		1,900
4. Cash	1,500	
Unearned Revenue		1,500
5. Dividends	900	
Cash		900

in advance of services, 1500

Required:

Provide an explanation for each transaction.

E2–10 Sun Devil Hair Design has the following transactions during the month of February.   *Record transactions* **(LO4)**

February 2	Pay $600 for radio advertising for February.
February 7	Purchase beauty supplies of $1,200 on account.
February 14	Provide beauty services of $2,400 to customers and receive cash.
February 15	Pay workers' salaries for the current month of $800.
February 25	Provide beauty services of $900 to customers on account.
February 28	Pay utility bill for the current month of $200.

Required:

Record each transaction. Sun Devil uses the following accounts: Cash, Accounts Receivable, Supplies, Accounts Payable, Service Revenue, Advertising Expense, Salaries Expense, and Utilities Expense.

E2–11 Bearcat Construction begins operations in March and has the following transactions.   *Record transactions* **(LO4)**

March 1	Issue common stock for $16,000.
March 5	Obtain $8,000 loan from the bank by signing a note.
March 10	Purchase construction equipment for $20,000 cash.
March 15	Purchase advertising for the current month for $1,000 cash.
March 22	Provide construction services for $17,000 on account.
March 27	Receive $12,000 cash on account from March 22 services.
March 28	Pay salaries for the current month of $5,000.

Required:

Record each transaction. Bearcat uses the following accounts: Cash, Accounts Receivable, Notes Payable, Common Stock, Service Revenue, Advertising Expense, and Salaries Expense.

E2–12 Consider the recorded transactions below.   *Post transactions to T-accounts* **(LO5)**

	Debit	Credit
1. Accounts Receivable	7,400	
Service Revenue		7,400
2. Supplies	1,800	
Accounts Payable		1,800
3. Cash	9,200	
Accounts Receivable		9,200
4. Advertising Expense	1,200	
Cash		1,200
5. Accounts Payable	2,700	
Cash		2,700
6. Cash	1,000	
Unearned Revenue		1,000

Required:

Post each transaction to T-accounts and compute the ending balance of each account. The beginning balance of each account before the transactions is: Cash, $2,400; Accounts Receivable, $3,200; Supplies, $300; Accounts Payable, $2,500; Unearned Revenue, $200. Service Revenue and Advertising Expense each have a beginning balance of zero.

Prepare a trial balance (LO6)

E2–13 Below is the complete list of accounts of Sooner Company and the related balance at the end of April. All accounts have their normal debit or credit balance. Cash, $2,900; Prepaid Rent, $6,400; Accounts Payable $3,300; Common Stock, $30,000; Service Revenue, $24,400; Salaries Expense, $7,200; Accounts Receivable, $5,100; Land, $50,000; Unearned Revenue, $1,800; Retained Earnings, $20,500; Supplies Expense, $8,400.

Required:

Prepare a trial balance with the list of accounts in the following order: assets, liabilities, stockholders' equity, revenues, and expenses.

Prepare a trial balance (LO6)

E2–14 Below is the complete list of accounts of Fightin' Blue Hens Incorporated and the related balance at the end of March. All accounts have their normal debit or credit balance. Supplies, $1,200; Buildings, $45,000; Salaries Payable, $400; Common Stock, $25,000; Accounts Payable, $1,700; Utilities Expense, $2,700; Prepaid Insurance, $1,300; Service Revenue, $18,500; Accounts Receivable, $3,200; Cash, $2,500; Salaries Expense, $5,400; Retained Earnings, $15,700.

Required:

Prepare a trial balance with the list of accounts in the following order: assets, liabilities, stockholders' equity, revenues, and expenses.

Record transactions, post to T-accounts, and prepare a trial balance (LO4, 5, 6)

E2–15 Green Wave Company plans to own and operate a storage rental facility. For the first month of operations, the company has the following transactions.

1. Issue 10,000 shares of common stock in exchange for $32,000 in cash.
2. Purchase land for $19,000. A note payable is signed for the full amount.
3. Purchase storage container equipment for $8,000 cash.
4. Hire three employees for $2,000 per month.
5. Receive cash of $12,000 in rental fees for the current month.
6. Purchase office supplies for $2,000 on account.
7. Pay employees $6,000 for the first month's salaries.

Required:

1. Record each transaction. Green Wave uses the following accounts: Cash, Supplies, Land, Equipment, Common Stock, Accounts Payable, Notes Payable, Service Revenue, and Salaries Expense.
2. Post each transaction to T-accounts and compute the ending balance of each account. Since this is the first month of operations, all T-accounts have a beginning balance of zero.
3. After calculating the ending balance of each account, prepare a trial balance.

Record transactions, post to T-accounts, and prepare a trial balance (LO4, 5, 6)

E2–16 Boilermaker House Painting Company incurs the following transactions for September.

1. Paint houses in the current month for $15,000 on account.
2. Purchase painting equipment for $16,000 cash.
3. Purchase office supplies on account for $2,500.
4. Pay workers' salaries of $3,200 for the current month.
5. Purchase advertising to appear in the current month for $1,200 cash.
6. Pay office rent of $4,400 for the current month.
7. Receive $10,000 from customers in (1) above.
8. Receive cash of $5,000 in advance from a customer who plans to have his house painted in the following month.

Required:

1. Record each transaction. Boilermaker uses the following accounts: Cash, Accounts Receivable, Supplies, Equipment, Accounts Payable, Unearned Revenue, Common Stock, Retained Earnings, Service Revenue, Salaries Expense, Advertising Expense, and Rent Expense.
2. Post each transaction to T-accounts and compute the ending balance of each account. At the beginning of September, the company had the following account balances: Cash, $21,100; Accounts Receivable, $1,200; Supplies, $400; Equipment, $6,400; Accounts Payable, $1,100; Common Stock, $20,000; Retained Earnings, $8,000. All other accounts had a beginning balance of zero.
3. After calculating the ending balance of each account, prepare a trial balance.

*For additional exercises, visit **www.mhhe.com/succeed** for Exercises: Set B.*

PROBLEMS: SET A

P2–1A Below is a list of activities for Jayhawk Corporation.

Analyze the impact of transactions on the accounting equation **(LO2)**

Transaction	Assets	=	Liabilities	+	Stockholders' Equity
1. Issue common stock in exchange for cash.	Increase	=	No effect	+	Increase
2. Purchase business supplies on account.					
3. Pay for legal services for the current month.					
4. Provide services to customers on account.					
5. Pay employee salaries for the current month.					
6. Provide services to customers for cash.					
7. Pay for advertising for the current month.					
8. Repay loan from the bank.					
9. Pay dividends to stockholders.					
10. Receive cash from customers in (4) above.					
11. Pay for supplies purchased in (2) above.					

Required:

For each activity, indicate whether the transaction increases, decreases, or has no effect on assets, liabilities, and stockholders' equity.

P2–2A Below is a list of activities for Purple Cow Incorporated.

Analyze the impact of transactions on the accounting equation **(LO2)**

Transaction	Assets	=	Liabilities	+	Stockholders' Equity
1. Provide services to customers on account, $1,600.	+$1,600	=	$0	+	+$1,600
2. Pay $400 for current month's rent.					
3. Hire a new employee, who will be paid $500 at the end of each month.					

(continued)

(concluded)

Transaction	Assets	=	Liabilities	+	Stockholders' Equity
4. Pay $100 for advertising aired in the current period.					
5. Purchase office supplies for $400 cash.					
6. Receive cash of $1,000 from customers in (1) above.					
7. Obtain a loan from the bank for $7,000.					
8. Receive a bill of $200 for utility costs in the current period.					
9. Issue common stock for $10,000 cash.					
10. Pay $500 to employee in (3) above.					
Totals	———	=	———	+	———

Required:

For each activity, indicate the impact on the accounting equation. After doing so for all transactions, ensure that the accounting equation remains in balance.

Identify the type of account and its normal debit or credit balance (LO3)

P2–3A Below is a list of typical accounts.

Accounts	Type of Account	Normal Balance (Debit or Credit)
1. Salaries Payable		
2. Common Stock		
3. Prepaid Rent		
4. Buildings		
5. Utilities Expense		
6. Equipment		
7. Rent Expense		
8. Notes Payable		
9. Salaries Expense		
10. Insurance Expense		
11. Cash		
12. Service Revenue		

Required:

For each account, indicate (1) the type of account and (2) whether the normal account balance is a debit or credit. For the type of account, choose from asset, liability, stockholders' equity, dividend, revenue, or expense.

Correct recorded transactions (LO4)

P2–4A Below are several transactions for Scarlet Knight Corporation. A junior accountant, recently employed by the company, proposes to record the following transactions.

External Transaction	Accounts	Debit	Credit
1. Owners invest $10,000 in the company and receive common stock.	~~Common Stock~~ *Cash* ~~Cash~~ *Common Stock*	10,000	10,000
2. Receive cash of $3,000 for services provided in the current period.	Cash Service Revenue	3,000	3,000
3. Purchase office supplies on account, $200.	Supplies ~~Cash~~ *Account Payable*	200	200
4. Pay $500 for next month's rent.	~~Rent Expense~~ *Prepaid rent* Cash	500	500
5. Purchase office equipment with cash of $1,700.	~~Cash~~ *Equipment* ~~Equipment~~ *cash.*	1,700	1,700

Required:

Assess whether the junior accountant correctly proposes how to record each transaction. If incorrect, provide the correction.

P2–5A Jake owns a lawn maintenance company, and Luke owns a machine repair shop. For the month of July, the following transactions occurred.

Record transactions **(LO4)**

Flip Side of P2–6A

July 3	Jake provides lawn services to Luke's repair shop on account, $400.
July 6	One of Jake's mowers malfunctions. Luke provides repair services to Jake on account, $350.
July 9	Luke pays $400 to Jake for lawn services provided on July 3.
July 14	Luke borrows $500 from Jake by signing a note.
July 18	Jake purchases advertising in a local newspaper for the remainder of July and pays cash, $100.
July 20	Jake pays $350 to Luke for services provided on July 6.
July 27	Luke performs repair services for other customers for cash, $700.
July 30	Luke pays employees' salaries for the month, $200.
July 31	Luke pays $500 to Jake for money borrowed on July 14.

Required:

Record the transactions for Jake's Lawn Maintenance Company.

P2–6A Refer to the transactions described in P2–5A.

Analyze the impact of transactions on the accounting equation and record transactions **(LO2, 4)**

Flip Side of P2–5A

	Jake's Lawn Maintenance Company				Luke's Repair Shop		
	Assets	= Liabilities +	Stockholders' Equity		Assets	= Liabilities +	Stockholders' Equity
July 3	+$400 =	$0 +	+$400		$0 =	+$400 +	−$400
6							
9							
14							
18							
20							
27							
30							
31							

Required:

1. Record each transaction for Luke's Repair Shop.
2. Using the format shown above, indicate the impact of each transaction on the accounting equation for each company.

P2–7A Below are the account balances of Bruins Company at the end of November.

Prepare a trial balance **(LO6)**

Accounts	Balances	Accounts	Balances
Cash	$30,000	Common Stock	$40,000
Accounts Receivable	40,000	Retained Earnings	25,000
Supplies	1,000	Dividends	1,000
Prepaid Rent	2,000	Service Revenue	55,000
Equipment	?	Salaries Expense	20,000
Accounts Payable	16,000	Rent Expense	11,000
Salaries Payable	4,000	Interest Expense	2,000
Interest Payable	2,000	Supplies Expense	6,000
Unearned Revenue	8,000	Utilities Expense	5,000
Notes Payable	20,000		

Required:

Prepare a trial balance by placing amounts in the appropriate debit or credit column and determining the balance of the Equipment account.

Complete the steps in the measurement of external transactions **(LO4, 5, 6)**

P2–8A Below are the transactions for Ute Sewing Shop for March, the first month of operations.

March 1	Issue common stock in exchange for cash of $2,000.
March 3	Purchase sewing equipment by signing a note with the local bank, $1,700.
March 5	Pay rent of $500 for March.
March 7	Martha, a customer, places an order for alterations to several dresses. Ute estimates that the alterations will cost Martha $700. Martha is not required to pay for the alterations until the work is complete.
March 12	Purchase sewing supplies for $120 on account. This material will be used to provide services to customers.
March 15	Martha receives altered dresses and pays $700 to Ute.
March 19	Bob needs 100 pairs of overalls expanded as he purchased too many small and medium sizes. He pays $600 to Ute for services and expects the overalls to be completed by March 25.
March 25	Bob receives his completed overalls.
March 30	Pay utilities of $85 for the current period.
March 31	Pay dividends of $100 to stockholders.

Required:

1. Record each transaction.
2. Post each transaction to the appropriate T-accounts.
3. Calculate the balance of each account at March 31.
4. Prepare a trial balance as of March 31.

Ute uses the following accounts: Cash, Supplies, Equipment, Accounts Payable, Unearned Revenue, Notes Payable, Common Stock, Dividends, Service Revenue, Rent Expense, and Utilities Expense.

Complete the steps in the measurement of external transactions **(LO4, 5, 6)**

QB

P2–9A Pirates Incorporated had the following balances at the beginning of September.

PIRATES INCORPORATED Trial Balance		
Accounts	**Debits**	**Credits**
Cash	$ 5,500	
Accounts Receivable	1,500	
Supplies	6,600	
Land	10,200	
Accounts Payable		$6,500
Notes Payable		2,000
Common Stock		8,000
Retained Earnings		7,300

Cash Debit
Cash service R Credit.

The following transactions occur in September.

September 1	Provide services to customers for cash, $3,700.
September 2	Purchase land with a long-term note for $5,400 from Crimson Company. *Land Debit, Case cre Note*
September 4	Receive an invoice for $400 from the local newspaper for an advertisement that appeared on September 2. *AcE → Debit ACcount −C Sornic R−*
September 8	Provide services to customers on account for $5,000. *Re → B*
September 10	Purchase supplies on account for $1,000. *Supplies →D Note Paro −7C*
September 13	Pay $3,000 to Crimson Company for a long-term note. *Notes Parable − D Cash −D C*

cash — D
A R → C

September 18   Receive $4,000 from customers on account.
September 20   Pay $800 for September's rent.   *R → D , cash → C*
September 30   Pay September's utility bill of $1,500.   *U → D , Cash → C*
September 30   Pay employees $3,000 for salaries for the month of September.   *S → D, C → C*
September 30   Pay a cash dividend of $1,000 to shareholders.   *D → P , C → C*

Required:

1. Record each transaction.
2. Post each transaction to the appropriate T-accounts.
3. Calculate the balance of each account at September 30. (*Hint:* Be sure to include the balance at the beginning of September in each T-account.)
4. Prepare a trial balance as of September 30.

PROBLEMS: SET B

Mc Graw Hill **connect**
|ACCOUNTING

P2–1B Below is a list of activities for Tigers Corporation.

Analyze the impact of transactions on the accounting equation **(LO2)**

Transaction	Assets	=	Liabilities	+	Stockholders' Equity
1. Obtain a loan at the bank.	Increase	=	Increase	+	No effect
2. Purchase a machine to use in operations for cash.					
3. Provide services to customers for cash.					
4. Pay workers' salaries for the current month.					
5. Repay loan from the bank in (1) above.					
6. Customers pay cash in advance of services.					
7. Pay for maintenance costs in the current month.					
8. Pay for advertising in the current month.					
9. Purchase office supplies on account.					
10. Provide services to customers on account.					
11. Pay dividends to stockholders.					

Required:

For each activity, indicate whether the transaction increases, decreases, or has no effect on assets, liabilities, and stockholders' equity.

P2–2B Below is a list of activities for Vikings Incorporated.

Analyze the impact of transactions on the accounting equation **(LO2)**

Transaction	Assets	=	Liabilities	+	Stockholders' Equity
1. Issue common stock in exchange for cash, $15,000.	+ $15,000	=	$0	+	+$15,000
2. Obtain a loan from the bank for $9,000.					
3. Receive cash of $1,200 in advance from customers.					
4. Purchase supplies on account, $2,400.					

(continued)

(concluded)

Transaction	Assets	=	Liabilities	+	Stockholders' Equity
5. Pay one year of rent in advance, $12,000.					
6. Provide services to customers on account, $3,000.					
7. Repay $4,000 of the loan in (2) above.					
8. Pay the full amount for supplies purchased in (4) above.					
9. Provide services to customers in (3) above.					
10. Pay cash dividends of $1,000 to stockholders.					
Totals		=		+	

Required:

For each activity, indicate the impact on the accounting equation. After doing all the transactions, ensure that the accounting equation remains in balance.

Identify the type of account and its normal debit or credit balance (LO3)

P2–3B Below is a list of typical accounts.

Accounts	Type of Account	Normal Balance (Debit or Credit)
1. Supplies		
2. Advertising Expense		
3. Prepaid Insurance		
4. Supplies Expense		
5. Accounts Payable		
6. Equipment		
7. Dividends		
8. Accounts Receivable		
9. Retained Earnings		
10. Unearned Revenue		
11. Service Revenue		
12. Utilities Payable		

Required:

For each account, indicate (1) the type of account and (2) whether the normal account balance is a debit or credit. For type of account, choose from asset, liability, stockholders' equity, dividend, revenue, or expense.

Correct recorded transactions (LO4)

P2–4B Below are several transactions for Crimson Tide Corporation. A junior accountant, recently employed by the company, proposes to record the following transactions.

External Transaction	Accounts	Debit	Credit
1. Pay cash dividends of $700 to stockholders.	Cash	700	
	Dividends		700
2. Provide services on account for customers, $2,400.	Cash	2,400	
	Service Revenue		2,400
3. Pay a $400 utilities bill for the current period.	Utilities Expense	400	
	Cash		400
4. Receive cash of $300 from previously billed customers.	Cash	300	
	Service Revenue		300
5. Pay for supplies previously purchased on account, $1,100.	Supplies Expense	1,100	
	Cash		1,100

Required:

Assess whether the junior accountant correctly proposes how to record each transaction. If incorrect, provide the correction.

P2–5B Eli owns an insurance office, while Olivia operates a maintenance service that provides basic custodial duties. For the month of May, the following transactions occurred.

Record transactions (LO4)

Flip Side of P2–6B

May 2	Olivia decides that she will need insurance for a one-day special event at the end of the month and pays Eli $200 in advance.
May 5	Olivia provides maintenance services to Eli's insurance offices on account, $375.
May 7	Eli borrows $400 from Olivia by signing a note.
May 14	Olivia purchases maintenance supplies from Spot Corporation, paying cash of $150.
May 19	Eli pays $375 to Olivia for maintenance services provided on May 5.
May 25	Eli pays the utility bill for the month of May, $125.
May 28	Olivia receives insurance services from Eli equaling the amount paid on May 2.
May 31	Eli pays $400 to Olivia for money borrowed on May 7.

Required:

Record each transaction for Eli's Insurance Services.

P2–6B Refer to the transactions described in P2–5B.

Analyze the impact of transactions on the accounting equation and record transactions (LO2, 4)

Flip Side of P2–5B

	Eli's Insurance Services				Olivia's Maintenance Services			
	Assets	= Liabilities	+	Stockholders' Equity	Assets	= Liabilities	+	Stockholders' Equity
May 2	+$200	= +$200	+	$0	+$200 −$200	= $0	+	$0
5								
7								
14								
19								
25								
28								
31								

Required:

Record transactions for Olivia's Maintenance Services. Then, using the format shown, indicate the impact of each transaction on the accounting equation for each company.

P2–7B Below are account balances of Ducks Company at the end of September.

Prepare a trial balance (LO6)

Accounts	Balances	Accounts	Balances
Cash	$20,000	Retained Earnings	$12,000
Accounts Receivable	13,000	Dividends	3,000
Supplies	6,000	Service Revenue	?
Prepaid Insurance	4,000	Salaries Expense	8,000
Equipment	23,000	Insurance Expense	7,000
Accounts Payable	6,000	Advertising Expense	1,000
Salaries Payable	3,000	Supplies Expense	9,000
Utilities Payable	1,000	Entertainment Expense	5,000
Unearned Revenue	8,000	Utilities Expense	1,000
Common Stock	24,000		

Required:

Prepare a trial balance by placing amounts in the appropriate debit or credit column and determining the balance of the Service Revenue account.

Complete the steps in the measurement of external transactions **(LO4, 5, 6)**

P2–8B Below are the transactions for Salukis Car Cleaning for June, the first month of operations.

June 1   Obtain a loan of $60,000 from the bank by signing a note.
June 2   Issue common stock in exchange for cash of $30,000.
June 7   Purchase car wash equipment for $65,000 cash.
June 10   Purchase cleaning supplies of $7,000 on account.
June 12   Wash 400 cars for $10 each. All customers pay cash.
June 16   Pay employees $800 for work performed.
June 19   Pay for advertising in a local newspaper, costing $400.
June 23   Wash 500 cars for $10 each on account.
June 29   Pay employees $850 for work performed.
June 30   A utility bill of $1,300 for the current month is paid.
June 30   Pay dividends of $500 to stockholders.

Required:

1. Record each transaction.
2. Post each transaction to the appropriate T-accounts.
3. Calculate the balance of each account.
4. Prepare a trial balance for June.

Salukis uses the following accounts: Cash, Accounts Receivable, Supplies, Equipment, Accounts Payable, Notes Payable, Common Stock, Dividends, Service Revenue, Salaries Expense, Advertising Expense, and Utilities Expense.

Complete the steps in the measurement of external transactions **(LO4, 5, 6)**

P2–9B Buckeye Incorporated had the following trial balance at the beginning of November.

BUCKEYE INCORPORATED Trial Balance		
Accounts	**Debits**	**Credits**
Cash	$2,200	
Accounts Receivable	500	
Supplies	600	
Equipment	8,400	
Accounts Payable		$1,500
Notes Payable		3,000
Common Stock		6,000
Retained Earnings		1,200

The following transactions occur in November.

November 1   Issue common stock in exchange for $12,000 cash.
November 2   Purchase equipment with a long-term note for $2,500 from Spartan Corporation.
November 4   Purchase supplies for $1,200 on account.
November 10   Provide services to customers on account for $8,000.
November 15   Pay creditors on account, $1,000.
November 20   Pay employees $2,000 for the first half of the month.
November 22   Provide services to customers for $10,000 cash.
November 24   Pay $1,000 on the note from Spartan Corporation.
November 26   Collect $6,000 on account from customers.
November 28   Pay $1,000 to the local utility company for November gas and electricity.
November 30   Pay $4,000 rent for November.

Required:
1. Record each transaction.
2. Post each transaction to the appropriate T-accounts.
3. Calculate the balance of each account at November 30. (*Hint:* Be sure to include the balance at the beginning of November in each T-account.)
4. Prepare a trial balance as of November 30.

For additional problems, visit **www.mhhe.com/succeed** *for Problems: Set C.*

ADDITIONAL PERSPECTIVES

Great Adventures

(This is a continuation of the Great Adventures problem from Chapter 1.)

Continuing Problem

AP2–1 Tony and Suzie graduate from college in May 2012 and begin developing their new business. They begin by offering clinics for basic outdoor activities such as mountain biking or kayaking. Upon developing a customer base, they'll hold their first adventure races. These races will involve four-person teams that race from one checkpoint to the next using a combination of kayaking, mountain biking, orienteering, and trail running. In the long run, they plan to sell outdoor gear and develop a ropes course for outdoor enthusiasts.

On July 1, 2012, Tony and Suzie organize their new company as a corporation, Great Adventures Inc. The articles of incorporation state that the corporation will sell 20,000 shares of common stock for $1 each. Each share of stock represents a unit of ownership. Tony and Suzie will act as co-presidents of the company. The following business activities occur during July.

July 1	Suzie purchases $10,000 of Great Adventures' common stock using cash she saved during college.
1	Tony purchases $10,000 of Great Adventures' common stock by borrowing from a local bank using his personal vehicle as collateral.
1	Suzie purchases a one-year insurance policy for $4,800 ($400 per month) to cover injuries to participants during outdoor clinics.
2	The company pays legal fees of $1,500 associated with incorporation.
4	Suzie purchases office supplies of $1,800 on account.
7	Suzie pays advertising of $300 to a local newspaper for an upcoming mountain biking clinic to be held on July 15. Attendees will be charged $50 the day of the clinic.
8	Tony purchases 10 mountain bikes, paying $12,000 cash.
15	On the day of the clinic, Great Adventures receives cash of $2,000 from 40 bikers. Tony conducts the mountain biking clinic.
22	Because of the success of the first mountain biking clinic, Tony holds another mountain biking clinic and the company receives $2,300.
24	Suzie pays advertising of $700 to a local radio station for a kayaking clinic to be held on August 10. Attendees can pay $100 in advance or $150 on the day of the clinic.
30	Great Adventures receives cash of $4,000 in advance from 40 kayakers for the upcoming kayak clinic.

Required:
1. Record each transaction in July.
2. Post each transaction to T-accounts.
3. Prepare a trial balance.

Financial Analysis

American Eagle Outfitters, Inc.

AP2–2 Financial information for **American Eagle** is presented in Appendix A at the end of the book.

Required:

1. Is American Eagle's company size increasing? To answer, calculate the percentage change in total assets and percentage change in net sales for the most recent year.
2. Is American Eagle's total profitability increasing? Determine your answer by calculating the percentage change in net income for the most recent year.
3. Did American Eagle issue any common stock in the most recent year?
4. Do you see the term *debit* or *credit* listed in the balance sheet? Which account types in the balance sheet increase with a debit and which ones increase with a credit?
5. Do you see the term *debit* or *credit* listed in the income statement? Which account types in the income statement increase with a debit? Which increase with a credit?

Financial Analysis

The Buckle, Inc.

AP2–3 Financial information for **The Buckle** is presented in Appendix B at the end of the book.

Required:

1. Is The Buckle's company size increasing? Determine your answer by calculating the percentage change in total assets and percentage change in net sales for the most recent year.
2. Is The Buckle's total profitability increasing? Determine your answer by calculating the percentage change in net income for the most recent year.
3. Did The Buckle issue any common stock in the most recent year?
4. Do you see the term *debit* or *credit* listed in the balance sheet? Which account types in the balance sheet increase with a debit and which ones increase with a credit?
5. Do you see the term *debit* or *credit* listed in the income statement? Which account types in the income statement increase with a debit? Which increase with a credit?

Comparative Analysis

American Eagle Outfitters, Inc., vs. The Buckle, Inc.

AP2–4 Financial information for **American Eagle** is presented in Appendix A at the end of the book, and financial information for **The Buckle** is presented in Appendix B at the end of the book.

Required:

Determine which company's growth rate in total assets, net sales, and net income is greater. Why do you think this might be the case?

Ethics

AP2–5 Larry has been the chief financial officer (CFO) of Maxima Auto Service for the past 10 years. The company has reported profits each year it's been in business. However, this year has been a tough one. Increased competition and the rising costs of labor have reduced the company's profits. On December 30, Larry informs Robert, the company's president and Larry's closest friend for the past 10 years, that it looks like the company will report a net loss (total expenses will be greater than total revenues) of about $50,000 this year.

The next day, December 31, while Larry is preparing the year-end reports, Robert stops by Larry's office to tell him that an additional $75,000 of revenues needs to be reported and that the company can now report a profit. When Larry asks about the source of the $75,000, Robert tells him, "Earlier in the month some customers paid for auto services with cash, and with this cash I bought additional assets for the company. That's why the $75,000 never showed up in the bank statement. I just forgot to tell you about this earlier." When Larry asks for more specifics about these transactions, Robert mumbles, "I can't recall where I placed the customer sales invoices or the purchase receipts for the assets, but don't worry; I know they're here.

We've been friends for a lot of years and you can trust me. Now, let's hurry and finish those reports and I'll treat you to dinner tonight at the restaurant of your choice."

Required:
Discuss the ethical dilemma Larry faces.

Internet Research

AP2–6 Obtain a copy of the annual report of **Apple Inc.** for the most recent year. You can find the annual report at the company's website (*www.apple.com*) in the investor information section or at the Securities and Exchange Commission's website (*www.sec .gov*) using EDGAR (Electronic Data Gathering, Analysis, and Retrieval). Form 10-K, which includes the annual report, is required to be filed on EDGAR. Search or scroll within the annual report to find the financial statements.

Required:
Determine the following from the company's financial statements:
1. What amount does the company report for accounts receivable? What does this amount represent?
2. What amount does the company report for accounts payable? What does this amount represent?
3. The company reports a single amount for accrued expenses in the liability section of the balance sheet. What are some possible liabilities included in this amount?
4. What amount does the company report for common stock? What does this amount represent?
5. Determine whether the company's total assets equal total liabilities plus total stockholders' (or shareholders') equity.
6. Apple refers to its income statement as the statement of operations. What amount does the company report for net sales? This amount represents sales of the company's products over what period of time?
7. What are some of the expenses listed in the income statement?
8. Do the company's total revenues exceed total expenses? By how much?

Written Communication

AP2–7 Barth Interior provides decorating advice to its clients. Three recent transactions of the company include:
a. Providing decorating services of $500 on account to one of its clients.
b. Paying $1,200 for an employee's salary in the current period.
c. Purchasing office equipment for $2,700.

Required:
Write a memo to your instructor describing each step of the six-step measurement process presented in Illustration 2–1 for each of the three transactions.

Answers to the Self-Study Questions
1. c   2. d   3. c   4. c   5. c   6. a   7. d   8. a   9. c   10. d

The Financial Reporting Process

3

Learning Objectives

AFTER STUDYING THIS CHAPTER, YOU SHOULD BE ABLE TO:

- **LO1** Record revenues using the revenue recognition principle and expenses using the matching principle.
- **LO2** Distinguish between accrual-basis and cash-basis accounting.
- **LO3** Demonstrate the purposes and recording of adjusting entries.
- **LO4** Post adjusting entries and prepare an adjusted trial balance.
- **LO5** Prepare financial statements using the adjusted trial balance.
- **LO6** Demonstrate the purposes and recording of closing entries.
- **LO7** Post closing entries and prepare a post-closing trial balance.

FEDERAL EXPRESS: DELIVERING PROFITS TO INVESTORS

Wouldn't it be great to put $1,000 into the stock market and watch your investment really grow? As a student, you may not have a lot of extra money right now, but someday you will. Which stock should you buy? Where should you buy it?

The largest stock exchange in the world in terms of value traded each day is the New York Stock Exchange (NYSE), nicknamed the "Big Board." The value of shares traded on the NYSE was approximately $20 trillion in 2009. Another popular place to find stocks is the NASDAQ (an acronym for National Association of Securities Dealers Automated Quotations system). This is an electronic stock exchange in the United States that lists more companies and, on average, trades more shares per day than any other securities market in the world. Together, the NYSE and NASDAQ offer investors thousands of stocks from which to choose. Thousands more are listed on other stock exchanges throughout the world.

With so many choices, how do you tell the winning stocks from the losing stocks? The single piece of information that best distinguishes them is *net income*. Recall that net income equals revenues minus expenses for each reporting period. It measures how profitable the business is. Since stockholders are the owners of the business, any profits of the company belong solely to them (and not to creditors). Therefore, as net income increases, so does the value of the company to its stockholders.

To see the power of net income in explaining movements in stock prices, consider the following information for **Federal Express (FedEx)**. Over the 20-year period from 1990–2009, FedEx's net income increased in 14 of 20 years. For the other six years, net income decreased. What happened to FedEx's stock price in each of these years? In the years that net income increased, FedEx's stock price *rose* an average of 21.0%. In contrast, in the years that net income decreased, FedEx's stock price *fell* an average of 9.6%. The goal is clear: Predict the direction of the change in net income and you'll predict the change in stock prices.

PART A

ACCRUAL-BASIS ACCOUNTING

Net income, while certainly not the only consideration, is an essential aspect of good investment decisions. Investors know that any information they gather to help in predicting net income will lead to more profitable investments. Given the importance of net income to investors, standard setters have devoted considerable attention to the proper measurement of the two primary components of net income—revenues and expenses. In this section, we look at important principles behind reporting of revenues and expenses and at their effect on accounting.

Revenue and Expense Reporting

■ **LO1**
Record revenues using the revenue recognition principle and expenses using the matching principle.

If accounting information is to be useful in making decisions, accountants must measure and report revenues and expenses in a way that clearly reflects the ability of the company to create value for its owners, the stockholders. To do this, we use **accrual-basis accounting**, in which we record revenues when we earn them (the revenue recognition principle) and we record expenses with related revenues (the matching principle). We discuss these two principles next.

REVENUE RECOGNITION PRINCIPLE

A company records revenues when it sells its product or provides its service to a customer. For example, revenues are recorded when **Federal Express** delivers a package, **Reebok** sells a pair of shoes, **AMC Theatres** sells a movie ticket, **American Eagle** sells a shirt, or **GEICO** provides insurance coverage. The overriding concept in understanding how to properly record revenue is the revenue recognition principle. The revenue recognition principle states that we record revenue in the period in which we *earn* it. If a company sells products or provides services to a customer in 2012, the firm should report the revenue in its 2012 income statement. If the company sells products or provides services to a customer in 2013, it should report the revenue in the 2013 income statement, and so on.

Recognize revenue when it is earned.

To illustrate, suppose Calvin wants to surprise his wife Ruby with a 12-day, Hawaiian cruise to celebrate their 35th wedding anniversary. He books the cruise with **Carnival Cruise Lines**. He makes reservations and pays for the cruise in November 2012, but the cruise is not scheduled to sail until April 2013. When does Carnival report revenue from the ticket sale? Although the company receives Calvin's cash from the ticket sale in November 2012, it does not report revenue at this time because it has not substantially fulfilled its obligation to Calvin. It has not yet provided the services. Carnival will recognize the revenue in April 2013 when the cruise occurs.

It works the other way, too. Suppose that, anticipating the cruise, Calvin buys a Jimmy Buffett CD from **Best Buy**. Rather than paying cash, Calvin uses his Best Buy card to buy the CD on account. Even though Best Buy doesn't receive cash immediately from Calvin, it still records the revenue at the time it sells the CD.

 KEY POINT

The revenue recognition principle states that we should recognize revenue in the period in which we *earn* it, not necessarily in the period in which we receive cash.

MATCHING PRINCIPLE

You've heard it said, "It takes money to make money." That's true for all businesses. To make money from the sale of goods and services, companies must spend money on such essentials as advertising, workers' salaries, utilities, office rent, equipment, and business supplies. We've discussed how use of the revenue recognition principle

affects when we record revenues. Now let's discuss when we record *expenses,* the costs associated with producing these revenues.

The matching principle states that we recognize expenses *in the same period as the revenues they help to generate.* Implied in this principle is a *cause-and-effect* relationship between revenue and expense recognition. In a given period, we report revenue as it is earned, according to the revenue recognition principle. It's logical, then, that in the same period we should also record all expenses incurred to generate that revenue. The result is a measure—net income—that matches current period accomplishments (revenues) and sacrifices (expenses). That's the matching principle.

> Expenses are reported with the revenues they help to generate.

To see how the matching principle is applied, let's look back at Calvin and Ruby's Hawaiian cruise. What costs does Carnival Cruise Lines incur in order to generate the revenue from providing a cruise in April 2013? Some of the costs necessary to operate a cruise ship include:

1. The purchase of supplies the month before the cruise to prepare for sailing.
2. The purchase of fuel in the month of the cruise.
3. The payment of the captain's and other crew members' salaries in the month after the cruise.

Regardless of when Carnival actually pays the cash for these costs, the company should "expense the costs"—report the costs as expenses—in April. By doing this, Carnival reports the expenses in the same period as the revenue the expenses helped to generate. Illustration 3–1 shows how these costs would be expensed using the matching principle.

ILLUSTRATION 3–1
Matching Principle

Matching Principle – The cost of generating revenue in April (ship supplies, the fuel used, and crew members' salaries) should be expensed in April even though the cash flows occur in March, April, and May.

It's easy to see how these costs helped to generate the ticket revenue in April. Purchasing ship supplies is necessary for providing a cruise. Likewise, fuel is necessary for the ship to sail. Salaries are necessary to pay workers to operate the ship and serve the guests. All three costs are necessary to generate the ticket revenue in April, so we record them as expenses in April.

Of course, these are but a few of the costs of a cruise. Some costs are only indirectly related to producing revenue. For example, salaries paid in April 2013 to an office worker at Carnival's executive offices in Miami, Florida, are not directly related to the ticket revenue. But even such indirect costs contribute to overall operations, including cruise revenue, and so are expensed in April.

Sometimes it's impossible to determine in which period or periods, if any, revenues will occur. For example, consider the cost of advertising. Calvin may have booked the April 2013 cruise because of an advertisement (television, radio, print, Internet, cell phone) by Carnival back in November 2012. In theory, it would be ideal for Carnival to record the cost of this advertisement as an expense in April at the same time it records the revenue the advertisement helped to generate. However, it's difficult to determine when, how much, or even whether additional revenues occur as a result of a particular series of ads. Because of this obstacle, firms generally recognize advertising expenditures as expenses *in the period the ads are provided,* with no attempt made to match them with related revenues.

 KEY POINT

The matching principle states that we recognize expenses in the same period as the revenues they help to generate. Expenses include those directly and indirectly related to producing revenues.

Decision Point

Question ?	Accounting information 📄	Analysis 🔍
Can the company earn revenues that exceed the cost of doing so?	Revenues and expenses reported in the income statement	Revenues measure the amount earned during the year. Expenses measure the cost of earning those revenues. Together, these two combine to measure net income, or profitability.

Accrual-Basis Compared with Cash-Basis Accounting

■ LO2
Distinguish between accrual-basis and cash-basis accounting.

In the preceding section, we discovered the following about accrual-basis accounting:

1. We record revenues when we earn them (the revenue recognition principle) and *not necessarily when we receive cash.*
2. We record expenses with related revenues (the matching principle) and *not necessarily when we pay cash.*

Under accrual-basis accounting, we record revenue and expense transactions *at the time the earnings-related activities occur.*

Cash-basis accounting is not part of generally accepted accounting principles (GAAP).

Cash-basis accounting provides an alternative way of recording revenues and expenses. Under **cash-basis accounting**, we record *revenues at the time we receive cash and expenses at the time we pay cash.* For example, recall in our Carnival example that Calvin purchased tickets in November 2012, for a Hawaiian cruise in April 2013. Under cash-basis accounting, the cruise line would report revenue in November 2012, at the time Calvin pays cash for the cruise, and it would record expenses as it pays cash for them over several months (rather than recording revenue in April 2013 in accord with the revenue recognition principle and related expenses in April 2013 in accord with the matching principle).

Cash-basis accounting may seem appealing because it is essentially how we think about the inflow and outflow of cash from our bank accounts. However, **because cash-basis accounting violates both the revenue recognition principle and the matching principle, it is generally not accepted in preparing financial statements.** We briefly study cash-basis accounting, though, to help provide a better understanding of the advantages and disadvantages of accrual-basis accounting.

Illustrations 3–2 and 3–3 demonstrate the timing difference between accrual-basis and cash-basis accounting by referring back to our example in Illustration 3–1 involving Ruby and Calvin's Hawaiian cruise.

		Recognize Revenue?	
		Accrual-Basis	Cash-Basis
November 2012	Company receives cash from Ruby and Calvin for Hawaiian cruise next April.	No	Yes
April 2013	Company provides cruise services to Ruby and Calvin.	Yes	No

ILLUSTRATION 3–2

Accrual-Basis Revenue versus Cash-Basis Revenue

		Recognize Expense?	
		Accrual-Basis	Cash-Basis
March 2013	Company pays cash for supplies to be used *next* month.	No	Yes
April 2013	Company uses supplies purchased *last* month.	Yes	No
	Company pays cash for fuel used during the cruise *this* month.	Yes	Yes
	Employees earn salaries but will not be paid until *next* month.	Yes	No
May 2013	Company pays cash to employees for salaries earned *last* month.	No	Yes

ILLUSTRATION 3–3

Accrual-Basis Expense versus Cash-Basis Expense

Under both accrual-basis and cash-basis accounting, all revenues and expenses are eventually recorded for the same amount. In fact, over the life of the company, accrual-basis net income equals cash-basis net income. **The difference between the two methods is in the timing of when we record those revenues and expenses.** Under accrual-basis accounting, we record revenues when earned and expenses when we incur them. Under cash-basis accounting, we record revenues and expenses at the time we receive or pay cash.

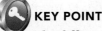

KEY POINT

The difference between accrual-basis accounting and cash-basis accounting is *timing*. Under accrual-basis accounting, we record revenues when we earn them (revenue recognition principle) and record expenses with the revenue they help to generate (matching principle). Under cash-basis accounting, we record revenues when we receive cash and expenses when we pay cash. Cash-basis accounting is not allowed for financial reporting purposes.

Let's Review

Cavalier Company experienced the following set of events:

May: *Receives cash* from customers for services to be provided in June.
June: *Provides services* to customers who prepaid in May.
May: *Pays cash* for supplies but does not use them.
June: *Uses the supplies* purchased in May.

Required:

1. Indicate in which month Cavalier records revenues under:
   a. Accrual-basis accounting *June*
   b. Cash-basis accounting *May*

2. Indicate in which month Cavalier records expenses under:
   a. Accrual-basis accounting *June*
   b. Cash-basis accounting *May*

Suggested Homework:
BE3-4, BE3-5;
E3-3, E3-4;
P3-1A&B; P3-2A&B

Solution:

1a. June   1b. May   2a. June   2b. May

PART B   THE MEASUREMENT PROCESS

In Chapter 2, we discussed the initial part of the accounting cycle process, measurement of external transactions. In this chapter, we will complete the accounting cycle process summarized in Illustration 3–4. First we continue the measurement process by recording adjusting entries (or internal transactions). Following adjusting entries, we will prepare financial statements and then close the books at the end of the period.

ILLUSTRATION 3–4

Steps in the
Accounting Cycle

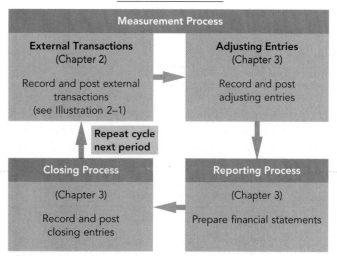

ACCOUNTING CYCLE

Adjusting Entries

■ **LO3**
Demonstrate the purposes and recording of adjusting entries.

At the end of a reporting period, even if we've accurately recorded every external transaction that occurred and accurately posted those transactions to appropriate accounts, our account balances are not updated for preparing financial statements. Before we can prepare the financial statements, we need to bring several of the accounts up-to-date. That's the purpose of adjusting entries. We use adjusting entries to record events that have occurred but that we have not yet recorded.

To envision the process, think of your auto insurance. Insurance companies require you to pay for insurance in advance. On the day you purchased the insurance, you actually bought an *asset* representing insurance coverage over a future period. With each passing day, however, the length of your policy is lapsing, decreasing your insurance asset. Tomorrow you will have one day less insurance coverage than you do today.

The same holds true for a business and its insurance coverage. Although it's true that the company's asset is declining daily, it is unnecessary (and in fact impractical) to record the lapsing of the insurance coverage each day. Recording the expense is necessary, though, when it's time to prepare financial statements at the end of the reporting period. Thus, we use an end-of-period *adjusting entry*. In the case of the insurance coverage, the business adjusts downward the balance of the asset (prepaid insurance) and records insurance expense for the amount of the policy that has lapsed.

If we do not record the adjusting entry for the part of the insurance policy that has lapsed, then total assets will be overstated and expenses will be understated, causing net income to be overstated. This kind of misstatement can mislead users of financial statements. Because adjusting entries allow for proper application of the revenue recognition principle (revenues) or the matching principle (expenses), they are a *necessary part of accrual-basis accounting*. They must be recorded at the end of each period before the company prepares its financial statements.

KEY POINT ────────────────────────────────

Adjusting entries are a necessary part of accrual-basis accounting. They help to record revenues in the period earned and expenses in the period they are incurred to generate those revenues. Another benefit is that, by properly recording revenues and expenses, we correctly state assets and liabilities.

It is useful to group adjusting entries into two broad categories—prepayments and accruals—that can be further divided into four subcategories: prepaid expenses, unearned revenues, accrued expenses, and accrued revenues. These four occur as follows.

Prepayments
Prepaid expenses—We paid cash (or had an obligation to pay cash) for the purchase of an asset *before* we incurred the expense.
Unearned revenues—We received cash and recorded a liability *before* we earned the revenue.

Accruals
Accrued expenses—We paid cash *after* we incurred the expense and recorded a liability.
Accrued revenues—We received cash *after* we earned the revenue and recorded an asset.

Let's consider each of these situations. The easiest way to understand adjusting entries is to look at some examples. So, look back to the external transactions of Eagle Golf Academy from Chapter 2. For easy reference, we've restated these transactions in Illustration 3–5 (next page). We will prepare all adjusting entries on January 31, to account for revenue and expense transactions that have not been recorded by the end of the month.

PREPAID EXPENSES

Prepaid expenses are the costs of assets acquired in one period that will be expensed in a future period (like the insurance coverage mentioned previously). The cash outflow (or obligation to pay cash, in the case of assets bought on account)

ILLUSTRATION 3–5	Transaction	Date	External Transactions in January	Type of Activity
External Transactions of Eagle Golf Academy	(1)	Jan. 1	Sell shares of common stock for $25,000 to obtain the funds necessary to start the business.	Financing
	(2)	Jan. 1	Borrow $10,000 from the local bank and sign a note promising to repay the full amount of the debt in three years.	Financing
	(3)	Jan. 1	Purchase equipment necessary for giving golf training, $24,000 cash.	Investing
	(4)	Jan. 1	Pay one year of rent in advance, $6,000 ($500 per month).	Operating
	(5)	Jan. 6	Purchase supplies on account, $2,300.	Operating
	(6)	Jan. 12	Provide golf training to customers for cash, $3,600.	Operating
	(7)	Jan. 17	Provide golf training to customers on account, $2,500.	Operating
	(8)	Jan. 23	Receive cash in advance for 10 golf training sessions to be given in the future, $600.	Operating
	(9)	Jan. 28	Pay salaries to employees, $2,800.	Operating
	(10)	Jan. 30	Pay cash dividends of $200 to shareholders.	Financing

from the purchase of an asset occurs before we record the expense. Examples are the purchase of equipment or supplies and the payment of rent or insurance in advance. These payments *create future benefits,* so we record them as assets at the time of purchase. The benefits provided by these assets *expire in future periods,* so we expense their cost in those future periods. **The adjusting entry for a prepaid expense always includes a debit to an expense account (increase an expense) and a credit to an asset account (decrease an asset).**

Eagle Golf Academy has three prepaid expenses during January: It purchases rent, supplies, and equipment. Each of these items provides future benefits and was recorded as an asset at the time of purchase. By the end of January, the company has used a portion of each asset, and that portion no longer represents a future benefit. The amount of the asset used represents an expense as well as a reduction of the asset. We'll look at each prepaid expense in turn.

Prepaid rent. Let's begin with transaction (4) in which Eagle Golf Academy purchases one year of rent in advance for $6,000 ($500 per month). The benefits from using the rented space occur evenly over time, with one month's cost attributable to January, one month to February, and so on. Therefore, we need to record one month of the asset's cost as an expense in January and include it in that month's income statement, along with the revenue it helped to produce. At the same time, the asset account has one month's less benefit with each passing month, requiring us to reduce the balance of the asset.

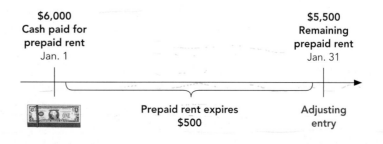

	$6,000 Cash paid for prepaid rent Jan. 1		$5,500 Remaining prepaid rent Jan. 31
		Prepaid rent expires $500	Adjusting entry

The end-of-period **adjusting entry** for expiration of prepaid rent is below.

January 31	Debit	Credit
Rent Expense (+E, −SE)	500	
Prepaid Rent (−A)		500
(*Reduce prepaid rent due to the passage of time*)		

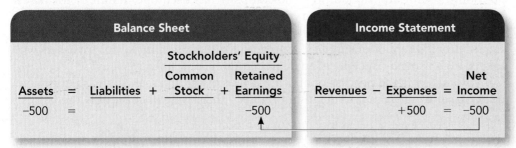

Balance Sheet					Income Statement		
			Stockholders' Equity				
			Common	**Retained**			**Net**
Assets	=	**Liabilities** +	**Stock** +	**Earnings**	**Revenues** −	**Expenses** =	**Income**
−500	=			−500		+500 =	−500

User's Guide At this point in the book, below each journal entry we begin to include simple accounting equation analyses, to show the effects of the journal entry on the balance sheet and income statement.

Notice that the adjusting entry includes a $500 expense (+E), which reduces net income and stockholders' equity (−SE). At the same time, the balance in the asset account, Prepaid Rent, decreases (−A) by $500 and will now have a balance of $5,500 (= $6,000 − $500). We adjust any other assets that expire over time (such as prepaid insurance) in a similar manner.

Supplies.   In transaction (5), Eagle purchases supplies for $2,300 on account on January 6. Even though cash will be paid later, the cost of supplies (or obligation to pay cash for supplies) is incurred on January 6. Suppose that at the end of January a count of supplies reveals that only $1,500 of supplies remains. What happened to the other $800 of supplies? Apparently, this is the amount of supplies used during the month. Since it's not cost-efficient to record the consumption of supplies every day, we make a single adjusting entry at the end of the month for the total amount used during the period.

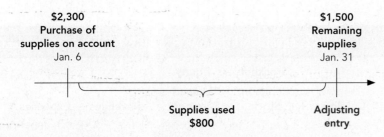

The end-of-period **adjusting entry** for supplies is below.

January 31	Debit	Credit
Supplies Expense (+E, −SE)	800	
Supplies (−A)		800
(*Consume supplies during the current period*)		

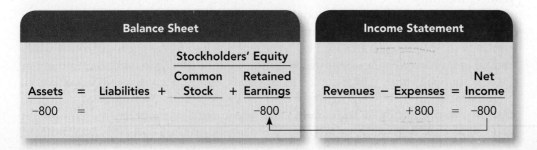

Balance Sheet					Income Statement		
			Stockholders' Equity				
			Common	**Retained**			**Net**
Assets	=	**Liabilities** +	**Stock** +	**Earnings**	**Revenues** −	**Expenses** =	**Income**
−800	=			−800		+800 =	−800

This entry simultaneously records the $800 of supplies used as an expense and reduces the balance of the Supplies account to the $1,500 amount that still remains.

Depreciable assets. In transaction (3), Eagle purchases equipment for $24,000 cash. Let's assume that, at the time of purchase, Eagle estimates the equipment will be useful for the next five years (60 months). Because one month (January) has passed since the purchase of this asset, Eagle has used one month of the asset's estimated 60-month useful life. In addition, the company has used one month of the asset's cost to produce revenue in January. Therefore, we should *match* the cost (expense) with the revenue it helps to produce. Although this creates a situation much like that of prepaid rent or of supplies, we record the reduction in the cost of assets with longer lives using a concept called depreciation.

Depreciation is the process of allocating the cost of an asset, such as equipment, to expense. We discuss it in detail in Chapter 7; here we will cover only the basics.

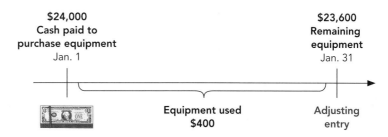

The end-of-period **adjusting entry** to record one month of depreciation for equipment is below.

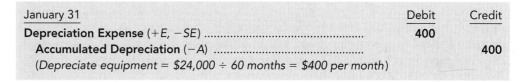

January 31	Debit	Credit
Depreciation Expense (+E, −SE)	400	
Accumulated Depreciation (−A)		400
(*Depreciate equipment = $24,000 ÷ 60 months = $400 per month*)		

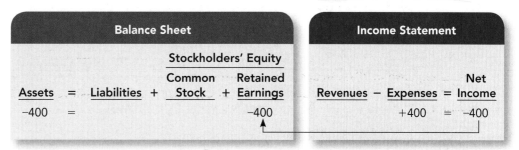

This entry reduces the Equipment account by $400. Notice, however, that we didn't reduce Equipment directly, by crediting the asset account itself. Instead, we reduced the asset *indirectly* by crediting an account called *Accumulated Depreciation*. The Accumulated Depreciation account is called a *contra account*. A **contra account** is an account with a balance that is opposite, or "contra," to that of its related accounts.

The normal balance in the Accumulated Depreciation contra asset account is a *credit*, which is opposite to the normal *debit* balance in an asset account. The reason we use a contra account is to keep the original balance of the asset intact while reducing its current balance indirectly. In the balance sheet, we report equipment at its current *book value*, which equals its original cost less accumulated depreciation.

Illustration 3–6 shows how **American Airlines** records accumulated depreciation for its property and equipment. The net amount of property and equipment represents the book value, or amount of the assets' original costs less accumulated

depreciation. As you will see in Chapter 7, depreciation is an *estimate* based on expected useful life and is an attempt to *allocate the cost of the asset over the useful life*. It is a calculation internal to the company and does not necessarily represent market value (what the asset could be sold for in the market).

AMERICAN AIRLINES Balance Sheet (partial) ($ in millions)		
Assets		
Flight equipment, at cost	$19,601	
Less: Accumulated depreciation	(7,147)	
Book value of flight equipment		$12,454
Other equipment and property, at cost	5,132	
Less: Accumulated depreciation	(2,762)	
Book value of other equipment and property		2,370

ILLUSTRATION 3–6

Reporting Depreciation of Property and Equipment for American Airlines

 ETHICAL DILEMMA

 You have recently been employed by a large retail chain that sells sporting goods. One of your tasks is to help prepare financial statements for external distribution. The chain's largest creditor, National Savings & Loan, requires that financial statements be prepared according to generally accepted accounting principles (GAAP). During the months of November and December 2012, the company spent $1 million on a major TV advertising campaign. The $1 million included the costs of producing the commercials as well as the broadcast time purchased to run them. Because the advertising will be aired in 2012 only, you decide to charge all the costs to advertising expense in 2012, in accordance with requirements of GAAP.

The company's chief financial officer (CFO), who hired you, asks you for a favor. Instead of charging the costs to advertising expense, he asks you to set up an asset called prepaid advertising and to wait until 2013 to record any expense. The CFO explains, "This ad campaign has produced significant sales in 2012; but I think it will continue to bring in customers throughout 2013. By recording the ad costs as an asset, we can match the cost of the advertising with the additional sales in 2013. Besides, if we expense the advertising in 2012, we will show an operating loss in our income statement. The bank requires that we continue to show profits in order to maintain our loan in good standing. Failure to remain in good standing could mean we'd have to fire some of our recent hires." What should you do?

UNEARNED REVENUES

We record **unearned revenues** when a company receives cash in advance from a customer for products or services to be provided in the future. When customers pay cash in advance, we debit cash and credit a liability. This liability reflects the company's obligation to provide goods or services to the customer in the future. Once

it has provided these products or services, the company can record revenue earned and reduce its obligation to the customer. **The adjusting entry for an unearned revenue always includes a debit to a liability account (decrease a liability) and a credit to a revenue account (increase a revenue).**

In transaction (8), Eagle receives $600 in advance from customers who will be given 10 golf lessons ($60 per lesson) in the future. Later, as Eagle provides that training to customers, it reduces the liability to customers and can record the service revenue because it now has earned it. Assume that by the end of January Eagle has provided one of the 10 training sessions paid for in advance.

$600 Cash received in advance Jan. 23		$540 Unearned revenue remains Jan. 31
	Services provided $60	Adjusting entry

The end-of-period **adjusting entry** to account for the revenue earned is below.

January 31	Debit	Credit
Unearned Revenue (−*L*)	60	
Service Revenue (+*R*, +*SE*)		60
(*Provide services to customers who paid in advance*)		

Balance Sheet					Income Statement		
			Stockholders' Equity				
			Common	Retained			Net
Assets	=	Liabilities +	Stock	+ Earnings	Revenues	− Expenses =	Income
	=	−60		+60	+60	=	+60

Illustration 3–7 shows an example of unearned revenue for **Apple Inc.**

ILLUSTRATION 3–7

Reporting Unearned Revenues and Other Current Liabilities for Apple Inc.

Common Terms
Another common name for unearned revenue is *deferred revenue*.

APPLE INC. Balance Sheet (partial) ($ in thousands)	
Current liabilities:	
Accounts payable	$ 5,601
Unearned revenue	10,305
Other current liabilities*	3,376
Total current liabilities	$19,282

*Includes amounts owed for taxes, salaries, advertising, and other operating costs.

Most of Apple's unearned revenue comes from sales of the popular iPhone. When you purchase an iPhone, Apple does not immediately record revenue from the sale. Instead, the company spreads this revenue over the next 24 months (the life of a typical iPhone contract). In other words, if you purchase an iPhone today, Apple

initially records the entire sale as unearned revenue and then begins to recognize revenue (and decrease unearned revenue) as the company earns this revenue each month for the next 24 months.

Now that we've discussed prepaid expenses and unearned revenues (prepayments), let's look at the two other categories of adjusting entries—accrued expenses and accrued revenues. Accruals are the opposite of prepayments. **Accruals occur when the cash flow occurs *after* either the expense is incurred or the revenue is earned.** Walking through some examples using our Eagle Golf Academy illustration will demonstrate both types of accruals.

ACCRUED EXPENSES

When a company has incurred an expense but hasn't yet paid cash or recorded an obligation to pay, it still should record the expense. This is referred to as an accrued expense. **The adjusting entry for an accrued expense always includes a debit to an expense account (increase an expense) and a credit to a liability account (increase a liability).**

Accrued salaries. Eagle pays total salaries to its employees of $100 per day. For the first four weeks (28 days), Eagle pays $2,800 cash to employees. For simplicity, we combined each of these four weeks in transaction (9) in Illustration 3–5. For the remaining three days in January, employees earn additional salaries of $300, but Eagle doesn't plan to pay the employees until the end of the week, February 4. However, Eagle must record the $300 salaries expense in the month employees worked (January). Stated differently, the salaries expense *accrues* during January even though the company won't pay the expense until February.

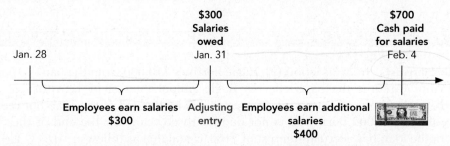

The end-of-period **adjusting entry** for accrued salaries is below.

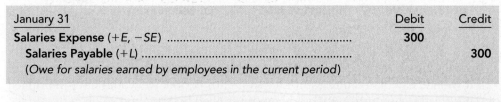

January 31	Debit	Credit
Salaries Expense (+E, −SE)	300	
Salaries Payable (+L)		300
(Owe for salaries earned by employees in the current period)		

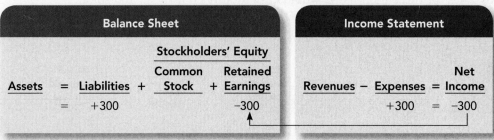

Balance Sheet					Income Statement		
			Stockholders' Equity				
			Common	Retained			Net
Assets	=	Liabilities +	Stock +	Earnings	Revenues −	Expenses =	Income
	=	+300		−300		+300 =	−300

Accrued utility costs. At the end of January, Eagle receives a utility bill for $960 associated with operations in January. Eagle plans to pay the bill on February 6. Even though it won't pay the cash until February, Eagle must record the utility costs

for January as an expense in January. The firm records the corresponding obligation to the utility company at the same time.

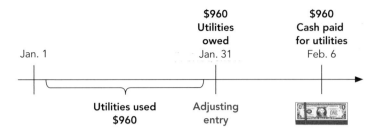

The end-of-period **adjusting entry** is below.

January 31	Debit	Credit
Utilities Expense (+E, −SE)	960	
Utilities Payable (+L)		960
(*Owe for utilities costs in the current period*)		

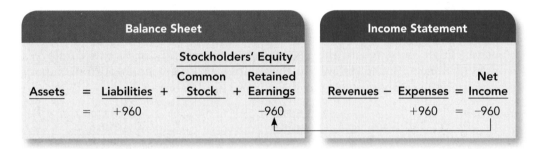

Balance Sheet						Income Statement		
				Stockholders' Equity				
				Common	**Retained**			**Net**
Assets	=	**Liabilities**	+	**Stock**	+ **Earnings**	**Revenues** −	**Expenses** =	**Income**
	=	+960			−960		+960 =	−960

Accrued interest. In transaction (2), Eagle borrows $10,000 from the bank to begin operations. Assume the bank charges Eagle annual interest of 12% (or 1% per month) on the borrowed amount. Interest is due by the end of the year, but repayment of the $10,000 borrowed is not due for three years. By the end of the first month, the loan has accrued interest of $100, calculated as follows:

Amount of note payable	×	**Annual interest rate**	×	**Fraction of the year**	=	**Interest**
$10,000	×	12%	×	1/12	=	$100

Notice that we multiplied by 1/12 to calculate the interest for one month (out of 12). If we had calculated interest for a two-month period, we would have multiplied by 2/12; for three months we would have multiplied by 3/12; and so on.

Although Eagle won't pay the $100 until the end of the year, it is a cost of using the borrowed funds during January and therefore is an expense for January.

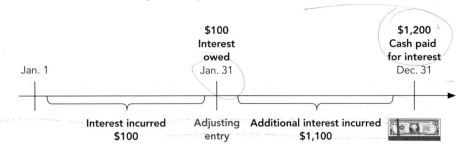

CHAPTER 3   The Financial Reporting Process   **121**

The end-of-period **adjusting entry** for interest payable is below.

January 31	Debit	Credit
Interest Expense (+E, −SE)	100	
Interest Payable (+L)		100
(Owe for interest charges in the current period)		

Balance Sheet				Income Statement		
		Stockholders' Equity				
		Common	**Retained**			**Net**
Assets =	**Liabilities** +	**Stock** +	**Earnings**	**Revenues** −	**Expenses** =	**Income**
=	+100		−100		+100 =	−100

COMMON MISTAKE

When recording the interest payable on a borrowed amount, students sometimes mistakenly credit the liability associated with the principal amount (Notes Payable). We record interest payable in a *separate account* (Interest Payable), to keep the balance owed for principal separate from the balance owed for interest.

ACCRUED REVENUES

When a company has earned revenue but hasn't yet received cash or recorded an amount receivable, it still should record the revenue. This is referred to as an **accrued revenue**. **The adjusting entry for an accrued revenue always includes a debit to an asset account (increase an asset) and a credit to a revenue account (increase a revenue).**

Interest receivable.   We can see an example of accrued revenues if we review the flip side of transaction (2), which we discussed in the previous section. The bank lends Eagle Golf Academy $10,000 and charges Eagle annual interest of 12% (or 1% per month) on the borrowed amount. By the end of the month, interest has been earned each day, but the bank has not yet recorded the interest because it is impractical to record interest on a daily basis. At the end of January, the bank records interest revenue earned of $100 (= $10,000 × 12% × 1/12). The bank's adjusting entry for January will include a debit to Interest Receivable and a credit to Interest Revenue for $100. Note that this is the same amount that Eagle Golf Academy, the borrower, records as Interest Expense.

Flip Side

Accounts receivable.   Revenue also accrues when a firm performs services but has not yet collected cash or billed the customer. Suppose, for instance, that Eagle provides $200 of golf training to customers from January 28 to January 31. However, it usually takes Eagle one week to mail bills to customers and another week for customers to pay. Therefore, Eagle expects to receive cash from these customers during February 8–14. Because Eagle earned the revenue in January (regardless of when cash receipt takes place), Eagle should recognize in January the service revenue and the amount receivable from those customers.

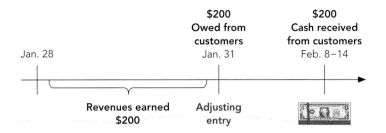

The end-of-period **adjusting entry** is below.

January 31	Debit	Credit
Accounts Receivable (+A)	**200**	
Service Revenue (+R, +SE)		**200**
(Bill customers for services provided during the current period)		

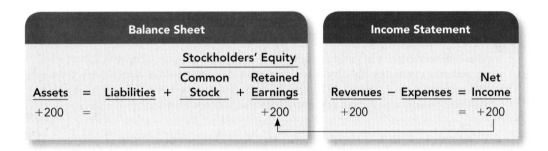

 KEY POINT

> Adjusting entries are needed when cash flows or obligations occur *before* the earnings-related activity (prepayment) or when cash flows occur *after* the earnings-related activity (accrual).

NO ADJUSTMENT NECESSARY

Notice that we did not make any adjusting entries associated with transaction (1) or (10) for Eagle Golf Academy. Transaction (1) is the sale of common stock, and transaction (10) is the payment of dividends to common stockholders. **Neither of these transactions involves the recognition of revenues or expenses and therefore will not require month-end adjusting entries.**

Similarly, **transactions in which we (1) receive cash at the same time we earn revenue or (2) pay cash at the same time we incur an expense will not require adjusting entries.** For example, when Eagle provides golf training to customers for cash [transaction (6)], the company records revenue at the same time it records the cash received, and no corresponding month-end adjusting entry is needed.

 KEY POINT

> Adjusting entries are *unnecessary* in two cases: (1) for transactions that do not involve revenue or expense activities and (2) for transactions that result in revenues or expenses being recorded at the same time as the cash flow.

漠 戻·l/伝

Below are four scenarios for a local **Midas Muffler** shop for the month of September.

Scenario 1: On September 1, the balance of maintenance supplies totals $400. On September 15, the shop purchases an additional $200 of maintenance supplies. By the end of September, only $100 of maintenance supplies remains.

Scenario 2: On September 4, Midas receives $6,000 cash from a local moving company in an agreement to provide truck maintenance of $1,000 each month for the next six months, beginning in September.

Scenario 3: Mechanics have worked the final four days in September, earning $600, but have not yet been paid. Midas plans to pay its mechanics on October 2.

Scenario 4: Customers receiving $250 of maintenance services from Midas on September 29 have not been billed as of the end of the month. These customers will be billed on October 3 and are expected to pay the full amount owed on October 6.

Required:

For each of the scenarios:

1. Indicate the type of adjusting entry needed.
2. Record the transaction described and the month-end adjusting entry.

Solution:

Scenario 1: Adjusting entry type: Prepaid expense.

September 15 (external transaction)	Debit	Credit
Supplies (+A)	200	
Cash (−A)		200
(Purchase maintenance supplies for cash)		

September 30 (month-end adjusting entry)	Debit	Credit
Supplies Expense (+E, −SE)	500	
Supplies (−A)		500
(Consume supplies)		
($400 + $200 − $100 = $500)		

Scenario 2: Adjusting entry type: Unearned revenue.

September 4 (external transaction)	Debit	Credit
Cash (+A)	6,000	
Unearned Revenue (+L)		6,000
(Receive cash in advance from customers)		

September 30 (month-end adjusting entry)	Debit	Credit
Unearned Revenue (−L)	1,000	
Service Revenue (+R, +SE)		1,000
(Provide first of six months of services)		

Scenario 3: Adjusting entry type: Accrued expense.

September 30 (month-end adjusting entry)	Debit	Credit
Salaries Expense (+E, −SE)	600	
Salaries Payable (+L)		600
(*Owe for salaries earned by employees in the current period*)		

October 2 (external transaction)	Debit	Credit
Salaries Payable (−L)	600	
Cash (−A)		600
(*Pay salaries owed*)		

Scenario 4: Adjusting entry type: Accrued revenue.

September 30 (month-end adjusting entry)	Debit	Credit
Accounts Receivable (+A)	250	
Service Revenue (+R, +SE)		250
(*Provide maintenance service on account*)		

October 6 (external transaction)	Debit	Credit
Cash (+A)	250	
Accounts Receivable (−A)		250
(*Collect cash from customers previously billed*)		

Suggested Homework:
BE3-6, BE3-10;
E3-7, E3-8;
P3-3A&B, P3-4A&B

Post Adjusting Entries

■ LO4
Post adjusting entries and prepare an adjusted trial balance.

To complete the measurement process, we need to update balances of assets, liabilities, revenues, and expenses for adjusting entries. In Illustration 3–8, we summarize the eight adjusting entries of Eagle Golf Academy recorded earlier. To update balances, we post the adjustments to the appropriate accounts in the general ledger, as demonstrated in Illustration 3–9.

ILLUSTRATION 3–8

Summary of Adjusting Entries for Eagle Golf Academy

January 31	Debit	Credit
(a) **Rent Expense** (+E, −SE)	500	
Prepaid Rent (−A)		500
(*Reduce prepaid rent due to the passage of time*)		
(b) **Supplies Expense** (+E, −SE)	800	
Supplies (−A)		800
(*Consume supplies during the current period*)		
(c) **Depreciation Expense** (+E, −SE)	400	
Accumulated Depreciation (−A)		400
(*Depreciate equipment*)		
($24,000 ÷ 60 months = $400 per month)		
(d) **Unearned Revenue** (−L)	60	
Service Revenue (+R, +SE)		60
(*Provide services to customers who paid in advance*)		
(e) **Salaries Expense** (+E, −SE)	300	
Salaries Payable (+L)		300
(*Owe for salaries earned by employees in the current period*)		

ILLUSTRATION 3–8
Summary of Adjusting Entries for Eagle Golf Academy *(continued)*

(f) **Utilities Expense** (+E, −SE)	960	
Utilities Payable (+L)		960
(Owe for utilities costs in the current period)		
(g) **Interest Expense** (+E, −SE)	100	
Interest Payable (+L)		100
(Owe for interest charges in the current period)		
(h) **Accounts Receivable** (+A)	200	
Service Revenue (+R, +SE)		200
(Bill customers for services provided during the month)		

ILLUSTRATION 3–9 Posting Adjusting Entries (in red) of Eagle Golf Academy to General Ledger Accounts

Assets = Liabilities + Stockholders' Equity

Cash

(1)	25,000	(3)	24,000
(2)	10,000	(4)	6,000
(6)	3,600	(9)	2,800
(8)	600	(10)	200
Bal.	**6,200**		

Accounts Receivable

(7)	2,500	
(h)	200	
Bal.	**2,700**	

Supplies

(5)	2,300		
		(b)	800
Bal.	**1,500**		

Prepaid Rent

(4)	6,000		
		(a)	500
Bal.	**5,500**		

Equipment

(3)	24,000	
Bal.	**24,000**	

Accumulated Depreciation

		(c)	400
		Bal.	**400**

Accounts Payable

		(5)	2,300
		Bal.	**2,300**

Unearned Revenue

		(8)	600
(d)	60		
		Bal.	**540**

Salaries Payable

		(e)	300
		Bal.	**300**

Utilities Payable

		(f)	960
		Bal.	**960**

Interest Payable

		(g)	100
		Bal.	**100**

Notes Payable

		(2)	10,000
		Bal.	**10,000**

Common Stock

		(1)	25,000
		Bal.	**25,000**

Dividends

(10)	200	
Bal.	**200**	

Supplies Expense

(b)	800	
Bal.	**800**	

Depreciation Expense

(c)	400	
Bal.	**400**	

Utilities Expense

(f)	960	
Bal.	**960**	

Retained Earnings

			0
		Bal.	**0**

Service Revenue

		(6)	3,600
		(7)	2,500
		(d)	60
		(h)	200
		Bal.	**6,360**

Rent Expense

(a)	500	
Bal.	**500**	

Salaries Expense

(9)	2,800	
(e)	300	
Bal.	**3,100**	

Interest Expense

(g)	100	
Bal.	**100**	

- Amounts in black represent external transactions in January. Numbers in parentheses refer to transaction numbers in Illustration 3–5.
- Amounts in red represent month-end adjusting entries. Letters in parentheses refer to adjusting entries in Illustration 3–8.
- Amounts in **bold** represent ending balances.

COMMON MISTAKE

Students sometimes mistakenly include the Cash account in an adjusting entry. An adjusting entry will never include the Cash account. Note that no adjusting entries are posted to the Cash account in Illustration 3–9.

KEY POINT

We post adjusting entries to the T-accounts in the general ledger to update the account balances.

ADJUSTED TRIAL BALANCE

After we have posted the adjusting entries to the general ledger accounts, we're ready to prepare an *adjusted* trial balance. An adjusted trial balance is a list of all accounts and their balances *after we have updated account balances for adjusting entries*. Illustration 3–10 shows the relationship between an unadjusted trial

ILLUSTRATION 3–10

Unadjusted Trial Balance and Adjusted Trial Balance for Eagle Golf Academy

	EAGLE GOLF ACADEMY Unadjusted Trial Balance and Adjusted Trial Balance January 31						
Accounts	**Unadjusted Trial Balance**		**Adjustments**		**Adjusted Trial Balance**		
	Debit	**Credit**	**Debit**	**Credit**	**Debit**	**Credit**	
Cash	$ 6,200				$ 6,200		
Accounts Receivable	2,500		(h) 200		2,700		
Supplies	2,300			(b) 800	1,500		
Prepaid Rent	6,000			(a) 500	5,500		
Equipment	24,000				24,000		
Accumulated Depreciation				(c) 400		$ 400	
Accounts Payable		$ 2,300				2,300	
Unearned Revenue		600	(d) 60			540	
Salaries Payable				(e) 300		300	
Utilities Payable				(f) 960		960	
Interest Payable				(g) 100		100	
Notes Payable		10,000				10,000	
Common Stock		25,000				25,000	
Retained Earnings		0				0	
Dividends	200				200		
Service Revenue		6,100		(d and h) 260		6,360	
Supplies Expense			(b) 800		800		
Rent Expense			(a) 500		500		
Depreciation Expense			(c) 400		400		
Salaries Expense	2,800		(e) 300		3,100		
Utilities Expense			(f) 960		960		
Interest Expense			(g) 100		100		
Totals	**$44,000**	**$44,000**			**$45,960**	**$45,960**	

Total debits equal total credits.

balance (before adjustments) and an adjusted trial balance (after adjustments). The unadjusted trial balance is the one shown in Chapter 2 in Illustration 2–26. The adjusted trial balance includes the adjusted balances of all general ledger accounts shown in Illustration 3–9.

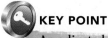

KEY POINT

An adjusted trial balance is a list of all accounts and their balances at a particular date, after we have updated account balances for adjusting entries.

THE REPORTING PROCESS: FINANCIAL STATEMENTS

Once the adjusted trial balance is complete, we prepare financial statements. Illustration 3–11 describes the relationship between the adjusted trial balance and the financial statements. Notice the color coding of the accounts, to indicate their relationships to the financial statements.

PART C

■ **LO5**
Prepare financial statements using the adjusted trial balance.

ILLUSTRATION 3–11
Relationship between Adjusted Trial Balance and Financial Statements

EAGLE GOLF ACADEMY Adjusted Trial Balance January 31		
Accounts	**Debit**	**Credit**
Cash	$ 6,200	
Accounts Receivable	2,700	
Supplies	1,500	
Prepaid Rent	5,500	
Equipment	24,000	
Accumulated Depreciation		$ 400
Accounts Payable		2,300
Unearned Revenue		540
Salaries Payable		300
Interest Payable		100
Utilities Payable		960
Notes Payable		10,000
Common Stock		25,000
Retained Earnings		0
Dividends	200	
Service Revenue		6,360
Supplies Expense	800	
Rent Expense	500	
Depreciation Expense	400	
Salaries Expense	3,100	
Utilities Expense	960	
Interest Expense	100	
Totals	$45,960	$45,960

BALANCE SHEET
Assets
=
Liabilities
+
Stockholders' Equity

STATEMENT OF STOCKHOLDERS' EQUITY

Common Stock
+
Retained Earnings
(= RE, Jan. 1 + NI − Divs)
=
Stockholders' Equity

INCOME STATEMENT
Revenues
−
Expenses
=
Net Income

Revenue and expense accounts are reported in the income statement. The difference between total revenues and total expenses equals net income. All asset, liability, and stockholders' equity accounts are reported in the balance sheet. The balance sheet confirms the equality of the basic accounting equation.

Income Statement

Illustration 3–12 shows the income statement of Eagle Golf Academy for the month of January. Note that, unlike the income statements shown in Chapter 1, this income statement has a *multicolumn* format: Amounts for individual items are placed in the left column, and subtotals are placed in the right column. Presenting the income statement in this manner makes it easier to see that net income equals the difference between total revenues and total expenses.

The income statement demonstrates that Eagle Golf Academy earned a profit of **$500** in the month of January. The revenues earned from providing training to customers exceed the costs of providing that training.

ILLUSTRATION 3–12

Income Statement for Eagle Golf Academy

Revenues minus expenses equal net income.

EAGLE GOLF ACADEMY Income Statement For the month ended January 31		
Revenues:		
Service revenue		$6,360
Expenses:		
Salaries expense	$3,100	
Rent expense	500	
Supplies expense	800	
Depreciation expense	400	
Interest expense	100	
Utilities expense	960	
Total expenses		5,860
Net income		$ 500

Statement of Stockholders' Equity

The statement of stockholders' equity summarizes the changes in each stockholders' equity account as well as in total stockholders' equity and the accounting value of the company to stockholders (owners). Illustration 3–13 shows the statement of stockholders' equity for Eagle Golf Academy.

ILLUSTRATION 3–13

Statement of Stockholders' Equity for Eagle Golf Academy

Retained earnings includes net income from the income statement.

EAGLE GOLF ACADEMY Statement of Stockholders' Equity For the month ended January 31	Common Stock	Retained Earnings	Total Stockholders' Equity
Balance at January 1	$ -0-	$ -0-	$ -0-
Issuance of common stock	25,000		25,000
Add: Net income for January		500	500
Less: Dividends		(200)	(200)
Balance at January 31	$25,000	$300	$25,300

Total stockholders' equity increases from **$0** at the beginning of January to **$25,300** by the end of January. The increase occurs as a result of a **$25,000** investment by the owners (stockholders) when they bought common stock plus an increase of **$300** when the company earned a profit of **$500** on behalf of its stockholders and distributed $200 of dividends.

You've seen that retained earnings has three components: revenues, expenses, and dividends. In the adjusted trial balance, the balance of the Retained Earnings account is its balance at the beginning of the accounting period—the balance *before* all revenue, expense, and dividend transactions. For Eagle Golf Academy, the beginning balance of Retained Earnings equals $0 since this is the first month of operations. Ending Retained Earnings equals its beginning balance of $0 plus the effects of all revenue and expense transactions (net income of **$500**) less dividends of **$200** paid to stockholders. Since dividends represent the payment of company resources (cash), they will have a negative effect on the stockholders' equity (retained earnings) of the company.

Classified Balance Sheet

The balance sheet you saw in Chapter 1 contained the key asset, liability, and stockholders' equity accounts, presented as a rather simple list. Here, we introduce a slightly more complex form of the balance sheet, with many more accounts. To put those accounts in an order that enables ease of understanding, we use a format called the classified balance sheet.

Common Terms Another common name for current assets and liabilities is *short-term assets and liabilities.*

A **classified balance sheet** groups a company's assets, liabilities, and stockholders' equity accounts into several standard categories: We can separate assets into those that provide a benefit over the next year (*current assets*) and those that provide a benefit for more than one year (*long-term assets*). More precisely, the distinction between current and long-term assets is whether the asset will benefit the firm for more than one year or an *operating cycle*, whichever is longer. The **operating cycle** is the average time between purchasing or acquiring inventory and receiving cash proceeds from its sale. For nearly all firms, the operating cycle is shorter than one year. Similarly, we can divide liabilities into those due during the next year (*current liabilities*) and those due in more than one year (*long-term liabilities*).

Illustration 3–14 (next page) presents a classified balance sheet for Eagle Golf Academy. As we discuss later in the book, long-term assets are further classified into groups. Long-term asset categories include investments; property, plant, and equipment; and intangible assets:

- *Long-term investments* involve a company paying cash to invest in another company's debt or stock. We discuss long-term investments in debt and equity securities in Appendix D.

- *Property, plant, and equipment* items include long-term productive assets used in the normal course of business, such as land, buildings, equipment, and machinery. Eagle's purchase of training equipment is an example of a purchase of property, plant, and equipment. We discuss property, plant, and equipment in Chapter 7.

- *Intangible assets* are assets that lack physical substance but have long-term value to a company, such as patents, copyrights, franchises, and trademarks. We discuss intangible assets in Chapter 7.

ILLUSTRATION 3–14

Classified Balance Sheet for Eagle Golf Academy

Total assets equal current plus long-term assets.

Total liabilities equal current plus long-term liabilities.

Total stockholders' equity includes common stock and retained earnings from the statement of stockholders' equity.

Total assets must equal total liabilities plus stockholders' equity.

EAGLE GOLF ACADEMY Classified Balance Sheet January 31				
Assets			**Liabilities**	
Current assets:			Current liabilities:	
Cash	$ 6,200		Accounts payable	$ 2,300
Accounts receivable	2,700		Unearned revenue	540
Supplies	1,500		Salaries payable	300
Prepaid rent	5,500		Utilities payable	960
Total current assets	15,900		Interest payable	100
			Total current liabilities	4,200
Long-term assets:				
Equipment	24,000		Long-term liabilities:	
Less: Accum. depr.	(400)		Notes payable	10,000
			Total liabilities	14,200
Total long-term assets	23,600			
			Stockholders' Equity	
			Common stock	25,000
			Retained earnings	300
			Total stockholders' equity	25,300
Total assets	$39,500		Total liabilities and stockholders' equity	$39,500

In Illustration 3–14, notice that total assets of **$39,500** equal total liabilities and stockholders' equity of **$39,500**. We achieve this equality only by including the correct balance of **$300** for retained earnings from the statement of stockholders' equity, *not* the balance of $0 from the adjusted trial balance.

 KEY POINT

We prepare the income statement, statement of stockholders' equity, and balance sheet from the adjusted trial balance. The income statement provides a measure of net income (profitability), calculated as revenues minus expenses. The balance sheet demonstrates that assets equal liabilities plus stockholders' equity (the basic accounting equation).

Statement of Cash Flows

The final financial statement we need to prepare is the statement of cash flows. As discussed in Chapter 1, the statement of cash flows measures activities involving cash receipts and cash payments, reflecting a company's operating, investing, and financing activities. We'll take another brief look at the statement of cash flows in the next chapter and then discuss it in detail in Chapter 11.

THE CLOSING PROCESS

PART D

Recall that revenues, expenses, and dividends are components of retained earnings. Notice that Eagle's balance sheet reports retained earnings of $300, as if all net income transactions (revenues and expenses) and dividend transactions had been recorded directly in Retained Earnings. However, instead of recording revenue, expense, and dividend transactions directly to the Retained Earnings account during the period, we recorded them to the three component accounts. This allows us to maintain individual measures of revenues, expenses, and dividends for preparing financial statements at the end of the period.

After we have reported revenues and expenses in the income statement and dividends in the statement of stockholders' equity, it's time to transfer these amounts to the Retained Earnings account itself. These three accounts—revenues, expenses, and dividends—are termed **temporary accounts**: We keep them for each period and then transfer the balances of revenues, expenses, and dividends to the Retained Earnings account. All accounts that appear in the balance sheet, including Retained Earnings, are **permanent accounts**, and we carry forward their balances from period to period. We treat only revenues, expenses, and dividends as temporary, *so it will appear as if we had recorded all these types of transactions directly in Retained Earnings* during the year. We accomplish this with closing entries.

■ **LO6**
Demonstrate the purposes and recording of closing entries.

Closing Entries

Closing entries transfer the balances of all temporary accounts (revenues, expenses, and dividends) to the balance of the Retained Earnings account. Here's how:

- All revenue accounts have credit balances. To transfer these balances to the Retained Earnings account, we debit each of these revenue accounts for its balance and credit Retained Earnings for the total.
- Similarly, all expense and dividend accounts have debit balances. So, we credit each of these accounts for its balance and debit Retained Earnings for the total.

By doing this, we accomplish two necessary tasks: First, we *update the balance in the Retained Earnings account to reflect transactions related to revenues, expenses, and dividends in the current period.* Second, we *reduce the balances of all revenue, expense, and dividend accounts to zero* so we can start from scratch in measuring those amounts in the next accounting period. After all, revenues, expenses, and dividends are temporary accounts, which means their balances each period must start at zero.

Closing entries serve two purposes.

KEY POINT

Closing entries serve two purposes: (1) to transfer the balances of temporary accounts (revenues, expenses, and dividends) to the Retained Earnings account, and (2) to reduce the balances of these temporary accounts to zero to prepare them for measuring activity in the next period.

For demonstration, refer back to Eagle Golf Academy. We can transfer the balances of all revenue, expense, and dividend accounts to the balance of the Retained Earnings account with the closing entries shown in Illustration 3–15.

ILLUSTRATION 3–15

Closing Entries for
Eagle Golf Academy

January 31	Debit	Credit
(a) Service Revenue	6,360	
Retained Earnings		6,360
(Close revenues to retained earnings)		
(b) Retained Earnings	5,860	
Supplies Expense		800
Rent Expense		500
Depreciation Expense		400
Salaries Expense		3,100
Utilities Expense		960
Interest Expense		100
(Close expenses to retained earnings)		
(c) Retained Earnings	200	
Dividends		200
(Close dividends to retained earnings)		

Note that closing entries transfer the balances of the components of retained earnings (revenues, expenses, and dividends) to the balance of Retained Earnings itself. Retained Earnings is credited (increased) in the first entry and then debited (decreased) in the second and third entries. Posting these amounts to the Retained Earnings account will result in the following ending balance:

	Retained Earnings		
		0	Beginning balance
		6,360	Total revenues
Total expenses	5,860		
Total dividends	200		
		300	Ending balance

The ending balance of Retained Earnings now includes all transactions affecting the components of the account. The ending balance of **$300** represents all revenues and expenses over the life of the company (just the first month of operations in this example) less dividends. Another way to think about the balance of Retained Earnings is that it's the amount of net income earned by the company for its owners but that has not been paid to owners in the form of dividends.

The ending balance of Retained Earnings in January will be its beginning balance in February. Then we'll close February's revenues, expenses, and dividends to Retained Earnings, and this cycle will continue each period.

 COMMON MISTAKE

Students sometimes believe that closing entries are meant to reduce the balance of Retained Eearnings to zero. Retained Earnings is a *permanent account*, representing the accumulation of all revenues, expenses, and dividends over the life of the company.

In summary, the key points about closing entries are as follows.

- We *transfer the balance of all revenue, expense, and dividend accounts to the balance of Retained Earnings.* Dollar-for-dollar, every credit to revenues is now a credit to Retained Earnings, and every debit to expenses or dividends is now a debit to Retained Earnings.
- Closing entries *increase the Retained Earnings account by the amount of revenues and decrease Retained Earnings by the amount of expenses and dividends.*
- The balance of *each revenue, expense, and dividend account equals zero after closing entries.* These accounts have temporary balances and must be closed, or "zeroed out," to prepare them for measuring activity in the next period.
- Closing entries *do not affect the balances of permanent accounts* (assets, liabilities, and permanent stockholders' equity accounts) *other than retained earnings.* Permanent accounts carry a cumulative balance throughout the life of the company.

Illustration 3–16 shows retained earnings, net income, and dividends for **Coca-Cola** over a three-year period. Notice that the balance of retained earnings increases each year by the amount of net income less dividends. Retained earnings is a permanent account and represents the cumulative total of net income less dividends over the life of the company.

CAREER CORNER

In practice, accountants do not prepare closing entries. Virtually all companies have accounting software packages that automatically update the Retained Earnings account and close the temporary accounts at the end of the year. Of course, accounting information systems go far beyond automatic closing entries. In today's competitive global environment, businesses demand information systems that can eliminate redundant tasks and quickly gather, process, and disseminate information to decision makers. Ordinary business processes—such as selling goods to customers, purchasing supplies, managing employees, and managing inventory—can be handled more efficiently with customized information systems. Employers recognize that individuals with strong information technology skills mixed with accounting knowledge add value to the company.

	THE COCA-COLA COMPANY ($ in millions)						
Year	Beginning Retained Earnings*	+	Net Income**	−	Dividends	=	Ending Retained Earnings
2005							$31,299
2006	$31,299	+	$5,080	−	$2,911	=	33,468
2007	33,468	+	5,981	−	3,149	=	36,300
2008	36,300	+	5,807	−	3,521	=	38,586

*Beginning retained earnings is the ending retained earnings from the previous year.
**Net income equals total revenues minus total expenses.

ILLUSTRATION 3–16

Relation between Retained Earnings, Net Income, and Dividends for Coca-Cola

KEY POINT

Closing entries increase retained earnings by the amount of revenues for the period and decrease retained earnings by the amount of expenses and dividends for the period.

Post Closing Entries

■ LO7
Post closing entries and prepare a post-closing trial balance.

After we have prepared closing entries, we post amounts to the accounts in the general ledger. Illustration 3–17 demonstrates the process of posting the closing entries. The current balance of each account reflects transactions during the period (in black), adjusting entries (in red), and closing entries (in blue).

ILLUSTRATION 3–17 Posting Closing Entries to Adjusted Balances of Ledger Accounts

Assets = **Liabilities** + **Stockholders' Equity**

Cash

(1)	25,000	(3)	24,000
(2)	10,000	(4)	6,000
(6)	3,600	(9)	2,800
(8)	600	(10)	200
Bal.	6,200		

Accounts Payable

		(5)	2,300
		Bal.	2,300

Common Stock

		(1)	25,000
		Bal.	25,000

Retained Earnings

			0
		(a)	6,360
(b)	5,860		
(c)	200		
		Bal.	300

Accounts Receivable

(7)	2,500		
(h)	200		
Bal.	2,700		

Unearned Revenue

		(8)	600
(d)	60		
		Bal.	540

Dividends

(10)	200		
		(c)	200
Bal.	0		

Service Revenue

		(6)	3,600
		(7)	2,500
		(d)	60
		(h)	200
(a)	6,360		
		Bal.	0

Supplies

(5)	2,300		
		(b)	800
Bal.	1,500		

Salaries Payable

		(e)	300
		Bal.	300

Supplies Expense

(b)	800		
		(b)	800
Bal.	0		

Rent Expense

(a)	500		
		(b)	500
Bal.	0		

Prepaid Rent

(4)	6,000		
		(a)	500
Bal.	5,500		

Utilities Payable

		(f)	960
		Bal.	960

Depreciation Expense

(c)	400		
		(b)	400
Bal.	0		

Salaries Expense

(9)	2,800		
(e)	300		
		(b)	3,100
Bal.	0		

Equipment

(3)	24,000		
Bal.	24,000		

Interest Payable

		(g)	100
		Bal.	100

Utilities Expense

(f)	960		
		(b)	960
Bal.	0		

Interest Expense

(g)	100		
		(b)	100
Bal.	0		

Accumulated Depreciation

		(c)	400
		Bal.	400

Notes Payable

		(2)	10,000
		Bal.	10,000

- Amounts in black represent external transactions during January. Numbers in parentheses refer to transaction numbers in Illustration 3–5.
- Amounts in red represent month-end adjusting entries. Letters in parentheses refer to adjusting entries in Illustration 3–8.
- Amounts in blue represent month-end closing entries. Letters in parentheses refer to closing entries in Illustration 3–15.

After we post the closing entries, the **$300** balance of Retained Earnings now equals the amount shown in the balance sheet. In addition, the ending balances of all revenue, expense, and dividend accounts are now zero and ready to begin the next period.

After we post the closing entries to the ledger accounts, we can prepare a post-closing trial balance. The post-closing trial balance is a list of all accounts and their balances at a particular date *after we have updated account balances for closing entries*. The post-closing trial balance helps to verify that we prepared and posted closing entries correctly and that the accounts are now ready for the next period's transactions.

Illustration 3–18 shows the post-closing trial balance for Eagle Golf Academy as of January 31.

Amounts in bold represent ending balances.

ILLUSTRATION 3–18

Post-Closing Trial Balance for Eagle Golf Academy

EAGLE GOLF ACADEMY
Post-Closing Trial Balance
January 31

Accounts	Debit	Credit
Cash	$ 6,200	
Accounts Receivable	2,700	
Supplies	1,500	
Prepaid Rent	5,500	
Equipment	24,000	
Accumulated Depreciation		$ 400
Accounts Payable		2,300
Unearned Revenue		540
Salaries Payable		300
Interest Payable		100
Utilities Payable		960
Notes Payable		10,000
Common Stock		25,000
Retained Earnings		300
Totals	$39,900	$39,900

Notice that the post-closing trial balance does not include any revenues, expenses, or dividends, because these accounts all have zero balances after closing entries. The balance of Retained Earnings has been updated from the adjusted trial balance to include all revenues, expenses, and dividends for the period.

Decision Point

Question	Accounting information	Analysis
The amounts reported for revenues and expenses represent activity over what period of time?	Income statement	Revenue and expense accounts measure activity only for the current reporting period (usually a month, quarter, or year). At the end of each period, they are closed and begin the next period at zero.

Let's Review   Below is the adjusted trial balance of Beckham Soccer Academy for October 31.

BECKHAM SOCCER ACADEMY Adjusted Trial Balance October 31		
Accounts	**Debit**	**Credit**
Cash	$ 2,600	
Supplies	3,900	
Accounts Payable		$ 1,000
Salaries Payable		300
Common Stock		3,000
Retained Earnings		1,700
Dividends	200	
Service Revenue		4,300
Salaries Expense	2,400	
Supplies Expense	700	
Rent Expense	500	
Totals	$10,300	$10,300

Required:

1. Prepare closing entries.
2. Prepare a post-closing trial balance.
3. Compare the balances of Retained Earnings in the adjusted trial balance and the post-closing trial balance.

Solution:

1. Closing entries.

October 31	Debit	Credit
Service Revenue	4,300	
Retained Earnings		4,300
(Close revenues to retained earnings)		
Retained Earnings	3,600	
Salaries Expense		2,400
Supplies Expense		700
Rent Expense		500
(Close expenses to retained earnings)		
Retained Earnings	200	
Dividends		200
(Close dividends to retained earnings)		

2. Post-closing trial balance.

BECKHAM SOCCER ACADEMY Post-Closing Trial Balance October 31		
Accounts	Debit	Credit
Cash	$2,600	
Supplies	3,900	
Accounts Payable		$1,000
Salaries Payable		300
Common Stock		3,000
Retained Earnings		2,200
Totals	$6,500	$6,500

3. The balance of Retained Earnings increases by $500 from the adjusted trial balance to the post-closing trial balance. The balance increases by the amount of net income ($700) and decreases by the amount of dividends ($200).

Suggested Homework:
**BE3-19, BE3-20;
E3-17, E3-18;
P3-7A&B; P3-8A&B**

KEY POINT

After we post the closing entries to the T-accounts in the general ledger, the balance of Retained Earnings equals the amount shown in the balance sheet. The balances of all revenue, expense, and dividend accounts are zero at that point.

KEY POINTS BY LEARNING OBJECTIVE

LO1 Record revenues using the revenue recognition principle and expenses using the matching principle.

The revenue recognition principle states that we should recognize revenue in the period in which we *earn* it, not necessarily in the period in which we receive cash.

The matching principle states that we recognize expenses in the same period as the revenues they help to generate. Expenses include those directly and indirectly related to producing revenues.

LO2 Distinguish between accrual-basis and cash-basis accounting.

The difference between accrual-basis accounting and cash-basis accounting is *timing*. Under accrual-basis accounting, we record revenues when we earn them (revenue recognition principle) and record expenses with the revenue they help to generate (matching

principle). Under cash-basis accounting, we record revenues when we receive cash and expenses when we pay cash. Cash-basis accounting is not allowed for financial reporting purposes.

LO3 Demonstrate the purposes and recording of adjusting entries.

Adjusting entries are a necessary part of accrual-basis accounting. They help to record revenues in the period earned and expenses in the period they are incurred to generate those revenues. Another benefit is that, by properly recording revenues and expenses, we correctly state assets and liabilities.

Adjusting entries are needed when cash flows or obligations occur *before* the earnings-related activity (prepayment) or when cash flows occur *after* the earnings-related activity (accrual).

Adjusting entries are unnecessary in two cases: (1) for transactions that do not

involve revenue or expense activities and (2) for transactions that result in revenues or expenses being recorded at the same time as the cash flow.

LO4 Post adjusting entries and prepare an adjusted trial balance.

We post adjusting entries to the T-accounts in the general ledger to update the account balances.

An adjusted trial balance is a list of all accounts and their balances at a particular date after we have updated account balances for adjusting entries.

LO5 Prepare financial statements using the adjusted trial balance.

We prepare the income statement, statement of stockholders' equity, and balance sheet from the adjusted trial balance. The income statement provides a measure of net income (profitability), calculated as revenues minus expenses. The balance sheet demonstrates that assets equal liabilities plus stockholders' equity (the basic accounting equation).

LO6 Demonstrate the purposes and recording of closing entries.

Closing entries serve two purposes: (1) to transfer the balances of temporary accounts (revenues, expenses, and dividends) to the retained earnings account and (2) to reduce the balances of these temporary accounts to zero to prepare them for measuring activity in the next period.

Closing entries increase the balance of retained earnings by the amount of revenues for the period and decrease retained earnings by the amount of expenses and dividends for the period.

LO7 Post closing entries and prepare a post-closing trial balance.

After we post the closing entries to the T-accounts in the general ledger, the balance of Retained Earnings equals the amount shown in the balance sheet. The balances of all revenue, expense, and dividend accounts are zero at that point.

GLOSSARY

Accrual-basis accounting: Record revenues when earned (the revenue recognition principle) and expenses with related revenues (the matching principle). **p. 108**

Accrued expense: When a company has incurred an expense but hasn't yet paid cash or recorded an obligation to pay. **p. 119**

Accrued revenue: When a company has earned revenue but hasn't yet received cash or recorded an amount receivable. **p. 121**

Adjusted trial balance: A list of all accounts and their balances after we have updated account balances for adjusting entries. **p. 126**

Adjusting entries: Entries used to record events that occur during the period but that have not yet been recorded by the end of the period. **p. 112**

Cash-basis accounting: Record revenues at the time cash is received and expenses at the time cash is paid. **p. 110**

Classified balance sheet: Balance sheet that groups a company's assets into current assets and long-term assets and that separates liabilities into current liabilities and long-term liabilities. **p. 129**

Closing entries: Entries that transfer the balances of all temporary accounts (revenues, expenses, and dividends) to the balance of the Retained Earnings account. **p. 131**

Contra account: An account with a balance that is opposite, or "contra," to that of its related accounts. **p. 116**

Matching principle: Recognize expenses in the same period as the revenues they help to generate. **p. 109**

Operating cycle: The average time between purchasing or acquiring inventory and receiving cash proceeds from its sale. **p. 129**

Permanent accounts: All accounts that appear in the balance sheet; account balances are carried forward from period to period. **p. 131**

Post-closing trial balance: A list of all accounts and their balances at a particular date after we have updated account balances for closing entries. **p. 135**

Prepaid expenses: The costs of assets acquired in one period that will be expensed in a future period. **p. 113**

Revenue recognition principle: Record revenue in the period in which it's earned. **p. 108**

Temporary accounts: All revenue, expense, and dividend accounts; account balances are maintained for a single period and then closed (or zeroed out) and transferred to the balance of the Retained Earnings account at the end of the period. **p. 131**

Unearned revenues: When a company receives cash in advance from a customer for products or services to be provided in the future. **p. 117**

SELF-STUDY QUESTIONS

1. On May 5, Johnson Plumbing receives a phone call from a customer needing a new water heater and schedules a service visit for May 7. On May 7, Johnson installs the new water heater. The customer pays for services on May 10. According to the *revenue recognition principle*, on which date should Johnson record service revenue?   ■ LO1
   a. May 5 (date of phone call).
   b. May 7 (date of service).
   c. May 10 (date of cash receipt).
   d. Evenly over the three dates.

2. On January 17, Papa's Pizza signs a contract with Bug Zappers for exterminating services related to a recent sighting of cockroaches in the restaurant. Papa's pays for the extermination service on January 29, and Bug Zappers sprays for bugs on February 7. According to the *matching principle*, on which date should Papa's Pizza record the extermination expense?   ■ LO1
   a. January 17 (date of the contract).
   b. January 29 (date of cash payment).
   c. February 7 (date of extermination service).
   d. Evenly over the three dates.

3. Refer to the information in self-study question 1. Using *cash-basis accounting*, on which date should Johnson record service revenue?   ■ LO2
   a. May 5 (date of phone call).
   b. May 7 (date of service).
   c. May 10 (date of cash receipt).
   d. Evenly over the three dates.

4. Refer to the information in self-study question 2. Using *cash-basis accounting*, on which date should Papa's Pizza record the extermination expense?   ■ LO2
   a. January 17 (date of the contract).
   b. January 29 (date of cash payment).
   c. February 7 (date of extermination service).
   d. Evenly over the three dates.

5. Which of the following is *not* a characteristic of adjusting entries?   ■ LO3
   a. Reduce the balances of revenue, expense, and dividend accounts to zero.
   b. Allow for proper application of the revenue recognition principle (revenues) or the matching principle (expenses).
   c. Are part of accrual-basis accounting.
   d. Are recorded at the end of the accounting period.

6. Ambassador Hotels purchases one year of fire insurance coverage on December 1 for $24,000 ($2,000 per month), debiting prepaid insurance. On December 31, Ambassador would record the following year-end adjusting entry: ■ LO3

	Debit	Credit
a. Insurance Expense	24,000	
Prepaid Insurance		24,000
b. Insurance Expense	2,000	
Prepaid Insurance		2,000
c. Insurance Expense	22,000	
Prepaid Insurance		22,000

d. No entry is required on December 31 because full cash payment was made on December 1 and the insurance does not expire until the following November 30.

■ LO4   7. An adjusted trial balance:
a. Lists all accounts and their balances at a particular date after updating ✓
   account balances for adjusting entries.
b. Is used to prepare the financial statements.
c. Includes balances for revenues, expenses, and dividends.
d. All the above.

■ LO5   8. Which of the following describes the information reported in the statement
of stockholders' equity?
a. Net income for the period calculated as revenues minus expenses. ✗
b. Equality of total assets with total liabilities plus stockholders' equity. ✗
c. Change in stockholders' equity through changes in common stock and
   retained earnings.
d. Net cash flows from operating, investing, and financing activities.

■ LO6   9. Which of the following describes the purpose(s) of closing entries?
a. Adjust the balances of asset and liability accounts for unrecorded activity
   during the period.
b. Transfer the balances of temporary accounts (revenues, expenses, and
   dividends) to Retained Earnings.
c. Reduce the balances of the temporary accounts to zero to prepare them for
   measuring activity in the next period.
d. Both *b*. and *c*.

■ LO7   10. Which of the following accounts is *not* listed in a post-closing trial balance?
a. Prepaid Rent.
b. Accounts Payable.
c. Salaries Expense.
d. Retained Earnings.

Check out
www.mhhe.com/succeed
for more multiple-choice
questions.

Note: For answers, see the last page of the chapter.

REVIEW QUESTIONS

■ LO1   1. Discuss the major principle that describes recording revenues.

■ LO1   2. Discuss the major principle that describes recording expenses.

■ LO1   3. Samantha is a first-year accounting student. She doesn't think it matters that
expenses are reported in the same period's income statement with the related
revenues (matching principle). She feels that "as long as revenues and expenses
are recorded in any period, that's good enough." Help her understand why the
matching principle is important.

■ LO2   4. Describe when revenues and expenses are recognized using cash-basis accounting.
How does this differ from accrual-basis accounting?

■ LO2
Flip Side of Question 7

5. Executive Lawn provides $100 of landscape maintenance to Peterson Law on
April 10. Consider three scenarios:

a. Peterson pays for the lawn service in advance on March 28.
b. Peterson pays for the lawn service on April 10, the day of service.
c. Peterson pays for the lawn service the following month on May 2.

If Executive Lawn uses accrual-basis accounting, on which date would Executive
Lawn record the $100 revenue for each scenario?

6. Consider the information in question 5. Using cash-basis accounting, on which date would Executive Lawn record the $100 revenue for each scenario?

■ LO2
Flip Side of Question 8

7. Peterson Law asks Executive Lawn to provide $100 of landscape maintenance. Executive Lawn provides the service on April 10. Consider three scenarios:

   a. Peterson pays for the lawn service in advance on March 28.
   b. Peterson pays for the lawn service on April 10, the day of service.
   c. Peterson pays for the lawn service the following month on May 2.

   If Peterson Law uses accrual-basis accounting, on which date would Peterson Law record the $100 expense for each scenario?

■ LO2
Flip Side of Question 5

8. Consider the information in question 7. Using cash-basis accounting, on which date would Peterson Law record the $100 expense for each scenario?

■ LO2
Flip Side of Question 6

9. Why are adjusting entries necessary under accrual-basis accounting?

10. There are two basic types of adjusting entries—prepayments and accruals. Describe each in terms of the timing of revenue and expense recognition versus the flow of cash.

■ LO3
■ LO3

11. Provide an example of a prepaid expense. The adjusting entry associated with a prepaid expense always includes a debit and credit to which account classifications?

■ LO3

12. Provide an example of an unearned revenue. The adjusting entry associated with an unearned revenue always includes a debit and credit to which account classifications?

■ LO3

13. Provide an example of an accrued expense. The adjusting entry associated with an accrued expense always includes a debit and credit to which account classifications?

■ LO3

14. Provide an example of an accrued revenue. The adjusting entry associated with an accrued revenue always includes a debit and credit to which account classifications?

■ LO3

15. Sequoya Printing purchases office supplies for $75 on October 2. The staff uses the office supplies continually on a daily basis throughout the month. By the end of the month, office supplies of $25 remain. Record the month-end adjusting entry for office supplies (assuming the balance of Office Supplies at the beginning of October was $0). *Supply Expense   50*
   Supplies   50

■ LO3

16. Jackson Rental receives its September utility bill of $320 on September 30 but does not pay the bill until October 10. Jackson's accountant records the utility expense of $320 on October 10 at the time of payment. Will this cause any of Jackson's accounts to be misstated at the end of September? If so, indicate which ones and the direction of the misstatement.

■ LO3

17. Global Printing publishes several types of magazines. Customers are required to pay for magazines in advance. On November 5, Global receives cash of $120,000 for prepaid subscriptions. By the end of November, Global has distributed $20,000 of magazines to customers. Record the month-end adjusting entry.

■ LO3

Debit
Unearned Revenue   20000
service Revenue
Credit
20000

18. At the end of May, Robertson Corporation has provided services to customers, but it has not yet billed these customers nor have any of them paid for those services. If Robertson makes no adjusting entry associated with these unpaid services provided, will any accounts be misstated? If so, indicate which ones and the direction of the misstatement.

■ LO3

19. Fill in the blank associated with each adjusting entry:

   a. *Prepaid expense:* Debit Supplies Expense; credit _____.
   b. *Unearned revenue:* Debit _____; credit Service Revenue.
   c. *Accrued expense:* Debit _____; credit Salaries Payable.
   d. *Accrued revenue:* Debit Accounts Receivable; credit _____.

■ LO3

■ **LO4**   20. What is the purpose of the adjusted trial balance? How do the adjusted trial balance and the (unadjusted) trial balance differ?

■ **LO5**   21. Explain what is meant by the term *classified* when referring to a balance sheet.

■ **LO5**   22. At the end of the period, Sanders Company reports the following amounts: Assets = $12,000; Liabilities = $8,000; Revenues = $5,000; Expenses = $3,000. Calculate stockholders' equity.

■ **LO6**   23. What are the two purposes of preparing closing entries?

■ **LO6**   24. What does it mean to close temporary accounts? Which of the following account types are closed: assets, liabilities, dividends, revenues, and expenses?

■ **LO6**   25. Describe the debits and credits for the three closing entries required at the end of a reporting period.

■ **LO6**   26. In its first four years of operations, Chance Communications reports net income of $300, $900, $1,500, and $2,400, respectively, and pays dividends of $200 per year. What would be the balance of Retained Earnings at the end of the fourth year?

■ **LO6**   27. Matt has been told by his instructor that dividends reduce retained earnings (and therefore stockholders' equity). However, since he knows that stockholders are receiving the dividend, Matt doesn't understand how paying a dividend would *decrease* stockholders' equity. Explain this to Matt.

■ **LO7**   28. How do the adjusted trial balance and the post-closing trial balance differ? Which accounts are shown in the adjusted trial balance but not in the post-closing trial balance? Which account is shown in both trial balances but with a different balance on each?

BRIEF EXERCISES

Determine revenues to be recognized **(LO1)**

BE3–1 Below are transactions for Lobos, Inc., during the month of December. Calculate the amount of revenue to recognize in December. If the transaction does not require the company to recognize a revenue, indicate how it would report the transaction.

a. Receive $1,200 cash from customers for services to be provided next month.

b. Perform $900 of services during the month and bill customers. Customers are expected to pay next month.

c. Perform $2,300 of services during the month and receive full cash payment from customers at the time of service.

Determine expenses to be recognized **(LO1)**

BE3–2 Below are transactions for Bronco Corporation during the month of June. Calculate the amount of expense to recognize in June. If the transaction does not require an expense to be recognized, indicate how the transaction would be reported.

a. Pay $600 cash to employees for work performed during June.

b. Receive a $200 telephone bill for the month of June, but Bronco does not plan to pay the bill until early next month.

c. Pay $500 on account for supplies purchased last month. All supplies were used last month.

Calculate net income **(LO1)**

BE3–3 Hoya Corporation reports the following amounts: Assets = $12,000; Liabilities = $2,000; Stockholders' equity = $10,000; Dividends = $2,000; Revenues = $15,000; and Expenses = $11,000. What amount is reported for net income?

Analyze the impact of transactions on the balance of cash, cash-basis net income, and accrual-basis net income **(LO1, 2)**

BE3–4 Consider the following set of transactions occurring during the month of May for Bison Consulting Company. For each transaction, indicate the impact on (1) the balance of cash, (2) cash-basis net income, and (3) accrual-basis net income for May. The first answer is provided as an example.

	Cash Balance	Cash-Basis Net Income	Accrual-Basis Net Income
(a) Receive $1,500 from customers who were billed for services in April.	+$1,500	+$1,500	$0
(b) Provide $3,200 of consulting services to a local business. Payment is not expected until June.			
(c) Purchase office supplies for $400 on account. All supplies are used by the end of May.			
(d) Pay $600 to workers. $400 is for work in May and $200 is for work in April.			
(e) Pay $200 to advertise in a local newspaper in May.			
Totals			

BE3–5 Rebel Technology maintains its records using cash-basis accounting. During the year, the company received cash from customers, $40,000, and paid cash for salaries, $22,000. At the beginning of the year, customers owe Rebel $1,000. By the end of the year, customers owe $6,000. At the beginning of the year, Rebel owes salaries of $5,000. At the end of the year, Rebel owes salaries of $3,000. Determine cash-basis net income and accrual-basis net income for the year.

Determine accrual-basis and cash-basis net income (LO1, 2)

BE3–6 At the beginning of May, Golden Gopher Company reports a balance in Supplies of $400. On May 15, Golden Gopher purchases an additional $2,300 of supplies for cash. By the end of May, only $200 of supplies remains. (1) Record the purchase of supplies on May 15. (2) Record the adjusting entry on May 31. (3) Calculate the balances after adjustment on May 31 of Supplies and Supplies Expense.

Record the adjusting entry for supplies (LO3)

BE3–7 Suppose Hoosiers, a specialty clothing store, rents space at a local mall for one year, paying $19,200 ($1,600/month) in advance on October 1. (1) Record the purchase of rent in advance on October 1. (2) Record the adjusting entry on December 31. (3) Calculate the year-end adjusted balances of prepaid rent and rent expense (assuming the balance of Prepaid Rent at the beginning of the year is $0).

Record the adjusting entry for prepaid rent (LO3)

BE3–8 Mountaineer Excavation operates in a low-lying area that is subject to heavy rains and flooding. Because of this, Mountaineer purchases one year of flood insurance in advance on March 1, paying $30,000 ($2,500/month). (1) Record the purchase of insurance in advance on March 1. (2) Record the adjusting entry on December 31. (3) Calculate the year-end adjusted balances of Prepaid Insurance and Insurance Expense (assuming the balance of Prepaid Insurance at the beginning of the year is $0).

Record the adjusting entry for prepaid insurance (LO3)

BE3–9 Beaver Construction purchases new equipment for $36,000 cash on April 1, 2012. At the time of purchase, the equipment is expected to be used in operations for six years (72 months) and have no resale or scrap value at the end. Beaver depreciates equipment evenly over the 72 months ($500/month). (1) Record the purchase of equipment on April 1. (2) Record the adjusting entry for depreciation on December 31, 2012. (3) Calculate the year-end adjusted balances of Accumulated Depreciation and Depreciation Expense (assuming the balance of Accumulated Depreciation at the beginning of 2012 is $0).

Record the adjusting entry for depreciation (LO3)

BE3–10 Suppose a customer rents a vehicle for three months from Commodores Rental on November 1, paying $4,500 ($1,500/month). (1) Record the rental for Commodores on November 1. (2) Record the adjusting entry on December 31. (3) Calculate the year-end adjusted balances of the Unearned Revenue and Service Revenue accounts (assuming the balance of Unearned Revenue at the beginning of the year is $0).

Record the adjusting entry for unearned revenue (LO3)

BE3–11 Fighting Irish Incorporated pays its employees $4,200 every two weeks ($300/day). The current two-week pay period ends on December 28, 2012, and employees are paid $4,200. The next two-week pay period ends on January 11, 2013, and

Record the adjusting entry for salaries payable (LO3)

employees are paid $4,200. (1) Record the adjusting entry on December 31, 2012. (2) Record the payment of salaries on January 11, 2013. (3) Calculate the 2012 year-end adjusted balance of Salaries Payable (assuming the balance of Salaries Payable before adjustment in 2012 is $0).

Record the adjusting entry for interest payable (LO3)

Flip Side of BE3–13

BE3–12 Midshipmen Company borrows $10,000 from Falcon Company on July 1, 2012. Midshipmen repays the amount borrowed and pays interest of 12% (1%/month) on June 30, 2013. (1) Record the borrowing for Midshipmen on July 1, 2012. (2) Record the adjusting entry for Midshipmen on December 31, 2012. (3) Calculate the 2012 year-end adjusted balances of Interest Payable and Interest Expense (assuming the balance of Interest Payable at the beginning of the year is $0).

Record the adjusting entry for interest receivable (LO3)

Flip Side of BE3–12

BE3–13 Refer to the information in BE3–12. (1) Record the lending for Falcon on July 1, 2012. (2) Record the adjusting entry for Falcon on December 31, 2012. (3) Calculate the 2012 year-end adjusted balances of Interest Receivable and Interest Revenue (assuming the balance of Interest Receivable at the beginning of the year is $0).

Assign accounts to financial statements (LO5)

BE3–14 For each of the following accounts, indicate whether the account is shown in the income statement or the balance sheet:

Accounts	Financial Statement
1. Accounts Receivable	_____
2. Unearned Revenue	_____
3. Supplies Expense	_____
4. Salaries Payable	_____
5. Depreciation Expense	_____
6. Service Revenue	_____

Understand the purpose of financial statements (LO5)

BE3–15 Below are the four primary financial statements. Match each financial statement with its primary purpose to investors.

Financial Statements	Purposes
1. _____ Income statement	a. Provides measures of resources and claims to those resources at the end of the year.
2. _____ Statement of stockholders' equity	b. Provides an indication of the company's ability to make a profit during the current year.
3. _____ Balance sheet	c. Provides a measure of net increases and decreases in cash for the current year.
4. _____ Statement of cash flows	d. Shows changes in owners' claims to resources for the current year.

Prepare an income statement (LO5)

BE3–16 The following account balances appear in the 2012 adjusted trial balance of Beavers Corporation: Service Revenue, $225,000; Salaries Expense, $100,000; Supplies Expense, $15,000; Rent Expense, $21,000; Depreciation Expense, $34,000; and Delivery Expense, $13,000. Prepare an income statement for the year ended December 31, 2012.

Prepare a statement of stockholders' equity (LO5)

BE3–17 The following account balances appear in the 2012 adjusted trial balance of Bulldog Corporation: Common Stock, $20,000; Retained Earnings, $7,000; Dividends, $1,000; Service Revenue, $25,000; Salaries Expense, $15,000; and Rent Expense, $8,000. No common stock was issued during the year. Prepare the statement of stockholders' equity for the year ended December 31, 2012.

Prepare a classified balance sheet (LO5)

BE3–18 The following account balances appear in the 2012 adjusted trial balance of Blue Devils Corporation: Cash, $4,000; Accounts Receivable, $8,000; Supplies, $18,000; Equipment, $110,000; Accumulated Depreciation, $40,000; Accounts Payable, $25,000;

Salaries Payable, $15,000; Common Stock, $50,000; and Retained Earnings, _____.
Prepare the December 31, 2012, classified balance sheet including the correct balance
for retained earnings.

BE3–19 The year-end adjusted trial balance of Aggies Corporation included the
following account balances: Retained Earnings, $220,000; Service Revenue, $850,000;
Salaries Expense, $380,000; Rent Expense, $140,000; Interest Expense, $75,000; and
Dividends, $50,000. Record the necessary closing entries.

Record closing
entries (LO6)

BE3–20 The year-end adjusted trial balance of Hilltoppers Corporation included the
following account balances: Cash, $4,000; Equipment, $16,000; Accounts Payable,
$2,000; Common Stock, $10,000; Retained Earnings, $7,000; Dividends, $1,000;
Service Revenue, $15,000; Salaries Expense, $10,000; and Utilities Expense, $3,000.
Prepare the post-closing trial balance.

Prepare a post-closing
trial balance (LO7)

EXERCISES

E3–1 Consider the following situations:

Determine the timing of
revenue recognition (LO1)

1. **American Airlines** collects cash on June 12 from the sale of a ticket to a customer.
   The flight occurs on August 16.
2. A customer purchases sunglasses from **Eddie Bauer** on January 27 on account.
   Eddie Bauer receives payment from the customer on February 2.
3. On March 30, a customer preorders 10 supreme pizzas (without onions) from
   Pizza Hut for a birthday party. The pizzas are prepared and delivered on April 2.
   The company receives cash at the time of delivery.
4. A customer pays in advance for a three-month subscription to **Sports Illustrated**
   on July 1. Issues are scheduled for delivery each week from July 1 through
   September 30.

Required:

For each situation, determine the date for which the company recognizes the revenue
under accrual-basis accounting.

E3–2 Consider the following situations:

Determine the
timing of expense
recognition (LO1)

1. **American Airlines** operates a flight from Dallas to Los Angeles on August 16. The
   pilots' salaries associated with the flight are paid on September 2.
2. **Eddie Bauer** pays cash on January 6 to purchase sunglasses from a wholesale
   distributor. The sunglasses are sold to customers on January 27.
3. On January 1, **Pizza Hut** pays for a one-year property insurance policy with
   coverage starting immediately.
4. **Sports Illustrated** signs an agreement with CBS on January 12 to provide television
   advertisements during the Super Bowl. Payment is due within 3 weeks after February 4,
   the day of the Super Bowl. Sports Illustrated makes the payment on February 23.

Required:

For each situation, determine the date for which the company recognizes the expense
under accrual-basis accounting.

E3–3 Refer to the situations discussed in E3–1.

Differentiate cash-basis
revenues from accrual-
basis revenues (LO2)

Required:

For each situation, determine the date for which the company recognizes revenue
using cash-basis accounting.

E3–4 Refer to the situation discussed in E3–2.

Differentiate cash-basis
expenses from accrual-
basis expenses (LO2)

Required:

For each situation, determine the date for which the company recognizes the expense
using cash-basis accounting.

HW

E3–5 During the course of your examination of the financial statements of Trojan Corporation for the year ended December 31, 2012, you come across several items needing further consideration. Currently, net income is $90,000.

a. An insurance policy covering 12 months was purchased on October 1, 2012, for $18,000. The entire amount was debited to Prepaid Insurance and no adjusting entry was made for this item in 2012.

b. During 2012, the company received a $3,000 cash advance from a customer for services to be performed in 2013. The $3,000 was incorrectly credited to Service Revenue.

c. There were no supplies listed in the balance sheet under assets. However, you discover that supplies costing $2,250 were on hand at December 31, 2012.

d. Trojan borrowed $60,000 from a local bank on September 1, 2012. Principal and interest at 12% will be paid on August 31, 2013. No accrual was made for interest in 2012.

Handwritten margin notes: 7200; 22,400; 600+; $600 × 4 =; 6000+; (600×4 = 2400)

Required:

Using the information in *a.* through *d.* above, determine the proper amount of net income as of December 31, 2012.

HW 12

E3–6 Listed below are all the steps in the accounting cycle.

Handwritten order notes: (i), (g), (h), (c), (b), (f), (a), (d), (e)

(a) Record and post adjusting entries.
(b) Post the transaction to the T-account in the general ledger.
(c) Record the transaction.
(d) Prepare financial statements (income statement, statement of stockholders' equity, balance sheet, and statement of cash flows).
(e) Record and post closing entries.
(f) Prepare a trial balance.
(g) Analyze the impact of the transaction on the accounting equation.
(h) Assess whether the transaction results in a debit or a credit to the account balance.
(i) Use source documents to identify accounts affected by external transactions.

Required:

List the steps in proper order.

E3–7 Golden Eagle Company prepares monthly financial statements for its bank. The November 30 and December 31 adjusted trial balances include the following account information:

	November 30		December 31	
	Debit	Credit	Debit	Credit
Supplies	1,500		3,000	
Prepaid Insurance	6,000		4,500	
Salaries Payable		10,000		15,000
Unearned Revenue		2,000		1,000

The following information also is known:

a. Purchases of supplies in December total $3,500.

b. No insurance payments are made in December.

c. $10,000 is paid to employees during December for November salaries.

d. On November 1, a tenant pays Golden Eagle $3,000 in advance rent for the period November through January. Unearned Revenue is credited.

Required:

Show the adjusting entries that were made for supplies, prepaid insurance, salaries payable, and unearned revenue on December 31.

E3–8 Consider the following transactions for Huskies Insurance Company:

a. Equipment costing $36,000 is purchased at the beginning of the year for cash. Depreciation on the equipment is $6,000 per year.

b. On June 30, the company lends its chief financial officer $40,000; principal and interest at 6% are due in one year.

c. On October 1, the company receives $12,000 from a customer for a one-year property insurance policy. Unearned Revenue is credited.

Required:

For each item, record the necessary adjusting entry for Huskies Insurance at its year-end of December 31. No adjusting entries were made during the year.

E3–9 Refer to the information in E3–8.

Required:

For each of the adjustments in E3–8, indicate by how much net income in the income statement is higher or lower if the adjustment is not recorded.

E3–10 Consider the following situations for Shocker:

a. On November 28, 2012, Shocker receives a $3,000 payment from a customer for services to be rendered evenly over the next three months. Unearned Revenue is credited.

b. On December 1, 2012, the company pays a local radio station $2,400 for 30 radio ads that were to be aired, 10 per month, throughout December, January, and February. Prepaid Advertising is debited.

c. Employee salaries for the month of December totaling $7,000 will be paid on January 7, 2013.

d. On August 31, 2012, Shocker borrows $60,000 from a local bank. A note is signed with principal and 8% interest to be paid on August 31, 2013.

Required:

Record the necessary adjusting entries for Shocker at December 31, 2012. No adjusting entries were made during the year.

E3–11 Refer to the information in E3–10.

Required:

For each of the adjustments recorded in E3–10, indicate by how much the assets, liabilities, and stockholders' equity in the December 31, 2012, balance sheet is higher or lower if the adjustment is not recorded.

E3–12 Below are transactions for Wolverine Company during 2012.

a. On December 1, 2012, Wolverine receives $3,000 cash from a company that is renting office space from Wolverine. The payment, representing rent for December and January, is credited to Unearned Revenue.

b. Wolverine purchases a one-year property insurance policy on July 1, 2012, for $12,000. The payment is debited to Prepaid Insurance for the entire amount. *120*

c. Employee salaries of $2,000 for the month of December will be paid in early January 2013.

d. On November 1, 2012, the company borrows $10,000 from a bank. The loan requires principal and interest at 12% to be paid on October 30, 2013.

e. Office supplies at the beginning of 2012 total $900. On August 15, Wolverine purchases an additional $2,400 of office supplies, debiting the Supplies account. By the end of the year, $400 of office supplies remains. *900*

Required:

Record the necessary adjusting entries at December 31, 2012, for Wolverine Company. You do not need to record transactions made during the year. Assume that no financial statements were prepared during the year and no adjusting entries were recorded.

Record year-end adjusting entries **(LO3)**

Calculate the effects of adjusting entries on net income **(LO3)**

Record year-end adjusting entries **(LO3)**

Calculate the effects of adjusting entries on the accounting equation **(LO3, 4)**

Record year-end adjusting entries **(LO3)**

Record year-end adjusting entries (LO3)

E3–13 Below are transactions for Hurricane Company during 2012.

a. On October 1, 2012, Hurricane lends $8,000 to another company. The other company signs a note indicating principal and 8% interest will be paid to Hurricane on September 30, 2013.

b. On November 1, 2012, Hurricane pays its landlord $3,000 representing rent for the months of November through January. The payment is debited to Prepaid Rent for the entire amount.

c. On August 1, 2012, Hurricane collects $12,000 in advance from another company that is renting a portion of Hurricane's factory. The $12,000 represents one year's rent and the entire amount is credited to Unearned Revenue.

d. Depreciation on machinery is $4,500 for the year.

e. Salaries for the year earned by employees but not paid to them or recorded are $4,000.

f. Hurricane begins the year with $1,000 in supplies. During the year, the company purchases $4,500 in supplies and debits that amount to Supplies. At year-end, supplies costing $2,500 remain on hand.

Required:

Record the necessary adjusting entries at December 31, 2012, for Hurricane Company for each of the situations. Assume that no financial statements were prepared during the year and no adjusting entries were recorded.

Prepare an adjusted trial balance (LO3, 4)

E3–14 The December 31, 2012, unadjusted trial balance for Demon Deacons Corporation is presented below.

Accounts	Debit	Credit
Cash	$ 9,000	
Accounts Receivable	14,000	
Prepaid Rent	6,000	
Supplies	3,000	
Unearned Revenue		$ 2,000
Common Stock		10,000
Retained Earnings		5,000
Service Revenue		45,000
Salaries Expense	30,000	
	$62,000	$62,000

At year-end, the following additional information is available:

a. The balance of Prepaid Rent, $6,000, represents payment on October 31, 2012, for rent from November 1, 2012, to April 30, 2013.

b. The balance of Unearned Revenue, $2,000, represents payment in advance from a customer. By the end of the year, $500 of the services have been provided.

c. An additional $600 in salaries is owed to employees at the end of the year but will not be paid until January 4, 2013.

d. The balance of Supplies, $3,000, represents the amount of office supplies on hand at the beginning of the year of $1,200 plus an additional $1,800 purchased throughout 2012. By the end of 2012, only $700 of supplies remains.

Required:

1. Update account balances for the year-end information by recording any necessary adjusting entries. No prior adjustments have been made in 2012.

2. Prepare an adjusted trial balance as of December 31, 2012.

E3–15 Below are the restated amounts of net income and retained earnings for Volunteers Inc. and Raiders Inc. for the period 2003–2012. Volunteers began operations in 2004.

Calculate the balance of retained earnings (LO5)

	VOLUNTEERS INC. ($ in millions)		RAIDERS INC. ($ in millions)	
Year	Net Income (Loss)	Retained Earnings	Net Income (Loss)	Retained Earnings
2003	—	$0	$ 25	$10
2004	$ 20		(53)	
2005	(6)		51	
2006	31		53	
2007	125		92	
2008	20		125	
2009	(141)		(52)	
2010	567		64	
2011	349		100	
2012	350		152	

Required:

Calculate the balance of retained earnings each year for each company. Neither company paid dividends during this time.

E3–16 The December 31, 2012, adjusted trial balance for Blue Hens Corporation is presented below.

Prepare financial statements from an adjusted trial balance (LO5)

Accounts	Debit	Credit
Cash	$ 11,000	
Accounts Receivable	140,000	
Prepaid Rent	5,000	
Supplies	25,000	
Equipment	300,000	
Accumulated Depreciation		$125,000
Accounts Payable		11,000
Salaries Payable		10,000
Interest Payable		4,000
Notes Payable (due in two years)		30,000
Common Stock		200,000
Retained Earnings		50,000
Service Revenue		400,000
Salaries Expense	300,000	
Rent Expense	15,000	
Depreciation Expense	30,000	
Interest Expense	4,000	
Totals	$830,000	$830,000

Required:

1. Prepare an income statement for the year ended December 31, 2012.
2. Prepare a classified balance sheet as of December 31, 2012.

Record closing entries (LO6)

E3–17 Seminoles Corporation's fiscal year-end is December 31, 2012. The following is a partial adjusted trial balance as of December 31.

Accounts	Debit	Credit
Retained Earnings		$20,000
Dividends	$ 2,000	
Service Revenue		40,000
Interest Revenue		5,000
Salaries Expense	14,000	
Rent Expense	5,000	
Advertising Expense	2,000	
Depreciation Expense	10,000	
Interest Expense	4,000	

Required:

Prepare the necessary closing entries.

Record closing entries (LO6)

E3–18 Laker Incorporated's fiscal year-end is December 31, 2012. The following is an adjusted trial balance as of December 31.

Accounts	Debit	Credit
Cash	$ 11,000	
Supplies	34,000	
Prepaid Rent	25,000	
Accounts Payable		$ 2,000
Notes Payable		20,000
Common Stock		35,000
Retained Earnings		8,000
Dividends	3,000	
Service Revenue		55,000
Salaries Expense	19,000	
Advertising Expense	12,000	
Rent Expense	9,000	
Utilities Expense	7,000	
Totals	$120,000	$120,000

Required:

Prepare the necessary closing entries.

Record closing entries and a post-closing trial balance (LO6, 7)

E3–19 Refer to the adjusted trial balance in E3–16.

Required:

1. Record the necessary closing entries at December 31, 2012.
2. Prepare a post-closing trial balance.

For additional exercises, visit www.mhhe.com/succeed for Exercises: Set B.

P3–1A Consider the following transactions.

Determine accrual-basis and cash-basis revenues and expenses **(LO1, 2)**

Transaction	Accrual-basis Revenue	Accrual-basis Expense	Cash-basis Revenue	Cash-basis Expense
1. Receive cash from customers in advance, $500.				
2. Pay utilities bill for the previous month, $100.				
3. Pay for insurance one year in advance, $1,500.				
4. Pay workers' salaries for the current month, $700.				
5. Record depreciation of building, $900.				
6. Receive cash from customers at the time of service, $1,200.				
7. Purchase office supplies on account, $230.				
8. Borrow cash from the bank, $3,000.				
9. Receive cash from customers for services performed last month, $650.				
10. Pay for advertising to appear in the current month, $350.				

Required:

For each transaction, determine the amount of revenue or expense, if any, that is recorded under accrual-basis accounting and under cash-basis accounting in the current period.

P3–2A Minutemen Law Services maintains its books using cash-basis accounting. However, the company decides to borrow $100,000 from a local bank, and the bank requires Minutemen to provide annual financial statements prepared using accrual-basis accounting as part of the creditworthiness verification. During 2012, the company records the following cash flows:

Convert cash-basis accounting to accrual-basis accounting **(LO1, 2)**

Cash collected from customers		$60,000
Cash paid for:		
Salaries	$35,000	
Supplies	3,000	
Rent	4,000	
Insurance	6,000	
Utilities	2,000	50,000
Net cash flows		$10,000

You are able to determine the following information:

	January 1, 2012	December 31, 2012
Accounts Receivable	$20,000	$22,000
Prepaid Insurance	-0-	3,200
Supplies	4,000	1,500
Salaries Payable	2,200	3,400

In addition, depreciation on the company's equipment is $8,000 for the year.

Required:

Prepare an accrual-basis income statement for the year ended December 31, 2012. (Ignore income taxes.)

Record adjusting entries and determine their effect on net income **(LO3)**

P3–3A The information necessary for preparing the 2012 year-end adjusting entries for Gamecock Advertising Agency appears below. Gamecock's fiscal year-end is December 31.

a. On July 1, 2012, Gamecock receives $5,000 from a customer for advertising services to be given evenly over the next 10 months. Gamecock credits Unearned Revenue.

b. At the beginning of the year, Gamecock's depreciable equipment has a cost of $30,000, a five-year life, and no salvage value. The equipment is depreciated evenly (straight-line depreciation method) over the five years.

c. On May 1, 2012, the company pays $3,600 for a two-year fire and liability insurance policy and debits Prepaid Insurance.

d. On September 1, 2012, the company borrows $10,000 from a local bank and signs a note. Principal and interest at 12% will be paid on August 31, 2013.

e. At year-end there is a $2,200 debit balance in the Supplies (asset) account. Only $900 of supplies remains on hand.

Required:

Record the necessary adjusting entries on December 31, 2012. No prior adjustments have been made during 2012.

Record adjusting entries **(LO3)**

P3–4A Crimson Tide Music Academy offers lessons in playing a wide range of musical instruments. The *unadjusted* trial balance as of December 31, 2012, appears below. December 31 is the company's fiscal year-end.

Accounts	Debits	Credits
Cash	$ 9,300	
Accounts Receivable	8,500	
Supplies	1,500	
Prepaid Rent	6,000	
Equipment	75,000	
Accumulated Depreciation		$ 10,000
Accounts Payable		6,700
Salaries Payable		-0-
Interest Payable		-0-
Utilities Payable		-0-
Notes Payable		15,000
Common Stock		35,000
Retained Earnings		14,000
Service Revenue		45,000
Salaries Expense	23,500	
Interest Expense	-0-	
Rent Expense	-0-	
Supplies Expense	-0-	
Utilities Expense	1,900	
Depreciation Expense	-0-	
Totals	$125,700	$125,700

Information necessary to prepare the year-end adjusting entries appears below.

a. Depreciation of equipment for the year is $5,000.

b. Accrued salaries at year-end should be $1,600.

c. Crimson Tide borrows $15,000 on September 1, 2012. The principal is due to be repaid in four years. Interest is payable each August 31 at an annual rate of 10%.

d. Unused supplies at year-end total $600. Crimson Tide debits Supplies at the time supplies are purchased.

e. Crimson Tide opens a second studio by purchasing one year of rent in advance on April 1, 2012, for $6,000 ($500 per month) debiting Prepaid Rent.

f. Unpaid utilities for December total $100.

Required:

Record the necessary adjusting entries on December 31, 2012.

P3–5A Boilermaker Unlimited specializes in building new homes and remodeling existing homes. Remodeling projects include adding game rooms, changing kitchen cabinets and countertops, and updating bathrooms. Below is the year-end adjusted trial balance of Boilermaker Unlimited.

Prepare financial statements from an adjusted trial balance when net income is positive **(LO5)**

BOILERMAKER UNLIMITED
Adjusted Trial Balance
December 31, 2012

Accounts	Debits	Credits
Cash	$ 15,000	
Accounts Receivable	24,000	
Supplies	31,000	
Prepaid Insurance	6,000	
Equipment	500,000	
Accumulated Depreciation		$ 160,000
Accounts Payable		30,000
Salaries Payable		27,000
Utilities Payable		4,000
Notes Payable (due in 5 years)		100,000
Common Stock		150,000
Retained Earnings		79,000
Dividends	25,000	
Service Revenue—new construction		400,000
Service Revenue—remodeling		250,000
Salaries Expense	150,000	
Supplies Expense	275,000	
Depreciation Expense	40,000	
Insurance Expense	24,000	
Utilities Expense	41,000	
Interest Expense	6,000	
Service Fee Expense	63,000	
Totals	$1,200,000	$1,200,000

Required:

Prepare an income statement, statement of stockholders' equity, and classified balance sheet. In preparing the statement of stockholders' equity, note that during the year the company issued additional common stock for $20,000. This amount is included in the amount for Common Stock in the adjusted trial balance.

P3–6A The year-end financial statements of Blue Devil Tax Services are provided below.

Record closing entries and prepare a post-closing trial balance **(LO6, 7)**

BLUE DEVIL TAX SERVICES
Income Statement

Service revenue		$72,500
Expenses:		
Salaries	$45,000	
Utilities	7,200	
Insurance	4,800	
Supplies	1,600	58,600
Net income		$13,900

BLUE DEVIL TAX SERVICES
Statement of Stockholders' Equity

	Common Stock	Retained Earnings	Total S. Equity
Beg. bal., Jan. 1	$50,000	$23,500	$ 73,500
Issue stock	20,000		20,000
Net income		13,900	13,900
Dividends		(5,000)	(5,000)
Ending bal., Dec. 31	$70,000	$32,400	$102,400

BLUE DEVIL TAX SERVICES				
Balance Sheet				

Assets			Liabilities		
Cash	$ 3,700		Accounts payable		$ 7,500
Accounts receivable	6,200		**Stockholders' Equity:**		
Land	100,000		Common stock	$70,000	
			Retained earnings	32,400	102,400
Total assets	$109,900		Total liabs. and equities		$109,900

Required:
1. Record year-end closing entries.
2. Prepare a post-closing trial balance. (*Hint:* The balance of Retained Earnings will be the amount shown in the balance sheet.)

Complete the accounting cycle after adjusting entries (LO4, 5, 6, 7)

P3–7A Refer to P3–4A.

Required:
Complete the following steps:
1. Enter the unadjusted balances from the trial balance into T-accounts.
2. Post the adjusting entries prepared in P3–4A to the accounts.
3. Prepare an adjusted trial balance.
4. Prepare an income statement and a statement of shareholders' equity for the year ended December 31, 2012, and a classified balance sheet as of December 31, 2012. Assume that no common stock is issued during the year.
5. Record closing entries.
6. Post closing entries to the accounts.
7. Prepare a post-closing trial balance.

Complete the full accounting cycle (LO3, 4, 5, 7)

P3–8A The general ledger of Red Storm Cleaners at January 1, 2012, includes the following account balances:

Accounts	Debits	Credits
Cash	$15,000	
Accounts Receivable	7,000	
Supplies	3,000	
Equipment	10,000	
Accumulated Depreciation		$ 3,000
Salaries Payable		5,000
Common Stock		20,000
Retained Earnings		7,000
Totals	$35,000	$35,000

The following is a summary of the transactions for the year:
a. Sales of services, $50,000, of which $20,000 is on account.
b. Collect on accounts receivable, $17,000.
c. Issue shares of common stock in exchange for $5,000 cash.
d. Pay salaries, $25,000 (of which $5,000 is for salaries payable in 2011).
e. Pay repairs and maintenance expenses, $12,000.
f. Purchase equipment for $7,000 cash.
g. Pay $1,000 cash dividends to stockholders.

Required:
1. Set up the necessary T-accounts and enter the beginning balances from the trial balance. In addition to the accounts shown, the company also has accounts for Dividends, Service Revenue, Salaries Expense, Repairs and Maintenance Expense, Depreciation Expense, and Supplies Expense.

2. Record each of the summary transactions listed above.
3. Post the transaction to the accounts.
4. Prepare an unadjusted trial balance.
5. Record adjusting entries. Accrued salaries at year-end amounted to $1,000. Depreciation for the year on the equipment is $4,000. Office supplies remaining on hand at the end of the year equal $1,000.
6. Post adjusting entries.
7. Prepare an adjusted trial balance.
8. Prepare an income statement for 2012 and a classified balance sheet as of December 31, 2012.
9. Record closing entries.
10. Post closing entries.
11. Prepare a post-closing trial balance.

PROBLEMS: SET B

P3–1B Consider the following transactions.

Determine accrual-basis and cash-basis revenues and expenses (LO1, 2)

Transaction	Accrual-Basis		Cash-Basis	
	Revenue	Expense	Revenue	Expense
1. Receive cash from customers at the time of service, $2,700.				
2. Issue common stock for cash, $5,000.				
3. Receive cash from customers who were previously billed, $1,200.				
4. Record depreciation of equipment, $500.				
5. Pay workers' salaries for the current month, $600.				
6. Pay for rent one year in advance, $2,400.				
7. Repay a long-term note to the bank, $2,000.				
8. Pay workers' salaries for the previous month, $750.				
9. Pay dividends to stockholders, $400.				
10. Purchase office supplies for cash, $440.				

Required:
For each transaction, determine the amount of revenue or expense, if any, that is recorded under accrual-basis accounting and under cash-basis accounting.

P3–2B Horned Frogs Fine Cooking maintains its books using cash-basis accounting. However, the company recently borrowed $50,000 from a local bank, and the bank requires the company to provide annual financial statements prepared using accrual-basis accounting as part of the creditworthiness verification. During 2012, the company records the following cash flows:

Convert cash-basis accounting to accrual-basis accounting (LO1, 2)

Cash collected from customers		$55,000
Cash paid for:		
Salaries	$22,000	
Supplies	8,000	
Repairs and maintenance	7,000	
Insurance	3,000	
Advertising	5,000	45,000
Net cash flows		$10,000

You are able to determine the following information:

	January 1, 2012	December 31, 2012
Accounts Receivable	$16,000	$12,000
Prepaid Insurance	1,200	3,200
Supplies	-0-	1,500
Salaries Payable	3,200	2,300

In addition, depreciation on the company's building is $6,000 for the year.

Required:

Prepare an accrual-basis income statement for 2012. (Ignore income taxes.)

Record adjusting entries and determine their effect on net income (LO3)

P3–3B The information necessary for preparing the 2012 year-end adjusting entries for Bearcat Personal Training Academy appears below. Bearcat's fiscal year-end is December 31.

a. Depreciation on the equipment for the year is $6,000.

b. Salaries earned (but not paid) from December 16 through December 31, 2012, are $3,000.

c. On March 1, 2012, Bearcat lends an employee $15,000. The employee signs a note requiring principal and interest at 8% to be paid on February 28, 2013.

d. On April 1, 2012, Bearcat pays an insurance company $12,000 for a two-year fire insurance policy. The entire $12,000 is debited to Prepaid Insurance at the time of the purchase.

e. Bearcat uses $1,200 of supplies in 2012.

f. A customer pays Bearcat $2,400 on October 31, 2012, for three months of personal training to begin November 1, 2012. Bearcat credits Unearned Revenue at the time of cash receipt.

g. On December 1, 2012, Bearcat pays $4,500 rent to the owner of the building. The payment represents rent for December 2012 through February 2013, at $1,500 per month. Prepaid Rent is debited at the time of the payment.

Required:

Record the necessary adjusting entries at December 31, 2012. No prior adjustments have been made during 2012.

Prepare adjusting entries (LO3)

P3–4B Jaguar Auto Company provides general car maintenance to customers. The company's fiscal year-end is December 31. The December 31, 2012, trial balance (before any adjusting entries) appears below.

Accounts	Debits	Credits
Cash	$ 17,000	
Accounts Receivable	14,000	
Supplies	22,000	
Prepaid Insurance	18,000	
Equipment	85,000	
Accumulated Depreciation		$ 27,000
Accounts Payable		11,000
Salaries Payable		-0-
Utilities Payable		-0-
Interest Payable		-0-
Notes Payable		30,000
Common Stock		25,000
Retained Earnings		9,000
Dividends	2,000	
Service Revenue		220,000

(continued)

(concluded)	Accounts	Debits	Credits
	Salaries Expense	153,000	
	Depreciation Expense	-0-	
	Insurance Expense	-0-	
	Supplies Expense	-0-	
	Utilities Expense	11,000	
	Interest Expense	-0-	
	Totals	$322,000	$322,000

Information necessary to prepare the year-end adjusting entries appears below.

a. Depreciation on the machines for the year is $9,000.

b. Employee salaries are paid every two weeks. The last pay period ended on December 23. Salaries earned from December 24 through December 31, 2012, are $3,000.

c. On September 1, 2012, Jaguar borrows $30,000 from a local bank and signs a note. The note requires interest to be paid annually on August 31 at 9%. The principal is due in five years.

d. On March 1, 2012, the company purchases insurance for $18,000 for a one-year policy to cover possible injury to mechanics. The entire $18,000 is debited to Prepaid Insurance at the time of the purchase.

e. $4,000 of supplies remains on hand at December 31, 2012.

f. On December 30, Jaguar receives a utility bill of $1,700 for the month. The bill will not be paid until early January 2013, and no entry is recorded when the bill is received.

Required:

Prepare the necessary adjusting entries on December 31, 2012.

P3–5B Orange Designs provides consulting services related to home decoration. Orange Designs provides customers with recommendations for a full range of home décor, including window treatments, carpet and wood flooring, paint colors, furniture, and much more. Below is the year-end adjusted trial balance of Orange Designs.

Prepare financial statements from an adjusted trial balance (LO5)

ORANGE DESIGNS
Adjusted Trial Balance
December 31, 2012

Accounts	Debits	Credits
Cash	$ 5,000	
Accounts Receivable	4,000	
Supplies	2,000	
Prepaid Rent	6,000	
Buildings	110,000	
Accumulated Depreciation		$ 21,000
Accounts Payable		3,000
Salaries Payable		4,000
Utilities Payable		1,000
Notes Payable		20,000
Common Stock		50,000
Retained Earnings		15,000
Service Revenues		115,000
Salaries Expense	42,000	
Rent Expense	18,000	
Depreciation Expense	7,000	
Supplies Expense	8,000	
Advertising Expense	13,000	
Utilities Expense	12,000	
Interest Expense	2,000	
Totals	$229,000	$229,000

Required:

Prepare an income statement, statement of stockholders' equity, and classified balance sheet. In preparing the statement of stockholders' equity, note that during the year the company issued additional common stock of $10,000. This amount is included in the amount for Common Stock in the adjusted trial balance.

Record closing entries and prepare a post-closing trial balance **(LO6, 7)**

P3–6B The year-end financial statements of Fighting Illini Financial Services are provided below.

FIGHTING ILLINI
Income Statement

Service revenue		$84,700
Expenses:		
Salaries	$49,000	
Supplies	9,100	
Rent	7,500	
Delivery	3,700	69,300
Net income		$15,400

FIGHTING ILLINI
Statement of Stockholders' Equity

	Common Stock	Retained Earnings	Total S. Equity
Beg. bal., Jan. 1	$60,000	$32,300	$ 92,300
Issue stock	15,000		15,000
Net income		15,400	15,400
Dividends		(6,000)	(6,000)
Ending bal., Dec. 31	$75,000	$41,700	$116,700

FIGHTING ILLINI
Balance Sheet

Assets			Liabilities		
Cash		$ 6,600	Accounts payable		$ 9,100
Accounts receivable		9,200	**Stockholders' Equity**		
Land		110,000	Common stock	$75,000	
			Retained earnings	41,700	116,700
Total assets		$125,800	Total liabs. and equities		$125,800

Required:

1. Record year-end closing entries.
2. Prepare a post-closing trial balance. (*Hint:* The balance of retained earnings will be the amount shown in the balance sheet.)

Complete the accounting cycle after adjusting entries **(LO4, 5, 6, 7)**

P3–7B Refer to P3–4B.

Required:

Complete the following steps:

1. Enter the unadjusted balances from the trial balance into T-accounts.
2. Post the adjusting entries prepared in P3–4B to the accounts.
3. Prepare an adjusted trial balance.
4. Prepare an income statement and a statement of shareholders' equity for the year ended December 31, 2012, and a classified balance sheet as of December 31, 2012. Assume that no common stock is issued during the year.
5. Record closing entries.
6. Post closing entries to the accounts.
7. Prepare a post-closing trial balance.

Complete the full accounting cycle **(LO3, 4, 5 6, 7)**

P3–8B The general ledger of Pipers Plumbing at January 1, 2012, includes the following account balances:

QB

Accounts	Debits	Credits
Cash	$ 4,000	
Accounts Receivable	9,000	
Supplies	3,000	
Equipment	26,000	
Accumulated Depreciation		$ 6,000
Accounts Payable		4,000
Utilities Payable		5,000
Unearned Revenue		-0-
Common Stock		18,000
Retained Earnings		9,000
Totals	$42,000	$42,000

The following is a summary of the transactions for the year:

a. Provide plumbing services for cash, $15,000, and on account, $60,000.
b. Collect on accounts receivable, $48,000.
c. Issue shares of common stock in exchange for $10,000 cash.
d. Pay salaries for the current year, $32,000.
e. Pay for utilities expenses, $12,000, of which $5,000 represents costs for 2011.
f. Receive cash in advance from customers, $8,000.
g. Pay $2,000 cash dividends to stockholders.

Required:

1. Set up the necessary T-accounts and enter the beginning balances from the trial balance. In addition to the accounts shown, the company has accounts for Dividends, Service Revenue, Salaries Expense, Utilities Expense, Supplies Expense, and Depreciation Expense.
2. Record each of the summary transactions listed above.
3. Post the transactions to the accounts.
4. Prepare an unadjusted trial balance.
5. Record adjusting entries. Depreciation for the year on the machinery is $6,000. Plumbing supplies remaining on hand at the end of the year equal $1,000. Of the $8,000 paid in advance by customers, $6,000 of the work has been completed by the end of the year.
6. Post adjusting entries.
7. Prepare an adjusted trial balance.
8. Prepare an income statement for 2012 and a classified balance sheet as of December 31, 2012.
9. Record closing entries.
10. Post closing entries
11. Prepare a post-closing trial balance.

For additional problems, visit www.mhhe.com/succeed for Problems: Set C.

ADDITIONAL PERSPECTIVES

Great Adventures

(This is a continuation of the Great Adventures problem from earlier chapters. To complete the requirements for this problem, be sure to account for the July transactions presented in AP2–1 on p. 103.)

Continuing Problem

AP3–1 The following transactions occur over the remainder of the year.

Aug. 1   Suzie applies for and obtains a $30,000 low-interest loan for the company from the city council, which has recently passed an initiative encouraging business development related to outdoor activities. The loan is due in three years, and 6% annual interest is due each year on July 31.

Aug. 4   The company purchases 14 kayaks, costing $28,000.

Aug. 10   Twenty additional kayakers pay $3,000 ($150 each), in addition to the $4,000 that was paid in advance on July 30, on the day of the clinic. Tony conducts the first kayak clinic.

Aug. 17   Tony conducts a second kayak clinic and receives $10,500 cash.

Aug. 24   Office supplies of $1,800 purchased on July 4 are paid in full.

Sep. 1   To provide better storage of mountain bikes and kayaks when not in use, the company rents a storage shed, purchasing a one-year rental policy for $2,400 ($200 per month).

Sep. 21   Tony conducts a rock-climbing clinic. The company receives $13,200 cash.

Oct. 17   Tony conducts an orienteering clinic. Participants practice how to understand a topographical map, read an altimeter, use a compass, and orient through heavily wooded areas. Clinic fees total $17,900.

Dec. 1   Tony decides to hold the company's first adventure race on December 15. Four-person teams will race from checkpoint to checkpoint using a combination of mountain biking, kayaking, orienteering, trail running, and rock-climbing skills. The first team in each category to complete all checkpoints in order wins. The entry fee for each team is $500.

Dec. 5   To help organize and promote the race, Tony hires his college roommate, Victor. Victor will be paid $50 in salary for each team that competes in the race. His salary will be paid after the race.

Dec. 8   The company pays $1,200 to purchase a permit from a state park where the race will be held. The amount is recorded as a miscellaneous expense.

Dec. 12   The company purchases racing supplies for $2,800 on account due in 30 days. Supplies include trophies for the top-finishing teams in each category, promotional shirts, snack foods and drinks for participants, and field markers to prepare the racecourse.

Dec. 15   Forty teams pay a total of $20,000 to race. The race is held.

Dec. 16   The company pays Victor's salary of $2,000.

Dec. 31   The company pays a dividend of $4,000 ($2,000 to Tony and $2,000 to Suzie).

Dec. 31   Using his personal money, Tony purchases a diamond ring for $4,500. Tony surprises Suzie by proposing that they get married. Suzie accepts!

The following information relates to year-end adjusting entries as of December 31, 2012.

a. Depreciation of the mountain bikes purchased on July 8 and kayaks purchased on August 4 totals $8,000.

b. Six months' worth of insurance has expired.

c. Four months' worth of rent has expired.

d. Of the $1,800 of office supplies purchased on July 4, $300 remains.

e. Interest expense on the $30,000 loan obtained from the city council on August 1 should be recorded.

f. Of the $2,800 of racing supplies purchased on December 12, $200 remains.

g. Suzie calculates that the company owes $14,000 in income taxes.

Required:

1. Record transactions from August 1 through December 31.
2. Record adjusting entries as of December 31, 2012.
3. Post transactions from August 1 through December 31 and adjusting entries on December 31 to T-accounts.
4. Prepare an adjusted trial balance as of December 31, 2012.
5. For the period July 1 to December 31, 2012, prepare an income statement and statement of stockholders' equity. Prepare a classified balance sheet as of December 31, 2012.

6. Record closing entries as of December 31, 2012.
7. Post closing entries to T-accounts.
8. Prepare a post-closing trial balance as of December 31, 2012.

American Eagle Outfitters, Inc.

Financial Analysis

AP3–2 Financial information for **American Eagle** is presented in Appendix A at the end of the book.

Required:
1. For the most recent year, what amount does American Eagle report for current assets? What assets are listed as current assets? What is the ratio of current assets to total assets?
2. For the most recent year, what amount does American Eagle report for current liabilities? What liabilities are listed as current liabilities? What is the ratio of current liabilities to total liabilities?
3. List any current assets or current liabilities that likely relate to adjusting entries.
4. What is the change in retained earnings reported in the balance sheet?
5. For the most recent year, what is the amount of net income reported in the income statement?
6. Using your answers in 4 and 5, calculate the amount of dividends paid during the year. Verify your answer by looking at the retained earnings column in the statement of stockholders' equity.

The Buckle, Inc.

Financial Analysis

AP3–3 Financial information for **The Buckle** is presented in Appendix B at the end of the book.

Required:
1. For the most recent year, what amount does The Buckle, Inc., report for current assets? What assets are listed as current assets? What is the ratio of current assets to total assets?
2. For the most recent year, what amount does The Buckle, Inc., report for current liabilities? What liabilities are listed as current liabilities? What is the ratio of current liabilities to total liabilities?
3. List any current assets or current liabilities that likely relate to adjusting entries.
4. For the most recent year, what is the change in retained earnings reported in the balance sheet?
5. For the most recent year, what is the amount of net income reported in the income statement?
6. Using your answers in parts 4 and 5 above, calculate the amount of dividends paid during the year. Verify your answer by looking at the retained earnings column in the statement of stockholders' equity.

American Eagle Outfitters, Inc. vs. The Buckle, Inc.

Comparative Analysis

AP3–4 Financial information for **American Eagle** is presented in Appendix A at the end of the book, and financial information for **The Buckle** is presented in Appendix B at the end of the book.

Required:
1. Determine which company maintains a higher ratio of current assets to total assets. How might this be an advantage for the company?
2. Determine which company maintains a higher ratio of current liabilities to total liabilities. How might this be a disadvantage for the company?
3. The dividend payout ratio equals dividends paid during the year divided by net income. Determine which company has a higher dividend payout ratio. Why might this be the case?

Ethics

AP3–5 You have recently been hired as the assistant controller for Stanton Temperton Corporation, which rents building space in major metropolitan areas. Customers are required to pay six months of rent in advance. At the end of 2012, the company's president, Jim Temperton, notices that net income has fallen compared to last year. In 2011, the company reported before-tax profit of $330,000, but in 2012 the before-tax profit is only $280,000. This concerns Jim for two reasons. First, his year-end bonus is tied directly to before-tax profits. Second, shareholders may see a decline in profitability as a weakness in the company and begin to sell their stock. With the sell-off of stock, Jim's personal investment in the company's stock, as well as his company-operated retirement plan, will be in jeopardy of severe losses.

After close inspection of the financial statements, Jim notices that the balance of the Unearned Revenue account is $120,000. This amount represents payments in advance from long-term customers ($80,000) and from relatively new customers ($40,000). Jim comes to you, the company's accountant, and suggests that the firm should recognize as revenue in 2012 the $80,000 received in advance from long-term customers. He offers the following explanation: "First, we have received these customers' cash by the end of 2012, so there is no question about their ability to pay. Second, we have a long-term history of fulfilling our obligation to these customers. We have always stood by our commitments to our customers and we always will. We earned that money when we got them to sign the six-month contract."

Required:
Discuss the ethical dilemma you face.

Internet Research

AP3–6 Obtain a copy of the annual report of **McDonald's Corporation** for the most recent year. You can find the annual report at the company's website (***www.mcdonalds.com***) in the investor information section or at the Securities and Exchange Commission's website (***www.sec.gov***) using EDGAR (Electronic Data Gathering, Analysis, and Retrieval). Form 10-K, which includes the annual report, is required to be filed on EDGAR. Search or scroll within the annual report to find the financial statements.

Required:
Determine the following from the company's financial statements:

1. Do the company's revenues exceed expenses? What is the amount of net income?
2. Did net income increase in the most recent year compared to the previous year?
3. Which assets are listed as current assets? Why are other assets not listed as current assets?
4. Which liabilities are listed as current liabilities? Why are other liabilities not listed as current liabilities?
5. By how much did retained earnings increase/decrease in the most recent year compared to the previous year?
6. What is the amount of dividends paid to common stockholders? This information can be found in the statement of shareholders' equity or the statement of cash flows.
7. Explain the relationship between the change in retained earnings, net income, and dividends.

Written Communication

AP3–7 You are a tutor for introductory financial accounting. You tell the students, "Recording adjusting entries is a critical step in the accounting cycle, and the two major classifications of adjusting entries are prepayments and accruals." Chris, one of the students in the class, says, "I don't understand."

Required:

Respond to Chris.

1. When do prepayments occur? When do accruals occur?
2. Describe the appropriate adjusting entry for prepaid expenses and for unearned revenues. What is the effect on net income, assets, liabilities, and stockholders' equity of not recording a required adjusting entry for prepayments?
3. Describe the required adjusting entry for accrued expenses and for accrued revenues. What is the effect on net income, assets, liabilities, and shareholders' equity of not recording a required adjusting entry for accruals?

Answers to the Self-Study Questions

1. b   2. c   3. c   4. b   5. a   6. b   7. d   8. c   9. d   10. c

Cash and Internal Controls

AFTER STUDYING THIS CHAPTER, YOU SHOULD BE ABLE TO:

- ■ **LO1** Discuss the impact of accounting scandals and the passage of the Sarbanes-Oxley Act.
- ■ **LO2** Identify the components, responsibilities, and limitations of internal control.
- ■ **LO3** Define cash and cash equivalents.
- ■ **LO4** Understand controls over cash receipts and cash disbursements.
- ■ **LO5** Reconcile a bank statement.
- ■ **LO6** Account for petty cash.
- ■ **LO7** Identify the major inflows and outflows of cash.

Analysis

- ■ **LO8** Assess earnings quality by comparing net income and cash flows.

REGAL ENTERTAINMENT: INTERNAL CONTROLS ARE A BOX-OFFICE HIT

According to research conducted by the Association of Certified Fraud Examiners (ACFE, *www.acfe.com*), U.S. organizations lose an estimated $1 *trillion* (or 7% of their total revenue) to employee fraud each year. This occurs despite increased corporate emphasis on antifraud controls and recent legislation to combat fraud. While some employees steal office supplies, inventory, and equipment, the asset most often targeted is cash. Cash fraud includes skimming cash receipts before they are recorded, stealing cash that has already been recorded, and falsely disbursing cash through fraudulent billing, expense reimbursement, or payroll.

Companies that rely heavily on cash transactions are especially susceptible to employee fraud. For example, consider a company like **Regal Entertainment Group** (NYSE: **RGC**), one of the world's largest motion picture exhibitors. The company operates almost 7,000 screens and sells about 250 million tickets per year, generating revenues each year of nearly $3 billion. The company states, "Revenues are generated principally through admissions and concessions sales with proceeds received in cash at the point of sale." The primary way a company like RGC can minimize cash losses due to employee fraud is to establish strong systems for internal control.

Toward that end, RGC makes extensive use of its point-of-service information technology for managing its theatres. The revenue streams generated by admissions and concessions are fully supported by information systems to monitor cash flow and to detect fraud and inventory theft. Simpler approaches to internal control include *separation of duties:* For example, one person sells tickets, and another collects the tickets. This prevents the ticket seller from pocketing a moviegoer's cash and then allowing admission without a ticket being produced by the ticket machine. At the end of the day, the number of tickets produced by the machine should exactly match the cash collected.

We discuss much more about fraud and ways to prevent it in this chapter. At the end of the chapter (in Problem 4-1A), you can apply your newly learned skills in preventing and detecting fraud at a movie theatre.

PART A

INTERNAL CONTROLS

We're all familiar, more or less, with the concept of fraud. Fraud occurs when a person intentionally deceives another person for personal gain or to damage that person. More specifically related to business activities, the Association of Certified Fraud Examiners (ACFE) defines occupational fraud as the use of one's occupation for personal enrichment through the deliberate misuse or misapplication of the employing organization's resources. As discussed in the chapter-opening Feature Story, occupational fraud is big business, with companies expecting to lose on average 7% of their total revenues to fraud each year. For a company like **Regal Entertainment Group**, 7% of total revenues would equal nearly $200 million lost to fraud in a single year. Given the high cost of occupational fraud, it's not surprising that companies are willing to spend significant amounts to prevent it.

To minimize occupational fraud, companies implement formal procedures known as internal controls. These represent a company's plan to (1) safeguard the company's assets and (2) improve the accuracy and reliability of accounting information. To accomplish this broad goal, all companies institute a variety of specific internal controls, which we discuss in this chapter.

The ACFE, the world's largest antifraud organization (*www.acfe.com*), reports that theft or the misuse of the company's resources occurs in 90% of all fraud cases. Common examples include stealing cash or inventory or using the company's resources for non–work-related purposes. Because cash is the asset most commonly misappropriated, a significant portion of this chapter discusses the procedures implemented by businesses to maintain control over cash receipts and cash disbursements. We'll also work through two specific examples of cash controls: the bank reconciliation and the petty cash fund.

A second source of occupational fraud involves financial statement manipulation. Here, those in charge of communicating financial accounting information falsify reports. You may have heard the phrase "cooking the books." The phrase implies that the accounting records ("books") have been presented in an altered form ("cooked"). Managers have a variety of reasons for manipulating the numbers in financial statements, such as maximizing their compensation, increasing the company's stock price, and preserving their jobs. Strong internal controls help to minimize financial statement manipulation.

To set the stage for the importance of internal controls in general, we discuss the impact of recent accounting scandals, and the response by Congress.

Recent Accounting Scandals and Response

■ **LO1**
Discuss the impact of accounting scandals and the passage of the Sarbanes-Oxley Act.

Managers are entrusted with the resources of both the company's lenders (liabilities) and its owners (stockholders' equity). In this sense, managers of the company act as stewards or caretakers of the company's assets. However, in recent years some managers shirked their ethical responsibilities and misused or misreported the company's funds. In many cases, top executives misreported accounting information to cover up their company's poor operating performance. Such fraudulent activity is costly: The ACFE reports that the median loss caused by fraudulent financial statement schemes, for example, is $2,000,000 per instance. As you become more familiar with specific accounting topics throughout the remainder of this book, you'll begin to understand how amounts reported in the financial statements can be manipulated by managers.

Two of the highest-profile cases of accounting fraud in U.S. history are the collapses of **Enron** and **WorldCom**. Enron used questionable accounting practices to avoid reporting billions in debt and losses in its financial statements. WorldCom misclassified certain expenditures to overstate assets and profitability by $11 billion. Both companies hoped to fool investors into overvaluing the company's stock. Other common types of financial statement fraud include creating fictitious revenues from

a fake customer, improperly valuing assets, hiding liabilities, and mismatching revenues and expenses.

As the Enron and WorldCom frauds (as well as several others) were being uncovered in 2001 and 2002, the stock prices of these companies plummeted. Investors lost nearly $200 billion as a result. Employees of these companies also suffered. Both firms declared bankruptcy, resulting in employee termination; reduced salaries and increased workloads for those who were left; and loss of employee retirement funds, stock options, and health benefits.

Recall from Chapter 1 that all public companies are required to have an independent party, an auditor, provide reasonable assurance that financial statements are free of material misstatements. So where were the auditors in the cases of Enron and WorldCom, when the external audits failed to detect billions of dollars of fraud? Both companies had the same audit firm, **Arthur Andersen**. At the time, many would have argued that Arthur Andersen was the most prestigious and most trusted audit firm in the world. How did billions of dollars of fraud go unreported?

The high-profile scandals led to an extensive investigation of Arthur Andersen by the Securities and Exchange Commission (SEC). This action, along with subsequent events, damaged the auditor's reputation so severely that most of its clients fled to other auditors to avoid being associated with the Andersen name. By the end of 2002, Arthur Andersen was no longer in business.

SARBANES-OXLEY ACT OF 2002

In response to these corporate accounting scandals and to public outrage over seemingly widespread unethical behavior of top executives, Congress passed the Sarbanes-Oxley Act, also known as the *Public Company Accounting Reform and Investor Protection Act of 2002* and commonly referred to as *SOX*. SOX applies to all companies that are required to file financial statements with the SEC and represents one of the greatest reforms in business practices in U.S. history. The act established a variety of new guidelines related to auditor-client relations and internal control procedures. Illustration 4–1 lists and discusses some of the major provisions of SOX.

ILLUSTRATION 4–1

Major Provisions of the Sarbanes-Oxley Act of 2002

Oversight board. The Public Company Accounting Oversight Board (PCAOB) has the authority to establish standards dealing with auditing, quality control, ethics, independence, and other activities relating to the preparation of audited financial reports. The board consists of five members who are appointed by the Securities and Exchange Commission.

Corporate executive accountability. Corporate executives must personally certify the company's financial statements and financial disclosures. Severe financial penalties and the possibility of imprisonment are consequences of fraudulent misstatement.

Nonaudit services. It's unlawful for the auditors of public companies to also perform certain nonaudit services, such as consulting, for their clients.

Retention of work papers. Auditors of public companies must retain all work papers for seven years or face a prison term for willful violation.

Auditor rotation. The lead auditor in charge of auditing a particular company (referred to as the *audit partner*) must rotate off that company within five years and allow a new audit partner to take the lead.

Conflicts of interest. Audit firms are not allowed to audit public companies whose chief executives worked for the audit firm and participated in that company's audit during the preceding year.

Hiring of auditor. Audit firms are hired by the audit committee of the board of directors of the company, not by company management.

Internal control. Section 404 of the act requires (a) that company management document and assess the effectiveness of all internal control processes that could affect financial reporting and (b) that company auditors express an opinion on whether management's assessment of the effectiveness of internal control is fairly stated.

The last provision listed in Illustration 4–1, internal controls under Section 404, is worth pausing over for a moment, given the topic of this chapter. Section 404 requires company management and auditors to document and assess the effectiveness of a company's internal controls—processes that could affect financial reporting. PCAOB chairman William McDonough explained the significance of this part of the law: "In the past, internal controls were merely considered by auditors; now they will have to be tested and examined in detail" (*PCAOBUS.org*, June 18, 2004). Whether you are an investor, an employee, a manager, or an auditor, understanding a company's internal controls is important.

KEY POINT

The accounting scandals in the early 2000s prompted passage of the Sarbanes-Oxley Act (SOX). Among other stipulations, SOX sets forth a variety of new guidelines related to auditor-client relations and additional internal controls. Section 404, in particular, requires company management and auditors to document and assess the effectiveness of a company's internal controls.

Framework for Internal Control

■ LO2
Identify the components, responsibilities, and limitations of internal control.

As noted above, internal control is a company's plan to (1) safeguard the company's assets and (2) improve the accuracy and reliability of accounting information. Effective internal control builds a wall to prevent misuse of company funds by employees and fraudulent or errant financial reporting. Strong internal control systems allow greater reliance by investors on reported financial statements.

COMPONENTS OF INTERNAL CONTROL

A framework for designing an internal control system was provided by the *Committee of Sponsoring Organizations (COSO)* of the Treadway Commission. Formed in 1985, COSO (*www.coso.org*) is dedicated to improving the quality of financial reporting through, among other things, effective internal controls. COSO suggests that internal control consists of five components, displayed in Illustration 4–2.

ILLUSTRATION 4–2

Components of Internal Control

Methods for collection of relevant **information and communication** in a timely manner, enabling people to carry out their responsibilities.

Continual **monitoring** of internal activities and reporting of deficiencies is required. Monitoring includes formal procedures for reporting control deficiencies.

Control activities are the policies and procedures that help ensure that management's directives are being carried out. These activities include authorizations, reconciliations, and separation of duties.

Risk assessment identifies and analyzes internal and external risk factors that could prevent a company's objectives from being achieved.

The **control environment** sets the overall ethical tone of the company with respect to internal control. It includes formal policies related to management's philosophy, assignment of responsibilities, and organizational structure.

The components of internal control are built on the foundation of the ethical tone set by top management in its control environment. From there, management assesses risks, implements specific control activities, and continuously monitors all systems. Running throughout this structure is the need for timely information and communication. Employees at all levels must understand the importance of high-quality information. Lower-level employees must report information accurately and in a timely manner to those higher in the organization. Top executives of a company then must effectively communicate this information to external parties such as investors and creditors through financial statements.

To see an example of how internal controls are linked to the information provided in financial statements, let's look at the description given by Regal Entertainment Group in its annual report (see Illustration 4–3).

REGAL ENTERTAINMENT GROUP
Notes to the Financial Statements (excerpt)

A company's internal control over financial reporting includes those policies and procedures that (1) pertain to the maintenance of records that, in reasonable detail, accurately and fairly reflect the transactions and dispositions of the assets of the company; (2) provide reasonable assurance that transactions are recorded as necessary to permit preparation of financial statements in accordance with generally accepted accounting principles, and that receipts and expenditures of the company are being made only in accordance with authorizations of management and directors of the company; and (3) provide reasonable assurance regarding prevention or timely detection of unauthorized acquisition, use, or disposition of the company's assets that could have a material effect on the financial statements.

ILLUSTRATION 4–3

Regal Entertainment's Discussion of Internal Controls and Financial Reporting

---

Movie theatre example. Let's look at how the five components of internal control apply in actual practice. Here, we apply them to operating a movie theatre.

The overall attitudes and actions of management greatly affect the *control environment.* If employees notice unethical behavior or comments by management, they are more likely to behave in a similar manner, wasting the company's resources. Wouldn't you be more comfortable investing in or lending to a movie theatre if it were run by a highly ethical person, rather than someone of questionable character?

Risk assessment includes careful consideration of internal and external risk factors. Internal risks include issues such as unsafe lighting, faulty video projectors, unsanitary bathrooms, and employee incompetence with regard to food preparation. Common examples of external risks include a vendor supplying lower-grade or unsafe popcorn, moviegoers' security in the parking lot, or perhaps the decline in customer demand from DVD rentals or On Demand at home. These internal and external risk factors put the company's objectives in jeopardy.

Control activities include a variety of policies and procedures used to protect a company's assets. There are two general types of control activities: preventive and detective. *Preventive controls* are designed to keep errors or fraud from occurring in the first place. *Detective controls* are designed to detect errors or fraud that already have occurred.

Common examples of preventive controls include:

1. **Separation of duties.** Authorizing transactions, recording transactions, and maintaining control of the related assets should be separated among employees. The employee selling the movie ticket should not also be the employee in charge of collecting the tickets. The accountant at the movie theatre should not also have direct access to company cash by filling in as a ticket cashier or being

responsible for the daily cash deposits. Employees who have physical control of theatre inventory (candy bars, T-shirts, and so on) should not also be in charge of accounting for that inventory.

2. **Physical controls** over assets and accounting records. Each night, money from ticket sales should be placed in the theatre's safe or deposited at the bank. Important documents should be kept in fireproof files, and electronic records should be backed up daily and require user-ID and password for access. Concession supplies should be kept in a locked room with access allowed only to authorized personnel.

3. **Proper authorization** to prevent improper use of the company's resources. The theatre should establish formal guidelines on how to handle cash receipts and make purchases. For example, only management should be authorized to make purchases over a certain amount.

4. **Employee management.** The company should provide employees with appropriate guidance to ensure they have the knowledge necessary to carry out their job duties. Employees should be made fully aware of the company's internal control procedures, ethical responsibilities, and channels for reporting irregular activities.

Some examples of detective controls include:

1. **Reconciliations.** Management should periodically determine whether the amount of physical assets of the company (cash, supplies, inventory, and other property) match—reconcile with—the accounting records. For example, accounting personnel should routinely reconcile the company's cash records with those of its bank, and any discrepancy should be investigated. Later in this chapter we'll see an example of how to prepare a bank reconciliation for Starlight Drive-In.

2. **Performance reviews.** The actual performance of individuals or processes should be checked against their expected performance. For example, the amount of food sold should be compared to the number of tickets sold over a period of time. If food sales are lower than expected for a given number of tickets, employees could be wasting food, stealing food, or giving it to their friends for free. Alternatively, vendors may be supplying lower-quality food, driving down sales. Management may also wish to evaluate the overall performance of the theatre by comparing ticket sales for the current year with ticket sales for the previous year.

Monitoring of internal controls needs to occur on an ongoing basis. The theatre manager needs to actively review daily operations to ensure that control procedures work effectively. For instance, the manager should compare daily cash from ticket sales with the number of tickets issued, compare concession sales with units purchased, and make sure employees are paid only for actual hours worked.

Information and communication depend on the reliability of the accounting information system itself. If the accountant's office has papers scattered everywhere, and you learn the company still does all its accounting by hand without a computer, wouldn't you, as an investor or lender, be a bit worried? A system should be in place to ensure that current transactions of the company are reflected in current reports. Employees also should be aware of procedures in place to deal with any perceived internal control failures. For example, an anonymous tip hotline should be in place to encourage communication about unethical activities, such as an employee giving concession items for free to her friends. Employee tips historically have been the most common means of detecting employee fraud.

RESPONSIBILITIES FOR INTERNAL CONTROL

Everyone in a company has an impact on the operation and effectiveness of internal controls, but **the top executives are the ones who must take final responsibility for their establishment and success.** The CEO and CFO sign a report each year assessing whether the internal controls are adequate. Section 404 of SOX requires not only that companies document their internal controls and assess their adequacy, but that the company's auditors provide an opinion on management's assessment. A recent survey by the Financial Executives Institute of 247 executives reports that the total cost to a company of complying with Section 404 averages nearly $4 million.

The Public Company Accounting Oversight Board (PCAOB) further requires the auditor to express its own opinion on whether the company has maintained effective internal control over financial reporting. To see how this information gets reported, look at Illustration 4–4, which provides an excerpt from Regal Entertainment's auditor's report.

REGAL ENTERTAINMENT GROUP
Auditor's Report (excerpt)

In our opinion, management's assessment that Regal Entertainment Group maintained effective internal control over financial reporting is fairly stated, in all material respects, based on criteria established in *Internal Control—Integrated Framework* issued by the Committee of Sponsoring Organizations of the Treadway Commission (COSO). Also, in our opinion, Regal Entertainment Group maintained, in all material respects, effective internal control over financial reporting, based on criteria established in *Internal Control—Integrated Framework* issued by the Committee of Sponsoring Organizations of the Treadway Commission (COSO).

ILLUSTRATION 4–4

Excerpt from Regal Entertainment's Auditor's Report Related to Effectiveness of Internal Controls

LIMITATIONS OF INTERNAL CONTROL

Unfortunately, even with the best internal control systems, financial misstatements can occur. While better internal control systems will more likely detect operating and reporting errors, no internal control system can turn a bad employee into a good one.

Internal control systems are especially susceptible to collusion. Collusion occurs when two or more people act in coordination to circumvent internal controls. Going back to our movie theatre example, if the ticket cashier and the ticket taker, or the ticket cashier and the accountant, decide to work together to steal cash, theft will be much more difficult to detect. Fraud cases that involve collusion are typically several times more severe than are fraud cases involving a single perpetrator. This suggests that collusion is effective in circumventing control procedures.

Top-level employees who have the ability to override internal control features also have opportunity to commit fraud. For example, managers may be required to obtain approval from the chief financial officer (CFO) for all large purchases. However, if the CFO uses the company's funds to purchase a boat for personal use at a lake home, fewer controls are in place to detect this misappropriation. Even if lower-level employees suspect wrongdoing, they may feel intimidated to confront the issue.

Finally, because there are natural risks to running any business, **effective internal controls and ethical employees alone cannot ensure a company's success, or even survival.** Regal Entertainment recognizes the limitations of internal controls and provides an explicit discussion of this issue in its annual report, as shown in Illustration 4–5 (next page).

ILLUSTRATION 4–5

Regal Entertainment's Discussion of Limitations of Internal Controls

> **REGAL ENTERTAINMENT GROUP**
> **Management Discussion and Analysis (excerpt)**
>
> Management recognizes that there are inherent limitations in the effectiveness of any internal control over financial reporting, including the possibility of human error and the circumvention or overriding of internal control. Accordingly, even effective internal control over financial reporting can provide only reasonable assurance with respect to financial statement preparation. Further, because of changes in conditions, the effectiveness of internal control over financial reporting may vary over time.

 KEY POINT

Internal control refers to a company's plan to improve the accuracy and reliability of accounting information and safeguard the company's assets. Five key components to an internal control system are (1) control environment, (2) risk assessment, (3) control activities, (4) monitoring, and (5) information and communication.

Decision Point

Question ?	Accounting information 📄	Analysis 🔍
Does the company maintain adequate internal controls?	Management's discussion, auditor's opinion	If management or the auditor notes any deficiencies in internal controls, financial accounting information may be unreliable.

PART B

CASH

Among all of the company's assets, cash is the one most susceptible to employee fraud. The obvious way that employees steal cash is by physically removing it from the company, such as pulling it out of the cash register and walking out the door. However, there are other, less obvious ways to commit fraud with a company's cash. An employee could falsify documents, causing the company to overreimburse the employee for certain expenses, to issue an inflated paycheck, or to make payment to a fictitious company. Because of these possibilities, companies develop strict procedures to maintain control of cash. Before discussing some of these controls, let's first get a good understanding of what "cash" includes.

Cash and Cash Equivalents

■ LO3

Define cash and cash equivalents.

The amount of **cash** recorded in a company's balance sheet includes currency, coins, and balances in savings and checking accounts, as well as items acceptable for deposit in these accounts, such as checks received from customers. *Checks* are written instruments instructing a bank to pay a specific amount from the check maker's account.

The balance of cash also includes **cash equivalents**, which are defined as short-term investments that have a maturity date no longer than three months *from the date of purchase*. Common examples of such investments are money market funds, Treasury bills, and certificates of deposit. The important point to understand is that

cash and cash equivalents usually are combined and reported as a single asset in the balance sheet of most companies.

KEY POINT

Cash includes not only currency, coins, balances in checking accounts, and checks and money orders received from customers, but also cash equivalents, defined as investments that mature within three months (such as money market funds, Treasury bills, and certificates of deposit).

Whether a customer uses cash or a check to make a purchase, the company records the transaction as a cash sale. Let's assume a local theatre sells tickets for the entire day totaling $3,000. Some customers pay cash for those tickets, while others use a check. (Others will use credit cards or debit cards, which we discuss later.) Regardless of which method of payment customers use, the theatre records all of those ticket sales as cash sales.

User's Guide Below is a shorthand way of showing the effects of transactions on assets, liabilities, and stockholders' equity. We use these throughout the book.

	Debit	Credit
Cash	3,000	
Service Revenue		3,000
(Sell tickets with cash or check)		

A	=	L	+	SE
+3,000				
				+3,000 Rev↑

How Much Cash Is Enough?

Investors and creditors closely monitor the amount of cash a company holds. The company needs enough cash, or enough other assets that can quickly be converted to cash, to pay obligations as they become due. Available cash also helps a company respond quickly to new, profitable opportunities before competitors do. On the other hand, having too much cash leads to inefficient use of funds and could be a signal that a company's management does not see additional opportunities for profitable expansion. Investors usually view excess cash as a negative. ●

Decision Maker's Perspective

Cash Controls

Management must safeguard all assets against possible misuse. Again, because cash is especially susceptible to theft, internal control of cash is a key issue.

CONTROLS OVER CASH RECEIPTS

Most businesses receive payment from the sale of products and services either in the form of cash or as a check received immediately or through the mail. Internal control over cash receipts could include the following steps:

■ **LO4**
Understand controls over cash receipts and cash disbursements.

1. Record all cash receipts as soon as possible. Theft is more difficult once a record of the cash receipt has been made.
2. Open mail each day, and make a list of checks received, including the amount and payer's name.
3. Designate an employee to deposit cash and checks into the company's bank account each day, different from the person who receives cash and checks.
4. Have another employee record cash receipts in the accounting records. Verify cash receipts by comparing the bank deposit slip with the accounting records.
5. Accept credit cards or debit cards, to limit the amount of cash employees handle.

Because acceptance of credit cards and debit cards is so widespread, let's look at those controls in a bit more detail.

Acceptance of credit cards.   The acceptance of credit cards provides an additional control by reducing employees' need to directly handle cash. The term *credit card* is derived from the fact that the issuer, such as **Visa** or **MasterCard**, extends credit (lends money) to the cardholder each time the cardholder uses the card. Cash in the amount of the sale automatically is deposited in the company's bank.

Credit card companies earn revenues primarily in two ways. First, the cardholder has a specified grace period before he or she has to pay the credit card balance in full. If the balance is not paid by the end of the grace period, the issuing company will charge a fee (interest). Second, credit card companies charge the *retailer*, not the customer, for the use of the credit card. This charge generally ranges from 2% to 4% of the amount of the sale.

For example, suppose a movie theatre accepts MasterCard as payment for $2,000 worth of movie tickets, and MasterCard charges the movie theatre a service fee of 3% (or $60 on sales of $2,000). Moviegoers don't pay cash to the theatre at the time of sale, but MasterCard deposits cash, less the service fee expense, into the theatre's account usually within 24 hours. Therefore, the theatre records the $2,000 credit card transaction as $1,940 cash received and $60 service fee expense.

A = L + SE		Debit	Credit
+1,940	Cash	1,940	
−60 Exp↑	Service Fee Expense	60	
+2,000 Rev↑	Service Revenue		2,000
	(Sell tickets with credit card and 3% service fee)		

From the seller's perspective, the only difference between a cash sale and a credit card sale is that the seller must pay a fee to the credit card company for allowing the customer to use a credit card.

Decision Point

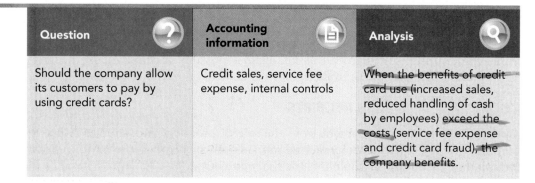

Question	Accounting information	Analysis
Should the company allow its customers to pay by using credit cards?	Credit sales, service fee expense, internal controls	When the benefits of credit card use (increased sales, reduced handling of cash by employees) exceed the costs (service fee expense and credit card fraud), the company benefits.

Acceptance of debit cards.   *Debit cards* also provide an additional control for cash receipts. Like credit cards, debit cards offer customers a way to purchase goods and services without a physical exchange of cash. They differ, however, in that most debit cards (sometimes referred to as *check cards*) work just like a check and withdraw funds directly from the cardholder's bank account at the time of use. (Recall that credit cards don't remove cash from the cardholder's account after each transaction.)

Similar to credit cards, the use of debit cards by customers results in a fee being charged to the retailer. However, the fees charged for debit cards are typically much lower than those charged for credit cards. Debit card transactions are recorded similar to credit card transactions.

COMMON MISTAKE

The term *debit card* can cause some confusion for someone in the first accounting course. Throughout this course, we refer to an increase in cash as a *debit* to cash. However, using your *debit card* will result in a decrease in your cash account. It's the *merchant's* cash account, not yours, that increases and is debited. Don't let this confuse you.

ETHICAL DILEMMA

Jill is starting her sophomore year of college. The only way she can pay for tuition and school supplies is to take out a student loan. To make living costs more affordable, she shares an apartment with two other students. One week after Jill starts classes, her car breaks down. She pays a $120 towing bill to get the car to the service station, and the mechanic tells her the car has suffered major engine failure. The cost to fix the car will be $1,600, which is a fair price for such damage. Jill has enough money from her student loan to pay the bill, but she knows this will put her behind for the next several months' rent. The mechanic tells her that if she pays cash, instead of writing a check or paying with a debit card or credit card, he will charge her only $1,300. When she asks the reason for the $300 discount, he tells her, "If you pay cash, there's no record of our transaction, and I won't have to pay taxes. This will save money for both of us." What should Jill do? Another mechanic is likely to charge her full price, and she would have to pay an additional towing charge to get the car to a different mechanic.

CONTROLS OVER CASH DISBURSEMENTS

Managers should design proper controls for cash disbursements to prevent any unauthorized payments and ensure proper recording. Consistent with our discussion of cash receipts, cash disbursements include not only disbursing physical cash, but also writing checks and using credit cards and debit cards to make payments. All these forms of payment constitute cash disbursement and require formal internal control procedures. Important elements of a cash disbursement control system include the following steps:

1. Make all disbursements, other than very small ones, by check, debit card, or credit card. This provides a permanent record of all disbursements.
2. Authorize all expenditures before purchase and verify the accuracy of the purchase itself. The employee who authorizes payment should not also be the employee who prepares the check.

3. Make sure checks are serially numbered and signed only by authorized employees. Require two signatures for larger checks.

4. Periodically check amounts shown in the debit card and credit card statements against purchase receipts. The employee verifying the accuracy of the debit card and credit card statements should not also be the employee responsible for actual purchases.

5. Set maximum purchase limits on debit cards and credit cards. Give approval to purchase above these amounts only to upper-level employees.

6. Employees responsible for making cash disbursements should not also be in charge of cash receipts.

When the movie theatre pays $1,000 to advertise its show times, it records the following transaction, regardless of whether it pays with cash, a check, or a debit card.

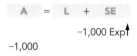

	Debit	Credit
Advertising Expense	1,000	
Cash		1,000
(Purchase advertising with cash, check, or debit card)		

A = L + SE

−1,000 Exp

−1,000

Because credit cards allow the purchaser to delay payment for several weeks or even months, if the theatre uses a credit card to pay for the $1,000 worth of advertising, it would record the purchase as follows.

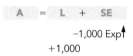

	Debit	Credit
Advertising Expense	1,000	
Accounts Payable		1,000
(Purchase advertising with credit card)		

A = L + SE

−1,000 Exp

+1,000

 KEY POINT

Because cash is the asset of a company most susceptible to employee fraud, controls over cash receipts and cash disbursements are an important part of a company's overall internal control system. Important controls over cash receipts include separation of duties for those who handle cash and independent verification of cash receipts. Important controls over cash disbursements include payment by check, credit card, or debit card, separation of duties, and various authorization and documentation procedures.

Bank Reconciliation 调解

■ LO5
Reconcile a bank statement.

Another important control used by nearly all companies to help maintain control of cash is a bank reconciliation. A bank reconciliation matches the balance of cash in the bank account with the balance of cash in the company's own records. If you have your own checking account, you know that the balance of cash in your checkbook often does not equal the balance of cash in your bank account. Why is that? One possibility is that you (or your bank) made a recording error. More likely, though, you've written a check or have cash receipts that haven't yet reached the bank, or maybe the bank has made an adjustment you haven't yet recorded.

It's the same for a business. A company's cash balance as recorded in its books rarely equals the cash balance reported in the bank statement. The reasons for the differences are the same as those for your personal checking account: Differences in these balances most often occur because of either timing differences or errors. It is the *possibility* of these errors, or even outright fraudulent activities, that makes the bank reconciliation a useful cash control tool.

Timing differences in cash occur when the company records transactions either before or after the bank records the same transaction. For example, when a movie theatre pays its popcorn supplier $200 by check, the company records a decrease in cash immediately, but the bank doesn't record a decrease in cash until the popcorn supplier later deposits the check. If the supplier waits a week before depositing the check, the balance of cash in the company's records will be reduced one week earlier than will the bank's.

Other times, the bank is the first to record a transaction. The bank could charge a $50 service fee for processing the company's transaction, immediately reducing the bank's record of the company's balance for cash. However, the company may not be immediately aware of this fee. Only when the monthly bank statement is sent will the company become aware of the cash reduction. In this case, the bank's balance for cash reflects a cash transaction before the company's balance can reflect the same transaction.

Errors can be made either by the company or its bank and may be accidental or intentional. An *accidental* error might occur if the company mistakenly were to record a check being written for $117 as $171 in its records, or if the bank improperly processed a deposit of $1,100 as a $1,010 deposit. An *intentional* error is the result of theft. If the company records a daily deposit of $5,000 but an employee deposits only $500 into the bank account and pockets the rest, the bank reconciliation will reveal the missing $4,500.

A bank reconciliation connects the company's cash balance to the bank's cash balance by identifying differences due to timing and errors. This concept is shown in Illustration 4–6.

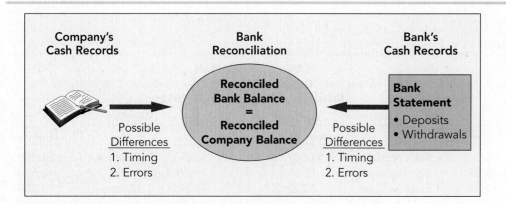

ILLUSTRATION 4–6

Bank Reconciliation

To see how a bank reconciliation is prepared, let's start by examining the bank statement of Starlight Drive-In. At the end of March, First Bank sends the bank statement in Illustration 4–7 (next page) to Starlight. Compare the bank statement with Starlight's own records of cash activity over the same period, as shown in Illustration 4–8 (next page).

First Bank's ending balance of cash ($4,100) differs from Starlight's ending balance of cash ($2,880). To understand why these two cash balances differ, we need to identify (1) timing differences created by cash activity reported by either First Bank or Starlight but not recorded by the other and (2) any errors.

ILLUSTRATION 4–7

Bank Statement

P.O. Box 26788
Odessa, TX 79760
(432) 799-BANK

First Bank
A Name You Can Trust

Member FDIC

Account Holder:	Starlight Drive-In	Account Number:	4061009619
	221B Baker Street		
	Odessa, TX 79760	Statement Date:	March 31, 2012

Account Summary

Beginning Balance March 1, 2012	Deposits and Credits No.	Total	Withdrawals and Debits No.	Total	Ending Balance March 31, 2012
$3,800	4	$8,600	7	$8,300	$4,100

Account Details

Deposits and Credits			Withdrawals and Debits				Daily Balance	
Date	Amount	Desc.	Date	No.	Amount	Desc.	Date	Amount
3/5	$3,600	DEP	3/8	293	$2,100	CHK	3/5	$7,400
3/9	3,000	NOTE	3/12	294	2,900	CHK	3/8	5,300
3/22	1,980	DEP	3/15		400	EFT	3/9	8,300
3/31	20	INT	3/22		750	NSF	3/12	5,400
			3/26	296	1,900	CHK	3/15	5,000
			3/28		200	DC	3/22	6,230
			3/31		50	SF	3/26	4,330
							3/28	4,130
	$8,600				$8,300		3/31	$4,100

Desc.	**DEP** Customer deposit	**INT** Interest earned	**SF** Service fees
	NOTE Note collected	**CHK** Customer check	**NSF** Nonsufficient funds
	EFT Electronic funds transfer	**DC** Debit card	

ILLUSTRATION 4–8

Company Records of
Cash Activities

STARLIGHT DRIVE-IN
Cash Account Records
March 1, 2012, to March 31, 2012

Deposits			Checks			
Date	Desc.	Amount	Date	No.	Desc.	Amount
3/5	Sales receipts	$3,600	3/6	293	Salaries	$2,100
3/22	Sales receipts	1,980	3/11	294	Rent	2,600
3/31	Sales receipts	2,200	3/21	295	Utilities	1,200
			3/24	296	Insurance	1,900
			3/30	297	Supplies	900
		$7,780				$8,700

SUMMARY OF TRANSACTIONS

Beginning Cash Balance March 1, 2012	+	Deposits	−	Checks	=	Ending Cash Balance March 31, 2012
$3,800		$7,780		$8,700		$2,880

COMMON MISTAKE

Notice that bank statements refer to an increase (or deposit) in the cash balance as a *credit* and a decrease (or withdrawal) as a *debit*. This terminology is the opposite of that used in financial accounting, where *debit* refers to an increase in cash and *credit* refers to a decrease in cash. The reason for the difference in terminology is a difference in perspective: The financial accounting records are prepared *from a company's perspective*, while the bank statement is prepared *from a bank's perspective*. When a company makes a deposit, the bank's liability to the company (a credit account) increases. When a company withdraws cash from its bank account, the bank's liability to the company decreases.

Reconciling the bank account involves three steps: (1) reconciling the bank's cash balance, (2) reconciling the company's cash balance, and (3) adjusting the company's cash balance. In the first two steps, we should catch timing differences (such as for deposits outstanding, checks outstanding, and bank memoranda) as well as errors made by either the company or the bank. In the third step, we update the company's accounting records for cash transactions that have occurred but have not yet been recorded.

STEP 1: RECONCILING THE BANK'S CASH BALANCE

First, we will reconcile the bank's cash balance. Cash transactions recorded by a company, but not yet recorded by its bank, include deposits outstanding and checks outstanding. Deposits outstanding are cash receipts of the company that have not been added to the bank's record of the company's balance. Checks outstanding are checks the company has written that have not been subtracted from the bank's record of the company's balance.

Timing differences

For example, comparing cash receipts recorded by Starlight (Illustration 4–8) to those reported as deposits in the bank statement (Illustration 4–7) reveals that cash sales receipts of $2,200 on March 31 are not yet reflected in the bank's balance by the end of March. This is a deposit outstanding.

Comparing the checks written by Starlight to those reported in the bank statement shows that the bank received checks #293, #294, and #296 by the end of March. This means checks #295 (for $1,200) and #297 (for $900) remain outstanding and are not yet reflected in the bank's balance.

Once the bank receives the deposits outstanding, the bank's cash balance will increase. Similarly, once the bank receives the checks outstanding, the bank's cash balance will decrease. We also need to check for and correct any bank errors.

The reconciled bank balance is calculated on the left side of Illustration 4–9 (next page).

STEP 2: RECONCILING THE COMPANY'S CASH BALANCE

Next, we need to reconcile the company's cash balance. What are some examples of cash transactions recorded by the bank but not yet recorded by the company? These would include items such as interest earned by the company, collections made by the bank on the company's behalf, service fees, and charges for NSF checks—customers' checks written on "nonsufficient funds," otherwise known as "bad" checks. In addition, we adjust the company's balance for any recording errors made by the company.

Six cash transactions recorded by First Bank (Illustration 4–7) are not reported in Starlight's cash records (Illustration 4–8) by the end of March:

1. Note received by First Bank on Starlight's behalf ($3,000 consisting of $2,800 plus related interest received of $200).
2. Interest earned by Starlight on its bank account ($20).

Timing differences

3. NSF check ($750).

4. Debit card purchase of office equipment by an employee ($200).

5. Electronic funds transfer (EFT) related to the payment of advertising ($400).

6. Service fee ($50).

 COMMON MISTAKE

Students sometimes mistake an NSF check as a bad check written *by* the company instead of one written *to* the company. When an NSF check occurs, the company must adjust its balance of cash downward to reverse the increase in cash it recorded at the time it received the check from the customer, because the customer did not have enough funds to cover the check. This bounced check will create an account receivable for the company until the customer pays the funds it owes.

Company error

In addition to the amounts related to timing differences, we need to address one other reconciling item. Comparing Starlight's record of checks written to those in the bank statement reveals an error by Starlight. Check #294 for rent was written for $2,900, but Starlight's accountant recorded it incorrectly as $2,600. First Bank processed the check for the correct amount of $2,900. This means Starlight needs to reduce its cash balance by an additional $300 for rent expense. The reconciled company balance is calculated on the right side of Illustration 4–9. (Note that the illustration shows additions to the company's account in green and subtractions from the account in red.)

ILLUSTRATION 4–9

Reconciling the Bank Statement

STARLIGHT DRIVE-IN
Bank Reconciliation
March 31, 2012

Bank's Cash Balance		*Company's* Cash Balance	
Before reconciliation	$4,100	Before reconciliation	$2,880
Deposits outstanding:	+2,200	Note received	+2,800
3/31 = $2,200		Interest earned from note	+200
		Interest earned on bank account	+20
Checks outstanding:	−2,100	NSF check	−750
#295 = $1,200		Debit card for office equipment	−200
#297 = $ 900		EFT for advertising	−400
		Service fee	−50
		Corrected rent expense error	−300
After reconciliation	$4,200	After reconciliation	$4,200

Reconciled

If the bank were aware of all deposits made and all checks written by the company, the bank's cash balance would be $4,200. Similarly, once the company adjusts its balance for information revealed in the bank statement, its cash balance is $4,200. The fact that the two balances match provides some indication that cash is not being mishandled by employees.

STEP 3: ADJUSTING THE COMPANY'S CASH BALANCE

As a final step in the reconciliation process, a company must update the balance in its Cash account, to adjust for the items used to reconcile the *company's* cash balance. We record these adjustments once the bank reconciliation is complete. Remember, these are amounts the company didn't know until it received the bank statement.

We record items that increase the company's cash by a debit to Cash. Similarly, we record items that decrease the company's cash by a credit to Cash. The entries needed to adjust Starlight's cash balance for reconciliation items are as follows.

March 31, 2012	Debit	Credit	A	=	L	+	SE
Cash	3,020		+3,020				
Notes Receivable		2,800	−2,800				
Interest Revenue		220					+220 Rev↑
(Reconcile cash increases)			A	=	L	+	SE
Accounts Receivable	750		+750				
Equipment	200		+200				
Advertising Expense	400						−400 Exp↑
Service Fee Expense	50						−50 Exp↑
Rent Expense	300						−300 Exp↑
Cash		1,700	−1,700				
(Reconcile cash decreases)							

Most of the accounts are easy to understand. We credit Notes Receivable because the note has been received, decreasing that asset account (−$2,800). We recognize interest revenue (+$220) as earned. We need to record cash outflows related to expenses (advertising, service fee, and rent) and asset purchases need to be recorded. Finally, we debit Accounts Receivable, increasing that asset account (+$750) to show that the customer who paid with an NSF check still owes the company money.

COMMON MISTAKE

Some students try to prepare adjusting entries for deposits outstanding, checks outstanding, or a bank error. The company does *not* need to adjust for these items related to reconciling the bank's balance because they are already properly recorded in the company's accounting records.

In the uncommon event that the two reconciled balances do not equal, management investigates the discrepancy to check for wrongdoing or errors by company employees or the bank. If the company cannot resolve the discrepancy, it records the difference to either Miscellaneous Expense or Miscellaneous Revenue, depending on whether it has a debit or credit balance. For example, suppose a company is unable to account for $100 of missing cash. In this event, the company records the following transaction, increasing Miscellaneous Expense and decreasing Cash.

	Debit	Credit	A	=	L	+	SE
Miscellaneous Expense	100						−100 Exp↑
Cash		100	−100				
(Record loss of $100 cash)							

KEY POINT

In a bank reconciliation we adjust the *bank's* balance for (1) cash transactions already recorded by the company but not yet recorded by the bank and (2) bank errors. Similarly, we adjust the *company's* balance for (1) cash transactions already recorded by the bank but not yet recorded by the company and (2) company errors. After we adjust both the bank balance and the company balance, the two should equal.

Let's Review

At the end of April 2012, Showtime Theatre's accounting records show a cash balance of $4,800. The April bank statement reports a cash balance of $3,700. The following information is gathered from the bank statement and company records:

Checks outstanding	$1,900	Customer's NSF check	$1,300
Deposits outstanding	1,600	Service fee	200
Interest earned	70		

In addition, Showtime discovered it correctly paid for advertising with a check for $220 but incorrectly recorded the check in the company's records for $250. The bank correctly processed the check for $220.

Required:

1. Prepare a bank reconciliation for the month of April 2012.
2. Prepare entries to adjust the balance of cash in the company's records.

Solution:

1. Bank reconciliation:

SHOWTIME THEATRE
Bank Reconciliation
April 30, 2012

Bank's Cash Balance		*Company's Cash Balance*	
Before reconciliation	$3,700	Before reconciliation	$4,800
Deposits outstanding	+1,600	Interest earned	+70
		Company error	+30
Checks outstanding	−1,900	Service fee	−200
		NSF check	−1,300
After reconciliation	$3,400	After reconciliation	$3,400

2. Entries to adjust cash balance:

April 30, 2012	Debit	Credit
Cash	100	
Interest Revenue		70
Advertising Expense		30
(Reconcile cash increases)		
Service Fee Expense	200	
Accounts Receivable	1,300	
Cash		1,500
(Reconcile cash decreases)		

Suggested Homework:
BE4-8, BE4-9;
E4-12, E4-13;
P4-2A&B, P4-3A&B

Petty Cash

■ **LO6**
Account for petty cash.

You probably pay for most of your purchases with a debit card, credit card, or check. However, it's nice to have a little cash in your wallet for emergency or impulse expenditures. For example, you might decide to buy a box of Girl Scout cookies from your neighbor or soda from a machine. In the same way, most companies like to keep a small amount of cash on hand at the company's location for

minor purchases such as postage, office supplies, delivery charges, and entertainment expenses. If the office manager orders a $10 pizza for a staff meeting, it would be inconvenient and costly to write and process a check for such a small amount. Furthermore, it would be time-consuming to run to the bank for a $10 cash withdrawal. To pay for these minor purchases, companies keep some minor amount of cash on hand in a petty cash fund.

Accounting for the petty cash fund involves recording transactions to (1) establish the fund, (2) recognize expenditures from the fund, and (3) replenish the fund as the cash balance becomes sufficiently low. Management establishes a petty cash fund by writing a check for cash against the company's checking account and putting that amount of withdrawn cash in the hands of an employee who becomes responsible for it. This employee is often referred to as the *petty-cash custodian*. The fund should have just enough cash to make minor expenditures over a reasonable period (such as a week or a month). Given appropriate documentation, such as a receipt for the purchase of the $10 pizza for the staff meeting or of office supplies, the petty-cash custodian will disburse cash to reimburse the purchaser. At any given time, the cash remaining in the fund plus all receipts should equal the amount of the fund. The receipts are important to ensure proper use of the funds and for recording expenditures each time the fund is replenished.

Suppose that at the beginning of May, Starlight Drive-In establishes a petty cash fund of $500 to pay for minor purchases. Starlight establishes the fund by recording:

May 1	Debit	Credit		A	=	L	+	SE
Petty Cash (on hand)	500			+500				
Cash (checking account)		500		−500				
(Establish the petty cash fund)								

Assume Starlight has the following expenditures from the petty cash fund during May:

Date	Expenditure	Amount
May 7	Postage	$ 75
May 16	Delivery charges	85
May 20	Office group lunch	50
May 26	Office supplies	120
		$330

By the end of May, the petty cash fund has distributed $330, leaving $170 in the fund, along with receipts for $330. However, the company did not record these transactions at the time these expenditures were made. By the end of the period, the expenditures from the petty cash fund must be recorded.

May 31	Debit	Credit		A	=	L	+	SE
Postage Expense	75							−75 Exp
Delivery Expense	85							−85 Exp
Entertainment Expense	50							−50 Exp
Supplies	120			+120				
Petty Cash (on hand)		330		−330				
(Recognize expenditures from the petty cash fund)								

Also at the end of the period, the petty cash fund may need to be replenished. Management can withdraw cash of $330 from the checking account and give it to the petty-cash custodian so the fund's balance will once again be $500.

A = L + SE	May 31	Debit	Credit
+330	**Petty Cash** (on hand)	330	
−330	**Cash** (checking account)		330
	(Replenish the petty cash fund at the end of the period)		

To maintain the control objective of separation of duties, the petty-cash custodian should not be involved in accounting for, nor in the process of writing or approving, replenishment checks.

What if only $150 is left in the petty cash fund, when there should be $170? It could be that $20 was stolen from the fund, or the fund could be missing a receipt for $20. If the question is not resolved, the firm will likely charge the $20 to Miscellaneous Expense.

KEY POINT

To pay for minor purchases, companies keep some cash on hand in a petty cash fund. At the end of the period, expenditures from the petty cash fund are recorded, and the fund is replenished.

Reporting Cash

To this point, we've considered several internal controls related to cash. Here, we discuss how companies report cash activities. Cash activities of a business enterprise are the most fundamental events upon which investors and lenders base their decisions: Where does a company get its cash? Where does a company usually spend its cash? These are important issues in determining management's efficient use of a company's resources and in predicting future performance. Companies report cash in two ways—in the balance sheet and in the statement of cash flows.

BALANCE SHEET

As we discussed in Chapter 3, companies report cash as an asset in the balance sheet. The amount is typically reported as a current asset and represents cash available for spending at the end of the reporting period. The balance sheet provides only the final balance for cash. It does not provide any details regarding cash receipts and payments during the period.

STATEMENT OF CASH FLOWS

■ LO7
Identify the major inflows and outflows of cash.

Companies report information about cash receipts and payments during the period in a statement of cash flows. **From the statement of cash flows, investors know a company's cash inflows and cash outflows related to (1) operating activities, (2) investing activities, and (3) financing activities.** We'll provide a complete discussion of the statement of cash flows in Chapter 11. Here, we briefly introduce the basics of the statement to help you understand that its purpose is to report activity related to the key topic of this chapter—cash.

Recall from Chapter 1 the three fundamental types of business activities relating to cash:

- *Operating activities* include cash transactions involving revenue and expense events during the period. In other words, operating activities include the cash effect of the same activities that are reported in the income statement.
- *Investing activities,* as the name implies, include cash investments in long-term assets and investment securities. When the firm later sells those assets, we consider those transactions investing activities also. So, investing activities tend to involve long-term assets.

- *Financing activities* include transactions designed to raise cash or finance the business. There are two ways to do this: borrow cash from lenders or raise cash from stockholders. We also consider cash outflows to repay debt and cash dividends to stockholders to be financing activities. So, financing activities involve liabilities and stockholders' equity.

It's easiest to understand cash flow information by looking at the underlying transactions. To do this, we'll refer back to the external transactions of Eagle Golf Academy introduced in Chapters 1 through 3. For convenience, Illustration 4–10 lists those transactions and analyzes their effects on the company's cash.

Transaction	External Transactions in January	Type of Activity	Is Cash Involved?	Inflow or Outflow?
(1)	Sell shares of common stock for $25,000 to obtain the funds necessary to start the business.	Financing	Yes	Inflow
(2)	Borrow $10,000 from the local bank and sign a note promising to repay the full amount of the debt in three years.	Financing	Yes	Inflow
(3)	Purchase equipment necessary for giving golf training, $24,000 cash.	Investing	Yes	Outflow
(4)	Pay one year of rent in advance, $6,000 ($500 per month).	Operating	Yes	Outflow
(5)	Purchase supplies on account, $2,300.	Operating	No	—
(6)	Provide golf training to customers for cash, $3,600.	Operating	Yes	Inflow
(7)	Provide golf training to customers on account, $2,500.	Operating	No	—
(8)	Receive cash in advance for 10 golf training sessions to be given in the future, $600.	Operating	Yes	Inflow
(9)	Pay salaries to employees, $2,800.	Operating	Yes	Outflow
(10)	Pay cash dividends of $200 to shareholders.	Financing	Yes	Outflow

ILLUSTRATION 4–10

External Transactions of Eagle Golf Academy

Which transactions involve the exchange of cash?

Which transactions involve the exchange of cash? All transactions except (5) and (7) involve either the receipt (inflow) or payment (outflow) of cash. **Only transactions involving *cash* affect a company's *cash* flows.**

Illustration 4–11 (next page) presents the statement of cash flows for Eagle Golf Academy using what's called the *direct method* of reporting operating activities. Corresponding transaction numbers are in brackets. (In Chapter 11 we'll discuss the *indirect method.*)

From the statement of cash flows, investors and creditors can see that the major source of cash inflow for Eagle is the issuance of common stock, a financing activity. Eagle has also received cash from bank borrowing, which must be repaid. The company is also investing heavily in its future by purchasing equipment. Eagle reports this amount as an investing outflow.

With regard to the three types of business activities, the cash flow that's related most directly to the company's profitability is net cash flows from operating activities. For Eagle Golf Academy, net cash flows from operating activities are –$4,600. This means that cash *outflows* related to operating activities exceed inflows. Stated another way, cash outflows related to expense activities exceed cash inflows related to revenue activities. While Eagle reports net income of $500 in its income statement (see Illustration 3–12 in Chapter 3), these same activities are not able to generate positive cash flows for the company. Ultimately, companies must be able to generate positive operating cash flows to maintain long-term success.

ILLUSTRATION 4–11

Statement of Cash Flows for Eagle Golf Academy

Numbers in brackets correspond to the external transaction numbers of Eagle Golf Academy in Illustration 4–10.

Only transactions that involve the exchange of cash are included in the statement of cash flows.

EAGLE GOLF ACADEMY Statement of Cash Flows For the month ended January 31, 2012		
Cash Flows from Operating Activities		
Cash inflows:		
From customers [6 and 8]	$ 4,200	
Cash outflows:		
For salaries [9]	(2,800)	
For rent [4]	(6,000)	
Net cash flows from operating activities		$ (4,600)
Cash Flows from Investing Activities		
Purchase equipment [3]	(24,000)	
Net cash flows from investing activities		(24,000)
Cash Flows from Financing Activities		
Issue common stock [1]	25,000	
Borrow from bank [2]	10,000	
Pay dividends [10]	(200)	
Net cash flows from financing activities		34,800
Net increase in cash		6,200
Cash at the beginning of the month		-0-
Cash at the end of the month		$ 6,200

The final amount reported in the statement of cash flows, **$6,200**, is the same amount of cash reported in the balance sheet. You can verify this is the case for Eagle Golf Academy by referring back to the balance sheet reported in Illustration 3–14 in Chapter 3.

KEY POINT

The statement of cash flows reports all cash activities for the period. *Operating activities* include those transactions involving revenue and expense activities. *Investing activities* include cash investments in long-term assets and investment securities. *Financing activities* include transactions designed to finance the business through borrowing and owner investment.

Decision Point

Question	Accounting information	Analysis
Is the company able to generate enough cash from internal sources to sustain daily operations?	Statement of cash flows	Cash flows generated from internal sources include operating and investing activities. For established companies, the sum of these amounts should be positive. Otherwise, the company will need to rely on external funding (lenders and stockholders), which is not sustainable in the long term.

A company reports in its current year each of the transactions listed below.

Let's Review

Required:

Indicate whether each transaction should be reported as an operating, investing, or financing cash flow in the company's statement of cash flows, and whether each is a cash inflow or outflow.

Transaction	Type of Cash Flow	Inflow or Outflow
1. Pay employees' salaries.	Operating Yes	outflow
2. Obtain a loan at the bank.	Financing	inflow
3. Purchase a building with cash.	Investing	outflow
4. Purchase equipment with a note payable.	No Cash flow	

Solution:

1. Operating—outflow.   2. Financing—inflow.   3. Investing—outflow.
4. Not reported as a cash flow because no cash is involved in the transaction.

Suggested Homework:
**BE4-11, BE4-12;
E4-16, E4-17;
P4-4A&B, P4-5A&B**

CASH ANALYSIS
Krispy Kreme vs. Starbucks

ANALYSIS

We now look at how decision makers analyze and use information about cash. Krispy Kreme and Starbucks provide some interesting comparisons.

The difference between revenues and expenses—net income—provides an accrual-basis measure of the company's ability to create wealth for its stockholders. In general, the greater a company's net income, the greater will be the value of the company to stockholders. However, the *timing* of revenues and expenses recorded under accrual-basis accounting may differ from the timing of operating cash flows.

Earlier, we discussed an example of such a timing difference, by comparing the net income of Eagle Golf Academy ($500) to its net cash flows from operations (−$4,600). If you were considering an investment in Eagle Golf Academy, would you consider net income of $500 to be a reliable indicator of the profit-generating potential of the company, given that it has net cash flows from operating activities of −$4,600? Which number is more useful in helping us to predict the long-term profitability of the company? We refer to the ability of current net income to help us predict the future performance of a company as **earnings quality**. When net income does not provide a good indicator of future performance, its earnings quality is said to be low.

COMPARING NET INCOME TO CASH FLOW

One of the more common techniques used by investors for measuring earnings quality relies on comparing the trend in a company's reported net income to its trend in free cash flow. A simple way to calculate a company's **free cash flow** is to consider its operating cash flows plus investing cash flows during the period. This measure represents the cash that is *free* to repay debt and distribute to stockholders. Companies whose free cash flow is declining relative to the trend in net income are likely to have lower-quality earnings.

Let's look at an example: In 1937, Vernon Rudolph bought a secret doughnut recipe from a French chef in New Orleans, rented a building in Winston-Salem, North Carolina, and began selling doughnuts. Since then, Mr. Rudolph's company,

■ LO8
Assess earnings quality by comparing net income and cash flows.

Financial analysts offer investment advice to their clients—banks, insurance companies, mutual funds, securities firms, and individual investors. This advice usually comes in the form of a formal recommendation (buy, hold, or sell). Before giving an opinion, analysts develop a detailed understanding of a company's operations through discussions with management, analysis of competitors, and projections of industry trends. They also develop a detailed understanding of a company's financial statements, including its earnings quality. Analysts typically do not recommend companies with lower-quality earnings.

Understanding a company's earnings quality comes from having a good grasp of accrual-basis accounting. This is why many finance majors and MBA students, pursuing careers as financial analysts, take additional accounting-related courses when earning their degrees and even after graduation.

Comparing free cash flow with net income can help in measuring the quality of earnings.

Krispy Kreme, grew into a leading branded specialty retailer across the country, producing over a billion doughnuts a year. To illustrate the preference of not relying on a single measure like net income in isolation, we compare Krispy Kreme with **Starbucks Corporation**.

As Illustrations 4–12 and 4–13 show, both Krispy Kreme and Starbucks enjoyed explosive increases in net income over the 1999–2004 period. However, their free cash flows (or strict cash-basis net incomes) tell a very different story. Notice that Krispy Kreme's free cash was falling through 2004, while Starbucks' was increasing. The pattern should have raised concerns about the long-term profit-generating ability of Krispy Kreme. Indeed, in 2005, Krispy Kreme's growth in net income could no longer be sustained and decreased dramatically because the company did not have sufficient cash to maintain profitable operations.

In comparison, Starbucks' upward trend in net income through 2004 showed no signs of slowing. However, that trend would last for only a few more years. Notice that Starbucks' free cash flow began falling in 2006, while net income continued to rise. Again, the difference in trends between net income and free cash flow should have been a warning to investors.

ILLUSTRATION 4–12

Net Income and Free Cash Flow for Krispy Kreme, 1999–2009

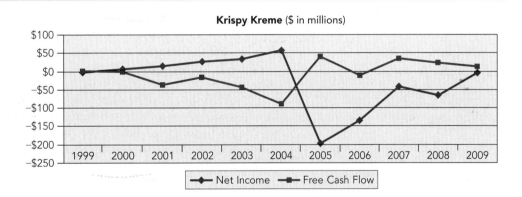

ILLUSTRATION 4–13

Net Income and Free Cash Flow for Starbucks Corporation, 1999–2009

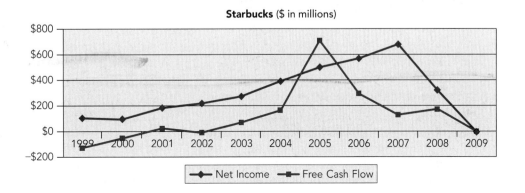

An upward trend in net income cannot be sustained indefinitely without a sufficient supply of cash. As predicted by the falling trend in free cash flow in 2006 and 2007, Starbucks' net income experienced a sharp decline beginning in 2008. These examples demonstrate the predictive ability of comparing a company's trend in net income and free cash flow. **When the trend in net income is upward while the trend in free cash flow is downward, a company is more likely to experience falling profits in the coming years.**

KEY POINT

Companies whose free cash flow is decreasing relative to net income are likely to have lower earnings quality than are other companies, all else being equal.

Question	Accounting information	Analysis	Decision Point
How does free cash flow predict a company's net income?	Net income from the income statement and free cash flow (operating and investing) from the statement of cash flows	When free cash flow and net income have similar trends, net income is more likely to continue that trend in the future.	

KEY POINTS BY LEARNING OBJECTIVE

LO1 Discuss the impact of accounting scandals and the passage of the Sarbanes-Oxley Act.

The accounting scandals in the early 2000s prompted passage of the Sarbanes-Oxley Act (SOX). Among other stipulations, SOX sets forth a variety of new guidelines related to auditor-client relations and additional internal controls. Section 404, in particular, requires company management and auditors to document and assess the effectiveness of a company's internal controls.

LO2 Identify the components, responsibilities, and limitations of internal control.

Internal control refers to a company's plan to improve the accuracy and reliability of accounting information and safeguard the company's assets. Five key components to an internal control system are (1) control environment, (2) risk assessment, (3) control activities, (4) monitoring, and (5) information and communication.

LO3 Define cash and cash equivalents.

Cash includes not only currency, coins, balances in checking accounts, and checks and money orders received from customers, but also cash equivalents, defined as investments that mature within three months (such as money

market funds, Treasury bills, and certificates of deposit).

LO4 Understand controls over cash receipts and cash disbursements.

Because cash is the asset of a company most susceptible to employee fraud, controls over cash receipts and cash disbursements are an important part of a company's overall internal control system. Important controls over cash receipts include segregation of duties for those who handle cash and independent verification of cash receipts. Important controls over cash disbursements include payment by check, credit card, or debit card, segregation of duties, and various authorization and documentation procedures.

LO5 Reconcile a bank statement.

In a bank reconciliation we adjust the *bank's* balance for (1) cash transactions already recorded by the company but not yet recorded by the bank and (2) bank errors. Similarly, we adjust the *company's* balance for (1) cash transactions already recorded by the bank but not yet recorded by the company and (2) company errors. After we adjust both the bank balance and the company balance, the two should equal.

LO6 Account for petty cash.

To pay for minor purchases, companies keep some cash on hand in a petty cash fund. At the end of the period, expenditures from the petty cash fund are recorded, and the fund is replenished.

LO7 Identify the major inflows and outflows of cash.

The statement of cash flows reports all cash activities for the period. *Operating activities* include those transactions and events involving revenues and expenses. *Investing activities* include cash investments in long-term assets

and investment securities. *Financing activities* include transactions designed to finance the business through borrowing and owner investment.

Analysis

LO8 Assess earnings quality by comparing net income and cash flows.

Companies whose free cash flow is decreasing relative to net income are likely to have lower earnings quality than are other companies, all else being equal.

GLOSSARY

Bank reconciliation: Matching the balance of cash in the bank account with the balance of cash in the company's own records. **p. 176**

Cash: Currency, coins, balances in savings and checking accounts, items acceptable for deposit in these accounts (such as checks received from customers), and cash equivalents. **p. 172**

Cash equivalents: Short-term investments that have a maturity date no longer than three months from the date of purchase. **p. 172**

Checks outstanding: Checks the company has written that have not been subtracted from the bank's record of the company's balance. **p. 179**

Collusion: Two or more people acting in coordination to circumvent internal controls. **p. 171**

Deposits outstanding: Cash receipts of the company that have not been added to the bank's record of the company's balance. **p. 179**

Earnings quality: The ability of net income to help predict future performance of the company. **p. 187**

Free cash flow: Operating cash flows plus investing cash flows during the period. **p. 187**

Internal controls: A company's plans to (1) safeguard the company's assets and (2) improve the accuracy and reliability of accounting information. **p. 166**

NSF checks: Checks drawn on nonsufficient funds, or "bad" checks from customers. **p. 179**

Occupational fraud: The use of one's occupation for personal enrichment through the deliberate misuse or misapplication of the employing organization's resources. **p. 166**

Petty cash fund: Small amount of cash kept on hand to pay for minor purchases. **p. 183**

Sarbanes-Oxley Act: Known as the *Public Company Accounting Reform and Investor Protection Act of 2002* and commonly referred to as *SOX*; the act established a variety of new guidelines related to auditor-client relations and internal control procedures. **p. 167**

Separation of duties: Authorizing transactions, recording transactions, and maintaining control of the related assets should be separated among employees. **p. 169**

SELF-STUDY QUESTIONS

■ **LO1**   1. Fraudulent reporting by management could include:
       a. Fictitious revenues from a fake customer.
       b. Improper asset valuation.
       c. Mismatching revenues and expenses.
       d. All of the above.

■ **LO1**   2. The Sarbanes-Oxley Act (SOX) mandates which of the following?
       a. Increased regulations related to auditor-client relations.
       b. Increased regulations related to internal control.
       c. Increased regulations related to corporate executive accountability.
       d. All of the above.

3. What is the concept behind *separation of duties* in establishing internal control?   ■ LO2
   a. Employee fraud is less likely to occur when access to assets and access to accounting records are separated.
   b. The company's financial accountant should not share information with the company's tax accountant.
   c. Duties of middle-level managers of the company should be clearly separated from those of top executives.
   d. The external auditors of the company should have no contact with managers while the audit is taking place.

4. Which of the following is considered cash for financial reporting purposes?   ■ LO3
   a. Accounts receivable.
   b. Investments with maturity dates greater than three months.
   c. Checks received from customers.
   d. Accounts payable.

5. Which of the following generally would *not* be considered good internal control of cash receipts?   ■ LO4
   a. Allowing customers to pay with a debit card.
   b. Requiring the employee receiving the cash from the customer to also deposit the cash into the company's bank account.
   c. Recording cash receipts as soon as they are received.
   d. Allowing customers to pay with a credit card.

6. Which of the following adjusts the bank's balance of cash in a bank reconciliation?   ■ LO5
   a. NSF checks.
   b. Service fees.
   c. An error by the company.
   d. Checks outstanding.

7. Which of the following adjusts the company's balance of cash in a bank reconciliation?   ■ LO5
   a. Interest earned.
   b. Checks outstanding.
   c. Deposits outstanding.
   d. An error by the bank.

8. The purpose of a petty cash fund is to: ■ LO6
   a. Provide a convenient form of payment for the company's customers.
   b. Pay employee salaries at the end of each period.
   c. Provide cash on hand for minor expenditures.
   d. Allow the company to save cash for major future purchases.

9. Operating cash flows would include which of the following?   ■ LO7
   a. Repayment of borrowed money.
   b. Payment for employee salaries.
   c. Services provided to customers on account.
   d. Payment for a new operating center.

10. A company's free cash flow is calculated as: ■ LO8
    a. The amount of cash reporting in the balance sheet.
    b. Net income less investing cash flows.
    c. Operating cash flows plus investing cash flows.
    d. Net income plus operating cash flows.

Note: For answers, see the last page of the chapter.

Check out www.mhhe.com/succeed for more multiple-choice questions.

REVIEW QUESTIONS

■ LO1   1. Define occupational fraud. Describe two common means of occupational fraud.

■ LO1   2. What is internal control? Why should a company establish an internal control system?

■ LO1   3. "Managers are stewards of the company's assets." Discuss what this means.

■ LO1   4. Why are some managers motivated to manipulate amounts reported in the financial statements?

■ LO1   5. What are some of the consequences to employees when managers engage in fraudulent financial reporting?

■ LO1   6. What are some of the major provisions of the Sarbanes-Oxley Act?

■ LO2   7. Briefly describe the five components of internal control outlined by the Committee of Sponsoring Organizations (COSO).

■ LO2   8. Describe the difference between preventive controls and detective controls. What are examples of each?

■ LO2   9. What is meant by separation of duties?

■ LO2   10. Who has responsibility for internal control in an organization? According to guidelines set forth in Section 404 of the Sarbanes-Oxley Act, what role does the auditor play in internal control?

■ LO2   11. What are some limitations of internal control?

■ LO2   12. To what does collusion refer?

■ LO2   13. Is fraud more likely to occur when it is being committed by top-level employees? Explain.

■ LO3   14. Define cash and cash equivalents.

■ LO3   15. Describe how the purchase of items with a check is recorded.

■ LO4   16. Discuss basic controls for cash receipts.

■ LO4   17. What is a credit card? How are credit card sales reported?

■ LO4   18. What is a debit card? How are debit card sales reported?

■ LO4   19. Discuss basic controls for cash disbursements.

■ LO4   20. How are credit card purchases reported?

■ LO5   21. What is a bank reconciliation? How can it help in determining whether proper control of cash has been maintained?

■ LO5   22. What are two primary reasons that the company's balance of cash will differ between its own records and those of the bank?

■ LO5   23. Give some examples of timing differences in cash transactions that firms need to account for in a bank reconciliation.

■ LO5   24. After preparing a bank reconciliation, what adjustments does the company need to make to its records?

■ LO6   25. What is a petty cash fund?

■ LO6   26. Describe how management maintains control over the petty cash fund.

■ LO7   27. The change in cash for the year can be calculated by comparing the balance of cash reported in this year's and last year's balance sheet. Why is the statement of cash flows needed?

■ LO7   28. Describe the operating, investing, and financing sections of the statement of cash flows.

29. How does the relationship between net income and cash flows for the period provide an indication of the quality of earnings?   ■ **LO8**

30. We compared **Krispy Kreme** and **Starbucks** at the end of this chapter. What was the difference between the two companies, and why did that matter?   ■ **LO8**

BRIEF EXERCISES

BE4–1 Match each of the following provisions of the Sarbanes-Oxley Act (SOX) with its description.

Identify terms associated with the Sarbanes-Oxley Act **(LO1)**

Major Provisions of the Sarbanes-Oxley Act

C	1. Oversight board	
a	2. Corporate executive accountability	
d	3. Auditor rotation	
b	4. Nonaudit services	
e	5. Internal control	

Descriptions

a. Executives must personally certify the company's financial statements.

b. Audit firm cannot provide a variety of other services to its client, such as consulting.

c. PCAOB establishes standards related to the preparation of audited financial reports.

d. Lead audit partners are required to change every five years.

e. Management must document the effectiveness of procedures that could affect financial reporting.

BE4–2 Match each of the following components of internal control with its description.

Identify terms associated with components of internal control **(LO2)**

Components of Internal Control

e	1. Control environment e
d	2. Risk assessment d
a	3. Control activities a
c	4. Information and communication
b	5. Monitoring b

Descriptions

a. Procedures for maintaining separation of duties.

b. Routine activities that are meant to continually observe internal control activities.

c. Transfer of data from lower managers to top executives for accurate financial reporting.

d. Formal policies to evaluate internal and external threats to achieving company objectives.

e. Overall attitude of the company with respect to internal controls.

BE4–3 Match each of the following control activities with its definition.

Define control activities associated with internal control **(LO2)**

Control Activities

e	1. Separation of duties
a	2. Physical controls
f	3. Proper authorization
c	4. Employee management
b	5. Reconciliations
d	6. Performance reviews

Definitions

a. The company should maintain security over assets and accounting records.

b. Management should periodically determine whether the amounts of physical assets of the company match the accounting records.

c. The company should provide employees with appropriate guidance to ensure they have the knowledge necessary to carry out their job duties.

d. The actual performance of individuals or processes should be checked against their expected performance.

e. Authorizing transactions, recording transactions, and maintaining control of the related assets should be separated among employees.

f. To prevent improper use of the company's resources, only certain employees are allowed to carry out certain business activities.

Identify cash and cash equivalents (LO3)

BE4–4 Determine whether the firm reports each of the following items as part of cash and cash equivalents in the balance sheet.

Item	Cash or Cash Equivalent? (yes/no)
1. Currency	_____
2. Inventory for sale to customers	_____
3. Balance in savings account	_____
4. Checks	_____
5. Accounts receivable	_____
6. Investments with maturities of less than three months	_____

Determine cash sales (LO4)

BE4–5 During the year, the following sales transactions occur. There is a charge of 3% on all credit card transactions. Calculate total cash sales recorded for the year.
1. Total cash sales = $400,000
2. Total check sales = $250,000
3. Total credit card sales = $500,000

Record cash expenditures (LO4)

BE4–6 Record the following transactions.
1. Pay employee salaries of $500 by issuing checks.
2. Purchase computer equipment of $900 using a credit card.
3. Pay for maintenance of $300 for a company vehicle using a debit card.

Identify terms associated with a bank reconciliation (LO5)

BE4–7 Match each term associated with a bank reconciliation with its description.

Terms		Descriptions
__d__	1. Checks outstanding	a. Cash receipts received by the company but not yet recorded by the bank.
__c__	2. NSF checks	b. Fees imposed by the bank to the company for providing routine services.
__f__	3. Company error	c. Checks written to the company that are returned by the bank as not having adequate funds.
__e__	4. Interest earned	d. Checks written by the company but not yet recorded by the bank.
__a__	5. Deposits outstanding	e. Money earned on the average daily balance of the checking account.
__b__	6. Bank service fees	f. The company recorded a deposit twice.

Prepare a bank reconciliation (LO5)

BE4–8 Indicate whether the firm should add or subtract each item below from its balance of cash or the bank's balance of cash in preparing a bank reconciliation. The first answer is provided as an example.

Reconciliation Items	Bank Balance	Company Balance
1. *Checks outstanding*	*Subtract*	
2. NSF checks		
3. Deposit recorded twice by company		
4. Interest earned		
5. Deposits outstanding		
6. Bank service fees		

BE4–9 Brangelina Adoption Agency's general ledger shows a cash balance of $4,583. The balance of cash in the March-end bank statement is $7,325. The bank statement reveals the following information: checks outstanding of $2,793, bank service fees of $75, and interest earned of $24. Calculate the correct balance of cash at the end of March.

Calculate the correct balance of cash (LO5)

BE4–10 Clooney Corp. establishes a petty cash fund for $200. By the end of the month, employees made the following expenditures from the fund: postage, $50; delivery, $75; supplies expense, $40; entertainment, $20. Record the expenditures from the petty cash fund, and record the entry to replenish the petty cash fund.

Record petty cash expenditures (LO6)

BE4–11 Match each type of cash flow to its definition.

Match types of cash flows with their definitions (LO7)

Types of Cash Flows	Definitions
_____ 1. Operating cash flows	a. Cash flows related to long-term assets and short-term investments.
_____ 2. Investing cash flows	b. Cash flows related to long-term liabilities and stockholders' equity.
_____ 3. Financing cash flows	c. Cash flows related to revenues and expenses.

BE4–12 Eastwood Enterprises offers horseback riding lessons. During the month of June, the company provides lessons on account totaling $4,100. By the end of the month, the company received on account $3,500 of this amount. In addition, Eastwood received $400 on account from customers who were provided lessons in May. Determine the amount of operating cash flows Eastwood will report as received from customers in June.

Determine operating cash flows (LO7)

BE4–13 On January 12, Ferrell Incorporated obtains a permit to start a comedy club, which will operate only on Saturday nights. To prepare the club for the grand opening, Ferrell purchases tables, chairs, ovens, and other related equipment for $55,000 on January 16. Ferrell pays 20% of this amount (= $11,000) in cash at the time of purchase and signs a note with Live Bank for the remaining amount. Determine the amount of investing cash flows Ferrell would report in January.

Determine investing cash flows (LO7)

BE4–14 Smith Law Firm specializes in the preparation of wills for estate planning. On October 1, 2012, the company begins operations by issuing stock for $10,000 and obtaining a loan from a local bank for $25,000. By the end of 2012, the company provides will preparation services of $32,000 cash and pays employee salaries of $23,000. In addition, Smith pays $2,000 in cash dividends to stockholders on December 31, 2012. Determine the amount of financing cash flows Smith would report in 2012.

Determine financing cash flows (LO7)

BE4–15 For each company, calculate free cash flow. Amounts in parentheses represent negative cash flows.

Calculate free cash flow (LO8)

	Operating Cash Flows	Investing Cash Flows	Financing Cash Flows
Tuohy Incorporated	$17,200	$(5,800)	$2,300
Oher Corporation	12,500	6,400	(7,100)

EXERCISES

E4–1 Below are several statements about occupational fraud.
1. For most large companies, occupational fraud is minimal and internal control procedures are unnecessary.
2. Managers have a variety of reasons for manipulating the numbers in financial statements, such as maximizing their compensation, increasing the company's stock price, and preserving their jobs.

Answer true-or-false questions about occupational fraud (LO1)

3. Internal control procedures include formal policies and procedures related to (1) safeguarding the company's assets and (2) improving the accuracy and reliability of accounting information.
4. "Cooking the books" is a phrase used by accountants to indicate the preparation of financial statements that are free of manipulation.
5. Most occupational fraud cases involve misuse of the company's resources.
6. Common types of financial statement fraud include creating fictitious revenues from a fake customer, improperly valuing assets, hiding liabilities, and mismatching revenues and expenses.

Required:

State whether the answer to each of the statements is true or false.

Answer true-or-false questions about the Sarbanes-Oxley Act (LO1)

E4–2 Below are several statements about the Sarbanes-Oxley Act (SOX).
1. SOX represents legislation passed in response to several accounting scandals in the early 2000s.
2. The requirements outlined in SOX apply only to those companies expected to have weak internal controls or to have manipulated financial statements in the past.
3. Section 404 of SOX requires both company management and auditors to document and assess the effectiveness of a company's internal control processes that could affect financial reporting.
4. Severe financial penalties and the possibility of imprisonment are consequences of fraudulent misstatement.
5. With the establishment of SOX, management now has primary responsibility for hiring an external audit firm.
6. The lead auditor in charge of auditing a particular company must rotate off that company only when occupational fraud is suspected.

Required:

State whether the answer to each of the statements is true or false.

Answer true-or-false questions about internal controls (LO2)

E4–3 Below are several statements about internal controls.
1. The components of internal control are built on the foundation of the ethical tone set by top management.
2. Once every three months, managers need to review operations to ensure that control procedures work effectively.
3. Collusion refers to the act of a single individual circumventing internal control procedures.
4. Detective control procedures are designed to detect errors or fraud that have already occurred, while preventive control procedures are designed to keep errors or fraud from occurring in the first place.
5. Fraud committed by top-level employees is more difficult to detect because those employees more often have the ability to override internal control features.
6. A good example of separation of duties would be having one person collect cash from customers and account for it, while having another person order inventory and maintain control over it.
7. Employee tips historically have been the most common means of detecting employee fraud.
8. Detective controls include reconciling the physical assets of the company with the accounting records and comparing actual performance of individuals or processes against their expected performance.
9. Effective internal controls and ethical employees ensure a company's success.

Required:

State whether the answer to each of the statements is true or false.

Determine control activity violations (LO2)

E4–4 Below are several scenarios related to control activities of a company.
1. A manufacturing company compares total sales in the current year to those in the previous year but does not compare the cost of production.

2. So that employees can have easy access to office supplies, a company keeps supplies in unlocked cabinets in multiple locations.
3. At the end of each day, a single employee collects all cash received from customers, records the total, and makes the deposit at the bank.
4. At the end of the year only, the company compares its cash records to the bank's records of cash deposited and withdrawn during the year.
5. A company encourages employees to call an anonymous hotline if they believe other employees are circumventing internal control features.
6. All employees have the authority to refund a customer's money.

Required:

For each scenario, determine which control activity is violated. Control activities include separation of duties, physical controls, proper authorization, employee management, reconciliations, and performance reviews. If no control activity is violated, state "none."

E4–5 Below are several amounts reported at the end of the year.

Currency located at the company	$ 800
Supplies	2,200
Short-term investments that mature within three months	1,700
Accounts receivable	2,500
Balance in savings account	7,500
Checks received from customers but not yet deposited	400
Prepaid rent	1,200
Coins located at the company	100
Equipment	8,400
Balance in checking account	5,200

Calculate the amount of cash to report (LO3)

Required:

Calculate the amount of cash to report in the balance sheet.

E4–6 Douglas and Son, Inc., uses the following process for its cash receipts: The company typically receives cash and check sales each day and places them in a single drawer. Each Friday, the cash clerk records the amount of cash received and deposits the money in the bank account. Each quarter, the controller requests information from the bank necessary to prepare a bank reconciliation.

Discuss internal control procedures related to cash receipts (LO4)

Required:

Discuss Douglas and Son's internal control procedures related to cash receipts, noting both weaknesses and strengths.

E4–7 Goldie and Kate operate a small clothing store that has annual revenues of about $100,000. The company has established the following procedures related to cash disbursements: The petty cash fund consists of $10,000. Employees place a receipt in the fund when making expenditures from it and obtain the necessary cash. For any expenditure not made with the petty cash fund, the employee writes a check. Employees are not required to obtain permission to write a check but are asked to use good judgment. Any check written for more than $5,000 can be signed only by Goldie or Kate.

Discuss internal control procedures related to cash disbursements (LO4)

Required:

Discuss Goldie and Kate's internal control procedures related to cash disbursements, noting both weaknesses and strengths.

E4–8 Janice Dodds opens the mail for Ajax Plumbing Company. She lists all customer checks on a spreadsheet that includes the name of the customer and the check amount. The checks, along with the spreadsheet, are then sent to Jim Seymour in the accounting department, who records the checks and deposits them daily in the company's checking account.

Discuss internal control procedures related to cash receipts (LO4)

Required:

Describe how the company could improve its internal control procedure for the handling of its cash receipts.

Reconcile timing differences in the bank's balance (LO5)

E4–9 Damon Company receives its monthly bank statement, which reports a balance of $1,750. After comparing this to the company's cash records, Damon's accountants determine that deposits outstanding total $3,200 and checks outstanding total $3,450.

Required:

Calculate the reconciled bank balance for cash.

Reconcile timing differences in the company's balance (LO5)

E4–10 Bourne Incorporated reports a cash balance at the end of the month of $2,370. A comparison of the company's cash records with the monthly bank statement reveals several additional cash transactions: bank service fees ($75), an NSF check from a customer ($250), a customer's note receivable collected by the bank ($1,100), and interest earned ($25).

Required:

Calculate the reconciled company balance for cash.

Record adjustments to the company's cash balance (LO5)

E4–11 Refer to the information in E4–10.

Required:

Prepare the necessary entries to adjust the balance of cash.

Calculate the balance of cash using a bank reconciliation (LO5)

E4–12 Spielberg Company's general ledger shows a checking account balance of $22,870 on July 31, 2012. The July cash receipts of $1,785, included in the general ledger balance, are placed in the night depository at the bank on July 31 and processed by the bank on August 1. The bank statement dated July 31 shows bank service fees of $45. The bank processes all checks written by the company by July 31 and lists them on the bank statement, except for one check totaling $1,360. The bank statement shows a balance of $22,400 on July 31.

Required:

Prepare a bank reconciliation to calculate the correct ending balance of cash on July 31, 2012.

Calculate the balance of cash using a bank reconciliation (LO5)

E4–13 On August 31, 2012, the general ledger of The Dean Acting Academy shows a balance for cash of $7,844. Cash receipts yet to be deposited into the checking account total $3,238, and checks written by the academy but not yet processed by the bank total $1,325. The company's balance of cash does not reflect a bank service fee of $25 and interest earned on the checking account of $36. These amounts are included in the balance of cash of $5,942 reported by the bank as of the end of August.

Required:

Prepare a bank reconciliation to calculate the correct ending balance of cash on August 31, 2012.

Record transactions for the petty cash fund (LO6)

E4–14 Halle's Berry Farm establishes a $400 petty cash fund on September 4 to pay for minor cash expenditures. The fund is replenished at the end of each month. At the end of September, the fund contains $70 in cash and the following receipts:

Office party decorations	$ 80
Lawn maintenance	110
Postage	65
Fuel for delivery	75

Required:

Record the establishment of the petty cash fund on September 4, the expenditures made during the month, and the replenishment of the fund on September 30.

E4–15 T. L. Jones Trucking Services establishes a petty cash fund on April 3 for $500. By the end of April, the fund has a cash balance of $72 and has receipts for the following items:

Utilities	$125
Pizza delivery (entertainment)	34
Stamps	49
Plumbing repair services	220

Record transactions for the petty cash fund (LO6)

Required:

Record the establishment of the petty cash fund on April 3, the expenditures made during the month, and the replenishment of the fund on April 30.

E4–16 Below are several transactions for Witherspoon Incorporated, a small manufacturer of decorative glass designs.

Classify cash flows (LO7)

Transaction	Cash Involved? (yes or no)	Operating, Investing, or Financing? (if cash involved)	Inflow or Outflow?
a. Borrow cash from the bank.	Yes	Financing	Inflow
b. Purchase supplies on account.	No	In	Inflow
c. Purchase equipment with cash.	Yes	Investing	out
d. Provide services on account.	No		
e. Pay cash on account for *b.* above.	Yes	O	out
f. Sell for cash a warehouse no longer in use.	Yes	Investing	in
g. Receive cash on account for *d.* above.	Yes	O	in
h. Pay cash to workers for salaries.	Yes	O	out

Required:

For each transaction, indicate (1) whether cash is involved (yes or no), and, if cash is involved, (2) whether Witherspoon should classify it as operating, investing, or financing in a statement of cash flows, and (3) whether the cash is an inflow or outflow.

E4–17 Below are several transactions for Meyers Corporation for 2012.

Calculate net cash flows (LO7)

Transaction	Inflow or Outflow of Cash?	Operating, Investing, or Financing?
a. Issue common stock for cash, $50,000.		
b. Purchase building and land with cash, $35,000.		
c. Provide services to customers on account, $7,000.		
d. Pay utilities on building, $1,000.		
e. Collect $5,000 on account from customers.		
f. Pay employee salaries, $9,000.		
g. Pay dividends to stockholders, $4,000.		
Net cash flows for the year		

Required:

1. For each transaction, determine the amount of the inflow or outflow of cash (indicate inflows with a "+" and outflows with a "−"). If cash is involved in the transaction, indicate whether Meyers should classify it as operating, investing, or financing in a statement of cash flows.
2. Calculate net cash flows for the year.

3. Assuming the balance of cash on January 1, 2012, equals $4,400, calculate the balance of cash on December 31, 2012.

Calculate operating cash flows (LO7)

E4–18 Below are cash transactions for Goldman Incorporated, which provides consulting services related to mining of precious metals.
a. Cash used for purchase of office supplies, $1,900.
b. Cash provided from consulting to customers, $45,600.
c. Cash used for purchase of mining equipment, $73,000.
d. Cash provided from long-term borrowing, $60,000.
e. Cash used for payment of employee salaries, $24,000.
f. Cash used for payment of office rent, $12,000.
g. Cash provided from sale of equipment purchased in *c*. above, $22,500.
h. Cash used to repay a portion of the long-term borrowing in *d*. above, $40,000.
i. Cash used to pay office utilities, $4,300.
j. Purchase of company vehicle, paying $10,000 cash and borrowing $15,000.

Required:
Calculate cash flows from operating activities.

Calculate investing cash flows (LO7)

E4–19 Refer to the information in E4–18.

Required:
Calculate cash flows from investing activities.

Calculate financing cash flows (LO7)

E4–20 Refer to the information in E4–18.

Required:
Calculate cash flows from financing activities.

Determine earnings quality (LO8)

E4–21 Below are amounts (in millions) for Glasco Company and Sullivan Company.

	GLASCO COMPANY		**SULLIVAN COMPANY**	
Year	Net Income	Free Cash Flow	Net Income	Free Cash Flow
1	$350	$420	$250	$300
4	470	630	330	210

Required:
Referring to the relation between net income and free cash flow, discuss each company's quality of earnings. Make a prediction as to which firm will have the larger increase in net income in year 5.

For additional exercises, visit www.mhhe.com/succeed for Exercises: Set B.

PROBLEMS: SET A

Discuss control procedures for cash receipts (LO4)

P4–1A The Carmike 8 Cinema is a modern theatre located close to a college campus. The cashier, located in a box office at the entrance to the theatre, receives cash from customers and operates a machine that ejects serially numbered tickets for each film. Customers then enter the theatre lobby where they can purchase refreshments at the concession stand. To gain admission to the movie, a customer hands the ticket to a ticket taker stationed some 50 feet from the box office at the entrance to the theatre lobby. The ticket taker tears the ticket in half, returns the stub to the customer, and

allows the customer to enter the theatre hallway through a turnstile. The ticket taker drops the other half of the ticket stub into a locked box.

Required:
1. What internal controls are present in the handling of cash receipts?
2. What steps should the theatre manager take regularly to give maximum effectiveness to these controls?
3. Assume the cashier and the ticket taker decide to work together in an effort to steal from the movie theatre. What action(s) might they take?
4. For each idea proposed in number 3 above, what additional control features could Carmike 8 Cinema add to catch the thieves and reduce the risk of future thefts?

P4–2A Oscar's Red Carpet Store maintains a checking account with Academy Bank. Oscar's sells carpet each day but makes bank deposits only once per week. The following provides information from the company's cash ledger for the month ending February 28, 2012.

Prepare the bank reconciliation and record cash adjustments **(LO5)**

	Date	Amount		No.	Date	Amount
Deposits:	2/4	$ 2,200	Checks:	321	2/2	$ 4,200
	2/11	1,800		322	2/8	500
	2/18	2,700		323	2/12	2,000
	2/25	3,600		324	2/19	1,700
Cash receipts:	2/26–2/28	1,100		325	2/27	300
		$11,400		326	2/28	800
				327	2/28	1,400
						$10,900

Balance on February 1	$ 6,300
Receipts	11,400
Disbursements	(10,900)
Balance on February 28	$ 6,800

Information from February's bank statement and company records reveals the following additional information:
a. The ending cash balance recorded in the bank statement is $10,350.
b. Cash receipts of $1,100 from 2/26–2/28 are outstanding.
c. Checks 325 and 327 are outstanding.
d. The deposit on 2/11 includes a customer's check for $300 that did not clear the bank (NSF check).
e. Check 323 was written for $2,800 for advertising in February. The bank properly recorded the check for this amount.
f. An automatic withdrawal for Oscar's February rent was made on February 4 for $1,200.
g. Oscar's checking account earns interest based on the average daily balance. The amount of interest earned for February is $150.
h. In January, one of Oscar's suppliers, Titanic Fabrics, borrowed $5,000 from Oscar. On February 24, Titanic paid $5,200 ($5,000 borrowed amount plus $200 interest) directly to Academy Bank in payment for January's borrowing.
i. Academy Bank charged the following service fees to Oscar's: $50 for NSF check, $10 for automatic withdrawal for rent payment, and $40 for collection of the loan amount from Titanic.

Required:
1. Prepare a bank reconciliation for Oscar's checking account on February 28, 2012.
2. Record the necessary cash adjustments.

Prepare the bank reconciliation and record cash adjustments (LO5)

P4–3A The cash records and bank statement for the month of May for Diaz Entertainment are shown below.

DIAZ ENTERTAINMENT
Cash Account Records
May 1, 2012, to May 31, 2012

Cash Balance May 1, 2012	+	Deposits	−	Checks	=	Cash Balance May 31, 2012
$5,380		$11,540		$11,620		$5,300

	Deposits				Checks		
Date	Desc.	Amount	Date	No.	Desc.		Amount
5/3	Sales	$ 1,360	5/7	471	Legal fees		$ 1,200
5/10	Sales	1,790	5/12	472	Property tax		1,570
5/17	Sales	2,420	5/15	473	Salaries		3,500
5/24	Sales	2,890	5/22	474	Advertising		1,400
5/31	Sales	3,080	5/30	475	Supplies		450
			5/31	476	Salaries		3,500
		$11,540					$11,620

P.O. Box 162647
Bowlegs, OK 74830
(405) 369-CASH

Midwest Bank
Looking Out For You

Member FDIC

Account Holder:	Diaz Entertainment 124 Saddle Blvd. Bowlegs, OK 74830	Account Number:	7772854360
		Statement Date:	May 31, 2012

Beginning Balance May 1, 2012	Deposits and Credits		Withdrawals and Debits		Ending Balance May 31, 2012
	No.	Total	No.	Total	
$6,160	7	$9,530	9	$9,290	$6,400

Deposits and Credits			Withdrawals and Debits				Daily Balance	
Date	Amount	Desc.	Date	No.	Amount	Desc.	Date	Amount
5/4	$1,360	DEP	5/1	469	$ 450	CHK	5/1	$5,710
5/11	1,790	DEP	5/2	470	330	CHK	5/2	5,380
5/18	2,420	DEP	5/9	471	1,200	CHK	5/4	6,740
5/20	1,000	NOTE	5/11		300	NSF	5/9	5,540
5/20	50	INT	5/12	472	1,570	CHK	5/11	7,030
5/25	2,890	DEP	5/18	473	3,500	CHK	5/12	5,460
5/31	20	INT	5/20		500	EFT	5/18	4,380
			5/25	474	1,400	CHK	5/20	4,930
			5/31		40	SF	5/25	6,420
	$9,530				$9,290		5/31	$6,400

Desc.	**DEP** Customer deposit	**INT** Interest earned	**SF** Service fees
	NOTE Note collected	**CHK** Customer check	**NSF** Nonsufficient funds
	EFT Electronic funds transfer		

Additional information:

a. The difference in the beginning balances in the company's records and the bank statement relates to checks #469 and #470, which are outstanding as of April 30, 2012.

b. The bank made the EFT on May 20 in error. The bank accidentally charged Diaz for payment that should have been made on another account.

Required:
1. Prepare a bank reconciliation for Diaz's checking account on May 31, 2012.
2. Record the necessary cash adjustments.

P4–4A Below is a summary of all transactions of Pixar Toy Manufacturing for the month of August 2012.

Prepare the statement of cash flows **(LO7)**

Cash Transactions	
Cash collections from:	
Customers	$ 92,500
Sale of unused warehouse	35,000
Bank borrowing	25,000
Cash payments for:	
Employee salaries	(64,300)
Office rent	(18,000)
Manufacturing equipment	(44,000)
Office utilities	(10,800)
Dividends to stockholders	(4,700)
Materials to make toys	(26,700)
Noncash Transactions	
Sales to customers on account	15,400
Purchase of materials on account	12,900
Purchase equipment with promissory note to pay later	17,500

Required:
Prepare a statement of cash flows for the month of August 2012, properly classifying each of the transactions into operating, investing, and financing activities. The cash balance at the beginning of August is $24,500.

P4–5A Rocky owns and operates Balboa's Gym located in Philadelphia. The following transactions occur for the month of October:

Record transactions, post to the Cash T-account, and prepare the statement of cash flows **(LO7)**

October 2	Receive membership dues for the month of October totaling $7,500.
October 5	Issue common stock in exchange for cash, $10,000.
October 9	Purchase additional boxing equipment for $8,600, paying one-half of the amount in cash and the other one-half due by the end of the year.
October 12	Pay $1,000 for advertising regarding a special membership rate available during the month of October.
October 19	Pay dividends to stockholders, $3,400.
October 22	Pay liability insurance to cover accidents to members for the next six months, starting November 1, $6,000.
October 25	Receive cash in advance for November memberships, $4,600.
October 30	Receive, but do not pay, utilities bill for the month, $4,200.
October 31	Pay employees' salaries for the month, $6,300.

Required:
1. Record each transaction.
2. Identify the transactions involving cash.
3. Assuming the balance of cash at the beginning of October is $15,600, post each cash transaction to the Cash T-account and compute the ending cash balance.
4. Prepare a statement of cash flows for the month of October, properly classifying each of the cash transactions into operating, investing, and financing activities.
5. Verify that the net cash flows reported in the statement of cash flows equal the change in the cash balance for the month.

PROBLEMS: SET B

Mc Graw Hill **connect**
|ACCOUNTING

Prepare a bank reconciliation and discuss cash procedures (LO4, 5)

P4–1B At the end of February, Howard Productions' accounting records reveal a balance for cash equal to $19,175. However, the balance of cash in the bank at the end of February is only $2,235. Howard is concerned and asks the company's accountant to reconcile the two balances. Examination of the bank statement and company records at the end of February reveals the following information:

NSF checks	$5,228	Service fees	$149
Deposits outstanding	7,642	Checks outstanding	479

In addition, during February the company's accountant wrote a check to one of its suppliers for $100. The check was recorded correctly in the company's records for $100 but processed incorrectly by the bank for $1,000. Howard has contacted the bank, which has agreed to fix the error. Finally, a petty cash fund of $3,500 was established during February. This amount was withdrawn from the checking account but not recorded.

Required:
1. Calculate the correct ending balance of cash at the end of February.
2. Discuss any problems you see with the company's cash procedures.

Prepare the bank reconciliation and record cash adjustments (LO5)

P4–2B On October 31, 2012, the bank statement for the checking account of Blockwood Video shows a balance of $12,630, while the company's records show a balance of $12,331. Information that might be useful in preparing a bank reconciliation is as follows:

a. Outstanding checks are $1,230.

b. The October 31 cash receipts of $785 are not deposited in the bank until November 2.

c. One check written in payment of utilities for $137 is correctly recorded by the bank but is recorded by Blockwood as a disbursement of $173.

d. In accordance with prior authorization, the bank withdraws $650 directly from the checking account as payment on a note payable. The interest portion of that payment is $50 and the principal portion is $600. Blockwood has not recorded the direct withdrawal.

e. Bank service fees of $24 are listed on the bank statement.

f. A deposit of $567 is recorded by the bank on October 13, but it did not belong to Blockwood. The deposit should have been made to the checking account of Hollybuster Video, a separate company.

g. The bank statement includes a charge of $75 for an NSF check. The check is returned with the bank statement, and the company will seek payment from the customer.

Required:
1. Prepare a bank reconciliation for the Blockwood checking account on October 31, 2012.
2. Record the necessary cash adjustments.

Prepare the bank reconciliation and record cash adjustments (LO5)

P4–3B The cash records and bank statement for the month of July for Glover Incorporated are shown below.

GLOVER INCORPORATED
Cash Account Records
July 1, 2012, to July 31, 2012

Cash Balance July 1, 2012	+	Deposits	−	Checks	=	Cash Balance July 31, 2012
$7,110		$8,420		$9,160		$6,370

Deposits				Checks			
Date	Desc.	Amount	Date	No.	Desc.	Amount
7/9	Sales	$2,560	7/7	531	Rent	$1,500
7/21	Sales	3,140	7/12	532	Salaries	1,960
7/31	Sales	2,720	7/19	533	Equipment	3,500
			7/22	534	Utilities	900
			7/30	535	Advertising	1,300
		$8,420				$9,160

P.O. Box 123878 **Fidelity Union** Member FDIC
Gotebo, OK 73041 *You Can Bank On Us*
(580) 377-OKIE

Account Holder:	Glover Incorporated	Account Number:	2252790471
	519 Main Street		
	Gotebo, OK 73041	Statement Date:	July 31, 2012

| Beginning Balance | Deposits and Credits | | Withdrawals and Debits | | Ending Balance |
July 1, 2012	No.	Total	No.	Total	July 31, 2012
$7,700	3	$5,750	7	$8,800	$4,650

Deposits and Credits			Withdrawals and Debits				Daily Balance	
Date	Amount	Desc.	Date	No.	Amount	Desc.	Date	Amount
7/10	$2,560	DEP	7/2	530	$ 590	CHK	7/2	$7,110
7/22	3,140	DEP	7/10	531	1,500	CHK	7/10	8,170
7/31	50	INT	7/14	532	1,960	CHK	7/14	6,210
			7/18		400	NSF	7/18	5,810
			7/22	533	3,800	CHK	7/22	5,150
			7/26		500	EFT	7/26	4,650
			7/30		50	SF	7/30	4,600
	$5,750				$8,800		7/31	$4,650

Desc.	**DEP** Customer deposit	**INT** Interest earned	**SF** Service fees
	NOTE Note collected	**CHK** Customer check	**NSF** Nonsufficient funds
	EFT Electronic funds transfer		

Additional information:

a. The difference in the beginning balances in the company's records and the bank statement relates to check #530, which is outstanding as of June 30, 2012.

b. Check #533 is correctly processed by the bank.

c. The EFT on July 26 relates to the purchase of office supplies.

Required:

1. Prepare a bank reconciliation for Glover's checking account on July 31, 2012.
2. Record the necessary cash adjustments.

P4–4B Below is a summary of all transactions of Dreamworks Bedding Supplies for the month of August 2012.

Prepare the statement of cash flows (LO7)

Cash Transactions

Cash collections from:	
Customers	$ 85,400
Sale of unused land	14,700
Issuance of common stock	20,000
Interest earned on savings account	200
Cash payments for:	
Employee salaries	(46,100)
Delivery truck	(32,500)
Advertising expense	(4,900)
Office supplies	(2,800)
Repayment of borrowing	(8,000)
Bedding material	(16,200)

Noncash Transactions

Sales to customers on account	11,300
Purchase of materials on account	7,400
Exchange common stock for building	82,000

Required:

Prepare a statement of cash flows for the month of August, properly classifying each of the transactions into operating, investing, and financing activities. The cash balance at the beginning of August is $7,300.

Record transactions, post to the Cash T-account, and prepare the statement of cash flows (LO 7)

P4–5B Peter loves dogs and cats. For the past several years, he has owned and operated Homeward Bound, which temporarily houses pets while their owners go on vacation. For the month of June, the company has the following transactions:

June	2	Obtain cash by borrowing $20,000 from the bank by signing a note.
June	3	Pay rent for the current month, $1,000.
June	7	Provide services to customers, $4,200 for cash and $2,500 on account.
June	11	Purchase cages and equipment necessary to maintain the animals, $7,400 cash.
June	17	Pay employees' salaries for the first half of the month, $5,500.
June	22	Pay dividends to stockholders, $1,300.
June	25	Receive cash in advance from a customer who wants to house his two dogs (Chance and Shadow) and cat (Sassy) while he goes on vacation the month of July, $1,600.
June	28	Pay utilities for the month, $2,300.
June	30	Record salaries earned by employees for the second half of the month, $5,500. Payment will be made on July 2.

Required:

1. Record each transaction.
2. Identify the transactions involving cash.
3. Assuming the balance of cash at the beginning of June is $13,700, post each cash transaction to the Cash T-account and compute the ending cash balance.
4. Prepare a statement of cash flows for the month of June, properly classifying each of the cash transactions into operating, investing, and financing activities.
5. Verify that the net cash flows reported in the statement of cash flows equal the change in the cash balance for the month.

*For additional problems, visit **www.mhhe.com/succeed** for Problems: Set C.*

ADDITIONAL PERSPECTIVES

Continuing Problem

Great Adventures

(This is a continuation of the Great Adventures problem from earlier chapters.)

AP4–1 An examination of the cash activities during the year shows the following.

GREAT ADVENTURES
Cash Account Records
July 1, 2012, to December 31, 2012

	Deposits			Checks/Debit Cards		
Date	Desc.	Amount	Date	No.	Desc.	Amount
7/1	Stock sale	$ 20,000	7/1	101	Insurance	$ 4,800
7/15	Clinic receipts	2,000	7/2	102	Legal fees	1,500
7/22	Clinic receipts	2,300	7/7	DC	Advertising	300
7/30	Clinic receipts	4,000	7/8	103	Bikes	12,000
8/1	Borrowing	30,000	7/24	DC	Advertising	700
8/10	Clinic receipts	3,000	8/4	104	Kayaks	28,000

(continued)

(concluded)

Deposits			Checks/Debit Cards			
Date	Desc.	Amount	Date	No.	Desc.	Amount
8/17	Clinic receipts	10,500	8/24	DC	Office supplies	1,800
9/21	Clinic receipts	13,200	9/1	105	Rent	2,400
10/17	Clinic receipts	17,900	12/8	106	Race permit	1,200
12/15	Race receipts	20,000	12/16	107	Salary	2,000
			12/31	108	Dividend	2,000
			12/31	109	Dividend	2,000
		$122,900				$58,700

SUMMARY OF TRANSACTIONS

Beginning Cash Balance July 1, 2012	+	Deposits	−	Checks	=	Ending Cash Balance December 31, 2012
$0		$122,900		$58,700		$64,200

Suzie has not reconciled the company's cash balance with that of the bank since the company was started. She asks Summit Bank to provide her with a six-month bank statement. To save time, Suzie makes deposits at the bank only on the first day of each month.

Summit Bank
Leading You to the Top

Member FDIC

Account Holder: Great Adventures, Inc.

Account Number: 1124537774

Statement Date: Dec. 31, 2012

Account Summary

Beginning Balance July 1, 2012	Deposits and Credits		Withdrawals and Debits		Ending Balance December 31, 2012
	No.	Total	No.	Total	
$0	8	$103,400	11	$52,900	$50,500

Account Details

Deposits and Credits			Withdrawals and Debits				Daily Balance	
Date	Amount	Desc.	Date	No.	Amount	Desc.	Date	Amount
7/1	$ 20,000	DEP	7/1	101	$ 4,800	CHK	7/1	$15,200
8/1	8,300	DEP	7/7	102	1,500	CHK	7/7	13,400
8/1	30,000	DEP	7/7		300	DC	7/14	1,400
9/1	13,500	DEP	7/14	103	12,000	CHK	7/24	700
9/30	200	INT	7/24		700	DC	8/1	39,000
10/1	13,200	DEP	8/9	104	28,000	CHK	8/9	11,000
11/1	17,900	DEP	8/24		1,800	DC	8/24	9,200
12/31	300	INT	9/2	105	2,400	CHK	9/1	22,700
			9/30		100	SF	9/2	20,300
			12/10	106	1,200	CHK	9/30	20,400
			12/31		100	SF	10/1	33,600
							11/1	51,500
							12/10	50,300
	$103,400				$52,900		12/31	$50,500

Desc.	DEP Customer deposit	INT Interest earned	SF Service fees
	CHK Customer check	DC Debit card	

After comparing the two balances, Suzie has some concern because the bank's balance of $50,500 is substantially less than the company's balance of $64,200.

Required:

1. Discuss any problems you see with Great Adventures' internal control procedures related to cash.
2. Prepare Great Adventures' bank reconciliation for the six-month period ended December 31, 2012, and any necessary entries to adjust cash.
3. How did failure to reconcile the bank statement affect the reported amounts for assets, liabilities, stockholders' equity, revenues, and expenses?

Financial Analysis

American Eagle Outfitters, Inc.

AP4–2 Financial information for American Eagle  is presented in Appendix A at the end of the book.

Required:

1. What does the Report of Independent Registered Public Accounting Firm indicate about American Eagle's internal controls?
2. In the summary of significant accounting policies, how does American Eagle define cash equivalents?
3. What is the amount of cash reported in the two most recent years? By how much has cash increased/decreased?
4. Determine the amounts American Eagle reports for net cash flows from operating activities, investing activities, and financing activities in its statement of cash flows for the most recent year. What are total cash flows for the year?
5. Compare your answers in question 4 to the increase/decrease you calculated in question 3. (Note: Include any effect of exchange rates on cash as an additional cash flow in question 4.)
6. What does American Eagle's trend in net income versus free cash flows over the three most recent years suggest about the company's earnings quality?

Financial Analysis

Buckle ⊖

The Buckle, Inc.

AP4–3 Financial information for **The Buckle** is presented in Appendix B at the end of the book.

Required:

1. What does the Report of Independent Registered Public Accounting Firm indicate about The Buckle's internal controls?
2. In the summary of significant accounting policies, how does The Buckle define cash equivalents?
3. What is the amount of cash reported in the two most recent years? By how much has cash increased/decreased?
4. Determine the amounts The Buckle reports for net cash flows from operating activities, investing activities, and financing activities in its statement of cash flows for the most recent year. What are total cash flows for the year?
5. Compare your answers in question 4 to the increase/decrease you calculated in question 3. (Note: Include any effect of exchange rates on cash as an additional cash flow in question 4.)
6. What does The Buckle's trend in net income versus free cash flows over the three most recent years suggest about the company's earnings quality?

American Eagle Outfitters, Inc., vs. The Buckle, Inc.

Comparative Analysis

AP4–4 Financial information for **American Eagle** is presented in Appendix A at the end of the book, and financial information for **The Buckle** is presented in Appendix B at the end of the book.

Required:

1. Which company has a greater amount of cash relative to total assets? What might this mean about the two companies' potential growth opportunities?
2. Based on the trend in net income versus free cash flows over the three most recent years, which company would you predict to have a greater percentage increase in net income in the following year? Why?

Ethics

AP4–5 Between his freshman and sophomore years of college, Jack takes a job as ticket collector at a local movie theatre. Moviegoers purchase a ticket from a separate employee outside the theatre and then enter through a single set of doors. Jack takes half their ticket, and they proceed to the movie of their choice.

Besides trying to earn enough money for college the next year, Jack loves to watch movies. One of the perks of working for the movie theatre is that all employees are allowed to watch one free movie per day. However, in the employee handbook it states that friends and family of employees are not allowed to watch free movies. In addition, employees must pay full price for all concession items.

Soon after starting work at the theatre, Jack notices that most other employees regularly bring their friends and family to the movie without purchasing a ticket. When Jack stops them at the door to ask for their ticket, they say, "Jack, no one really follows that policy. Just be cool and let us in. You can do the same." Jack even notices that upper management does not follow the policy of no family and friends watching free movies. Furthermore, employees commonly bring their own cups to get free soft drinks and their own containers to eat free popcorn.

Jack considers whether he should also start bringing friends and family and enjoying the free popcorn and beverages. He reasons, "Why should I be the only one following the rules? If everyone else is doing it, including upper management, what harm would it be for me to do it too? After all, when you watch a movie you aren't really stealing anything, and popcorn and drinks cost hardly anything. Plus, I really need to save for college."

Required:

Discuss the ethical dilemma Jack faces.

Internet Research

AP4–6 Financial accounting information can often be found at financial websites. These websites are useful for collecting information about a company's stock price, analysts' forecasts, dividend history, historical financial accounting information, and much more. One such site is Yahoo! Finance (*finance.yahoo.com*).

Required:

1. Visit Yahoo! Finance and get a stock quote for **Google**. To do this, type "GOOG" in the "Get Quotes" box. Under "Financials" click on the "Cash Flow" link. Calculate Google's free cash flows for the three most recent years.
2. Calculate **IBM**'s free cash flows in the same way by typing "IBM" in the "Get Quotes" box.

3. Compare the trends in free cash flows between the companies. What would explain differences between these two companies' free cash flows?

4. Click on "Historical Prices" and compare the trend in these companies' stock prices over the same three-year period used to calculate free cash flows.

Written Communication

AP4–7 Consider the following independent situations:

1. John Smith is the petty-cash custodian. John approves all requests for payment out of the $200 fund, which is replenished at the end of each month. At the end of each month, John submits a list of all accounts and amounts to be charged, and a check is written to him for the total amount. John is the only person ever to tally the fund.

2. All of the company's cash disbursements are made by check. Each check must be supported by an approved voucher, which is in turn supported by the appropriate invoice and, for purchases, a receiving document. The vouchers are approved by Dean Leiser, the chief accountant, after reviewing the supporting documentation. Betty Hanson prepares the checks for Leiser's signature. Leiser also maintains the company's check register (the cash disbursements journal) and reconciles the bank account at the end of each month.

3. Fran Jones opens the company's mail and lists all checks and cash received from customers. A copy of the list is sent to Jerry McDonald who maintains the general ledger accounts. Fran prepares and makes the daily deposit at the bank. Fran also maintains the subsidiary ledger for accounts receivable, which is used to generate monthly statements to customers.

Required:

Write a memo to your instructor indicating the apparent internal control weaknesses and suggest alternative procedures to eliminate the weaknesses.

Answers to the Self-Study Questions

1. d   2. d   3. a   4. c   5. b   6. d   7. a   8. c   9. b   10. c

Receivables and Sales

Learning Objectives

AFTER STUDYING THIS CHAPTER, YOU SHOULD BE ABLE TO:

- ■ **LO1** Recognize accounts receivable.
- ■ **LO2** Calculate net revenues using discounts, returns, and allowances.
- ■ **LO3** Record an allowance for future uncollectible accounts.
- ■ **LO4** Apply the procedure to write off accounts receivable as uncollectible.
- ■ **LO5** Use the aging method to estimate future uncollectible accounts.
- ■ **LO6** Contrast the allowance method and direct write-off method when accounting for uncollectible accounts.
- ■ **LO7** Apply the procedure to account for notes receivable, including interest calculation.

Analysis

- ■ **LO8** Calculate key ratios investors use to monitor a company's effectiveness in managing receivables.

Appendix

- ■ **LO9** Estimate uncollectible accounts using the percentage-of-credit-sales method.

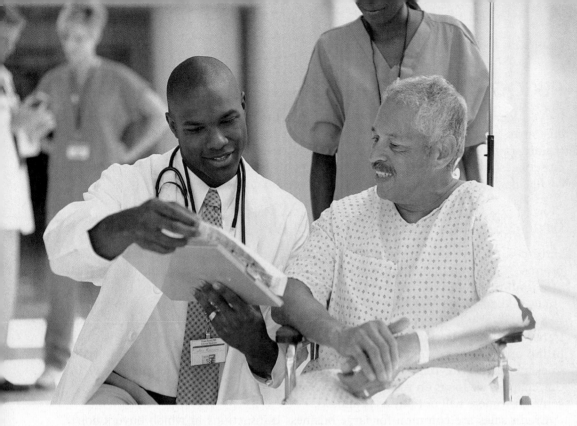

TENET HEALTHCARE: BAD DEBTS CAUSE PAIN TO INVESTORS

Tenet Healthcare Corporation is one of the largest hospital chains in the United States. The company operates 50 hospitals in 12 states, employs over 57,000 people, admits more than 500,000 patients, and has nearly 4,000,000 outpatient visits each year. For the period 2007–2009, the company reported net operating revenues of $26 billion. Everything seems fine, right?

Wrong. Over this same period, Tenet reported profits of only $145 million. That's a profit of only one-half of a penny for every dollar of revenue. One of the reasons for Tenet's poor operating performance was the cost of "uncompensated care." Uncompensated care occurs when patients receive services but are either unwilling or unable to pay. Though hospitals try to minimize these costs, federal law requires that patients not be denied emergency treatment due to inability to pay. Uncompensated care is a problem for the entire health-care industry.

Tenet reports uncompensated care in three ways: (1) as charity care, (2) as discounted services, and (3) as provisions for bad debts. For patients who are financially unable to pay for their health-care services, Tenet does not pursue collection of amounts that qualify as charity care. Also, it offers discounted services to patients who have no insurance or are underinsured. The company instituted a program of discounted services to reduce the reported amounts of bad debts. Bad debts occur when customers have been billed but never pay, and the company decides to recognize that fact in its accounting records. In reality, the three types of uncompensated care are difficult to separate, and all have a negative economic impact on the company's operations.

Over the period 2007–2009, Tenet reported the following amounts (in millions) for each of these categories of uncompensated care:

Year	Charity Care	Discounted Services	Provision for Bad Debts	Total
2007	$121	$ 342	$ 555	$1,018
2008	113	359	628	1,100
2009	118	365	697	1,180
Total	$352	$1,066	$1,880	$3,298

Tenet's profits would have been dramatically higher without the cost of more than $3 billion in uncompensated care. Tenet states in its annual report, ". . . unless our business mix shifts toward a greater number of insured patients or the trend of higher co-payments and deductibles reverses, we anticipate this high level of uncollectible accounts to continue." In 2010, health-care industry troubles, such as Tenet's, sparked a heated national debate over the need for health-care reform in the United States.

PART A

RECOGNIZING ACCOUNTS RECEIVABLE

As you learned in Chapter 2, companies sometimes provide goods or services to customers, not for cash, but on account. Formally, accounts receivable represent the amount of cash owed to a company by its customers from the sale of products or services on account. To understand accounts receivable, we need to start with *credit sales*, from which accounts receivable originate.

Credit Sales and Accounts Receivable

■ **LO1**
Recognize accounts receivable.

Have you ever sold a product or service to someone and accepted that person's promise to pay you in the future? For example, did you ever sell a candy bar as part of a fund-raiser and have the person promise to pay you later? If so, you made a credit sale. Credit sales transfer products and services to a customer today while bearing the risk of collecting payment from that customer in the future. Credit sales transactions are also known as *sales on account* or *services on account*. As we saw in the opening story, Tenet Healthcare provides a considerable number of credit sales for health care–related services, but many of its credit customers never pay. In this chapter, we focus on recording credit sales and dealing with the likelihood that some customers will not pay as promised.

Credit sales are common for large business transactions in which buyers don't have sufficient cash available or in which credit cards cannot be used because the transaction amount exceeds typical credit card limits. They typically include an informal credit agreement supported by an invoice and require payment within 30 to 60 days after the sale. **Even though the seller does not receive cash at the time of the credit sale, the firm records revenue immediately, as long as future collection from the customer is reasonably certain.**

Along with the recognized revenue, at the time of sale the seller also obtains a legal right to receive cash from the buyer. **The legal right to *receive* cash is valuable and represents an asset of the company.** This asset is referred to as accounts receivable (sometimes called *trade receivables*), and the firm records it at the time of a credit sale.

To see how companies record credit sales, consider an example. Suppose Link's Dental charges $500 for teeth whitening. Dee Kay decides to have her teeth whitened on March 1 but doesn't pay cash at the time of service. She promises to pay the $500 whitening fee to Link by March 31. Link's Dental records the following at the time of the whitening.

A = L + SE	March 1	Debit	Credit
+500	**Accounts Receivable**	500	
+500 Rev↑	**Service Revenue**		500
	(*Provide services on account*)		

Notice that instead of debiting Cash, as in a cash sale, Link's Dental debits another asset—Accounts Receivable—for the credit sale.

 KEY POINT

Companies record an asset (accounts receivable) and revenue when they sell products and services to their customers on account, expecting payment in the future.

As you study receivables, realize that one company's right to *collect* cash corresponds to another company's (or individual's) obligation to *pay* cash. One company's

account receivable is the flip side of another company's account payable. In Chapter 6 we discuss accounts payable in the context of inventory purchases on account. In Chapter 8 we again discuss accounts payable, but in the context of current liabilities.

Flip Side

OTHER TYPES OF RECEIVABLES

Other types of receivables are less common than accounts receivable. *Nontrade receivables* are receivables that originate from sources other than customers. They include tax refund claims, interest receivable, and loans by the company to other entities, including stockholders and employees. When receivables are accompanied by formal credit arrangements made with written debt instruments (or notes), we refer to them as *notes receivable*. We'll consider notes receivable later in this chapter.

Net Revenues

From time to time, companies offer discounts to customers. These discounts offer ways to quickly sell old inventory, attract new customers, reward long-term loyal customers, and encourage customers to pay quickly on their accounts. However, while these discounts may be beneficial to the company's long-term success, they can reduce the amount of revenue reported in the current period. In addition, the company's revenues are reduced when customers return unsatisfactory products or demand allowances for inferior services. Therefore, it is important for managers to consider not only their companies' total revenues, but also net revenues. Net revenues refer to a company's total revenues less any amounts for discounts, returns, and allowances. We discuss these items next.

■ **LO2**
Calculate net revenues using discounts, returns, and allowances.

TRADE DISCOUNTS

Trade discounts represent a reduction in the listed price of a product or service. Companies typically use trade discounts to provide incentives to larger customers or consumer groups to purchase from the company. Trade discounts also can be a way to change prices without publishing a new price list or to disguise real prices from competitors.

When recording a transaction, companies don't recognize trade discounts *directly*. Instead, they recognize trade discounts *indirectly* by recording the sale at the discounted price. For example, let's go back to Link's Dental, which typically charges $500 for teeth whitening. Assume that in order to entice more customers, Dr. Link offers a 20% discount on teeth whitening to any of his regular patients. Since Dee Kay is one of Dr. Link's regular patients, she can take advantage of the special discount and have her teeth whitened for only $400.

March 1	Debit	Credit
Accounts Receivable	400	
Service Revenue		400
(Make credit sale of $500 with a 20% trade discount)		

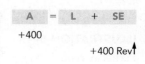

A	=	L	+	SE
+400				
				+400 Rev↑

Notice that Link's Dental records the trade discount *indirectly* by recognizing revenue equal to the discounted price, which is $500 less the trade discount of $100 (= $500 × 20%).

SALES DISCOUNTS

Unlike a trade discount, a sales discount represents a reduction, not in the selling price of a product or service, but in the amount to be paid by a credit customer if payment is made within a specified period of time. It's a discount intended to provide incentive for quick payment.

Discount terms, such as 2/10, n/30, are a shorthand way to communicate the amount of the discount and the time period within which it's available. The term "2/10," pronounced "two ten," for example, indicates the customer will receive a 2% discount if the amount owed is paid within 10 days. The term "n/30," pronounced "net thirty," means that if the customer does *not* take the discount, full payment is due within 30 days.

Assume Link's Dental wants Dee to pay quickly on her teeth whitening bill and offers her terms of 2/10, n/30. This means that if Dee pays within 10 days, the amount due ($400 after the trade discount) will be reduced by 2% (or $8 = $400 × 2%). Let's consider two alternatives—taking or not taking the sales discount.

With the sales discount. Let's see what happens when Dee pays within 10 days: Assume that Dee pays on March 10, which is within the 10-day discount period. Link's Dental records the following transaction when it receives payment.

March 10	Debit	Credit
Cash	392	
Sales Discounts	8	
Accounts Receivable		400
(Collect cash on account with a 2% sales discount)		

Balance Sheet						Income Statement		
			Stockholders' Equity					
			Common	**Retained**				**Net**
Assets	**=**	**Liabilities +**	**Stock**	**+ Earnings**		**Revenues**	**− Expenses =**	**Income**
+392	=			−8		−8	=	−8
−400								
−8								

Notice that Link receives only $392 cash, the full amount owed less the 2% sales discount. **We record the sales discount as a contra revenue account.** A contra revenue account is an account with a balance that is opposite, or "contra," to that of its related revenue account. The reason we use a contra revenue account is to be able to keep a record of the total revenue separate from the reduction in that revenue due to quick payment. In this case, Service Revenue has a credit balance of $400, and its related contra revenue account—Sales Discounts—has a debit balance of $8. The net effect is that sales discounts increase, reducing net revenues of the company to $392. It's easier to see the relationship between these two accounts by looking at the partial income statement of Link's Dental in Illustration 5–1.

ILLUSTRATION 5–1

Partial Income Statement Reporting Revenues Net of Sales Discounts

LINK'S DENTAL		
Income Statement (partial)		
Service revenues	$400	
Less: Sales discounts	(8)	
Net service revenues		$392

Link provides a service with a normal price of $500. However, after the trade discount of $100 and the sales discount of $8, Link's income statement reports net revenue of $392.

Also notice that Link's Dental credits Accounts Receivable for $400, even though it receives only $392 cash. The reason is that the $400 balance in Accounts Receivable

is "paid in full" by the combination of the $392 cash payment and the $8 sales discount. Dee owes $0 after paying $392. The balance of Accounts Receivable now equals $0, as demonstrated in Illustration 5–2.

	Accounts Receivable		
Credit sale	Mar. 1 400		Collection of $392 on account
		Mar. 10 400	
Ending balance	Bal. 0		

Without the sales discount.   For our second scenario, assume that Dee waits until March 31 to pay, which is *not* within the 10-day discount period. Link's Dental records the following transaction at the time it collects cash from Dee.

March 31	Debit	Credit
Cash	400	
Accounts Receivable		400
(Collect cash on account)		

A	=	L	+	SE
+400				
−400				

Notice that there is no indication in recording the transaction that the customer does not take the sales discount. This is the typical way to record a cash collection on account when no sales discounts are involved. Accounts Receivable is credited for $400 to reduce its balance to $0, representing the amount owed by the customer after payment.

SALES RETURNS AND ALLOWANCES

In some cases, customers may not be satisfied with a product or service purchased. If a customer returns a product, we call that a sales return. After a sales return, (a) we reduce the customer's account balance if the sale was on account or (b) we issue a cash refund if the sale was for cash.

Sometimes, because of a deficiency in the company's product or service, the seller reduces the customer's balance owed or provides at least a partial refund while allowing the customer to keep the product. Such a reduction or partial refund is called a sales allowance. Suppose on March 5, after she gets her teeth whitened but before she pays, Dee notices that another local dentist is offering the same procedure for $350, which is $50 less than Link's discounted price of $400. Dee brings this to Dr. Link's attention and because his policy is to match any competitor's pricing, he offers to reduce Dee's account balance by $50. Link's Dental records the following sales allowance.

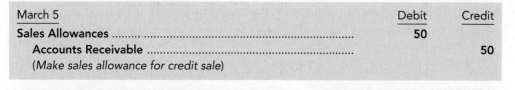

March 5	Debit	Credit
Sales Allowances	50	
Accounts Receivable		50
(Make sales allowance for credit sale)		

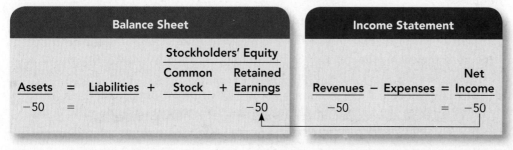

Balance Sheet					Income Statement		
			Stockholders' Equity				
			Common	**Retained**			**Net**
Assets	=	**Liabilities** +	**Stock** +	**Earnings**	**Revenues** −	**Expenses** =	**Income**
−50	=			−50	−50	=	−50

This reduction of accounts receivable indicates that Dee owes less after the allowance—she now owes only $350.

Firms sometimes combine their sales returns and sales allowances in a *single* Sales Returns and Allowances account. **Like sales discounts, sales returns and allowances are contra revenue accounts.** We report both sales discounts and sales returns and allowances as reductions in the related revenue account, causing a reduction in net income.

KEY POINT

Sales discounts, returns, and allowances are contra revenue accounts. We subtract the balances in these accounts from total revenues when calculating net revenues.

Decision Point

Question	Accounting information	Analysis
Does a company have a recurring problem with customer satisfaction?	Total sales and sales returns and allowances	If sales returns and allowances are routinely high relative to total sales, this might indicate that customers are not satisfied with the company's products or services.

COMMON MISTAKE

Students sometimes misclassify contra revenue accounts—sales discounts, returns, and allowances—as expenses. Like expenses, contra revenues have normal debit balances and reduce the reported amount of net income. However, contra revenues represent *direct reductions* of revenues, whereas expenses represent the separate costs of generating revenues. Misclassifying contra revenue accounts as expenses overstates revenues and expenses but leaves bottom-line net income unaffected.

Let's Review

Snap-Crackle-Pop (SCP) Chiropractic normally charges $120 for a full spinal adjustment. Currently, the company is offering a $20 discount to senior citizens. In addition, SCP offers terms 2/10, n/30 to all customers receiving services on account. The following events occur.

June 18   David, age 72, calls to set up an appointment.

June 20   David visits SCP and receives a spinal adjustment for the discounted price.

June 29   David pays for his office visit.

Required:

1. On what date should SCP record patient revenue?
2. Record patient revenue for SCP.
3. Record the cash collection for SCP assuming SCP receives David's payment in full on June 29 (within the discount period).
4. Calculate the balance of Accounts Receivable using a T-account format, and then calculate the balance of net revenue as shown in the income statement after the cash payment is received.

Solution:

1. SCP should record patient revenue on June 20—the date the service is provided.

2. Record patient revenue:

June 20	Debit	Credit
Accounts Receivable	100	
Service Revenue		100
(Provide services on account)		
(Revenue = $120 less $20 trade discount)		

3. Record receipt of David's payment in full within the discount period:

June 29	Debit	Credit
Cash	98	
Sales Discounts	2	
Accounts Receivable		100
(Collect cash on account with a 2% sales discount)		
(Sales discount = $100 × 2%)		

4. Balance of Accounts Receivable and calculation of net revenue after receipt of cash payment:

Accounts Receivable		
Jun. 20 100		
	Jun. 29 100	
Bal. 0		

Service revenue (from *Requirement 2*)	$100	
Less: Sales discounts (from *Requirement 3*)	(2)	
Net revenue	$ 98	

Suggested Homework:
BE5-1, BE5-2;
E5-2, E5-3;
P5-2A&B

VALUING ACCOUNTS RECEIVABLE

PART B

The right to receive cash from a customer is a valuable resource for the company. **This is why accounts receivable is an asset, reported in the company's balance sheet.** If the company expects to receive the cash within one year, it classifies the receivable as a current asset; otherwise it classifies the receivable as a long-term asset.

What, though, is the *value* of being owed $100? If you are confident the person will actually pay you $100 in the near future, then you might consider the right to receive the money to be worth $100. However, if the person is unable to pay you anything, then your right to collect $100 is worth $0. Of course there are many possibilities in between. To be useful to decision makers, accounts receivable should be reported at the amount of cash the firm *expects* to collect, an amount known as net realizable value.

KEY POINT

We recognize accounts receivable as assets in the balance sheet and report them at their *net realizable value*, that is, the amount of cash we expect to collect.

Allowance Method

■ **LO3**
Record an allowance
for future uncollectible
accounts.

We know that companies often are not able to collect all of their accounts receivable from customers. Rather than accept only cash payment at the time of sale, should companies extend credit to their customers by allowing them to purchase on account? **The upside of extending credit to customers is that it boosts sales by allowing customers the ability to purchase on account and pay cash later.** Just think of how many times you wanted to buy food, clothes, electronics, or other items that you could afford, but you didn't have cash with you. You're not alone. Many customers may not have cash readily available to make a purchase or, for other reasons, simply prefer to buy on credit.

The downside of extending credit to customers is that not all customers will pay fully on their accounts. Even the most well-meaning customers may find themselves in difficult financial circumstances beyond their control, limiting their ability to repay debt. Customers' accounts that we no longer consider collectible are **uncollectible accounts**, or *bad debts*.

We account for uncollectible accounts using what's called the **allowance method**. This method involves *allowing for the possibility* that some accounts will be uncollectible at some point in the future.[1] Be sure to understand this key point. Using the allowance method we account for events (customers' bad debts) that have *not yet* occurred but that are likely to occur. This is different from other transactions you've learned about to this point. Those earlier transactions involved recording events that have already occurred, such as purchasing supplies, paying employees, and providing services to customers. **Under the allowance method, companies are required to *estimate* future uncollectible accounts and record those estimates in the current year.**

The allowance method estimates future uncollectible accounts.

Before seeing exactly how to record the allowance method, let's first think about the effects that uncollectible accounts should have on the financial position of the company. Uncollectible accounts have the effect of (1) reducing assets (accounts receivable) by an estimate of the amount we don't expect to collect and (2) increasing expenses (bad debt expense) to reflect the cost of offering credit to customers. Illustration 5–3 demonstrates how the effects of uncollectible accounts should therefore be reflected in the financial statements.

ILLUSTRATION 5–3

The Financial Statement Effects of Accounting for Future Uncollectible Accounts

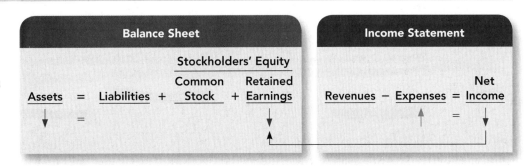

An account we do not expect to collect has no value. Thus, we need to reduce assets because we don't expect to collect the entire accounts receivable (assets). At the same time, failure to collect a customer's cash represents a cost inherent in using credit sales. The cost of uncollectible accounts is an operating expense, decreasing net income by the uncollectible amount. Next, let's see how to record bad debts so that both of these effects are captured in the financial statements—the reduction in assets and the increase in operating expenses.

[1]Later in the chapter, we'll look at a second method—the direct write-off method. The direct write-off method is used for tax purposes but is generally not permitted for financial reporting.

 **KEY POINT**

Under the allowance method, companies are required to *estimate* future uncollectible accounts and record those estimates in the current year. Estimated uncollectible accounts reduce assets and increase expenses.

ESTIMATING UNCOLLECTIBLE ACCOUNTS

Now that we have discussed the impact of uncollectible accounts in the financial statements, let's see how we record them. To use the allowance method, a company first estimates at the end of the *current* year how much in uncollectible accounts will occur in the *following* year. Consider an example of future uncollectible accounts for Kimzey Medical Clinic, which specializes in emergency outpatient care. Because it doesn't verify the patient's health insurance before administering care, Kimzey knows that a high proportion of fees for emergency care provided will not be collected.

In 2012, Kimzey bills customers $50 million for emergency care it provided. By the end of the year, $20 million remains due from customers, but how much of this amount does Kimzey expect *not* to collect in the following year? Let's suppose that in previous years approximately 30% of accounts receivable were not collected; Kimzey decides to base this year's estimate on that same percentage. Estimating uncollectible accounts based on the percentage of accounts receivable expected not to be collected is known as the **percentage-of-receivables method**. This method sometimes is referred to as the *balance sheet method*, because we base the estimate of bad debts on a balance sheet amount—accounts receivable.[2]

Using the 30% estimate, Kimzey expects that $6 million of its accounts receivable (or 30% of $20 million) likely will never be collected. It makes the following year-end adjustment to allow for these future uncollectible accounts.

December 31, 2012 ($ in millions)	Debit	Credit
Bad Debt Expense	6	
Allowance for Uncollectible Accounts		6
(*Estimate future bad debts*)		
($20 million × 30% = $6 million)		

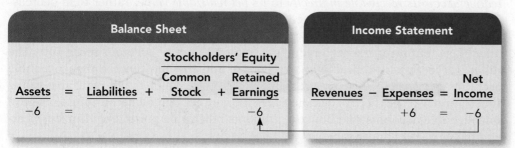

The effect of the adjustment in the financial statements reflects the impact of the transaction on the financial position of the company. Because the nature of the accounts in this adjusting entry differs somewhat from those in other year-end adjusting entries we covered in Chapter 3, let's look closer.

Bad debt expense. First, bad debt expense represents the cost of the estimated future bad debts. Kimzey estimates that it will not collect 30% of its accounts receivable, and so records Bad Debt Expense of $6 million. We include this expense

Common Terms Bad debt expense sometimes is referred to as *uncollectible accounts expense.*

---

[2]In the appendix to this chapter, we'll consider a second method, the *percentage-of-credit-sales method* (also referred to as the *income statement method*). In practice, companies are required to follow the percentage-of-receivables method, so that will be our focus here.

in the same income statement as the credit sales with which these bad debts are associated. By doing so, we properly "match" expenses (bad debts) with the revenues (credit sales) they help to generate. Illustration 5–4 shows the partial income statement for Kimzey Medical Clinic after estimating bad debt expense.

ILLUSTRATION 5–4

Partial Income Statement Showing Estimated Bad Debt Expense

> **KIMZEY MEDICAL CLINIC**
> **Income Statement (partial)**
> **For the year ended 2012**
>
> | ($ in millions) | |
> |---|---|
> | Credit sales | $50 |
> | Bad debt expense | (6) |
> | | $44 |

Match expenses with their related revenues.

In the 2012 income statement, we reduce the $50 million of revenue from credit sales by $6 million for estimated future bad debts. Even though the company reports credit sales of $50 million, the expected profits on these sales, after considering the cost of future bad debts, is only $44 million.

 KEY POINT

Adjusting for estimates of future uncollectible accounts matches expenses (bad debts) in the same period as the revenues (credit sales) they help to generate.

Common Terms The allowance for uncollectible accounts is sometimes referred to as the *allowance for doubtful accounts.*

Allowance for uncollectible accounts.   Second, we adjust for future bad debts by making an allowance for uncollectible accounts. The contra asset account Allowance for Uncollectible Accounts represents the amount of accounts receivable we do not expect to collect. Earlier in the chapter, we discussed *contra revenue* accounts— sales discounts, returns, and allowances. Recall that these accounts provide a way to *reduce revenue indirectly.* In the same way, the allowance account provides a way to *reduce accounts receivable indirectly* to its *net realizable value,* rather than decreasing the accounts receivable balance itself.

We report the allowance for uncollectible accounts in the asset section of the balance sheet, but it represents a reduction in the balance of accounts receivable. The difference between total accounts receivable and the allowance for uncollectible accounts is referred to as *net accounts receivable,* which is net realizable value. Illustration 5–5 (next page) demonstrates the concept behind accounting for future uncollectible accounts and how the accounts receivable portion of Kimzey's year-end balance sheet appears.

Report accounts receivable at net realizable value.

After we estimate uncollectible accounts to be $6 million, we reduce the $20 million balance of accounts receivable and report them at their net realizable value of $14 million. But is this estimate correct? Only time will tell. Kimzey's prediction of $6 million for uncollectible accounts might be too high, or it might be too low. In either case, it's generally more informative than making no estimate at all. (Later in the chapter, we'll find out how close the estimate is.)

 KEY POINT

Recording an allowance for uncollectible accounts correctly reports accounts receivable at their net realizable value.

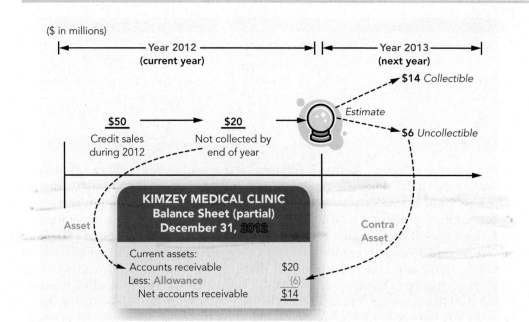

ILLUSTRATION 5–5
Accounting for
Uncollectible Accounts
and the Accounts
Receivable Portion of
the Balance Sheet

 COMMON MISTAKE

Because Allowance for Uncollectible Accounts has a normal credit balance, students sometimes misclassify this account as a liability, which also has a normal credit balance. Instead, a contra asset represents a reduction in a related asset.

Decision Point

Question	Accounting information	Analysis
Are the company's credit sales policies too lenient?	Accounts receivable and the allowance for uncollectible accounts	A high ratio of the allowance for uncollectible accounts to total accounts receivable could be an indication that the company extends too much credit to high-risk customers.

WRITING OFF ACCOUNTS RECEIVABLE

To continue with our example of Kimzey Medical Clinic, let's suppose that on February 23, 2013 (the following year), Kimzey receives notice that one of its former patients, Bruce Easley, has filed for bankruptcy protection against all creditors. Based on this information, Kimzey believes it is unlikely Bruce will pay his account of $4,000. Remember, Kimzey previously allowed for the likelihood that *some* of its customers would not pay, though it didn't know which ones. Now that it *knows* a specific customer will not pay, it can adjust the allowance and reduce the accounts receivable balance itself. Upon receiving news of this *actual* bad debt, Kimzey records the following.

■ **LO4**
Apply the procedure to write off accounts receivable as uncollectible.

February 23, 2013	Debit	Credit
Allowance for Uncollectible Accounts	4,000	
Accounts Receivable		4,000
(*Write off a customer's account*)		

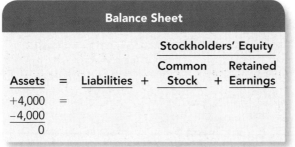

Balance Sheet					Income Statement		
			Stockholders' Equity				
			Common	Retained			Net
Assets	=	Liabilities +	Stock	+ Earnings	Revenues	− Expenses =	Income
+4,000	=						
−4,000							
0							

What is the effect in Kimzey's financial statements when writing off Bruce's account receivable? **Overall, the write-off of the account receivable has no effect on total amounts reported in the balance sheet or in the income statement.** Notice that there is no decrease in total assets and no decrease in net income with the write-off. Here's why: **We have already recorded the negative effects of the bad news.** Kimzey recorded those effects when it *estimated* future bad debts at the end of 2012 and both reduced assets and recorded the bad debt expense. Now, when Bruce declares bankruptcy in the following year, 2013, we have already established the allowance for this bad debt. The write-off on February 23, 2013, reduces both an asset account (Accounts Receivable) and its contra asset account (Allowance for Uncollectible Accounts), leaving the *net* receivable unaffected. Thus, the write-off results in no change to total assets.

COMMON MISTAKE

Students often mistakenly record bad debt expense when they write off an uncollectible account. The bad debt expense was recorded in a prior year at the time of estimating uncollectible accounts.

COLLECTION OF ACCOUNTS PREVIOUSLY WRITTEN OFF

Later in 2013, on September 8, Bruce's bankruptcy proceedings are complete. Kimzey had expected to receive none of the $4,000 Bruce owed. However, after liquidating all assets, Bruce is able to pay each of his creditors 25% of the amount due them. So, when Kimzey receives payment of $1,000 (= $4,000 × 25%), it makes the following two entries.

September 8, 2013	Debit	Credit
Accounts Receivable	1,000	
Allowance for Uncollectible Accounts		1,000
(*Reestablish portion of account previously written off*)		
Cash	1,000	
Accounts Receivable		1,000
(*Collect cash on account*)		

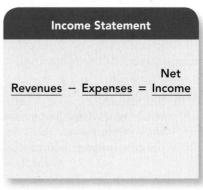

Balance Sheet					Income Statement		
			Stockholders' Equity				
			Common	Retained			Net
Assets	=	Liabilities +	Stock	+ Earnings	Revenues	− Expenses =	Income
+1,000	=						
−1,000							
+1,000							
−1,000							
0							

The first entry simply reverses a portion of the previous entry that Kimzey made on February 23 to write off the account. The second entry records the collection of the account receivable. Notice that in both entries the debit entry increases total assets by the same amount that the credit entry decreases total assets. **Therefore, collecting cash on an account previously written off has no effect on total assets and no effect on net income.**

Let's assume that total accounts written off by Kimzey during 2013 equaled $5 million but that $1 million of this amount was ultimately collected by the end of the year. The time line of events related to accounts receivable of Kimzey during 2012 and 2013 is this:

1. At the end of 2012, accounts receivable total $20 million.
2. Kimzey makes an adjustment at the end of 2012 for *estimated* bad debts of $6 million.
3. In 2013, *actual* accounts Kimzey writes off as uncollectible total $5 million.
4. Of the $5 million in accounts written off earlier, $1 million later appears receivable.
5. Kimzey receives $1 million cash for the accounts reestablished in (4).

Illustration 5–6 summarizes the impact of each of these events (also numbered 1–5 there) in calculating net accounts receivable.

ILLUSTRATION 5–6

Balance of Kimzey's Net Accounts Receivable

($ in millions)	2012		2013		
				(4)	**(5)**
	(1)	**(2)**	**(3)**	**Reestablish**	**Collect Cash**
	Accounts	*Estimate*	**Write Off**	**Previous**	**from Previous**
	Receivable	**Bad Debts in**	*Actual* **Bad**	**Write-offs**	**Write-offs**
	Total $20	**2013 to Be $6**	**Debts of $5**	**of $1**	**of $1**
Accts. receiv.	$20	$20	$15	$16	$15
Less: Allowance	(0)	(6)	(1)	(2)	(2)
Net accts. receiv.	$20	$14	$14	$14	$13

Net accounts receivable decline for two of these events. First, as we *estimate* future bad debts, we recognize the likelihood that we will not collect cash for some accounts. Second, once the company receives payment from customers, their account balances are no longer receivable.

On the other hand, writing off *actual* bad debts and reestablishing those previous write-offs when it appears that customers will pay has no effect on net accounts receivable.

Notice that the balance of the allowance account is $2 million at the end of 2013. Does the fact that the allowance account has a nonzero ending balance mean that Kimzey's estimate of uncollectible accounts for 2013 was *wrong*? Perhaps. On the other hand, it may only mean that some of the $15 million in accounts receivable has not yet proven uncollectible but eventually will. In any case, when we make estimates in accounting, it's highly unlikely they will prove exactly correct.

Users of financial statements must realize that some of the amounts reported in financial statements are estimates, and estimating the future almost always results in some inaccuracy. Illustration 5–7 (next page) provides an excerpt from the annual report of **Tenet Healthcare Corporation**.

KEY POINT

Writing off a customer's account as uncollectible reduces the balance of accounts receivable but also reduces the contra asset—allowance for uncollectible accounts. The net effect is that there is no change in the *net* receivable (accounts receivable less the allowance) or in total assets. We recorded the decrease to assets as a result of the bad debt when we established the allowance for uncollectible accounts in a prior year.

ILLUSTRATION 5–7

Excerpt from Tenet Healthcare Corporation's Annual Report

TENET HEALTHCARE CORPORATION
Notes to the Financial Statements (excerpt)

The preparation of financial statements, in conformity with accounting principles generally accepted in the United States of America, requires us to make estimates and assumptions that affect the amounts reported in the Consolidated Financial Statements and these accompanying notes. We regularly evaluate the accounting policies and estimates we use. In general, we base the estimates on historical experience and on assumptions that we believe to be reasonable given the particular circumstances in which we operate. Although we believe all adjustments considered necessary for fair presentation have been included, actual results may vary from those estimates.

ESTIMATING UNCOLLECTIBLE ACCOUNTS IN THE FOLLOWING YEAR

At the end of 2013, Kimzey must once again estimate uncollectible accounts and make a year-end adjustment. Suppose that in 2013 Kimzey bills customers for services totaling $80 million, and $30 million is still receivable at the end of the year. Of the $30 million still receivable, let's say Kimzey again uses the percentage-of-receivables method and estimates 30% (or $9 million) will not be collected. For what amount would Kimzey record the year-end adjustment for bad debts in 2013? Before answering, let's first examine the current balance of the allowance account, as shown in Illustration 5–8.

ILLUSTRATION 5–8

Balance of Kimzey's Allowance for Uncollectible Accounts

Allowance for Uncollectible Accounts ($ in millions)		
Write off account 5	6	Beginning balance for 2013
	1	Collection of previous write-off
	2	Balance before adjustment
	?	Year-end adjustment
	9	Estimated ending balance for 2013

Notice that the balance before the year-end adjustment in this example is a $2 million *credit*. **A credit balance before adjustment indicates that last year's estimate of uncollectible accounts may have been too high.** However, it's possible that some of the estimated uncollectible accounts have not proven bad yet. **A *debit* balance before adjustment indicates that last year's estimate was too low.**

Based on all available information at the end of 2013, Kimzey estimates that the allowance for uncollectible accounts should be $9 million. This means the allowance account needs to increase from its current balance of $2 million credit to the estimated ending balance of $9 million credit. Kimzey can accomplish this by adjusting the account for $7 million as follows:

A = L + SE		Debit	Credit
−7 Exp↑	**December 31, 2013**		
−7	**Bad Debt Expense**	7	
	Allowance for Uncollectible Accounts		7
	(*Estimate future bad debts*)		

In its 2013 income statement, Kimzey will report bad debt expense of $7 million along with other operating expenses of, say, $50 million. This is shown in Illustration 5–9.

KIMZEY MEDICAL CLINIC Income Statement For the year ended 2013		
($ in millions)		
Revenue from credit sales		$80
Expenses:		
Bad debt expense	$ 7	
Other operating expenses	50	57
Net income		$23

ILLUSTRATION 5–9

Bad Debt Expense in the Income Statement

In the 2013 balance sheet, Kimzey will report the allowance account at the best estimate of its appropriate balance, $9 million. This is shown in Illustration 5–10.

KIMZEY MEDICAL CLINIC Balance Sheet (partial) December 31, 2013		
Assets		
Current assets ($ in millions):		
Accounts receivable	$30	
Less: Allowance for uncollectible accounts	(9)	
Net accounts receivable		$21

ILLUSTRATION 5–10

Accounts Receivable Portion of the Balance Sheet

The process of estimating an allowance for uncollectible accounts, writing off bad debts in the following period, and then reestimating the allowance at the end of the period is one that occurs throughout the company's life.

AGING OF ACCOUNTS RECEIVABLE

In our example for Kimzey Medical Clinic, we estimated future uncollectible accounts by applying a *single* estimated percentage to total accounts receivable (30%). Management can estimate this percentage using historical averages, current economic conditions, industry comparisons, or other analytical techniques. A more accurate method than assuming a single percentage uncollectible for all accounts is to consider the *age* of various accounts receivable, and use a higher percentage for "old" accounts than for "new" accounts. This is known as the aging method. For instance, accounts that are 60 days past due are older than accounts that are 30 days past due. **The older the account, the less likely it is to be collected.**

■ **LO5**
Use the aging method to estimate future uncollectible accounts.

Let's return to Kimzey Medical Clinic to see how an aging of accounts receivable can be used to estimate uncollectible accounts. Recall that accounts receivable at the end of 2013 totaled $30 million. Illustration 5–11 (next page) shows Kimzey's accounts receivable aging schedule at the end of 2013.

Each age group has its own estimate of the percent uncollectible. Summing the estimated allowance for each age group results in a total estimated allowance of **$8** million. Because the allowance has a balance of $2 million before adjustment at the end of 2013 (refer back to Illustration 5–8), it needs a **$6** million adjustment. In other words, the $2 million current balance in the allowance account needs an upward adjustment of $6 million to reach the $8 million estimated ending balance for 2013. Illustration 5–12 (next page) demonstrates this calculation.

ILLUSTRATION 5–11

Kimzey's Accounts Receivable Aging Schedule

($ in millions)

Age Group (days past due)	Accounts Receivable	×	Estimated Percent Uncollectible	=	Estimated Allowance
0–60	$20		20%		$4.0
61–120	5		30%		1.5
121–180	4		40%		1.6
More than 180	1		90%		0.9
Total	$30				$8.0

ILLUSTRATION 5–12

Balance of Kimzey's Allowance for Uncollectible Accounts

Allowance for Uncollectible Accounts
($ in millions)

Write off account	5		6	Beginning balance for 2013
			1	Collection of previous write-off
			2	Balance before adjustment
			?	**Year-end adjustment**
			8	Estimated ending balance for 2013

To adjust the allowance from its current balance of $2 million credit to the estimated balance of $8 million credit, we record the following:

A	=	L	+	SE
				−6 Exp↑
−6				

December 31, 2013	Debit	Credit
Bad Debt Expense	6	
Allowance for Uncollectible Accounts		6
(*Estimate future bad debts*)		

Illustration 5–13 presents **Tenet Healthcare**'s policy of estimating uncollectible accounts.

ILLUSTRATION 5–13

Excerpt from Tenet Healthcare Corporation's Annual Report

TENET HEALTHCARE CORPORATION
Notes to the Financial Statements (excerpt)

We provide for an allowance against accounts receivable that could become uncollectible by establishing an allowance to reduce the carrying value of such receivables to their estimated net realizable value. We estimate this allowance based on the aging of our accounts receivable by hospital, our historical collection experience by hospital and for each type of payer over an 18-month look-back period, and other relevant factors. There are various factors that can impact collection trends, such as changes in the economy, which in turn have an impact on unemployment rates and the number of uninsured and underinsured patients, the volume of patients through the emergency department, the increased burden of co-payments and deductibles to be made by patients with insurance, and business practices related to collection efforts. These factors continuously change and can have an impact on collection trends and our estimation process.

The following tables present the approximate aging by payer of our continuing operations' net accounts receivable.

Age	Medicare	Medicaid	Managed Care	Indemnity, Self-pay, and Other	Total
0–60 days	94%	63%	78%	26%	69%
61–120 days	3	24	12	27	15
121–180 days	3	11	5	13	6
Over 180 days	0	2	5	34	10
Total	100%	100%	100%	100%	100%

KEY POINT

~~Using the aging method to estimate uncollectible accounts is more accurate than~~ ~~applying a single percentage to all accounts receivable.~~ The aging method recognizes that the longer accounts are past due, the less likely they are to be collected.

Decision Point

Question	Accounting information	Analysis
How likely is it that the company's accounts receivable will be collected?	Notes to the financial statements detailing the age of individual accounts receivable	Older accounts are less likely to be collected.

Let's Review

Community Medical is an outpatient health facility that provides minor surgical and other health-related services to the local community. Many of the patients do not have medical insurance. These customers are required to pay for services within 30 days of receiving treatment. At the beginning of 2012, Community Medical's allowance for uncollectible accounts was a $100,000 credit.

Required:

1. Record the write-off of $120,000 of accounts receivable during 2012.
2. Estimate the allowance for future uncollectible accounts using the following ages and estimated percentage uncollectible at the end of 2012:

Age Group	Amount Receivable	Estimated Percent Uncollectible	Estimated Amount Uncollectible
Not yet due	$600,000	10%	
1–45 days past due	200,000	20	
More than 45 days past due	50,000	60	
Total	$850,000		

3. Use a T-account to determine the year-end adjustment to the allowance account.
4. Record the year-end adjustment for bad debts expense.
5. Prepare a partial balance sheet showing accounts receivable and the allowance for uncollectible accounts.

Solution:

1. Write-off of accounts receivable during 2012:

	Debit	Credit
Allowance for Uncollectible Accounts	120,000	
Accounts Receivable		120,000

2. Estimate of the allowance for future uncollectible accounts:

Age Group	Amount Receivable	Estimated Percent Uncollectible	Estimated Amount Uncollectible
Not yet due	$600,000	10%	$ 60,000
1–45 days past due	200,000	20%	40,000
More than 45 days past due	50,000	60%	30,000
Total	$850,000		$130,000

3. Year-end adjustment to the allowance account:

Allowance for Uncollectible Accounts			
		100,000	Beginning balance
Write-offs	120,000		
Balance before adjustment	20,000		
		?	Year-end adjustment
		130,000	Estimated ending balance

4. Year-end adjustment for bad debt expense:

December 31, 2012	Debit	Credit
Bad Debt Expense	**150,000**	
Allowance for Uncollectible Accounts		**150,000***

*Notice from the T-account in *Requirement* 3 that the balance of the allowance account before adjustment is a $20,000 *debit*. Based on the estimated allowance of a $130,000 *credit*, we need a credit adjustment of $150,000. Of this adjustment, $20,000 is needed to get the allowance account to a zero balance, and the remaining $130,000 credit adjusts the account to the estimated ending balance.

5. Balance sheet:

COMMUNITY MEDICAL		
Balance Sheet (partial)		
December 31, 2012		
Assets		
Current assets:		
Accounts receivable	$850,000	
Less: Allowance for uncollectible accounts	(130,000)	
Net accounts receivable		$720,000

Suggested Homework:
**BE5-5, BE5-8;
E5-11, E5-12;
P5-4A&B, P5-6A&B**

Direct Write-Off Method

■ **LO6**
Contrast the allowance method and direct write-off method when accounting for uncollectible accounts.

We've just seen how the allowance method of accounting for uncollectible accounts works. However, if uncollectible accounts are not anticipated or are immaterial, or if it's not possible to reliably estimate them, we need not make an allowance for them. **In these rare situations, we do not estimate uncollectible accounts, but we write off any bad debts that do arise as bad debt expense at that time.**

For example, suppose a company provides services for $10,000 on account in 2012, but makes no allowance for uncollectible accounts at the end of the year. On September 17, 2013, an account of $2,000 is considered uncollectible. The company records the write-off as follows.

A	=	L	+	SE
				−2,000 Exp↑
−2,000				

September 17, 2013	Debit	Credit
Bad Debt Expense	**2,000**	
Accounts Receivable		**2,000**
(*Write off uncollectible account directly*)		

The direct write-off method typically is not acceptable for financial reporting.

Recording bad debt expense at the time we know the account to be uncollectible is known as the direct write-off method. **The direct write-off method is used for tax purposes but is generally not permitted for financial reporting.** Can you guess why? Accounts receivable generated from the credit sales in 2012 are recorded in 2012, but no allowance is made for the possibility that some of these accounts will not be collected. As a result, in 2012 assets are overstated and operating expenses are understated. This is why the direct write-off method of accounting

for uncollectible accounts is not permitted for financial reporting purposes except in limited circumstances. Specifically, **a firm must use the allowance method if it is probable that the firm will not collect a material amount of receivables and it can reasonably estimate that amount.**

Illustration 5–14 highlights the difference between the allowance method and the direct write-off method for our example.

	2012 (Year-end estimated bad debts = $2,000)		2013 (Actual bad debts = $2,000)	
	Year-end adjustment		Write-off	
Allowance method (estimate)	Bad Debt Expense	2,000	Allowance	2,000
	Allowance	2,000	Accounts Receivable	2,000
Direct write-off method	No Adjustment		Bad Debt Expense	2,000
			Accounts Receivable	2,000

ILLUSTRATION 5–14

Comparing the Allowance Method and the Direct Write-off Method for Recording Uncollectible Accounts

Assume that at the end of 2012 we *estimate* $2,000 of accounts receivable won't be collected. For simplicity, also assume that our estimate of future bad debts turns out to be correct, and actual bad debts in 2013 total $2,000.

Under the allowance method, future bad debts are *estimated* and recorded as an expense and a reduction in assets in 2012. Under the direct write-off method, though, we make no attempt to estimate future bad debts. We record bad debt expense in the period the account proves uncollectible. In this case, we report the bad debt expense and reduction in assets in 2013. Notice that, either way, the ultimate effect is a $2,000 debit to Bad Debt Expense and a $2,000 credit to Accounts Receivable. **The difference is in the timing.**

COMMON MISTAKE

Some students erroneously think firms should reduce total assets and record bad debt expense at the time the bad debt actually occurs. However, companies *anticipate* future bad debts and establish an allowance for those estimates.

KEY POINT

The direct write-off method reduces accounts receivable and records bad debt expense at the time the account receivable proves uncollectible. If the credit sale occurs in a prior reporting period, bad debt expense is not properly matched with revenues (credit sales). Also, accounts receivable will be overstated in the prior period. The direct write-off method typically is not acceptable for financial reporting.

Managing Bad Debt Estimates

While the allowance method is conceptually superior to the direct write-off method and more accurately reports assets and matches revenues and expenses, it does have one disadvantage. This disadvantage arises from the fact that reported amounts under the allowance method represent management estimates. If so inclined, management could use these estimates to manipulate reported earnings.[3] For example, if management wants to boost earnings in the current year, it can intentionally

Decision Maker's Perspective

---

[3]M. McNichols, G. P. Wilson, and L. De Angelo. 1988. Evidence of Earnings Management from the Provision for Bad Debts. *Journal of Accounting Research* (26): 1–40.

underestimate future uncollectible accounts. Similarly, if a company is having an especially good year and management wants to "reserve" earnings for the future, it can intentionally *overestimate* future uncollectible accounts. Having a large expense in the current year means there is less of a charge to bad debt expense in a future year, increasing future earnings. Other expenses, such as rent expense, are much more difficult to manipulate because their reported amounts don't rely on management estimates. These expenses are evidenced by past transactions, and their amounts are verifiable to the penny using a receipt or an invoice.

HealthSouth Corporation appears to have used estimates of uncollectible accounts to manipulate earnings. In the early 1990s, HealthSouth reported large amounts of bad debt expense, building large reserves in the allowance account. Then in the mid-1990s, as additional earnings were needed to meet analysts' expectations, HealthSouth was able to report low amounts for bad debt expense because of the previously inflated allowance account. In 1999, when it became apparent that HealthSouth's earnings were falling dramatically, the company took a "big bath" by reporting a very large charge to bad debt expense. Some companies feel that if they are going to have a bad year, they might as well release all the bad news at once. This makes it possible to report better news in future years. ●

 ETHICAL DILEMMA

 Philip Stanton, the executive manager of Thomson Pharmaceutical, receives a bonus if the company's net income in the current year exceeds net income in the past year. By the end of 2012, it appears that net income for 2012 will easily exceed net income for 2011. Philip has asked Mary Beth Williams, the company's controller, to try to reduce this year's income and "bank" some of the profits for future years. Mary Beth suggests that the company's bad debt expense as a percentage of accounts receivable for 2012 be increased from 10% to 15%. She believes 10% is the more accurate estimate but knows that both the corporation's internal and external auditors allow some flexibility in estimates. What is the effect of increasing the estimate of bad debts from 10% to 15% of accounts receivable? Does Mary Beth's proposal present an ethical dilemma?

PART C

NOTES RECEIVABLE

Notes receivable are similar to accounts receivable but are more formal credit arrangements evidenced by a written debt instrument, or *note*. Notes receivable typically arise from loans to other entities (including affiliated companies); loans to stockholders and employees; and occasionally the sale of merchandise, other assets, or services.

Accounting for Notes Receivable

■ **LO7**
Apply the procedure to account for notes receivable, including interest calculation.

Like accounts receivable, notes receivable are assets and therefore have a normal debit balance. We classify notes receivable as either *current* or *noncurrent*, depending on the expected collection date. If the time to maturity is longer than one year, the note receivable is a long-term asset.

As an example, let's say that, on February 1, 2012, Kimzey Medical Clinic provides services of $10,000 to a patient, Justin Payne, who is not able to pay immediately. In place of payment, Justin offers Kimzey a six-month, 12% promissory note. Because of the large amount of the receivable, Kimzey agrees to accept the promissory note as a way to increase the likelihood of eventually receiving payment. In addition, because of the delay in payment, Kimzey would like to charge interest on the outstanding balance. A formal promissory note provides an explicit statement of the interest charges. Illustration 5–15 shows an example of a typical note receivable.

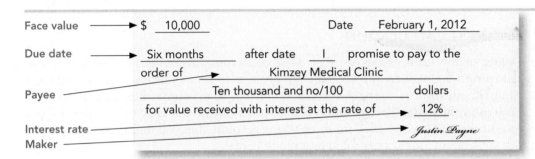

Face value ⟶	$ 10,000	Date February 1, 2012
Due date ⟶	Six months	after date I promise to pay to the
	order of	Kimzey Medical Clinic
Payee	Ten thousand and no/100	dollars
	for value received with interest at the rate of ⟶	12% .
Interest rate		⟶ Justin Payne
Maker		

ILLUSTRATION 5–15
Note Receivable

Kimzey records the note as follows.

February 1, 2012	Debit	Credit
Notes Receivable	10,000	
Service Revenue		10,000
(Accept a six-month, 12% note receivable for services provided)		

A	=	L	+	SE
+10,000				
				+10,000 Rev↑

Another example of the use of notes receivable is to replace existing accounts receivable. For example, suppose that Justin received $10,000 of services on account, but Kimzey originally recorded the amount due as a typical account receivable. Over time, it became apparent that Justin would not be able to pay quickly, so Kimzey required Justin to sign a six-month, 12% promissory note on February 1, 2012. When Justin signs the note, Kimzey records the following transaction to reclassify the existing account receivable as a note receivable.

February 1, 2012	Debit	Credit
Notes Receivable	10,000	
Accounts Receivable		10,000
(Reclassify an existing account receivable as a six-month, 12% note receivable)		

A	=	L	+	SE
+10,000				
−10,000				

Recognize that the transaction has no impact on the accounting equation; it is simply a matter of reclassifying assets. One asset (notes receivable) increases, while another asset (accounts receivable) decreases.

How would the patient, Justin Payne, record the previous transaction? By signing the note, Justin has an account payable that becomes reclassified as a note payable. He records the issuance of the note payable on February 1 as follows.

Flip Side

February 1, 2012	Debit	Credit
Accounts Payable	10,000	
Notes Payable		10,000
(Reclassify account payable as a six-month, 12% note payable)		

A	=	L	+	SE
		−10,000		
		+10,000		

Flip Side

Just as one company's account payable is another company's account receivable, there is also a note payable for every note receivable. For every dollar a company earns in interest revenue, another company incurs a dollar of interest expense. We address notes payable in Chapter 8, but if you have a good understanding of notes receivable, then you have a head start with its flip side—notes payable.

 KEY POINT

Notes receivable are similar to accounts receivable except that notes receivable are more formal credit arrangements made with a written debt instrument, or *note*.

INTEREST CALCULATION

Many of the same issues we discussed concerning accounts receivable, such as allowing for uncollectible accounts, apply also to notes receivable. The one issue that usually applies to notes receivable but not to accounts receivable is interest. You're probably familiar with the concept of interest. You may be earning interest on money in a savings account or checking account, and you might be paying interest on student loans, a car loan, or a credit card.

In the previous example, Kimzey issued a six-month, 12% promissory note. The "12%" indicates the *annual* interest rate charged by the payee. The terms of the six-month note mean that Kimzey will charge Justin Payne one-half year of interest, or 6%, on the face value. Interest on Kimzey's note receivable is calculated as follows.

Interest calculation

		Face value		Annual interest rate		Fraction of the year
Interest	=	value	×	interest rate	×	of the year
$600	=	$10,000	×	12%	×	6/12

 KEY POINT

We calculate interest as the face value of the note multiplied by the stated annual interest rate multiplied by the appropriate fraction of the year that the note is outstanding.

COLLECTION OF NOTES RECEIVABLE

We record the collection of notes receivable the same way as collection of accounts receivable, except that we also record interest earned as interest revenue in the income statement.

Continuing the previous example, suppose that on August 1, 2012, the maturity date, Justin repays the note and interest in full as promised. Kimzey will record the following.

A = L + SE	August 1, 2012	Debit	Credit
+10,600	**Cash**	**10,600**	
−10,000	Notes Receivable		10,000
+600 Rev↑	Interest Revenue		600
	(Collect note receivable and interest)		
	(Interest revenue = $10,000 × 12% × 6/12)		

Over the six-month period, Kimzey earns interest revenue of $600. The credit to Notes Receivable reduces the balance in that account to $0, which is the amount Justin owes after payment to Kimzey.

ACCRUED INTEREST

It frequently happens that a note is issued in one year and the maturity date occurs in the following year. For example, what if Justin Payne issued the previous six-month note to Kimzey on November 1, 2012, instead of February 1, 2012? In that case, the $10,000 face value (principal) and $600 interest on the six-month note are not due until May 1, 2013. The length of the note (six months) and interest rate (12%) remain the same, and so the total interest charged to Justin remains the same. However, Kimzey will earn interest revenue in two separate accounting periods (assuming Kimzey uses a calendar year): for two months of the six-month note in 2012 (November and December), and for four months in the next year (January through April). Illustration 5–16 demonstrates the calculation of interest revenue over time. Interest receivable from Kimzey's six-month, $10,000, 12% note is $100 per month (= $10,000 × 12% × 1/12).

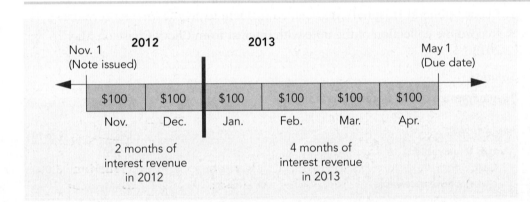

ILLUSTRATION 5–16

Calculating Interest Revenue over Time for Kimzey Medical Clinic

Because Kimzey earns two months of interest in 2012, it must accrue that interest as revenue on December 31, 2012 (even though no cash has been collected). The adjustment to accrue interest revenue follows.

December 31, 2012	Debit	Credit	
Interest Receivable	**200**		A = L + SE
Interest Revenue		200	+200
(Accrue interest revenue)			+200 Rev↑
(Interest revenue = $10,000 × 12% × 2/12)			

On May 1, 2013, the maturity date, Kimzey records the collection of the note receivable and interest receivable from 2012 as well as the revenue related to the remaining four months' interest earned in 2013.

May 1, 2013	Debit	Credit	
Cash	**10,600**		A = L + SE
Notes Receivable		10,000	+10,600
Interest Receivable		200	−10,000
Interest Revenue		400	−200
(Collect note receivable and interest)			+400 Rev↑
(Interest revenue = $10,000 × 12% × 4/12)			

On May 1, 2013, Kimzey has received the note receivable recorded on November 1, 2012, and the interest receivable recorded on December 31, 2012, and has eliminated their balances. The remaining four months' interest occurs in 2013, and Kimzey recognizes it as revenue in 2013.

KEY POINT

We record interest earned on notes receivable but not yet collected by the end of the year as interest receivable and interest revenue.

Let's Review

General Hospital has a policy of lending any employee up to $3,000 for a period of 12 months at a fixed interest rate of 9%. Chevy Chase has worked for General Hospital for more than 10 years and wishes to take his family on a summer vacation. On May 1, 2012, he borrows $3,000 from General Hospital to be repaid in 12 months.

Required:

1. Record the loan of cash and acceptance of the note receivable by General Hospital.
2. Record General Hospital's year-end adjustment to accrue interest revenue.
3. Record the collection of the note with interest from Chevy Chase on May 1, 2013.

Solution:

1. Acceptance of the note receivable:

May 1, 2012	Debit	Credit
Notes Receivable	3,000	
Cash		3,000
(*Accept note receivable*)		

2. Year-end adjustment to accrue interest revenue:

December 31, 2012	Debit	Credit
Interest Receivable	180	
Interest Revenue (8 months' interest)		180
(*Accrue interest revenue*)		
(*Interest revenue = $3,000 × 9% × 8/12*)		

3. Collection of the note with interest:

May 1, 2013	Debit	Credit
Cash	3,270	
Notes Receivable		3,000
Interest Receivable		180
Interest Revenue (4 months' interest)		90
(*Collect note receivable and interest*)		
(*Interest revenue = $3,000 × 9% × 4/12*)		

Suggested Homework:
BE5-10, BE5-11;
E5-15, E5-17;
P5-8A&B

ANALYSIS

RECEIVABLES ANALYSIS
Tenet vs. LifePoint

The amount of a company's accounts receivable is influenced by a variety of factors, including the level of sales, the nature of the product or service sold, and credit and collection policies. These factors are, of course, related. For example, a change

in credit policies could affect sales. More liberal credit policies—allowing customers a longer time to pay or offering cash discounts for early payment—often are initiated with the specific objective of increasing sales volume.

Management's choice of credit and collection policies results in trade-offs. For example, when a company attempts to boost sales by allowing customers more time to pay, that policy also creates an increase in the required investment in receivables and may increase bad debts because older accounts are less likely to be collected. Offering discounts for early payment may increase sales volume, accelerate customer payment, and reduce bad debts, but at the same time it reduces the amount of cash collected from customers who take advantage of the discounts.

CAREER CORNER

Companies that make large amounts of credit sales often employ credit analysts. These analysts are responsible for deciding whether to extend credit to potential customers. To make this decision, credit analysts focus on the customer's credit history (such as delinquency in paying bills) and information about current financial position, generally found using amounts in the financial statements. When the credit risk is too high, the analyst will advise management to reject the customer's request for goods and services, or perhaps limit the amount of credit extended. Management must then face a difficult trade-off: the potential gains from additional customer revenues versus the risk of an eventual uncollectible account. Credit analysts are most commonly employed by financial institutions ranging from banks to credit rating agencies and investment companies.

Investors, creditors, and financial analysts can gain important insights by monitoring a company's investment in receivables. Two important ratios that help in understanding the company's effectiveness in managing receivables are the *receivables turnover ratio* and the *average collection period*. We discuss those measures and then compare them for **Tenet Healthcare Corporation** and **LifePoint Hospitals**.

■ **LO8**
Calculate key ratios investors use to monitor a company's effectiveness in managing receivables.

RECEIVABLES TURNOVER RATIO

The **receivables turnover ratio** shows the number of times during a year that the average accounts receivable balance is collected (or "turns over"). We calculate it as follows:

$$\text{Receivables turnover ratio} = \frac{\text{Net credit sales}}{\text{Average accounts receivable}}$$

Let's say net credit sales are $400,000 for the year and the average accounts receivable balance is $40,000. In that case, we could say the turnover ratio is 10 ($400,000/$40,000), or that average receivables were collected 10 times during the year.

Note that the lower half of the receivables turnover ratio—average accounts receivable—is typically measured as the beginning accounts receivable plus the ending accounts receivable divided by two. So, our average of $40,000 might be the result of having a $35,000 balance at the beginning of the year and a $45,000 balance at the end of the year.

$$\text{Receivables turnover ratio} = \frac{\$400,000}{(\$35,000 + \$45,000)/2} = 10$$

AVERAGE COLLECTION PERIOD

The **average collection period** is another way to express the same efficiency measure. We calculate the average collection period as:

$$\text{Average collection period} = \frac{\text{365 days}}{\text{Receivables turnover ratio}}$$

It shows the approximate number of days the average accounts receivable balance is outstanding. If the turnover is 10 times a year (365 days), then the average balance is collected every 36.5 days.

$$\text{Average collection period} = \frac{365 \text{ days}}{10} = 36.5 \text{ days}$$

Companies typically strive for a high receivables turnover ratio and a correspondingly low average collection period. As a company's sales increase, receivables also likely will increase. If the percentage increase in receivables is greater than the percentage increase in sales, the receivables turnover ratio will decline (and the average collection period will increase). This could indicate that customers are dissatisfied with the product or that the company's payment terms for attracting new customers are too generous, which, in turn, could increase sales returns and bad debts.

Of course, what's "high" and what's "low" for these ratios depends on the situation. Companies may wish to evaluate these ratios relative to the prior year's ratios, ratios of other firms in the same industry, or specific targets set by management.

Decision Point

Question	Accounting information	Analysis
Is the company effectively managing its receivables?	Receivables turnover ratio and average collection period	A high receivables turnover ratio (or low average collection period) generally indicates that the company's credit sales and collection policies are effective.

Now let's compare **Tenet Healthcare Corporation** to **LifePoint Hospitals**. The calculations of the receivables turnover ratio and average collection period for each company for 2008 and 2009, along with their net income for those years, are shown in Illustration 5–17.

ILLUSTRATION 5–17

Comparison of Receivables Ratios between Tenet Healthcare Corporation and LifePoint Hospitals

TENET HEALTHCARE CORPORATION

	Net Sales (in millions)	Average Accounts Receivable (in millions)	Receivables Turnover Ratio	Average Collection Period	Net Income
2008	$8,585	$1,361	$\frac{\$8,585}{\$1,361} = 6.31$	$\frac{365}{6.31} = 57.8$	$ 32
2009	$9,014	$1,248	$\frac{\$9,014}{\$1,248} = 7.22$	$\frac{365}{7.22} = 50.6$	$197

LIFEPOINT HOSPITALS

	Net Sales (in millions)	Average Accounts Receivable (in millions)	Receivables Turnover Ratio	Average Collection Period	Net Income
2008	$2,701	$ 310	$\frac{\$2,701}{\$310} = 8.71$	$\frac{365}{8.71} = 41.9$	$103
2009	$2,963	$ 321	$\frac{\$2,963}{\$321} = 9.23$	$\frac{365}{9.23} = 39.5$	$134

More profitable operations.

More efficiently collects cash

From Illustration 5–17, we see that LifePoint has a much higher receivables turn-over, indicating that the company more efficiently collects cash from patients than does Tenet. The average collection period is much longer for Tenet. Better management of receivables by LifePoint may help explain the company's more profitable operations. Over the two-year period, LifePoint's net income is greater than that of Tenet, even though its revenue is only about one-third.

Having enough cash is important to running any business. The more quickly a company can collect its receivables, the more quickly it can use that cash to generate even more cash by reinvesting in the business and generating additional sales.

 KEY POINT

The receivables turnover ratio and average collection period can provide an indication of management's ability to collect cash from customers in a timely manner.

PERCENTAGE-OF-CREDIT-SALES METHOD

> **APPENDIX**

In the chapter, we estimated uncollectible accounts based on a percentage of accounts receivable at the end of the period. You learned that this method is the *percentage-of-receivables* method or the *balance sheet method,* because we base the estimate of bad debts on a balance sheet amount—accounts receivable.

As an alternative, we can estimate uncollectible accounts based on the percentage of credit sales for the year, aptly referred to as the *percentage-of-credit-sales method* or the *income statement method,* because we base the estimate of bad debts on an income statement amount—credit sales. In this appendix, we consider the percentage-of-credit-sales method.

Let's rework the example in the chapter for Kimzey Medical Clinic (see Illustrations 5–8 to 5–10 and their discussion). During 2013, Kimzey bills customers $80 million for services, with $30 million in accounts receivable remaining at the end of the year. The balance of the allowance account, before adjustment, is a $2 million credit. For the percentage-of-receivables method, we'll use the estimate for uncollectible accounts used in the chapter—30% of receivables. For the percentage-of-credit-sales method, let's assume Kimzey expects 10% of credit sales to be uncollectible. Kimzey bases the 10% estimate on a number of factors, such as the average percentage of uncollectibles each year over the past several years.

Illustration 5–18 demonstrates the differences in the two methods when adjusting for estimates of uncollectible accounts.

■ LO9
Estimate uncollectible accounts using the percentage-of-credit-sales method.

Percentage-of-Receivables Method (repeated from chapter)		Percentage-of-Credit Sales Method	
Estimate of Uncollectible Accounts		Estimate of Uncollectible Accounts	
• 30% of ending accounts receivable will not be collected.		• 10% of credit sales will not be collected.	
• 30% of $30 million = $9 million.		• 10% of $80 million = $8 million.	
• Adjust from $2 million existing balance.		• Ignore $2 million existing balance.	
Adjustment ($ in millions)		Adjustment ($ in millions)	
Bad Debt Expense	7	Bad Debt Expense	8
Allowance for Uncoll. Accts.	7	Allowance for Uncoll. Accts.	8

ILLUSTRATION 5–18

Adjusting for Estimates of Uncollectible Accounts

Notice that the two methods for estimating uncollectible accounts result in different adjustments. Because the amounts of the adjustments differ, the effects on the financial statements differ. Recall that the balance of the allowance account before adjustment is a $2 million credit. After adjustment, the balance of the allowance account will differ between the two methods, as will the amount of bad debt expense. Illustration 5–19 summarizes the differences in financial statement effects.

ILLUSTRATION 5–19

Financial Statement Effects of Estimating Uncollectible Accounts

Percentage-of-Receivables Method
($ in millions)

Income Statement Effect

Revenues	$80
Bad debt expense	(7)
Net income	$73

Balance Sheet Effect

Accounts receivable	$30
Less: Allowance	(9)*
Net accounts receivable	$21

* $9 = $2 + $7 (adjustment)

Percentage-of-Credit-Sales Method
($ in millions)

Income Statement Effect

Revenues	$80
Bad debt expense	(8)
Net income	$72

Balance Sheet Effect

Accounts receivable	$30
Less: Allowance	(10)*
Net accounts receivable	$20

* $10 = $2 + $8 (adjustment)

From an income statement perspective, some argue that the percentage-of-credit-sales method provides a better method for estimating bad debts because expenses (bad debts) are better matched with revenues (credit sales). A better matching of expenses and revenues results in a more accurate measure of net income for the period. From a balance sheet perspective, though, the percentage-of-receivables method is preferable because assets (net accounts receivable) are reported closer to their net realizable value.

The current emphasis on better measurement of assets (balance sheet focus) outweighs the emphasis on better measurement of net income (income statement focus). **This is why the percentage-of-receivables method (balance sheet method) is the preferable method, while the percentage-of-credit-sales method (income statement method) is allowed only if amounts do not differ significantly from estimates using the percentage-of-receivables method.**

 KEY POINT

When applying the percentage-of-credit-sales method, we adjust the allowance for uncollectible accounts for the current year's credit sales that we don't expect to collect (rather than adjusting at the end of the year for the percentage of accounts receivable we don't expect to collect).

 KEY POINTS BY LEARNING OBJECTIVE

LO1 Recognize accounts receivable.

Companies record an asset (accounts receivable) and revenue when they sell products and services to their customers on account, expecting payment in the future.

LO2 Calculate net revenues using discounts, returns, and allowances.

Sales discounts, returns, and allowances are contra revenue accounts. We subtract the balances in these accounts from total revenues when calculating net revenues.

LO3 Record an allowance for future uncollectible accounts.

We recognize accounts receivable as assets in the balance sheet and record them at their net

realizable values, that is, the amount of cash we expect to collect.

Under the allowance method, companies are required to *estimate* future uncollectible accounts and record those estimates in the current year. Estimated uncollectible accounts reduce assets and increase expenses.

Adjusting for estimates of future uncollectible accounts matches expenses (bad debts) in the same period as the revenues (credit sales) they help to generate.

Recording an allowance for uncollectible accounts correctly reports accounts receivable at their net realizable value.

LO4 Apply the procedure to write off accounts receivable as uncollectible.

Writing off a customer's account as uncollectible reduces the balance of accounts receivable but also reduces the contra asset—allowance for uncollectible accounts. The net effect is that there is no change in the *net* receivable (accounts receivable less the allowance) or in total assets. We recorded the decrease to assets as a result of the bad debt when we established the allowance for uncollectible accounts in a prior year.

LO5 Use the aging method to estimate future uncollectible accounts.

Using the aging method to estimate uncollectible accounts is more accurate than applying a single percentage to all accounts receivable. The aging method recognizes that the longer accounts are past due, the less likely they are to be collected.

LO6 Contrast the allowance method and direct write-off method when accounting for uncollectible accounts.

The direct write-off method reduces accounts receivable and records bad debt expense at the time the account receivable proves

uncollectible. If the credit sale occurs in a prior reporting period, bad debt expense is not properly matched with revenues (credit sales). Also, accounts receivable will be overstated in the prior period. The direct write-off method typically is not acceptable for financial reporting.

LO7 Apply the procedure to account for notes receivable, including interest calculation.

Notes receivable are similar to accounts receivable except that notes receivable are more formal credit arrangements made with a written debt instrument, or *note*.

We calculate interest as the face value of the note multiplied by the stated annual interest rate multiplied by the appropriate fraction of the year.

We record interest earned on notes receivable but not yet collected by the end of the year as interest receivable and interest revenue.

Analysis

LO8 Calculate key ratios investors use to monitor a company's effectiveness in managing receivables.

The receivables turnover ratio and average collection period can provide an indication of management's ability to collect cash from customers in a timely manner.

Appendix

LO9 Estimate uncollectible accounts using the percentage-of-credit-sales method.

When applying the percentage-of-credit-sales method, we adjust the allowance for uncollectible accounts for the current year's credit sales that we don't expect to collect (rather than adjusting at the end of the year for the percentage of accounts receivable we don't expect to collect).

GLOSSARY

Accounts receivable: The amount of cash owed to the company by its customers from the sale of products or services on account. **p. 214**

Aging method: Using a higher percentage for "old" accounts than for "new" accounts when estimating uncollectible accounts. **p. 227**

Allowance for uncollectible accounts: Contra asset account representing the amount of accounts receivable that we do not expect to collect. **p. 222**

Allowance method: Recording an adjustment at the end of each period to allow for the possibility of

future uncollectible accounts. The adjustment has the effects of reducing assets and increasing expenses. **p. 220**

Average collection period: Approximate number of days the average accounts receivable balance is outstanding. It equals 365 divided by the receivables turnover ratio. **p. 237**

Bad debt expense: The amount of the adjustment to the allowance for uncollectible accounts, representing the cost of estimated future bad debts charged to the current period. **p. 221**

Contra revenue account: An account with a balance that is opposite, or "contra," to that of its related revenue account. **p. 216**

Credit sales: Transfer of products and services to a customer today while bearing the risk of collecting payment from that customer in the future. Also known as *sales on account* or *services on account*. **p. 214**

Direct write-off method: Recording bad debt expense at the time we know the account is uncollectible. **p. 230**

Net accounts receivable: The difference between total accounts receivable and the allowance for uncollectible accounts. **p. 222**

Net realizable value: The amount of cash the firm expects to collect. **p. 219**

Net revenues: A company's total revenues less any discounts, returns, and allowances. **p. 215**

Notes receivable: Formal credit arrangements evidenced by a written debt instrument, or *note*. **p. 232**

Percentage-of-receivables method: Method of estimating uncollectible accounts based on the percentage of accounts receivable expected not to be collected. **p. 221**

Receivables turnover ratio: Number of times during a year that the average accounts receivable balance is collected (or "turns over"). It equals net credit sales divided by average accounts receivable. **p. 237**

Sales allowance: Seller reduces the customer's balance owed or provides at least a partial refund because of some deficiency in the company's product or service. **p. 217**

Sales discount: Reduction in the amount to be paid by a credit customer if payment on account is made within a specified period of time. **p. 215**

Sales return: Customer returns a product. **p. 217**

Trade discount: Reduction in the listed price of a product or service. **p. 215**

Uncollectible accounts: Customers' accounts that no longer are considered collectible. **p. 220**

SELF-STUDY QUESTIONS

■ **LO1**

1. Accounts receivable are best described as:
   a. Liabilities of the company that represent the amount owed to suppliers.
   b. Amounts that have previously been received from customers.
   c. Assets of the company representing the amount owed by customers.
   d. Amounts that have previously been paid to suppliers.

■ **LO2**

2. On March 17, Fox Lumber sells materials to Whitney Construction for $12,000, terms 2/10, n/30. Whitney pays for the materials on March 23. What amount would Fox record as revenue on March 17?
   a. $12,400.
   b. $11,760.
   c. $12,000.
   d. $12,240.

■ **LO2**

3. Refer to the information in the previous question. What is the amount of net revenues (sales minus sales discounts) as of March 23?
   a. $0.
   b. $11,760.
   c. $12,000.
   d. $12,240.

■ **LO3**

4. Suppose the balance of Allowance for Uncollectible Accounts at the end of the current year is $400 (*credit*) before any adjustment. The company estimates future uncollectible accounts to be $3,200. At what amount would bad debt expense be reported in the current year's income statement?
   a. $400.
   b. $2,800.
   c. $3,200.
   d. $3,600.

■ **LO3**

5. Suppose the balance of Allowance for Uncollectible Accounts at the end of the current year is $400 (*debit*) before any adjustment. The company estimates future

uncollectible accounts to be $3,200. At what amount would bad debt expense be reported in the current year's income statement?

d.

a. $400.
b. $2,800.
c. $3,200.
d. $3,600.

6. The entry to record a write-off of accounts receivable will include: ■ LO4
   a. A debit to Bad Debt Expense.
   b. A debit to Allowance for Uncollectible Accounts.
   c. No entry because an allowance for uncollectible accounts was established in an earlier period.
   d. A debit to Service Revenue.

7. Kidz Incorporated reports the following aging schedule of its accounts receivable ■ LO5
   with the estimated percent uncollectible. What is the total estimate of uncollectible accounts using the aging method?

Age Group	Amount Receivable	Estimated Percent Uncollectible	
0–60 days	$20,000	2%	400
61–90 days	6,000	15%	900
More than 90 days past due	2,000	50%	1000
Total	$28,000		2300

C

a. $1,150.
b. $1,900.
c. $2,300.
d. $5,900.

8. The direct write-off method is generally not permitted for financial reporting ■ LO6
   purposes because:
   a. Compared to the allowance method, it would allow greater flexibility to managers in manipulating reported net income.
   b. This method is primarily used for tax purposes.
   c. It is too difficult to accurately estimate future bad debts.
   d. Expenses (bad debts) are not properly matched with the revenues (credit sales) they help to generate.

9. On January 1, 2012, Roberson Supply borrows $10,000 from Nees Manufacturing ■ LO7
   by signing a 9% note due in eight months. Calculate the amount of interest revenue Nees will record on September 1, 2012, the date that the note is due.
   a. $300.
   b. $600.
   c. $900.
   d. $1,000.

10. At the beginning of 2012, Clay Ventures has total accounts receivable of $100,000. ■ LO8
    By the end of 2012, Clay reports net credit sales of $900,000 and total accounts receivable of $200,000. What is the receivables turnover ratio for Clay Ventures?
    a. 2.0.
    b. 4.5.
    c. 6.0.
    d. 9.0.

Note: For answers, see the last page of the chapter.

Check out
www.mhhe.com/succeed
for more multiple-choice
questions.

REVIEW QUESTIONS

■ LO1   1. When recording a credit sale, what account do we debit? Describe where this account is reported in the financial statements.

■ LO1   2. What is the difference between a trade receivable and a nontrade receivable?

■ LO2   3. Explain the difference between a trade discount and a sales discount. Where are sales discounts reported in the income statement?

■ LO2   4. Briefly explain the accounting treatment for sales returns and allowances. Where are these accounts reported in the income statement?

■ LO2   5. Revenue can be earned at one point or over a period. Provide an example of each.

■ LO3   6. Explain the correct way companies should account for uncollectible accounts receivable (bad debts).

■ LO3   7. What two purposes do firms achieve by estimating future uncollectible accounts?

■ LO3   8. How does accounting for uncollectible accounts conform to the concept of the matching principle?

■ LO3   9. What are the financial statement effects of establishing an allowance for uncollectible accounts?

■ LO3   10. Describe the year-end adjustment to record the allowance for uncollectible accounts.

■ LO3   11. Allowance for Uncollectible Accounts is a contra asset account, which means that its normal balance is a credit. However, it is possible for the account to have a debit balance before year-end adjustments are recorded. Explain how this could happen.

■ LO3   12. We report accounts receivable in the balance sheet at their *net realizable value*. Explain what this term means.

■ LO4   13. When we have established an allowance for uncollectible accounts, how do we write off an account receivable as uncollectible? What effect does this write-off have on the reported amount of total assets and net income at the time of the write-off?

■ LO4   14. If at the end of the year Allowance for Uncollectible Accounts has a credit balance before any adjustment, what might that tell us about last year's estimate of future uncollectible accounts?

■ LO5   15. What does the *age* of accounts receivable refer to? How can we use an aging method to estimate uncollectible accounts receivable?

■ LO6   16. Discuss the differences between the allowance method and the direct write-off method for recording uncollectible accounts. Which of the two is acceptable under financial accounting rules?

■ LO7   17. Notes receivable differ from accounts receivable in that notes receivable represent *written* debt instruments. What is one other common difference between notes receivable and accounts receivable?

■ LO7   18. With respect to notes receivable, explain what each of these represent: (a) face value, (b) annual interest rate, and (c) fraction of the year.

■ LO7   19. What will be the total interest earned on a 6%, $2,000 note receivable that is due in nine months?

■ LO7   20. Interest on a note receivable typically is due along with the face value at the note's maturity date. If the end of the accounting period occurs before the maturity date, how do we record interest earned but not yet collected?

■ LO8   21. How is the receivables turnover ratio measured? What does this ratio indicate? Is a higher or lower receivables turnover preferable?

22. How is the average collection period of receivables measured? What does this ratio indicate? Is a higher or lower average collection period preferable? ■ **LO8**

23. How can effectively managing receivables benefit a company? ■ **LO8**

24. Which method, the percentage-of-receivables method or the percentage-of-credit-sales method, is typically used in practice? Why? ■ **LO9**

25. Explain why the percentage-of-receivables method is referred to as the *balance sheet method* and the percentage-of-credit-sales method is referred to as the *income statement method*. ■ **LO9**

BRIEF EXERCISES

BE5–1 The Giles Agency offers a 10% trade discount when providing advertising services of $1,000 or more to its customers. Audrey's Antiques decides to purchase advertising services of $2,500 (not including the trade discount), while Michael's Motors purchases only $600 of advertising. Both services are provided on account. Record both transactions for The Giles Agency, accounting for any trade discounts.

Record accounts receivable and trade discount (LO2)

BE5–2 Kelly's Jewelry reported the following amounts at the end of the year: total jewelry sales = $650,000; sales discounts = $15,000; sales returns = $40,000; sales allowances = $20,000. Compute net sales.

Calculate net sales (LO2)

BE5–3 At the end of the year, Mercy Cosmetics' balance of Allowance for Uncollectible Accounts is $500 (*credit*) before adjustment. The balance of Accounts Receivable is $20,000. The company estimates that 15% of accounts will not be collected over the next year. What adjustment would Mercy Cosmetics record for Allowance for Uncollectible Accounts?

Record the adjustment for uncollectible accounts (LO3)

BE5–4 At the end of the year, Dahir Incorporated's balance of Allowance for Uncollectible Accounts is $2,000 (*credit*) before adjustment. The company estimates future uncollectible accounts to be $10,000. What adjustment would Dahir record for Allowance for Uncollectible Accounts?

Record the adjustment for uncollectible accounts (LO3)

BE5–5 Refer to the information in BE5–4, but now assume that the balance of Allowance for Uncollectible Accounts before adjustment is $2,000 (*debit*). The company still estimates future uncollectible accounts to be $10,000. What is the adjustment Dahir would record for Allowance for Uncollectible Accounts?

Record the adjustment for uncollectible accounts (LO3)

BE5–6 At the beginning of the year, Mitchum Enterprises allows for estimated uncollectible accounts of $14,000. By the end of the year, actual bad debts total $15,000. Record the write–off to uncollectible accounts. Following the write-off, what is the balance of Allowance for Uncollectible Accounts?

Record the write-off of uncollectible accounts (LO4)

BE5–7 Barnes Books allows for possible bad debts. On May 7, Barnes writes off a customer account of $6,000. On September 9, the customer unexpectedly pays the $6,000 balance. Record the cash collection on September 9.

Record collection of account previously written off (LO4)

BE5–8 Williamson Distributors separates its accounts receivable into three age groups for purposes of estimating the percentage of uncollectible accounts.
1. Accounts not yet due = $30,000; estimated uncollectible = 5%.
2. Accounts 1–30 days past due = $10,000; estimated uncollectible = 20%.
3. Accounts more than 30 days past due = $4,000; estimated uncollectible = 30%.
Compute the total estimated uncollectible accounts.

Calculate uncollectible accounts using the aging method (LO5)

BE5–9 Brady is hired in 2012 to be the accountant for Anderson Manufacturing, a private company. At the end of 2012, the balance of Accounts Receivable is $24,000. In the past, Anderson has used only the direct write-off method to account for bad debts. Based on a detailed analysis of amounts owed, Brady believes the best estimate of future bad debts is $8,000. If Anderson continues to use the direct write-off method to account for uncollectible accounts, what adjustment, if any, would Brady record

Use the direct write-off method to account for uncollectible accounts (LO6)

at the end of 2012? What adjustment, if any, would Brady record if Anderson instead uses the allowance method to account for uncollectible accounts?

Calculate amounts related to interest (LO7)

BE5–10 Calculate the missing amount for each of the following notes receivable.

Face Value	Annual Interest Rate	Fraction of the Year	Interest
$10,000	6%	4 months	(a)
$20,000	4%	(b)	$800
$25,000	(c)	6 months	$500
(d)	8%	6 months	$600

Calculate interest revenue on notes receivable (LO7)

BE5–11 On October 1, 2012, Oberley Corporation loans one of its employees $30,000 and accepts a 12-month, 8% note receivable. Calculate the amount of interest revenue Oberley will recognize in 2012 and 2013.

Use the percentage-of-credit-sales method to adjust for uncollectible accounts (LO9)

BE5–12 At the end of the year, Brinkley Incorporated's balance of Allowance for Uncollectible Accounts is $3,000 (*credit*) before adjustment. The company estimates future uncollectible accounts to be 4% of credit sales for the year. Credit sales for the year total $125,000. What is the adjustment Brinkley would record for Allowance for Uncollectible Accounts using the percentage-of-credit-sales method?

Use the percentage-of-credit-sales method to adjust for uncollectible accounts (LO9)

BE5–13 Refer to the information in BE5–12, but now assume that the balance of Allowance for Uncollectible Accounts before adjustment is $3,000 (*debit*). The company still estimates future uncollectible accounts to be 4% of credit sales for the year. What adjustment would Brinkley record for Allowance for Uncollectible Accounts using the percentage-of-credit-sales method?

EXERCISES

Record credit sale (LO1)

E5–1 On May 7, Juanita Construction provides services on account to Michael Wolfe for $3,000. Michael pays for those services on May 13.

Required:
For Juanita Construction, record the service on account on May 7 and the collection of cash on May 13.

Record cash sales with a trade discount (LO2)

E5–2 Merry Maidens Cleaning generally charges $200 for a detailed cleaning of a normal-size home. However, to generate additional business, Merry Maidens is offering a new-customer discount of 10%. On May 1, Ms. E. Pearson has Merry Maidens clean her house and pays cash equal to the discounted price.

Required:
Record the revenue earned by Merry Maidens Cleaning on May 1.

Record credit sale and cash collection with a sales discount (LO1, 2)

E5–3 On March 12, Medical Waste Services provides services on account to Grace Hospital for $10,000, terms 3/10, n/30. Grace pays for those services on March 20.

Required:
For Medical Waste Services, record the service on account on March 12 and the collection of cash on March 20.

Record credit sale and cash collection (LO1, 2)

E5–4 Refer to the information in E5–3, but now assume that Grace does not pay for services until March 31, missing the 3% sales discount.

Flip Side of E5–5

Required:
For Medical Waste Services, record the service on account on March 12 and the collection of cash on March 31.

E5–5 Refer to the information in E5–4.

Required:

For Grace Hospital, record the purchase of services on account on March 12 and the payment of cash on March 31.

Record credit purchase and cash payment **(LO1, 2)**

Flip Side of E5–4

Record credit sales with a sales allowance **(LO1, 2)**

E5–6 On April 25, Foreman Electric installs wiring in a new home for $2,500 on account. However, on April 27, Foreman's electrical work does not pass inspection, and Foreman grants the customer an allowance of $500 because of the problem. The customer makes full payment of the balance owed, excluding the allowance, on April 30.

Required:
1. Record the credit sale on April 25.
2. Record the sales allowance on April 27.
3. Record the cash collection on April 30.
4. Calculate net sales associated with these transactions.

E5–7 During 2012, its first year of operations, Pave Construction provides services on account of $140,000. By the end of 2012, cash collections on these accounts total $100,000. Pave estimates that 30% of the uncollected accounts will be bad debts.

Required:
1. Record the adjustment for uncollectible accounts on December 31, 2012.
2. Calculate the net realizable value of accounts receivable.

Record the adjustment for uncollectible accounts and calculate net realizable value **(LO3)**

E5–8 Physicians' Hospital has the following balances on December 31, 2012, before any adjustment: Accounts Receivable = $50,000; Allowance for Uncollectible Accounts = $1,000 (credit). On December 31, 2012, Physicians' estimates uncollectible accounts to be 20% of accounts receivable.   50000 × 20% = 10000

Required:
1. Record the adjustment for uncollectible accounts on December 31, 2012.
2. Determine the amount at which bad debt expense is reported in the income statement and the allowance for uncollectible accounts is reported in the balance sheet.
3. Calculate the net realizable value of accounts receivable.

Record the adjustment for uncollectible accounts and calculate net realizable value **(LO3)**

E5–9 Southwest Pediatrics has the following balances on December 31, 2012, before any adjustment: Accounts Receivable = $120,000; Allowance for Uncollectible Accounts = $2,000 (*debit*). On December 31, 2012, Southwest estimates uncollectible accounts to be 10% of accounts receivable.

Required:
1. Record the adjustment for uncollectible accounts on December 31, 2012.
2. Determine the amount at which bad debt expense is reported in the income statement and the allowance for uncollectible accounts is reported in the balance sheet.
3. Calculate the net realizable value of accounts receivable.

Record the adjustment for uncollectible accounts and calculate net realizable value **(LO3)**

E5–10 Consider the following transactions associated with accounts receivable and the allowance for uncollectible accounts.

Identify the financial statement effects of transactions related to accounts receivable and allowance for uncollectible accounts **(LO3, 4)**

Credit Sales Transaction Cycle	Assets	Liabilities	Stockholders' Equity	Revenues	Expenses
1. Provide services on account					
2. Estimate uncollectible accounts					
3. Write off accounts as uncollectible					
4. Collect on account previously written off					

Required:

For each transaction, indicate whether it would increase (I), decrease (D), or have no effect (NE) on the account totals. (*Hint:* Make sure the accounting equation, Assets = Liabilities + Stockholders' Equity, remains in balance after each transaction.)

Record the adjustment for uncollectible accounts using the aging method (LO5)

E5–11 Mercy Hospital has the following balances on December 31, 2012, before any adjustment: Accounts Receivable = $60,000; Allowance for Uncollectible Accounts = $1,500 (credit). Mercy estimates uncollectible accounts based on an aging of accounts receivable as shown below.

Age Group	Amount Receivable	Estimated Percent Uncollectible
Not yet due	$40,000	10%
0–30 days past due	10,000	20%
31–90 days past due	7,000	50%
More than 90 days past due	3,000	90%
Total	$60,000	

Required:
1. Estimate the amount of uncollectible receivables.
2. Record the adjustment for uncollectible accounts on December 31, 2012.
3. Calculate the net realizable value of accounts receivable.

Record the adjustment for uncollectible accounts using the aging method (LO5)

E5–12 The Physical Therapy Center specializes in helping patients regain motor skills after serious accidents. The center has the following balances on December 31, 2012, before any adjustment: Accounts Receivable = $100,000; Allowance for Uncollectible Accounts = $3,000 (*debit*). The center estimates uncollectible accounts based on an aging of accounts receivable as shown below.

Age Group	Amount Receivable	Estimated Percent Uncollectible	
Not yet due	$ 50,000	5%	2500
0–60 days past due	25,000	10%	2500
61–120 days past due	15,000	20%	3000
More than 120 days past due	10,000	70%	7000
Total	$100,000		$15000

Required:
1. Estimate the amount of uncollectible receivables. *15000*
2. Record the adjustment for uncollectible accounts on December 31, 2012.
3. Calculate the net realizable value of accounts receivable.

Compare the allowance method and the direct write-off method (LO6)

E5–13 At the beginning of 2012, Brad's Heating & Air (BHA) has a balance of $25,000 in accounts receivable. Because BHA is a privately owned company, the company has used only the direct write-off method to account for uncollectible accounts. However, at the end of 2012, BHA wishes to obtain a loan at the local bank, which requires the preparation of proper financial statements. This means that BHA now will need to use the allowance method. The following transactions occur during 2012 and 2013.
a. During 2012, install air conditioning systems on account, $180,000.
b. During 2012, collect $175,000 from customers on account.
c. At the end of 2012, estimate that uncollectible accounts total 20% of ending accounts receivable.
d. In 2013, customers' accounts totaling $7,000 are written off as uncollectible.

Required:
1. Record each transaction using the allowance method.
2. Record each transaction using the direct write-off method.
3. Calculate the difference in net income (before taxes) in 2012 and 2013 between the two methods.

E5–14 During 2012, LeBron Corporation accepts the following notes receivable.

a. On April 1, LeBron provides services to a customer on account. The customer signs a four-month, 9% note for $6,000.

b. On June 1, LeBron lends cash to one of the company's executives by accepting a six-month, 10% note for $10,000.

c. On November 1, LeBron accepts payment for prior services by having a customer with a past-due account receivable sign a three-month, 8% note for $5,000.

Record notes receivable (LO7)

Required:
Record the acceptance of each of the notes receivable.

E5–15 On March 1, Terrell & Associates provides legal services to Whole Grain Bakery regarding some recent food poisoning complaints. Legal services total $10,000. In payment for the services, Whole Grain Bakery signs a 10% note requiring the payment of the face amount and interest to Terrell & Associates on September 1.

Record notes receivable and interest revenue (LO7)

Flip Side of E5–16

Required:
For Terrell & Associates, record the acceptance of the note receivable on March 1 and the cash collection on September 1.

E5–16 Refer to the information in E5–15.

Record notes payable and interest expense (LO7)

Flip Side of E5–15

Required:
For Whole Grain Bakery, record the issuance of the note payable on March 1 and the cash payment on September 1.

E5–17 On April 1, 2012, Shoemaker Corporation realizes that one of its main suppliers is having difficulty meeting delivery schedules, which is hurting Shoemaker's business. The supplier explains that it has a temporary lack of funds that is slowing its production cycle. Shoemaker agrees to lend $500,000 to its supplier using a 12-month, 12% note.

Record notes receivable and interest revenue (LO7)

Required:
Record the following transactions for Shoemaker Corporation.
1. The loan of $500,000 and acceptance of the note receivable on April 1, 2012.
2. The adjustment for accrued interest on December 31, 2012.
3. Cash collection of the note and interest on April 1, 2013.

E5–18 Below are amounts (in millions) from three companies' annual reports.

Calculate receivables ratios (LO8)

	Beginning Accounts Receivable (net)	Ending Accounts Receivable (net)	Net Sales
Walmart	$1,715	$2,662	$312,427
Target	$5,666	$6,194	$ 57,878
Costco Wholesale	$ 529	$ 565	$ 58,963

Required:
For each company, calculate the receivables turnover ratio and the average collection period (rounded to one decimal place). Which company appears most efficient in collecting cash from sales?

E5–19 Suzuki Supply reports the following amounts at the end of 2012 (before adjustment).

Compare the percentage-of-receivables method and the percentage-of-credit-sales method (LO9)

Credit Sales for 2012	$250,000
Accounts Receivable, December 31, 2012	45,000
Allowance for Uncollectible Accounts, December 31, 2012	1,000 (credit)

Required:
1. Record the adjustment for uncollectible accounts using the percentage-of-receivables method. Suzuki estimates 10% of receivables will not be collected.

2. Record the adjustment for uncollectible accounts using the percentage-of-credit-sales method. Suzuki estimates 2% of credit sales will not be collected.

3. Calculate the effect on net income (before taxes) and total assets in 2012 for each method.

Compare the percentage-of-receivables method and the percentage-of-credit-sales method (LO9)

E5–20 Refer to the information in E5–19, but now assume that the balance of the Allowance for Uncollectible Accounts on December 31, 2012, is $1,000 *(debit)* (before adjustment).

Required:

1. Record the adjustment for uncollectible accounts using the percentage-of-receivables method. Suzuki estimates 10% of receivables will not be collected.

2. Record the adjustment for uncollectible accounts using the percentage-of-credit-sales method. Suzuki estimates 2% of credit sales will not be collected.

3. Calculate the effect on net income (before taxes) and total assets in 2012 for each method.

For additional exercises, visit www.mhhe.com/succeed for Exercises: Set B.

PROBLEMS: SET A

Calculate the amount of revenue to recognize (LO1)

P5–1A Assume the following scenarios.

Scenario 1: During 2012, **IBM** provides consulting services on its mainframe computer for $10,000 on account. The customer does not pay for those services until 2013.

Scenario 2: On January 1, 2012, **Gold's Gym** sells a one-year membership for $1,200 cash. Normally, this type of membership would cost $1,500, but the company is offering a 20% "New Year's Resolution" discount.

Scenario 3: During 2012, **The Manitowoc Company** provides shipbuilding services to the U.S. Navy for $300,000. The U.S. Navy will pay $100,000 at the end of each year for the next three years, beginning in 2012.

Scenario 4: During 2012, **Goodyear** sells tires to customers on account for $24,000. By the end of the year, collections total $20,000. At the end of 2013, it becomes apparent that the remaining $4,000 will never be collected from customers.

Required:

For each scenario, calculate the amount of revenue to be recognized in 2012.

Record transactions related to credit sales and contra revenues (LO1, 2)

P5–2A Outdoor Expo provides guided fishing tours. The company charges $200 per person but offers a 10% discount to parties of four or more. Consider the following transactions during the month of May.

May   2   Charlene books a fishing tour with Outdoor Expo for herself and four friends at the group discount price ($900 = $180 × 5). The tour is scheduled for May 7.

May   7   The fishing tour occurs. Outdoor Expo asks that payment be made within 30 days of the tour and offers a 5% discount for payment within 15 days.

May   9   Charlene is upset that no one caught a single fish and asks management for a discount. Outdoor Expo has a strict policy of no discounts related to number of fish caught.

May 15   Upon deeper investigation, management of Outdoor Expo discovers that Charlene's tour was led by a new guide who did not take the group to some of the better fishing spots. In concession, management offers a sales allowance of 40% of the amount due.

May 20   Charlene pays for the tour after deducting the sales allowance.

Required:

1. Record the necessary transaction(s) for Outdoor Expo on each date.

2. Calculate net sales.

3. Show how Outdoor Expo would present net sales in its income statement.

P5–3A The following events occur for The Underwood Corporation during 2012 and 2013, its first two years of operations.

Record transactions related to accounts receivable (**LO3, 4**)

June 12, 2012	Provide services to customers on account for $35,000.
September 17, 2012	Receive $20,000 from customers on account.
December 31, 2012	Estimate that 40% of accounts receivable at the end of the year will not be received.
March 4, 2013	Provide services to customers on account for $50,000.
May 20, 2013	Receive $10,000 from customers for services provided in 2012.
July 2, 2013	Write off the remaining amounts owed from services provided in 2012.
October 19, 2013	Receive $40,000 from customers for services provided in 2013.
December 31, 2013	Estimate that 40% of accounts receivable at the end of the year will not be received.

Required:

1. Record transactions for each date.
2. Post transactions to the following accounts: Cash, Accounts Receivable, and Allowance for Uncollectible Accounts.
3. Calculate the net realizable value of accounts receivable at the end of 2012 and 2013.

P5–4A Pearl E. White Orthodontist specializes in correcting misaligned teeth. During 2012, Pearl provides services on account of $580,000. Of this amount, $70,000 remains receivable at the end of the year. An aging schedule as of December 31, 2012, is provided below.

Record transactions related to uncollectible accounts (**LO3, 4, 5**)

Age Group	Amount Receivable	Estimated Percent Uncollectible	
Not yet due	$30,000	5%	*1500*
0–90 days past due	15,000	10%	*1500*
91–180 days past due	10,000	30%	*3000*
More than 180 days past due	15,000	80%	*12000*
Total	$70,000		*18,000.*

Required:

1. Calculate the allowance for uncollectible accounts.
2. Record the December 31, 2012, adjustment, assuming the balance of Allowance for Uncollectible Accounts before adjustment is $4,000 (*credit*).
3. On July 19, 2013, a customer's account balance of $7,000 is written off as uncollectible. Record the write-off.
4. On September 30, 2013, the customer whose account was written off in *Requirement 3* unexpectedly pays the full amount. Record the cash collection.

P5–5A In an effort to boost sales in the current year, Roy's Gym has implemented a new program where members do not have to pay for their annual membership until the end of the year. The program seems to have substantially increased membership and revenues. Below are year-end amounts.

Compare the direct write-off method to the allowance method (**LO3, 6**)

	Membership Revenues	Accounts Receivable
Last year	$100,000	$ 5,000
Current year	300,000	160,000

Arnold, the owner, realizes that many members have not paid their annual membership fees by the end of the year. However, Arnold believes that no allowance for uncollectible accounts should be reported in the current year because none of the nonpaying members' accounts have proven uncollectible. Arnold wants to use the direct

write-off method to record bad debts, waiting until the end of next year before writing off any accounts.

Required:

1. Do you agree with Arnold's reasoning for not reporting any allowance for future uncollectible accounts? Explain.
2. Suppose that similar programs in the past have resulted in uncollectible accounts of approximately 75%. If Arnold uses the allowance method, what should be the balance of Allowance for Uncollectible Accounts at the end of the current year?
3. Based on your answer in *Requirement* 2, for what amount will total assets and expenses be misstated in the current year if Arnold uses the direct write-off method? Ignore tax effects.

Using estimates of uncollectible accounts to overstate income (LO3)

P5–6A Willie Cheetum is the CEO of Happy Foods, a distributor of produce to grocery store chains throughout the Midwest. At the end of the year, the company's accounting manager provides Willie with the following information, before any adjustment.

Accounts receivable	$1,000,000
Estimated percentage uncollectible	10%
Allowance for uncollectible accounts	$30,000 (*credit*)
Operating income	$250,000

Willie's compensation contract states that if the company generates operating income of at least $200,000, he will get a salary bonus early next year.

Required:

1. Record the adjustment for uncollectible accounts using the accountant's estimate of 10% of accounts receivable.
2. After the adjustment is recorded in *Requirement* 1, what is the revised amount of operating income? Will Willie get his salary bonus?
3. Willie instructs the accountant to record the adjustment for uncollectible accounts using 7% rather than 10% of accounts receivable. Now will Willie get his salary bonus? Explain.
4. By how much would total assets and operating income be misstated using the 7% amount?

Overestimating future uncollectible accounts (LO3, 4)

P5–7A Humanity International sells medical and food supplies to those in need in underdeveloped countries. Customers in these countries are often very poor and must purchase items on account. At the end of 2012, total accounts receivable equal $1,200,000. The company understands that it's dealing with high credit risk clients. These countries are often in the middle of a financial crisis, civil war, severe drought, or some other difficult circumstance. Because of this, Humanity International typically estimates the percentage of uncollectible accounts to be 40% (= $480,000). Actual write-offs in 2013 total only $200,000, which means that the company significantly overestimated uncollectible accounts in 2012. It appears that efforts by the International Monetary Fund (IMF) and the United Nations (UN), and a mild winter mixed with adequate spring rains, have provided for more stable economic conditions than were expected, helping customers to pay on their accounts.

Required:

1. Record the adjustment for uncollectible accounts at the end of 2012, assuming there is no balance in Allowance for Uncollectible Accounts at the end of 2012 before any adjustment.
2. By the end of 2013, Humanity International has the benefit of hindsight to know that estimates of uncollectible accounts in 2012 were too high. How did this overestimation affect the reported amounts of total assets and expenses at the end of 2012? Ignore tax effects.

3. Should Humanity International prepare new financial statements for 2012 to show the correct amount of uncollectible accounts? Explain.

P5–8A On December 1, 2012, Liang Chemical provides services to a customer for $80,000. In payment for the services, the customer signs a three-year, 12% note. The face amount and all interest are due at the end of the third year.

annual rate

1 %

 HW

Record long-term notes receivable and interest revenue **(LO7)**

Required:

1. Record the acceptance of the note on December 1, 2012.
2. Record the adjustment for interest revenue on December 31, 2012, 2013, and 2014.
3. Record the cash collection on December 1, 2015.

PROBLEMS: SET B

P5–1B Assume the following scenarios.

Scenario 1: During 2012, **The Hubbard Group** provides services of $800,000 for repair of a state highway. The company receives an initial payment of $200,000 with the balance to be received the following year.

Scenario 2: **Rolling Stone** magazine typically charges $60 for a one-year subscription. On January 1, 2012, Herman, age 72, purchases a one-year subscription to the magazine and receives a 10% senior citizen discount.

Scenario 3: During 2012, **Waste Management** provides services on account for $20,000. The customer pays for those services in 2013.

Scenario 4: During 2012, **Sysco Corporation** sells grocery items to one of its customers for $250,000 on account. Cash collections on those sales are $170,000 in 2012 and $50,000 in 2013. The remaining $30,000 is written off as uncollectible in 2013.

Calculate the amount of revenue to recognize **(LO1)**

Required:

For each scenario, calculate the amount of revenue to be recognized in 2012.

P5–2B Data Recovery Services (DRS) specializes in data recovery from crashed hard drives. The price charged varies based on the extent of damage and the amount of data being recovered. DRS offers a 20% discount to students and faculty at educational institutions. Consider the following transactions during the month of June.

Record transactions related to credit sales and contra revenues **(LO1, 2)**

June 10   Rashid's hard drive crashes and he sends it to DRS.
June 12   After initial evaluation, DRS e-mails Rashid to let him know that full data recovery will cost $2,000.
June 13   Rashid informs DRS that he would like them to recover the data and that he is a student at UCLA, qualifying him for a 20% educational discount and reducing the cost by $400 (= $2,000 × 20%).
June 16   DRS performs the work and claims to be successful in recovering all data. DRS asks Rashid to pay within 30 days of today's date, offering a 3% discount for payment within 10 days.
June 19   When Rashid receives the hard drive, he notices that DRS did not successfully recover all data. Approximately 25% of the data has not been recovered and he informs DRS.
June 20   DRS reduces the amount Rashid owes by 25%.
June 30   Rashid pays the amount owed.

Required:

1. Record the necessary transaction(s) for Data Recovery Services on each date.
2. Calculate net sales.
3. Show how net sales would be presented in the income statement.
4. Calculate net sales if Rashid had paid his bill on June 25.

Record transactions
related to accounts
receivable (LO3, 4)

P5–3B The following events occur for Morris Engineering during 2012 and 2013, its first two years of operations.

February 2, 2012	Provide services to customers on account for $32,000.
July 23, 2012	Receive $22,000 from customers on account.
December 31, 2012	Estimate that 30% of uncollected accounts will not be received.
April 12, 2013	Provide services to customers on account for $45,000.
June 28, 2013	Receive $6,000 from customers for services provided in 2012.
September 13, 2013	Write off the remaining amounts owed from services provided in 2012.
October 5, 2013	Receive $40,000 from customers for services provided in 2013.
December 31, 2013	Estimate that 30% of uncollected accounts will not be received.

Required:
1. Record transactions for each date.
2. Post transactions to the following accounts: Cash, Accounts Receivable, and Allowance for Uncollectible Accounts.
3. Calculate the net realizable value of accounts receivable at the end of 2012 and 2013.

Record transactions
related to uncollectible
accounts (LO3, 4, 5)

P5–4B Facial Cosmetics provides plastic surgery primarily to hide the appearance of unwanted scars and other blemishes. During 2012, the company provides services of $400,000 on account. Of this amount, $50,000 remains uncollected at the end of the year. An aging schedule as of December 31, 2012, is provided below.

Age Group	Amount Receivable	Estimated Percent Uncollectible	
Not yet due	$30,000	2%	600
0–30 days past due	10,000	5%	500
31–60 days past due	7,000	10%	700 1200
More than 60 days past due	3,000	20%	600 1200
Total	$50,000		

$2,400

Required:
1. Calculate the allowance for uncollectible accounts.
2. Record the December 31, 2012, adjustment, assuming the balance of Allowance for Uncollectible Accounts before adjustment is $300 (*debit*).
3. On April 3, 2013, a customer's account balance of $400 is written off as uncollectible. Record the write-off.
4. On July 17, 2013, the customer whose account was written off in *Requirement* 3 unexpectedly pays $100 of the amount but does not expect to pay any additional amounts. Record the cash collection.

Compare the direct
write-off method
to the allowance
method (LO3, 6)

P5–5B Letni Corporation engages in the manufacture and sale of semiconductor chips for the computing and communications industries. During the past year, operating revenues remained relatively flat compared to the prior year but management notices a big increase in accounts receivable. The increase in receivables is largely due to the recent economic slowdown in the computing and telecommunications industries. Many of the company's customers are having financial difficulty, lengthening the period of time it takes to collect on account. Below are year-end amounts.

Age Group	Operating Revenue	Accounts Receivable	Average Age	Accounts Written Off
Two years ago	$1,200,000	$140,000	5 days	$ 0
Last year	1,500,000	150,000	7 days	1,000
Current year	1,600,000	320,000	40 days	0

Paul, the CEO of Letni, notices that accounts written off over the past three years have been minimal and, therefore, suggests that no allowance for uncollectible accounts be

established in the current year. Any account proving uncollectible can be charged to next year's financial statements (the direct write-off method).

Required:

1. Do you agree with Paul's reasoning? Explain.
2. Suppose that other companies in these industries have had similar increasing trends in accounts receivable aging. These companies also had very successful collections in the past but now estimate uncollectible accounts to be 20% because of the significant downturn in the industries. If Letni uses the allowance method estimated at 20% of accounts receivable, what should be the balance of Allowance for Uncollectible Accounts at the end of the current year?
3. Based on your answer in *Requirement* 2, for what amount will total assets and expenses be misstated in the current year if Letni uses the direct write-off method? Ignore tax effects.

P5–6B Wanda B. Rich is the CEO of Outlet Flooring, a discount provider of carpet, tile, wood, and laminate flooring. At the end of the year, the company's accountant provides Wanda with the following information, before any adjustment.

Using estimates of uncollectible accounts to understate income (LO3)

Accounts receivable	$10,000,000
Estimated percentage uncollectible	3%
Allowance for uncollectible accounts	$100,000 (*credit*)
Operating income	$2,400,000

Wanda has significant stock ownership in the company and, therefore, would like to keep the stock price high. Analysts on Wall Street expect the company to have operating income of $1,800,000. The fact that actual operating income is well above this amount will make investors happy and help maintain a high stock price. Meeting analysts' expectations will also help Wanda keep her job.

Required:

1. Record the adjustment for uncollectible accounts using the accountant's estimate of 3% of accounts receivable.
2. After the adjustment is recorded in *Requirement* 1, what is the revised amount of operating income? Will Outlet Flooring still meet analysts' expectations?
3. Wanda instructs the accountant to instead record $600,000 as bad debt expense so that operating income will exactly meet analysts' expectations. By how much would total assets and operating income be misstated if the accountant records this amount?
4. Why would Wanda be motivated to manage operating income in this way?

P5–7B By the end of its first year of operations, Previts Corporation has credit sales of $650,000 and accounts receivable of $250,000. Given it's the first year of operations, Previts' management is unsure how much allowance for uncollectible accounts it should establish. One of the company's competitors, which has been in the same industry for an extended period, estimates uncollectible accounts to be 4% of ending accounts receivable, so Previts decides to use that same amount. However, actual write-offs in the following year were 20% of the $250,000 (= $50,000). Previts' inexperience in the industry led to making sales to high credit risk customers.

Underestimating future uncollectible accounts (LO3, 4)

Required:

1. Record the adjustment for uncollectible accounts at the end of the first year of operations using the 4% estimate of accounts receivable.
2. By the end of the second year, Previts has the benefit of hindsight to know that estimates of uncollectible accounts in the first year were too low. By how much did Previts underestimate uncollectible accounts in the first year? How did this underestimation affect the reported amounts of total assets and expenses at the end of the first year? Ignore tax effects.
3. Should Previts prepare new financial statements for the first year of operations to show the correct amount of uncollectible accounts? Explain.

Record long-term notes receivable and interest revenue **(LO7)**

P5–8B On April 15, 2012, Sampson Consulting provides services to a customer for $100,000. To pay for the services, the customer signs a three-year, 9% note. The face amount and all interest are due at the end of the third year. [*Hint:* Because the note is accepted during the middle of the month, Sampson plans to recognize one-half month of interest revenue in April 2012, and one-half month of interest revenue in April 2015.]

Required:
1. Record the acceptance of the note on April 15, 2012.
2. Record the adjustment for interest revenue on December 31, 2012, 2013, and 2014.
3. Record the cash collection on April 15, 2015.

For additional problems, visit **www.mhhe.com/succeed** *for Problems: Set C.*

ADDITIONAL PERSPECTIVES

Continuing Problem

Great Adventures

(This is a continuation of the Great Adventures problem from earlier chapters.)

AP5–1 Tony and Suzie are ready to expand Great Adventures even further in 2013. Tony believes that many groups in the community (for example, Boy Scouts, church groups, civic groups, and local businesses) would like to hold one-day outings for their members. Groups would engage in outdoor activities such as rock climbing, fishing, capture the flag, paintball, treasure hunts, scavenger hunts, nature hikes, and so on. The purpose of these one-day events would be for each member of the group to learn the importance of TEAM (Together Everyone Achieves More).

Tony knows that most people are not familiar with these types of activities, so to encourage business he allows groups to participate in the event before paying. He offers a 5% quick-payment discount to those that pay within 10 days after the event. He also guarantees that at least eight hours of outdoor activities will be provided or the customer will receive a 20% discount. For the first six months of the year, the following activities occur for TEAM operations.

Jan.	24	Great Adventures purchases outdoor gear such as ropes, helmets, harnesses, compasses, and other miscellaneous equipment for $5,000 cash.
Feb.	25	Mr. Kendall's Boy Scout troop participates in a one-day TEAM adventure. Normally, Tony would charge a group of this size $3,500, but he wants to encourage kids to exercise more and enjoy the outdoors so he charges the group only $3,000.
Feb.	28	The Boy Scout troop pays the full amount owed, less the 5% quick-payment discount.
Mar.	19	Reynold's Management has its employees participate in a one-day TEAM adventure. Great Adventures charges $4,000, and Reynold's agrees to pay within 30 days.
Mar.	27	Reynold's pays the full amount owed, less the 5% quick-payment discount.
Apr.	7	Several men from the Elks Lodge decide to participate in a TEAM adventure. They pay $7,500, and the event is scheduled for the following week.
Apr.	14	The TEAM adventure is held for members of the Elks Lodge.
May	9	Myers Manufacturing participates in a TEAM adventure. Great Adventures charges $6,000, and Myers agrees to pay within 30 days.
Jun. 1–30		Several MBA groups participate in TEAM adventures during June. Great Adventures charges $24,000 to these groups, with payment due in July.
Jun.	30	Myers Manufacturing fails to pay the amount owed within the specified period and agrees to sign a three-month, 8% note receivable to replace the existing account receivable.

Required:

1. Record TEAM adventure transactions occurring during the first six months of 2013.
2. As of June 30, 2013, Great Adventures finishes its first 12 months of operations. If Suzie wants to prepare financial statements, part of the process would involve allowing for uncollectible accounts receivable.
   a. Suppose Suzie estimates uncollectible accounts to be 10% of accounts receivable (which does not include the $6,000 note receivable from Myers Manufacturing). Record the adjustment for uncollectible accounts on June 30, 2013.
   b. Prepare a partial balance sheet showing the net accounts receivable section.

American Eagle Outfitters, Inc.

Financial Analysis

AP5–2 Financial information for **American Eagle** is presented in Appendix A at the end of the book.

Required:

1. Determine whether the trend in net sales has been increasing or decreasing for the past three years.
2. Where is accounts receivable reported? Explain why using net sales to calculate the receivables turnover ratio might not be a good indicator of a company's ability to efficiently manage receivables for a retail company like American Eagle, which typically sells clothing for cash.
3. Does American Eagle report an allowance for uncollectible accounts in the balance sheet? If so, how much is reported for the most recent year?

The Buckle, Inc.

Financial Analysis

AP5–3 Financial information for **The Buckle** is presented in Appendix B at the end of the book.

Required:

1. Determine whether the trend in net sales has been increasing or decreasing for the past three years.
2. Where is accounts receivable reported? Explain why using net sales to calculate the receivables turnover ratio might not be a good indicator of a company's ability to efficiently manage receivables for a retail company like The Buckle, which typically sells clothing for cash.
3. Does The Buckle report an allowance for uncollectible accounts in the balance sheet? If so, how much is reported for the most recent year?

American Eagle Outfitters, Inc., vs. The Buckle, Inc.

Comparative Analysis

AP5–4 Financial information for **American Eagle** is presented in Appendix A at the end of the book, and financial information for **The Buckle** is presented in Appendix B at the end of the book.

Required:

Try to estimate each company's ratio of total current receivables to total current assets. Do you see problems with either company's management of receivables?

Ethics

AP5–5 You have recently been hired as the assistant controller for Stanton Industries. Your immediate superior is the controller who, in turn, reports to the vice president of finance.

The controller has assigned you the task of preparing the year-end adjustments. For receivables, you have prepared an aging of accounts receivable and have applied

historical percentages to the balances of each of the age categories. The analysis indicates that an appropriate balance for Allowance for Uncollectible Accounts is $180,000. The existing balance in the allowance account prior to any adjustment is a $20,000 credit balance.

After showing your analysis to the controller, he tells you to change the aging category of a large account from over 120 days to current status and to prepare a new invoice to the customer with a revised date that agrees with the new aging category. This will change the required allowance for uncollectible accounts from $180,000 to $135,000. Tactfully, you ask the controller for an explanation for the change and he tells you, "We need the extra income; the bottom line is too low."

Required:

1. What is the effect on income before taxes of the change requested by the controller?
2. Discuss the ethical dilemma you face. Consider your options and responsibilities along with the possible consequences of any action you might take.

Internet Research

AP5–6 Obtain a copy of the annual report of **Avon Products, Inc.,** for the most recent year. You can find the annual report at the company's website (*www.avon.com*) in the investor information section or at the Securities and Exchange Commission's website (*www.sec.gov*) using EDGAR (Electronic Data Gathering, Analysis, and Retrieval). Form 10-K, which includes the annual report, is required to be filed on EDGAR. Search or scroll within the annual report to find the financial statements.

Required:

Answer the following questions related to the company's accounts receivable and bad debts:

1. What is the amount of net accounts receivable at the end of the year? What is the amount of total accounts receivable?
2. What is the amount of bad debt expense for the year? (*Hint:* Check the statement of cash flows.)
3. Determine the amount of actual bad debt write-offs made during the year. Assume that all bad debts relate only to trade accounts receivable. Did the company underestimate or overestimate bad debts?
4. Calculate the receivables turnover ratio and average collection period for the most recent year. Assuming the industry averages for the receivables turnover ratio and average collection period are 10.5 times and 34.8 days, respectively, what do you conclude about the receivables of Avon?

Written Communication

AP5–7 You have been hired as a consultant by a parts manufacturing firm to provide advice as to the proper accounting methods the company should use in some key areas. In the area of receivables, the company president does not understand your recommendation to use the allowance method for uncollectible accounts. She stated, "Financial statements should be based on objective data rather than the guesswork required for the allowance method. Besides, since my uncollectibles are fairly constant from period to period, with significant variations occurring infrequently, the direct write-off method is just as good as the allowance method."

Required:

Draft a one-page response in the form of a memo to the president in support of your recommendation for the company to use the allowance method.

Earnings Management

AP5–8 Ernie Upshaw is the supervising manager of Sleep Tight Bedding. At the end of the year, the company's accounting manager provides Ernie with the following information, before any adjustment.

Accounts receivable	$500,000
Estimated percent uncollectible	9%
Allowance for uncollectible accounts	$20,000 (*debit*)
Operating income	$320,000

In the previous year, Sleep Tight Bedding reported operating income (after adjustment) of $275,000. Ernie knows that it's important to report an upward trend in earnings. This is important not only for Ernie's compensation and employment, but also for the company's stock price. If investors see a decline in earnings, the stock price could drop significantly, and Ernie owns a large amount of the company's stock. This has caused Ernie many sleepless nights.

Required:
1. Record the adjustment for uncollectible accounts using the accounting manager's estimate of 9% of accounts receivable.
2. After the adjustment is recorded in *Requirement* 1, what is the revised amount of operating income? Does operating income increase or decrease compared to the previous year?
3. Ernie instructs the accounting manager to record the adjustment for uncollectible accounts using 4% rather than 9% of accounts receivable. After this adjustment, does operating income increase or decrease compared to the previous year?
4. By how much would total assets and expenses be misstated using the 4% amount?

Answers to the Self-Study Questions
1. c   2. c   3. b   4. b   5. d   6. b   7. c   8. d   9. b   10. c

Inventory and Cost of Goods Sold

Learning Objectives

AFTER STUDYING THIS CHAPTER, YOU SHOULD BE ABLE TO:

- ■ **LO1** Trace the flow of inventory costs from manufacturing companies to merchandising companies.
- ■ **LO2** Calculate cost of goods sold.
- ■ **LO3** Determine the cost of goods sold and ending inventory using different inventory cost methods.
- ■ **LO4** Explain the financial statement effects and tax effects of inventory cost flow assumptions.
- ■ **LO5** Record inventory transactions using a perpetual inventory system.
- ■ **LO6** Prepare a multiple-step income statement.
- ■ **LO7** Apply the lower-of-cost-or-market method for inventories.

Analysis

- ■ **LO8** Analyze management of inventory using the inventory turnover ratio and gross profit ratio.

Appendix

- ■ **LO9** Record inventory transactions using a periodic inventory system.
- ■ **LO10** Determine the financial statement effects of inventory errors.

BEST BUY: TAKING INVENTORY OF ELECTRONICS SOLD

Best Buy Co., Inc., is the largest specialty retailer of consumer goods in the United States, accounting for 17% of the specialty retail market. You are probably familiar with most of the products offered by Best Buy—computers, computer software, video games, music, DVDs, mobile phones, digital and video cameras, home appliances (washing machines, dryers, and refrigerators), and other related merchandise.

Merchandise inventory for sale to customers is the single largest asset owned by Best Buy, as it is for many retail companies. At any given time, Best Buy holds about $3 billion in inventory, or about 30% of the company's total assets. Proper management of inventory is key to the company's success.

Management of Best Buy knows there is a fine line between having too little and too much inventory. Having too little inventory reduces the selection of products available to customers, ultimately reducing sales revenue. On the other hand, in a technology-based industry where changes occur rapidly, having too much inventory can leave the store holding outdated inventory. Just think of what happens to the value of computers when the next generation becomes available. Managers don't want to get stuck with old inventory that is decreasing in value. Besides obsolescence, other costs associated with holding large inventories are storage, insurance, and shrinkage (theft). Holding less inventory provides access to money that can be invested elsewhere within the company.

For now, Best Buy seems to be taking the right steps with its inventory. Look below at the company's revenues from inventory sales compared to the cost of the inventory sold. These amounts are reported in the company's income statement. The difference between revenues and cost of goods sold (an expense) is called *gross profit,* and it has been steadily increasing over time.

	2006	2007	2008	2009
Revenues	$30,848	$35,934	$40,023	$45,015
Cost of goods sold	23,122	27,165	30,477	34,017
Gross profit	$ 7,726	$ 8,769	$ 9,546	$10,998

In this chapter, we explore how to account for the purchase and sale of inventory items. We'll see how inventory (an asset in the balance sheet) turns into cost of goods sold (an expense in the income statement) once it is sold, and how these amounts can affect business decisions.

PART A

UNDERSTANDING INVENTORY AND COST OF GOODS SOLD

In preceding chapters, we dealt mostly with companies that provide a service. *Service companies* such as **UPS**, **United Healthcare**, **Allstate Insurance**, and **Marriott Hotels** earn revenues by providing services to their customers. UPS delivers your packages, United Healthcare treats your medical needs, Allstate provides insurance coverage, and Marriott offers you a place to stay the night. Many companies, though, earn revenues by selling inventory rather than a service.

Part A of this chapter introduces the concept of inventory and demonstrates the different methods used to calculate the cost of inventory for external reporting. Once you understand this, then you're ready to see, in Part B and Part C, how companies actually maintain their own (internal) records of inventory transactions and the adjustments that are sometimes needed to prepare financial statements.

Inventory 清单，储备/存货

■ LO1
Trace the flow of inventory costs from manufacturing companies to merchandising companies.

Companies that earn revenue by selling inventory are either *manufacturing* or *merchandising companies*. Inventory includes items a company intends for sale to customers. You already are familiar with several types of inventory—clothes at **The Limited**, shoes at **Payless ShoeSource**, grocery items at **Publix Super Markets**, digital equipment at **Best Buy**, building supplies at **The Home Depot**, and so on. Inventory also includes items that are not yet finished products. For instance, lumber at a cabinet manufacturer, steel at a construction firm, and rubber at a tire manufacturer are part of inventory because the firm will use them to make a finished product for sale to customers.

We report inventory as a current asset in the balance sheet—an *asset* because it represents a valuable resource the company owns, and *current* because the company expects to convert it to cash in the near term. At the end of the period, the amount the company reports for inventory is the cost of inventory *not yet sold*. What happens to the cost of the inventory sold during the period? The company reports the cost of the inventory it sold as cost of goods sold in the income statement.

Common Terms Cost of goods sold is also referred to as *cost of sales, cost of merchandise sold,* or *cost of products sold.*

As we'll see, determining these two amounts is a critical task in accounting for inventory. For companies that earn revenues by selling inventory, cost of goods sold often is the largest expense in the income statement. Before we explore how companies calculate cost of goods sold, we first need to consider the differences between merchandising and manufacturing companies, so that we understand the types of inventory each holds.

MERCHANDISING COMPANIES

Merchandising companies purchase inventories that are primarily in finished form for resale to customers. These companies may assemble, sort, repackage, redistribute, store, refrigerate, deliver, or install the inventory, but they do not manufacture it. They simply serve as intermediaries in the process of moving inventory from the manufacturer, the company that actually makes the inventory, to the end user.

We can broadly classify merchandising companies as wholesalers or retailers. *Wholesalers* resell inventory to retail companies or to professional users. For example, a wholesale food service company like **Sysco Corporation** supplies food to restaurants, schools, and sporting events but generally does not sell food directly to the public. Also, Sysco does not transform the food prior to sale; it just stores the food, repackages it as necessary, and delivers it.

Retailers purchase inventory from manufacturers or wholesalers and then sell this inventory to end users. You probably are more familiar with retail companies because these are the companies from which you buy products. **Best Buy**, **Target**,

Lowe's, Macy's, Gap, Sears, and McDonald's are retailers. Merchandising companies typically hold their inventories in a single category simply called *inventory*.

MANUFACTURING COMPANIES

Manufacturing companies manufacture the inventories they sell, rather than buying them in finished form from suppliers. **Apple Inc.**, **Coca-Cola**, **Sara Lee**, **Harley-Davidson**, **ExxonMobil**, **Ford**, **Sony**, and **Dell** are manufacturers. Manufacturing companies buy the inputs for the products they manufacture. Thus, we classify inventory for a manufacturer into three categories: (1) raw materials, (2) work in process, and (3) finished goods:

- **Raw materials** inventory includes the cost of components that will become part of the finished product but have not yet been used in production. (Raw materials sometimes are called *direct materials*.)
- **Work-in-process** inventory refers to the products that have started the production process but are not yet complete at the end of the period.
- **Finished goods** inventory consists of items for which the manufacturing process is complete.

Each of these inventory accounts includes its own costs. For example, Dell's raw materials inventory includes the costs of the semiconductors, circuit boards, and plastic parts that go into the production of personal computers. For its work-in-process inventory, Dell includes the cost of *raw materials* used in production, the cost of *direct labor* that we can trace directly to the goods in process, and an allocated portion of other manufacturing costs, called *overhead*. Overhead costs include costs to operate the manufacturing facility, depreciation of manufacturing equipment, and many other costs that we cannot directly link to the production of specific inventories. Once the manufacturing process is complete, Dell transfers to finished goods inventory the total cost of fully assembled but unshipped computers at the end of the reporting period. Illustration 6–1 shows inventory amounts for **Dell Computers**.

DELL COMPUTERS Notes to the Financial Statements (excerpt)		
($ in millions)	**2009**	**2008**
Raw materials	$454	$ 714
Work in process	150	144
Finished products	263	322
Total inventories	$867	$1,180

ILLUSTRATION 6–1

Types of Inventory for Dell Computers

At any given time, Dell holds around 70% of its inventory in a form other than finished products ready for sale to customers. Once inventory products are finished, Dell hopes to sell them as soon as possible.

KEY POINT

Service companies earn revenues by providing services to customers. Merchandising and manufacturing companies earn revenues by selling inventory to customers.

FLOW OF INVENTORY COSTS

As you might guess, the flow of inventory costs differs depending on the type of company. Illustration 6–2 (next page) shows the flow of inventory costs for the three types of companies—service, merchandising, and manufacturing.

ILLUSTRATION 6–2

Types of Companies
and Flow of Inventory
Costs

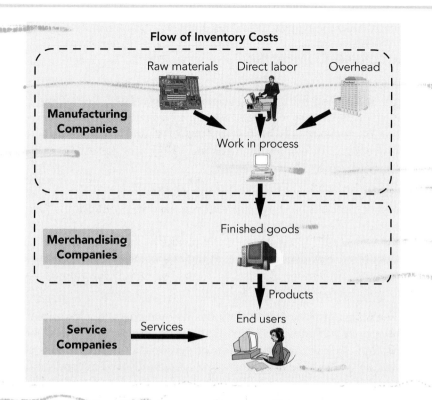

Inventory's journey begins when manufacturing companies purchase raw materials, hire workers, and incur manufacturing overhead during production. Once the products are finished, manufacturers normally pass inventories to merchandising companies, whether wholesalers or retailers. Merchandising companies then sell inventories to you, the end user. In some cases, manufacturers may sell directly to end users.

Some companies provide both services and inventories to customers. For example, **IBM** generates about half its revenues from selling its inventories of hardware and software, and the other half from providing services like consulting, systems maintenance, and financing.

In this chapter, we focus on merchandising companies, both wholesalers and retailers. Still, most of the accounting principles and procedures discussed here also apply to manufacturing companies. We do not attempt to address all the unique problems of accumulating the direct costs of raw materials and labor and allocating manufacturing overhead. We leave those details for managerial and cost accounting courses. In this course, we focus on the financial reporting implications of inventory cost flows.

Cost of Goods Sold

■ **LO2**
Calculate cost of goods
sold.

Let's think a little more about the relationship between ending inventory in the balance sheet and cost of goods sold in the income statement. Remember that inventory represents the cost of inventory *not sold*, and cost of goods sold represents the cost of inventory *sold*. Thus, we can see that, once the inventory is sold, the amount reported for inventory becomes the amount reported for cost of goods sold. This relationship is depicted at the bottom of Illustration 6–3. Note, too, the two inventory inputs at the top of the figure: beginning inventory and purchases during the year. **The costs of *beginning inventory* plus the *additional purchases during the year* make up the cost of inventory (cost of goods) available for sale.**

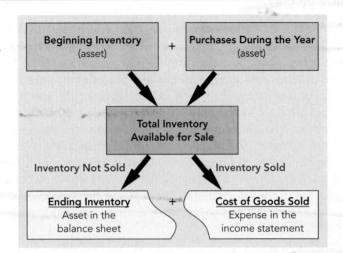

ILLUSTRATION 6–3
Relationship between
Inventory and Cost of
Goods Sold

To demonstrate these relationships using numbers, assume a local **Best Buy** store begins the year with $20,000 of DVD player inventory. That amount represents how much Best Buy spent to purchase the inventory of DVD players on hand at the beginning of the year. During the year, the company purchases additional DVD players for $90,000. What is the total cost of goods (DVD players) available for sale? Illustration 6–4 shows the answer: $110,000 (= $20,000 + $90,000). Now, assume that by the end of the year, the purchase cost of the remaining DVD player inventory is $30,000. What is the cost of goods sold? As Illustration 6–4 shows, the cost of the DVD players sold is $80,000 (= $110,000 − $30,000).

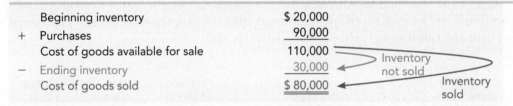

	Beginning inventory	$ 20,000
+	Purchases	90,000
	Cost of goods available for sale	110,000
−	Ending inventory	30,000
	Cost of goods sold	$ 80,000

Inventory not sold

Inventory sold

ILLUSTRATION 6–4
Numerical Illustration
of the Relationship
between Inventory and
Cost of Goods Sold

Of the $110,000 of goods available for sale during the year, some were not sold (ending inventory = $30,000) and some were sold (cost of goods sold = $80,000). The cost of the inventory sold (cost of goods sold) is an expense, which the company reports in the income statement (as we will see in more detail later).

 KEY POINT

Inventory is a current asset reported in the balance sheet and represents the cost of inventory *not yet sold* at the end of the period. Cost of goods sold is an expense reported in the income statement and represents the cost of inventory *sold*.

Inventory Cost Methods

To this point, we've discussed the cost of inventory without considering how we determine that cost. We do that now by considering four methods for inventory costing:

1. Specific identification
2. First-in, first-out (FIFO)
3. Last-in, first-out (LIFO)
4. Weighted-average cost

■ LO3
Determine the cost
of goods sold and
ending inventory using
different inventory cost
methods.

SPECIFIC IDENTIFICATION

The specific identification method is the method you might think of as the most logical. It matches—identifies—each unit of inventory with its actual cost. For example, an automobile has a unique serial number that we can match to an invoice identifying the actual purchase price. Fine jewelry and pieces of art are other possibilities. Specific identification works well in such cases. However, the specific identification method is practicable only for companies selling unique, expensive products. Consider the inventory at **The Home Depot** or **Sally Beauty Supply**: numerous items, many of which are relatively inexpensive. Specific identification would be very difficult for such merchandisers. Although bar codes and RFID tags now make it possible to identify and track each unit of inventory, the costs of doing so outweigh the benefits for multiple, small inventory items. For that reason, the specific identification method is used primarily by companies with unique, expensive products with low sales volume.

FIRST-IN, FIRST-OUT

For practical reasons, most companies use one of the other three inventory cost flow assumptions—FIFO, LIFO, or weighted-average cost—to determine cost of goods sold and inventory. Note the use of the word *assumptions.* Each of these three inventory cost methods *assumes* a particular pattern of inventory cost flows. However, the *actual* flow of inventory does not need to match the *assumed* cost flow in order for the company to use a particular method.

To see how the three cost flow assumptions work, let's begin with FIFO. We'll examine the inventory transactions in Illustration 6–5 for Mario's Game Shop, which sells video game cartridges. Mario has 100 units of inventory at the beginning of the year and then makes two purchases during the year—one on April 25 and one on October 19. (Note the different unit costs at the time of each purchase.) There are **1,000** game cartridges available for sale.

ILLUSTRATION 6–5
Inventory Transactions for Mario's Game Shop

Date	Transaction	Number of Units	Unit Cost	Total Cost
Jan. 1	Beginning inventory	100	$ 7	$ 700
Apr. 25	Purchase	300	9	2,700
Oct. 19	Purchase	600	11	6,600
	Total goods available for sale	1,000		$10,000
Jan. 1–Dec. 31	Total sales to customers	800		
Dec. 31	Ending inventory	200		

During the year, Mario sells **800** video game cartridges for $15 each. This means that **200** cartridges remain in ending inventory at the end of the year. But which 200? Do they include some of the $7 units from beginning inventory? Are they 200 of the $9 units from the April 25 purchase? Or, do they include some $11 units from the October 19 purchase? We consider these questions below.

Using the **first-in, first-out (FIFO) method**, we assume that the first units purchased (the first in) are the first ones sold (the first out). We assume that beginning inventory sells first, followed by the inventory from the first purchase during the year, followed by the inventory from the second purchase during the year, and so on.

In our example, which 800 units did Mario's Game Shop sell? Using the FIFO method, we *assume* they were the *first* 800 units purchased, and that all other units remain in ending inventory. These calculations are shown in Illustration 6–6.

We assume that all units from beginning inventory (100 units) and the April 25 purchase (300 units) were sold. For the final 400 units sold, we split the October 19

Inventory Transactions for Mario's Game Shop—FIFO METHOD

Purchases	Number of Units	×	Unit Cost	=	Total Cost		Cost of Goods Sold	+	Ending Inventory
	Cost of Goods Available for Sale			**=**					
Jan. 1	100		$ 7		$ 700	Sold first	$ 700		
Apr. 25	300		9		2,700	800 units	2,700		
Oct. 19	400		11		4,400		4,400		
	200		11		2,200	Not sold			$2,200
	1,000				$10,000	**=**	$7,800	**+**	$2,200

ILLUSTRATION 6–6

Inventory Calculation Using the FIFO Method

purchase of 600 units into two groups—400 units assumed sold and 200 units assumed not sold. We calculate cost of goods sold as the units of inventory assumed sold times their respective unit costs. [That is: $(100 \times \$7) + (300 \times \$9) + (400 \times \$11)$ in our example.] Similarly, ending inventory equals the units assumed not sold times *their* respective unit costs $(200 \times \$11$ in our example). The amount of cost of goods sold Mario reports in the income statement will be **$7,800**. The amount of ending inventory in the balance sheet will be **$2,200**.

You may have realized that we don't actually need to directly calculate both cost of goods sold and inventory. Once we calculate one, the other is apparent. Because the two amounts always add up to the cost of goods available for sale (**$10,000** in our example), knowing either amount allows us to subtract to find the other.

Realize, too, that the amounts reported for ending inventory and cost of goods sold do *not* represent the actual cost of inventory sold and not sold. That's okay. **Companies are allowed to report inventory costs by *assuming* which units of inventory are sold and not sold, even if this does not match the *actual* flow.**

LAST-IN, FIRST-OUT

Using the last-in, first-out (LIFO) method, we assume that the last units purchased (the last in) are the first ones sold (the first out). If Mario sold 800 units, we assume all the 600 units purchased on October 19 (the last purchase) were sold, along with 200 units from the April 25 purchase. That leaves 100 of the units from the April 25 purchase and all 100 units from beginning inventory assumed to remain in ending inventory (not sold). Illustration 6–7 shows calculations of cost of goods sold and ending inventory for the LIFO method.

Inventory Transactions for Mario's Game Shop—LIFO METHOD

Purchases	Number of Units	×	Unit Cost	=	Total Cost		Cost of Goods Sold	+	Ending Inventory
	Cost of Goods Available for Sale			**=**					
Jan. 1	100		$ 7		$ 700	Not sold			$ 700
Apr. 25	100		9		900				900
	200		9		1,800	Sold last 800 units	$1,800		
Oct. 19	600		11		6,600		6,600		
	1,000				$10,000		$8,400	**+**	$1,600

ILLUSTRATION 6–7

Inventory Calculation Using the LIFO Method

COMMON MISTAKE

Many students find it surprising that companies are allowed to report inventory costs using assumed amounts rather than actual amounts. Nearly all companies sell their actual inventory in a FIFO manner, but they are allowed to report it as if they sold it in a LIFO manner. Later, we'll see why that's advantageous.

WEIGHTED-AVERAGE COST

Using the weighted-average cost method, we assume that both cost of goods sold and ending inventory consist of a random mixture of all the goods available for sale. We assume each unit of inventory has a cost equal to the weighted-average unit cost of all inventory items. We calculate that cost at the end of the year as:

$$\text{Weighted-average unit cost} = \frac{\text{Cost of goods available for sale}}{\text{Number of units available for sale}}$$

Illustration 6–8 demonstrates the calculation of cost of goods sold and ending inventory using the weighted-average cost method. Notice that the weighted-average cost of each game cartridge is $10, even though none of the game cartridges actually cost $10. However, on average, all the game cartridges cost $10, and this is the amount we use to calculate cost of goods sold and ending inventory under the weighted-average cost method.

ILLUSTRATION 6–8

Inventory Calculation Using the Weighted-Average Cost Method

Inventory Transactions for Mario's Game Shop— WEIGHTED-AVERAGE COST METHOD

| | | Cost of Goods Available for Sale | | |
| | | Number of Units | × Unit Cost = | Total Cost |
Date	Transaction			
Jan. 1	Beginning inventory	100	$ 7	$ 700
Apr. 25	Purchase	300	9	2,700
Oct. 19	Purchase	600	11	6,600
		1,000		$10,000

$$\text{Weighted-average unit cost} = \frac{\$10,000}{1,000 \text{ units}} = \$10 \text{ per unit}$$

Cost of goods sold	=	800 sold	×	$10	= $ 8,000
Ending inventory	=	200 not sold	×	10	= 2,000
					$10,000

 COMMON MISTAKE

In calculating the weighted-average unit cost, be sure to use a *weighted* average of the unit cost instead of the *simple* average. In the example above, there are three unit costs: $7, $9, and $11. A simple average of these amounts is $9 [= (7 + 9 + 11) ÷ 3]. The simple average, though, fails to take into account that several more units were purchased at $11 than at $7 or $9. So we need to *weight* the unit costs by the number of units purchased. We do that by taking the total cost of goods available for sale ($10,000) divided by total number of units available for sale (1,000) for a weighted average of $10.

Illustration 6–9 depicts the concept behind the three inventory cost flow assumptions. A company begins the year with one unit of inventory and then purchases three units of inventory during the year. If the company sells two units of inventory, which two are they? Using FIFO, we assume inventory is sold in the order

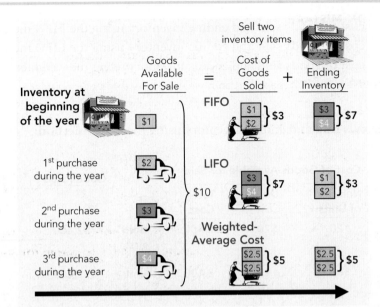

ILLUSTRATION 6–9

Comparison of Cost of Goods Sold and Ending Inventory under the Three Inventory Cost Flow Assumptions

purchased: Beginning inventory is sold first, and then the first purchase during the year is sold second. Using LIFO, we assume inventory is sold in the *opposite* order that we purchased it: The last unit purchased is sold first, and the second-to-last unit purchased is sold second. Using average cost, we assume inventory is sold using an average of all inventory purchased, including the beginning inventory.

 COMMON MISTAKE

Students sometimes answer FIFO and LIFO backwards when calculating ending inventory. The reason is that these acronyms describe more directly the calculation of *cost of goods sold,* rather than ending inventory. For example, FIFO (first-in, first-out) directly suggests which inventory units are assumed sold (the first ones in) and therefore used to calculate cost of goods sold. It is implicit that the inventory units *not* sold are the last ones in and are used to calculate ending inventory.

 KEY POINT

Companies are allowed to report inventory costs by *assuming* which specific units of inventory are sold and not sold, even if this does not match the *actual* flow. The three major inventory cost flow assumptions are FIFO (first-in, first-out), LIFO (last-in, first-out), and weighted-average cost.

Let's Review

NASCAR Unlimited sells remote-control cars. For 2012, the company has the following beginning inventory and purchase.

Date	Transaction	Number of Units	Unit Cost	Total Cost
Jan. 1	Beginning inventory	120	$20	$2,400
Aug. 15	Purchase	180	15	2,700
	Total	300		$5,100

Because of technological advances, NASCAR Unlimited has seen a decrease in the unit cost of its inventory. Throughout the year, the company maintained a selling price of $30 for each remote-control car and sold a total of 280 units, which leaves 20 units in ending inventory.

Required:

1. Calculate cost of goods sold and ending inventory using the FIFO method.
2. Calculate cost of goods sold and ending inventory using the LIFO method.
3. Calculate cost of goods sold and ending inventory using the weighted-average cost method.

Solution:

1. Cost of goods sold and ending inventory using the **FIFO method:**

Purchases	Number of Units	×	Unit Cost	=	Total Cost		Cost of Goods Sold	+	Ending Inventory
	Cost of Goods Available for Sale					=			
Jan. 1	120		$20		$2,400	Sold first 280 units	$2,400		
Aug. 15	160		15		2,400		2,400		
	20		15		300	Not sold			$300
	300				$5,100	=	$4,800	+	$300

2. Cost of goods sold and ending inventory using the **LIFO method:**

Purchases	Number of Units	×	Unit Cost	=	Total Cost		Cost of Goods Sold	+	Ending Inventory
	Cost of Goods Available for Sale					=			
Jan. 1	20		$20		$ 400	Not sold			$400
Aug. 15	100		20		2,000	Sold last 280 units	$2,000		
	180		15		2,700		2,700		
	300				$5,100	=	$4,700	+	$400

3. Cost of goods sold and ending inventory using the **weighted-average cost method:**

$$\text{Weighted-average unit cost} = \frac{\$5,100}{300} = \$17$$

Cost of goods sold	= 280 sold × $17 =	$4,760
Ending inventory	= 20 not sold × 17 =	340
	300	$5,100

Suggested Homework:
BE6-4, BE6-5;
E6-2, E6-3;
P6-1A&B, P6-2A&B

Effects of Managers' Choice of Inventory Reporting Methods

■ **LO4**
Explain the financial statement effects and tax effects of inventory cost flow assumptions.

Companies are free to choose FIFO, LIFO, or weighted-average cost to report inventory and cost of goods sold. However, because inventory costs generally change over time, the reported amounts for ending inventory and cost of goods sold will not be the same across inventory reporting methods. These differences could cause investors and creditors to make bad decisions if they are not aware of differences in inventory assumptions.

Illustration 6–10 compares the FIFO, LIFO, and weighted-average cost methods for Mario's Game Shop (assuming rising costs). (Recall from the Feature Story at the start of the chapter, that *gross profit* is a key measure of profitability, calculated as the difference between revenues and cost of goods sold.)

	FIFO	LIFO	Weighted-Average
Balance sheet:			
Ending inventory	$ 2,200	$ 1,600	$ 2,000
Income statement:			
Sales revenue (800 × $15)	$12,000	$12,000	$12,000
Cost of goods sold	7,800	8,400	8,000
Gross profit	$ 4,200	$ 3,600	$ 4,000

ILLUSTRATION 6–10

Comparison of Inventory Cost Flow Assumptions, When Costs Are Rising

When inventory costs are rising, Mario's Game Shop will report both higher inventory in the balance sheet and higher gross profit in the income statement if it chooses FIFO. The reason is that FIFO assumes the lower costs of the earlier purchases become cost of goods sold first, leaving the higher costs of the later purchases in ending inventory. Under the same assumption (rising inventory costs), LIFO will produce the *opposite* effect: LIFO will report both the lowest inventory and the lowest gross profit. The weighted-average cost method typically produces amounts that fall between the FIFO and LIFO amounts for both cost of goods sold and ending inventory.

Accountants often call FIFO the *balance-sheet approach:* The amount it reports for ending inventory (which appears in the *balance sheet*) better approximates the current cost of inventory. The ending inventory amount reported under LIFO, in contrast, generally includes "old" inventory costs that do not realistically represent the cost of today's inventory.

FIFO has a balance-sheet focus.

Accountants often call LIFO the *income-statement approach:* The amount it reports for cost of goods sold (which appears in the *income statement*) more realistically matches the current costs of inventory needed to produce current revenues. Recall that LIFO assumes the last purchases are sold first, reporting the most recent inventory cost in cost of goods sold. However, also note that the most recent cost is not the same as the actual cost. FIFO better approximates actual cost of goods sold for most companies, since most companies' actual physical flow follows FIFO.

LIFO has an income-statement focus.

FIFO or LIFO?

Management must weigh the benefits of FIFO and LIFO when deciding which inventory cost flow assumption will produce a better outcome for the company. Here we review the logic behind that decision.

Decision Maker's Perspective

Why Choose FIFO?

Most companies' actual physical flow follows FIFO. Think about a supermarket, car dealership, clothing shop, electronics store, or just about any company you're familiar with. These companies generally sell their oldest inventory first (first-in, first-out). If a company wants to choose an inventory method that most closely approximates its *actual physical flow* of inventory, then for most companies FIFO makes the most sense.

FIFO matches physical flow for most companies.

Another reason managers may want to use FIFO relates to its effect on the financial statements. **During periods of rising costs, which is the case for most companies (including our example for Mario's Game Shop), FIFO results in a (1) *higher* ending inventory, (2) *lower* cost of goods sold, and**

FIFO generally results in higher assets and higher net income when inventory costs are rising.

Many career opportunities are available in tax accounting. Because tax laws constantly change and are complex, tax accountants provide services to their clients not only through income tax statement preparation but also by formulating tax strategies to minimize tax payments. The choice of LIFO versus FIFO is one such example.

Tax accountants need a thorough understanding of legal matters, business transactions, and the tax code. Large corporations increasingly are looking to hire individuals with both an accounting and a legal background in tax. For example, someone who is a Certified Public Accountant (CPA) and has a law degree is especially desirable in the job market. In addition, people in nonaccounting positions also benefit greatly from an understanding of tax accounting. Whether you work in a large corporation or own a small business, virtually all business decisions have tax consequences.

LIFO generally results in tax savings.

(3) _higher_ reported profit than does LIFO. Managers may want to report higher assets and profitability to increase their bonus compensation, decrease unemployment risk, satisfy shareholders, meet lending agreements, or increase stock price.

Why Choose LIFO?

If FIFO results in higher total assets and higher net income and produces amounts that most closely follow the actual flow of inventory, why would any company choose LIFO? **The primary benefit of choosing LIFO is tax savings.** LIFO results in the lowest amount of reported profits (when inventory costs are rising). While that might not look so good in the income statement, it's a welcome outcome in the tax return. When taxable income is lower, the company owes less in taxes to the Internal Revenue Service (IRS).

Can a company have its cake and eat it too by using FIFO for the income statement and LIFO for the tax return? No. The IRS established the **LIFO conformity rule**, which requires a company that uses LIFO for tax reporting to also use LIFO for financial reporting. ●

REPORTING THE LIFO DIFFERENCE

As Mario's Game Shop demonstrates, the choice between FIFO and LIFO results in different amounts for ending inventory in the balance sheet and cost of goods sold in the income statement. This complicates the way we compare financial statements: One company may be using FIFO, while a competing company may be using LIFO. To determine which of the two companies is more profitable, investors must adjust for the fact that managers' choice of inventory method has an effect on reported performance.

Because of the financial statement effects of different inventory methods, companies that choose LIFO must report the difference in the amount of inventory a company would report _if_ it used FIFO instead of LIFO. (This difference is sometimes referred to as the LIFO reserve.) For some companies that have been using LIFO for a long time or for companies that have seen dramatic increases in inventory costs, the LIFO difference can be substantial. For example, Illustration 6–11 shows the effect of the LIFO difference reported by **Rite Aid Corporation**, which uses LIFO to account for most of its inventory.

ILLUSTRATION 6–11

Impact of the LIFO Difference on Reported Inventory of Rite Aid Corporation

RITE AID CORPORATION Notes to the Financial Statements (partial)		
($ in millions)	2009	2008
Reported inventory under LIFO	$3,509	$3,937
LIFO difference	746	563
Inventory assuming FIFO	$4,255	$4,500

If Rite Aid had used FIFO instead of LIFO, reported inventory amounts would have been $746 million greater and $563 million greater in 2009 and 2008, respectively. The magnitude of these effects can have a significant influence on investors' decisions.

Decision Point

Question	Accounting information	Analysis
When comparing inventory amounts between two companies, does the choice of inventory method matter?	The LIFO difference reported in the footnotes to the financial statements	When inventory costs are rising, FIFO results in a *higher* reported inventory. The LIFO difference can be used to compare inventory of two companies if one uses FIFO and the other uses LIFO.

CONSISTENCY IN REPORTING

Companies can choose which inventory method they prefer, even if the method does not match the actual physical flow of goods. However, once the company chooses a method, it is not allowed to frequently change to another one.[1] For example, a retail store cannot use FIFO in the current year because inventory costs are rising and then switch to LIFO in the following year because inventory costs are now falling.

However, a company need not use the same method for all its inventory. **International Paper Company**, for instance, uses LIFO for its raw materials and finished pulp and paper products, and both FIFO and weighted-average cost for other inventories. Because of the importance of inventories and the possible differential effects of different methods on the financial statements, a company informs its stockholders of the inventory method(s) being used in a note to the financial statements.

KEY POINT

Generally, FIFO more closely resembles the actual physical flow of inventory. When inventory costs are rising, FIFO results in higher reported inventory in the balance sheet and higher reported income in the income statement. Conversely, LIFO results in a lower reported inventory and net income, reducing the company's income tax obligation.

INTERNATIONAL FINANCIAL REPORTING STANDARDS (IFRS)

LIFO is not allowed under IFRS because it tends not to match the actual physical flow of inventory. FIFO and weighted-average cost are allowable inventory cost methods under IFRS. This distinction will become increasingly important as the United States moves closer to accepting IFRS for financial reporting. Will LIFO eventually disappear as a permitted inventory cost flow method? Perhaps so . . . stay tuned.

For more discussion, see Appendix E.

---

[1]When a company changes from LIFO for tax purposes, it cannot change back to LIFO until it has filed five tax returns using the non-LIFO method.

PART B

RECORDING INVENTORY TRANSACTIONS

So far, we've talked about purchases and sales of inventories and how to track their costs. We have not yet discussed how to *record* inventory transactions. We turn to that topic now.

Most companies, with the help of scanners and bar codes, keep a continual record of inventory using a **perpetual inventory system**. The continual—that is, perpetual—tracking of inventory helps a company to better manage its inventory levels. Just think of the losses that might occur at a video game store if the manager has no clear idea of the store's inventory and orders too many of a particular game that soon becomes obsolete when the next version or next hottest game comes out.

In contrast, a **periodic inventory system** does not continually modify inventory amounts, but instead *periodically* adjusts for purchases and sales of inventory at the end of the reporting period, based on a physical count of inventory on hand. Because this system does not provide a useful, continuing record of inventory, very few companies actually use the periodic inventory system in practice to maintain their own (internal) records of inventory transactions. Therefore, in this section, we will focus on how to record inventory transactions using a perpetual inventory system. Appendix A to the chapter covers the periodic system.

Perpetual Inventory System

■ LO5
Record inventory transactions using a perpetual inventory system.

To see how to record inventory transactions using a perpetual inventory system, we will look again at the inventory transactions for Mario's Game Shop. Recall that from January 1 through December 31, Mario sold 800 games. Now let's modify the example by giving exact dates for the sale of the 800 games—300 on July 17 and 500 on December 15. Illustration 6–12 shows the order of inventory transactions for Mario's Game Shop, including the total cost of the inventory and the total revenue from the sale of the 800 games.

ILLUSTRATION 6–12

Inventory Transactions for Mario's Game Shop

Date	Transaction	Details	Total Cost	Total Revenue
Jan. 1	Beginning inventory	100 units for $7 each	$ 700	
Apr. 25	Purchase	300 units for $9 each	2,700	
Jul. 17	Sale	300 units for $15 each		$ 4,500
Oct. 19	Purchase	600 units for $11 each	6,600	
Dec. 15	Sale	500 units for $15 each		7,500
	Totals		$10,000	$12,000

Using this information, let's see how Mario would record purchases and sales of inventory.

INVENTORY PURCHASES AND SALES

To record the purchase of new inventory, we debit Inventory (an asset) to show that the company's balance of this asset account has increased. At the same time, if the purchase was paid in cash, we credit Cash. Or more likely, if the company made the purchase on account, we credit Accounts Payable, increasing total liabilities. Thus, Mario records the first purchase of 300 units for $2,700 on April 25 as:

April 25	Debit	Credit
Inventory	2,700	
Accounts Payable		2,700
(*Purchase inventory on account*)		

Balance Sheet						Income Statement		
				Stockholders' Equity				
				Common	Retained			Net
Assets	=	Liabilities	+	Stock	+ Earnings	Revenues	– Expenses =	Income
+2,700	=	+2,700						

On July 17, Mario sold 300 units of inventory on account for $15 each, resulting in total sales of $4,500. We make two entries to record the sale: (1) The first entry shows an increase to the asset account (in this case, Accounts Receivable) and an increase to Sales Revenue. (2) The second entry adjusts the Inventory and Cost of Goods Sold accounts.

Mario records as revenue the $4,500 from the July 17 sale. That amount is the price Mario charges to customers, but what did that inventory *cost* Mario? (That is, what is the cost of the goods sold?) Under the assumption that Mario uses FIFO to calculate inventory, the cost of the *first* 300 units purchased is $2,500, which is $700 of beginning inventory (100 units × $7) plus $1,800 of the April 25 purchase (200 units × $9). We record this amount as the cost of goods sold for the July 17 sale. At the same time, we maintain a continual (perpetual) record of inventory by reducing the Inventory balance by the cost of the amount sold, $2,500, as shown below.

July 17	Debit	Credit
Accounts Receivable	4,500	
Sales Revenue		4,500
(*Sell inventory on account*)		
($4,500 = 300 units × $15)		
Cost of Goods Sold	2,500	
Inventory		2,500
(*Record cost of inventory sold*)		
($2,500 = [100 units × $7] + [200 units × $9])		

Balance Sheet						Income Statement		
				Stockholders' Equity				
				Common	Retained			Net
Assets	=	Liabilities	+	Stock	+ Earnings	Revenues	– Expenses =	Income
+4,500	=				+2,000	+4,500	– +2,500 =	+2,000
–2,500								
+2,000								

By recording the sales revenue and the cost of goods sold at the same time, we can see that Mario's profit on the sale is $2,000.

On October 19, Mario purchased 600 additional units of inventory for $6,600 on account. We record that purchase as:

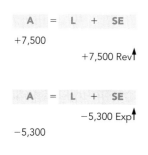

October 19	Debit	Credit
Inventory	**6,600**	
Accounts Payable		**6,600**
(Purchase inventory on account)		

A = L + SE
+6,600
       +6,600

On December 15, Mario sold another 500 units for $15 each on account. Again, we make two entries to record the sale. The first increases Accounts Receivable and Sales Revenue. The second adjusts the Cost of Goods Sold and Inventory accounts. What did the inventory sold on December 15 cost Mario? On the FIFO basis, the cost of goods sold is $5,300 (100 units × $9 plus 400 units × $11). Mario increases Cost of Goods Sold and decreases Inventory by that amount. Thus, we record the sale on December 15 as:

December 15	Debit	Credit
Accounts Receivable	**7,500**	
Sales Revenue		**7,500**
(Sell inventory on account)		
($7,500 = 500 units × $15)		
Cost of Goods Sold	**5,300**	
Inventory		**5,300**
(Record cost of inventory sold)		
($5,300 = [100 units × $9] + [400 units × $11])		

A = L + SE
+7,500
       +7,500 Rev↑

A = L + SE
       −5,300 Exp↑
−5,300

After recording all purchases and sales of inventory for the year, we can determine the ending balance of Inventory by examining the postings to the account. Thus, Mario's ending Inventory balance is $2,200, as shown in Illustration 6–13.

ILLUSTRATION 6–13

Inventory Account for Mario's Game Shop

Inventory			
Jan. 1 Beginning	700		
Apr. 25 Purchase	2,700	2,500	Jul. 17 Sale
Oct. 19 Purchase	6,600	5,300	Dec. 15 Sale
	10,000	7,800	
Dec. 31 Ending FIFO amount	Bal. 2,200		

KEY POINT

The perpetual inventory system maintains a continual—or *perpetual*—record of inventory purchased and sold. When companies *purchase* inventory using a perpetual inventory system, they increase the Inventory account and either decrease Cash or increase Accounts Payable. When companies *sell* inventory, they make two entries: (1) They increase an asset account (Cash or Accounts Receivable) and increase Sales Revenue, and (2) they increase Cost of Goods Sold and decrease Inventory.

Simple adjustment from FIFO to LIFO.   In the example above, we recorded inventory transactions using the FIFO assumption. Thus, Mario assumed that the 800 units sold during the year came from the first 800 units purchased. **In practice, virtually all companies maintain their own inventory records using the FIFO assumption, because that's how they typically sell their actual inventory.** However, as discussed earlier in the chapter, for preparing financial statements, many companies choose to report their inventory using the LIFO assumption. So, how does a company adjust its own inventory records maintained on a FIFO basis to a LIFO basis for preparing financial statements? The adjustment is referred to as the LIFO adjustment, and you'll see that this involves a *very simple* adjustment.

To see how easy the LIFO adjustment can be, let's refer back to our example involving Mario's Game Shop. As summarized in Illustration 6–13, Mario's ending balance of Inventory using FIFO is $2,200. Under LIFO, it is only $1,600 (see Illustration 6–7). As a result, if Mario's wants to adjust its FIFO inventory records to LIFO for preparing financial statements, it needs to adjust Inventory downward by $600 (decreasing the balance from $2,200 to $1,600). In this case, we record the LIFO adjustment at the end of the period through a decrease to Inventory and an increase to Cost of Goods Sold:

December 31	Debit	Credit
Cost of Goods Sold	600	
Inventory		600
(Record the LIFO adjustment)		

A	=	L	+	SE
				−600 Exp
−600				

In rare situations where the LIFO Inventory balance is *greater* than the FIFO Inventory balance (such as when inventory costs are declining), the entry for the LIFO adjustment would be reversed.

Illustration 6–14 shows the Inventory account for Mario's Game Shop after the LIFO adjustment. Notice that the balance of Inventory has decreased to reflect the amount reported under the LIFO method.

Inventory				
Jan. 1 Beginning	700			
Apr. 25 Purchase	2,700	2,500	Jul. 17 Sale	
Oct. 19 Purchase	6,600	5,300	Dec. 15 Sale	
	10,000	7,800		
FIFO amount	2,200			
		600	LIFO	
Dec. 31 Ending			adjustment	
LIFO amount	Bal. 1,600			

ILLUSTRATION 6–14

Inventory Account for Mario's Game Shop, after LIFO Adjustment

KEY POINT

Nearly all companies maintain their own inventory records on a FIFO basis, and then some prepare financial statements on a LIFO basis. To adjust their FIFO inventory records to LIFO for financial reporting, companies use a simple LIFO adjustment at the end of the period.

ADDITIONAL INVENTORY TRANSACTIONS

To this point, we've recorded inventory purchases and inventory sales transactions. So that we can discuss additional inventory topics, let's add three more inventory-related transactions to our Mario's example. Let's assume Mario also:

1. On April 25, pays freight charges of $300 for inventory purchased on April 25.
2. On April 30, pays for the units purchased on April 25, less a 2% purchase discount.
3. On October 22, returns 50 defective units from the October 19 purchase.

Next, we discuss how to record each of these three transactions.

Freight charges.   A significant cost associated with inventory for most merchandising companies includes freight (also called shipping) charges. This includes the cost of shipments of inventory from suppliers, as well as the cost of shipments to customers. When goods are shipped, they are shipped with terms *FOB shipping point* or *FOB destination.* FOB stands for "free on board" and indicates *when* title (ownership) passes from the seller to the buyer. FOB *shipping point* means title passes when the seller *ships* the inventory, not when the buyer receives it. The fact that a buyer does not have actual physical possession of the inventory does not prevent transfer of title to the buyer's inventory. In contrast, if the seller ships the inventory FOB *destination,* then title does not transfer to the buyer when the inventory is shipped. The buyer would not record the purchase transaction until the shipped inventory reached its *destination,* the buyer's location.

Freight charges on incoming shipments from suppliers are commonly referred to as freight-in. **We add the cost of freight-in to the balance of Inventory.** In this case, the cost of freight is considered a cost of the purchased inventory. When Mario pays $300 for freight charges associated with the purchase of inventory on April 25, those charges would be recorded as part of the inventory cost.

A = L + SE	April 25	Debit	Credit
+300	Inventory	300	
−300	Cash		300
	(Pay freight-in charges)		

Later, when that inventory is sold, those freight charges become part of the cost of goods sold. In Mario's case, all of the units purchased on April 25 are sold by the end of the year, so the $300 freight charge would be reported as part of cost of goods sold in the income statement at the end of the year.

The cost of freight on shipments *to* customers is called freight-out. Shipping charges for outgoing inventory are reported in the income statement either as part of cost of goods sold or as an operating expense, usually among selling expenses. If a company adopts a policy of not including shipping charges in cost of goods sold, both the amounts incurred during the period as well as the income statement classification of the expense must be disclosed.[2]

To see an example of how **Amazon.com** accounts for freight charges, look at Illustration 6–15 (next page).

Purchase discounts.   As discussed in Chapter 5, sellers often encourage prompt payment by offering *discounts* to buyers. From the seller's point of view, these are sales

[2]FASB ASC 605–45–50–2: Revenue Recognition–Principal Agent Considerations–Disclosure–Shipping and Handling Fees and Costs (previously "Accounting for Shipping and Handling Fees and Costs," *EITF Issue No. 00-10* [Norwalk, Conn.: FASB, 2000] par. 6).

ILLUSTRATION 6–15
Accounting for
Shipping Costs by
Amazon.com

AMAZON.COM, INC.
Notes to the Financial Statements (excerpt)

Shipping charges to receive products from our suppliers are included in our inventory, and recognized as "Cost of sales.". . . Outbound shipping-related costs are included in "Cost of sales" and totaled $1.5 billion, $1.2 billion, and $884 million for 2008, 2007, and 2006.

discounts; from the buyer's point of view, they are *purchase discounts*. Purchase discounts allow buyers to trim a portion of the cost of the purchase in exchange for payment within a certain period of time. Buyers are not required to take purchase discounts, but many find it advantageous to do so.

Let's assume that Mario's supplier, Luigi Software, Inc., offers terms 2/10, n/30 for the April 25 purchase on account. This means that Mario can receive a 2% discount if payment is made within 10 days, but the total invoice is due within 30 days. Mario's policy is to take advantage of discounts offered.

For a review of credit terms, look back at page 216.

Recall that on April 25 Mario purchased 300 units on account for $9 each (or $2,700 total). When Mario makes payment on April 30, the discount would be $54 (= $2,700 × 2%). Mario has to pay only $2,646 (= $2,700 − $54) to eliminate the $2,700 amount owed. To account for the purchase discount, we subtract the discount from the balance in the Inventory account:

April 30	Debit	Credit	A	=	L	+	SE
Accounts Payable	2,700				−2,700		
Inventory		54	−54				
Cash		2,646	−2,646				
(Pay on account with a 2% purchase discount of $54)							
($54 = $2,700 × 2%)							

Just as freight charges *add* to the cost of inventory and therefore increase the cost of goods sold once those items are sold, purchase discounts *subtract* from the cost of inventory and therefore reduce cost of goods sold once those items are sold. When Mario sells the 300 units purchased on April 25, the cost of goods sold associated with those items will be the cost of the actual units ($2,700) plus freight charges ($300) less the purchase discount ($54), totaling $2,946.

Purchase returns. Occasionally, a company will find inventory items to be unacceptable for some reason—perhaps they are damaged or are different from what was ordered. In those cases, the company returns the items to the supplier and records the purchase return as a reduction in both Inventory and Accounts Payable. For example, when Mario decides on October 22 to return 50 defective units from the 600 units purchased on October 19 for $11 each, the company would record the following transaction:

October 22	Debit	Credit	A	=	L	+	SE
Accounts Payable	550				−550		
Inventory		550	−550				
(Return inventory previously purchased on account)							
($550 = 50 defective units × $11)							

Let's Review

Camcorder Central sells high-end **Sony** camcorders and accounts for its inventory using FIFO with a perpetual system. At the beginning of March 2012, the company has camcorder inventory of $24,000 (= $240 × 100 units).

Required:

Record the following inventory transactions for Camcorder Central.

1. On March 7, Camcorder Central purchases on account 210 camcorders from Sony Corporation for $250 each, terms 2/10, n/30.
2. On March 8, Camcorder Central pays $2,000 for freight charges associated with the 210 camcorders purchased on March 7.
3. On March 10, Camcorder Central returns to Sony 10 defective camcorders from the March 7 purchase, receiving a credit of $250 for each camcorder.
4. On March 16, Camcorder Central makes full payment for inventory purchased on March 7, excluding the 10 defective camcorders returned and the 2% discount received.
5. On March 20, Camcorder Central sells 300 camcorders for $90,000 ($300 each). All sales are for cash.

Solution:

1. Camcorder Central's March 7 purchase on account of 210 camcorders from Sony Corporation for $250 each, terms 2/10, n/30:

March 7	Debit	Credit
Inventory	52,500	
Accounts Payable		52,500
(*Purchase camcorders on account*)		
(*$52,500 = $250 × 210 camcorders*)		

2. Camcorder's March 8 payment for freight charges associated with the camcorders purchased on March 7:

March 8	Debit	Credit
Inventory	2,000	
Cash		2,000
(*Pay for freight charges*)		

3. Camcorder's March 10 return of 10 defective camcorders from the March 7 purchase, for a credit of $250 per camcorder:

March 10	Debit	Credit
Accounts Payable	2,500	
Inventory		2,500
(*Return defective camcorders*)		

4. Camcorder's March 16 payment for inventory purchased on March 7, excluding the returned camcorders and less the 2% discount:

March 16	Debit	Credit
Accounts Payable	50,000	
Inventory		1,000
Cash		49,000
(*Make full payment for March 7 purchase*)		
(*$1,000 = $50,000 × 2%*)		

5. Camcorder's cash sale on March 20 of 300 camcorders for $300 each:

March 20	Debit	Credit
Cash	90,000	
Sales Revenue		90,000
(Sell 300 camcorders for cash)		
($90,000 = $300 × 300 camcorders)		
Cost of Goods Sold	75,000	
Inventory		75,000
(Record cost of camcorders sold)		
(Cost of 100 camcorders in beginning inventory = $24,000)		
(Cost of 200 camcorders purchased = $52,500 + $2,000 − $2,500 − $1,000 = $51,000)		

Suggested Homework:
BE6-9, BE6-11;
E6-7, E6-8;
P6-3A&B, P6-6A&B

SALES TRANSACTIONS: THE OTHER SIDE OF PURCHASE TRANSACTIONS

Flip Side

For every purchase transaction, there is a sales transaction for another party. Sometimes, seeing the other side of the transaction helps us understand the economic events we are recording. In the Let's Review exercise above, Camcorder Central made a $52,500 purchase of inventory on account from Sony Corporation. Camcorder Central then returned inventory of $2,500 and received a $1,000 purchase discount for quick payment. Camcorder Central is the purchaser and Sony is the seller. We discussed returns and discounts from the seller's viewpoint in Chapter 5; here, let's briefly reexamine the transactions between Sony and Camcorder Central so we can see a side-by-side comparison of purchase and sales transactions. Illustration 6–16 shows these entries.

Purchaser			**Seller**		
Camcorder Central			Sony Corporation		
Purchase on Account			**Sale on Account***		
Inventory	52,500		Accounts Receivable	52,500	
Accounts Payable		52,500	Sales Revenue		52,500
Purchase Return			**Sales Return**		
Accounts Payable	2,500		Sales Return	2,500	
Inventory		2,500	Accounts Receivable		2,500
Payment on Account with Discount			**Receipt on Account with Discount**		
Accounts Payable	50,000		Cash	49,000	
Inventory		1,000	Sales Discounts	1,000	
Cash		49,000	Accounts Receivable		50,000

ILLUSTRATION 6–16

Comparison of Purchase and Sale of Inventory Transactions

*In practice, Sony also records the cost of inventory sold at the time of the sale. For simplicity, we omit this part of the transaction since Camcorder Central has no comparable transaction. We have also omitted Camcorder Central's March 20 sale of camcorders, since Sony is not party to that transaction.

 KEY POINT

For most companies, freight charges are added to the cost of inventory, whereas purchase returns and purchase discounts are deducted from the cost of inventory. Some companies choose to report freight charges on outgoing shipments as part of selling expenses instead of cost of goods sold.

Multiple-Step Income Statement

In Chapters 1 through 5, we presented a form of the income statement with two main categories: total revenues and total expenses. Look back at Illustration 3–12 (page 128) for an example. That format involves essentially a single calculation—total revenues minus total expenses—to get to net income. Not surprisingly, such an income statement is called a *single-step income statement*.

In this chapter, we have seen that sales and purchases of inventory typically are the most important transactions for a merchandising company. As a result, in their income statements, merchandisers report revenues and expenses from these transactions separately from other revenues and expenses. Because of this separate reporting, merchandising companies usually use a different format, called a **multiple-step income statement**, referring to the fact that the income statement reports *multiple* levels of income (or profitability).

Gross profit.   The multiple-step income statement begins by reporting that a company's sales revenue minus cost of goods sold equals gross profit. Illustration 6–17 shows these amounts for our continuing example of Mario's Game Shop. Recall that Mario sold 800 units during the year for $15 each (or $12,000 total). This amount is reported as sales revenue.

ILLUSTRATION 6–17

Multiple-Step Income Statement

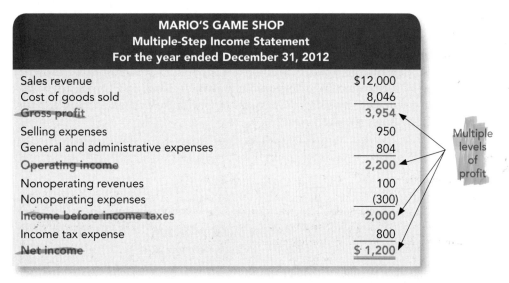

MARIO'S GAME SHOP
Multiple-Step Income Statement
For the year ended December 31, 2012

Sales revenue	$12,000
Cost of goods sold	8,046
Gross profit	3,954
Selling expenses	950
General and administrative expenses	804
Operating income	2,200
Nonoperating revenues	100
Nonoperating expenses	(300)
Income before income taxes	2,000
Income tax expense	800
Net income	$ 1,200

Multiple levels of profit

From sales revenue, we subtract the cost of the 800 units sold. Again, to calculate this balance, we can look back to our transactions involving goods sold, including the cost of freight charges and the purchase discount associated with the purchase on April 25. The 800 units sold consist of the following:

	Units Sold	Unit Cost	Total Cost
Beginning inventory	100	$ 7	$ 700
Purchase on April 25	300	9	2,700
Freight charges			300
Purchase discount			(54)
Purchase on October 19	400	11	4,400
	800		$8,046

Mario would report $8,046 as the cost of goods sold.

The difference between sales of inventory and the cost of that inventory is the company's *gross profit*. Gross profit is one of the profitability measures investors use to evaluate the performance of a merchandising company. As Illustration 6–17 shows, Mario's gross profit is $3,954.

Operating income.   After gross profit, the next items reported are selling expenses and general and administrative expenses, often referred to as **operating expenses**. We discussed several types of operating expenses in earlier chapters—salaries, utilities, advertising, supplies, rent, insurance, and bad debts. These costs are normal for operating most companies. Gross profit reduced by these operating expenses is referred to as operating income (or sometimes referred to as *income from operations*). It measures profitability from *normal* operations, a key performance measure for predicting the future profit-generating ability of the company.

After operating income, a company reports **nonoperating revenues and expenses**. Nonoperating revenues and expenses arise from activities that are *not* part of the company's primary operations. Interest revenue and interest expense are examples. (In Chapter 7, we will discuss another common nonoperating item—gains and losses on the sale of long-term assets.) Investors focus less on nonoperating items than on income from operations, as these nonoperating activities often do not have long-term implications on the company's profitability.

Income before income taxes.   Combining operating income with nonoperating revenues and expenses yields income before income taxes. For Mario's Game Shop, the amount of nonoperating expenses exceeds the amount of nonoperating revenues, so income before income taxes is lower than operating income.

Net income.   Next, the company subtracts income tax expense to find its bottom-line net income. At the bottom line, net income represents the difference between all revenues and all expenses for the period. Note in Illustration 6–17 that the multiple-step income statement, unlike the single-step format, reports *multiple levels of profit*—gross profit, operating income, income before income taxes, and net income. We'll examine the multiple-step income statement again in Chapter 12, when we discuss additional income statement activities such as discontinued operations and extraordinary items.

KEY POINT

A multiple-step income statement reports multiple levels of profitability. **Gross profit** equals sales revenue minus cost of goods sold. **Operating income** equals gross profit minus operating expenses. **Income before income taxes** equals operating income plus nonoperating revenues and minus nonoperating expenses. **Net income** equals all revenues minus all expenses.

Illustration 6–18 presents an example of a multiple-step income statement for **hhgregg, Inc.**, a specialty retailer of consumer electronics and home appliances.

hhgregg, INC. Multiple-Step Income Statement For the year ended March 31, 2009 ($ in millions)	
Sales revenue, net	$1,397
Cost of goods sold	962
Gross profit	435
Selling, general, and administrative expenses	287
Advertising expenses	62
Other operating expenses	16
Operating income	70
Interest expense	7
Income before income taxes	63
Income tax expense	26
Net income	$ 37

ILLUSTRATION 6–18

Multiple-Step Income Statement for hhgregg, Inc.

The company has sales revenue of $1,397 million and cost of goods sold of $962 million, resulting in a gross profit of $435 million. After subtracting normal operating expenses, operating income is $70 million. Income before taxes equals $63 million after subtracting interest expense. The company's after-tax net income equals $37 million.

PART C

LOWER-OF-COST-OR-MARKET METHOD

■ **LO7**

Apply the lower-of-cost-or-market method for inventories.

Think about the store where you usually buy your clothes. You've probably noticed the store selling leftover inventory at deeply discounted prices after the end of each selling season to make room for the next season's clothing line. The value of the company's old clothing inventory has likely fallen below its original cost. Is it appropriate to report the reduced-value inventory at its original cost? The answer to that question has motivated accountants to use the lower-of-cost-or-market method.

When the market value of inventory falls below its original cost, companies are required to report inventory at the lower market value. Normally, the market value of inventory is considered to be the replacement cost of that inventory. In other words, what is the cost to replace the inventory item in its identical form? The cost of inventory is the amount initially recorded in the accounting records based on methods we discussed in the previous section (specific identification, FIFO, LIFO, or weighted-average cost). Once it has determined both the cost and market value of inventory, the company reports ending inventory in the balance sheet at the *lower* of the two amounts. This is known as the lower-of-cost-or-market (LCM) method to valuing inventory.

Illustration 6–19 demonstrates the concept behind the lower-of-cost-or-market method.

ILLUSTRATION 6–19

Lower-of-Cost-or-Market Method

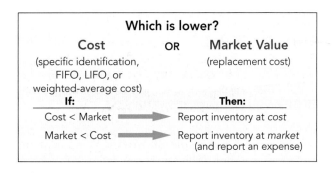

To see how we apply the lower-of-cost-or-market method to inventory amounts, assume Mario's Game Shop sells FunStation 2 and FunStation 3. Illustration 6–20 shows information related to ending inventory at the end of 2012.

ILLUSTRATION 6–20

Calculating the Lower-of-Cost-or-Market

Inventory Items	Cost per Unit	Market per Unit	Lower-of-Cost-or-Market per Unit		Quantity		Total Lower-of-Cost-or-Market
FunStation 2	$300	$200	→ $200	×	15	=	$ 3,000
FunStation 3	400	450	→ 400	×	20	=	8,000
			Reported ending inventory			=	$11,000

Mario reports the FunStation 2 in ending inventory at market value ($200 per unit) because that's lower than its original cost ($300 per unit). The 15 FunStation 2s were originally reported in inventory at their cost of $4,500 (= 15 × $300). To reduce the inventory from that original cost of $4,500 to its lower market value of $3,000 (= 15 × $200), Mario records a $1,500 reduction in inventory with the following year-end adjustment.

December 31, 2012	Debit	Credit
Cost of Goods Sold	1,500	
Inventory		1,500
(Adjust inventory down to market value)		

Balance Sheet					Income Statement			
			Stockholders' Equity					
			Common	Retained				Net
Assets	=	**Liabilities** +	**Stock** +	**Earnings**	**Revenues**	− **Expenses**	=	**Income**
−1,500	=			−1,500		+1,500	=	−1,500

Notice that the write-down of inventory has the effect not only of reducing total assets, but also of reducing net income and retained earnings.

The FunStation 3 inventory, on the other hand, remains on the books at its original cost of $8,000 (= $400 × 20), since cost is less than market value. Mario does not need to make any adjustment for these inventory items.

After adjusting inventory to the lower-of-cost-or-market, the store calculates its ending Inventory balance as:

	Inventory		
Balance before LCM adjustment	12,500		
		1,500	LCM adjustment
Ending balance	Bal. 11,000		

Conservatism and the Lower-of-Cost-or-Market Method

Firms are required to report the falling value of inventory, but they are not allowed to report any increasing value of inventory. Why is this? The answer lies in the conservative nature of some accounting procedures. A *conservative* approach in accounting implies that there is more potential harm to users of financial statements if estimated *gains* turn out to be wrong than if estimated *losses* turn out to be wrong. It also guides companies, when faced with a choice, to select accounting methods that are less likely to overstate assets and net income. Therefore, companies typically do not report estimated gains. ●

Decision Maker's Perspective

KEY POINT

We report inventory at the lower-of-cost-or-market; that is, at cost (specific identification, FIFO, LIFO, or weighted-average cost) or market value (replacement cost), whichever is lower. When market value falls below cost, we adjust downward the balance of inventory from cost to market value.

Let's Review

Auto Adrenaline provides specialty car products—satellite radios, GPS navigation systems, and subwoofers. At the end of 2012, the company's records show the following amounts in ending inventory.

Inventory Items	Quantity	Cost per Unit	Market per Unit
Satellite radios	10	$100	$120
GPS navigators	20	300	350
Subwoofers	40	70	50

Required:

1. Determine ending inventory using the lower-of-cost-or-market method.

2. Record any necessary year-end adjustment entry associated with the lower-of-cost-or-market method.

Solution:

1. Ending inventory, lower-of-cost-or-market:

Inventory Items	Cost per Unit	Market per Unit	Lower-of-Cost-or-Market per Unit		Quantity		Total Lower-of-Cost-or-Market
Satellite radios	$100	$120 →	$100	×	10	=	$1,000
GPS navigators	300	350 →	300	×	20	=	6,000
Subwoofers	70	50 →	50	×	40	=	2,000
							$9,000

Cost is lower than market for satellite radios and GPS navigators. We get lower-of-cost-or-market by multiplying the *cost* per unit times the quantity. However, market is lower than cost for subwoofers. In that case, we get lower-of-cost-or-market by multiplying the *market* per unit times quantity.

2. Year-end adjustment associated with the lower-of-cost-or-market method:

December 31, 2012	Debit	Credit
Cost of Goods Sold	800	
Inventory		800
(*Adjust inventory down to market value*)		
($800 = 40 subwoofers × $20 decline in market below cost)		

Suggested Homework:
BE6-14, BE6-15;
E6-13, E6-14;
P6-4A&B

We need the $800 adjustment to reduce the reported Inventory balance of the 40 subwoofers by $20 each (from $70 to $50).

ETHICAL DILEMMA

Diamond Computers, which is owned and operated by Dale Diamond, manufactures and sells different types of computers. The company has reported profits every year since its inception in 2000 and has applied for a bank loan near the end of 2012 to upgrade manufacturing facilities. These upgrades should significantly boost future productivity and profitability.

In preparing the financial statements for the year, the chief accountant, Sandy Walters, mentions to Dale that approximately $80,000 of computer inventory has become obsolete and a write-down of inventory should be recorded in 2012.

Dale understands that the write-down would result in a net loss being reported for company operations in 2012. This could jeopardize the company's application for the bank loan, which would lead to employee layoffs. Dale is a very kind, older gentleman who cares little for his personal wealth but who is deeply devoted to his employees' well-being. He truly believes the loan is necessary for the company's sustained viability. Dale suggests Sandy wait until 2013 to write down the inventory so that profitable financial statements can be presented to the bank this year.

What should Sandy do?

INVENTORY ANALYSIS
Best Buy vs. Radio Shack

ANALYSIS

■ **LO8**
Analyze management of inventory using the inventory turnover ratio and gross profit ratio.

As discussed in the previous section, if managers purchase too much inventory, the company runs the risk of the inventory becoming obsolete and market value falling below cost, resulting in inventory write-downs. Outside analysts as well as managers often use the *inventory turnover ratio* to evaluate a company's effectiveness in managing its investment in inventory. In addition, investors often rely on the *gross profit ratio* to determine the core profitability of a merchandising company's operations. We discuss these ratios next.

INVENTORY TURNOVER RATIO

The inventory turnover ratio shows the number of times the firm sells its average inventory balance during a reporting period. It is calculated as cost of goods sold divided by average inventory.

$$\text{Inventory turnover ratio} = \frac{\text{Cost of goods sold}}{\text{Average inventory}}$$

The more frequently a business is able to sell or "turn over" its average inventory balance, the less the company needs to invest in inventory for a given level of sales. Other things equal, a higher ratio indicates greater effectiveness of a company in managing its investment in inventory.

AVERAGE DAYS IN INVENTORY

Another way to measure the same activity is to calculate the average days in inventory. This ratio indicates the approximate number of days the average inventory is held. It is calculated as 365 days divided by the inventory turnover ratio.

$$\text{Average days in inventory} = \frac{365}{\text{Inventory turnover ratio}}$$

We can analyze the inventory of **Best Buy** and **Radio Shack Corporation** by calculating these ratios for both companies. Best Buy sells a large volume of commonly purchased products. In contrast, Radio Shack sells more distinct electronic items. Below are relevant amounts for each company as of February 2009 for Best Buy and December 2008 for Radio Shack.

($ in millions)	Cost of Goods Sold	Beginning Inventory	Ending Inventory
Best Buy	$34,017	$4,708	$4,753
Radio Shack	2,302	705	636

To compute the inventory turnover ratio we need the *average* inventory, which is the beginning amount of inventory plus the ending amount, divided by 2.

Best Buy   Average inventory = ($4,708 + $4,753) ÷ 2 = $4,730.5

Radio Shack   Average inventory = ($705 + $636) ÷ 2 = $670.5

We put average inventory in the denominator to compute the inventory turnover ratio, as shown in Illustration 6–21.

ILLUSTRATION 6–21

Inventory Turnover Ratios for Best Buy and Radio Shack

	Inventory Turnover Ratio	Average Days in Inventory
Best Buy	$34,017 ÷ $4,730.5 = 7.2 times	$\frac{365}{7.2}$ = 51 days
Radio Shack	$2,302 ÷ $670.5 = 3.4 times	$\frac{365}{3.4}$ = 107 days

The turnover ratio is more than twice as high for Best Buy. On average, it takes Radio Shack an additional 56 days to sell its inventory. If the two companies had the same business strategies, this would indicate that Best Buy is better at managing inventory. In this case, though, the difference in inventory turnover more likely is related to the products the two stores sell. Specialty items are not expected to sell as quickly. As we see in the next section, Radio Shack offsets its relatively low inventory turnover with a relatively high profit margin.

Decision Point

Question	Accounting information	Analysis
Is the company effectively managing its inventory?	Inventory turnover ratio and average days in inventory	A high inventory turnover ratio (or low average days in inventory) generally indicates that the company's inventory policies are effective.

COMMON MISTAKE

Many students use ending inventory rather than average inventory in calculating the inventory turnover ratio. Generally, when you calculate a ratio that includes an income statement item (an amount generated over a period) with a balance sheet item (an amount at a particular date), the balance sheet item needs to be converted to an amount *over the same period*. This is done by averaging the beginning and ending balances of the balance sheet item.

GROSS PROFIT RATIO

Another important indicator of the company's successful management of inventory is the gross profit ratio. It measures the amount by which the sale price of inventory exceeds its cost per dollar of sales. We calculate the gross profit ratio as gross profit divided by net sales. (Net sales equal total sales revenue less sales discounts, returns, and allowances).

$$\text{Gross profit ratio} = \frac{\text{Gross profit}}{\text{Net sales}}$$

The higher the gross profit ratio, the higher is the "markup" a company is able to achieve on its inventories. Best Buy and Radio Shack report the following information.

($ in millions)	Net Sales	–	Cost of Goods Sold	=	Gross Profit
Best Buy	$45,015		$34,017		$10,998
Radio Shack	4,225		2,302		1,923

Illustration 6–22 shows calculation of the gross profit ratio for Best Buy and Radio Shack.

	Gross Profit ÷ Net Sales	=	Gross Profit Ratio
Best Buy	$10,998 ÷ $45,015	=	24%
Radio Shack	$1,923 ÷ $4,225	=	46%

ILLUSTRATION 6–22

Gross Profit Ratios for Best Buy and Radio Shack

For Best Buy, this means that for every $1 of sales revenue, the company spends $0.76 on inventory, resulting in a gross profit of $0.24. In contrast, the gross profit ratio for Radio Shack is 46%. We saw earlier that Radio Shack's inventory turnover is about half that of Best Buy. But, we see now that Radio Shack makes up for that lower turnover with a gross profit margin about twice that of Best Buy. The products Best Buy sells are familiar goods, and competition from companies like **Dell**, **Target**, and **Walmart** for these high-volume items keeps sale prices low compared to costs. Because Radio Shack specializes in unique lower-volume products, there is less competition, allowing greater price markups.

As products become more highly specialized, gross profit ratios typically increase even further. For example, consider a company like **Blue Coat Systems**, a company that specializes in unique products and services that optimize and secure information sent over business networks or the Internet. In 2009, the company reported gross profit of $314 million on net sales of $445 million—a gross profit ratio of 71%.

KEY POINT

The inventory turnover ratio indicates the number of times the firm sells, or turns over, its average inventory balance during a reporting period. The gross profit ratio measures the amount by which the sale price of inventory exceeds its cost per dollar of sales.

Decision Point

Question	Accounting information	Analysis
For how much is a company able to sell a product above its cost?	Gross profit and net sales	The ratio of gross profit to net sales indicates how much the sales price exceeds inventory cost for each $1 of sales.

APPENDIX A

RECORDING INVENTORY TRANSACTIONS USING A PERIODIC INVENTORY SYSTEM

■ **LO9**
Record inventory transactions using a periodic inventory system.

In this chapter, we discussed how to record inventory transactions using a *perpetual* inventory system. Here we discuss how to record inventory transactions using a *periodic* inventory system.

Recall that under a **perpetual inventory system** we maintain a continual—or *perpetual*—record of inventory purchased and sold. In contrast, using a **periodic inventory system** we do not continually modify inventory amounts. Instead, we *periodically* adjust for purchases and sales of inventory at the end of the reporting period, based on a physical count of inventory on hand.

To demonstrate the differences in these two systems, let's record inventory transactions under the periodic system using the same information (from Illustration 6–12) that we used to demonstrate the perpetual inventory system. We repeat those transactions in Illustration 6–23.

ILLUSTRATION 6–23
Inventory Transactions for Mario's Game Shop

Date	Transaction	Details	Total Cost	Total Revenue
Jan. 1	Beginning inventory	100 units for $7 each	$ 700	
Apr. 25	Purchase	300 units for $9 each	2,700	
Jul. 17	Sale	300 units for $15 each		$ 4,500
Oct. 19	Purchase	600 units for $11 each	6,600	
Dec. 15	Sale	500 units for $15 each		7,500
	Totals		$10,000	$12,000

To make the distinction between the perpetual system and periodic system easier, let's look at side-by-side comparisons. The perpetual entries are repeated from those in the chapter.

INVENTORY PURCHASES AND SALES

The first transaction on April 25 involves the purchase of $2,700 of inventory on account. Under the periodic system, instead of debiting the Inventory account, we debit a Purchases account. Remember, we're not continually adjusting the Inventory account under the periodic method. We use the Purchases account to temporarily track increases in inventory.

Purchase inventory on account

Perpetual System			Periodic System		
Inventory	2,700		Purchases	2,700	
Accounts Payable		2,700	Accounts Payable		2,700

The transaction on July 17 involves the sale on account of 300 units of inventory for $4,500. We record that transaction as follows.

Perpetual System			Periodic System			
Accounts Receivable	4,500		Accounts Receivable	4,500		Sell inventory on
Sales Revenue		4,500	Sales Revenue		4,500	account
Cost of Goods Sold	2,500					
Inventory		2,500	No entry for cost of goods sold			

Notice that under the periodic system, we record the revenue earned, but we don't record the reduction in inventory or the increase in cost of goods sold at the time of the sale. Instead, we will record these at the end of the period.

The final two transactions are (1) the purchase of 600 additional units of inventory for $6,600 on account on October 19 and (2) the sale of 500 units for $7,500 on account on December 15.

Perpetual System			Periodic System			
Inventory	6,600		Purchases	6,600		Purchase inventory on
Accounts Payable		6,600	Accounts Payable		6,600	account

Perpetual System			Periodic System			
Accounts Receivable	7,500		Accounts Receivable	7,500		Sell inventory on
Sales Revenue		7,500	Sales Revenue		7,500	account
Cost of Goods Sold	5,300					
Inventory		5,300	No entry for cost of goods sold			

In addition to purchases and sales of inventory, we also looked at additional inventory transactions for Mario's Game Shop that related to freight charges, purchase discounts, and purchase returns:

1. On April 25, Mario pays freight charges of $300 for inventory purchased on April 25.
2. On April 30, Mario pays for the units purchased on April 25, less a 2% purchase discount.
3. On October 22, Mario returns 50 defective units from the October 19 purchase.

Next, let's compare the perpetual system and periodic system for these transactions.

FREIGHT CHARGES

Under the perpetual system discussed in the chapter, we saw that freight charges are included as an additional cost of inventory. Here we'll see that under the periodic system, we record these charges in a separate account called Freight-in. That account will later be closed in a period-end adjustment. For freight charges of $300 associated with the April 25 purchase, we record the following transaction.

Perpetual System			Periodic System			
Inventory	300		Freight-in	300		Pay freight-in charges
Cash		300	Cash		300	

PURCHASE DISCOUNTS AND RETURNS

Under the perpetual system, purchase discounts and purchase returns are recorded as a reduction in inventory cost. Under the periodic system, these transactions are recorded in separate accounts—Purchase Discounts and Purchase Returns. In the

perpetual system, we credit purchase returns and purchase discounts to Inventory. The Purchase Returns and Purchase Discounts accounts used in the periodic system are referred to as *contra purchases accounts*.

For our examples in the chapter, Mario (1) makes payment on April 30 for inventory purchased on April 25 for $2,700, receiving a $54 discount and (2) returns 50 defective units on October 22 from the 600 units purchased on account on October 19 for $11 each.

Pay on account with a 2% purchase discount of $54

Perpetual System			Periodic System		
Accounts Payable	2,700		Accounts Payable	2,700	
Inventory		54	Purchase Discounts		54
Cash		2,646	Cash		2,646

Return inventory previously purchased on account

Perpetual System		Periodic System	
Accounts Payable	550	Accounts Payable	550
Inventory	550	Purchase Returns	550

PERIOD-END ADJUSTMENT

A period-end adjustment is needed only under the periodic system. The adjustment serves the following purposes:

1. Adjusts the balance of inventory to its proper ending balance.
2. Records the cost of goods sold for the period, to match inventory costs with the related sales revenue.
3. Closes (or zeros out) the temporary purchases accounts (Purchases, Freight-in, Purchase Discounts, and Purchase Returns).

Let's see what the period-end adjustment would look like for Mario's Game Shop using the transactions described in this appendix. In addition, recall that beginning inventory equals $700 (= 100 units × $7 unit cost) and ending inventory equals $1,650 (= 150 units × $11 unit cost).

Adjust inventory and cost of goods sold at the end of the period

Perpetual System	Periodic System		
No entry	Inventory (ending)	1,650	
	Cost of Goods Sold	8,046	
	Purchase Discounts	54	
	Purchase Returns	550	
	Purchases		9,300
	Freight-In		300
	Inventory (beginning)		700

Temporary accounts closed

Notice that (1) the balance of Inventory is updated for its ending amount of $1,650, while its beginning balance of $700 is eliminated, (2) Cost of Goods Sold is recorded for $8,046, and (3) temporary accounts related to purchases are closed to zero.

If you look carefully, you may notice that the amount of cost of goods sold above calculated under the periodic system is the same as that calculated under the perpetual system (in Illustration 6–17). To see a detailed example of this, let's reexamine the first section of the multiple-step income statement, shown again in Illustration 6–24.

The periodic system and perpetual system will always produce the same amounts for cost of goods sold and inventory when the FIFO inventory method is used.

MARIO'S GAME SHOP
Multiple-Step Income Statement (partial)
For the year ended December 31, 2012

Sales revenue		$12,000
Cost of goods sold:		
Beginning inventory	$ 700	
Add: Purchases	9,300	
Freight-in	300	
Less: Purchase discounts	(54)	
Purchase returns	(550)	
Cost of goods available for sale	9,696	
Less: Ending inventory	(1,650)	
Cost of goods sold		8,046
Gross profit		**$ 3,954**

ILLUSTRATION 6–24

Calculation of Gross Profit in a Multiple-Step Income Statement

However, when using LIFO, the amounts for cost of goods sold and ending inventory may differ between the two systems. The reason for this difference is discussed further in more advanced accounting courses; it occurs because determining which "last" units of inventory are sold first occurs multiple times using a perpetual system but just once using a periodic system.

In practice, very few companies report inventory and cost of goods sold using the LIFO perpetual system. Instead, as discussed in Part B of the chapter, nearly all companies that report using LIFO maintain their own records on a FIFO basis and then adjust for the LIFO difference for preparing financial statements. **The inventory recording and reporting procedures discussed in Part B of the chapter reflect those used in actual practice.**

 KEY POINT

Using the periodic inventory system, we record purchases of inventory, freight-in, purchase returns, and purchase discounts to *temporary accounts* rather than directly to Inventory. These temporary accounts are closed in a period-end adjustment. In addition, at the time inventory is sold, we do not record a decrease in inventory sold; instead, we update the balance of Inventory in the period-end adjustment.

INVENTORY ERRORS

Nobody's perfect, and even accountants make mistakes. When we discover accounting errors, we always correct them. However, we don't always know when we've made an error. Errors can unknowingly occur in inventory amounts if there are mistakes in a physical count of inventory or in the pricing of inventory quantities.

EFFECTS IN THE CURRENT YEAR

To understand the effects of an inventory error in the financial statements, let's think again about the formula for cost of goods sold, shown in Illustration 6–25.

APPENDIX B

■ **LO10**
Determine the financial statement effects of inventory errors.

	Beginning Inventory
+	Purchases
−	Ending Inventory → Asset; Balance sheet
	Cost of Goods Sold → Expense; Income statement

ILLUSTRATION 6–25

Calculation of Cost of Goods Sold

Notice that an error in calculating ending inventory (an asset in the balance sheet) causes an error in calculating cost of goods sold (an expense in the income statement). If cost of goods sold is misstated, gross profit will be misstated as well, but in the opposite direction. This is true because gross profit equals sales *minus* cost of goods sold. The effect of the inventory error in the current year is summarized in Illustration 6–26.

ILLUSTRATION 6–26

Summary of Effects of Inventory Error in the Current Year

Inventory Error	Ending Inventory	Cost of Goods Sold	Gross Profit
Overstate ending inventory	Overstate	Understate	Overstate
Understate ending inventory	Understate	Overstate	Understate

EFFECTS IN THE FOLLOWING YEAR

To understand the effects of a current-year inventory error on financial statements in the following year, remember that the amount of ending inventory this year is the amount of beginning inventory next year. An error in ending inventory this year will create an error in beginning inventory next year. This is demonstrated in Illustration 6–27.

ILLUSTRATION 6–27

Relationship between Cost of Goods Sold in the Current Year and the Following Year

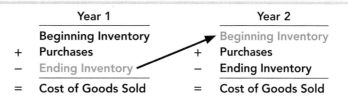

Notice that ending inventory is *subtracted* in calculating cost of goods sold in year 1 (the year of the inventory error). That same amount becomes beginning inventory in the following year and is *added* in calculating cost of goods sold. Because of this, **an error in calculating ending inventory in the current year will automatically affect cost of goods sold in the following year** *in the opposite direction.*

Consider a simple example to see how this works. Illustration 6–28 shows the correct inventory amounts for 2012 and 2013.

ILLUSTRATION 6–28

Correct Inventory Amounts

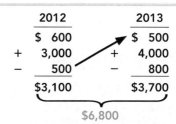

Now, assume the company mistakenly reports ending inventory in 2012 as $400, instead of $500. The effect of the mistake is shown in Illustration 6–29.

ILLUSTRATION 6–29

Incorrect Inventory Amounts

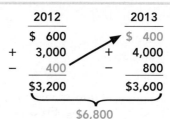

Notice three things: First, the amount reported for inventory is correct by the end of the second year, $800. This is true *even if the company had never discovered its inventory mistake* in 2012.

Second, the total amount reported for cost of goods sold over the two-year period from 2012 to 2013 is the same ($6,800) whether the error occurs or not. That's because the overstatement to cost of goods sold of $100 in 2012 is offset by an understatement of $100 in 2013. This also means that the inventory error affects gross profit in each of the two years, but the combined two-year gross profit amount is unaffected.

Third, if the combined two-year gross profit is correct, then retained earnings will also be correct by the end of 2013. Thus, the inventory error in 2012 has no effect on the accounting equation at the end of 2013. Assets (inventory) and stockholders' equity (retained earnings) are correctly stated.

KEY POINT

In the current year, inventory errors affect the amounts reported for inventory and retained earnings in the balance sheet and amounts reported for cost of goods sold and gross profit in the income statement. At the end of the following year, the error has no effect on ending inventory or retained earnings but reverses for cost of goods sold and gross profit.

KEY POINTS BY LEARNING OBJECTIVE

LO1 Trace the flow of inventory costs from manufacturing companies to merchandising companies.

Service companies earn revenues by providing services to customers. Manufacturing and merchandising companies earn revenues by selling inventory to customers.

LO2 Calculate cost of goods sold.

Inventory is a current asset reported in the balance sheet and represents the cost of inventory *not yet sold* at the end of the period. Cost of goods sold is an expense reported in the income statement and represents the cost of inventory *sold*.

LO3 Determine the cost of goods sold and ending inventory using different inventory cost methods.

Companies are allowed to report inventory costs by *assuming* which units of inventory are sold and not sold, even if this does not match the *actual* flow. The three major inventory cost flow assumptions are FIFO (first-in, first-out), LIFO (last-in, first-out), and weighted-average cost.

LO4 Explain the financial statement effects and tax effects of inventory cost flow assumptions.

Generally, FIFO more closely resembles the actual physical flow of inventory. When inventory costs are rising, FIFO results in higher reported inventory in the balance sheet

and higher reported income in the income statement. Conversely, LIFO results in a lower reported inventory and net income, reducing the company's income tax obligation.

LO5 Record inventory transactions using a perpetual inventory system.

The perpetual inventory system maintains a continual—or *perpetual*—record of inventory purchased and sold. When companies *purchase* inventory using a perpetual inventory system, they increase the Inventory account and either decrease Cash or increase Accounts Payable. When companies *sell* inventory, they make two entries: (1) They increase an asset account (Cash or Accounts Receivable) and increase Sales Revenue, and (2) they increase Cost of Goods Sold and decrease Inventory.

Nearly all companies maintain their own inventory records on a FIFO basis, and then some prepare financial statements on a LIFO basis. To adjust their FIFO inventory records to LIFO for financial reporting, companies use a simple LIFO adjustment at the end of the period.

For most companies, freight charges are added to the cost of inventory, whereas purchase returns and purchase discounts are deducted from the cost of inventory. Some companies choose to report freight charges on outgoing shipments as part of selling expenses instead of cost of goods sold.

LO6 Prepare a multiple-step income statement.

A multiple-step income statement reports multiple levels of profitability. *Gross profit* equals sales revenue minus cost of goods sold. *Operating income* equals gross profit minus operating expenses. *Income before income taxes* equals operating income plus nonoperating revenues and minus nonoperating expenses. *Net income* equals all revenues minus all expenses.

LO7 Apply the lower-of-cost-or-market method for inventories.

We report inventory at the lower-of-cost-or-market; that is, at cost (specific identification, FIFO, LIFO, or weighted-average cost) or market value (replacement cost), whichever is lower. When market value falls below cost, we adjust downward the balance of inventory from cost to market value.

Analysis

LO8 Analyze management of inventory using the inventory turnover ratio and gross profit ratio.

The inventory turnover ratio indicates the number of times the firm sells, or turns over, its average inventory balance during a reporting period. The gross profit ratio measures the amount by which the sale price of inventory exceeds its cost per dollar of sales.

Appendixes

LO9 Record inventory transactions using a periodic inventory system.

Using the periodic inventory system, we record purchases of inventory, freight-in, purchase returns, and purchase discounts to *temporary accounts* rather than directly to Inventory. These temporary accounts are closed in a period-end adjustment. In addition, at the time inventory is sold, we do not record a decrease in inventory sold; instead, we update the balance of Inventory in the period-end adjustment.

LO10 Determine the financial statement effects of inventory errors.

In the current year, inventory errors affect the amounts reported for inventory and retained earnings in the balance sheet and amounts reported for cost of goods sold and gross profit in the income statement. At the end of the following year, the error has no effect on ending inventory or retained earnings but reverses for cost of goods sold and gross profit.

GLOSSARY

Average days in inventory: Approximate number of days the average inventory is held. It equals 365 days divided by the inventory turnover ratio. **p. 288**

Cost of goods sold: Cost of the inventory that was sold during the period. **p. 262**

Finished goods: Inventory items for which the manufacturing process is complete. **p. 263**

First-in, first-out method (FIFO): Inventory costing method that assumes the first units purchased (the first in) are the first ones sold (the first out). **p. 266**

Freight-in: Cost to transport inventory to the company, which is included as part of inventory cost. **p. 278**

Freight-out: Cost of freight on shipments to customers, which is included in the income statement either as part of cost of goods sold or as a selling expense. **p. 278**

Gross profit: The difference between sales revenue and cost of goods sold. **p. 282**

Gross profit ratio: Measure of the amount by which the sale price of inventory exceeds its cost per dollar of sales. It equals gross profit divided by net sales. **p. 289**

Income before income taxes: Operating income plus nonoperating revenues less nonoperating expenses. **p. 283**

Inventory: Items a company intends for sale to customers. **p. 262**

Inventory turnover ratio: The number of times a firm sells its average inventory balance during a reporting period. It equals cost of goods sold divided by average inventory. **p. 287**

Last-in, first-out method (LIFO): Inventory costing method that assumes the last units purchased (the last in) are the first ones sold (the first out). **p. 267**

LIFO adjustment: An adjustment used to convert a company's own inventory records maintained on a FIFO basis to LIFO basis for preparing financial statements. **p. 277**

LIFO conformity rule: IRS rule requiring a company that uses LIFO for tax reporting to also use LIFO for financial reporting. **p. 272**

Lower-of-cost-or-market (LCM) method: Method where companies report inventory in the balance sheet at the lower of cost or market value, where market value equals replacement cost. **p. 284**

Multiple-step income statement: An income statement that reports *multiple* levels of income (or profitability). **p. 282**

Net income: Difference between all revenues and all expenses for the period. **p. 283**

Operating income: Profitability from normal operations that equals gross profit less operating expenses. **p. 283**

Periodic inventory system: Inventory system that periodically adjusts for purchases and sales of inventory at the end of the reporting period based on a physical count of inventory on hand. **p. 274**

Perpetual inventory system: Inventory system that maintains a continual record of inventory purchased and sold. **p. 274**

Raw materials: Components that will become part of the finished product but have not yet been used in production. **p. 263**

Replacement cost: The cost to replace an inventory item in its identical form. **p. 284**

Specific identification method: Inventory costing method that matches or identifies each unit of inventory with its actual cost. **p. 266**

Weighted-average cost method: Inventory costing method that assumes both cost of goods sold and ending inventory consist of a random mixture of all the goods available for sale. **p. 268**

Work-in-process: Products that have started the production process but are not yet complete at the end of the period. **p. 263**

SELF-STUDY QUESTIONS

1. Which of following companies earn revenues by selling inventory?　　■ LO1
   a. Service companies.
   b. Manufacturing companies.
   c. Merchandising companies.
   d. Both manufacturing and merchandising companies.

2. At the beginning of the year, Bennett Supply has inventory of $3,500. During the year, the company purchases an additional $12,000 of inventory. An inventory count at the end of the year reveals remaining inventory of $4,000. What amount will Bennett report for cost of goods sold?　　■ LO2
   a. $11,000.
   b. $11,500.
   c. $12,000.
   d. $12,500.

3. Madison Outlet has the following inventory transactions for the year:　　■ LO3

Date	Transaction	Number of Units	Unit Cost	Total Cost
Jan. 1	Beginning inventory	10	$200	$2,000
Mar. 14	Purchase	15	300	4,500
				$6,500
Jan. 1–Dec. 31	Total sales to customers	12		

What amount would Madison report for *cost of goods sold* using FIFO?
   a. $2,600.
   b. $2,900.
   c. $3,600.
   d. $3,900.

4. Which inventory cost flow assumption generally results in the lowest reported amount for cost of goods sold when inventory costs are rising?　　■ LO4
   a. Lower-of-cost-or-market.
   b. First-in, first-out (FIFO).
   c. Last-in, first-out (LIFO).
   d. Weighted-average cost.

5. Using a *perpetual* inventory system, the purchase of inventory on account would be recorded as:　　■ LO5
   a. Debit Cost of Goods Sold; credit Inventory.
   b. Debit Inventory; credit Sales Revenue.

      c. Debit Purchases; credit Accounts Payable.

      d. Debit Inventory; credit Accounts Payable.

■ LO6

6. Which of the following levels of profitability in a multiple-step income statement represents revenues from the sale of inventory less the cost of that inventory?

      a. Gross profit.

      b. Operating income.

      c. Income before income taxes.

      d. Net income.

■ LO7

7. At the end of a reporting period, Maxwell Corporation determines that its ending inventory has a cost of $1,000 and a market value of $800. What would be the effect(s) of the adjustment to write down inventory to market value?

      a. Decrease total assets.

      b. Decrease net income.

      c. Decrease retained earnings.

      d. All of the above.

■ LO8

8. For the year, Simmons Incorporated reports net sales of $100,000, cost of goods sold of $80,000, and an average inventory balance of $40,000. What is Simmons' gross profit ratio?

      a. 20%.

      b. 25%.

      c. 40%.

      d. 50%.

■ LO9

9. Using a *periodic* inventory system, the purchase of inventory on account would be recorded as:

      a. Debit Cost of Goods Sold; credit Inventory.

      b. Debit Inventory; credit Sales Revenue.

      c. Debit Purchases; credit Accounts Payable.

      d. Debit Inventory; credit Accounts Payable.

■ LO10

10. Suppose Ajax Corporation overstates its ending inventory amount. What effect will this have on the reported amount of cost of goods sold in the year of the error?

      a. Overstate cost of goods sold.

      b. Understate cost of goods sold.

      c. Have no effect on cost of goods sold.

      d. Not possible to determine with information given.

Check out
www.mhhe.com/succeed
for more multiple-choice
questions.

Note: For answers, see the last page of the chapter.

REVIEW QUESTIONS

■ LO1

1. What is inventory? Where in the financial statements is inventory reported?

■ LO1

2. What is the primary distinction between a service company and a manufacturing or merchandising company?

■ LO1

3. What is the difference among raw materials inventory, work-in-process inventory, and finished goods inventory?

■ LO2

4. Define the cost of goods available for sale. How does it relate to cost of goods sold and ending inventory?

■ LO2

5. For a company like **Radio Shack**, what does the balance of Cost of Goods Sold in the income statement represent? What does the balance of Inventory in the balance sheet represent?

6. Cheryl believes that companies report cost of goods sold and ending inventory based on *actual* units sold and not sold. Her accounting instructor explains that most companies account for cost of goods sold and ending inventory based on *assumed* units sold and not sold. Help her understand why companies are allowed to do this.   ■ LO3

7. What are the three primary cost flow assumptions? How does the specific identification method differ from these three primary cost flow assumptions?   ■ LO3

8. Which cost flow assumption generally results in the highest reported amount for ending inventory when inventory costs are rising? Explain.   ■ LO4

9. Which cost flow assumption generally results in the highest reported amount of net income when inventory costs are rising? Explain.   ■ LO4

10. What does it mean that FIFO has a balance-sheet focus and LIFO has an income-statement focus?   ■ LO4

11. Explain how LIFO generally results in lower income taxes payable when inventory costs are increasing. What is the LIFO conformity rule?   ■ LO4

12. What is the difference between the *timing* of recording inventory transactions under the perpetual and periodic inventory systems?   ■ LO5

13. Explain how freight charges, purchase returns, and purchase discounts affect the cost of inventory.   ■ LO5

14. What is a multiple-step income statement? What information does it provide beyond "bottom-line" net income?   ■ LO6

15. Explain the lower-of-cost-or-market method of reporting inventory.   ■ LO7

16. How is cost determined under the lower-of-cost-or-market method? How is market value determined for this purpose?   ■ LO7

17. Describe the entry to adjust from cost to market for inventory write-downs. What effects does this adjustment have on (a) assets, (b) liabilities, (c) stockholders' equity (or retained earnings), (d) revenues, (e) expenses, and (f) net income?   ■ LO7

18. What is meant by the assertion that the lower-of-cost-or-market method is an example of conservatism in accounting?   ■ LO7

19. What is the inventory turnover ratio? What is it designed to measure?   ■ LO8

20. How is gross profit calculated? What is the gross profit ratio? What is it designed to measure?   ■ LO8

21. Explain how the sale of inventory on account is recorded under a periodic system. How does this differ from the recording under a perpetual system?   ■ LO9

22. What are the purposes of the period-end adjustment under the periodic inventory system?   ■ LO9

23. Jeff is the new inventory manager for Alan Company. During the year-end inventory count, Jeff forgets that the company stores additional inventory in a back room, causing his final ending inventory count to be understated. Explain what effect this error will have on the reported amounts for (a) assets, (b) liabilities, (c) stockholders' equity (or retained earnings), (d) revenues, (e) expenses, and (f) net income in the current year.   ■ LO10

24. Refer to the inventory error in *Question* 23. Explain what effect Jeff's error will have on reported amounts at the end of the following year, assuming the mistake is not corrected and no further mistakes are made.   ■ LO10

BRIEF EXERCISES

Understand terms related to types of companies (LO1)

BE6–1 Match each of the following types of companies with its definition.

Types of Companies	Definitions
1. _____ Service company	a. Purchases goods that are primarily in finished form for resale to customers.
2. _____ Merchandising company	b. Earns revenues by providing services to customers.
3. _____ Manufacturing company	c. Produces the goods they sell to customers.

Understand terms related to inventory (LO1)

BE6–2 Match each of the following inventory classifications with its definition.

Inventory Classifications	Definitions
1. _____ Raw materials	a. Cost of items not yet complete by the end of the period.
2. _____ Work-in-process	b. Inventory that has been substantially completed.
3. _____ Finished goods	c. Basic components used to build a product.

Calculate cost of goods sold (LO2)

BE6–3 At the beginning of 2012, Bryers Incorporated reports inventory of $7,000. During 2012, the company purchases additional inventory for $22,000. At the end of 2012, the cost of inventory remaining is $9,000. Calculate cost of goods sold for 2012.

Calculate ending inventory and cost of goods sold using FIFO (LO3)

BE6–4 During 2012, Wright Company sells 320 remote control airplanes for $100 each. The company has the following inventory purchase transactions for 2012.

Date	Transaction	Number of Units	Unit Cost	Total Cost
Jan. 1	Beginning inventory	50	$72	$ 3,600
May. 5	Purchase	200	75	15,000
Nov. 3	Purchase	100	80	8,000
		350		$26,600

Calculate ending inventory and cost of goods sold for 2012 assuming the company uses FIFO.

Calculate ending inventory and cost of goods sold using LIFO (LO3)

BE6–5 Refer to the information in BE6–4. Calculate ending inventory and cost of goods sold for 2012, assuming the company uses LIFO.

Calculate ending inventory and cost of goods sold using weighted-average cost (LO3)

BE6–6 Refer to the information in BE6–4. Calculate ending inventory and cost of goods sold for 2012, assuming the company uses weighted-average cost.

Calculate ending inventory and cost of goods sold using specific identification (LO3)

BE6–7 Refer to the information in BE6–4. Calculate ending inventory and cost of goods sold for 2012, assuming the company uses specific identification. Actual sales by the company include its entire beginning inventory, 180 units of inventory from the May 5 purchase, and 90 units from the November 3 purchase.

Identify financial statement effects of FIFO and LIFO (LO4)

BE6–8 For each item below, indicate whether FIFO or LIFO will generally result in a higher reported amount when inventory costs are rising versus falling. The first answer is provided as an example.

Inventory Costs	Higher Total Assets	Higher Cost of Goods Sold	Higher Net Income
Rising	FIFO		
Declining			

BE6–9 Shankar Company uses a perpetual system to record inventory transactions. The company purchases inventory on account on February 2, 2012, for $30,000 and then sells this inventory on account on March 17, 2012, for $50,000. Record transactions for the purchase and sale of inventory.

Record inventory purchases and sales using a perpetual system (LO5)

BE6–10 Shankar Company uses a perpetual system to record inventory transactions. The company purchases inventory on account on February 2, 2012, for $30,000. In addition to the cost of inventory, the company also pays $500 for freight charges associated with the purchase on the same day. Record the purchase of inventory on February 2, including the freight charges.

Record freight charges for inventory using a perpetual system (LO5)

BE6–11 Shankar Company uses a perpetual system to record inventory transactions. The company purchases 1,000 units of inventory on account on February 2, 2012, for $30,000 ($30 per unit) but then returns 50 defective units on February 5, 2012. Record the inventory purchase on February 2 and the inventory return on February 5.

Record purchase returns of inventory using a perpetual system (LO5)

BE6–12 Shankar Company uses a perpetual system to record inventory transactions. The company purchases inventory on account on February 2, 2012, for $30,000, with terms 2/10, n/30. On February 10, the company pays on account for the inventory. Record the inventory purchase on February 2 and the payment on February 10.

Record purchase discounts of inventory using a perpetual system (LO5)

BE6–13 For each company, calculate the missing amount.

Calculate amounts related to the multiple-step income statement (LO6)

Company	Sales Revenue	Cost of Goods Sold	Gross Profit	Operating Expenses	Net Income
Lennon	$16,000	(a)	$7,000	$3,000	$4,000
Harrison	17,000	$10,000	(b)	5,000	2,000
McCartney	11,000	8,000	3,000	(c)	1,000
Starr	14,000	5,000	9,000	6,000	(d)

BE6–14 Powder Ski Shop reports inventory using lower-of-cost-or-market. Below is information related to its year-end inventory. Calculate the amount to be reported for ending inventory.

Calculate ending inventory using lower-of-cost-or-market (LO7)

Inventory	Quantity	Cost	Market
Ski jackets	15	$120	$100
Skis	20	350	400

BE6–15 Creative Technology reports inventory using lower-of-cost-or-market. Below is information related to its year-end inventory. Calculate the amount to be reported for ending inventory.

Calculate ending inventory using lower-of-cost-or-market (LO7)

Inventory	Quantity	Cost	Market
Optima cameras	100	$50	$80
Inspire speakers	40	60	50

BE6–16 Using the amounts below, calculate the inventory turnover ratio, average days in inventory, and gross profit ratio.

Calculate inventory ratios (LO8)

Net sales	$200,000
Cost of goods sold	140,000
Beginning inventory	45,000
Ending inventory	35,000

BE6–17 Refer to the information in BE6–9, but now assume that Shankar uses a periodic system to record inventory transactions. Record transactions for the purchase and sale of inventory.

Record inventory purchases and sales using a periodic system (LO9)

Record freight charges for inventory using a periodic system (LO9)

BE6–18 Refer to the information in BE6–10, but now assume that Shankar uses a periodic system to record inventory transactions. Record the purchase of inventory on February 2, including the freight charges.

Record purchase returns of inventory using a periodic system (LO9)

BE6–19 Refer to the information in BE6–11, but now assume that Shankar uses a periodic system to record inventory transactions. Record the inventory purchase on February 2 and the inventory return on February 5.

Record purchase discounts of inventory using a periodic system (LO9)

BE6–20 Refer to the information in BE6–12, but now assume that Shankar uses a periodic system to record inventory transactions. Record the inventory purchase on February 2 and the payment on February 10.

Find income statement effects of overstatement in ending inventory (LO10)

BE6–21 Ebbers Corporation overstated its ending inventory balance by $10,000 in 2012. What impact will this error have on cost of goods sold and gross profit in 2012 and 2013?

Find balance sheet effects of overstatement in ending inventory (LO10)

BE6–22 Refer to the information in BE6–21. What impact will this error have on ending inventory and retained earnings in 2012 and 2013? Ignore any tax effects.

EXERCISES

🅜 **connect**™
|ACCOUNTING

Calculate cost of goods sold (LO2)

E6–1 Russell Retail Group begins the year with inventory of $45,000 and ends the year with inventory of $35,000. During the year, the company has four purchases for the following amounts.

Purchase on February 17	$200,000
Purchase on May 6	120,000
Purchase on September 8	150,000
Purchase on December 4	400,000

Required:
Calculate cost of goods sold for the year.

Calculate inventory amounts when costs are rising (LO3)

E6–2 During 2012, TRC Corporation has the following inventory transactions.

Date	Transaction	Number of Units	Unit Cost	Total Cost
Jan. 1	Beginning inventory	40	$32	$ 1,280
Apr. 7	Purchase	120	34	4,080
Jul. 16	Purchase	190	37	7,030
Oct. 6	Purchase	100	38	3,800
		450		$16,190

For the entire year, the company sells 400 units of inventory for $50 each.

Required:
1. Using **FIFO**, calculate (a) ending inventory, (b) cost of goods sold, (c) sales revenue, and (d) gross profit.
2. Using **LIFO**, calculate (a) ending inventory, (b) cost of goods sold, (c) sales revenue, and (d) gross profit.
3. Using weighted-average cost, calculate (a) ending inventory, (b) cost of goods sold, (c) sales revenue, and (d) gross profit.
4. Determine which method will result in higher profitability when inventory costs are rising.

E6–3 During 2012, Trombley Incorporated has the following inventory transactions.

Calculate inventory amounts when costs are declining (LO3)

Date	Transaction	Number of Units	Unit Cost	Total Cost
Jan. 1	Beginning inventory	10	$12	$120
Mar. 4	Purchase	15	11	165
Jun. 9	Purchase	20	10	200
Nov. 11	Purchase	20	8	160
		65		$645

For the entire year, the company sells 50 units of inventory for $20 each.

Required:
1. Using FIFO, calculate (a) ending inventory, (b) cost of goods sold, (c) sales revenue, and (d) gross profit.
2. Using LIFO, calculate (a) ending inventory, (b) cost of goods sold, (c) sales revenue, and (d) gross profit.
3. Using weighted-average cost, calculate (a) ending inventory, (b) cost of goods sold, (c) sales revenue, and (d) gross profit.
4. Determine which method will result in higher profitability when inventory costs are declining.

E6–4 Bingerton Industries uses a perpetual inventory system. The company began the year with inventory of $75,000. Purchases of inventory on account during the year totaled $300,000. Inventory costing $325,000 was sold on account for $500,000.

Record inventory transactions using a perpetual system (LO5)

Required:
Record transactions for the purchase and sale of inventory.

E6–5 On June 5, Staley Electronics purchases 100 units of inventory on account for $10 each. After closer examination, Staley determines 20 units are defective and returns them to its supplier for full credit on June 9. All remaining inventory is sold on account on June 16 for $15 each.

Record inventory purchase and purchase return using a perpetual system (LO5)

Required:
Record transactions for the purchase, return, and sale of inventory.

E6–6 On June 5, Staley Electronics purchases 100 units of inventory on account for $10 each, with terms 2/10, n/30. Staley pays for the inventory on June 12.

Record inventory purchase and purchase discount using a perpetual system (LO5)

Required:
1. Record transactions for the purchase of inventory and payment on account.
2. Now assume payment is made on June 22. Record the payment on account.

E6–7 Littleton Books has the following transactions during May.

Record transactions using a perpetual system (LO5)

May 2   Purchases books on account from Readers Wholesale for $2,300, terms 2/10, n/30.
May 3   Pays freight costs of $100 on books purchased from Readers.
May 5   Returns books with a cost of $300 to Readers because part of the order is incorrect.
May 10 Pays the full amount due to Readers.
May 30 Sells all books purchased on May 2 (less those returned on May 5) for $3,000 on account.

Required:
1. Record the transactions of Littleton Books, assuming the company uses a perpetual inventory system.
2. Assume that payment to Readers is made on May 24 instead of May 10. Record this payment.

Record transactions using a perpetual system (LO5)

E6–8 Sundance Systems has the following transactions during July.

July 5   Purchases 20 laptop computers on account from Red River Supplies for $1,500 each, terms 3/10, n/30.

July 8   Returns to Red River two laptops that had defective hard drives.

July 13   Pays the full amount due to Red River.

July 28   Sells remaining 18 laptops purchased on July 5 for $2,000 each on account.

Required:

Record the transactions of Sundance Systems, assuming the company uses a perpetual inventory system.

Record transactions using a perpetual system (LO5)

Flip Side of E6–10

E6–9 DS Unlimited has the following transactions during August.

August 6   Purchases 50 handheld game devices on account from GameGirl, Inc., for $100 each, terms 1/10, n/60.

August 7   Pays $300 to Sure Shipping for freight charges associated with the August 6 purchase.

August 10   Returns to GameGirl five game devices that were defective.

August 14   Pays the full amount due to GameGirl.

August 23   Sells 30 game devices purchased on August 6 for $120 each to customers on account. The total cost of the 30 game devices sold is $3,170.

Required:

Record the transactions of DS Unlimited, assuming the company uses a perpetual inventory system.

Record transactions using a perpetual system (LO5)

Flip Side of E6–9

E6–10 Refer to the transactions in E6–9.

Required:

Prepare the transactions for GameGirl, Inc., assuming the company uses a perpetual inventory system. Assume the 50 game devices sold on August 6 to DS Unlimited had a cost to GameGirl of $80 each. The items returned on August 10 were considered worthless to GameGirl and were discarded.

Prepare a multiple-step income statement (LO6)

E6–11 Wayman Corporation reports the following amounts in its December 31, 2012, income statement.

Sales revenue	$320,000	Income tax expense	$ 40,000
Interest expense	10,000	Cost of goods sold	120,000
Salaries expense	30,000	Advertising expense	20,000
Utilities expense	40,000		

Required:

Prepare a multiple-step income statement.

Prepare a multiple-step income statement and analyze profitability (LO6)

E6–12 Tisdale Incorporated reports the following amount in its December 31, 2012, income statement.

Sales revenue	$250,000	Income tax expense	$ 20,000
Gain on land sale*	100,000	Cost of goods sold	180,000
Selling expenses	50,000	Administrative expenses	30,000
General expenses	40,000		

*On July 12, 2012, the company sold land for $400,000 that it had previously purchased for $300,000, resulting in a $100,000 gain. This is the only land owned by the company.

Required:

1. Prepare a multiple-step income statement.
2. Explain how analyzing the multiple levels of profitability can help in understanding the future profit-generating potential of Tisdale Incorporated.

E6–13 Home Furnishings reports inventory using the lower-of-cost-or-market method. Below is information related to its year-end inventory.

Inventory	Quantity	Cost	Market
Furniture	100	$ 75	$ 90
Electronics	40	300	250

Calculate inventory using lower-of-cost-or-market **(LO7)**

Required:
1. Calculate ending inventory under lower-of-cost-or-market.
2. Record any necessary adjustment to inventory.
3. Explain the impact of the adjustment in the financial statements.

E6–14 A company like **Golf USA** that sells golf-related inventory typically will have inventory items such as golf clothing and golf equipment. As technology advances the design and performance of the next generation of drivers, the older models become less marketable and therefore decline in value. Suppose that in 2012, **Ping** (a manufacturer of golf clubs) introduces the MegaDriver II, the new and improved version of the MegaDriver. Below are amounts related to Golf USA's inventory at the end of 2012.

Calculate inventory using lower-of-cost-or market **(LO7)**

Inventory	Quantity	Cost	Market
Shirts	25	$ 50	$ 60
MegaDriver	5	260	200
MegaDriver II	20	300	320

Required:
1. Calculate ending inventory under lower-of-cost-or-market.
2. Record any necessary adjustment to inventory.
3. Explain the impact of the adjustment in the financial statements.

E6–15 Lewis Incorporated and Clark Enterprises report the following amounts for 2012.

Calculate cost of goods sold, the inventory turnover ratio, and average days in inventory **(LO2, 8)**

	Lewis	Clark
Inventory (beginning)	$ 14,000	$ 40,000
Inventory (ending)	8,000	50,000
Purchases	120,000	150,000
Purchase returns	5,000	50,000

Required:
1. Calculate cost of goods sold for each company.
2. Calculate the inventory turnover ratio for each company.
3. Calculate the average days in inventory for each company.
4. Explain which company appears to be managing its inventory more efficiently.

E6–16 Below are amounts found in the income statements of three companies.

Calculate levels of profitability for a multiple-step income statement and the gross profit ratio **(LO6, 8)**

Company	Sales Revenue	Cost of Goods Sold	Operating Expenses	Nonoperating Expenses	Income Tax Expense
Henry	$12,000	$ 3,000	$4,000	$1,000	$1,000
Grace	15,000	10,000	6,000	3,000	0
James	20,000	12,000	2,000	0	2,000

Required:
1. For each company, calculate (a) gross profit, (b) operating income, (c) income before income taxes, and (d) net income.
2. For each company, calculate the gross profit ratio and indicate which company has the most favorable ratio.

Record transactions using a periodic system (LO9)

E6–17 Refer to the transactions in E6–7.

Required:

1. Record the transactions of Littleton Books, assuming the company uses a periodic inventory system.
2. Record the period-end adjustment to cost of goods sold on May 31, assuming the company has no beginning or ending inventory.

Record transactions using a periodic system (LO9)

E6–18 Refer to the transactions in E6–8.

Required:

1. Record the transactions of Sundance Systems, assuming the company uses a periodic inventory system.
2. Record the period-end adjustment to cost of goods sold on July 31, assuming the company has no beginning inventory.

Record transactions using a periodic system (LO9)

E6–19 Refer to the transactions in E6–9.

Required:

1. Record the transactions of DS Unlimited, assuming the company uses a periodic inventory system.
2. Record the period-end adjustment to cost of goods sold on August 31, assuming the company has no beginning inventory and ending inventory has a cost of $1,585.

Find financial statement effects of understatement in ending inventory (LO10)

E6–20 Mulligan Corporation purchases inventory on account with terms FOB shipping point. The goods are shipped on December 30, 2012, but do not reach the company until January 5, 2013. Mulligan correctly records accounts payable associated with the purchase but does not include this inventory in its 2012 ending inventory count.

Required:

1. If an error has been made, explain why.
2. If an error has been made, indicate whether there is an understatement (U), overstatement (O), or no effect (N) on the reported amount of each financial statement element in the current year and following year. Ignore any tax effects.

	Balance Sheet			Income Statement		
Year	Assets	Liabilities	Stockholders' Equity	Revenues	Cost of Goods Sold	Gross Profit
Current						
Following						

For additional exercises, visit www.mhhe.com/succeed for Exercises: Set B.

PROBLEMS: SET A

Mc Graw Hill **connect**
|ACCOUNTING

Calculate ending inventory and cost of goods sold for four inventory methods (LO3)

P6–1A Sandra's Purse Boutique has the following transactions related to its top-selling Gucci purse for the month of October 2012.

Date	Transactions	Units	Cost per Unit	Total Cost
October 1	Beginning inventory	6	$800	$ 4,800
October 4	Sale	4		
October 10	Purchase	5 11+4=15	810	4,050
October 13	Sale	3		
October 20	Purchase	4 1	820	3,280
October 28	Sale	7		
October 30	Purchase	6	830	4,980
		7		$17,110

Required:

1. Calculate ending inventory and cost of goods sold at October 31, 2012, using the specific identification method. The October 4 sale consists of purses from beginning inventory, the October 13 sale consists of one purse from beginning inventory and two purses from the October 10 purchase, and the October 28 sale consists of three purses from the October 10 purchase and four purses from the October 20 purchase.
2. Using FIFO, calculate ending inventory and cost of goods sold at October 31, 2012.
3. Using LIFO, calculate ending inventory and cost of goods sold at October 31, 2012.
4. Using weighted-average cost, calculate ending inventory and cost of goods sold at October 31, 2012.

P6–2A Greg's Bicycle Shop has the following transactions related to its top-selling **Mongoose** mountain bike for the month of March 2012:

Calculate ending inventory, cost of goods sold, sales revenue, and gross profit for four inventory methods (LO3, 4, 5)

Date	Transactions	Units	Cost per Unit	Total Cost
March 1	Beginning inventory	20	$200	$ 4,000
March 5	Sale ($300 each)	15		
March 9	Purchase	10	220	2,200
March 17	Sale ($350 each)	8		
March 22	Purchase	10	230	2,300
March 27	Sale ($375 each)	12		
March 30	Purchase	8	250	2,000
				$10,500

Required:

1. Calculate ending inventory and cost of goods sold at March 31, 2012, using the specific identification method. The March 5 sale consists of bikes from beginning inventory, the March 17 sale consists of bikes from the March 9 purchase, and the March 27 sale consists of four bikes from beginning inventory and eight bikes from the March 22 purchase.
2. Using FIFO, calculate ending inventory and cost of goods sold at March 31, 2012.
3. Using LIFO, calculate ending inventory and cost of goods sold at March 31, 2012.
4. Using weighted-average cost, calculate ending inventory and cost of goods sold at March 31, 2012.
5. Calculate sales revenue and gross profit under each of the four methods.
6. Comparing FIFO and LIFO, which one provides the more meaningful measure of ending inventory? Explain.
7. If Greg's Bicycle Shop chooses to report inventory using LIFO instead of FIFO, record the LIFO adjustment.

P6–3A At the beginning of July, CD City has a balance in inventory of $2,900. The following transactions occur during the month of July.

Record transactions and prepare a partial income statement using a perpetual inventory system (LO5, 6)

July 3 Purchase CDs on account from Wholesale Music for $1,800, terms 2/10, n/30.
July 4 Pay freight charges related to the July 3 purchase from Wholesale Music, $100.
July 9 Return incorrectly ordered CDs to Wholesale Music and receive credit, $300.
July 11 Pay Wholesale Music in full.
July 12 Sell CDs to customers on account, $4,800, that had a cost of $2,500.
July 15 Receive full payment from customers related to the sale on July 12.
July 18 Purchase CDs on account from Music Supply for $2,600, terms 1/10, n/30.
July 22 Sell CDs to customers for cash, $3,700, that had a cost of $2,000.
July 28 Return CDs to Music Supply and receive credit of $200.
July 30 Pay Music Supply in full.

Required:

1. Assuming that CD City uses a perpetual inventory system, record the transactions.
2. Prepare the top section of the multiple-step income statement through gross profit for the month of July.

Report inventory
using lower-of-cost-or-
market **(LO7)**

P6–4A A local **Chevrolet** dealership carries the following types of vehicles:

Inventory Items	Quantity	Cost per Unit	Market (replacement cost) per Unit	Lower-of-Cost-or-Market
Vans	3	$22,000	$20,000	_____
Trucks	6	17,000	16,000	_____
2-door sedans	2	12,000	14,000	_____
4-door sedans	7	16,000	19,000	_____
Sports cars	3	32,000	35,000	_____
SUVs	5	28,000	23,000	_____

Because of recent increases in gasoline prices, the car dealership has noticed a reduced demand for its SUVs, vans, and trucks.

Required:
1. Compute the total cost of the entire inventory.
2. Determine whether each inventory item would be reported at cost or market. Multiply the quantity of each inventory item by the appropriate cost or market amount and place the total in the "Lower-of-Cost-or-Market" column. Then determine the total for that column.
3. Compare your answers in *Requirement* 1 and *Requirement* 2 and then record any necessary adjustment to write down inventory from cost to market value.
4. Discuss the financial statement effects of using lower-of-cost-or-market to report inventory.

Calculate ending
inventory and cost of
goods sold using FIFO
and LIFO and adjust
inventory using the
lower-of-cost-or-market
method **(LO3, 7)**

P6–5A For 2012, Parker Games has the following inventory transactions related to its traditional board games.

Date	Transaction	Units	Cost	Total Cost
Jan. 1	Beginning inventory	100	$20	$2,000
Mar. 12	Purchase	80	15	1,200
Sep. 17	Purchase	50	8	400
		230		$3,600
Jan. 1–Dec. 31	Sales	160		

Because of the increasing popularity of electronic video games, Parker Games continues to see a decline in the demand for board games. Sales prices have decreased by over 50% during 2012. At the end of the year, Parker estimates the total cost to replace the 70 units of unsold inventory is only $400.

Required:
1. Using FIFO, calculate ending inventory and cost of goods sold.
2. Using LIFO, calculate ending inventory and cost of goods sold.
3. Determine the amount of ending inventory to report using lower-of-cost-or-market. Record any necessary adjustment under (a) FIFO and (b) LIFO.

Record transactions
using a perpetual system,
prepare a partial income
statement, and adjust
for the lower-of-cost-or-
market method
(LO2, 3, 4, 5, 6, 7)

P6–6A At the beginning of October, Bowser Co.'s inventory consists of 60 units with a cost per unit of $40. The following transactions occur during the month of October.

October 4   Purchase 120 units of inventory on account from Waluigi Co. for $50 per unit, terms 2/10, n/30.
October 5   Pay freight charges related to the October 4 purchase, $600.
October 9   Return 20 defective units from the October 4 purchase and receive credit.
October 12   Pay Waluigi Co. in full.
October 15   Sell 150 units of inventory to customers on account, $12,000. [*Hint:* The cost of units sold from the October 4 purchase includes $50 unit cost plus $6 per unit for freight less $1 per unit for the purchase discount, or $55 per unit.]
October 19   Receive full payment from customers related to the sale on October 15.

October 20   Purchase 100 units of inventory from Waluigi Co. for $60 per unit, terms 1/10, n/30.

October 22   Sell 90 units of inventory to customers for cash, $7,200.

Required:

1. Assuming that Bowser Co. uses a FIFO perpetual inventory system to maintain its inventory records, record the transactions.
2. Assuming for preparing financial statements that Bowser Co. reports inventory using LIFO, record the LIFO adjustment.
3. Suppose by the end of October that the remaining inventory is estimated to have a market value per unit of $35, record any necessary adjustment for the lower-of-cost-or-market method after the LIFO adjustment.
4. Prepare the top section of the multiple-step income statement through gross profit for the month of October after the lower-of-cost-or-market adjustment.

P6–7A Baskin-Robbins is one of the world's largest specialty ice cream shops. The company offers dozens of different flavors, from Very Berry Strawberry to lowfat Espresso 'n Cream. Assume that a local Baskin-Robbins in Raleigh, North Carolina, has the following amounts for the month of July 2012.

Prepare a multiple-step income statement and calculate the inventory turnover ratio and gross profit ratio (LO6, 8)

Salaries expense	$12,700	Sales revenue	$64,800
Inventory (July 1, 2012)	1,800	Interest income	2,300
Sales returns	1,200	Cost of goods sold	28,200
Utilities expense	3,100	Rent expense	5,700
Income tax expense	5,000	Interest expense	500
		Inventory (July 31, 2012)	1,200

Required:

1. Prepare a multiple-step income statement for the month ended July 31, 2012.
2. Calculate the inventory turnover ratio for the month of July. Would you expect this ratio to be higher or lower in December 2012? Explain.
3. Calculate the gross profit ratio for the month of July.

P6–8A Wawa Food Markets is a convenience store chain located primarily in the Northeast. The company sells gas, candy bars, drinks, and other grocery-related items. **St. Jude Medical Incorporated** sells medical devices related to cardiovascular needs. Suppose a local Wawa Food Market and St. Jude sales office report the following amounts in the same year (company names are disguised):

Use the inventory turnover ratio and gross profit ratio to analyze companies (LO8)

	Company 1	Company 2
Net sales	$300,000	$300,000
Cost of goods sold	90,000	240,000
Gross profit	$210,000	$ 60,000
Average inventory	$ 30,000	$ 20,000

Required:

1. For Company 1 and Company 2, calculate the inventory turnover ratio.
2. For Company 1 and Company 2, calculate the gross profit ratio.
3. After comparing the inventory turnover ratios and gross profit ratios, which company do you think is Wawa and which is St. Jude? Explain.

P6–9A Refer to the transactions of CD City in P6–3A.

Record transactions and prepare a partial income statement using a periodic inventory system (LO9)

Required:

1. Assuming that CD City uses a periodic inventory system, record the transactions.
2. Record the month-end adjustment to inventory, assuming that a final count reveals ending inventory with a cost of $2,370.
3. Prepare the top section of the multiple-step income statement through gross profit for the month of July.

Correct inventory
understatement and
calculate gross profit
ratio (LO8, 10)

P6–10A Over a four-year period, Jackie Corporation reported the following series of gross profits.

	2009	2010	2011	2012
Net sales	$50,000	$56,000	$64,000	$80,000
Cost of goods sold	25,000	39,000	21,000	41,000
Gross profit	$25,000	$17,000	$43,000	$39,000

In 2012, the company performed a comprehensive review of its inventory accounting procedures. Based on this review, company records reveal that ending inventory was understated by $10,000 in 2010. Inventory in all other years is correct.

Required:

1. Calculate the gross profit ratio for each of the four years based on amounts originally reported.
2. Calculate the gross profit ratio for each of the four years based on corrected amounts. Describe the trend in the gross profit ratios based on the original amounts versus the corrected amounts.
3. Total gross profit over the four-year period based on the amounts originally reported equals $124,000 (= $25,000 + $17,000 + $43,000 + $39,000). Compare this amount to total gross profit over the four-year period based on the corrected amounts.

PROBLEMS: SET B

Calculate ending
inventory and cost of
goods sold for four
inventory methods (LO3)

P6–1B Jimmie's Fishing Hole has the following transactions related to its top-selling **Shimano** fishing reel for the month of June 2012:

Date	Transactions	Units	Cost per Unit	Total Cost
June 1	Beginning inventory	16	$250	$ 4,000
June 7	Sale	11		
June 12	Purchase	10	240	2,400
June 15	Sale	12		
June 24	Purchase	10	230	2,300
June 27	Sale	8		
June 29	Purchase	10	220	2,200
				$10,900

Required:

1. Calculate ending inventory and cost of goods sold at June 30, 2012, using the specific identification method. The June 7 sale consists of fishing reels from beginning inventory, the June 15 sale consists of three fishing reels from beginning inventory and nine fishing reels from the June 12 purchase, and the June 27 sale consists of one fishing reel from beginning inventory and seven fishing reels from the June 24 purchase.
2. Using FIFO, calculate ending inventory and cost of goods sold at June 30, 2012.
3. Using LIFO, calculate ending inventory and cost of goods sold at June 30, 2012.
4. Using weighted-average cost, calculate ending inventory and cost of goods sold at June 30, 2012.

Calculate ending
inventory, cost of
goods sold, sales
revenue, and gross
profit for four inventory
methods (LO3, 4, 5)

P6–2B Pete's Tennis Shop has the following transactions related to its top-selling **Wilson** tennis racket for the month of August 2012:

Date	Transactions	Units	Cost per Unit	Total Cost
August 1	Beginning inventory	8	$150	$1,200
August 4	Sale ($175 each)	5		
August 11	Purchase	10	140	1,400
August 13	Sale ($190 each)	8		
August 20	Purchase	10	130	1,300
August 26	Sale ($200 each)	11		
August 29	Purchase	12	120	1,440
				$5,340

Required:

1. Calculate ending inventory and cost of goods sold at August 31, 2012, using the specific identification method. The August 4 sale consists of rackets from beginning inventory, the August 13 sale consists of rackets from the August 11 purchase, and the August 26 sale consists of one racket from beginning inventory and 10 rackets from the August 20 purchase.
2. Using FIFO, calculate ending inventory and cost of goods sold at August 31, 2012.
3. Using LIFO, calculate ending inventory and cost of goods sold at August 31, 2012.
4. Using weighted-average cost, calculate ending inventory and cost of goods sold at August 31, 2012.
5. Calculate sales revenue and gross profit under each of the four methods.
6. Comparing FIFO and LIFO, which one provides the more meaningful measure of ending inventory? Explain.
7. If Pete's chooses to report inventory using LIFO, record the LIFO adjustment.

P6–3B At the beginning of June, Circuit Country has a balance in inventory of $2,500. The following transactions occur during the month of June.

> Record transactions and prepare a partial income statement using a perpetual inventory system (LO5, 6)

June 2   Purchase radios on account from Radio World for $2,200, terms 2/15, n/45.
June 4   Pay freight charges related to the June 2 purchase from Radio World, $300.
June 8   Return defective radios to Radio World and receive credit, $200.
June 10   Pay Radio World in full.
June 11   Sell radios to customers on account, $4,000, that had a cost of $2,700.
June 18   Receive payment on account from customers, $3,000.
June 20   Purchase radios on account from Sound Unlimited for $3,300, terms 3/10, n/30.
June 23   Sell radios to customers for cash, $4,800, that had a cost of $3,100.
June 26   Return damaged radios to Sound Unlimited and receive credit of $400.
June 28   Pay Sound Unlimited in full.

Required:

1. Assuming that Circuit Country uses a perpetual inventory system, record transactions using the following account titles: Cash, Accounts Receivable, Inventory, Accounts Payable, Sales, and Cost of Goods Sold.
2. Prepare the top section of the multiple-step income statement through gross profit for the month of June.

P6–4B A home improvement store, like **Lowe's**, carries the following items:

> Report inventory using lower-of-cost-or-market (LO7)

Inventory Items	Quantity	Cost per Unit	Market (replacement cost) per Unit	Lower-of-Cost-or-Market
Hammers	100	$ 7.00	$ 7.50	
Saws	50	10.00	9.00	
Screwdrivers	130	2.00	2.60	
Drills	40	25.00	22.00	
1-gallon paint cans	160	5.50	5.00	
Paintbrushes	180	6.00	6.50	

Required:
1. Compute the total cost of inventory.
2. Determine whether each inventory item would be reported at cost or market. Multiply the quantity of each inventory item by the appropriate cost or market amount and place the total in the "Lower-of-Cost-or-Market" column. Then determine the total of that column.
3. Compare your answers in *Requirement* 1 and *Requirement* 2 and then record any necessary adjustment to write down inventory from cost to market value.
4. Discuss the financial statement effects of using lower-of-cost-or-market to report inventory.

P6–5B Trends by Tiffany sells high-end leather purses. During 2012, the company has the following inventory transactions.

Date	Transaction	Units	Cost	Total Cost
Jan. 1	Beginning inventory	10	$400	$ 4,000
Apr. 9	Purchase	20	420	8,400
Oct. 4	Purchase	16	450	7,200
		46		$19,600
Jan. 1–Dec. 31	Sales	42		

Because trends in purses change frequently, Trends by Tiffany estimates that the remaining four purses have a current replacement cost at December 31 of only $250 each.

Required:
1. Using FIFO, calculate ending inventory and cost of goods sold.
2. Using LIFO, calculate ending inventory and cost of goods sold.
3. Determine the amount of ending inventory to report using lower-of-cost-or-market. Record any necessary adjustment under (a) FIFO and (b) LIFO.

P6–6B At the beginning of November, Yoshi Inc.'s inventory consists of 50 units with a cost per unit of $95. The following transactions occur during the month of November.

November 2   Purchase 80 units of inventory on account from Toad Inc. for $100 per unit, terms 2/10, n/30.
November 3   Pay freight charges related to the November 2 purchase, $210.
November 9   Return 10 defective units from the November 2 purchase and receive credit.
November 11   Pay Toad Inc. in full.
November 16   Sell 100 units of inventory to customers on account, $13,000. [*Hint:* The cost of units sold from the November 2 purchase includes $100 unit cost plus $3 per unit for freight less $2 per unit for the purchase discount, or $101 per unit.]
November 20   Receive full payment from customers related to the sale on November 16.
November 21   Purchase 60 units of inventory from Toad Inc. for $105 per unit, terms 1/10, n/30.
November 24   Sell 70 units of inventory to customers for cash, $8,100.

Required:
1. Assuming that Yoshi Inc. uses a FIFO perpetual inventory system to maintain its internal inventory records, record the transactions.
2. Assuming for preparing financial statements that Yoshi Inc. reports inventory using LIFO, record the LIFO adjustment.
3. Suppose by the end of November that the remaining inventory is estimated to have a market value per unit of $80, record any necessary adjustment for the lower-of-cost-or-market method after the LIFO adjustment.
4. Prepare the top section of the multiple-step income statement through gross profit for the month of November after the lower-of-cost-or-market adjustment.

P6–7B Toys "R" Us sells a variety of children's toys, games, books, and accessories. Assume that a local store has the following amounts for the month of March 2012.

Sales revenue	$72,300	Cost of goods sold	$35,300
Purchase discounts	2,200	Inventory (Mar. 31, 2012)	1,100
Advertising expense	5,400	Insurance expense	1,800
Rent expense	3,300	Sales discounts	2,500
Gain on sale of building	6,500	Salaries expense	8,400
Inventory (Mar. 1, 2012)	2,300	Income tax expense	3,200

Prepare a multiple-step income statement and calculate the inventory turnover ratio and gross profit ratio (LO6, 8)

Required:

1. Prepare a multiple-step income statement for the month ended March 31, 2012.
2. Calculate the inventory turnover ratio for the month of March. Would you expect this ratio to be higher or lower in December 2012? Explain.
3. Calculate the gross profit ratio for the month of March.

P6–8B Payless ShoeSource and **Dillard's** both offer men's formal footwear. Payless offers lower- to middle-priced footwear, whereas Dillard's offers more specialized, higher-end footwear. The average price for a pair of shoes in Payless may be about $50, whereas the average price in Dillard's may be about $175. The types of shoes offered by Dillard's are not sold by many other stores. Suppose a Payless store and a Dillard's store report the following amounts for men's shoes in the same year (company names are disguised):

Use the inventory turnover ratio and gross profit ratio to analyze companies (LO8)

	Company 1	Company 2
Net sales	$100,000	$100,000
Cost of goods sold	40,000	75,000
Gross profit	$ 60,000	$ 25,000
Average inventory	$ 25,000	$ 10,000

Required:

1. For Company 1 and Company 2, calculate the inventory turnover ratio.
2. For Company 1 and Company 2, calculate the gross profit ratio.
3. After comparing the inventory turnover ratios and gross profit ratios, which company do you think is Payless and which is Dillard's? Explain.

P6–9B Refer to the transactions of Circuit Country in P6–3B.

Record transactions and prepare a partial income statement using a periodic inventory system (LO9)

Required:

1. Assuming that Circuit Country uses a periodic inventory system, record the transactions.
2. Record the month-end adjustment to inventory, assuming that a final count reveals ending inventory with a cost of $1,860.
3. Prepare the top section of the multiple-step income statement through gross profit for the month of June.

P6–10B Sylvester has a bird shop that sells canaries. Sylvester maintains accurate records on the number of birds purchased from its suppliers and the number sold to customers. The records show the following purchases and sales during 2012.

Determine the effects of inventory errors using FIFO (LO3, 10)

Date	Transactions	Units	Cost per Unit	Total Cost
January 1	Beginning inventory	25	$30	$ 750
April 14	Purchase	70	32	2,240
August 22	Purchase	120	34	4,080
October 29	Purchase	85	36	3,060
		300		$10,130
Jan. 1–Dec. 31	Sales ($50 each)	270		

Sylvester uses a periodic inventory system and believes there are 30 birds remaining in ending inventory. However, Sylvester neglects to make a final inventory count at the end of the year. An employee accidentally left one of the cages open one night and 10 birds flew away, leaving only 20 birds in ending inventory. Sylvester is not aware of the lost canaries.

Required:
1. What amount will Sylvester calculate for ending inventory and cost of goods sold using FIFO, assuming he erroneously believes 30 canaries remain in ending inventory?
2. What amount would Sylvester calculate for ending inventory and cost of goods sold using FIFO if he knew that only 20 canaries remain in ending inventory?
3. What effect will the inventory error have on reported amounts for (a) ending inventory, (b) retained earnings, (c) cost of goods sold, and (d) net income (ignoring tax effects) in 2012?
4. Assuming that ending inventory is correctly counted at the end of 2013, what effect will the inventory error in 2012 have on reported amounts for (a) ending inventory, (b) retained earnings, (c) cost of goods sold, and (d) net income (ignoring tax effects) in 2013?

For additional problems, visit **www.mhhe.com/succeed** *for Problems: Set C.*

ADDITIONAL PERSPECTIVES

Continuing Problem

Great Adventures

(This is a continuation of the Great Adventures problem from earlier chapters.)

AP6–1 Now that operations for outdoor clinics and TEAM events are running smoothly, Suzie thinks of another area for business expansion. She notices that a few clinic participants wear multiuse (MU) watches. Beyond the normal timekeeping features of most watches, MU watches are able to report temperature, altitude, and barometric pressure. MU watches are waterproof, so moisture from kayaking, rain, fishing, or even diving up to 100 feet won't damage them. Suzie decides to have MU watches available for sale at the start of each clinic. The following transactions relate to purchases and sales of watches during the second half of 2013. All watches are sold for $300 each.

Jul. 17   Purchased 50 watches for $7,500 ($150 per watch) on account.
Jul. 31   Sold 40 watches for $12,000 cash.
Aug. 12   Purchased 40 watches for $6,400 ($160 per watch) cash.
Aug. 22   Sold 30 watches for $9,000 on account.
Sep. 19   Paid for watches ordered on July 17.
Sep. 27   Received full payment for watches sold on account on August 22.
Oct. 27   Purchased 80 watches for $13,600 ($170 per watch) cash.
Nov. 20   Sold 90 watches for $27,000 cash.
Dec.   4   Purchased 100 watches for $18,000 ($180 per watch) cash.
Dec.   8   Sold 40 watches for $12,000 on account.

Required:
1. (a) Calculate sales revenue, cost of goods sold, and ending inventory as of December 31, 2013, assuming Suzie uses FIFO to account for inventory.
   (b) Prepare the gross profit section of a partial income statement for transactions related to MU watches.
2. Late in December, the next generation of multiuse (MU II) watches is released. In addition to all of the features of the MU watch, the MU II watches are equipped with a global positioning system (GPS) and have the ability to download and play songs and videos off the Internet. The demand for the original MU watches is

greatly reduced. As of December 31, the estimated market value of MU watches is only $100 per watch.

(a) Record any necessary adjustment on December 31, 2013, related to this information.

(b) For what amount would MU inventory be reported in the December 31, 2013, balance sheet?

(c) Prepare an updated gross profit section of a partial income statement accounting for this additional information. Compare your answer to *Requirement* 1(b).

American Eagle Outfitters, Inc.

Financial Analysis

AP6–2 Financial information for **American Eagle** is presented in Appendix A at the end of the book.

Required:

1. In the summary of significant accounting policies, what is American Eagle's procedure in accounting for inventory?
2. For the most recent year, what is the amount of inventory in the balance sheet? What does this amount represent?
3. American Eagle refers to its cost of goods sold using a different name. What is it?
4. For the most recent year, what is the amount of cost of goods sold in the income statement? What does this amount represent?
5. Calculate American Eagle's inventory turnover ratio and average days in inventory for the most recent year.
6. Calculate American Eagle's gross profit ratio for each of the three years. Do you notice any trend?
7. For the most recent year, calculate American Eagle's ratio of operating expenses to net sales.

The Buckle, Inc.

Financial Analysis

Buckle

AP6–3 Financial information for **The Buckle** is presented in Appendix B at the end of the book.

Required:

1. In the summary of significant accounting policies, what is The Buckle's procedure in accounting for inventory?
2. For the most recent year, what is the amount of inventory in the balance sheet? What does this amount represent?
3. The Buckle refers to its cost of goods sold using a different name. What is it?
4. For the most recent year, what is the amount of cost of goods sold in the income statement? What does this amount represent?
5. Calculate The Buckle's inventory turnover ratio and average days in inventory for the most recent year.
6. Calculate The Buckle's gross profit ratio for each of the three years. Do you notice any trend?
7. For the most recent year, calculate The Buckle's ratio of operating expenses to net sales.

American Eagle, Inc., vs. The Buckle, Inc.

Comparative Analysis

Buckle

AP6–4 Financial information for **American Eagle** is presented in Appendix A at the end of the book, and financial information for **The Buckle** is presented in Appendix B at the end of the book.

Required:

1. Which company carries a greater inventory balance as a percentage of total assets?
2. Analyze each company's inventory using the inventory turnover ratio and average days in inventory.

3. Determine which company's operations are more profitable using the gross profit ratio.
4. Considering the companies' ratio of operating expenses to net sales, does your answer to *Requirement* 3 change? Explain.

Ethics

AP6–5 Horizon Corporation manufactures personal computers. The company began operations in 2003 and reported profits for the years 2003 through 2010. Due primarily to increased competition and price slashing in the industry, 2011's income statement reported a loss of $20 million. Just before the end of the 2012 fiscal year, a memo from the company's chief financial officer to Jim Fielding, the company controller, included the following comments:

> If we don't do something about the large amount of unsold computers already manufactured, our auditors will require us to record a write down. The resulting loss for 2012 will cause a violation of our debt covenants and force the company into bankruptcy. I suggest that you ship half of our inventory to J.B. Sales, Inc., in Oklahoma City. I know the company's president, and he will accept the inventory and acknowledge the shipment as a purchase. We can record the sale in 2012 which will boost our loss to a profit. Then J.B. Sales will simply return the inventory in 2013 after the financial statements have been issued.

Required:
Discuss the ethical dilemma faced by Jim Fielding.

Internet Research

AP6–6 Obtain copies of the annual reports of **The Coca-Cola Company** and **PepsiCo Corporation** for the most recent year. You can find the annual reports at the companies' websites (*www.coca-cola.com* and *www.pepsico.com*) in the investor information section or at the Securities and Exchange Commission's website (*www.sec.gov*) using EDGAR (Electronic Data Gathering, Analysis, and Retrieval). The SEC requires Form 10-K, which includes the annual report, to be filed on EDGAR. Search or scroll within the annual reports to find the financial statements.

Required:
1. For each company, calculate the gross profit ratio, inventory turnover ratio, and average days in inventory.
2. Compare the management of each company's investment in inventory.

Written Communication

AP6–7 You have just been hired as a consultant to Gilbert Industries, a newly formed company. The company president, Mindy Grayson, is seeking your advice as to the appropriate inventory method Gilbert should use to value its inventory and cost of goods sold. Ms. Grayson has narrowed the choice to LIFO and FIFO. She has heard that LIFO might be better for tax purposes, but FIFO has certain advantages for financial reporting to investors and creditors. You have been told that the company will be profitable in its first year and for the foreseeable future.

Required:
Prepare a report for the president describing the factors that should be considered by Gilbert in choosing between LIFO and FIFO.

Earnings Management

AP6–8 Eddie's Galleria sells billiard tables. The company has the following purchases and sales for 2012.

Date	Transactions	Units	Cost per Unit	Total Cost
January 1	Beginning inventory	150	$540	$ 81,000
March 8	Purchase	120	570	68,400
August 22	Purchase	100	600	60,000
October 29	Purchase	80	640	51,200
		450		$260,600
Jan. 1–Dec. 31	Sales ($700 each)	400		

Eddie is worried about the company's financial performance. He has noticed an increase in the purchase cost of billiard tables, but at the same time, competition from other billiard table stores and other entertainment choices have prevented him from increasing the sales price. Eddie is worried that if the company's profitability is too low, stockholders will demand he be replaced. Eddie does not want to lose his job. Since 60 of the 400 billiard tables sold have not yet been picked up by the customers as of December 31, 2012, Eddie decides incorrectly to include these tables in ending inventory. He appropriately includes the sale of these 60 tables as part of total revenues in 2012.

Required:

1. What amount will Eddie calculate for ending inventory and cost of goods sold using FIFO, assuming he erroneously reports that 110 tables remain in ending inventory?
2. What amount would Eddie calculate for cost of goods sold using FIFO if he correctly reports that only 50 tables remain in ending inventory?
3. What effect will the inventory error have on reported amounts for (a) ending inventory, (b) retained earnings, (c) cost of goods sold, and (d) net income (ignoring tax effects) in 2012?
4. Assuming that ending inventory is correctly counted at the end of 2013, what effect will the inventory error in 2012 have on reported amounts for (a) ending inventory, (b) retained earnings, (c) cost of goods sold, and (d) net income (ignoring tax effects) in 2013?

Answers to the Self-Study Questions
1. d   2. b   3. a   4. b   5. d   6. a   7. d   8. a   9. c   10. b

Long-Term Assets

AFTER STUDYING THIS CHAPTER, YOU SHOULD BE ABLE TO:

- ■ **LO1** Identify and record the major types of property, plant, and equipment.
- ■ **LO2** Identify and record the major types of intangible assets.
- ■ **LO3** Discuss the accounting treatment of expenditures after acquisition.
- ■ **LO4** Calculate depreciation of property, plant, and equipment.
- ■ **LO5** Calculate amortization of intangible assets.
- ■ **LO6** Account for the disposal of long-term assets.

Analysis

- ■ **LO7** Describe the relationship among return on assets, profit margin, and asset turnover.

Appendix

- ■ **LO8** Identify impairment situations and describe the two-step impairment process.

WORLDCOM: EXPENSES CALLED ASSETS

WorldCom was the parent company of **MCI** and recognized as the leading telecommunications company in North America. Then in 2002, a routine internal audit uncovered massive accounting fraud. The firm had recorded assets in the balance sheet that should have been recorded as *expenses* in the income statement. Although this kind of fraudulent reporting was not new, the sheer volume of the fraud set new records. By failing to record expenses, WorldCom overstated its income and assets by about $11 billion (not $11 million, but $11 *billion!*). Estimates of investor losses from the resulting bankruptcy exceeded $100 billion.

How was the fraud accomplished? When WorldCom used the telecommunication lines of another company, it paid a fee. This fee is part of normal operating costs, and it should have been recorded as an expense of the current period, to properly match the expense with the revenues it helped to generate. Instead, WorldCom recorded these operating expenses as long-term assets in the balance sheet. Failure to report these operating expenses caused net income to be overstated by billions; operating expenses were purposely misstated as assets.

What motivated WorldCom's management to commit this fraud? It appears the intention was to hide operating losses and maintain a strong stock price. If investors had known the true operating performance of WorldCom, the stock price would have tumbled.

For his role in the accounting scandal that led to the largest bankruptcy in U.S. history, Bernard Ebbers, the 63-year-old CEO of WorldCom, was sentenced to 25 years in a low-security federal prison.[1] Ebbers, who took the stand in his own defense, insisted that he knew nothing of WorldCom's fraudulent accounting, but had left the accounting to Scott Sullivan, the company's former chief financial officer (CFO). The jury did not buy Ebbers's hands-off defense. They concluded that the CEO, as head of the company, is ultimately responsible for the firm's accounting.

---

[1]J. Sandberg, D. Solomon, and R. Blumenstein. "Inside WorldCom's Unearthing of a Vast Accounting Scandal." *The Wall Street Journal* (June 27, 2002); K. Eichenwald and S. Romero. "Inquiry Finds Effort to Delay at WorldCom." *The New York Times* (July 4, 2002); K. Crawford. "Ex-WorldCom CEO Ebbers Guilty." *CNNMoney.com* (March 15, 2005); and "Bernard Ebbers Given 25-year Prison Sentence." CBC News (July 13, 2005).

Winnebago cannot make campers without its manufacturing facilities and the equipment in those facilities. In contrast, it's not physical assets, but copyrights on its computer software that give **Google** the ability to generate billions of dollars in revenue each year. Both of these types of revenue-producing assets are considered *long-term assets*, the topic of this chapter.

We classify long-term assets into two major categories:

Common Terms Tangible assets are also called *property, plant, and equipment; plant assets; or fixed assets.*

1. **Tangible assets.** Assets in this category include land, land improvements, buildings, equipment, and natural resources. Winnebago's land, buildings, and equipment fall into this category.
2. **Intangible assets.** Assets in this category include patents, trademarks, copyrights, franchises, and goodwill. We distinguish these assets from property, plant, and equipment by their lack of physical substance. The evidence of their existence often is based on a legal contract. Google's copyrights are intangible assets.

Long-term assets often represent a significant portion of the total assets of a company. Illustration 7–1 presents a breakdown of the total assets for **Darden Restaurants**, a publicly traded company that owns and operates restaurant chains such as Red Lobster, Olive Garden, and Longhorn Steakhouse. Notice that current assets represent only about 11% of total assets, and long-term assets make up the remaining 89%. Accounting for long-term assets, both tangible (property, plant, and equipment) and intangible, is important and is the primary focus in this chapter.

ILLUSTRATION 7–1

Balance Sheet for Darden Restaurants

DARDEN RESTAURANTS Balance Sheet (partial) May 31, 2009 and 2008 ($ in thousands)		
	2009	**2008**
Cash	$ 62,900	$ 43,200
Receivables	147,500	161,300
Inventory	247,000	216,700
Other current assets	97,400	46,700
Total current assets	554,800	467,900
Property, plant, and equipment	3,306,700	3,066,000
Intangible assets	1,058,200	1,040,800
Other long-term assets and investments	105,500	155,900
Total assets	$5,025,200	$4,730,600

To properly report both tangible and intangible assets, we need to address a variety of issues including (1) which amounts to include in their cost, (2) how to expense their costs while using them, and (3) how to record their sale or disposal at the end of their useful life. These three are the basis for the three major parts of the chapter.

PART A

ACQUISITIONS

The first issue to consider in accounting for long-term assets is how to identify them and measure their costs. To do this, we need to understand the major types of tangible and intangible assets. We begin with tangible assets, also referred to as property, plant, and equipment.

Property, Plant, and Equipment

The property, plant, and equipment category consists of land, land improvements, buildings, equipment, and natural resources. The general rule for recording all such long-term assets can be stated rather simply: **We record a long-term asset at its cost *plus* all expenditures necessary to get the asset ready for use.** Thus, the initial cost of a long-term asset might be more than just its purchase price; it also will include any additional amounts the firm paid to bring the asset to its desired condition and location for use. We use the term capitalize to describe recording an expenditure as an asset.

When we make an expenditure, we have the choice of recording it as an expense of the current period or recording it as an asset and then allocating that cost as an expense over future periods. The choice depends on when the company benefits from having the asset: in the current period or over future periods. Determining which costs to record as expenses and which to record as long-term assets is crucial. Several infamous accounting frauds were the result of inflating net income by improperly recording current expenses as long-term assets.

We look at the proper recording of land, land improvements, buildings, basket purchases, equipment, and natural resources next.

■ **LO1**
Identify and record the major types of property, plant, and equipment.

LAND

The Land account represents land a company is using in its operations. (In contrast, land purchased for investment purposes is recorded in a separate investment account.) We capitalize to Land all expenditures necessary to get the land ready for its intended use.

Such capitalized costs include the purchase price of the land plus closing costs such as fees for the attorney, real estate agent commissions, title, title search, and recording fees. If the property is subject to back taxes or other obligations, we include these amounts as well. In fact, any additional expenditure such as clearing, filling, and draining the land, or even removing old buildings to prepare the land for its intended use, become part of the land's capitalized cost. If we receive any cash from selling salvaged materials from old buildings torn down, we reduce the cost of land by that amount.

Assume, for instance, that Kyoto's Sushi Bar purchases a two-acre tract of land and an existing building for $500,000. The company plans to remove the old building and construct a new restaurant on the site. In addition to the purchase price, the company pays a sales commission of $30,000 to the real estate agent and title insurance of $3,000. Kyoto also pays $8,000 in property taxes, which includes $6,000 of back taxes (unpaid taxes from previous years) paid by Kyoto on behalf of the seller and $2,000 due for the current fiscal year after the purchase date. Shortly after closing, the company pays a contractor $50,000 to tear down the old building and remove it from the site. Kyoto is able to sell salvaged materials from the old building for $5,000 and pays an additional $6,000 to level the land.

Using the guideline of **cost *plus* all expenditures necessary to get the asset ready for use,** at what amount should Kyoto record as the cost of the land? Illustration 7–2 (next page) shows the computation for the cost of Kyoto's land.

You may wonder why Kyoto recorded only $6,000 for property taxes. That was the amount required to get the asset ready for use—Kyoto could not use the land until it paid the back taxes. The additional $2,000 in property taxes, though, relates only to the current period, and so Kyoto records that amount as an expense in the current period. All of the other costs, including the $6,000 in back property taxes, are necessary to acquire the land, so Kyoto capitalizes them. Note that the salvaged materials that were sold for $5,000 reduce the overall cost of the land.

ILLUSTRATION 7–2

Computation of the
Cost of Land

Purchase price of land (and building to be removed)	$500,000
Commissions	30,000
Back property taxes	6,000
Title insurance	3,000
Cost of removing old building	50,000
Less: Salvaged materials from old building	(5,000)
Cost of leveling the land	6,000
Total cost	$590,000

COMMON MISTAKE

Many students incorrectly add or ignore the cash received from the sale of salvaged materials. Cash received from the sale of salvaged materials *reduces* the total cost of land.

LAND IMPROVEMENTS

Beyond the cost of the land, Kyoto likely will spend additional amounts to improve the land by adding a parking lot, sidewalks, driveways, landscaping, lighting systems, fences, sprinklers, and similar additions. These are **land improvements**.

In Chapter 3, we briefly discussed *depreciation* as the process of allocating the cost of an asset over its life. We will discuss depreciation in detail later in this chapter. When we do so, you will discover that land is an asset we do not depreciate because its life is indefinite. However, we do depreciate land improvements. For example, the paved parking lot Kyoto adds to its new property will eventually deteriorate and be replaced. Because land improvements have limited lives, we record them separately from the land itself.

BUILDINGS

Buildings include administrative offices, retail stores, manufacturing facilities, and storage warehouses. The cost of acquiring a building usually includes realtor commissions and legal fees in addition to the purchase price. The new owner sometimes needs to remodel or otherwise modify the building to suit its needs. These additional costs are part of the building's acquisition cost.

Unique accounting issues arise when a firm constructs a building rather than purchasing it. Of course the cost of construction includes architect fees, material costs, and construction labor. New building construction likely also includes costs such as officer supervision, overhead (costs indirectly related to the construction), and capitalized interest.

Capitalized interest refers to interest costs we add to the asset account rather than recording them as interest expense. In keeping with the idea that the cost of an asset includes *all* costs of making the asset ready for its intended use, if a company borrows money to finance the construction of an asset, the interest paid to borrow the funds logically is part of the asset's cost. Capitalizing interest also is in keeping with the *matching principle*. The matching principle states that expenses are to be matched with (included on the same income statement as) the revenues they help to create. During construction of a building, no revenues are created. Revenues won't be created until after the asset is fully constructed and placed into service. Therefore, interest represents a cost similar to materials, labor, and overhead necessary in preparing an asset for use.

EQUIPMENT

Equipment is a broad term that includes machinery used in manufacturing, computers and other office equipment, vehicles, furniture, and fixtures. The cost of equipment is the actual purchase price plus all other costs necessary to prepare the

asset for use. These can be any of a variety of other costs including sales tax, shipping, delivery insurance, assembly, installation, testing, and even legal fees incurred to establish title.

What about recurring costs related to equipment, such as annual property insurance and annual property taxes on vehicles? Rather than including recurring costs as part of the cost of the equipment, we expense them as we incur them, in order to properly match them with revenues generated during the same period. The question to ask yourself when deciding whether to add a cost to the asset account or record it as an expense of the current period is, *"Is this a cost of acquiring this asset and getting it ready for use, or is it a recurring cost that benefits the company in the current period?"*

Assume now that Kyoto's Sushi Bar purchases new restaurant equipment for $82,000 plus $6,500 in sales tax. Kyoto pays a freight company $800 to transport the equipment and $200 shipping insurance. The firm also pays $1,600 for one year of liability insurance on the equipment in advance. The equipment was also installed at an additional cost of $1,500. Illustration 7–3 shows the calculation of the amount at which Kyoto should record the cost of the equipment.

Purchase price	$82,000
Sales tax	6,500
Transportation	800
Shipping insurance	200
Installation	1,500
Total cost	$91,000

ILLUSTRATION 7–3

Computation of the Cost of Equipment

Thus, Kyoto should record the equipment at a total cost of $91,000. With the exception of the $1,600 annual insurance on the equipment, each of the expenditures described was necessary to bring the equipment to its condition and location for use. Kyoto will report the $1,600 insurance amount as insurance expense over the first year of coverage.

BASKET PURCHASES

Sometimes companies purchase more than one asset at the same time for one purchase price. This is known as a **basket purchase**. For example, assume Kyoto purchases land, building, and equipment together for $900,000. How much should we record in the separate accounts for the land, the building, and the equipment? The simple answer is that we allocate the total purchase price of $900,000 based on the estimated fair values of each of the individual assets.

The difficulty, though, is that the estimated fair values of the individual assets often exceed the total purchase price, in this case, $900,000. Let's say the estimated fair values of the land, buildings, and equipment are $200,000, $700,000, and $100,000, respectively, for a total estimated fair value of $1 million. In that case, Kyoto's total purchase of $900,000 will be allocated to the separate accounts for Land, Building, and Equipment based on their relative fair values as shown in Illustration 7–4.

	Estimated Fair Value	Allocation Percentage	Amount of Basket Purchase	Recorded Amount
Land	$ 200,000	$200,000/$1,000,000 = 20% ×	$900,000	$180,000
Building	700,000	$700,000/$1,000,000 = 70% ×	$900,000	630,000
Equipment	100,000	$100,000/$1,000,000 = 10% ×	$900,000	90,000
Total	$1,000,000			$900,000

ILLUSTRATION 7–4

Allocation of Cost in a Basket Purchase

NATURAL RESOURCES

In addition to land, buildings, and equipment, many companies depend heavily on natural resources, such as oil, natural gas, timber, and even salt. **ExxonMobil**, for example, maintains oil and natural gas deposits on six of the world's seven continents. **Weyerhaeuser** is one of the largest pulp and paper companies in the world with major investments in soft timber forests. Even salt is a natural resource, with the largest supply in the United States mined directly under the Great Lakes of North America.

We can distinguish natural resources from other property, plant, and equipment by the fact that we can physically use up, or *deplete*, natural resources. ExxonMobil's oil reserves are a natural resource that decreases as the firm extracts oil. Similarly, timber is used extensively to provide materials in the construction industry. Salt is used as a food additive and to melt icy roads in the winter.

A primary concern with regard to natural resources is sustainability. A common definition of sustainability is "meeting the needs of the present without compromising the ability of future generations to meet their own needs." The oil and gas industry is developing new sources of energy based on solar, wind, and hydro power. Another example is the timber industry, in which companies plant three new trees for every tree cut down. Companies need to find ways of replenishing the natural resources used so that we do not leave future generations without these valuable resources.

KEY POINT

Tangible assets include land, land improvements, buildings, equipment, and natural resources.

Intangible Assets

■ **LO2**
Identify and record the major types of intangible assets.

The other major category of long-term assets, intangible assets, have no physical substance. Assets in this category include patents, trademarks, copyrights, franchises, and goodwill.

Despite their lack of physical substance, intangible assets can be very valuable indeed. One of the most valuable intangible assets for many companies is their trademark or brand. *BusinessWeek* publishes an annual list of the 100 most valuable brands. Illustration 7–5 summarizes the top 10 most valuable brands in 2009. As you can see, the **Coca-Cola** brand has an estimated value of $68.7 billion. Despite this value, Coca-Cola reports trademarks on its balance sheet at only $2 billion. Later, we'll see why many intangible assets are *not* recorded on the balance sheet at their estimated values.

ILLUSTRATION 7–5

World's Top 10 Brands

Rank	Company	Country	Estimated Value
1	Coca-Cola	United States	$68.7 billion
2	IBM	United States	60.2 billion
3	Microsoft	United States	56.6 billion
4	GE	United States	47.8 billion
5	Nokia	Finland	34.9 billion
6	McDonald's	United States	32.3 billion
7	Google	United States	32.0 billion
8	Toyota	Japan	31.3 billion
9	Intel	United States	30.6 billion
10	Disney	United States	28.4 billion

Source: *BusinessWeek* (September 2009), *http://businessweek.com/go/brand/*.

Companies acquire intangible assets in two ways: (1) They *purchase* intangible assets like patents, copyrights, trademarks, or franchise rights from other entities, or (2) they *create* intangible assets internally, by developing a new product or process and obtaining a protective patent. The reporting rules for intangible assets vary depending on whether the company purchased or acquired the asset.

Reporting *purchased* intangibles is similar to reporting purchased property, plant, and equipment. **We record purchased intangible assets at their original cost plus all other costs, such as legal and filing fees, necessary to get the asset ready for use.** Filing fees include items such as the fee to record a copyright with the U.S. Copyright Office or the various fees to record a patent with the U.S. Patent and Trademark Office.

Reporting intangible assets that are *developed internally* is quite different. Rather than recording these on the balance sheet as intangible assets, **we expense to the income statement most of the costs for internally developed intangible assets as we incur those costs.** For example, the research and development (R&D) costs incurred in developing a patent internally are not recorded as an intangible asset in the balance sheet. Instead, they are expensed directly in the income statement. The reason we expense all R&D costs is the difficulty in determining the portion of R&D that benefits future periods. Conceptually, we should record as an intangible asset the portion that benefits future periods. Due to the difficulties in arriving at this estimate, current U.S. accounting rules require firms to expense all R&D costs as incurred.

INTERNATIONAL FINANCIAL REPORTING STANDARDS (IFRS)

International accounting standards differ from U.S. accounting standards in the treatment of R&D costs. U.S. GAAP requires that we expense all research and development expenditures in the period incurred. IFRS makes a distinction between *research* activities and *development* activities. Under IFRS, research expenditures are expensed in the period incurred, consistent with U.S. GAAP. However, development costs that benefit future periods can be recorded as an intangible asset.

For more discussion, see Appendix E.

A similar argument about the difficulty of estimating benefits in future periods can be made for advertising expenses. Advertising at **Coca-Cola** clearly has made its trademark more valuable. Because we cannot tell what portion of today's advertising benefits future periods and how many periods it might benefit, advertising costs are not recorded as an intangible asset on the balance sheet. Instead, advertising costs are recorded as expenses in the income statement.

KEY POINT

We record (capitalize) purchased intangible assets at their purchase price plus all costs necessary to get the asset ready for use. We expense internally generated intangible assets, such as R&D and advertising costs, as we incur them.

Let's look in more detail at how we report specific types of intangible assets.

PATENTS

A **patent** is an exclusive right to manufacture a product or to use a process. The U.S. Patent and Trademark Office grants this right for a period of 20 years. When a firm *purchases* a patent, it records the patent at its purchase price plus such other costs as legal and filing fees to secure the patent.

In contrast, when a firm *develops a patent internally*, it expenses the research and development costs as it incurs them. An exception to this rule is legal fees. The firm will record in the Patent asset account the legal and filing fees to secure the patent, even if it developed the patented item or process internally.

Holders of patents often need to defend their exclusive rights in court. For example, The **J.M. Smucker Company** obtained a patent on a round, crustless, frozen peanut butter and jelly sandwich sealed in an airtight foil wrapper, marketed under the name "Uncrustables." Smucker's later had to defend its patent by attempting to stop another company from making similar sandwiches. The costs of successfully defending a patent, including attorneys' fees, are added to the Patent account.

COPYRIGHTS

A **copyright** is an exclusive right of protection given by the U.S. Copyright Office to the creator of a published work such as a song, film, painting, photograph, book, or computer software. Copyrights are protected by law and give the creator (and his or her heirs) the exclusive right to reproduce and sell the artistic or published work for the life of the creator plus 70 years. A copyright also allows the copyright holder to pursue legal action against anyone who attempts to infringe the copyright. Accounting for the costs of copyrights is virtually identical to that of patents.

TRADEMARKS

A **trademark**, like the name **Coca-Cola**, is a word, slogan, or symbol that distinctively identifies a company, product, or service. The firm can register its trademark with the U.S. Patent and Trademark Office to protect it from use by others for a period of 10 years. The registration can be renewed for an indefinite number of 10-year periods, so a trademark is an example of an intangible asset whose useful life can be indefinite.

Firms often acquire trademarks through acquisition. As an example, **Hewlett-Packard (HP)** acquired all the outstanding stock of **Compaq Computer Corporation** for $24 billion, of which $1.4 billion was assigned to the Compaq trademark.

Advertising costs can factor into the cost of a trademark in a big way. For example, **Subway** aired a series of commercials featuring Jared Fogle, a student at Indiana University who lost 245 pounds eating Subway sandwiches. Certainly these ads benefited Subway. But what was the value to the company of the advertising? And for how many years will Subway receive that value? These are difficult questions. Thus, when a firm develops a trademark internally through advertising, it doesn't record the advertising costs as part of the cost of the intangible asset. Instead, it expenses the advertising costs in the income statement. Even though some advertising costs meet the definition of an asset by providing future benefits, due to the difficulty in estimating these amounts, financial accounting rules require advertising costs to be expensed as incurred.

A firm can record attorney fees, registration fees, design costs, successful legal defense, and other costs directly related to securing the trademark as an intangible asset in the Trademark asset account. This is how Coca-Cola can have a trademark valued at $67 billion, but reported in the balance sheet at only $2 billion. The estimated value of the trademark is not recorded on the balance sheet; instead, only the legal, registration, and design fees are recorded. The advertising costs that create value for the trademark are recorded as advertising expense.

FRANCHISES

The last time you ordered a sandwich at Subway, you probably dealt with a franchise. Many popular retail businesses such as restaurants, auto dealerships, and hotels are set up as franchises. These are local outlets that pay for the exclusive right to use the franchisor company's name and to sell its products within a specified geographical area. Many franchisors provide other benefits to the franchisee,

Names can lose their trademarked status if their owners fail to prevent improper use by others. All of the following were once valuable trademarks in the United States: *aspirin, escalator, cellophane, zipper, shredded wheat, corn flakes,* and *kerosene.*

such as participating in the construction of the retail outlet, training employees, and purchasing national advertising.

To record the cost of a franchise, the franchisee records the initial fee as an intangible asset and then expenses that cost over the life of the franchise agreement. Additional periodic payments to the franchisor usually are for services the franchisor provides on a continuing basis, and the franchisee will expense them as incurred.

GOODWILL 信誉

Goodwill often is the largest, yet the most confusing, intangible asset recorded in the balance sheet. While most long-term assets, even intangible ones, can be separated from the company and sold individually, goodwill cannot. Goodwill represents the value of a company as a whole, over and above the value of its identifiable net assets. That value can emerge from a company's reputation, its trained employees and management team, its favorable business location, and any other unique features of the company that we are unable to associate with a specific asset.

We record goodwill as an intangible asset in the balance sheet *only* when we purchase it as part of the acquisition of another company. In this case, the acquiring company records goodwill equal to the purchase price less the fair value of the net assets acquired. The fair value of the net assets is equal to the value of all identifiable assets acquired, minus the value of all liabilities assumed.

To see how this works, assume that Enriched White Bread Company (EWB) acquires Whole Wheat Bread Company (WWB) by paying $36 million in cash. The fair values of all identifiable assets acquired are as follows ($ in millions):

Receivables	$10
Inventory	14
Property, plant, and equipment	18
Patent	8
Total	$50

In the purchase, EWB also assumes all of WWB's long-term debt, which has a fair value of $24 million at the date of acquisition. Illustration 7–6 shows how to calculate the amount EWB would report as goodwill ($10 million).

($ in millions)		
Purchase price		$36
Less:		
Fair value of assets acquired	$ 50	
Less: Fair value of liabilities assumed	(24)	
Fair value of identifiable net assets		(26)
Goodwill		$10

ILLUSTRATION 7–6

Business Acquisition with Goodwill

EWB records the acquisition as follows:

	Debit	Credit	A	=	L	+	SE
Receivables (at fair value)........................	10		+10				
Inventory (at fair value)	14		+14				
Property, Plant, and Equipment (at fair value)	18		+18				
Patent (at fair value)	8		+8				
Goodwill (remaining purchase price)	10		+10				
Long-Term Debt (at fair value)		24			+24		
Cash (at purchase price)		36	−36				
(*Acquire Whole Wheat Bread Company*)							

Most companies also create goodwill to some extent through advertising, training, and other efforts. However, as it does for other internally generated intangibles, a company must *expense* any costs it incurs in the internal generation of goodwill. Imagine how difficult it would be to estimate the amount and future benefits of internally generated goodwill. Due to this difficulty, we record goodwill only when it is acquired as part of the purchase of another business.

 KEY POINT

Intangible assets include patents, copyrights, trademarks, franchises, and goodwill.

Expenditures after Acquisition

■ LO3
Discuss the accounting treatment of expenditures after acquisition.

Over the life of a long-term asset, the owners often incur additional expenditures for repairs and maintenance, additions, improvements, or litigation costs. We credit these costs to Cash or perhaps to Accounts Payable or Notes Payable, but what account do we debit? As with any other expenditure, the choice is to debit either an asset or an expense. Recall that an asset is a probable future benefit. **We capitalize an expenditure as an asset if it increases future benefits. We expense an expenditure if it benefits only the current period.** To see the choice more clearly, let's look at repairs and maintenance, additions, improvements, and litigation costs in more detail.

REPAIRS AND MAINTENANCE

The cost of an engine tune-up or the repair of an engine part for a delivery truck allows the truck to continue its productive activity. We expense repairs and maintenance expenditures like these because they maintain a given level of benefits in the period incurred. We capitalize as assets more extensive repairs that *increase* the future benefits of the delivery truck, such as a new transmission or an engine overhaul.

ADDITIONS

An addition occurs when we add a new major component to an existing asset. We should capitalize the cost of additions because they increase, rather than maintain, the future benefits from the expenditure. For example, adding a refrigeration unit to a delivery truck increases the capability of the truck beyond that originally anticipated, thus increasing its future benefits.

IMPROVEMENTS

An improvement is the cost of replacing a major component of an asset. The replacement can be a new component with the same characteristics as the old component, or a new component with enhanced operating capabilities. For example, we could replace an existing refrigeration unit in a delivery truck with a new but similar unit or with a new and improved refrigeration unit. In either case, the cost of the improvement usually increases future benefits, and we should capitalize it to the Equipment account.

LEGAL DEFENSE OF INTANGIBLE ASSETS

The expenditures after acquisition mentioned so far—repairs and maintenance, additions, and improvements—generally relate to property, plant, and equipment. Intangible assets, though, also can require expenditures after their acquisition, the most frequent being the cost of legally defending the right that gives the asset its value. For example, when The J.M. Smucker Company attempted to prevent

another company from copying its pea- nut butter and jelly sandwich patent, it incurred legal costs. If a firm suc- cessfully defends an intangible right, it should capitalize the litigation costs and amortize them over the remaining use- ful life of the related intangible. How- ever, if the defense of an intangible right is unsuccessful, then the firm should expense the litigation costs as incurred because they provide no future benefit.

MATERIALITY

Materiality relates to the size of an item that is likely to influence a decision. An item is said to be material if it is large enough to influence a decision. Mate-

riality is an important consideration in the "capitalize versus expense" decision. There often are practical problems in capitalizing small expenditures. For example, a stapler may have a 20-year service life, but it would not be practical to capitalize and then allocate that small of a cost to expense over 20 years. Companies generally expense all costs under a certain dollar amount, say $1,000, regardless of whether future benefits are increased. It's important for a company to establish a policy for treating these expenditures and apply the policy consistently.

Illustration 7–7 provides a summary of expenditures after acquisition.

Type of Expenditure	Definition	Period Benefited	Usual Accounting Treatment
Repairs and maintenance	Maintaining a given level of benefits	Current	**Expense**
Repairs and maintenance	Making major repairs that increase future benefits	Future	**Capitalize**
Additions	Adding a new major component	Future	**Capitalize**
Improvements	Replacing a major component	Future	**Capitalize**
Legal defense of intangible assets	Incurring litigation costs to defend the legal right to the asset	Future	**Capitalize** (Expense if defense is unsuccessful)

ILLUSTRATION 7–7

Expenditures after Acquisition

KEY POINT

Capital expenditures (recorded as assets) benefit *future* periods. Expenses typically benefit only the *current* period.

COST ALLOCATION

PART B

When people talk about a car depreciating, they usually are talking about how much the value of the car has decreased. Depreciation in accounting, though, is dif- ferent. The primary dictionary definition of depreciation differs from the definition of depreciation used in accounting:

Dictionary definition = Decrease in value (or selling price) of an asset.

Accounting definition = Allocation of an asset's cost to an expense over time.

 COMMON MISTAKE

Students sometimes mistake accounting depreciation as recording the decrease in value of an asset. Depreciation in accounting is *not* a valuation process. Rather, depreciation in accounting is an allocation of an asset's cost to expense over time.

In this section, we discuss the allocation of an asset's cost over time. We use the term *depreciation* to describe that process when it applies to property, plant, and equipment. You will see that we use a different term, *depletion*, to describe the cost allocation process when it applies to natural resources. For intangible assets, the term we use is *amortization*.

Depreciation of Property, Plant, and Equipment

■ LO4
Calculate depreciation of property, plant, and equipment.

Depreciation in accounting is the process of allocating to an expense the cost of an asset over its service life. An asset provides benefits (revenues) to a company in future periods. To properly match the cost (expense) with the revenues it helps to generate, we allocate a portion of the asset's cost to an expense in each year that the asset provides a benefit. If the asset will provide benefits to the company for four years, for example, then we allocate a portion of the asset's cost to depreciation expense in each year for four years. Illustration 7–8 portrays this concept of depreciating an asset's original purchase cost over the periods benefited.

ILLUSTRATION 7–8
Depreciation of Long-Term Assets

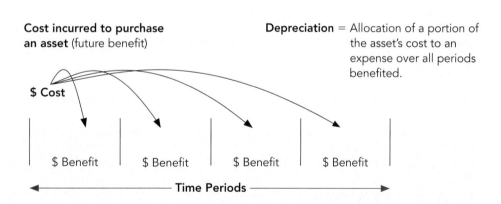

For demonstration, let's assume the local **Starbucks** pays $1,200 for equipment— say, an espresso machine. The machine is expected to have a useful life of four years. We record annual depreciation as shown below.

				Debit	Credit
Depreciation Expense				300	
Accumulated Depreciation					300
(Depreciate equipment)					
($300 = $1,200 ÷ 4 years)					

ACCUMULATED DEPRECIATION

The credit portion of the entry requires some explanation. **Accumulated Depreciation** is a contra asset account, meaning that it reduces an asset account. Rather than credit the Equipment account directly, we instead credit its contra account,

which we offset against the Equipment account in the balance sheet. The name of the account comes from the fact that the depreciation we record each period *accumulates* in the account. After one year, for instance, we have:

Equipment (cost)	$1,200
Less: Accumulated depreciation ($300 × 1 year)	(300)
= Book value	$ 900

Book value equals the original cost of the asset minus the current balance in Accumulated Depreciation. Note that by increasing accumulated depreciation each period, we are reducing the book value of equipment. The Accumulated Depreciation account allows us to reduce the book value of assets through depreciation, while maintaining the original cost of each asset in the accounting records.

Common Terms Book value sometimes is called *carrying value.*

After two years, we have:

Equipment (cost)	$1,200
Less: Accumulated depreciation ($300 × 2 years)	(600)
= Book value	$ 600

 KEY POINT

Depreciation refers to the allocation of the asset's original cost to an expense during the periods benefited. Depreciation does *not* refer to the change in value or selling price.

Depreciation requires accountants to estimate the *service life* of the asset, or its *useful life*, as well as its residual value at the end of that life. The **service life** is how long the company expects to receive benefits from the asset before disposing of it. We can measure service life in units of time or in units of activity. For example, the estimated service life of a delivery truck might be either five years or 100,000 miles. We use the terms service life and useful life interchangeably, because both terms are used in practice.

Common Terms Service life often is called *useful life.*

Depreciation also requires accountants to estimate what an asset's value will be at the end of its service life. Called **residual value**, or *salvage value*, it is the amount the company expects to receive from selling the asset at the end of its service life. A company might estimate residual value from prior experience or by researching the resale values of similar types of assets. Due to the difficulty in estimating residual value, it's not uncommon to assume a residual value of zero.

Common Terms Residual value often is called *salvage value.*

Remember: We record depreciation for land improvements, buildings, and equipment, but we *don't* record depreciation for land. Unlike other long-term assets, land is not "used up" over time.

 COMMON MISTAKE

A common mistake is to depreciate land. Land is *not* depreciated, because its service life never ends.

Generally accepted accounting principles allow us to use various methods to calculate depreciation. In the following sections, we illustrate the three most common depreciation methods used in practice: straight-line, declining-balance, and

activity-based.[2] All three illustrations are based on the same business situation: Little King Sandwiches, a local submarine sandwich restaurant, purchased a new delivery truck. The specific details of that purchase are described in Illustration 7–9.

ILLUSTRATION 7–9

Data for Little King Sandwiches's Delivery Truck Purchase, to Illustrate Depreciation Methods

Cost of the new truck	$40,000
Estimated residual value	$5,000
Estimated service life	5 years or 100,000 miles

STRAIGHT-LINE DEPRECIATION

By far the most easily understood and widely used depreciation method is straight-line. With the **straight-line method** we allocate an *equal* amount of the depreciable cost to each year of the asset's service life. The *depreciable cost* is the asset's cost minus its estimated residual value. We simply divide the depreciable cost by the number of years in the asset's life, as shown in Illustration 7–10.

ILLUSTRATION 7–10

Formula for Straight-Line Method

$$\text{Depreciation expense} = \frac{\text{Asset's cost} - \text{Residual value}}{\text{Service life}} = \frac{\text{Depreciable cost}}{\text{Service life}}$$

$$\text{Depreciation expense} = \frac{\$40,000 - \$5,000}{5 \text{ years}} = \$7,000 \text{ per year}$$

Note that dividing the depreciable cost each year by five is the same as multiplying the depreciable cost each year by 20% (1/5 = 0.20).

Illustration 7–11 provides a depreciation schedule using the straight-line method.

ILLUSTRATION 7–11

Straight-Line Depreciation Schedule

LITTLE KING SANDWICHES
Depreciation Schedule—Straight-Line

		Calculation			End-of-Year Amounts	
Year	Depreciable Cost	× Depreciation Rate	=	Depreciation Expense	Accumulated Depreciation	Book Value*
						$40,000
1	$35,000	0.20		$ 7,000	$ 7,000	33,000
2	35,000	0.20		7,000	14,000	26,000
3	35,000	0.20		7,000	21,000	19,000
4	35,000	0.20		7,000	28,000	12,000
5	35,000	0.20		7,000	35,000	5,000
Total				$35,000		

*Book value is the cost of the asset ($40,000) minus accumulated depreciation. Book value of $33,000 at the end of year 1, for example, is $40,000 minus $7,000 in accumulated depreciation.

---

[2]Some introductory financial accounting textbooks illustrate a fourth depreciation method called *sum-of-the-years'-digits*. However, use of this method has decreased dramatically over the years to the point that this method is now rarely seen in actual practice. A recent survey of depreciation methods used by large public companies is provided in Illustration 7–17.

Partial-year depreciation. We assume Little King Sandwiches bought the delivery truck at the beginning of year 1. What if it bought the truck sometime during the year instead? Then, it will record depreciation for only the portion of the first year that it owned the truck. For example, if Little King bought the truck on November 1 and its year-end is December 31, it will record depreciation for only two of the 12 months in year 1. So, depreciation expense in year 1 is $1,167 (= $7,000 × 2/12). If instead Little King bought the truck back on March 1, it will record depreciation for 10 of the 12 months in year 1. In that case, depreciation expense in year 1 is $5,833 (= $7,000 × 10/12).

In both cases, depreciation for the second, third, fourth, and fifth years still is $7,000. The partial-year depreciation for the first year does not affect the depreciation in those subsequent years. However, it does affect the depreciation treatment in the asset's final year of service life: Since the firm didn't take a full year of depreciation in year 1, it needs to record a partial year of depreciation in year 6 in order to fully depreciate the truck from its cost of $40,000 down to its residual value of $5,000. Depreciation in year 6 is $5,833 for the truck purchased on November 1 (= $7,000 − $1,167). For the truck purchased on March 1, depreciation in year 6 is $1,167 (= $7,000 − $5,833).

 COMMON MISTAKE

Many students think March 1 to the end of the year is nine months because December is the twelfth month and March is the third month. March 1 to the end of the year is actually *ten* months; it is every month except January and February.

Change in depreciation estimate. Depreciation is an *estimate*. Remember that the amount of depreciation allocated to each period is produced by two estimates—management's estimates of service life and of residual value—as well as the depreciation method chosen. Management needs to periodically review these estimates. When a change in estimate is required, the company changes depreciation in current and future years, but not in prior periods.

For example, assume that at the end of the third year Little King Sandwiches estimates the remaining service life of the delivery truck to be four more years, for a total service life of seven years rather than the original five. At this time, Little King also changes the estimated residual value to $3,000 from the original estimate of $5,000. How much should Little King record each year for depreciation in years 4 to 7? Take the book value at the end of year 3 ($19,000), subtract the new estimated residual value ($3,000), and then divide by the new remaining service life (four more years). Little King Sandwiches will record depreciation in years 4 to 7 as $4,000 per year. Illustration 7–12 shows the calculations.

Book value, end of year 3	$19,000
− New residual value	(3,000)
New depreciable cost	16,000
÷ Remaining service life	÷ 4
Annual depreciation in years 4 to 7	$ 4,000

ILLUSTRATION 7–12

Change in Depreciation Estimate

Notice that Little King Sandwiches makes all the changes in years 4 to 7. The company does not go back and change the calculations for depreciation already recorded in years 1 to 3.

ETHICAL DILEMMA

James Wright is the chief financial officer (CFO) for The Butcher Block, a major steakhouse restaurant chain. As CFO, James has the final responsibility for all aspects of financial reporting. The company is publicly traded and followed closely by the investment community. James holds regular teleconference discussions with financial analysts; in the most recent teleconference, he indicated the company is emerging nicely from the economic recession. He told the analysts that The Butcher Block should post earnings per share (net income divided by the number of shares of common stock) of at least $1.25. The analysts now expect that amount.

A couple months later, James is examining the preliminary year-end numbers. He notices that earnings per share are coming in at $1.23, two cents per share under target. He also is aware that The Butcher Block has been depreciating most of its restaurant equipment conservatively over a five-year useful life. In some cases, the equipment is used by the company for 10 years or more. He proposes to change the estimated useful life for a subset of the equipment to a more reasonable useful life of seven, rather than five, years. By depreciating over a longer useful life, depreciation expense will be lower in the current year, increasing earnings per share for the year to $1.26. It looks like The Butcher Block is going to meet analyst expectations after all.

Do you think James Wright's proposal to more accurately reflect the true depreciable life of assets is ethical? What concerns might you have?

Straight-line depreciation assumes that the benefits we derive from the use of an asset are the same each year. In some situations it might be more reasonable to assume that the asset will provide greater benefits in the earlier years of its life than in the later years. In these cases, we achieve a better matching of depreciation with revenues by using an accelerated depreciation method, with higher depreciation in the earlier years of the asset's life and lower depreciation in later years. We look at one such method next.

DECLINING-BALANCE DEPRECIATION

The declining-balance method is an accelerated depreciation method. Declining-balance depreciation will be higher than straight-line depreciation in earlier years, but lower in later years. **However, both declining-balance and straight-line will result in the same total depreciation over the asset's service life.** No matter what allocation method we use, total depreciation over the asset's service life will be equal to the depreciable cost (asset cost minus residual value).

The depreciation rate we use under the declining-balance method is a multiple of the straight-line rate, such as 125%, 150%, or 200% of the straight-line rate. The most common declining-balance rate is 200%, which we refer to as the *double-* declining-balance method since the rate is double the straight-line rate. In our illustration for Little King Sandwiches, the double-declining-balance rate would be 40% (two times the straight-line rate of 20%). Illustration 7–13 provides a depreciation schedule using the double-declining-balance method.

LITTLE KING SANDWICHES
Depreciation Schedule—Double-Declining-Balance

ILLUSTRATION 7–13
Double-Declining-Balance Depreciation Schedule

		Calculation			End-of-Year Amounts	
Year	Beginning Book Value	× Depreciation Rate	=	Depreciation Expense	Accumulated Depreciation	Book Value*
						$40,000
1	$40,000	0.40		$16,000	$16,000	24,000
2	24,000	0.40		9,600	25,600	14,400
3	14,400	0.40		5,760	31,360	8,640
4	8,640	0.40		3,456	34,816	5,184
5	5,184			184**	35,000	**5,000**
Total				$35,000		

*Book value is the cost of the asset minus accumulated depreciation. Book value at the end of year 1 is $24,000, equal to the cost of $40,000 minus accumulated depreciation of $16,000. Book value at the end of **year 1** in the last column is equal to book value at the beginning of **year 2** in the second column of the schedule.
**Amount necessary to reduce book value to residual value.

A simple way to get the depreciation rate for double-declining-balance is to divide the number 2 by the estimated service life (2/5 year service life = 0.40). If the service life had been four years instead of five, what depreciation rates would we use under straight-line and under double-declining-balance? The straight-line rate is 1 divided by the four-year service life, or 1/4 = 0.25. The double-declining-balance rate is 2 divided by the four-year service life, or 2/4 = 0.50.

Notice two unusual features of declining-balance depreciation. First, we multiply the rate by *book value* (cost minus accumulated depreciation), rather than by the depreciable cost (cost minus residual value). Second, in year 5 we are not able to record depreciation expense for the entire $5,184 times 0.40, because doing so would cause the book value to fall below the expected residual value. Instead, depreciation expense in the final year is the amount that reduces book value to the expected residual value (book value beginning of year, $5,184, minus estimated residual value, $5,000, = $184).

 COMMON MISTAKE

Mistakes are commonly made in the first and last year of the calculation. In the first year, students sometimes calculate depreciation incorrectly as cost minus residual value times the depreciation rate. The correct way in the first year is to simply multiply cost times the depreciation rate. In the final year, some students incorrectly calculate depreciation expense in the same manner as in earlier years, multiplying book value by the depreciation rate. However, under the declining-balance method, depreciation expense in the final year is the amount necessary to reduce book value down to residual value.

If the estimated residual value is high enough, the asset will reach its residual value in fewer years than its expected service life. For instance, if the estimated residual value had been $10,000 rather than $5,000, the delivery truck would be fully depreciated under the double-declining-balance method in only three years, even though we used a five-year life in determining the depreciation rate.

ACTIVITY-BASED DEPRECIATION

Straight-line and declining-balance methods measure depreciation based on time. In an **activity-based method**, we instead allocate an asset's cost based on its *use.* For example, we could measure the service life of a machine in terms of its output

Common Terms
Activity-based depreciation is also called *units of production* or *units of output.*

(units, pounds, barrels). This method also works for vehicles such as our delivery truck, whose use we measure in miles.

We first compute the average *depreciation rate per unit* by dividing the depreciable cost (cost minus residual value) by the number of units expected to be produced. In our illustration, the depreciation rate is $0.35 per mile, calculated as shown in Illustration 7–14.

ILLUSTRATION 7–14

Formula for Depreciation Rate per Unit in Activity-Based Method

$$\text{Depreciation rate per unit} = \frac{\text{Depreciable cost}}{\text{Total units expected to be produced}}$$

$$\text{Depreciation rate} = \frac{\$40{,}000 - \$5{,}000}{100{,}000 \text{ expected miles}} = \$0.35 \text{ per mile}$$

To calculate the depreciation expense for the reporting period, we then multiply the per-unit rate by the number of units of activity each period. Illustration 7–15 shows a depreciation schedule using the activity-based method. The actual miles driven in years 1 to 5 were 30,000, 22,000, 15,000, 20,000, and 13,000. Notice that the activity-based method is very similar to the straight-line method, except that rather than dividing the depreciable cost by the service life in years, we divide it by the service life in expected miles.

ILLUSTRATION 7–15

Activity-Based Depreciation Schedule

LITTLE KING SANDWICHES
Depreciation Schedule—Activity-Based

Year	Miles Driven	×	Depreciation Rate	=	Depreciation Expense	Accumulated Depreciation	Book Value*
							$40,000
1	30,000		$0.35		**$10,500**	$10,500	29,500
2	22,000		0.35		**7,700**	18,200	21,800
3	15,000		0.35		**5,250**	23,450	16,550
4	20,000		0.35		**7,000**	30,450	9,550
5	13,000		0.35		**4,550**	35,000	**5,000**
Total	100,000				**$35,000**		

*Book value is the cost of the asset ($40,000) minus accumulated depreciation. Book value of $29,500 in year 1 is $40,000 minus $10,500 in accumulated depreciation.

In our illustration, the delivery truck is driven exactly 100,000 miles over the five years. What if we drive the delivery truck *less than* 100,000 miles by the end of the fifth year? Then we will continue to depreciate the truck past five years until we reach 100,000 miles. Similarly, if we drive the delivery truck more than 100,000 miles in less than five years, we will stop depreciating the truck at 100,000 miles before the five years are up. In either case, we need to depreciate the asset until the book value (cost minus accumulated depreciation) declines to the estimated residual value.

Decision Maker's Perspective

Selecting a Depreciation Method

Assume you are the chief financial officer (CFO) responsible for your company's accounting and reporting policies. Which depreciation method would you choose? Illustration 7–16 compares annual depreciation under the three alternatives we discussed.

Year	Straight-Line	Double-Declining-Balance	Activity-Based
1	$ 7,000	$16,000	$10,500
2	7,000	9,600	7,700
3	7,000	5,760	5,250
4	7,000	3,456	7,000
5	7,000	184	4,550
Total	$35,000	$35,000	$35,000

ILLUSTRATION 7–16

Comparison of Depreciation Methods

Comparing methods, we see that all three alternatives result in total depreciation of $35,000 ($40,000 cost minus $5,000 residual value). Straight-line creates an equal amount of depreciation each year. Double-declining-balance creates more depreciation in earlier years and less depreciation in later years. Activity-based depreciation varies depending on the miles driven each year.

Companies are free to choose the depreciation method they believe best reflects the pattern of an asset's use and the revenues it creates. Illustration 7–17 shows the results of a recent survey of depreciation methods used by large public companies.

ILLUSTRATION 7–17

Use of Various Depreciation Methods

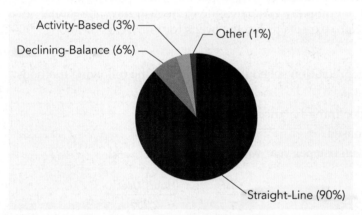

Activity-Based (3%)

Declining-Balance (6%)

Other (1%)

Straight-Line (90%)

Source: Accounting Trends and Techniques (New York: AICPA, 2009).

Why do so many companies use the straight-line method? Many probably believe they realize benefits from their plant assets approximately evenly over these assets' service lives. Certainly another motivating factor is that straight-line is the easiest method to apply. One more important motivation is straight-line's positive effect on reported income. Straight-line produces a higher net income than accelerated methods in the earlier years of an asset's life. Higher net income can improve bonuses paid to management, increase stock prices, and reduce the likelihood of violating debt agreements with lenders. ●

DEPLETION

Earlier in the chapter we discussed natural resources like oil, natural gas, and timber. We allocate natural resources to expense through a process known as **depletion**. The process of recording depletion expense for natural resources is nearly identical to the activity-based method of recording depreciation. Specific details for recording depletion are covered in more advanced accounting courses.

TAX DEPRECIATION

Conflicting with the desire to report higher net income is the desire to reduce taxes by *reducing* taxable income. An accelerated method serves this objective by reducing taxable income more in the earlier years of an asset's life than does straight-line.

As a result, most companies use the straight-line method for financial reporting and the Internal Revenue Service's prescribed accelerated method (called MACRS[3]) for income tax purposes. Thus, companies record higher net income using straight-line depreciation and lower taxable income using MACRS depreciation. MACRS combines declining-balance methods in earlier years with straight-line in later years to allow for a more advantageous tax depreciation deduction. Congress, not accountants, approved MACRS rules to encourage greater investment in long-term assets by U.S. companies.

 KEY POINT

Straight-line, declining-balance, and activity-based depreciation all are acceptable depreciation methods for financial reporting. Most companies use straight-line depreciation for financial reporting and an accelerated method called MACRS for tax reporting.

Let's Review

University Hero purchases new bread ovens at a cost of $110,000. On the date of purchase, the company estimates the ovens will have a residual value of $20,000. University Hero expects to use the ovens for four years or about 9,000 total hours.

Required:

Prepare a depreciation schedule using each of the following methods:

1. Straight-line.
2. Double-declining-balance.
3. Activity-based.

Actual oven use per year was as follows:

Year	Hours Used
1	2,200
2	2,600
3	2,300
4	2,100
Total	9,200

Solution:

1. Straight-line:

UNIVERSITY HERO
Depreciation Schedule—Straight-Line

	Calculation				End-of-Year Amounts	
Year	Depreciable Cost	×	Depreciation Rate*	=	Depreciation Expense	Accumulated Depreciation	Book Value**
1	$90,000		0.25		**$22,500**	$22,500	$87,500
2	90,000		0.25		**22,500**	45,000	65,000
3	90,000		0.25		**22,500**	67,500	42,500
4	90,000		0.25		**22,500**	90,000	**20,000**
Total					**$90,000**		

*1 ÷ 4 years = 0.25 per year
**$110,000 cost minus accumulated depreciation.

[3]Modified Accelerated Cost Recovery System.

2. Double-declining-balance:

UNIVERSITY HERO
Depreciation Schedule—Double-Declining-Balance

	Calculation				End-of-Year Amounts	
Year	Beginning Book Value	× Depreciation Rate*	=	Depreciation Expense	Accumulated Depreciation	Book Value**
1	$110,000	0.50		$55,000	$55,000	$55,000
2	55,000	0.50		27,500	82,500	27,500
3	27,500	0.50		7,500***	90,000	20,000
4				0	90,000	20,000
Total				$90,000		

*2 ÷ 4 years = 0.50 per year
**$110,000 cost minus accumulated depreciation.
***Amount needed to reduce book value to residual value.

3. Activity-based:

UNIVERSITY HERO
Depreciation Schedule—Activity-Based

	Calculation				End-of-Year Amounts	
Year	Hours Used	× Depreciation Rate*	=	Depreciation Expense	Accumulated Depreciation	Book Value**
1	2,200	$10		$22,000	$22,000	$88,000
2	2,600	10		26,000	48,000	62,000
3	2,300	10		23,000	71,000	39,000
4	2,100			19,000***	90,000	20,000
Total	9,200			$90,000		

*$90,000 ÷ 9,000 hours = $10/hour
**$110,000 cost minus accumulated depreciation.
***Amount needed to reduce book value to residual value.

Suggested Homework:
BE7-7, BE7-8;
E7-10, E7-11;
P7-5A&B, P7-7A&B

Amortization of Intangible Assets

Allocating the cost of property, plant, and equipment to expense is called depreciation. Allocating the cost of natural resources to expense is called depletion. Similarly, allocating the cost of *intangible* assets to expense is called **amortization**. 偿还

INTANGIBLE ASSETS SUBJECT TO AMORTIZATION

Most intangible assets have a finite useful life that we can estimate. For these, we allocate the asset's cost less any estimated residual value to periods in which we expect the intangible asset to contribute to the company's revenue-generating activities. This requires that we estimate the intangible asset's service life and its residual value.

The service life of an intangible asset usually is limited by legal, regulatory, or contractual provisions. For example, the legal life of a patent is 20 years. However, the estimated useful life of a patent often is less than 20 years if the benefits are not expected to continue for the patent's entire legal life. The patent for **Apple**'s iPad, for example, is amortized over fewer than 20 years, since new technology will cause the iPad to become outdated in a much shorter period.

The expected residual value of most intangible assets is zero. This might not be the case, though, if at the end of its useful life to the reporting entity the asset will

■ LO5
Calculate amortization of intangible assets.

benefit another entity. For example, if **Microsoft** has a commitment from another company to purchase one of its patents at the end of the patent's useful life at a determinable price, we use that price as the patent's residual value.

The method of amortization should reflect the pattern of use of the asset in generating benefits. Most companies use *straight-line amortization* for intangibles. Also, many companies credit amortization to the intangible asset account itself rather than to accumulated amortization. However, using a contra account such as Accumulated Amortization also is acceptable.

Let's look at an example: In early January, Little King Sandwiches acquires franchise rights from University Hero for $800,000. The franchise agreement is for a period of 20 years. In addition, Little King purchases a patent for a meat-slicing process for $72,000. The original legal life of the patent was 20 years, and there are 12 years remaining. However, due to expected technological obsolescence, the company estimates that the useful life of the patent is only 8 more years. Little King uses straight-line amortization for all intangible assets. The company's fiscal year-end is December 31. Little King records the amortization expense for the franchise and the patent as follows.

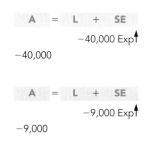

	Debit	Credit
Amortization Expense	40,000	
Franchises		40,000
(Amortize franchise)		
($40,000 = $800,000 ÷ 20 years)		
Amortization Expense	9,000	
Patents		9,000
(Amortize patent)		
($9,000 = $72,000 ÷ 8 years)		

INTANGIBLE ASSETS NOT SUBJECT TO AMORTIZATION

We don't depreciate land because it has an unlimited life. Similarly, we do *not* amortize intangible assets with indefinite useful lives. An asset's useful life is indefinite if there is no foreseeable limit on the period of time over which we expect it to contribute to the cash flows of the entity. For example, suppose Little King acquired a trademark for a line of sandwiches. Registered trademarks have a legal life of 10 years, but the trademark registration is renewable for an indefinite number of 10-year periods. We consider the life of Little King's trademark to be indefinite, so we don't amortize it.

Goodwill is the most common intangible asset with an indefinite useful life. Recall that we measure goodwill as the difference between the purchase price of a company and the fair value of all its identifiable net assets (tangible and intangible assets minus the fair value of liabilities assumed). Does this mean that goodwill and other intangible assets with indefinite useful lives will remain on a company's balance sheet at their original cost forever? Probably not. Management must review long-term assets for a potential write-down when events or changes in circumstances indicate the amount recorded for an asset in the accounting records might not be recoverable. All long-term assets are subject to these "impairment" rules, which we discuss in more detail in the appendix to this chapter.

 KEY POINT

Amortization is a process, similar to depreciation, in which we allocate the cost of intangible assets over their estimated service lives. Intangible assets with an indefinite useful life (goodwill and most trademarks) are *not* amortized.

ASSET DISPOSITION: SALE, RETIREMENT, OR EXCHANGE

Few things last forever. In this section we discuss what to do when we no longer use a long-term asset. A *sale* is a possibility. When a long-term asset is no longer useful but cannot be sold, we have a *retirement*. For example, Little King Sandwiches might physically remove a baking oven that no longer works and also remove it from the accounting records through a retirement entry. An *exchange* occurs when two companies trade assets. In a trade, we often use cash to make up for any difference in fair value between the assets.

■ **LO6**
Account for the disposal of long-term assets.

Selling a long-term asset can result in either a gain or a loss. We record a *gain* if we sell the asset for *more* than its book value. Similarly, we record a *loss* if we sell the asset for *less* than its book value. A gain is a credit balance account like other revenue accounts; a loss is a debit balance account like other expense accounts. Remember, book value is the cost of the asset minus accumulated depreciation. In order to have the correct book value, it's important to record depreciation up to the date of the sale.

 COMMON MISTAKE

Some students forget to update depreciation prior to recording the disposal of the asset. Depreciation must be recorded up to the date of the sale, retirement, or exchange. Otherwise, the book value will be overstated, and the resulting gain or loss on disposal will be in error as well.

To illustrate the recording of disposals, let's return to our delivery truck example for Little King Sandwiches. Assume Little King uses straight-line depreciation and records the delivery truck in the Equipment account. The specific details are summarized again in Illustration 7–18.

Original cost of the truck	$40,000
Estimated residual value	$5,000
Estimated service life	5 years

ILLUSTRATION 7–18

Data for Little King Sandwiches's Delivery Truck Purchase, to Illustrate Long-Term Asset Disposals

Sale of Long-Term Assets

If we assume that Little King sells the delivery truck at the end of year 3 for $22,000, we can calculate the gain as $3,000. Note that both the delivery truck and the related accumulated depreciation are removed. Illustration 7–19 shows the calculation.

Sale amount		$22,000
Less:		
Original cost of the truck	$40,000	
Less: Accumulated depreciation (3 years × $7,000/year)	(21,000)	
Book value at the end of year 3		19,000
Gain on sale		$ 3,000

ILLUSTRATION 7–19

Gain on Sale

We record the gain on sale as:

	Debit	Credit
Cash	22,000	
Accumulated Depreciation	21,000	
Equipment		40,000
Gain		3,000
(*Sell equipment for a gain*)		

A	=	L	+	SE
+22,000				
+21,000				
−40,000				
				+3,000 Rev↑

COMMON MISTAKE

Be careful not to combine the delivery truck ($40,000) and accumulated depreciation ($21,000) and credit the $19,000 difference to the Equipment account. Instead, remove the delivery truck and accumulated depreciation from the accounting records separately. Otherwise, the Equipment and the Accumulated Depreciation accounts will incorrectly have a remaining balance after the asset has been sold.

If we assume that Little King sells the delivery truck at the end of year 3 for only $17,000 instead of $22,000, we have a $2,000 loss as calculated in Illustration 7–20.

ILLUSTRATION 7–20

Loss on Sale

Sale amount		$17,000
Less:		
Original cost of the truck	$40,000	
Less: Accumulated depreciation (3 years × $7,000/year)	(21,000)	
Book value at the end of year 3		19,000
Loss on sale		$ (2,000)

We record the loss on sale as:

A = L + SE		Debit	Credit
+17,000	Cash	17,000	
+21,000	Accumulated Depreciation	21,000	
−2,000 Exp↑	Loss	2,000	
−40,000	Equipment		40,000
	(Sell equipment for a loss)		

Decision Point

Question ?	Accounting information 📄	Analysis 🔍
How different is the company's recorded book value from its actual fair value?	Gain or loss on sale	A gain on sale indicates the actual fair value is more than the recorded book value. A loss on sale indicates the opposite.

Retirement of Long-Term Assets

Now assume that Little King retires the delivery truck instead of selling it. If, for example, the truck is totaled in an accident at the end of year 3, we have a $19,000 loss on retirement as calculated in Illustration 7–21.

ILLUSTRATION 7–21

Loss on Retirement

Sale amount		$ 0
Less:		
Original cost of the truck	$40,000	
Less: Accumulated depreciation (3 years × $7,000/year)	(21,000)	
Book value at the end of year 3		19,000
Loss on retirement		$(19,000)

We record the loss on retirement as:

	Debit	Credit
Accumulated Depreciation	21,000	
Loss	19,000	
Equipment		40,000
(*Retire equipment for a loss*)		

A = L + SE
+21,000
−19,000 Exp↑
−40,000

The above entry assumes Little King did not have collision insurance coverage. If Little King had insured the truck and collected $17,000 in insurance money for the totaled vehicle, the entry would be identical to the sale for $17,000 in Illustration 7–20.

Exchange of Long-Term Assets

Now assume that Little King exchanges the delivery truck at the end of year 3 for a new truck valued at $45,000. The dealership gives Little King a trade-in allowance of $23,000 on the exchange, with the remaining $22,000 paid in cash. We have a $4,000 gain, as calculated in Illustration 7–22.

Trade-in allowance		$23,000
Less:		
Original cost of the truck	$40,000	
Less: Accumulated depreciation (3 years × $7,000/year)	(21,000)	
Book value at the end of year 3		19,000
Gain on exchange		$ 4,000

ILLUSTRATION 7–22

Gain on Exchange

We record the gain on exchange as:

	Debit	Credit
Equipment (new)	45,000	
Accumulated Depreciation	21,000	
Cash		22,000
Equipment (old)		40,000
Gain		4,000
(*Exchange equipment for a gain*)		

A = L + SE
+45,000
+21,000
−22,000
−40,000
+4,000 Rev↑

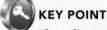

KEY POINT

If we dispose of an asset for *more* than book value, we record a gain. If we dispose of an asset for *less* than book value, we record a loss.

ASSET ANALYSIS
Walmart vs. Abercrombie

We have discussed the purchase, depreciation, and disposal of long-term assets. In this final section, we see how to use actual financial statement information to analyze the profitability of a company's assets. Illustration 7–23 (next page) provides selected financial data reported by **Walmart** and **Abercrombie** for use in our analysis.

ANALYSIS

■ LO7
Describe the relation among return on assets, profit margin, and asset turnover.

ILLUSTRATION 7–23

Selected Financial Data for Walmart and Abercrombie

($ in millions) Walmart	2009	2008
Net sales	$405,607	$378,799
Net income	13,400	12,731
Total assets	163,429	163,514

Abercrombie	2009	2008
Net sales	$3,540	$3,750
Net income	272	476
Total assets	2,848	2,568

RETURN ON ASSETS

Common Terms Return on assets is often just called *ROA*.

Walmart had net income of $13,400 million and Abercrombie had net income of $272 million in 2009. Since Walmart's net income is so much larger, does that mean Walmart is more profitable? Not necessarily. Walmart is also a much larger company, as indicated by total assets. Walmart's total assets were $163,429 million compared to $2,848 million for Abercrombie. A more comparable measure of profitability than income is **return on assets**, which equals net income divided by *average* total assets. Dividing net income by average total assets adjusts net income for differences in company size.

 COMMON MISTAKE

Students sometimes divide by ending total assets rather than by *average* total assets. We measure net income over time, whereas we measure total assets at a *point* in time. Therefore, whenever we divide a number in the income statement by a number in the balance sheet, it's more meaningful to use an *average* balance sheet number.

The return on assets ratio is calculated for Walmart and Abercrombie in Illustration 7–24.

ILLUSTRATION 7–24

Return on Assets for Walmart and Abercrombie

($ in millions)	Net Income	÷	Average Total Assets	=	Return on Assets
Walmart	$13,400	÷	($163,429 + $163,514)/2	=	8.2%
Abercrombie	$ 272	÷	($2,848 + $2,568)/2	=	10.0%

Although Walmart has a much higher net income, Abercrombie actually is more profitable, with a higher return on assets. Return on assets indicates the amount of net income generated for each dollar invested in assets.

Decision Point

Question	Accounting information	Analysis
How effectively is the company using its assets?	Return on assets ratio	A higher return on assets generally indicates a more effective use of assets.

PROFIT MARGIN AND ASSET TURNOVER

We can explore profitability further by separating return on assets into two components: profit margin and asset turnover, as shown in Illustration 7–25.

$$\underset{\text{Average total assets}}{\text{Return on assets}} = \underset{\text{Net sales}}{\text{Profit margin}} \times \underset{\text{Average total assets}}{\text{Asset turnover}}$$

Return on assets	=	Profit margin	×	Asset turnover
$\dfrac{\text{Net income}}{\text{Average total assets}}$	=	$\dfrac{\text{Net income}}{\text{Net sales}}$	×	$\dfrac{\text{Net sales}}{\text{Average total assets}}$

ILLUSTRATION 7–25
Components of Return on Assets

Profit margin is net income divided by net sales. This ratio indicates the earnings per dollar of sales. **Asset turnover** is net sales divided by average total assets. This ratio measures the sales per dollar of assets invested.

Strategies for Increasing Return on Assets

Decision Maker's Perspective

Companies have two primary strategies for increasing their return on assets. Some companies, like Walmart, pursue a high sales volume by charging *lower prices*. Walmart is profitable as long as it can maintain or increase its asset turnover. Other companies, like Abercrombie, pursue a higher profit margin through *product differentiation* and *premium pricing*. Abercrombie is profitable as long as it can maintain or increase its high profit margins. In Illustrations 7–26 and 7–27 we calculate profit margin and asset turnover, respectively, for both companies. We then can see if our expectations regarding Walmart and Abercrombie are supported.

($ in millions)	Net Income	÷	Net Sales	=	Profit Margin
Walmart	$13,400	÷	$405,607	=	3.3%
Abercrombie	$272	÷	$ 3,540	=	7.7%

ILLUSTRATION 7–26
Profit Margin for Walmart and Abercrombie

($ in millions)	Net Sales	÷	Average Total Assets	=	Asset Turnover
Walmart	$405,607	÷	($163,429 + $163,514)/2	=	2.5 times
Abercrombie	$3,540	÷	($2,848 + $2,568)/2	=	1.3 times

ILLUSTRATION 7–27
Asset Turnover for Walmart and Abercrombie

Illustration 7–26 indicates that Abercrombie's profit margin is more than twice that for Walmart. Illustration 7–27, however, shows that Walmart has the higher asset turnover. These accounting ratios support our expectations regarding the different business strategies Walmart and Abercrombie are pursuing. To maximize profitability, a company ideally strives to increase *both* net income per dollar of sales (profit margin) and sales per dollar invested in assets (asset turnover). ●

 KEY POINT

Return on assets indicates the amount of net income generated for each dollar invested in assets. Return on assets can be separated to examine two important business strategies: profit margin and asset turnover.

Decision Point

Question	Accounting information	Analysis
How much profit is being generated from sales?	Profit margin	A higher profit margin indicates a company generates a higher net income per dollar of sales.
Is the company effectively generating sales from its assets?	Asset turnover ratio	A higher asset turnover indicates a company generates a higher sales volume per dollar of assets invested.

APPENDIX

ASSET IMPAIRMENT

损害，损伤

■ **LO8**
Identify impairment situations and describe the two-step impairment process.

Management must review long-term assets for impairment when events or changes in circumstances indicate that book value might not be recoverable. **Impairment** occurs when the future cash flows (future benefits) generated for a long-term asset fall below its book value (cost minus accumulated depreciation). The relationship among future cash flows, fair value, and book value can be confusing. Illustration 7–28 displays the normal relationship and the impaired relationship among these three values.

ILLUSTRATION 7–28

Relationship among Future Cash Flows, Fair Value, and Book Value

	Normal Relationship		Impaired Relationship
Largest:	Future cash flows	*Largest:*	Book value
Middle:	Fair value	*Middle:*	Future cash flows
Smallest:	Book value	*Smallest:*	Fair value

Note that future cash flows always exceed fair value. This is true since the present value of future cash flows are used in determining fair value and the present value of an amount is always less than the total of its future cash flows. If estimated future cash flows from the asset are below the book value (as in the impaired relationship column), we record an impairment loss. The *impairment loss* is equal to the difference between the asset's book value and its fair value. Thus, reporting for impairment losses is a two-step process summarized in Illustration 7–29.

ILLUSTRATION 7–29

Two-Step Impairment Process

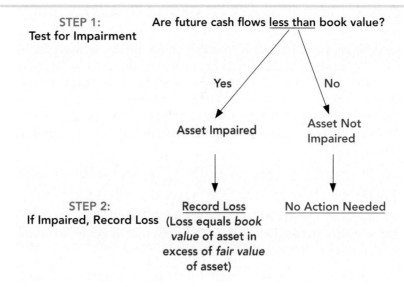

STEP 1:
Test for Impairment — Are future cash flows <u>less than</u> book value?

Yes → Asset Impaired
No → Asset Not Impaired

STEP 2:
If Impaired, Record Loss

<u>Record Loss</u> (Loss equals *book value* of asset in excess of *fair value* of asset)

<u>No Action Needed</u>

To illustrate asset impairment, suppose Little King pays $50,000 for the trademark rights to a line of specialty sandwiches. This intangible asset is not amortized because management assumes the trademark has an indefinite useful life. After several years, sales for this line of specialty sandwiches are disappointing, and management estimates the total future cash flows from sales will be only $20,000. Due to the disappointing sales, the estimated fair value of the trademark is now about $12,000. Here's how Little King determines and records the impairment loss.

STEP 1: TEST FOR IMPAIRMENT

The long-term asset is impaired since future cash flows ($20,000) are less than book value ($50,000).

STEP 2: IF IMPAIRED, RECORD THE LOSS

The loss is $38,000, calculated as the amount by which book value ($50,000) exceeds fair value ($12,000). We record the impairment loss as follows:

	Debit	Credit
Loss	38,000	
Trademarks		38,000
(*Record impairment of trademark*)		

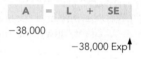

A = L + SE
−38,000
−38,000 Exp↑

 COMMON MISTAKE

Some students forget step 1 when considering impairment. Record an impairment loss only when book value exceeds *both* future cash flows and fair value.

What is the overall financial statement effect of an impairment loss? The impairment entry reduces net income in the income statement by $38,000 and reduces total assets in the balance sheet by $38,000. The new balance in the Trademarks account is $12,000, which equals its current fair value. We can write down the trademark further through impairment in future years, but we cannot write it back up under current accounting rules.

 INTERNATIONAL FINANCIAL REPORTING STANDARDS (IFRS)

International accounting standards also record impairments based on a two-step impairment process. The details are covered in more advanced accounting courses. However, one important difference is this: Impairments under U.S. GAAP are permanent—the asset cannot be written back up in future periods. In contrast, impairments under IFRS rules can be reversed. Thus, under IFRS a company can record an impairment loss in one period and then write the asset back up with a corresponding gain in a later period.

For more discussion, see Appendix E.

 KEY POINT

Impairment is a two-step process: **Step 1: Test for impairment:** The long-term asset is impaired if future cash flows are less than book value. **Step 2: If impaired, record impairment loss:** The impairment loss is the amount by which book value exceeds fair value.

Decision Maker's Perspective

Taking a Big Bath

In practice, determining impairment losses can be subjective. Accounting research suggests that managers sometimes use the recording of impairment losses to their advantage. Some companies time their impairment losses with other one-time losses such as losses on sales of assets, inventory write-downs, and restructuring charges, to record a big loss in one year. We refer to this practice as taking a big bath—recording all losses in one year to make a bad year even worse. Management thus cleans its slate and is able to report higher earnings in future years. Future earnings are higher because the write-down of assets in this year results in lower depreciation and amortization charges in the future. When analyzing financial statements, investors should be alert to this kind of manipulation. ●

KEY POINTS BY LEARNING OBJECTIVE

LO1 Identify and record the major types of property, plant, and equipment.

Tangible assets include land, land improvements, buildings, equipment, and natural resources.

LO2 Identify and record the major types of intangible assets.

We record (capitalize) purchased intangible assets at their purchase price plus all costs necessary to get the asset ready for use. We expense internally generated intangible assets, such as R&D and advertising costs, as we incur those costs.

Intangible assets include patents, copyrights, trademarks, franchises, and goodwill.

LO3 Discuss the accounting treatment of expenditures after acquisition.

Capital items (recorded as assets) benefit *future* periods. Expenses benefit only the *current* period.

LO4 Calculate depreciation of property, plant, and equipment.

Depreciation refers to the allocation of an asset's original cost to an expense during the periods benefited. Depreciation does *not* refer to the change in value or selling price.

Straight-line, declining-balance, and activity-based depreciation all are acceptable depreciation methods for financial reporting. Most companies use straight-line depreciation for financial reporting and an accelerated method called MACRS for tax reporting.

LO5 Calculate amortization of intangible assets.

Amortization is a process, similar to depreciation, in which we allocate the cost of intangible assets over their estimated service life. Intangible assets with an indefinite useful life (goodwill and most trademarks) are *not* amortized.

LO6 Account for the disposal of long-term assets.

If we dispose of an asset for more than book value, we record a gain. If we dispose of an asset for less than book value, we record a loss.

Analysis

LO7 Describe the relationship among return on assets, profit margin, and asset turnover.

Return on assets indicates the amount of net income generated for each dollar invested in assets. Return on assets can be separated to examine two important business strategies: profit margin and asset turnover.

Appendix

LO8 Identify impairment situations and describe the two-step impairment process.

Impairment is a two-step process. **Step 1: Test for impairment:** The long-term asset is impaired if future cash flows are less than book value. **Step 2: If impaired, record loss:** The impairment loss is the amount book value exceeds fair value.

GLOSSARY

Accelerated depreciation method: Allocates a higher depreciation in the earlier years of the asset's life and lower depreciation in later years. **p. 334**

Accumulated Depreciation: A contra asset account representing the total depreciation taken to date. **p. 330**

Activity-based method: Allocates an asset's cost based on its use. **p. 335**

Addition: Occurs when a new major component is added to an existing asset. **p. 328**

Amortization: Allocation of the cost of an intangible asset over its service life. **p. 339**

Asset turnover: Net sales divided by average total assets, which measures the sales per dollar of assets invested. **p. 345**

Basket purchase: Purchase of more than one asset at the same time for one purchase price. **p. 323**

Big bath: Recording all losses in one year to make a bad year even worse. **p. 348**

Book value: Equal to the original cost of the asset minus the current balance in Accumulated Depreciation. **p. 331**

Capitalize: Record an expenditure as an asset. **p. 321**

Capitalized interest: Interest costs recorded as assets rather than interest expense. **p. 322**

Copyright: An exclusive right of protection given to the creator of a published work such as a song, film, painting, photograph, book, or computer software. **p. 326**

Declining-balance method: An accelerated depreciation method that records more depreciation in earlier years and less depreciation in later years. **p. 334**

Depletion: Allocation of the cost of a natural resource over its service life. **p. 337**

Depreciation: Allocation of the cost of a tangible asset over its service life. **p. 330**

Franchise: Local outlets that pay for the exclusive right to use the franchisor company's name and to sell its products within a specified geographical area. **p. 326**

Goodwill: The value of a company as a whole, over and above the value of its identifiable net assets. Goodwill equals the purchase price less the fair value of the net assets acquired. **p. 327**

Impairment: Occurs when the future cash flows (future benefits) generated for a long-term asset fall below its book value (cost minus accumulated depreciation). **p. 346**

Improvement: The cost of replacing a major component of an asset. **p. 328**

Intangible assets: Long-term assets that lack physical substance, and whose existence is often based on a legal contract. **p. 324**

Land improvements: Improvements to land such as paving, lighting, and landscaping that, unlike land itself, are subject to depreciation. **p. 322**

Material: Large enough to influence a decision. **p. 329**

Natural resources: Assets like oil, natural gas, and timber that we can physically use up or deplete. **p. 324**

Patent: An exclusive right to manufacture a product or to use a process. **p. 325**

Profit margin: Net income divided by net sales; indicates the earnings per dollar of sales. **p. 345**

Repairs and maintenance: Expenses that maintain a given level of benefits in the period incurred. **p. 328**

Residual value: The amount the company expects to receive from selling the asset at the end of its service life; also referred to as *salvage value*. **p. 331**

Return on assets: Net income divided by average total assets; measures the amount of net income generated for each dollar invested in assets. **p. 344**

Service life: How long the company expects to receive benefits from the asset before disposing of it; also referred to as *useful life*. **p. 331**

Straight-line method: Allocates an equal amount of depreciation to each year of the asset's service life. **p. 332**

Trademark: A word, slogan, or symbol that distinctively identifies a company, product, or service. **p. 326**

SELF-STUDY QUESTIONS

1. We normally record a long-term asset at the: ■ **LO1**
   a. Cost of the asset only.
   b. Cost of the asset plus all costs necessary to get the asset ready for use.
   c. Appraised value.
   d. Cost of the asset, but subsequently adjust it up or down to appraised value.

2. Sandwich Express incurred the following costs related to its purchase of a bread machine.   ■ **LO1**

Cost of the equipment	$20,000
Sales tax (8%)	1,600
Shipping	2,200
Installation	1,400
Total costs	$25,200

At what amount should Sandwich Express record the bread machine?
a. $20,000.
b. $21,600.
c. $23,800.
d. $25,200.

■ LO2   3. Research and development costs generated internally:
a. Are recorded as research and development assets.
b. Are capitalized and then amortized.
c. Should be included in the cost of the patent they relate to.
d. Should be expensed.

■ LO3   4. Which of the following expenditures should be recorded as an expense?
a. Repairs and maintenance that maintain current benefits.
b. Adding a major new component to an existing asset.
c. Replacing a major component of an existing asset.
d. Successful legal defense of an intangible asset.

■ LO4   5. Which of the following will maximize net income by minimizing depreciation expense in the first year of the asset's life?
a. Short service life, high residual value, and straight-line depreciation.
b. Long service life, high residual value, and straight-line depreciation.
c. Short service life, low residual value, and double-declining-balance depreciation.
d. Long service life, high residual value, and double-declining-balance depreciation.

■ LO4   6. The book value of an asset is equal to the:
a. Replacement cost.
b. Asset's cost less accumulated depreciation.
c. Asset's fair value less its historical cost.
d. Historical cost plus accumulated depreciation.

■ LO4   7. The balance in the Accumulated Depreciation account represents:
a. The amount charged to expense in the current period.
b. A contra expense account.
c. A cash fund to be used to replace plant assets.
d. The amount charged to depreciation expense since the acquisition of the plant asset.

■ LO5   8. Which of the following statements is *true* regarding the amortization of intangible assets?
a. Intangible assets with a limited useful life are not amortized.
b. The service life of an intangible asset is always equal to its legal life.
c. The expected residual value of most intangible assets is zero.
d. In recording amortization, Accumulated Amortization is always credited.

■ LO6   9. Equipment originally costing $95,000 has accumulated depreciation of $30,000. If it sells the equipment for $55,000, the company should record:
a. No gain or loss.
b. A gain of $10,000.
c. A loss of $10,000.
d. A loss of $40,000.

■ LO7   10. The return on assets is equal to the:
a. Profit margin plus asset turnover.
b. Profit margin minus asset turnover.
c. Profit margin times asset turnover.
d. Profit margin divided by asset turnover.

Check out
www.mhhe.com/succeed
for more multiple-choice
questions.

Note: For answers, see the last page of the chapter.

REVIEW QUESTIONS

1. **WorldCom** committed the largest fraud in U.S. history. What was the primary method WorldCom's management used to carry out the fraud?   ■ LO1

2. What are the two major categories of long-term assets? How do these two categories differ?   ■ LO1

3. Explain how we initially record a long-term asset.   ■ LO1

4. If University Hero initially records an expense incorrectly as an asset, how does this mistake affect the income statement and the balance sheet?   ■ LO1

5. Little King acquires land and an old building across the street from Northwestern State University. Little King intends to remove the old building and build a new sandwich shop on the land. What costs might the firm incur to make the land ready for its intended use?   ■ LO1

6. Why don't we depreciate land? What are land improvements? Why do we record land and land improvements separately?   ■ LO1

7. Equipment includes machinery used in manufacturing, computers and other office equipment, vehicles, furniture, and fixtures. What costs might we incur to get equipment ready for use?   ■ LO1

8. Where in the balance sheet do we report natural resources? Provide at least three examples of natural resource assets.   ■ LO1

9. Explain how the accounting treatment differs between purchased and internally developed intangible assets.   ■ LO2

10. What are the differences among a patent, a copyright, and a trademark?   ■ LO2

11. What is goodwill and how do we measure it? Can we sell goodwill separately from the business?   ■ LO2

12. How do we decide whether to capitalize (record as an asset) or expense a particular cost?   ■ LO3

13. Explain the usual accounting treatment for repairs and maintenance, additions, and improvements.   ■ LO3

14. Are litigation costs to defend an intangible asset capitalized or expensed? Explain your answer.   ■ LO3

15. How is the dictionary definition different from the accounting definition of depreciation?   ■ LO4

16. What factors must we estimate in allocating the cost of a long-term asset over its service life?   ■ LO4

17. What is the service life of an asset? How do we determine service life under the straight-line and the activity-based depreciation methods?   ■ LO4

18. What is residual value? How do we use residual value in calculating depreciation under the straight-line method?   ■ LO4

19. Contrast the effects of the straight-line, declining-balance, and activity-based methods on annual depreciation expense.   ■ LO4

20. Assume that Little King Sandwiches uses straight-line depreciation and University Hero uses double-declining-balance depreciation. Explain the difficulties in comparing the income statements and balance sheets of the two companies.   ■ LO4

21. Assume Little King Sandwiches depreciates a building over 40 years and University Hero depreciates a similar building over 20 years, and both companies use the straight-line depreciation method. Explain the difficulties in comparing the income statements and balance sheets of the two companies.   ■ LO4

■ LO4   22. Which depreciation method is most common for financial reporting? Which depreciation method is most common for tax reporting? Why do companies choose these methods?

■ LO5   23. Justin Time is confident that firms amortize all intangible assets. Is he right? If amortized, are intangible assets always amortized over their legal life? Explain.

■ LO6   24. What is book value? How do we compute the gain or loss on the sale of long-term assets?

■ LO7   25. Describe return on assets, profit margin, and asset turnover.

■ LO7   26. Provide an example of a company like **Abercrombie** with a high profit margin. Provide an example of a company like **Walmart** with high asset turnover.

■ LO8   27. What is an asset impairment? Describe the two-step process for recording impairments. How does recording an impairment loss affect the income statement and the balance sheet?

■ LO8   28. How do companies take a *big bath?* Explain the effect of a big bath on the current year's and future years' net income.

BRIEF EXERCISES   Mc Graw Hill **connect** | ACCOUNTING

Determine the initial cost of land (**LO1**)

BE7–1 Fresh Veggies, Inc. (FVI), purchases land and a warehouse for $500,000. In addition to the purchase price, FVI makes the following expenditures related to the acquisition: broker's commission, $30,000; title insurance, $2,000; and miscellaneous closing costs, $5,000. The warehouse is immediately demolished at a cost of $30,000 in anticipation of building a new warehouse. Determine the amount FVI should record as the cost of the land.

Determine the initial cost of equipment (**LO1**)

BE7–2 Whole Grain Bakery purchases an industrial bread machine for $25,000. In addition to the purchase price, the company makes the following expenditures: freight, $1,500; installation, $3,000; testing, $1,000; and property tax on the machine for the first year, $500. What is the initial cost of the bread machine? *Not including*

Calculate goodwill (**LO2**)

BE7–3 Kosher Pickle Company acquires all the outstanding stock of Midwest Produce for $14 million. The fair value of Midwest's assets is $11.3 million. The fair value of Midwest's liabilities is $1.5 million. Calculate the amount paid for goodwill. *14 – 9.8 = 4.2*   *14 12.8 4.2 million*

Compute research and development expense (**LO2**)

BE7–4 West Coast Growers incurs the following costs during the year related to the creation of a new disease-resistant tomato plant.

Salaries for R&D	$440,000
Depreciation on R&D facilities and equipment	135,000
Utilities incurred for the R&D facilities	6,000
Patent filing and related legal costs	22,000
Payment to another company for part of the development work	110,000

What amount should West Coast Growers report as research and development (R&D) expense in its income statement?

Account for expenditures after acquisition (**LO3**)

BE7–5 Hanoi Foods incurs the following expenditures during the current fiscal year: (1) annual maintenance on its machinery, $8,900; (2) remodeling of offices, $42,000; (3) improvement of the shipping and receiving area, resulting in an increase in productivity, $25,000; and (4) addition of a security system to the manufacturing facility, $35,000. How should Hanoi account for each of these expenditures?

BE7–6 Early in the fiscal year, The Beanery purchases a delivery vehicle for $40,000. At the end of the year, the machine has a fair value of $33,000. The company controller records depreciation expense of $7,000 for the year, the decline in the vehicle's value. Explain why the controller's approach to recording depreciation expense is not correct.

Explain depreciation (**LO4**)

BE7–7 El Tapitio purchased restaurant furniture on September 1, 2012, for $35,000. Residual value at the end of an estimated 10-year service life is expected to be $5,000. Calculate depreciation expense for 2012 and 2013, using the straight-line method, and assuming a December 31 year-end.

Calculate partial-year depreciation (**LO4**)

BE7–8 Hawaiian Specialty Foods purchased equipment for $20,000. Residual value at the end of an estimated four-year service life is expected to be $2,000. The machine operated for 2,200 hours in the first year, and the company expects the machine to operate for a total of 10,000 hours. Calculate depreciation expense for the first year using each of the following depreciation methods: (1) straight-line, (2) double-declining-balance, and (3) activity-based.

Calculate depreciation (**LO4**)

BE7–9 In early January, Burger Mania acquired 100% of the common stock of the Crispy Taco restaurant chain. The purchase price allocation included the following items: $4 million, patent; $3 million, trademark considered to have an indefinite useful life; and $5 million, goodwill. Burger Mania's policy is to amortize intangible assets with finite useful lives using the straight-line method, no residual value, and a five-year service life. What is the total amount of amortization expense that would appear in Burger Mania's income statement for the first year ended December 31 related to these items?

Calculate amortization expense (**LO5**)

BE7–10 Granite Stone Creamery sold ice cream equipment for $12,000. Granite Stone originally purchased the equipment for $80,000, and depreciation through the date of sale totaled $66,000. What was the gain or loss on the sale of the equipment?

Account for the sale of long-term assets (**LO6**)

BE7–11 China Inn and Midwest Chicken exchanged assets. China Inn received a delivery truck and gave equipment. The fair value and book value of the equipment were $17,000 and $10,000 (original cost of $35,000 less accumulated depreciation of $25,000), respectively. To equalize market values of the exchanged assets, China Inn paid $8,000 in cash to Midwest Chicken. At what amount did China Inn record the delivery truck? How much gain or loss did China Inn recognize on the exchange?

Account for the exchange of long-term assets (**LO6**)

Flip Side of BE7–12

BE7–12 China Inn and Midwest Chicken exchanged assets. Midwest Chicken received equipment and gave a delivery truck. The fair value and book value of the delivery truck given were $25,000 and $28,000 (original cost of $33,000 less accumulated depreciation of $5,000), respectively. To equalize market values of the exchanged assets, Midwest Chicken received $8,000 in cash from China Inn. At what amount did Midwest Chicken record the equipment? How much gain or loss did Midwest Chicken recognize on the exchange?

Account for the exchange of long-term assets (**LO6**)

Flip Side of BE7–11

BE7–13 The balance sheet of Cedar Crest Resort reports total assets of $740,000 and $940,000 at the beginning and end of the year, respectively. The return on assets for the year is 20%. Calculate Cedar Crest's net income for the year.

Use the return on assets ratio (**LO7**)

BE7–14 Vegetarian Delights has been experiencing declining market conditions for its specialty foods division. Management decided to test the operational assets of the division for possible impairment. The test revealed the following: book value of division's assets, $28.5 million; fair value of division's assets, $20 million; sum of estimated future cash flows generated from the division's assets, $30 million. What amount of impairment loss, if any, should Vegetarian Delights record?

Determine the impairment loss (**LO8**)

BE7–15 Refer to the situation described in BE 7–14. Assume the sum of estimated future cash flows is $26 million instead of $30 million. What amount of impairment loss should Vegetarian Delights record?

Determine the impairment loss (**LO8**)

EXERCISES

Record purchase of
land **(LO1)**

E7–1 McCoy's Fish House purchases a tract of land and an existing building for $900,000. The company plans to remove the old building and construct a new restaurant on the site. In addition to the purchase price, McCoy pays closing costs, including title insurance of $2,000. The company also pays $12,000 in property taxes, which includes $8,000 of back taxes (unpaid taxes from previous years) paid by McCoy on behalf of the seller and $4,000 due for the current fiscal year after the purchase date. Shortly after closing, the company pays a contractor $45,000 to tear down the old building and remove it from the site. McCoy is able to sell salvaged materials from the old building for $3,000 and pays an additional $10,000 to level the land.

Required:
Determine the amount McCoy's Fish House should record as the cost of the land.

Record purchase of
equipment **(LO1)**

E7–2 Orion Flour Mills purchased a new machine and made the following expenditures:

Purchase price	$65,000
Sales tax	5,500
Shipment of machine	900
Insurance on the machine for the first year	600
Installation of machine	1,800

The machine, including sales tax, was purchased on account, with payment due in 30 days. The other expenditures listed above were paid in cash.

Required:
Record the above expenditures for the new machine.

Allocate costs in a basket
purchase **(LO1)**

E7–3 Red Rock Bakery purchases land, building, and equipment for a single purchase price of $400,000. However, the estimated fair values of the land, building, and equipment are $150,000, $300,000, and $50,000, respectively, for a total estimated fair value of $500,000.

Required:
Determine the amounts Red Rock should record in the separate accounts for the land, the building, and the equipment.

Reporting intangible
assets **(LO2)**

E7–4 Brick Oven Corporation was organized early in 2012. The following expenditures were made during the first few months of the year:

Attorneys' fees to organize the corporation	$ 8,000
Purchase of a patent	30,000
Legal and other fees for transfer of the patent	2,000
Preopening employee salaries	70,000
Total	$110,000

Required:
Record the $110,000 in cash expenditures.

Determine acquisition
costs of land, equipment,
and patents **(LO1, 2)**

E7–5 Determine the response that best completes the following statements or questions.

1. On December 1, 2012, Bar S purchased a $500,000 tract of land for a factory site. Bar S removed an old building on the property and sold the materials it salvaged

from the demolition. Bar S incurred additional costs and realized salvage proceeds during December 2012 as follows:

Demolition of old building	$40,000
Legal fees for purchase contract and recording of ownership	13,000
Title guarantee insurance	8,000
Proceeds from sale of salvaged materials	3,000

In its December 31, 2012, balance sheet, Bar S should report a balance in the Land account of

a. $558,000.

b. $561,000.

c. $564,000.

d. $521,000.

2. On October 1, 2012, Manning Corp. purchased a machine for $126,000 that was placed in service on November 30, 2012. Manning incurred additional costs for this machine, as follows:

Shipping	$3,000
Installation	4,000
Testing	5,000

In Manning's December 31, 2012, balance sheet, the machine's cost should be reported as:

a. $126,000.

b. $129,000.

c. $133,000.

d. $138,000.

3. Hanner Corp. bought Patent A for $40,000 and Patent B for $60,000. Hanner also paid acquisition costs of $5,000 for Patent A and $7,000 for Patent B. Both patents were challenged in legal actions. Hanner paid $20,000 in legal fees for a successful defense of Patent A and $30,000 in legal fees for an unsuccessful defense of Patent B. Due to the unsuccessful defense, Patent B was taken off the books. What amount should Hanner capitalize for patents?

a. $162,000.

b. $ 65,000.

c. $112,000.

d. $ 45,000.

E7–6 On March 31, 2012, Mainline Produce Corporation acquired all the outstanding common stock of Iceberg Lettuce Corporation for $34,000,000 in cash. The book values and fair values of Iceberg's assets and liabilities were as follows:

Calculate the amount of goodwill **(LO2)**

	Book Value	Fair Value
Current assets	$12,000,000	$15,000,000
Property, plant, and equipment	22,000,000	28,000,000
Other assets	2,000,000	3,000,000
Current liabilities	8,000,000	8,000,000
Long-term liabilities	12,000,000	11,000,000

Required:

Calculate the amount paid for goodwill.

Record patent and
research and development
expense (LO2)

E7–7 In 2012, Satellite Systems modified its model Z2 satellite to incorporate a new communication device. The company made the following expenditures:

Basic research to develop the technology	$4,000,000
Engineering design work	1,360,000
Development of a prototype device	600,000
Testing and modification of the prototype	400,000
Legal fees for patent application	80,000
Legal fees for successful defense of the new patent	40,000
Total	$6,480,000

During your year-end review of the accounts related to intangibles, you discover that the company has capitalized all the above as costs of the patent. Management contends that the device represents an improvement of the existing communication system of the satellite and, therefore, should be capitalized.

Required:

1. Which of the above costs should Satellite Systems capitalize to the Patent account in the balance sheet?
2. Which of the above costs should Satellite Systems report as research and development expense in the income statement?
3. What are the basic criteria for determining whether to capitalize or expense intangible related costs?

Match terms used in the
chapter (LO2, 4)

E7–8 Listed below are several terms and phrases associated with operational assets. Pair each item from List A (by letter) with the item from List B that is most appropriately associated with it.

List A	List B
_f_ 1. Depreciation	a. Exclusive right to display a word, a symbol, or an emblem.
_e_ 2. Goodwill	
_g_ 3. Amortization	b. Exclusive right to benefit from a creative work.
_d_ 4. Natural resources	c. Assets that represent contractual rights.
_c_ 5. Intangible assets	d. Oil and gas deposits, timber tracts, and mineral deposits.
_b_ 6. Copyright	
_a_ 7. Trademark	e. Purchase price less fair value of net identifiable assets.
	f. The allocation of cost for plant and equipment.
	g. The allocation of cost for intangible assets.

Record expenditures after
acquisition (LO3)

E7–9 Sub Sandwiches of America made the following expenditures related to its restaurant:

1. Replaced the heating equipment at a cost of $250,000.
2. Covered the patio area with a clear plastic dome and enclosed it with glass for use during the winter months. The total cost of the project was $750,000.
3. Performed annual building maintenance at a cost of $24,000.
4. Paid for annual insurance for the facility at $8,800.
5. Built a new sign above the restaurant, putting the company name in bright neon lights, for $9,900.
6. Paved a gravel parking lot at a cost of $65,000.

Required:

Sub Sandwiches of America credits Cash for each of these expenditures. Indicate the account it debits for each.

Determine depreciation
for the first year under
three methods (LO4)

E7–10 Super Saver Groceries purchased store equipment for $21,000. Super Saver estimates that at the end of its 10-year service life, the equipment will be worth $1,000. During the 10-year period, the company expects to use the equipment for a total of 10,000 hours. Super Saver used the equipment for 1,500 hours the first year.

Required:

Calculate depreciation expense of the equipment for the first year, using each of the following methods. Round all amounts to the nearest dollar.

1. Straight-line.
2. Double-declining-balance.
3. Activity-based.

E7–11 Speedy Delivery Company purchases a delivery van for $28,000. Speedy estimates that at the end of its four-year service life, the van will be worth $4,000. During the four-year period, the company expects to drive the van 120,000 miles.

Determine depreciation under three methods (LO4)

Required:

Calculate annual depreciation for the four-year life of the van using each of the following methods. Round all amounts to the nearest dollar.

1. Straight-line.
2. Double-declining-balance.
3. Activity-based.

Actual miles driven each year were 33,000 miles in year 1; 36,000 miles in year 2; 28,000 miles in year 3; and 30,000 miles in year 4. Note that actual total miles of 127,000 exceed expectations by 7,000 miles.

E7–12 Togo's Sandwiches acquired equipment on April 1, 2012, for $13,000. The company estimates a residual value of $1,000 and a five-year service life.

Determine straight-line depreciation for partial periods (LO4)

Required:

Calculate depreciation expense using the straight-line method for 2012 and 2013, assuming a December 31 year-end.

E7–13 Tasty Subs acquired a delivery truck on October 1, 2012, for $16,500. The company estimates a residual value of $1,500 and a six-year service life.

Determine straight-line depreciation for partial periods (LO4)

Required:

Calculate depreciation expense using the straight-line method for 2012 and 2013, assuming a December 31 year-end.

E7–14 The Donut Stop acquired equipment for $25,000. The company uses straight-line depreciation and estimates a residual value of $5,000 and a four-year service life. At the end of the second year, the company estimates that the equipment will be useful for four additional years, for a total service life of six years rather than the original four. At the same time, the company also changed the estimated residual value to $3,000 from the original estimate of $5,000.

Determine depreciation expense for a change in depreciation estimate (LO4)

Required:

Calculate how much The Donut Stop should record each year for depreciation in years 3 to 6.

E7–15 Tasty Subs acquired a delivery truck on October 1, 2012, for $16,500. The company estimates a residual value of $1,500 and a six-year service life. It expects to drive the truck 100,000 miles. Actual mileage was 4,000 miles in 2012 and 17,000 miles in 2013.

Determine activity-based depreciation (LO4)

Required:

Calculate depreciation expense using the activity-based method for 2012 and 2013, assuming a December 31 year-end.

E7–16 On January 1, 2012, Weaver Corporation purchased a patent for $240,000. The remaining legal life is 20 years, but the company estimates the patent will be useful for only six more years. In January 2014, the company incurred legal fees of $60,000 in successfully defending a patent infringement suit. The successful defense did not change the company's estimate of useful life. Weaver Corporation's year-end is December 31.

Record amortization expense (LO5)

Required:

1. Record the purchase in 2012; amortization in 2012; amortization in 2013; legal fees in 2014; and amortization in 2014.
2. What is the balance in the Patent account at the end of 2014?

Record the sale of equipment (LO6)

E7–17 Abbott Landscaping purchased a tractor at a cost of $32,000 and sold it three years later for $16,000. Abbott recorded depreciation using the straight-line method, a five-year service life, and a $2,000 residual value. Tractors are included in the Equipment account.

Required:

1. Record the sale.
2. Assume the tractor was sold for $10,000 instead of $16,000. Record the sale.

Record an exchange of land (LO6)

E7–18 Salad Express exchanged land it had been holding for future plant expansion for a more suitable parcel of land along distribution routes. Salad Express reported the old land on the previously issued balance sheet at its original cost of $60,000. According to an independent appraisal, the old land currently is worth $112,000. Salad Express paid $14,000 in cash to complete the transaction.

Required:

1. What is the fair value of the new parcel of land received by Salad Express?
2. Record the exchange.

Calculate ratios (LO7)

E7–19 Under Armour, Inc., reported sales of $725,244 and net income of $38,229 in its 2008 income statement. Under Armour also reported total assets of $487,555 in its 2008 balance sheet and $390,613 in its 2007 balance sheet. All amounts are reported in thousands of dollars. (For example, "$725,244" indicates $725,244,000.)

Required:

Calculate the return on assets, the profit margin, and the asset turnover ratio for Under Armour in 2008.

Calculate impairment loss (LO8)

E7–20 Midwest Services, Inc., operates several restaurant chains throughout the Midwest. One restaurant chain has experienced sharply declining profits. The company's management has decided to test the operational assets of the restaurants for possible impairment. The relevant information for these assets is presented below.

Book value	$8.5 million
Estimated total future cash flows	7.5 million
Fair value	6.0 million

Required:

1. Determine the amount of the impairment loss, if any.
2. Repeat *Requirement* 1 assuming that the estimated total future cash flows are $9.5 million and the fair value is $8 million.

For additional exercises, visit www.mhhe.com/succeed for Exercises: Set B.

PROBLEMS: SET A

Determine the acquisition cost of land and building (LO1)

P7–1A Italian Bread Company purchased land as a factory site for $60,000. An old building on the property was demolished, and construction began on a new building. Costs incurred during the first year are listed on the next page:

Demolition of old building	$ 8,000
Sale of salvaged materials	(1,000)
Architect fees (for new building)	15,000
Legal fees (for title investigation of land)	2,000
Property taxes on the land (for the first year)	3,000
Building construction costs	500,000
Interest costs related to the construction	18,000

Required:

Determine the amounts that the company should record in the Land and the Building accounts.

P7–2A Great Harvest Bakery purchased bread ovens from New Morning Bakery. New Morning Bakery was closing its bakery business and sold its two-year-old ovens at a discount for $600,000. Great Harvest incurred and paid freight costs of $30,000, and its employees ran special electrical connections to the ovens at a cost of $4,000. Labor costs were $32,800. Unfortunately, one of the ovens was damaged during installation, and repairs cost $4,000. Great Harvest then consumed $800 of bread dough in testing the ovens. It installed safety guards on the ovens at a cost of $1,400 and placed the machines in operation.

Determine the acquisition cost of equipment (**LO1**)

Flip Side of P7–8A

Required:

1. Prepare a schedule showing the amount at which the ovens should be recorded in Great Harvest's Equipment account.
2. Indicate where any amounts not included in the Equipment account should be recorded.

P7–3A Fresh Cut Corporation purchased all the outstanding common stock of Premium Meats for $11,000,000 in cash. The book value of Premium Meats' net assets (assets minus liabilities) was $7,800,000. The book values and fair values of Premium Meats' assets and liabilities were:

Calculate and record goodwill (**LO2**)

	Book Value	Fair Value
Receivables	$1,300,000	$ 1,100,000
Property, plant, and equipment	8,000,000	9,400,000
Intangible assets	200,000	1,200,000
Liabilities	(1,700,000)	(1,700,000)
Net assets	$7,800,000	$10,000,000

Required:

1. Calculate the amount Fresh Cut paid for goodwill.
2. Record Fresh Cut's acquisition of Premium Meats.

P7–4A Several years ago, Health Services acquired a helicopter for use in emergency situations. Health Services incurred the following expenditures related to the helicopter delivery operations in 2012:   Captilized

Record expenditures after acquisition (**LO3**)

1. Overhauled the engine at a cost of $7,500. Health Services estimated the work would increase the service life for an additional five years.
2. Painted the Health Services company logo on the helicopter at a cost of $6,000.   Captilized
3. Added new emergency health equipment to the helicopter for $25,000.   Captilized.
4. Modified the helicopter to reduce cabin noise by installing new sound barrier technology at a cost of $15,000.   Captilized
5. Paid insurance on the helicopter for 2012, which increased 15% over the prior year to $9,000.   Current   expense   every year.
6. Performed annual maintenance and repairs at a cost of $39,000.   Expense   current

Required:

Indicate whether Health Services should capitalize or expense each of these expenditures. How could Health Services use expenditures like these to increase reported earnings?

Determine depreciation under three methods **(LO4)**

P7–5A University Car Wash built a deluxe car wash across the street from campus. The new machines cost $240,000 including installation. The company estimates that the equipment will have a residual value of $30,000. University Car Wash also estimates it will use the machine for six years or about 12,000 total hours.

Required:

Prepare a depreciation schedule for six years using the following methods:

1. Straight-line.
2. Double-declining-balance.
3. Activity-based.

Actual use per year was as follows:

Year	Hours Used
1	2,600
2	2,100
3	2,200
4	1,800
5	1,600
6	1,700

Record amortization and prepare the intangible assets section **(LO5)**

P7–6A The following information relates to the intangible assets of University Testing Services (UTS):

a. On January 1, 2012, UTS completed the purchase of Heinrich Corporation for $3,000,000 in cash. The fair value of the net identifiable assets of Heinrich was $2,700,000.

b. Included in the assets purchased from Heinrich was a patent valued at $90,000. The original legal life of the patent was 20 years; there are 12 years remaining, but UTS believes the patent will be useful for only eight more years.

c. UTS acquired a franchise on July 1, 2012, by paying an initial franchise fee of $350,000. The contractual life of the franchise is 10 years.

Required:

1. Record amortization expense for the intangible assets at December 31, 2012.
2. Prepare the intangible asset section of the December 31, 2012, balance sheet.

Compute depreciation, amortization, and book value of long-term assets **(LO4, 5)**

P7–7A Solich Sandwich Shop had the following long-term asset balances as of December 31, 2012:

	Cost	Accumulated Depreciation	Book Value
Land	$ 85,000	–	$ 85,000
Building	450,000	$(85,500)	364,500
Equipment	250,000	(48,000)	202,000
Patent	200,000	(80,000)	120,000

Solich purchased all the assets at the beginning of 2010 (3 years ago). The building is depreciated over a 20-year service life using the double-declining-balance method and estimating no residual value. The equipment is depreciated over a 10-year useful life using the straight-line method with an estimated residual value of $10,000. The patent is estimated to have a five-year service life with no residual value and is amortized using the straight-line method.

Required:

1. For the year ended December 31, 2012, record depreciation expense for buildings and equipment. Land is not depreciated.
2. For the year ended December 31, 2012, record amortization expense for the patent.
3. Calculate the book value for each of the four long-term assets at December 31, 2012.

P7–8A New Morning Bakery is in the process of closing its operations. It sold its two-year-old bakery ovens to Great Harvest Bakery for $600,000. The ovens originally cost $800,000, had an estimated service life of 10 years, and an estimated residual value of $50,000. New Morning Bakery uses the straight-line depreciation method for all equipment.

Record the disposal of equipment **(LO6)**

Required:

1. Calculate the balance in the Accumulated Depreciation account at the end of the second year.
2. Calculate the book value of the ovens at the end of the second year.
3. What is the gain or loss on the sale of the ovens at the end of the second year?
4. Record the sale of the ovens at the end of the second year.

Flip Side of P7–2A

P7–9A **Dell Corporation** and **Apple Inc.** reported the following information in their 2009 annual financial statements ($ in millions):

Calculate and interpret ratios **(LO7)**

Dell Corporation	2009	2008
Net sales	$61,101	$61,133
Net income	2,478	2,947
Total assets	26,500	27,561

Apple Inc.	2009	2008
Net sales	$36,537	$32,479
Net income	5,704	4,834
Total assets	53,581	39,572

Required:

1. Calculate Dell's return on assets, profit margin, and asset turnover ratio for 2009.
2. Calculate Apple's return on assets, profit margin, and asset turnover ratio for 2009.
3. Which company has the higher profit margin and which company has the higher asset turnover? Is this consistent with the primary business strategies of these two companies?

P7–10A University Hero is considering expanding operations beyond its healthy sandwiches. Jim Axelrod, vice president of marketing, would like to add a line of smoothies with a similar health emphasis. Each smoothie would include two free health supplements such as vitamins, antioxidants, and protein. Jim believes smoothie sales should help fill the slow mid-afternoon period. Adding the line of smoothies would require purchasing additional freezer space, machinery, and equipment. Jim provides the following projections of net sales, net income, and average total assets in support of his proposal.

Calculate and interpret ratios **(LO7)**

	Sandwiches Only	Sandwiches and Smoothies
Net sales	$800,000	$1,400,000
Net income	100,000	160,000
Average total assets	400,000	800,000

Required:

1. Calculate University Hero's return on assets, profit margin, and asset turnover for sandwiches only.
2. Calculate University Hero's return on assets, profit margin, and asset turnover for sandwiches and smoothies.
3. Based on these ratios, what recommendation would you make?

PROBLEMS: SET B

Determine the acquisition cost of land and building **(LO1)**

P7–1B Italian Pizza Company purchased land as a factory site for $80,000. Prior to construction of the new building, the land had to be cleared of trees and brush. Construction costs incurred during the first year are listed below:

Land clearing costs	$ 4,000
Sale of firewood to a worker	(500)
Architect fees (for new building)	20,000
Title investigation of land	2,500
Property taxes on land (for the first year)	2,000
Building construction costs	300,000

Required:

Determine the amounts that the company should record in the Land and the New Building accounts.

Determine the acquisition cost of equipment **(LO1)**

Flip Side of P7–8B

P7–2B Sicily Pizza purchased baking ovens from New World Deli. New World Deli was closing its bakery business and sold its three-year-old ovens for $300,000. In addition to the purchase price, Sicily Pizza paid shipping costs of $15,000. Employees of Sicily Pizza installed the ovens; labor costs were $16,000. An outside contractor performed some of the electrical work for $2,800. Sicily Pizza consumed pizza dough with a cost of $1,200 in testing the ovens. It then installed new timers on the ovens at a cost of $700 and placed the machines in operation.

Required:

1. Prepare a schedule showing the amount at which Sicily Pizza should record the ovens in the Equipment account.
2. Indicate where any amounts not included in the Equipment account should be recorded.

Calculate and record goodwill **(LO2)**

P7–3B Northern Equipment Corporation purchased all the outstanding common stock of Pioneer Equipment Rental for $5,500,000 in cash. The book value of Pioneer's net assets (assets minus liabilities) was $3,900,000. The book values and fair values of Pioneer's assets and liabilities were:

	Book Value	Fair Value
Receivables	$ 650,000	$ 550,000
Property, plant, and equipment	4,000,000	4,700,000
Intangible assets	100,000	600,000
Liabilities	(850,000)	(850,000)
Net assets	$3,900,000	$5,000,000

Required:

1. Calculate the amount paid for goodwill.
2. Record Northern Equipment's acquisition of Pioneer Equipment Rental.

Record expenditures after acquisition **(LO3)**

P7–4B Stillwater Youth Programs (SYP) purchased a used school bus to use in transporting children for its after-school program. SYP incurred the following expenses related to the bus in 2012:

1. Painted the SYP logo on the bus for $3,000 to help promote the after-school *Ca* program.
2. Installed new seats on the bus at a cost of $5,000. *Ca*
3. Installed a DVD player and sound system to entertain the children in-transit and announce upcoming events at a cost of $1,000. *Ca*
4. Paid insurance on the school bus for 2012, which increased 10% over the prior year to an annual premium of $2,800. *ex*
5. Performed annual maintenance and repairs for $1,400. *ex*
6. Overhauled the engine at a cost of $6,500, increasing the service life of the bus by an estimated three years. *Ca*

Required:

Indicate whether SYP should capitalize or expense each of these expenditures.
How could SYP use expenditures like these to increase reported earnings?

P7–5B Cheetah Copy purchased a new copy machine. The new machine cost $120,000 including installation. The company estimates the equipment will have a residual value of $30,000. Cheetah Copy also estimates it will use the machine for four years or about 8,000 total hours.

Determine depreciation under three methods (LO4)

Required:

Prepare a depreciation schedule for four years using the following methods:

1. Straight-line.
2. Double-declining-balance. (*Hint:* The asset will be depreciated in only two years.)
3. Activity-based.

Actual use per year was as follows:

Year	Hours Used
1	2,500
2	2,200
3	1,900
4	2,000

P7–6B The following information relates to the intangible assets of Lettuce Express:

Record amortization and prepare the intangible assets section (LO5)

a. On January 1, 2012, Lettuce Express completed the purchase of Farmers Produce, Inc., for $1,500,000 in cash. The fair value of the identifiable net assets of Farmers Produce was $1,350,000.
b. Included in the assets purchased from Farmers Produce was a patent for a method of processing lettuce valued at $45,000. The original legal life of the patent was 20 years. There are still 17 years left on the patent, but Lettuce Express estimates the patent will be useful for only 10 more years.
c. Lettuce Express acquired a franchise on July 1, 2012, by paying an initial franchise fee of $175,000. The contractual life of the franchise is seven years.

Required:

1. Record amortization expense for the intangible assets at December 31, 2012.
2. Prepare the intangible asset section of the December 31, 2012, balance sheet.

P7–7B Togo's Sandwich Shop had the following long-term asset balances as of January 1, 2012:

Compute depreciation, amortization, and book value of long-term assets (LO4, 5)

	Cost	Accumulated Depreciation	Book Value
Land	$ 75,000	–	$ 75,000
Building	550,000	$(104,500)	445,500
Equipment	150,000	(28,000)	122,000
Patent	100,000	(40,000)	60,000

Togo's purchased all the assets at the beginning of 2010 (3 years ago). The building is depreciated over a 20-year service life using the double-declining-balance method and estimating no residual value. The equipment is depreciated over a 10-year useful life using the straight-line method with an estimated residual value of $10,000. The patent is estimated to have a five-year service life with no residual value and is amortized using the straight-line method.

Required:

1. For the year ended December 31, 2012, record depreciation expense for buildings and equipment. Land is not depreciated.
2. For the year ended December 31, 2012, record amortization expense for the patent.
3. Calculate the book value for each of the four long-term assets at December 31, 2012.

Record the disposal of equipment (LO6)

Flip Side of P7–2B

P7–8B New Deli is in the process of closing its operations. It sold its three-year-old ovens to Sicily Pizza for $300,000. The ovens originally cost $400,000 and had an estimated service life of 10 years and an estimated residual value of $25,000. New Deli uses straight-line depreciation for all equipment.

Required:

1. Calculate the balance in the Accumulated Depreciation account at the end of the third year.
2. Calculate the book value of the ovens at the end of the third year.
3. What is the gain or loss on the sale of the ovens at the end of the third year?
4. Record the sale of the ovens at the end of the third year.

Calculate and interpret ratios (LO7)

P7–9B **Nike** is the market leader and **Under Armour** is an up-and-coming player in the highly competitive athletic apparel market. Reported below is selected financial information from their 2008 annual financial statements ($ in millions):

Nike Corporation	2008	2007
Net sales	$19,176.1	$18,627.0
Net income	1,486.7	1,883.4
Total assets	13,249.6	12,442.7

Under Armour	2008	2007
Net sales	$725.2	$606.6
Net income	38.2	52.6
Total assets	487.6	390.6

Required:

1. Calculate Nike's return on assets, profit margin, and asset turnover ratio for 2008.
2. Calculate Under Armour's return on assets, profit margin, and asset turnover ratio for 2008.
3. Which company has the higher profit margin and which company has the higher asset turnover?

Calculate and interpret ratios (LO7)

P7–10B Barry Sanders, likely the best running back to ever play football, has opened a successful used-car dealership. He has noted a higher than normal percentage of sales for trucks and SUVs with hauling capacity at his dealership. He is also aware that several of the best recreational lakes in the state are located nearby. Barry is considering expanding his dealership to include the sale of recreational boats. Barry provides the following projections of net sales, net income, and average total assets in support of his proposal.

	Cars Only	Cars and Boats
Net sales	$6,400,000	$7,600,000
Net income	400,000	600,000
Average total assets	1,600,000	1,800,000

Required:

1. Calculate Barry's return on assets, profit margin, and asset turnover for cars only.
2. Calculate Barry's return on assets, profit margin, and asset turnover for cars and boats.
3. Based on these ratios, what recommendation would you make?

*For additional problems, visit **www.mhhe.com/succeed** for Problems: Set C.*

ADDITIONAL PERSPECTIVES

Great Adventures

(This is a continuation of the Great Adventures problem from earlier chapters.)

Continuing Problem

AP7–1 Tony and Suzie see the need for a rugged all-terrain vehicle to transport participants and supplies. They would love to buy a Hummer, but it is just too expensive and too small for their needs, so they settle on a used Suburban. The cost of the Suburban is $12,000. The vehicle is purchased in late June and will be put into use on July 1, 2013. Annual insurance from **GEICO** runs $1,800 per year. The paint is starting to fade, so they spend an extra $3,000 to repaint the vehicle, placing the Great Adventures logo on the front hood, back, and both sides. An additional $2,000 is spent on a deluxe roof rack and a trailer hitch. They expect to use the Suburban for five years and then sell the vehicle for $4,500.

Required:

1. Determine the amount that should be recorded for the new vehicle.
2. Indicate where any amounts not included in the Equipment account should be recorded.
3. Prepare a depreciation schedule using the straight-line method. Follow the example in Illustration 7–11, except the first and last years will have a half-year of depreciation to reflect the beginning of its service life on July 1, 2013.
4. Record the sale of the vehicle two years later on July 1, 2015, for $10,000.

American Eagle Outfitters, Inc.

Financial Analysis

AP7–2 Financial information for **American Eagle** is presented in Appendix A at the end of the book.

Required:

1. The summary of significant accounting polices is located in footnote 2 to the financial statements. Locate the section on property and equipment. What depreciation method does American Eagle use? What are the estimated useful lives for buildings, leasehold improvements, and fixtures and equipment?
2. Find footnote 7 entitled Property and Equipment. What are the cost and the book value of property and equipment? What is the trend in depreciation expense for the past three years?
3. Find footnote 9 entitled Leases. Retail stores, like American Eagle, tend to lease rather than buy their stores. What is the most common term for the store leases? What are the future minimum lease obligations under operating leases at January 30, 2010?

Financial Analysis

The Buckle, Inc.

AP7–3 Financial information for **The Buckle** is presented in Appendix B at the end of the book.

Required:

1. The summary of significant accounting polices is located in footnote A to the financial statements. Locate the section on property and equipment. What depreciation method does The Buckle use? What are the estimated useful lives for buildings, leasehold improvements, and property and equipment?
2. Find footnote D entitled Property and Equipment. What is the cost of property and equipment? What is the trend in property and equipment for the past two years?
3. Find footnote H entitled Commitments. Retail stores, like The Buckle, tend to lease rather than buy their stores. What is the most common term for the leases? What are the future minimum rental commitments under operating leases at February 6, 2010?

Comparative Analysis

American Eagle Outfitters, Inc., vs. The Buckle, Inc.

AP7–4 Financial information for **American Eagle** is presented in Appendix A at the end of the book, and financial information for **The Buckle** is presented in Appendix B at the end of the book.

Required:

1. Calculate American Eagle's return on assets, profit margin, and asset turnover ratio.
2. Calculate The Buckle's return on assets, profit margin, and asset turnover ratio.
3. Which company is doing better based on return on assets? Which company has the higher profit margin? Which company has the higher asset turnover?

Ethics

AP7–5 Companies often are under pressure to meet or beat Wall Street earnings projections in order to increase stock prices and also to increase the value of stock options. Some resort to earnings management practices to artificially create desired results.

Required:

1. How can a company increase earnings by changing its depreciation method?
2. How can a company increase earnings by changing the estimated service lives of depreciable assets?
3. How can a company increase earnings by changing the estimated residual value of depreciable assets?

Internet Research

AP7–6 Companies are increasingly making their accounting information, especially their annual reports, available through their websites. Select a well-known publicly traded company and go to its website. Look for the investment section, and then click on annual reports. Select the most recent annual report. If you have difficulty, try another company. Answer the following questions based on the company's most recent annual report.

Required:

1. What is the official name of the company?
2. What is its fiscal year-end?
3. At the end of the year, what is the net balance in property, plant, and equipment? (*Hint: Requirements* 3 and 4 are reported in the balance sheet.)

4. Does the company have any intangible assets? If so, how much is reported for intangible assets?
5. What is the balance in accumulated depreciation? (*Hint:* This is either in the balance sheet or in a note about property, plant, and equipment.)
6. Which method of depreciation is used? (*Hint:* It's usually disclosed in the notes under summary of accounting policies.)

Written Communication

AP7–7 At a recent luncheon, you were seated next to Mr. Fogle, the president of a local company that manufactures food processors. He heard that you were in a financial accounting class and asked:

> Why is it that I'm forced to record depreciation expense on my property when I could sell it for more than I originally paid? I thought that the purpose of the balance sheet is to reflect the value of my business and that the purpose of the income statement is to report the net change in value or wealth of a company. It just doesn't make sense to penalize my profits when the building hasn't lost any value.

At the conclusion of the luncheon, you promised to send him a short explanation of the rationale for current depreciation practices.

Required:

Prepare a memo to Mr. Fogle. Explain the accounting concept of depreciation and contrast this with the dictionary definition of depreciation.

Earnings Management

AP7–8 Edward L. Vincent is CFO of Energy Resources, Inc. The company specializes in the exploration and development of natural gas. It's near year-end, and Edward is feeling terrific. Natural gas prices have risen throughout the year, and Energy Resources is set to report record-breaking performance that will greatly exceed analysts' expectations. However, during an executive meeting this morning, management agreed to "tone down" profits due to concerns that reporting excess profits could encourage additional government regulations in the industry, hindering future profitability.

Edward decides to adjust the estimated service life of development equipment from 10 years to six years. He also plans to adjust estimated residual values on development equipment to zero as it is nearly impossible to accurately estimate residual values on equipment like this anyway.

Required:

1. Explain how the adjustment of estimated service life from 10 years to six years will affect depreciation expense and net income.
2. Explain how the adjustment of estimated residual values to zero will affect depreciation expense and net income.
3. In addition to heading off additional government regulations, why might Energy Resources have an incentive to report lower profits in the current period?

Answers to the Self-Study Questions
1. b   2. d   3. d   4. a   5. b   6. b   7. d   8. c   9. c   10. c

8

Current Liabilities

Learning Objectives

AFTER STUDYING THIS CHAPTER, YOU SHOULD BE ABLE TO:

- ■ **LO1** Distinguish between current and long-term liabilities.
- ■ **LO2** Account for notes payable and interest expense.
- ■ **LO3** Account for employee and employer payroll liabilities.
- ■ **LO4** Demonstrate the accounting for other current liabilities.
- ■ **LO5** Apply the appropriate accounting treatment for contingencies.

Analysis

- ■ **LO6** Assess liquidity using current liability ratios.

UNITED AIRLINES: A FUTURE UP IN THE AIR

Have you ever considered buying stock in an airline? Do you think companies like **American**, **Delta**, or **United** would be a good investment? Think again. Warren Buffett, a self-made billionaire based in Omaha, Nebraska, is regarded as one of the world's top investors. In 1991 he observed that the airline industry had not made a dime for investors in a century of manned flight. Buffett acknowledged his mistake in buying stock in **US Airways**, which later filed for Chapter 11 bankruptcy along with Delta, **Northwest**, United, and others.

Companies must file for bankruptcy protection when they no longer are able to pay their liabilities as they become due. By carefully examining information in financial statements, investors and creditors can assess a company's profitability and its *liquidity*—its ability to pay currently maturing debt. Both profitability and liquidity help indicate a company's risk of filing for bankruptcy. Wise investors, like Warren Buffett, pay careful attention to these warning signs.

What are some of the current liabilities reported by companies in the airline industry? The airline industry is very labor-intensive, resulting in extensive payroll liabilities. Another substantial current liability for airlines is advance ticket sales. This liability, representing tickets sold for future flights, is in the billions of dollars for several major U.S. airlines. Airlines are well known for their frequent-flier programs. These programs have created liabilities for frequent-flier incentives exceeding $100 million. Finally, a somewhat different type of liability airlines face is contingent liabilities. A *contingent liability* is a possible liability for which payment is contingent upon another event. An example is pending litigation. All of the major airlines report contingent liabilities related to unsettled litigation.

With airlines incurring so many types of liabilities, it is no wonder many airlines have filed for bankruptcy. However, there is one shining star among companies in the airline industry—**Southwest Airlines**. Known as the airline where your "bags fly free," it is recognized in the investment community for its strong financial performance. At the end of the chapter, we compare liquidity ratios between United Airlines and Southwest Airlines, to explore whether the financial reputation of Southwest Airlines is for real.

■ **LO1**
Distinguish between current and long-term liabilities.

CURRENT LIABILITIES

In the four preceding chapters, we worked our way down the asset side of the balance sheet, examining cash, accounts receivable, inventory, and long-term assets. We now turn to the liabilities side of the balance sheet. In the next three chapters, we discuss how companies finance their operations through borrowing (liabilities) or additional investment by owners (stockholders' equity). Chapter 8 focuses on current liabilities and Chapter 9 on long-term liabilities. In Chapter 10, we look at stockholders' equity.

Liabilities have three essential characteristics. Liabilities are: (1) probable *future* sacrifices of economic benefits, (2) arising from *present* obligations to other entities, (3) resulting from *past* transactions or events.[1] The definition of liabilities touches on the present, the future, and the past: A **liability** is a present responsibility to sacrifice assets in the future due to a transaction or other event that happened in the past.

Recall that assets represent probable future *benefits.* In contrast, liabilities represent probable future *sacrifices* of benefits. What benefits are sacrificed? Most liabilities require the future sacrifice of cash. For instance, accounts payable, notes payable, and salaries payable usually are paid in cash.

Can you think of a liability that requires paying something other than cash? One such liability is unearned revenue. Remember (from Chapter 3) that this liability arises when a company receives payment in advance of providing the product or service it's selling. This obligation requires giving up inventory or services rather than cash to satisfy the debt.

Current vs. Long-Term Classification

In a classified balance sheet, we categorize liabilities as either current or long-term. **In most cases, current liabilities are payable within one year, and long-term liabilities are payable more than one year from now.**

Common Terms Current liabilities are also sometimes called *short-term liabilities.*

COMMON MISTAKE

Current liabilities are *usually,* but not always, due within one year. But for some companies (a winery, for example), it takes longer than a year to perform the activities that produce revenue. We call the time it takes to produce revenue—from "cash to cash" as the saying goes (i.e., initial investment to revenue)—the *operating cycle.* If a company has an operating cycle longer than one year, its current liabilities are defined by the operating cycle rather than by the length of a year. For now, remember that in most cases (but not all) current liabilities are due within one year.

Distinguishing between current and long-term liabilities is important in helping investors and creditors assess risk. Given a choice, most companies would prefer to report a liability as long-term rather than current, because doing so may cause the firm to appear less risky. In turn, less-risky firms may enjoy lower interest rates on borrowing and command higher stock prices for new stock listings.

The Feature Story at the beginning of this chapter pointed out that the U.S. airline industry has experienced financial difficulties in recent years, resulting in greater risk to investors. Several major airlines have been forced into bankruptcy because they were unable to pay current liabilities as they became due. In Illustration 8–1 an excerpt from the annual report of **United Airlines** discusses the problem.

---

[1]"Elements of Financial Statements." 1985. *Statement of Financial Accounting Concepts No. 6* (Stamford, Conn.: FASB), par. 38.

ILLUSTRATION 8–1
Bankruptcy of United
Airlines

UNITED AIRLINES
Management Discussion and Analysis (excerpt)

Over the past several years, United and indeed the entire airline industry have faced severe business challenges and fundamental industry changes which have produced material adverse impacts on earnings, financial position and liquidity. The Company had been operating under Chapter 11 bankruptcy protection since December 9, 2002, and emerged on February 1, 2006.

Operating revenues for the airline industry in general, as well as for United, have been adversely impacted by several factors. The growth of low cost carriers; excess seat capacity; pricing transparency; reduced demand for high-yield business travel; global events such as the war in Iraq, the outbreak of disease as well as the fear of terrorist attacks since September 11, 2001; and the enactment of federal taxes on ticket sales to fund additional airport security measures, have caused earnings to decline.

What obligations do firms most frequently report as current liabilities? Notes payable, accounts payable, and payroll liabilities are three main categories. In addition, companies report a variety of other current liabilities, including unearned revenue, sales tax payable, and the current portion of long-term debt.

There is no prescribed order for presenting accounts within the current liabilities section of the balance sheet. However, many companies list notes payable first, followed by accounts payable, and then other current liabilities from largest to smallest. *Follow this order when preparing your homework assignments.* In keeping with this order, we discuss notes payable in the next section.

 KEY POINT

In most cases, current liabilities are payable within one year, and long-term liabilities are payable more than one year from now.

Notes Payable

In Chapter 5, we saw how companies account for notes receivable. Here, we discuss the flip side of notes receivable—notes payable. Recall that notes receivable is an asset that creates interest revenue. In contrast, notes payable is a *liability* that creates interest *expense*.

Very often, small firms are unable to tap into the major sources of long-term financing (such as bonds) to the extent necessary to provide for their capital needs, so they must rely heavily on short-term financing. When a company borrows cash from a bank, the bank requires the firm to sign a note promising to repay the amount borrowed plus interest. The borrower reports its liability as **notes payable**. About two-thirds of bank loans are short-term. Even large companies use short-term debt as a significant part of their capital structure. A major reason is that short-term funds usually offer lower interest rates than long-term debt.

Assume **Southwest Airlines** borrows $100,000 from **Bank of America** on September 1, 2012, signing a 6%, six-month note for the amount borrowed plus accrued interest due six months later on March 1, 2013. On September 1, 2012, Southwest will receive $100,000 in cash and record the following:

■ **LO2**
Account for notes payable and interest expense.

September 1, 2012	Debit	Credit
Cash	100,000	
Notes Payable		100,000
(*Issue notes payable*)		

A	=	L	+	SE
+100,000				
		+100,000		

When a company borrows money, it pays the lender **interest** in return for using the lender's money during the term of the loan. Interest is stated in terms of an annual percentage rate to be applied to the face value of the loan. Because the stated interest rate is an *annual* rate, when calculating interest for a current note payable we must adjust for the fraction of the annual period the loan spans. We calculate interest on notes as:

$$\textbf{Interest} = \textbf{Face value} \times \frac{\textbf{Annual}}{\textbf{interest rate}} \times \frac{\textbf{Fraction}}{\textbf{of the year}}$$

In the example above, how much interest cost does Southwest incur for the six-month period of the note from September 1, 2012, to March 1, 2013?

$$\$3,000 = \$100,000 \times 6\% \times 6/12$$

However, if Southwest's reporting period ends on December 31, 2012, the company can't wait until March 1, 2013, to record interest. Instead, the company records the four months' interest incurred during 2012 in an adjustment prior to preparing the 2012 financial statements. Since the firm will not pay the 2012 interest until the note becomes due (March 1, 2013), it records the $2,000 interest as **interest payable,** as follows:

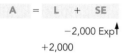

December 31, 2012	Debit	Credit
Interest Expense (= $100,000 × 6% × 4/12)	2,000	
Interest Payable		2,000
(*Record interest incurred, but not paid*)		

−2,000 Exp↑
+2,000

 COMMON MISTAKE

When calculating the number of months of interest, students sometimes mistakenly subtract December (month 12) from September (month 9) and get three months. However, the time from September 1 to December 31 includes both September and December, so there are four months. If you are ever in doubt, count out the months on your fingers. Your fingers never lie.

The purpose of the adjusting entry is to report four months' interest (September, October, November, and December) in 2012. Southwest will report the remaining $1,000 of interest (for January and February) in 2013. Since the firm won't actually pay the 2012 interest until March 1, 2013, its financial statements for the year ended December 31, 2012, will show interest payable of $2,000 along with notes payable of $100,000 as a current liability on the balance sheet, and the "other expenses" section of the income statement will report interest expense of $2,000.

When the note comes due on March 1, 2013, Southwest Airlines will pay the face value of the loan ($100,000) plus the entire $3,000 interest incurred ($100,000 × 6% × 6/12). The $3,000 represents six months of interest—the four months of interest ($2,000) in 2012 previously recorded as interest payable and two months of interest ($1,000) in 2013. Southwest records these transactions on March 1, 2013, as follows:

A = L + SE
−100,000
−1,000 Exp↑
−2,000
−103,000

March 1, 2013	Debit	Credit
Notes Payable (face value)	100,000	
Interest Expense (= $100,000 × 6% × 2/12)	1,000	
Interest Payable (= $100,000 × 6% × 4/12)	2,000	
Cash		103,000
(*Pay notes payable and interest*)		

The entry on March 1 does the following:

- Removes the note payable ($100,000).
- Records interest expense for January and February 2013 ($1,000).
- Removes the interest payable recorded in the December 31, 2012, entry ($2,000).
- Reduces cash ($103,000).

Notice that we record interest expense incurred for four months in 2012 and two months in 2013, rather than recording all six months' interest expense in 2013 when we pay it. This is consistent with the matching principle.

KEY POINT

We record interest expense in the period in which we *incur* it, rather than in the period in which we pay it.

How would the lender, Bank of America, record this note? For the bank it's a **note receivable** rather than a note payable, and it generates **interest revenue** rather than interest expense. (You may want to review the discussion on notes receivable in Chapter 5.) The entries for Bank of America's loan are as follows:

Flip Side

September 1, 2012	Debit	Credit		A	=	L	+	SE
Notes Receivable	100,000			+100,000				
Cash		100,000		−100,000				
(Issue notes receivable)								

December 31, 2012	Debit	Credit		A	=	L	+	SE
Interest Receivable	2,000			+2,000				
Interest Revenue (= $100,000 × 6% × 4/12)		2,000						+2,000 Rev↑
(Record interest earned, but not received)								

March 1, 2013	Debit	Credit		A	=	L	+	SE
Cash	103,000			+103,000				
Interest Revenue (= $100,000 × 6% × 2/12)		1,000						+1,000 Rev↑
Interest Receivable (= $100,000 × 6% × 4/12)		2,000		−2,000				
Notes Receivable (face value)		100,000		−100,000				
(Collect notes receivable and interest)								

Let's Review

Assume **Delta Airlines** borrows $500,000 from **Chase Bank** on November 1, 2012, signing a 9%, six-month note payable.

Required:

1. Record the issuance of the note payable.
2. Record the adjustment for the note payable on December 31, 2012.
3. Record the payment of the note payable at maturity.

Solution:

1. Issuance of note payable:

November 1, 2012	Debit	Credit
Cash	**500,000**	
Notes Payable		**500,000**
(*Issue note payable*)		

2. Adjustment for interest expense at the end of the period:

December 31, 2012	Debit	Credit
Interest Expense (= $500,000 \times 9\% \times 2/12$)	**7,500**	
Interest Payable		**7,500**
(*Record interest incurred, but not paid*)		

3. Payment of note at maturity:

Suggested Homework:
BE8-1, BE8-2;
E8-2, E8-3;
P8-2A&B

May 1, 2013	Debit	Credit
Notes Payable	**500,000**	
Interest Expense (= $500,000 \times 9\% \times 4/12$)	**15,000**	
Interest Payable (= $500,000 \times 9\% \times 2/12$)	**7,500**	
Cash		**522,500**
(*Pay note payable and interest*)		

Rather than wait until borrowing becomes necessary, many companies pre-arrange the terms of a note payable by establishing a line of credit with a bank. A line of credit is an informal agreement that permits a company to borrow up to a prearranged limit without having to follow formal loan procedures and prepare paperwork. The line of credit works like a note payable except the company is able to borrow without having to go through a formal loan approval process each time it borrows money. Banks sometimes require the company to maintain a cash balance on deposit with the bank, say, 5% of the line of credit. The recording for a line of credit is exactly the same as the recording for notes payable described earlier.

Decision Point

Question ?	Accounting information 📄	Analysis 🔍
How can you tell the amount and interest rate of a company's line of credit?	Notes to the financial statements	Companies are required to disclose the terms of available lines of credit such as the amounts, maturity dates, and interest rates.

If a company borrows from another company rather than from a bank, the note is referred to as commercial paper. Commercial paper is sold with maturities ranging from 30 to 270 days. (Beyond 270 days, the issuing firm is required to file a registration statement with the SEC.) Since a company is borrowing directly from another company, the interest rate on commercial paper is usually lower than on a bank loan. Commercial paper has thus become an increasingly popular way for large companies to raise funds, so much so that the total dollar value of commercial paper loans outstanding has multiplied five times in the last decade.

KEY POINT

Many short-term loans are arranged under an existing line of credit with a bank, or for larger corporations in the form of commercial paper, a loan from one company to another.

Accounts Payable

Accounts payable, sometimes called *trade accounts payable*, are amounts the company owes to suppliers of merchandise or services that it has bought on credit. We discussed accounting for this very common form of current liability when we discussed inventory purchases in Chapter 6. Briefly, recall that when a company purchases items on account (if it does not pay immediately with cash), it increases a liability called Accounts Payable. Later, when the company pays the amount owed, it decreases both Cash and Accounts Payable.

Payroll Liabilities

Many companies, including those in the airline industry, are very labor-intensive. Payroll liabilities make up a significant portion of current liabilities for these companies. Here, we will look at how payroll is calculated for both the employee and the employer.

■ **LO3**
Account for employee and employer payroll liabilities.

Let's assume you are hired at a $60,000 annual salary with salary payments of $5,000 per month. Before you make any spending plans, though, you need to realize that your payroll check will be much *less* than $5,000 a month. Before depositing your monthly payroll check in your bank account, your employer will "withhold" amounts for (1) federal and state income taxes; (2) Social Security and Medicare; (3) health, dental, disability, and life insurance premiums; and (4) *employee* investments to retirement or savings plans. Realistically, then, your $5,000 monthly salary translates to less than $4,000 in actual take-home pay.

Now assume you are an employer. You hire an employee at a starting annual salary of $60,000. Your costs for this employee will be much *more* than $5,000 per month. Besides the $5,000 monthly salary, you will incur significant costs for (1) federal and state unemployment taxes; (2) the *employer* portion of Social Security and Medicare; (3) *employer* contributions for health, dental, disability, and life insurance; and (4) *employer* contributions to retirement or savings plans. With these additional costs, a $5,000 monthly salary could very easily create total costs in excess of $6,000 per month. Illustration 8–2 summarizes payroll costs for employees and employers. We discuss these costs below.

Employee Payroll Costs	Employer Payroll Costs
Federal and state income taxes	Federal and state unemployment taxes
Employee portion of Social Security and Medicare	Employer matching portion of Social Security and Medicare
Employee contributions for health, dental, disability, and life insurance	Employer contributions for health, dental, disability, and life insurance
Employee investments in retirement or savings plans	Employer contributions to retirement or savings plans

ILLUSTRATION 8–2

Payroll Costs for Employees and Employers

EMPLOYEE COSTS

Employers are required by law to withhold federal and state income taxes from employees' paychecks and remit these taxes to the government. The amount withheld varies according to the amount the employee earns and the number of exemptions

CAREER CORNER

When comparing compensation among different career opportunities, don't base your final decision on salary alone. Fringe benefits can sometimes make up for a lower annual salary. Various employers offer *fringe benefits*—also called "perquisites," or "perks"—that catch the attention of would-be employees: a pound of coffee every month at Starbucks, free skiing for employees at Vail Ski Resort, or scuba and kayaking in the pool at Nike's Athletic Village in Beaverton, Oregon. More common fringe benefits, and ones that many people appreciate in the long run, include employer coverage of family health insurance, educational benefits, and contributions to retirement plans.

However, remember that even more important than either salary *or* benefits are the training and experience the position offers. Training and experience can provide you with the skills necessary to land that big promotion or dream job in the future.

the employee claims. The IRS furnishes tax tables that assist in determining the amount withheld. If you are able to claim more exemptions, you will have less tax withheld from your paycheck. Not all states require the payment of personal income taxes: Alaska, Florida, Nevada, South Dakota, Texas, Washington, and Wyoming have no state income tax. Two others, New Hampshire and Tennessee, tax only dividend and interest income.

Employers also withhold Social Security and Medicare taxes from employees' paychecks. Collectively, Social Security and Medicare taxes are referred to as **FICA taxes**, named for the Federal Insurance Contribution Act (FICA). This act requires employers to withhold a 6.2% Social Security tax up to a maximum base amount plus a 1.45% Medicare tax with no maximum. Therefore, the total FICA tax is 7.65% (6.2% + 1.45%) on income up to a base amount ($106,800 in 2010) and 1.45% on all income above the base amount. For example, if you earn less than $106,800, you will have 7.65% withheld from your check all year. However, if you earn, let's say, $156,800, you would have 7.65% withheld for FICA on the first $106,800 of your annual salary and then only 1.45% withheld on the remaining $50,000 earned during the rest of the year.

Besides the required deductions for income tax and FICA taxes, employees may opt to have additional amounts withheld from their paychecks. These might include the employee portion of insurance premiums, employee investments in retirement or savings plans, and contributions to charitable organizations such as **United Way**. The employer records the amounts deducted from employee payroll as liabilities until it pays them to the appropriate organizations.

EMPLOYER COSTS

By law, the employer pays an additional (matching) FICA tax on behalf of the employee. The employer's limits on FICA tax are the same as the employee's. Thus, the government actually collects 15.3% (7.65% employee + 7.65% employer) on each employee's salary.

In addition to FICA, the employer also must pay federal and state **unemployment taxes** on behalf of its employees. The *Federal Unemployment Tax Act* (FUTA) requires a tax of 6.2% on the first $7,000 earned by each employee. This amount is reduced by a 5.4% (maximum) credit for contributions to state unemployment programs, so the net federal rate often is 0.8%. Under the *State Unemployment Tax Act* (SUTA), in many states the maximum state unemployment tax rate is 5.4%, but many companies pay a lower rate based on past employment history.

 COMMON MISTAKE

Many people think FICA taxes are paid only by the employee. The employer is required to match the amount withheld for each employee, effectively doubling the amount paid into Social Security.

Additional employee benefits paid for by the employer are referred to as **fringe** 部分
benefits. Employers often pay all or part of employees' insurance premiums and make contributions to retirement or savings plans. Many companies provide additional fringe benefits specific to the company or the industry, as discussed in the nearby Career Corner. For instance, an important additional fringe benefit in the airline industry is the ability for the employee and family to fly free.

To understand how employee and employer payroll costs are recorded, assume that Hawaiian Travel Agency has a total payroll for the month of January of $100,000 for its 20 employees. Its withholdings and payroll taxes are shown in Illustration 8–3.

Federal and state income tax withheld	$24,000	
Health insurance premiums (Blue Cross) paid by employer	5,000	
Contribution to retirement plan (Fidelity) paid by employer	10,000	
FICA tax rate (Social Security and Medicare)	7.65%	
Federal and state unemployment tax rate	6.2%	

ILLUSTRATION 8–3

Payroll Example, Hawaiian Travel Agency

Hawaiian Travel Agency records the *employee* salary expense, withholdings, and salaries payable on January 31 as follows:

January 31	Debit	Credit		A	=	L	+	SE
Salaries Expense	100,000							−100,000 Exp
Income Tax Payable		24,000				+24,000		
FICA Tax Payable (= 0.0765 × $100,000)		7,650				+7,650		
Salaries Payable (to balance)		68,350				+68,350		
(*Record employee salary expense and withholdings*)								

Hawaiian Travel Agency records its employer-provided fringe benefits as follows:

January 31	Debit	Credit		A	=	L	+	SE
Salaries Expense (fringe benefits)	15,000							−15,000 Exp
Accounts Payable (to Blue Cross)		5,000				+5,000		
Accounts Payable (to Fidelity)		10,000				+10,000		
(*Record employer-provided fringe benefits*)								

Hawaiian Travel Agency pays employer's FICA taxes at the same rate that the employees pay (7.65%) and also pays unemployment taxes at the rate of 6.2%. The agency records its *employer's* payroll taxes as follows:

January 31	Debit	Credit		A	=	L	+	SE
Payroll Tax Expense (total)	13,850							−13,850 Exp
FICA Tax Payable (= 0.0765 × $100,000)		7,650				+7,650		
Unemployment Tax Payable (= 0.062 × $100,000)		6,200				+6,200		
(*Record employer payroll taxes*)								

Hawaiian Travel Agency incurred an additional $28,850 in expenses ($15,000 for fringe benefits plus $13,850 for employer payroll taxes) beyond the $100,000 salary expense. Also notice that the FICA tax payable in the *employee* withholding is the same amount recorded for *employer* payroll tax. That's because the employee

pays 7.65% and the employer matches this amount with an additional 7.65%. The amounts withheld are then transferred at regular intervals, monthly or quarterly, to their designated recipients. Income taxes, FICA taxes, and unemployment taxes are transferred to various government agencies, and fringe benefits are paid to the company's contractual suppliers.

 KEY POINT

Employee salaries are reduced by withholdings for federal and state income taxes, FICA taxes, and the employee portion of insurance and retirement contributions. The employer, too, incurs additional payroll expenses for unemployment taxes, the employer portion of FICA taxes, and employer insurance and retirement contributions.

Other Current Liabilities

■ LO4
Demonstrate the accounting for other current liabilities.

Additional current liabilities companies might report include unearned revenues, sales tax payable, the current portion of long-term debt, and deferred taxes. We explore each of these in more detail below.

UNEARNED REVENUES

United Airlines sells tickets and collects the cash price several days, weeks, or sometimes months before the actual flight. When does United Airlines record the revenue—when it sells the ticket, or when the flight actually takes place? Illustration 8–4 provides the answer, in United's disclosure of its revenue recognition policies.

ILLUSTRATION 8–4
Revenue Recognition Policy of United Airlines

> **UNITED AIRLINES**
> **Notes to the Financial Statements (excerpt)**
>
> *Airline Revenues*—We record passenger fares and cargo revenues as operating revenues when the transportation is provided. The value of unused passenger tickets is included in current liabilities as advance ticket sales. We periodically evaluate the balance in advance ticket sales and record any adjustments in the period the evaluation is completed.

As you can see, United waits until the actual flight occurs to record the revenues. Since the flights have not taken place, the airline has not yet earned the revenue.

United's situation is not unique. It's not uncommon for companies to require advance payments from customers that will be applied to the purchase price when they deliver goods or provide services. You've likely been one of these customers. Examples of advance payments are gift cards from clothing stores like **American Eagle** or restaurants like **Chili's**, movie tickets from **Fandango**, room deposits at hotels like **Embassy Suites**, and subscriptions for magazines like *Sports Illustrated*.

How do these companies account for the cash they receive in advance? We initially discussed unearned revenue in Chapter 3, but let's review with an example. Assume **Apple Inc.** sells an iTunes gift card to a customer for $100. Apple records the sale of the gift card as follows:

A	=	L	+	SE		Debit	Credit
+100					**Cash**	**100**	
		+100			**Unearned Revenue**		**100**
					(*Receive cash for gift card*)		

As you can see, Apple Inc. records the receipt of cash, but does not credit Sales Revenue. Rather, since the iTunes have not been downloaded yet, the company credits Unearned Revenue, a liability account. While it may seem unusual for an account called Unearned Revenue to be a liability, think of it this way: Having already collected the cash, the company now has the obligation to earn it.

When the customer purchases and downloads, say, $15 worth of music, Apple records the following:

	Debit	Credit
Unearned Revenue	15	
Sales Revenue		15
(Earn revenue from music downloaded)		

A	=	L	+	SE
		−15		
				+15 Rev↑

As the company earns revenue from music downloads, it decreases (debits) Unearned Revenue and increases (credits) Sales Revenue. The customer has a balance of $85 on his gift card, and Apple Inc. has a balance in Unearned Revenue, a liability account, of $85 for music downloads.

 KEY POINT

> When a company receives cash in advance, it debits Cash and credits Unearned Revenue, a current liability account. When it earns the revenue, the company debits Unearned Revenue and credits Sales Revenue.

Let's Review

The new **Dallas Cowboys** football stadium has a seating capacity of 80,000, expandable to 111,000 with standing-room-only capacity. The new stadium cost $1.15 billion, making it one of the most expensive sports stadiums ever built. The Cowboys hold eight regular season games at home; an average ticket sells for about $100 a game. Assume the Cowboys collect $48 million in season ticket sales prior to the beginning of the season. For eight home games, that's $6 million per game ($48 million ÷ 8 games).

Required:

1. Record the sale of $48 million in season tickets prior to the beginning of the season.

2. Record the $6 million in revenue recognized after the first game.

Solution:

1. Sale of $48 million in season ticket sales:

($ in millions)	Debit	Credit
Cash	48	
Unearned Revenue		48
(Sell season tickets prior to the beginning of the season)		

2. $6 million in revenue recognized after the first game:

($ in millions)	Debit	Credit
Unearned Revenue	6	
Sales Revenue		6
(Earn revenue for each home game played)		

Suggested Homework:
BE8-6,
E8-10;
P8-5A&B

The Cowboys would make similar entries after each home game.

SALES TAX PAYABLE

Most states impose a state sales tax, and many areas include a local sales tax as well. Yet, some states do not have a sales tax. Upon arriving in Oregon for the first time, Don ordered lunch at a fast-food restaurant. His meal cost $4.99. When the employee at the counter said, "You're not from Oregon, are you?", Don wondered aloud how the sales clerk could tell. The clerk politely replied, "You have five dollars and some change in your hand, but in Oregon there's no sales tax." States that currently don't impose a general state sales tax are Alaska, Delaware, Montana, New Hampshire, and Oregon. However, many cities in Alaska have *local* sales taxes. The other four states impose sales-type taxes on specific transactions such as lodging, tobacco, or gasoline sales.

Each company selling products subject to sales tax is responsible for collecting the sales tax directly from customers and periodically sending the sales taxes collected to the state and local governments. The selling company records sales revenue in one account and sales tax payable in another. **When the company collects the sales taxes, it increases (debits) Cash and increases (credits) Sales Tax Payable.**

Suppose you buy lunch in the airport for $15 plus 9% sales tax. The airport restaurant records the transaction this way:

	Debit	Credit
Cash	16.35	
Sales Revenue		15.00
Sales Tax Payable (= $15 × 0.09)		1.35
(Record sales and sales tax)		

A = L + SE
+16.35
+15.00 Rev↑
+1.35

Some companies don't separately record sales and sales tax with each sale. Instead, they choose to separate the two amounts later. Suppose you buy lunch in the airport for $21.80 that includes a 9% sales tax. How much did the restaurant charge you for the lunch, and how much does it owe the state for sales tax? If we divide the total cash paid by 1.09 (1 + 9% sales tax rate), we get $20 (= $21.80 ÷ 1.09) as the sales price, leaving $1.80 as sales tax payable. If the entire amount collected is recorded initially as sales, at some point the company will separate the sales tax portion from sales and record that amount as sales tax payable.

 KEY POINT

Sales taxes collected from customers by the seller are not an expense. Instead, they represent current liabilities payable to the government.

CURRENT PORTION OF LONG-TERM DEBT

Distinguishing between the current portion of long-term debt and long-term debt is important to management, investors, and lenders. The current portion of long-term debt is the amount that will be paid within the next year. Management needs to know this amount in order to budget the cash flow necessary to pay the current portion as it becomes due. Investors and lenders also pay attention to current debt because it provides information about a company's liquidity, a useful indicator of risk.

Long-term obligations (notes, mortgages, bonds) usually are reclassified and reported as current liabilities when they become payable within the upcoming year (or operating cycle, if longer than a year). For example, a firm reports a 10-year note payable as a long-term liability for nine years but as a current liability on the balance

sheet prepared during the tenth year of its term to maturity. As another example, **Southwest Airlines** had total borrowings of $3,515 million at December 31, 2009, of which $190 million was payable in 2010 and the remaining $3,325 million is due after 2010. In its 2009 balance sheet, the company records the $3,515 million in current and long-term debt, as shown in Illustration 8–5.

ILLUSTRATION 8–5
Current Portion of
Long-Term Debt

SOUTHWEST AIRLINES	
Balance Sheet (partial)	
December 31, 2009	
($ in millions)	
Current liabilities:	
Current portion of long-term debt	$ 190
Long-term liabilities:	
Long-term debt	3,325
Total borrowings	$3,515

KEY POINT

We report the currently maturing portion of a long-term debt as a current liability on the balance sheet.

Current or Long-Term?

Decision Maker's Perspective

Given a choice, do you suppose management would prefer to report an obligation as a current liability or a long-term liability? Other things being equal, most managers would choose the long-term classification. The reason is that outsiders like banks, bondholders, and shareholders usually consider debt that is due currently to be riskier than debt that is not due for some time. Riskier debt means paying higher interest rates for borrowing. So, be aware that management has incentives to report current obligations as long-term. ●

DEFERRED TAXES   →延其月的，推迟

Net income in the income statement is *not* the same amount as taxable income reported to the Internal Revenue Service (IRS). Net income is based on financial accounting rules, while taxable income in the corporate tax return is based on tax accounting rules. There are many differences between financial accounting rules and tax accounting rules. For instance, most companies use straight-line depreciation in financial accounting, but a different depreciation method (called MACRS) for tax accounting. You will learn more about tax accounting rules in an individual or corporate income tax class.

Differences between financial accounting and tax accounting can result in a company recording financial income now, but deferring payment of some of its income tax expense to future years. In such a case, it will report a *deferred tax liability*. (Or the company may record an expense now, but deduct it for taxes in future years, in which case it will report a deferred tax asset.) As you might guess, deferred taxes can get pretty complex. For now, just remember that there are differences between net income reported on the income statement and taxable income reported on the tax return, and these differences can result in deferred tax liabilities, both current and long-term.

KEY POINT

Net income and taxable income often differ because of differences in financial accounting and tax accounting rules. These differences can result in deferred tax liabilities, in which income is reported now but the tax on the income will not be paid until future years.

PART B

■ **LO5**
Apply the appropriate accounting treatment for contingencies.

CONTINGENCIES

Many companies are involved in litigation disputes, in which the final outcome is uncertain. In its financial statements, does the company wait until the lawsuit is settled, or does it go ahead and report the details of the unsettled case? In this section, we discuss how to report these uncertain situations, which are broadly called **contingencies**. We look at both contingent liabilities and their flip side, contingent gains.

Contingent Liabilities

A **contingent liability** may not be a liability at all. Whether it is depends on whether an uncertain event that might result in a loss occurs or not. Examples include lawsuits, product warranties, environmental problems, and premium offers. **Philip Morris**'s tobacco litigation, **Motorola**'s cell phone warranties, **BP**'s environmental obligations, and **United**'s frequent-flier program are all contingent liabilities. To demonstrate, let's consider a litigation example.

LITIGATION AND OTHER CAUSES

Deloitte was the auditor for a client we'll call Jeeps, Inc. The client sold accessories for jeeps, such as tops, lights, cargo carriers, and hitches. One of the major issues that appeared in Deloitte's audit of Jeeps, Inc., was outstanding litigation. Several lawsuits against the company alleged that the jeep top (made of vinyl) did not hold during a major collision. The jeep manufacturer, **Chrysler**, also was named in the lawsuits. The damages claimed were quite large, about $100 million. Although the company had litigation insurance, there was some question whether the insurance company could pay because the insurance carrier was undergoing financial difficulty. The auditor discussed the situation with the outside legal counsel representing Jeeps, Inc. Legal counsel indicated that the possibility of payment was remote and that if the case went to trial, Jeeps, Inc., would almost surely win.

As the auditor, you could choose one of three options to report the situation. You could: (1) report a liability for the full $100 million or for some lesser amount, (2) provide full disclosure in a note to the financial statements but not report a liability in the balance sheet, or (3) provide no disclosure at all.

Whether we report a contingent liability (option 1) depends on two criteria: (1) the likelihood of payment and (2) the ability to estimate the amount of payment. Let's look at the options for each:

1. The likelihood of payment can be:
   a. *Probable*—likely to occur;
   b. *Reasonably possible*—more than remote but less than probable; or
   c. *Remote*—the chance is slight.

2. The ability to estimate the payment amount is either:
   a. Known or reasonably estimable; or
   b. Not reasonably estimable.

A contingent liability is recorded only if a loss is *probable* **and** the amount can be *reasonably estimated*. We record this with a debit to Loss (which acts like an expense account) and a credit to Contingent Liability.

	Debit	Credit
Loss	x,xxx	
Contingent Liability		x,xxx
(Record a contingent liability)		

INTERNATIONAL FINANCIAL REPORTING STANDARDS (IFRS)

We record a contingent liability under U.S. GAAP if it's both probable and can be reasonably estimated. IFRS rules are similar, but the threshold is "more likely than not." This is a lower threshold than "probable," and thus, contingent liabilities are more likely to be recorded under IFRS rules than under U.S. GAAP.

For more discussion, see Appendix E.

If the likelihood of payment is probable and if one amount within a range appears more likely, we record that amount. When no amount within the range appears more likely than others, we record the *minimum* amount and disclose the potential additional loss. If the likelihood of payment is *reasonably possible* rather than probable, we record no entry but make full disclosure in a note to the financial statements to describe the contingency. Finally, if the likelihood of payment is *remote,* disclosure usually is not required. Illustration 8–6 provides a summary of the accounting for contingent liabilities.

If payment is:	Known or Reasonably Estimable	Not Reasonably Estimable
Probable	Liability recorded and disclosure required	Disclosure required
Reasonably possible	Disclosure required	Disclosure required
Remote	Disclosure not required	Disclosure not required

ILLUSTRATION 8–6

Accounting Treatment of Contingent Liabilities

KEY POINT

A contingent liability is recorded only if a loss is *probable* **and** the amount can be *reasonably estimated.*

Back to the example of Jeeps, Inc.: How do you think **Deloitte**, as the auditor of Jeeps, Inc., treated the litigation described earlier? Based on the response of legal counsel, the likelihood of the payment occurring was considered to be remote, so disclosure was not required. However, because the amount was so large, and because there were concerns about the firm's primary insurance carrier undergoing financial difficulty, Deloitte insisted on full disclosure of the litigation in the notes to the financial statements.

Decision Point

Question ?	Accounting information 📄	Analysis 🔍
Is the company involved in any litigation?	Notes to the financial statements	Companies are required to disclose all contingencies, including litigation, with at least a reasonable possibility of payment. This information can then be used to help estimate their potential financial impact.

Illustration 8–7 provides excerpts from the disclosure of contingencies made by **United Airlines**.

ILLUSTRATION 8–7

Disclosure of Contingencies by United Airlines

UNITED AIRLINES
Notes to the Financial Statements (excerpts)

Legal and Environmental Contingencies. United Airlines has certain contingencies resulting from litigation and claims (including environmental issues) incident to the ordinary course of business. Management believes, after considering a number of factors, including (but not limited to) the views of legal counsel, the nature of contingencies to which we are subject and prior experience, that the ultimate disposition of these contingencies will not materially affect the Company's consolidated financial position or results of operations.

Contingency for Frequent-Flyer Program Awards. United's Mileage Plus frequent-flyer program awards mileage credits to passengers who fly on United, United Express, and certain other airlines that participate in the program. When a travel award level is attained by a Mileage Plus member, we record a liability for the estimated cost of such awards. The Company had recorded a liability and deferred revenue for its frequent-flyer program totaling $1.6 billion (consisting of $679 million for prepaid miles and $923 million related to award travel).

WARRANTIES

Warranties are perhaps the most common example of contingent liabilities. When you buy a new **Dell** notebook, it comes with a warranty covering the hardware from defect for either a 90-day, one-year, or two-year period depending on the product. Why does Dell offer a warranty? To increase sales, of course.

Based on the matching principle, the company needs to record the warranty expense in the same accounting period in which it sells you the product. The warranty for the computer represents an expense and a liability for Dell at the time of the sale because it meets the criteria for recording a contingent liability: Because warranties almost always entail an eventual expenditure, it's *probable* that a cost will be incurred. And even though Dell doesn't know exactly what that cost will be, it can, based on experience, *reasonably estimate* the amount. Let's look at a warranty example in more detail.

Dell introduces a new notebook computer in December that carries a one-year warranty against manufacturer's defects. Based on industry experience with similar product introductions, Dell expects warranty costs will be an amount equal to approximately 3% of sales. New notebook sales for the month of December are $1.5 million. Dell records the warranty liability on December 31 as follows:

December 31	Debit	Credit
Warranty Expense ($1.5 million × 3%)	45,000	
Warranty Liability		45,000
(Record liability for warranties)		

A = L + SE

−45,000 Exp↑

+45,000

When customers make warranty claims and Dell incurs costs to satisfy those claims, the liability is reduced. Let's say that customers make claims costing $12,000 in December. We record the warranty expenditures as follows:

December 31	Debit	Credit
Warranty Liability	12,000	
Cash		12,000
(Record actual warranty expenditures)		

A = L + SE

−12,000

−12,000

Any time you need to calculate a balance, it's often helpful to make a T-account and record the transactions. Remember, journal entries show the transaction, while T-accounts give you the balance. The balance in the Warranty Liability account at the end of December is $33,000 as follows:

	Warranty Liability		
Payment	12,000	45,000	Expense
		33,000	Balance

COMMON MISTAKE

Some students think the balance in the Warranty Liability account is equal to Warranty Expense, $45,000 in this example. Remember, the liability is increased by warranty expense but then is reduced over time by actual warranty expenditures.

Contingent Gains

Flip Side

A **contingent gain** is an existing uncertain situation that might result in a gain, which often is the flip side of contingent liabilities. In a pending lawsuit, one side—the defendant—faces a contingent liability, while the other side—the plaintiff—has a contingent gain. For example, **Polaroid** sued **Kodak** for patent infringement of its instant photography technology. Polaroid had a potential gain, while Kodak faced a potential loss.

As discussed earlier, we record contingent liabilities when the loss is probable and the amount is reasonably estimable. However, **we do not record contingent gains until the gain is certain.** The nonparallel treatment of contingent gains follows the same conservative reasoning that motivates reporting some assets (like inventory) at lower-of-cost-or-market. Specifically, it's desirable to anticipate losses, but recognizing gains should await their final settlement. Though firms do not record contingent gains in the accounts, they sometimes disclose them in notes to the financial statements.

KEY POINT

Unlike contingent liabilities, contingent gains are not recorded until the gain is certain and no longer a contingency.

沒金流动性 ·

ANALYSIS

LO6
Assess liquidity using current liability ratios.

LIQUIDITY ANALYSIS
United vs. Southwest

Liquidity refers to having sufficient cash (or other current assets convertible to cash in a relatively short time) to pay currently maturing debts. Because a lack of liquidity can result in financial difficulties or even bankruptcy, it is critical that managers as well as outside investors and lenders maintain close watch on this aspect of a company's well-being. Here we look at three liquidity measures: working capital, the current ratio, and the acid-test ratio. All three measures are calculated using current assets and current liabilities.

WORKING CAPITAL

The concept of **working capital** is straightforward. It is simply the difference between current assets and current liabilities:

$$\text{Working capital} = \text{Current assets} - \text{Current liabilities}$$

Working capital answers the question, "After paying our current obligations, how much will we have to work with?" For example, if you have $20 in your pocket and you know that you still owe $10 to your friend and $3 for parking, your working capital is $7. A large positive working capital is an indicator of liquidity—whether a company will be able to pay its current debts on time.

However, working capital is not the best measure of liquidity when comparing one company with another, since it does not control for the relative size of each company. In comparing companies, the current ratio and the acid-test ratio are better measures of a company's ability to pay its debts on time.

CURRENT RATIO

We calculate the **current ratio** by dividing current assets by current liabilities:

$$\text{Current ratio} = \frac{\text{Current assets}}{\text{Current liabilities}}$$

A current ratio greater than 1 implies more current assets than current liabilities. Recall that current assets include cash, current investments, accounts receivable, inventories, and prepaid expenses. As a rule of thumb, a current ratio of 1 or higher often reflects an acceptable level of liquidity. A current ratio of 1 indicates that for every dollar of current liabilities, the company has an equal amount of current assets. A current ratio of, say, 1.5 indicates that for every dollar of current liabilities, the company has $1.50 of current assets.

In general, the higher the current ratio, the greater the company's liquidity. But we should evaluate the current ratio, like other ratios, in the context of the industry in which the company operates and other specific circumstances. Keep in mind, though, that not all current assets are equally liquid, which leads us to another, more specific ratio for measuring liquidity.

ACID-TEST RATIO

Common Terms The acid-test ratio is also called the *quick ratio*.

The **acid-test ratio**, or *quick ratio,* is similar to the current ratio but is based on a more conservative measure of current assets available to pay current liabilities. We calculate it by dividing "quick assets" by current liabilities. **Quick assets** include only cash, current investments, and accounts receivable. By eliminating current assets, such as inventory and prepaid expenses, that are less readily convertible into cash, the acid-test ratio may provide a better indication of a company's liquidity than does the current ratio.

$$\text{Acid-test ratio} = \frac{\text{Cash} + \text{Current investments} + \text{Accounts receivable}}{\text{Current liabilities}}$$

We interpret the acid-test ratio much like the current ratio, with one difference: We know that the current assets in the top half of the ratio are only those that can be quickly converted to cash. Thus, an acid-test ratio of, say, 1.5 would indicate that for every dollar of current liabilities, the company has $1.50 of current assets that are easily convertible to cash that might be used to help pay the current liabilities as they come due. As is true for other ratios, be sure to evaluate the acid-test ratio in the context of the industry in which the company operates.

KEY POINT

Working capital is the difference between current assets and current liabilities. The current ratio is equal to current assets divided by current liabilities. The acid-test ratio is equal to quick assets (cash, current investments, and accounts receivable) divided by current liabilities. Each measures a company's liquidity, its ability to pay currently maturing debts.

Decision Point

Question	?	Accounting information		Analysis	
Does the company have enough cash to pay current liabilities as they come due?		Working capital, current ratio, and acid-test ratio		A high working capital, current ratio, or acid-test ratio generally indicates the ability to pay current liabilities on a timely basis.	

Let's compare **United Airlines**'s liquidity ratios to those of **Southwest Airlines**, considered by many to be the airline industry leader in profitability and overall financial condition.

Let's Review

Selected financial data regarding current assets and current liabilities for United and Southwest Airlines are as follows.

($ in millions)	United	Southwest
Current assets:		
Cash and cash equivalents	$3,046	$1,368
Current investments		435
Net receivables	977	574
Inventory	237	203
Other current assets	601	313
Total current assets	$4,861	$2,893
Current liabilities:		
Accounts payable	$3,231	$2,643
Short/current long-term debt	1,808	163
Other current liabilities	2,242	
Total current liabilities	$7,281	$2,806

Required:

1. Calculate working capital for United Airlines and Southwest Airlines. Is working capital adequate for each company?

2. Calculate the current ratio for United Airlines and Southwest Airlines. Which company has a better current ratio?

3. Calculate the acid-test (quick) ratio for United Airlines and Southwest Airlines. Which company has a better acid-test ratio?

Solution:

1. Working capital:

($ in millions)	Total Current Assets	−	Total Current Liabilities	=	Working Capital
United	$4,861	−	$7,281	=	$(2,420)
Southwest	$2,893	−	$2,806	=	$ 87

United Airlines actually has a negative working capital, in which its current liabilities exceed its current assets by $2.4 billion. Southwest Airlines, with positive working capital, has more liquidity.

2. Current ratio:

($ in millions)	Total Current Assets	÷	Total Current Liabilities	=	Current Ratio
United	$4,861	÷	$7,281	=	0.67
Southwest	$2,893	÷	$2,806	=	1.03

Southwest Airlines also has a higher current ratio, which would indicate better liquidity than United. Southwest has just above the "acceptable" liquidity level of 1.0.

3. Acid-test (quick) ratio:

Remember that *quick assets* equal cash + current investments + net receivables.

($ in millions)	Quick Assets	÷	Total Current Liabilities	=	Acid-Test Ratio
United	$4,023	÷	$7,281	=	0.55
Southwest	$2,377	÷	$2,806	=	0.85

Suggested Homework:
BE8-15;
E8-16;
P8-9A&B

By eliminating less-liquid current assets such as inventory, the acid-test ratio often provides a better indicator of liquidity. Once again, Southwest Airlines "wins" with an acid-test ratio of 0.85, compared to 0.55 for United Airlines.

What do the liquidity measures for United and Southwest tell us? Together, they provide an indication of a company's ability to pay its currently maturing debts. Looking at working capital, the current ratio, and the acid-test ratio, it appears that Southwest Airlines is in a better position than United to meet its current debt obligations. But remember that we should evaluate liquidity measures in the context of an industry. The airlines have faced tough times recently, between dampened demand resulting from 9/11, increasing fuel costs, and the recent recession. So, while Southwest has fared better than United, its liquidity still may not compare well with other industries.

Decision Maker's Perspective   Indicators of Liquidity

If the firm's current ratio or acid-test ratio is lower than that of the industry as a whole, does that mean liquidity is a problem? Perhaps, but perhaps not. It does, though, raise a red flag that suggests caution when assessing other aspects of the company.

It's important to remember that each ratio is but one piece of the puzzle. For example, profitability is probably the best long-run indicator of liquidity. It is

difficult to maintain liquidity over a string of consecutive loss years. Another consideration is that management may be very efficient in managing current assets so that some current assets—receivables or inventory—remain at minimum amounts. This is good for the company overall, but it may result in less-impressive current and acid-test ratios. The turnover ratios we discussed in Chapters 5 and 6, such as receivables turnover and inventory turnover, help measure the efficiency of asset management in this regard. ●

COMMON MISTAKE

As a general rule, a higher current ratio is better. However, a high current ratio is not always a positive signal. Companies having difficulty collecting receivables or holding excessive inventory will also have a higher current ratio. Managers must balance the incentive for strong liquidity (yielding a high current ratio) with the need to minimize levels of receivables and inventory (yielding a lower current ratio).

Effect of Transactions on Liquidity Ratios

It also is important to understand the effect of specific transactions on the current ratio and acid-test ratio. Both ratios have the same denominator, current liabilities, so a decrease in current liabilities will increase the ratios (dividing by a smaller number makes the ratio bigger). Likewise, an increase in current liabilities will decrease the ratios (dividing by a bigger number makes the ratio smaller).

How are the ratios affected by changes in current assets? It depends on which current asset changes. Both ratios include cash, current investments, and accounts receivable. An increase in any of those will increase *both* ratios. However, only the current ratio includes inventory and other current assets. An increase to inventory or other current assets will increase the current ratio, but not the acid-test ratio.

Liquidity Management

Can management influence the ratios that measure liquidity? Yes, at least to some extent. A company can influence the timing of accounts payable recognition by asking suppliers to change their delivery schedules. For example, a large airplane manufacturer like **Boeing** or **McDonnell Douglas** might delay the shipment and billing of certain inventory parts from late December to early January, reducing accounts payable at its December year-end. Because accounts payable is included in calculating the current ratio, the timing of accounts payable recognition could mean the difference between an unacceptable ratio and an acceptable one, or between violating and complying with a debt covenant.

Suppose, for instance, a company with a current ratio of 1.25 (current assets of $5 million and current liabilities of $4 million) has entered into a *debt covenant* with its bank that requires a minimum current ratio of 1.25. A **debt covenant** is an agreement between a borrower and a lender that requires that certain minimum financial measures be met or the lender can recall the debt. By delaying the delivery of $1 million of inventory purchased on account, the company can increase the ratio to 1.33 (current assets of $4 million and current liabilities of $3 million). Investors and creditors should be aware of managerial activities that increase liquidity ratios, such as misclassification of current liabilities or unusual variations in accounts payable levels.

ETHICAL DILEMMA

Airport Accessories (AA) has several loans outstanding with a local bank. The loan contract contains an agreement that AA must maintain a current ratio of at least 0.90. Micah, the assistant controller, estimates that the year-end current assets and current liabilities will be $2,100,000 and $2,400,000, respectively. These estimates provide a current ratio of only 0.875. Violation of the debt agreement will increase AA's borrowing costs because the loans will be renegotiated at higher interest rates.

Micah proposes that AA purchase inventory of $600,000 on credit before year-end. This will cause both current assets and current liabilities to increase by the same amount, but the current ratio will increase to 0.90. The extra $600,000 in inventory will be used over the next year. However, the purchase will cause warehousing costs and financing costs to increase.

Micah is concerned about the ethics of his proposal. What do you think?

 KEY POINTS BY LEARNING OBJECTIVE

LO1 Distinguish between current and long-term liabilities.

In most cases, current liabilities are payable within one year and long-term liabilities are payable more than one year from now.

LO2 Account for notes payable and interest expense.

We record interest expense in the period we incur it, rather than in the period in which we pay it.

Many short-term loans are arranged under an existing line of credit with a bank, or for larger corporations in the form of commercial paper, a loan from one company to another.

LO3 Account for employee and employer payroll liabilities.

Employee salaries are reduced by withholdings for federal and state income taxes, FICA taxes, and the employee portion of insurance and retirement contributions. The employer, too, incurs additional payroll expenses for unemployment taxes, the employer portion of FICA taxes, and employer insurance and retirement contributions.

LO4 Demonstrate the accounting for other current liabilities.

When a company receives cash in advance, it debits Cash and credits Unearned Revenue, a current liability account. When it earns the revenue, the company debits Unearned Revenue and credits Sales Revenue.

Sales taxes collected from customers by the seller are not an expense. Instead, they represent current liabilities payable to the government.

We report the currently maturing portion of a long-term debt as a current liability on the balance sheet.

Net income and taxable income often differ because of differences between financial accounting and tax accounting rules. These differences can result in *deferred tax liabilities*, in which income is reported now but the tax on the income will not be paid until future years.

LO5 Apply the appropriate accounting treatment for contingencies.

A contingent liability is recorded only if a loss is *probable* **and** the amount can be *reasonably estimated*.

Unlike contingent liabilities, contingent gains are not recorded until the gain is certain and no longer a contingency.

Analysis

LO6 Assess liquidity using current liability ratios.

Working capital is the difference between current assets and current liabilities. The current ratio is equal to current assets divided by current liabilities. The acid-test ratio is equal to quick assets (cash, short-term investments, and accounts receivable) divided by current liabilities. Each measures a company's liquidity, its ability to pay currently maturing debts.

GLOSSARY

Acid-test ratio: Cash, current investments, and accounts receivable divided by current liabilities; measures the availability of liquid current assets to pay current liabilities. **p. 386**

Commercial paper: Borrowing from another company rather than from a bank. **p. 374**

Contingencies: Uncertain situations that can result in a gain or a loss for a company. **p. 382**

Contingent gain: An existing uncertain situation that might result in a gain. **p. 385**

Contingent liability: An existing uncertain situation that might result in a loss. **p. 382**

Current liabilities: Debts that, in most cases, are due within one year. However, when a company has an operating cycle of longer than a year, its current liabilities are defined by the length of the operating cycle, rather than by the length of one year. **p. 370**

Current portion of long-term debt: Debt that will be paid within the next year. **p. 380**

Current ratio: Current assets divided by current liabilities; measures the availability of current assets to pay current liabilities. **p. 386**

Debt covenant: An agreement between a borrower and a lender that requires that certain minimum financial measures be met or the lender can recall the debt. **p. 389**

FICA taxes: Based on the Federal Insurance Contribution Act; tax withheld from employees' paychecks and matched by employers for Social Security and Medicare. **p. 376**

Fringe benefits: Additional employee benefits paid for by the employer. **p. 377**

Liability: A present responsibility to sacrifice assets in the future due to a transaction or other event that happened in the past. **p. 370**

Line of credit: An informal agreement that permits a company to borrow up to a prearranged limit without having to follow formal loan procedures and prepare paperwork. **p. 374**

Liquidity: Having sufficient cash (or other assets convertible to cash in a relatively short time) to pay currently maturing debts. **p. 386**

Notes payable: Written promises to repay amounts borrowed plus interest. **p. 371**

Quick assets: Includes only cash, current investments, and accounts receivable. **p. 386**

Sales tax payable: Sales tax collected from customers by the seller, representing current liabilities payable to the government. **p. 380**

Unearned revenue: A liability account used to record cash received in advance of the sale or service. **p. 378**

Unemployment taxes: A tax to cover federal and state unemployment costs paid by the employer on behalf of its employees. **p. 376**

Working capital: The difference between current assets and current liabilities. **p. 386**

SELF-STUDY QUESTIONS

1. Which of the following statements regarding liabilities is *not* true?　　　　■ LO1
   a. Liabilities can be for services rather than cash.
   b. Liabilities are reported in the balance sheet for almost every business.
   c. Liabilities result from future transactions.
   d. Liabilities represent probable future sacrifices of benefits.

2. Current liabilities:　　　　■ LO1
   a. May include contingent liabilities.
   b. Include obligations payable within one year or one operating cycle, whichever is shorter.
   c. Can be satisfied only with the payment of cash.
   d. Are preferred by most companies over long-term liabilities.

3. If Express Jet borrows $100 million on October 1, 2012, for one year at 6% interest, how much interest expense does it record for the year ended December 31, 2012?　　　　■ LO2
   a. $0.
   b. $1 million.
   c. $1.5 million.
   d. $6 million.

4. We record interest expense on a note payable in the period in which:　　　　■ LO2
   a. We pay cash for interest.
   b. We incur interest.

c. We pay cash and incur interest.

d. We pay cash or incur interest.

■ LO3

5. Which of the following is *not* deducted from an employee's salary?

a. FICA taxes.

b. Unemployment taxes.

c. Income taxes.

d. Employee portion of insurance and retirement payments.

■ LO4

6. The seller collects sales taxes from the customer at the time of sale and reports the sales taxes as:

a. Sales tax expense.

b. Sales tax revenue.

c. Sales tax receivable.

d. Sales tax payable.

■ LO5

7. Management can estimate the amount of loss that will occur due to litigation against the company. If the likelihood of loss is reasonably possible, a contingent liability should be:

a. Disclosed but not reported as a liability.

b. Disclosed and reported as a liability.

c. Neither disclosed nor reported as a liability.

d. Reported as a liability but not disclosed.

■ LO5

8. Smith Co. filed suit against Western, Inc., seeking damages for patent infringement. Western's legal counsel believes it is probable that Western will settle the lawsuit for an estimated amount in the range of $75,000 to $175,000, with all amounts in the range considered equally likely. How should Western report this litigation?

a. As a liability for $75,000 with disclosure of the range.

b. As a liability for $125,000 with disclosure of the range.

c. As a liability for $175,000 with disclosure of the range.

d. As a disclosure only. No liability is reported.

■ LO6

9. The acid-test ratio is:

a. Current assets divided by current liabilities.

b. Cash and current investments divided by current liabilities.

c. Cash, current investments, and accounts receivable divided by current liabilities.

d. Cash, current investments, accounts receivable, and inventory divided by current liabilities.

■ LO6

10. Assuming a current ratio of 1.0 and an acid-test ratio of 0.75, how will the purchase of inventory with cash affect each ratio?

a. Increase the current ratio and increase the acid-test ratio.

b. No change to the current ratio and decrease the acid-test ratio.

c. Decrease the current ratio and decrease the acid-test ratio.

d. Increase the current ratio and decrease the acid-test ratio.

Check out
www.mhhe.com/succeed
for more multiple-choice
questions.

Note: For answers, see the last page of the chapter.

REVIEW QUESTIONS

■ LO1

1. What are the essential characteristics of liabilities for purposes of financial reporting?

■ LO1

2. How do we define current liabilities? Long-term liabilities?

■ LO1

3. Why is it important to distinguish between current and long-term liabilities?

4. **United Airlines** served as an example throughout the chapter. Provide several examples of current liabilities in the airline industry.   ■ LO1

5. Explain why we record interest in the period in which we incur it rather than in the period in which we pay it.   ■ LO2

6. Bank loans often are arranged under existing lines of credit. What is a line of credit? How does a line of credit work?   ■ LO2

7. How does commercial paper differ from a normal bank loan? Why is the interest rate often less for commercial paper?   ■ LO2

8. Name at least four items withheld from employee payroll checks. Which deductions are required by law and which are voluntary?   ■ LO3

9. Name at least four employer costs in addition to the employee's salary. Which costs are required by law and which are voluntary?   ■ LO3

10. Who pays Social Security taxes: the employer, the employee, or both? How is the deduction for Social Security and Medicare (FICA) computed?   ■ LO3

11. Retailers like **McDonald's**, **American Eagle**, and **Apple Inc.** sell quite a few gift cards. Explain how these companies account for the sale of gift cards.   ■ LO4

12. *BusinessWeek* sells magazine subscriptions in advance of their distribution. (a) What journal entry would the company make at the time it sells subscriptions? (b) What journal entry would the company make each time it distributes a magazine?   ■ LO4

13. Like all retailers, **Hollister** is required to collect sales tax to be remitted to state and local government authorities. Assume a local store has cash proceeds from sales of $5,325, including $325 in sales tax. What is the sales tax rate? Provide the journal entry to record the proceeds.   ■ LO4

14. If $10 million of **Dell Computer Corporation**'s $130 million notes payable is due in the next year, how will the firm present this debt within the current and long-term liabilities sections of the current year's balance sheet?   ■ LO4

15. Is net income reported in the income statement the same amount as taxable income in the corporate tax return? Why or why not?   ■ LO4

16. Define contingent liability. Provide three common examples.   ■ LO5

17. List and briefly describe the three categories of likelihood that a payment for a contingent liability will need to be made.   ■ LO5

18. Under what circumstances should a firm report a contingent liability?   ■ LO5

19. Suppose the firm's analysis of a contingent liability indicates that an obligation is not probable. What accounting treatment, if any, is warranted?   ■ LO5

20. If a contingent liability is probable but estimable only within a range, what amount, if any, should the firm report?   ■ LO5

21. Your company is the plaintiff in a lawsuit. Legal counsel advises you that your eventual victory is inevitable. "You will be awarded $2 million," your attorney confidently asserts. Describe the appropriate accounting treatment.   ■ LO5

22. Current liabilities affect a company's liquidity. What is liquidity, and how do we evaluate it?   ■ LO6

23. Explain the differences among working capital, the current ratio, and the acid-test ratio.   ■ LO6

24. How would the following transactions affect the current ratio and the acid-test ratio? (a) Purchase of inventory with cash; and (b) sale of inventory for more than its cost. Assume that prior to these transactions the current ratio and acid-test ratio are both less than one.   ■ LO6

BRIEF EXERCISES

Record notes payable (LO2)

Flip Side of BE8–2

BE8–1 On November 1, Bahama Cruise Lines borrows $3 million and issues a six-month, 6% note payable. Interest is payable at maturity. Record the issuance of the note and the appropriate adjustment for interest expense at December 31, the end of the reporting period.

Record notes receivable (LO2)

Flip Side of BE8–1

BE8–2 On November 1, Bahama National Bank lends $3 million and accepts a six-month, 6% note receivable. Interest is due at maturity. Record the acceptance of the note and the appropriate adjustment for interest revenue at December 31, the end of the reporting period.

Determine interest expense (LO2)

BE8–3 On July 1, Alaskan Adventures issues a $100,000, eight-month, 6% note. Interest is payable at maturity. What is the amount of interest expense that the company would record in a year-end adjustment on December 31?

Record commercial paper (LO2)

BE8–4 On April 1, Online Travel issues $12 million of commercial paper with a maturity on December 31 and an 8% interest rate. Record the issuance of the commercial paper and its repayment at maturity.

Calculate FICA taxes (LO3)

BE8–5 Mike Samson is a college football coach making a base salary of $640,800 a year ($53,400 per month). Employers are required to withhold a 6.2% Social Security tax up to a maximum base amount and a 1.45% Medicare tax with no maximum. Assuming the FICA base amount is $106,800, compute how much will be withheld during the year for Coach Samson's Social Security and Medicare. Through what month will Social Security be withheld? What additional amount will the employer need to contribute?

Record unearned revenues (LO4)

BE8–6 On December 18, **Intel** receives $250,000 from a customer toward a cash sale of $2.5 million for computer chips to be completed on January 23. The computer chips had a total production cost of $1.5 million. What journal entries should Intel record on December 18 and January 23? Assume Intel uses the perpetual inventory system.

Record sales tax (LO4)

BE8–7 During December, Far West Services makes a $1,200 credit sale. The state sales tax rate is 6% and the local sales tax rate is 2.5%. Record sales and sales tax payable.

Report current portion of long-term debt (LO4)

BE8–8 On September 1, 2012, **Southwest Airlines** borrows $40 million, of which $8 million is due next year. Show how Southwest Airlines would record the $40 million debt on its December 31, 2012, balance sheet.

Calculate warranty liability (LO5)

BE8–9 **Sony** introduces a new compact music player to compete with **Apple**'s iPod that carries a two-year warranty against manufacturer's defects. Based on industry experience with similar product introductions, warranty costs are expected to be approximately 2% of sales. By the end of the first year of selling the product, total sales are $30 million and actual warranty expenditures are $200,000. What amount (if any) should Sony report as a liability at the end of the year?

Determine the financial statement effect of a contingent liability (LO5)

BE8–10 Consultants notify management of Discount Pharmaceuticals that a stroke medication poses a potential health hazard. Counsel indicates that a product recall is probable and is estimated to cost the company $8 million. How will this affect the company's income statement and balance sheet this period?

Account for a contingent liability (LO5)

Flip Side of BE8–12

BE8–11 Electronic Innovators is the defendant in a $10 million lawsuit filed by one of its customers, Aviation Systems. The litigation is in final appeal, and legal counsel advises that it is probable that Electronic Innovators will lose the lawsuit. The estimated amount is somewhere between $6 and $10 million. How should Electronic Innovators account for this event?

Account for a contingent gain (LO5)

Flip Side of BE8–11

BE8–12 Aviation Systems is involved in a $10 million lawsuit filed against one of its suppliers, Electronic Innovators. The litigation is in final appeal, and legal counsel advises that it is probable that Aviation Systems will win the lawsuit and be awarded somewhere between $6 and $10 million. How should Aviation Systems account for this event?

BE8–13 The Environmental Protection Agency (EPA) is in the process of investigating a possible water contamination issue at the manufacturing facility of Northwest Forest Products. The EPA has not yet proposed a penalty assessment. Management feels an assessment is reasonably possible, and if an assessment is made, an unfavorable settlement is estimated between $20 and $30 million. How should Northwest Forest Products report this situation in its current financial statements?

Determine the financial statement effect of a contingent liability **(LO5)**

BE8–14 Motorola is a world leader in the development of cellular phone technology. During the year, the company becomes aware of potential costs due to (1) a product defect that is reasonably possible and can be reasonably estimated, (2) a safety hazard that is probable and cannot be reasonably estimated, and (3) a new product warranty that is probable and can be reasonably estimated. Which of these potential costs, if any, should Motorola record?

Account for contingent liabilities **(LO5)**

BE8–15 Under Armour has the following current assets: cash, $102 million; receivables, $94 million; inventory, $182 million; and other current assets, $18 million. Under Armour has the following liabilities: accounts payable, $98 million; current portion of long-term debt, $35 million; and long-term debt, $23 million. Based on these amounts, calculate the current ratio and the acid-test ratio for Under Armour.

Calculate current and acid-test ratios **(LO6)**

EXERCISES

E8–1 Match (by letter) the correct reporting method for each of the items listed below.

Determine proper classification of liabilities **(LO1)**

Reporting Method

C = Current liability
L = Long-term liability
D = Disclosure note only
N = Not reported

Item

_____ 1. Accounts payable.
_____ 2. Current portion of long-term debt.
_____ 3. Sales tax collected from customers.
_____ 4. Notes payable due next year.
_____ 5. Notes payable due in two years.
_____ 6. Customer advances.
_____ 7. Commercial paper.
_____ 8. Unused line of credit.
_____ 9. A contingent liability with a *probable* likelihood of occurring within the next year and can be estimated.
_____ 10. A contingent liability with a *reasonably possible* likelihood of occurring within the next year and can be estimated.

E8–2 On November 1, 2012, Aviation Training Corp. borrows $50,000 cash from Community Savings and Loan. Aviation Training signs a three-month, 6% note payable. Interest is payable at maturity. Aviation's year-end is December 31.

Record notes payable **(LO2)**

Required:
1. Record the note payable by Aviation Training.
2. Record the appropriate adjustment for the note by Aviation Training on December 31, 2012.
3. Record the payment of the note at maturity.

E8–3 On August 1, 2012, Trico Technologies, an aeronautic electronics company, borrows $20 million cash to expand operations. The loan is made by FirstBanc Corp. under a short-term line of credit arrangement. Trico signs a six-month, 8% promissory note. Interest is payable at maturity. Trico's year-end is December 31.

Record notes payable **(LO2)**
Flip Side of E8–4

Required:

1. Record the issuance of the note by Trico Technologies.
2. Record the appropriate adjustment for the note by Trico on December 31, 2012.
3. Record the payment of the note by Trico at maturity.

Record notes receivable (LO2)

Flip Side of E8–3

E8–4 On August 1, 2012, Trico Technologies, an aeronautic electronics company, borrows $20 million cash to expand operations. The loan is made by FirstBanc Corp. under a short-term line of credit arrangement. Trico signs a six-month, 8% promissory note. Interest is payable at maturity. FirstBanc Corp.'s year-end is December 31.

Required:

1. Record the acceptance of the note by FirstBanc Corp.
2. Record the appropriate adjustment for the note by FirstBanc Corp., on December 31, 2012.
3. Record the receipt of cash by FirstBanc Corp. at maturity.

Determine interest expense (LO2)

E8–5 OS Environmental provides cost-effective solutions for managing regulatory requirements and environmental needs specific to the airline industry. Assume that on July 1, 2012, the company issues a one-year note for the amount of $5 million. Interest is payable at maturity.

Required:

Determine the amount of interest expense that should be recorded in a year-end adjusting entry under each of the following independent assumptions:

Interest Rate	Fiscal Year-End
1. 12%	December 31
2. 10%	September 30
3. 9%	October 31
4. 6%	January 31

Record a line of credit (LO2)

E8–6 The following selected transactions relate to liabilities of Rocky Mountain Adventures. Rocky Mountain's fiscal year ends on December 31.

January 13	Negotiate a revolving credit agreement with First Bank that can be renewed annually upon bank approval. The amount available under the line of credit is $10 million at the bank's prime rate.
February 1	Arrange a three-month bank loan of $4 million with First Bank under the line of credit agreement. Interest at the prime rate of 7% is payable at maturity.
May 1	Pay the 7% note at maturity.

Required:

Record the appropriate entries, if any, on January 13, February 1, and May 1.

Calculate payroll withholdings and payroll taxes (LO3)

E8–7 Aspen Ski Resorts has 100 employees, each working 40 hours per week and earning $10 an hour. Although the company does not pay any health or retirement benefits, one of the perks of working at Aspen is that employees are allowed free skiing on their days off. Federal income taxes are withheld at 15% and state income taxes at 5%. FICA taxes are 7.65% of the first $106,800 earned per employee and 1.45% thereafter. Unemployment taxes are 6.2% of the first $7,000 earned per employee.

Required:

1. Compute the total salary expense, the total withholdings from employee salaries, and the actual direct deposit of payroll for the first week of January.
2. Compute the total payroll tax expense Aspen Ski Resorts will pay for the first week of January in addition to the total salary expense and employee withholdings calculated in *Requirement* 1.
3. How should Aspen Ski Resorts account for the free skiing given to employees on their days off?

E8–8 During January, Luxury Cruise Lines pays employee salaries of $2 million. Withholdings in January are $153,000 for the employee portion of FICA, $300,000 for federal income tax, $125,000 for state income tax, and $20,000 for the employee portion of health insurance (payable to **Blue Cross/Blue Shield**). The company incurs an additional $124,000 for federal and state unemployment tax and $60,000 for the employer portion of health insurance.

Record payroll (LO3)

Required:

1. Record the employee salary expense, withholdings, and salaries payable.
2. Record the employer-provided fringe benefits.
3. Record the employer payroll taxes.

E8–9 Airline Temporary Services (ATS) pays employees monthly. Payroll information is listed below for January, the first month of ATS's fiscal year. Assume that none of the employees exceeds the federal unemployment tax maximum salary of $7,000 in January.

Record payroll (LO3)

Salaries expense	$500,000
Federal and state income tax withheld	100,000
Federal unemployment tax rate	0.80%
State unemployment tax rate (after FUTA deduction)	5.40%
Social Security (FICA) tax rate	7.65%

Required:

Record salaries expense and payroll tax expense for the January pay period.

E8–10 Apple Inc. is the number one online music retailer through its iTunes music store. Apple sells iTunes gift cards in $15, $25, and $50 increments. Assume Apple sells $20 million in iTunes gift cards in December, and customers redeem $13 million of the gift cards.

Analyze and record unearned revenues (LO4)

Required:

1. Record the advance collection of $20 million for iTunes gift cards.
2. Record the revenue earned when $13 million in gift cards is redeemed.

E8–11 Two competing travel agencies provide similar services, but they record sales using different methods.

Record unearned revenue (LO4)

1. Eastern Travel records sales and sales tax in separate accounts. For the month of January, cash sales total $20,000, and sales tax is $1,600.
2. Western Travel records sales and sales tax together. For the month of January, cash sales total $10,800, including an 8% sales tax.

Required:

Record cash sales and the related sales tax for (1) Eastern Travel and (2) Western Travel.

E8–12 Top Sound International designs and sells high-end stereo equipment for auto and home use. Engineers notified management in December 2012 of a circuit flaw in an amplifier that poses a potential fire hazard. Further investigation indicates that a product recall is probable, estimated to cost the company $3 million. The fiscal year ends on December 31.

Analyze and record a contingent liability (LO5)

Required:

1. Should this contingent liability be reported, disclosed in a note only, or neither? Explain.
2. What loss, if any, should Top Sound report in its 2012 income statement?
3. What liability, if any, should Top Sound report in its 2012 balance sheet?
4. What entry, if any, should be recorded?

Determine proper treatment of a contingent liability (LO5)

E8–13 Pacific Cruise Lines is a defendant in litigation involving a swimming accident on one of its three cruise ships.

Required:

For each of the following scenarios, determine the appropriate way to report the situation. Explain your reasoning and record any necessary entry.

1. The likelihood of a payment occurring is probable, and the estimated amount is $1.2 million.
2. The likelihood of a payment occurring is probable, and the amount is estimated to be in the range of $1 to $1.5 million.
3. The likelihood of a payment occurring is reasonably possible, and the estimated amount is $1.2 million.
4. The likelihood of a payment occurring is remote, while the estimated potential amount is $1.2 million.

Record warranties (LO5)

E8–14 Computer Wholesalers restores and resells notebook computers on **eBay**. It originally acquires the notebook computers from corporations upgrading their computer systems, and it backs each notebook it sells with a 90-day warranty against defects. Based on previous experience, Computer Wholesalers expects warranty costs to be approximately 5% of sales. By the end of the first year, sales and actual warranty expenditures are $500,000 and $18,000, respectively.

Required:

1. Does this situation represent a contingent liability? Why or why not?
2. Record warranty expense and warranty liability for the year based on 5% of sales.
3. Record the reduction in the warranty liability and the reduction in cash of $18,000 incurred during the year.
4. What is the balance in the Warranty Liability account after the entries in *Requirements* 2 and 3?

Analyze disclosure of contingent liabilities (LO5)

E8–15 **Dow Chemical Company** provides chemical, plastic, and agricultural products and services to various consumer markets. The following excerpt is taken from the disclosure notes of Dow's annual report.

> **DOW CHEMICAL**
> **Notes to the Financial Statements (excerpt)**
>
> Dow Chemical had accrued obligations of $381 million for environmental remediation and restoration costs, including $40 million for the remediation of Superfund sites. This is management's best estimate of the costs for remediation and restoration with respect to environmental matters for which the Company has accrued liabilities, although the ultimate cost with respect to these particular matters could range up to twice that amount. Inherent uncertainties exist in these estimates primarily due to unknown conditions, changing governmental regulations and legal standards regarding liability, and evolving technologies for handling site remediation and restoration.

Required:

1. Does the excerpt describe a contingent liability?
2. Under what conditions would Dow record such a contingency?
3. How did Dow record the $381 million?

Calculate and analyze liquidity ratios (LO6)

E8–16 Selected financial data regarding current assets and current liabilities for **Royal Caribbean Cruises, Ltd.**, a leader in the cruise line industry, is provided:

($ in millions)	
Current assets:	
Cash and cash equivalents	$ 403
Current investments	82
Net receivables	271
Inventory	96
Other current assets	125
Total current assets	$ 977
Current liabilities:	
Accounts payable	$1,061
Short-term debt	644
Other current liabilities	969
Total current liabilities	$2,674

Required:

1. Calculate the current ratio and the acid-test ratio for Royal Caribbean.
2. Compare your calculations with those for United Airlines and Southwest Airlines reported in the chapter text. Which company appears more likely to have difficulty paying its currently maturing debts?

For additional exercises, visit www.mhhe.com/succeed for Exercises: Set B.

PROBLEMS: SET A

P8–1A Listed below are several terms and phrases associated with current liabilities. Pair each item from List A (by letter) with the item from List B that is most appropriately associated with it.

Review current liability terms and concepts (LO1)

List A	List B
_____ 1. An IOU promising to repay the amount borrowed plus interest.	a. Recording of a contingent liability.
_____ 2. Payment amount is reasonably possible and can be reasonably estimated.	b. Unearned revenues.
_____ 3. Mixture of liabilities and equity a business uses.	c. The riskiness of a business's obligations.
_____ 4. Payment amount is probable and can be reasonably estimated.	d. Disclosure of a contingent liability.
_____ 5. A liability that requires the sacrifice of something other than cash.	e. Interest on debt.
_____ 6. Long-term debt maturing within one year.	f. Payroll taxes.
_____ 7. FICA and FUTA.	g. Line of credit.
_____ 8. Informal agreement that permits a company to borrow up to a prearranged limit.	h. Capital structure.
_____ 9. Classifying liabilities as either current or long-term helps investors and creditors assess this.	i. Note payable.
_____ 10. Amount of note payable × annual interest rate × fraction of the year.	j. Current portion of long-term debt.

Record notes payable and notes receivable (LO2)

P8–2A Precision Castparts, a manufacturer of processed engine parts in the automotive and airline industries, borrows $40 million cash on October 1, 2012, to provide working capital for anticipated expansion. Precision signs a one-year, 8% promissory note to Midwest Bank under a prearranged short-term line of credit. Interest on the note is payable at maturity. Each firm has a December 31 year-end.

Required:

1. Prepare the journal entries on October 1, 2012, to record (a) the notes payable for Precision Castparts and (b) the notes receivable for Midwest Bank.
2. Record the adjustments on December 31, 2012, for (a) Precision Castparts and (b) Midwest Bank.
3. Prepare the journal entries on September 30, 2013, to record payment of (a) the notes payable for Precision Castparts and (b) the notes receivable for Midwest Bank.

Record payroll (LO3)

P8–3A Caribbean Tours' total payroll for the month of January was $500,000. The following withholdings, fringe benefits, and payroll taxes apply:

Federal and state income tax withheld	$50,000
Health insurance premiums (**Blue Cross**) paid by employer	9,000
Contribution to retirement plan (**Fidelity**) paid by employer	20,000
FICA tax rate (Social Security and Medicare)	7.65%
Federal and state unemployment tax rate	6.20%

Assume that none of the withholdings or payroll taxes has been paid by the end of January (record them as payables), and no employee's cumulative wages exceed the relevant wage bases.

Required:

1. Record the employee salary expense, withholdings, and salaries payable.
2. Record the employer-provided fringe benefits.
3. Record the employer payroll taxes.

Record payroll (LO3)

P8–4A Vacation Destinations offers its employees the option of contributing up to 6% of their salaries to a voluntary retirement plan, with the employer matching their contribution. The company also pays 100% of medical and life insurance premiums. Assume that no employee's cumulative wages exceed the relevant wage bases. Payroll information for the first biweekly payroll period ending February 14 is listed below.

Wages and salaries	$1,000,000
Employee contribution to voluntary retirement plan	42,000
Medical insurance premiums	21,000
Life insurance premiums	4,000
Federal and state income tax withheld	250,000
Social Security tax rate	6.20%
Medicare tax rate	1.45%
Federal and state unemployment tax rate	6.20%

Required:

1. Record the employee salary expense, withholdings, and salaries payable.
2. Record the employer-provided fringe benefits.
3. Record the employer payroll taxes.

Record unearned revenues (LO4)

P8–5A The University of Michigan football stadium, built in 1927, is the largest college stadium in America, with a seating capacity of 107,500 fans. Assume the stadium sells

out all six home games before the season begins, and the athletic department collects $64.5 million in ticket sales.

Required:

1. What is the average price per season ticket and average price per individual game ticket sold?
2. Record the advance collection of $64.5 million in ticket sales.
3. Record the revenue earned after the first home game is completed.

P8–6A Texas Roadhouse opened a new restaurant in October. During its first three months of operation, the restaurant sold gift cards in various amounts totaling $2,500. The cards are redeemable for meals within one year of the purchase date. Gift cards totaling $728 were presented for redemption during the first three months of operation prior to year-end on December 31. The sales tax rate on restaurant sales is 4%, assessed at the time meals (not gift cards) are purchased. Texas Roadhouse will remit sales taxes in January.

Record unearned revenues and sales taxes (LO4)

Required:

1. Record (in summary form) the $2,500 in gift cards sold (keeping in mind that, in actuality, the firm would record each sale of a gift card individually).
2. Record the $728 in gift cards redeemed, including the 4% sales tax assessed.
3. Determine the balance in the Unearned Revenue account (remaining liability for gift cards) Texas Roadhouse will report on the December 31 balance sheet.

P8–7A The ink-jet printing division of Environmental Printing has grown tremendously in recent years. Assume the following transactions related to the ink-jet division occur during the year ended December 31, 2012.

Record contingencies (LO5)

Required:

Record any amounts as a result of each of these contingencies.

1. Environmental Printing was sued for $10 million by Addamax. Plaintiff alleges that the defendants formed an unlawful joint venture and drove it out of business. The case is expected to go to trial later this year. The likelihood of payment is reasonably possible.
2. Environmental Printing is the plaintiff in an $8 million lawsuit filed against a competitor in the high-end color-printer market. Environmental Printing expects to win the case and be awarded between $5.5 and $8 million.
3. Environmental Printing recently became aware of a design flaw in one of its ink-jet printers. A product recall appears probable. Such an action would likely cost the company between $400,000 and $800,000.

P8–8A Dinoco Petroleum faces three potential contingency situations, described below. Dinoco's fiscal year ends December 31, 2012, and it issues its 2012 financial statements on March 15, 2013.

Record contingencies (LO5)

Required:

Determine the appropriate means of reporting each situation for the year ended December 31, 2012, and record any necessary entries. Explain your reasoning.

1. In the initial trial, Dinoco lost a $120 million lawsuit resulting from a dispute with a supplier. The case is under appeal. Although Dinoco is unable to predict the outcome, it does not expect the case to have a material adverse effect on the company.
2. In November 2011, the state of Texas filed suit against Dinoco, seeking civil penalties and injunctive relief for violations of environmental laws regulating hazardous waste. On January 12, 2013, Dinoco reached a settlement with state authorities. Based upon discussions with legal counsel, it is probable that it will require $140 million to cover the cost of violations.
3. Dinoco is the plaintiff in a $200 million lawsuit filed against a customer for damages due to lost profits from rejected contracts and for unpaid receivables. The case is in final appeal, and legal counsel advises that it is probable Dinoco will prevail and be awarded $100 million.

Calculate and analyze
ratios **(LO6)**

P8–9A Selected financial data regarding current assets and current liabilities for
The Home Depot and **Lowe's**, two close competitors in the building supply industry,
are as follows:

($ in millions)	The Home Depot	Lowe's
Current assets:		
Cash and cash equivalents	$ 519	$ 245
Current investments	6	416
Net receivables	972	166
Inventory	10,673	8,209
Other current assets	1,192	215
Total current assets	$13,362	$9,251
Current liabilities:		
Accounts payable	$ 8,221	$4,543
Short-term debt	1,767	1,021
Other current liabilities	1,165	2,458
Total current liabilities	$11,153	$8,022

Required:

1. Calculate the current ratio for The Home Depot and Lowe's. Which company has
   the better ratio? Compare your calculations with those for **United Airlines** and
   Southwest Airlines reported in the chapter text. Which industry maintains a higher
   current ratio?
2. Calculate the acid-test (quick) ratio for The Home Depot and Lowe's. Which
   company has the better ratio? Compare your calculations with those for United
   Airlines and Southwest Airlines reported in the chapter text. Which industry
   maintains a higher acid-test ratio?
3. How would the purchase of additional inventory on credit affect the current ratio?
   How would it affect the acid-test ratio?

PROBLEMS: SET B

Review current liability
terms and concepts **(LO1)**

P8–1B Listed below are several terms and phrases associated with current liabilities.
Pair each item from List A (by letter) with the item from List B that is most
appropriately associated with it.

List A

_____ 1. Interest expense is recorded in the period
interest is incurred rather than in the period
interest is paid.

_____ 2. Payment is reasonably possible and can be
reasonably estimated.

_____ 3. Cash, current investments, and accounts
receivable all divided by current liabilities.

_____ 4. Payment is probable and can be reasonably
estimated.

_____ 5. Gift certificates.

_____ 6. Long-term debt maturing within one year.

_____ 7. Social Security and Medicare.

_____ 8. Unsecured notes sold in minimum
denominations of $25,000 with
maturities up to 270 days.

_____ 9. Classifying liabilities as either current or long-
term helps investors and creditors assess this.

_____ 10. Incurred on notes payable.

List B

a. The riskiness
   of a business's
   obligations.
b. Current portion of
   long-term debt.
c. Recording a
   contingent liability.
d. Disclosure of a
   contingent liability.
e. Interest expense.
f. FICA.
g. Commercial paper.
h. Acid-test ratio.
i. Accrual accounting.
j. Unearned revenues.

P8–2B **Eskimo Joe's**, designer of the world's second best-selling T-shirt (just behind **Hard Rock Cafe**), borrows $20 million cash on November 1, 2012. Eskimo Joe's signs a six-month, 9% promissory note to Stillwater National Bank under a prearranged short-term line of credit. Interest on the note is payable at maturity. Each firm has a December 31 year-end.

Record notes payable and notes receivable **(LO2)**

QB

Required:

1. Prepare the journal entries on November 1, 2012, to record (a) the notes payable for Eskimo Joe's and (b) the notes receivable for Stillwater National Bank.
2. Record the adjustment on December 31, 2012, for (a) Eskimo Joe's and (b) Stillwater National Bank.
3. Prepare the journal entries on April 30, 2013, to record payment of (a) the notes payable for Eskimo Joe's and (b) the notes receivable for Stillwater National Bank.

P8–3B **Kashi Sales, L.L.C.**, produces healthy, whole-grain foods such as breakfast cereals, frozen dinners, and granola bars. Assume payroll for the month of January was $400,000 and the following withholdings, fringe benefits, and payroll taxes apply:

Record payroll **(LO3)**

Federal and state income tax withheld	$125,000
Health insurance premiums (**Blue Cross**) paid by employer	12,000
Contribution to retirement plan (**Fidelity**) paid by employer	50,000
FICA tax rate (Social Security and Medicare)	7.65%
Federal and state unemployment tax rate	6.20%

Assume that Kashi has paid none of the withholdings or payroll taxes by the end of January (record them as payables).

Required:

1. Record the employee salary expense, withholdings, and salaries payable.
2. Record the employer-provided fringe benefits.
3. Record the employer payroll taxes.

P8–4B Emily Turnbull, president of Aerobic Equipment Corporation, is concerned about her employees' well-being. The company offers its employees free medical, dental, and life insurance coverage. It also matches employee contributions to a voluntary retirement plan up to 5% of their salaries. Assume that no employee's cumulative wages exceed the relevant wage bases. Payroll information for the biweekly payroll period ending January 24 is listed below.

Record payroll **(LO3)**

Wages and salaries	$2,000,000
Employee contribution to voluntary retirement plan	100,000
Medical insurance premiums	40,000
Dental insurance premiums	14,000
Life insurance premiums	7,000
Federal and state income tax withheld	430,000
FICA tax rate	7.65%
Federal and state unemployment tax rate	6.20%

Required:

1. Record the employee salary expense, withholdings, and salaries payable.
2. Record the employer-provided fringe benefits.
3. Record the employer payroll taxes.

P8–5B Named in honor of the late Dr. F. C. "Phog" Allen, the Kansas Jayhawks' head coach for 39 years, Allen Fieldhouse is labeled by many as one of the best places in America to watch a college basketball game. Allen Fieldhouse has a seating capacity of 16,300. Assume the basketball arena sells out all 15 home games before the season begins, and the athletic department collects $12,225,000 in ticket sales.

Record unearned revenues **(LO4)**

Required:

1. What is the average price per season ticket and average price per individual game ticket sold?
2. Record the advance collection of $12,225,000 in ticket sales.
3. Record the revenue earned after the first home game is completed.

P8–6B Logan's Roadhouse opened a new restaurant in November. During its first two months of operation, the restaurant sold gift cards in various amounts totaling $1,800. The cards are redeemable for meals within one year of the purchase date. Gift cards totaling $689 were presented for redemption during the first two months of operation prior to year-end on December 31. The sales tax rate on restaurant sales is 6%, assessed at the time meals (not gift cards) are purchased. Logan's will remit sales taxes in January.

Required:

1. Record (in summary form) the $1,800 in gift cards sold (keeping in mind that, in actuality, each sale of a gift card or a meal would be recorded individually).
2. Record the $689 in gift cards redeemed, including the 6% sales tax assessed.
3. Determine the balance in the Unearned Revenue account (remaining liability for gift cards) to be reported on the December 31 balance sheet.

P8–7B Compact Electronics is a leading manufacturer of digital camera equipment. Assume the following transactions occur during the year ended December 31, 2012.

Required:

Record any amounts as a result of each of these contingencies.

1. Sales were $28 million (all credit) for 2012. Although no customer accounts have been shown to be uncollectible, the company estimates that 2% of credit sales will eventually prove uncollectible.
2. Compact Electronics is the plaintiff in a $4 million lawsuit filed against a supplier. The suit is in final appeal, and attorneys advise it is virtually certain that Compact Electronics will win and be awarded $2.5 million.
3. In November 2012, Compact Electronics became aware of a design flaw in one of its digital camera models. A product recall appears probable and would likely cost the company $500,000.
4. Compact Electronics is the defendant in a patent infringement lawsuit brought by a competitor. It appears reasonably likely Compact Electronics will lose the case, and potential losses are estimated to be in the range of $1.5 to $2.5 million.

P8–8B Authors Academic Publishing faces three potential contingency situations, described below. Authors' fiscal year ends December 31, 2012.

Required:

Determine the appropriate means of reporting each situation for the year ended December 31, 2012, and record any necessary entries. Explain your reasoning.

1. In August 2012, a worker was injured in an accident, partially as a result of his own negligence. The worker has sued the company for $1 million. Legal counsel believes it is reasonably possible that the outcome of the suit will be unfavorable, and that the settlement would cost the company from $250,000 to $500,000.
2. A suit for breach of contract seeking damages of $2,000,000 was filed by an author on October 4, 2012. Legal counsel believes an unfavorable outcome is probable. A reasonable estimate of the award to the plaintiff is between $1 million and $1.5 million. No amount within this range is a better estimate of potential damages than any other amount.
3. Authors is the plaintiff in a pending court case. Its lawyers believe it is probable that Authors will be awarded damages of $2 million.

P8–9B Selected financial data regarding current assets and current liabilities for **American Airlines** and **Delta Airlines** are provided as follows:

($ in millions)	American	Delta
Current assets:		
Cash and cash equivalents	$1,225	$ 4,684
Current investments	3,104	1,351
Net receivables	811	1,844
Inventory	525	388
Other current assets	270	637
Total current assets	$5,935	$ 8,904
Current liabilities:		
Accounts payable	$6,702	$ 6,991
Short-term debt	2,672	2,407
Other current liabilities		1,604
Total current liabilities	$9,374	$11,002

Required:

1. Calculate the current ratio for American Airlines and Delta Airlines. Compare your calculations with those for **United Airlines** and **Southwest Airlines** reported in the chapter text. Which of the four airlines has the best current ratio?
2. Calculate the acid-test (quick) ratio for American Airlines and Delta Airlines. Compare your calculations with those for United Airlines and Southwest Airlines reported in the chapter text. Which of the four airlines has the best acid-test ratio?
3. How would the cash purchase of additional inventory affect the current ratio? How would it affect the acid-test ratio?

*For additional problems, visit **www.mhhe.com/succeed** for Problems: Set C.*

ADDITIONAL PERSPECTIVES

Great Adventures

(This is a continuation of the Great Adventures problem from earlier chapters.)

AP8–1 Great Adventures is a defendant in litigation involving a biking accident during one of its adventure races. The front tire on one of the bikes came off during the race, resulting in serious injury to the rider. However, Great Adventures can document that each bike was carefully inspected prior to the race. It may have been that the rider loosened the wheel during the race and then forgot to tighten the quick-release mechanism.

Continuing Problem

Required:

For each of the following scenarios, determine the appropriate way to report the situation. Explain your reasoning and record any necessary entry.

1. The likelihood of a payment occurring is probable, and the estimated amount is $120,000.
2. The likelihood of a payment occurring is probable, and the amount is estimated to be in the range of $100,000 to $150,000.
3. The likelihood of a payment occurring is reasonably possible, and the estimated amount is $120,000.
4. The likelihood of a payment occurring is remote, while the estimated potential amount is $120,000.

American Eagle Outfitters, Inc.

AP8–2 Financial information for **American Eagle** is presented in Appendix A at the end of the book.

Financial Analysis

Required:

1. Calculate the current ratio for the past two years. Did the current ratio improve or weaken in the more recent year?
2. Calculate the acid-test (quick) ratio for the past two years. Did the acid-test ratio improve or weaken in the more recent year?
3. If American Eagle used $100 million in current investments to pay $100 million in accounts payable, how would its current ratio and acid-test ratio change? Show your calculations.

Financial Analysis

The Buckle, Inc.

AP8–3 Financial information for **The Buckle** is presented in Appendix B at the end of the book.

Required:

1. Calculate the current ratio for the past two years. Did the current ratio improve or weaken in the more recent year?
2. Calculate the acid-test (quick) ratio for the past two years. Did the acid-test ratio improve or weaken in the more recent year?
3. If The Buckle purchased $50 million of inventory by debiting Inventory and crediting Accounts Payable, how would its current ratio and acid-test ratio change? Show your calculations.

Comparative Analysis

American Eagle Outfitters, Inc., vs. The Buckle, Inc.

AP8–4 Financial information for **American Eagle** is presented in Appendix A at the end of the book, and financial information for **The Buckle** is presented in Appendix B at the end of the book.

Required:

1. Calculate the current ratio for both companies for the year ended January 30, 2010. Which company has the better ratio? Compare your calculations with those for **United Airlines** and **Southwest Airlines** reported in the chapter text. Which industry maintains a higher current ratio?
2. Calculate the acid-test (quick) ratio for both companies for the year ended January 30, 2010. Which company has the better ratio? Compare your calculations with those for United Airlines and Southwest Airlines reported in the chapter text. Which industry maintains a higher acid-test ratio?
3. How would the purchase of additional inventory with accounts payable affect the current ratio for these two companies? Why is the answer for American Eagle and The Buckle opposite that for United Airlines?

Ethics

AP8–5 Eugene Wright is CFO of Caribbean Cruise Lines. The company designs and manufactures luxury boats. It's near year-end, and Eugene is feeling kind of queasy. The economy is in a recession, and demand for luxury boats is way down. Eugene did some preliminary liquidity analysis and noted the company's current ratio is slightly below the 1.2 minimum stated in its debt covenant with First Federal Bank. Eugene realizes that if the company reports a current ratio below 1.2 at year-end, the company runs the risk that First Federal will call its $10 million loan. He just cannot let that happen.

Caribbean Cruise Lines has current assets of $12 million and current liabilities of $10.1 million. Eugene decides to delay the delivery of $1 million in inventory

purchased on account from the originally scheduled date of December 26 to a new arrival date of January 3. This maneuver will decrease inventory and accounts payable by $1 million at December year-end. Eugene believes the company can somehow get by without the added inventory, as manufacturing slows down some during the holiday season.

Required:

1. How will the delay in the delivery of $1 million in inventory purchased on account affect the company's current ratio on December 31? Provide supporting calculations of the current ratio before and after this proposed delivery delay.
2. Is this practice ethical? Provide arguments both for and against.

Internet Research

AP8–6 A very helpful site to learn about individual publicly traded companies is *finance.yahoo.com*. Go to this website and look up a well-known publicly traded company. Once you find the company page, perform the following tasks.

Required:

1. Click on "Basic Chart." How has the stock price changed over the past year?
2. Click on "Profile." In what industry does the company operate?
3. Click on "Key Statistics." What is the current ratio for the company?
4. Click on "SEC Filings." When was the most recent 10-K, also called the annual report, submitted?
5. Click on "Competitors." Who are the company's primary competitors?

Written Communication

AP8–7 Western Manufacturing is involved with several potential contingent liabilities. Your assignment is to draft the appropriate accounting treatment for each situation described below. Western's fiscal year-end is December 31, 2012, and the financial statements will be issued in early February 2013.

  a. During 2012, Western experienced labor disputes at three of its plants. Management hopes an agreement will soon be reached. However, negotiations between the company and the unions have not produced an acceptable settlement, and employee strikes are currently under way. It is virtually certain that material costs will be incurred, but the amount of possible costs cannot be reasonably estimated.
  b. Western warrants most products it sells against defects in materials and workmanship for a period of a year. Based on its experience with previous product introductions, warranty costs are expected to approximate 2% of sales. A new product introduced in 2012 had sales of $2 million, and actual warranty expenditures incurred so far on the product are $25,000. The only entry made so far relating to warranties on this new product was to debit Warranty Expense $25,000 and credit Cash $25,000.
  c. Western is involved in a suit filed in January 2013 by Crump Holdings seeking $88 million, as an adjustment to the purchase price in connection with the company's sale of its textile business in 2012. The suit alleges that Western misstated the assets and liabilities used to calculate the purchase price for the textile division. Legal counsel advises that it is reasonably possible that Western could lose up to $88 million.

Required:

In a memo, describe the appropriate means of reporting each situation and explain your reasoning.

Earnings Management

AP8–8 Quattro Technologies, a hydraulic manufacturer in the aeronautics industry, has reported steadily increasing earnings over the past few years. The company reported net income of $120 million in 2010 and $140 million in 2011. The stock is receiving increasing analyst attention because many investors expect the steady earnings growth to continue well into the future.

One of the factors increasing sales is the superior warranty Quattro offers. Based on experience, warranty expense in 2012 should be around $40 million. However, in a recent executive meeting it was suggested that the CFO report a larger, more conservative, estimate of warranty expense. Income before warranty expense in 2012 is $210 million. By recording a warranty expense of $50 million this year, Quattro could maintain its steady earnings growth and be in a better position to maintain earnings growth again next year.

Required:

1. Can Quattro use warranty expense to manage its earnings? How?
2. Assume income before warranty expense is $210 million in 2012 and 2013, and total warranty expense over the two years is $80 million. What is the impact of the executive meeting suggestion on income in 2012? In 2013?
3. Is the executive meeting suggestion ethical? What would you do if you were the CFO?

Answers to the Self-Study Questions
1. c   2. a   3. c   4. b   5. b   6. d   7. a   8. a   9. c   10. b

9

Long-Term Liabilities

SIX FLAGS: THE UPS AND DOWNS OF BORROWING

Can you name the largest chain of amusement parks in the world? Would you guess **Disney**? **Six Flags** actually is larger, with over 20 amusement and water parks across North America. The first Six Flags amusement park, *Six Flags Over Texas,* was built in 1961 in Arlington, between Dallas and Fort Worth. The park is named for the six different flags that have flown over the state of Texas during its history—the flags of Spain, France, Mexico, the Republic of Texas, the United States, and the Confederate States of America.

What is the top-rated amusement park in the world? Six Flags? Disney? Guess again. Cedar Point, in Sandusky, Ohio, is known as the roller-coaster capital of the world and was rated the *Best Amusement Park in the World* for eleven consecutive years (***www.amusementtoday.com***). The park boasts an unheard-of 17 roller coasters! With a lineup that includes three of the top 10 steel roller coasters, Cedar Point is a coaster lover's dream come true. Its parent firm, **Cedar Fair Entertainment Company**, currently owns and operates 12 amusement parks in North America.

Comparing the financial information for Six Flags and Cedar Fair is revealing. Both companies are listed on the New York Stock Exchange, Six Flags under the ticker symbol SIX and Cedar Fair under the ticker symbol FUN. Both carry a very high level of long-term debt. However, the profitability of the two companies is quite different. From 2006–2008, Six Flags reported an average net loss each year of $238 million, and in 2009 Six Flags entered into bankruptcy proceedings. During this same time, Cedar Fair reported an average annual net income of about $30 million.

As you will learn in this chapter, assuming more debt can be either good or bad. If a company earns a rate of return higher than the interest rate on its debt, borrowing additional funds can increase overall profitability. On the other hand, if a company earns a rate of return lower than the interest rate on its debt, borrowing additional funds will further reduce profitability and may even result in bankruptcy proceedings.

PART A

OVERVIEW OF LONG-TERM DEBT

In the previous chapter, we discussed current liabilities. In this chapter we focus on long-term liabilities, primarily bonds. Parts A, B, and C deal with various aspects of bonds. Part D discusses other long-term liabilities such as installment notes and leases. We conclude the chapter by looking at how debt affects the riskiness and profitability of **Coca-Cola** and **Pepsi**.

Suppose you are the chief financial officer (CFO) for RC Enterprises, a company that designs, manufactures, and installs steel roller coasters. The executives at your company have an idea for a new ride that could revolutionize the amusement park industry. A ride like this could spur a huge increase in sales volume and create the opportunity to expand the idea to amusement parks around the world. But growth requires funding. What are RC Enterprises's choices? To answer that question, let's consider the financing alternatives available.

Financing Alternatives

■ LO1
Explain financing alternatives.

Some of the financing needed to fund a company's growth can come from the profits generated by operations. Frequently, though, companies must find additional external financing to meet their needs for cash. Let's look back at the basic accounting equation:

$$\text{Assets} = \text{Liabilities} + \text{Stockholders' Equity}$$

(resources) = (claims to resources)

The right side of the accounting equation reveals the two sources of external financing available to RC Enterprises: Debt financing refers to borrowing money (liabilities). Equity financing refers to obtaining additional investment from stockholders (stockholders' equity).

Companies in the auto industry, like **Ford**, typically lean toward liabilities for their financing. Companies in the computer industry, like **Microsoft**, use stockholders' equity to a greater extent to finance their asset growth. The mixture of liabilities and stockholders' equity a business uses is called its capital structure.

Decision Point

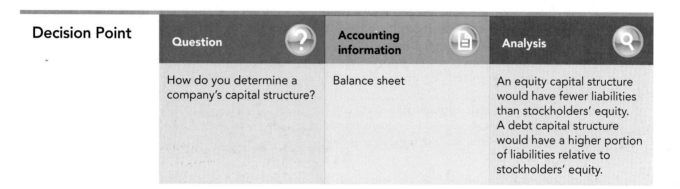

Question	Accounting information	Analysis
How do you determine a company's capital structure?	Balance sheet	An equity capital structure would have fewer liabilities than stockholders' equity. A debt capital structure would have a higher portion of liabilities relative to stockholders' equity.

Why would a company choose to borrow money rather than issue additional stock in the company? One of the primary reasons relates to taxes. **Interest expense incurred when borrowing money is tax-deductible, whereas dividends paid to stockholders are *not* tax-deductible.** Interest expense incurred on debt reduces taxable income; paying dividends to stockholders does not reduce taxable income because dividends are not an expense. Therefore, debt can be a less costly source of external financing.

KEY POINT

Companies obtain external funds through debt financing (liabilities) and equity financing (stockholders' equity). One advantage of debt financing is that interest on borrowed funds is tax-deductible.

Companies have three primary sources of long-term debt financing: bonds, notes, and leases. Medium- and large-sized corporations often choose to borrow cash by issuing bonds. In fact, **bonds are the most common form of corporate debt.** A company also can borrow cash from a bank or other financial institution through notes payable. A third source of debt financing that continues to grow in popularity is leasing. We discuss each of these sources of long-term debt financing in this chapter.

What Are Bonds?

A **bond** is a formal debt instrument that obligates the borrower to repay a stated amount, referred to as the *principal* or *face amount,* at a specified maturity date. In return for the use of the money borrowed, the borrower also agrees to pay *interest* over the life of the bond. Sound familiar? It should. That's the way we described notes payable in the preceding chapter. Bonds are very similar to notes. Bonds, though, usually are issued to many lenders, while notes most often are issued to a single lender such as a bank. Traditionally, interest on bonds is paid twice a year (semiannually) on designated interest dates, beginning six months after the original bond issue date.

Perhaps your local school board issued bonds to build a new football stadium for the high school, or maybe your hometown issued bonds to build a new library. To build the stadium or library, a city needs external financing, so it borrows money from people in the community. Bonds provide a way to borrow the money needed from many community members, each willing to lend a small amount. In return, those investing in the bonds receive interest over the life of the bonds, say 20 years, and repayment of the principal amount at the end of the bonds' life.

For most large corporations, bonds are sold, or *underwritten,* by investment houses. The three largest bond underwriters are **JPMorgan**, **Citibank**, and **Bank of America**. The issuing company—the borrower—pays a fee for these underwriting services. Other costs include legal, accounting, registration, and printing fees. To keep costs down, the issuing company may choose to sell the debt securities directly to a single investor, such as a large investment fund or an insurance company. This is referred to as a **private placement**. Issue costs for private placements are lower because these bonds are not subject to the costly and lengthy process of registering with the SEC that is required of all public offerings.

Why do some companies issue bonds rather than borrow money directly from a bank? A company that borrows by issuing bonds is effectively bypassing the bank and borrowing directly from the investing public—usually at a lower interest rate than it would in a bank loan. However, issuing bonds entails significant bond issue costs that can exceed 5% of the amount borrowed. For smaller loans, the additional bond issuance costs exceed the savings from a lower interest rate, making it more economical to borrow from a bank. For loans of $20 million or more, the interest rate savings often exceed the additional bond issuance costs, making a bond issue more attractive.

A bond issue, in effect, breaks down a large debt into manageable parts—usually $1,000 units. This avoids the necessity of finding a single investor who is both willing and able to loan a large amount of money at a reasonable interest rate. So rather than signing a $50 million note to borrow cash, a company may find it more practicable to sell $1,000 bonds to as many as 50,000 separate investors.

CAREER CORNER

Financing alternatives, capital structure, bonds, notes, and leases are topics covered in both accounting and finance. How do you decide whether to major in accounting or finance? Some students choose finance because they consider accounting more of a "desk job" and finance more "people-oriented." This just isn't true! Both accounting and finance positions require strong communication and interpersonal skills. Some students choose finance because they consider it easier to obtain a degree in finance than a degree in accounting. While there may be some truth to this, remember **Nike**'s famous slogan "No pain, no gain." Accounting majors can apply for almost any entry-level finance position, while finance majors do not have the accounting coursework to apply for many entry-level accounting positions. The extra work for an accounting degree is likely to pay additional dividends in the future.

Bond Characteristics

A **bond indenture** is a contract between a firm issuing bonds to borrow money (the issuer) and the corporations or individuals who purchase the bonds as investments (the investors). Because it would not be practical for the corporation to enter into a direct agreement with each of the many bondholders, the bond indenture is held by a trustee, usually a commercial bank or other financial institution, appointed by the issuing firm to represent the rights of the bondholders. If the firm fails to live up to the terms of the bond indenture, the trustee may bring legal action against the company on behalf of the bondholders.

For any particular bond, the bond may be secured or unsecured, term or serial, callable, or convertible. We'll discuss each of these characteristics below.

SECURED AND UNSECURED BONDS

■ **LO2**
Identify the characteristics of bonds.

When you buy a house and finance your purchase with a bank loan, you sign a mortgage agreement assigning your house as collateral. If later you are unable to make the payments, the bank is entitled to take your house. **Secured bonds** are similar. They are supported by specific assets the issuer has pledged as collateral. For instance, mortgage bonds are backed by specific real estate assets. If the borrower defaults on the payments, the lender is entitled to the real estate pledged as collateral.

However, **most bonds are unsecured. Unsecured bonds**, also referred to as *debentures*, are not backed by a specific asset. These bonds are secured only by the "full faith and credit" of the borrower.

TERM AND SERIAL BONDS

Term bonds require payment of the full principal amount of the bond at a single maturity date (the end of the loan term). Most bonds have this characteristic. Borrowers often plan ahead for the repayment by setting aside funds throughout the term to maturity. For example, let's say a city borrows $20 million to build a new sports park by issuing 7% term bonds due in 10 years. To ensure that sufficient funds are available to pay the $20 million 10 years later, the borrower sets aside money in a "sinking fund." A **sinking fund** is a designated fund to which an organization makes payments each year over the life of its outstanding debt. The city might put $2 million each year for 10 years into a sinking fund, so that $20 million is available to pay the bonds when they become due.

Serial bonds require payments in installments over a series of years. Rather than issuing $20 million in bonds that will be due at the *end* of the 10th year, the city may issue $20 million worth of 7% serial bonds, of which $2 million is due *each year* for the next 10 years. This makes it easier for the city to meet its bond obligations as they become due. Since **most bonds are term bonds,** we focus on term bonds in this chapter.

CALLABLE BONDS

Suppose your company issued bonds a few years ago that pay 10% interest. Now market interest rates have declined to 6%, but you're obligated to pay 10%

interest for the remaining time to maturity. How can you avoid this unfortunate situation?

Most corporate bonds are **callable**, or redeemable. This feature allows the borrower to repay the bonds before their scheduled maturity date at a specified call price. The *call price* is stated in the bond contract and usually exceeds the bond's face amount.

A call feature helps protect the borrower against future decreases in interest rates. If interest rates decline, the borrower can buy back the high-interest-rate bonds at a fixed price and issue new bonds at the new, lower interest rate. Just think about any loans that you may currently have, maybe a car loan or credit card balance. If interest rates drop, wouldn't it be nice to pay off your debt and reestablish it at the lower interest rate? Many home loans, in fact, provide the option to pay the loan early and refinance at a lower rate.

CONVERTIBLE BONDS

While a bond could be both callable and convertible, **a call feature is more common than a conversion feature.** Another important distinction is that callable bonds are designed to benefit the borrower, whereas convertible bonds benefit both the borrower and the lender. **Convertible** bonds allow the lender (the investor) to convert each bond into a specified number of shares of common stock. For example, let's say a $1,000 convertible bond can be converted into 20 shares of common stock. In this case, convertible bondholders benefit if the market price of the common stock goes above $50 per share (= $1,000 ÷ 20 shares), assuming the current market price of the bond is $1,000. If the company's stock price goes to $60 per share, the convertible bondholder can trade the $1,000 bond for 20 shares of stock worth $60 per share (or $1,200). Prior to conversion, the bondholder still receives interest on the convertible bond. The borrower also benefits. Convertible bonds sell at a higher price and require a lower interest rate than bonds without a conversion feature.

 INTERNATIONAL FINANCIAL REPORTING STANDARDS (IFRS)

Using IFRS, we would divide the issue price of convertible debt into its liability (bonds) and equity (conversion option) elements. Under U.S. GAAP, the entire issue price is recorded as a liability.

For more discussion, see Appendix E.

Illustration 9–1 summarizes bond characteristics.

Bond Characteristic	Definition
Secured	Bonds are backed by collateral.
Unsecured	Bonds are not backed by collateral.
Term	Bond issue matures on a single date.
Serial	Bond issue matures in installments.
Callable	Borrower can pay off bonds early.
Convertible	Lender can convert bonds to common stock.

ILLUSTRATION 9–1

Summary of Bond Characteristics

 KEY POINT

The distinguishing characteristics of bonds include whether they are backed by collateral (secured or unsecured), become due at a single specified date or over a series of years (term or serial), can be redeemed prior to maturity (callable), or can be converted into common stock (convertible).

Corporations normally issue bonds in the millions of dollars. However, to simplify the illustrations in this chapter, we drop three digits and illustrate the issuance of bonds in thousands rather than in millions. We begin with the following example and build upon it as we progress through the chapter.

Assume that on January 1, 2012, RC Enterprises decides to raise money for development of its new roller coaster by issuing $100,000 of bonds paying a stated interest rate of 7%. The bonds are due in 10 years, with interest payable semiannually on June 30 and December 31 each year. **In practice, most corporate bonds pay interest semiannually (every six months) rather than paying interest monthly, quarterly, or annually.** Thus, investors in RC Enterprises's bonds will receive (1) the *face amount* of $100,000 at the end of 10 years and (2) *interest payments* of $3,500 (= $100,000 × 7% × 1/2 year) every six months for 10 years. That's a total of 20 interest payments of $3,500 each (= $70,000). Illustration 9–2 provides a timeline of the cash flows related to the bond issue.

ILLUSTRATION 9–2

Timeline of a
Bond Issue

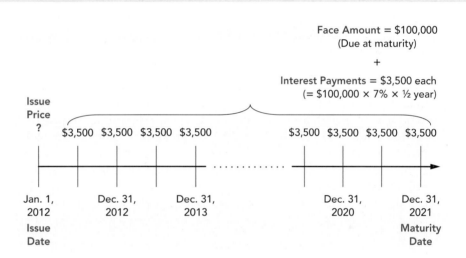

Over the 10-year period, bondholders will receive a total of $170,000, which is the face amount of $100,000 due at maturity plus semiannual interest payments totaling $70,000. How much are investors willing to pay the company today (January 1, 2012) for the right to receive $170,000 over the next 10 years? Certainly less than $170,000, because the cash flows are in the future. In the next section we see how to determine that price.

PART B

■ LO3
Determine the price
of a bond issue.

PRICING A BOND

We can calculate the issue price of a bond as the present value of the face amount *plus* the present value of the periodic interest payments. To calculate the issue price of RC Enterprises's $100,000 bonds, we need to determine the face amount of the bonds, the interest payment each period, the market interest rate per period, and the number of periods to maturity.

Bonds Issued at Face Amount

Common Terms The market rate is also known as the *effective interest rate* or *yield rate*.

For RC, the face amount equals $100,000. The interest payment every six months is $3,500 (= $100,000 × 7% × 1/2 year). The market interest rate represents the true interest rate used by investors to value RC's bond issue. The market rate can be equal to, less than, or greater than the stated 7% interest rate paid to investors. As we will see later, the market rate is determined for each bond issue by the forces of supply and demand. The stated interest rate is the rate quoted in the bond contract used to calculate the cash payments for interest.

Let's first assume the market interest rate is 7%, the same as the stated interest rate. (Later we will calculate the bond issue price when the market interest rate is less than or greater than the stated interest rate.) The number of periods to maturity is the number of years to maturity multiplied by the number of interest payments per year. Since RC's bonds pay interest semiannually (twice per year) for 10 years, there are 20 periods to maturity.

One way to determine the issue price of bonds is to use your financial calculator. Illustration 9–3 shows the calculator inputs used to obtain an issue price at the face amount of $100,000.

ILLUSTRATION 9–3

Pricing Bonds Issued at Face Amount Using a Financial Calculator

CALCULATOR INPUT

Bond Characteristics	Key	Amount
1. Face amount	FV	$100,000
2. Interest payment each period	PMT	$3,500 = $100,000 × 7% × 1/2 year
3. Market interest rate each period	I	3.5% = 7% ÷ 2 semiannual periods
4. Periods to maturity	N	20 = 10 years × 2 periods each year

CALCULATOR OUTPUT

Issue price	PV	$100,000

368004.5 +
9200

An alternative to using a financial calculator is to calculate the price of bonds in Excel. Illustration 9–4 demonstrates the inputs and the formula used to calculate the issue price.

ILLUSTRATION 9–4

Pricing Bonds Issued at Face Amount Using Excel

	C7			f_x	=-PV(C4, C5, C3, C2, 0)	
	A	B	C	D	E	F
1						
2	Face amount		$100,000.00			
3	Interest payment		$3,500.00			
4	Market interest rate		3.5%			
5	Number of periods		20			
6						
7	Issue price		$100,000.00			
8						
9						

Sheet1 / Sheet2 / Sheet3   Ready   100%

A third alternative is to calculate the price of the bonds using present value tables. In Illustration 9–5 we calculate the price of the bonds using the present value tables provided at the back of the textbook.

ILLUSTRATION 9–5

Pricing Bonds Issued at Face Amount Using Present Value Tables

Present value of face amount	= $100,000 × 0.50257*	= $ 50,257
Present value of interest payments	= $3,500[1] × 14.21240**	= 49,743
Issue price of the bonds		$100,000

[1]$100,000 × 7% × 1/2 year = $3,500
*Table 2, i = 3.5%, n = 20
**Table 4, i = 3.5%, n = 20

We use Table 2, the present value of $1, to calculate the present value of the face amount since it's just one amount ($100,000) due at maturity. We use Table 4, the present value of an ordinary annuity of $1, to calculate the present value of the interest payments since they are a series of equal amounts ($3,500 each) paid every semiannual interest period.

Using any of these three alternatives, the issue price of the bonds is equal to $100,000. All three methods have their advantages. A financial calculator and Excel are simple to use and provide greater flexibility regarding the choice of different interest rates and time periods. On the other hand, present value tables provide a better conceptual understanding of how bond prices are determined.

We assumed a market rate of 7%, which is exactly equal to the 7% stated rate of interest on the bond contract. The market rate is the interest rate investors determine for each bond issue through the forces of supply and demand. Market rates change continuously. Announcements by the Federal Reserve regarding its intentions to increase the federal funds rate (the interest rate the Federal Reserve charges to banks), political unrest, an increase in the price of oil, and fears of growing inflation, to name a few, can cause an increase in market interest rates.

Another important point to remember is that the market rate is not the same for all companies issuing bonds. Market rates vary based on the default risk of the company issuing the bonds. **Default risk** refers to the possibility that a company will be unable to pay the bond's face amount or interest payments as they become due. As a company's default risk increases, investors demand a higher market interest rate on their bond investments. For example, would you pay the same for a $1,000 bond paying 7% interest issued by **Six Flags** as you would for a $1,000 bond paying 7% interest issued by **Cedar Fair**? Probably not. As we discussed earlier, Six Flags lost money in each of the past three years. This means there is a greater chance of default by Six Flags. By paying less for Six Flags' $1,000, 7% bond, investors are effectively increasing their market rate of return. **The higher the market interest rate, the lower the bond issue price will be.**

Bonds Issued at a Discount

Now let's assume that RC Enterprises issues the same $100,000 of 7% bonds when other bonds of similar risk and maturity are paying 8%. RC's bonds are less attractive to investors, because investors can purchase bonds of similar risk that are paying the higher 8% rate. Because of this, to make the bonds more attractive, RC will have to issue its 7% bonds *below* its $100,000 face amount. Bonds issued *below* face amount are said to be issued at a discount.

In this instance, the bonds will be issued for less than the $100,000 face amount. How much less? Let's calculate the bond issue price using I = 4% (= 8% ÷ 2) rather than the 3.5% used in the previous example. In Illustration 9–6 we recalculate the issue price of the bonds, assuming the market rate of interest is now 8% per year (4% every semiannual period).

ILLUSTRATION 9–6

Pricing Bonds Issued at a Discount Using a Financial Calculator

CALCULATOR INPUT

Bond Characteristics	Key	Amount
1. Face amount	FV	$100,000
2. Interest payment each period	PMT	$3,500 = $100,000 × 7% × 1/2 year
3. Market interest rate each period	I	4% = 8% ÷ 2 semiannual periods
4. Periods to maturity	N	20 = 10 years × 2 periods each year

CALCULATOR OUTPUT

Issue price	PV	$93,205

Illustration 9–7 demonstrates how to use Excel to determine the issue price.

	C7		▼		f_x	20		
	A	B	C		D	E	F	
1								
2	Face amount		$100,000.00					
3	Interest payment		$3,500.00					
4	Market interest rate		4%					
5	Number of periods		20					
6								
7	Issue price		$93,205.00					
8								
9								

Sheet1 / Sheet2 / Sheet3

Ready   100%

ILLUSTRATION 9–7

Pricing Bonds Issued at a Discount Using Excel

In Illustration 9–8 we calculate the price of the bonds using the present value tables provided at the back of the textbook, assuming the market rate of interest is 8% per year, or 4% every semiannual period.

Present value of principal	= $100,000 × 0.45639*	= $45,639
Present value of interest payments	= $3,500[1] × 13.59033**	= 47,566
Issue price of the bonds		$93,205

[1]$100,000 × 7% × 1/2 year = $3,500
*Table 2, i = 4%, n = 20
**Table 4, i = 4%, n = 20

ILLUSTRATION 9–8

Pricing Bonds Issued at a Discount Using Present Value Tables

In practice, investors might refer to the bonds as being "issued at 93.2." This means the bonds were issued at approximately 93.2% of the $100,000 face value, or $93,200.

We see that in this instance the bond issue price is below the face amount of $100,000. The issuing company receives only $93,205 from investors, but will pay back $100,000 when the bonds mature in 10 years. Why? Because the bonds pay only 7% interest when the market rate for bonds of similar risk and maturity is 8%. By issuing the bonds for only $93,205, the issuer is effectively raising the interest earned by investors from the stated rate of 7% to the market rate of 8%. In other words, an investor paying $93,205 for the 7% bonds will earn the same rate of return on the investment (8%) as if he paid $100,000 for 8% bonds.

 COMMON MISTAKE

The interest rate we use to calculate the bond issue price is always the *market* rate, never the stated rate. Some students get confused and incorrectly use the stated rate to calculate present value. Use the stated rate to calculate the interest payment each period, but use the market rate to calculate the present value of the cash flows.

Bonds Issued at a Premium

Now let's assume that RC Enterprises issues $100,000 of 7% bonds when other bonds of similar risk and maturity are paying only 6%. Investors will pay *more* than $100,000 for these 7% bonds since they look relatively attractive compared

with bonds paying only 6%. These bonds will sell at a premium. A **premium** occurs when the issue price of a bond is *above* its face amount. In this case, RC's bonds will sell for more than $100,000. How much more? In Illustration 9–9 we recalculate the issue price using a market rate of 6% (3% semiannually).

ILLUSTRATION 9–9

Pricing Bonds Issued at a Premium Using a Financial Calculator

		CALCULATOR INPUT	
Bond Characteristics	**Key**	**Amount**	
1. Face amount	FV	$100,000	
2. Interest payment each period	PMT	$3,500 = $100,000 × 7% × 1/2 year	
3. Market interest rate each period	I	3% = 6% ÷ 2 semiannual periods	
4. Periods to maturity	N	20 = 10 years × 2 periods each year	
		CALCULATOR OUTPUT	
Issue price	PV	$107,439	

Illustration 9–10 demonstrates how to use Excel to determine the issue price.

ILLUSTRATION 9–10

Pricing Bonds Issued at a Premium Using Excel

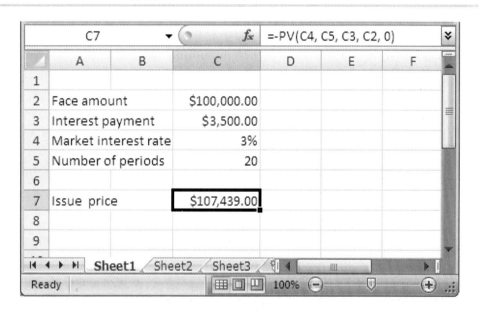

Illustration 9–11 calculates the price of the bonds using the present value tables provided at the back of the textbook, again assuming the market rate of interest is 6% (3% semiannually).

ILLUSTRATION 9–11

Pricing Bonds Issued at a Premium Using Present Value Tables

Present value of principal	= $100,000 × 0.55368*	= $ 55,368
Present value of interest payments	= $3,500[1] × 14.87747**	= 52,071
Issue price of the bonds		$107,439

[1]$100,000 × 7% × 1/2 year = $3,500
*Table 2, i = 3%, n = 20
**Table 4, i = 3%, n = 20

In practice, investors might refer to these bonds as being "issued at 107.4." This means the bonds were issued at approximately 107.4% of the $100,000 face value, or $107,400.

Here, we see that the bond issue price is above the face amount of $100,000. RC Enterprises receives $107,439 from investors, but will need to pay back only $100,000 when the bonds mature in 10 years. Why? Because the bonds pay 7% interest when the market rate for bonds of similar risk is only 6%. By issuing the bonds for $107,439, the company is effectively lowering the interest earned by investors from the stated rate of 7% to the market rate of 6%.

Illustration 9–12 shows the relation between the stated interest rate, the market interest rate, and the bond issue price.

Stated Interest Rate		Market Interest Rate	Bonds Issued at
7%	<	8%	Discount
7%	=	7%	Face amount
7%	>	6%	Premium

ILLUSTRATION 9–12

Stated Rate, Market Rate, and the Bond Issue Price

If the bonds' stated interest rate is less than the market interest rate, then the bonds will issue below face amount (discount). If the bonds' stated interest rate equals the market interest rate, then the bonds will issue at face amount. Finally, if the bonds' stated interest rate is more than the market interest rate, the bonds will issue above face amount (premium).

Which is most common in practice—bonds issued at face amount, a discount, or a premium? Most bonds initially are issued at a slight discount. Because there is a delay between when the company determines the characteristics of the bonds and when the bonds actually are issued, the company must estimate the market rate of interest. Bond issuers usually adopt a stated interest rate that is close to, but just under, the expected market interest rate. However, in future periods, the bonds may trade at either a discount or a premium depending on changes in market interest rates.

KEY POINT

The price of a bond is equal to the present value of the face amount (principal) payable at maturity, plus the present value of the periodic interest payments. Bonds can be issued at face amount, below face amount (at a discount), or above face amount (at a premium).

Assume that on January 1, 2012, Wally World issues $200,000 of 9% bonds, due in 10 years, with interest payable semiannually on June 30 and December 31 each year.

Let's Review

Required:

1. If the market rate is 9%, will the bonds issue at face amount, a discount, or a premium? Calculate the issue price.

2. If the market rate is 10%, will the bonds issue at face amount, a discount, or a premium? Calculate the issue price.

3. If the market rate is 8%, will the bonds issue at face amount, a discount, or a premium? Calculate the issue price.

Solution:

1. If the market rate is 9%, the bonds will issue at face amount.

CALCULATOR INPUT

Bond Characteristics	Key	Amount
1. Face amount	FV	$200,000
2. Interest payment each period	PMT	$9,000 = $200,000 × 9% × 1/2 year
3. Market interest rate each period	I	4.5% = 9% ÷ 2 semiannual periods
4. Periods to maturity	N	20 = 10 years × 2 periods each year

CALCULATOR OUTPUT

Issue price	PV	$200,000

	C7		f_x	=-PV(C4, C5, C3, C2, 0)
	A	B	C	D	E	F
1						
2	Face amount		$200,000.00			
3	Interest payment		$9,000.00			
4	Market interest rate		4.5%			
5	Number of periods		20			
6						
7	Issue price		$200,000.00			
8						
9						

PRESENT VALUE TABLES

Present value of principal	= $200,000 × 0.41464*	=	$ 82,928
Present value of interest payments	= $9,000[1] × 13.00794**	=	117,072
Issue price of the bonds			$200,000

[1]$200,000 × 9% × 1/2 year = $9,000
*Table 2, *i* = 4.5%, *n* = 20
**Table 4, *i* = 4.5%, *n* = 20

2. If the market rate is 10%, the bonds will issue at a discount. The only change we make in the calculation is that now I = 5% rather than 4.5%.

CALCULATOR INPUT

Bond Characteristics	Key	Amount
1. Face amount	FV	$200,000
2. Interest payment each period	PMT	$9,000 = $200,000 × 9% × 1/2 year
3. Market interest rate each period	I	5% = 10% ÷ 2 semiannual periods
4. Periods to maturity	N	20 = 10 years × 2 periods each year

CALCULATOR OUTPUT

Issue price	PV	$187,538

	C7		f_x	=-PV(C4, C5, C3, C2, 0)	
	A	B	C	D	E	F
1						
2	Face amount		$200,000.00			
3	Interest payment		$9,000.00			
4	Market interest rate		5%			
5	Number of periods		20			
6						
7	Issue price		$187,538.00			
8						
9						

Sheet1 / Sheet2 / Sheet3

Ready   100%

PRESENT VALUE TABLES

Present value of principal	= $200,000 × 0.37689*	=	$ 75,378
Present value of interest payments	= $9,000[1] × 12.46221**	=	112,160
Issue price of the bonds			$187,538

[1]$200,000 × 9% × 1/2 year = $9,000
*Table 2, $i = 5\%$, $n = 20$
**Table 4, $i = 5\%$, $n = 20$

3. If the market rate is 8%, the bonds will issue at a premium. The only change we make in the calculation is that now I = 4%.

CALCULATOR INPUT

Bond Characteristics	Key	Amount
1. Face amount	FV	$200,000
2. Interest payment each period	PMT	$9,000 = $200,000 × 9% × 1/2 year
3. Market interest rate each period	I	4% = 8% ÷ 2 semiannual periods
4. Periods to maturity	N	20 = 10 years × 2 periods each year

CALCULATOR OUTPUT

Issue price	PV	$213,590

	C7		f_x	=-PV(C4, C5, C3, C2, 0)	
	A	B	C	D	E	F
1						
2	Face amount		$200,000.00			
3	Interest payment		$9,000.00			
4	Market interest rate		4%			
5	Number of periods		20			
6						
7	Issue price		$213,590.00			
8						
9						

Sheet1 / Sheet2 / Sheet3

Ready   100%

Suggested Homework:
BE9-3, BE9-4;
E9-3, E9-4;
P9-1A&B

PRESENT VALUE TABLES

Present value of principal	= $200,000 × 0.45639*	= $ 91,278
Present value of interest payments	= $9,000[1] × 13.59033**	= 122,312
Issue price of the bonds		$213,590

[1]$200,000 × 9% × 1/2 year = $9,000
*Table 2, i = 4%, n = 20
**Table 4, i = 4%, n = 20

PART C

RECORDING BONDS PAYABLE

Now that we have seen how companies price bonds, let's look at how they record the bond issue and the related interest.

Accounting for a Bond Issue

■ **LO4**
Account for the issuance of bonds.

To see how to record the issuance of bonds, let's return to our initial example. On January 1, 2012, RC Enterprises issues $100,000 of 7% bonds, due in 10 years, with interest payable semiannually on June 30 and December 31 each year.

RECORDING BONDS ISSUED AT FACE VALUE

The bonds issue for exactly $100,000, assuming a 7% market interest rate. RC Enterprises records the bond issue as:

A = L + SE
+100,000
      +100,000

January 1, 2012	Debit	Credit
Cash	100,000	
Bonds Payable		100,000
(Issue bonds at face amount)		

RC Enterprises reports bonds payable in the long-term liabilities section of the balance sheet. Nine years from now, when the bonds are within one year of maturity, the firm will reclassify the bonds as current liabilities.

On June 30, 2012, RC Enterprises records the first semiannual interest payment:

A = L + SE
      −3,500 Exp↑
−3,500

June 30, 2012	Debit	Credit
Interest Expense	3,500	
Cash		3,500
(Pay semiannual interest)		
($3,500 = $100,000 × 7% × 1/2)		

The firm will record another semiannual interest payment on December 31, 2012. In fact, it will record semiannual interest payments at the end of every six-month period for the next 10 years.

RECORDING BONDS ISSUED AT A DISCOUNT

In the preceding example we assumed the stated interest rate (7%) and the market interest rate (7%) were the same. How will the entries differ if the stated interest rate is less than the market rate of, say, 8%? The bonds will issue at only $93,205. This is less than $100,000 because the bonds are paying only 7%, while investors can purchase bonds of similar risk paying 8%. When bonds issue at less than face value, we say they issue at a discount. RC Enterprises records the bond issue at a discount as:

January 1, 2012	Debit	Credit
Cash	93,205	
Bonds Payable		93,205
(Issue bonds at a discount)		

A = L + SE
+93,205
+93,205

We initially record the Bonds Payable account at $93,205.[1] The balance in the Bonds Payable account is the **carrying value**. The carrying value will increase from the amount originally borrowed ($93,205) to the amount due at maturity ($100,000) over the 10-year life of the bonds.

 INTERNATIONAL FINANCIAL REPORTING STANDARDS (IFRS)

Including the discount or premium as part of the carrying value of bonds payable (called the *net method*) is the preferred method of reporting under IFRS. This is also how companies in the United States report bonds payable on the balance sheet. An alternative approach (referred to as the *gross method*), in which bonds payable is recorded at face value and the discount or premium is recorded in a separate account, is covered in more advanced accounting courses.

For more discussion, see Appendix E.

We calculate each period's interest expense as the carrying value (the amount actually owed during that period) times the market rate (4% semiannually or 8% annually, in our example).[2] For the first interest payment, interest expense is:

$$\underset{\text{expense}}{\text{Interest}} = \underset{\text{of bond}}{\text{Carrying value}} \times \underset{\text{rate per period}}{\text{Market interest}}$$

$$\$3,728 \quad = \quad \$93,205 \quad \times \quad 8\% \times 1/2$$

However, the bond agreement specifies that cash paid for interest is equal to the face amount times the stated rate (3.5% semiannually or 7% annually, in our example):

$$\underset{\text{for interest}}{\text{Cash paid}} = \underset{\text{of bond}}{\text{Face amount}} \times \underset{\text{rate per period}}{\text{Stated interest}}$$

$$\$3,500 \quad = \quad \$100,000 \quad \times \quad 7\% \times 1/2$$

Notice that when the bond sells at a discount, interest expense ($3,728) is *more* than the cash paid for interest ($3,500). (The opposite is true when the bond sells at a premium: Interest expense is less than the cash paid for interest.) On June 30, 2012, RC Enterprises records interest expense, an increase in the carrying value of bonds payable, and the cash paid for interest as follows:

June 30, 2012	Debit	Credit
Interest Expense (= $93,205 × 8% × 1/2)	3,728	
Bonds Payable (difference)		228
Cash (= $100,000 × 7% × 1/2)		3,500
(Pay semiannual interest)		

A = L + SE
−3,728 Exp
+228
−3,500

---

[1]Recording bonds payable, net of the discount or plus the premium, is how companies report bonds payable on the balance sheet. Companies also record the flip side, investment in bonds, net of the discount or plus the premium. Using the net method to record both bonds payable and the investment in bonds is (1) consistent with the actual reporting used by companies in practice and (2) easier to understand than recording the discount or premium separately.

[2]We cover the effective interest method, as this is the generally accepted method under both U.S. GAAP and IFRS. The straight-line amortization method, which is allowed only if it does not materially differ from the effective interest method, is discussed as an alternative approach in more advanced accounting courses.

COMMON MISTAKE

Students sometimes incorrectly record interest expense using the stated rate rather than the market rate. Remember that interest expense is the carrying value times the market rate, while the cash paid for interest is the face amount times the stated rate.

Because the carrying value of debt issued at a discount increases over time, interest expense also will increase each semiannual interest period. We record interest for the next semiannual interest period on December 31, 2012, as:

A = L + SE

−3,737 Exp↑

+237

−3,500

December 31, 2012	Debit	Credit
Interest Expense (= [$93,205 + $228] × 8% × 1/2).................	3,737	
Bonds Payable (difference)...		237
Cash (= $100,000 × 7% × 1/2)...		3,500
(Pay semiannual interest)		

到期付款

An **amortization schedule** provides a convenient summary of the cash interest payments, interest expense, and changes in carrying value for each semiannual interest period. Illustration 9–13 provides an amortization schedule for the bonds issued at a discount. Note that the amounts for the June 30, 2012, and the December 31, 2012, semiannual interest payments shown above can be taken directly from the amortization schedule.

ILLUSTRATION 9–13

Amortization Schedule for Bonds Issued at a Discount

(1) Date	(2) Cash Paid for Interest	(3) Interest Expense	(4) Increase in Carrying Value	(5) Carrying Value
	Face Amount × Stated Rate	Carrying Value × Market Rate	(3)−(2)	Prior Carrying Value + (4)
1/1/12				$ 93,205
6/30/12	$3,500	$3,728	$228	93,433
12/31/12	3,500	3,737	237	93,670
*	*	*	*	*
*	*	*	*	99,057
6/30/21	3,500	3,962	462	99,519
12/31/21	3,500	3,981	481	100,000

The amortization schedule shows interest calculations every six months because interest is paid semiannually. The entire amortization schedule would be 20 rows long. To save space, we show only the amortization for the first and last years. The eight years in the middle are represented by asterisks. Cash paid is $3,500 (= $100,000 × 7% × 1/2) every six months. Interest expense is the carrying value times the market rate. Interest expense for the six months ended June 30, 2012, is $3,728 (= $93,205 × 4%). The difference between interest expense and the cash paid increases the carrying value of the bonds. At the maturity date, the carrying value will equal the face amount of $100,000.

Decision Maker's Perspective

Carrying Value and Market Value

Is the carrying value of bonds payable reported on the balance sheet really what the bonds are worth? Yes, but only on the date issued and on the final maturity date. Between these two dates, the carrying value of bonds payable reported on the balance sheet can vary considerably from the true underlying market value of the liability.

The reason is that the market interest rate is constantly changing. The market value of bonds moves in the opposite direction of interest rates: When market interest rates go up, the market value of bonds goes down. However, the carrying value of bonds is not adjusted for changes in market interest rates after the issue date.

Refer back to the amortization schedule for the bonds issued at a discount by RC Enterprises. The carrying value of $93,205 on the date of issue equals the market value of the bonds. However, the carrying value one year later on December 31, 2012 ($93,670), will equal market value *only* if the market rate of interest continues to be 8%. If market interest rates go up during the year, the value of bonds payable will fall. Similarly, if market rates go down during the year, the value of bonds payable will increase.

Current generally accepted accounting principles allow the option to report some or all of a company's financial assets and liabilities at fair value. If a company chooses to report a financial liability such as bonds payable at fair value, then it reports changes in fair value as gains and losses in the income statement. ●

RECORDING BONDS ISSUED AT A PREMIUM

Now assume RC Enterprises issues $100,000 of 7% bonds when other bonds of similar risk are paying only 6%. The bonds will issue at $107,439. Investors will pay more than $100,000 for these 7% bonds because bonds of similar risk are paying only 6% interest. When bonds issue at more than face value, we say they issue at a premium. RC Enterprises records the bond issue at a premium as:

January 1, 2012	Debit	Credit
Cash	107,439	
Bonds Payable		107,439
(Issue bonds at a premium)		

A	=	L	+	SE
+107,439				+107,439

Initially, we record the Bonds Payable account at $107,439. However, RC Enterprises will need to pay back only $100,000 when the bonds mature in 10 years. Therefore, the carrying value will decrease from $107,439 (issue price) to $100,000 (face amount) over the 10-year life of the bonds. We still calculate interest expense as the carrying value times the market rate (3% semiannually). On June 30, 2012, RC Enterprises records interest, assuming the bonds were issued at a premium, as follows:

June 30, 2012	Debit	Credit
Interest Expense (= $107,439 × 6% × 1/2).................................	3,223	
Bonds Payable (difference)..	277	
Cash (= $100,000 × 7% × 1/2)..		3,500
(Pay semiannual interest)		

A	=	L	+	SE
				−3,223 Exp↑
		−277		
−3,500				

When bonds are issued at a premium, the carrying value of the debt decreases over time. That's why we *debit* Bonds Payable, because Bonds Payable is decreasing over time. Since the carrying value of the debt decreases over time, interest expense will also decrease each semiannual interest period. RC Enterprises records interest for the next semiannual interest period on December 31, 2012, as:

December 31, 2012	Debit	Credit
Interest Expense (= [$107,439 − $277] × 6% × 1/2).................	3,215	
Bonds Payable (difference)..	285	
Cash (= $100,000 × 7% × 1/2)..		3,500
(Pay semiannual interest)		

A	=	L	+	SE
				−3,215 Exp↑
		−285		
−3,500				

The amortization schedule in Illustration 9–14 summarizes the recording of interest expense for the bonds issued at a premium.

ILLUSTRATION 9–14

Amortization Schedule for Bonds Issued at a Premium

(1) Date	(2) Cash Paid for Interest	(3) Interest Expense	(4) Decrease in Carrying Value	(5) Carrying Value
	Face Amount × Stated Rate	Carrying Value × Market Rate	(2) − (3)	Prior Carrying Value − (4)
1/1/12				$107,439
6/30/12	$3,500	$3,223	$277	107,162
12/31/12	3,500	3,215	285	106,877
*	*	*	*	*
*	*	*	*	100,956
6/30/21	3,500	3,029	471	100,485
12/31/21	3,500	3,015	485	100,000

Just as in the discount example, the amounts for the June 30, 2012, and the December 31, 2012, semiannual interest payments can be obtained directly from the amortization schedule. Now, however, with a bond premium, the difference between cash paid and interest expense *decreases* the carrying value each period from $107,439 at bond issue down to $100,000 (the face amount) at bond maturity.

Illustration 9–15 shows how carrying value changes as a bond approaches its maturity date.

ILLUSTRATION 9–15

Changes in Carrying Value over Time

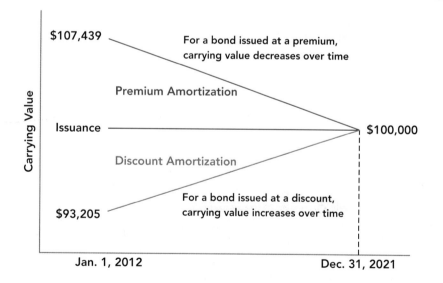

 KEY POINT

When bonds issue at face amount, the carrying value and the corresponding interest expense *remain constant* over time. When bonds issue at a discount (below face amount), the carrying value and the corresponding interest expense *increase* over time. When bonds issue at a premium (above face amount), the carrying value and the corresponding interest expense *decrease* over time.

Assume that on January 1, 2012, Wally World issues $200,000 of 9% bonds, due in 10 years, with interest payable semiannually on June 30 and December 31 each year.

Let's Review

Required:

1. If the market rate is 9%, the bonds will issue at $200,000. Record the bond issue on January 1, 2012, and the first two semiannual interest payments on June 30, 2012, and December 31, 2012.

2. If the market rate is 10%, the bonds will issue at $187,538. Record the bond issue on January 1, 2012, and the first two semiannual interest payments on June 30, 2012, and December 31, 2012.

3. If the market rate is 8%, the bonds will issue at $213,590. Record the bond issue on January 1, 2012, and the first two semiannual interest payments on June 30, 2012, and December 31, 2012.

Solution:

1. Record the bonds issued at face amount and the first two semiannual interest payments:

January 1, 2012	Debit	Credit
Cash	200,000	
Bonds Payable		200,000
(Issue bonds at face amount)		
June 30, 2012		
Interest Expense	9,000	
Cash (= $200,000 × 9% × 1/2)		9,000
(Pay semiannual interest)		
December 31, 2012		
Interest Expense	9,000	
Cash (= $200,000 × 9% × 1/2)		9,000
(Pay semiannual interest)		

2. Record the bonds issued at a discount and the first two semiannual interest payments:

January 1, 2012	Debit	Credit
Cash	187,538	
Bonds Payable		187,538
(Issue bonds at a discount)		
June 30, 2012		
Interest Expense (= $187,538 × 10% × 1/2)	9,377	
Bonds Payable (difference)		377
Cash (= $200,000 × 9% × 1/2).................................		9,000
(Pay semiannual interest)		
December 31, 2012		
Interest Expense (= [$187,538 + $377] × 10% × 1/2)	9,396	
Bonds Payable (difference)		396
Cash (= $200,000 × 9% × 1/2).................................		9,000
(Pay semiannual interest)		

3. Record the bonds issued at a premium and the first two semiannual interest payments:

January 1, 2012	Debit	Credit
Cash	213,590	
Bonds Payable		213,590
(Issue bonds at a premium)		
June 30, 2012		
Interest Expense (= $213,590 × 8% × 1/2)	8,544	
Bonds Payable (difference)	456	
Cash (= $200,000 × 9% × 1/2)...		9,000
(Pay semiannual interest)		
December 31, 2012		
Interest Expense (= [$213,590 − $456] × 8% × 1/2).................	8,525	
Bonds Payable (difference)	475	
Cash (= $200,000 × 9% × 1/2)...		9,000
(Pay semiannual interest)		

Suggested Homework:
BE9-6, BE9-7;
E9-6, E9-7;
P9-2A&B, P9-4A&B

Accounting for Bond Retirements

LO5
Record the retirement of bonds.

When the issuing corporation buys back its bonds from the investors, we say the company has **retired** those bonds. The corporation can wait until the bonds mature to retire them, or frequently (for reasons we describe below), the issuer will choose to buy the bonds back from the bondholders early.

BOND RETIREMENTS AT MATURITY

Regardless of whether bonds are issued at face amount, a discount, or a premium, **their carrying value at maturity will equal their face amount.** RC Enterprises records the retirement of its bonds at maturity (December 31, 2021) as:

A	=	L	+	SE
		−100,000		
−100,000				

December 31, 2021	Debit	Credit
Bonds Payable	100,000	
Cash		100,000
(Retire bonds at maturity)		

BOND RETIREMENTS BEFORE MATURITY

Earlier we noted that a call feature accompanies most bonds, allowing the issuer to buy back bonds at a fixed price. Even when bonds are not callable in this way, the issuing company can retire bonds early by purchasing them on the open market. Regardless of the method, when the issuer retires debt of any type before its scheduled maturity date, the transaction is an **early extinguishment of debt**.

Let's return to our example of RC Enterprises issuing $100,000 of 7% bonds maturing in 10 years when other bonds of similar risk are paying 8%. The bonds were issued on January 1, 2012, below face amount (at a discount) at $93,205. Let's assume that market interest rates drop from 8% to 6% during 2012 and RC Enterprises decides to repurchase the bonds one year after issuance on December 31,

2012, when the carrying value of the bonds is now $93,670 (see the amortization table in Illustration 9–13).

When interest rates go down, bond prices go up. If the market rate drops to 6%, it will now cost $106,877 to retire the bonds on December 31, 2012.[3] The bonds have a carrying value on December 31, 2012, of only $93,670, but it will cost the issuing company $106,877 to retire them. RC Enterprises will record a loss for the difference. RC Enterprises records the retirement as:

December 31, 2012	Debit	Credit
Bonds Payable (account balance)	93,670	
Loss (difference)	13,207	
Cash (amount paid)		106,877
(Retire bonds before maturity)		

A	=	L	+	SE
		−93,670		
				−13,207 Exp↑
−106,877				

Losses (and gains) on the early extinguishment of debt are reported as nonoperating items (similar to losses and gains on the sale of long-term assets) in the income statement. Losses have the effect of reducing net income, while gains increase net income.

Why Buy Back Debt Early?

Decision Maker's Perspective

In the example above, RC Enterprises recorded a loss of $13,207 due to a decrease in market interest rates of 2%. One way a company can protect itself from decreases in interest rates is to include a call feature allowing the company to repurchase bonds at a fixed price (such as 2% over face amount, which in our example would be $102,000). When interest rates decrease, companies with a call provision are more likely to repurchase higher-cost debt and then reissue debt at new, lower interest rates. This type of buyback and reissue lowers future interest expense.

Another reason to repay debt early is to improve the company's debt ratios (discussed later in the chapter). **Six Flags** sold seven amusement parks for just over $300 million and used the proceeds to reduce its overall debt.

Early extinguishment of debt can also be timed to manage reported earnings. Since bonds payable are reported at carrying values and not market values, firms can time their repurchase of bonds to help meet earnings expectations. For instance, when interest rates go up, bond prices go down. In this case, RC Enterprises will record a gain rather than a loss on early extinguishment. ●

KEY POINT

No gain or loss is recorded on bonds retired at maturity. For bonds retired before maturity, we record a gain or loss on early extinguishment equal to the difference between the price paid to repurchase the bonds and the bonds' carrying value.

---

[3]The repurchase price of $106,877 is based on the following financial calculator inputs: future value, $100,000; interest payment each period, $3,500; market interest rate each period, 3% (6% ÷ 2 semiannual periods); and periods to maturity, 18 (9 years left × 2 periods each year).

ETHICAL DILEMMA

On January 1, 2012, West-Tex Oil issued $50 million of 8% bonds maturing in 10 years. The market interest rate on the issue date was 9%, which resulted in the bonds being issued at a discount. In December 2013, Tex Winters, the company CFO, notes that in the two years since the bonds were issued, interest rates have fallen almost 3%. Tex suggests that West-Tex might consider repurchasing the 8% bonds and reissuing new bonds at the lower current interest rates.

Another executive, Will Bright, asks, "Won't the repurchase result in a large loss to our financial statements?" Tex agrees, indicating that West-Tex is likely to just meet earnings targets for 2013. It would probably not meet them with an added loss on bond repurchase in the millions. However, 2014 looks to be a record-breaking year. They decide that maybe they should wait until 2014 to repurchase the bonds.

How could the repurchase of debt cause a loss to be reported in net income? Explain how the repurchase of debt might be timed to manage reported earnings. Is it ethical to time the repurchase of bonds to help meet earnings targets?

PART D

■ **LO6**
Identify other major long-term liabilities.

OTHER LONG-TERM LIABILITIES

Companies report many long-term liabilities other than bonds payable. In this section, we briefly discuss two of them: installment notes and leases. (Deferred taxes, a third long-term liability, discussed in Chapter 8, are classified as either current or long-term.) The emphasis in this discussion is on the big picture, saving the details for more advanced accounting courses.

Installment Notes

You may have purchased a car, or maybe even a house. If so, unless you paid cash, you signed a note promising to pay the purchase price over, say, four years for the car or 30 years for the house. Car and house loans usually call for payment in monthly installments rather than by a single amount at maturity. Companies, too, often borrow using installment notes. **Each installment payment includes both an amount that represents interest and an amount that represents a reduction of the outstanding loan balance.** The periodic reduction of the balance is enough that at maturity the note is completely paid.

To illustrate, assume that RC Enterprises obtains a $25,000, 6%, four-year loan for a new truck on January 1, 2012. Payments of $587.13 are required at the end of each month for 48 months.[4] Illustration 9–16 (next page) provides an amortization schedule for the loan.

Notice that the carrying value begins at $25,000 and decreases each month to a final carrying value of $0 at the end of the four-year loan. Also, notice that interest

---

[4]The monthly payment of $587.13 is based on the following financial calculator inputs: future value, $0; present value, $25,000; market interest rate, 0.5% (6% ÷ 12 periods each year); periods to maturity, 48 (4 years × 12 periods each year)—and solving for the monthly payment (PMT).

(1) Date	(2) Cash Paid for Interest	(3) Interest Expense	(4) Decrease in Carrying Value	(5) Carrying Value
		Carrying Value × Market Rate	(2) – (3)	Prior Carrying Value – (4)
1/1/12				$25,000.00
1/31/12	$587.13	$125.00	$462.13	24,537.87
2/28/12	587.13	122.69	464.44	24,073.43
*	*	*	*	*
*	*	*	*	*
11/30/15	587.13	5.83	581.30	584.21
12/31/15	587.13	2.92	584.21	0

ILLUSTRATION 9–16

Amortization Schedule for an Installment Note

expense decreases with each monthly payment. In each of the following months, the amount that goes to interest expense becomes less and the amount that goes to decreasing the carrying value (referred to as the principal) becomes more. Why is this? Interest expense decreases over time because the carrying value decreases over time, and interest is a constant percentage of carrying value.

We record the note and the first two monthly installment payments as follows:

January 1, 2012	Debit	Credit
Cash	25,000	
Notes Payable		25,000
(Issue a note payable)		
January 31, 2012		
Interest Expense (= $25,000 × 6% × 1/12)	125.00	
Notes Payable (difference)	462.13	
Cash (monthly payment)		587.13
(Pay monthly installment on note)		
February 28, 2012		
Interest Expense (= $24,537.87 × 6% × 1/12)	122.69	
Notes Payable (difference)	464.44	
Cash (monthly payment)		587.13
(Pay monthly installment on note)		

A	=	L	+	SE
+25,000				
		+25,000		

A	=	L	+	SE
				−125.00 Exp↑
		−462.13		
−587.13				

A	=	L	+	SE
				−122.69 Exp↑
		−464.44		
−587.13				

 KEY POINT

Most notes payable require periodic installment payments. Each installment payment includes an amount that represents interest expense and an amount that represents a reduction of the outstanding loan balance.

Leases

If you have ever leased a car or an apartment, you are familiar with leasing. A **lease** is a contractual arrangement by which the *lessor* (owner) provides the *lessee* (user) the right to use an asset for a specified period of time. For accounting purposes, we have two basic types of leases: operating leases and capital leases.

Operating leases are like rentals. If you lease a car for a week, you really have no intention of owning the car. Short-term car rentals and most apartment leases are operating leases. The lessor owns the asset, and the lessee simply uses the asset temporarily. Over the lease term, the lessee records rent expense and the lessor records rent revenue.

However, not all leases are simply rentals. Capital leases occur when the lessee essentially buys an asset and borrows the money through a lease to pay for the asset. For example, let's say RC Enterprises leases rather than buys a truck, signing a four-year lease at 6% interest that automatically transfers ownership of the car to RC Enterprises at the end of the lease term. The dealership (the lessor) calculates the lease payments to cover the purchase price of the truck and 6% interest. In substance, RC Enterprises (the lessee) bought the car and borrowed the money at 6% interest to pay for it, even though RC signed a so-called lease agreement. RC would record the lease just as if it had bought the car and borrowed the money from the dealer—except "notes payable" would be labeled "lease payable." In turn, the dealership records the sale like other sales on credit.[5]

Decision Maker's Perspective

Why Do Some Companies Lease Rather Than Buy?

Leasing continues to grow in popularity. Approximately one-third of all debt financing in the United States is through leasing. Why do so many companies choose to lease rather than buy?

1. ***Leasing improves cash flows through up to 100% financing.*** In a purchase, most lenders require a down payment up to 20%. In contrast, leasing may allow you to finance up to the entire purchase price, freeing cash for other uses.

2. ***Leasing improves the balance sheet by reducing long-term debt.*** As long as the lessee can structure the lease as an operating lease, the lessee reports only rent expense, avoiding the reporting of long-term debt in a purchase with debt financing.

3. ***Leasing can lower income taxes.*** Many companies today find that purchasing equipment causes them to be faced with an extra income tax burden under the alternative minimum tax (AMT) calculations. Leasing is one way to help avoid these additional taxes. ●

 KEY POINT

An operating lease is recorded just like a rental. In a capital lease, the lessee essentially "buys" the asset and borrows the money to pay for it.

Decision Point

Question ?	Accounting information 📄	Analysis 🔍
Does the company have significant obligations related to operating leases?	Disclosure of lease commitments in the notes to the financial statements	Operating lease commitments are not reported as liabilities on the balance sheet, but are disclosed in the notes to the financial statements. They need to be considered when calculating important debt ratios such as the debt to equity ratio.

[5]Lease accounting can be complex. Therefore, the details regarding the accounting for capital leases are covered in more advanced accounting classes.

DEBT ANALYSIS
Coca-Cola vs. PepsiCo

Business decisions include risk. Failure to properly consider risk in those decisions is one of the most costly, yet most common, mistakes investors and creditors make. Long-term debt is one of the first places decision makers should look when trying to get a handle on risk. As stated in the feature story at the beginning of the chapter, **Six Flags** entered into bankruptcy proceedings in 2009 due to difficulties in repaying its long-term debt. Illustration 9–17 describes steps taken by Six Flags to reduce its long-term debt.

<table>
<tr><td>

SIX FLAGS, INC.
Notes to the Financial Statements (excerpt)

Six Flags, Inc., has entered into an agreement to sell three of its water parks and four of its theme parks to PARC 7F-Operations Corporation (PARC) of Jacksonville, Florida, for $312 million, consisting of $275 million in cash and a note receivable for $37 million.

    The disposition of these seven parks is a key component of the Company's overall strategy to reduce debt and enhance operational and financial flexibility. Company management stated that its intent was to reduce debt by several hundred million dollars over the next several years.

</td></tr>
</table>

■ **LO7**
Make financial decisions using long-term liability ratios.

ILLUSTRATION 9–17
Six Flags's Disclosure of Long-Term Debt

"HZ" → "3+4"

Here, we look at two ratios frequently used to measure financial risk related to long-term liabilities: (1) debt to equity and (2) times interest earned.

DEBT TO EQUITY RATIO

To measure a company's risk, we often calculate the **debt to equity ratio**:

$$\text{Debt to equity ratio} = \frac{\text{Total liabilities}}{\text{Stockholders' equity}}$$

Debt requires payment on specific dates. Failure to repay debt or the interest associated with the debt on a timely basis may result in default and perhaps even bankruptcy. Other things being equal, the higher the debt to equity ratio, the higher the risk of bankruptcy. When a company assumes more debt, risk increases.

Debt also can be an advantage. It can enhance the return to stockholders. If a company earns a return in excess of the cost of borrowing the funds, shareholders are provided with a total return greater than what could have been earned with equity funds alone. Unfortunately, borrowing is not always favorable. Sometimes the cost of borrowing the funds exceeds the returns they generate. This illustrates the risk–reward trade-off faced by shareholders.

Have you ever ordered a Pepsi and then found out the place serves only Coke products? Amusement parks often have exclusive contracts for soft drinks. The official soft drink of **Six Flags** is Coca-Cola, while **Cedar Point** serves only Pepsi products. Illustration 9–18 provides selected financial data for **Coca-Cola** and **PepsiCo**.

ILLUSTRATION 9–18

Financial Information for Coca-Cola and PepsiCo

Selected Balance Sheet Data
December 31, 2008 and 2007
($ in millions)

	Coca-Cola		PepsiCo	
	2008	**2007**	**2008**	**2007**
Total assets	$40,519	$43,269	$35,994	$34,628
Total liabilities	$20,047	$21,525	$23,888	$17,394
Stockholders' equity	20,472	21,744	12,106	17,234
Total liabilities and equity	$40,519	$43,269	$35,994	$34,628

Income Statements
For the year ended December 31, 2008
($ in millions)

	Coca-Cola	PepsiCo
Net sales	$31,944	$43,251
Cost of goods sold	11,374	20,351
Gross profit	20,570	22,900
Operating expenses	12,693	15,550
Interest expense	438	329
Tax expense	1,632	1,879
Net income	$ 5,807	$ 5,142

Illustration 9–19 compares the 2008 debt to equity ratio for Coca-Cola and PepsiCo.

ILLUSTRATION 9–19

Debt to Equity Ratio for Coca-Cola and PepsiCo

($ in millions)	Total Liabilities	÷	Stockholders' Equity	=	Debt to Equity Ratio
Coca-Cola	$20,047	÷	$20,472	=	0.98
PepsiCo	$23,888	÷	$12,106	=	1.97

The debt to equity ratio is higher for PepsiCo. Debt to equity is a measure of financial leverage. Thus, PepsiCo has higher leverage than Coca-Cola. Leverage enables a company to earn a higher return using debt than without debt, in the same way a person can lift more weight with a lever than without it.

Decision Point

Question	Accounting information	Analysis
Which company has higher leverage?	Debt to equity ratio	Debt to equity is a measure of financial leverage. Companies with more debt will have a higher debt to equity ratio and higher leverage.

PepsiCo is assuming more debt, and therefore its investors are assuming more risk. Remember, this added debt could be good or bad depending on whether the company earns a return in excess of the cost of borrowed funds. Let's explore this further by revisiting the return on assets introduced in Chapter 7. Recall that **return on assets** measures the amount of income generated for each dollar invested in assets. In Illustration 9–20 we calculate the return on assets for Coca-Cola and PepsiCo.

$$\text{Return on assets} = \frac{\text{Net income}}{\text{Average total assets}}$$

($ in millions)	Net Income	÷	Average Total Assets	=	Return on Assets
Coca-Cola	$5,807	÷	$41,894*	=	13.9%
PepsiCo	$5,142	÷	$35,311**	=	14.6%

ILLUSTRATION 9–20

Return on Assets for Coca-Cola and PepsiCo

*($40,519 + $43,269) ÷ 2
**($35,994 + $34,628) ÷ 2

The return on assets indicates a company's overall profitability, ignoring specific sources of financing. PepsiCo's profitability slightly exceeds Coca-Cola's. Note that both Coca-Cola and PepsiCo have a strong return on assets.

What happens when we compare the companies' **return on equity**, which indicates their ability to generate earnings from the resources that *owners* provide? Illustration 9–21 shows the calculation for return on equity.

$$\text{Return on equity} = \frac{\text{Net income}}{\text{Average stockholders' equity}}$$

($ in millions)	Net Income	÷	Average Stockholders' Equity	=	Return on Equity
Coca-Cola	$5,807	÷	$21,108*	=	27.5%
PepsiCo	$5,142	÷	$14,670**	=	35.1%

ILLUSTRATION 9–21

Return on Equity for Coca-Cola and PepsiCo

*($20,472 + $21,744) ÷ 2
**($12,106 + $17,234) ÷ 2

The difference between the return on assets and return on equity measures is due to the difference in leverage: PepsiCo's higher leverage results in a 7.6% higher return on equity compared to only a 0.7% higher return on assets. PepsiCo increased its return on equity 2.4 times (35.1% ÷ 14.6%) the return on assets. Coca-Cola increased its return on equity only 2.0 times (27.5% ÷ 13.9%) the return on assets. So, as long as both companies have strong returns in excess of the rate charged on borrowed funds, the greater leverage of PepsiCo will result in a higher return to investors. However, if returns should fall below the rate charged on borrowed funds, PepsiCo's greater leverage will result in lower overall returns to PepsiCo than to Coca-Cola. That's where the risk comes in.

Decision Point

Question	Accounting information	Analysis
How does leverage affect a company's return on equity?	Debt to equity ratio; return on equity ratio	Leverage increases risk. In good times, higher leverage results in higher return on equity. In down times, higher leverage results in lower return on equity.

TIMES INTEREST EARNED RATIO

Lenders require interest payments in return for the use of their money. Failure to pay interest when it is due may invoke penalties, possibly leading to bankruptcy. A ratio often used to measure this risk is the times interest earned ratio. This ratio compares interest expense with income available to pay those charges.

At first glance, you might think we can calculate this simply by dividing net income by interest expense. But remember, interest is one of the expenses subtracted in determining net income. So to measure the amount available to pay interest, we need to add interest back to net income. Similarly, because interest is deductible for income tax purposes, we need to add back tax expense as well.

To illustrate the need to add back interest expense and tax expense, assume a company has the following income statement:

Income before interest and taxes	$100,000
Interest expense	(20,000)
Income before taxes	80,000
Income tax expense (40%)	(32,000)
Net income	$ 48,000

What's the maximum amount of interest the company *could have incurred* and still break even? Is it $48,000? No, it's $100,000:

Income before interest and taxes	$100,000
Interest expense	(100,000)
Income before taxes	0
Income tax expense (40%)	(0)
Net income	$ 0

Notice that the $100,000 is equal to net income plus income tax expense plus interest expense.

We compute the times interest earned ratio as:

$$\text{Times interest earned ratio} = \frac{\text{Net income} + \text{Interest expense} + \text{Tax expense}}{\text{Interest expense}}$$

Illustration 9–22 compares the times interest earned ratios for Coca-Cola and PepsiCo to see which company is better able to meet interest payments.

ILLUSTRATION 9–22

Times Interest Earned Ratio for Coca-Cola and PepsiCo

($ in millions)	Net Income + Interest Expense + Tax Expense	÷	Interest Expense	=	Times Interest Earned Ratio
Coca-Cola	$7,877	÷	$438	=	18.0
PepsiCo	$7,350	÷	$329	=	22.3

PepsiCo has a higher times interest earned ratio than Coca-Cola. However, both companies exhibit strong earnings in relation to their interest expense, and both companies appear well able to meet interest payments as they become due.

KEY POINT

The debt to equity ratio is a measure of financial leverage. Taking on more debt (higher leverage) can be good or bad depending on whether the company earns a return in excess of the cost of borrowed funds. **The times interest earned ratio measures a company's ability to meet interest payments as they become due.**

Question		Accounting information		Analysis		**Decision Point**
Can a company meet its interest obligations?		Times interest earned ratio		A high times interest earned ratio indicates the ability of a company to meet its interest obligations.		

KEY POINTS BY LEARNING OBJECTIVE

LO1 Explain financing alternatives.

Companies obtain external funds through debt financing (liabilities) and equity financing (stockholders' equity). One advantage of debt financing is that interest on borrowed funds is tax-deductible.

LO2 Identify the characteristics of bonds.

The distinguishing characteristics of bonds include whether they are backed by collateral (secured or unsecured), become due at a single specified date or over a series of years (term or serial), can be redeemed prior to maturity (callable), or can be converted into common stock (convertible).

LO3 Determine the price of a bond issue.

The price of a bond is equal to the present value of the face amount (principal) payable at maturity, plus the present value of the periodic interest payments. Bonds can be issued at face amount, below face amount (at a discount), or above face amount (at a premium).

LO4 Account for the issuance of bonds.

When bonds issue at face amount, the carrying value and the corresponding interest expense *remain constant* over time. When bonds issue at a discount (below face amount), the carrying value and the corresponding interest expense *increase* over time. When bonds issue at a

premium (above face amount), the carrying value and the corresponding interest expense *decrease* over time.

LO5 Record the retirement of bonds.

No gain or loss is recorded on bonds retired at maturity. For bonds retired before maturity, we record a gain or loss on early extinguishment equal to the difference between the price paid to repurchase the bonds and the bonds' carrying value.

LO6 Identify other major long-term liabilities.

Most notes payable require periodic installment payments. Each installment payment includes an amount that represents interest expense and an amount that represents a reduction of the outstanding loan balance.

An operating lease is recorded just like a rental. In a capital lease, the lessee essentially "buys" the asset and borrows the money to pay for it.

Analysis

LO7 Make financial decisions using long-term liability ratios.

The debt to equity ratio is a measure of financial leverage. Assuming more debt (higher leverage) can be good or bad depending on whether the company earns a return in excess of the cost of borrowed funds. The times interest earned ratio measures a company's ability to meet interest payments as they become due.

GLOSSARY

Amortization schedule: Provides a summary of the cash interest payments, interest expense, and changes in carrying value for debt instruments. **p. 426**

Bond: A formal debt instrument that obligates the borrower to repay a stated amount, referred to as the principal or face amount, at a specified maturity date. **p. 413**

Bond indenture: A contract between a firm issuing bonds and the corporations or individuals who purchase the bonds. **p. 414**

Callable: A bond feature that allows the borrower to repay the bonds before their scheduled maturity date at a specified call price. **p. 415**

Capital lease: Contract in which the lessee essentially buys an asset and borrows the money through a lease to pay for the asset. **p. 434**

Capital structure: The mixture of liabilities and stockholders' equity in a business. **p. 412**

Carrying value: The balance in the bonds payable account, which equals the face value of bonds payable minus the discount or the face value plus the premium. **p. 425**

Convertible: A bond feature that allows the lender (or investor) to convert each bond into a specified number of shares of common stock. **p. 415**

Debt financing: Obtaining additional funding from lenders. **p. 412**

Debt to equity ratio: Total liabilities divided by total stockholders' equity; measures a company's risk. **p. 435**

Default risk: The risk that a company will be unable to pay the bond's face amount or interest payments as it becomes due. **p. 418**

Discount: A bond's issue price is below the face amount. **p. 418**

Early extinguishment of debt: The issuer retires debt before its scheduled maturity date. **p. 430**

Equity financing: Obtaining additional funding from stockholders. **p. 412**

Installment payment: Includes both an amount that represents interest and an amount that represents a reduction of the outstanding balance. **p. 432**

Lease: A contractual arrangement by which the lessor (owner) provides the lessee (user) the right to use an asset for a specified period of time. **p. 433**

Market interest rate: Represents the true interest rate used by investors to value a bond. **p. 416**

Operating lease: Contract in which the lessor owns the asset and the lessee simply uses the asset temporarily. **p. 433**

Premium: A bond's issue price is above the face amount. **p. 420**

Private placement: Sale of debt securities directly to a single investor. **p. 413**

Return on assets: Net income divided by average total assets; measures the income generated per dollar of assets. **p. 437**

Return on equity: Net income divided by average stockholders' equity; measures the income generated per dollar of equity. **p. 437**

Secured bonds: Bonds that are supported by specific assets pledged as collateral. **p. 414**

Serial bonds: Bonds that require payment of the principal amount of the bond over a series of maturity dates. **p. 414**

Sinking fund: An investment fund used to set aside money to be used to pay debts as they come due. **p. 414**

Stated interest rate: The rate quoted in the bond contract used to calculate the cash payments for interest. **p. 416**

Term bonds: Bonds that require payment of the full principal amount of the bond at a single maturity date. **p. 414**

Times interest earned ratio: Ratio that compares interest expense with income available to pay those charges. **p. 438**

Unsecured bonds: Bonds that are *not* supported by specific assets pledged as collateral. **p. 414**

SELF-STUDY QUESTIONS

■ **LO1**

1. Which of the following is *not* a primary source of corporate debt financing?

    a. Bonds.
    b. Notes.
    c. Leases.
    d. Receivables.

■ **LO2**

2. Serial bonds are:

    a. Bonds backed by collateral.
    b. Bonds that mature in installments.

    c. Bonds the issuer can repurchase at a fixed price.

    d. Bonds issued below the face amount.

3. Convertible bonds: ■ **LO2**

    a. Provide potential benefits only to the issuer.

    b. Provide potential benefits only to the investor.

    c. Provide potential benefits to both the issuer and the investor.

    d. Provide no potential benefits.

4. The price of a bond is equal to: ■ **LO3**

    a. The present value of the face amount plus the present value of the stated interest payments.

    b. The future value of the face amount plus the future value of the stated interest payments.

    c. The present value of the face amount only.

    d. The present value of the interest only.

5. Which of the following is true for bonds issued at a discount?   ■ **LO4**

    a. The stated interest rate is greater than the market interest rate.

    b. The market interest rate is greater than the stated interest rate.

    c. The stated interest rate and the market interest rate are equal.

    d. The stated interest rate and the market interest rate are unrelated.

6. Interest expense on bonds payable is calculated as: ■ **LO4**

    a. Face amount times the stated interest rate.

    b. Carrying value times the market interest rate.

    c. Face amount times the market interest rate.

    d. Carrying value times the stated interest rate.

7. When bonds are issued at a discount, what happens to the carrying value and   ■ **LO4**
interest expense over the life of the bonds?

    a. Carrying value and interest expense increase.

    b. Carrying value and interest expense decrease.

    c. Carrying value decreases and interest expense increases.

    d. Carrying value increases and interest expense decreases.

8. Lincoln County retires a $50 million bond issue when the carrying value of the   ■ **LO5**
bonds is $48 million, but the market value of the bonds is $54 million. Lincoln
County will record the retirement as:

    a. A debit of $6 million to Loss due to early extinguishment.

    b. A credit of $6 million to Gain due to early extinguishment.

    c. No gain or loss on retirement.

    d. A debit to Cash for $54 million.

9. Which of the following leases is essentially the purchase of an asset with debt   ■ **LO6**
financing?

    a. An operating lease.

    b. A capital lease.

    c. Both an operating lease and a capital lease.

    d. Neither an operating lease nor a capital lease.

10. Which of the following ratios measures financial leverage?   ■ **LO7**

    a. The return on assets ratio.

    b. The return on equity ratio.

    c. The times interest earned ratio.

    d. The debt to equity ratio.

Check out
www.mhhe.com/succeed
for more multiple-choice
questions.

Note: For answers, see the last page of the chapter.

REVIEW QUESTIONS

■ **LO1**   1. What is capital structure? How do the capital structures of **Ford** and **Microsoft** differ?

■ **LO1**   2. Why would a company choose to borrow money rather than issue additional stock?

■ **LO1**   3. What are bond issue costs? What is an underwriter?

■ **LO1**   4. Why do some companies issue bonds rather than borrow money directly from a bank?

■ **LO2**   5. Contrast the following types of bonds:
       a. Secured and unsecured.
       b. Term and serial.
       c. Callable and convertible.

■ **LO2**   6. What are convertible bonds? How do they benefit both the investor and the issuer?

■ **LO3**   7. How do we calculate the issue price of bonds? Is it equal to the present value of the principal? Explain.

■ **LO3**   8. Explain the difference in each of these terms used for bonds:
       a. Face amount and carrying value.
       b. Stated interest rate and market interest rate.

■ **LO3**   9. If bonds issue at a *discount,* is the stated interest rate less than, equal to, or more than the market interest rate? Explain.

■ **LO3**   10. If bonds issue at a *premium,* is the stated interest rate less than, equal to, or more than the market interest rate? Explain.

■ **LO3**   11. Extreme Motion issues $500,000 of 6% bonds due in 20 years with interest payable semiannually on June 30 and December 31. What is the amount of the cash payment for interest every six months? How many interest payments will there be?

■ **LO3**   12. Extreme Motion issues $500,000 of 6% bonds due in 20 years with interest payable semiannually on June 30 and December 31. Calculate the issue price of the bonds assuming a market interest rate of:
       a. 5%
       b. 6%
       c. 7%

■ **LO4**   13. If bonds issue at a *discount,* what happens to the carrying value of bonds payable and the amount recorded for interest expense over time?

■ **LO4**   14. If bonds issue at a *premium,* what happens to the carrying value of bonds payable and the amount recorded for interest expense over time?

■ **LO4**   15. Explain how each of the columns in an amortization schedule is calculated, assuming the bonds are issued at a discount. How is the amortization schedule different if bonds are issued at a premium?

■ **LO5**   16. Why would a company choose to buy back bonds before their maturity date?

■ **LO5**   17. If bonds with a carrying value of $280,000 are retired early at a cost of $330,000, is a gain or loss recorded by the issuer retiring the bonds? How does the issuer record the retirement?

■ **LO6**   18. How do interest expense and the carrying value of the note change over time for an installment note with fixed monthly loan payments?

■ **LO6**   19. Explain the difference between an operating lease and a capital lease.

■ **LO7**   20. What are the potential risks and rewards of carrying additional debt?

BRIEF EXERCISES

BE9–1 Water Emporium issues $20 million of 4% convertible bonds that mature in 10 years. Each $1,000 bond is convertible into 20 shares of common stock. The current market price of Water Emporium stock is $40 per share.
1. Explain why Water Emporium might choose to issue convertible bonds.
2. Explain why investors might choose Water Emporium's convertible bonds.

Explain the conversion feature of bonds (LO2)

BE9–2 Ultimate Butter Popcorn issues 6%, 20-year bonds with a face amount of $50,000. The market interest rate for bonds of similar risk and maturity is 6%. Interest is paid semiannually. At what price will the bonds issue?

Calculate the issue price of bonds (LO3)

BE9–3 Ultimate Butter Popcorn issues 6%, 10-year bonds with a face amount of $50,000. The market interest rate for bonds of similar risk and maturity is 7%. Interest is paid semiannually. At what price will the bonds issue?

Calculate the issue price of bonds (LO3)

BE9–4 Ultimate Butter Popcorn issues 6%, 15-year bonds with a face amount of $50,000. The market interest rate for bonds of similar risk and maturity is 5%. Interest is paid semiannually. At what price will the bonds issue?

Calculate the issue price of bonds (LO3)

BE9–5 Pretzelmania, Inc., issues 6%, 10-year bonds with a face amount of $60,000 for $60,000 on January 1, 2012. The market interest rate for bonds of similar risk and maturity is 6%. Interest is paid semiannually on June 30 and December 31.
1. Record the bond issue.
2. Record the first interest payment on June 30, 2012.

Record bond issue and related semiannual interest (LO4)

BE9–6 Pretzelmania, Inc., issues 6%, 10-year bonds with a face amount of $60,000 for $55,736 on January 1, 2012. The market interest rate for bonds of similar risk and maturity is 7%. Interest is paid semiannually on June 30 and December 31.
1. Record the bond issue.
2. Record the first interest payment on June 30, 2012.

Record bond issue and related semiannual interest (LO4)

BE9–7 Pretzelmania, Inc., issues 6%, 10-year bonds with a face amount of $60,000 for $64,676 on January 1, 2012. The market interest rate for bonds of similar risk and maturity is 5%. Interest is paid semiannually on June 30 and December 31.
1. Record the bond issue.
2. Record the first interest payment on June 30, 2012.

Record bond issue and related semiannual interest (LO4)

BE9–8 Pretzelmania, Inc., issues 6%, 10-year bonds with a face amount of $60,000 for $60,000 on January 1, 2012. The market interest rate for bonds of similar risk and maturity is 6%. Interest is paid *annually* on December 31.
1. Record the bond issue.
2. Record the first interest payment on December 31, 2012.

Record bond issue and related annual interest (LO4)

BE9–9 Pretzelmania, Inc., issues 6%, 10-year bonds with a face amount of $60,000 for $55,786 on January 1, 2012. The market interest rate for bonds of similar risk and maturity is 7%. Interest is paid *annually* on December 31.
1. Record the bond issue.
2. Record the first interest payment on December 31, 2012. (*Hint:* Interest expense is 7% times the carrying value of $55,786.)

Record bond issue and related annual interest (LO4)

BE9–10 Pretzelmania, Inc., issues 6%, 10-year bonds with a face amount of $60,000 for $64,633 on January 1, 2012. The market interest rate for bonds of similar risk and maturity is 5%. Interest is paid *annually* on December 31.
1. Record the bond issue.
2. Record the first interest payment on December 31, 2012. (*Hint:* Interest expense is 5% times the carrying value of $64,633.)

Record bond issue and related annual interest (LO4)

BE9–11 On January 1, 2012, Lizzy's Lemonade issues 7%, 15-year bonds with a face amount of $90,000 for $82,219, priced to yield 8%. Interest is paid semiannually. What amount of interest expense will be recorded on June 30, 2012, the first interest payment date?

Calculate interest expense (LO4)

Calculate interest expense (LO4)

BE9–12 On January 1, 2012, Lyle's Limeade issues 3%, 20-year bonds with a face amount of $80,000 for $69,034, priced to yield 4%. Interest is paid semiannually. What amount of interest expense will be recorded in the December 31, 2012, annual income statement?

Interpret a bond amortization schedule (LO4)

BE9–13 Presented below is a partial amortization schedule for Discount Pizza.

(1) Period	(2) Cash Paid for Interest	(3) Interest Expense	(4) Increase in Carrying Value	(5) Carrying Value
Issue date				$55,736
1	$1,800	$1,951	$151	55,887
2	1,800	1,956	156	56,043

1. Record the bond issue.
2. Record the first interest payment.
3. Explain why interest expense increases each period.

Interpret a bond amortization schedule (LO4)

BE9–14 Presented below is a partial amortization schedule for Premium Pizza.

(1) Period	(2) Cash Paid for Interest	(3) Interest Expense	(4) Decrease in Carrying Value	(5) Carrying Value
Issue date				$64,677
1	$1,800	$1,617	$183	64,494
2	1,800	1,612	188	64,306

1. Record the bond issue.
2. Record the first interest payment.
3. Explain why interest expense decreases each period.

Record early retirement of bonds issued at a discount (LO5)

BE9–15 Discount Pizza retires its 6% bonds for $58,000 before their scheduled maturity. At the time, the bonds have a carrying value of $56,043. Record the early retirement of the bonds.

Record early retirement of bonds issued at a premium (LO5)

BE9–16 Premium Pizza retires its 6% bonds for $62,000 before their scheduled maturity. At the time, the bonds have a carrying value of $64,306. Record the early retirement of the bonds.

Record installment notes (LO6)

BE9–17 On January 1, 2012, Corvallis Carnivals borrows $20,000 to purchase a delivery truck by agreeing to a 7%, four-year loan with the bank. Payments of $478.92 are due at the end of each month, with the first installment due on January 31, 2012. Record the issuance of the note payable and the first monthly payment.

Calculate ratios (LO7)

BE9–18 **CEC Entertainment**, which owns the Chuck E. Cheese pizza chain, has the following selected data ($ in millions):

CEC ENTERTAINMENT Selected Balance Sheet Data		
	2008	**2007**
Total assets	$747	$738
Total liabilities	618	520
Total stockholders' equity	129	218

CEC ENTERTAINMENT Selected Income Statement Data	
Sales revenue	$815
Interest expense	17
Tax expense	34
Net income	56

Based on these amounts, calculate the following ratios for 2008:
1. Debt to equity ratio.
2. Return on assets ratio.
3. Return on equity ratio.
4. Times interest earned ratio.

Why is the return on equity higher than the return on assets?

EXERCISES

E9–1 Penny Arcades, Inc., is trying to decide between the following two alternatives to finance its new $25 million gaming center:

a. Issue $25 million of 6% bonds at face amount.

b. Issue 1 million shares of common stock for $25 per share.

Compare financing alternatives (LO1)

	Issue Bonds	Issue Stock
Operating income	$10,000,000	$10,000,000
Interest expense (bonds only)		
Income before tax		
Income tax expense (30%)		
Net income	$	$
Number of shares	3,000,000	4,000,000
Earnings per share (Net income/# of shares)	$	$

Required:

1. Assuming bonds or shares of stock are issued at the beginning of the year, complete the income statement for each alternative.
2. Which alternative results in the highest earnings per share?

E9–2 Listed below are terms and definitions associated with bonds.

Match bond terms with their definitions (LO2)

Terms

_____ e 1. Bond indenture.
_____ g 2. Secured bond.
_____ c 3. Unsecured bond.
_____ f 4. Term bond.
_____ b 5. Serial bond.
_____ a 6. Callable bond.
_____ d 7. Convertible bond.
_____ h 8. Bond issue costs.

Definitions

a. Allows the issuer to pay off the bonds early at a fixed price.
b. Matures in installments.
c. Secured only by the "full faith and credit" of the issuing corporation.
d. Allows the investor to transfer each bond into shares of common stock.
e. A contract between the issuer and the investor.
f. Matures on a single date.
g. Supported by specific assets pledged as collateral by the issuer.
h. Includes underwriting, legal, accounting, registration, and printing fees.

Required:

Match (by letter) the bond terms with their definitions. Each letter is used only once.

E9–3 On January 1, 2012, Frontier World issues $40 million of 8% bonds, due in 15 years, with interest payable semiannually on June 30 and December 31 each year. The proceeds will be used to build a new ride that combines a roller coaster, a water ride, a dark tunnel, and the great smell of outdoor barbeque, all in one ride.

Calculate the issue price of bonds (LO3)

Required:

1. If the market rate is 7%, will the bonds issue at face amount, a discount, or a premium? Calculate the issue price.
2. If the market rate is 8%, will the bonds issue at face amount, a discount, or a premium? Calculate the issue price.

3. If the market rate is 9%, will the bonds issue at face amount, a discount, or a premium? Calculate the issue price.

Calculate the issue price of bonds (LO3)

E9–4 On January 1, 2012, Water World issues $25 million of 6% bonds, due in 20 years, with interest payable semiannually on June 30 and December 31 each year. Water World intends to use the funds to build the world's largest water avalanche and the "tornado"— a giant outdoor vortex in which riders spin in progressively smaller and faster circles until they drop through a small tunnel at the bottom.

Required:

1. If the market rate is 5%, will the bonds issue at face amount, a discount, or a premium? Calculate the issue price.
2. If the market rate is 6%, will the bonds issue at face amount, a discount, or a premium? Calculate the issue price.
3. If the market rate is 7%, will the bonds issue at face amount, a discount, or a premium? Calculate the issue price.

Record bonds issued at face amount (LO4)

E9–5 On January 1, 2012, Splash City issues $400,000 of 8% bonds, due in 15 years, with interest payable semiannually on June 30 and December 31 each year.

Required:

Assuming the market interest rate on the issue date is 8%, the bonds will issue at $400,000. Record the bond issue on January 1, 2012, and the first two semiannual interest payments on June 30, 2012, and December 31, 2012.

Record bonds issued at a discount (LO4)

E9–6 On January 1, 2012, Splash City issues $400,000 of 8% bonds, due in 15 years, with interest payable semiannually on June 30 and December 31 each year.

Required:

Assuming the market interest rate on the issue date is 9%, the bonds will issue at $367,422.

1. Complete the first three rows of an amortization table.
2. Record the bond issue on January 1, 2012, and the first two semiannual interest payments on June 30, 2012, and December 31, 2012.

Record bonds issued at a premium (LO4)

E9–7 On January 1, 2012, Splash City issues $400,000 of 8% bonds, due in 15 years, with interest payable semiannually on June 30 and December 31 each year.

Required:

Assuming the market interest rate on the issue date is 7%, the bonds will issue at $436,784.

1. Complete the first three rows of an amortization table.
2. Record the bond issue on January 1, 2012, and the first two semiannual interest payments on June 30, 2012, and December 31, 2012.

Record bonds issued at face amount (LO4)

E9–8 On January 1, 2012, White Water issues $500,000 of 6% bonds, due in 20 years, with interest payable semiannually on June 30 and December 31 each year.

Required:

Assuming the market interest rate on the issue date is 6%, the bonds will issue at $500,000. Record the bond issue on January 1, 2012, and the first two semiannual interest payments on June 30, 2012, and December 31, 2012.

Record bonds issued at a discount (LO4)

E9–9 On January 1, 2012, White Water issues $500,000 of 6% bonds, due in 20 years, with interest payable semiannually on June 30 and December 31 each year.

Required:

Assuming the market interest rate on the issue date is 7%, the bonds will issue at $446,612.

1. Complete the first three rows of an amortization table.
2. Record the bond issue on January 1, 2012, and the first two semiannual interest payments on June 30, 2012, and December 31, 2012.

E9–10 On January 1, 2012, White Water issues $500,000 of 6% bonds, due in 20 years, with interest payable semiannually on June 30 and December 31 each year.

Record bonds issued at a premium (LO4)

Required:

Assuming the market interest rate on the issue date is 5%, the bonds will issue at $562,757.

1. Complete the first three rows of an amortization table.
2. Record the bond issue on January 1, 2012, and the first two semiannual interest payments on June 30, 2012, and December 31, 2012.

E9–11 On January 1, 2012, White Water issues $500,000 of 6% bonds, due in 20 years, with interest payable annually on December 31 each year.

Record bonds issued at face amount with interest payable annually (LO4)

Required:

Assuming the market interest rate on the issue date is 6%, the bonds will issue at $500,000. Record the bond issue on January 1, 2012, and the first two interest payments on December 31, 2012, and December 31, 2013.

E9–12 On January 1, 2012, White Water issues $500,000 of 6% bonds, due in 20 years, with interest payable annually on December 31 each year.

Record bonds issued at a discount with interest payable annually (LO4)

Required:

Assuming the market interest rate on the issue date is 7%, the bonds will issue at $447,030.

1. Complete the first three rows of an amortization table. (*Hint:* Use Illustration 9–13, except the dates for the first three rows will be 1/1/12, 12/31/12, and 12/31/13 since interest is payable *annually* rather than semiannually. Interest expense for the period ended December 31, 2012, is calculated as the carrying value of $447,030 times the market rate of 7%.)
2. Record the bond issue on January 1, 2012, and the first two interest payments on December 31, 2012, and December 31, 2013.

E9–13 On January 1, 2012, White Water issues $500,000 of 6% bonds, due in 20 years, with interest payable annually on December 31 each year.

Record bonds issued at a premium with interest payable annually (LO4)

Required:

Assuming the market interest rate on the issue date is 5%, the bonds will issue at $562,311.

1. Complete the first three rows of an amortization table. (*Hint:* Use Illustration 9–14, except the dates for the first three rows will be 1/1/12, 12/31/12, and 12/31/13 since interest is payable *annually* rather than semiannually. Interest expense for the period ended December 31, 2012, is calculated as the carrying value of $562,311 times the market rate of 5%.)
2. Record the bond issue on January 1, 2012, and the first two interest payments on December 31, 2012, and December 31, 2013.

E9–14 On January 1, 2012, Splash City issues $400,000 of 8% bonds, due in 15 years, with interest payable semiannually on June 30 and December 31 each year. The market interest rate on the issue date is 9% and the bonds issued at $367,422.

Record the retirement of bonds (LO5)

Required:

1. Using an amortization schedule, show that the bonds have a carrying value of $369,706 on December 31, 2013.
2. If the market interest rate drops to 7% on December 31, 2013, it will cost $433,781 to retire the bonds. Record the retirement of the bonds on December 31, 2013.

E9–15 On January 1, 2012, White Water issues $500,000 of 6% bonds, due in 20 years, with interest payable semiannually on June 30 and December 31 each year. The market interest rate on the issue date is 5% and the bonds issued at $562,757.

Record the retirement of bonds (LO5)

Required:

1. Using an amortization schedule, show that the bonds have a carrying value of $556,810 on December 31, 2014.
2. If the market interest rate increases to 7% on December 31, 2014, it will cost $450,748 to retire the bonds. Record the retirement of the bonds on December 31, 2014.

Record installment notes (LO6)

E9–16 On January 1, 2012, Tropical Paradise borrows $40,000 by agreeing to a 6%, five-year note with the bank. The funds will be used to purchase a new BMW convertible for use in promoting resort properties to potential customers. Loan payments of $773.31 are due at the end of each month with the first installment due on January 31, 2012.

Required:
Record the issuance of the installment note payable and the first two monthly payments.

Calculate and analyze ratios (LO7)

E9–17 Two leading online travel companies are **Expedia** and **Priceline**. Selected financial data for these two close competitors are as follows:

($ in thousands)	Expedia	Priceline
Total assets	$5,937,156	$1,834,224
Total liabilities	3,254,475	476,610
Total stockholders' equity	2,682,681	1,357,614
Sales revenue	$2,955,426	$2,338,212
Interest expense	84,233	24,084
Tax expense	154,400	47,168
Net income	299,526	489,472

Required:
1. Calculate the debt to equity ratio for Expedia and Priceline. Which company has the higher ratio? Compare your calculations with those for **Coca-Cola** and **PepsiCo** reported in the chapter. Which industry maintains a higher debt to equity ratio?
2. Calculate the times interest earned ratio for Expedia and Priceline. Which company is better able to meet interest payments as they become due? Compare your calculations with those for Coca-Cola and PepsiCo reported in the chapter. Which industry has a better times interest earned ratio?

For additional exercises, visit www.mhhe.com/succeed for Exercises: Set B.

PROBLEMS: SET A

Calculate the issue price of a bond and prepare amortization schedules (LO3, 4)

P9–1A Coney Island Entertainment issues $1,000,000 of 6% bonds, due in 15 years, with interest payable semiannually on June 30 and December 31 each year.

Required:
Calculate the issue price of a bond and complete the first three rows of an amortization schedule when:
1. The market interest rate is 6% and the bonds issue at face amount.
2. The market interest rate is 7% and the bonds issue at a discount.
3. The market interest rate is 5% and the bonds issue at a premium.

Record bond issue and related interest (LO4)

P9–2A On January 1, 2012, Twister Enterprises, a manufacturer of a variety of transportable spin rides, issues $500,000 of 7% bonds, due in 20 years, with interest payable semiannually on June 30 and December 31 each year.

Required:
1. If the market interest rate is 7%, the bonds will issue at $500,000. Record the bond issue on January 1, 2012, and the first two semiannual interest payments on June 30, 2012, and December 31, 2012.
2. If the market interest rate is 8%, the bonds will issue at $450,518. Record the bond issue on January 1, 2012, and the first two semiannual interest payments on June 30, 2012, and December 31, 2012.

3. If the market interest rate is 6%, the bonds will issue at $557,787. Record the bond issue on January 1, 2012, and the first two semiannual interest payments on June 30, 2012, and December 31, 2012.

P9–3A On January 1, 2012, Vacation Destinations issues bonds that pay interest semiannually on June 30 and December 31. Portions of the bond amortization schedule appear below:

Understand a bond amortization schedule (**LO4**)

(1) Date	(2) Cash Paid for Interest	(3) Interest Expense	(4) Increase in Carrying Value	(5) Carrying Value
1/1/2012				$28,048,810
6/30/2012	$1,200,000	$1,262,196	$ 62,196	28,111,006
12/31/2012	1,200,000	1,264,995	64,995	28,176,001
*	*	*	*	*
*	*	*	*	29,719,099
6/30/2021	1,200,000	1,337,360	137,360	29,856,459
12/31/2021	1,200,000	1,343,541	143,541	30,000,000

Required:

1. Were the bonds issued at face amount, a discount, or a premium?
2. What is the original issue price of the bonds?
3. What is the face amount of the bonds?
4. What is the term to maturity in years?
5. What is the stated annual interest rate?
6. What is the market annual interest rate?
7. What is the total cash interest paid over the term to maturity?

P9–4A On January 1, 2012, Universe of Fun issues $800,000, 9% bonds that mature in 10 years. The market interest rate for bonds of similar risk and maturity is 10%, and the bonds issue for $750,151. Interest is paid semiannually on June 30 and December 31.

Prepare a bond amortization schedule and record transactions for the bond issuer (**LO4**)

Required:

1. Complete the first three rows of an amortization schedule.
2. Record the issuance of the bonds on January 1, 2012.
3. Record the interest payments on June 30, 2012, and December 31, 2012.

P9–5A On January 1, 2012, Gundy Enterprises purchases an office for $250,000, paying $50,000 down and borrowing the remaining $200,000, signing an 8%, 30-year mortgage. Installment payments of $1,467.53 are due at the end of each month, with the first payment due on January 31, 2012.

Record and analyze installment notes (**LO6**)

Required:

1. Record issuance of the mortgage installment note on January 1, 2012.
2. Complete the first three rows of an amortization schedule similar to Illustration 9–16.
3. Record the first monthly mortgage payment on January 31, 2012. How much of the first payment goes to interest expense and how much goes to reducing the carrying value of the loan?
4. Total payments over the 30 years are $528,311 ($1,467.53 × 360 monthly payments). How much of this is interest expense and how much is actual payment of the loan?

P9–6A Thrillville has $40 million in bonds payable. One of the contractual agreements in the bond indenture is that the debt to equity ratio cannot exceed 2.0. Thrillville's total assets are $80 million, and its liabilities other than the bonds payable are $10 million. The company is considering some additional financing through leasing.

Explore the impact of leases on the debt to equity ratio (**LO6, 7**)

Required:

1. Calculate total stockholders' equity using the balance sheet equation.
2. What is the debt to equity ratio?
3. Explain the difference between an operating lease and a capital lease.
4. The company enters a lease agreement requiring lease payments with a present value of $15 million. Will this lease agreement affect the debt to equity ratio differently if the lease is recorded as an operating lease versus a capital lease?
5. Will entering into the lease cause the debt to equity ratio to be in violation of the contractual agreement in the bond indenture? Show your calculations (a) assuming an operating lease and (b) assuming a capital lease.

Calculate and analyze
ratios **(LO7)**

P9–7A Two leading hotel chains in the United States are **Starwood Hotels and Resorts** (owners of Sheraton, Westin, etc.) and **Marriott**. Selected financial data for these two close competitors are as follows:

($ in millions)	Starwood		Marriott	
	2008	**2007**	**2008**	**2007**
Total assets	$9,703	$9,622	$ 8,903	$8,942
Total liabilities	8,082	7,546	7,523	7,513
Total stockholders' equity	1,621	2,076	1,380	1,429
Sales revenue	$5,907		$12,879	
Interest expense	210		163	
Tax expense	76		350	
Net income	329		362	

Required:

1. Calculate the debt to equity ratio for Starwood and Marriott for the most recent year. Which company has the higher ratio? Compare your calculations with those for **Coca-Cola** and **PepsiCo** reported in the chapter. Which industry maintains a higher debt to equity ratio?
2. Calculate the return on assets and the return on equity for Starwood and Marriott. Which company has the better profitability ratios? How do they compare with those for Coca-Cola and PepsiCo reported in the chapter?
3. Calculate the times interest earned ratio for Starwood and Marriott. Which company is better able to meet interest payments as they become due? Compare your calculations with those for Coca-Cola and PepsiCo reported in the chapter. Which industry has a better times interest earned ratio?

PROBLEMS: SET B

Calculate the issue
price of a bond and
prepare amortization
schedules **(LO3, 4)**

P9–1B Christmas Anytime issues $750,000 of 7% bonds, due in 10 years, with interest payable semiannually on June 30 and December 31 each year.

Required:

Calculate the issue price of a bond and complete the first three rows of an amortization schedule when:

1. The market interest rate is 7% and the bonds issue at face amount.
2. The market interest rate is 8% and the bonds issue at a discount.
3. The market interest rate is 6% and the bonds issue at a premium.

Record bond issue and
related interest **(LO4)**

P9–2B Viking Voyager specializes in the design and production of replica Viking boats. On January 1, 2012, the company issues $2,000,000 of 8% bonds, due in 10 years, with interest payable semiannually on June 30 and December 31 each year.

Required:

1. If the market interest rate is 8%, the bonds will issue at $2,000,000. Record the bond issue on January 1, 2012, and the first two semiannual interest payments on June 30, 2012, and December 31, 2012.
2. If the market interest rate is 9%, the bonds will issue at $1,869,921. Record the bond issue on January 1, 2012, and the first two semiannual interest payments on June 30, 2012, and December 31, 2012.
3. If the market interest rate is 7%, the bonds will issue at $2,142,124. Record the bond issue on January 1, 2012, and the first two semiannual interest payments on June 30, 2012, and December 31, 2012.

P9–3B Temptation Vacations issues bonds on January 1, 2012, that pay interest semiannually on June 30 and December 31. Portions of the bond amortization schedule appear below:

Understand a bond amortization schedule (LO4)

(1) Date	(2) Cash Paid for Interest	(3) Interest Expense	(4) Decrease in Carrying Value	(5) Carrying Value
1/1/2012				$55,338,768
6/30/2012	$2,000,000	$1,936,857	$ 63,143	55,275,625
12/31/2012	2,000,000	1,934,647	65,353	55,210,272
*	*	*	*	*
*	*	*	*	50,474,924
6/30/2031	2,000,000	1,766,622	233,378	50,241,546
12/31/2031	2,000,000	1,758,454	241,546	50,000,000

Required:

1. Were the bonds issued at face amount, a discount, or a premium?
2. What is the original issue price of the bonds?
3. What is the face amount of the bonds?
4. What is the term to maturity in years?
5. What is the stated annual interest rate?
6. What is the market annual interest rate?
7. What is the total cash interest paid over the term to maturity?

8. final entry at maturity date

P9–4B Super Splash issues $900,000, 8% bonds on January 1, 2012, that mature in 20 years. The market interest rate for bonds of similar risk and maturity is 7%, and the bonds issue for $996,098. Interest is paid semiannually on June 30 and December 31.

premium

Prepare a bond amortization schedule and record transactions for the bond issuer (LO4)

Required:

1. Complete the first three rows of an amortization schedule.
2. Record the issuance of the bonds on January 1, 2012.
3. Record the interest payments on June 30, 2012, and December 31, 2012.

P9–5B On January 1, 2012, Stoops Entertainment purchases a building for $500,000, paying $100,000 down and borrowing the remaining $400,000, signing a 7%, 15-year mortgage. Installment payments of $3,595.31 are due at the end of each month, with the first payment due on January 31, 2012.

Record and analyze installment notes (LO6)

Required:

1. Record issuance of the mortgage installment note on January 1, 2012.
2. Complete the first three rows of an amortization schedule similar to Illustration 9–16.
3. Record the first monthly mortgage payment on January 31, 2012. How much of the first payment goes to interest expense and how much goes to reducing the carrying value of the loan?
4. Total payments over the 15 years are $647,156 ($3,595.31 × 180 monthly payments). How much of this is interest expense and how much is actual payment of the loan?

Explore the impact of leases on the debt to equity ratio **(LO6, 7)**

P9–6B Chunky Cheese Pizza has $60 million in bonds payable. The bond indenture states that the debt to equity ratio cannot exceed 3.0. Chunky's total assets are $200 million, and its liabilities other than the bonds payable are $90 million. The company is considering some additional financing through leasing.

Required:

1. Calculate total stockholders' equity using the balance sheet equation.
2. What is the debt to equity ratio?
3. Explain the difference between an operating and a capital lease.
4. The company enters a lease agreement requiring lease payments with a present value of $5 million. Will this lease agreement affect the debt to equity ratio differently if the lease is recorded as an operating lease versus a capital lease?
5. Will entering into the lease cause the debt to equity ratio to be in violation of the contractual agreement in the bond indenture? Show your calculations (a) assuming an operating lease and (b) assuming a capital lease.

Calculate and analyze ratios **(LO7)**

P9–7B Two of the world's leading cruise lines are **Royal Caribbean Cruises** and **Carnival Corporation**. Selected financial data for these two close competitors are as follows:

($ in millions)	Royal Caribbean		Carnival	
	2008	**2007**	**2008**	**2007**
Total assets	$16,463	$14,982	$33,400	$34,181
Total liabilities	9,660	8,225	14,302	14,218
Total stockholders' equity	6,803	6,757	19,098	19,963
Sales revenue	$ 6,533		$14,646	
Interest expense	327		414	
Tax expense	–		47	
Net income	574		2,330	

Required:

1. Calculate the debt to equity ratio for Royal Caribbean and Carnival for the most recent year. Which company has the higher ratio? Compare your calculations with those for **Coca-Cola** and **PepsiCo** reported in the chapter.
2. Calculate the return on assets and the return on equity for Royal Caribbean and Carnival. Which company has the better profitability ratios? How do they compare with those for Coca-Cola and PepsiCo reported in the chapter?
3. Calculate the times interest earned ratio for Royal Caribbean and Carnival. Which company is better able to meet interest payments as they become due? Compare your calculations with those for Coca-Cola and PepsiCo reported in the chapter. Which industry has a better times interest earned ratio?

For additional problems, visit www.mhhe.com/succeed for Problems: Set C.

ADDITIONAL PERSPECTIVES

Continuing Problem

Great Adventures

(This is a continuation of the Great Adventures problem from earlier chapters.)

AP9–1 Tony's favorite memories of his childhood were the times he spent with his dad at camp. Tony was daydreaming of those days a bit as he and Suzie jogged along a nature trail and came across a wonderful piece of property for sale. He turned to Suzie and said, "I've always wanted to start a camp where families could get away and spend

some quality time together. If we just had the money, I know this would be the perfect place." They called several banks and on January 1, 2014, Great Adventures obtained a $500,000, 6%, 10-year installment loan from Summit Bank. Monthly payments of $5,551 are required at the end of each month over the life of the 10-year loan. Each monthly payment of $5,551 includes both interest expense and principal payments (i.e., reduction of the loan amount.)

Late that night Tony exclaimed, "$500,000 for our new camp, this has to be the best news ever." Suzie snuggled close and said, "There's something else I need to tell you, Tony, I'm expecting!" They decided right then, if it was a boy, they would name him Venture.

Required:

1. Complete the first three rows of an amortization table.
2. Record the note payable on January 1, 2014, and the first two payments on January 31, 2014, and February 28, 2014.

American Eagle Outfitters, Inc.

AP9–2 Financial information for **American Eagle** is presented in Appendix A at the end of the book.

Required:

1. Calculate the debt to equity ratio for the past two years. Did the ratio improve or weaken in the more recent year?
2. Calculate the return on equity. Would investors obtain a higher return on equity if American Eagle borrowed more money?
3. *Review the balance sheet and note 8 to the financial statements.* Based on this information, how would you rate the bankruptcy risk of American Eagle?

Financial Analysis

The Buckle, Inc.

AP9–3 Financial information for **The Buckle** is presented in Appendix B at the end of the book.

Required:

1. Calculate the debt to equity ratio for the past two years. Did the ratio improve or weaken in the more recent year?
2. Calculate the return on equity. Would investors obtain a higher return on equity if The Buckle borrowed more money?
3. *Review the balance sheet and note E to the financial statements.* Based on this information, how would you rate the bankruptcy risk of The Buckle?

Financial Analysis

American Eagle Outfitters, Inc., vs. The Buckle, Inc.

AP9–4 Financial information for **American Eagle** is presented in Appendix A at the end of the book, and financial information for **The Buckle** is presented in Appendix B at the end of the book.

Required:

1. Calculate the debt to equity ratio for American Eagle and The Buckle for the most recent year. Which company has the better ratio? Compare your calculations with those for **Coca-Cola** and **PepsiCo** reported earlier in the chapter. Which industry maintains a higher debt to equity ratio?
2. Calculate the return on assets and the return on equity for American Eagle and The Buckle for the most recent year. Which company has the better profitability ratios?

Comparative Analysis

Ethics

AP9–5 The Tony Hawk Skate Park was built in early 2010. The construction was financed by $10 million of 5% bonds issued at face value, due in 10 years, with interest payable on June 30 and December 31 each year. The park did well initially, reporting net income in both 2010 and 2011. However, the discussion at the executive board meeting in late 2012 focused on falling skate-park revenues and increasing maintenance expenses. While several ideas were proposed, Jim Trost, the VP of finance, had an intriguing short-term solution. Jim stated, "Interest rates have steadily climbed the past three years. At the current market interest rate of 9%, we could repurchase our bonds for just under $8 million, recording a gain of over $2 million on the repurchase. We could then reissue new bonds at the current 9% rate."

Required:

1. Calculate the actual repurchase price on December 31, 2012, assuming the 10-year, 5% bonds paying interest semiannually were initially issued at a face value of $10 million three years earlier on January 1, 2010. (*Hint:* The periods to maturity (n) will now be 14, calculated as 7 years remaining times 2 periods each year.)
2. Record the bond retirement on December 31, 2012.
3. Is it ethical to time the repurchase of bonds in 2012 in order to include a $2 million gain on repurchase in a bad year? What if the transaction is fully disclosed?
4. From a business standpoint, is the retirement of 5% bonds and the reissue of 9% bonds a good idea? Explain why or why not.

Internet Research

AP9–6 Standard & Poor's is a global leader in credit ratings and credit risk analysis. Go to its website at *standardandpoors.com*. Select "U.S." Click on "Products and Services."

Required:

1. Begin on the homepage. Click on "About S&P" listed at the top right of the page. About how much debt is covered by Standard & Poor's credit ratings?
2. Go back to the homepage. Click on "Ratings." Click on "Learn About Corporate Ratings." Click on "Corporates: News & Commentary" at the bottom of the page. Briefly summarize an item in the news today.
3. Go back to the homepage. Click on "Indices." Click on "S&P 500." When did the S&P 500 begin?
4. Go back to the homepage. Click on "Products and Services." Briefly summarize one of the products listed.

Written Communication

AP9–7 Western Entertainment is considering issuing bonds to finance its business expansion. The company contacts you, a business consultant charging $200 an hour, to answer the following questions.
1. What are the advantages of issuing bonds over borrowing funds from a bank?
2. What are the advantages of issuing bonds over issuing common stock?
3. How is a bond price determined?

Required:

Write a memo providing answers worthy of your billing rate.

Earnings Management

AP9–8 Adrenaline Entertainment is struggling financially and its CFO, David Plesko, is starting to feel the heat. Back on January 1, 2010, Adrenaline Entertainment issued $100 million of 6% bonds, due in 15 years, with interest payable semiannually on June 30 and December 31 each year. The market interest rate on the date of issue was 5%.

It is now the end of 2014, and David has a plan to increase reported net income in 2014. The market interest rate has risen to 9% by the end of 2014. David wants to retire the $100 million, 6% bonds and reissue new 9% bonds instead.

Required:

1. Show that the bonds originally were issued on January 1, 2010, for $110,465,146.
2. Calculate the carrying value of the bonds five years later on December 31, 2014. (*Hint:* Use a market rate of 2.5% (5% ÷ 2), and the number of periods is now 20 semiannual periods.)
3. Calculate the market value of the bonds five years later on December 31, 2014. (*Hint:* The market rate is now 4.5% (9% ÷ 2) rather than 2.5% (5% ÷ 2), and the number of periods is now 20 semiannual periods.)
4. Record the early retirement of the bonds on December 31, 2014. Does the transaction increase net income? By how much (ignoring any tax effect)?
5. Is David Plesko's plan ethical? Do you think investors would agree with David Plesko that the retirement of the 6% bonds and the reissue of 9% bonds is a good idea? Explain why or why not.

Answers to the Self-Study Questions
1. d   2. b   3. c   4. a   5. b   6. b   7. a   8. a   9. b   10. d

Stockholders' Equity

AFTER STUDYING THIS CHAPTER, YOU SHOULD BE ABLE TO:

- **LO1** Identify the advantages and disadvantages of the corporate form of ownership.
- **LO2** Record the issuance of common stock.
- **LO3** Contrast preferred stock with common stock and bonds payable.
- **LO4** Account for treasury stock.
- **LO5** Describe retained earnings and record cash dividends.
- **LO6** Explain the effect of stock dividends and stock splits.
- **LO7** Prepare and analyze the stockholders' equity section of a balance sheet and the statement of stockholders' equity.

Analysis

- **LO8** Evaluate company performance using information on stockholders' equity.

DECKERS OUTDOOR: FROM DOWN UNDER TO TOP TEN

David Letterman has made the "Top Ten" list famous. His top ten things you *don't* want to hear from your accountant include, "Listen, I'm not good with math," "The good news is you're getting a huge refund—the bad news is you'll have to hide in Costa Rica for a while," "Do you have any dedemptions or exuptions or whatever?," and "Relax, everything here will be fine—I used to work for Enron."

Wouldn't it be nice to know the top ten best stock investments for the future? Although we can't predict the future, we can learn from the past. The ten best stock investments and their investment return over the past decade from 2000 through 2009 were:

Company	Main Product or Service	Return, 2000–2009
Green Mountain Coffee	Coffee	7,434%
Hansen Natural	Beverages	6,455%
Terra Nitrogen	Fertilizers	6,156%
Bally	Slot machines	5,965%
Southwestern Energy	Natural gas	5,411%
Clean Harbors	Hazardous waste disposal	5,464%
Amedisys	Home health care	4,452%
Quality Systems	Accounting and other financial software	3,592%
Deckers Outdoor	Footwear	3,549%
XTO Energy	Oil and natural gas	3,533%

Green Mountain Coffee was the top investment over the past decade. You may be more familiar with Starbucks, but Green Mountain was the better investment. If you had invested $1,000 in the company in 2000, your investment would have grown to over $74,000 by the end of 2009. The second-place finisher, **Hansen Natural**, provides a variety of all-natural beverages such as soda, energy drinks like the Monster brand, juice, and tea. A $1,000 investment in Hansen Natural would have grown to over $64,000 ten years later. Another company you might be familiar with is **Deckers Outdoor**. The company designs and manufactures trendy footwear like Teva sandals and UGG sheepskin boots, available in most shopping malls.

What do these great stock investments have in common? They all were very profitable in relation to the initial investment made by stockholders. In this chapter you will learn how to compare earnings in relation to equity—both the stockholders' equity recorded in the company balance sheet and the market value of equity as determined by the price per share times the number of shares.

Recall from the accounting equation that assets equal liabilities plus stockholders' equity.

$$\underbrace{\text{Assets}}_{\text{(resources)}} = \underbrace{\text{Liabilities} + \text{Stockholders' Equity}}_{\text{(claims to resources)}}$$

Common Terms
Stockholders' equity sometimes is referred to as *shareholders' equity.*

In Chapters 4–7 we focused on assets and in Chapters 8–9 on liabilities. Here, in Chapter 10, we focus on the third component of the accounting equation—stockholders' equity. Because assets represent resources of the company and liabilities are creditors' claims to those resources, equity represents the owners' residual claim to those resources. Stated another way, equity is equal to what we own (assets) minus what we owe (liabilities). We use the term *stockholders'* equity (as opposed to *owners'* equity) because our focus throughout the book is on corporations.

Stockholders' equity consists of three primary classifications: paid-in capital, retained earnings, and treasury stock. **Paid-in capital** is the amount stockholders have invested in the company. **Retained earnings** is the amount of earnings the corporation has kept or retained—that is, the earnings not paid out in dividends. **Treasury stock** is the corporation's own stock that it has reacquired. Illustration 10–1 shows those components in the stockholders' equity section of the balance sheet for **American Eagle**.

ILLUSTRATION 10–1

Stockholders' Equity Section for American Eagle

AMERICAN EAGLE Balance Sheet January 31, 2009	
(Dollars and number of shares in thousands)	
Total assets	$1,963,676
Total liabilities	$ 554,645
Stockholders' equity:	
Preferred stock, $0.01 par value	–0–
Common stock, $0.01 par value	2,485
Additional paid-in capital	513,574
Total paid-in capital	516,059
Retained earnings	1,679,772
Treasury stock, 43,248 (thousand) shares	(786,800)
Total stockholders' equity	$1,409,031
Total liabilities and stockholders' equity	$1,963,676

At this point, simply note that total stockholders' equity for American Eagle consists of total paid-in capital, retained earnings, and treasury stock. It is increased by paid-in capital and retained earnings and reduced by treasury stock. We'll fill in the details as we progress through the chapter.

In Part A of the chapter, we discuss transactions involving paid-in capital. A better description might be "invested capital" since it's the amount stockholders invest when they purchase a company's stock. In Part B, we examine transactions involving retained earnings. A better description might be "earned capital," since it's the amount the company has *earned* for the stockholders. In Part C, we look at the reporting of stockholders' equity.

INVESTED CAPITAL

PART A

Invested capital is the amount of money paid into a company by its owners. The owners of a corporation are its stockholders. Recall from Chapter 1 that a company can be formed as a sole proprietorship, a partnership, or a corporation. A sole proprietorship is a business owned by one person, whereas a partnership is a business owned by two or more persons. A **corporation** is an entity that is legally separate from its owners and even pays its own income taxes. Most corporations are owned by many stockholders, although some corporations are owned entirely by one individual.

■ **LO1**
Identify the advantages and disadvantages of the corporate form of ownership.

While sole proprietorships are the most common form of business, corporations dominate in terms of total sales, assets, earnings, and employees. That's why we focus on corporations in this book. To better understand the composition of invested capital, it is helpful to know more about the corporate form of ownership.

Corporations

Corporations are formed in accordance with the laws of individual states. For instance, **American Eagle** is based in Pennsylvania but incorporated in the state of Delaware. Many corporations choose to incorporate in Delaware due to the favorable incorporation laws found there. State incorporation laws share many similarities, thanks to the widespread adoption of the **Model Business Corporation Act**. This act serves as a guide to states in the development of their corporate statutes.

The state incorporation laws, in turn, guide corporations as they write their **articles of incorporation** (sometimes called the *corporate charter*). The articles of incorporation describe (a) the nature of the firm's business activities, (b) the shares of stock to be issued, and (c) the initial board of directors. The board of directors establishes corporate policies and appoints officers who manage the corporation. Illustration 10–2 presents an **organization chart** tracing the line of authority for a typical corporation.

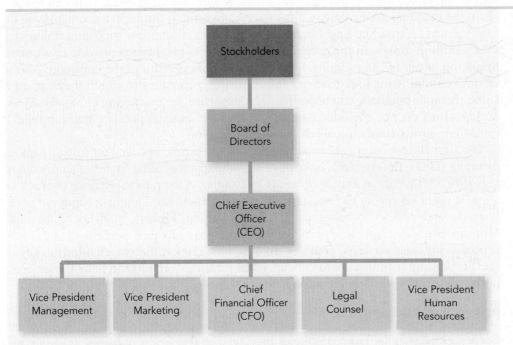

ILLUSTRATION 10–2
Organization Chart

Ultimately, a corporation's stockholders control the company. They are the owners of the corporation. By voting their shares, stockholders determine the makeup of the board of directors—which in turn appoints the management to run the company.

STAGES OF EQUITY FINANCING

Most corporations that end up selling stock to the general public don't begin that way. Instead, there's usually a progression of equity financing stages leading to a public offering, as summarized in Illustration 10–3.

ILLUSTRATION 10–3

Stages of Equity Financing

Stages of Equity Financing

The progression leading to a public offering might include some or all of these steps:

(1) Investment by the founders of the business. ➡ (2) Investment by friends and family of the founders.

(3) Outside investment by "angel" investors and venture capital firms. ➡ (4) Initial public offering (IPO).

Most corporations first raise money by selling stock to the founders of the business and to their friends and family. As the equity financing needs of the corporation grow, companies prepare a business plan and seek outside investment from "angel" investors and venture capital firms. Angel investors are wealthy individuals in the business community willing to risk investment funds on a promising business venture. Individual angel investors may invest from a few thousand dollars to over a million dollars in the corporation. Venture capital firms provide additional financing, often in the millions, for a percentage ownership in the company. Many venture capital firms look to invest in promising companies to which they can add value through business contacts, financial expertise, or marketing channels. Most corporations do not consider issuing stock to the general public ("going public") until their equity financing needs exceed $20 million.

The first time a corporation issues stock to the public is called an **initial public offering (IPO)**. Future stock issues by the company are called *seasoned equity offerings (SEOs)*. Like the issuance of bonds in Chapter 9, the public issuance of stock is a major event requiring the assistance of an investment banking firm (underwriter), lawyers, and public accountants. Major investment bankers, such as **Citigroup**, **Morgan Stanley**, and **Goldman Sachs**, can charge up to 6 percent of the issue proceeds for their services. That's $6 million for a $100 million stock offering. Legal and accounting fees also are not cheap, often running over $200 an hour for services performed in preparation for a public stock offering.

PUBLIC OR PRIVATE

Corporations may be either public or private. The stock of a publicly held corporation trades on the New York Stock Exchange (NYSE) or National Association of Securities Dealers Automated Quotations (NASDAQ), or by over-the-counter (OTC)

trading. Many of the largest companies in the world such as **Walmart**, **Exxon-Mobil**, and **General Electric** are traded on the NYSE. The NASDAQ is home to many of the largest high-tech companies, including **Microsoft**, **Intel**, and **Cisco**. Over-the-counter trading takes place outside one of the major stock exchanges. Because these trades are not on any major stock exchange and there is less research done on them in the financial market, they are considered to be more risky. All publicly held corporations are regulated by the Securities and Exchange Commission (SEC), resulting in significant additional reporting and filing requirements.

A **privately held corporation** does not allow investment by the general public and normally has fewer stockholders than a public corporation. Three of the largest private corporations in the United States are **Cargill** (agricultural commodities), **Koch Industries** (oil and gas), and **Chrysler** (cars). Corporations whose stock is privately held do not need to file financial statements with the SEC.

Frequently, companies begin as smaller, privately held corporations. Then, as success broadens opportunities for expansion, the corporation goes public. For example, **Google** was a private corporation until it decided to take the company public in order to raise large amounts of outside investment funds. The result was the largest technology IPO ever.

STOCKHOLDER RIGHTS

Whether public or private, stockholders are the owners of the corporation and have certain rights: the right to vote on certain matters (including electing the board of directors), the right to receive dividends, the right to share in the distribution of assets if the company is liquidated, and (sometimes) the right to maintain their percentage share of ownership (the *preemptive right*). Illustration 10–4 further explains these stockholder rights.

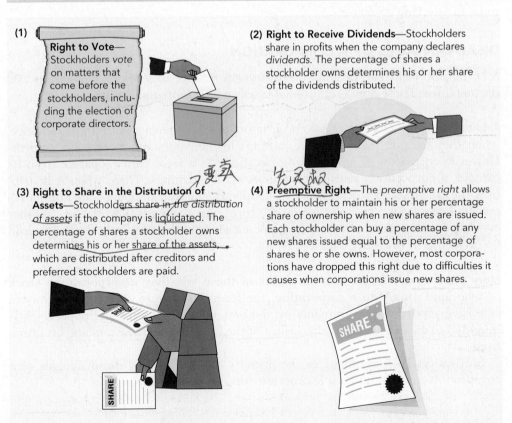

ILLUSTRATION 10–4

Stockholder Rights

(1) Right to Vote—Stockholders *vote* on matters that come before the stockholders, including the election of corporate directors.

(2) Right to Receive Dividends—Stockholders share in profits when the company declares *dividends*. The percentage of shares a stockholder owns determines his or her share of the dividends distributed.

(3) Right to Share in the Distribution of Assets—Stockholders share in the distribution of assets if the company is liquidated. The percentage of shares a stockholder owns determines his or her share of the assets, which are distributed after creditors and preferred stockholders are paid.

(4) Preemptive Right—The *preemptive right* allows a stockholder to maintain his or her percentage share of ownership when new shares are issued. Each stockholder can buy a percentage of any new shares issued equal to the percentage of shares he or she owns. However, most corporations have dropped this right due to difficulties it causes when corporations issue new shares.

ADVANTAGES OF A CORPORATION

A corporation offers three primary advantages over sole proprietorships and partnerships. These are: (1) limited liability, (2) ability to raise capital, and (3) lack of mutual agency.

Limited liability.   Limited liability guarantees that stockholders in a corporation can lose no more than the amount they invested in the company, even in the event of bankruptcy. In contrast, owners in a sole proprietorship or a partnership can be held personally liable for debts the company has incurred, above and beyond the investment they have made.

Ability to raise capital.   A corporation is better suited to raising capital than is a sole proprietorship or a partnership. Because corporations sell ownership interest in the form of shares of stock, ownership rights are easily transferred. An investor can sell his or her ownership interest (shares of stock) at any time and without affecting the structure of the corporation or its operations. As a result, attracting outside investment is easier for a corporation than for a sole proprietorship or a partnership.

Lack of mutual agency.   Another favorable aspect of investing in a corporation is the *lack of mutual agency*. Mutual agency means that individual partners in a partnership each have the power to bind the business to a contract. Therefore, an investor in a partnership must be very careful to investigate the character and business savvy of his or her fellow partners. In contrast, stockholders' participation in the affairs of a corporation is limited to voting at stockholders' meetings (unless the stockholder also is a manager). For example, owning shares of **Microsoft** stock doesn't allow you to transact business or enter into a contract in Microsoft's name. Consequently, a stockholder needn't exercise the same degree of care that partners must in selecting co-owners.

DISADVANTAGES OF A CORPORATION

A corporation has two primary disadvantages relative to sole proprietorships and partnerships. These are (1) additional taxes and (2) more paperwork.

Additional taxes.   Owners of sole proprietorships and partnerships are taxed once, when they include their share of earnings in their personal income tax returns. However, corporations have **double taxation**: As a legal entity separate from its owners, a corporation pays income taxes on its earnings. Then, when it distributes the earnings to stockholders in dividends, the stockholders—the company's owners—pay taxes a second time on the corporate dividends they receive. In other words, corporate income is taxed once on earnings at the corporate level and again on dividends at the individual level.

More paperwork.   To protect the rights of those who buy a corporation's stock or who lend money to a corporation, the federal and state governments impose extensive reporting requirements on the company. The additional paperwork is intended to ensure adequate disclosure of the information investors and creditors need.

Illustration 10–5 summarizes the primary advantages and disadvantages of a corporation compared to a sole proprietorship or partnership.

ILLUSTRATION 10–5
Advantages and
Disadvantages of a
Corporation

Advantages

(1) Limited liability
A stockholder can lose no more than the amount invested.

(2) Ability to raise capital
Attracting outside investment is easier for a corporation.

(3) Lack of mutual agency
Stockholders cannot legally bind the corporation to a contract.

Disadvantages

(1) Additional taxes
Corporate earnings are taxed twice—at the corporate level and individual stockholder level.

(2) More paperwork
Federal and state governments impose additional reporting requirements.

Limited Liability *and* Beneficial Tax Treatment

Decision Maker's Perspective

Wouldn't it be nice to get the best of both worlds—enjoy the limited liability of a corporation and the tax benefits of a sole proprietorship or partnership? An S corporation allows a company to enjoy limited liability as a corporation, but tax treatment as a partnership. Because of these benefits, many companies that qualify choose to incorporate as S corporations. One of the major restrictions is that the corporation cannot have more than 100 stockholders, so S corporations appeal more to smaller, less widely held businesses.

Two additional business forms have evolved in response to liability issues and tax treatment—*limited liability companies* (LLCs) and *limited liability partnerships* (LLPs). Most accounting firms in the United States adopt one of these two business forms because they offer limited liability and avoid double taxation, but with no limits on the number of owners as in an S corporation. ●

 KEY POINT

The primary advantages of the corporate form of business are limited liability, ability to raise capital, and lack of mutual agency. The primary disadvantages are additional taxes and more paperwork.

Common Stock

If a corporation has only one kind of stock, it usually is labeled as common stock. We can think of the common stockholders as the "true owners" of the business. The number of shares of common stock in a corporation are described as being authorized, issued, or outstanding.

AUTHORIZED, ISSUED, AND OUTSTANDING STOCK

Authorized stock is the total number of shares available to sell, stated in the company's articles of incorporation. The authorization of stock is not recorded in the accounting records. However, the corporation is required to disclose the number of shares authorized. **Issued stock** is the number of shares that have been sold to investors. A company usually does not issue all its authorized stock. **Outstanding stock** is the number of shares held *by investors*. Issued and outstanding are the same amounts as long as the corporation has not repurchased any of its own shares. Repurchased shares, called *treasury stock*, are included as part of shares issued, but excluded from shares outstanding. We discuss treasury stock in more detail later in the chapter. Illustration 10–6 summarizes the differences between authorized, issued, and outstanding shares.

ILLUSTRATION 10–6

Authorized, Issued, and Outstanding Stock

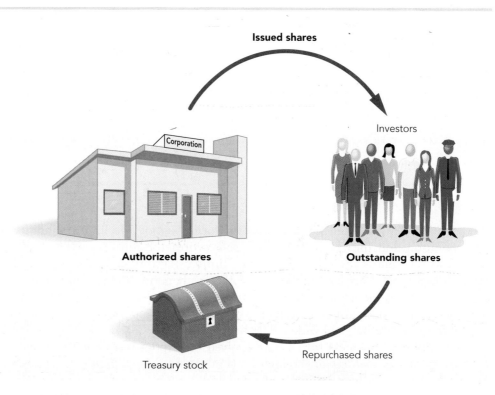

Type of Stock	Definition
Authorized	Shares available to sell (issued and unissued)
Issued	Shares actually sold (includes treasury stock)
Outstanding	Shares held by investors (excludes treasury stock)

$$\text{Authorized} - \text{Unissued} = \text{Issued}$$
$$\text{Issued} - \text{Treasury Stock} = \text{Outstanding}$$

Decision Point

Question	Accounting information	Analysis
How many of a company's shares are authorized, issued, and outstanding?	Balance sheet	The number of authorized, issued, and outstanding shares is normally reported in the stockholders' equity section of the balance sheet. If the number of issued and outstanding shares differs, look for a separate line in the equity section called *treasury stock*.

PAR VALUE 票面价值，面值

Par value is the legal capital per share of stock that's assigned when the corporation is first established. Par value originally indicated the real value of a company's shares of stock. During the late 19th and early 20th centuries, many cases of selling shares for *less* than par value (known as *watered shares*) triggered a number of lawsuits. To escape potential litigation, companies began issuing shares with very low par values—often pennies. Today, **par value has no relationship to the market value of the common stock.** For instance, **American Eagle**'s common stock has a par value of $0.01 per share but a market value over $15 per share.

Laws in some states permit corporations to issue no-par stock. No-par value stock is common stock that has not been assigned a par value. Most new corporations, and even some established corporations such as **Nike** or **Procter & Gamble**, issue no-par value common stock. In some cases, a corporation assigns a stated value to the shares. Stated value is treated and recorded in the same manner as par value shares.

 COMMON MISTAKE

Some students confuse par value with market value. Par value is the legal capital per share that is set when the corporation is first established and actually is unrelated to "value." The market value per share is equal to the current share price. In most cases, the market value per share will far exceed the par value.

ACCOUNTING FOR COMMON STOCK ISSUES

When a company receives cash from issuing common stock, it debits Cash. If it issues no-par value stock, the corporation credits the equity account entitled Common Stock. For example, let's assume Canadian Falcon, a specialty retailer of casual apparel and accessories, issues 1,000 shares of no-par value common stock at $30 per share. We record this transaction as:

	Debit	Credit
Cash (= 1,000 shares × $30)	30,000	
Common Stock		30,000
(*Issue no-par value common stock*)		

A	=	L	+	SE
+30,000				
				+30,000

If the company issues par value stock rather than no-par value stock, we record the transaction slightly differently. In that case, we credit two equity accounts. We credit the Common Stock account for the number of shares issued times the par value per share (as before), *and* we credit Additional Paid-in Capital for the portion of the cash proceeds above par value.

For example, assume that Canadian Falcon issues 1,000 shares of $0.01 par value common stock at $30 per share. The company credits the Common Stock account for par value. One thousand shares issued times $0.01 per share is $10. The company credits Additional Paid-in Capital for the portion of the cash proceeds above par value.

	Debit	Credit
Cash (= 1,000 shares × $30)	30,000	
Common Stock (= 1,000 shares × $0.01)		10
Additional Paid-in Capital (difference).................................		29,990
(Issue common stock above par)		

A = L + SE

+30,000

+10
+29,990

What if the common stock had a *stated value* of $0.01, rather than a *par value* of $0.01? We would record the same entry as in the par value example. For accounting purposes, **stated value is treated in the same manner as par value.**

Occasionally, a company will issue shares of stock in exchange for noncash goods or services. For example, what if 1,000 shares of common stock were issued to an attorney in payment for $30,000 in legal services? We would record the transaction in the same way as above, except we debit Legal Fees Expense, rather than Cash, for $30,000. The noncash exchange of stock, in this case for legal services, must be recorded at the fair value of the goods or services received.

 KEY POINT

If no-par value stock is issued, the corporation debits Cash and credits Common Stock. If par value or stated value stock is issued, the corporation debits Cash and credits two equity accounts—Common Stock at the par value or stated value per share and Additional Paid-in Capital for the portion above par or stated value.

Preferred Stock 优先股

In order to attract wider investment, some corporations issue preferred stock in addition to common stock. **American Eagle** has been authorized to issue 5 million shares of preferred stock, but the company has yet to issue any of these shares. Preferred stock is "preferred" over common stock in two ways:

1. Preferred stockholders usually have first rights to a specified amount of dividends (a stated dollar amount per share or a percentage of par value per share). If the board of directors declares dividends, preferred shareholders will receive the designated dividend before common shareholders receive any.

2. Preferred stockholders receive preference over common stockholders in the distribution of assets in the event the corporation is dissolved.

However, unlike common stock, most preferred stock does not have voting rights, leaving control of the company to common stockholders.

COMPARISON OF FINANCING ALTERNATIVES

Preferred stock actually has a mixture of attributes somewhere between common stock (equity) and a bond (liability). Investors in common stock are the owners of the corporation because they have voting rights. Investors in bonds are creditors

who have loaned money to the corporation. Preferred stockholders have characteristics of both. Illustration 10–7 provides a comparison of common stock, preferred stock, and bonds along several dimensions. Note that preferred stock falls in the middle between common stock and bonds for each of these factors.

Factor	Common Stock	Preferred Stock	Bonds
Voting rights	Yes	Usually no	No
Risk to the investor	Highest	Middle	Lowest
Expected return to the investor	Highest	Middle	Lowest
Risk of contract violations	Lowest	Middle	Highest
Preference for payments	Lowest	Middle	Highest
Tax deductibility of payments	No	Usually no	Yes

ILLUSTRATION 10–7
Comparison of Financing Alternatives

FEATURES OF PREFERRED STOCK

Preferred stock is especially interesting due to the flexibility allowed in its contractual provisions. For instance, preferred stock might be convertible, redeemable, and/or cumulative:

Convertible Shares can be exchanged for common stock.

Redeemable Shares can be returned to the corporation at a fixed price.

Cumulative Shares receive priority for future dividends, if dividends are not paid in a given year.

Preferred stock may be **convertible**, which allows the stockholder to exchange shares of preferred stock for common stock at a specified conversion ratio. **Xerox Corporation** at one time had outstanding 6.4 million shares of convertible preferred stock.

Occasionally, preferred stock is **redeemable** at the option of either stockholders or the corporation. A redemption privilege might allow preferred stockholders the option, under specified conditions, to return their shares for a predetermined redemption price. Similarly, shares may be redeemable at the option of the issuing corporation.

INTERNATIONAL FINANCIAL REPORTING STANDARDS (IFRS)

Under U.S. accounting rules, we usually record preferred stock in the stockholders' equity section of the balance sheet just above common stock. However, sometimes preferred stock shares features with debt. Redeemable preferred stock with a fixed redemption date (called *mandatorily redeemable*) is reported, like bonds payable, in the liability section of the balance sheet.[1] However, under IFRS, most preferred stock is reported as debt, with the dividends reported in the income statement as interest expense. Under U.S. GAAP, that's the case only for "mandatorily redeemable" preferred stock.

For more discussion, see Appendix E.

Preferred stock usually is **cumulative**: If the specified dividend is not paid in a given year, unpaid dividends (called **dividends in arrears**) accumulate, and the firm must pay them in a later year before paying any dividends on common stock. For instance, assume that a company issues 1,000 shares of 8%, $30 par value cumulative

---
[1]FASB ASC Topic 480: Distinguishing Liabilities from Equity.

preferred stock and 1,000 shares of $1 par value common stock. The company owes a dividend on the preferred stock of $2,400 each year (= 1,000 shares × 8% × $30 par value). If the dividend is not paid in 2010 or 2011, dividends in arrears for the two years will total $4,800. Now, let's say the company declares a dividend of $10,000 in 2012. Before it can pay dividends to common stockholders, it must pay the $4,800 in unpaid dividends for 2010 and 2011, and then the current dividend on preferred stock of $2,400 in 2012. After paying the preferred stock dividends, the company can pay the remaining balance of $2,800 (= $10,000 − $4,800 − $2,400) in dividends on common stock. However, if the preferred stock is noncumulative, any dividends in arrears are lost. The dividend of $10,000 in 2012 will be split, with $2,400 paid to preferred stockholders for the current year and the remaining $7,600 paid to common stockholders.

Because dividends are not an actual liability until they are declared by the board of directors, dividends in arrears are not reported as a liability in the balance sheet. However, information regarding any dividends in arrears is disclosed in the notes to the financial statements.

ACCOUNTING FOR PREFERRED STOCK ISSUES

We record the issuance of preferred stock similar to the way we did for the issue of common stock. Assume that Canadian Falcon issues 1,000 shares of $30 par value preferred stock for $40 per share. We record the transaction as:

A = L + SE		Debit	Credit
+40,000	Cash (= 1,000 shares × $40)	40,000	
+30,000	Preferred Stock (= 1,000 shares × $30)................................		30,000
+10,000	Additional Paid-in Capital (difference)....................................		10,000
	(Issue preferred stock above par)		

Illustration 10–8 displays the stockholders' equity section of the balance sheet for Canadian Falcon following the issuance of both common and preferred stock. We discuss the retained earnings balance later in the chapter.

ILLUSTRATION 10–8

Stockholders' Equity Section

CANADIAN FALCON Balance Sheet (partial) December 31, 2012	
Stockholders' equity:	
Preferred stock, $30 par value; 100,000 shares authorized; 1,000 shares issued and outstanding	$ 30,000
Common stock, $0.01 par value; 1 million shares authorized; 1,000 shares issued and outstanding	10
Additional paid-in capital	39,990
Total paid-in capital	70,000
Retained earnings	30,000
Total stockholders' equity	$100,000

KEY POINT

Preferred stock has features of both common stock and bonds and is usually included in stockholders' equity. However, some preferred stock (mandatorily redeemable) is so similar to bonds that we include it with bonds payable in the liability section of the balance sheet.

Treasury Stock 库存股份

■ **LO4**
Account for treasury stock.

We just examined the issuance of common and preferred stock. Next, we look at what happens when companies reacquire shares they have previously issued. Most medium- and large-size companies buy back some of their own shares. Many have formal share repurchase plans. **Treasury stock** is the name given to a corporation's own stock that it has reacquired.

Just as issuing shares increases stockholders' equity, buying those shares back decreases stockholders' equity. Buying back shares is quite different from buying the shares of another corporation. For example, when **Gap** buys its own stock, it decreases stockholders' equity and records the repurchase as treasury stock. On the other hand, if Gap purchases shares of **The Limited**, it records this transaction as an investment (an asset) and not as treasury stock (a reduction of stockholders' equity). We discuss equity investments in Appendix D.

Share buybacks are more common than ever. Over two-thirds of all publicly traded companies report treasury stock in their balance sheets. What would motivate a company to buy back its own stock?

Why Corporations Repurchase Their Stock

Decision Maker's Perspective

Companies buy back their own stock for various reasons:

1. **To boost underpriced stock.** When company management feels the market price of its stock is too low, it may attempt to support the price by decreasing the supply of stock in the marketplace. A **Johnson & Johnson** announcement that it planned to buy up to $5 billion of its outstanding shares triggered a public buying spree that pushed the stock price up by more than 3%.
2. **To distribute surplus cash without paying dividends.** While dividends usually are a good thing, investors do pay personal income tax on them. Another way for a firm to distribute surplus cash to shareholders without giving them taxable *dividend* income is to use the excess cash to repurchase its own stock.
3. **To boost earnings per share.** Earnings per share is calculated as earnings divided by the number of shares outstanding. Stock repurchases reduce the number of shares outstanding, thereby increasing earnings per share. However, with less cash in the company, it's more difficult for companies to maintain the same level of earnings following a share repurchase.
4. **To satisfy employee stock ownership plans.** Perhaps the primary motivation for stock repurchases is to acquire shares used in employee stock award and stock option compensation programs. **Microsoft**, for example, reported that its board of directors had approved a program to repurchase shares of its common stock to offset the increase in shares from stock option and stock purchase plans. ●

American Eagle reported its treasury stock transactions in the notes to its financial statements as shown in Illustration 10–9.

AMERICAN EAGLE OUTFITTERS, INC.
Notes to the Financial Statements (excerpt)

ILLUSTRATION 10–9

Disclosure of Treasury Stock Transactions by American Eagle

The Company's Board authorized an additional 60.0 million shares of its common stock to be repurchased under the Company's share repurchase program. Subsequent to this authorization, the Company repurchased 18.7 million shares of its common stock. The shares were repurchased for approximately $438.3 million, at a weighted average share price of $23.38. As of March 25, 2010, the Company had 30.0 million shares remaining authorized for repurchase.

ACCOUNTING FOR TREASURY STOCK

Treasury stock is the repurchase of a company's own issued stock. As noted above, buying back stock decreases stockholders' equity. Rather than reducing the stock accounts directly, though, we record treasury stock as a "negative" or "contra" account. Recall that liability and stockholders' equity accounts normally have credit balances. So, treasury stock is included in the stockholders' equity section of the balance sheet with an opposite, or debit, balance. When a corporation repurchases its own stock, it increases (debits) Treasury Stock, while it decreases (credits) Cash.

 COMMON MISTAKE

Sometimes students confuse the purchase of treasury stock with investments in another company. An equity investment is the purchase of stock *in another corporation,* and we record it as an increase in assets. Treasury stock is the repurchase of a *corporation's own stock,* and we record it as a reduction in stockholders' equity. It is not an asset; a company cannot invest in itself.

We record treasury stock at the *cost* of the shares reacquired. For example, let's assume that Canadian Falcon repurchases 100 shares of its own $0.01 par value common stock at $30 per share. We record this transaction as:

	Debit	Credit
Treasury Stock (= 100 shares × $30)..	3,000	
Cash		3,000
(Repurchase treasury stock)		

A = L + SE
−3,000
−3,000

Notice that the stock's par value has no effect on the entry to record treasury stock. We record treasury stock at its cost, which is $30 per share in this example. The debit to Treasury Stock reduces stockholders' equity. Illustration 10–10 displays the stockholders' equity section of the balance sheet following the repurchase of treasury stock.

ILLUSTRATION 10–10

Stockholders' Equity after Purchase of Treasury Stock

CANADIAN FALCON Balance Sheet (partial)	
Stockholders' equity:	
Preferred stock, $30 par value; 100,000 shares authorized; 1,000 shares issued and outstanding	$30,000
Common stock, $0.01 par value; 1 million shares authorized; 1,000 shares issued and 900 shares outstanding	10
Additional paid-in capital	39,990
Total paid-in capital	70,000
Retained earnings	30,000
Treasury stock, 100 shares	(3,000)
Total stockholders' equity	$97,000

Treasury stock is reported as a contra equity, or negative amount, since treasury stock reduces total stockholders' equity.

Now let's assume that Canadian Falcon later reissues the 100 shares of treasury stock for $35. Recall that these shares originally were purchased for $30 per share, so the $35 reissue price represents a $5 per share increase in additional

paid-in capital. It's *not* recorded as a $5 per share gain in the income statement, as we would for the sale of an investment in another company, since the company is reissuing its own stock. We record this transaction as:

	Debit	Credit
Cash (= 100 shares × $35)	**3,500**	
Treasury Stock (= 100 shares × $30)		**3,000**
Additional Paid-in Capital[2] (= 100 shares × $5)		**500**
(Reissue treasury stock above cost)		

A	=	L	+	SE
+3,500				
				+3,000
				+500

We debit Cash at $35 per share to record the inflow of cash from reissuing treasury stock. We recorded the 100 shares of treasury stock in the accounting records at a cost of $30 per share at the time of purchase. Now, when we reissue the treasury shares, we must reduce the Treasury Stock account at the same $30 per share. We record the $500 difference (= 100 shares × $5 per share) as Additional Paid-in Capital. Illustration 10–11 presents the stockholders' equity section of the balance sheet immediately after the sale of treasury stock.

ILLUSTRATION 10–11
Stockholders' Equity after Sale of Treasury Stock

CANADIAN FALCON
Balance Sheet (partial)

Stockholders' equity:	
Preferred stock, $30 par value; 100,000 shares authorized; 1,000 shares issued and outstanding	$ 30,000
Common stock, $0.01 par value; 1 million shares authorized; 1,000 shares issued and outstanding	10
Additional paid-in capital	40,490
Total paid-in capital	70,500
Retained earnings	30,000
Treasury stock	0
Total stockholders' equity	$100,500

What if the stock price goes down, and we reissue the treasury stock for less than we paid to buy back the shares? Let's assume Canadian Falcon later reissues the 100 shares of treasury stock for only $25 rather than $35. It records this transaction as:

	Debit	Credit
Cash (= 100 × $25)	**2,500**	
Additional Paid-in Capital[3] (= 100 × $5)	**500**	
Treasury Stock (= 100 × $30)...		**3,000**
(Reissue treasury stock below cost)		

A	=	L	+	SE
+2,500				
				−500
				+3,000

By repurchasing 100 shares of its own stock for $30 per share and reselling them for only $25 per share, Canadian Falcon experienced a decrease in additional

---

[2]Some companies credit "Additional Paid-in Capital from Treasury Stock Transactions" as a separate account from "Additional Paid-in Capital from Common Stock Transactions." We combine all additional paid-in capital entries into one "Additional Paid-in Capital" account, similar to how most companies report additional paid-in capital on the balance sheet.
[3]Companies debit Retained Earnings rather than Additional Paid-in Capital if there is not a sufficient prior credit balance in Additional Paid-in Capital from treasury stock transactions. The details are covered in more advanced financial accounting courses.

paid-in capital. This is reflected in the entry as a debit to the Additional Paid-in Capital account. It's not recorded as a $5 per share loss in the income statement, as we would for the sale of an investment in another company, since the company is reissuing its own stock.

KEY POINT

We include treasury stock in the stockholders' equity section of the balance sheet as a reduction in stockholders' equity. When we reissue treasury stock, we report the difference between its cost and the cash received as an increase or decrease in additional paid-in capital.

PART B

EARNED CAPITAL

■ **LO5**
Describe retained earnings and record cash dividends.

In Part A of the chapter, we discussed transactions involving "invested capital," because when investors buy a corporation's stock, they are investing in the company. Here, in Part B, we examine transactions involving retained earnings. Similarly, we might refer to this source of stockholders' equity as "earned capital," because it represents the net assets of the company that have been *earned* for the stockholders rather than *invested* by the stockholders.

Retained Earnings and Dividends

As noted at the beginning of the chapter, retained earnings represent the earnings retained in the corporation—earnings not paid out as dividends to stockholders. In other words, the amount of retained earnings equals all net income, less all dividends, since the company began.

In a company's early years, the amount of retained earnings tends to be small, and total paid-in capital—money invested into the corporation—tends to be large. As the years go by, the earnings retained in the business continue to grow and, for many profitable companies, can exceed the total amount originally invested in the corporation. Unfortunately, for some companies, expenses sometimes are more than revenues, so a net loss rather than net income is recorded. Just as net income increases retained earnings, a net loss *decreases* retained earnings.

Retained Earnings has a normal credit balance, consistent with other stockholders' equity accounts. However, if losses exceed income since the company began, Retained Earnings will have a debit balance. A debit balance in Retained Earnings is called an accumulated deficit. We subtract an accumulated deficit from total paid-in capital in the balance sheet to arrive at total stockholders' equity. Many companies in the start-up phase or when experiencing financial difficulties report an accumulated deficit. For instance, **Amazon.com** had an accumulated deficit of $730 million at the end of 2008 due to net losses reported in earlier years.

COMMON MISTAKE

Some students think, incorrectly, that retained earnings represents a *cash* balance set aside by the company. In fact, the size of retained earnings has no relationship to the balance in the Cash account. **American Eagle** reported $1.3 billion in retained earnings, but only $60 million in cash.

Dividends are distributions by a corporation to its stockholders. Investors pay careful attention to cash dividends. A change in the quarterly or annual cash dividend paid by a company can provide useful information about its future prospects.

For instance, an increase in dividends often is perceived as good news. Companies tend to increase dividends when the company is doing well and future prospects look bright.

Many investors choose to automatically reinvest their dividends. Automatic dividend reinvestment works similar to compound interest in a savings account. The investor does not receive dividends directly as cash; instead, his or her dividends are directly reinvested into more shares of the company. This allows the investment to grow at a faster rate.

Why Don't Some Companies Pay Dividends?

Decision Maker's Perspective

Some companies are unprofitable and, therefore, unable to pay cash dividends. However, many profitable companies *choose* not to pay cash dividends. Companies with large expansion plans, called *growth companies*, prefer to reinvest earnings in the growth of the company rather than distribute earnings back to investors in the form of cash dividends. **Starbucks** is a nice example. As companies mature and their growth opportunities diminish, they tend to pay out more dividends. **Microsoft** and **Walmart** did not pay dividends in their early growth years, but began paying them in more recent years. ●

Why do investors buy stock in companies like **Starbucks** if they do not receive dividends? Investors make money through dividends, but they also make money when a company's share price increases. **American Eagle** has experienced tremendous increases in share price, but it has paid relatively small dividends. For instance, investors holding American Eagle stock in 2009 enjoyed a total return of 73%. This return includes a share price increase of about 71% and dividends of about 2%. Thus, the gains to American Eagle investors have come almost entirely from share price increases rather than dividend payments. Illustration 10–12 presents the disclosure of American Eagle's dividend policy.

ILLUSTRATION 10–12

American Eagle's Dividend Policy

AMERICAN EAGLE OUTFITTERS, INC.
Notes to the Financial Statements (excerpt)

Subsequent to the fourth quarter, our Board declared a quarterly cash dividend of $0.075 per share, payable on April 13, to stockholders of record at the close of business on March 30. The payment of future dividends is at the discretion of our Board and is based on future earnings, cash flow, financial condition, capital requirements, changes in U.S. taxation and other relevant factors. It is anticipated that any future dividends paid will be declared on a quarterly basis.

Note that it is the board of directors that declares the cash dividend to be paid. The day this occurs is known as the **declaration date**. The declaration of a cash dividend creates a binding legal obligation for the company declaring the dividend. On that date, we (a) increase Dividends, a temporary account that is closed into Retained Earnings at the end of each period, and (b) increase the liability account, Dividends Payable. The board of directors also indicates a specific date on which the company will determine the registered owners of stock and therefore who will receive the dividend. This date is called the **record date**. Investors who own stock on the date of record are entitled to receive the dividend. The date of the actual cash distribution is the **payment date**.

To illustrate the payment of a cash dividend, assume that on March 15 Canadian Falcon declares a $0.25 per share dividend on its 2,000 outstanding shares—1,000

shares of common stock and 1,000 shares of preferred stock. We record the declaration of cash dividends as:

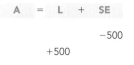

March 15 (declaration date)	Debit	Credit
Dividends (= 2,000 shares × $0.25)	**500**	
Dividends Payable		500
(*Declare cash dividends*)		

The Dividends account is a *temporary* stockholders' equity account that is closed into Retained Earnings at the end of each period, as discussed in Chapter 3.

Let's continue our example and assume that the dividend declared by Canadian Falcon is paid on April 15 to stockholders of record at the close of business on March 31. We make no entry on March 31, the date of record. We record the payment of cash dividends on April 15 as:

April 15 (payment date)	Debit	Credit
Dividends Payable (= 2,000 shares × $0.25)	**500**	
Cash		500
(*Pay cash dividends*)		

As we will show in Part C later in the chapter, the amount of cash dividends the company declares and pays will be reported in the statement of stockholders' equity.

 KEY POINT

The declaration of cash dividends decreases Retained Earnings and increases Dividends Payable. The payment of cash dividends decreases Dividends Payable and decreases Cash. The net effect, then, is a reduction in both retained earnings and cash.

Decision Point	Question ?	Accounting information 📄	Analysis 🔍
	How much did the company pay in cash dividends?	Statement of stockholders' equity	The statement of stockholders' equity provides a summary of the activity in each equity account during the period. Any dividends declared and paid during the year will be reported in this statement.

Let's Review

Slacks 5th Avenue has two classes of stock authorized: $100 par preferred and $1 par common. As of the beginning of 2012, 1,000 shares of common stock and no preferred shares have been issued. The following transactions affect stockholders' equity during 2012:

January	15	Issue 2,000 additional shares of common stock for $20 per share.
February	1	Issue 100 shares of preferred stock for $110 per share.
June	1	Declare a cash dividend of $5 per share on preferred stock and $1 per share on common stock to all stockholders of record on June 15.
June	30	Pay the cash dividend declared on June 1.
October	1	Repurchase 200 shares of treasury stock for $25 per share.
November	1	Reissue 100 shares of the treasury stock purchased on October 1 for $28 per share.

Slacks 5th Avenue has the following beginning balances in its stockholders' equity accounts on January 1, 2012: Preferred Stock, $0: Common Stock, $1,000; Paid-in Capital, $14,000; and Retained Earnings, $5,000.

Required:

1. Record each transaction.
2. Indicate whether each transaction increases (+), decreases (−), or has no effect (NE), on total assets, total liabilities, and total stockholders' equity.

Solution:

1. Entries to record each transaction:

	Debit	Credit
January 15, 2012		
Cash (= 2,000 × $20)	40,000	
Common Stock (= 2,000 × $1)		2,000
Additional Paid-in Capital (difference)...............................		38,000
(*Issue common stock above par*)		
February 1, 2012		
Cash (= 100 × $110)	11,000	
Preferred Stock (= 100 × $100)..		10,000
Additional Paid-in Capital (difference)		1,000
(*Issue preferred stock above par*)		
June 1, 2012		
Dividends*	3,500	
Dividends Payable		3,500
(*Declare cash dividends*)		
*=(100 preferred shares × $5) + (3,000 common shares × $1)		
June 30, 2012		
Dividends Payable	3,500	
Cash		3,500
(*Pay cash dividends*)		
October 1, 2012		
Treasury Stock (= 200 shares × $25)	5,000	
Cash		5,000
(*Repurchase treasury stock*)		
November 1, 2012		
Cash (= 100 shares × $28)	2,800	
Treasury Stock (= 100 shares × $25)		2,500
Additional Paid-in Capital (= 100 × $3)		300
(*Reissue treasury stock above cost*)		

2. Effects of transactions on the components of the accounting equation:

Transaction	Total Assets	Total Liabilities	Total Stockholders' Equity
Issue common stock	+	NE	+
Issue preferred stock	+	NE	+
Declare cash dividends	NE	+	−
Pay cash dividends	−	−	NE
Purchase treasury stock	−	NE	−
Reissue treasury stock	+	NE	+

Suggested Homework:
BE10-3, BE10-4;
E10-5, E10-6;
P10-2A&B

Stock Dividends and Stock Splits

■ **LO6**
Explain the effect of
stock dividends and
stock splits.

Sometimes corporations distribute to shareholders additional shares of the companies' own stock rather than cash. These are known as stock dividends or stock splits depending on the size of the stock distribution. Suppose you own 100 shares of stock. Assuming a 10% stock dividend, you'll get 10 additional shares. If it's a 20% stock dividend, you'll get 20 more shares. A 100% stock dividend, equivalent to a 2-for-1 stock split, means 100 more shares.

Large stock dividends (25% or higher) and stock splits are declared primarily due to the effect they have on stock prices. Let's say that before the 100% stock dividend, your shares are trading at $40 a share, so your 100 shares are worth $4,000. After the 100% stock dividend, you will have twice as many shares. It sounds good, but let's look closer. Since the company as a whole still has the same value, each share of stock is now worth one-half what it was worth before the stock dividend. Your 200 shares still have a value of $4,000, the same as your 100 shares before the stock dividend. However, now each share is worth half as much—$20 rather than $40 per share.

Think of the company as a pizza. A 100% stock dividend is like changing an 8-slice pizza into 16 slices by cutting each slice in half. You are no better off with 16 half-slices than with the original 8 slices. Whether it's cut in 8 large slices or 16 smaller slices, it's still the same-sized pizza. Whether a company is represented by 1 million shares worth $40 each or 2 million shares worth $20 each, it's the same $40 million company. **Total assets, total liabilities, and total stockholders' equity do not change as a result of a stock dividend.**

 COMMON MISTAKE

Unfortunately, people often misuse the term *stock dividends* to refer to cash dividends on stock. Stock dividends, though, as you've learned, are distributions of additional shares of stock to shareholders, unlike cash dividends, which are distributions of cash to shareholders.

STOCK DIVIDENDS

Accounting standards distinguish between stock splits, large stock dividends, and small stock dividends (less than 25%). We look first at the accounting for stock splits and large stock dividends because they are more common in practice.

Stock splits/Large stock dividends. When a company declares a stock split, we do not record a transaction. After a 2-for-1 stock split, the Common Stock account balance (total par value) represents twice as many shares. For instance, assume Canadian Falcon declares a 2-for-1 stock split on its 1,000 shares of $0.01 par value common stock. The balance in the Common Stock account is 1,000 shares times $0.01 par value per share, which equals $10. With no journal entry, the balance remains $10 despite the number of shares doubling. As a result, the par value *per share* is reduced by one-half to $0.005 (2,000 shares times $0.005 par per share still equals $10).

As you might expect, having the par value per share change in this way is cumbersome and expensive. All records, printed or electronic, that refer to the previous amount must be changed to reflect the new amount. Fortunately there is an alternative: To avoid the inconvenience and added cost, a company can choose to account for the large stock distribution as a stock *dividend* rather than a stock *split*. We account for a large stock dividend by recording an increase in the Common

Stock account in the amount of the par value of the additional shares distributed, as presented below:

	Debit	Credit
Stock Dividends (= 1,000 shares × $0.01)	10	
Common Stock		10
(*Declare 100% [large] stock dividend*)		

A	=	L	+	SE
				−10
				+10

So, to avoid changing the par value per share, most companies report a 100% stock distribution as a stock split to be recorded as a stock dividend.

Similar to cash dividends, the Stock Dividends account is a temporary stockholders' equity account that is closed into Retained Earnings. Because an increase to stock dividends reduces retained earnings, we decrease one equity account, Retained Earnings, and increase another equity account, Common Stock. Note that the above entry does not change total assets, total liabilities, or total stockholders' equity. Illustration 10–13 presents the stockholders' equity section of the balance sheet for Canadian Falcon before and after the 2-for-1 stock split accounted for as a 100% stock dividend.

ILLUSTRATION 10–13

Stockholders' Equity before and after a 2-for-1 Stock Split Accounted for as a 100% Stock Dividend

CANADIAN FALCON Balance Sheet (partial)	Before 100% Stock Dividend	After 100% Stock Dividend
Stockholders' equity:		
Preferred stock, $30 par value	$ 30,000	$ 30,000
Common stock, $0.01 par value	10	20
Additional paid-in capital	40,490	40,490
Total paid-in capital	70,500	70,510
Retained earnings	29,500	29,490
Total stockholders' equity	$100,000	$100,000
Common shares outstanding	1,000	2,000
Par value per share	$0.01	$0.01
Share price	$30	$15

Notice that total stockholders' equity remains at **$100,000** before and after the stock distribution. Common stock increased by $10, while retained earnings decreased by $10.

Why Declare a Stock Split?

Decision Maker's Perspective

Why would a company declare a 2-for-1 stock split when the stockholders are not really receiving anything of substance? The primary reason is to lower the trading price of the stock to a more acceptable trading range, making it attractive to a larger number of potential investors. Many companies like their stock to trade under $100 per share—$20 to $40 per share is common. For instance, after a company declares a 2-for-1 stock split with a per share market price of $80, it then has twice the number of shares outstanding, each with an approximate market value reduced to a more marketable trading range of $40.

However, there are exceptions to the normal trading range. **Google's** stock trades in the several-hundred-dollars-per-share range. **Berkshire Hathaway's** "A" shares trade at over $100,000 per share, making it accessible only to wealthier investors. Berkshire Hathaway is founded by billionaire investor Warren Buffett. While still an outspoken critic of stock dividends and stock splits, even Warren Buffett is giving in a little. In January 2010, Berkshire Hathaway's "B" shares, designed for general public investment, were split 50 to 1. The shares had a value of about $3,500 before the split and a value in a more acceptable trading range of about $70 ($3,500 ÷ 50) after the stock split. ●

Small stock dividends.   Let's also look briefly at small stock dividends. Recall that we record large stock dividends at the *par value* per share. We record small stock dividends at the *market value*, rather than the par value, per share. Assume, for example, the market value of Canadian Falcon common stock is $30 per share when Canadian Falcon declares a 10% dividend on its 1,000 shares outstanding of $0.01 par value common stock. After the 10% stock dividend, Canadian Falcon will have 1,100 shares outstanding. The company records this small stock dividend as:

A = L + SE	June 30, 2012	Debit	Credit
−3,000	**Stock Dividends** (= 1,000 × 10% × $30)	3,000	
+1	**Common Stock** (= 1,000 × 10% × $0.01)................................		1
+2,999	**Additional Paid-in Capital** (difference)....................................		2,999
	(Pay 10% [small] stock dividend)		

So, small stock dividends are recorded at the market value per new share, while large stock dividends are recorded at the par value per share. Why the inconsistency? Some believe that a small stock dividend will have little impact on the market price of shares currently outstanding, arguing for the recording of small stock dividends at market value. However, this reasoning is contrary to research evidence, which finds the market price adjusts for both large and small stock dividends.[4] A 10% stock dividend will result in 10% more shares, but each share will be worth 10% less, so the investor is no better off. Note that the above entry still does not change total assets, total liabilities, or total stockholders' equity. The debit to Stock Dividends simply decreases one equity account, Retained Earnings, while the credits increase two other equity accounts, Common Stock and Additional Paid-in Capital.

American Eagle is a prime candidate for stock splits since its share price has risen dramatically in prior years. Illustration 10–14 presents the disclosure of American Eagle's 3-for-2 stock split.

ILLUSTRATION 10–14

American Eagle's Stock Split

AMERICAN EAGLE OUTFITTERS, INC.
Notes to the Financial Statements

On November 13, the Company's Board approved a 3-for-2 stock split. This stock split was distributed on December 18, to stockholders of record on November 24. All share amounts and per share data presented herein have been restated to reflect this stock split.

---

[4]Taylor W. Foster and Don Vickrey. 1978. "The Information Content of Stock Dividend Announcements." *Accounting Review 53*, no. 2 (April), pp. 360–70; and J. David Spiceland and Alan J. Winters. 1986. "The Market Reaction to Stock Distributions: The Effect of Market Anticipation and Cash Returns." *Accounting and Business Research 16*, no. 63 (Summer), pp. 211–25.

ETHICAL DILEMMA

Intercontinental Clothing Distributors has paid cash dividends every year since the company was founded in 1990. The dividends have steadily increased from $0.05 per share to the latest dividend declaration of $1.00 per share. The board of directors is eager to continue this trend despite the fact that earnings fell significantly during the recent quarter as a result of worsening economic conditions and increased competition. The chair of the board proposes a solution. She suggests a 5% stock dividend in lieu of a cash dividend, to be accompanied by the following press announcement: "In place of our regular $1.00 per share cash dividend, Intercontinental will distribute a 5% stock dividend on its common shares, currently trading at $20 per share. Changing the form of the dividend will permit the company to direct available cash resources to the modernization of facilities in order to better compete in the 21st century."

Is a 5% stock dividend equivalent to a $1.00 per share cash dividend when shares are trading at $20 per share? Is the chair's suggestion ethical?

KEY POINT

Declaring stock dividends and stock splits is like cutting a pizza into more slices. Everyone has more shares, but each share is worth proportionately less than before.

REPORTING STOCKHOLDERS' EQUITY

PART C

We now can apply what we've learned so far in the chapter to analyze the stockholders' equity of an actual company—**American Eagle**. In this section, we show the financial statement presentation of stockholders' equity in the balance sheet and differentiate it from the statement of stockholders' equity.

Stockholders' Equity in the Balance Sheet

Illustration 10–15 (next page) presents the stockholders' equity section of the balance sheet for **American Eagle**, introduced briefly at the beginning of the chapter.

Preferred stock is listed before common stock in the balance sheet. American Eagle has 5 million shares of preferred stock authorized but has not yet issued any preferred shares. Can you determine how many shares of common stock the company has issued? Common stock is reported at its par value of $0.01 per share. If we take the Common Stock account balance of $2,485,000 ($2,485 in thousands) and divide it by $0.01 per share, we find that the company has issued just under 250 million shares (248,500,000). The number of shares outstanding is equal to the number of shares issued (248,500,000) minus the number of shares bought back (the 43,248,000 treasury shares), or 205,252,000 shares.

Notice that the Additional Paid-in Capital account balance is much larger than the Common Stock account balance. This is to be expected. Remember, American Eagle has a par value of only $0.01 per share, so most of the money invested in the company was credited to Additional Paid-in Capital rather than Common Stock.

■ **LO7**
Prepare and analyze the stockholders' equity section of a balance sheet and the statement of stockholders' equity.

ILLUSTRATION 10–15

Stockholders' Equity Section of American Eagle's Balance Sheet

AMERICAN EAGLE
Balance Sheet (partial)
January 31, 2009

(Dollars and number of shares in thousands)

Total assets	$ 1,963,676
Total liabilities	$ 554,645
Stockholders' equity:	
Preferred stock, $0.01 par value	–0–
Common stock, $0.01 par value	2,485
Additional paid-in capital	513,574
Total paid-in capital	516,059
Retained earnings	1,679,772
Treasury stock, 43,248 (thousand) shares	(786,800)
Total stockholders' equity	$1,409,031
Total liabilities and stockholders' equity	$ 1,963,676

Now look at retained earnings. When a company is started, most of the equity is in the paid-in capital section because that's the amount invested by stockholders. But then, if a company is profitable, like American Eagle, and pays little in dividends, the retained earnings section of equity grows and often exceeds the amount invested by stockholders. For American Eagle, the amount of retained earnings is so large that it actually exceeds total stockholders' equity. How can this happen? American Eagle has been very profitable over the years, building retained earnings. It has used a portion of the company's earnings to buy back treasury shares, which decreases stockholders' equity. American Eagle has applied this strategy to such an extent that the balance in treasury stock (representing the cost of shares repurchased by the company) now exceeds total paid-in capital (representing the total cost of shares originally issued).

American Eagle has been very active in acquiring treasury shares. Has it benefited from the treasury stock repurchases? Dividing the treasury stock balance of $786,800 by the 43,248 shares repurchased, we can estimate an average purchase cost of $18.19 per share. That average repurchase price is nearly double the current trading price of $9 per share at January 31, 2009. Thus, at this point in time, it looks like American Eagle has not benefited from the treasury stock repurchase. However, if stock prices should again rise above $18.19 per share, the company could sell the treasury shares for more than the average purchase price.

Statement of Stockholders' Equity

The stockholders' equity section of the balance sheet, like the one we just examined for American Eagle, shows the balance in each equity account *at a point in time*. In contrast, the **statement of stockholders' equity** summarizes the *changes* in the balance in each stockholders' equity account *over a period of time*.

To contrast the stockholders' equity section of the balance sheet and the statement of stockholders' equity, let's compare both statements for our continuing example company—Canadian Falcon. Illustration 10–16 (next page) shows the stockholders' equity section reported in Canadian Falcon's balance sheet.

Compare that snapshot of stockholders' equity at the end of 2012 with Illustration 10–17 (next page) showing the statement of stockholders' equity for Canadian Falcon.

CANADIAN FALCON
Balance Sheet (partial)
December 31, 2012

Stockholders' equity:

Preferred stock, $30 par value; 100,000 shares authorized; 1,000 shares issued and outstanding	$ 30,000
Common stock, $0.01 par value; 1 million shares authorized; 2,000 shares issued and outstanding	20
Additional paid-in capital	40,490
Total paid-in capital	70,510
Retained earnings	29,490
Treasury stock	–0–
Total stockholders' equity	$100,000

ILLUSTRATION 10–16

Stockholders' Equity Section—Canadian Falcon

CANADIAN FALCON
Statement of Stockholders' Equity
For the year ended December 31, 2012

	Preferred Stock	Common Stock	Additional Paid-in Capital	Retained Earnings	Treasury Stock	Total Stockholders' Equity
Balance, January 1	$ –0–	$–0–	$ –0–	$ –0–	$ –0–	$ –0–
Issued common stock		10	29,990			30,000
Issued preferred stock	30,000		10,000			40,000
Repurchase of treasury stock					(3,000)	(3,000)
Sale of treasury stock			500		3,000	3,500
Cash dividends				(500)		(500)
100% stock dividend		10		(10)		–0–
Net income				30,000		30,000
Balance, December 31	$30,000	$20	$40,490	$29,490	$ –0–	$100,000

ILLUSTRATION 10–17

Statement of Stockholders' Equity—Canadian Falcon

Each of the beginning balances in Illustration 10–17 is zero because this is the first year of operations. (The beginning balances for the following year, January 1, 2013, are the same as the ending balance this year, December 31, 2012.)

The statement of stockholders' equity reports how each equity account changed during the year. For instance, the Common Stock account increased because Canadian Falcon issued common stock and declared a 100% stock dividend. The Additional Paid-in Capital account increased from the issuance of common stock, the issuance of preferred stock, and the sale of treasury stock for more than its original cost. Retained Earnings increased due to net income and decreased due to both cash and stock dividends. The repurchase of treasury stock is shown as a reduction because treasury stock reduces total stockholders' equity. The ending balance in Treasury Stock is zero, since all the treasury stock purchased was resold by the end of the year.

KEY POINT

The stockholders' equity section of the balance sheet presents the balance of each equity account *at a point in time*. The statement of stockholders' equity shows the change in each equity account balance *over time*.

Let's Review

This exercise is a continuation of the Let's Review exercise presented earlier. Recall that Slacks 5th Avenue has two classes of stock authorized: $100 par preferred and $1 par value common. As of the beginning of 2012, 1,000 shares of common stock have been issued and no shares of preferred stock have been issued. The following transactions affect stockholders' equity during 2012:

January	15	Issue 2,000 additional shares of common stock for $20 per share.
February	1	Issue 100 shares of preferred stock for $110 per share.
June	1	Declare a cash dividend of $5 per share on preferred stock and $1 per share on common stock to all stockholders of record on June 15.
June	30	Pay the cash dividend declared on June 1.
October	1	Repurchase 200 shares of common treasury stock for $25 per share.
November	1	Reissue 100 shares of treasury stock purchased on October 1 for $28 per share.

Slacks 5th Avenue has the following beginning balances in its stockholders' equity accounts on January 1, 2012: Preferred Stock, $0; Common Stock, $1,000; Paid-in Capital, $14,000; and Retained Earnings, $5,000. Net income for the year ended December 31, 2012, is $4,000.

Required:

Taking into consideration all of the transactions during 2012, prepare the following for Slacks 5th Avenue:

1. The stockholders' equity section as of December 31, 2012.

2. The statement of stockholders' equity for the year ended December 31, 2012.

Solution:

1. Stockholders' equity section:

SLACKS 5TH AVENUE
Balance Sheet (partial)
December 31, 2012

Stockholders' equity:	
Preferred stock, $100 par value	$10,000
Common stock, $1 par value	3,000
Additional paid-in capital	53,300
Total paid-in capital	66,300
Retained earnings	5,500
Treasury stock	(2,500)
Total stockholders' equity	$69,300

2. Statement of stockholders' equity:

	Preferred Stock	Common Stock	Additional Paid-in Capital	Retained Earnings	Treasury Stock	Total Stockholders' Equity
SLACKS 5TH AVENUE						
Statement of Stockholders' Equity						
For the year ended December 31, 2012						
Balance, January 1	$ –0–	$1,000	$14,000	$5,000	$ –0–	$20,000
Issued common stock		2,000	38,000			40,000
Issued preferred stock	10,000		1,000			11,000
Cash dividends				(3,500)		(3,500)
Repurchase of treasury stock					(5,000)	(5,000)
Sale of treasury stock			300		2,500	2,800
Net income				4,000		4,000
Balance, December 31	$10,000	$3,000	$53,300	$5,500	$(2,500)	$69,300

Suggested Homework:
BE10-13, BE10-14;
E10-10, E10-11;
P10-5A&B

EQUITY ANALYSIS

Deckers Outdoor vs. Timberland

ANALYSIS

■ **LO8**
Evaluate company performance using information on stockholders' equity.

Earnings are the key to a company's long-run survival. However, we need to evaluate earnings in comparison to the size of the investment. For instance, earnings of $500,000 may be quite large for a small business, but would be a rather disappointing outcome for a major corporation like **American Eagle**. A useful summary measure of earnings that considers the relative size of the business is the return on equity.

RETURN ON EQUITY

The **return on equity** (ROE) measures the ability of company management to generate earnings from the resources that owners provide. We compute the ratio by dividing net income by average stockholders' equity.

$$\text{Return on equity} = \frac{\text{Net income}}{\text{Average stockholders' equity}}$$

Deckers Outdoor was listed at the beginning of the chapter as one of the top ten investments of the past decade. The company is probably best known for its footwear products such as Teva sandals and UGG sheepskin boots. We can compare its profitability with a close competitor in the footwear industry, **Timberland**. Illustration 10–18 (next page) provides selected financial data for Deckers Outdoor and Timberland.

ILLUSTRATION 10–18

Financial Information for Deckers Outdoor and Timberland

Selected Balance Sheet Data
December 31, 2009 and 2008
($ in thousands)

	Deckers Outdoor		Timberland	
	2009	2008	2009	2008
Total assets	$599,043	$483,721	$859,907	$849,399
Total liabilities	$107,685	$ 99,469	$264,290	$272,861
Stockholders' equity	491,358	384,252	595,617	576,538
Total liabilities and equity	$599,043	$483,721	$859,907	$849,399
Stock price, ending	$101.72		$17.83	
Shares outstanding (in thousands)	12,868		85,660	

Selected Income Statement Data
For the year ended December 31, 2009
($ in thousands)

	Deckers Outdoor	Timberland
Net sales	$813,177	$1,285,876
Net income	$116,786	$56,644

The return on equity for both companies is calculated in Illustration 10–19.

ILLUSTRATION 10–19

Return on Equity for Deckers Outdoor and Timberland

($ in thousands)	Net Income	÷	Average Stockholders' Equity	=	Return on Equity
Deckers Outdoor	$116,786	÷	($384,252 + $491,358)/2	=	26.7%
Timberland	$56,644	÷	($576,538 + $595,617)/2	=	9.7%

As might be expected for a top-10 investment, Deckers Outdoor has a significantly higher return on equity of 26.7% compared to a respectable 9.7% for Timberland. A return on equity of 26.7% suggests that for every $1 of investors' resources, the company has earned almost $0.27 for its investors. Similarly, a return on equity of 9.7% suggests that for every $1 of investors' resources, the company has earned almost $0.10 for its investors. Although the return on equity is useful when comparing the effectiveness of management in employing resources provided by owners, analysts must be careful not to view it in isolation or without considering how the ratio is derived.

RETURN ON THE MARKET VALUE OF EQUITY

To supplement the return on equity ratio, analysts often relate earnings to the market value of equity, which is calculated as the ending stock price times the number of shares outstanding. The return on the market value of equity is computed as net income divided by the market value of equity, as shown in Illustration 10–20 (next page).

Once again, Deckers Outdoor has a higher return than Timberland. Notice that the return on the market value of equity for both companies is much lower than their return on equity. The reason is that the average stockholders' equity for Deckers Outdoor and Timberland is much lower than the market value of equity. For

($ in thousands)	Net Income	÷	Market Value of Equity (Ending stock price × Number of shares)	=	Return on the Market Value of Equity
Deckers Outdoor	$116,786	÷	($101.72 × 12,868)	=	8.9%
Timberland	$56,644	÷	($17.83 × 85,660)	=	3.7%

ILLUSTRATION 10–20

Return on the Market Value of Equity for Deckers Outdoor and Timberland

some companies, the return on equity is a meaningful measure of earnings performance. For others, the return on the market value of equity is a better measure, especially when the recorded balance in stockholders' equity and the market value of equity differ greatly.

Why Doesn't Stockholders' Equity Equal the Market Value of Equity?

Decision Maker's Perspective

The *market* value of equity is the price investors are willing to pay for a company's stock. The market value of equity equals the stock price times the number of shares outstanding. On the other hand, the *book* value of equity equals total stockholders' equity reported in the balance sheet. Market value and book value generally are not the same, and often are vastly different. For example, Deckers Outdoor reported total stockholders' equity of $491 million in 2009, yet its market value at this same time was over $1.3 billion. Why?

Keep in mind that stockholders' equity is equal to assets minus liabilities. An asset's book value usually equals its market value *on the date it's purchased*. However, the two aren't necessarily the same after that. For instance, an asset such as a building might increase in value over time, but it continues to be reported in the balance sheet at historical cost minus accumulated depreciation. Consider another example: **Deckers Outdoor** creates brand awareness and increases market value through advertising, but under accounting rules, it expenses all its advertising costs as it incurs them. This causes the true market value of assets and stockholders' equity to be greater than the amount recorded for assets and stockholders' equity in the accounting records. ●

Decision Point

Question	Accounting information	Analysis
What is a company's return on investment?	Return on equity and return on market value of equity	A high return on equity or market value of equity in relation to industry competitors indicates a strong return on investment. Note the return on market value of equity will normally be lower than the return on equity.

EARNINGS PER SHARE

Earnings per share (EPS) measures the net income earned per share of common stock. We calculate earnings per share as net income minus dividends on preferred stock divided by the average shares of common stock outstanding during the period:

$$\text{Earnings per share} = \frac{\text{Net income} - \text{Dividends on preferred stock}}{\text{Average shares of common stock outstanding}}$$

The upper half of the fraction measures the income available to common stockholders. We subtract any dividends paid to preferred stockholders from net income to arrive at the income available to the true owners of the company—the common stockholders. If a company does not issue preferred stock, the top half of the fraction is simply net income. We then divide income available to common stockholders by the average shares outstanding during the period to calculate earnings per share.

Earnings per share is useful in comparing earnings performance for the same company over time. It is *not* useful for comparing earnings performance of one company with another because of wide differences in the number of shares outstanding among companies. For instance, assume two companies, Alpha and Beta, both report net income of $1 million and are valued by the market at $20 million. Quite comparable, right? But, if Alpha has one million shares outstanding and Beta has two million shares outstanding, their earnings per share amounts will not be comparable. Alpha will have a share price of $20 (= $20 million ÷ 1 million shares) and an EPS of $1.00 (= $1 million in earnings ÷ 1 million shares). Beta, on the other hand, will have a share price of $10 (= $20 million ÷ 2 million shares) and an EPS of $0.50 (= $1 million in earnings ÷ 2 million shares). Is the earnings performance for Alpha better than that for Beta? Of course not. They both earned $1 million. Alpha's earnings per share is higher simply because it has half as many shares outstanding. (Same pizza, fewer slices.)

If Alpha declared a 2-for-1 stock split, its earnings per share would match Beta's exactly. The key point is that earnings per share is useful in comparing either Alpha's earnings over time, or Beta's earnings over time, but it is not useful in comparing the companies *with each other*.

Investors use earnings per share extensively in evaluating the earnings performance of a company over time. Investors are looking for companies with the potential to increase earnings per share. Analysts also forecast earnings on a per share basis. If reported earnings per share fall short of analysts' forecasts, this is considered negative news, usually resulting in a decline in a company's stock price.

PRICE-EARNINGS RATIO

Another measure analysts use extensively is the price-earnings ratio (PE ratio). It indicates how the stock is trading in relationship to current earnings. We calculate the PE ratio as the stock price divided by earnings per share, so that both stock price and earnings are expressed on a per share basis:

$$\text{Price-earnings ratio} = \frac{\text{Stock price}}{\text{Earnings per share}}$$

Price-earnings ratios are commonly in the range of 15 to 20. A high PE ratio indicates that the market has high hopes for a company's stock and has bid up the price. Growth stocks are stocks whose future earnings investors expect to be higher. Their stock prices are high in relation to current earnings because investors expect future earnings to be higher. On the other hand, value stocks are stocks that are priced low in relation to current earnings. The low price in relation to earnings may be justified due to poor future prospects, or it might suggest an underpriced "sleeper" stock. Illustration 10–21 calculates the price-earnings ratio for **Deckers Outdoor** and **Timberland**.

ILLUSTRATION 10–21 Price-Earnings Ratios for Deckers Outdoor and Timberland	($ in thousands)	Stock Price	÷	Earnings per Share	=	Price-Earnings Ratio
	Deckers Outdoor	$101.72	÷	$116,786/12,868	=	11.2
	Timberland	$ 17.83	÷	$ 56,644/85,660	=	27.0

490

The price-earnings ratio for Deckers Outdoor and Timberland is 11.2 and 27.0, respectively. A low price-earnings ratio indicates to investors that a stock is priced low in relation to its current earnings. Deckers Outdoor has a much lower stock price in relation to its current earnings, making it a potentially more attractive investment.

 KEY POINT

The return on equity measures the ability to generate earnings from the owners' investment. It is calculated as net income divided by average stockholders' equity. The return on the market value of equity is another useful measure, especially when the recorded balance in stockholders' equity and the market value of equity differ substantially. Earnings per share measures the net income earned per share of common stock. The price-earnings ratio indicates how the stock is trading in relationship to current earnings.

Decision Point

Question	Accounting information	Analysis
Do investors expect future earnings to grow?	Price-earnings ratio (PE ratio)	A high PE ratio indicates investors expect future earnings to be higher. A low PE ratio indicates investors' lack of confidence in future earnings growth.

 ## KEY POINTS BY LEARNING OBJECTIVE

LO1 Identify the advantages and disadvantages of the corporate form of ownership.

The primary advantages of the corporate form of business are limited liability, ability to raise capital, and lack of mutual agency. The primary disadvantages are additional taxes and more paperwork.

LO2 Record the issuance of common stock.

If no-par value stock is issued, the corporation debits Cash and credits Common Stock. If par value or stated value stock is issued, the corporation debits Cash and credits two equity accounts—Common Stock at the par value or stated value per share and Additional Paid-in Capital for the portion above par or stated value.

LO3 Contrast preferred stock with common stock and bonds payable.

Preferred stock has features of both common stock and bonds and is usually included in stockholders' equity. However, mandatorily redeemable preferred stock is so similar to bonds that we include it with bonds payable in the liability section of the balance sheet.

LO4 Account for treasury stock.

We include treasury stock in the stockholders' equity section of the balance sheet as a reduction in stockholders' equity. When we reissue treasury stock, we report the difference between its cost and the cash received as an increase or decrease in Additional Paid-in Capital.

LO5 Describe retained earnings and record cash dividends.

The declaration of cash dividends decreases Retained Earnings and increases Dividends Payable. The payment of dividends decreases Dividends Payable and decreases Cash. The net effect, then, is a reduction in both retained earnings and cash.

LO6 Explain the effect of stock dividends and stock splits.

Declaring stock dividends and stock splits is like cutting a pizza into more slices. Everyone has more shares, but each share is worth proportionately less than before.

LO7 Prepare and analyze the stockholders' equity section of a balance sheet and the statement of stockholders' equity.

The stockholders' equity section of the balance sheet presents the balance of each equity account *at a point in time*. The statement of stockholders' equity shows the change in each equity account balance *over time*.

Analysis

LO8 Evaluate company performance using information on stockholders' equity.

The return on equity measures the ability to generate earnings from the owners' investment. It is calculated as net income divided by average stockholders' equity. The return on the market value of equity is another useful measure, especially when the recorded balance in stockholders' equity and the market value of equity differ substantially. Earnings per share measures the net income earned per share of common stock. The price-earnings ratio indicates how the stock is trading in relationship to current earnings.

GLOSSARY

Accumulated deficit: A debit balance in Retained Earnings. **p. 472**

Additional paid-in capital: The portion of the cash proceeds above par value. **p. 458**

Angel investors: Wealthy individuals in the business community willing to risk investment funds on a promising business venture. **p. 460**

Articles of incorporation: Describes the nature of the firm's business activities, the shares to be issued, and the composition of the initial board of directors. **p. 459**

Authorized stock: The total number of shares available to sell, stated in the company's articles of incorporation. **p. 464**

Convertible: Shares can be exchanged for common stock. **p. 467**

Cumulative: Shares receive priority for future dividends, if dividends are not paid in a given year. **p. 467**

Declaration date: The day on which the board of directors declares the cash dividend to be paid. **p. 473**

Dividends: Distributions by a corporation to its stockholders. **p. 472**

Dividends in arrears: Unpaid dividends on cumulative preferred stock. **p. 467**

Double taxation: A corporation pays income taxes on its earnings, and when dividends are distributed to stockholders, the stockholders pay taxes a second time on the corporate dividends they receive. **p. 462**

Earnings per share: Measures the net income earned per share of common stock. **p. 485**

Growth stocks: Stocks that tend to have higher price-earnings ratios and are expected to have higher future earnings. **p. 486**

Initial public offering: The first time a corporation issues stock to the public. **p. 460**

Issued stock: The number of shares sold to investors; includes treasury shares. **p. 464**

Limited liability: Stockholders in a corporation can lose no more than the amount they invested in the company. **p. 462**

Model Business Corporation Act: Serves as a guide to states in the development of their corporate statutes. **p. 459**

Mutual agency: Individual partners each have power to bind the partnership to a contract. **p. 462**

No-par value stock: Common stock that has not been assigned a par value. **p. 465**

Organization chart: Traces the line of authority for a typical corporation. **p. 459**

Outstanding stock: The number of shares held by investors; excludes treasury shares. **p. 464**

Paid-in capital: The amount stockholders have invested in the company. **p. 458**

Par value: The legal capital assigned per share of stock. **p. 465**

Payment date: The date of the actual cash distribution of dividends. **p. 473**

Preferred stock: Stock with preference over common stock in the payment of dividends and the distribution of assets. **p. 466**

Price-earnings ratio: The stock price divided by earnings per share so that both stock price and earnings are expressed on a per share basis. **p. 486**

Privately held corporation: Does not allow investment by the general public and normally has fewer stockholders. **p. 461**

Publicly held corporation: Allows investment by the general public and is regulated by the Securities and Exchange Commission. **p. 460**

Record date: A specific date on which the company will determine the registered owners of stock and, therefore, who will receive the dividend. **p. 473**

Redeemable: Shares can be returned to the corporation at a fixed price. **p. 467**

Retained earnings: Represents all net income, less all dividends, since the company began. **pp. 458, 472**

Return on equity: Net income divided by average stockholders' equity; measures the income generated per dollar of equity. **p. 483**

Return on the market value of equity: Net income divided by the market value of equity. **p. 484**

S corporation: Allows a company to enjoy limited liability as a corporation, but tax treatment as a partnership. **p. 463**

Stated value: The legal capital assigned per share to no-par stock. **p. 465**

Statement of stockholders' equity: Summarizes the changes in the balance in each stockholders' equity account over a period of time. **p. 480**

Stock dividends: Additional shares of a company's own stock given to stockholders. **p. 476**

Stock split: A large stock dividend that includes a reduction in the par or stated value per share. **p. 476**

Treasury stock: A corporation's own stock that it has reacquired. **p. 458**

Value stocks: Stocks that tend to have lower price-earnings ratios and are priced low in relation to current earnings. **p. 486**

Venture capital firms: Provide additional financing, often in the millions, for a percentage ownership in the company. **p. 460**

SELF-STUDY QUESTIONS

1. Which of the following is a publicly traded company? ■ **LO1**
   a. American Eagle.
   b. Cargill. ✗
   c. Ernst & Young. ✗
   d. Koch Industries. ✗

2. The disadvantages of owning a corporation include: ■ **LO1**
   a. Lack of mutual agency.
   b. Additional taxes.
   c. Limited liability.
   d. Ability to raise capital.

3. The correct order from the smallest number of shares to the largest number of shares is: ■ **LO2**
   a. Authorized, issued, and outstanding.
   b. Outstanding, issued, and authorized.
   c. Issued, outstanding, and authorized.
   d. Issued, authorized, and outstanding.

4. Preferred stock: ■ **LO3**
   a. Is always recorded as a liability.
   b. Is always recorded as part of stockholders' equity.
   c. Can have features of both liabilities and stockholders' equity.
   d. Is not included in either liabilities or stockholders' equity.

5. Treasury stock: ■ **LO4**
   a. Has a normal credit balance.
   b. Decreases stockholders' equity.
   c. Is recorded as an investment.
   d. Increases stockholders' equity.

6. Retained earnings: ■ **LO5**
   a. Has a normal debit balance. ✗
   b. Decreases stockholders' equity.
   c. Is equal to the balance in cash. ✗
   d. Increases stockholders' equity.

7. We record cash dividends on the:
   a. Declaration date, record date, and payment date.
   b. Record date and payment date.
   c. Declaration date and payment date.
   d. Declaration date and record date.

8. Both cash dividends and stock dividends: ■ **LO6**
   a. Reduce total assets.
   b. Reduce total liabilities.
   c. Reduce total stockholders' equity.
   d. Reduce retained earnings.

■ **LO7**

9. How does the stockholders' equity section in the balance sheet differ from the statement of stockholders' equity?
   a. The stockholders' equity section shows balances at a point in time, whereas the statement of stockholders' equity shows activity over a period of time.
   b. The stockholders' equity section shows activity over a period of time, whereas the statement of stockholders' equity is at a point in time.
   c. There are no differences between them.
   d. The stockholders' equity section is more detailed than the statement of stockholders' equity.

■ **LO8**

Check out
www.mhhe.com/succeed
for more multiple-choice
questions.

10. The PE ratio:
    a. Tends to be lower for growth stocks.
    b. Tends to be higher for value stocks.
    c. Indicates how a stock is trading in relation to current earnings.
    d. Typically is less than 1.

Note: For answers, see the last page of the chapter.

REVIEW QUESTIONS

■ **LO1**   1. Corporations typically do not first raise capital by issuing stock to the general public. What are the common stages of equity financing leading to an initial public offering (IPO)?

■ **LO1**   2. What is the difference between a public and a private corporation? Provide an example of each.

■ **LO1**   3. What are the four basic ownership rights of common stockholders?

■ **LO1**   4. Which form of business organization is most common? Which form of business organization is larger in terms of total sales, total assets, earnings, and number of employees?

■ **LO1**   5. Describe the primary advantages and disadvantages of a corporation.

■ **LO1**   6. Explain how an LLC or an S corporation represents the "best of both worlds" in terms of business ownership.

■ **LO2**   7. Explain the difference between authorized, issued, and outstanding shares.

■ **LO2**   8. The articles of incorporation allow for the issuance of 1 million shares of common stock. During its first year, California Clothing issued 100,000 shares and reacquired 10,000 shares it held as treasury stock. At the end of the first year, how many shares are authorized, issued, and outstanding?

■ **LO2**   9. What is par value? How is it related to market value? How is it used in recording the issuance of stock?

■ **LO3**   10. What are the three potential features of preferred stock? Indicate whether each feature makes the preferred stock appear more like stockholders' equity or more like long-term liabilities.

■ **LO3**   11. Explain why preferred stock often is said to be a mixture of attributes somewhere between common stock and bonds.

■ **LO4**   12. What would motivate a company to buy back its own stock?

■ **LO4**   13. How is the accounting for a repurchase of a company's own stock (treasury stock) different from the purchase of stock in another corporation?

■ **LO5**   14. Explain why some companies choose not to pay cash dividends. Why do investors purchase stock in companies that do not pay cash dividends?

15. Describe the declaration date, record date, and payment date for a cash dividend. ■ LO5

16. How does a 100% stock dividend or a 2-for-1 stock split affect total assets, total liabilities, and total stockholders' equity? ■ LO6

17. Contrast the effects of a cash dividend and a stock dividend on total assets, total liabilities, and total stockholders' equity. ■ LO6

18. What happens to the par value, the share's trading price, and the number of shares outstanding in a 2-for-1 stock split? ■ LO6

19. Indicate the correct order in which to report the following accounts in the stockholders' equity section of the balance sheet: Additional Paid-in Capital, Common Stock, Preferred Stock, Treasury Stock, and Retained Earnings. ■ LO7

20. How is the stockholders' equity section of the balance sheet different from the statement of stockholders' equity? ■ LO7

21. Why doesn't total stockholders' equity equal the market value of the firm? ■ LO8

22. Which tends to be larger, the return on equity or the return on the market value of equity? Explain why. ■ LO8

23. What does "PE" stand for in the PE ratio, and how do investors use this ratio? ■ LO8

BRIEF EXERCISES

BE10–1 Waldo is planning to start a clothing store helping big and tall men blend in with the crowd. Explain to Waldo the advantages and disadvantages of a corporation in comparison to a sole proprietorship or partnership.

Cite advantages and disadvantages of a corporation (LO1)

BE10–2 Renaldo heard that an S corporation combines the benefits of a corporation with the benefits of a partnership. Explain to Renaldo the specific benefits of an S corporation and any drawbacks to organizing as an S corporation.

Understand an S corporation (LO1)

BE10–3 Western Wear Clothing issues 2,000 shares of its $0.01 par value common stock to provide funds for further expansion. Assuming the issue price is $12 per share, record the issuance of common stock.

Record issuance of common stock (LO2)

BE10–4 Gothic Architecture is a new chain of clothing stores specializing in the color black. Gothic issues 1,000 shares of its $1 par value common stock at $20 per share. Record the issuance of the stock. How would the entry differ if Gothic issued no-par value stock?

Record issuance of common stock (LO2)

BE10–5 Equinox Outdoor Wear issues 1,000 shares of its $0.01 par value preferred stock for cash at $22 per share. Record the issuance of the preferred shares.

Record issuance of preferred stock (LO3)

BE10–6 Match each of the following preferred stock features with its description.

Recognize preferred stock features (LO3)

Preferred Stock Features	Description
_____ 1. Convertible	a. Shares receive dividend priority, if a dividend is not paid.
_____ 2. Redeemable	b. Shares can be sold at a predetermined price.
_____ 3. Cumulative	c. Shares can be exchanged for common stock.

BE10–7 Rachel's Designs has 1,000 shares of 6%, $50 par value cumulative preferred stock issued at the beginning of 2010. All remaining shares are common stock. Due to cash flow difficulties, the company was not able to pay dividends in 2010 or 2011. The company plans to pay total dividends of $10,000 in 2012. How much of the $10,000 dividend will be paid to preferred stockholders and how much will be paid to common stockholders?

Determine the amount of preferred stock dividends (LO3)

Record purchase of treasury stock (LO4)

BE10–8 California Surf Clothing Company issues 1,000 shares of $1 par value common stock at $25 per share. Later in the year, the company decides to repurchase 100 shares at a cost of $28 per share. Record the purchase of treasury stock.

Record sale of treasury stock (LO4)

BE10–9 Refer to the situation described in BE10–8. Record the transaction if California Surf reissues the 100 shares of treasury stock at $30 per share. How would it be different if the shares reissue at $26 per share rather than at $30 per share?

Record cash dividends (LO5)

BE10–10 Divine Apparel has 3,000 shares of common stock outstanding. On October 1, the company declares a $0.50 per share dividend to stockholders of record on October 15. The dividend is paid on October 31. Record all transactions on the appropriate dates for cash dividends.

Record stock dividends (LO6)

BE10–11 On June 30, the board of directors of Sandals, Inc., declares a 100% stock dividend on its 20,000, $1 par, common shares. The market price of Sandals common stock is $25 on June 30. Record the stock dividend.

Analyze a stock split (LO6)

BE10–12 Refer to the situation described in BE10–11, but assume a 2-for-1 stock split instead of the 100% stock dividend. Explain why Sandals did not record a 2-for-1 stock split. What are the number of shares, par value per share, and market price per share immediately after the 2-for-1 stock split?

Indicate effects on total stockholders' equity (LO7)

BE10–13 Indicate whether each of the following transactions increases (+), decreases (−), or has no effect (NE) on total assets, total liabilities, and total stockholders' equity. The first transaction is completed as an example.

Transaction	Total Assets	Total Liabilities	Total Stockholders' Equity
Issue common stock	+	NE	+
Issue preferred stock	+	NE	+
Purchase treasury stock	−	NE	−
Sale of treasury stock	+	NE	+

Prepare the stockholders' equity section (LO7)

BE10–14 Silk Station has the following accounts at December 31: Common Stock, $1 par value, 1,000,000 shares; Paid-in Capital, $17 million; Retained Earnings, $10 million; and Treasury Stock, 50,000 shares, $1.1 million. Prepare the stockholders' equity section of the balance sheet.

Calculate the return on equity (LO8)

BE10–15 The financial statements of **Limited Brands, Inc.**, include the following selected data ($ in millions): sales, $9,043; net income, $220; beginning stockholders' equity, $2,219; and ending stockholders' equity, $1,874. Calculate the return on equity.

EXERCISES

Match terms with their definitions (LO1)

E10–1 Match (by letter) the following terms with their definitions. Each letter is used only once.

Terms

_____ 1. Publicly held corporation.
_____ 2. Model Business Corporation Act.
_____ 3. Articles of incorporation.
_____ 4. Limited liability.
_____ 5. Mutual agency.
_____ 6. Double taxation.
_____ 7. S corporation.
_____ 8. Limited liability company.

Definitions

a. Shareholders can lose no more than the amount they invest in the company.

b. Corporate earnings are taxed twice—at the corporate level and individual shareholder level.

c. Like an S corporation, but there are no limitations on the number of owners as in an S corporation.

d. Designed to serve as a guide to states in the development of their corporate statutes.

e. Allows for legal treatment as a corporation, but tax treatment as a partnership.

f. Has stock traded on a stock exchange such as the New York Stock Exchange (NYSE).

g. Individual partners in a partnership have the power to bind the business to a contract.

h. Describes (a) the nature of the firm's business activities, (b) the shares to be issued, and (c) the composition of the initial board of directors.

E10–2 Your friend, Jonathon Fain, is an engineering major with an entrepreneurial spirit. He wants to start his own corporation and needs your accounting expertise. He has no idea what the following terms mean: (1) authorized stock, (2) issued stock, (3) outstanding stock, (4) preferred stock, and (5) treasury stock.

Explain the meaning of terms used in stockholders' equity (LO2, 3, 4)

Required:

Write a note to Jonathon carefully explaining what each term means and how they are different from each other.

E10–3 Clothing Frontiers began operations on January 1, 2012, and engages in the following transactions during the year related to stockholders' equity.

Record the issuance of common stock (LO2)

January 1   Issues 600 shares of common stock for $40 per share.
April   1   Issues 100 additional shares of common stock for $44 per share.

Required:

1. Record the transactions, assuming Clothing Frontiers has no-par common stock.
2. Record the transactions, assuming Clothing Frontiers has $1 par value common stock.
3. Record the transactions, assuming Clothing Frontiers' common stock has a $1 stated value, rather than a $1 par value.

E10–4 Nathan's Athletic Apparel has 1,000 shares of 7%, $100 par value preferred stock the company issued at the beginning of 2011. All remaining shares are common stock. The company was not able to pay dividends in 2011, but plans to pay dividends of $15,000 in 2012.

Determine the amount of preferred stock dividends (LO3)

Required:

1. Assuming the preferred stock is cumulative, how much of the $15,000 dividend will be paid to preferred stockholders and how much will be paid to common stockholders in 2012?
2. Assuming the preferred stock is noncumulative, how much of the $15,000 dividend will be paid to preferred stockholders and how much will be paid to common stockholders in 2012?

E10–5 Italian Stallion has the following transactions during the year related to stockholders' equity.

Record common stock, preferred stock, and dividend transactions (LO2, 3, 5)

February 1   Issues 5,000 shares of no-par common stock for $15 per share.
May   15   Issues 500 shares of $10 par value preferred stock for $12 per share.
October 1   Declares a cash dividend of $0.75 per share to all stockholders of record (both common and preferred) on October 15.
October 15   Date of record.
October 31   Pays the cash dividend declared on October 1.

Required:

Record each of these transactions.

Record issuance of stock and treasury stock transactions (LO2, 3, 4)

E10–6 Finishing Touches has two classes of stock authorized: 8%, $10 par preferred, and $1 par value common. The following transactions affect stockholders' equity during 2012, its first year of operations:

January	2	Issues 100,000 shares of common stock for $25 per share.
February	6	Issues 2,000 shares of 8% preferred stock for $12 per share.
September	10	Repurchases 10,000 shares of its own common stock for $30 per share.
December	15	Reissues 5,000 shares of treasury stock at $35 per share.

Required:

Record each of these transactions.

Prepare the stockholders' equity section (LO7)

E10–7 Refer to the information in E10–6. In its first year of operations, Finishing Touches has income of $150,000 and pays dividends at the end of the year of $95,000 ($1 per share) on all common shares outstanding and $1,600 on all preferred shares outstanding.

Required:

Prepare the stockholders' equity section of the balance sheet for Finishing Touches as of December 31, 2012.

Record cash dividends (LO5)

E10–8 On March 15, **American Eagle** declares a quarterly cash dividend of $0.075 per share payable on April 13 to all stockholders of record on March 30.

Required:

Record American Eagle's declaration and payment of cash dividends for its 220 million shares.

Record common stock, treasury stock, and cash dividends (LO2, 4, 5)

E10–9 Power Drive Corporation designs and produces a line of golf equipment and golf apparel. Power Drive has 100,000 shares of common stock outstanding as of the beginning of 2012. Power Drive has the following transactions affecting stockholders' equity in 2012.

March	1	Issues 55,000 additional shares of $1 par value common stock for $52 per share.
May	10	Repurchases 5,000 shares of treasury stock for $55 per share.
June	1	Declares a cash dividend of $1.50 per share to all stockholders of record on June 15. (*Hint:* Dividends are not paid on treasury stock.)
July	1	Pays the cash dividend declared on June 1.
October	21	Reissues 2,500 shares of treasury stock purchased on May 10 for $60 per share.

Required:

Record each of these transactions.

Prepare the stockholders' equity section (LO7)

E10–10 Refer to the information in E10–9. Power Drive Corporation has the following beginning balances in its stockholders' equity accounts on January 1, 2012: Common Stock, $100,000; Paid-in Capital, $4,500,000; and Retained Earnings, $2,000,000. Net income for the year ended December 31, 2012, is $600,000.

Required:

Taking into consideration all of the transactions recorded in E10–9, prepare the stockholders' equity section of the balance sheet for Power Drive Corporation as of December 31, 2012.

Prepare a statement of stockholders' equity (LO7)

E10–11 Refer to the information in E10–9. Power Drive Corporation has the following beginning balances in its stockholders' equity accounts on January 1, 2012: Common

Stock, $100,000; Paid-in Capital, $4,500,000; and Retained Earnings, $2,000,000. Net income for the year ended December 31, 2012, is $600,000.

Required:

Taking into consideration all the transactions recorded in E10–9, prepare the statement of stockholders' equity for Power Drive Corporation for the year ended December 31, 2012, using the format provided.

POWER DRIVE CORPORATION
Statement of Stockholders' Equity
For the year ended December 31, 2012

	Common Stock	Additional Paid-in Capital	Retained Earnings	Treasury Stock	Total Stockholders' Equity
Balance, January 1	$100,000	$4,500,000	$2,000,000	$ -0-	$6,600,000
Issued common stock					
Repurchased treasury stock					
Cash dividends					
Sold treasury stock					
Net income					
Balance, December 31					

E10–12 Indicate whether each of the following transactions increases (+), decreases (−), or has no effect (NE) on total assets, total liabilities, and total stockholders' equity. The first transaction is completed as an example.

Indicate effects on total stockholders' equity (LO7)

Transaction	Total Assets	Total Liabilities	Total Stockholders' Equity
Issue common stock	+	*NE*	+
Issue preferred stock			
Repurchase treasury stock			
Sale of treasury stock			
Declare cash dividend			
Pay cash dividend			
100% stock dividend			
2-for-1 stock split			

E10–13 United Apparel has the following balances in its stockholders' equity accounts on December 31, 2012: Treasury Stock, $750,000; Common Stock, $500,000; Preferred Stock, $2,600,000; Retained Earnings, $1,700,000; and Additional Paid-in Capital, $7,800,000.

Prepare the stockholders' equity section (LO7)

Required:

Prepare the stockholders' equity section of the balance sheet for United Apparel as of December 31, 2012.

E10–14 The financial statements of **Limited Brands, Inc.**, include the following selected data (in millions):

Calculate and analyze ratios (LO8)

($ in millions)	2009	2008
Sales	$9,043	$10,134
Net income	$220	$718
Stockholders' equity	$1,874	$2,219
Shares outstanding (in millions)	321	–
Stock price	$7.92	–

Required:

1. Calculate the return on equity in 2009. Compare it with the amount calculated for **Deckers Outdoor** and **Timberland** in the chapter.
2. Calculate the return on the market value of equity in 2009. Compare it with the amount calculated for Deckers Outdoor and Timberland in the chapter.
3. Calculate earnings per share in 2009. Why is it not reasonable to compare it with the earnings per share for Deckers Outdoor and Timberland?
4. Calculate the price-earnings ratio in 2009. Compare it with the amount calculated for Deckers Outdoor and Timberland in the chapter.

Calculate and analyze ratios (LO8)

E10–15 Financial information for Forever 18 includes the following selected data (in millions):

($ in millions)	2012	2011
Net income	$210	$180
Dividends on preferred stock	$25	$20
Shares outstanding (in millions)	240	220
Stock price	$11.52	$10.47

Required:

1. Calculate earnings per share in 2011 and 2012. Did earnings per share increase in 2012?
2. Calculate the price-earnings ratio in 2011 and 2012. In which year is the stock priced lower in relation to reported earnings?

For additional exercises, visit www.mhhe.com/succeed for Exercises: Set B.

PROBLEMS: SET A

Match terms with their definitions (LO1)

P10–1A Match (by letter) the following terms with their definitions. Each letter is used only once.

Terms

———— 1. Cumulative.
———— 2. Retained earnings.
———— 3. Outstanding stock.
———— 4. Limited liability.
———— 5. Treasury stock.
———— 6. Issued stock.
———— 7. Angel investors.
———— 8. Paid-in capital.
———— 9. Authorized stock.
———— 10. Redeemable.

Definitions

a. The amount invested by stockholders.
b. Shares available to sell.
c. Shares can be returned to the corporation at a predetermined price.
d. The earnings not paid out in dividends.
e. Shares actually sold.
f. Shares receive priority for future dividends, if dividends are not paid in a given year.
g. Shares held by investors.
h. Shareholders can lose no more than the amount they invested in the company.
i. Wealthy individuals in the business community willing to risk investment funds on a promising business venture.
j. The corporation's own stock that it reacquired.

P10–2A Donnie Hilfiger has two classes of stock authorized: $1 par preferred and $0.01 par value common. As of the beginning of 2012, 200 shares of preferred stock and 3,000 shares of common stock have been issued. The following transactions affect stockholders' equity during 2012:

Record equity transactions and indicate the effect on the balance sheet equation (LO2, 3, 4, 5)

March	1	Issues 1,000 shares of common stock for $32 per share.
May	15	Repurchases 600 shares of treasury stock for $25 per share.
July	10	Reissues 100 shares of treasury stock purchased on May 15 for $30 per share.
October	15	Issues 100 shares of preferred stock for $35 per share.
December	1	Declares a cash dividend on both common and preferred stock of $0.75 per share to all stockholders of record on December 15. (*Hint:* Dividends are not paid on treasury stock.)
December	31	Pays the cash dividends declared on December 1.

Donnie Hilfiger has the following beginning balances in its stockholders' equity accounts on January 1, 2012: Preferred Stock, $200; Common Stock, $30; Additional Paid-in Capital, $66,000; and Retained Earnings, $25,500. Net income for the year ended December 31, 2012, is $9,800.

Required:

1. Record each of these transactions.
2. Indicate whether each of these transactions would increase (+), decrease (−), or have no effect (NE) on total assets, total liabilities, and total stockholders' equity by completing the following chart.

Transaction	Total Assets	Total Liabilities	Total Stockholders' Equity
Issue common stock			
Repurchase treasury stock			
Reissue treasury stock			
Issue preferred stock			
Declare cash dividends			
Pay cash dividends			

P10–3A Sammy's Sportshops has been very profitable in recent years and has seen its stock price steadily increase to over $100 per share. The CFO thinks the company should consider either a 100% stock dividend or a 2-for-1 stock split.

Indicate effect of stock dividends and stock splits (LO6)

4

Required:

1. Complete the following chart comparing the effects of a 100% stock dividend versus a 2-for-1 stock split on the stockholders' equity accounts, shares outstanding, par value, and share price.

	Before	After 100% Stock Dividend	After 2-for-1 Stock Split
Common stock, $1 par value	$ 1,000	2,000	1000
Additional paid-in capital	49,000	48,000	49,000
Total paid-in capital	50,000		
Retained earnings	22,850	21,850	22,850
Total stockholders' equity	$72,850	72,850	72,850
Shares outstanding	1,000	2,000	2,000
Par value per share	$1	$1.0	50¢
Share price	$110	$55	$55

2. What is the primary reason companies declare a large stock dividend or a stock split?

Analyze the stockholders'
equity section (LO7)

P10–4A The stockholders' equity section of Velcro World is presented here.

VELCRO WORLD Balance Sheet (partial)	
($ in thousands)	
Stockholders' equity:	
Preferred stock, $1 par value	$ 5,000
Common stock, $1 par value	20,000
Additional paid-in capital	575,000
Total paid-in capital	600,000
Retained earnings	278,000
Treasury stock, 10,000 common shares	(220,000)
Total stockholders' equity	$658,000

Required:

Based on the stockholders' equity section of Velcro World, answer the following questions. Remember that all amounts are presented in thousands.

1. How many shares of preferred stock have been issued?
2. How many shares of common stock have been issued?
3. If the common shares were issued at $20 per share, at what price per share were the preferred shares issued?
4. If retained earnings at the beginning of the period was $240 million and $20 million was paid in dividends during the year, what was the net income for the year?
5. What was the average cost per share of the treasury stock acquired?

Understand stockholders'
equity and the statement
of stockholders'
equity (LO7)

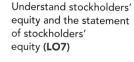

P10–5A Refer to the information provided in P10–2A.

Required:

Taking into consideration all the transactions during 2012, respond to the following for Donnie Hilfiger:

1. Prepare the stockholders' equity section of the balance sheet as of December 31, 2012.
2. Prepare the statement of stockholders' equity for the year ended December 31, 2012.
3. Explain how *Requirements* 1 and 2 are similar and how they are different.

Record equity
transactions and prepare
the stockholders' equity
section (LO2, 3, 4, 5, 7)

P10–6A Major League Apparel has two classes of stock authorized: 5%, $10 par preferred, and $1 par value common. The following transactions affect stockholders' equity during 2012, its first year of operations:

January	2	Issue 100,000 shares of common stock for $60 per share.
February	14	Issue 50,000 shares of preferred stock for $11 per share.
May	8	Repurchase 10,000 shares of its own common stock for $50 per share.
May	31	Reissue 5,000 shares of treasury stock for $55 per share.
December	1	Declare a cash dividend on its common stock of $0.50 per share and a $25,000 (5% of par value) cash dividend on its preferred stock payable to all stockholders of record on December 15. The dividend is payable on December 30. (*Hint:* Dividends are not paid on treasury stock.)
December	30	Pay the cash dividends declared on December 1.

Required:

1. Record each of these transactions.
2. Prepare the stockholders' equity section of the balance sheet as of December 31, 2012. Net income for the year was $480,000.

Calculate and analyze
ratios (LO8)

P10–7A Abercrombie & Fitch is a close competitor of **Deckers Outdoor** and **Timberland** in the apparel industry. Selected financial data for Abercrombie is provided as follows:

($ in millions)	2009	2008
Sales	$3,540	$3,750
Net income	272	476
Total assets	$2,848	$2,568
Total liabilities	$1,003	$ 949
Stockholders' equity	1,845	1,619
Total liabilities and stockholders' equity	$2,848	$2,568
Shares outstanding (in millions)	103	–
Stock price	$29	–

Required:

1. Calculate the return on equity for Abercrombie in 2009. How does it compare with the return on equity for Deckers Outdoor and Timberland reported in the chapter?
2. Calculate the return on the market value of equity for Abercrombie in 2009. How does it compare with the return on the market value of equity for Deckers Outdoor and Timberland reported in the chapter?
3. Why is the return on the market value of equity for Abercrombie, Deckers Outdoor, and Timberland so much lower than the return on equity?
4. Calculate the price-earnings ratio for Abercrombie in 2009. How does it compare with the price-earnings ratio for Deckers Outdoor and Timberland reported in the chapter? Which is trading at a lower price per dollar of earnings?

PROBLEMS: SET B

P10–1B Match (by letter) the following terms with their definitions. Each letter is used only once.

Match terms with their definitions **(LO1 to 8)**

Terms

_____ 1. PE ratio.
_____ 2. Stockholders' equity section of the balance sheet.
_____ 3. Accumulated deficit.
_____ 4. Growth stocks.
_____ 5. 100% stock dividend.
_____ 6. Statement of stockholders' equity.
_____ 7. Treasury stock.
_____ 8. Value stocks.
_____ 9. Return on equity.
_____ 10. Retained earnings.

Definitions

a. A debit balance in Retained Earnings.
b. Priced high in relation to current earnings as investors expect future earnings to be higher.
c. Effectively the same as a 2-for-1 stock split.
d. The earnings not paid out in dividends.
e. The stock price divided by earnings per share.
f. Summarizes the *changes* in the balance in each stockholders' equity account *over a period of time.*
g. Priced low in relation to current earnings.
h. Measures the ability of company management to generate earnings from the resources that owners provide.
i. Shows the balance in each equity account *at a point in time.*
j. The corporation's own stock that it reacquired.

Record equity transactions and indicate the effect on the balance sheet equation (LO2, 3, 4, 5)

P10–2B Nautical has two classes of stock authorized: $10 par preferred, and $1 par value common. As of the beginning of 2012, 100 shares of preferred stock and 2,000 shares of common stock have been issued. The following transactions affect stockholders' equity during 2012:

March 1 Issue 2,000 additional shares of common stock for $15 per share.
April 1 Issue 200 additional shares of preferred stock for $30 per share.
June 1 Declare a cash dividend on both common and preferred stock of $0.50 per share to all stockholders of record on June 15.
June 30 Pay the cash dividends declared on June 1.
August 1 Repurchase 200 shares of common treasury stock for $12 per share.
October 1 Reissue 100 shares of treasury stock purchased on August 1 for $14 per share.

Nautical has the following beginning balances in its stockholders' equity accounts on January 1, 2012: Preferred Stock, $1,000; Common Stock, $2,000; Paid-in Capital, $18,500; and Retained Earnings, $10,500. Net income for the year ended December 31, 2012, is $7,150.

Required:
1. Record each of these transactions.
2. Indicate whether each of these transactions would increase (+), decrease (−), or have no effect (NE) on total assets, total liabilities, and total stockholders' equity by completing the following chart.

Transaction	Total Assets	Total Liabilities	Total Stockholders' Equity
Issue common stock	+	NE	+
Issue preferred stock	+	NE	+
Declare cash dividends	NE	+	−
Pay cash dividends	−	−	NE
Repurchase treasury stock	−	NE	−
Reissue treasury stock	+	NE	+

Indicate effect of stock dividends and stock splits (LO6)

P10–3B The Athletic Village has done very well the past year, and its stock price is now trading at $82 per share. Management is considering either a 100% stock dividend or a 2-for-1 stock split.

Required:
Complete the following chart comparing the effects of a 100% stock dividend versus a 2-for-1 stock split on the stockholders' equity accounts, shares outstanding, par value, and share price.

	Before	After 100% Stock Dividend	After 2-for-1 Stock Split
Common stock, $0.01 par value	$ 10		
Additional paid-in capital	24,990		
Total paid-in capital	25,000		
Retained earnings	15,000		
Total stockholders' equity	$40,000		
Shares outstanding	1,000		
Par value per share	$0.01		
Share price	$82		

Analyze the stockholders' equity section (LO7)

P10–4B The stockholders' equity section of The Seventies Shop is presented here.

THE SEVENTIES SHOP
Balance Sheet (partial)

($ in thousands)	
Stockholders' equity:	
Preferred stock, $50 par value	$ –0–
Common stock, $5 par value	15,000
Additional paid-in capital	45,000
Total paid-in capital	60,000
Retained earnings	48,000
Treasury stock	(2,700)
Total stockholders' equity	$105,300

Required:

Based on the stockholders' equity section of The Seventies Shop, answer the following questions. Remember that all amounts are presented in thousands.

1. How many shares of preferred stock have been issued?
2. How many shares of common stock have been issued?
3. Total paid-in capital is $60 million. At what price per share were the common shares issued?
4. If retained earnings at the beginning of the period was $40 million and net income during the year was $10,850,000, how much was paid in dividends for the year?
5. If the treasury stock was reacquired at $18 per share, how many shares were reacquired?
6. How much was the dividend per share? (*Hint:* Dividends are not paid on treasury stock.)

P10–5B Refer to the information provided in P10–2B.

Required:

Taking into consideration all the transactions during 2012, respond to the following for Nautical:

1. Prepare the stockholders' equity section of the balance sheet as of December 31, 2012.
2. Prepare the statement of stockholders' equity for the year ended December 31, 2012.
3. Explain how *Requirements* 1 and 2 are similar and how they are different.

> Understand stockholders' equity and the statement of stockholders' equity (LO7)

P10–6B National League Gear has two classes of stock authorized: 6%, $20 par preferred, and $5 par value common. The following transactions affect stockholders' equity during 2012, National League's first year of operations:

> Record equity transactions and prepare the stockholders' equity section (LO2, 3, 4, 5, 7)

February	2	Issue 1 million shares of common stock for $25 per share.
February	4	Issue 500,000 shares of preferred stock for $22 per share.
June	15	Repurchase 100,000 shares of its own common stock for $20 per share.
August	15	Reissue 75,000 shares of treasury stock for $35 per share.
November	1	Declare a cash dividend on its common stock of $1 per share and a $600,000 (6% of par value) cash dividend on its preferred stock payable to all stockholders on record on November 15. (*Hint:* Dividends are not paid on treasury stock.)
November	30	Pay the dividends declared on November 1.

Required:

1. Record each of these transactions.
2. Prepare the stockholders' equity section of the balance sheet as of December 31, 2012. Net income for the year was $4,800,000.

P10–7B **Gap** is a close competitor of **Deckers Outdoor** and **Timberland** in the teenage apparel industry. Gap also owns the **Old Navy** and **Banana Republic** clothing chains. Gap reported higher earnings than Deckers Outdoor and Timberland in 2009.

> Calculate and analyze ratios (LO8)

Does that mean Gap is more profitable? Maybe, but we need to control for the differences in company size in order to accurately compare the profitability of the companies. Selected financial data for Gap is provided as follows:

($ in millions)	2009	2008
Sales	$14,526	$15,763
Net income	967	833
Total assets	$ 7,564	$ 7,838
Total liabilities	$ 3,177	$ 3,564
Stockholders' equity	4,387	4,274
Total liabilities and stockholders' equity	$ 7,564	$ 7,838
Shares outstanding (in millions)	694	–
Stock price	$16	–

Required:

1. Calculate the return on equity for Gap in 2009. How does it compare with the return on equity for Deckers Outdoor and Timberland reported in the chapter?
2. Calculate the return on the market value of equity for Gap in 2009. How does it compare with the return on the market value of equity for Deckers Outdoor and Timberland reported in the chapter?
3. Why is the return on the market value of equity for Gap so much lower than the return on equity?
4. Calculate the price-earnings ratio for Gap in 2009. How does it compare with the price-earnings ratio for Deckers Outdoor and Timberland reported in the chapter? Which is trading at a lower price per dollar of earnings?

For additional problems, visit www.mhhe.com/succeed for Problems: Set C.

ADDITIONAL PERSPECTIVES

Continuing Problem

Great Adventures

(This is a continuation of the Great Adventures problem from earlier chapters.)

AP10–1 Tony and Suzie purchased land costing $500,000 for a new camp in January 2014. Now they need money to build the cabins, dining facility, a ropes course, and an outdoor swimming pool. Tony and Suzie first checked with Summit Bank to see if they could borrow another million dollars, but unfortunately the bank turned them down as too risky. Undeterred, they promoted their idea to close friends they had made through the outdoor clinics and TEAM events. They decided to go ahead and sell shares of stock in the company to raise the additional funds for the camp. Great Adventures has two classes of stock authorized: 8%, $10 par preferred, and $1 par value common.

When the company began on July 1, 2012, Tony and Suzie each purchased 10,000 shares of $1 par value common stock at $1 per share. The following transactions affect stockholders' equity during 2014, its third year of operations:

Jul.	2	Issue an additional 100,000 shares of common stock for $12 per share.
Sep.	10	Repurchase 10,000 shares of its own common stock (i.e., treasury stock) for $15 per share.
Nov.	15	Reissue 5,000 shares of treasury stock at $16 per share.
Dec.	1	Declare a cash dividend on its common stock of $115,000 ($1 per share) to all stockholders of record on December 15. The dividend is payable on December 31.

Required:
1. Record each of these transactions.
2. Great Adventures has net income of $150,000 in 2014. Retained earnings at the beginning of 2014 was $140,000. Prepare the stockholders' equity section of the balance sheet for Great Adventures as of December 31, 2014.

American Eagle Outfitters, Inc.

Financial Analysis

AP10–2 Financial information for the year ended January 31, 2009, is presented in the text of the chapter. Financial information for **American Eagle** for the year ended January 31, 2010, is presented in Appendix A at the end of the book. Using the financial information presented in Appendix A, answer the following.

Required:
1. What is the par value per share for the common stock?
2. How many common shares were issued at the end of the most recent year?
3. Did the company have any treasury stock? How many shares?
4. How much did the company pay in cash dividends in the most recent year?

The Buckle, Inc.

Financial Analysis

AP10–3 Financial information for **The Buckle** is presented in Appendix B at the end of the book.

Required:
1. What is the par value per share for the common stock?
2. How many common shares were issued at the end of the most recent year?
3. Did the company have any treasury stock? How many shares?
4. How much did the company pay in cash dividends in the most recent year?
5. Has the company ever issued a stock dividend or stock split? If so, describe.

American Eagle Outfitters, Inc., vs. The Buckle, Inc.

Comparative Analysis

AP10–4 Financial information for **American Eagle** is presented in Appendix A at the end of the book, and financial information for **The Buckle** is presented in Appendix B at the end of the book. The stock prices as of January 30, 2010, for American Eagle and The Buckle were $15.89 and $30.34, respectively.

Required:
1. Calculate the return on equity for American Eagle and The Buckle in 2010. Which company has a higher return on equity?
2. Calculate the return on the market value of equity for American Eagle and The Buckle in 2010. Which company has a higher return on the market value of equity?
3. Why is the return on the market value of equity for American Eagle and The Buckle so much lower than the return on equity?
4. Calculate the price-earnings ratio for American Eagle and The Buckle. Which is trading at a lower price per dollar of earnings?

Ethics

AP10–5 Put yourself in the shoes of a company president: The extremely successful launch of a new product has resulted in an additional $5 million in unexpected operating cash flows. You can think of several ways to use the extra $5 million.

One alternative is to pay out a special dividend to the shareholders. As president, you are accountable to the board of directors, which is elected by the shareholders. Rather than pay a dividend, you could repurchase shares of the company's own stock. The stock seems currently to be underpriced, and by purchasing treasury shares you are distributing surplus cash to shareholders without giving them taxable dividend income.

You could also pay a special year-end bonus to your employees. With 500 employees, that would average $10,000 per employee, quite a nice holiday bonus. After all, it was the employees' hard work and dedication that earned the money in the first place.

Or you could use the money to reinvest in the company. By reinvesting the money, it might be easier to continue the upward earnings trend in the future.

Finally, you could approach the board of directors for a compensation adjustment of your own. It's been a great year, and you are the president of the company. Shouldn't you at least share in the success?

Required:

Determine how you would allocate the additional $5 million. Are there other areas in which to spend the money not mentioned in the above case? Is it ethical for the president to be directly compensated based on the company's performance each year?

Internet Research

AP10–6 EDGAR, the Electronic Data Gathering, Analysis, and Retrieval system, is a giant database of documents the U.S. Securities and Exchange Commission (SEC) requires that companies submit. All publicly traded domestic companies use EDGAR to make the majority of their filings. (Filings by foreign companies are not required to be filed on EDGAR, but many of these companies do so voluntarily.) Form 10-K, which includes the annual report, is an important document required to be filed on EDGAR. The SEC makes this information available, free to the public, on the Internet.

Required:
1. Access EDGAR on the Internet. The web address is *www.sec.gov*.
2. Search for a public company with which you are familiar. Access its most recent 10-K filing, and search or scroll to find the statement of stockholders' equity.
3. Determine from the statement the transactions that affected common stock during the past year.
4. Determine from the statement the transactions that affected retained earnings during the past year.
5. Explain how the totals on the statement of stockholders' equity agree with the amounts reported in the stockholders' equity section in the balance sheet.

Written Communication

AP10–7 Preferred stock has characteristics of both liabilities and stockholders' equity. Convertible bonds are another example of a financing arrangement that blurs the line between liabilities and stockholders' equity. Items like these have led some to conclude that the present distinction between liabilities and equity should be eliminated. Under this approach, liabilities and equity would be combined into one category that includes both creditor and owner claims to resources.

Required:
1. Define liabilities and stockholders' equity.
2. Provide arguments in support of maintaining the distinction between liabilities and stockholders' equity in the balance sheet.
3. Provide arguments in support of eliminating the distinction between liabilities and stockholders' equity in the balance sheet.
4. Which do you recommend? Why?

Earnings Management

AP10–8 Renegade Clothing is struggling to meet analysts' forecasts. It's early December 2012, and the year-end projections are in. Listed below are the projections for the year ended 2012 and the comparable actual amounts for 2011.

	Projected 2012	Actual 2011
Sales	$14,000,000	$16,023,000
Net income	878,000	1,113,000
Total assets	$ 6,500,000	$ 6,821,000
Total liabilities	$ 2,500,000	$ 2,396,000
Stockholders' equity	4,000,000	4,425,000
Total liabilities and stockholders' equity	$ 6,500,000	$ 6,821,000
Shares outstanding	950,000	950,000

Analysts forecast earnings per share for 2012 to be $0.95 per share. It looks like earnings per share will fall short of expectations in 2012.

Ronald Outlaw, the director of marketing, has a creative idea to improve earnings per share and the return on equity for 2012. He proposes the company borrow additional funds and use the proceeds to repurchase some of its own stock—treasury shares. Is this a good idea?

Required:

1. Calculate the projected earnings per share and return on equity for 2012 before any repurchase of stock.

Now assume Renegade Clothing purchases 100,000 shares of its own stock at $10 per share. The projections for 2012 will change as follows:

	2012	2011
Sales	$14,000,000	$16,023,000
Net income	878,000	1,113,000
Total assets	$ 6,500,000	$ 6,821,000
Total liabilities	$ 3,500,000	$ 2,396,000
Stockholders' equity	3,000,000	4,425,000
Total liabilities and stockholders' equity	$ 6,500,000	$ 6,821,000
Shares outstanding	850,000	950,000

2. Calculate the new projected earnings per share and return on equity for 2012, assuming the company goes through with the treasury stock repurchase.
   (*Hint:* In computing earnings per share, average shares outstanding is now 900,000 = (850,000 + 950,000) ÷ 2.)
3. Explain how the repurchase of treasury stock near year-end improves earnings per share and the return on equity ratio.

Answers to the Self Study Questions
1. a   2. b   3. b   4. c   5. b   6. d   7. c   8. d   9. a   10. c

Statement of Cash Flows

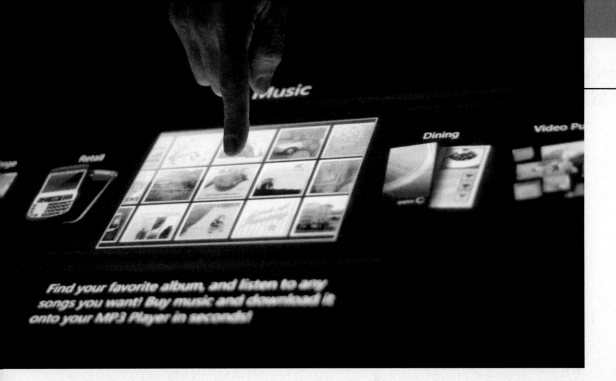

APPLE, INC.: CASH FLOWS AT THE CORE

Net income represents all revenues less expenses of a company during a reporting period. Operating cash flows represent the cash inflows less cash outflows related to the very same revenue and expense activities. Although you might expect these two amounts to be similar, fairly large differences sometimes exist. For instance, here are the 2009 net income and operating cash flows for three well-known companies in the electronics industry ($ in millions):

Company Name	Net Income	Operating Cash Flows
Apple	$ 5,704	$10,159
Hewlett-Packard	7,660	13,379
Microsoft	14,569	19,037

All three companies report higher operating cash flows than net income. For **Apple** and **Hewlett-Packard**, operating cash flow is almost twice net income. One reason may be that certain items, like depreciation expense, decrease net income but have no effect on operating cash flows. Both net income and operating cash flows are important indicators in explaining stock prices. Which is more important to investors—net income or operating cash flows? The financial press discusses net income more than cash flows, but many finance courses emphasize that "cash is king."

However, in comparing net income with operating cash flows, research consistently finds that net income, not cash, is king. Net income works better than operating cash flow in forecasting not only future net income, but also future cash flow.[1] The research also finds that stock returns (the change in stock price plus dividends) are more closely related to net income than to operating cash flow.[2] Net income helps smooth out the unevenness or lumpiness in year-to-year operating cash flow, producing a better estimate of ongoing company profitability.

While net income may win in a direct competition with operating cash flow, it's important to remember that both net income and operating cash flow provide important information. An investor or creditor who analyzes both net income and operating cash flow will do better than one who focuses solely on net income. For instance, a company with increasing earnings but decreasing operating cash flow is probably not as good an investment as a company with increasing earnings and increasing operating cash flow. Net income and operating cash flows are each so valuable that we might think of them both as financial royalty.

[1]M. Barth, C. Cram, and K. Nelson. 2001. "Accruals and the Prediction of Future Cash Flows." *The Accounting Review* 76 (January), pp. 27–58; and C. Finger. 1994. "The Ability of Earnings to Predict Future Earnings and Cash Flow." *Journal of Accounting Research* 32 (Autumn), pp. 210–23.
[2]P. Dechow. 1994. "Accounting Earnings and Cash Flow as Measures of Firm Performance: The Role of Accounting Accruals." *Journal of Accounting and Economics* (July), pp. 3–42.

PART A

FORMATTING THE STATEMENT OF CASH FLOWS

A **statement of cash flows** provides a summary of cash inflows and cash outflows during the reporting period. Illustration 11–1 presents the statement of cash flows for E-Games, Inc.

ILLUSTRATION 11–1

Statement of Cash Flows

E-GAMES, INC. Statement of Cash Flows For the year ended December 31, 2012		
Cash Flows from Operating Activities		
Net income	$42,000	
Adjustments for noncash effects:		
Depreciation expense	9,000	
Loss on sale of land	4,000	
Changes in current assets and current liabilities:		
Increase in accounts receivable	(7,000)	
Decrease in inventory	10,000	
Increase in prepaid rent	(2,000)	
Decrease in accounts payable	(5,000)	
Increase in interest payable	1,000	
Decrease in income tax payable	(2,000)	
Net cash flows from operating activities		$50,000
Cash Flows from Investing Activities		
Purchase of investment	(35,000)	
Sale of land	6,000	
Net cash flows from investing activities		(29,000)
Cash Flows from Financing Activities		
Issuance of common stock	5,000	
Payment of cash dividends	(12,000)	
Net cash flows from financing activities		(7,000)
Net increase (decrease) in cash		14,000
Cash at the beginning of the period		48,000
Cash at the end of the period		$62,000
Note: Noncash Activities		
Purchased equipment by issuing a note payable		$20,000

We will use this statement as an example throughout the chapter. Don't be concerned about the details just yet. That's what the rest of the chapter is all about.

Classification of Transactions

■ **LO1**
Classify cash transactions as operating, investing, or financing activities.

The three primary categories of cash flows are (1) cash flows from operating activities, (2) cash flows from investing activities, and (3) cash flows from financing activities. Classifying each cash flow by source (operating, investing, or financing activities) is more informative than simply listing the various cash flows.

REPORTING CASH FLOW ACTIVITIES

Operating activities include cash receipts and cash payments for transactions relating to revenue and expense activities. These are essentially the very same activities reported on the income statement. In other words, cash flows from operating activities include the elements of net income, but reported on a cash basis. Common examples of operating activities include the collection of cash from customers or the payment of cash for inventory purchases, salaries, and rent.

Investing activities include cash transactions involving the purchase and sale of long-term assets and current investments. Companies periodically invest cash

to replace or expand productive facilities such as buildings, land, and equipment. They might also invest in other assets, such as stocks or bonds of other firms, with the expectation of a return on those investments. Eventually, many of these assets are sold. Investment in and sale of long-term assets and investments are common examples of investing activities.

Financing activities are both inflows and outflows of cash resulting from the external financing of a business. A major portion of financing for many companies comes from external sources, specifically stockholders and lenders. Common financing activities are borrowing and repaying debt, issuing and repurchasing stock, and paying dividends.

INTERNATIONAL FINANCIAL REPORTING STANDARDS (IFRS)

In a joint project on financial reporting presentation with the FASB, the IASB recently proposed extending the operating, investing, and financing classifications used in the statement of cash flows to the income statement and the balance sheet. If the proposal goes through, all the major financial statements will be organized along the lines of operating, investing, and financing activities.

For more discussion, see Appendix E.

Illustration 11–2 lists common cash receipts and cash payments for operating, investing, and financing activities. **Review this illustration carefully** (you may even want to bookmark it); it will come in handy in solving many of the questions, exercises, problems, and cases at the end of the chapter.

ILLUSTRATION 11–2
Operating, Investing, and Financing Activities

Cash Flows from Operating Activities

Cash Inflows	Cash Outflows
Sale of goods or services	Purchase of inventory
Receipt of interest and dividends	For operating expenses
	For interest
	For income taxes

Cash Flows from Investing Activities

Cash Inflows	Cash Outflows
Sale of investments	Purchase of investments
Sale of property, plant, and equipment or intangibles	Purchase of property, plant, and equipment or intangibles
Collection of notes receivable	Lending with notes receivable

Cash Flows from Financing Activities

Cash Inflows	Cash Outflows
Issuance of bonds or notes payable	Repayment of bonds or notes payable
Issuance of stock	Reacquisition of stock (treasury stock)
	Payment of dividends

Let's look at a few of the cash flows. For example, we report interest and dividends received from investments with operating activities rather than investing activities. Similarly, we report interest paid on bonds or notes payable with operating activities rather than financing activities. Why are these classified as operating activities? They are included in operating activities because each is a cash flow from an activity reported in the income statement—interest revenue, dividend revenue, and interest expense. As we discussed earlier, operating activities are those we report on the income statement.

On the other hand, we record dividends paid as a financing activity. Recall that dividends are not an expense and, therefore, paying dividends has no effect on net

income. The payment of dividends simply reduces assets (cash) and stockholders' equity (retained earnings).

COMMON MISTAKE

Students sometimes misclassify dividends in preparing the statement of cash flows. Dividends *received* are included in operating activities. Dividends *paid* are included in financing activities.

As we saw in Chapter 3, we prepare the income statement, the statement of stockholders' equity, and the balance sheet directly from the adjusted trial balance. Unfortunately, though, the accounts listed on the adjusted trial balance do not directly provide the cash inflows and cash outflows we report on the statement of cash flows. We need to rely on other sources to determine the amounts necessary to prepare the statement of cash flows. Illustration 11–3 outlines the three primary sources.

ILLUSTRATION 11–3

Information Sources for Preparing the Statement of Cash Flows

Information Sources	Explanation
1. Income statement	The income statement provides important information in determining cash flows from operating activities.
2. Balance sheet	We look at the change in asset, liability, and stockholders' equity accounts from the end of the last period to the end of this period to find cash flows from operating, investing, and financing activities.
3. Detailed accounting records	Sometimes we need additional information from the accounting records to determine specific cash inflows or cash outflows for the period.

KEY POINT

Operating activities relate to income statement items. Investing activities primarily involve changes in long-term assets. Financing activities primarily involve changes in long-term liabilities and stockholders' equity.

Illustration 11–4 summarizes the relationship of the income statement and balance sheet to the operating, investing, and financing sections in the statement of cash flows.

ILLUSTRATION 11–4

Relationship of the Income Statement and Balance Sheet to the Statement of Cash Flows

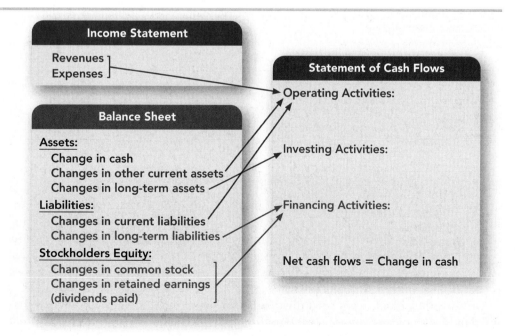

REPORTING NONCASH ACTIVITIES

Suppose a company borrows $200,000 cash from a bank, issuing a long-term note payable for that amount. The firm reports this transaction in a statement of cash flows as a *financing activity*. Now suppose the company uses that cash to purchase new equipment. It reports this second transaction as an *investing activity*. But what if, instead of two separate transactions, the company acquired $200,000 of new equipment by issuing a $200,000 long-term note payable in a *single transaction?* Since this transaction does not affect cash, it is excluded from the statement of cash flows.

However, undertaking a significant investing activity and a significant financing activity as two parts of a single transaction does not lessen the value of reporting these activities. For that reason, transactions that do not increase or decrease cash, but that result in significant investing and financing activities, are reported as **noncash activities** either directly after the cash flow statement or in a note to the financial statements. Examples of significant noncash investing and financing activities include:

1. Purchase of long-term assets by issuing debt.
2. Purchase of long-term assets by issuing stock.
3. Conversion of bonds payable into common stock.
4. Exchange of long-term assets.

Having a better overall picture of total investing and financing activities is important for investors and creditors. Thus, they should consider both the investing and financing activities reported in the statement of cash flows and the noncash investing and financing activities reported in the notes to the financial statements.

Decision Point

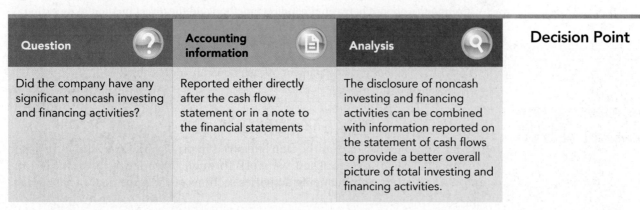

Question ?	Accounting information 🗎	Analysis 🔍
Did the company have any significant noncash investing and financing activities?	Reported either directly after the cash flow statement or in a note to the financial statements	The disclosure of noncash investing and financing activities can be combined with information reported on the statement of cash flows to provide a better overall picture of total investing and financing activities.

Let's Review

Indicate whether each of the following items is classified as an operating activity, investing activity, financing activity, or a significant noncash activity.
1. Dividends received from an investment.
2. Dividends paid to shareholders.
3. Property, plant, and equipment purchased for cash.
4. Property, plant, and equipment purchased by issuing stock.
5. Notes receivable accepted for lending cash.
6. Notes payable issued for borrowing cash.

Solution:
1. Operating.
2. Financing.
3. Investing.
4. Noncash.
5. Investing.
6. Financing.

Suggested Homework:
BE11-1, BE11-2;
E11-3, E11-4;
P11-1A&B

OPERATING ACTIVITIES—INDIRECT AND DIRECT METHODS

We have two ways to determine and report cash flows from operating activities in a statement of cash flows—the indirect method and the direct method. The methods differ only in the presentation format for operating activities. **The total net cash flows from operating activities are identical under both methods.** Also, the two methods affect only the operating section. We report investing, financing, and noncash activities identically under both methods.

Using the indirect method, we begin with net income and then list adjustments to net income, in order to arrive at operating cash flows. The indirect method is more popular because it is generally easier and less costly to prepare. In fact, nearly all major companies in the United States (about 99%) prepare the statement of cash flows using the indirect method.[3] For this reason, we emphasize the indirect method.

Using the direct method, we adjust the items on the income statement to directly show the cash inflows and outflows from operations such as cash received from customers and cash paid for inventory, salaries, rent, interest, and taxes. If a company decides to use the direct method to report operating activities, it must also report the indirect method either along with the statement of cash flows or in a separate note to the financial statements.

We discuss the indirect method in the next section. We present the direct method using the same example in an appendix to this chapter.

 KEY POINT

Companies choose between the indirect method and the direct method in reporting operating activities in the statement of cash flows. The indirect method is less costly to prepare and is used in practice by the majority of companies. The direct method more logically presents the cash inflows and outflows from operations. The investing and financing sections of the statement of cash flows are identical under both methods.

PART B

PREPARING THE STATEMENT OF CASH FLOWS

In this section, we first look at the steps involved in preparing the statement of cash flows, and its basic format. Then we work through these steps in preparing the operating, investing, and financing activities sections of the statement of cash flows.

Steps in Preparing the Statement of Cash Flows

Illustration 11–5 summarizes the four basic steps in preparing the statement of cash flows.

ILLUSTRATION 11–5

Steps in Preparing the Statement of Cash Flows

Step 1. Calculate net cash flows from *operating activities*, using information from the income statement and changes in current assets (other than cash) and current liabilities from the balance sheet.

Step 2. Determine the net cash flows from *investing activities*, by analyzing changes in long-term asset accounts from the balance sheet.

Step 3. Determine the net cash flows from *financing activities*, by analyzing changes in long-term liabilities and stockholders' equity accounts from the balance sheet.

Step 4. Combine the operating, investing, and financing activities, and make sure the total change from these three activities agrees with the net increase (decrease) in cash shown at the bottom of the statement of cash flows.

---

[3]*Accounting Trends and Techniques—2009*. 2009. (New York: American Institute of Certified Public Accountants).

Illustration 11–6 provides the income statement, balance sheet, and additional information for E-Games, Inc. We will use this information to prepare the statement of cash flows following the four basic steps.

ILLUSTRATION 11–6

Income Statement, Balance Sheet, and Additional Information for E-Games, Inc.

E-GAMES, INC.
Income Statement
For the year ended December 31, 2012

Revenues		$1,012,000
Expenses:		
Cost of goods sold	$650,000	
Operating expenses (salaries, rent, utilities)	286,000	
Depreciation expense	9,000	
Loss on sale of land	4,000	
Interest expense	5,000	
Income tax expense	16,000	
Total expenses		970,000
Net income		$ 42,000

E-GAMES, INC.
Balance Sheet
December 31, 2012 and 2011

	2012	2011	Increase (I) or Decrease (D)
Assets			
Current assets:			
Cash	$ 62,000	$ 48,000	$14,000 (I)
Accounts receivable	27,000	20,000	7,000 (I)
Inventory	35,000	45,000	10,000 (D)
Prepaid rent	4,000	2,000	2,000 (I)
Long-term assets:			
Investments	35,000	0	35,000 (I)
Land	70,000	80,000	10,000 (D)
Equipment	90,000	70,000	20,000 (I)
Accumulated depreciation	(23,000)	(14,000)	9,000 (I)
Total assets	$300,000	$251,000	
Liabilities and Stockholders' Equity			
Current liabilities:			
Accounts payable	$ 22,000	$ 27,000	$ 5,000 (D)
Interest payable	2,000	1,000	1,000 (I)
Income tax payable	5,000	7,000	2,000 (D)
Long-term liabilities:			
Notes payable	95,000	75,000	20,000 (I)
Stockholders' equity:			
Common stock	105,000	100,000	5,000 (I)
Retained earnings	71,000	41,000	30,000 (I)
Total liabilities and stockholders' equity	$300,000	$251,000	

(*continued*)

ILLUSTRATION 11–6
(concluded)

Additional Information for 2012:

1. Purchased stock in Intendo Corporation for $35,000.
2. Sold land originally costing $10,000 for $6,000, resulting in a $4,000 loss on sale of land.
3. Purchased $20,000 in equipment by issuing a $20,000 note payable due in three years. No cash was exchanged in the transaction.
4. Issued common stock for $5,000 cash.
5. Declared and paid a cash dividend of $12,000.

Basic Format

In preparing the statement of cash flows, it's helpful to first set up the basic format. As Illustration 11–7 shows, the last three lines of the statement of cash flows include amounts for the net increase (decrease) in cash, cash at the beginning of the period, and cash at the end of the period obtained from the E-Games balance sheet. Cash at the beginning of the period is $48,000 (the balance for cash in the 2011 balance sheet column), and cash at the end of the period is $62,000 (the balance for cash in the 2012 balance sheet column). The $14,000 change in the cash balance will be our "check figure," which means the cash inflows and cash outflows we identify must net to this amount. After all, the purpose of the statement of cash flows is to explain *why* cash increased by $14,000.

ILLUSTRATION 11–7

Basic Format for the Statement of Cash Flows

E-GAMES, INC.
Statement of Cash Flows
For the year ended December 31, 2012

Cash Flows from Operating Activities	$_____
Cash Flows from Investing Activities	_____
Cash Flows from Financing Activities	_____
Net increase (decrease) in cash	14,000
Cash at the beginning of the period	48,000
Cash at the end of the period	$62,000
Note: Noncash Activities	
List of noncash transactions	_____

Operating Activities—Indirect Method

■ **LO2**
Prepare the operating activities section of the statement of cash flows using the indirect method.

As we learned in Illustration 11–5, the first step in preparing the statement of cash flows is to calculate net cash flows from *operating activities* using information from the income statement and changes in current assets (other than cash) and current liabilities from the balance sheet.

The key to understanding the operating activities section of the statement of cash flows is to understand that both net income and cash flows from operating activities represent the same operating activities: The income statement reports net income on an *accrual basis*. That is, we report revenues when we earn them, regardless of when cash is received, and expenses when we incur them, regardless of when cash is paid. On the other hand, the statement of cash flows reports the very same activities on a *cash basis*—revenues when we receive cash, and expenses when we pay cash.

Net income includes both cash and noncash components. *Our task, when preparing a statement of cash flows, is to convert net income from an accrual basis to*

a cash basis. In other words, we remove noncash components from net income so that what's left is cash flows only. We can classify the noncash components as:

(a)   revenues and expenses that don't affect cash at all (adjustments for non-cash components of net income), and

(b)   revenues and expenses that do affect cash, but not by the amount reported as the revenue or expense (adjustments for changes in current assets and current liabilities).

We look at each of those two adjustments for noncash components in the sections that follow.

Question ❓	Accounting information 🗎	Analysis 🔍
Is a company's net income supported by strong operating cash flows?	Operating activities section of the statement of cash flows using the indirect method	The operating activities section using the indirect method reconciles net income to operating cash flows. Net income is considered to be of higher quality when backed by strong operating cash flows.

Decision Point

ADJUSTMENTS FOR NONCASH COMPONENTS OF NET INCOME

Using the indirect method, we first adjust net income for revenues and expenses that don't affect cash at all. Here are two common examples.

Depreciation expense.   Depreciation expense reduces net income. Remember, though, depreciation expense does not correspond to a cash outflow in the current period. Recording depreciation expense results in increases to the Depreciation Expense and Accumulated Depreciation accounts. In recording depreciation, we're simply allocating the cost of an asset over the periods the asset is used. But since we deducted this noncash expense in the determination of net income, we need to add it back in order to eliminate it. Amortization of intangible assets is treated the same way as depreciation of tangible assets. We add back both depreciation expense and amortization expense to net income in arriving at cash flows from operating activities.

E-Games, Inc., reports net income of $42,000 and depreciation expense of $9,000 in its income statement. Since depreciation expense reduces net income by $9,000, E-Games will add the $9,000 back to net income as a step in arriving at net cash flows from operations. Illustration 11–8 shows how E-Games reports depreciation expense in the statement of cash flows under the indirect method.

ILLUSTRATION 11–8

Adjustment for Depreciation Expense

E-GAMES, INC. Statement of Cash Flows (partial)	
Cash Flows from Operating Activities	
Net income	$42,000
Adjustments for noncash effects:	
Depreciation expense	9,000

Loss on sale of land.   Gains on the sale of long-term assets increase net income, while losses on the sale of those assets decrease net income. E-Games, Inc., reports a $4,000 loss on sale of land in its income statement. To see how to treat the loss,

let's re-create how E-Games recorded the sale of land. We see from additional-information item (2) that E-Games sold land originally costing $10,000 for only $6,000, resulting in a $4,000 loss.

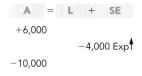

		Debit	Credit
Cash		6,000	
Loss		4,000	
Land			10,000
(Record loss on sale of land)			

A = L + SE
+6,000
−4,000 Exp↑
−10,000

The cash effect of this transaction is a cash increase of $6,000. The sale of land, though, is an investing activity, so this cash inflow is reported in the investing section of the statement of cash flows. Note that the loss is simply the difference between cash received in the sale of land (reported as an investing activity) and the cost of the land. It is not a cash inflow or cash outflow. And yet, we subtracted the $4,000 loss on the income statement in the determination of net income, so we need to add it back in order to eliminate this noncash component of net income. Illustration 11–9 shows how E-Games adds back the loss on sale of land to net income in arriving at net cash flows from operating activities.

ILLUSTRATION 11–9

Adjustment for Loss on Sale of Land

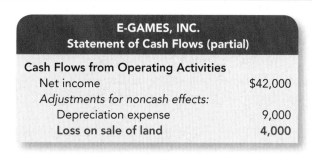

E-GAMES, INC.
Statement of Cash Flows (partial)

Cash Flows from Operating Activities
Net income	$42,000
Adjustments for noncash effects:	
Depreciation expense	9,000
Loss on sale of land	**4,000**

What if E-Games, Inc., had a gain of $4,000, rather than a loss, on the sale of land? Since we would have added the $4,000 gain in the determination of net income, we would need to subtract it from net income to eliminate it.

 COMMON MISTAKE

Students sometimes are unsure whether to add or subtract a loss on the sale of assets. Just remember that a loss is like an expense—both reduce net income. Treat a loss on the sale of assets like depreciation expense and add it back to net income. A gain on the sale of long-term assets is the opposite of an expense, so we subtract it from net income to arrive at net cash flows from operating activities.

ADJUSTMENTS FOR CHANGES IN CURRENT ASSETS AND CURRENT LIABILITIES

For components of net income that increase or decrease cash, but *by an amount different from that reported on the income statement,* we adjust net income for changes in the balances of related balance sheet accounts to convert the effects of those items to a cash basis. For example, E-Games reports sales revenue of $1,012,000 in its income statement. This does not mean, however, that E-Games collected $1,012,000 cash from its customers during the reporting period. Since accounts receivable increased during the year, some of the sales revenue the company earned

must not yet have been collected. We need, then, to make an adjustment to net income for the change in accounts receivable to convert the sales revenue number to a cash basis. To similarly convert other income statement components from accrual basis to cash basis, we adjust net income for changes in all current assets (other than cash) and current liabilities. Let's look at the changes in current assets and current liabilities for E-Games to see how this works.

Increase in accounts receivable.   E-Games' accounts receivable increased $7,000 during the year (from $20,000 in 2011 to $27,000 in 2012). This tells us that the company must not have collected all of its $1,012,000 sales revenue in cash. Why? Because customers owe the company $7,000 more than before. Let's confirm this by recording the selling and collection activities during the year:

	Debit	Credit		A	=	L	+	SE
Cash (to balance)	1,005,000			+1,005,000				
Accounts Receivable (= $27,000 − $20,000)	7,000			+7,000				
Revenues (from income statement)		1,012,000						+1,012,000 Rev↑
(Record increase in accounts receivable)								

We record an increase in Revenues with a credit and an increase in Accounts Receivable with a debit. Cash received from customers of $1,005,000 is the number we need for the debits and credits to equal.

The $7,000 increase in accounts receivable represents $7,000 of credit sales that E-Games reported as part of net income but that did not result in operating cash inflows. Therefore, to adjust net income to operating cash flows, we need to eliminate $7,000 from net income, as shown in Illustration 11–10.

E-GAMES, INC.
Statement of Cash Flows (partial)

Cash Flows from Operating Activities	
Net income	$42,000
Adjustments for noncash effects:	
Depreciation expense	9,000
Loss on sale of land	4,000
Changes in current assets and current liabilities:	
Increase in accounts receivable	(7,000)

ILLUSTRATION 11–10

Adjustment for Change in Accounts Receivable

A decrease in accounts receivable would have the opposite effect. We would *add* a decrease in accounts receivable to net income to arrive at net cash flows from operating activities. A decrease in accounts receivable indicates that we collected more cash from customers than we recorded as credit sales.

Decrease in inventory.   E-Games' inventory balance decreased by $10,000 during the year. This tells us that the company purchased $10,000 less inventory than is reflected in cost of goods sold in the income statement. In other words, $10,000 of E-Games' cost of goods sold was a result of reducing its inventory, rather than a purchase of new inventory and a corresponding cash outflow. Therefore, we need to eliminate the noncash portion of cost of goods sold from net income as part of our conversion of net income to operating cash flows. To eliminate the effect of this $10,000 expense, we add the $10,000 decrease in inventory to net income. Illustration 11–11 shows this adjustment.

ILLUSTRATION 11–11

Adjustment for Change in Inventory

E-GAMES, INC. Statement of Cash Flows (partial)	
Cash Flows from Operating Activities	
Net income	$42,000
Adjustments for noncash effects:	
Depreciation expense	9,000
Loss on sale of land	4,000
Changes in current assets and current liabilities:	
Increase in accounts receivable	(7,000)
Decrease in inventory	**10,000**

Increase in prepaid rent. E-Games' prepaid rent increased $2,000 during the year. The company paid $2,000 cash for an asset (prepaid rent) for which there is no corresponding expense (rent expense). In other words, the cash outflow for prepaid rent caused cash to decrease by $2,000, but net income remained unaffected. To adjust for this, we subtract the $2,000 increase in prepaid rent from net income to reflect the $2,000 cash outflow not reflected in net income. Illustration 11–12 shows this adjustment.

ILLUSTRATION 11–12

Adjustment for Change in Prepaid Rent

E-GAMES, INC. Statement of Cash Flows (partial)	
Cash Flows from Operating Activities	
Net income	$42,000
Adjustments for noncash effects:	
Depreciation expense	9,000
Loss on sale of land	4,000
Changes in current assets and current liabilities:	
Increase in accounts receivable	(7,000)
Decrease in inventory	10,000
Increase in prepaid rent	**(2,000)**

Decrease in accounts payable. E-Games' accounts payable decreased $5,000 during the year. Reducing the amount owed to suppliers means the company paid $5,000 more cash than the cost of goods purchased. The decrease in accounts payable indicates that the company paid $5,000 cash to reduce its liability (accounts payable) but reported no corresponding expense (cost of goods sold) during the period. In other words, total cash outflows to reduce accounts payable were $5,000 greater than total related expenses. To adjust for the greater cash outflows, we subtract the $5,000 decrease in accounts payable from net income, as shown in Illustration 11–13.

ILLUSTRATION 11–13

Adjustment for Change in Accounts Payable

E-GAMES, INC. Statement of Cash Flows (partial)	
Cash Flows from Operating Activities	
Net income	$42,000
Adjustments for noncash effects:	
Depreciation expense	9,000
Loss on sale of land	4,000
Changes in current assets and current liabilities:	
Increase in accounts receivable	(7,000)
Decrease in inventory	10,000
Increase in prepaid rent	(2,000)
Decrease in accounts payable	**(5,000)**

Increase in interest payable. E-Games' interest payable increased $1,000 during the year. That means the company owes $1,000 more than previously, so it must have paid $1,000 less cash than the interest expense included in net income. As shown in Illustration 11–14, the company adds the increase in interest payable to net income to adjust for the fact that cash outflows are less than interest expense, increasing overall cash flows.

Decrease in income tax payable. E-Games' income tax payable decreased $2,000 during the year. A change in income tax payable indicates a difference between income tax expense and income taxes paid. A $2,000 decrease in income tax payable indicates E-Games paid $2,000 more to reduce its tax liability (income tax payable) than it recorded as an expense (income tax expense) in net income. To adjust for the fact that cash outflow is greater than tax expense, we subtract $2,000 from net income to calculate operating cash flows. Illustration 11–15 shows this adjustment and calculates total net cash flows from operating activities of $50,000.

CAREER CORNER

Are you good at analyzing information? If so, you might consider a career as a financial analyst. A career in this field involves understanding the operations of companies, assessing the reasonableness of their stock price, and predicting their future performance. Investment analysts rely heavily on financial statements as a source of information in predicting stock price movements. Since financial statements, including the cash flow statement covered in this chapter, are accounting-based, it is no surprise that a strong background in accounting is necessary for a career as a financial analyst. A background in accounting is useful, not only in preparing accounting information, but analyzing and interpreting that information as well.

E-GAMES, INC.
Statement of Cash Flows (partial)

Cash Flows from Operating Activities	
Net income	$42,000
Adjustments for noncash effects:	
Depreciation expense	9,000
Loss on sale of land	4,000
Changes in current assets and current liabilities:	
Increase in accounts receivable	(7,000)
Decrease in inventory	10,000
Increase in prepaid rent	(2,000)
Decrease in accounts payable	(5,000)
Increase in interest payable	1,000

ILLUSTRATION 11–14

Adjustment for Change in Interest Payable

E-GAMES, INC.
Statement of Cash Flows (partial)

Cash Flows from Operating Activities		
Net income		$42,000
Adjustments for noncash effects:		
Depreciation expense		9,000
Loss on sale of land		4,000
Changes in current assets and current liabilities:		
Increase in accounts receivable		(7,000)
Decrease in inventory		10,000
Increase in prepaid rent		(2,000)
Decrease in accounts payable		(5,000)
Increase in interest payable		1,000
Decrease in income tax payable		(2,000)
Net cash flows from operating activities		$50,000

ILLUSTRATION 11–15

Adjustment for Change in Income Tax Payable

Illustration 11–16 provides a summary of the adjustments we make to convert net income to net cash flows from operating activities.

ILLUSTRATION 11–16

Summary of Adjustments to Net Income

Cash Flows from Operating Activities

Net income

Adjustments for noncash effects:

For noncash components of income:
+ Depreciation expense
+ Amortization expense
+ Loss on sale of assets
− Gain on sale of assets

For changes in current assets and current liabilities:
− Increase in a current asset
+ Decrease in a current asset
+ Increase in a current liability
− Decrease in a current liability

= Net cash flows from operating activities

This illustration is a helpful reference when completing the homework exercises at the end of the chapter. Remember that for noncash components of income, we add back expenses and losses and subtract gains. For changes in current liabilities, we add an increase in a current liability and subtract a decrease. We do just the opposite for changes in current assets.

KEY POINT

Using the indirect method, we start with net income and adjust this number for (a) revenue and expense items that do not represent cash and (b) changes in current assets and current liabilities.

Investing and Financing Activities

■ **LO3**
Prepare the investing activities section and the financing activities section of the statement of cash flows.

As noted earlier, we prepare the investing and financing activities in the statement of cash flows the same whether we use the indirect or the direct method. Here, we take a detailed look at how investing and financing activities are determined in our E-Games, Inc., example.

INVESTING ACTIVITIES

As we learned in Illustration 11–5, the second step in preparing the statement of cash flows is to determine the net cash flows from *investing* activities by analyzing changes in long-term asset accounts from the balance sheet. The long-term assets section of the balance sheet is the place to look for investing activities.[4] Looking at that section of E-Games' balance sheet, we determine the following cash flows from investing activities.

---

[4]Although not used as an example in this chapter, it's also possible to have investing activities related to changes in current investments or current notes receivable.

Increase in investments. E-Games' investments in stock increased $35,000 during the year (from $0 in 2011 to $35,000 in 2012). In the absence of contrary evidence, it's logical to assume the increase is due to the purchase of investments during the year. Additional-information item (1) in Illustration 11–6 confirms this assumption. As Illustration 11–17 (see below) shows, we report the purchase of Intendo Corporation stock as a cash outflow of $35,000 from investing activities.

Decrease in land. The Land account decreased $10,000 during the year, indicating that E-Games sold land costing $10,000. Additional-information item (2) in Illustration 11–6 indicates that we originally recorded the land at a cost of $10,000 but sold it for only $6,000 (resulting in a loss on the sale of land of $4,000, as recorded in the operating activities section). We report $6,000 as a cash inflow from investing activities—the actual amount of cash proceeds received from the sale. (See Illustration 11–17, below.)

 COMMON MISTAKE

Some students mistakenly record a cash inflow from investing activities equal to the change in the asset account, $10,000 in this case. Remember, though, that the statement of cash flows reports the *actual* cash received or paid, which is not always the same as the change in the balance sheet accounts.

Increase in equipment. E-Games' Equipment account increased by $20,000 during the year. If E-Games purchased the equipment with cash, we would record a cash outflow from investing activities of $20,000. However, additional-information item (3) in Illustration 11–6 indicates that the firm paid for the equipment by issuing a $20,000 note payable. No cash was exchanged in the transaction. The increase in equipment therefore represents a noncash activity, which is disclosed in the cash flow footnote. Illustration 11–17 provides a summary of the cash flows from investing activities and disclosure of the noncash activity.

ILLUSTRATION 11–17

Cash Flows from Investing Activities

E-GAMES, INC. **Statement of Cash Flows (partial)**	
Cash Flows from Investing Activities	
Purchase of investment	$(35,000)
Sale of land	6,000
Net cash flows from investing activities	$ (29,000)
Note: Noncash Activities	
Purchased equipment by issuing a note payable	$ 20,000

FINANCING ACTIVITIES

The third step in preparing the statement of cash flows is to determine the net cash flows from *financing* activities. We can find a firm's financing activities by examining changes in long-term liabilities and stockholders' equity accounts from the balance sheet.[5] Referring back to E-Games' balance sheet, we find the following cash flows from financing activities.

---

[5]Although not used as an example in this chapter, it is also possible for financing activities to be indicated by changes in current liability accounts, such as current notes payable.

Increase in notes payable. E-Games has only one long-term liability. The company reports an increase in notes payable of $20,000. As we saw earlier, this was in payment for equipment and represents a noncash activity disclosed in a note to the cash flow statement.

Increase in common stock. Common stock increased by $5,000 during the year. Item (4) of the additional information in Illustration 11–6 confirms that this was the result of issuing $5,000 of common stock. As Illustration 11–18 (see below) shows, the $5,000 inflow of cash is reported as a financing activity.

Increase in retained earnings. E-Games' Retained Earnings balance increased by $30,000 during the year. Recall from earlier chapters that the balance of Retained Earnings increases with net income and decreases with dividends:

Retained Earnings

		41,000	Beginning balance
Dividends	?	42,000	Net income
(decreases RE)			(increases RE)
		71,000	Ending balance

Since net income is $42,000 and retained earnings increased by only $30,000, the company must have declared dividends of $12,000 during the year:

Retained earnings, beginning balance	$41,000
+ Net income	42,000
− Dividends	(12,000)
Retained earnings, ending balance	$71,000

Additional-information item (5) in Illustration 11–6 confirms that E-Games declared and paid dividends of $12,000 during the year. As shown in Illustration 11–18, we report the payment of cash dividends as a cash outflow from financing activities.

ILLUSTRATION 11–18

Cash Flows from Financing Activities

E-GAMES, INC.
Statement of Cash Flows (partial)

Cash Flows from Financing Activities		
Issuance of common stock	$ 5,000	
Payment of cash dividends	(12,000)	
Net cash flows from financing activities		(7,000)

Only the dividends actually paid in cash during the year are reported in the statement of cash flows. If the company declares dividends in 2012 but does not pay them until 2013, it will report the dividends paid as a cash outflow in 2013, not in 2012.

KEY POINT

Most investing activities can be explained by changes in long-term asset accounts. Most financing activities can be explained by changes in long-term liability and stockholders' equity accounts.

The fourth and final step in preparing the statement of cash flows (see Illustration 11–5) is to combine the operating, investing, and financing activities and make sure the total of these three activities *agrees* with the net increase (decrease) in cash. Illustration 11–19 shows the complete statement of cash flows for E-Games, with all three sections—operating, investing, and financing—included along with the note for noncash activities.

E-GAMES, INC. Statement of Cash Flows—Indirect Method For the year ended December 31, 2012		
Cash Flows from Operating Activities		
Net income	$42,000	
Adjustments for noncash effects:		
Depreciation expense	9,000	
Loss on sale of land	4,000	
Changes in current assets and current liabilities:		
Increase in accounts receivable	(7,000)	
Decrease in inventory	10,000	
Increase in prepaid rent	(2,000)	
Decrease in accounts payable	(5,000)	
Increase in interest payable	1,000	
Decrease in income tax payable	(2,000)	
Net cash flows from operating activities		$50,000
Cash Flows from Investing Activities		
Purchase of investment	(35,000)	
Sale of land	6,000	
Net cash flows from investing activities		(29,000)
Cash Flows from Financing Activities		
Issuance of common stock	5,000	
Payment of cash dividends	(12,000)	
Net cash flows from financing activities		(7,000)
Net increase (decrease) in cash		14,000
Cash at the beginning of the period		48,000
Cash at the end of the period		$62,000
Note: Noncash Activities		
Purchased equipment by issuing a note payable		$20,000

ILLUSTRATION 11–19

Complete Statement of Cash Flows for E-Games, Inc.

This is the moment of truth. The sum of the net cash flows from operating, investing, and financing activities should equal the net increase (decrease) in cash for the period. In Illustration 11–19, we see that the total of the cash flows from operating (+$50,000), investing (−$29,000), and financing (−$7,000) activities equals the net increase in cash of $14,000 for the year. This amount was the increase in cash from the balance sheet in Illustration 11–6.

Let's Review

Provided below are the income statement, balance sheet, and additional information for E-Phones, Inc.

E-PHONES, INC.
Income Statement
For the year ended December 31, 2012

Revenues		$2,200,000
Gain on sale of investment		5,000
Expenses:		
Cost of goods sold	$1,100,000	
Operating expenses	450,000	
Depreciation expense	25,000	
Income tax expense	217,000	
Total expenses		1,792,000
Net income		$ 413,000

E-PHONES, INC.
Balance Sheet
December 31, 2012 and 2011

	2012	2011	Increase (I) or Decrease (D)
Assets			
Current assets:			
Cash	$ 32,000	$ 48,000	$ 16,000 (D)
Accounts receivable	32,000	40,000	8,000 (D)
Inventory	100,000	70,000	30,000 (I)
Long-term assets:			
Investments	0	50,000	50,000 (D)
Land	280,000	180,000	100,000 (I)
Equipment	200,000	140,000	60,000 (I)
Accumulated depreciation	(53,000)	(28,000)	25,000 (I)
Total assets	$591,000	$500,000	
Liabilities and Stockholders' Equity			
Current liabilities:			
Accounts payable	$ 52,000	$ 62,000	$ 10,000 (D)
Income tax payable	55,000	12,000	43,000 (I)
Long-term liabilities:			
Bonds payable	0	200,000	200,000 (D)
Stockholders' equity:			
Common stock	200,000	100,000	100,000 (I)
Retained earnings	284,000	126,000	158,000 (I)
Total liabilities and stockholders' equity	$591,000	$500,000	

Additional Information for 2012:

1. Sold an investment in stock costing $50,000 for $55,000, resulting in a $5,000 gain
   on sale of investment.
2. Purchased $100,000 in land, issuing $100,000 of common stock as payment. No cash
   was exchanged in the transaction.
3. Purchased equipment for $60,000 cash.
4. Retired the $200,000 balance in bonds payable at the beginning of the year.
5. Declared and paid a cash dividend of $255,000.

Required:

Prepare the statement of cash flows using the *indirect method*. Disclose any non-cash transactions in an accompanying note.

Solution:

E-PHONES, INC.
Statement of Cash Flows—Indirect Method
For the year ended December 31, 2012

Cash Flows from Operating Activities		
Net income	$413,000	
Adjustments for noncash effects:		
Depreciation expense	25,000	
Gain on sale of investment	(5,000)	
Changes in current assets and current liabilities:		
Decrease in accounts receivable	8,000	
Increase in inventory	(30,000)	
Decrease in accounts payable	(10,000)	
Increase in income tax payable	43,000	
Net cash flows from operating activities		$444,000
Cash Flows from Investing Activities		
Sale of investment	55,000	
Purchase of equipment	(60,000)	
Net cash flows from investing activities		(5,000)
Cash Flows from Financing Activities		
Retirement of bonds payable	(200,000)	
Payment of cash dividends	(255,000)	
Net cash flows from financing activities		(455,000)
Net increase (decrease) in cash		(16,000)
Cash at the beginning of the period		48,000
Cash at the end of the period		$ 32,000
Note: Noncash Activities		
Purchased land by issuing common stock		$100,000

Suggested Homework:
BE11-4, BE11-5;
E11-7, E11-8;
P11-2A&B; P11-4A&B

ANALYSIS

CASH FLOW ANALYSIS
Apple vs. Dell

Throughout this text, we have emphasized the analysis of financial statements from a decision maker's perspective. Often that analysis includes the development and comparison of financial ratios. Each of the ratios discussed in Chapters 5 through 10 is based on income statement and balance sheet amounts.

■ **LO4**
Perform financial analysis using the statement of cash flows.

Cash Flow Ratios

Decision Maker's Perspective

Analysts often supplement their investigation of income statement and balance sheet amounts with cash flow ratios. Some cash flow ratios are derived by substituting net cash flows from operating activities in place of net income—not to replace those ratios but to complement them. Substituting cash flow from operations in place of net income offers additional insight in the evaluation of a company's

profitability and financial strength.[6] Positive cash flow from operations is important to a company's survival in the long run. ●

Now we reexamine the financial ratios introduced in Chapter 7—return on assets, profit margin, and asset turnover—substituting net cash flows from operating activities, also called **operating cash flows**, in place of net income. Illustration 11–20 provides selected financial data for **Apple** and **Dell**.

ILLUSTRATION 11–20

Selected Financial Data for Apple and Dell

($ in millions)	2009	2008
Apple		
Net sales	$36,537	$32,479
Net income	5,704	4,834
Operating cash flows	10,159	9,596
Total assets	53,851	39,572
Dell		
Net sales	$61,101	$61,133
Net income	2,478	2,947
Operating cash flows	1,894	3,949
Total assets	26,500	27,561

RETURN ON ASSETS

Return on assets, introduced in Chapter 7, is calculated as net income divided by average total assets. Illustration 11–21 presents return on assets for Apple and Dell.

ILLUSTRATION 11–21

Return on Assets for Apple and Dell

($ in millions)	Net Income	÷	Average Total Assets	=	Return on Assets
Apple	$5,704	÷	($53,851 + $39,572)/2	=	12.2%
Dell	$2,478	÷	($26,500 + $27,561)/2	=	9.2%

Both Apple and Dell report strong return on assets, with Apple's return on assets of 12.2% being higher than Dell's at 9.2%. Thus, Apple generated more income for each dollar invested in assets.

CASH RETURN ON ASSETS

We can gain additional insights by examining a similar measure called the cash return on assets. We calculate it as:

Cash return on assets = Operating cash flows ÷ Average total assets

Illustration 11–22 presents the cash return on assets for Apple and Dell.

ILLUSTRATION 11–22

Cash Return on Assets for Apple and Dell

($ in millions)	Operating Cash Flows	÷	Average Total Assets	=	Cash Return on Assets
Apple	$10,159	÷	($53,851 + $39,572)/2	=	21.7%
Dell	$1,894	÷	($26,500 + $27,561)/2	=	7.0%

[6]Proposals for informative sets of cash flow ratios are offered by Charles A. Carslaw and John R. Mills. 1991. "Developing Ratios for Effective Cash Flow Statement Analysis." *Journal of Accountancy* 172 (November), pp. 63–70; Don E. Giacomino and David E. Mielke. 1993. "Cash Flows: Another Approach to Ratio Analysis." *Journal of Accountancy* 174 (March), pp. 55–58; and John Mills and Jeanne H. Yamamura. 1998. "The Power of Cash Flow Ratios." *Journal of Accountancy* 186 (October), pp. 53–61.

Apple's cash return on assets of 21.7% is much higher than Dell's cash return on assets of only 7.0%. Note that operating cash flows exceed net income for Apple, while operating cash flows are less than net income for Dell. This causes a greater difference in *cash* return on assets for Apple and Dell, in comparison to the spread between the two companies for return on assets presented in Illustration 11–21. Apple's net income is supported by even higher operating cash flows, while Dell's is not.

COMPONENTS OF CASH RETURN ON ASSETS

Let's explore the cash return on assets further by separating the ratio into two separate parts, as shown in Illustration 11–23.

$$\text{Cash return on assets} = \text{Cash flow to sales} \times \text{Asset turnover}$$

$$\frac{\text{Operating cash flows}}{\text{Average total assets}} = \frac{\text{Operating cash flows}}{\text{Net sales}} \times \frac{\text{Net sales}}{\text{Average total assets}}$$

ILLUSTRATION 11–23

Components of Cash Return on Assets

Cash return on assets can be separated into cash flow to sales and asset turnover. **Cash flow to sales** measures the operating cash flows generated for each dollar of sales. (It is the cash flow equivalent to profit margin, introduced in Chapter 7.) **Asset turnover**, also covered in Chapter 7, measures the sales revenue generated per dollar of assets. Cash flow to sales and asset turnover represent two primary strategies that companies have for increasing their cash return on assets. One strategy, used by Apple, is to sell highly innovative products that yield very high cash inflows from customers in relationship to the cash outflows to produce their products. Another strategy, which Dell uses, is to pursue high asset turnover by selling at lower prices than the competition. In Illustrations 11–24 and 11–25, we calculate cash flow to sales and asset turnover for both companies. We then can see whether our expectations regarding Apple and Dell are supported.

($ in millions)	Operating Cash Flows	÷	Net Sales	=	Cash Flow to Sales
Apple	$10,159	÷	$36,537	=	27.8%
Dell	$1,894	÷	$61,101	=	3.1%

ILLUSTRATION 11–24

Cash Flow to Sales for Apple and Dell

($ in millions)	Net Sales	÷	Average Total Assets	=	Asset Turnover
Apple	$36,537	÷	($53,851 + $39,572)/2	=	0.8 times
Dell	$61,101	÷	($26,500 + $27,561)/2	=	2.3 times

ILLUSTRATION 11–25

Asset Turnover for Apple and Dell

The cash flow ratios support our expectations regarding the different business strategies of Apple and Dell. Apple, with its innovative products such as the iPod, iPad, and the iPhone, generates higher cash flow from each dollar of sales than Dell, as Illustration 11–24 shows. However, Dell, with its innovative marketing, distribution, and discount pricing strategies, generates nearly three times the asset turnover of Apple, as Illustration 11–25 shows. To maximize cash flow from operations, a company strives to increase *both* cash flow per dollar of sales (cash flow to sales) and sales per dollar of assets invested (asset turnover).

KEY POINT

Cash return on assets indicates the amount of operating cash flow generated for each dollar invested in assets. We can separate cash return on assets into two components—cash flow to sales and asset turnover—to examine two important business strategies.

Decision Point

Question ?	Accounting information 📄	Analysis 🔍
Are the company's cash flows based more on selling at higher prices or on increasing sales volume?	Cash flow to sales and asset turnover ratios	Companies with high cash flow to sales ratios obtain high cash inflows from sales to customers in relation to the cash outflows to produce the products. Companies with high asset turnover ratios may not make as much on each sale, but they make money through higher sales volume.

ETHICAL DILEMMA

Ebenezer is CEO of a successful small business. One day he stops by to see Tim Cratchit, the new branch manager at First National Bank. Ebenezer would like to double the size of his loan with the bank from $500,000 to $1 million. Ebenezer explains, "Business is booming, sales and earnings are up each of the past three years, and we could certainly use the funds for further business expansion." Tim Cratchit has a big heart, and Ebenezer has been a close friend of the family. He thinks to himself this loan decision will be easy, but he asks Ebenezer to e-mail the past three years' financial statements as required by bank policy.

In looking over the financial statements sent by Ebenezer, Tim becomes concerned. Sales and earnings have increased just as Ebenezer said. However, receivables, inventory, and accounts payable have grown at a much faster rate than sales. Furthermore, he notices a steady decrease in operating cash flows over the past three years, with negative operating cash flows in each of the past two years.

Who are the stakeholders, and what is the ethical dilemma? Do you think Tim should go ahead and approve the loan?

APPENDIX

LO5

Prepare the operating section of the statement of cash flows using the direct method.

OPERATING ACTIVITIES—DIRECT METHOD

The presentation of cash flows from operating activities in the chapter is referred to as the indirect method. By this method, we determine the cash effect of each operating activity or income statement item indirectly, starting with reported net income and working backward to convert to a cash basis.

An alternative is the **direct method,** by which we report the cash inflows and cash outflows directly on the statement of cash flows. For instance, we report *cash received from customers* as the cash effect of sales activities, and *cash paid to suppliers* as the cash effect of cost of goods sold. Income statement items that have *no* cash effect—such as depreciation expense or gains and losses on the sale of assets—are simply not reported under the direct method.

Here, we repeat the example for E-Games, Inc., this time presenting cash flows from operating activities using the direct method. For convenience, the income statement, balance sheet, and additional information for E-Games, Inc., are repeated in Illustration 11–26.

ILLUSTRATION 11–26

Income Statement, Balance Sheet, and Additional Information for E-Games, Inc.

E-GAMES, INC.
Income Statement
For the year ended December 31, 2012

Revenues		$1,012,000
Expenses:		
Cost of goods sold	$650,000	
Operating expenses (salaries, rent, utilities)	286,000	
Depreciation expense	9,000	
Loss on sale of land	4,000	
Interest expense	5,000	
Income tax expense	16,000	
Total expenses		970,000
Net income		$ 42,000

E-GAMES, INC.
Balance Sheet
December 31, 2012 and 2011

	2012	2011	Increase (I) or Decrease (D)
Assets			
Current assets:			
Cash	$ 62,000	$ 48,000	$14,000 (I)
Accounts receivable	27,000	20,000	7,000 (I)
Inventory	35,000	45,000	10,000 (D)
Prepaid rent	4,000	2,000	2,000 (I)
Long-term assets:			
Investments	35,000	0	35,000 (I)
Land	70,000	80,000	10,000 (D)
Equipment	90,000	70,000	20,000 (I)
Accumulated depreciation	(23,000)	(14,000)	9,000 (I)
Total assets	$300,000	$251,000	
Liabilities and Stockholders' Equity			
Current liabilities:			
Accounts payable	$ 22,000	$ 27,000	$ 5,000 (D)
Interest payable	2,000	1,000	1,000 (I)
Income tax payable	5,000	7,000	2,000 (D)
Long-term liabilities:			
Notes payable	95,000	75,000	20,000 (I)
Stockholders' equity:			
Common stock	105,000	100,000	5,000 (I)
Retained earnings	71,000	41,000	30,000 (I)
Total liabilities and stockholders' equity	$300,000	$251,000	

(continued)

ILLUSTRATION 11–26
(*concluded*)

Additional Information for 2012:
1. Purchased stock in Intendo Corporation for $35,000.
2. Land costing $10,000 was sold for only $6,000, resulting in a $4,000 loss on sale of land.
3. Purchased $20,000 in equipment by issuing a $20,000 note payable due in three years. No cash was exchanged in the transaction.
4. Issued common stock for $5,000 cash.
5. The company declared and paid a cash dividend of $12,000.

Remember from Illustration 11–5 that the first step in preparing the statement of cash flows is to calculate net cash flows from *operating* activities using information from the income statement and changes in current assets and current liabilities from the balance sheet.

The income statement reports revenues earned during the year, *regardless of when cash is received,* and the expenses incurred in generating those revenues, *regardless of when cash is paid.* This is the *accrual concept* of accounting that we've discussed throughout the book. Cash flows from operating activities, on the other hand, are both inflows and outflows of cash that result from activities reported in the income statement. In other words, it's the elements of net income, but **reported on a cash basis.** Using the direct method, we examine each account in the income statement and convert it from an accrual amount to a cash amount. We directly report the cash inflows and cash outflows from operations as shown in Illustration 11–27.

ILLUSTRATION 11–27

Operating Activities Using the Direct Method

Cash Flows from Operating Activities
Cash inflows:
    Cash received from customers
    Cash received from interest
    Cash received from dividends
Cash outflows:
    Cash paid to suppliers
    Cash paid for operating expenses
    Cash paid for interest
    Cash paid for income taxes

= Net cash flows from operating activities

The best way to apply the direct method is to convert each revenue and expense item to its cash-basis amount. We do this by considering how each income statement account is affected by related changes in current asset and current liability accounts.

Cash received from customers.   E-Games reports revenues of $1,012,000 as the first item in its income statement. Did E-Games receive $1,012,000 in cash from those revenues? We can answer this by looking at the change in accounts receivable. If accounts receivable increases, this indicates that revenues exceed cash receipts from customers. That's why customers owe more than they did before. If accounts receivable decreases, the opposite will be true. Recall that accounts receivable increased $7,000. Therefore, we deduct the $7,000 increase in accounts receivable from revenues to obtain cash received from customers of $1,005,000, as shown in Illustration 11–28.

Revenues	$ 1,012,000
− Increase in accounts receivable	(7,000)
Cash received from customers	**$1,005,000**

ILLUSTRATION 11–28

Cash Received from Customers

Let's consider this again from a couple of different perspectives. Accounts receivable increases when customers buy on credit and decreases when we receive cash from customers. We can compare sales and the change in accounts receivable during the year to determine the amount of cash we received from customers. In T–account format the relationship looks like this:

Accounts Receivable

Beginning balance	20,000		
Credit sales	1,012,000	?	Cash received
(*increases A/R*)			(*decreases A/R*)
Ending balance	27,000		

We see from this analysis that *cash received from customers* must have been $1,005,000. Still another way to view the situation is to think about how E-Games recorded these selling and collection activities during the year:

	Debit	Credit		A	=	L	+	SE
Cash (to balance)	**1,005,000**			+1,005,000				
Accounts Receivable (= $27,000 − $20,000)	**7,000**					+7,000		
Revenues (from income statement)		**1,012,000**						+1,012,000 Rev↑
(*Receive cash from customers*)								

We record an increase in Revenues with a credit and an increase in Accounts Receivable with a debit. Cash received from customers must be $1,005,000 for debits to equal credits.

Cash paid to suppliers. Moving down the income statement, we see that E-Games reports cost of goods sold of $650,000. Did E-Games pay cash of $650,000 to suppliers of those goods during the year? To answer this, we look to the two current balance sheet accounts affected by merchandise purchases—Inventory and Accounts Payable.

First, compare cost of goods sold with the change in inventory to determine the cost of goods purchased (not necessarily cash paid) during the year. Inventory decreased by $10,000. We can visualize the relationship in T-account format:

Inventory

Beginning balance	45,000		
Cost of goods purchased	?	650,000	Cost of goods sold
(*increases inventory*)			(*decreases inventory*)
Ending balance	35,000		

The number needed to explain the change is $640,000. That's the cost of goods *purchased* during the year. It's not necessarily true, though, that E-Games paid $640,000 cash to suppliers of these goods. We need to look at the change in accounts payable to determine the cash paid to suppliers:

Accounts Payable

		27,000	Beginning balance
Cash paid to suppliers	?	640,000	Cost of goods purchased
(*decreases A/P*)			(*increases A/P*)
		22,000	Ending balance

We now see that cash paid to suppliers is $645,000. We can confirm this by looking at how E-Games recorded inventory purchases and sales during the year:

A = L + SE		Debit	Credit
−650,000 Exp↑	Cost of Goods Sold (from income statement)	650,000	
−5,000	Accounts Payable (= $27,000 − $22,000)	5,000	
−10,000	Inventory (= $45,000 − $35,000)		10,000
−645,000	Cash (to balance)		645,000
	(Pay cash for inventory)		

We record an increase in Cost of Goods Sold with a debit, a decrease in Inventory with a credit, and a decrease in Accounts Payable with a debit. Cash paid to suppliers is the "plug" figure we need for debits to equal credits in the journal entry.

Alternatively, we can analyze the situation this way: Inventory decreased $10,000 for the year, so E-Games needed to purchase only $640,000 of goods in order to sell $650,000 of goods; $10,000 came from existing inventory. Because accounts payable decreased by $5,000, cash paid to suppliers must have been $5,000 more than purchases, so we add the decrease in accounts payable to purchases of $640,000 to arrive at cash paid to suppliers of $645,000, as shown in Illustration 11–29.

ILLUSTRATION 11–29

Cash Paid to Suppliers

Cost of goods sold	$ 650,000
− Decrease in inventory	(10,000)
= Purchases	640,000
+ Decrease in accounts payable	5,000
= Cash paid to suppliers	$645,000

Cash paid for operating expenses.   Operating expenses of $286,000 appear next in the income statement. We examine the changes in current assets and current liabilities for any accounts related to operating expenses. Rent expense is included in operating expenses, so we must consider the change in prepaid rent. Increasing prepaid rent takes additional cash. Prepaid rent increased by $2,000, so we need to add this change to operating expenses to determine the cash paid for operating expenses, as shown in Illustration 11–30.

ILLUSTRATION 11–30

Cash Paid for
Operating Expenses

Operating expenses	$ 286,000
+ Increase in prepaid rent	2,000
= Cash paid for operating expenses	$288,000

We see no current assets or current liabilities associated with other operating expenses such as salaries expense or utilities expense, so we make no adjustments to these expenses. Therefore, the amounts we report for these expenses in the income statement must equal the amount of cash we paid for these items.

Let's check our calculation by recording the payment for operating expenses during the year:

	Debit	Credit	A	=	L	+	SE
Operating Expenses (from the income statement).....................	**286,000**						−286,000 Exp↑
Prepaid Rent (= $4,000 − $2,000)...	**2,000**		+2,000				
Cash (to balance)..		**288,000**	−288,000				
(*Pay operating expenses*)							

Depreciation expense and loss on sale of land.   The next expense listed in the income statement is depreciation expense of $9,000. Depreciation expense has no effect on cash flows. It is merely an allocation in the current period of a prior cash expenditure (to acquire the depreciable asset). Therefore, unlike the other expenses to this point, depreciation is *not* reported on the statement of cash flows under the direct method.

Similar to depreciation expense, the loss on sale of land is *not* reported because it, too, has no effect on *operating* cash flows. Additional-information item (2) in Illustration 11–26 indicates that land we originally purchased at a cost of $10,000 was sold for $6,000, resulting in a loss on the sale of land of $4,000. E-Games records the sale as:

	Debit	Credit	A	=	L	+	SE
Cash (selling price)..	**6,000**		+6,000				
Loss (difference)...	**4,000**						−4,000 Exp↑
Land (cost)...		**10,000**	−10,000				
(*Receive cash from sale of land*)							

As we discussed previously, we report the $6,000 cash inflow as an investing activity, because both investing in land and later selling it are considered investing activities. The original cost of the land, and thus the loss, has no effect on operating cash flows.

Cash paid for interest.   E-Games next reports interest expense of $5,000 in the income statement. The related current asset or current liability in the balance sheet is interest payable. If interest payable increases, interest expense exceeds cash paid for interest. Interest payable increases $1,000. As shown in Illustration 11–31, we deduct the increase in interest payable from interest expense to arrive at cash paid for interest.

Interest expense	$ 5,000
− Increase in interest payable	(1,000)
= Cash paid for interest	$4,000

ILLUSTRATION 11–31
Cash Paid for Interest

We can check our calculation by recording the payment for interest during the year:

	Debit	Credit	A	=	L	+	SE
Interest Expense (from income statement).................................	**5,000**						−5,000 Exp↑
Interest Payable (= $2,000 − $1,000)......................................		**1,000**			+1,000		
Cash (to balance)...		**4,000**	−4,000				
(*Pay interest*)							

Cash paid for income taxes. The final item reported in the income statement is income tax expense of $16,000. The related current asset or current liability in the balance sheet is income tax payable. Income tax payable decreased $2,000. This means that E-Games paid $2,000 more than the income tax expense recorded. As shown in Illustration 11–32, we add the decrease in income tax payable to income tax expense to calculate cash paid for income taxes.

ILLUSTRATION 11–32

Cash Paid for Income Taxes

Income tax expense	$ 16,000
+ Decrease in income tax payable	2,000
= **Cash paid for income taxes**	**$18,000**

Recording the payment of taxes during the year confirms this:

A = L + SE		Debit	Credit
−16,000 Exp↑	**Income Tax Expense** (from income statement)...........................	**16,000**	
−2,000	**Income Tax Payable** (= $7,000 − $5,000)....................................	**2,000**	
−18,000	**Cash** (to balance)..		**18,000**
	(*Pay income taxes*)		

Illustration 11–33 shows the completed operating activities section using the direct method.

ILLUSTRATION 11–33

Operating Activities Using the Direct Method

E-GAMES, INC. Statement of Cash Flows (partial)—Direct Method	
Cash Flows from Operating Activities	
Cash received from customers	$1,005,000
Cash paid to suppliers	(645,000)
Cash paid for operating expenses	(288,000)
Cash paid for interest	(4,000)
Cash paid for income taxes	(18,000)
Net cash flows from operating activities	$50,000

Note that the net cash flows from operating activities is $50,000—**the same amount we calculated earlier in Illustration 11–15 using the indirect method.** This will always be the case. The indirect method begins with net income, whereas the direct method considers each of the individual accounts that make up net income. Both methods take into consideration the *same changes* in current asset and current liability accounts.

 KEY POINT

The indirect method and direct method differ only in the presentation of operating activities. In the indirect method, we start with net income and make adjustments to arrive at net cash flows from operating activities. In the direct method, we convert each individual line item in the income statement to its cash basis and directly list the cash inflows and cash outflows from operating activities. The net cash flows from operating activities are *the same under both methods.*

The income statement, balance sheet, and additional information from the accounting records of E-Phones, Inc., are provided below.

Let's Review

E-PHONES, INC.
Income Statement
For the year ended December 31, 2012

Revenues		$2,200,000
Gain on sale of investment		5,000
Expenses:		
Cost of goods sold	$1,100,000	
Operating expenses	450,000	
Depreciation expense	25,000	
Income tax expense	217,000	
Total expenses		1,792,000
Net income		$ 413,000

E-PHONES, INC.
Balance Sheet
December 31, 2012 and 2011

	2012	2011	Increase (I) or Decrease (D)
Assets			
Current assets:			
Cash	$ 32,000	$ 48,000	$ 16,000 (D)
Accounts receivable	32,000	40,000	8,000 (D)
Inventory	100,000	70,000	30,000 (I)
Long-term assets:			
Investments	0	50,000	50,000 (D)
Land	280,000	180,000	100,000 (I)
Equipment	200,000	140,000	60,000 (I)
Accumulated depreciation	(53,000)	(28,000)	25,000 (I)
Total assets	$591,000	$500,000	
Liabilities and Stockholders' Equity			
Current liabilities:			
Accounts payable	$ 52,000	$ 62,000	$ 10,000 (D)
Income tax payable	55,000	12,000	43,000 (I)
Long-term liabilities:			
Bonds payable	0	200,000	200,000 (D)
Stockholders' equity:			
Common stock	200,000	100,000	100,000 (I)
Retained earnings	284,000	126,000	158,000 (I)
Total liabilities and stockholders' equity	$591,000	$500,000	

Additional Information for 2012:

1. Sold an investment in stock costing $50,000 for $55,000, resulting in a $5,000 gain on sale of investment.
2. Purchased $100,000 in land issuing $100,000 of common stock as payment. No cash was exchanged in the transaction.
3. Purchased equipment for $60,000 cash.
4. Retired the $200,000 balance in bonds payable at the beginning of the year.
5. Declared and paid a cash dividend of $255,000.

Required:

Prepare the statement of cash flows using the *direct method* for reporting operating activities. Disclose any noncash transactions in a note to the statement of cash flows.

Solution:

E-PHONES, INC. Statement of Cash Flows—Direct Method For the year ended December 31, 2012		
Cash Flows from Operating Activities		
Cash received from customers	$2,208,000	
Cash paid to suppliers	(1,140,000)	
Cash paid for operating expenses	(450,000)	
Cash paid for income taxes	(174,000)	
Net cash flows from operating activities		$444,000
Cash Flows from Investing Activities		
Sale of investment	55,000	
Purchase of equipment	(60,000)	
Net cash flows from investing activities		(5,000)
Cash Flows from Financing Activities		
Retire bonds payable	(200,000)	
Payment of cash dividends	(255,000)	
Net cash flows from financing activities		(455,000)
Net increase (decrease) in cash		(16,000)
Cash at the beginning of the period		48,000
Cash at the end of the period		$ 32,000
Note: Noncash Activities		
Purchased land by issuing common stock		$100,000

Here are the supporting calculations for cash flows from operating activities under the direct method:

Revenues	$ 2,200,000
+ Decrease in accounts receivable	8,000
= Cash received from customers	$2,208,000
Cost of goods sold	$ 1,100,000
+ Increase in inventory	30,000
= Purchases	1,130,000
+ Decrease in accounts payable	10,000
= Cash paid to suppliers	$1,140,000
Cash paid for operating expenses	$ 450,000
Income tax expense	$ 217,000
− Increase in income tax payable	(43,000)
= Cash paid for income taxes	$ 174,000

Suggested Homework:
**BE11-12, BE11-13;
E11-13, E11-14;
P11-6A&B; P11-7A&B**

KEY POINTS BY LEARNING OBJECTIVE

LO1 Classify cash transactions as operating, investing, or financing activities.

Operating activities relate to income statement items. Investing activities primarily involve changes in long-term assets. Financing activities primarily involve changes in long-term liabilities and stockholders' equity.

Companies choose between the indirect method and direct method in reporting operating activities in the statement of cash flows. The indirect method is less costly to prepare, and most companies use it. The direct method more logically presents the cash inflows and outflows from operations. The investing and financing sections of the statement of cash flows are identical under both methods.

LO2 Prepare the operating activities section of the statement of cash flows using the indirect method.

Using the indirect method, we start with net income and adjust this number for (a) revenue and expense items that do not represent cash and (b) changes in current assets and current liabilities.

LO3 Prepare the investing activities section and the financing activities section of the statement of cash flows.

Most investing activities can be explained by changes in long-term asset accounts. Most financing activities can be explained by changes in long-term liability and stockholders' equity accounts.

Analysis

LO4 Perform financial analysis using the statement of cash flows.

Cash return on assets indicates the amount of operating cash flow generated for each dollar invested in assets. We can separate cash return on assets to two components—cash flow to sales and asset turnover—to examine two important business strategies.

Appendix

LO5 Prepare the operating activities section of the statement of cash flows using the direct method.

The indirect method and direct method differ only in the presentation of operating activities. In the indirect method, we start with net income and make adjustments to arrive at net cash flows from operating activities. In the direct method, we convert each individual line item in the income statement to its cash basis and directly list the cash inflows and cash outflows from operating activities. The net cash flows from operating activities are *the same* under both methods.

GLOSSARY

Asset turnover: Sales revenue divided by average total assets; measures the sales revenue generated per dollar of assets. **p. 527**

Cash flow to sales: Net cash flows from operating activities divided by sales revenue; measures the operating cash flow generated per dollar of sales. **p. 527**

Cash return on assets: Net cash flows from operating activities divided by average total assets; measures the operating cash flow generated per dollar of assets. **p. 526**

Direct method: Adjusts the items on the income statement to directly show the cash inflows and outflows from operations, such as cash received from customers and cash paid for inventory, salaries, rent, interest, and taxes. **p. 512**

Financing activities: Includes cash transactions resulting from the external financing of a business. **p. 509**

Indirect method: Begins with net income and then lists adjustments to net income in order to arrive at operating cash flows. **p. 512**

Investing activities: Includes cash transactions involving the purchase and sale of long-term assets and current investments. **p. 508**

Noncash activities: Significant investing and financing activities that do not affect cash. **p. 511**

Operating activities: Includes cash receipts and cash payments for transactions relating to revenue and expense activities. **p. 508**

Statement of cash flows: A summary of cash inflows and cash outflows during the reporting period sorted by operating, investing, and financing activities. **p. 508**

SELF-STUDY QUESTIONS

■ **LO1**   1. The purchase of a long-term asset is classified in the statement of cash flows as a(n):
a. Operating activity.
b. Investing activity.
c. Financing activity.
d. Noncash activity.

■ **LO1**   2. The issuance of common stock is classified in the statement of cash flows as a(n):
a. Operating activity.
b. Investing activity.
c. Financing activity.
d. Noncash activity.

■ **LO1**   3. The payment of bonds payable is classified in the statement of cash flows as a(n):
a. Operating activity.
b. Investing activity.
c. Financing activity.
d. Noncash activity.

■ **LO1**   4. Which of the following is an example of a noncash activity?
a. Sale of land for more than its cost.
b. Purchase of land by issuing common stock.
c. Sale of land for less than its cost.
d. Purchase of land using cash proceeds from issuance of common stock.

■ **LO2**   5. We can identify operating activities from income statement information and changes in:
a. Current asset and current liability accounts.
b. Long-term asset accounts.
c. Long-term liability accounts.
d. Stockholders' equity accounts.

■ **LO2**   6. The indirect and direct methods:
a. Are used by companies about equally in actual practice.
b. Affect the presentations of operating, investing, and financing activities.
c. Arrive at different amounts for net cash flows from operating activities.
d. Are two allowable methods to present operating activities in the statement of cash flows.

■ **LO3**   7. Which of the following is an example of a cash inflow from an investing activity?
a. Receipt of cash from the issuance of common stock.
b. Receipt of cash from the sale of equipment.
c. Receipt of cash from the issuance of a note payable.
d. Receipt of cash from the sale of inventory.

■ **LO3**   8. Which of the following is an example of a cash outflow from a financing activity?
a. Payment of interest.
b. Purchase of an intangible asset.
c. Payment of cash dividends.
d. Purchase of land.

■ **LO4**   9. We can separate cash return on assets into:
a. Cash flow to sales and return on assets.
b. Profit margin and asset turnover.
c. Cash flow to sales and profit margin.
d. Cash flow to sales and asset turnover.

10. Which of the following items do we report in the statement of cash flows using the direct method?
    a. Depreciation expense.
    b. Gain on sale of an asset.
    c. Cash paid to suppliers.
    d. Loss on sale of an asset.

■ LO5

Note: For answers, see the last page of the chapter.

Check out
www.mhhe.com/succeed
for more multiple-choice
questions.

REVIEW QUESTIONS

1. Identify and briefly describe the three categories of cash flows reported in the statement of cash flows.

■ LO1

2. Changes in current assets and current liabilities are used in determining net cash flows from operating activities. Changes in which balance sheet accounts are used in determining net cash flows from investing activities? Changes in which balance sheet accounts are used in determining net cash flows from financing activities?

■ LO1

3. Explain what we mean by noncash activities and provide an example.

■ LO1

4. Why is it necessary to use an income statement, balance sheet, and additional information to prepare a statement of cash flows?

■ LO1

5. Describe the basic format used in preparing a statement of cash flows, including the heading, the three major categories, and what is included in the last three lines of the statement.

■ LO1

6. Briefly describe the four steps outlined in the text for preparing a statement of cash flows.

■ LO1

7. Distinguish between the indirect method and the direct method for reporting net cash flows from operating activities. Which method is more common in practice? Which method provides a more logical presentation of cash flows?

■ LO1

8. Describe the most common adjustments we use to convert net income to net cash flows from operations under the indirect method.

■ LO2

9. The executives at Peach, Inc., are confused. The company reports a net loss of $200,000, and yet its net cash flow from operating activities increased $300,000 during the same period. Is this possible? Explain.

■ LO2

10. Explain how we report depreciation expense in the statement of cash flows using the indirect method. Why do we report it this way?

■ LO2

11. Describe how we report a gain or loss on the sale of an asset in the statement of cash flows using the indirect method. Why do we report it this way?

■ LO2

12. Indicate whether we add or subtract each of the following items from net income in preparing the statement of cash flows using the indirect method: (a) an increase in current assets, (b) a decrease in current assets, (c) an increase in current liabilities, and (d) a decrease in current liabilities.

■ LO2

13. How does an increase in accounts receivable affect net income in relation to operating cash flows? Why? How does a decrease in accounts receivable affect net income in relation to operating cash flows? Why?

■ LO2

14. Bell Corporation purchases land by issuing its own common stock. How do we report this transaction, if at all?

■ LO3

■ **LO2, 3**   15. A $10,000 investment on the books of a company is sold for $9,000. Under the indirect method, how does this transaction affect operating, investing, and financing activities?

■ **LO3**   16. Provide three examples of financing activities reported in the statement of cash flows.

■ **LO4**   17. Explain the difference between the calculation of return on assets and cash return on assets. How can cash-based ratios supplement the analysis of ratios based on income statement and balance sheet information?

■ **LO4**   18. Describe the two primary strategies firms use to increase cash return on assets. Which strategy does Apple use, and which does Dell use?

■ **LO5**   19. What are the primary cash inflows and cash outflows under the direct method for determining net cash flows from operating activities?

■ **LO5**   20. Why do we exclude depreciation expense and the gain or loss on sale of an asset from the operating activities section of the statement of cash flows under the direct method?

BRIEF EXERCISES

Determine proper classification (LO1)

BE11–1 Classify each of the following items as an operating, investing, or financing activity.
1. Dividends paid.
2. Repayment of notes payable.
3. Payment for inventory.
4. Purchase of equipment.
5. Interest paid.

Determine proper classification (LO1)

BE11–2 The following selected transactions occur during the first year of operations. Determine how each should be reported in the statement of cash flows.
1. Issued one million shares of common stock at $20 per share.
2. Paid $75,000 to suppliers for inventory.
3. Paid a dividend of $1 per share to common stockholders.
4. Loaned $50,000 to an employee and accepted a note receivable.

Understand the basic format for the statement of cash flows (LO2)

BE11–3 Place the following items in the correct order as they would appear in the statement of cash flows.
1. Financing activities.
2. Net increase (decrease) in cash.
3. Operating activities.
4. Beginning cash balance.
5. Ending cash balance.
6. Investing activities.

Calculate operating activities—indirect method (LO2)

BE11–4 Laser World reports net income of $550,000. Depreciation expense is $40,000, accounts receivable increases $10,000, and accounts payable decreases $20,000. Calculate net cash flows from operating activities using the indirect method.

Calculate operating activities—indirect method (LO2)

BE11–5 Macrosoft Company reports net income of $65,000. The accounting records reveal depreciation expense of $80,000 as well as increases in prepaid rent, accounts payable, and income tax payable of $60,000, $12,000, and $18,000, respectively. Prepare the operating activities section of Macrosoft's statement of cash flows using the indirect method.

Calculate operating activities—indirect method (LO2)

BE11–6 Hi-Tech, Inc., reports net income of $60 million. Included in that number are depreciation expense of $5 million and a loss on the sale of equipment of $1 million. Records reveal increases in accounts receivable, accounts payable, and inventory of

$2 million, $3 million, and $4 million, respectively. What are Hi-Tech's net cash flows from operating activities?

BE11–7 Engineering Wonders reports net income of $60 million. Included in that number is building depreciation expense of $5 million and a gain on the sale of land of $1 million. Records reveal decreases in accounts receivable, accounts payable, and inventory of $2 million, $3 million, and $4 million, respectively. What are Engineering Wonders' net cash flows from operating activities?

Calculate operating activities—indirect method **(LO2)**

BE11–8 Creative Sound Systems sold investments, land, and its own common stock for $30 million, $15 million, and $40 million, respectively. Creative Sound Systems also purchased treasury stock, equipment, and a patent for $21 million, $25 million, and $12 million, respectively. What amount should the company report as net cash flows from investing activities?

Calculate net cash flows from investing activities **(LO3)**

BE11–9 Refer to the situation described in BE11–8. What amount should Creative Sound Systems report as net cash flows from financing activities?

Calculate net cash flows from financing activities **(LO3)**

BE11–10 The balance sheet of Cranium Gaming reports total assets of $400,000 and $700,000 at the beginning and end of the year, respectively. Sales revenues are $1.1 million, net income is $65,000, and operating cash flows are $55,000. Calculate the cash return on assets, cash flow to sales, and asset turnover for Cranium Gaming.

Calculate the cash return on assets **(LO4)**

BE11–11 The balance sheet of Innovative Products reports total assets of $520,000 and $720,000 at the beginning and end of the year, respectively. The cash return on assets for the year is 20%. Calculate Innovative Products' net cash flows from operating activities (operating cash flows) for the year.

Calculate the net cash flows from operating activities **(LO4)**

BE11–12 Video Shack's accounts receivable decreases during the year by $8 million. What is the amount of cash received from customers during the reporting period if its sales are $63 million?

Determine cash received from customers **(LO5)**

BE11–13 Electronic Superstore's inventory increases during the year by $4 million, and its accounts payable to suppliers increases by $6 million during the same period. What is the amount of cash paid to suppliers of merchandise during the reporting period if its cost of goods sold is $35 million?

Determine cash paid to suppliers **(LO5)**

BE11–14 Wireless Solutions reports operating expenses of $885,000. Operating expenses include both rent expense and salaries expense. Prepaid rent increases during the year by $20,000 and salaries payable increases by $15,000. What is the cash paid for operating expenses during the year?

Determine cash paid for operating expenses **(LO5)**

BE11–15 Computer World reports income tax expense of $240,000. Income taxes payable at the beginning and end of the year are $55,000 and $65,000, respectively. What is the cash paid for income taxes during the year?

Determine cash paid for income taxes **(LO5)**

EXERCISES

E11–1 Match (by letter) the following items with the description or example that best fits. Each letter is used only once.

Match terms with their definitions **(LO1, 2, 3, 4, 5)**

Terms

_____ 1. Operating activities.
_____ 2. Investing activities.
_____ 3. Financing activities.
_____ 4. Noncash activities.
_____ 5. Indirect method.
_____ 6. Direct method.
_____ 7. Depreciation expense.
_____ 8. Cash return on assets.

Descriptions

a. Begins with net income and then lists adjustments to net income in order to arrive at operating cash flows.

b. Item included in net income, but excluded from net operating cash flows.

c. Net cash flows from operating activities divided by average total assets.

d. Cash transactions involving lenders and investors.

e. Cash transactions involving net income.

f. Cash transactions for the purchase and sale of long-term assets.

g. Purchase of long-term assets by issuing stock.

h. Shows the cash inflows and outflows from operations such as cash received from customers and cash paid for inventory, salaries, rent, interest, and taxes.

Determine proper classification (LO1)

E11–2 Discount Computers is in its second year of business providing computer repair services in the local community and reselling used computers on the Internet. The company is owned by 10 investors, each investing $100,000. Justin Lake was hired as president and CEO, with one stipulation: He would receive no salary unless the company achieved annual operating cash flows exceeding $200,000. If the $200,000 was achieved, Justin would receive a $100,000 bonus, and each of the 10 investors would receive a dividend of $10,000.

At the end of the year, Justin had Nicole Roberts, one of the business interns from the local college, calculate a preliminary statement of cash flows. Operating cash flows were $185,000. Justin carefully looked over the calculations that night and then met with Nicole in the morning. Justin starts out: "Nicole, you did an excellent job in preparing the statement of cash flows. The only change I could find is that we need to move the $25,000 increase in notes payable to the bank from financing activities to operating activities. We borrowed that money three months ago and plan to pay it back within a year. After you finish the changes, round up the rest of the interns. Lunch is on me."

Required:

Do you agree with the change recommended by Justin Lake? Is there anything unethical about his actions? What should Nicole do in this situation?

Determine proper classification (LO1)

E11–3 Analysis of an income statement, balance sheet, and additional information from the accounting records of Gadgets, Inc., reveals the following items.

1. Purchase of a patent.
2. Depreciation expense.
3. Decrease in accounts receivable.
4. Issuance of a note payable.
5. Increase in inventory.
6. Collection of notes receivable.
7. Purchase of equipment.
8. Exchange of long-term assets.
9. Decrease in accounts payable.
10. Payment of dividends.

Required:

Indicate in which section of the statement of cash flows each of these items would be reported: operating activities (indirect method), investing activities, financing activities, or a separate noncash activities note.

Determine proper classification (LO1)

E11–4 Wi-Fi, Inc., has the following selected transactions during the year.

1. Issues $20 million in bonds.
2. Purchases equipment for $80,000.
3. Pays a $20,000 account payable.
4. Collects a $15,000 account receivable.
5. Exchanges land for a new patent. Both are valued at $300,000.
6. Declares and pays a cash dividend of $100,000.
7. Loans $50,000 to a customer, accepting a note receivable.
8. Pays $75,000 to suppliers for inventory.

Required:

Indicate in which section of the statement of cash flows each of these items would be reported: operating activities (indirect method), investing activities, financing activities, or a separate noncash activities note.

E11–5 Ernie's Electronics had the following transactions with Bert's Bargain House:

1. Ernie sold Bert land, originally purchased for $180,000, at a sales price of $195,000, resulting in a gain on sale of land of $15,000.
2. Ernie borrowed $100,000 from Bert, signing a three-year note payable.
3. Ernie purchased $1 million in common stock in Bert's Bargain House through a private placement.
4. Ernie received a dividend of $40,000 from the common stock investment in Bert's Bargain House.

Determine proper classification **(LO1)**

Flip Side of E11–6

Required:

Analyze each of the four transactions from the perspective of Ernie's Electronics. Indicate in which section of the statement of cash flows each of these items would be reported for Ernie's Electronics: operating activities (indirect method), investing activities, financing activities, or a separate noncash activities note.

E11–6 Refer to the transactions between Ernie's Electronics and Bert's Bargain House recorded in E11–5.

Determine proper classification **(LO1)**

Flip Side of E11–5

Required:

Analyze each of the four transactions from the perspective of Bert's Bargain House. Indicate in which section of the statement of cash flows each of these items would be reported for Bert's Bargain House: operating activities (indirect method), investing activities, financing activities, or a separate noncash activities note.

E11–7 Technology Solutions' format for the statement of cash flows was corrupted by a computer virus, as follows:

Prepare the basic format for the statement of cash flows **(LO2, 3)**

TECHNOLOGY SOLUTIONS Statement of Cash Flows For the year ended December 31, 2012	
Cash at the beginning of the period	$$$
Cash at the end of the period	$$$
Net increase (decrease) in cash	$$$
Cash Flows from Financing Activities	
List of cash inflows and outflows from financing activities	
Net cash flows from financing activities	$$$
Noncash Activities	
List of noncash transactions	$$$
Cash Flows from Investing Activities	
List of cash inflows and outflows from investing activities	
Net cash flows from investing activities	$$$
Cash Flows from Operating Activities	
List of items adjusting net income to operating cash flows	
Adjustments	
Net income	
Net cash flows from operating activities	$$$

Required:

Prepare a correct format for Technology Solutions to use in preparing the statement of cash flows.

Calculate operating
activities—indirect
method (LO2)

E11–8 Hardware Suppliers reports net income of $155,000. Included in net income is a gain on the sale of land of $15,000. A comparison of this year's and last year's balance sheets reveals an increase in accounts receivable of $25,000, an increase in inventory of $15,000, and a decrease in accounts payable of $45,000.

Required:
Prepare the operating activities section of the statement of cash flows using the indirect method. Do you see a pattern in Hardware Suppliers' adjustments to net income to arrive at operating cash flows? What might this imply?

Calculate operating
activities—indirect
method (LO2)

E11–9 Software Distributors reports net income of $55,000. Included in that number is depreciation expense of $10,000 and a loss on the sale of land of $5,000. A comparison of this year's and last year's balance sheets reveals a decrease in accounts receivable of $25,000, a decrease in inventory of $15,000, and an increase in accounts payable of $45,000.

Required:
Prepare the operating activities section of the statement of cash flows using the indirect method. Do you see a pattern in Software Distributors' adjustments to net income to arrive at operating cash flows? What might this imply?

Prepare a statement
of cash flows—indirect
method (LO2, 3)

E11–10 The balance sheet for Plasma Screens Corporation along with additional information is provided below:

PLASMA SCREENS CORPORATION
Balance Sheet
December 31, 2012 and 2011

	2012	2011
Assets		
Current assets:		
Cash	$ 112,000	$ 120,000
Accounts receivable	78,000	92,000
Inventory	95,000	80,000
Prepaid rent	4,000	2,000
Long-term assets:		
Land	480,000	480,000
Equipment	790,000	670,000
Accumulated depreciation	(428,000)	(268,000)
Total assets	$1,131,000	$1,176,000
Liabilities and Stockholders' Equity		
Current liabilities:		
Accounts payable	$ 99,000	$ 85,000
Interest payable	6,000	12,000
Income tax payable	8,000	5,000
Long-term liabilities:		
Notes payable	100,000	200,000
Stockholders' equity:		
Common stock	700,000	700,000
Retained earnings	218,000	174,000
Total liabilities and stockholders' equity	$1,131,000	$1,176,000

Additional Information for 2012:
1. Net income is $69,000.
2. The company purchases $120,000 in equipment.
3. Depreciation expense is $160,000.
4. The company repays $100,000 in notes payable.
5. The company declares and pays a cash dividend of $25,000.

Required:

Prepare the statement of cash flows using the indirect method.

E11–11 Portions of the financial statements for Peach Computer are provided below.

Calculate operating activities—indirect method **(LO2)**

PEACH COMPUTER
Income Statement
For the year ended December 31, 2012

Revenues		$1,800,000
Expenses:		
Cost of goods sold	$1,050,000	
Operating expenses	560,000	
Depreciation expense	50,000	
Income tax expense	40,000	
Total expenses		1,700,000
Net income		$ 100,000

PEACH COMPUTER
Selected Balance Sheet Data
December 31

	2012	2011	Increase (I) or Decrease (D)
Cash	$102,000	$85,000	$17,000 (I)
Accounts receivable	45,000	49,000	4,000 (D)
Inventory	75,000	55,000	20,000 (I)
Prepaid rent	3,000	5,000	2,000 (D)
Accounts payable	45,000	37,000	8,000 (I)
Income tax payable	5,000	10,000	5,000 (D)

Required:

Prepare the operating activities section of the statement of cash flows for Peach Computer using the *indirect* method.

E11–12 Google has the following selected data ($ in millions):

Calculate financial ratios **(LO4)**

	2009	2008
Net sales	$23,651	$21,796
Net income	6,520	4,227
Operating cash flows	9,316	7,853
Total assets	40,497	31,768

Required:

1. Calculate the return on assets. Compare it with the amounts calculated for **Apple** and **Dell** in Illustration 11–21.
2. Calculate the cash return on assets. Compare it with the amounts calculated for Apple and Dell in Illustration 11–22.
3. Calculate the cash flow to sales ratio and the asset turnover ratio. Compare the ratios with those calculated for Apple and Dell in Illustrations 11–24 and 11–25. Is Google's business strategy closer to Apple's or to Dell's?

E11–13 Refer to the information provided for Peach Computer in E11–11.

Calculate operating activities—direct method **(LO5)**

Required:

Prepare the operating activities section of the statement of cash flows for Peach Computer using the *direct* method.

Calculate operating
activities—direct
method **(LO5)**

E11–14 Mega Screens, Inc., reports sales revenue of $2,700,000, cost of goods sold of $1,500,000, and income tax expense of $140,000 for the year ended December 31, 2012. Selected balance sheet accounts are as follows:

MEGA SCREENS, INC. Selected Balance Sheet Data December 31			
	2012	**2011**	**Increase (I) or Decrease (D)**
Cash	$145,000	$185,000	$40,000 (D)
Accounts receivable	275,000	225,000	50,000 (I)
Inventory	120,000	155,000	35,000 (D)
Accounts payable	115,000	127,000	12,000 (D)
Income tax payable	20,000	15,000	5,000 (I)

Required:
Calculate cash received from customers, cash paid to suppliers, and cash paid for income taxes.

Calculate operating
activities—direct
method **(LO5)**

E11–15 The income statement for **Hewlett-Packard** reports revenues of $91,658 million and cost of goods sold of $69,178 million. An examination of balance sheet amounts indicates accounts receivable increased $1,723 million, inventory increased $873 million, and accounts payable to suppliers decreased $1,957 million.

Required:
Using the direct method, calculate (1) cash received from customers and (2) cash paid to suppliers.

*For additional exercises, visit **www.mhhe.com/succeed** for Exercises: Set B.*

PROBLEMS: SET A

Determine proper
classification **(LO1)**

P11–1A Listed below are several transactions. For each transaction, indicate by letter whether the cash effect of each transaction is reported in a statement of cash flows as an operating (O), investing (I), financing (F), or noncash (NC) activity. Also, indicate whether the transaction is a cash inflow (CI) or cash outflow (CO), or has no effect on cash (NE). The first answer is provided as an example.

Transaction	Type of Activity	Cash Inflow or Outflow
1. *Payment of employee salaries.*	*O*	*CO*
2. Sale of land for cash.		
3. Purchase of rent in advance.		
4. Collection of an account receivable.		
5. Issuance of common stock.		
6. Purchase of inventory.		
7. Collection of notes receivable.		
8. Payment of income taxes.		
9. Sale of equipment for a note receivable.		
10. Issuance of bonds.		
11. Loan to another firm.		
12. Payment of a long-term note payable.		
13. Purchase of treasury stock.		
14. Payment of an account payable.		
15. Sale of equipment for cash.		

P11–2A Seth Erkenbeck, a recent college graduate, has just completed the basic format to be used in preparing the statement of cash flows (indirect method) for ATM Software Developers. All amounts are in thousands (000s).

Basic format for the statement of cash flows (LO2, 3)

ATM SOFTWARE DEVELOPERS
Statement of Cash Flows
For the year ended December 31, 2012

Cash Flows from Operating Activities	
Net income	$
Adjustments for noncash effects:	
Net cash flows from operating activities	_____
Cash Flows from Investing Activities	
Net cash flows from investing activities	_____
Cash Flows from Financing Activities	
Net cash flows from financing activities	_____
Net increase (decrease) in cash	$2,565
Cash at the beginning of the period	7,410
Cash at the end of the period	$9,975

Listed below in random order are line items to be included in the statement of cash flows.

Cash received from the sale of land	$ 8,550
Issuance of common stock	12,825
Depreciation expense	5,415
Increase in accounts receivable	3,990
Decrease in accounts payable	1,710
Issuance of long-term notes payable	16,245
Purchase of equipment	39,615
Decrease in inventory	1,425
Decrease in prepaid rent	855
Payment of dividends	6,270
Net income	11,400
Purchase of treasury stock	2,565

Required:

Prepare the statement of cash flows for ATM Software Developers using the *indirect* method.

P11–3A Portions of the financial statements for Alliance Technologies are provided below.

Calculate operating activities—indirect method (LO2)

ALLIANCE TECHNOLOGIES
Income Statement
For the year ended December 31, 2012

Revenues		$305,000
Expenses:		
Cost of goods sold	$185,000	
Operating expenses	60,000	
Depreciation expense	16,000	
Income tax expense	22,000	
Total expenses		283,000
Net income		$ 22,000

ALLIANCE TECHNOLOGIES
Selected Balance Sheet Data
December 31, 2012, compared to December 31, 2011

Decrease in accounts receivable	$ 6,000
Increase in inventory	13,000
Decrease in prepaid rent	9,000
Increase in operating expenses payable	5,000
Decrease in accounts payable	8,000
Increase in income tax payable	20,000

Required:

Prepare the operating activities section of the statement of cash flows for Alliance Technologies using the *indirect* method.

P11–4A The income statement, balance sheet, and additional information for Video Phones, Inc., are provided.

Prepare a statement of cash flows—indirect method (LO2, 3)

VIDEO PHONES, INC.
Income Statement
For the year ended December 31, 2012

Revenues		$3,036,000
Expenses:		
Cost of goods sold	$1,950,000	
Operating expenses	858,000	
Depreciation expense	27,000	
Loss on sale of land	8,000	
Interest expense	15,000	
Income tax expense	48,000	
Total expenses		2,906,000
Net income		$ 130,000

VIDEO PHONES, INC.
Balance Sheet
December 31

	2012	2011
Assets		
Current assets:		
Cash	$186,000	$144,000
Accounts receivable	81,000	60,000
Inventory	105,000	135,000
Prepaid rent	12,000	6,000
Long-term assets:		
Investments	105,000	0
Land	210,000	240,000
Equipment	270,000	210,000
Accumulated depreciation	(69,000)	(42,000)
Total assets	$900,000	$753,000
Liabilities and Stockholders' Equity		
Current liabilities:		
Accounts payable	$ 66,000	$ 81,000
Interest payable	6,000	10,000
Income tax payable	15,000	14,000
Long-term liabilities:		
Notes payable	285,000	225,000
Stockholders' equity:		
Common stock	300,000	300,000
Retained earnings	228,000	123,000
Total liabilities and stockholders' equity	$900,000	$753,000

Additional Information for 2012:
1. Purchase investment in bonds for $105,000.
2. Sell land costing $30,000 for only $22,000, resulting in an $8,000 loss on sale of land.
3. Purchase $60,000 in equipment by borrowing $60,000 with a note payable due in three years. No cash is exchanged in the transaction.
4. Declare and pay a cash dividend of $25,000.

Required:
Prepare the statement of cash flows using the *indirect* method. Disclose any noncash transactions in an accompanying note.

P11–5A Google and **Yahoo** are competitors in the Internet search engine business. Selected financial data for Google and Yahoo are as follows:

Calculate and analyze ratios (LO4)

($ in millions)	2009	2008
Google		
Net sales	$23,651	$21,796
Net income	6,520	4,227
Operating cash flows	9,316	7,853
Total assets	40,497	31,768
Yahoo		
Net sales	$ 6,460	$ 7,209
Net income	598	424
Operating cash flows	1,310	1,880
Total assets	14,936	13,690

Required:
1. Calculate the return on assets for both companies. Compare the ratios with those calculated for **Apple** and **Dell** in Illustration 11–21.
2. Calculate the cash return on assets for both companies. Compare the ratios with those calculated for Apple and Dell in Illustration 11–22.
3. Calculate the cash flow to sales ratio and the asset turnover ratio for both companies. Compare the ratios with those calculated for Apple and Dell in Illustrations 11–24 and 11–25. Are Google's and Yahoo's business strategies closer to Apple's or to Dell's?

P11–6A Refer to the information provided in P11–3A for Alliance Technologies.

Calculate operating activities—direct method (LO5)

Required:
Prepare the operating activities section of the statement of cash flows for Alliance Technologies using the *direct* method.

P11–7A Data for Video Phones, Inc., is provided in P11–4A.

Calculate operating activities—direct method (LO5)

Required:
Prepare the statement of cash flows for Video Phones, Inc., using the *direct* method. Disclose any noncash transactions in an accompanying note.

P11–8A Cash flows from operating activities for both the indirect and direct methods are presented for Reverse Logic. All amounts are in thousands (000s).

Prepare an income statement using operating cash flow information—indirect and direct methods (LO2, 5)

Cash Flows from Operating Activities (Indirect method)	
Net income	$164
Adjustments for noncash effects:	
Depreciation expense	52
Changes in current assets and current liabilities:	
Increase in accounts receivable	(28)
Decrease in inventory	40
Increase in prepaid rent	(4)
Decrease in accounts payable	(16)
Decrease in income tax payable	(8)
Net cash flows from operating activities	$200

(continued)

(concluded)

Cash Flows from Operating Activities (Direct method)

Cash received from customers	$ 4,020
Cash paid to suppliers	(2,580)
Cash paid for operating expenses	(1,152)
Cash paid for income taxes	(88)
Net cash flows from operating activities	$200

Required:

Complete the following income statement for Reverse Logic. Assume all accounts payable are to suppliers.

REVERSE LOGIC
Income Statement
For the year ended December 31, 2012

Revenues		$?
Expenses:		
Cost of goods sold	$?	
Operating expenses	?	
Depreciation expense	52	
Income tax expense	?	
Total expenses		?
Net income		$164

[Hint: Use the following calculations and work backwards from bottom (in red) to top for each item.]

Revenues
± Change in accounts receivable
= Cash received from customers   _____

Cost of goods sold
± Change in inventory
= Purchases
± Change in accounts payable
= Cash paid to suppliers   _____

Operating expenses
± Change in prepaid rent
= Cash paid for operating expenses   _____

Income tax expense
± Change in income tax payable
= Cash paid for income taxes   _____

PROBLEMS: SET B

Determine proper classification **(LO1)**

P11–1B Listed below are several transactions. For each transaction, indicate by letter whether the cash effect of each transaction is reported in a statement of cash flows as an operating (O), investing (I), financing (F), or noncash (NC) activity. Also, indicate whether the transaction is a cash inflow (CI) or cash outflow (CO), or has no effect on cash (NE). The first answer is provided as an example.

Transaction	Type of Activity	Cash Inflow or Outflow
1. *Issuance of common stock.*	*F*	*CI*
2. Sale of land for cash.		
3. Purchase of treasury stock.		
4. Collection of an account receivable.		
5. Issuance of a note payable.		
6. Purchase of inventory.		
7. Repayment of a note payable.		
8. Payment of employee salaries.		
9. Sale of equipment for a note receivable.		
10. Issuance of bonds.		
11. Investment in bonds.		
12. Payment of interest on bonds payable.		
13. Payment of a cash dividend.		
14. Purchase of a building.		
15. Collection of a note receivable.		

P11–2B Natalie Daniels has completed the basic format to be used in preparing the statement of cash flows (indirect method) for CPU Hardware Designers. All amounts are in thousands (000s).

Basic format for the statement of cash flows (LO2, 3)

CPU HARDWARE DESIGNERS
Statement of Cash Flows
For the year ended December 31, 2012

Cash Flows from Operating Activities	
Net income	
Adjustments for noncash effects:	
Net cash flows from operating activities	_____
Cash Flows from Investing Activities	
Net cash flows from investing activities	_____
Cash Flows from Financing Activities	
Net cash flows from financing activities	_____
Net increase (decrease) in cash	$(50,000)
Cash at the beginning of the period	80,000
Cash at the end of the period	$ 30,000

Below, in random order, are line items to be included in the statement of cash flows.

Cash received from the sale of land	$ 3,000
Issuance of common stock	250,000
Depreciation expense	20,000
Increase in accounts receivable	60,000
Increase in accounts payable	10,000
Loss on sale of land	7,000
Purchase of equipment	220,000
Increase in inventory	30,000
Increase in prepaid rent	10,000
Payment of dividends	40,000
Net income	70,000
Repayment of notes payable	50,000

Required:

Prepare the statement of cash flows for CPU Hardware Designers using the *indirect* method.

Calculate operating activities—indirect method (**LO2**)

P11–3B Portions of the financial statements for Software Associates are provided below.

SOFTWARE ASSOCIATES		
Income Statement		
For the year ended December 31, 2012		
Revenues		$610,000
Expenses:		
Cost of goods sold	$370,000	
Operating expenses	120,000	
Depreciation expense	32,000	
Income tax expense	44,000	
Total expenses		566,000
Net income		$ 44,000

SOFTWARE ASSOCIATES	
Selected Balance Sheet Data	
December 31, 2012, compared to December 31, 2011	
Decrease in accounts receivable	$ 9,000
Decrease in inventory	12,000
Increase in prepaid rent	2,000
Decrease in operating expenses payable	3,000
Increase in accounts payable	6,000
Increase in income tax payable	7,000

Required:

Prepare the operating activities section of the statement of cash flows for Software Associates using the *indirect* method.

Prepare a statement of cash flows—indirect method (**LO2, 3**)

P11–4B The income statement, balance sheet, and additional information for Virtual Gaming Systems are provided.

VIRTUAL GAMING SYSTEMS		
Income Statement		
For the year ended December 31, 2012		
Revenues		$2,500,000
Gain on sale of land		2,000
Total revenues		2,502,000
Expenses:		
Cost of goods sold	$1,600,000	
Operating expenses	605,000	
Depreciation expense	23,000	
Interest expense	24,000	
Income tax expense	70,000	
Total expenses		2,322,000
Net income		$ 180,000

VIRTUAL GAMING SYSTEMS
Balance Sheet
December 31

	2012	2011
Assets		
Current assets:		
Cash	$199,000	$144,000
Accounts receivable	75,000	90,000
Inventory	145,000	135,000
Prepaid rent	4,000	6,000
Long-term assets:		
Investments	185,000	100,000
Land	210,000	260,000
Equipment	230,000	210,000
Accumulated depreciation	(128,000)	(105,000)
Total assets	$920,000	$840,000
Liabilities and Stockholders' Equity		
Current liabilities:		
Accounts payable	$ 30,000	$ 88,000
Interest payable	4,000	3,000
Income tax payable	21,000	24,000
Long-term liabilities:		
Notes payable	245,000	225,000
Stockholders' equity:		
Common stock	350,000	300,000
Retained earnings	270,000	200,000
Total liabilities and stockholders' equity	$920,000	$840,000

Additional Information for 2012:

1. Purchase additional investment in stocks for $85,000.
2. Sell land costing $50,000 for $52,000, resulting in a $2,000 gain on sale of land.
3. Purchase $20,000 in equipment by borrowing $20,000 with a note payable due in three years. No cash is exchanged in the transaction.
4. Declare and pay a cash dividend of $110,000.
5. Issue common stock for $50,000.

Required:

Prepare the statement of cash flows using the *indirect* method. Disclose any noncash transactions in an accompanying note.

P11–5B Hewlett-Packard and **IBM** are close competitors in the sale of computer products and technology consulting. Selected financial data for Hewlett-Packard and IBM are as follows:

Calculate and analyze ratios (LO4)

($ in millions)	2009	2008
Hewlett-Packard		
Net sales	$114,552	$118,364
Net income	7,660	8,329
Operating cash flows	13,379	14,591
Total assets	114,799	113,331
IBM		
Net sales	$ 95,758	$103,630
Net income	13,425	12,334
Operating cash flows	20,773	18,812
Total assets	109,022	109,524

Required:

1. Calculate the return on assets for both companies. Compare the ratios with those calculated for **Apple** and **Dell** in Illustration 11–21.
2. Calculate the cash return on assets for both companies. Compare the ratios with those calculated for Apple and Dell in Illustration 11–22.
3. Calculate the cash flow to sales ratio and the asset turnover ratio for both companies. Which company has the better ratios, Hewlett-Packard or IBM? Are Hewlett-Packard's and IBM's business strategies closer to Apple's or to Dell's?

Calculate operating activities—direct method **(LO5)**

P11–6B Refer to the information provided in P11–3B for Software Associates.

Required:

Prepare the operating activities section of the statement of cash flows for Software Associates using the *direct* method.

Calculate operating activities—direct method **(LO5)**

P11–7B Data for Virtual Gaming Systems is provided in P11–4B.

Required:

Prepare the statement of cash flows for Virtual Gaming Systems using the *direct* method. Disclose any noncash transactions in an accompanying note.

Prepare an income statement using operating cash flow information—indirect and direct methods **(LO2, 5)**

P11–8B Cash flows from operating activities for both the indirect and direct methods are presented for Electronic Transformations.

Cash Flows from Operating Activities (Indirect method)

Net income		$35,000
Adjustments for noncash effects:		
Depreciation expense		8,000
Changes in current assets and current liabilities:		
Increase in accounts receivable		(12,000)
Increase in accounts payable		7,000
Increase in income tax payable		5,000
Net cash flows from operating activities		$43,000

Cash Flows from Operating Activities (Direct method)

Cash received from customers		$78,000
Cash paid for operating expenses		(25,000)
Cash paid for income taxes		(10,000)
Net cash flows from operating activities		$43,000

Required:

Complete the following income statement for Electronic Transformations. Assume all accounts payable are to suppliers.

ELECTRONIC TRANSFORMATIONS
Income Statement
For the year ended December 31, 2012

Revenues		$?
Expenses:		
Operating expenses	$?	
Depreciation expense	8,000	
Income tax expense	?	
Total expenses		?
Net income		$35,000

[*Hint:* Use the calculations on the next page and work backwards from bottom (in red) to top for each item.]

    Revenues
± Change in accounts receivable   _____
= **Cash received from customers**   ══════════════

    Operating expenses
± Change in accounts payable   _____
= **Cash paid for operating expenses**   ══════════════

    Income tax expense
± Change in income tax payable   _____
= **Cash paid for income taxes**   ══════════════

*For additional problems, visit **www.mhhe.com/succeed** for Problems: Set C.*

ADDITIONAL PERSPECTIVES

Great Adventures

(This is a continuation of the Great Adventures problem from earlier chapters.)

Continuing Problem

AP11–1 The income statement, balance sheet, and additional information for Great Adventures, Inc., are provided below.

GREAT ADVENTURES, INC.
Income Statement
For the year ended December 31, 2014

Revenues:		
Service revenue (clinic, racing, TEAM)	$543,000	
Sales revenue (MU watches)	118,000	
Total revenues		$661,000
Expenses:		
Cost of goods sold (watches)	70,000	
Operating expenses	304,276	
Depreciation expense	50,000	
Interest expense	29,724	
Income tax expense	57,000	
Total expenses		511,000
Net income		$150,000

GREAT ADVENTURES, INC.
Balance Sheet
December 31, 2014 and 2013

	2014	2013	Increase (I) or Decrease (D)
Assets			
Current assets:			
Cash	$ 322,362	$138,000	$ 184,362 (I)
Accounts receivable	45,000	35,000	10,000 (I)
Inventory	17,000	14,000	3,000 (I)
Other current assets	13,000	11,000	2,000 (I)

(continued)

(concluded)

GREAT ADVENTURES, INC.
Balance Sheet
December 31, 2014 and 2013

	2014	2013	Increase (I) or Decrease (D)
Long-term assets:			
Land	$ 500,000	$ 0	$ 500,000 (I)
Buildings	1,000,000	0	1,000,000 (I)
Equipment	65,000	65,000	
Accumulated depreciation	(75,250)	(25,250)	50,000 (I)
Total assets	$1,887,112	$237,750	
Liabilities and Stockholders' Equity			
Current liabilities:			
Accounts payable	$ 12,000	$ 9,000	$ 3,000 (I)
Interest payable	750	750	
Income tax payable	57,000	38,000	19,000 (I)
Long-term liabilities:			
Notes payable	492,362	30,000	462,362 (I)
Stockholders' equity:			
Common stock	120,000	20,000	100,000 (I)
Paid-in capital	1,105,000	0	1,105,000 (I)
Retained earnings	175,000	140,000	35,000 (I)
Treasury stock	(75,000)	0	(75,000) (I)
Total liabilities and stockholders' equity	$1,887,112	$237,750	

Additional Information for 2014:
1. Borrowed $500,000 in January 2014. Made 12 monthly payments during the year, reducing the balance of the loan by $37,638.
2. Issued common stock for $1.2 million.
3. Purchased 10,000 shares of treasury stock for $15 per share.
4. Reissued 5,000 shares of treasury stock at $16 per share.
5. Declared and paid a cash dividend of $115,000.

Required:
Prepare the statement of cash flows for the year ended December 31, 2014, using the *indirect* method.

Financial Analysis

American Eagle Outfitters, Inc.

AP11–2 Financial information for **American Eagle** is presented in Appendix A at the end of the book.

Required:
1. What was the amount of increase or decrease in cash and cash equivalents for the most recent year?
2. What was net cash from operating activities for the most recent year? Is net cash from operating activities increasing each year? What is the largest reconciling item between net income and net operating cash flows during the most recent year?
3. What was net cash from investing activities for the most recent year? Is it positive or negative? What is the largest investing activity during the most recent year?

4. What was net cash from financing activities for the most recent year? Is negative financing activities a good sign or a bad sign? What is the largest financing activity during the most recent year?

The Buckle, Inc.

AP11–3 Financial information for **The Buckle** is presented in Appendix B at the end of the book.

Required:

1. What was the amount of increase or decrease in cash and cash equivalents for the most recent year?
2. What was net cash from operating activities for the most recent year? Is net cash from operating activities increasing each year? What is the largest reconciling item between net income and net operating cash flows during the most recent year?
3. What was net cash from investing activities for the most recent year? Is it positive or negative? What is the largest investing activity during the most recent year?
4. What was net cash from financing activities for the most recent year? Is negative financing activities a good sign or a bad sign? What is the largest financing activity during the most recent year?

American Eagle Outfitters, Inc., vs. The Buckle, Inc.

AP11–4 Financial information for **American Eagle** is presented in Appendix A at the end of the book, and financial information for **The Buckle** is presented in Appendix B at the end of the book.

Required:

1. Calculate American Eagle's cash return on assets, cash flow to sales, and asset turnover ratio.
2. Calculate The Buckle's cash return on assets, cash flow to sales, and asset turnover ratio.
3. Which company is doing better based on cash return on assets? Which company has the higher cash flow to sales? Which company has the higher asset turnover?

Ethics

AP11–5 Aggressive Corporation approaches Matt Taylor, a loan officer for Oklahoma State Bank, seeking to increase the company's borrowings with the bank from $100,000 to $150,000. Matt has an uneasy feeling as he examines the loan application from Aggressive Corporation, which just completed its first year of operations. The application included the following financial statements.

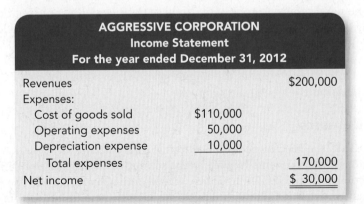

AGGRESSIVE CORPORATION
Income Statement
For the year ended December 31, 2012

Revenues		$200,000
Expenses:		
Cost of goods sold	$110,000	
Operating expenses	50,000	
Depreciation expense	10,000	
Total expenses		170,000
Net income		$ 30,000

AGGRESSIVE CORPORATION Balance Sheet December 31		
	2012	**2011**
Assets		
Current assets:		
Cash	$ 10,000	$0
Accounts receivable	60,000	0
Inventory	40,000	0
Long-term assets:		
Equipment	100,000	0
Accumulated depreciation	(10,000)	0
Total assets	$200,000	$0
Liabilities and Stockholders' Equity		
Current liabilities:		
Accounts payable	$ 20,000	$0
Interest payable	10,000	0
Long-term liabilities:		
Note payable	100,000	0
Stockholders' equity:		
Common stock	40,000	0
Retained earnings	30,000	0
Total liabilities and stockholders' equity	$200,000	$0

The income statement submitted with the application shows net income of $30,000 in the first year of operations. Referring to the balance sheet, this net income represents a more-than-acceptable 15% rate of return on assets of $200,000.

Matt's concern stems from his recollection that the $100,000 note payable reported on the balance sheet is a three-year loan from his bank, approved earlier this year. He recalls another promising new company that, just recently, defaulted on its loan due to its inability to generate sufficient cash flows to meet its loan obligations.

Seeing Matt's hesitation, Larry Bling, the CEO of Aggressive Corporation, closes the door to the conference room and shares with Matt that he owns several other businesses. He says he will be looking for a new CFO in another year to run Aggressive Corporation along with his other businesses and Matt is just the kind of guy he is looking for. Larry mentions that as CFO, Matt would receive a significant salary. Matt is flattered and says he will look over the loan application and get back to Larry concerning the $50,000 loan increase by the end of the week.

Required:
1. Prepare a statement of cash flows for Aggressive Corporation.
2. Explain how Aggressive Corporation can have positive net income but negative operating cash flows. How does the finding of negative operating cash flows affect your confidence in the reliability of the net income amount?
3. Why do you think Larry mentioned the potential employment position? Should the potential employment position with Aggressive Corporation have any influence on the loan decision?

Internet Research

AP11–6 EDGAR, the Electronic Data Gathering, Analysis, and Retrieval system, is a giant database of documents required to be submitted to the U.S. Securities and Exchange Commission (SEC). All publicly traded domestic companies use EDGAR to make the majority of their filings. (Filings by foreign companies are not required to be filed on EDGAR, but many of these companies do so voluntarily.) Form 10-K, which

includes the annual report, is an important document required to be filed on EDGAR. The SEC makes this information available, free to the public, on the Internet.

Required:

1. Access EDGAR on the Internet. The web address is ***www.sec.gov***.
2. Search for a public company with which you are familiar. Access its most recent 10-K filing. Search or scroll to find the statement of cash flows.
3. Is the direct or indirect method used to report operating activities? What is the largest adjustment to net income in reconciling net income and cash flows from operations in the most recent year?
4. What has been the most significant investing activity for the company in the most recent three years?
5. What has been the most significant financing activity for the company in the most recent three years?

Written Communication

AP11–7 "Why can't we pay our shareholders a dividend?" shouts your new boss at Polar Opposites. "This income statement you prepared for me says we earned $5 million in our first year!" You recently prepared the financial statements below.

POLAR OPPOSITES Income Statement For the year ended December 31, 2012	
	($ in millions)
Sales revenue	$65
Cost of goods sold	(35)
Depreciation expense	(4)
Operating expenses	(21)
Net income	$ 5

POLAR OPPOSITES Balance Sheet December 31, 2012	
	($ in millions)
Cash	$ 1
Accounts receivable (net)	16
Merchandise inventory	14
Machinery (net)	44
Total	$75
Accounts payable	$ 7
Accrued expenses payable	9
Notes payable	29
Common stock	25
Retained earnings	5
Total	$75

Although net income was $5 million, cash flow from operating activities was a negative $5 million. This just didn't make any sense to your boss.

Required:

Prepare a memo explaining how net income could be positive and operating cash flows negative. Include in your report a determination of operating cash flows of negative $5 million using the *indirect* method.

Earnings Management

AP11–8 Bryan Eubank began his accounting career as an auditor for a Big 4 CPA firm. He focused on clients in the high-technology sector, becoming an expert on topics such as inventory write-downs, stock options, and business acquisitions. Impressed with his technical skills and experience, General Electronics, a large consumer electronics chain, hired Bryan as the company controller responsible for all of the accounting functions within the corporation. Bryan was excited about his new position—for about a week, until he took the first careful look at General Electronics' financial statements.

The cause of Bryan's change in attitude is the set of financial statements he's been staring at for the past few hours. For some time prior to his recruitment, he had been aware that his new employer had experienced a long trend of moderate profitability. The reports on his desk confirm the slight but steady improvements in net income in recent years. The disturbing trend Bryan is now noticing, though, is a decline in cash flows from operations. Bryan has sketched out the following comparison ($ in millions):

	2012	2011	2010	2009
Operating income	$1,400	$1,320	$1,275	$1,270
Net income	385	350	345	295
Cash flows from operations	16	110	120	155

Profits? Yes. Increasing profits? Yes. So what is the cause of his distress? The trend in cash flows from operations, which is going in the opposite direction of net income. Upon closer review, Bryan noticed a couple events that, unfortunately, seem related:
a. The company's credit policy has been loosened, credit terms relaxed, and payment periods lengthened. This has resulted in a large increase in accounts receivable.
b. Several of the company's salary arrangements, including that of the CEO and CFO, are based on reported net income.

Required:
1. What is likely causing the increase in accounts receivable? How does an increase in accounts receivable affect net income differently than operating cash flows?
2. Explain why salary arrangements for officers, such as the CEO and CFO, might increase the risk of earnings management.
3. Why is the trend in cash flows from operations, combined with the additional events, such a concern for Bryan?
4. What course of action, if any, should Bryan take?

Answers to the Self-Study Questions
1. b   2. c   3. c   4. b   5. a   6. d   7. b   8. c   9. d   10. c

Financial Statement Analysis

Learning Objectives

AFTER STUDYING THIS CHAPTER, YOU SHOULD BE ABLE TO:

■ **LO1** Perform vertical analysis.

■ **LO2** Perform horizontal analysis.

■ **LO3** Use ratios to analyze a company's risk.

■ **LO4** Use ratios to analyze a company's profitability.

■ **LO5** Distinguish persistent earnings from one-time items.

■ **LO6** Explain quality of earnings and distinguish between conservative and aggressive accounting practices.

UNDER ARMOUR: MAKING THE COMPETITION SWEAT

It started with a simple plan to make a superior T-shirt—a shirt that provides compression and removes perspiration from your skin rather than absorbs it. Founded in 1996 by former University of Maryland football player Kevin Plank, **Under Armour** is now widely recognized for its performance apparel—clothing designed to keep athletes cool, dry, and light. With its introduction of football cleats, Under Armour has joined **Nike** and **Reebok** as one of only three authorized footwear suppliers for the National Football League. The company has expanded beyond football to supply athletic apparel for nearly every major sport. The Under Armour name is even stretching overseas with a strong market presence in the United Kingdom, Canada, Europe, Japan, Australia, New Zealand, and South Africa.

Under Armour sold over 12 million shares of stock to the general public in its initial public offering (IPO) in November 2005. The IPO, on the NASDAQ stock exchange, was a memorable one. The stock had one of the highest share price increases ever for the first day of trading, beginning at $13 and doubling to close the day at just over $26 per share. The stock has continued to do well. In December 2006, the company moved its listing to the New York Stock Exchange (under the ticker symbol UA).

Investors are very enthusiastic about Under Armour's growth potential. Some think the company is poised to become the next Nike. Why has Under Armour stock performed so well? Will it continue that success? What are the risks of investing in a company like Under Armour?

To find answers to questions like these, we use the tools described in this chapter to analyze financial statements—the same statements you've learned to prepare in the preceding chapters. The techniques we introduce here—such as vertical analysis, horizontal analysis, and ratio analysis—help analysts evaluate the riskiness and profitability of potential investments in companies such as Under Armour and compare them to industry leaders like Nike.

PART A

COMPARISON OF FINANCIAL ACCOUNTING INFORMATION

We use ratios to make comparisons every day. Consider major sports. Batting averages provide feedback in baseball about how well a player is hitting. Basketball and football use points per game to compare teams' offensive and defensive performance. In each case, the ratio is more meaningful than a single number by itself. For example, are 50 hits in baseball a good number? It depends on the number of at-bats. Similarly, 500 points are more informative about a team's performance when divided by the number of games played.

Likewise, we can use ratios to help evaluate a firm's performance and financial position. Is net income of $10 million a cause for shareholders to celebrate? Probably not, if shareholders' equity is $1 billion, because $10 million is then only a 1% return on equity. But if shareholders' equity is $20 million, net income of $10 million is a 50% return on equity and something for shareholders to celebrate. Ratios are most useful when compared to some standard. That standard of comparison may be the performance of a competing company, last year's performance by the same company, or an industry average. Illustration 12–1 provides a summary of these three different types of comparisons.

ILLUSTRATION 12–1

Three Types of Comparisons

| | Type of Comparison | Example |

1. Comparisons between companies

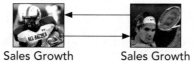

Sales Growth   Sales Growth

Compare sales growth for **Under Armour** with sales growth for **Nike**.

2. Comparisons over time

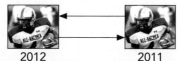

2012   2011

Compare Under Armour's earnings this year with its earnings last year.

3. Comparisons to industry

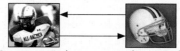

Company Risk   Industry Risk

Compare Under Armour's level of risk with the average degree of risk for the sports apparel industry.*

*Industry averages can be obtained from websites such as Yahoo Finance or from financial ratings agencies such as Dun & Bradstreet, Moody's, and Standard & Poor's.

Vertical Analysis

■ **LO1**
Perform vertical analysis.

Common Terms Vertical analysis is also known as *common-size analysis.*

In performing **vertical analysis**, we express each item in a financial statement as a percentage of the same base amount. For instance, we can express each line item in an income statement as a percentage of sales. In a balance sheet, we can express each item as a percentage of total assets. Let's look at an example to see the benefits of vertical analysis.

VERTICAL ANALYSIS OF THE INCOME STATEMENT

Illustration 12–2 provides common-size income statements for **Under Armour** and **Nike**. Notice that the two companies end their fiscal years on different dates. Under

ILLUSTRATION 12–2
Common-Size Income
Statements

UNDER ARMOUR AND NIKE
Common-Size Income Statements
For the years ended December 31, 2009, and May 31, 2009
($ in millions)

For the year ended:	UNDER ARMOUR December 31, 2009		NIKE May 31, 2009	
	Amount	%	Amount	%
Net sales*	$856.4	100.0	$19,176.1	100.0
Cost of goods sold	443.4	51.8	10,571.7	55.1
Gross profit	413.0	48.2	8,604.4	44.9
Operating expenses	327.7	38.3	6,745.9	35.2
Operating income	85.3	9.9	1,858.5	9.7
Other income (expense)	(2.9)	(0.3)	98.0	0.5
Income before tax	82.4	9.6	1,956.5	10.2
Income tax expense	35.6	4.1	469.8	2.4
Net income	$ 46.8	5.5	$ 1,486.7	7.8

*Net sales equal total sales revenue less sales returns, allowances, and discounts.

Common Terms Income
tax expense is also
called *provision for
income taxes.*

Armour's year-end is December 31 while Nike's is May 31. Even though the year-ends do not exactly match, we can still make meaningful comparisons between the two companies.

What do we learn from this comparison? Nike reports net income of almost $1.5 billion while Under Armour reports only $46.8 million. Does this mean Nike's operations are over 30 times more profitable than Under Armour's? Not necessarily. Nike is a much larger company, reporting sales over $19 billion compared to $856.4 million for Under Armour. Because of its greater size, we expect Nike to report a greater *amount* of net income. To better compare the performance of the two companies, we can use vertical analysis to express each income statement item as a *percentage of sales.*

Under Armour's gross profit equals 48.2% of sales (= $413.0 ÷ $856.4) compared to Nike's 44.9%. This means that Under Armour earns a slightly higher gross profit for each item sold, consistent with its business strategy of focusing on high-quality performance apparel. However, Under Armour's higher gross profit is offset almost entirely by its proportionately higher operating expenses, 38.3% of sales compared to 35.2% for Nike. The net result is that operating income, as a percentage of sales, is quite similar for the two companies. Nike's net income, as a percentage of sales, exceeds Under Armour's, though. The reason: Nike reports $98 million in other income while Under Armour reports $2.9 million in other *expense,* and Nike has a lower portion of income reduced for income tax expense.

Decision Point

Question	Accounting information	Analysis
How do we compare income between companies of different size?	Common-size income statements	A vertical analysis using common-size income statements allows for the comparison of income statement items between companies of different size.

VERTICAL ANALYSIS OF THE BALANCE SHEET

Vertical analysis of the balance sheet is useful, too. For this, we divide each balance sheet item by total assets to get an idea of its relative significance. Illustration 12–3 provides common-size balance sheets for Under Armour and Nike.

ILLUSTRATION 12–3

Common-Size Balance Sheets

UNDER ARMOUR AND NIKE Common-Size Balance Sheets December 31, 2009, and May 31, 2009 ($ in millions)				
	UNDER ARMOUR		**NIKE**	
	December 31, 2009		May 31, 2009	
	Amount	%	Amount	%
Assets				
Current assets	$448.0	82.1	$ 9,734.0	73.4
Property and equipment	72.9	13.4	1,957.7	14.8
Intangible assets	5.7	1.0	660.9	5.0
Other assets	19.0	3.5	897.0	6.8
Total assets	$545.6	100.0	$13,249.6	100.0
Liabilities and Stockholders' Equity				
Current liabilities	$120.2	22.0	$ 3,277.0	24.7
Long-term liabilities	25.4	4.7	1,279.2	9.7
Common stock	197.8	36.3	3,242.0	24.5
Retained earnings	202.2	37.0	5,451.4	41.1
Total liabilities and stockholders' equity	$545.6	100.0	$13,249.6	100.0

What can we learn by analyzing the common-size balance sheets? Focusing on the asset portion of the balance sheet, we discover that Under Armour has a higher percentage of current assets than Nike and a slightly lower share of assets invested in property and equipment. Looking at liabilities and stockholders' equity, we see that the two companies maintain a similar proportion of current liabilities but differ in their proportion of long-term liabilities. Under Armour is financed more by equity than by debt; its long-term liabilities represent only 4.7% of total assets. In comparison, Nike reports a higher level of long-term liabilities at 9.7%.

Finally, it's interesting to note the relative contributions of common stock and retained earnings for the two companies. Under Armour reports a higher proportion of common stock and a lower proportion of retained earnings in comparison to Nike. Newer companies, like Under Armour, tend to have a greater portion of equity from investment in the company (common stock) than from earnings retained in the company (retained earnings). Just the opposite is true for many well-established companies, like Nike. Profitable operations over many years have created a retained earnings balance for Nike that exceeds the original investment in the company.

 KEY POINT

For vertical analysis, we express each item as a percentage of the same base amount, such as a percentage of sales in the income statement or as a percentage of total assets in the balance sheet.

Horizontal Analysis

We use horizontal analysis to analyze trends in financial statement data for a single company over time. For example, are sales growing faster than cost of goods sold? Are operating expenses growing faster than sales? Are any specific expenses increasing at a greater rate than others? Questions such as these can help identify areas of concern or, perhaps, indications of better things to come.

■ **LO2**
Perform horizontal analysis.

Common Terms
Horizontal analysis is also known as *trend analysis* or *time-series analysis.*

HORIZONTAL ANALYSIS OF THE INCOME STATEMENT

Illustration 12–4 provides income statements over two years for Under Armour. The final two columns show the dollar amount and percentage changes.

ILLUSTRATION 12–4
Horizontal Analysis of Under Armour's Income Statement

UNDER ARMOUR
Income Statement
For the years ended December 31
($ in millions)

	Year		Increase (Decrease)	
	2009	**2008**	**Amount**	**%**
Net sales	$856.4	$725.2	$131.2	18.1
Cost of goods sold	443.4	370.3	73.1	19.7
Gross profit	413.0	354.9	58.1	16.4
Operating expenses	327.7	278.0	49.7	17.9
Operating income	85.3	76.9	8.4	10.9
Other expense	2.9	7.0	(4.1)	(58.6)
Income before tax	82.4	69.9	12.5	17.9
Income tax expense	35.6	31.7	3.9	12.3
Net income	$ 46.8	$ 38.2	$ 8.6	22.5

We calculate the *amount* of the increases or decreases by simply subtracting the 2008 balance from the 2009 balances. A positive difference indicates the amount increased in 2009. A negative amount represents a decrease, which we record in parentheses. We calculate the *percentage* increase or decrease based on the following formula:

$$\% \text{ Increase (Decrease)} = \frac{\text{Current-year amount} - \text{Prior-year amount}}{\text{Prior-year amount}}$$

In our example, the calculation would be:

$$\% \text{ Increase (Decrease)} = \frac{2009 \text{ amount} - 2008 \text{ amount}}{2008 \text{ amount}}$$

For example, the *amount* of sales increased $131.2 million—equal to sales of $856.4 million in 2009 minus sales of $725.2 million in 2008. We calculate the *percentage* increase of 18.1% by dividing the $131.2 million increase in sales by 2008 sales of $725.2 million. If the base-year amount (2008 in our example) is ever zero, we can't calculate a percentage. Also, if the base year is negative, a percentage change is not meaningful.

The horizontal analysis of Under Armour's income statement demonstrates steady growth in company operations. Gross profit increased 16.4% (= $58.1 ÷ $354.9), operating income increased 10.9% (= $8.4 ÷ $76.9), income before tax increased

17.9% (= $12.5 ÷ $69.9), and net income increased 22.5% (= $8.6 ÷ $38.2). The growth in these income measures definitely is a positive sign.

However, note that gross profit did not grow as quickly as sales. Under Armour did increase sales, but the cost of those sales (cost of goods sold) grew at an even greater rate. Another negative sign is that the company's operating expenses increased at a faster rate than its gross profit (17.9% vs. 16.4%). While sales are increasing, similar or even larger increases in the cost of goods sold and operating expenses raise some concerns.

HORIZONTAL ANALYSIS OF THE BALANCE SHEET

Illustration 12–5 provides balance sheet information for Under Armour for 2009 and 2008, with amount and percentage changes in the final two columns.

ILLUSTRATION 12–5

Horizontal Analysis of Under Armour's Balance Sheet

UNDER ARMOUR Balance Sheet December 31 ($ in millions)				
	Year		**Increase (Decrease)**	
	2009	**2008**	**Amount**	**%**
Assets				
Current assets	$ 448.0	$396.4	$ 51.6	13.0
Property and equipment	72.9	73.5	(0.6)	(0.8)
Intangible assets	5.7	5.5	0.2	3.6
Other assets	19.0	12.2	6.8	55.7
Total assets	$ 545.6	$487.6	$ 58.0	11.9
Liabilities and Stockholders' Equity				
Current liabilities	$ 120.2	$133.1	$(12.9)	(9.7)
Long-term liabilities	25.4	23.4	2.0	8.5
Common stock	197.8	175.1	22.7	13.0
Retained earnings	202.2	156.0	46.2	29.6
Total liabilities and stockholders' equity	$ 545.6	$487.6	$ 58.0	11.9

Using horizontal analysis, it's important to look at both the *amount* and the *percentage* changes. For example, if we focused solely on the percentage changes, "other assets" would receive the greatest attention due to the 55.7% increase in this account. However, in dollar amount, the increase in "other assets" is only $6.8 million, which is small compared to the company's total assets of $545.6 million.

The horizontal analysis of Under Armour's balance sheet further reflects its growth in operations during the year. Each of the asset categories increased, with the exception of a slight decrease in property and equipment. Under Armour had a stock offering again in 2009, as reflected in the $22.7 million increase in common stock. The company used some of the proceeds from the stock offering to reduce short-term debt. Retained earnings increased $46.2 million, or 29.6%, due primarily to net income of $46.8 million during the year.

 KEY POINT

We use horizontal analysis to analyze trends in financial statement data, such as the amount of change and the percentage change, for one company over time.

The income statement for **Nike** for the years ending May 31, 2009 and 2008, is as follows:

Let's Review

NIKE
Income Statement
For the years ended May 31
($ in millions)

	2009	2008	Increase (Decrease) Amount	%
Net sales	$19,176.1	$18,627.0		
Cost of goods sold	10,571.7	10,239.6		
Gross profit	8,604.4	8,387.4		
Operating expenses	6,745.9	5,953.7		
Operating income	1,858.5	2,433.7		
Other income (expense)	98.0	69.2		
Income before tax	1,956.5	2,502.9		
Income tax expense	469.8	619.5		
Net income	$ 1,486.7	$ 1,883.4		

Required:

Complete the "Amount" and "%" columns in a horizontal analysis of Nike's income statement. Discuss the meaning of the major fluctuations during the year.

Solution:

NIKE
Income Statement
For the years ended May 31
($ in millions)

	2009	2008	Increase (Decrease) Amount	%
Net sales	$19,176.1	$18,627.0	$549.1	2.9
Cost of goods sold	10,571.7	10,239.6	332.1	3.2
Gross profit	8,604.4	8,387.4	217.0	2.6
Operating expenses	6,745.9	5,953.7	792.2	13.3
Operating income	1,858.5	2,433.7	(575.2)	(23.6)
Other income (expense)	98.0	69.2	28.8	41.6
Income before tax	1,956.5	2,502.9	(546.4)	21.8
Income tax expense	469.8	619.5	(149.7)	(24.2)
Net income	$ 1,486.7	$ 1,883.4	(396.7)	(21.1)

Both Nike's sales and cost of goods sold increased slightly over the previous year. The largest fluctuation relates to operating expenses that increased $792.2 million, or 13.3%, over the prior year. While "other income" had the largest percentage change (41.6%), the overall amount of change is only $28.8 million. It is primarily the increase in operating expenses that caused the decrease in net income in comparison to the previous year.

Suggested Homework:
**BE12-1, BE12-2;
E12-2, E12-3;
P12-2A&B, P12-3A&B**

PART B

USING RATIOS TO ASSESS RISK AND PROFITABILITY

Beginning in Chapter 4, we provided an example of ratio analysis between two competing companies at the end of each chapter. Let's now apply what we learned in those separate ratio analyses in a detailed examination of **Under Armour**, comparing the results to the sports apparel industry leader—**Nike**. The income statement and balance sheet for Under Armour for the years ended December 31, 2009 and 2008, are presented in Illustration 12–6.

ILLUSTRATION 12–6

Under Armour's Financial Statements

UNDER ARMOUR
Income Statement
For the years ended December 31
($ in millions)

	2009	2008
Net sales	$856.4	$725.2
Cost of goods sold	443.4	370.3
Gross profit	413.0	354.9
Operating expenses	327.7	278.0
Operating income	85.3	76.9
Other income (expense)	2.9	7.0
Income before tax	82.4	69.9
Income tax expense	35.6	31.7
Net income	$ 46.8	$ 38.2

UNDER ARMOUR
Balance Sheet
December 31
($ in millions)

	2009	2008
Assets		
Current assets:		
Cash	$187.3	$102.0
Net receivables	92.2	94.1
Inventory	148.5	182.2
Other current assets	20.0	18.1
Total current assets	448.0	396.4
Property and equipment	72.9	73.5
Intangible assets	5.7	5.5
Other assets	19.0	12.2
Total assets	$545.6	$487.6
Liabilities and Stockholders' Equity		
Current liabilities	$120.1	$133.1
Long-term liabilities	25.4	23.4
Stockholders' equity	400.1	331.1
Total liabilities and stockholders' equity	$545.6	$487.6

We'll review 14 ratios classified into two categories: risk ratios and profitability ratios. When calculating ratios, remember how income statement accounts differ from balance sheet accounts: We measure income statement accounts over a *period* of time (like a video). We measure balance sheet accounts at a *point* in time (like a photograph). Therefore, ratios that compare an income statement account with a balance sheet account should express the balance sheet account as an *average* of the beginning and ending balances.

 COMMON MISTAKE

In comparing an income statement account with a balance sheet account, some students incorrectly use the balance sheet account's ending balance, rather than the *average* of its beginning and ending balances. Since income statement accounts are measured over a period of time, comparisons to related balance sheet accounts also need to be over time by taking the average of the beginning and ending balances.

Risk Analysis

Illustration 12–7 summarizes eight risk ratios, the chapters in which we discussed them, and how they're calculated. We divide the eight risk ratios into six liquidity ratios and two solvency ratios. **Liquidity** refers to a company's ability to pay its *current* liabilities. The accounts used to calculate liquidity ratios are located in the current assets and current liabilities sections of the balance sheet. **Solvency** refers to a company's ability to pay its *long-term* liabilities as well.

■ **LO3**
Use ratios to analyze a company's risk.

Risk Ratios	Chapter	Calculations
Liquidity		
Receivables turnover ratio	5	$\dfrac{\text{Net credit sales}}{\text{Average accounts receivable}}$
Average collection period	5	$\dfrac{365 \text{ days}}{\text{Receivables turnover ratio}}$
Inventory turnover ratio	6	$\dfrac{\text{Cost of goods sold}}{\text{Average inventory}}$
Average days in inventory	6	$\dfrac{365 \text{ days}}{\text{Inventory turnover ratio}}$
Current ratio	8	$\dfrac{\text{Current assets}}{\text{Current liabilities}}$
Acid-test ratio	8	$\dfrac{\text{Cash} + \text{Current investments} + \text{Accounts receivable}}{\text{Current liabilities}}$
Solvency		
Debt to equity ratio	9	$\dfrac{\text{Total liabilities}}{\text{Stockholders' equity}}$
Times interest earned ratio	9	$\dfrac{\text{Net income} + \text{Interest expense} + \text{Tax expense}}{\text{Interest expense}}$

ILLUSTRATION 12–7
Risk Ratios

CAREER CORNER

Investors and creditors, as well as suppliers, customers, employees, and the government among others, rely heavily on financial accounting information. Who checks big companies like Under Armour and Nike to make sure they are reporting accurately? Auditors. Many accounting majors begin their careers in auditing. They then use the experience they gain in auditing to obtain management and accounting positions in private industry, sometimes even with a company they previously audited.

However, auditing is not just for accounting majors. Finance majors are hired as auditors in the banking and insurance industries. Management information systems (MIS) majors are hired to audit computer systems. Management majors are hired to audit the effectiveness and efficiency of management operations. There even are marketing auditors, who identify strengths and weaknesses in marketing strategy and overall marketing structures.[1] Analysis skills, like those covered in this chapter, are the types of skills necessary for a successful career in the auditing profession as well as in many other business careers.

Let's calculate each of the eight risk ratios for Under Armour and then compare the results with Nike's. **We show the detailed calculations for Nike in a review problem at the end of this section.**

RECEIVABLES TURNOVER RATIO

The receivables turnover ratio measures how many times, on average, a company collects its receivables during the year. A low receivables turnover ratio may indicate that the company is having trouble collecting its accounts receivable. A high receivables turnover ratio is a positive sign that a company can quickly turn its receivables into cash. Illustration 12–8 shows the calculation of the receivables turnover ratio for Under Armour and compares it to Nike's.

ILLUSTRATION 12–8
Receivables Turnover Ratio

Receivables Turnover Ratio	Under Armour	Nike
$\dfrac{\text{Net credit sales}}{\text{Average accounts receivable}}$	$\dfrac{\$856.4}{(\$94.1 + \$92.2)/2} = 9.2$ times	6.2 times

In calculating the receivables turnover ratio, we have assumed that Under Armour's sales are all credit sales, typical of sporting goods stores such as **Academy Sports** or **Dick's Sporting Goods**. The bottom half of the fraction is the *average* accounts receivable during the year, calculated as beginning receivables plus ending receivables divided by two. Under Armour's receivables turnover ratio is 9.2, indicating that receivables turn over (are collected) 9.2 times per year. This is much higher than Nike's receivables turnover ratio of 6.2.

AVERAGE COLLECTION PERIOD

We often convert the receivables turnover ratio into days and call it the average collection period. The shorter the average collection period, the better. Illustration 12–9 displays the average collection period for Under Armour and Nike.

ILLUSTRATION 12–9
Average Collection Period

Average Collection Period	Under Armour	Nike
$\dfrac{\text{365 days}}{\text{Receivables turnover ratio}}$	$\dfrac{365}{9.2} = 39.7$ days	58.9 days

---

[1]J. Mylonakis. 2003. "Functions and Responsibilities of Marketing Auditors in Measuring Organizational Performance." *International Journal of Technology Management 25*, no. 8, pp. 814–25.

Under Armour's average collection period of 39.7 days is 365 days divided by the receivables turnover ratio of 9.2. It takes Under Armour an average of over one month (39.7 days) to collect its accounts receivable. Nike's average collection period, at 58.9 days, is about 20 days longer.

INVENTORY TURNOVER RATIO

The **inventory turnover ratio** measures how many times, on average, a company sells its entire inventory during the year. A high inventory turnover ratio usually is a positive sign. It indicates that inventory is selling quickly, less cash is tied up in inventory, and the risk of outdated inventory is lower. However, an extremely high inventory turnover ratio might be a signal that the company is losing sales due to inventory shortages. Illustration 12–10 provides the inventory turnover ratios for Under Armour and Nike.

Inventory Turnover Ratio	Under Armour	Nike
$\dfrac{\text{Cost of goods sold}}{\text{Average inventory}}$	$\dfrac{\$443.4}{(\$182.2 + \$148.5)/2} = 2.7$ times	4.4 times

ILLUSTRATION 12–10

Inventory Turnover Ratio

Inventory at Under Armour turns over, on average, about 2.7 times per year compared to 4.4 times per year at Nike. The slower inventory turnover at Under Armour is a negative sign, indicating a greater risk of slow-moving inventory items.

AVERAGE DAYS IN INVENTORY

We can convert the inventory turnover ratio into days and call it the **average days in inventory**. As you can imagine, companies try to minimize the number of days they hold inventory. We calculate the average days in inventory in Illustration 12–11.

Average Days in Inventory	Under Armour	Nike
$\dfrac{365 \text{ days}}{\text{Inventory turnover ratio}}$	$\dfrac{365}{2.7} = 135.2$ days	83.0 days

ILLUSTRATION 12–11

Average Days in Inventory

Under Armour's average days in inventory is 135.2 days, calculated as 365 days divided by the inventory turnover ratio of 2.7. In comparison, Nike's average days in inventory is much lower at 83.0 days.

Inventory turnover ratios and the resulting average days in inventory vary significantly by industry. For example, compared with the sporting goods apparel industry, the dairy industry with its perishable products has a much higher inventory turnover, and car dealerships have a lower inventory turnover. Inventory turnover might even vary by product within the same industry. The inventory turnover for milk, for instance, is much higher than for aged cheddar cheese within the dairy industry. Similarly, the inventory turnover for Honda Civics is much higher than for the higher-priced Honda Crosstour.

ETHICAL DILEMMA

Michael Hechtner was recently hired as an assistant controller for Athletic Persuasions, a recognized leader in the promotion of athletic events. However, the past year has been a difficult one for the company's operations. In order to help with slowing sales, the company has extended credit to more customers and accepted payment over longer time periods, resulting in a significant increase in accounts receivable. Similarly, with slowing sales, its inventory of promotional supplies has increased dramatically.

One afternoon, Michael joined the controller, J.P. Sloan, for a visit with Citizens State Bank. Athletic Persuasions had used up its line of credit and was looking to borrow additional funds. In meeting with the loan officer at the bank, Michael was surprised at the positive spin J.P. Sloan put on the company operations. J.P. exclaimed, "Athletic Persuasions continues to prosper in a difficult environment. Our current assets have significantly increased in relation to current liabilities, resulting in a much improved current ratio over the prior year. It seems wherever I look, the company has been successful."

What do you think are Michael's ethical concerns in this situation? Is there anything truly unethical in the controller's statement to the banker? What should Michael do in this situation? Is it acceptable for Michael just to keep quiet?

CURRENT RATIO

The **current ratio** compares current assets to current liabilities. It's probably the most widely used of all liquidity ratios. A high current ratio indicates that a company has sufficient current assets to pay current liabilities as they become due. Illustration 12–12 presents the current ratios for Under Armour and Nike.

ILLUSTRATION 12–12

Current Ratio

Current Ratio	Under Armour	Nike
$\dfrac{\text{Current assets}}{\text{Current liabilities}}$	$\dfrac{\$448.0}{\$120.1} = 3.7 \text{ to } 1$	3.0 to 1

Under Armour's current ratio of 3.7 means the firm has $3.70 in current assets for each $1 in current liabilities. Under Armour's current ratio is higher than Nike's current ratio of 3.0. A company needs to maintain sufficient current assets to pay current liabilities as they become due. Thus, a higher current ratio usually indicates less risk.

However, a high current ratio is not always a good signal. A high current ratio might occur when a company has difficulty collecting receivables or carries too much inventory. Analysts become concerned if a company reports an increasing

current ratio combined with either a lower receivables turnover ratio or a lower inventory turnover ratio.

ACID-TEST RATIO

The acid-test ratio is similar to the current ratio but is a more conservative measure of current assets available to pay current liabilities. Specifically, the top half of the fraction includes only cash, current investments, and accounts receivable. Because it eliminates current assets such as inventories and prepaid expenses that are less readily convertible into cash, the acid-test ratio may provide a better indication of a company's liquidity than does the current ratio. We calculate the acid-test ratio in Illustration 12–13.

Acid-Test Ratio	Under Armour	Nike
Cash + Current investments + Accounts receivable / Current liabilities	$\dfrac{\$187.3 + 0 + \$92.2}{\$120.1} = 2.3 \text{ to } 1$	2.0 to 1

ILLUSTRATION 12–13
Acid-Test Ratio

Under Armour's acid-test ratio is 2.3 to 1 and compares favorably with Nike's ratio of 2.0 to 1. Both companies appear to have more than enough liquid assets available to pay current liabilities as they become due.

DEBT TO EQUITY RATIO

Other things being equal, the higher the debt to equity ratio, the higher the risk of bankruptcy. The reason is that, unlike shareholders, debt holders have the ability to force a company into bankruptcy for failing to pay interest or repay the debt in a timely manner. Illustration 12–14 shows the calculation of the debt to equity ratio for Under Armour and Nike.

Debt to Equity Ratio	Under Armour	Nike
Total liabilities / Stockholders' equity	$\dfrac{\$120.1 + \$25.4}{\$400.1} = 36.4\%$	52.4%

ILLUSTRATION 12–14
Debt to Equity Ratio

Under Armour has a debt to equity ratio of 36.4%, or $0.36 in liabilities for each $1 in stockholders' equity. Nike's debt to equity ratio is higher, at 52.4%.

Additional debt can be good for investors, as long as a company earns a return on borrowed funds in excess of interest costs. However, taking on additional debt can also be bad for investors, if a company earns less on borrowed funds than interest costs. This highlights the risk-return trade-off of debt. More debt increases the risk of bankruptcy, but it also increases the potential returns investors can enjoy.

TIMES INTEREST EARNED RATIO

We use the times interest earned ratio to compare interest payments with a company's income available to pay those charges. Interest payments are more often associated with long-term liabilities than with current liabilities such as wages, taxes, and utilities. That's why we classify this ratio as a solvency ratio rather than a liquidity ratio.

We calculate the times interest earned ratio by dividing net income *before* interest expense and income taxes by interest expense. To get to this amount, we just add interest expense and tax expense back to net income. We use net income before interest expense and income taxes as a reliable indicator of the amount available to pay the interest. Illustration 12–15 shows how the ratio is calculated.

ILLUSTRATION 12–15

Times Interest Earned Ratio

Times Interest Earned Ratio	Under Armour	Nike
$\dfrac{\text{Net income} + \text{Interest expense} + \text{Tax expense}}{\text{Interest expense}}$	$\dfrac{\$46.8 + \$2.4 + \$35.6}{\$2.4} = 35.3$	42.9

Under Armour's interest expense of $2.4 million is not listed separately on the income statement, but rather, is obtained from the notes to the financial statements. The times interest earned ratio for Under Armour is 35.3. That means Under Armour's net income before interest and taxes was 35.3 times the amount it needed for interest expense alone. In comparison, Nike has an even better times interest earned ratio of 42.9. Both Under Armour and Nike generate more than enough income to cover their interest payments.

 KEY POINT

We categorize risk ratios into liquidity ratios and solvency ratios. Liquidity ratios focus on the company's ability to pay *current* liabilities, whereas solvency ratios focus more on *long-term* liabilities.

Let's Review

The income statement and balance sheet for **Nike** for the years ending May 31, 2009 and 2008, are shown below.

NIKE Income Statement For the years ended May 31 ($ in millions)		
	2009	**2008**
Net sales	$19,176.1	$18,627.0
Cost of goods sold	10,571.7	10,239.6
Gross profit	8,604.4	8,387.4
Operating expenses	6,745.9	5,953.7
Operating income	1,858.5	2,433.7
Other income (expense)	98.0*	69.2
Income before tax	1,956.5	2,502.9
Income tax expense	469.8	619.5
Net income	$ 1,486.7	$ 1,883.4

*Includes interest expense of $46.7

NIKE
Balance Sheet
May 31
($ in millions)

	2009	2008
Assets		
Current assets:		
Cash	$ 2,291.1	$ 2,133.9
Net receivables	3,156.3	3,022.5
Current investments	1,164.0	642.2
Inventory	2,357.0	2,438.4
Other current assets	765.6	602.3
Total current assets	$ 9,734.0	8,839.3
Property and equipment	1,957.7	1,891.1
Intangible assets	660.9	1,191.9
Other assets	897.0	520.4
Total assets	$13,249.6	$12,442.7
Liabilities and Stockholders' Equity		
Current liabilities	$ 3,277.0	$ 3,321.5
Long-term liabilities	1,279.2	1,295.6
Stockholders' equity	8,693.4	7,825.6
Total liabilities and stockholders' equity	$13,249.6	$12,442.7

Required:

Calculate the eight risk ratios we've discussed for Nike for the year ended May 31, 2009.

Solution:

Risk Ratios	Calculations	
Liquidity		
Receivables turnover ratio	$\dfrac{\$19,176.1}{(\$3,022.5 + \$3,156.3)/2}$	= 6.2 times
Average collection period	$\dfrac{365}{6.2}$	= 58.9 days
Inventory turnover ratio	$\dfrac{\$10,571.7}{(\$2,438.4 + \$2,357.0)/2}$	= 4.4 times
Average days in inventory	$\dfrac{365}{4.4}$	= 83.0 days
Current ratio	$\dfrac{\$9,734.0}{\$3,277.0}$	= 3.0 to 1
Acid-test ratio	$\dfrac{\$2,291.1 + \$1,164.0 + \$3,156.3}{\$3,277.0}$	= 2.0 to 1
Solvency		
Debt to equity ratio	$\dfrac{\$3,277.0 + \$1,279.2}{\$8,693.4}$	= 52.4%
Times interest earned ratio	$\dfrac{\$1,486.7 + \$46.7 + \$469.8}{\$46.7}$	= 42.9 times

Suggested Homework:
BE12-6, BE12-7;
E12-5, E12-7;
P12-4A&B, P12-6A&B

Profitability Analysis

■ LO4
Use ratios to analyze a
company's profitability.

Our next six ratios focus on profitability, the primary measure of company success. Profitability ratios measure the earnings or operating effectiveness of a company. Not only is profitability necessary just to survive as a company, it's the primary indicator used by investors and creditors in making financial decisions. Illustration 12–16 summarizes the six profitability ratios we have examined, the chapters in which we discussed them, and how we calculate them.

ILLUSTRATION 12–16
Profitability Ratios

Profitability Ratios	Chapter	Calculations
Gross profit ratio	6	$\dfrac{\text{Gross profit}}{\text{Net sales}}$
Return on assets	7	$\dfrac{\text{Net income}}{\text{Average total assets}}$
Profit margin	7	$\dfrac{\text{Net income}}{\text{Net sales}}$
Asset turnover	7	$\dfrac{\text{Net sales}}{\text{Average total assets}}$
Return on equity	10	$\dfrac{\text{Net income}}{\text{Average stockholders' equity}}$
Price-earnings ratio	10	$\dfrac{\text{Stock price}}{\text{Earnings per share}}$

GROSS PROFIT RATIO

Common Terms Gross profit is also called *gross margin* or *gross profit margin*.

The gross profit ratio indicates the portion of each dollar of sales above its cost of goods sold. We calculate this ratio as gross profit (net sales minus cost of goods sold) divided by net sales. Gross profit ratios vary by industry. For example, consider the average gross profit ratio for the following major industries: retail grocery stores (27%), apparel stores (35%), and major drug manufacturers (68%). Illustration 12–17 presents the calculation of the gross profit ratio for Under Armour and a comparison with Nike. **We'll calculate Nike's profitability ratios in a review problem at the end of this section.**

ILLUSTRATION 12–17
Gross Profit Ratio

Gross Profit Ratio	Under Armour	Nike
$\dfrac{\text{Gross profit}}{\text{Net sales}}$	$\dfrac{\$413.0}{\$856.4} = 48.2\%$	44.9%

With a gross profit ratio of 48.2%, Under Armour sells its merchandise for about twice what it costs to produce. In comparison, Nike has a gross profit ratio of 44.9%. Nike's gross profit is still quite high, but not as high as Under Armour's.

Gross profit ratios normally decline as competition increases. For example, a patented drug can sell for many times its production cost. However, when the patent expires, competition from generic drug companies drives down selling prices, resulting in lower gross profit ratios.

How Warren Buffett Interprets Financial Statements

Warren Buffett is one of the world's wealthiest individuals, with investments in the billions. As founder and CEO of **Berkshire Hathaway**, an investment company located in Omaha, Nebraska, he is also highly regarded as one of the world's top investment advisors. So, what's the secret to his success? Warren Buffett is best known for his attention to details, carefully examining each line in the financial statements.

Warren Buffett seeks to invest in companies with a "durable competitive advantage." That means he is looking for profitable companies that can maintain their profitability over time. To find these companies, he carefully studies their income statements for evidence of above-average profits that can be sustained despite actions taken by competing companies. He also studies their balance sheets looking for financially healthy companies. Some of his major investments include **GEICO** insurance, **Burlington Northern** railroads, **Goldman Sachs**, **Pampered Chef**, **See's Candies**, and **Fruit of the Loom**. Warren Buffett uses nearly identical ratios to the ones covered in this chapter, but it's his unique ability to interpret those ratios in selecting the best possible investments that sets him apart. ●

RETURN ON ASSETS

Return on assets measures the income the company earns on each dollar invested in assets. We calculate it as net income divided by *average* (not *ending*) total assets. Average total assets are calculated as beginning total assets plus ending total assets divided by 2. Illustration 12–18 provides the calculation of return on assets for Under Armour and a comparison to Nike.

Common Terms Return on assets is referred to as *ROA*.

Return on Assets	Under Armour	Nike
$\dfrac{\text{Net income}}{\text{Average total assets}}$	$\dfrac{\$46.8}{(\$487.6 + \$545.6)/2} = 9.1\%$	11.6%

ILLUSTRATION 12–18
Return on Assets

Under Armour earned a return on assets of 9.1%, which is lower than Nike's return on assets of 11.6%. As we learned in Chapter 7, we can further separate return on assets into two ratios: profit margin and asset turnover. Illustration 12–19 shows the calculations.

Return on assets	=	Profit margin	×	Asset turnover
$\dfrac{\text{Net income}}{\text{Average total assets}}$	=	$\dfrac{\text{Net income}}{\text{Net sales}}$	×	$\dfrac{\text{Net sales}}{\text{Average total assets}}$

ILLUSTRATION 12–19
Components of Return on Assets

Some companies, like **Saks Fifth Avenue**, rely more on high profit margins, while other companies, like **Dollar General**, rely more on asset turnover. Investors are especially intrigued by companies that can obtain both—high profit margins and high asset turnover. For example, **Apple, Inc.** introduced several extremely popular products such as the iPod and the iPhone that generated both high profit margin and high asset turnover for the company.

PROFIT MARGIN

Profit margin measures the income earned on each dollar of sales. We calculate it by dividing net income by net sales. Illustration 12–20 provides the calculation of profit margin for Under Armour and Nike.

ILLUSTRATION 12–20
Profit Margin

Profit Margin	Under Armour	Nike
$\dfrac{\text{Net income}}{\text{Net sales}}$	$\dfrac{\$46.8}{\$856.4} = 5.5\%$	7.8%

Under Armour has a profit margin of 5.5%, meaning that for every dollar of sales, 5.5 cents goes toward net income. Nike has a higher profit margin of 7.8%. Now let's look at asset turnover, the second factor influencing return on assets.

ASSET TURNOVER

Asset turnover measures sales volume in relation to the investment in assets. We calculate asset turnover as sales divided by *average* (not *ending*) total assets. Illustration 12–21 presents the calculation of asset turnover.

ILLUSTRATION 12–21
Asset Turnover

Asset Turnover	Under Armour	Nike
$\dfrac{\text{Net sales}}{\text{Average total assets}}$	$\dfrac{\$856.4}{(\$487.6 + \$545.6)/2} = 1.7 \text{ times}$	1.5 times

Under Armour's asset turnover is 1.7. Under Armour generates $1.70 in sales for every dollar it invests in assets. Nike's asset turnover is just slightly lower at 1.5.

RETURN ON EQUITY

Common Terms Return on equity is referred to as *ROE*.

Return on equity measures the income earned for each dollar in stockholders' equity. Return on equity relates net income to the investment made by owners of the business. The ratio is calculated by dividing net income by *average* stockholders' equity. Average stockholders' equity is calculated as beginning stockholders' equity plus ending stockholders' equity divided by 2. Illustration 12–22 shows the calculation of return on equity.

ILLUSTRATION 12–22
Return on Equity

Return on Equity	Under Armour	Nike
$\dfrac{\text{Net income}}{\text{Average stockholders' equity}}$	$\dfrac{\$46.8}{(\$331.1 + \$400.1)/2} = 12.8\%$	18.0%

Under Armour has a return on equity of 12.8%. Its net income is 12.8 cents for every dollar invested in equity. Nike has an even higher return on equity of 18.0%.

Why is Nike's return on assets 2.5 percentage points higher than Under Armour's, while Nike's return on equity is over 5 percentage points higher than Under Armour's? The answer relates to *financial leverage*—the amount of debt each company carries. Recall that Nike has a higher debt to equity ratio. Remember, too, that debt can be good for the company as long as the return on investment exceeds the interest cost of borrowing. Both Under Armour and Nike enjoy returns well in excess of the interest cost on borrowed funds. By carrying greater debt, Nike is able to provide a higher return on equity in relationship to its return on assets, further benefiting the investors in the company.

PRICE-EARNINGS RATIO

The price-earnings (PE) ratio compares a company's share price with its earnings per share. The PE ratio is an indication of investors' expectations of future earnings for the company. Illustration 12–23 presents the PE ratios for Under Armour and Nike.

Price-Earnings Ratio	Under Armour	Nike
$\dfrac{\text{Stock price}}{\text{Earnings per share}}$	$\dfrac{\$27.27}{\$0.94} = 29.0$	18.6

ILLUSTRATION 12–23

Price-Earnings Ratio

At the end of 2009, Under Armour's closing stock price is $27.27, and the company reports earnings per share for 2009 of $0.94. This represents a PE ratio of 29.0. The stock price is trading at 29 times earnings. In contrast, the PE ratio for Nike is 18.6. Stocks commonly trade at a PE ratio somewhere between 15 and 20, similar to Nike's. At 29.0, Under Armour has a very high PE ratio. It appears that, at least at this point in time, investors are more optimistic about Under Armour's future earnings potential than Nike's, as shown by the price they are willing to pay for **Under Armour** stock.

As we discussed in Chapter 10, investors pursue two basic types of stock investments: growth stocks and value stocks. Growth stocks, like Under Armour, have high expectations of future earnings growth and therefore usually trade at higher PE ratios. Growth stocks are said to be *great* stocks at a *good* price. Value stocks have lower share prices in relationship to their fundamental ratios and therefore trade at lower (bargain) PE ratios. Value stocks are said to be *good* stocks at a *great* price. Some investors take the strategy of picking the stocks with the best future potential (growth stocks); other investors shop for the best bargains (value stocks); while most investors take a combined approach, searching for stocks based on both future potential and current stock price.

 KEY POINT

Profitability ratios measure the earnings or operating effectiveness of a company over a period of time, such as a year. Investors view profitability as the number one measure of company success.

Let's Review

The income statement and balance sheet for **Nike** for the years ending May 31, 2009 and 2008, follow. In addition, Nike reported earnings per share for the year ended May 31, 2009, of $3.07, and the closing stock price on May 31, 2009, was $57.05.

Required:

Calculate the six profitability ratios we've discussed for the year ended May 31, 2009.

NIKE Income Statement For the years ended May 31 ($ in millions)	2009	2008
Net sales	$19,176.1	$18,627.0
Cost of goods sold	10,571.7	10,239.6
Gross profit	8,604.4	8,387.4
Operating expenses	6,745.9	5,953.7
Operating income	1,858.5	2,433.7
Other income (expense)	98.0*	69.2
Income before tax	1,956.5	2,502.9
Income tax expense	469.8	619.5
Net income	$ 1,486.7	$ 1,883.4

NIKE Balance Sheet May 31 ($ in millions)	2009	2008
Assets		
Current assets:		
Cash	$ 2,291.1	$ 2,133.9
Net receivables	3,156.3	3,022.5
Current investments	1,164.0	642.2
Inventory	2,357.0	2,438.4
Other current assets	765.6	602.3
Total current assets	9,734.0	8,839.3
Property and equipment	1,957.7	1,891.1
Intangible assets	660.9	1,191.9
Other assets	897.0	520.4
Total assets	$13,249.6	$12,442.7
Liabilities and Stockholders' Equity		
Current liabilities	$ 3,277.0	$ 3,321.5
Long-term liabilities	1,279.2	1,295.6
Stockholders' equity	8,693.4	7,825.6
Total liabilities and stockholders' equity	$13,249.6	$12,442.7

Solution:

Profitability Ratios	Calculations	
Gross profit ratio	$\dfrac{\$8,604.4}{\$19,176.1}$	= 44.9%
Return on assets	$\dfrac{\$1,486.7}{(\$12,442.7 + \$13,249.6)/2}$	= 11.6%
Profit margin	$\dfrac{\$1,486.7}{\$19,176.1}$	= 7.8%
Asset turnover	$\dfrac{\$19,176.1}{(\$12,442.7 + \$13,249.6)/2}$	= 1.5 times
Return on equity	$\dfrac{\$1,486.7}{(\$7,825.6 + \$8,693.4)/2}$	= 18.0%
Price-earnings ratio	$\dfrac{\$57.05}{\$3.07}$	= 18.6

Suggested Homework:
**BE12-10, BE12-11;
E12-6, E12-8;
P12-5A&B, P12-6A&B**

EARNINGS PERSISTENCE AND EARNINGS QUALITY

PART C

■ **LO5**
Distinguish persistent earnings from one-time items.

As we just saw when analyzing the PE ratio, investors predict Under Armour's earnings will grow more than Nike's. That's why Under Armour's stock price is higher relative to its current earnings. If for some reason investors see Under Armour's growth in earnings begin to slow, the stock price will fall. Investors are interested in whether earnings will remain strong and in the quality of those earnings. We look at those topics in this section.

Earnings Persistence and One-Time Income Items

To make predictions of future earnings, investors look for the current earnings that will continue or *persist* into future years. Some items that are part of net income in the current year are not expected to persist. We refer to these as *one-time income items*. The prime examples are (1) discontinued operations and (2) extraordinary items.

DISCONTINUED OPERATIONS

A **discontinued operation** is the sale or disposal of a significant component of a company's operations. For example, **IBM** reported a $515 million loss on discontinued operations on the sale of its hard-disk drive business to **Hitachi**. Sometimes a company will dispose of one of its business activities by ending operations and selling the individual assets. **We report any profits or losses on discontinued operations in the current year, separately from profits and losses on the portion of the business that will continue.** This allows investors the opportunity to exclude discontinued operations in their estimate of income that will persist into future years.

For an example of accounting for discontinued operations, let's consider Federer Sports Apparel, which has two business activities: a very profitable line of tennis apparel and a less profitable line of tennis shoes. Let's say that during 2012, the company decides to sell the tennis shoe business to a competitor, and the loss from discontinued operations is $2.5 million. We report the $2.5 million loss "net of tax,"

which means the $2.5 million includes the effect of taxes. Illustration 12–24 shows the income statement presentation of discontinued operations for Federer Sports Apparel.

ILLUSTRATION 12–24

Presentation of a Discontinued Operation

FEDERER SPORTS APPAREL Income Statement For the year ended December 31, 2012	
Sales revenue	$15,500,000
Cost of goods sold	7,000,000
Gross profit	8,500,000
Operating expenses	1,200,000
Depreciation expense	1,000,000
Other revenues and expenses	300,000
Income before tax	6,000,000
Income tax expense	2,000,000
Income from continuing operations	4,000,000
Discontinued operation:	
Loss from disposal of tennis shoe segment, net of tax	2,500,000
Net income	$ 1,500,000

With discontinued operations reported separately in the income statement, investors can clearly see the reported net income *excluding* the effects of the discontinued tennis shoe segment, $4.0 million in this situation. Investors then can use the income excluding discontinued operations, $4.0 million, to estimate income that persists into future periods.

EXTRAORDINARY ITEMS

Sometimes, companies have gains or losses that do not reflect normal operations and that are not likely to happen again. Because of the one-time, unusual nature of these items, we don't want to combine their effects on net income with those of normal operations. These items are referred to as extraordinary items.

To be an extraordinary item, an event that produces a gain or loss must meet two conditions. It must be (1) *unusual* in nature and (2) *infrequent* in occurrence. Unusual in nature means that the event is not normal for that type of company. Infrequent in occurrence means the company does not expect the event to happen again in the near future.

A company must consider the definition of extraordinary in the context of the environment in which it operates. For example, uninsured losses from a natural disaster such as a flood, earthquake, or hurricane would normally be reported as an extraordinary loss in the income statement. However if, due to lower land prices, a grower planted in a flood zone with the expectation of periodic flood losses, the loss would be included as part of operating costs and not categorized separately as an extraordinary item.

We report extraordinary items separately, net of taxes, near the bottom of the income statement just below discontinued operations. To illustrate, let's assume Federer Sports Apparel suffers an uninsured loss to property and equipment from an earthquake. This event meets both criteria for an extraordinary item—it is unusual in nature and infrequent in occurrence. If the loss (net of taxes) is $600,000, we would report it separately as an extraordinary item in the income statement as shown in Illustration 12–25.

ILLUSTRATION 12–25
Presentation of an
Extraordinary Item

FEDERER SPORTS APPAREL
Income Statement
For the year ended December 31, 2012

Sales revenue	$15,500,000
Cost of goods sold	7,000,000
Gross profit	8,500,000
Operating expenses	1,200,000
Depreciation expense	1,000,000
Other revenues and expenses	300,000
Income before tax	6,000,000
Income tax expense	2,000,000
Income from continuing operations	4,000,000
Discontinued operation:	
Loss from disposal of tennis shoe segment, net of tax	2,500,000
Extraordinary item:	
Loss from earthquake damage, net of tax	600,000
Net income	$ 900,000

As we do with discontinued operations, we report extraordinary items separately near the bottom of the income statement to allow investors to see that these are one-time items that should be excluded in estimating income that will persist into future periods.

Decision Point

Question ?	Accounting information 🖹	Analysis 🔍
Are any parts of the company's earnings not expected to persist into the future?	One-time items reported near the bottom of the income statement	Investors should normally exclude discontinued operations and extraordinary items in estimating future earnings performance

INTERNATIONAL FINANCIAL REPORTING STANDARDS (IFRS)

The FASB and the IASB work closely together in developing new standards. Discontinued operations are a good example. Rather than coming up with separate rules, the IASB reviewed the FASB's extensive work in the area and adopted nearly identical standards for the reporting of discontinued operations.

Unfortunately, the FASB and IASB do not always agree. Extraordinary items are a good example of that. The IASB does not allow the reporting of extraordinary items, due to the difficulty in determining across cultures what is unusual in nature and infrequent in occurrence. Hopefully, differences like this will be resolved as both standard setters continue their work toward global convergence of accounting standards.

For more discussion, see Appendix E.

OTHER REVENUES AND EXPENSES

The sale or disposal of a significant component of a company's operations is recorded as discontinued operations. However, the sale or disposal of most assets is reported, not as discontinued operations, but rather as other revenues and expenses. For example, **Marie Callender's** has both a restaurant business and a frozen-food business with its products sold in grocery stores. The sale of either the restaurant business or the frozen-food business would likely qualify as discontinued operations. On the other hand, the sale of a single restaurant or a single frozen-food product to another company would not be recorded as discontinued operations. Rather, the gain or loss on the sale of the asset would be included as "other revenues and expenses" (just below operating expenses) in the income statement.

Similarly, many items meet one, but not both, criteria for extraordinary item treatment. In that case, they are correctly excluded from extraordinary items. Common examples include losses due to the write-down of receivables, inventory, or long-term assets; gains or losses on the sale of long-term assets; losses due to an employee strike; or losses due to business restructuring. Each of these items is reported in the income statement as "other revenues and expenses" rather than as extraordinary items. Illustration 12–26 provides a summary.

ILLUSTRATION 12–26 Comparison of Extraordinary Items with Other Revenues and Expenses	**Extraordinary Items** **"Unusual in nature"** *and* **"Infrequent"** **Examples** 1. Uninsured losses from a natural disaster such as a flood, earthquake, or hurricane. 2. Takeover of property by a foreign government.	**Other Revenues and Expenses** **"Unusual in nature"** *or* **"Infrequent"** **Examples** 1. Losses due to the write-down of receivables, inventory, or long-term assets. 2. Gains or losses on the sale of long-term assets. 3. Losses due to an employee strike. 4. Losses due to business restructuring.

Decision Maker's Perspective

Does Location in the Income Statement Matter?

As manager of a company, would you prefer to show a loss as part of other expenses or as an extraordinary item in the income statement? Your first response might be that it really doesn't matter, since the choice affects only the location in the income statement and has no effect on the final net income number. This is true, yet many managers still prefer to show a loss near the bottom of the income statement as extraordinary, rather than placing it higher on the income statement as part of other expenses. Why?

One use of an income statement by investors is to estimate income that will persist into future years. Understandably, a manager might want to report a loss as extraordinary as a way to signal to investors that it is a one-time item and they should exclude it in estimating income for future years. Doing so would result in the appearance of a more profitable company, potentially boosting the company's stock price. So, at least in some situations, it's not just the final net income number that matters, but also the location of the item in the income statement that matters as well. ●

KEY POINT

When using a company's current earnings to estimate future earnings performance, investors normally should exclude discontinued operations and extraordinary items.

Quality of Earnings

Quality of earnings refers to the ability of reported earnings to reflect the company's true earnings, as well as the usefulness of reported earnings to predict future earnings. To illustrate the concept, we continue our example of Federer Sports Apparel.

FINANCIAL STATEMENTS BY MR. SAMPRAS

Let's move one year forward to 2013 for our example company, Federer Sports Apparel. Mr. Sampras, as chief financial officer (CFO), is responsible for all the accounting, finance, and MIS operations of the business. He has developed a reputation for his conservative, calm, laid-back management style. Illustration 12–27 presents the preliminary financial statements for 2013, prepared under the supervision of Mr. Sampras.

■ LO6
Explain quality of earnings and distinguish between conservative and aggressive accounting practices.

ILLUSTRATION 12–27
Financial Statements Prepared by Mr. Sampras

FEDERER SPORTS APPAREL
Income Statement
For the year ended December 31, 2013

Sales revenue	$ 18,800,000
Cost of goods sold	13,200,000
Gross profit	5,600,000
Operating expenses	1,600,000
Depreciation expense	1,000,000
Inventory write-down	200,000
Loss (litigation)	1,500,000
Income before tax	1,300,000
Income tax expense	450,000
Net income	$ 850,000

FEDERER SPORTS APPAREL
Balance Sheet
December 31

	2013	2012
Cash	$ 2,300,000	$ 800,000
Accounts receivable	1,500,000	1,200,000
Inventory	2,800,000	1,700,000
Buildings	11,000,000	11,000,000
Less: Accumulated depreciation	(2,000,000)	(1,000,000)
Total assets	$15,600,000	$13,700,000
Accounts payable	$ 1,450,000	$ 1,700,000
Contingent liability	1,500,000	0
Common stock	8,000,000	8,000,000
Retained earnings	4,650,000	4,000,000
Total liabilities and stockholders' equity	$15,600,000	$13,700,000

(continued)

ILLUSTRATION 12–27
(concluded)

FEDERER SPORTS APPAREL Statement of Cash Flows For the year ended December 31, 2013		
Cash Flows from Operating Activities		
Net income	$ 850,000	
Adjustments:		
Depreciation expense	1,000,000	
Increase in accounts receivable	(300,000)	
Increase in inventory	(1,100,000)	
Decrease in accounts payable	(250,000)	
Increase in contingent liability	1,500,000	
Net cash flows from operating activities		$1,700,000
Cash Flows from Investing Activities		
Net cash flows from investing activities		0
Cash Flows from Financing Activities		
Payment of cash dividends	(200,000)	
Net cash flows from financing activities		(200,000)
Net increase (decrease) in cash		1,500,000
Cash at the beginning of the period		800,000
Cash at the end of the period		$2,300,000

SAMPRAS RETIRES AND McENROE IS HIRED

After completing the preliminary financial statements for 2013, Mr. Sampras retires, and the company hires a new CFO, Mr. McEnroe. In contrast to Mr. Sampras, Mr. McEnroe has a more aggressive, in-your-face management style. Mr. McEnroe has made it clear that he is now in charge and some changes will need to be made. Illustration 12–28 outlines four accounting changes Mr. McEnroe proposed. They are based on accounting topics we discussed in Chapters 5, 6, 7, and 8.

ILLUSTRATION 12–28

Mr. McEnroe's
Proposed Changes

Mr. McEnroe's Proposed Changes

1. Estimate of bad debts. At the end of 2013, Mr. Sampras estimated that future bad debts will be 6% to 10% of current accounts receivable. He decided to play it safe and recorded an allowance equal to 10% of accounts receivable, or $150,000. Mr. McEnroe proposes changing the estimate to be 6% of accounts receivable, or $90,000. This change would increase net accounts receivable and decrease bad debt expense by $60,000.

2. Write-down of inventory. Mr. Sampras recorded a $200,000 write-down of inventory as follows:

December 31, 2013	Debit	Credit
Loss	200,000	
Inventory		200,000
(Write-down inventory)		

Mr. McEnroe insists the write-down was not necessary because the decline in inventory value was only temporary. Therefore, he proposes eliminating this entry, which would increase inventory and decrease loss on inventory write-down by $200,000.

3. Change in depreciation estimate. For the building purchased for $11 million at the beginning of 2012, Mr. Sampras recorded depreciation expense of $1 million in 2012 and 2013, using the straight-line method over 10 years with an estimated salvage value of $1 million. Beginning in 2013, Mr. McEnroe proposes calculating depreciation over 20 years instead of 10 and using an estimated salvage value of $500,000. That change decreases accumulated depreciation and depreciation expense in 2013 by $500,000.

(continued)

4. Loss contingency. At the end of 2013, the company's lawyer advised Mr. Sampras that there was a 70% chance of losing a litigation suit of $1,500,000 filed against the company. Mr. Sampras recorded the possible loss as follows:

December 31, 2013	Debit	Credit
Loss	1,500,000	
Contingent Liability		1,500,000
(Record litigation against the company)		

ILLUSTRATION 12–28

(concluded)

Mr. McEnroe argues that a 70% likelihood of losing the litigation is reasonably possible, but not probable. Therefore, he proposes removing the litigation entry from the accounting records. The change would remove the loss and decrease liabilities by $1,500,000.

FINANCIAL STATEMENTS BY MR. McENROE

How will the proposed accounting changes affect net income? Illustration 12–29 presents the preliminary income statement prepared by Mr. Sampras, the effect of the accounting changes, and the updated income statement prepared by Mr. McEnroe.

FEDERER SPORTS APPAREL
Income Statement
For the year ended December 31, 2013

	Sampras	Changes	McEnroe
Sales revenue	$18,800,000		$18,800,000
Cost of goods sold	13,200,000		13,200,000
Gross profit	5,600,000		5,600,000
Operating expenses	1,600,000	$ (60,000)	1,540,000
Depreciation expense	1,000,000	(500,000)	500,000
Inventory write-down	200,000	(200,000)	0
Loss (litigation)	1,500,000	(1,500,000)	0
Income before tax	1,300,000	2,260,000	3,560,000
Income tax expense	450,000		450,000
Net income	$ 850,000	$2,260,000	$ 3,110,000

ILLUSTRATION 12–29

Income Statement
Revised by
Mr. McEnroe

The four proposed accounting changes cause net income to more than triple, from $850,000 to $3,110,000. Notice that all four changes proposed by Mr. McEnroe increase net income: The change in the estimated allowance for uncollectible accounts increases net income $60,000; the elimination of the inventory write-down increases net income $200,000; the change in useful life to calculate depreciation method increases net income $500,000; and the elimination of the litigation liability increases net income $1,500,000. Note that income tax expense did not change because all of these changes affect financial income but not taxable income.

Look Out for Earnings Management at Year-End

Let's assume you're an auditor and all four of the final changes to the accounting records for the year increase income. Wouldn't you be just a little concerned? It may be that all four adjustments are perfectly legitimate, but it also may be an indication management is inflating earnings. Year-end adjustments, especially those with an increasing or decreasing pattern, should be investigated with greater skepticism. ●

Decision Maker's Perspective

How do positive changes to net income affect the balance sheet? Illustration 12–30 presents the balance sheet prepared by Mr. Sampras, the effect of the four accounting changes, and the updated balance sheet prepared by Mr. McEnroe.

ILLUSTRATION 12–30

Balance Sheet Revised by Mr. McEnroe

FEDERER SPORTS APPAREL Balance Sheet December 31	Sampras	Changes	McEnroe
Assets			
Cash	$ 2,300,000		$ 2,300,000
Accounts receivable	1,500,000	$ 60,000	1,560,000
Inventory	2,800,000	200,000	3,000,000
Buildings	11,000,000		11,000,000
Less: Accumulated depreciation	(2,000,000)	500,000	(1,500,000)
Total assets	$15,600,000	760,000	$16,360,000
Liabilities and Stockholders' Equity			
Accounts payable	$ 1,450,000		$ 1,450,000
Contingent liability	1,500,000	(1,500,000)	0
Common stock	8,000,000		8,000,000
Retained earnings	4,650,000	2,260,000	6,910,000
Total liabilities and stockholders' equity	$15,600,000	$ 760,000	$16,360,000

The balance sheet also improves from the proposed adjustments. Total assets increase due to increases in receivables and inventory plus a decrease in accumulated depreciation. Total liabilities decrease due to the elimination of the $1.5 million litigation liability. Stockholders' equity also goes up, due to the increase in retained earnings caused by the increase in reported net income for the year.

What about the effects of the proposed adjustments on the statement of cash flows? Illustration 12–31 provides the statement of cash flows as revised by Mr. McEnroe.

ILLUSTRATION 12–31

Statement of Cash Flows Revised by Mr. McEnroe

FEDERER SPORTS APPAREL Statement of Cash Flows For the year ended December 31, 2013	Sampras	Changes	McEnroe
Operating Activities			
Net income	$ 850,000	$2,260,000	$3,110,000
Adjustments:			
Depreciation expense	1,000,000	(500,000)	500,000
Increase in accounts receivable	(300,000)	(60,000)	(360,000)
Increase in inventory	(1,100,000)	(200,000)	(1,300,000)
Decrease in accounts payable	(250,000)		(250,000)
Increase in contingent liability	1,500,000	(1,500,000)	0
Net cash flows from operating activities	1,700,000	0	1,700,000
Investing Activities	0		0
Financing Activities			
Payment of cash dividends	(200,000)		(200,000)
Net cash flows from financing activities	(200,000)		(200,000)
Net increase (decrease) in cash	1,500,000		1,500,000
Cash at the beginning of the period	800,000		800,000
Cash at the end of the period	$2,300,000		$2,300,000

Interestingly, the proposed changes have **no effect at all on total operating cash flows or on the overall change in cash.** Net cash flows from operating activities remain at $1,700,000 after the four proposed transactions. The net increase in cash remains at $1,500,000. None of the proposed changes affects the underlying cash flows of the company. Rather, each improves the *appearance* of amounts reported in the income statement and the balance sheet.

SYMBOLISM REVEALED

By now you've probably guessed that Mr. Sampras and Mr. McEnroe are intended to symbolize an important accounting concept. Mr. Sampras represents conservative accounting practices. Conservative accounting practices are those that result in reporting lower income, lower assets, and higher liabilities. The larger estimation of the allowance for uncollectible accounts, the write-down of overvalued inventory, the use of a shorter useful life for depreciation, and the recording of a contingent litigation loss are all examples of conservative accounting.

In contrast, Mr. McEnroe represents aggressive accounting practices. Aggressive accounting practices result in reporting higher income, higher assets, and lower liabilities. Mr. McEnroe's lower estimation of the allowance for uncollectible accounts, waiting to report an inventory write-down, choosing a longer useful life for depreciation, and waiting to record a litigation loss all are examples of more aggressive accounting. Everyone involved in business, not just accountants, needs to recognize the difference between conservative and aggressive accounting practices.

KEY POINT

Changes in accounting estimates and practices alter the appearance of amounts reported in the income statement and the balance sheet. Changes in accounting estimates and practices usually have no effect on a company's underlying cash flows.

Classify each of the following accounting practices as conservative or aggressive.

1. Increase the allowance for uncollectible accounts.
2. When costs are going up, change from LIFO to FIFO.
3. Increase the useful life for calculating depreciation.
4. Record a larger expense for warranties.
5. Wait to record revenue until the earnings process is complete.

Solution:

1. Conservative.
2. Aggressive.
3. Aggressive.
4. Conservative.
5. Conservative.

Let's Review

Suggested Homework:
**BE12-14, BE12-15;
E12-14, E12-15**

ETHICAL DILEMMA

Late one Friday afternoon, Dana Woo, the controller at Horrocks Storage & Transport (HST), is reviewing the financial statements she just prepared.

For over a year, the economy has been in a down cycle, and the transportation industry has been particularly hard hit. As a result, Dana expected HST's financial results would not be pleasant news to shareholders. However, what Dana saw in the preliminary statements made her sigh aloud. Results were much worse than she feared.

"Stew (the company president) already is in the doghouse with shareholders," Dana thinks to herself. "When they see these numbers, they'll hang him out to dry."

"I wonder if he's considered some strategic accounting changes," she says to herself, after reflecting on the situation. "The bad news could be softened quite a bit by changing inventory methods from LIFO to FIFO or reconsidering some of the estimates used in depreciation."

Would Dana violate ethical standards by proposing her ideas to the company president? When do aggressive accounting practices become unethical accounting practices?

KEY POINTS BY LEARNING OBJECTIVE

LO1 Perform vertical analysis.

For vertical analysis, we express each item as a percentage of the same base amount, such as a percentage of sales in the income statement or as a percentage of total assets in the balance sheet.

LO2 Perform horizontal analysis.

We use horizontal analysis to analyze trends in financial statement data, such as the amount of change and the percentage change, for one company over time.

LO3 Use ratios to analyze a company's risk.

We categorize risk ratios into liquidity ratios and solvency ratios. Liquidity ratios focus on the company's ability to pay *current* liabilities, whereas solvency ratios focus more on *long-term* liabilities.

LO4 Use ratios to analyze a company's profitability.

Profitability ratios measure the earnings or operating effectiveness of a company over a period of time, such as a year. Investors view profitability as the number one measure of company success.

LO5 Distinguish persistent earnings from one-time items.

When using a company's current earnings to estimate future earnings performance, investors normally should exclude discontinued operations and extraordinary items.

LO6 Explain quality of earnings and distinguish between conservative and aggressive accounting practices.

Changes in accounting estimates and practices alter the appearance of amounts reported in the income statement and the balance sheet. Changes in accounting estimates and practices usually have no effect on a company's underlying cash flows.

GLOSSARY

Acid-test ratio: Cash, current investments, and accounts receivable divided by current liabilities; measures the availability of liquid current assets to pay current liabilities. **p. 575**

Aggressive accounting practices: Practices that result in reporting higher income, higher assets, and lower liabilities. **p. 591**

Asset turnover: Net sales divided by average total assets, which measures the sales per dollar of assets invested. **p. 580**

Average collection period: Approximate number of days the average accounts receivable balance is outstanding. It equals 365 divided by the receivables turnover ratio. **p. 572**

Average days in inventory: Approximate number of days the average inventory is held. It equals 365 days divided by the inventory turnover ratio. **p. 573**

Conservative accounting practices: Practices that result in reporting lower income, lower assets, and higher liabilities. **p. 591**

Current ratio: Current assets divided by current liabilities; measures the availability of current assets to pay current liabilities. **p. 574**

Debt to equity ratio: Total liabilities divided by stockholders' equity; measures a company's solvency risk. **p. 575**

Discontinued operation: The sale or disposal of a significant component of a company's operations. **p. 583**

Extraordinary item: An event that is (1) unusual in nature and (2) infrequent in occurrence. **p. 584**

Gross profit ratio: Gross profit divided by net sales; measures the amount by which the sale price of inventory exceeds its cost per dollar of sales. **p. 578**

Growth stocks: Stocks that have high expectations of future earnings growth and therefore usually trade at higher PE ratios. **p. 581**

Horizontal analysis: Analyzes trends in financial statement data for a single company over time. **p. 567**

Inventory turnover ratio: Cost of goods sold divided by average inventory; the number of times the firm sells its average inventory balance during a reporting period. **p. 573**

Liquidity: Refers to a company's ability to pay its current liabilities. **p. 571**

Price-earnings (PE) ratio: Compares a company's share price with its earnings per share. **p. 581**

Profit margin: Net income divided by net sales; indicates the earnings per dollar of sales. **p. 580**

Profitability ratios: Measure the earnings or operating effectiveness of a company. **p. 578**

Quality of earnings: Refers to the ability of reported earnings to reflect the company's true earnings, as well as the usefulness of reported earnings to predict future earnings. **p. 587**

Receivables turnover ratio: Net credit sales divided by average accounts receivable; the number of times during a year that the average accounts receivable balance is collected ("turns over"). **p. 572**

Return on assets: Net income divided by average total assets; measures the amount of net income generated for each dollar invested in assets. **p. 579**

Return on equity: Net income divided by average stockholders' equity; measures the income generated per dollar of equity. **p. 580**

Solvency: Refers to a company's ability to pay its long-term liabilities. **p. 571**

Times interest earned ratio: Ratio that compares interest expense with income available to pay those charges. **p. 575**

Value stocks: Stocks that have lower share prices in relationship to their fundamental ratios and therefore trade at lower (bargain) PE ratios. **p. 581**

Vertical analysis: Expresses each item in a financial statement as a percentage of the same base amount. **p. 564**

SELF-STUDY QUESTIONS

1. When using vertical analysis, we express income statement accounts as a percentage of: ■ **LO1**
   a. Net income.
   b. Sales.
   c. Gross profit.
   d. Total assets.

2. When using vertical analysis, we express balance sheet accounts as a percentage of: ■ **LO1**
   a. Total assets.
   b. Total liabilities.
   c. Total stockholders' equity.
   d. Sales.

3. Horizontal analysis examines trends in a company: ■ **LO2**
   a. Between income statement accounts in the same year.
   b. Between balance sheet accounts in the same year.
   c. Between income statement and balance sheet accounts in the same year.
   d. Over time.

■ LO2

4. Which of the following is an example of horizontal analysis?
   a. Comparing operating expenses with sales.
   b. Comparing the growth in sales with the growth in cost of goods sold.
   c. Comparing property, plant, and equipment with total assets.
   d. Comparing gross profit across companies.

■ LO3

5. Which of the following ratios is most useful in evaluating solvency?
   a. Receivables turnover ratio.
   b. Inventory turnover ratio.
   c. Debt to equity ratio.
   d. Current ratio.

■ LO3

6. Which of the following is a positive sign that a company can quickly turn its receivables into cash?
   a. A low receivables turnover ratio.
   b. A high receivables turnover ratio.
   c. A low average collection period.
   d. Both a high receivables turnover ratio and a low average collection period.

■ LO4

7. The Sports Shack reports net income of $120,000, sales of $1,200,000, and average assets of $960,000. The profit margin is:
   a. 10%.
   b. 12.5%.
   c. 80%.
   d. 125%.

■ LO4

8. The Sports Shack reports net income of $120,000, sales of $1,200,000, and average assets of $960,000. The asset turnover is:
   a. 0.10 times.
   b. 0.80 times.
   c. 8 times.
   d. 1.25 times.

■ LO5

9. An extraordinary item must meet which of the following criteria?
   a. Unusual in nature.
   b. Infrequent in occurrence.
   c. Unusual in nature *and* infrequent in occurrence.
   d. Unusual in nature *or* infrequent in occurrence.

■ LO6

Check out
www.mhhe.com/succeed
for more multiple-choice
questions.

10. Which of the following is an example of a conservative accounting practice?
   a. Adjust the allowance for uncollectible accounts to a larger amount.
   b. Record inventory at market rather than lower-of-cost-or-market.
   c. Change from double-declining-balance to straight-line depreciation.
   d. Record sales revenue before it is actually earned.

Note: For answers, see the last page of the chapter.

REVIEW QUESTIONS

■ LO1, 2

1. Identify the three types of comparisons commonly used in financial statement analysis.

■ LO1, 2

2. Explain the difference between vertical and horizontal analysis.

3. In performing vertical analysis, we express each item in a financial statement as a percentage of a base amount. What base amount is commonly used for income statement accounts? For balance sheet accounts?   ■ LO1

4. Two profitable companies in the same industry have similar total stockholders' equity. However, one company has most of its equity balance in common stock, while the other company has most of its equity balance in retained earnings. Neither company has ever paid a dividend. Which one is more likely to be an older and more established company? Why?   ■ LO1

5. Why, in performing horizontal analysis, is it important to look at both the amount and the percentage change?   ■ LO2

6. Explain why ratios that compare an income statement account with a balance sheet account should express the balance sheet account as an average of the beginning and ending balances.   ■ LO3

7. What is the difference between liquidity and solvency?   ■ LO3

8. Which risk ratios best answer each of the following financial questions?   ■ LO3
   a. How quickly is a company able to collect its receivables?
   b. How quickly is a company able to sell its inventory?
   c. Is the company able to make interest payments as they become due?

9. Determine whether each of the following changes in risk ratios is good news or bad news about a company.   ■ LO3
   a. Increase in receivables turnover.
   b. Decrease in inventory turnover.
   c. Increase in the current ratio.
   d. Increase in the debt to equity ratio.

10. Pro Leather, a supplier to sporting goods manufacturers, has a current ratio of 0.90, based on current assets of $450,000 and current liabilities of $500,000. How, if at all, will a $100,000 purchase of inventory on account affect the current ratio?   ■ LO3

11. Which profitability ratios best answer each of the following financial questions?   ■ LO4
   a. What is the income earned for each dollar invested in assets?
   b. What is the income earned for each dollar of sales?
   c. What is the amount of sales for each dollar invested in assets?

12. Determine whether each of the following changes in profitability ratios normally is good news or bad news about a company.   ■ LO4
   a. Increase in profit margin.
   b. Decrease in asset turnover.
   c. Decrease in return on equity.
   d. Increase in the price-earnings ratio.

13. Hash Mark, Inc., reports a return on assets of 8% and a return on equity of 12%. Why do the two rates differ?   ■ LO4

14. Define earnings persistence. How does earnings persistence relate to the reporting of discontinued operations and extraordinary items?   ■ LO5

15. Shifting Formations, Inc., reports earnings per share of $1.30. In the following year, it reports bottom-line earnings per share of $1.25 but earnings per share on income before extraordinary items of $1.50. Is this trend in earnings per share favorable or unfavorable? Explain why.   ■ LO5

16. Explain the difference between conservative and aggressive accounting practices.   ■ LO6

17. Provide an example of a conservative accounting practice. Why is this practice conservative?   ■ LO6

■ **LO6**   18. Provide an example of an aggressive accounting practice. Why is this practice aggressive?

■ **LO6**   19. Goal Line Products makes several year-end adjustments, including an increase in the allowance for uncollectible accounts, a write-down of inventory, a decrease in the estimated useful life for depreciation, and an increase in the liability reported for litigation. What, if anything, do all these adjustments have in common?

■ **LO6**   20. Provide an example of an adjustment that improves the income statement and the balance sheet, but has no effect on cash flows.

BRIEF EXERCISES

Prepare vertical analysis (LO1)

BE12–1 Perform a vertical analysis on the following information.

	2012	2011
Cash	$ 300,000	$ 800,000
Accounts receivable	500,000	200,000
Inventory	800,000	700,000
Long-term assets	3,400,000	2,300,000
Total assets	$5,000,000	$4,000,000

Prepare horizontal analysis (LO2)

BE12–2 Using the information presented in BE12–1, perform a horizontal analysis providing both the amount and percentage change.

Understand vertical analysis (LO1)

BE12–3 Athletic World reports the following vertical analysis percentages.

	2012	2011
Sales	100%	100%
Cost of goods sold	48%	56%
Operating expenses	35%	30%

Did Athletic World's income before tax as a percentage of sales increase, decrease, or stay the same? If net income as a percentage of sales increases, does that mean net income also increases? Explain.

Understand horizontal analysis (LO2)

BE12–4 Sales are $2.5 million in 2011, $2.6 million in 2012, and $2.4 million in 2013. What is the percentage change from 2011 to 2012? What is the percentage change from 2012 to 2013? Be sure to indicate whether the percentage change is an increase or a decrease.

Understand percentage change (LO2)

BE12–5 If sales are $1,026,000 in 2013 and this represents a 14% increase over sales in 2012, what were sales in 2012?

Calculate receivables turnover (LO3)

BE12–6 Universal Sports Supply began the year with an accounts receivable balance of $100,000 and a year-end balance of $120,000. Credit sales of $600,000 generate a gross profit of $200,000. Calculate the receivables turnover ratio for the year.

Calculate inventory turnover (LO3)

BE12–7 Universal Sports Supply began the year with an inventory balance of $80,000 and a year-end balance of $60,000. Sales of $600,000 generate a gross profit of $200,000. Calculate the inventory turnover ratio for the year.

Understand inventory turnover (LO3)

BE12–8 The Intramural Sports Club reports sales revenue of $550,000. Inventory at both the beginning and end of the year totals $100,000. The inventory turnover ratio for the year is 4.0. What amount of gross profit does the company report in its income statement?

Understand the current ratio (LO3)

BE12–9 Dungy Training Company has a current ratio of 0.80 to 1, based on current assets of $6 million and current liabilities of $7.5 million. How, if at all, will an $800,000 cash purchase of inventory affect the current ratio? How, if at all, will an $800,000 purchase of inventory on account affect the current ratio?

BE12–10 Peyton's Palace has net income of $14 million on sales revenue of $120 million. Total assets were $86 million at the beginning of the year and $94 million at the end of the year. Calculate Peyton's return on assets, profit margin, and asset turnover ratios.

Calculate profitability ratios (LO4)

BE12–11 LaDanion's Limos reports net income of $120,000, average total assets of $600,000, and average total liabilities of $240,000. Calculate LaDanion's return on assets and return on equity ratios.

Calculate profitability ratios (LO4)

BE12–12 Kobe's Clinics provides health services and career counseling. Net income from the health services business this year is $22 million after tax. During the year, Kobe's Clinics sold the career counseling side of the business at a loss after tax of $6.5 million. Show how Kobe's Clinics would report this loss in the income statement, beginning with income from continuing operations of $22 million.

Record discontinued operations (LO5)

BE12–13 Game Time Sports owns a recreational facility with basketball courts, pitching machines, and athletic fields. Determine whether the firm should report each of the following items as discontinued operations, extraordinary items, or other expenses.

Classify income statement items (LO5)

1. Due to insurance concerns, Game Time sells a trampoline basketball game for a loss of $1,500.
2. Game Time experiences water damage due to a flood. The company replaces the basketball floors at a cost of $75,000. Unfortunately, Game Time does not carry flood insurance.
3. Game Time has revenues from three sources: basketball, baseball, and football. It sells the baseball operations for a loss of $55,000 to focus on the more profitable basketball and football operations.

BE12–14 Classify each of the following accounting practices as conservative or aggressive.

Distinguish between conservative and aggressive accounting practices (LO6)

1. Increase the allowance for uncollectible accounts.
2. When costs are rising, change from LIFO to FIFO.
3. Change from declining-balance to straight-line depreciation in the second year of an asset depreciated over 20 years.

BE12–15 Classify each of the following accepted accounting practices as conservative or aggressive.

Distinguish between conservative and aggressive accounting practices (LO6)

1. Use lower-of-cost-or-market to value inventory.
2. Expense all research and development costs rather than recording some research and development costs as an asset.
3. Record loss contingencies when they are probable and can be reasonably estimated, but do not record gain contingencies until they are certain.

EXERCISES

E12–1 Match (by letter) the following items with the description or example that best fits. Each letter is used only once.

Match terms with their definitions (LO1, 2, 3, 4, 5, 6)

Items
_____ 1. Vertical analysis.
_____ 2. Horizontal analysis.
_____ 3. Liquidity.
_____ 4. Solvency.
_____ 5. Discontinued operation.
_____ 6. Extraordinary item.
_____ 7. Quality of earnings.
_____ 8. Conservative accounting practices.

Descriptions
a. A company's ability to pay its current liabilities.
b. Accounting choices that result in reporting lower income, lower assets, and higher liabilities.

c. A profit or loss unusual in nature and infrequent in occurrence.

d. The ability of reported earnings to reflect the company's true earnings as well as the usefulness of reported earnings to help investors predict future earnings.

e. A tool to analyze trends in financial statement data for a single company over time.

f. The sale or disposal of a significant component of a company's operations.

g. A means to express each item in a financial statement as a percentage of a base amount.

h. A company's ability to pay its long-term liabilities.

Prepare vertical analysis (LO1)

E12–2 The income statement for Federer Sports Apparel for 2013 and 2012 is presented below.

FEDERER SPORTS APPAREL
Income Statement
For the years ended December 31

	2013	2012
Sales revenue	$18,800,000	$15,500,000
Cost of goods sold	13,200,000	7,000,000
Gross profit	5,600,000	8,500,000
Operating expenses	1,600,000	1,200,000
Depreciation expense	1,000,000	1,000,000
Inventory write-down	200,000	
Loss (litigation)	1,500,000	300,000
Income before tax	1,300,000	6,000,000
Income tax expense	450,000	2,000,000
Net income	$ 850,000	$ 4,000,000

Required:

Prepare a vertical analysis of the data for 2013 and 2012.

Prepare horizontal analysis (LO2)

E12–3 Refer to the information provided in E12–2.

Required:

Prepare a horizontal analysis for 2013 using 2012 as the base year.

Prepare vertical and horizontal analyses (LO1, 2)

E12–4 The balance sheet for Federer Sports Apparel for 2013 and 2012 is presented below.

FEDERER SPORTS APPAREL
Balance Sheet
December 31

	2013	2012
Assets		
Cash	$ 2,300,000	$ 800,000
Accounts receivable	1,500,000	1,200,000
Inventory	2,800,000	1,700,000
Buildings	11,000,000	11,000,000
Less: Accumulated depreciation	(2,000,000)	(1,000,000)
Total assets	$15,600,000	$13,700,000
Liabilities and Stockholders' Equity		
Accounts payable	$ 1,450,000	$ 1,700,000
Contingent liability	1,500,000	0
Common stock	8,000,000	8,000,000
Retained earnings	4,650,000	4,000,000
Total liabilities and stockholders' equity	$15,600,000	$13,700,000

Required:
1. Prepare a vertical analysis of the balance sheet data for 2013 and 2012. Express each amount as a percentage of total assets.
2. Prepare a horizontal analysis for 2013 using 2012 as the base year.

E12–5 The 2012 income statement of Adrian Express reports sales of $16 million, cost of goods sold of $9.6 million, and net income of $1.6 million. Balance sheet information is provided in the following table. All amounts are in thousands.

Evaluate risk ratios (LO3)

ADRIAN EXPRESS
Balance Sheet
December 31, 2012 and 2011

($ in 000s)	2012	2011
Assets		
Current assets:		
Cash	$ 600	$ 760
Accounts receivable	1,400	1,000
Inventory	1,800	1,400
Long-term assets	4,800	4,240
Total assets	$8,600	$7,400
Liabilities and Stockholders' Equity		
Current liabilities	$2,020	$1,660
Long-term liabilities	2,300	2,400
Common stock	2,000	2,000
Retained earnings	2,280	1,340
Total liabilities and stockholders' equity	$8,600	$7,400

Industry averages for the following four risk ratios are as follows:

Average collection period	25 days
Average days in inventory	60 days
Current ratio	2 to 1
Debt to equity ratio	50%

Required:
1. Calculate the four risk ratios listed above for Adrian Express in 2012.
2. Do you think the company is more risky or less risky than the industry average? Explain your answer.

E12–6 Refer to the information for Adrian Express in E12–5. Industry averages for the following profitability ratios are as follows:

Evaluate profitability ratios (LO4)

Gross profit ratio	45%
Return on assets	25%
Profit margin	15%
Asset turnover	2.5 times
Return on equity	35%

Required:
1. Calculate the five profitability ratios listed above for Adrian Express.
2. Do you think the company is more profitable or less profitable than the industry average? Explain your answer.

Calculate risk ratios (LO3)   **E12–7** The balance sheet for Plasma Screens Corporation and additional information are provided below.

PLASMA SCREENS CORPORATION Balance Sheet December 31, 2012 and 2011		
	2012	**2011**
Assets		
Current assets:		
Cash	$ 112,000	$ 120,000
Accounts receivable	78,000	92,000
Inventory	95,000	80,000
Investments	4,000	2,000
Long-term assets:		
Land	480,000	480,000
Equipment	790,000	670,000
Less: Accumulated depreciation	(428,000)	(268,000)
Total assets	$1,131,000	$1,176,000
Liabilities and Stockholders' Equity		
Current liabilities:		
Accounts payable	$ 99,000	$ 85,000
Interest payable	6,000	12,000
Income tax payable	8,000	5,000
Long-term liabilities:		
Notes payable	100,000	200,000
Stockholders' equity:		
Common stock	700,000	700,000
Retained earnings	218,000	174,000
Total liabilities and stockholders' equity	$1,131,000	$1,176,000

Additional Information for 2012:
1. Net income is $69,000.
2. Sales on account are $1,520,000.
3. Cost of goods sold is $1,160,000.

Required:
1. Calculate the following risk ratios for 2012:
   a. Receivables turnover ratio.
   b. Inventory turnover ratio.
   c. Current ratio.
   d. Acid-test ratio.
   e. Debt to equity ratio.
2. When we compare two companies, can one have a higher current ratio while the other has a higher acid-test ratio? Explain your answer.

Calculate profitability ratios (LO4)   **E12–8** Refer to the information provided for Plasma Screens Corporation in E12–7.

Required:
1. Calculate the following profitability ratios for 2012:
   a. Gross profit ratio.
   b. Return on assets.
   c. Profit margin.
   d. Asset turnover.
   e. Return on equity.

2. When we compare two companies, can one have a higher return on assets while the other has a higher return on equity? Explain your answer.

E12–9 The following condensed information is reported by Sporting Collectibles.

Calculate profitability ratios (LO4)

	2013	2012
Income Statement Information		
Sales revenue	$10,400,000	$8,400,000
Cost of goods sold	6,800,000	5,900,000
Net income	360,000	248,000
Balance Sheet Information		
Current assets	$ 1,600,000	$1,500,000
Long-term assets	2,200,000	1,900,000
Total assets	$ 3,800,000	$3,400,000
Current liabilities	$ 1,200,000	$ 900,000
Long-term liabilities	1,500,000	1,500,000
Common stock	800,000	800,000
Retained earnings	300,000	200,000
Total liabilities and stockholders' equity	$ 3,800,000	$3,400,000

Required:
1. Calculate the following profitability ratios for 2013:
   a. Gross profit ratio.
   b. Return on assets.
   c. Profit margin.
   d. Asset turnover.
   e. Return on equity.
2. Determine the amount of dividends paid to shareholders in 2013.

E12–10 The income statement for Stretch-Tape Corporation reports revenue of $420,000 and net income of $50,000. Average total assets for the year are $800,000. Stockholders' equity at the beginning of the year was $500,000, and $20,000 was paid to stockholders as dividends during the year. There were no other stockholders' equity transactions that occurred during the year.

Calculate profitability ratios (LO4)

Required:
Calculate the return on assets, profit margin, asset turnover, and return on equity ratios.

E12–11 As an auditor for Bernard and Thomas, you are responsible for determining the proper classification of income statement items in the audit of California Sports Grill.

Classify income statement items (LO5)

a. One of the company's restaurants is destroyed in a forest fire that raged through Southern California. Uninsured losses from the fire are estimated to be $450,000.
b. California Sports Grill has three operating divisions: restaurants, catering, and frozen retail foods. The company sells the frozen retail foods division of the business for a profit of $2.4 million in order to focus more on the restaurant and catering business.
c. An employee strike to increase wages and benefits shut down operations for several days at an estimated cost of $200,000.
d. A restaurant waiter slipped on a wet floor and sued the company. The employee won a settlement for $100,000, but California Sports Grill has yet not paid the settlement.
e. The company owns and operates over 40 restaurants but sold one underperforming restaurant this year at a loss of $650,000.

Required:

Indicate whether each item should be classified as discontinued operations, extraordinary items, other revenues, or other expenses. Provide a brief justification for each answer.

Record discontinued operations **(LO5)**

E12–12 LeBron's Bookstores has two divisions: books and electronics. The electronics division had another great year in 2012 with sales of $10 million, cost of goods sold of $6 million, operating expenses of $2 million, and income tax expense of $500,000. The book division did not do as well and was sold during the year. The loss from operations and sale of the book division was $800,000 before taxes and $600,000 after taxes.

Required:

Prepare the income statement for LeBron's Bookstores, including the proper reporting for the discontinued book division.

Record discontinued operations and extraordinary items **(LO5)**

E12–13 Shaquille Corporation has income before tax of $1.2 million and income tax expense of $300,000 for the year ended December 31, 2012, before considering the following items: (1) a $225,000 gain, after tax, from the disposal of an operating segment, and (2) an extraordinary loss of $150,000, after tax, due to a plant explosion.

Required:

Prepare the 2012 income statement for Shaquille Corporation beginning with income before tax.

Distinguish between conservative and aggressive accounting practices **(LO6)**

E12–14 Dwight's Trophy Shop is considering the following accounting changes:

a. Increase the allowance for uncollectible accounts.
b. When costs are going up, change from LIFO to FIFO.
c. Change from the straight-line method of depreciation to declining-balance in the second year of equipment with a 10-year life.
d. Record a smaller expense for warranties.

Required:

Classify each accounting change as either conservative or aggressive.

Distinguish between conservative and aggressive accounting practices **(LO6)**

E12–15 Attached is a schedule of five proposed changes at the end of the year.

($ in 000s)	Before the Change	Proposed Change		After the Change
Sales revenue	$18,800,000	(a)	$200,000	$19,000,000
Cost of goods sold	13,200,000	(b)	400,000	13,600,000
Operating expenses	1,600,000	(c)	(100,000)	1,500,000
Other revenue	500,000	(d)	50,000	550,000
Other expense	450,000	(e)	(50,000)	400,000
Net income	$ 4,050,000			$ 4,050,000

Required:

1. Indicate whether each of the proposed changes is conservative, aggressive, or neutral.
2. Indicate whether the total effect of all the changes is conservative, aggressive, or neutral.

*For additional exercises, visit **www.mhhe.com/succeed** for Exercises: Set B.*

PROBLEMS: SET A

P12–1A Sports Emporium has two operating segments: sporting goods and sports apparel. The income statement for each operating segment is presented below.

Perform vertical analysis **(LO1)**

SPORTS EMPORIUM Income Statement For the year ended December 31, 2012				
	Sporting Goods		**Sports Apparel**	
	Amount	%	Amount	%
Sales revenue	$1,550,000		$870,000	
Cost of goods sold	940,000		390,000	
Gross profit	610,000		480,000	
Operating expenses	350,000		240,000	
Operating income	260,000		240,000	
Other income (expense)	15,000		(10,000)	
Income before tax	275,000		230,000	
Income tax expense	70,000		60,000	
Net income	$ 205,000		$170,000	

Required:
1. Complete the "%" columns to be used in a vertical analysis of Sports Emporium's two operating segments. Express each amount as a percentage of sales.
2. Use vertical analysis to compare the profitability of the two operating segments. Which segment is more profitable?

P12–2A The income statement for Sports Emporium for the years ending December 31, 2013 and 2012, is provided below.

Perform horizontal analysis **(LO2)**

SPORTS EMPORIUM Income Statement For the years ended December 31				
			Increase (Decrease)	
	2013	2012	Amount	%
Sales revenue	$3,200,000	$2,420,000		
Cost of goods sold	2,050,000	1,330,000		
Gross profit	1,150,000	1,090,000		
Operating expenses	760,000	590,000		
Operating income	390,000	500,000		
Other income (expense)	8,000	5,000		
Income before tax	398,000	505,000		
Income tax expense	95,000	130,000		
Net income	$ 303,000	$ 375,000		

Required:
1. Complete the "Amount" and "%" columns to be used in a horizontal analysis of Sports Emporium's income statement.
2. Discuss the major fluctuations in income statement items during the year.

P12–3A The balance sheet for Virtual Gaming Systems for 2012 and 2011 is provided below.

VIRTUAL GAMING SYSTEMS Balance Sheet For the years ended December 31, 2012 and 2011		
	2012	**2011**
Assets		
Current assets:		
Cash	$186,000	$144,000
Accounts receivable	81,000	60,000
Inventory	105,000	135,000
Prepaid rent	12,000	6,000
Long-term assets:		
Investment in bonds	105,000	0
Land	210,000	240,000
Equipment	270,000	210,000
Less: Accumulated depreciation	(69,000)	(42,000)
Total assets	$900,000	$753,000
Liabilities and Stockholders' Equity		
Current liabilities:		
Accounts payable	$ 66,000	$ 81,000
Interest payable	6,000	3,000
Income tax payable	15,000	14,000
Long-term liabilities:		
Notes payable	285,000	225,000
Stockholders' equity:		
Common stock	300,000	300,000
Retained earnings	228,000	130,000
Total liabilities and stockholders' equity	$900,000	$753,000

Required:
1. Prepare a vertical analysis of Virtual Gaming Systems' 2012 and 2011 balance sheets. Express each amount as a percentage of total assets for that year.
2. Prepare a horizontal analysis of Virtual Gaming Systems' 2012 balance sheet using 2011 as the base year.

P12–4A The following income statement and balance sheet for Virtual Gaming Systems are provided.

VIRTUAL GAMING SYSTEMS Income Statement For the year ended December 31, 2012		
Sales revenue		$3,036,000
Cost of goods sold		1,950,000
Gross profit		1,086,000
Expenses:		
Operating expenses	$858,000	
Depreciation expense	27,000	
Loss on sale of land	8,000	
Interest expense	15,000	
Income tax expense	48,000	
Total expenses		956,000
Net income		$ 130,000

VIRTUAL GAMING SYSTEMS
Balance Sheet
December 31

	2012	2011
Assets		
Current assets:		
Cash	$186,000	$144,000
Accounts receivable	81,000	60,000
Inventory	105,000	135,000
Prepaid rent	12,000	6,000
Long-term assets:		
Investment in bonds	105,000	0
Land	210,000	240,000
Equipment	270,000	210,000
Less: Accumulated depreciation	(69,000)	(42,000)
Total assets	$900,000	$753,000
Liabilities and Stockholders' Equity		
Current liabilities:		
Accounts payable	$ 66,000	$ 81,000
Interest payable	6,000	3,000
Income tax payable	15,000	14,000
Long-term liabilities:		
Notes payable	285,000	225,000
Stockholders' equity:		
Common stock	300,000	300,000
Retained earnings	228,000	130,000
Total liabilities and stockholders' equity	$900,000	$753,000

Required:

Assuming that all sales were on account, calculate the following risk ratios for 2012.

1. Receivables turnover ratio.
2. Average collection period.
3. Inventory turnover ratio.
4. Average days in inventory.
5. Current ratio.
6. Acid-test ratio.
7. Debt to equity ratio.
8. Times interest earned ratio.

P12–5A Data for Virtual Gaming Systems is provided in P12–4A. Earnings per share for the year ended December 31, 2012, are $1.30. The closing stock price on December 31, 2012, is $27.30.

Calculate profitability ratios (LO4)

Required:

Calculate the following profitability ratios for 2012.

1. Gross profit ratio.
2. Return on assets.
3. Profit margin.
4. Asset turnover.
5. Return on equity.
6. Price-earnings ratio.

Use ratios to analyze risk and profitability (LO3, 4)

P12–6A Income statement and balance sheet data for Virtual Gaming Systems are provided below.

VIRTUAL GAMING SYSTEMS Income Statement For the year ended December 31		
	2013	**2012**
Sales revenue	$3,510,000	$3,036,000
Cost of goods sold	2,480,000	1,950,000
Gross profit	1,030,000	1,086,000
Expenses:		
Operating expenses	955,000	858,000
Depreciation expense	30,000	27,000
Loss on sale of land	0	8,000
Interest expense	18,000	15,000
Income tax expense	8,000	48,000
Total expenses	1,011,000	956,000
Net income	$ 19,000	$ 130,000

VIRTUAL GAMING SYSTEMS Balance Sheet December 31			
	2013	**2012**	**2011**
Assets			
Current assets:			
Cash	$ 201,000	$186,000	$144,000
Accounts receivable	75,000	81,000	60,000
Inventory	125,000	105,000	135,000
Prepaid rent	14,000	12,000	6,000
Long-term assets:			
Investment in bonds	105,000	105,000	0
Land	300,000	210,000	240,000
Equipment	300,000	270,000	210,000
Less: Accumulated depreciation	(99,000)	(69,000)	(42,000)
Total assets	$1,021,000	$900,000	$753,000
Liabilities and Stockholders' Equity			
Current liabilities:			
Accounts payable	$ 78,000	$ 66,000	$ 81,000
Interest payable	9,000	6,000	3,000
Income tax payable	12,000	15,000	14,000
Long-term liabilities:			
Notes payable	400,000	285,000	225,000
Stockholders' equity:			
Common stock	300,000	300,000	300,000
Retained earnings	222,000	228,000	130,000
Total liabilities and stockholders' equity	$1,021,000	$900,000	$753,000

Required:

1. Calculate the following risk ratios for 2012 and 2013:
   a. Receivables turnover ratio.   c. Current ratio.
   b. Inventory turnover ratio.   d. Debt to equity ratio.

2. Calculate the following profitability ratios for 2012 and 2013:
   a. Gross profit ratio.   c. Profit margin.
   b. Return on assets.   d. Asset turnover.

3. Based on the ratios calculated, determine whether overall risk and profitability improved from 2012 to 2013.

PROBLEMS: SET B

P12–1B Game-On Sports operates in two distinct segments: athletic equipment and accessories. The income statement for each operating segment is presented below.

Perform vertical analysis (LO1)

GAME-ON SPORTS
Income Statement
For the year ended December 31, 2012

	Athletic Equipment		Accessories	
	Amount	%	Amount	%
Sales revenue	$2,800,000		$3,250,000	
Cost of goods sold	1,250,000		1,620,000	
Gross profit	1,550,000		1,630,000	
Operating expenses	650,000		700,000	
Operating income	900,000		930,000	
Other income (expense)	75,000		(10,000)	
Income before tax	975,000		920,000	
Income tax expense	225,000		200,000	
Net income	$ 750,000		$ 720,000	

Required:
1. Complete the "%" columns to be used in a vertical analysis of Game-On Sports' two operating segments. Express each amount as a percentage of sales.
2. Use vertical analysis to compare the profitability of the two operating segments. Which segment is more profitable?

P12–2B The income statement for Game-On Sports for the years ending December 31, 2013 and 2012, is provided below.

Perform horizontal analysis (LO2)

GAME-ON SPORTS
Income Statement
For the years ended December 31

			Increase (Decrease)	
	2013	2012	Amount	%
Sales revenue	$5,850,000	$6,050,000		
Cost of goods sold	2,750,000	2,870,000		
Gross profit	3,100,000	3,180,000		
Operating expenses	1,460,000	1,350,000		
Operating income	1,640,000	1,830,000		
Other income (expense)	50,000	65,000		
Income before tax	1,690,000	1,895,000		
Income tax expense	370,000	425,000		
Net income	$1,320,000	$1,470,000		

Required:
1. Complete the "Amount" and "%" columns to be used in a horizontal analysis of Game-On Sports' income statement.
2. Discuss the major fluctuations in income statement items during the year.

Perform vertical
and horizontal
analysis (LO1, 2)

P12–3B The balance sheet for The Athletic Attic for 2012 and 2011 is provided below.

THE ATHLETIC ATTIC
Balance Sheet
December 31

	2012	2011
Assets		
Current assets:		
Cash	$ 154,000	$ 204,000
Accounts receivable	740,000	760,000
Inventory	1,355,000	1,025,000
Supplies	100,000	75,000
Long-term assets:		
Equipment	1,100,000	1,100,000
Less: Accumulated depreciation	(400,000)	(200,000)
Total assets	$3,049,000	$2,964,000
Liabilities and Stockholders' Equity		
Current liabilities:		
Accounts payable	$ 105,000	$ 81,000
Interest payable	0	4,000
Income tax payable	35,000	30,000
Long-term liabilities:		
Notes payable	500,000	500,000
Stockholders' equity:		
Common stock	600,000	600,000
Retained earnings	1,809,000	1,749,000
Total liabilities and stockholders' equity	$3,049,000	$2,964,000

Required:
1. Prepare a vertical analysis of The Athletic Attic's 2012 and 2011 balance sheets. Express each amount as a percentage of total assets for that year.
2. Prepare a horizontal analysis of The Athletic Attic's 2012 balance sheet using 2011 as the base year.

Calculate risk ratios (LO3)

P12–4B The following income statement and balance sheet for The Athletic Attic are provided.

THE ATHLETIC ATTIC
Income Statement
For the year ended December 31, 2012

Sales revenue		$8,800,000
Cost of goods sold		5,400,000
Gross profit		3,400,000
Expenses:		
Operating expenses	$1,550,000	
Depreciation expense	200,000	
Interest expense	40,000	
Income tax expense	350,000	
Total expenses		2,140,000
Net income		$1,260,000

THE ATHLETIC ATTIC
Balance Sheet
December 31

	2012	2011
Assets		
Current assets:		
Cash	$ 154,000	$ 204,000
Accounts receivable	740,000	760,000
Inventory	1,355,000	1,025,000
Supplies	100,000	75,000
Long-term assets:		
Equipment	1,100,000	1,100,000
Less: Accumulated depreciation	(400,000)	(200,000)
Total assets	$3,049,000	$2,964,000
Liabilities and Stockholders' Equity		
Current liabilities:		
Accounts payable	$ 105,000	$ 81,000
Interest payable	0	4,000
Income tax payable	35,000	30,000
Long-term liabilities:		
Notes payable	500,000	500,000
Stockholders' equity:		
Common stock	600,000	600,000
Retained earnings	1,809,000	1,749,000
Total liabilities and stockholders' equity	$3,049,000	$2,964,000

Required:
Assuming that all sales were on account, calculate the following risk ratios for 2012:

1. Receivables turnover ratio.
2. Average collection period.
3. Inventory turnover ratio.
4. Average days in inventory.
5. Current ratio.
6. Acid-test ratio.
7. Debt to equity ratio.
8. Times interest earned ratio.

P12–5B Data for The Athletic Attic are provided in P12–4B. Earnings per share for the year ended December 31, 2012, are $1.26. The closing stock price on December 31, 2012, is $21.42.

Calculate profitability ratios **(LO4)**

Required:
Calculate the following profitability ratios for 2012:

1. Gross profit ratio.
2. Return on assets.
3. Profit margin.
4. Asset turnover.
5. Return on equity.
6. Price-earnings ratio.

Use ratios to analyze risk
and profitability (LO3, 4)

P12–6B Income statement and balance sheet data for The Athletic Attic are provided below.

THE ATHLETIC ATTIC Income Statement For the years ended December 31		
	2013	2012
Sales revenue	$10,400,000	$8,800,000
Cost of goods sold	6,800,000	5,400,000
Gross profit	3,600,000	3,400,000
Expenses:		
Operating expenses	1,600,000	1,550,000
Depreciation expense	200,000	200,000
Interest expense	40,000	40,000
Income tax expense	400,000	350,000
Total expenses	2,240,000	2,140,000
Net income	$ 1,360,000	$1,260,000

THE ATHLETIC ATTIC Balance Sheet December 31			
	2013	2012	2011
Assets			
Current assets:			
Cash	$ 225,000	$ 154,000	$ 204,000
Accounts receivable	990,000	740,000	760,000
Inventory	1,725,000	1,355,000	1,025,000
Supplies	130,000	100,000	75,000
Long-term assets:			
Equipment	1,100,000	1,100,000	1,100,000
Less: Accumulated depreciation	(600,000)	(400,000)	(200,000)
Total assets	$3,570,000	$3,049,000	$2,964,000
Liabilities and Stockholders' Equity			
Current liabilities:			
Accounts payable	$ 175,000	$ 105,000	$ 81,000
Interest payable	4,000	0	4,000
Income tax payable	40,000	35,000	30,000
Long-term liabilities:			
Notes payable	500,000	500,000	500,000
Stockholders' equity:			
Common stock	600,000	600,000	600,000
Retained earnings	2,251,000	1,809,000	1,749,000
Total liabilities and stockholders' equity	$3,570,000	$3,049,000	$2,964,000

Required:
1. Calculate the following risk ratios for 2012 and 2013:

   a. Receivables turnover ratio.   c. Current ratio.
   b. Inventory turnover ratio.   d. Debt to equity ratio.
2. Calculate the following profitability ratios for 2012 and 2013:

   a. Gross profit ratio.   c. Profit margin.
   b. Return on assets.   d. Asset turnover.

3. Based on the ratios calculated, determine whether overall risk and profitability improved from 2012 to 2013.

*For additional problems, visit **www.mhhe.com/succeed** for Problems: Set C.*

ADDITIONAL PERSPECTIVES

Great Adventures

(This is the conclusion of the Great Adventures problem from earlier chapters.)

AP12–1 Income statement and balance sheet data for Great Adventures, Inc., are provided below.

Continuing Problem

GREAT ADVENTURES, INC. Income Statement For the year ended December 31, 2014		
Revenues:		
Service revenue (clinic, racing, TEAM)	$543,000	
Sales revenue (MU watches)	118,000	
Total revenues		$661,000
Expenses:		
Cost of goods sold (MU watches)	70,000	
Operating expenses	304,276	
Depreciation expense	50,000	
Interest expense	29,724	
Income tax expense	57,000	
Total expenses		511,000
Net income		$150,000

GREAT ADVENTURES, INC. Balance Sheet December 31, 2014 and 2013			
	2014	2013	Increase (I) or Decrease (D)
Assets			
Current assets:			
Cash	$ 322,362	$138,000	$ 184,362 (I)
Accounts receivable	45,000	35,000	10,000 (I)
Inventory	17,000	14,000	3,000 (I)
Other current assets	13,000	11,000	2,000 (I)
Long-term assets:			
Land	500,000	0	500,000 (I)
Buildings	1,000,000	0	1,000,000 (I)
Equipment	65,000	65,000	
Less: Accumulated depreciation	(75,250)	(25,250)	50,000 (I)
Total assets	$1,887,112	$237,750	

(continued)

(concluded)

GREAT ADVENTURES, INC.
Balance Sheet
December 31, 2014 and 2013

	2014	2013	Increase (I) or Decrease (D)
Liabilities and Stockholders' Equity			
Current liabilities:			
Accounts payable	$ 12,000	$ 9,000	$ 3,000 (I)
Interest payable	750	750	
Income tax payable	57,000	38,000	19,000 (I)
Long-term liabilities:			
Notes payable	492,362	30,000	462,362 (I)
Stockholders' equity:			
Common stock	120,000	20,000	100,000 (I)
Paid-in capital	1,105,000	0	1,105,000 (I)
Retained earnings	175,000	140,000	35,000 (I)
Treasury stock	(75,000)	0	(75,000) (I)
Total liabilities and stockholders' equity	$1,887,112	$237,750	

As you can tell from the financial statements, 2014 was an especially busy year. Tony and Suzie were able to use the $1.2 million received from the issuance of 100,000 shares of stock and hire a construction company for $1 million to build the cabins, dining facilities, ropes course, and the outdoor swimming pool. They even put in a baby pool to celebrate the birth of their firstborn son, little Venture Matheson.

Required:
1. Calculate the following risk ratios for 2014.
   a. Receivables turnover ratio.   e. Current ratio.
   b. Average collection period.   f. Acid-test ratio.
   c. Inventory turnover ratio.   g. Debt to equity ratio.
   d. Average days in inventory.   h. Times interest earned ratio.
2. Calculate the following profitability ratios for 2014.
   a. Gross profit ratio (on the MU watches).   d. Asset turnover.
   b. Return on assets.   e. Return on equity.
   c. Profit margin.
3. Briefly comment on Great Adventures' risk and profitability in 2014.

Financial Analysis

American Eagle Outfitters, Inc.

AP12–2 Financial information for **American Eagle** is presented in Appendix A at the end of the book.

Required:
1. Complete the "Amount" and "%" columns to be used in a horizontal analysis of American Eagle's income statement for the year ended January 30, 2010. Discuss the major fluctuations during the year.
2. Calculate the following risk ratios for the year ended January 30, 2010:
   a. Receivables turnover ratio.   e. Current ratio.
   b. Average collection period.   f. Acid-test ratio.
   c. Inventory turnover ratio.   g. Debt to equity ratio.
   d. Average days in inventory.
3. Calculate the following profitability ratios for the year ended January 30, 2010:
   a. Gross profit ratio.   d. Asset turnover.
   b. Return on assets.   e. Return on equity.
   c. Profit margin.

The Buckle. Inc.

AP12–3 Financial information for **The Buckle** is presented in Appendix B at the end of the book.

Required:

1. Complete the "Amount" and "%" columns to be used in a horizontal analysis of The Buckle's income statement for the year ended January 30, 2010. Discuss the major fluctuations during the year.
2. Calculate the following risk ratios for the year ended January 30, 2010:
   a. Receivables turnover ratio.
   b. Average collection period.
   c. Inventory turnover ratio.
   d. Average days in inventory.
   e. Current ratio.
   f. Acid-test ratio.
   g. Debt to equity ratio.
3. Calculate the following profitability ratios for the year ended January 30, 2010:
   a. Gross profit ratio.
   b. Return on assets.
   c. Profit margin.
   d. Asset turnover.
   e. Return on equity.

American Eagle Outfitters, Inc., vs. The Buckle. Inc.

AP12–4 Financial information for **American Eagle** is presented in Appendix A at the end of the book, and financial information for **The Buckle** is presented in Appendix B at the end of the book.

Required:

1. Calculate the following risk ratios for both companies for the year ended January 30, 2010. Based on these calculations, which company appears to be more risky?
   a. Receivables turnover ratio.
   b. Average collection period.
   c. Inventory turnover ratio.
   d. Average days in inventory.
   e. Current ratio.
   f. Acid-test ratio.
   g. Debt to equity ratio.
2. Calculate the following profitability ratios for both companies for the year ended January 30, 2010. Based on these calculations, which company appears to be more profitable?
   a. Gross profit ratio.
   b. Return on assets.
   c. Profit margin.
   d. Asset turnover.
   e. Return on equity.

Ethics

AP12–5 After years of steady growth in net income, The Performance Drug Company sustained a loss of $1.6 million in 2012. The loss was primarily due to $5 million in expenses related to a product recall. The company designs and produces health supplements and had to recall a product in 2012 because of potential health risks.

The company controller, Joe Mammoth, suggests the loss be included in the 2012 income statement as an extraordinary item. "If we report it as an extraordinary item, our income from continuing operations will actually show an increase from the prior year. Investors will appreciate the continued growth in ongoing profitability and will discount the one-time loss." Joe further notes that executive bonuses are tied to income from continuing operations, not net income.

The CEO asks Joe to justify this treatment. "I know we have had product recalls before and, of course, they do occur in our industry," Joe replies, "but we have never had a recall of this magnitude, and have upgraded our quality control procedures so this should never happen again."

Required:

Discuss the ethical dilemma faced by Joe Mammoth and the CEO. Who are the stakeholders and how are they affected?

Internet Research

AP12–6 Companies like Reuters provide updated ratio analysis on publicly traded companies free of charge. Go to *www.investor.reuters.com*. Choose stocks in the left-hand margin. Look up a company's ticker symbol. For example, Pepsi's ticker symbol is PBG. Type in the ticker symbol and click on "Ratios."

Required:
1. Evaluate the company's risk (both liquidity and solvency) in relation to the industry and sector averages.
2. Evaluate the company's profitability in relation to the industry and sector averages.

Written Communication

AP12–7 Roseburg Corporation manufactures cardboard containers. In 2008, the company purchased several large tracts of timber for $20 million with the intention of harvesting its own timber rather than buying timber from outside suppliers. However, in 2012, Roseburg abandoned the idea, and sold all of the timber tracts for $30 million. Net income for 2012, before considering this event, was $12 million.

Required:

Write a memo providing your recommended income statement presentation of the gain on the sale of the timber tracts. Be sure to include a discussion of the alternatives that might be considered.

Earnings Management

AP12–8 Major League Products was founded in 1992 to provide high-quality merchandise carrying the logos of each fan's favorite major league team. In recent years, the company has struggled to compete against new Internet-based companies selling products at much lower prices. Andrew Ransom, in his second year out of college, was assigned to audit the financial statements of Major League Products. One of the steps in the auditing process is to examine the nature of year-end adjustments. Andrew's investigation reveals that the company has made several year-end adjustments, including (a) a decrease in the allowance for uncollectible accounts, (b) a reversal in the previous write-down of inventory, (c) an increase in the estimated useful life used to calculate depreciation expense, and (d) a decrease in the liability reported for litigation.

Required:
1. Classify each adjustment as conservative or aggressive.
2. What, if anything, do all these adjustments have in common?
3. How do these adjustments affect the company's cash balance?
4. Why might these year-end adjustments, taken together, raise concerns about earnings management?

Answers to the Self-Study Questions
1. b   2. a   3. d   4. b   5. c   6. d   7. a   8. d   9. c   10. a

AMERICAN EAGLE
OUTFITTERS
ae.com

UNITED STATES SECURITIES AND EXCHANGE COMMISSION
Washington, D.C. 20549

Form 10-K

☑ **ANNUAL REPORT PURSUANT TO SECTION 13 OR 15(d) OF THE SECURITIES EXCHANGE ACT OF 1934**

For the Fiscal Year Ended January 30, 2010

OR

☐ **TRANSITION REPORT PURSUANT TO SECTION 13 OR 15(d) OF THE SECURITIES EXCHANGE ACT OF 1934**

Commission File Number: 1-33338

American Eagle Outfitters, Inc.

(Exact name of registrant as specified in its charter)

Delaware	**No. 13-2721761**
(State or other jurisdiction of incorporation or organization)	*(I.R.S. Employer Identification No.)*
77 Hot Metal Street, Pittsburgh, PA	**15203-2329**
(Address of principal executive offices)	*(Zip Code)*

Registrant's telephone number, including area code: (412) 432-3300

Securities registered pursuant to Section 12(b) of the Act:

Common Shares, $0.01 par value	New York Stock Exchange
(Title of class)	*(Name of each exchange on which registered)*

Securities registered pursuant to Section 12(g) of the Act:
None

Indicate by check mark if the registrant is a well-known seasoned issuer, as defined in Rule 405 of the Securities Act.   YES ☑   NO ☐

Indicate by check mark if the registrant is not required to file reports pursuant to Section 13 or Sections 15(d) of the Act.   YES ☐   NO ☑

Indicate by check mark whether the registrant (1) has filed all reports required to be filed by Section 13 or 15(d) of the Securities Exchange Act of 1934 during the preceding 12 months (or for such shorter period that the registrant was required to submit and post such files), and (2) has been subject to the filing requirements for the past 90 days.   YES ☑   NO ☐

Indicate by check mark whether the registrant has submitted electronically and posted on its corporate Web site, if any, every Interactive Data File required to be submitted and posted pursuant to Rule 405 of Regulation S-T (§ 232.405 of this chapter) during the preceding 12 months (or for such shorter period that the registrant was required to submit and post such files).   YES ☐   NO ☐

Indicate by check mark if disclosure of delinquent filers pursuant to Item 405 of Regulation S-K (§ 229.405 of this chapter) is not contained herein, and will not be contained, to the best of registrant's knowledge, in definitive proxy or information statements incorporated by reference in Part III of this Form 10-K or any amendment to this Form 10-K.   ☐

Indicate by check mark whether the registrant is a large accelerated filer, an accelerated filer, a non-accelerated filer, or a smaller reporting company. See the definitions of "large accelerated filer," "accelerated filer" and "smaller reporting company" in Rule 12b-2 of the Exchange Act.

Large accelerated filer ☑   Accelerated filer ☐   Non-accelerated filer ☐   Smaller reporting company ☐
(Do not check if a smaller reporting company)

Indicate by check mark whether the registrant is a shell company (as defined in Rule 12b-2 of the Act).   YES ☐   NO ☑

The aggregate market value of voting and non-voting common equity held by non-affiliates of the registrant as of August 1, 2009 was $2,583,043,775.

Indicate the number of shares outstanding of each of the registrant's classes of common stock, as of the latest practicable date: 209,044,166 Common Shares were outstanding at March 19, 2010.

DOCUMENTS INCORPORATED BY REFERENCE

Part III — Proxy Statement for 2010 Annual Meeting of Stockholders, in part, as indicated.

Report of Independent Registered Public Accounting Firm

The Board of Directors and Stockholders of
American Eagle Outfitters, Inc.

We have audited the accompanying consolidated balance sheets of American Eagle Outfitters, Inc. (the Company) as of January 30, 2010 and January 31, 2009, and the related consolidated statements of operations, comprehensive income, stockholders' equity, and cash flows for each of the three years in the period ended January 30, 2010. These financial statements are the responsibility of the Company's management. Our responsibility is to express an opinion on these financial statements based on our audits.

We conducted our audits in accordance with the standards of the Public Company Accounting Oversight Board (United States). Those standards require that we plan and perform the audit to obtain reasonable assurance about whether the financial statements are free of material misstatement. An audit includes examining, on a test basis, evidence supporting the amounts and disclosures in the financial statements. An audit also includes assessing the accounting principles used and significant estimates made by management, as well as evaluating the overall financial statement presentation. We believe that our audits provide a reasonable basis for our opinion.

In our opinion, the financial statements referred to above present fairly, in all material respects, the consolidated financial position of American Eagle Outfitters, Inc. at January 30, 2010 and January 31, 2009, and the consolidated results of its operations and its cash flows for each of the three years in the period ended January 30, 2010, in conformity with U.S. generally accepted accounting principles.

As discussed in Note 13 to the consolidated financial statements, the Company changed its accounting for income tax uncertainties effective February 4, 2007.

We also have audited, in accordance with the standards of the Public Company Accounting Oversight Board (United States), American Eagle Outfitters, Inc.'s internal control over financial reporting as of January 30, 2010, based on criteria established in Internal Control — Integrated Framework issued by the Committee of Sponsoring Organizations of the Treadway Commission and our report dated March 26, 2010 expressed an unqualified opinion.

/s/   Ernst & Young LLP

Pittsburgh, Pennsylvania
March 26, 2010

AMERICAN EAGLE OUTFITTERS, INC.

CONSOLIDATED BALANCE SHEETS

	January 30, 2010	January 31, 2009
	(In thousands, except per share amounts)	

ASSETS

	January 30, 2010	January 31, 2009
Current assets:		
Cash and cash equivalents	$ 693,960	$ 473,342
Short-term investments	4,675	10,511
Merchandise inventory	326,454	294,928
Accounts receivable	34,746	41,471
Prepaid expenses and other	47,039	59,660
Deferred income taxes	60,156	45,447
Total current assets	1,167,030	925,359
Property and equipment, at cost, net of accumulated depreciation and amortization	713,142	740,240
Goodwill	11,210	10,706
Long-term investments	197,773	251,007
Non-current deferred income taxes	27,305	15,001
Other assets, net	21,688	21,363
Total assets	$2,138,148	$1,963,676

LIABILITIES AND STOCKHOLDERS' EQUITY

	January 30, 2010	January 31, 2009
Current liabilities:		
Accounts payable	$ 158,526	$ 152,068
Note payable	30,000	75,000
Accrued compensation and payroll taxes	55,144	29,417
Accrued rent	68,866	64,695
Accrued income and other taxes	20,585	6,259
Unredeemed gift cards and gift certificates	39,389	42,299
Current portion of deferred lease credits	17,388	13,726
Other liabilities and accrued expenses	19,057	18,299
Total current liabilities	408,955	401,763
Non-current liabilities:		
Deferred lease credits	89,591	88,314
Non-current accrued income taxes	38,618	39,898
Other non-current liabilities	22,467	24,670
Total non-current liabilities	150,676	152,882
Commitments and contingencies	—	—
Stockholders' equity:		
Preferred stock, $0.01 par value; 5,000 shares authorized; none issued and outstanding	—	—
Common stock, $0.01 par value; 600,000 shares authorized; 249,561 and 249,328 shares issued; 206,832 and 205,281 shares outstanding, respectively	2,486	2,485
Contributed capital	554,399	513,574
Accumulated other comprehensive income (loss)	16,838	(14,389)
Retained earnings	1,764,049	1,694,161
Treasury stock, 41,737 and 43,248 shares, respectively, at cost	(759,255)	(786,800)
Total stockholders' equity	1,578,517	1,409,031
Total liabilities and stockholders' equity	$2,138,148	$1,963,676

Refer to Notes to Consolidated Financial Statements

AMERICAN EAGLE OUTFITTERS, INC.
CONSOLIDATED STATEMENTS OF OPERATIONS

	For the Years Ended		
	January 30, 2010	January 31, 2009	February 2, 2008
	(In thousands, except per share amounts)		
Net sales	$2,990,520	$2,988,866	$3,055,419
Cost of sales, including certain buying, occupancy and warehousing expenses	1,832,471	1,814,765	1,632,281
Gross profit	1,158,049	1,174,101	1,423,138
Selling, general and administrative expenses	756,256	734,029	714,588
Loss on impairment of assets	17,992	6,713	592
Depreciation and amortization expense	145,408	131,219	109,203
Operating income	238,393	302,140	598,755
Other (expense) income, net	(5,062)	17,790	37,626
Total other-than-temporary impairment losses	(4,413)	(22,889)	—
Portion of loss recognized in other comprehensive income, before tax	3,473	—	—
Net impairment loss recognized in earnings	(940)	(22,889)	—
Income before income taxes	232,391	297,041	636,381
Provision for income taxes	63,369	117,980	236,362
Net income	$ 169,022	$ 179,061	$ 400,019
Basic income per common share	$ 0.82	$ 0.87	$ 1.85
Diluted income per common share	$ 0.81	$ 0.86	$ 1.82
Weighted average common shares outstanding — basic	206,171	205,169	216,119
Weighted average common shares outstanding — diluted	209,512	207,582	220,280

Refer to Notes to Consolidated Financial Statements

AMERICAN EAGLE OUTFITTERS, INC.
CONSOLIDATED STATEMENTS OF COMPREHENSIVE INCOME

	For the Years Ended		
	January 30, 2010	January 31, 2009	February 2, 2008
	(In thousands)		
Net income	$169,022	$179,061	$400,019
Other comprehensive income (loss):			
Temporary recovery (impairment) related to investment securities, net of tax	14,506	(22,795)	—
Reclassification adjustment for OTTI charges realized in net income related to ARS	940	751	—
Reclassification adjustment for losses realized in net income due to the sale of available-for-sale securities, net of tax	—	197	242
Unrealized (loss) gain on investments, net of tax	—	(378)	947
Foreign currency translation adjustment	15,781	(27,649)	12,582
Other comprehensive income (loss)	31,227	(49,874)	13,771
Comprehensive income	$200,249	$129,187	$413,790

Refer to Notes to Consolidated Financial Statements

AMERICAN EAGLE OUTFITTERS, INC.

CONSOLIDATED STATEMENTS OF STOCKHOLDERS' EQUITY

	Shares Outstanding (1)	Common Stock	Contributed Capital	Retained Earnings	Treasury Stock(2)	Accumulated Other Comprehensive Income (Loss)	Stockholders' Equity
			(In thousands, except per share amounts)				
Balance at February 3, 2007	221,284	2,461	453,418	1,302,345	(362,626)	21,714	1,417,312
Adoption of ASC 740 regarding accounting for unrecognized tax benefits	—	—	—	(13,304)	—	—	(13,304)
Balance at February 4, 2007	221,284	2,461	453,418	1,289,041	(362,626)	21,714	1,404,008
Stock awards	1,092	20	39,977	—	—	—	39,997
Repurchase of common stock as part of publicly announced programs	(18,750)	—	—	—	(438,291)	—	(438,291)
Repurchase of common stock from employees	(415)	—	—	—	(12,310)	—	(12,310)
Reissuance of treasury stock	1,269	—	—	(6,480)	20,546	—	14,066
Net income	—	—	—	400,019	—		400,019
Other comprehensive income, net of tax	—	—	—	—	—	13,771	13,771
Cash dividends ($0.38 per share)	—	—	—	(80,796)	—	—	(80,796)
Balance at February 2, 2008	204,480	$2,481	$493,395	$1,601,784	$(792,681)	$ 35,485	$1,340,464
Stock awards	453	4	20,179	420	—	—	20,603
Repurchase of common stock from employees	(164)	—	—	—	(3,432)	—	(3,432)
Reissuance of treasury stock	512	—	—	(4,710)	9,313	—	4,603
Net income	—	—	—	179,061	—	—	179,061
Other comprehensive loss, net of tax	—	—	—	—	—	(49,874)	(49,874)
Cash dividends ($0.40 per share)	—	—	—	(82,394)	—	—	(82,394)
Balance at January 31, 2009	205,281	$2,485	$513,574	$1,694,161	$(786,800)	$(14,389)	$1,409,031
Stock awards	41	1	40,825	—	—	—	40,826
Repurchase of common stock from employees	(18)	—	—	—	(247)	—	(247)
Reissuance of treasury stock	1,528	—	—	(15,228)	27,792	—	12,564
Net income	—	—	—	169,022	—	—	169,022
Other comprehensive income, net of tax	—	—	—	—	—	31,227	31,227
Cash dividends and dividend equivalents ($0.40 per share)	—	—	—	(83,906)	—	—	(83,906)
Balance at January 30, 2010	206,832	$2,486	$554,399	$1,764,049	$(759,255)	$ 16,838	$1,578,517

(1) 600,000 authorized, 249,561 issued and 206,832 outstanding (excluding 992 shares of non-vested restricted stock), $0.01 par value common stock at January 30, 2010; 600,000 authorized, 249,328 issued and 205,281 outstanding (excluding 799 shares of non-vested restricted stock), $0.01 par value common stock at January 31, 2009; 600,000 authorized, 248,763 issued and 204,480 outstanding (excluding 687 shares of non-vested restricted stock), $0.01 par value common stock at February 2, 2008; The Company has 5,000 authorized, with none issued or outstanding, $0.01 par value preferred stock at January 30, 2010, January 31, 2009 and February 2, 2008.

(2) 41,737 shares, 43,248 shares and 43,596 shares at January 30, 2010, January 31, 2009 and February 2, 2008, respectively. During Fiscal 2009 Fiscal 2008 and Fiscal 2007, 1,528 shares, 512 shares and 1,269 shares, respectively, were reissued from treasury stock for the issuance of share-based payments.

Refer to Notes to Consolidated Financial Statements

AMERICAN EAGLE OUTFITTERS, INC.

CONSOLIDATED STATEMENTS OF CASH FLOWS

	For the Years Ended		
	January 30, 2010	January 31, 2009	February 2, 2008
	(In thousands)		
Operating activities:			
Net income	$ 169,022	$ 179,061	$ 400,019
Adjustments to reconcile net income to net cash provided by operating activities			
Depreciation and amortization	147,483	133,141	110,753
Share-based compensation	36,900	20,296	33,670
Provision for deferred income taxes	(36,027)	24,469	(8,147)
Tax benefit from share-based payments	7,995	1,121	7,260
Excess tax benefit from share-based payments	(2,812)	(693)	(6,156)
Foreign currency transaction loss (gain)	6,477	(1,141)	1,221
Loss on impairment of assets	17,992	6,713	592
Net impairment loss recognized in earnings	940	22,889	—
Realized loss on sale of investment securities	2,749	1,117	393
Changes in assets and liabilities:			
Merchandise inventory	(27,994)	(13,735)	(19,074)
Accounts receivable	7,052	(10,094)	(5,660)
Prepaid expenses and other	13,063	(24,781)	(1,334)
Other assets, net	1,146	390	(3,242)
Accounts payable	4,992	(3,053)	(15,559)
Unredeemed gift cards and gift certificates	(3,430)	(11,392)	(699)
Deferred lease credits	4,173	18,887	4,640
Accrued compensation and payroll taxes	25,528	(19,799)	(9,144)
Accrued income and other taxes	12,862	(20,697)	(31,416)
Accrued liabilities	(1,649)	611	6,546
Total adjustments	217,440	124,249	64,644
Net cash provided by operating activities	**386,462**	**303,310**	**464,663**
Investing activities:			
Capital expenditures	(127,419)	(265,335)	(250,407)
Purchase of available-for-sale securities	—	(48,655)	(1,772,653)
Sale of available-for-sale securities	80,353	393,559	2,126,891
Other investing activities	(2,003)	(2,297)	(1,563)
Net cash (used for) provided by investing activities	**(49,069)**	**77,272**	**102,268**
Financing activities:			
Payments on capital leases	(2,015)	(2,177)	(1,912)
Proceeds from issuance of note payable	—	75,000	—
Partial repayment of note payable	(45,000)	—	—
Repurchase of common stock as part of publicly announced programs	—	—	(438,291)
Repurchase of common stock from employees	(247)	(3,432)	(12,310)
Net proceeds from stock options exercised	7,630	3,799	13,183
Excess tax benefit from share-based payments	2,812	693	6,156
Cash dividends paid	(82,985)	(82,394)	(80,796)
Net cash used for financing activities	**(119,805)**	**(8,511)**	**(513,970)**
Effect of exchange rates on cash	3,030	(14,790)	3,363
Net increase in cash and cash equivalents	**220,618**	**357,281**	**56,324**
Cash and cash equivalents — beginning of period	473,342	116,061	59,737
Cash and cash equivalents — end of period	$ 693,960	$ 473,342	$ 116,061

Refer to Notes to Consolidated Financial Statements

AMERICAN EAGLE OUTFITTERS, INC.

NOTES TO CONSOLIDATED FINANCIAL STATEMENTS
FOR THE YEAR ENDED JANUARY 30, 2010

1. Business Operations

American Eagle Outfitters, Inc., a Delaware corporation, (the "Company"), operates under the American Eagle® ("AE"), aerie® by American Eagle, 77kids by american eagle® and MARTIN+OSA® brands.

Founded in 1977, American Eagle Outfitters is a leading apparel and accessories retailer that operates more than 1,000 retail stores in the U.S. and Canada, and online at ae.com®. Through its family of brands, AEO, Inc. offers high quality, on-trend clothing, accessories and personal care products at affordable prices. The Company's online business, AEO Direct, ships to 75 countries worldwide.

American Eagle Outfitters® boasts a passionate and loyal customer base ranging from college students to Hollywood celebrities. The Company focuses on delivering the right product at the right price, combined with a philosophy of operational excellence and discipline across the organization.

AE Brand

The American Eagle Outfitters® brand targets 15- to 25-year old girls and guys, achieving the perfect combination of American prep and current fashion. Denim is the cornerstone of the American Eagle® product assortment, which is completed by other key categories including sweaters, graphic t-shirts, fleece, outerwear and accessories. The American Eagle® attitude is honest, real, individual and fun. American Eagle® is priced to be worn by everyone, everyday, delivering value through quality and style.

aerie by American Eagle

In the fall of 2006, the Company launched aerie® by American Eagle ("aerie"), a collection of Dormwear®, intimates, and personal care products for the 15- to 25-year-old AE® girl. The collection is available in 137 standalone aerie stores throughout the country, online at aerie.com, and at select American Eagle® stores. aerie® features a complete fitness line called aerie f.i.t.™, as well as a personal care collection that includes fragrance, body care and cosmetics to complement the aerie lifestyle. Designed to be sexy, comfortable and cozy, aerie® offers AE® customers a new way to express their personal style everyday.

77kids by american eagle

Introduced in October of 2008 as an online-only brand, 77kids® by american eagle® ("77kids") offers on-trend, high-quality clothing and accessories for kids ages two to 10. The Company plans to open five 77kids® brick-and-mortar stores in Fiscal 2010. The brand draws from the strong heritage of American Eagle Outfitters®, with a point-of-view that's thoughtful, playful and real. Like American Eagle® clothing, 77kids focuses on great fit, value and style.

MARTIN+OSA

MARTIN+OSA® ("M+O") provides clothing and accessories for 28- to 40-year old men and women at its 28 stores and online at www.martinandosa.com.

Refer to Note 15 to the Consolidated Financial Statements for additional information regarding the planned closure of MARTIN+OSA.

AEO Direct

We sell merchandise via our e-commerce operations, ae.com, aerie.com, 77kids.com and martinandosa.com, which are extensions of the lifestyle that we convey in our stores. We currently ship to 75 countries.

AMERICAN EAGLE OUTFITTERS, INC.

NOTES TO CONSOLIDATED FINANCIAL STATEMENTS — (Continued)

Merchandise Mix

The following table sets forth the approximate consolidated percentage of net sales attributable to each merchandise group for each of the periods indicated:

	For the Years Ended		
	January 30, 2010	January 31, 2009	February 2, 2008
Men's apparel and accessories....................	40%	42%	38%
Women's apparel and accessories (excluding aerie)	51%	50%	55%
aerie	9%	8%	7%
Total	100%	100%	100%

2. Summary of Significant Accounting Policies

Principles of Consolidation

The Consolidated Financial Statements include the accounts of the Company and its wholly-owned subsidiaries. All intercompany transactions and balances have been eliminated in consolidation. At January 30, 2010, the Company operated in one reportable segment.

Fiscal Year

The Company's financial year is a 52/53 week year that ends on the Saturday nearest to January 31. As used herein, "Fiscal 2010" refers to the 52 week periods ending January 29, 2011. "Fiscal 2009","Fiscal 2008" and "Fiscal 2007" refer to the 52 week periods ended January 30, 2010, January 31, 2009 and February 2, 2008, respectively. "Fiscal 2006" refers to the 53 week period ended February 3, 2007. "Fiscal 2005" refers to the 52 week periods ended January 28, 2006.

Estimates

The preparation of financial statements in conformity with accounting principles generally accepted in the United States of America ("GAAP") requires the Company's management to make estimates and assumptions that affect the reported amounts of assets and liabilities and disclosure of contingent assets and liabilities at the date of the financial statements and the reported amounts of revenues and expenses during the reporting period. Actual results could differ from those estimates. On an ongoing basis, our management reviews its estimates based on currently available information. Changes in facts and circumstances may result in revised estimates.

Recent Accounting Pronouncements

In July 2009, the Financial Accounting Standards Board ("FASB") issued Statement of Financial Accounting Standards ("SFAS") 168, *The FASB Accounting Standards Codification and the Hierarchy of Generally Accepted Accounting Principles*, a replacement of FASB Statement No. 162 *The Hierarchy of Generally Accepted Accounting Principles*. SFAS 168 establishes the FASB Accounting Standard Codification ("ASC") as the single source of authoritative accounting principles recognized by the FASB to be applied by nongovernmental entities in the preparation of financial statements in conformity with GAAP. Effective July 2009, the FASB ASC is considered the single source of authoritative U.S. accounting and reporting standards, except for additional authoritative rules and interpretive releases issued by the Securities and Exchange Commission ("SEC"). The Company adopted SFAS 168, as codified in ASC 105, *Generally Accepted Accounting Principles,* as of October 31, 2009. All accounting references within this Annual Report on Form 10-K have been updated and, therefore, previous references to GAAP have been replaced with references to GAAP as codified in the ASC.

AMERICAN EAGLE OUTFITTERS, INC.

NOTES TO CONSOLIDATED FINANCIAL STATEMENTS — (Continued)

In September 2009, the FASB approved the consensus on Emerging Issues Task Force ("EITF") 08-1, *Revenue Arrangements with Multiple Deliverables,* primarily codified under ASC 605, *Revenue Recognition,* as Accounting Standards Update ("ASU") 2009-13, *Revenue Recognition (Topic 605): Multiple-Deliverable Revenue Arrangements* ("ASU 2009-13"). ASU 2009-13 requires entities to allocate revenue in an arrangement using estimated selling prices of the delivered goods and services based on a selling price hierarchy. The amendments eliminate the residual method of revenue allocation and require revenue to be allocated among the various deliverables in a multi-element transaction using the relative selling price method. This guidance is effective for revenue arrangements entered into or materially modified in fiscal years beginning after June 15, 2010. The Company is currently evaluating the impact that the adoption of ASU 2009-13 will have on its Consolidated Financial Statements.

In January 2010, the FASB issued ASU 2010-06, *Fair Value Measurements and Disclosures Topic 820: Improving Disclosures about Fair Value Measurements* ("ASU 2010-06"). ASU 2010-06 requires new disclosures regarding transfers in and out of the Level 1 and 2 and activity within Level 3 fair value measurements and clarifies existing disclosures of inputs and valuation techniques for Level 2 and 3 fair value measurements. The new disclosures and clarifications of existing disclosures are effective for interim and annual reporting periods beginning after December 15, 2009, except for the disclosure of activity within Level 3 fair value measurements, which is effective for fiscal years beginning after December 15, 2010, and for interim reporting periods within those years. The Company is currently evaluating the impact that the adoption of ASU 2010-06 will have on its Consolidated Financial Statements and disclosures.

Foreign Currency Translation

The Canadian dollar is the functional currency for the Canadian business. In accordance with ASC 830, *Foreign Currency Matters*, assets and liabilities denominated in foreign currencies were translated into U.S. dollars (the reporting currency) at the exchange rate prevailing at the balance sheet date. Revenues and expenses denominated in foreign currencies were translated into U.S. dollars at the monthly average exchange rate for the period. Gains or losses resulting from foreign currency transactions are included in the results of operations, whereas, related translation adjustments are reported as an element of other comprehensive income in accordance with ASC 220, *Comprehensive Income* (refer to Note 10 to the Consolidated Financial Statements).

Cash and Cash Equivalents, Short-term Investments and Long-term Investments

Cash includes cash equivalents. The Company considers all highly liquid investments purchased with a maturity of three months or less to be cash equivalents.

As of January 30, 2010, short-term investments included auction rate securities ("ARS") classified as available for sale that the Company expects to be redeemed at par within 12 months, based on notice from the issuer.

As of January 30, 2010, long-term investments included investments with remaining maturities of greater than 12 months and consisted of ARS classified as available-for-sale that have experienced failed auctions or have long-term auction resets. The remaining contractual maturities of our long-term investments are approximately 17 months to 38 years. The weighted average contractual maturity for our long-term investments is approximately 25 years.

Unrealized gains and losses on the Company's available-for-sale securities are excluded from earnings and are reported as a separate component of stockholders' equity, within accumulated other comprehensive income, until realized. The components of other-than-temporary impairment ("OTTI") losses related to credit losses, as defined by ASC 320 *Investments — Debt and Equity Securities* ("ASC 320"), are considered by the Company to be realized losses. When available-for-sale securities are sold, the cost of the securities is specifically identified and is used to determine any realized gain or loss.

Refer to Note 3 to the Consolidated Financial Statements for information regarding cash and cash equivalents, short-term investments and long-term investments.

AMERICAN EAGLE OUTFITTERS, INC.

NOTES TO CONSOLIDATED FINANCIAL STATEMENTS — (Continued)

Other-than-Temporary Impairment

The Company evaluates its investments for impairment in accordance with ASC 320. ASC 320 provides guidance for determining when an investment is considered impaired, whether impairment is other-than-temporary, and measurement of an impairment loss. An investment is considered impaired if the fair value of the investment is less than its cost. If, after consideration of all available evidence to evaluate the realizable value of its investment, impairment is determined to be other-than-temporary, then an impairment loss is recognized in the Consolidated Statement of Operations equal to the difference between the investment's cost and its fair value. As of May 3, 2009, the Company adopted ASC 320-10-65, *Transition Related to FSP FAS 115-2 and FAS 124-2, Recognition and Presentation of Other-Than-Temporary-Impairments* ("ASC 320-10-65"), which modifies the requirements for recognizing OTTI and changes the impairment model for debt securities. In addition, ASC 320-10-65 requires additional disclosures relating to debt and equity securities both in the interim and annual periods as well as requires the Company to present total OTTI in the Consolidated Statements of Operations, with an offsetting reduction for any non-credit loss impairment amount recognized in other comprehensive income ("OCI"). During Fiscal 2009, the Company recorded net impairment loss recognized in earnings related to credit losses on its investment securities of $0.9 million. During Fiscal 2008, the Company recorded net impairment loss recognized in earnings of $22.9 million in earnings related to certain investment securities.

Refer to Notes 3 and 4 to the Consolidated Financial Statements for additional information regarding net impairment loss recognized in earnings.

Merchandise Inventory

Merchandise inventory is valued at the lower of average cost or market, utilizing the retail method. Average cost includes merchandise design and sourcing costs and related expenses. The Company records merchandise receipts at the time merchandise is delivered to the foreign shipping port by the manufacturer (FOB port). This is the point at which title and risk of loss transfer to the Company.

The Company reviews its inventory levels to identify slow-moving merchandise and generally uses markdowns to clear merchandise. Additionally, the Company estimates a markdown reserve for future planned permanent markdowns related to current inventory. Markdowns may occur when inventory exceeds customer demand for reasons of style, seasonal adaptation, changes in customer preference, lack of consumer acceptance of fashion items, competition, or if it is determined that the inventory in stock will not sell at its currently ticketed price. Such markdowns may have a material adverse impact on earnings, depending on the extent and amount of inventory affected. The Company also estimates a shrinkage reserve for the period between the last physical count and the balance sheet date. The estimate for the shrinkage reserve, based on historical results, can be affected by changes in merchandise mix and changes in actual shrinkage trends.

Property and Equipment

Property and equipment is recorded on the basis of cost with depreciation computed utilizing the straight-line method over the assets' estimated useful lives. The useful lives of our major classes of assets are as follows:

Buildings	25 years
Leasehold improvements	Lesser of 10 years or the term of the lease
Fixtures and equipment	5 years

In accordance with ASC 360, *Property, Plant, and Equipment*, the Company's management evaluates the value of leasehold improvements and store fixtures associated with retail stores, which have been open for a period of time sufficient to reach maturity. The Company evaluates long-lived assets for impairment at the individual store level, which is the lowest level at which individual cash flows can be identified. Impairment losses are recorded on long-lived assets used in operations when events and circumstances indicate that the assets might be impaired and the undiscounted cash flows estimated to be generated by those assets are less than the carrying amounts of the assets.

AMERICAN EAGLE OUTFITTERS, INC.

NOTES TO CONSOLIDATED FINANCIAL STATEMENTS — (Continued)

When events such as these occur, the impaired assets are adjusted to their estimated fair value and an impairment loss is recorded separately as a component of operating income under loss on impairment of assets.

During Fiscal 2009, the Company recorded asset impairment charges of $18.0 million related primarily to the impairment of 10 M+O stores. During Fiscal 2008 the Company recorded asset impairment charges of $6.7 million related primarily to the impairment of five M+O stores. Based on the Company's review of the operating performance and projections of future performance of these stores, the Company determined that these stores would not be able to generate sufficient cash flow over the life of the related leases to recover the Company's initial investment in them. During Fiscal 2007, the Company recognized impairment losses of $0.6 million related to AE stores.

When the Company closes, remodels or relocates a store prior to the end of its lease term, the remaining net book value of the assets related to the store is recorded as a write-off of assets. During Fiscal 2009, Fiscal 2008 and Fiscal 2007, the Company recorded $2.3 million, $4.9 million and $6.7 million related to asset write-offs within depreciation and amortization expense.

Refer to Note 15 to the Consolidated Financial Statements for additional information regarding the planned closure of MARTIN+OSA.

Goodwill

As of January 30, 2010, the Company had approximately $11.2 million of goodwill compared to $10.7 million as of January 31, 2009. The Company's goodwill is primarily related to the acquisition of its importing operations on January 31, 2000, as well as the acquisition of its Canadian business on November 29, 2000. The increase in goodwill is due to the fluctuation in the foreign exchange spot rate at which the Canadian goodwill is translated. In accordance with ASC 350, *Intangibles-Goodwill and Other,* the Company evaluates goodwill for possible impairment on at least an annual basis and last performed an annual impairment test as of January 30, 2010. Resulting from the Company's annual goodwill impairment test performed as of January 30, 2010, the Company concluded that its goodwill was not impaired.

Other Assets, Net

Other assets, net consist primarily of assets related to our deferred compensation plans and trademark costs, net of accumulated amortization. Trademark costs are amortized over five to 15 years.

Deferred Lease Credits

Deferred lease credits represent the unamortized portion of construction allowances received from landlords related to the Company's retail stores. Construction allowances are generally comprised of cash amounts received by the Company from its landlords as part of the negotiated lease terms. The Company records a receivable and a deferred lease credit liability at the lease commencement date (date of initial possession of the store). The deferred lease credit is amortized on a straight-line basis as a reduction of rent expense over the term of the original lease (including the pre-opening, build-out period) and any subsequent renewal terms. The receivable is reduced as amounts are received from the landlord.

Self-Insurance Liability

The Company is self-insured for certain losses related to employee medical benefits and worker's compensation. Costs for self-insurance claims filed and claims incurred but not reported are accrued based on known claims and historical experience. Management believes that it has adequately reserved for its self-insurance liability, which is capped through the use of stop loss contracts with insurance companies. However, any significant variation of future claims from historical trends could cause actual results to differ from the accrued liability.

AMERICAN EAGLE OUTFITTERS, INC.

NOTES TO CONSOLIDATED FINANCIAL STATEMENTS — (Continued)

Co-branded Credit Card and Customer Loyalty Program

The Company offers a co-branded credit card (the "AE Visa Card") and a private label credit card (the "AE Credit Card") under both the American Eagle and aerie brands. Both of these credit cards are issued by a third-party bank (the "Bank"), and the Company has no liability to the Bank for bad debt expense, provided that purchases are made in accordance with the Bank's procedures. Once a customer is approved to receive the AE Visa Card and the card is activated, the customer is eligible to participate in the Company's credit card rewards program. Under the rewards program that expired on December 31, 2009, points were earned on purchases made with the AE Visa Card at AE and aerie, and at other retailers where the card is accepted. Points earned under this credit card reward program resulted in the issuance of an AE gift card when a certain point threshold was reached. The AE gift card does not expire; however, points earned that have not been used towards the issuance of an AE gift card expire after 36 months of no purchase activity. On January 1, 2010, the Company modified the benefits on the AE Visa and AE Credit Card programs to make both credit cards a part of the rewards program. Customers who make purchases at AE, aerie and 77kids earn discounts in the form of savings certificates when certain purchase levels are reached. Also, AE Visa Card customers, who make purchases at other retailers where the card is accepted, earn additional discounts. Savings certificates are valid for 90 days from issuance.

Points earned under the credit card rewards program on purchases at AE and aerie are accounted for by analogy to ASC 605-25, *Revenue Recognition, Multiple Element Arrangements* ("ASC 605-25"). The Company believes that points earned under its point and loyalty programs represent deliverables in a multiple element arrangement rather than a rebate or refund of cash. Accordingly, the portion of the sales revenue attributed to the award points is deferred and recognized when the award is redeemed or when the points expire. Additionally, credit card reward points earned on non-AE or aerie purchases are accounted for in accordance with ASC 605-25. As the points are earned, a current liability is recorded for the estimated cost of the award, and the impact of adjustments is recorded in cost of sales.

Through December 31, 2009, the Company offered its customers the AE All-Access Pass, a customer loyalty program. On January 1, 2010, the Company replaced the Pass with the AEREWARD$^{sm} Loyalty Program (the "Program"). Under either loyalty program, customers accumulate points based on purchase activity and earn rewards by reaching certain point thresholds during three-month earning periods. Rewards earned during these periods are valid through the stated expiration date, which is approximately one month from the mailing date. These rewards can be redeemed for a discount on a purchase of merchandise. Rewards not redeemed during the one-month redemption period are forfeited. The Company determined that rewards earned using the Pass and the Program should be accounted for in accordance with ASC 605-25. Accordingly, the portion of the sales revenue attributed to the award credits is deferred and recognized when the awards are redeemed or expire.

Stock Repurchases

During Fiscal 2007, the Company's Board of Directors ("the Board") authorized a total of 60.0 million shares of its common stock for repurchase under its share repurchase program with expiration dates extending into Fiscal 2010. During Fiscal 2007, the Company repurchased 18.7 million shares as part of its publicly announced repurchase programs for approximately $438.3 million, at a weighted average price of $23.38 per share. The Company did not repurchase any common stock as part of its publicly announced repurchase program during Fiscal 2009 or Fiscal 2008. At January 30, 2010, the authorization to repurchase 11.3 million shares of the Company's common stock under its share repurchase program expired. As of March 26, 2010, the Company had 30.0 million shares remaining authorized for repurchase. These shares will be repurchased at the Company's discretion. The authorization relating to the remaining 30.0 million shares expires at the end of Fiscal 2010.

During Fiscal 2009 and Fiscal 2008, the Company repurchased approximately 18,000 and 0.2 million shares, respectively, from certain employees at market prices totaling $0.2 million and $3.4 million, respectively. These shares were repurchased for the payment of taxes in connection with the vesting of share-based payments, as permitted under the 2005 Stock Award and Incentive Plan, as amended (the "2005 Plan").

AMERICAN EAGLE OUTFITTERS, INC.

NOTES TO CONSOLIDATED FINANCIAL STATEMENTS — (Continued)

The aforementioned share repurchases have been recorded as treasury stock.

Income Taxes

The Company calculates income taxes in accordance with ASC 740, *Income Taxes* ("ASC 740"), which requires the use of the asset and liability method. Under this method, deferred tax assets and liabilities are recognized based on the difference between the Consolidated Financial Statement carrying amounts of existing assets and liabilities and their respective tax bases as computed pursuant to ASC 740. Deferred tax assets and liabilities are measured using the tax rates, based on certain judgments regarding enacted tax laws and published guidance, in effect in the years when those temporary differences are expected to reverse. A valuation allowance is established against the deferred tax assets when it is more likely than not that some portion or all of the deferred taxes may not be realized. Changes in the Company's level and composition of earnings, tax laws or the deferred tax valuation allowance, as well as the results of tax audits, may materially impact the Company's effective tax rate.

Effective February 4, 2007, the Company adopted the accounting pronouncement now codified in ASC 740 regarding accounting for unrecognized tax benefits. This pronouncement prescribes a comprehensive model for recognizing, measuring, presenting and disclosing in the financial statements tax positions taken or expected to be taken on a tax return, including a decision whether to file or not to file in a particular jurisdiction. Under ASC 740, a tax benefit from an uncertain position may be recognized only if it is "more likely than not" that the position is sustainable based on its technical merits.

The calculation of the deferred tax assets and liabilities, as well as the decision to recognize a tax benefit from an uncertain position and to establish a valuation allowance require management to make estimates and assumptions. The Company believes that its assumptions and estimates are reasonable, although actual results may have a positive or negative material impact on the balances of deferred tax assets and liabilities, valuation allowances or net income.

Revenue Recognition

Revenue is recorded for store sales upon the purchase of merchandise by customers. The Company's e-commerce operation records revenue upon the estimated customer receipt date of the merchandise. Shipping and handling revenues are included in net sales. Sales tax collected from customers is excluded from revenue and is included as part of accrued income and other taxes on the Company's Consolidated Balance Sheets.

Revenue is recorded net of estimated and actual sales returns and deductions for coupon redemptions and other promotions. The Company records the impact of adjustments to its sales return reserve quarterly within net sales and cost of sales. The sales return reserve reflects an estimate of sales returns based on projected merchandise returns determined through the use of historical average return percentages.

	For the Years Ended	
	January 30, 2010	January 31, 2009
	(In thousands)	
Beginning balance	$ 4,092	$ 4,683
Returns	(74,540)	(81,704)
Provisions	75,293	81,113
Ending balance	$ 4,845	$ 4,092

Revenue is not recorded on the purchase of gift cards. A current liability is recorded upon purchase, and revenue is recognized when the gift card is redeemed for merchandise. Additionally, the Company recognizes revenue on unredeemed gift cards based on an estimate of the amounts that will not be redeemed ("gift card breakage"), determined through historical redemption trends. Gift card breakage revenue is recognized in

AMERICAN EAGLE OUTFITTERS, INC.

NOTES TO CONSOLIDATED FINANCIAL STATEMENTS — (Continued)

proportion to actual gift card redemptions as a component of net sales. For further information on the Company's gift card program, refer to the Gift Cards caption below.

The Company sells off end-of-season, overstock, and irregular merchandise to a third-party. The proceeds from these sales are presented on a gross basis, with proceeds and cost of sell-offs recorded in net sales and cost of sales, respectively.

	For the Years Ended		
	January 30, 2010	January 31, 2009	February 2, 2008
	(In thousands)		
Proceeds from sell-offs.........................	$31,889	$38,240	$23,775
Marked-down cost of merchandise disposed of via sell-offs ..	$31,345	$38,012	$25,805

Cost of Sales, Including Certain Buying, Occupancy and Warehousing Expenses

Cost of sales consists of merchandise costs, including design, sourcing, importing and inbound freight costs, as well as markdowns, shrinkage and certain promotional costs (collectively "merchandise costs") and buying, occupancy and warehousing costs. Buying, occupancy and warehousing costs consist of compensation, employee benefit expenses and travel for our buyers and certain senior merchandising executives; rent and utilities related to our stores, corporate headquarters, distribution centers and other office space; freight from our distribution centers to the stores; compensation and supplies for our distribution centers, including purchasing, receiving and inspection costs; and shipping and handling costs related to our e-commerce operation. Merchandise margin is the difference between net sales and merchandise costs. Gross profit is the difference between net sales and cost of sales.

Selling, General and Administrative Expenses

Selling, general and administrative expenses consist of compensation and employee benefit expenses, including salaries, incentives and related benefits associated with our stores and corporate headquarters. Selling, general and administrative expenses also include advertising costs, supplies for our stores and home office, communication costs, travel and entertainment, leasing costs and services purchased. Selling, general and administrative expenses do not include compensation, employee benefit expenses and travel for our design, sourcing and importing teams, our buyers and our distribution centers as these amounts are recorded in cost of sales.

Advertising Costs

Certain advertising costs, including direct mail, in-store photographs and other promotional costs are expensed when the marketing campaign commences. As of January 30, 2010 and January 31, 2009, the Company had prepaid advertising expense of $5.4 million and $2.9 million, respectively. All other advertising costs are expensed as incurred. The Company recognized $68.9 million, $79.7 million and $74.9 million in advertising expense during Fiscal 2009, Fiscal 2008 and Fiscal 2007, respectively.

Design Costs

The Company has certain design costs, including compensation, rent, depreciation, travel, supplies and samples, which are included in cost of sales as the respective inventory is sold.

Store Pre-Opening Costs

Store pre-opening costs consist primarily of rent, advertising, supplies and payroll expenses. These costs are expensed as incurred.

AMERICAN EAGLE OUTFITTERS, INC.

NOTES TO CONSOLIDATED FINANCIAL STATEMENTS — (Continued)

Other (Expense) Income, Net

Other (expense) income, net consists primarily of a realized investment loss, interest income/expense and foreign currency transaction gain/loss.

Gift Cards

The value of a gift card is recorded as a current liability upon purchase and revenue is recognized when the gift card is redeemed for merchandise. Prior to July 8, 2007, if a gift card remained inactive for greater than 24 months, the Company assessed the recipient a one-dollar per month service fee, where allowed by law, which was automatically deducted from the remaining value of the card. For those jurisdictions where assessing a service fee was not allowable by law, the estimated breakage was recorded in a manner consistent with that described above, starting after 24 months of inactivity. Both gift card service fees and breakage estimates were recorded within other (expense) income, net.

On July 8, 2007, the Company discontinued assessing a service fee on active gift cards. As a result, the Company estimates gift card breakage and recognizes revenue in proportion to actual gift card redemptions as a component of net sales. The Company determines an estimated gift card breakage rate by continuously evaluating historical redemption data and the time when there is a remote likelihood that a gift card will be redeemed.

Legal Proceedings and Claims

The Company is subject to certain legal proceedings and claims arising out of the conduct of its business. In accordance with ASC 450, *Contingencies* ("ASC 450"), the Company records a reserve for estimated losses when the loss is probable and the amount can be reasonably estimated. If a range of possible loss exists and no anticipated loss within the range is more likely than any other anticipated loss, the Company records the accrual at the low end of the range, in accordance with ASC 450. As the Company believes that it has provided adequate reserves, it anticipates that the ultimate outcome of any matter currently pending against the Company will not materially affect the consolidated financial position, results of operations or consolidated cash flows of the Company.

Supplemental Disclosures of Cash Flow Information

The table below shows supplemental cash flow information for cash amounts paid during the respective periods:

	For the Years Ended		
	January 30, 2010	January 31, 2009	February 2, 2008
	(In thousands)		
Cash paid during the periods for:			
Income taxes	$61,869	$132,234	$260,615
Interest	$ 1,879	$ 1,947	$ —

Segment Information

In accordance with ASC 280, *Segment Reporting* ("ASC 280"), the Company has identified four operating segments (American Eagle Brand US and Canadian stores, aerie by American Eagle retail stores, MARTIN+OSA retail stores and AEO Direct) that reflect the basis used internally to review performance and allocate resources. All of the operating segments have been aggregated and are presented as one reportable segment, as permitted by ASC 280.

AMERICAN EAGLE OUTFITTERS, INC.

NOTES TO CONSOLIDATED FINANCIAL STATEMENTS — (Continued)

The following tables present summarized geographical information:

	For the Years Ended		
	January 30, 2010	January 31, 2009	February 2, 2008
	(In thousands)		
Net sales:			
United States	$2,715,583	$2,707,261	$2,770,119
Foreign(1)	274,937	281,605	285,300
Total net sales	$2,990,520	$2,988,866	$3,055,419

(1) Amounts represent sales from American Eagle and aerie Canadian retail stores, as well as AEO Direct sales, that are billed to and/or shipped to foreign countries.

	January 30, 2010	January 31, 2009
	(In thousands)	
Long-lived assets, net:		
United States	$678,385	$708,180
Foreign	45,967	42,766
Total long-lived assets, net	$724,352	$750,946

Reclassifications

Certain reclassifications have been made to the Consolidated Financial Statements for prior periods in order to conform to the current period presentation.

3. Cash and Cash Equivalents, Short-term Investments and Long-term Investments

The following table summarizes the fair market value of our cash and marketable securities, which are recorded as cash and cash equivalents on the Consolidated Balance Sheets, our short-term investments and our long-term investments:

	January 30, 2010		
	Balance	Unrealized Holding Gains	Unrealized Holding Losses
		(In thousands)	
Cash and cash equivalents:			
Cash	$144,391	$—	$ —
Commercial paper	25,420		
Treasury bills	119,988		
Money-market	404,161	—	—
Total cash and cash equivalents	$693,960	$—	$ —
Short-term investments:			
Student-loan backed ARS	$ 400	$—	$ —
State and local government ARS	4,275	—	—
Total short-term investments	$ 4,675	$—	$ —
Long-term investments:			
Student-loan backed ARS	$149,031	$—	$ (8,569)
State and local government ARS	35,969	—	(456)
Auction rate preferred securities	12,773	—	(1,287)
Total long-term investments	$197,773	$—	$(10,312)
Total	$896,408	$—	$(10,312)

AMERICAN EAGLE OUTFITTERS, INC.

NOTES TO CONSOLIDATED FINANCIAL STATEMENTS — (Continued)

	January 31, 2009		
	Balance	Unrealized Holding Gains	Unrealized Holding Losses
		(In thousands)	
Cash and cash equivalents:			
Cash	$ 61,355	$—	$ —
Money-market	411,987	—	—
Total cash and cash equivalents	$473,342	$—	$ —
Short-term investments:			
Preferred stock	$ 6,219	$—	$ —
Auction rate preferred securities	4,292	—	—
Total short-term investments	$ 10,511	$—	$ —
Long-term investments:			
Student-loan backed ARS	$169,254	$—	$(31,446)
State and local government ARS	69,970	—	(630)
Auction rate preferred securities	11,783	—	(3,217)
Total long-term investments	$251,007	$—	$(35,293)
Total	$734,860	$—	$(35,293)

Proceeds from the sale of available-for-sale securities were $80.4 million, $393.6 million and $2.127 billion for Fiscal 2009, Fiscal 2008 and Fiscal 2007, respectively. There were no purchases of investments during Fiscal 2009. The proceeds from the sale of available-for-sale securities for Fiscal 2008 and Fiscal 2007 are offset against purchases of $48.7 million and $1.773 billion, respectively. In addition to the net impairment loss recognized in earnings discussed below for Fiscal 2009 and Fiscal 2008, the Company recorded net realized losses related to the sale of available-for-sale securities of $2.7 million, $1.1 million and $0.4 million for Fiscal 2009, Fiscal 2008 and Fiscal 2007, respectively, in other (expense) income, net.

The following tables present the length of time available-for-sale securities were in continuous unrealized loss positions but were not deemed to be other-than-temporarily impaired:

	Less than 12 Months		Greater than or Equal to 12 Months	
	Gross Unrealized Holding Losses	Fair Value	Gross Unrealized Holding Losses	Fair Value
		(In thousands)		
January 30, 2010				
Student-loan backed ARS	$ (1,643)	$ 9,203	$(6,926)	$50,228
State and local government ARS	(273)	8,096	(183)	20,922
Auction rate preferred securities	—	—	(1,287)	12,773
Total(1)	$ (1,916)	$ 17,299	$(8,396)	$83,923
January 31, 2009				
Student-loan backed ARS	$(31,446)	$169,254	$ —	$ —
State and local government ARS	(630)	61,570	—	—
Auction rate preferred securities	(3,217)	11,783	—	—
Total(1)	$(35,293)	$242,607	$ —	$ —

AMERICAN EAGLE OUTFITTERS, INC.

NOTES TO CONSOLIDATED FINANCIAL STATEMENTS — (Continued)

(1) Fair value excludes $101.2 million as of January 30, 2010 and $8.4 million as of January 31, 2009 of investments whose fair value approximates par. Additionally, as of January 31, 2009, fair value excludes $10.5 million of securities on which net impairment loss recognized in earnings has been recorded.

As of January 30, 2010, we had a total of $896.4 million in cash and cash equivalents, short-term and long-term investments, which included $189.6 million of investments in ARS and $12.8 million of auction rate preferred securities ("ARPS"), net of $10.3 million ($6.4 million net of tax) of temporary impairment and $0.9 million in net impairment loss recognized in earnings. Our short-term and long-term investments consist of the following:

	No. of Issues	Par Value	Cumulative Unrealized Losses Recognized in OCI	Cumulative Losses Recognized in Earnings	Carrying Value as of January 30, 2010
			(In thousands, except no. of issues amount)		
Auction rate securities ("ARS"):					
Closed-end municipal fund ARS	5	$ 17,025	$ (9)	$ —	$ 17,016
Municipal Bond ARS	5	23,675	(447)	—	23,228
Auction rate preferred securities	2	15,000	(1,287)	(940)	12,773
Federally-insured student loan ARS	16	148,000	(6,012)	—	141,988
Private-insured student loan ARS	1	10,000	(2,557)	—	7,443
Total Auction rate securities	29	$213,700	$(10,312)	$(940)	$202,448

Lehman Brothers Holding, Inc. ("Lehman") acted as a broker and auction agent for all of the Company's ARPS. Lehman filed for Chapter 11 bankruptcy protection during September 2008, resulting in the dissolution of the investment trusts for most of the Company's ARPS. As a result, the Company received 760,000 preferred shares in Fiscal 2008 and an additional 576,000 preferred shares in Fiscal 2009. During the 13 weeks ended May 2, 2009, the Company liquidated all 1.3 million shares for $7.8 million and recorded an incremental loss of $2.7 million. The total realized loss on the sale of these securities was $25.6 million, of which $22.9 million was recorded as a net impairment loss recognized in earnings in Fiscal 2008.

The Company continues to monitor the market for ARS and ARPS and consider the impact, if any, on the fair value of its investments. If current market conditions deteriorate further, or the anticipated recovery in market values does not occur, we may be required to record additional impairment.

4. Fair Value Measurements

ASC 820, *Fair Value Measurement Disclosures* ("ASC 820"), defines fair value, establishes a framework for measuring fair value in accordance with GAAP, and expands disclosures about fair value measurements. Fair value is defined under ASC 820 as the exit price associated with the sale of an asset or transfer of a liability in an orderly transaction between market participants at the measurement date. The Company adopted the provisions of ASC 820 as of February 3, 2008, for items measured at fair value on a recurring basis, which consist of financial instruments including ARS and ARPS. The Company adopted the provisions of ASC 820-10-65 *Fair Value Measurements, Transition and Open Effective Date Information, Transition related to FASB Staff Position FAS 157-2, Effective Date of FASB Statement No. 157* as of February 1, 2009 for items measured at fair value on a nonrecurring basis, including goodwill and property and equipment. Additionally, the Company adopted the provisions of ASC 320-10-65 and ASC 820-10-65 *Fair Value Measurements, Transition and Open Effective Date Information, Transition related to FASB Staff Position 157-4, Determining Fair Value When the Volume and Level of Activity for the Asset or Liability*

AMERICAN EAGLE OUTFITTERS, INC.

NOTES TO CONSOLIDATED FINANCIAL STATEMENTS — (Continued)

Have Significantly Decreased and Identifying Transactions That Are Not Orderly as of May 3, 2009 for its financial instruments measured at fair value. The impact of adopting these was not significant on the Company's accompanying financial statements.

Financial Instruments

Valuation techniques used to measure fair value under ASC 820 must maximize the use of observable inputs and minimize the use of unobservable inputs. In addition, ASC 820 establishes this three-tier fair value hierarchy, which prioritizes the inputs used in measuring fair value. These tiers include:

- *Level 1* — Quoted prices in active markets for identical assets or liabilities.

- *Level 2* — Inputs other than Level 1 that are observable, either directly or indirectly, such as quoted prices for similar assets or liabilities; quoted prices in markets that are not active; or other inputs that are observable or can be corroborated by observable market data for substantially the full term of the assets or liabilities.

- *Level 3* — Unobservable inputs (i.e. projections, estimates, interpretations, etc.) that are supported by little or no market activity and that are significant to the fair value of the assets or liabilities.

As of January 30, 2010 and January 31, 2009, the Company held certain assets that are required to be measured at fair value on a recurring basis. These include cash equivalents and short and long-term investments, including ARS and ARPS.

In accordance with ASC 820, the following tables represent the fair value hierarchy for the Company's financial assets (cash equivalents and investments) measured at fair value on a recurring basis as of January 30, 2010 and January 31, 2009:

	Fair Value Measurements at January 30, 2010			
	Carrying Amount as of January 30, 2010	Quoted Market Prices in Active Markets for Identical Assets (Level 1)	Significant Other Observable Inputs (Level 2)	Significant Unobservable Inputs (Level 3)
	(In thousands)			
Cash and Cash Equivalents				
Cash	$144,391	$144,391	$ —	$ —
Commercial paper	25,420	25,420	—	—
Treasury bills	119,988	119,988	—	—
Money-market	404,161	404,161	—	—
Total cash and cash equivalents	$693,960	$693,960	$ —	$ —
Short-term Investments				
Student-loan backed ARS	$ 400	$ —	$ —	$ 400
State and local government ARS	4,275	—	—	4,275
Total Short-term Investments	$ 4,675	$ —	$ —	$ 4,675
Long-term Investments				
Student-loan backed ARS	$149,031	$ —	$ —	$149,031
State and local government ARS	35,969	—	—	35,969
Auction rate preferred securities	12,773	—	—	12,773
Total Long-term Investments	$197,773	$ —	$ —	$197,773
Total	$896,408	$693,960	$ —	$202,448
Percent to total	100.0%	77.4%	0.0%	22.6%

AMERICAN EAGLE OUTFITTERS, INC.

NOTES TO CONSOLIDATED FINANCIAL STATEMENTS — (Continued)

| | Fair Value Measurements at January 31, 2009 | | | |
	Carrying Amount as of January 31, 2009	Quoted Market Prices in Active Markets for Identical Assets (Level 1)	Significant Other Observable Inputs (Level 2)	Significant Unobservable Inputs (Level 3)
	(In thousands)			
Cash and Cash Equivalents				
Cash	$ 61,355	$ 61,355	$ —	$ —
Money-market	411,987	411,987	—	—
Total cash and cash equivalents	$473,342	$473,342	$ —	$ —
Short-term Investments				
Preferred Stock	$ 6,219	$ 6,219	$ —	$ —
Auction rate preferred securities . .	4,292	—	4,292	—
Total Short-term Investments	$ 10,511	$ 6,219	$4,292	$ —
Long-term Investments				
Student-loan backed ARS	$169,254	$ —	$ —	$169,254
State and local government ARS . .	69,970	—	—	69,970
Auction rate preferred securities . .	11,783	—	—	11,783
Total Long-term Investments	$251,007	$ —	$ —	$251,007
Total	$734,860	$479,561	$4,292	$251,007
Percent to total	100.0%	65.3%	0.6%	34.1%

The Company used a discounted cash flow ("DCF") model to value our Level 3 investments. For Fiscal 2009, the assumptions in the Company's model included different recovery periods, ranging from 0.5 year to 11 years, depending on the type of security and varying discount factors for yield, ranging from 0.3% to 6.6%, and illiquidity, ranging from 0.3% to 4.0%. For Fiscal 2008, the assumptions in the Company's model included different recovery periods, ranging from 1.1 years to 11 years, depending on the type of security and varying discount factors for yield, ranging from 1.7% to 18.8%, and illiquidity, ranging from 0.0% to 1.0%. These assumptions are subjective. They are based on the Company's current judgment and view of current market conditions. The use of different assumptions would result in a different valuation and related charge. As a result of the discounted cash flow analysis for Fiscal 2009, the Company recorded a net recovery of $25.0 million ($15.5 million, net of tax) which reduced the total cumulative impairment recognized in other comprehensive income ("OCI") as of January 30, 2010 to $10.3 million ($6.4 million, net of tax) from $35.3 million ($21.8 million, net of tax) at the end of Fiscal 2008. The reversal of temporary impairment was primarily driven by calls at par for the Company's private-insured student loan ARS. As a result of the calls, the securities which were previously impaired were revalued at par. These amounts were recorded in OCI and resulted in an increase in the investments' estimated fair values. The net increase in fair value was partially offset by $0.9 million of net impairment loss recognized in earnings during Fiscal 2009 as a result of credit rating downgrades.

AMERICAN EAGLE OUTFITTERS, INC.

NOTES TO CONSOLIDATED FINANCIAL STATEMENTS — (Continued)

The following table presents a rollforward of the amount of net impairment loss recognized in earnings related to credit losses:

	For the Year Ended January 30, 2010 (In thousands)
Beginning balance of credit losses previously recognized in earnings	$ —
Year-to-date OTTI credit losses recognized in earnings.	940
Ending balance of cumulative credit losses recognized in earnings	$940

The reconciliation of our assets measured at fair value on a recurring basis using unobservable inputs (Level 3) is as follows:

	Level 3 (Unobservable Inputs)			
	Total	Auction-Rate Municipal Securities	Student Loan-Backed Auction-Rate Securities	Auction-Rate Preferred Securities
Carrying value at February 2, 2008	$ —	$ —	$ —	$ —
Additions to Level 3 upon adoption of ASC 820(1)	340,475	84,575	212,000	43,900
Settlements.	(29,875)	(18,575)	(11,300)	—
Additions to Level 3(2).	4,600	4,600	—	—
Transfers out of Level 3(3)	(28,900)	—	—	(28,900)
Losses:				
Losses reported in OCI	(35,293)	(630)	(31,446)	(3,217)
Balance at January 31, 2009	$251,007	$ 69,970	$169,254	$ 11,783
Settlements.	(72,600)	(29,900)	(42,700)	—
Gains and (losses):				
Reported in earnings	(940)	—	—	(940)
Reported in OCI	24,981	174	22,877	1,930
Balance at January 30, 2010	$202,448	$ 40,244	$149,431	$ 12,773

(1) Represents amounts transferred upon the adoption of ASC 820 during the first quarter of Fiscal 2008.

(2) Additions to Level 3 include securities previously classified as Level 2, which were securities that had experienced partial calls prior to the fourth quarter of 2008 and were previously valued at par.

(3) Transfers out of Level 3 include preferred securities (into Level 1) and ARPS (into Level 2). The transfers to Level 1 occurred due to the Company acquiring exchange traded preferred shares as a result of the ARPS trusts liquidating. The transfers to Level 2 occurred as a result of the Company determining that it was more appropriate to value these investments using observable market prices of the underlying securities. The OTTI charge of $22.9 million that was reported in earnings was taken on Level 1 and Level 2 securities transferred from Level 3.

Non-Financial Assets

The Company's non-financial assets, which include goodwill and property and equipment, are not required to be measured at fair value on a recurring basis. However, if certain triggering events occur, or if an annual impairment test is required and the Company is required to evaluate the non-financial instrument for impairment, a resulting asset impairment would require that the non-financial asset be recorded at the estimated fair value.

AMERICAN EAGLE OUTFITTERS, INC.

NOTES TO CONSOLIDATED FINANCIAL STATEMENTS — (Continued)

Resulting from the Company's annual goodwill impairment test performed as of January 30, 2010, the Company concluded that its goodwill was not impaired.

Certain long-lived assets were measured at fair value on a nonrecurring basis using Level 3 inputs as defined in ASC 820. Based on the Company's review of the operating performance and projections of underperforming stores, the Company determined that certain underperforming stores would not be able to generate sufficient cash flow over the life of the related leases to recover the Company's initial investment in them. The fair value of those stores were determined by estimating the amount and timing of net future cash flows and discounting them using a risk-adjusted rate of interest. The Company estimates future cash flows based on its experience and knowledge of the market in which the store is located. During Fiscal 2009, certain long-lived assets with a carrying value of $18.0 million, primarily related to 10 M+O stores, were determined to be unable to recover their respective carrying values and, therefore, were written down to their fair value, resulting in a loss on impairment of assets of $18.0 million.

5. Earnings per Share

ASC 260-10-45, *Participating Securities and the Two-Class Method* ("ASC 260-10-45"), addresses whether awards granted in unvested share-based payment transactions that contain non-forfeitable rights to dividends or dividend equivalents (whether paid or unpaid) are participating securities and therefore are included in computing earnings per share under the two-class method, as described in ASC 260, *Earnings Per Share*. Participating securities are securities that may participate in dividends with common stock and the two-class method is an earnings allocation formula that treats a participating security as having rights to earnings that would otherwise have been available to common shareholders. Under the two-class method, earnings for the period are allocated between common shareholders and other shareholders, based on their respective rights to receive dividends. Restricted stock awards granted to certain employees under the Company's 2005 Plan are considered participating securities as these employees receive non-forfeitable dividends at the same rate as common stock. ASC 260-10-45 was adopted and retrospectively applied at the beginning of Fiscal 2009. For Fiscal 2009, Fiscal 2008 and Fiscal 2007, the application of ASC 260-10-45 resulted in no material change to basic EPS or diluted EPS.

The following is a reconciliation between basic and diluted weighted average shares outstanding:

	For the Years Ended		
	January 30, 2010	January 31, 2009	February 2, 2008
	(In thousands, except per share amounts)		
Weighted average common shares outstanding:			
Basic number of common shares outstanding	206,171	205,169	216,119
Dilutive effect of stock options and non-vested restricted stock	3,341	2,413	4,161
Dilutive number of common shares outstanding	209,512	207,582	220,280
Basic net income per common share			
Net income	$169,022	$179,061	$400,019
Less: Income allocated to participating securities	365	364	215
Net income available to common shareholders	$168,657	$178,697	$399,804
Basic net income per common share	$ 0.82	$ 0.87	$ 1.85
Dilutive net income per common share			
Net income	$169,022	$179,061	$400,019
Less: Income allocated to participating securities	360	360	210
Net income available to common shareholders	$168,662	$178,701	$399,809
Dilutive net income per common share	$ 0.81	$ 0.86	$ 1.82

AMERICAN EAGLE OUTFITTERS, INC.

NOTES TO CONSOLIDATED FINANCIAL STATEMENTS — (Continued)

Equity awards to purchase approximately 6.6 million, 7.6 million, and 2.5 million shares of common stock during the Fiscal 2009, Fiscal 2008 and Fiscal 2007, respectively, were outstanding, but were not included in the computation of weighted average diluted common share amounts as the effect of doing so would have been anti-dilutive.

Additionally, for Fiscal 2009 and Fiscal 2008, approximately 0.4 million and 0.8 million shares, respectively, of performance-based restricted stock were not included in the computation of weighted average diluted common share amounts because the number of shares ultimately issued is contingent on the Company's performance compared to pre-established annual performance goals.

6.   Accounts Receivable

Accounts receivable are comprised of the following:

	January 30, 2010	January 31, 2009
	(In thousands)	
Construction allowances	$11,132	$11,139
Merchandise sell-offs	8,063	17,057
Interest income	217	1,355
Marketing cost reimbursements	2,556	2,363
Credit card receivable	7,832	5,175
Merchandise vendor receivables	375	2,899
Gift card receivable	1,413	115
Franchise receivable	1,419	—
Other	1,739	1,368
Total	$34,746	$41,471

7.   Property and Equipment

Property and equipment consists of the following:

	January 30, 2010	January 31, 2009
	(In thousands)	
Land	$ 6,364	$ 6,364
Buildings	151,484	122,414
Leasehold improvements	645,794	605,299
Fixtures and equipment	590,610	536,009
Construction in progress	554	28,543
	$1,394,806	$1,298,629
Less: Accumulated depreciation and amortization	(681,664)	(558,389)
Net property and equipment	$ 713,142	$ 740,240

Depreciation expense is summarized as follows:

	For the Years Ended		
	January 30, 2010	January 31, 2009	February 2, 2008
	(In thousands)		
Depreciation expense	$144,883	$130,802	$108,919

AMERICAN EAGLE OUTFITTERS, INC.

NOTES TO CONSOLIDATED FINANCIAL STATEMENTS — (Continued)

8. Note Payable and Other Credit Arrangements

The Company has borrowing agreements with four separate financial institutions under which it may borrow an aggregate of $325.0 million United States dollars ("USD") and $25.0 million Canadian dollars ("CAD"). Of this amount, $200.0 million USD can be used for demand letter of credit facilities, $100.0 million USD and $25.0 million CAD can be used for demand line borrowings and the remaining $25.0 million USD can be used for either letters of credit or demand line borrowings at the Company's discretion. The $100.0 million USD of demand line credit is comprised of two facilities each with $50.0 million USD of borrowing capacity. The expiration dates of the two demand line facilities are April 21, 2010 and May 22, 2010. The $25.0 million CAD of demand line credit was established during Fiscal 2009, and is provided at the discretion of the lender.

During Fiscal 2009, the Company reduced the amount of credit available that could be used for either letters of credit or as a demand line from $100.0 million USD to $25.0 million USD. This request was made by the lender due to the Company's low utilization of this credit facility. The reduction was effective July 3, 2009 and had no material impact on the Company's Consolidated Financial Statements or on the Company's ability to fund its operations. Additionally, during Fiscal 2009, the Company increased its borrowing capacity for demand letters of credit from $150.0 million USD to $200.0 million USD.

As of January 30, 2010, the Company had outstanding trade and standby letters of credit of $51.5 million USD and demand line borrowings of $30.0 million USD, which reflects a $45.0 million USD reduction from January 31, 2009, as a result of a voluntary partial repayment made during Fiscal 2009. The outstanding amounts on the demand line borrowings can be called for repayment by the financial institutions at any time. Additionally, the availability of any remaining borrowings is subject to acceptance by the respective financial institutions. The average borrowing rate on the demand lines for Fiscal 2009 was 2.5% and the Company has incorporated the outstanding demand line borrowings into working capital.

9. Leases

The Company leases all store premises, some of its office space and certain information technology and office equipment. The store leases generally have initial terms of 10 years. Most of these store leases provide for base rentals and the payment of a percentage of sales as additional contingent rent when sales exceed specified levels. Additionally, most leases contain construction allowances and/or rent holidays. In recognizing landlord incentives and minimum rent expense, the Company amortizes the charges on a straight-line basis over the lease term (including the pre-opening build-out period). These leases are classified as operating leases.

A summary of fixed minimum and contingent rent expense for all operating leases follows:

	For the Years Ended		
	January 30, 2010	January 31, 2009	February 2, 2008
	(In thousands)		
Store rent:			
Fixed minimum	$229,428	$197,820	$167,051
Contingent	7,873	11,767	17,626
Total store rent, excluding common area maintenance charges, real estate taxes and certain other expenses	$237,301	$209,587	$184,677
Offices, distribution facilities, equipment and other	18,664	18,260	17,250
Total rent expense	$255,965	$227,847	$201,927

In addition, the Company is typically responsible under its store, office and distribution center leases for tenant occupancy costs, including maintenance costs, common area charges, real estate taxes and certain other expenses.

AMERICAN EAGLE OUTFITTERS, INC.

NOTES TO CONSOLIDATED FINANCIAL STATEMENTS — (Continued)

The table below summarizes future minimum lease obligations, consisting of fixed minimum rent, under operating leases in effect at January 30, 2010:

Fiscal years:	Future Minimum Lease Obligations (In thousands)
2010	$ 242,859
2011	226,699
2012	210,676
2013	194,613
2014	176,612
Thereafter	693,048
Total	$1,744,507

10.   Other Comprehensive Income (Loss)

The accumulated balances of other comprehensive income (loss) included as part of the Consolidated Statements of Stockholders' Equity follow:

	Before Tax Amount	Tax (Expense) Benefit	Accumulated Other Comprehensive Income (Loss)
	(In thousands)		
Balance at February 3, 2007	$ 21,201	$ 513	$ 21,714
Unrealized gain on investments	1,538	(591)	947
Reclassification adjustment for net losses realized in net income related to sale of available-for-sale securities	393	(151)	242
Foreign currency translation adjustment	12,582	—	12,582
Balance at February 2, 2008	$ 35,714	$ (229)	$ 35,485
Temporary impairment related to ARS	(36,825)	14,030	(22,795)
Reclassification adjustment for losses realized in net income related to sale of ARS	318	(121)	197
Reclassification adjustment for OTTI charges realized in net income related to ARS	1,214	(463)	751
Unrealized loss on investments	(607)	229	(378)
Foreign currency translation adjustment	(27,649)	—	(27,649)
Balance at January 31, 2009	$(27,835)	$13,446	$(14,389)
Temporary reversal of impairment related to ARS	24,041	(9,535)	14,506
Reclassification adjustment for OTTI charges realized in net income related to ARS	940	—	940
Foreign currency translation adjustment	15,781	—	15,781
Balance at January 30, 2010	$ 12,927	$ 3,911	$ 16,838

AMERICAN EAGLE OUTFITTERS, INC.

NOTES TO CONSOLIDATED FINANCIAL STATEMENTS — (Continued)

The components of accumulated other comprehensive income (loss) were as follows:

	For the Years Ended	
	January 30, 2010	January 31, 2009
	(In thousands)	
Net unrealized (loss) gain on available-for-sale securities, net of tax(1). . . .	$(6,401)	$(21,847)
Foreign currency translation adjustment	23,239	7,458
Accumulated other comprehensive (loss) income	$16,838	$(14,389)

(1) Amounts are shown net of tax of $3.9 million and $13.4 million for Fiscal 2009 and Fiscal 2008, respectively.

11. Share-Based Payments

At January 30, 2010, the Company had awards outstanding under three share-based compensation plans, which are described below.

The Company accounts for share-based compensation under the provisions of ASC 718, *Compensation — Stock Compensation* ("ASC 718"), which requires the Company to measure and recognize compensation expense for all share-based payments at fair value. Total share-based compensation expense included in the Consolidated Statements of Operations for Fiscal 2009, Fiscal 2008 and Fiscal 2007 was $36.9 million ($22.8 million, net of tax), $20.3 million ($12.5 million, net of tax) and $33.7 million ($20.7 million, net of tax), respectively.

ASC 718 requires recognition of compensation cost under a non-substantive vesting period approach. Accordingly, the Company recognizes compensation expense over the period from the grant date to the date retirement eligibility is achieved, if that is expected to occur during the nominal vesting period. Additionally, for awards granted to retirement eligible employees, the full compensation cost of an award must be recognized immediately upon grant.

Share-based compensation plans

1994 Stock Option Plan

On February 10, 1994, the Company's Board adopted the American Eagle Outfitters, Inc. 1994 Stock Option Plan (the "1994 Plan"). The 1994 Plan provided for the grant of 12.2 million incentive or non-qualified options to purchase common stock. The 1994 Plan was subsequently amended to increase the shares available for grant to 24.3 million shares. Additionally, the amendment provided that the maximum number of options that may be granted to any individual may not exceed 8.1 million shares. The options granted under the 1994 Plan were approved by the Compensation Committee of the Board, primarily vest over five years, and expire 10 years from the date of grant. The 1994 Plan terminated on January 2, 2004 with all rights of the optionees and all unexpired options continuing in force and operation after the termination.

1999 Stock Incentive Plan

The 1999 Stock Option Plan (the "1999 Plan") was approved by the stockholders on June 8, 1999. The 1999 Plan authorized 18.0 million shares for issuance in the form of stock options, stock appreciation rights ("SAR"), restricted stock awards, performance units or performance shares. The 1999 Plan was subsequently amended to increase the shares available for grant to 33.0 million. Additionally, the 1999 Plan provided that the maximum number of shares awarded to any individual may not exceed 9.0 million shares. The 1999 Plan allowed the Compensation Committee to determine which employees and consultants received awards and the terms and conditions of these awards. The 1999 Plan provided for a grant of 1,875 stock options quarterly (not to be adjusted for stock splits) to each director who is not an officer or employee of the Company starting in August 2003. The Company ceased making these quarterly stock option grants in June 2005. Under this plan, 33.2 million non-

AMERICAN EAGLE OUTFITTERS, INC.

NOTES TO CONSOLIDATED FINANCIAL STATEMENTS — (Continued)

qualified stock options and 6.7 million shares of restricted stock were granted to employees and certain non-employees (without considering cancellations to date of awards for 7.9 million shares). Approximately 33% of the options granted were to vest over eight years after the date of grant but were accelerated as the Company met annual performance goals. Approximately 34% of the options granted under the 1999 Plan vest over three years, 23% vest over five years and the remaining grants vest over one year. All options expire after 10 years. Performance-based restricted stock was earned if the Company met established performance goals. The 1999 Plan terminated on June 15, 2005 with all rights of the awardees and all unexpired awards continuing in force and operation after the termination.

2005 Stock Award and Incentive Plan

The 2005 Plan was approved by the stockholders on June 15, 2005. The 2005 Plan authorized 18.4 million shares for issuance, of which 6.4 million shares are available for full value awards in the form of restricted stock awards, restricted stock units or other full value stock awards and 12.0 million shares are available for stock options, SAR, dividend equivalents, performance awards or other non-full value stock awards. The 2005 Plan was subsequently amended and restated on June 16, 2009 to, among other things, increase the shares available for grant to 31.9 million effective as of January 31, 2009 without taking into consideration of 9.1 million non-qualified stock options, 2.9 million shares of restricted stock and 0.2 million shares of common stock that had been previously granted under the 2005 plan to employees and directors (without considering cancellations as of January 31, 2009 of awards for 2.9 million shares). The 2005 Plan provides that the maximum number of shares awarded to any individual may not exceed 6.0 million shares per year for options and SAR and no more than 4.0 million shares may be granted with respect to each of restricted shares of stock and restricted stock units plus any unused carryover limit from the previous year. The 2005 Plan allows the Compensation Committee of the Board to determine which employees receive awards and the terms and conditions of the awards that are mandatory under the 2005 Plan. The 2005 Plan provides for grants to directors who are not officers or employees of the Company, which are not to exceed 20,000 shares per year (not to be adjusted for stock splits). Through January 30, 2010, 12.6 million non-qualified stock options, 4.6 million shares of restricted stock and 0.2 million shares of common stock had been granted under the 2005 Plan to employees and directors (without considering cancellations to date of awards for 4.6 million shares). Approximately 99% of the options granted under the 2005 Plan vest over three years and 1% vest over five years. Options were granted for ten and seven year terms. Approximately 97% of the restricted stock awards are performance-based and are earned if the Company meets established performance goals. The remaining 3% of the restricted stock awards are time-based and vest over three years.

Stock Option Grants

The Company grants both time-based and performance-based stock options under the 2005 Plan. Time-based stock option awards vest over the requisite service period of the award or to an employee's eligible retirement date, if earlier. Performance-based stock option awards vest over three years and are earned if the Company meets pre-established performance goals during each year.

AMERICAN EAGLE OUTFITTERS, INC.

NOTES TO CONSOLIDATED FINANCIAL STATEMENTS — (Continued)

A summary of the Company's stock option activity under all plans for Fiscal 2009 follows:

| | For the Year Ended January 30, 2010 | | | |
	Options	Weighted-Average Exercise Price	Weighted-Average Remaining Contractual Life (In Years)	Aggregate Intrinsic Value (In thousands)
Outstanding — January 31, 2009	14,496,734	$15.25		
Granted.	3,402,609	$11.34		
Exercised(1)	1,463,897	$ 7.08		
Cancelled	1,530,504	$16.70	—	—
Outstanding — January 30, 2010	14,904,942	$15.01	3.8	$60,091
Vested and expected to vest — January 30, 2010.	14,546,241	$14.99	3.8	$58,809
Exercisable — January 30, 2010	5,031,264	$ 7.13	2.1	$44,063

(1) Options exercised during Fiscal 2009 ranged in price from $4.68 to $13.46.

The weighted-average grant date fair value of stock options granted during Fiscal 2009, Fiscal 2008 and Fiscal 2007 was $3.86, $7.16 and $10.64, respectively. The aggregate intrinsic value of options exercised during Fiscal 2009, Fiscal 2008 and Fiscal 2007 was $11.7 million, $3.9 million and $22.5 million, respectively. Cash received from the exercise of stock options and the actual tax benefit realized from stock option exercises were $7.6 million and $8.0 million, respectively, for Fiscal 2009. Cash received from the exercise of stock options and the actual tax benefit realized from stock option exercises were $3.8 million and $1.1 million, respectively, for Fiscal 2008. Cash received from the exercise of stock options and the actual tax benefit realized from stock option exercises were $13.2 million and $7.3 million, respectively, for Fiscal 2007.

The fair value of stock options was estimated at the date of grant using a Black-Scholes option pricing model with the following weighted-average assumptions:

| | For the Years Ended | | |
Black-Scholes Option Valuation Assumptions	January 30, 2010	January 31, 2009	February 2, 2008
Risk-free interest rates(1)	1.7%	2.5%	4.5%
Dividend yield	3.4%	1.7%	0.9%
Volatility factors of the expected market price of the Company's common stock(2)	56.9%	44.4%	39.2%
Weighted-average expected term(3).	4.1 years	4.3 years	4.4 years

(1) Based on the U.S. Treasury yield curve in effect at the time of grant with a term consistent with the expected life of our stock options.

(2) Based on a combination of historical volatility of the Company's common stock and implied volatility.

(3) Represents the period of time options are expected to be outstanding. The weighted average expected option term for the years ended January 30, 2010 and January 31, 2009 were determined based on historical experience. The weighted average expected option terms for the year ended February 2, 2008 was determined using a combination of the "simplified method" for plain vanilla options as allowed by ASC 718, and past behavior. The "simplified method" calculates the expected term as the average of the vesting term and original contractual term of the options.

AMERICAN EAGLE OUTFITTERS, INC.

NOTES TO CONSOLIDATED FINANCIAL STATEMENTS — (Continued)

As of January 30, 2010, there was $8.5 million of unrecognized compensation expense related to nonvested stock option awards that is expected to be recognized over a weighted average period of 1.4 years.

Restricted Stock Grants

Time-based restricted stock awards include two types of awards; time-based restricted stock and time-based restricted stock units. Time-based restricted stock awards vest over three years and participate in nonforfeitable dividends. Time-based restricted stock units vest over three years, however, they may be accelerated to vest over one year if the Company meets pre-established performance goals in the year of grant. Time-based restricted stock units receive dividend equivalents in the form of additional time-based restricted stock units, which are subject to the same restrictions and forfeiture provisions as the original award.

Performance-based restricted stock awards include two types of awards; performance-based restricted stock and performance-based restricted stock units. Performance-based restricted stock awards vest over one year based upon the Company's achievement of pre-established goals and participate in nonforfeitable dividends. Performance-based restricted stock units cliff vest at the end of a three year period based upon the Company's achievement of pre-established goals. Performance-based restricted stock units receive dividend equivalents in the form of additional performance-based restricted stock units, which are subject to the same restrictions as the original award.

The grant date fair value of restricted stock awards is based on the closing market price of the Company's common stock on the date of grant. Historically, the Company has granted only restricted stock awards that entitled the holders to receive nonforfeitable dividends prior to vesting. Beginning with the Fiscal 2009 restricted stock awards, the Company began to also grant restricted stock unit awards to its employees. The restricted stock unit awards differ from the restricted stock awards in that they do not contain nonforfeitable rights to dividends and are therefore not considered participating securities in accordance with ASC 260-10-45.

A summary of the activity of the Company's restricted stock is presented in the following tables.

	Time-Based Restricted Stock For the Year Ended January 30, 2010		Performance-Based Restricted Stock For the Year Ended January 30, 2010	
	Shares	Weighted-Average Grant Date Fair Value	Shares	Weighted-Average Grant Date Fair Value
Nonvested — January 31, 2009.....	41,000	$19.97	757,812	$21.26
Granted	1,883	13.28	989,664	9.66
Vested	(41,000)	19.97	—	—
Cancelled.....................	—	—	(757,812)	21.26
Nonvested — January 30, 2010.....	1,883	$13.28	989,664	$ 9.66

	Time-Based Restricted Stock Units For the Year Ended January 30, 2010		Performance-Based Restricted Stock Units For the Year Ended January 30, 2010	
	Shares	Weighted-Average Grant Date Fair Value	Shares	Weighted-Average Grant Date Fair Value
Nonvested — January 31, 2009....	—	$ —	—	$ —
Granted	1,855,618	9.79	417,101	9.82
Vested	—	—	—	—
Cancelled.....................	(187,526)	9.66	(10,870)	9.66
Nonvested — January 30, 2010....	1,668,092	$9.79	406,231	$9.82

AMERICAN EAGLE OUTFITTERS, INC.

NOTES TO CONSOLIDATED FINANCIAL STATEMENTS — (Continued)

As of January 30, 2010, there was $2.1 million of unrecognized compensation expense related to nonvested restricted stock awards that is expected to be recognized over a weighted average period of one month. The total fair value of restricted stock awards vested during Fiscal 2009, Fiscal 2008 and Fiscal 2007 was $0.6 million, $9.6 million and $32.6 million, respectively.

As of January 30, 2010, the Company had 28.4 million shares available for all equity grants.

12.   Retirement Plan and Employee Stock Purchase Plan

The Company maintains a profit sharing and 401(k) plan (the "Retirement Plan"). Under the provisions of the Retirement Plan, full-time employees and part-time employees are automatically enrolled to contribute 3% of their salary if they have attained 20½ years of age. In addition, full-time employee need to have completed 60 days of service and part-time employees must complete 1,000 hours worked to be eligible. Individuals can decline enrollment or can contribute up to 50% of their salary to the 401(k) plan on a pretax basis, subject to IRS limitations. After one year of service, the Company will match 100% of the first 3% of pay plus an additional 50% of the next 3% of pay that is contributed to the plan. Contributions to the profit sharing plan, as determined by the Board, are discretionary. The Company recognized $7.2 million, $6.3 million and $6.1 million in expense during Fiscal 2009, Fiscal 2008 and Fiscal 2007, respectively, in connection with the Retirement Plan.

The Employee Stock Purchase Plan is a non-qualified plan that covers all full-time employees and part-time employees who are at least 18 years old and have completed 60 days of service. Contributions are determined by the employee, with the Company matching 15% of the investment up to a maximum investment of $100 per pay period. These contributions are used to purchase shares of Company stock in the open market.

13.   Income Taxes

The components of income before income taxes were:

| | For the Years Ended | | |
	January 30, 2010	January 31, 2009	February 2, 2008
	(In thousands)		
U.S.	$197,948	$244,629	$568,519
Foreign	34,443	52,412	67,862
Total	$232,391	$297,041	$636,381

AMERICAN EAGLE OUTFITTERS, INC.

NOTES TO CONSOLIDATED FINANCIAL STATEMENTS — (Continued)

The significant components of the Company's deferred tax assets and liabilities were as follows:

	January 30, 2010	January 31, 2009
	(In thousands)	
Deferred tax assets:		
Deferred compensation	$ 36,018	$ 21,492
Tax credits	31,756	4,217
Rent	24,498	22,207
Inventories	11,422	14,828
Investment securities	10,677	8,721
Employee compensation and benefits	10,669	3,677
Foreign and state income taxes	7,484	12,984
Temporary impairment of investment securities	3,911	13,446
Other	8,384	10,158
Gross deferred tax assets	144,819	111,730
Valuation allowance	(15,688)	(12,933)
Total deferred tax assets	$129,131	$ 98,797
Deferred tax liabilities:		
Property and equipment	$ (37,896)	$ (36,641)
Prepaid expenses	(3,774)	(1,708)
Total deferred tax liabilities	$ (41,670)	$ (38,349)
Total deferred tax assets, net	$ 87,461	$ 60,448
Classification in the Consolidated Balance Sheet		
Current deferred tax assets	$ 60,156	$ 45,447
Noncurrent deferred tax assets	27,305	15,001
Total deferred tax assets	$ 87,461	$ 60,448

The net increase in deferred tax assets and liabilities was primarily due to an increase in the deferred tax asset for tax credit carryovers associated with the repatriation of earnings from Canada and an increase in the deferred tax asset for deferred compensation.

AMERICAN EAGLE OUTFITTERS, INC.

NOTES TO CONSOLIDATED FINANCIAL STATEMENTS — (Continued)

Significant components of the provision for income taxes were as follows:

	For the Years Ended		
	January 30, 2010	January 31, 2009	February 2, 2008
	(In thousands)		
Current:			
Federal................................	$ 73,095	$ 69,592	$172,604
Foreign taxes	14,526	16,341	24,030
State..................................	11,948	7,578	27,987
Total current................................	99,569	93,511	224,621
Deferred:			
Federal................................	(38,810)	21,927	10,306
Foreign taxes	6,513	(340)	(2,077)
State..................................	(3,903)	2,882	3,512
Total deferred................................	(36,200)	24,469	11,741
Provision for income taxes	$ 63,369	117,980	$236,362

As a result of additional tax deductions related to share-based payments, tax benefits have been recognized as contributed capital for Fiscal 2009, Fiscal 2008, and Fiscal 2007 in the amounts of $8.0 million, $1.1 million and $7.3 million, respectively.

During Fiscal 2009 the Company approved and repatriated $91.7 million from its Canadian subsidiaries. The proceeds from the repatriation were used for general corporate purposes. We plan to indefinitely reinvest accumulated earnings of our Canadian subsidiaries outside of the United States to the extent not repatriated in Fiscal 2009. Accordingly, no provision for U.S. income taxes has been provided thereon. Upon distribution of those earnings in the form of dividends or otherwise, we would be subject to income and withholding taxes offset by foreign tax credits. As of January 30, 2010, the unremitted earnings of our Canadian subsidiaries were $28.0 million.

As of January 30, 2010, the gross amount of unrecognized tax benefits was $31.6 million, of which $23.4 million would affect the effective income tax rate if recognized. The gross amount of unrecognized tax benefits as of January 31, 2009 was $41.1 million, of which $23.1 million would affect the effective income tax rate if recognized.

The following table summarizes the activity related to our unrecognized tax benefits:

	For the Years Ended		
	January 30, 2010	January 31, 2009	February 2, 2008
	(In thousands)		
Unrecognized tax benefits, beginning of the year balance..................................	$ 41,080	$42,953	$39,311
Increases in tax positions of prior periods	1,679	205	2,562
Decreases in tax positions of prior periods............	(13,471)	(1,705)	(5,026)
Increases in current period tax positions	14,842	4,221	8,057
Settlements..................................	(6,204)	(4,529)	(1,764)
Lapse of statute of limitations.....................	(6,291)	(30)	(187)
Translation adjustment	14	(35)	—
Unrecognized tax benefits, end of the year balance	$ 31,649	$41,080	$42,953

AMERICAN EAGLE OUTFITTERS, INC.

NOTES TO CONSOLIDATED FINANCIAL STATEMENTS — (Continued)

Unrecognized tax benefits decreased by $9.5 million and $1.9 million during Fiscal 2009 and 2008, respectively. The decreases were primarily due to federal and state income tax settlements and statute of limitation lapses. The Company does not anticipate any significant changes to the unrecognized tax benefits recorded at the balance sheet date over the next twelve months.

The Company records accrued interest and penalties related to unrecognized tax benefits in the provision for income taxes. Accrued interest and penalties related to unrecognized tax benefits included in the Consolidated Balance Sheet were $7.0 million and $11.4 million as of January 30, 2010 and January 31, 2009, respectively. During Fiscal 2009, the Company recognized a net benefit of $3.3 million in the provision for income taxes related to the reversal of accrued interest and penalties primarily due to federal and state income tax settlements. An immaterial amount of interest and penalties were recognized in the provision for income taxes during Fiscal 2008 and 2007.

The Company and its subsidiaries file income tax returns in the U.S. federal jurisdiction and various state and foreign jurisdictions. The Internal Revenue Service ("IRS") examination of the Company's U.S. federal income tax returns for the tax years ended July 2006 and July 2007 were completed in November of 2009. Additionally, the previously unagreed item for the tax years ended July 2003 to July 2005 was resolved through a review and agreement with IRS Appeals during Fiscal 2009. Accordingly, all years prior to July 2008 are no longer subject to U.S. federal income tax examinations by tax authorities. During Fiscal 2009, the Company changed its tax year end to a 52/53 week year that ends on the Saturday nearest January 31 from July 31 to conform to its financial statement year end. This change was effective for the tax year ended January 31, 2009. An IRS examination of the July 2008 and January 2009 federal income tax returns is scheduled to begin in the first quarter of Fiscal 2010. The Company does not anticipate that any adjustments will result in a material change to its financial position, results of operations or cash flow. With respect to state and local jurisdictions and countries outside of the United States, with limited exceptions, generally, the Company and its subsidiaries are no longer subject to income tax audits for tax years before 2003. Although the outcome of tax audits is always uncertain, the Company believes that adequate amounts of tax, interest and penalties have been provided for any adjustments that are expected to result from these years.

The Company has foreign tax credit carryovers associated with the repatriation of earnings from Canada in the amount of $26.8 million as of January 30, 2010. The foreign tax credit carryovers expire in Fiscal 2019 to the extent not utilized. No valuation allowance has been recorded on the foreign tax credit carryovers because we believe it is more likely than not the foreign tax credits will be utilized prior to expiration.

The Company has been certified to qualify for nonrefundable incentive tax credits in Kansas for additional expenditures related to the Ottawa, Kansas distribution center. As a result, the Company has a deferred tax asset related to Kansas tax credit carryforwards of $5.0 million (net of federal income taxes). These tax credits can be utilized to offset future Kansas income taxes and will generally expire in eight years. The use of these tax credits is dependent upon the level of income tax due to Kansas and the Company meeting certain requirements in future periods. Due to the contingencies related to the future use of these tax credits, we believe it is more likely than not that the full benefit of this asset will not be realized within the carryforward period. Thus, a valuation allowance of $5.0 million (net of federal income taxes) has been recorded as of January 30, 2010. The valuation allowance recorded as of January 31, 2009 was $3.8 million. The Company may earn additional tax credits or change its assessment of the valuation allowance if certain employment and training requirements are met.

During Fiscal 2009 and 2008, the Company recorded a valuation allowance against deferred tax assets arising from the other than temporary impairment or disposition of certain investment securities. The disposition of the investment securities results in a capital loss that can only be utilized to the extent of capital gains. These capital losses are subject to a three year carryback period and a five year carryforward period for tax purposes. The capital losses generally will expire in Fiscal 2014. Due to the contingencies related to the future use of these capital losses, we believe it is more likely than not that the full benefit of this asset will not be realized within the carryforward period. Thus, the Company has recorded a valuation allowance against the deferred tax assets arising from the other than temporary impairment or disposition of these investment securities. The valuation allowance related to these investment securities was $10.7 million and $9.1 million as of January 30, 2010 and January 31, 2009, respectively.

AMERICAN EAGLE OUTFITTERS, INC.

NOTES TO CONSOLIDATED FINANCIAL STATEMENTS — (Continued)

The Company has not recorded a valuation allowance on the temporary impairment of the investment securities recorded in other comprehensive income. The Company believes this treatment is consistent with the Company's intent and ability to hold the debt securities to recovery.

A reconciliation between the statutory federal income tax rate and the effective income tax rate from continuing operations follows:

	For the Years Ended		
	January 30, 2010	January 31, 2009	February 2, 2008
Federal income tax rate	35%	35%	35%
State income taxes, net of federal income tax effect........	3	3	3
Canadian earnings repatriation	(7)	—	—
Tax settlements	(5)	—	—
Valuation allowance on ARS and ARPS impairment	1	3	
Tax impact of tax exempt interest	—	(1)	(1)
	27%	40%	37%

14. Quarterly Financial Information — Unaudited

The sum of the quarterly EPS amounts may not equal the full year amount as the computations of the weighted average shares outstanding for each quarter and the full year are calculated independently.

	Fiscal 2009 Quarters Ended			
	May 2, 2009	August 1, 2009	October 31, 2009	January 30, 2010
	(In thousands, except per share amounts)			
Net sales	$611,986	$657,596	$748,962	$971,976
Gross profit	220,925	248,833	300,128	388,163
Net income..............................	21,967	28,572	59,159	59,324
Income per common share — basic	0.11	0.14	0.29	0.29
Income per common share — diluted..........	0.11	0.14	0.28	0.28

	Fiscal 2008 Quarters Ended			
	May 3, 2008	August 2, 2008	November 1, 2008	January 31, 2009
	(In thousands, except per share amounts)			
Net sales................................	$640,302	$688,815	$754,036	$905,713
Gross profit.............................	263,667	289,384	309,412	311,638
Net income	43,895	59,831	42,604	32,731
Income per common share — basic	0.21	0.29	0.21	0.16
Income per common share — diluted	0.21	0.29	0.21	0.16

15. Subsequent Event

On March 5, 2010, the Company's Board approved management's recommendation to proceed with the closure of the M+O brand. The Company notified employees and issued a press release announcing this decision on March 9, 2010. The decision to take this action resulted from an extensive evaluation of the brand and review of

AMERICAN EAGLE OUTFITTERS, INC.

NOTES TO CONSOLIDATED FINANCIAL STATEMENTS — (Continued)

strategic alternatives, which revealed that it was not achieving performance levels that warranted further investment.

As a result of this decision, the Company plans to close all 28 stores and cease all online and corporate operations of M+O in Fiscal 2010. The timing of the store closures is dependent on a number of factors that include negotiating third-party agreements, adherence to notification requirements and local laws.

In conjunction with the closing of M+O, the Company expects the Fiscal 2010 cash outflow, net of associated tax benefits, to be approximately $10 million to $40 million. This is comprised of estimated pre-tax charges of approximately $32 million to $77 million, which includes lease-related items of approximately $18 million to $63 million, severance of approximately $10 million and other charges of approximately $4 million. Additionally, the Company estimates approximately $29 million of non-cash, pre-tax impairment charges and inventory write downs. These charges are expected to be recognized primarily over the first half of Fiscal 2010.

The above estimates are preliminary and based on a number of significant assumptions and could change materially.

Refer to Note 2 to the Consolidated Financial Statements for additional information regarding M+O store impairments previously recorded.

The Company has evaluated the existence of subsequent events through the filing date of this Annual Report on Form 10-K.

ITEM 9. *CHANGES IN AND DISAGREEMENTS WITH ACCOUNTANTS ON ACCOUNTING AND FINANCIAL DISCLOSURE.*

None.

ITEM 9A. *CONTROLS AND PROCEDURES.*

Disclosure Controls and Procedures

We maintain disclosure controls and procedures that are designed to provide reasonable assurance that information required to be disclosed in our reports under the Securities Exchange Act of 1934, as amended (the "Exchange Act"), is recorded, processed, summarized and reported within the time periods specified in the SEC's rules and forms, and that such information is accumulated and communicated to the management of American Eagle Outfitters, Inc. (the "Management"), including our Principal Executive Officer and our Principal Financial Officer, as appropriate, to allow timely decisions regarding required disclosure. In designing and evaluating the disclosure controls and procedures, Management recognized that any controls and procedures, no matter how well designed and operated, can provide only reasonable assurance of achieving the desired control objectives.

In connection with the preparation of this Annual Report on Form 10-K as of January 30, 2010, an evaluation was performed under the supervision and with the participation of our Management, including the Principal Executive Officer and Principal Financial Officer, of the effectiveness of the design and operation of the Company's disclosure controls and procedures (as defined in Rule 13a-15(e) under the Exchange Act). Based upon that evaluation, our Principal Executive Officer and our Principal Financial Officer have concluded that our disclosure controls and procedures were effective at the reasonable assurance level as of the end of the period covered by this Annual Report on Form 10-K.

Management's Annual Report on Internal Control Over Financial Reporting

Our Management is responsible for establishing and maintaining adequate internal control over financial reporting (as defined in Rule 13a-15(f) under the Exchange Act). Our internal control over financial reporting is designed to provide a reasonable assurance to our Management and our Board regarding the preparation and fair presentation of published financial statements.

All internal control systems, no matter how well designed have inherent limitations. Therefore, even those systems determined to be effective can provide only reasonable assurance with respect to financial statement preparation and presentation.

Our Management assessed the effectiveness of our internal control over financial reporting as of January 30, 2010. In making this assessment, our Management used the criteria set forth by the Committee of Sponsoring Organizations of the Treadway Commission (COSO) in Internal Control — Integrated Framework. Based on this assessment, our Management concluded that we maintained effective internal control over financial reporting as of January 30, 2010.

The Company's independent registered public accounting firm that audited the financial statements included in this Annual Report issued an attestation report on the Company's internal control over financial reporting.

Changes in Internal Control Over Financial Reporting

There were no changes in our internal control over financial reporting during the three months ended January 30, 2010 that have materially affected, or are reasonably likely to materially affect, our internal control over financial reporting.

Buckle

2009 Annual Report

FINANCIAL HIGHLIGHTS

(Dollar Amounts In Thousands Except Per Share Amounts And Selected Operating Data)

	JANUARY 30, 2010	JANUARY 31, 2009	FEBRUARY 2, 2008
INCOME STATEMENT DATA			
Net sales	$ 898,287	$ 792,046	$ 619,888
Income before income taxes	$ 204,127	$ 164,868	$ 118,810
Provision for income taxes	$ 76,824	$ 60,459	$ 43,563
Net income	$ 127,303	$ 104,409	$ 75,247
Diluted earnings per share	$ 2.73	$ 2.24	$ 1.63
Net income as a percentage of net sales	14.2%	13.2%	12.1%
BALANCE SHEET DATA			
Working capital	$ 172,779	$ 197,539	$ 184,395
Long-term investments	$ 72,770	$ 56,213	$ 81,201
Total assets	$ 488,903	$ 465,340	$ 450,657
Long-term debt	$ —	$ —	$ —
Stockholders' equity	$ 354,259	$ 337,222	$ 338,320
SELECTED OPERATING DATA			
Number of stores open at year end	401	387	368
Average sales per square foot	$ 428	$ 401	$ 335
Average sales per store (000's)	$ 2,129	$ 1,995	$ 1,668
Comparable store sales change	7.8%	20.6%	13.2%

2009 BUCKLE HIGHLIGHTS

Opened 20 new stores and completed 22 substantial remodels; closed 1 store in April 2009, 1 store in October 2009, and 4 stores in January 2010 to end the fiscal year with 401 stores in 41 states.

Achieved average sales per store of $2.1 million, up from $2.0 million in fiscal 2008.

Average sales per square foot were $428, up from $401 in fiscal 2008.

Total denim sales increased for the tenth consecutive year, with the category representing approximately 43% of fiscal 2009 net sales.

Gross margin improved as a percentage of net sales for the seventh consecutive year, rising to 44.6% from 43.4% in fiscal 2008.

Average transaction value increased 6.4% to $93.85 and average price point increased 3.9% to $45.05.

NET SALES
(Amounts In Thousands)

2005	$ 501,101
2006 (a)	$ 530,074
2007	$ 619,888
2008	$ 792,046
2009	$ 898,287

DILUTED EARNINGS PER SHARE

2005	$ 1.13
2006 (a)	$ 1.24
2007	$ 1.63
2008	$ 2.24
2009	$ 2.73

(a) Consists of 53 weeks.

Fiscal 2009 marked another outstanding year for Buckle on a number of fronts. We achieved record sales of $898.3 million, a 13.4% increase over fiscal 2008. In addition, we reported record earnings of $127.3 million, or $2.73 per diluted share, a 21.9% increase over last year.

Reflecting our continued commitment to creating shareholder value, we returned more than $120.3 million to shareholders throughout the year. On top of our quarterly dividends of $0.20 per share, we paid a special cash dividend of $1.80 per share during the third quarter—marking our third special dividend in the last four fiscal years. This brings our total cash returned to shareholders over the past five years to $502.6 million, including $360.7 million in dividends and $141.9 million in share repurchases. As we look ahead, our balance sheet remains strong with $230.8 million in cash and investments, stockholders' equity of $354.3 million, and no long-term debt.

Our financial results are a function of our focused approach to creating the most enjoyable shopping experience possible for our guests. No matter what is happening in the marketplace, our commitment to delivering a wide selection of quality merchandise and outstanding service to our guests remains constant.

Store Performance – Through the end of 2009, Buckle achieved 13 consecutive quarters of positive comparable store sales. Driven by a 7.8% increase in comparable store sales, our average sales per store increased to $2.1 million from $2.0 million in 2008, and our average sales per square foot increased to $428 from $401. We also improved our gross margin to 44.6% from 43.4% and our operating margin to 22.2% from 20.5%.

Denim – Composing 43% of our total sales, denim continues to serve as the cornerstone of our business. Fiscal 2009 was no exception as we increased denim sales for the tenth year in a row—growing the category by 17.5% and selling a record-level 4.3 million pairs of jeans. Throughout the year, our skilled merchandising team expanded our selection of denim fits, brands, and styles—strengthening our reputation as a denim destination.

Merchandise – Our merchandising team, led by Pat Whisler and Bob Carlberg, did an exceptional job of providing newness by collaborating with an outstanding group of vendors to successfully anticipate trends, develop new styles, and update guests' favorites. Their talent and efforts enabled us to manage our inventory as we achieved record sales for the eighth consecutive year. For the fiscal year, the men's business grew 1.5% on top of growth of 25.5% and 20.5% in each of the past two years and the women's business grew 22.5% on top of growth of 29.5% and 14.0% in the past two years.

Shopping Experience – Led by Kari Smith and Michelle Hoffman, our sales team is driven by high expectations and is dedicated to meeting them. Our 20 district managers, each averaging 21 years with the company, have done a tremendous job of motivating their teams and finding new and innovative ways to educate our teammates—effectively raising the bar for service.

Real Estate – Expansion through carefully selected new store locations in regional malls and lifestyle shopping centers is also an important component of our overall growth. Led by Brett Milkie, our real estate team takes a practical approach to site selection driven by the economics of each individual location and the availability of an internal leader to successfully manage in a particular market. In 2009, we opened 20 new stores, including our first in New York and New Jersey, remodeled 22 stores, and closed 6, ending the year with 401 stores in 41 states. This year, we plan to open 20 new stores and remodel another 25 locations.

Building for the Future – Teammates in the home office and distribution center are essential to our success. Thanks to the efforts of our online team, we increased Buckle.com sales by 45% to $52.3 million. To support this growth, we invested $5.5 million during the year to expand our online fulfillment center. We also broke ground on a new distribution center that is estimated to cost $25-$27 million. Projected to be complete in July 2010, the new facility will be equipped to support more than 600 stores. Plans for 2010 also include the replacement of our point-of-sale software and hardware, allowing us to improve our customer loyalty program and better serve our guests.

As a specialty retailer, we are proud of what we've accomplished, but we're even more excited about where we are headed. Our progress is the collective result of 7,000+ teammates' efforts across all areas of the business. To each of you, I say thank you.

I would also like to take this opportunity to thank our loyal guests for choosing to shop with us. We never forget whom we are here to serve and will work hard to continue to earn your business.

Sincerely,

Dennis H. Nelson

Dennis H. Nelson
President and Chief Executive Officer

Following a disciplined real estate strategy, we continue to increase our geographic presence by opening new retail locations in regional malls and lifestyle centers across the United States. In 2009, we opened 20 new stores. Plans for 2010 include 20 new stores—including additional stores in New Jersey and New York.

Buckle continues to enhance the in-store shopping experience. Over the past year, we rolled out new mannequins, tables, and fixtures and renovated 22 stores, bringing the total number of locations featuring our signature store design to 222 as of January 30, 2010. Plans for 2010 include 25 additional remodels.

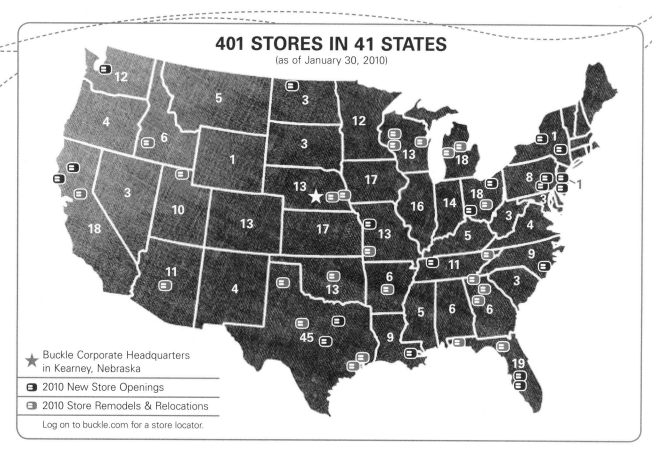

401 STORES IN 41 STATES
(as of January 30, 2010)

★ Buckle Corporate Headquarters in Kearney, Nebraska

☐ 2010 New Store Openings

☐ 2010 Store Remodels & Relocations

Log on to buckle.com for a store locator.

2010 NEW STORE OPENINGS

Mall	Location	Mall	Location
Montgomery Mall	North Wales, PA	Governor's Square Mall	Clarksville, TN
The Domain II	Austin, TX	Arden Fair Mall	Sacramento, CA
The Village at Fairview	Fairview, TX	Kenwood Towne Center	Cincinnati, OH
Northgate Mall	San Rafael, CA	Eastview Mall	Victor, NY
Bellevue Square	Bellevue, WA	Dakota Square	Minot, ND
Cherry Hill Mall	Cherry Hill, NJ	Beachwood Place	Beachwood, OH
The Florida Mall	Orlando, FL	Jacksonville Mall	Jacksonville, NC
Deptford Mall	Deptford, NJ	Park City Center	Lancaster, PA
The Esplanade	Kenner, LA	Waterford Lakes Town Center	Orlando, FL
Crossgate Mall	Albany, NY	Summit Fair	Lee's Summit, MO

UNITED STATES
SECURITIES AND EXCHANGE COMMISSION
WASHINGTON, D.C. 20549

FORM 10-K

☒   **ANNUAL REPORT PURSUANT TO SECTION 13 OR 15(d) OF**
THE SECURITIES EXCHANGE ACT OF 1934

For the Fiscal Year Ended **January 30, 2010**

☐   **TRANSITION REPORT PURSUANT TO SECTION 13 OR 15(d) OF**
THE SECURITIES EXCHANGE ACT OF 1934

For the Transition Period from _____ to _____

Commission File Number: 001-12951

THE BUCKLE, INC.

(Exact name of Registrant as specified in its charter)

Nebraska	**47-0366193**
(State or other jurisdiction of incorporation or organization)	(I.R.S. Employer Identification No.)

2407 West 24th Street, Kearney, Nebraska   68845-4915
(Address of principal executive offices)   (Zip Code)

Registrant's telephone number, including area code: **(308) 236-8491**

Securities registered pursuant to Section 12(b) of the Act:

<u>Title of class</u>	<u>Name of Each Exchange on Which Registered</u>
Common Stock, $0.01 par value	New York Stock Exchange

Securities registered pursuant to Section 12(g) of the Act: None

Indicate by check mark if the registrant is a well-known seasoned issuer, as defined in Rule 405 of the Securities Act. Yes ☐   No ☒

Indicate by check mark if the registrant is not required to file reports pursuant to Section 13 or 15(d) of the Act. Yes ☐   No ☒

Indicate by check mark whether the registrant (1) has filed all reports required to be filed by Section 13 or 15(d) of the Securities Exchange Act of 1934 during the preceding 12 months (or for such shorter period that the Registrant was required to file such reports) and (2) has been subject to such filing requirements for the past 90 days. Yes ☒ No ☐

Indicate by check mark whether the registrant has submitted electronically and posted on its corporate Web site, if any, every Interactive Data File required to be submitted and posted pursuant to Rule 405 of Regulation S-T during the preceding 12 months (or for a shorter period that the registrant was required to submit and post such files). Yes ☐ No ☐

Indicate by check mark if disclosure of delinquent filers pursuant to Item 405 of Regulation S-K is not contained herein, and will not be contained, to the best of the Registrant's knowledge, in definitive proxy or information statements incorporated by reference in Part III of this Form 10-K or any amendment to this Form 10-K ☐.

Indicate by check mark whether the registrant is a large accelerated filer, accelerated filer, non-accelerated filer, or smaller reporting company. (See definition of "large accelerated filer," "accelerated filer," and "smaller reporting company" in Rule 12b-2 of the Exchange Act). Check one.
        ☑ Large accelerated filer; ☐ Accelerated filer; ☐ Non-accelerated filer; ☐ Smaller Reporting Company

Indicate by check mark whether the registrant is a shell company (as defined in Rule 12b-2 of the Act). Yes ☐No ☒

The aggregate market value (based on the closing price of the New York Stock Exchange) of the common stock of the registrant held by non-affiliates of the registrant was $785,519,774 on July 31, 2009. For purposes of this response, executive officers and directors are deemed to be the affiliates of the Registrant and the holdings by non-affiliates was computed as 25,388,487 shares.

The number of shares outstanding of the Registrant's Common Stock, as of March 26, 2010, was 46,659,195.

DOCUMENTS INCORPORATED BY REFERENCE

Portions of the definitive Proxy Statement for the registrant's 2010 Annual Meeting of Shareholders to be held June 4, 2010 are incorporated by reference in Part III.

ITEM 6 - SELECTED FINANCIAL DATA

SELECTED FINANCIAL DATA

(Amounts in Thousands Except Share, Per Share Amounts, and Selected Operating Data)

	Fiscal Years Ended				
	January 30, 2010	January 31, 2009	February 2, 2008	February 3, 2007 (d)	January 28, 2006
Income Statement Data					
Net sales	$898,287	$792,046	$619,888	$530,074	$501,101
Cost of sales (including buying, distribution, and occupancy costs)	497,668	448,558	365,350	322,760	307,063
Gross profit	400,619	343,488	254,538	207,314	194,038
Selling expenses	168,741	151,251	118,699	107,592	100,148
General and administrative expenses	32,416	30,041	26,212	20,701	17,568
Income from operations	199,462	162,196	109,627	79,021	76,322
Other income, net	3,674	7,829	9,183	9,032	6,123
Gain (loss) - impairment of securities	991	(5,157)	-	-	-
Income before income taxes	204,127	164,868	118,810	88,053	82,445
Provision for income taxes	76,824	60,459	43,563	32,327	30,539
Net income	$127,303	$104,409	$75,247	$55,726	$51,906
Basic earnings per share	$2.79	$2.30	$1.69	$1.29	$1.17
Diluted earnings per share	$2.73	$2.24	$1.63	$1.24	$1.13
Dividends declared per share (a)	$2.60	$2.73	$0.60	$1.71	$0.27
Selected Operating Data					
Stores open at end of period	401	387	368	350	338
Average sales per square foot	$428	$401	$335	$302	$298
Average sales per store (000's)	$2,129	$1,995	$1,668	$1,493	$1,474
Comparable store sales change (b)	7.8%	20.6%	13.2%	0.0%	1.4%
Balance Sheet Data (c)					
Working capital	$172,779	$197,539	$184,395	$189,017	$193,428
Long-term investments	$72,770	$56,213	$81,201	$31,958	$41,654
Total assets	$488,903	$465,340	$450,657	$368,198	$374,266
Long-term debt	-	-	-	-	-
Stockholders' equity	$354,259	$337,222	$338,320	$286,587	$299,793

(a)   During fiscal 2005, cash dividends were $0.0533 per share in the first quarter, $0.0667 per share in the second quarter, and $0.0756 per share in the third and fourth quarters. During fiscal 2006, cash dividends were $0.0756 per share in the first and second quarters, $0.0889 per share in the third quarter, and $0.1333 per share in the fourth quarter. In addition, the Company paid a special one-time cash dividend of $1.3333 per share in the fourth quarter of fiscal 2006. During fiscal 2007, cash dividends were $0.1333 per share in the first and second quarters and $0.1667 per share in the third and fourth quarters. During fiscal 2008, cash dividends were $0.1667 per share in the first and second quarters and $0.20 per share in the third and fourth quarters. In addition, the Company paid a special one-time cash dividend of $2.00 per share in the third quarter of fiscal 2008. During fiscal 2009, cash dividends were $0.20 per share in each of the four quarters. The Company also paid a special one-time cash dividend of $1.80 per share in the third quarter of fiscal 2009. Dividend amounts prior to the Company's 3-for-2 stock split with distribution date of January 12, 2007 and 3-for-2 stock split with distribution date of October 30, 2008, have been adjusted to reflect the impact of these stock splits.

(b)   Stores are deemed to be comparable stores if they were open in the prior year on the first day of the fiscal period presented. Stores which have been remodeled, expanded, and/or relocated, but would otherwise be included as comparable stores, are not excluded from the comparable store sales calculation. Online sales are excluded from comparable store sales.

(c)   At the end of the period.

(d)   Consists of 53 weeks.

ITEM 8 - FINANCIAL STATEMENTS AND SUPPLEMENTARY DATA

REPORT OF INDEPENDENT REGISTERED PUBLIC ACCOUNTING FIRM

To the Board of Directors and Stockholders of
The Buckle, Inc.
Kearney, Nebraska

We have audited the accompanying balance sheets of The Buckle, Inc. (the "Company") as of January 30, 2010 and January 31, 2009, and the related statements of income, stockholders' equity, and cash flows for each of the three fiscal years in the period ended January 30, 2010. Our audits also included the financial statement schedule listed in the Index at Item 15. These financial statements and financial statement schedule are the responsibility of the Company's management. Our responsibility is to express an opinion on the financial statements and financial statement schedule based on our audits.

We conducted our audits in accordance with the standards of the Public Company Accounting Oversight Board (United States). Those standards require that we plan and perform the audit to obtain reasonable assurance about whether the financial statements are free of material misstatement. An audit includes examining, on a test basis, evidence supporting the amounts and disclosures in the financial statements. An audit also includes assessing the accounting principles used and significant estimates made by management, as well as evaluating the overall financial statement presentation. We believe that our audits provide a reasonable basis for our opinion.

In our opinion, such financial statements present fairly, in all material respects, the financial position of The Buckle, Inc. as of January 30, 2010 and January 31, 2009, and the results of its operations and its cash flows for each of the three fiscal years in the period ended January 30, 2010, in conformity with accounting principles generally accepted in the United States of America. Also, in our opinion, such financial statement schedule, when considered in relation to the basic financial statements taken as a whole, presents fairly, in all material respects, the information set forth therein.

We have also audited, in accordance with the standards of the Public Company Accounting Oversight Board (United States), the Company's internal control over financial reporting as of January 30, 2010, based on the criteria established in *Internal Control — Integrated Framework* issued by the Committee of Sponsoring Organizations of the Treadway Commission and our report, dated March 31, 2010, expressed an unqualified opinion on the Company's internal control over financial reporting.

/s/ Deloitte & Touche LLP

DELOITTE & TOUCHE LLP
Omaha, Nebraska
March 31, 2010

THE BUCKLE, INC.

BALANCE SHEETS
(Dollar Amounts in Thousands Except Share and Per Share Amounts)

ASSETS	January 30, 2010	January 31, 2009
CURRENT ASSETS:		
Cash and cash equivalents	$ 135,340	$ 162,463
Short-term investments (Notes A, B, and C)	22,687	19,150
Accounts receivable, net of allowance of $35 and $46, respectively	6,911	3,734
Inventory	88,187	83,963
Prepaid expenses and other assets (Note F)	11,684	17,655
Total current assets	264,809	286,965
PROPERTY AND EQUIPMENT (Note D):	305,974	264,154
Less accumulated depreciation and amortization	(159,392)	(147,460)
	146,582	116,694
LONG-TERM INVESTMENTS (Notes A, B, and C)	72,770	56,213
OTHER ASSETS (Notes F and G)	4,742	5,468
	$ 488,903	$ 465,340

LIABILITIES AND STOCKHOLDERS' EQUITY		
CURRENT LIABILITIES:		
Accounts payable	$ 24,364	$ 22,472
Accrued employee compensation	41,463	40,460
Accrued store operating expenses	8,866	7,701
Gift certificates redeemable	13,507	10,144
Income taxes payable	3,830	8,649
Total current liabilities	92,030	89,426
DEFERRED COMPENSATION (Note I)	5,957	4,090
DEFERRED RENT LIABILITY	36,657	34,602
Total liabilities	134,644	128,118
COMMITMENTS (Notes E and H)		
STOCKHOLDERS' EQUITY (Note J):		
Common stock, authorized 100,000,000 shares of $.01 par value; 46,381,263 and 45,906,265 shares issued and outstanding at January 30, 2010 and January 31, 2009, respectively	464	459
Additional paid-in capital	78,837	68,894
Retained earnings	275,751	268,789
Accumulated other comprehensive loss	(793)	(920)
Total stockholders' equity	354,259	337,222
	$ 488,903	$ 465,340

See notes to financial statements.

THE BUCKLE, INC.

STATEMENTS OF INCOME

(Dollar Amounts in Thousands Except Per Share Amounts)

	Fiscal Years Ended		
	January 30, 2010	January 31, 2009	February 2, 2008
SALES, Net of returns and allowances of $73,596, $54,973, and $42,087, respectively	$898,287	$792,046	$619,888
COST OF SALES (Including buying, distribution, and occupancy costs)	497,668	448,558	365,350
Gross profit	400,619	343,488	254,538
OPERATING EXPENSES:			
Selling	168,741	151,251	118,699
General and administrative	32,416	30,041	26,212
	201,157	181,292	144,911
INCOME FROM OPERATIONS	199,462	162,196	109,627
OTHER INCOME, Net (Note A)	3,674	7,829	9,183
GAIN (LOSS) - IMPAIRMENT OF SECURITIES (Note B)	991	(5,157)	-
INCOME BEFORE INCOME TAXES	204,127	164,868	118,810
PROVISION FOR INCOME TAXES (Note F)	76,824	60,459	43,563
NET INCOME	$127,303	$104,409	$ 75,247
EARNINGS PER SHARE (Note K):			
Basic	$ 2.79	$ 2.30	$ 1.69
Diluted	$ 2.73	$ 2.24	$ 1.63

See notes to financial statements.

THE BUCKLE, INC.

STATEMENTS OF STOCKHOLDERS' EQUITY
(Dollar Amounts in Thousands Except Share and Per Share Amounts)

	Number of Shares	Common Stock	Additional Paid-in Capital	Retained Earnings	Accumulated Other Comprehensive Loss	Total
BALANCE, February 4, 2007	29,408,576	$ 294	$ 43,493	$ 242,800	$ -	$ 286,587
Net income	-	-	-	75,247	-	75,247
Dividends paid on common stock,						
($.1333 per share - 1st and 2nd quarters)	-	-	-	(12,014)	-	(12,014)
($.1667 per share - 3rd and 4th quarters)	-	-	-	(14,988)	-	(14,988)
Common stock issued on exercise						
of stock options	937,247	9	12,015	-	-	12,024
Issuance of non-vested stock, net of forfeitures	138,345	1	(1)	-	-	-
Amortization of non-vested stock grants,						
net of forfeitures	-	-	3,886	-	-	3,886
Stock option compensation expense	-	-	293	-	-	293
Common stock purchased and retired	(642,500)	(6)	(21,571)	-	-	(21,577)
Income tax benefit related to						
exercise of stock options	-	-	8,862	-	-	8,862
BALANCE, February 2, 2008	29,841,668	298	46,977	291,045	-	338,320
Net income	-	-	-	104,409	-	104,409
Dividends paid on common stock,						
($.1667 per share - 1st and 2nd quarters)	-	-	-	(15,269)	-	(15,269)
($.20 per share - 3rd and 4th quarters)	-	-	-	(18,474)	-	(18,474)
($2.00 per share - 3rd quarter)	-	-	-	(92,922)	-	(92,922)
Common stock issued on exercise						
of stock options	994,555	10	12,714	-	-	12,724
Issuance of non-vested stock, net of forfeitures	139,635	1	(1)	-	-	-
Amortization of non-vested stock grants,						
net of forfeitures	-	-	4,879	-	-	4,879
Stock option compensation expense	-	-	289	-	-	289
Common stock purchased and retired	(557,100)	(5)	(9,354)	-	-	(9,359)
Income tax benefit related to						
exercise of stock options	-	-	13,545	-	-	13,545
3-for-2 stock split	15,487,507	155	(155)	-	-	-
Unrealized loss on investments, net of tax	-	-	-	-	(920)	(920)
BALANCE, January 31, 2009	45,906,265	459	68,894	268,789	(920)	337,222
Net income	-	-	-	127,303	-	127,303
Dividends paid on common stock,						
($.20 per share - 1st, 2nd, 3rd, and 4th quarters)	-	-	-	(37,011)	-	(37,011)
($1.80 per share - 3rd quarter)	-	-	-	(83,330)	-	(83,330)
Common stock issued on exercise						
of stock options	278,430	3	1,823	-	-	1,826
Issuance of non-vested stock, net of forfeitures	196,568	2	(2)	-	-	-
Amortization of non-vested stock grants,						
net of forfeitures	-	-	4,988	-	-	4,988
Stock option compensation expense	-	-	175	-	-	175
Income tax benefit related to exercise						
of stock options	-	-	2,959	-	-	2,959
Unrealized loss on investments, net of tax	-	-	-	-	127	127
BALANCE, January 30, 2010	46,381,263	$ 464	$ 78,837	$ 275,751	$ (793)	$ 354,259

See notes to financial statements.

THE BUCKLE, INC.

STATEMENTS OF CASH FLOWS
(Dollar Amounts in Thousands)

	Fiscal Years Ended		
	January 30, 2010	January 31, 2009	February 2, 2008
CASH FLOWS FROM OPERATING ACTIVITIES:			
Net income	$ 127,303	$ 104,409	$ 75,247
Adjustments to reconcile net income to net cash flows			
from operating activities:			
Depreciation and amortization	25,135	21,779	20,384
Amortization of non-vested stock grants, net of forfeitures	4,988	4,879	3,886
Stock option compensation expense	175	289	293
Gain on involuntary conversion of aircraft to monetary asset	-	(2,963)	-
(Gain) loss - impairment of securities	(991)	5,157	-
Deferred income taxes	414	(595)	(1,509)
Other	38	574	146
Changes in operating assets and liabilities:			
Accounts receivable	(1,967)	(895)	1,246
Inventory	(4,224)	(6,324)	(7,333)
Prepaid expenses and other assets	6,282	(2,478)	(1,542)
Accounts payable	(2,916)	(844)	8,903
Accrued employee compensation	1,003	12,624	10,036
Accrued store operating expenses	1,165	1,997	1,236
Gift certificates redeemable	3,363	1,633	1,802
Income taxes payable	(5,731)	906	5,576
Long-term liabilities and deferred compensation	3,922	3,581	2,709
Net cash flows from operating activities	157,959	143,729	121,080
CASH FLOWS FROM INVESTING ACTIVITIES:			
Purchase of property and equipment	(50,561)	(47,448)	(27,484)
Proceeds from sale of property and equipment	308	11,819	21
Change in other assets	(74)	(29)	167
Purchases of investments	(52,604)	(46,687)	(153,511)
Proceeds from sales / maturities of investments	33,703	148,818	117,079
Net cash flows from investing activities	(69,228)	66,473	(63,728)
CASH FLOWS FROM FINANCING ACTIVITIES:			
Proceeds from the exercise of stock options	1,826	12,724	12,024
Excess tax benefit from stock option exercises	2,661	11,268	7,744
Purchases of common stock	-	(9,359)	(21,577)
Payment of dividends	(120,341)	(126,665)	(27,002)
Net cash flows from financing activities	(115,854)	(112,032)	(28,811)
NET INCREASE (DECREASE) IN CASH AND CASH EQUIVALENTS	(27,123)	98,170	28,541
CASH AND CASH EQUIVALENTS, Beginning of year	162,463	64,293	35,752
CASH AND CASH EQUIVALENTS, End of year	$ 135,340	$ 162,463	$ 64,293

See notes to financial statements.

THE BUCKLE, INC.
NOTES TO FINANCIAL STATEMENTS
(Dollar Amounts in Thousands Except Share and Per Share Amounts)

A.   SUMMARY OF SIGNIFICANT ACCOUNTING POLICIES

Fiscal Year – The Buckle, Inc. (the "Company") has its fiscal year end on the Saturday nearest January 31. All references in these financial statements to fiscal years are to the calendar year in which the fiscal year begins. Fiscal 2009 represents the 52-week period ended January 30, 2010, fiscal 2008 represents the 52-week period ended January 31, 2009, and fiscal 2007 represents the 52-week period ended February 2, 2008.

Nature of Operations – The Company is a retailer of medium to better-priced casual apparel, footwear, and accessories for fashion conscious young men and women operating 401 stores located in 41 states throughout the continental United States as of January 30, 2010.

During fiscal 2009, the Company opened 20 new stores, substantially renovated 22 stores, and closed 6 stores. During fiscal 2008, the Company opened 21 new stores, substantially renovated 13 stores, and closed 2 stores. During fiscal 2007, the Company opened 20 new stores, substantially renovated 7 stores, and closed 2 stores.

Revenue Recognition – Retail store sales are recorded upon the purchase of merchandise by customers. Online sales are recorded when merchandise is delivered to the customer, with the time of delivery being based on estimated shipping time from the Company's distribution center to the customer. Shipping fees charged to customers are included in revenue and shipping costs are included in selling expenses. Shipping costs were $5,420, $3,813, and $1,882 during fiscal 2009, 2008, and 2007, respectively. Merchandise returns are estimated based upon the historical average sales return percentage and accrued at the end of the period. The reserve for merchandise returns was $647 and $526 as of January 30, 2010 and January 31, 2009, respectively. The Company accounts for layaway sales in accordance with FASB ASC 605, *Revenue Recognition*, recognizing revenue from sales made under its layaway program upon delivery of the merchandise to the customer. The Company has several sales incentives that it offers customers including a frequent shopper punch card, B-Rewards gift certificates, and occasional sweepstakes and gift with purchase offers. The frequent shopper punch card is recognized as a cost of goods sold at the time of redemption, using the actual amount tendered. The B-Rewards incentives, based upon $10 for each $300 in net purchases, are recorded as a liability and as a selling expense at the time the gift certificates are earned. Sweepstake prizes are recorded as cost of goods sold (if it is a merchandise giveaway) or as a selling expense at the time the prize is redeemed by the customer, using actual costs incurred, and gifts with purchase are recorded as a cost of goods sold at the time of the purchase and gift redemption, using the actual cost of the gifted item.

The Company records the sale of gift cards and gift certificates as a current liability and recognizes a sale when a customer redeems the gift card or gift certificate. The amount of the gift certificate liability is determined using the outstanding balances from the prior three years of issuance and the gift card liability is determined using the outstanding balances from the prior four years of issuance. The Company records breakage as other income when the probability of redemption, which is based on historical redemption patterns, is remote. Breakage reported for the fiscal years ended January 30, 2010, January 31, 2009, and February 2, 2008 was $434, $389, and $0, respectively. The Company recognizes a current liability for the down payment made when merchandise is placed on layaway and recognizes layaways as a sale at the time the customer makes final payment and picks up the merchandise.

Cash and Cash Equivalents – The Company considers all highly liquid debt instruments with an original maturity of three months or less when purchased to be cash equivalents.

Investments – The Company accounts for investments in accordance with FASB ASC 320, *Investments-Debt and Equity Securities*. Investments classified as short-term investments include securities with a maturity of greater than three months and less than one year, and a portion of the Company's investments in auction-rate securities ("ARS"), which are available-for-sale securities. Available-for-sale securities are reported at fair value, with unrealized gains and losses excluded from earnings and reported as a separate component of stockholders' equity (net of the effect of income taxes), using the specific identification method, until they are sold. The Company reviews impairments in accordance with FASB ASC 320 to determine the classification of potential impairments as either "temporary" or "other-than-temporary." A temporary impairment results in an unrealized loss being recorded in other comprehensive income. Impairments that are considered other-than-temporary are recognized as a loss in the statements of income. The Company considers various factors in reviewing impairments, including the length of time and extent to which the fair value has been less than the Company's cost basis, the financial condition and near-term prospects of the issuer, and the Company's intent and ability to hold the investments for a period of time sufficient to allow for any anticipated recovery in market value. Held-to-maturity securities are carried at amortized cost. The Company believes it has the ability and maintains its intent to hold these investments until recovery of market value occurs. Trading securities are reported at fair value, with unrealized gains and losses included in earnings, using the specific identification method.

Inventory – Inventory is stated at the lower of cost or market. Cost is determined using the average cost method. Management records a reserve for merchandise obsolescence and markdowns based on assumptions using calculations applied to current inventory levels by department within each of four different markdown levels. Management also reviews the levels of inventory in each markdown group, and the overall aging of inventory, versus the estimated future demand for such product and the current market conditions. The calculation for estimated markdowns and/or obsolescence reduced the Company's inventory valuation by $5,832 and $6,228 as of January 30, 2010 and January 31, 2009, respectively. The amount charged (credited) to cost of goods sold, resulting from changes in the markdown reserve balance, was $(396), $439, and $(581), for fiscal years 2009, 2008, and 2007, respectively.

Property and Equipment – Property and equipment are stated on the basis of historical cost. Depreciation is provided using a combination of accelerated and straight-line methods based upon the estimated useful lives of the assets. The majority of property and equipment have useful lives of five to ten years with the exception of buildings, which have estimated useful lives of 31.5 to 39 years. Leasehold improvements are stated on the basis of historical cost and are amortized over the shorter of the life of the lease or the estimated economic life of the assets. When circumstances indicate the carrying values of long-lived assets may be impaired, an evaluation is performed on current net book value amounts. Judgments made by the Company related to the expected useful lives of property and equipment and the ability to realize cash flows in excess of carrying amounts of such assets are affected by factors such as changes in economic conditions and changes in operating performance. As the Company assesses the expected cash flows and carrying amounts of long-lived assets, adjustments are made to such carrying values.

Pre-Opening Expenses – Costs related to opening new stores are expensed as incurred.

Advertising Costs – Advertising costs are expensed as incurred and were $8,521, $7,674, and $6,376 for fiscal years 2009, 2008, and 2007, respectively.

Health Care Costs - The Company is self-funded for health and dental claims up to $200 per individual per plan year. The Company's plan covers eligible employees, and management makes estimates at period end to record a reserve for unpaid claims based upon historical claims information. The accrued liability as a reserve for unpaid health care claims was $700 and $600 as of January 30, 2010 and January 31, 2009, respectively.

Operating Leases – The Company leases retail stores under operating leases. Most lease agreements contain tenant improvement allowances, rent holidays, rent escalation clauses, and/or contingent rent provisions. For purposes of recognizing lease incentives and minimum rental expenses on a straight-line basis over the terms of the leases, the Company uses the date of initial possession to begin expensing rent, which is generally when the Company enters the space and begins to make improvements in preparation of intended use.

For tenant improvement allowances and rent holidays, the Company records a deferred rent liability on the balance sheets and amortizes the deferred rent over the terms of the leases as reductions to rent expense on the statements of income.

For scheduled rent escalation clauses during the lease terms or for rental payments commencing at a date other than the date of initial occupancy, the Company records minimum rental expenses on a straight-line basis over the terms of the leases on the statements of income. Certain leases provide for contingent rents, which are determined as a percentage of gross sales in excess of specified levels. The Company records a contingent rent liability in "accrued store operating expenses" on the balance sheets and the corresponding rent expense when specified levels have been achieved or are reasonably probable to be achieved.

Other Income – The Company's other income is derived primarily from interest and dividends received on cash and investments, but also includes miscellaneous other sources of income.

Income Taxes – The Company records a deferred tax asset and liability for expected future tax consequences resulting from temporary differences between financial reporting and tax bases of assets and liabilities. The Company considers future taxable income and ongoing tax planning in assessing the value of its deferred tax assets. If the judgment of the Company's management determines that it is more than likely that these assets will not be realized, the Company would reduce the value of these assets to their expected realizable value, thereby decreasing net income. If the Company subsequently determined that the deferred tax assets, which had been written down, would be realized in the future, such value would be increased, thus increasing net income in the period such determination was made. The Company records tax benefits only for tax positions that are more than likely to be sustained upon examination by tax authorities. The amount recognized is measured as the largest amount of benefit that is greater than 50% likely to be realized upon ultimate settlement. Unrecognized tax benefits are tax benefits claimed in the Company's tax returns that do not meet these recognition and measurement standards.

Stock Splits – On September 15, 2008, the Company's Board of Directors approved a 3-for-2 stock split payable in the form of a stock dividend for shareholders of record as of October 15, 2008, with a distribution date of October 30, 2008. All share and per share data (except par value and historical stockholders' equity data) presented in the financial statements for all periods has been adjusted to reflect the impact of this stock split.

Financial Instruments and Credit Risk Concentrations – Financial instruments, which potentially subject the Company to concentrations of credit risk, are primarily cash, investments, and accounts receivable. The Company places its investments primarily in tax-free municipal bonds, auction-rate securities, or U.S. Treasury securities with short-term maturities and limits the amount of credit exposure to any one entity.

Of the Company's $230,797 in total cash and investments as of January 30, 2010, $22,792 was comprised of investments in auction-rate securities ("ARS"). ARS have a long-term stated maturity, but are reset through a "dutch auction" process that occurs every 7 to 49 days, depending on the terms of the individual security. Until February 2008, the ARS market was highly liquid. During February 2008, however, a significant number of auctions related to these securities failed, meaning that there was not enough demand to sell the entire issue at auction. The failed auctions have limited the current liquidity of certain of the Company's investments in ARS and the Company has reason to believe that certain of the underlying issuers of its ARS are currently at risk. The Company does not, however, anticipate that further auction failures will have a material impact on the Company's ability to fund its business.

Concentrations of credit risk with respect to accounts receivable are limited due to the nature of the Company's receivables, which include primarily employee receivables that can be offset against future compensation. The Company's financial instruments have a fair value approximating the carrying value.

Earnings Per Share – Basic earnings per share data are based on the weighted average outstanding common shares during the period. Diluted earnings per share data are based on the weighted average outstanding common shares and the effect of all dilutive potential common shares, including stock options. Basic and diluted earnings per share for fiscal 2007 have been adjusted to reflect the impact of the Company's 3-for-2 stock split paid in the form of a stock dividend on October 30, 2008.

Use of Estimates – The preparation of financial statements in conformity with accounting principles generally accepted in the United States of America requires management to make estimates and assumptions that affect the reported amounts of certain assets and liabilities, the disclosure of contingent assets and liabilities at the date of the financial statements, and the reported amounts of revenues and expenses during the reporting period. Actual results could differ from these estimates.

Comprehensive Income – Comprehensive income consists of net income and unrealized gains and losses on available-for-sale securities. Unrealized losses on the Company's investments in auction-rate securities have been included in accumulated other comprehensive loss and are separately included as a component of stockholders' equity, net of related income taxes.

	Fiscal Years Ended		
	January 30, 2010	January 31, 2009	February 2, 2008
Net income	$ 127,303	$ 104,409	$ 75,247
Changes in net unrealized losses on investments in auction-rate securities, net of taxes of $(75), $540, and $0, respectively	127	(920)	-
Comprehensive income	$ 127,430	$ 103,489	$ 75,247

Recently Issued Accounting Pronouncements – Effective February 3, 2008, the Company adopted the provisions of FASB ASC 820, *Fair Value Measurements and Disclosures*. FASB ASC 820 defines fair value, establishes a framework for measuring fair value, and expands disclosures about fair value measurements. The provisions of FASB ASC 820 apply to all financial instruments that are being measured and reported on a fair value basis. In addition, FASB ASC 820-10-15-1A delayed the effective date of FASB ASC 820 to fiscal years beginning after November 15, 2008, and interim periods within those fiscal years, for all non-financial assets and liabilities, except those that are recognized or disclosed at fair value in the financial statements on a recurring basis. The adoption of FASB ASC 820 during fiscal 2008 for all financial instruments and the adoption during fiscal 2009 for all non-financial assets and liabilities did not have any impact on the Company's financial position or results of operations.

Effective February 3, 2008, the Company adopted the provisions of FASB ASC 825, *Financial Instruments*. FASB ASC 825 provides an option for companies to report selected financial assets and liabilities at fair value. Although the Company adopted the provisions of FASB ASC 825 effective with the beginning of the Company's 2008 fiscal year, it did not elect the fair value option for any financial instruments or other items held by the Company. Therefore, the adoption of FASB ASC 825 did not have any impact on the Company's financial position or results of operations.

In May 2009, FASB issued FASB ASC 855, *Subsequent Events*. This guidance requires management to evaluate subsequent events through the date the financial statements are issued, or are available to be issued, and requires companies to disclose the date through which such subsequent events have been evaluated. FASB ASC 855 was effective for financial statements issued for interim or annual reporting periods ending after June 15, 2009. In February 2010, FASB issued Accounting Standards Update 2010-09 which removed the requirement for SEC filers to disclose the date through which subsequent events have been evaluated. The adoption of FASB ASC 855 did not have any impact on the Company's financial position or results of operations. The Company has determined that there were no subsequent events requiring recognition or disclosure in the financial statements presented herein.

In June 2009, FASB issued FASB ASC 105, *Generally Accepted Accounting Principles*, which establishes the FASB *Accounting Standards Codification* ("ASC") as the single source of GAAP recognized by FASB to be applied by nongovernmental entities. Rules and interpretive releases of the Securities and Exchange Commission ("SEC") under authority of federal securities laws are also sources of authoritative GAAP for SEC registrants. On the effective date of FASB ASC 105, the codification superseded all then-existing non-SEC accounting and reporting standards. All other non-grandfathered, non-SEC accounting literature not included in the codification became non-authoritative. FASB ASC 105 was effective for financial statements issued for interim or annual reporting periods ending after September 15, 2009. Therefore, the Company adopted the provisions of FASB ASC 105 on August 2, 2009. The adoption of FASB ASC 105 did not have any impact on the Company's financial position or results of operations.

Supplemental Cash Flow Information - The Company had non-cash investing activities during fiscal years 2009, 2008, and 2007 of $4,808, $1,839, and $1,582, respectively. The non-cash investing activity relates to unpaid purchases of property, plant, and equipment included in accounts payable as of the end of the year. Amounts reported as unpaid purchases are recorded as cash outflows from investing activities for purchases of property, plant, and equipment in the statement of cash flows in the period they are paid.

Additional cash flow information for the Company includes cash paid for income taxes during fiscal years 2009, 2008, and 2007 of $79,480, $48,879, and $31,730, respectively.

B.   INVESTMENTS

The following is a summary of investments as of January 30, 2010:

	Amortized Cost or Par Value	Gross Unrealized Gains	Gross Unrealized Losses	Other-than-Temporary Impairment	Estimated Fair Value
Available-for-Sale Securities:					
Auction-rate securities	$ 24,775	$ -	$ (1,258)	$ (725)	$ 22,792
Municipal bonds	8,116	14	(14)	-	8,116
Preferred stock	2,000	-	-	(1,974)	26
	$ 34,891	$ 14	$ (1,272)	$ (2,699)	$ 30,934
Held-to-Maturity Securities:					
State and municipal bonds	$ 47,036	$ 535	$ (10)	-	$ 47,561
Fixed maturities	8,890	92	-	-	8,982
Certificates of deposit	1,640	27	-	-	1,667
U.S. treasuries	1,000	1	-	-	1,001
	$ 58,566	$ 655	$ (10)	$ -	$ 59,211
Trading Securities:					
Mutual funds	$ 6,200	$ -	$ (243)	$ -	$ 5,957

The following is a summary of investments as of January 31, 2009:

	Amortized Cost or Par Value	Gross Unrealized Gains	Gross Unrealized Losses	Other-than-Temporary Impairment	Estimated Fair Value
Available-for-Sale Securities:					
Auction-rate securities	$ 35,495	$ -	$ (1,460)	$ (3,757)	$ 30,278
Preferred stock	2,000	-	-	(1,400)	600
	$ 37,495	$ -	$ (1,460)	$ (5,157)	$ 30,878
Held-to-Maturity Securities:					
State and municipal bonds	$ 31,965	$ 536	$ (90)	-	$ 32,411
Fixed maturities	2,500	37	(7)	-	2,530
Certificates of deposit	2,945	42	-	-	2,987
U.S. treasuries	2,985	19	(9)	-	2,995
	$ 40,395	$ 634	$ (106)	$ -	$ 40,923
Trading Securities:					
Mutual funds	$ 5,165	$ -	$ (1,075)	$ -	$ 4,090

The auction-rate securities and preferred stock were invested as follows as of January 30, 2010:

Nature	Underlying Collateral	Par Value
Municipal revenue bonds	92% insured by AAA/AA/A-rated bond insurers at January 30, 2010	$11,700
Municipal bond funds	Fixed income instruments within issuers' money market funds	9,325
Student loan bonds	Student loans guaranteed by state entities	3,750
Preferred stock	Underlying investments of closed-end funds	2,000
Total par value		$26,775

As of January 30, 2010, the Company's auction-rate securities portfolio was 57% AAA/Aaa-rated, 27% AA/Aa-rated, 9% A-rated, and 7% below A-rated.

The amortized cost and fair value of debt securities by contractual maturity as of January 30, 2010 is as follows:

	Amortized Cost	Fair Value
Available-for-sale securities		
Less than 1 year	$ 2,950	$ 2,950
1 - 5 years	1,452	1,454
5 - 10 years	1,206	1,209
Greater than 10 years	2,508	2,503
	$ 8,116	$ 8,116
Held-to-maturity securities		
Less than 1 year	$ 18,387	$ 18,520
1 - 5 years	35,802	36,234
5 - 10 years	1,926	1,978
Greater than 10 years	2,451	2,479
	$ 58,566	$ 59,211

At January 30, 2010 and January 31, 2009, $26,634 and $29,328 of available-for-sale securities and $40,179 and $22,795 of held-to-maturity investments are classified in long-term investments. Trading securities are held in a Rabbi Trust, intended to fund the Company's deferred compensation plan, and are classified in long-term investments.

The Company's investments in auction-rate securities ("ARS") are classified as available-for-sale and reported at fair market value. As of January 30, 2010, the reported investment amount is net of $1,258 of temporary impairment and $2,699 of other-than-temporary impairment ("OTTI") to account for the impairment of certain securities from their stated par value. The $1,258 temporary impairment is reported, net of tax, as an "accumulated other comprehensive loss" of $793 in stockholders' equity as of January 30, 2010. For the investments considered temporarily impaired, the Company believes that these ARS can be successfully redeemed or liquidated through future auctions at par value plus accrued interest. The Company believes it has the ability and maintains its intent to hold these investments until such recovery of market value occurs; therefore, the Company believes the current lack of liquidity has created the temporary impairment in valuation.

As of January 30, 2010, the Company had $24,775 invested in ARS and $2,000 invested in preferred securities, at par value, which are reported at their estimated fair value of $22,792 and $26, respectively. As of January 31, 2009, the Company had $35,495 invested in ARS and $2,000 invested in preferred securities, which were reported at their estimated fair value of $30,278 and $600, respectively. ARS have a long-term stated maturity, but are reset through a "dutch auction" process that occurs every 7 to 49 days, depending on the terms of the individual security. Until February 2008, the ARS market was highly liquid. During February 2008, however, a significant number of auctions related to these securities failed, meaning that there was not enough demand to sell the entire issue at auction. The failed auctions have limited the current liquidity of certain of the Company's investments in ARS and the Company has reason to believe that certain of the underlying issuers of its ARS are currently at risk. The Company does not, however, anticipate that further auction failures will have a material impact on the Company's ability to fund its business. During fiscal 2009, the Company was able to successfully liquidate $5,320 of its investments in ARS at par value. The Company also liquidated investments in preferred securities that were valued at $2,217 ($5,400 at par value) as of January 31, 2009 for $3,933, and recorded a gain of $1,716 in the statement of income for the fiscal year ended January 30, 2010. The Company reviews all investments for OTTI at least quarterly or as indicators of impairment exist and added $725 to OTTI during the fourth quarter of fiscal 2009. Indicators of impairment include the duration and severity of decline in market value. In addition, the Company considers qualitative factors including, but not limited to, the financial condition of the investee, the credit rating of the investee, and the current and expected market and industry conditions in which the investee operates.

As of January 30, 2010, $1,350 of the Company's investment in ARS and preferred securities was classified in short-term investments, due to known or anticipated subsequent redemptions, and $21,468 was classified in long-term investments. As of January 31, 2009, $1,550 of the Company's investment in ARS and preferred securities was classified in short-term investments and $29,328 was classified in long-term investments.

C.   FAIR VALUE MEASURMENTS

As defined by FASB ASC 820, *Fair Value Measurements and Disclosures*, fair value is the price that would be received to sell an asset or paid to transfer a liability in an orderly transaction between market participants at the measurement date. Financial assets and liabilities measured and reported at fair value are classified and disclosed in one of the following categories:

- Level 1 – Quoted market prices in active markets for identical assets or liabilities. Short-term and long-term investments with active markets or known redemption values are reported at fair value utilizing Level 1 inputs.
- Level 2 – Observable market-based inputs (either directly or indirectly) such as quoted prices for similar assets or liabilities, quoted prices in markets that are not active, or other inputs that are observable or inputs that are corroborated by market data.
- Level 3 – Unobservable inputs that are not corroborated by market data and are projections, estimates, or interpretations that are supported by little or no market activity and are significant to the fair value of the assets. The Company has concluded that certain of its ARS represent Level 3 valuation and should be valued using a discounted cash flow analysis. The assumptions used in preparing the discounted cash flow model include estimates for interest rates, timing and amount of cash flows, and expected holding periods of the ARS.

As of January 30, 2010 and January 31, 2009, the Company held certain assets that are required to be measured at fair value on a recurring basis including available-for-sale and trading securities. The Company's available-for-sale securities include its investments in ARS, as further described in Note B. The failed auctions, beginning in February 2008, related to certain of the Company's investments in ARS have limited the availability of quoted market prices. The Company has determined the fair value of its ARS using Level 1 inputs for known or anticipated subsequent redemptions at par value, Level 2 inputs using observable inputs, and Level 3 using unobservable inputs where the following criteria were considered in estimating fair value:

- Pricing was provided by the custodian of ARS;
- Pricing was provided by a third-party broker for ARS;
- Sales of similar securities;
- Quoted prices for similar securities in active markets;
- Quoted prices for publicly traded preferred securities;
- Quoted prices for similar assets in markets that are not active - including markets where there are few transactions for the asset, the prices are not current, or price quotations vary substantially either over time or among market makers, or in which little information is released publicly;
- Pricing was provided by a third-party valuation consultant (using Level 3 inputs).

In addition, the Company considers other factors including, but not limited to, the financial condition of the investee, the credit rating, insurance, guarantees, collateral, cash flows, and the current and expected market and industry conditions in which the investee operates. Management believes it has used information that was reasonably obtainable in order to complete its valuation process and determine if the Company's investments in ARS had incurred any temporary and/or other-than-temporary impairment as of January 30, 2010 and January 31, 2009.

Future fluctuations in fair value of ARS that the Company judges to be temporary, including any recoveries of previous write-downs, would be recorded as an adjustment to "accumulated other comprehensive loss." The value and liquidity of ARS held by the Company may be affected by continued auction-rate failures, the credit quality of each security, the amount and timing of interest payments, the amount and timing of future principal payments, and the probability of full repayment of the principal. Additional indicators of impairment include the duration and severity of the decline in market value. The interest rates on these investments will be determined by the terms of each individual ARS. The material risks associated with the ARS held by the Company include those stated above as well as the current economic environment, downgrading of credit ratings on investments held, and the volatility of the entities backing each of the issues.

The Company's financial assets measured at fair value on a recurring basis subject to the disclosure requirements of FASB ASC 820 were as follows:

	Fair Value Measurements at Reporting Date Using			
January 30, 2010	**Quoted Prices in Active Markets for Identical Assets (Level 1)**	**Significant Observable Inputs (Level 2)**	**Significant Unobservable Inputs (Level 3)**	**Total**
Available-for-sale securities				
Auction-rate securities	$ 1,261	$ 12,894	$ 8,637	$ 22,792
Municipal bonds	8,116	-	-	8,116
Preferred stock	26	-	-	26
Trading securities (including mutual funds)	5,957	-	-	5,957
Totals	$ 15,360	$ 12,894	$ 8,637	$ 36,891

	Fair Value Measurements at Reporting Date Using			
January 31, 2009	**Quoted Prices in Active Markets for Identical Assets (Level 1)**	**Significant Observable Inputs (Level 2)**	**Significant Unobservable Inputs (Level 3)**	**Total**
Available-for-sale securities				
Auction-rate securities	$ 1,550	$ 21,468	$ 7,260	$ 30,278
Preferred stock	600	-	-	600
Trading securities (including mutual funds)	4,090	-	-	4,090
Totals	$ 6,240	$ 21,468	$ 7,260	$ 34,968

ARS, municipal bonds, and preferred securities included in Level 1 represent securities which have a known or anticipated upcoming redemption as of January 30, 2010 and those that have publicly traded quoted prices. ARS included in Level 2 represent securities which have not experienced a successful auction subsequent to February 2, 2008. The fair market value for these securities was determined by applying a discount to par value based on auction prices for similar securities and by utilizing a discounted cash flow model, using market-based inputs, to determine fair value. The Company used a discounted cash flow model to value its Level 3 investments, using estimates regarding recovery periods, yield, and liquidity. The assumptions used are subjective based upon management's judgment and views on current market conditions, and resulted in $739 of the Company's recorded temporary impairment and $725 of the OTTI as of January 30, 2010. The use of different assumptions would result in a different valuation and related temporary impairment charge.

Changes in the fair value of the Company's financial assets measured at fair value on a recurring basis using significant unobservable inputs (Level 3), as defined in FASB ASC 820, are as follows:

	Fiscal Years Ended	
Available-for-Sale Auction-Rate Securities	January 30, 2010	January 31, 2009
Balance, beginning of year	$ 7,260	-
Total gains or losses (realized and unrealized):		
Included in net income	(725)	-
Included in other comprehensive income	(48)	(690)
Purchases, sales, issuances, and settlements (net)	(25)	-
Transfers in and/or out of Level 3	2,175	7,950
Balance, end of year	$ 8,637	$ 7,260

D.   PROPERTY AND EQUIPMENT

	January 30, 2010	January 31, 2009
Land	$ 1,959	$ 1,170
Building and improvements	14,678	13,447
Office equipment	6,105	6,043
Transportation equipment	19,005	18,997
Leasehold improvements	119,941	111,544
Furniture and fixtures	110,579	96,778
Shipping/receiving equipment	15,783	10,294
Screenprinting equipment	111	111
Construction-in-progress	17,813	5,770
	$ 305,974	$ 264,154

E.   FINANCING ARRANGEMENTS

The Company has available an unsecured line of credit of $17,500 of which $10,000 is available for letters of credit. During fiscal 2009, this line of credit was extended through July 31, 2012. Borrowings under the line of credit and letter of credit provide for interest to be paid at a rate equal to the prime rate as set by the Wells Fargo Bank, N.A. index on the date of the borrowings. There were no bank borrowings at January 30, 2010 and January 31, 2009. There were no bank borrowings during fiscal 2009, 2008, and 2007. The Company had outstanding letters of credit totaling $618 and $1,059 at January 30, 2010 and January 31, 2009, respectively.

F.   INCOME TAXES

The provision for income taxes consists of:

	Fiscal Years Ended		
	January 30, 2010	January 31, 2009	February 2, 2008
Current income tax expense (benefit):			
Federal	$ 66,059	$ 52,905	$ 38,224
State	10,351	8,149	6,849
Deferred income tax expense (benefit):	414	(595)	(1,509)
Total	$ 76,824	$ 60,459	$ 43,564

Total income tax expense for the year varies from the amount which would be provided by applying the statutory income tax rate to earnings before income taxes. The primary reasons for this difference (expressed as a percent of pre-tax income) are as follows:

	Fiscal Years Ended		
	January 30, 2010	January 31, 2009	February 2, 2008
Statutory rate	35.0 %	35.0 %	35.0 %
State income tax effect	3.4	3.6	4.0
Tax exempt interest income	(0.3)	(1.0)	(2.0)
Other	(0.5)	(0.9)	(0.3)
Effective tax rate	37.6 %	36.7 %	36.7 %

Deferred income tax assets and liabilities are comprised of the following:

	January 30, 2010	January 31, 2009
Deferred income tax assets (liabilities):		
Inventory	$ 3,641	$ 3,681
Stock-based compensation	3,337	3,112
Accrued compensation	3,373	2,547
Accrued store operating costs	390	262
Unrealized loss on securities	2,021	2,847
Gift certificates redeemable	550	495
Allowance for doubtful accounts	13	17
Deferred rent liability	13,563	12,803
Property and equipment	(15,841)	(14,228)
Net deferred income tax asset	$ 11,047	$ 11,536

At January 30, 2010 and January 31, 2009, respectively, the net current deferred income tax assets of $7,396 and $7,085 are classified in "prepaid expenses and other assets." The net non-current deferred income tax assets of $3,651 and $4,451 are classified in "other assets" at January 30, 2010 and January 31, 2009, respectively. There are no unrecognized tax benefits to be recorded in the Company's financial statements at January 30, 2010 or January 31, 2009. The Company has no open examinations with the Internal Revenue Service and fiscal years 2006, 2007, 2008, and 2009 remain subject to examination by the Internal Revenue Service as well as state taxing authorities.

G. RELATED PARTY TRANSACTIONS

Included in other assets is a note receivable of $1,035 at January 30, 2010 and $1,005 at January 31, 2009, respectively, from a life insurance trust fund controlled by the Company's Chairman. The note was created over three years, beginning in July 1994, when the Company paid life insurance premiums of $200 each year for the Chairman on a personal policy. The note accrues interest at 5% of the principal balance per year and is to be paid from the life insurance proceeds. The note is secured by a life insurance policy on the Chairman.

H. COMMITMENTS

Leases - The Company conducts its operations in leased facilities under numerous non-cancelable operating leases expiring at various dates through fiscal 2021. Most of the Company's stores have lease terms of approximately ten years and generally do not contain renewal options. Most lease agreements contain tenant improvement allowances, rent holidays, rent escalation clauses, and/or contingent rent provisions. For purposes of recognizing lease incentives and minimum rental expenses on a straight-line basis over the terms of the leases, the Company uses the date of initial possession to begin amortization, which is generally when the Company enters the space and begins to make improvements in preparation of intended use. For tenant improvement allowances and rent holidays, the Company records a deferred rent liability on the balance sheets and amortizes the deferred rent over the terms of the leases as reductions to rent expense on the statements of income. For scheduled rent escalation clauses during the lease terms or for rental payments commencing at a date other than the date of initial occupancy, the Company records minimum rental expenses on a straight-line basis over the terms of the leases on the statements of income. Certain leases provide for contingent rents, which are determined as a percentage of gross sales in excess of specified levels. The Company records a contingent rent liability on the balance sheets and the corresponding rent expense when specified levels have been achieved or are reasonably probable to be achieved. Operating lease base rental expense for fiscal 2009, 2008, and 2007 was $45,805, $41,687, and $38,298, respectively. Most of the rental payments are based on a minimum annual rental plus a percentage of sales in excess of a specified amount. Percentage rents for fiscal 2009, 2008, and 2007 were $4,153, $3,202, and $1,159, respectively.

Total future minimum rental commitments under these operating leases with remaining lease terms in excess of one year as of January 30, 2010 are as follows:

Fiscal Year	Minimum Rental Commitments
2010	$ 49,006
2011	43,806
2012	39,313
2013	35,644
2014	31,592
Thereafter	104,595
Total minimum rental commitments	$ 303,956

Litigation - From time to time, the Company is involved in litigation relating to claims arising out of its operations in the normal course of business. As of the date of these financial statements, the Company was not engaged in any legal proceedings that are expected, individually or in the aggregate, to have a material effect on the Company.

I.   EMPLOYEE BENEFITS

The Company has a 401(k) profit sharing plan covering all eligible employees who elect to participate. Contributions to the plan are based upon the amount of the employees' deferrals and the employer's discretionary matching formula. The Company may contribute to the plan at its discretion. The total expense under the profit sharing plan was $1,130, $1,022, and $887 for fiscal years 2009, 2008, and 2007, respectively.

The Buckle, Inc. Deferred Compensation Plan covers the Company's executive officers. The plan is funded by participant contributions and a specified annual Company matching contribution not to exceed 6% of the participant's compensation. The Company's contributions were $428, $341, and $390 for fiscal years 2009, 2008, and 2007, respectively.

J.   STOCK-BASED COMPENSATION

The Company has several stock option plans which allow for granting of stock options to employees, executives, and directors. The options are in the form of non-qualified stock options and are granted with an exercise price equal to the market value of the Company's common stock on the date of grant. The options generally expire ten years from the date of grant. The Company also has a restricted stock plan that allows for the granting of non-vested shares of common stock to employees and executives and a restricted stock plan that allows for the granting of non-vested shares of common stock to non-employee directors.

As of January 30, 2010, 641,748 shares were available for grant under the various stock option plans, of which 452,111 were available for grant to executive officers. Also as of January 30, 2010, 208,372 shares were available for grant under the various restricted stock plans, of which 129,248 were available for grant to executive officers.

The Company accounts for stock-based compensation in accordance with FASB ASC 718, *Compensation-Stock Compensation*. Compensation expense was recognized fiscal 2009, 2008, and 2007 for new awards, based on the grant date fair value, as well as for the portion of awards granted in fiscal years prior to FASB ASC 718 adoption that was not vested as of the beginning of fiscal 2006. The fair value of stock options is determined using the Black-Scholes option pricing model, while the fair value of grants of non-vested common stock awards is the stock price on the date of grant.

Information regarding the impact of stock-based compensation expense is as follows:

	Fiscal Years Ended		
	January 30, 2010	January 31, 2009	February 2, 2008
Stock-based compensation expense, before tax:			
Stock options	$ 175	$ 289	$ 293
Non-vested shares of common stock	4,988	4,879	3,886
Total stock-based compensation expense, before tax	$ 5,163	$ 5,168	$ 4,179
Total stock-based compensation expense, after tax	$ 3,253	$ 3,256	$ 2,633

FASB ASC 718 requires the benefits of tax deductions in excess of the compensation cost recognized for stock options exercised during the period to be classified as financing cash inflows. This amount is shown as "excess tax benefit from stock option exercises" on the statements of cash flows. For fiscal 2009, 2008, and 2007, the excess tax benefit realized from exercised stock options was $2,661, $11,268, and $7,744, respectively.

No stock options were granted during fiscal 2009. Stock options granted during fiscal 2008 and 2007 were granted under the Company's 1993 Director Stock Option Plan. Grants were made with an exercise price equal to the market value of the Company's common stock on the date of grant and a contractual term of ten years. Options granted under the 1993 Director Stock Option Plan typically vest over a period of three years.

The weighted average grant date fair value of options granted during the fiscal year was $8.41 and $8.54 per option for fiscal 2008 and 2007, respectively. The fair value of options granted was estimated at the date of grant using the Black-Scholes option pricing model with the following assumptions:

	Fiscal Years Ended	
	January 31, 2009	**February 2, 2008**
Risk-free interest rate *(1)*	3.10 %	4.80 %
Dividend yield *(2)*	2.40 %	2.40 %
Expected volatility *(3)*	33.00 %	39.00 %
Expected lives - years *(4)*	7.0	7.0

(1) Based on the U.S. Treasury yield curve in effect at the time of grant with a term consistent with the expected lives of stock options.

(2) Based on expected dividend yield as of the date of grant.

(3) Based on historical volatility of the Company's common stock over a period consistent with the expected lives of stock options.

(4) Based on historical and expected exercise behavior.

On September 15, 2008, the Board of Directors authorized a $3.00 per share ($2.00 per share after 3-for-2 stock split) special one-time cash dividend to be paid on October 27, 2008 to shareholders of record at the close of business on October 15, 2008. Additionally, on September 21, 2009, the Board of Directors authorized a $1.80 per share special one-time cash dividend to be paid on October 27, 2009 to shareholders of record at the close of business on October 15, 2009. To preserve the intrinsic value for option holders, the Board also approved on each occasion, pursuant to the terms of the Company's various stock option plans, a proportional adjustment to both the exercise price and the number of shares covered by each award for all outstanding stock options. This adjustment did not result in any incremental compensation expense.

A summary of the Company's stock-based compensation activity related to stock options for the fiscal year ended January 30, 2010 is as follows:

	Shares	Weighted Average Exercise Price	Weighted Average Remaining Contractual Life		Aggregate Intrinsic Value
Outstanding - beginning of year	1,635,163	$ 6.91			
Granted	-	-			
Other (1)	447	5.83			
Expired/forfeited	(5,069)	24.21			
Exercised	(278,430)	6.56			
Outstanding - end of year	1,352,111	$ 5.02	3.29	years	$ 34,237
Exercisable - end of year	1,331,816	$ 4.75	3.22	years	$ 34,076

(1) An adjustment was made to the exercise price and number of options outstanding for the special cash dividend paid during October 2009. "Other" represents additional options issued as a result of this adjustment in the third quarter of fiscal 2009.

The total intrinsic value of options exercised during fiscal 2009, 2008, and 2007, respectively, was $7,477, $35,447, and $23,135. As of January 30, 2010, there was $64 of unrecognized compensation expense related to non-vested stock options. It is expected that this expense will be recognized over a weighted average period of approximately 1.0 year.

Non-vested shares of common stock granted during fiscal 2007 and 2008 were granted pursuant to the Company's 2005 Restricted Stock Plan. Non-vested shares granted during fiscal 2009 were granted pursuant to the Company's 2005 Restricted Stock Plan and the Company's 2008 Director Restricted Stock Plan. Shares granted under the 2005 Plan typically vest over a period of four years, only upon certification by the Compensation Committee of the Board of Directors that the Company has achieved its pre-established performance targets for the fiscal year. Shares granted under the 2008 Director Plan vest 25% on the date of grant and then in equal portions on each of the first three anniversaries of the date of grant.

A summary of the Company's stock-based compensation activity related to grants of non-vested shares of common stock for the fiscal year ended January 30, 2010 is as follows:

	Shares	Weighted Average Grant Date Fair Value
Non-Vested - beginning of year	423,171	$ 23.84
Granted	243,800	21.20
Forfeited	(47,232)	22.66
Vested	(214,394)	22.14
Non-Vested - end of year	405,345	$ 23.29

As of January 30, 2010, there was $4,066 of unrecognized compensation expense related to grants of non-vested shares. It is expected that this expense will be recognized over a weighted average period of approximately 1.9 years. The total fair value of shares vested during fiscal 2009, 2008, and 2007 was $6,517, $5,128, and $4,398, respectively.

K. EARNINGS PER SHARE

The following table provides reconciliation between basic and diluted earnings per share:

	Fiscal Years Ended								
	January 30, 2010			January 31, 2009			February 2, 2008		
	Income	Weighted Average Shares	Per Share Amount	Income	Weighted Average Shares	Per Share Amount	Income	Weighted Average Shares	Per Share Amount
Basic EPS									
Net income	$ 127,303	45,699	$ 2.79	$ 104,409	45,367	$ 2.30	$ 75,247	44,551	$ 1.69
Effect of Dilutive Securities									
Stock options and non-vested shares	-	993	(0.06)	-	1,207	(0.06)	-	1,703	(0.06)
Diluted EPS	$ 127,303	46,692	$ 2.73	$ 104,409	46,574	$ 2.24	$ 75,247	46,254	$ 1.63

Stock options to purchase 72,637 shares of common stock were not included in the computation of diluted earnings per share for fiscal 2008 because the options would be considered anti-dilutive. No stock options were deemed anti-dilutive and excluded from the computation of diluted earnings per share for either fiscal 2009 or 2007.

L.   SEGMENT INFORMATION

The Company is a retailer of medium to better-priced casual apparel, footwear, and accessories. The Company operated 401 stores located in 41 states throughout the continental United States as of January 30, 2010. The Company operates its business as one segment.

The following is information regarding the Company's major product lines and is stated as a percentage of the Company's net sales:

	Fiscal Years Ended		
	January 30, 2010	January 31, 2009	February 2, 2008
Denims	42.9 %	41.4 %	43.2 %
Tops (including sweaters)	36.7	39.0	36.1
Accessories	7.7	7.7	7.7
Sportswear/fashions	5.0	4.6	4.3
Footwear	4.7	4.6	5.6
Outerwear	2.5	2.0	2.0
Casual bottoms	0.4	0.6	1.0
Other	0.1	0.1	0.1
	100.0 %	100.0 %	100.0 %

M.   SELECTED QUARTERLY FINANCIAL DATA (UNAUDITED)

Selected unaudited quarterly financial information for fiscal 2009 and 2008 are as follows:

	Quarter			
Fiscal 2009	First	Second	Third	Fourth
Net sales	$ 199,697	$ 192,906	$ 231,238	$ 274,446
Gross profit	$ 86,703	$ 82,278	$ 102,117	$ 129,521
Net income	$ 26,862	$ 24,994	$ 33,305	$ 42,142
Basic earnings per share	$ 0.59	$ 0.55	$ 0.73	$ 0.92
Diluted earnings per share	$ 0.58	$ 0.54	$ 0.71	$ 0.90

	Quarter			
Fiscal 2008	First	Second	Third	Fourth
Net sales	$ 160,300	$ 169,765	$ 210,567	$ 251,414
Gross profit	$ 65,622	$ 70,268	$ 91,805	$ 115,793
Net income	$ 18,717	$ 22,276	$ 29,076	$ 34,340
Basic earnings per share	$ 0.42	$ 0.49	$ 0.64	$ 0.75
Diluted earnings per share	$ 0.41	$ 0.48	$ 0.62	$ 0.74

Basic and diluted shares outstanding are computed independently for each of the quarters presented and, therefore, may not sum to the totals for the year.

ITEM 9 - CHANGES IN AND DISAGREEMENTS WITH ACCOUNTANTS ON ACCOUNTING AND FINANCIAL DISCLOSURE

None.

ITEM 9A - CONTROLS AND PROCEDURES

The Company maintains a system of disclosure controls and procedures that are designed to provide reasonable assurance that material information, which is required to be timely disclosed, is accumulated and communicated to management in a timely manner. An evaluation of the effectiveness of the design and operation of our disclosure controls and procedures (as defined in Rules 13a-15(e) of the Securities Exchange Act of 1934 (the "Exchange Act")) was performed as of the end of the period covered by this report. This evaluation was performed under the supervision and with the participation of the Company's Chief Executive Officer and Chief Financial Officer. Based upon that evaluation, the Chief Executive Officer and Chief Financial Officer concluded that, as of the end of the period covered by this report, the Company's disclosure controls and procedures are effective to provide reasonable assurance that information required to be disclosed by the Company in the Company's reports that it files or submits under the Exchange Act is accumulated and communicated to management, including its Chief Executive Officer and Chief Financial Officer, as appropriate, to allow timely decisions regarding required disclosure and are effective to provide reasonable assurance that such information is recorded, processed, summarized, and reported within the time periods specified by the SEC's rules and forms.

Change in Internal Control Over Financial Reporting – There were no changes in the Company's internal control over financial reporting that occurred during the Company's last fiscal quarter that have materially affected, or are reasonable likely to materially affect, the Company's internal control over financial reporting.

Management's Report on Internal Control Over Financial Reporting – Management of the Company is responsible for establishing and maintaining adequate internal control over financial reporting as defined in Rules 13a-15(f) and 15d-15(f) under the Securities Exchange Act of 1934. The Company's internal control over financial reporting is designed to provide reasonable assurance regarding the reliability of financial reporting and the preparation of financial statements for external purposes in accordance with accounting principles generally accepted in the United State of America ("GAAP").

All internal control systems, no matter how well designed, have inherent limitations. Therefore, even those systems determined to be effective can provide only reasonable assurance with respect to financial statement preparation and presentation. Because of its inherent limitations, internal control over financial reporting may not prevent or detect misstatements.

Management has assessed the effectiveness of the Company's internal control over financial reporting as of January 30, 2010, based on the criteria set forth by the Committee of Sponsoring Organizations ("COSO") of the Treadway Commission in their *Internal Control–Integrated Framework*. In making its assessment of internal control over financial reporting, management has concluded that the Company's internal control over financial reporting was effective as of January 30, 2010.

The Company's independent registered public accounting firm, Deloitte & Touche LLP, has audited the effectiveness of the Company's internal control over financial reporting. Their report appears herein.

REPORT OF INDEPENDENT REGISTERED PUBLIC ACCOUNTING FIRM

To the Board of Directors and Stockholders of
The Buckle, Inc.
Kearney, Nebraska

We have audited the internal control over financial reporting of The Buckle, Inc. (the "Company") as of January 30, 2010, based on criteria established in *Internal Control — Integrated Framework* issued by the Committee of Sponsoring Organizations of the Treadway Commission. The Company's management is responsible for maintaining effective internal control over financial reporting and for its assessment of the effectiveness of internal control over financial reporting, included in the accompanying *Management's Report on Internal Control Over Financial Reporting*. Our responsibility is to express an opinion on the Company's internal control over financial reporting based on our audit.

We conducted our audit in accordance with the standards of the Public Company Accounting Oversight Board (United States). Those standards require that we plan and perform the audit to obtain reasonable assurance about whether effective internal control over financial reporting was maintained in all material respects. Our audit included obtaining an understanding of internal control over financial reporting, assessing the risk that a material weakness exists, testing and evaluating the design and operating effectiveness of internal control based on the assessed risk, and performing such other procedures as we considered necessary in the circumstances. We believe that our audit provides a reasonable basis for our opinion.

A company's internal control over financial reporting is a process designed by, or under the supervision of, the company's principal executive and principal financial officers, or persons performing similar functions, and effected by the company's board of directors, management, and other personnel to provide reasonable assurance regarding the reliability of financial reporting and the preparation of financial statements for external purposes in accordance with generally accepted accounting principles. A company's internal control over financial reporting includes those policies and procedures that (1) pertain to the maintenance of records that, in reasonable detail, accurately and fairly reflect the transactions and dispositions of the assets of the company; (2) provide reasonable assurance that transactions are recorded as necessary to permit preparation of financial statements in accordance with generally accepted accounting principles, and that receipts and expenditures of the company are being made only in accordance with authorizations of management and directors of the company; and (3) provide reasonable assurance regarding prevention or timely detection of unauthorized acquisition, use or disposition of the company's assets that could have a material effect on the financial statements.

Because of the inherent limitations of internal control over financial reporting, including the possibility of collusion or improper management override of controls, material misstatements due to error or fraud may not be prevented or detected on a timely basis. Also, projections of any evaluation of the effectiveness of the internal control over financial reporting to future periods are subject to the risk that the controls may become inadequate because of changes in conditions, or that the degree of compliance with the policies or procedures may deteriorate.

In our opinion, the Company maintained, in all material respects, effective internal control over financial reporting as of January 30, 2010, based on the criteria established in *Internal Control — Integrated Framework* issued by the Committee of Sponsoring Organizations of the Treadway Commission.

We have also audited, in accordance with the standards of the Public Company Accounting Oversight Board (United States), the financial statements and financial statement schedule as of and for the fiscal year ended January 30, 2010, of the Company and our report dated March 31, 2010 expressed an unqualified opinion on those financial statements and financial statement schedule.

/s/ Deloitte & Touche LLP

DELOITTE & TOUCHE LLP
Omaha, Nebraska
March 31, 2010

ITEM 9B – OTHER INFORMATION

As required by Section 303A of the New York Stock Exchange's Corporate Governance Standards, the Company's Chief Executive Officer submitted a certification to the New York Stock Exchange in fiscal 2009 that he was not aware of any violation by the Company of the New York Stock Exchange's Corporate Governance Standards as of the date of the certification, June 29, 2009.

PART III

ITEM 10 – DIRECTORS, EXECUTIVE OFFICERS, AND CORPORATE GOVERNANCE

The information required by this item appears under the captions "Executive Officers of the Company" appearing on pages 10 and 11 of this report and "Election of Directors" in the Company's Proxy Statement for its 2010 Annual Shareholders' Meeting and is incorporated by reference.

ITEM 11- EXECUTIVE COMPENSATION

Information required by this item appears under the following captions in the Company's Proxy Statement for its 2010 Annual Shareholders' Meeting and is incorporated by reference: "Executive Compensation," "Director Compensation" (included under the "Election of Directors" section), and "Report of the Audit Committee."

ITEM 12 - SECURITY OWNERSHIP OF CERTAIN BENEFICIAL OWNERS AND MANAGEMENT AND RELATED STOCKHOLDER MATTERS

The information required by this item appears under the captions "Beneficial Ownership of Common Stock" and "Election of Directors" in the Company's Proxy Statement for its 2010 Annual Shareholders' Meeting and in the Notes to Financial Statements under Footnote J on pages 46 to 48 of this report and is incorporated by reference.

ITEM 13 - CERTAIN RELATIONSHIPS AND RELATED TRANSACTIONS AND DIRECTOR INDEPENDENCE

The information required by this item appears under the captions "Independence" and "Related Party Transactions" (included under the "Election of Directors" section) in the Company's Proxy for its 2010 Annual Shareholders' Meeting and is incorporated by reference.

ITEM 14 – PRINCIPAL ACCOUNTANT FEES AND SERVICES

Information regarding the fees billed by our independent registered public accounting firm and the nature of services comprising the fees for each of the two most recent fiscal years is set forth under the caption "Ratification of Independent Registered Public Accounting Firm" in the Company's Proxy Statement for its 2010 Annual Shareholders' Meeting and is incorporated by reference.

PART IV

ITEM 15 – EXHIBITS AND FINANCIAL STATEMENT SCHEDULE

(a) Financial Statement Schedule
Valuation and Qualifying Account. This schedule is on page 54.
All other schedules are omitted because they are not applicable or the required information is presented in the financial statements or notes thereto.

(b) Exhibits
See index to exhibits on pages 55 and 56.

Buckle Corporate Office
2407 W. 24th Street
Kearney, NE 68845
308.236.8491

Mixed Sources
Product group from well-managed
forests, controlled sources and
recycled wood or fiber
www.fsc.org   Cert no. SW-COC-001530
©1996 Forest Stewardship Council

FSC

Time Value of Money

Learning Objectives

AFTER STUDYING THIS APPENDIX, YOU SHOULD BE ABLE TO:

■ **LO1** Contrast simple and compound interest.

■ **LO2** Calculate the future value and present value of a single amount.

■ **LO3** Calculate the future value and present value of an annuity.

Congratulations! While at a local convenience store, you bought a lottery ticket and won $1,000. The ticket gives you the option of receiving (a) $1,000 today or (b) $1,000 one year from now. Which do you choose?

Probably, all of us would choose $1,000 today. Choosing to take the money today instead of one year from now just makes common sense. It also makes good economic sense. You could take your $1,000 winnings today, put it in a savings account, earn interest on it for one year, and have an amount greater than $1,000 a year from now. So, $1,000 today is not equal to $1,000 a year from now. This simple example demonstrates the time value of money, which means that interest causes the value of money received today to be greater than the value of that same amount of money received in the future.

Time value of money concepts are useful—in fact, essential—in solving many business decisions. These decisions include valuing assets and liabilities, making investment decisions, paying off debts, and establishing a retirement plan, to name just a few. We'll discuss some of these next.

Simple versus Compound Interest

Interest is the cost of borrowing money. If you borrow $1,000 today and agree to pay 10% interest, you will pay back $1,100 a year from now. It is this interest that gives money its time value.

Simple interest is interest you earn on the initial investment only. Calculate it as the initial investment times the applicable interest rate times the period of the investment or loan:

■ **LO1**
Contrast simple and compound interest.

Simple interest = Initial investment × Interest rate × Time

For example, suppose you put $1,000 into a savings account that pays simple interest of 10% and then withdraw the money at the end of three years. Illustration C–1 demonstrates that the amount of simple interest you earned on your $1,000 in each of the three years is $100 (= $1,000 × 10%).

With simple interest at 10% annually, the $1,000 initial investment generates $100 of interest each year and grows to **$1,300** by the end of the third year.

Time	Simple Interest (= Initial investment × Interest rate)	Outstanding Balance
Initial investment		$1,000
End of year 1	$1,000 × 10% = $100	$1,100
End of year 2	$1,000 × 10% = $100	$1,200
End of year 3	$1,000 × 10% = $100	$1,300

ILLUSTRATION C–1

Calculation of Simple Interest

Compound interest works differently. **Compound interest** is interest you earn on the initial investment *and on previous interest.* Because you are earning "interest on interest" each period, compound interest yields increasingly larger amounts of interest earnings for each period of the investment (unlike simple interest, which yielded the same $100 in each year of our example above). Illustration C–2 shows calculations of compound interest for a $1,000, three-year investment that earns 10%.

ILLUSTRATION C–2

Calculation of
Compound Interest

Time	Compound Interest (= Outstanding balance × Interest rate)	Outstanding Balance
Initial investment		$1,000
End of year 1	$1,000 × 10% = $100	$1,100
End of year 2	$1,100 × 10% = $110	$1,210
End of year 3	$1,210 × 10% = $121	$1,331

With compound interest at 10% annually, the $1,000 initial investment grows to **$1,331** at the end of three years. This compares to only **$1,300** for simple interest. The extra $31 represents *compounding,* or interest earned on interest. Nearly all business applications use compound interest, and compound interest is what we use in calculating the time value of money.

KEY POINT

Simple interest is interest we earn on the initial investment only. Compound interest is the interest we earn on the initial investment plus previous interest. We use compound interest in calculating the time value of money.

Time Value of a Single Amount

■ **LO2**
Calculate the future value and present value of a single amount.

To better understand how compound interest affects the time value of money, we'll examine this topic from two perspectives. First, we'll calculate how much an amount today will grow to be at some point in the future (*future value*), and then we'll take the opposite perspective and examine how much an amount in the future is worth today (*present value*).

FUTURE VALUE

In the example above, in which we invested $1,000 for three years at 10% compounded annually, we call $1,331 the future value. **Future value** is how much an amount today will grow to be in the future. The timeline in Illustration C–3 provides a useful way to visualize future values. Time $n = 0$ indicates today, the date of the initial investment.

ILLUSTRATION C–3

Future Value of a
Single Amount

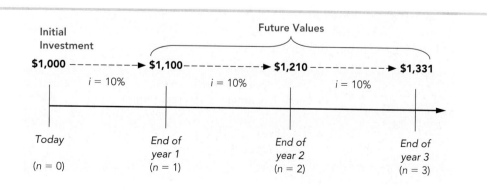

Notice that at the end of each year, the investment grows by 10%. The future value at the end of the first year is **$1,100** (= $1,000 × 1.10). After three years, the investment has a future value of **$1,331** (= $1,000 × 1.10 × 1.10 × 1.10), representing 10% growth of a growing base amount each year.

To calculate future value, we can use a mathematical formula, time value of money tables, a calculator, or a computer spreadsheet. We show all four methods below.

Formula. We can determine the future value of any amount with a formula, as follows:

$$FV = I\,(1 + i)^n$$

where:

FV = future value of the invested amount

I = initial investment

i = interest rate

n = number of compounding periods

Table 1. Instead of using a formula, we can also determine future value by using time value of money tables. Table 1, Future Value of $1, located at the end of this book, contains the future value of $1 invested for various periods of time, n, and various interest rates, i. With this table, it's easy to determine the future value of any invested amount. To do so, simply multiply the invested amount by the table value you find at the intersection of the *column* for the desired interest rate and the *row* for the number of periods. Illustration C–4 contains an excerpt from Table 1.

Periods (n)	Interest Rates (i)					
	7%	8%	9%	10%	11%	12%
1	1.07000	1.08000	1.09000	1.10000	1.11000	1.12000
2	1.14490	1.16640	1.18810	1.21000	1.23210	1.25440
3	1.22504	1.25971	1.29503	1.33100	1.36763	1.40493
4	1.31080	1.36049	1.41158	1.46410	1.51807	1.57352
5	1.40255	1.46933	1.53862	1.61051	1.68506	1.76234
6	1.50073	1.58687	1.67710	1.77156	1.87041	1.97382
7	1.60578	1.71382	1.82804	1.94872	2.07616	2.21068
8	1.71819	1.85093	1.99256	2.14359	2.30454	2.47596

ILLUSTRATION C–4

Future Value of $1 (excerpt from Table 1)

The table shows various values of $(1 + i)^n$ for different combinations of i and n. From the table you can find the future value factor for three periods ($n = 3$) at 10% interest to be 1.33100. This means that $1 invested at 10% compounded annually will grow to $1.331 (= $1 × 1.331) in three years. The table uses $1 as the initial investment, whereas our example used $1,000. Therefore, we need to multiply the future value factor by $1,000.

$$FV = I \times FV\ factor$$
$$FV = \$1,000 \times 1.33100^* = \$1,331$$
*Future value of $1; $n = 3$, $i = 10\%$

Calculator. Of course, you can do the same future value calculations by using a calculator. Future values are automatically stored in the memory of financial calculators. To compute a future value, you input three amounts: (1) initial investment, (2) interest rate per period, and (3) number of periods. Illustration C–5 shows the inputs and output using a financial calculator.

ILLUSTRATION C–5

Calculate the Future Value of a Single Amount Using a Financial Calculator

The key symbols used to input the interest rate and number of periods differ across calculators, so be sure to check which key is appropriate for your calculator.

CALCULATOR INPUTS

Inputs	Key	Amount
1. Present value (initial investment)	PV	$1,000
2. Interest rate per period	i	10%
3. Number of periods	n	3

CALCULATOR OUTPUT

Future value	FV	$1,331

Excel. Another option is to use an Excel spreadsheet, which has automatically stored the time value factors. To see how this is performed, see Illustration C–6.

ILLUSTRATION C–6

Calculate the Future Value of a Single Amount Using Excel

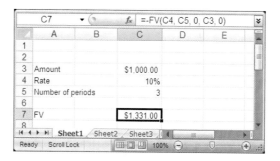

Interest compounding more than annually. In our example, interest was compounded annually (once per year). Remember that the n in the future value formula refers to the number of compounding *periods*—which is not necessarily the number of years. For example, suppose the three-year, $1,000 investment earns 10% compounded *semiannually*, or twice per year. The number of periods over three years is now six (= 3 years × 2 semiannual periods per year). The interest rate per period is 5% (= 10% annual rate ÷ 2).[1] The future value of the three-year, $1,000 investment that earns 10% compounded semiannually is calculated below.

$$FV = I \times FV \text{ factor}$$
$$FV = \$1,000 \times 1.34010^* = \$1,340$$
*Future value of $1; $n = 6$, $i = 5\%$

Notice that the future amount is slightly higher for semiannual compounding ($1,340) compared to annual compounding ($1,331). **The more frequent the rate of compounding, the more interest we earn on previous interest, resulting in a higher future value.**

To confirm your understanding, let's look at a couple of examples of how to calculate the future value of a single amount.

Example 1. Suppose a company's top executive, Shirley McDaniel, currently owns stock in the company worth $800,000. Shirley is ready to retire but will not do so until her stock is worth at least $1,000,000. Over the next three years, the company's stock is expected to grow 8% annually. Will Shirley be ready to retire in three years?

---

[1]The rate of compounding can be broken into any number of periods. For example, if we instead assume *quarterly* compounding (four times per year), the number of periods over three years would be 12 (= 3 years × 4 quarters) and the interest rate per period would be 2.5% (= 10% ÷ 4 quarters).

The future value of $800,000 in three years with an annual interest rate of 8% equals $1,007,768 (= $800,000 × 1.25971, time value factor from Table 1, Future Value of $1, with $n = 3$ and $i = 8\%$). With 8% growth, Shirley *will* be ready to retire in three years.

Example 2. Now suppose you are 20 years old and would like to retire by age 60. A goal of yours has always been to retire as a millionaire. You don't have any money to invest, but you do have a pretty nice car. If you sold your car for $28,000, bought a six-year-old car for $5,000, and invested the difference of $23,000 earning a 10% annual return, how much would you have at retirement?

The future value of $23,000 in 40 years (your proposed retirement age minus your present age) with an annual interest rate of 10% equals $1,040,963 (= $23,000 × 45.25926, time value factor from Table 1, Future Value of $1, with $n = 40$ and $i = 10\%$). With a 10% annual return, just $23,000 today will grow to over 1 million dollars in 40 years. If you swap your expensive wheels, you'll have that million-dollar nest egg.

PRESENT VALUE

Present value is precisely the opposite of future value. Instead of telling us how much some amount today will grow to be in the future, present value tells us the value today of receiving some larger amount in the future. What is it worth today to receive $1,331 in three years? To answer this, we need to determine the discount rate. The discount rate is the rate at which we would be willing to give up current dollars for future dollars. If you would be willing to give up $100 today to receive $108 in one year, then your discount rate, or time value of money, equals 8%.

Continuing with our example, let's assume that your discount rate is 10%. In this case, the present value of receiving $1,331 in three years is $1,000. We could have figured this from Illustration C–3 by working backwards from the future value. The timeline in Illustration C–7 depicts this relationship between present value and future value.

To calculate present value, we can use a formula, time value of money tables, a calculator, or a computer spreadsheet. We show all four methods below.

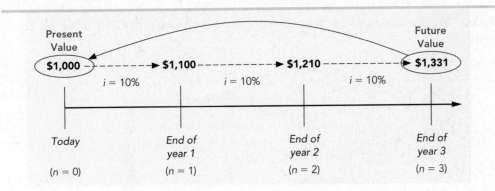

ILLUSTRATION C–7

Present Value of a Single Amount

Formula. We can calculate present values with the following formula:

$$PV = \frac{FV}{(1 + i)^n}$$

Table 2. Alternatively, we can use Table 2, Present Value of $1, located at the end of this book. Illustration C–8 shows an excerpt of Table 2.

ILLUSTRATION C–8

Present Value of $1
(excerpt from Table 2)

Periods (n)	Interest Rates (i)					
	7%	8%	9%	10%	11%	12%
1	.93458	.92593	.91743	.90909	.90090	.89286
2	.87344	.85734	.84168	.82645	.81162	.79719
3	.81630	.79383	.77218	.75131	.73119	.71178
4	.76290	.73503	.70843	.68301	.65873	.63552
5	.71299	.68058	.64993	.62092	.59345	.56743
6	.66634	.63017	.59627	.56447	.53464	.50663
7	.62275	.58349	.54703	.51316	.48166	.45235
8	.58201	.54027	.50187	.46651	.43393	.40388

From the table you can find the present value factor for three periods ($n = 3$) at 10% is 0.75131. This means that $1 received in three years where there is interest of 10% compounded annually is worth about $0.75 today. So, the present value of $1,331 is approximately $1,000.

$$\textbf{PV} = \textbf{FV} \times \textbf{PV factor}$$
$$\text{PV} = \$1,331 \times 0.75131 = \$1,000^*$$
*Rounded to the nearest whole dollar

Calculator. Illustration C–9 shows the same example worked out with a financial calculator.

ILLUSTRATION C–9

Calculate the Present
Value of a Single
Amount Using a
Financial Calculator

CALCULATOR INPUTS

Inputs	Key	Amount
1. Future value	FV	$1,331
2. Interest rate per period	i	10%
3. Number of periods	n	3

CALCULATOR OUTPUT

Present value	PV	$1,000

Excel. In Illustration C–10, we see the same example worked out using an Excel spreadsheet.

ILLUSTRATION C–10

Calculate the Present
Value of a Single
Amount Using Excel

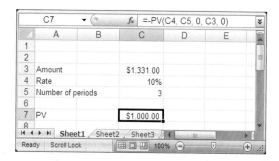

To confirm your understanding, let's look at a couple of examples of how to calculate the present value of a single amount.

Example 1. Suppose Fisher Realtors lists for sale a 2,500-square-foot business building for $500,000. Someone offers to purchase the building, taking occupancy

today, and then pay $575,000 in two years. If Fisher's discount rate is 7% compounded annually, should it accept the customer's offer?

The present value of receiving $575,000 in two years with an annual interest rate of 7% equals $502,228 (= $575,000 × 0.87344, time value factor from Table 2, Present Value of $1, with $n = 2$ and $i = 7\%$). The present value of the future $575,000 payment is $502,228, which is greater than the $500,000 listed selling price, so Fisher should accept the offer.

Example 2.   Let's assume you would like to be a millionaire in 40 years. Investing aggressively in higher-risk securities, you are pretty confident you can earn an average return of 12% a year. How much do you need to invest today to have $1,000,000 in 40 years?

The present value of $1,000,000 in 40 years with an annual interest rate of 12% equals $10,750 (= $1,000,000 × 0.01075, time value factor from Table 2, Present Value of $1, with $n = 40$ and $i = 12\%$). An investment of only $10,750 today would grow to $1,000,000 in 40 years, assuming a 12% annual interest rate.

If you could earn only 6% annually rather than 12%, you would have to invest quite a bit more. The present value of $1,000,000 in 40 years with an interest rate of 6% equals $97,220 (= $1,000,000 × 0.09722, time value factor from Table 2, Present Value of $1, with $n = 40$ and $i = 6\%$). Over longer periods, the investment return you can achieve really makes a difference in the wealth you can accumulate.

KEY POINT

The *future value* of a single amount is how much that amount today will grow to be in the future. The *present value* of a single amount is the value today of receiving that amount in the future.

Let's Review

Below are four scenarios related to the future value and present value of a single amount.

1. Manuel is saving for a new car. He puts $10,000 into an investment account today. He expects the account to earn 12% annually. How much will Manuel have in five years?
2. Ingrid would like to take her family to Disney World in three years. She expects the trip to cost $4,500 at that time. If she can earn 9% annually, how much should she set aside today so that she can pay for the trip in three years?
3. John puts $6,000 in a savings account today that earns 8% interest compounded semiannually. How much will John have in six years?
4. Anna purchases a ring with a selling price of $4,000 today but doesn't have to pay cash until one year from the purchase date. Assuming a discount rate of 16% compounded quarterly, what is Anna's actual cost of the ring today?

Required:
Calculate the time value of money for each scenario.

Solution:
(Rounded to the nearest whole dollar)
1. $10,000 × 1.76234 (FV of $1, $n = 5, i = 12\%$) = $17,623
2. $4,500 × 0.77218 (PV of $1, $n = 3, i = 9\%$) = $3,475
3. $6,000 × 1.60103 (FV of $1, $n = 12, i = 4\%$) = $9,606
4. $4,000 × 0.85480 (PV of $1, $n = 4, i = 4\%$) = $3,419

Suggested Homework:
BEC-2, BEC-4;
EC-1, EC-3;
PC-1A&B

Time Value of an Annuity

■ LO3
Calculate the future value and present value of an annuity.

Up to now, we've focused on calculating the future value and present value of a *single* amount. However, many business transactions are structured as a series of receipts and payments of cash rather than a single amount. If we are to receive or pay the same amount each period, we refer to the cash flows as an **annuity**. Familiar examples of annuities are monthly payments for a car loan, house loan, or apartment rent. Of course, payments need not be monthly. They could be quarterly, semiannually, annually, or any interval. **As long as the cash payments are of equal amounts over equal time intervals, we refer to the cash payments as an annuity.**

As with single amounts, we can calculate both the future value and the present value of an annuity.

FUTURE VALUE

Let's suppose that you decide to invest $1,000 at the end of *each year* for the next three years, earning 10% compounded annually. What will the value of these three $1,000 payments be at the end of the third year? The timeline in Illustration C–11 demonstrates how to calculate the future value of this annuity.

ILLUSTRATION C–11

Future Value of an Annuity

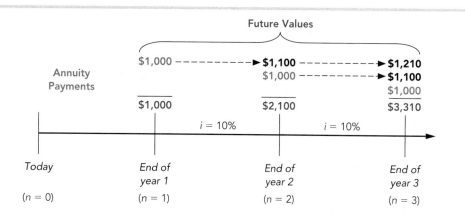

By the end of year 1, the investment's future value equals the $1,000 annuity payment. No interest has been earned because you invest the $1,000 at the *end* of the year. By the end of year 2, though, the first annuity payment has grown by 10% ($1,100 = $1,000 × 1.10), and you make the second $1,000 annuity payment. Adding these together, your total investment has grown to $2,100. By the end of the third year, the first annuity payment has grown by another 10% ($1,210 = $1,100 × 1.10), the second annuity payment has grown by 10% ($1,100 = $1,000 × 1.10), and you make the final $1,000 annuity payment. Add these together to find that the total investment has grown to $3,310. This is the future value of a $1,000 annuity for three years at 10% interest compounded annually.

Table 3. Since annuities consist of multiple payments, calculating the future value of an annuity can be time-consuming, especially as the length of the annuity increases. To make this task more efficient, we can calculate the future value of an annuity using the time value of money tables located at the end of this book, a financial calculator, or a computer spreadsheet.[2]

---

[2]The mathematical formula for calculating the future value of an annuity is a bit more complicated than are these other methods, so we'll focus on those.

Illustration C–12 shows an excerpt of Table 3, Future Value of an Annuity of $1.

Periods (n)	Interest Rates (i)					
	7%	8%	9%	10%	11%	12%
1	1.0000	1.0000	1.0000	1.0000	1.0000	1.0000
2	2.0700	2.0800	2.0900	2.1000	2.1100	2.1200
3	3.2149	3.2464	3.2781	3.3100	3.3421	3.3744
4	4.4399	4.5061	4.5731	4.6410	4.7097	4.7793
5	5.7507	5.8666	5.9847	6.1051	6.2278	6.3528
6	7.1533	7.3359	7.5233	7.7156	7.9129	8.1152
7	8.6540	8.9228	9.2004	9.4872	9.7833	10.0890
8	10.2598	10.6366	11.0285	11.4359	11.8594	12.2997

ILLUSTRATION C–12

Future Value of an Annuity of $1 (excerpt from Table 3)

We calculate the future value of an annuity (FVA) by multiplying the annuity payment by the factor corresponding to three periods and 10% interest:

$$FVA = \$1,000 \times 3.3100 = \$3,310$$

Calculator. You can also calculate the future value of an annuity using a financial calculator. To compute the future value of an annuity, you simply input three amounts: (1) payment amount, (2) interest rate per period, and (3) number of periods. Make sure the present value (PV) is set equal to zero. Illustration C–13 presents the inputs and output using a financial calculator.

CALCULATOR INPUTS		
Inputs	Key	Amount
1. Payment amount	PMT	$1,000
2. Interest rate per period	i	10%
3. Number of periods	n	3
CALCULATOR OUTPUT		
Future value	FV	$3,310

ILLUSTRATION C–13

Calculate the Future Value of an Annuity Using a Financial Calculator

Excel. Illustration C–14 shows the Excel method for calculating the future value of an annuity.

ILLUSTRATION C–14

Calculate the Future Value of an Annuity Using Excel

Again, let's look at two examples.

Example 1. Suppose **Pixar Productions** borrows $100 million to produce a sequel to *Toy Story 3* and is required to pay back this amount in five years. If, at the end

of each of the next five years, Pixar puts $16 million in an account that is expected to earn 12% interest compounded annually, will the company have enough cash set aside to pay its debt?

The future value of a $16 million annuity over five years that earns 12% annually equals $101,644,800 (= $16,000,000 × 6.3528, time value factor from Table 3, Future Value of an Annuity of $1, with $n = 5$ and $i = 12\%$). Pixar will have enough cash to pay its $100 million debt.

Example 2. You still have aspirations of being a millionaire in 40 years, but you do not have much money to invest right now. If you set aside just $2,500 at the end of each year with an average annual return of 10%, how much will you have at the end of 40 years?

The future value of a $2,500 annuity over 40 years that earns 10% annually equals $1,106,482 (= $2,500 × 442.5926, time value factor from Table 3, Future Value of an Annuity of $1, with $n = 40$ and $i = 10\%$). You will have quite a bit less assuming an average annual return of 8% ($647,641) and quite a bit more if you can achieve an average annual return of 12% ($1,917,729). Interest rates matter!

PRESENT VALUE

One application of the present value of an annuity relates back to Chapter 9. There, you learned that we report certain liabilities in financial statements at their present values. Most of these liabilities specify that the borrower must pay the lender periodic interest payments (or an annuity) over the life of the loan. As a result, we use the present value of an annuity to determine what portion of these future interest payments the borrower must report as a liability today.

To understand the idea behind the present value of an annuity, you need to realize that each annuity payment represents a single future amount. We calculate the present value of *each* of these future amounts and then add them together to determine the present value of an annuity. This idea is depicted in the timeline in Illustration C–15.

ILLUSTRATION C–15

Present Value of an Annuity

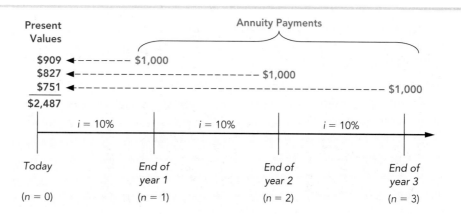

The present value of three **$1,000** annual payments discounted at 10% equals the present value of the first payment (**$909**), plus the present value of the second payment (**$827**), plus the present value of the third payment (**$751**). You can verify these amounts by looking at the present value factors in Table 2, Present Value of $1, with $n = 1, 2,$ and 3 and $i = 10\%$. The total present value of the annuity is **$2,487**.

Table 4. Instead of calculating the present value of each annuity payment, a more efficient method is to use time value of money tables. An excerpt of Table 4, Present Value of an Annuity of $1, located at the end of this book, is shown in Illustration C–16.

	Interest Rates (*i*)					
Periods (*n*)	7%	8%	9%	10%	11%	12%
1	0.93458	0.92593	0.91743	0.90909	0.90090	0.89286
2	1.80802	1.78326	1.75911	1.73554	1.71252	1.69005
3	2.62432	2.57710	2.53129	2.48685	2.44371	2.40183
4	3.38721	3.31213	3.23972	3.16987	3.10245	3.03735
5	4.10020	3.99271	3.88965	3.79079	3.69590	3.60478
6	4.76654	4.62288	4.48592	4.35526	4.23054	4.11141
7	5.38929	5.20637	5.03295	4.86842	4.71220	4.56376
8	5.97130	5.74664	5.53482	5.33493	5.14612	4.96764

ILLUSTRATION C–16

Present Value of an Annuity of $1 (excerpt from Table 4)

We calculate the present value of an annuity (PVA) by multiplying the annuity payment by the factor corresponding to three periods and 10% interest:

$$PVA = \$1,000 \times 2.48685 = \$2,487$$

Calculator.   Illustration C–17 shows the calculator solution.

CALCULATOR INPUTS

Inputs	Key	Amount
1. Payment amount	PMT	$1,000
2. Interest rate per period	*i*	10%
3. Number of periods	*n*	3

CALCULATOR OUTPUT

Present value	PV	$2,487

ILLUSTRATION C–17

Calculate the Present Value of an Annuity Using a Financial Calculator

Excel.   Illustration C–18 shows the Excel solution.

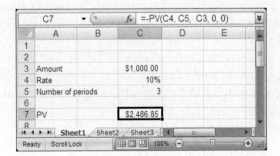

ILLUSTRATION C–18

Calculate the Present Value of an Annuity Using Excel

Again, let's look at some examples.

Example 1.   A movie theatre considers upgrading its concessions area at a cost of $10,000. The upgrades are expected to produce additional cash flows from concession sales of $2,000 per year over the next six years. Should the movie theatre upgrade its concessions area if its discount rate is 8% annually?

The present value of a $2,000 annuity over six years at 8% interest is $9,245.76 (= $2,000 × 4.62288, time value factor from Table 4, Present Value of an Annuity of $1, with $n = 6$ and $i = 8\%$). The $10,000 cost of the upgrade is greater than the present value of the future cash flows of $9,245.76 generated. The theatre will be better off *not* making the investment.

Example 2.   Each year you play the Monopoly game at **McDonald's**. This is your year: As you peel back the sticker, you realize you have both Park Place and Boardwalk. You have just won a million dollars payable in $50,000 installments over the next 20 years. Assuming a discount rate of 10%, how much did you really win?

The present value of a $50,000 annuity over 20 periods at 10% is $425,678 (= $50,000 × 8.51356, time value factor from Table 4, Present Value of an Annuity of $1, with $n = 20$ and $i = 10\%$). The value today of $50,000 per year for the next 20 years is actually less than half a million dollars, though you'd probably not be too disappointed with these winnings.

 KEY POINT

Cash payments of equal amounts over equal time intervals are called an annuity. The *future* value of an annuity is the sum of the future values of a series of cash payments. Similarly, the *present* value of an annuity is the sum of the present values of a series of cash payments.

Let's Review

Below are four scenarios related to the future value and present value of an annuity.

1. Manuel is saving for a new car. He puts $2,000 into an investment account at the end of each year for the next five years. He expects the account to earn 12% annually. How much will Manuel have in five years?

2. Ingrid would like to take her family to Disney World in three years. She decides to purchase a vacation package that requires her to make three annual payments of $1,500 at the end of each year for the next three years. If she can earn 9% annually, how much should she set aside today so that the three annual payments can be made?

3. John puts $500 in a savings account at the end of each six months for the next six years that earns 8% interest compounded semiannually. How much will John have in six years?

4. Anna purchases a ring with a selling price of $4,000 and will make four payments of $1,000 at the end of each quarter for the next four quarters. Assuming a discount rate of 16% compounded quarterly, what is Anna's actual cost of the ring today?

Required:

Calculate the time value of money for each scenario.

Solution:

(Rounded to the nearest whole dollar)

1. $2,000 × 6.3528 (FV of Annuity of $1, $n = 5$, $i = 12\%$) = $12,706
2. $1,500 × 2.53129 (PV of Annuity of $1, $n = 3$, $i = 9\%$) = $3,797
3. $500 × 15.0258 (FV of Annuity, $n = 12$, $i = 4\%$) = $7,513
4. $1,000 × 3.62990 (PV of Annuity, $n = 4$, $i = 4\%$) = $3,630

Suggested Homework:
BEC-6, BEC-8;
EC-6, EC-8;
PC-3A&B

KEY POINTS BY LEARNING OBJECTIVE

LO1 Contrast simple and compound interest.

Simple interest is interest we earn on the initial investment only. Compound interest is the interest we earn on the initial investment plus previous interest. We use compound interest in calculating the time value of money.

LO2 Calculate the future value and present value of a single amount.

The *future value* of a single amount is how much that amount today will grow to be in the future. The *present value* of a single amount is the value today of receiving that amount in the future.

LO3 Calculate the future value and present value of an annuity.

Cash payments of equal amounts over equal time intervals are called an annuity. The *future* value of an annuity is the sum of the future values of a series of cash payments. Similarly, the *present* value of an annuity is the sum of the present values of a series of cash payments.

GLOSSARY

Annuity: Cash payments of equal amounts over equal time intervals. **p. C–8**

Compound interest: Interest earned on the initial investment and on previous interest. **p. C–2**

Discount rate: The rate at which someone would be willing to give up current dollars for future dollars. **p. C–5**

Future value: How much an amount today will grow to be in the future. **p. C–2**

Present value: The value today of receiving some amount in the future. **p. C–5**

Simple interest: Interest earned on the initial investment only. **p. C–1**

Time value of money: The value of money today is greater than the value of that same amount of money in the future. **p. C–1**

SELF-STUDY QUESTIONS

1. How does simple interest differ from compound interest?   ■ **LO1**
   a. Simple interest includes interest earned on the initial investment plus interest earned on previous interest.
   b. Simple interest includes interest earned on the initial investment only.
   c. Simple interest is for a shorter time interval.
   d. Simple interest is for a longer time interval.

2. What is the future value of $100 invested in an account for eight years that earns   ■ **LO2**
   10% annual interest, compounded semiannually (rounded to the nearest whole dollar)?
   a. $214.
   b. $216.
   c. $218.
   d. $220.

3. Present value represents: ■ **LO2**
   a. The value today of receiving money in the future.
   b. The amount that an investment today will grow to be in the future.
   c. The difference between the initial investment and the growth of that investment over time.
   d. A series of equal payments.

4. Cooper wants to save for college. Assuming he puts $5,000 into an account at the   ■ **LO3**
   end of each year for five years and earns 12% compounded annually, how much

will he have saved by the end of the fifth year (rounded to the nearest whole dollar)?

a. $25,000.

b. $31,764.

c. $18,024.

d. $14,096.

Note: Answers appear at the end of the appendix.

REVIEW QUESTIONS

■ LO1   1. Define interest. Explain the difference between simple interest and compound interest.

■ LO2   2. Identify the three items of information necessary to calculate the future value of a single amount.

■ LO2   3. Define the present value of a single amount. What is the discount rate?

■ LO3   4. What is an annuity?

■ LO3   5. What is the relationship between the present value of a single amount and the present value of an annuity?

BRIEF EXERCISES

Understand simple versus compound interest (**LO1**)

BEC–1 Oprah is deciding between investment options. Both investments earn an interest rate of 7%, but interest on the first investment is compounded annually, while interest on the second investment is compounded semiannually. Which investment would you advise Oprah to choose? Why?

Calculate the future value of a single amount (**LO2**)

BEC–2 Dusty would like to buy a new car in five years. He currently has $10,000 saved. He's considering buying a car for around $14,000 but would like to add a Turbo engine to increase the car's performance. This would increase the price of the car to $18,000. If Dusty can earn 10% interest, compounded annually, will he be able to get a car with a Turbo engine in five years?

Calculate the future value of a single amount (**LO2**)

BEC–3 Arnold and Maria would like to visit Austria in three years to celebrate their 25th wedding anniversary. Currently, the couple has saved $22,000, but they expect the trip to cost $26,000. If they put $22,000 in an account that earns 6% interest, compounded annually, will they be able to pay for the trip in three years?

Calculate the future value of a single amount (**LO2**)

BEC–4 Calculate the future value of the following single amounts.

	Initial Investment	Annual Rate	Interest Compounded	Period Invested
1.	$7,000	9%	Annually	8 years
2.	5,000	10	Semiannually	5 years
3.	8,000	8	Quarterly	4 years

Calculate the present value of a single amount (**LO2**)

BEC–5 Maddy works at Burgers R Us. Her boss tells her that if she stays with the company for four years, she will receive a bonus of $5,000. With an annual discount rate of 7%, calculate the value today of receiving $5,000 in four years.

Calculate the present value of a single amount (**LO2**)

BEC–6 Ronald has an investment opportunity that promises to pay him $45,000 in five years. He could earn an 8% annual return investing his money elsewhere. What is the most he would be willing to invest today in this opportunity?

BEC–7 Calculate the present value of the following single amounts.

	Future Value	Annual Rate	Interest Compounded	Period Invested
1.	$9,000	5%	Annually	4 years
2.	6,000	6	Semiannually	7 years
3.	5,000	16	Quarterly	3 years

Calculate the present value of a single amount (LO2)

BEC–8 Tom and Katie were recently married and want to take a cruise. To do so, the couple needs to save $20,000. They plan to invest $3,000 at the end of each year for the next six years to earn 9% compounded annually. Determine whether Tom and Katie will reach their goal of $20,000 in six years.

Calculate the future value of an annuity (LO3)

BEC–9 Matt plans to start his own business once he graduates from college. He plans to save $2,000 each six months for the next four years. If his savings earn 8% annually (or 4% each six months), determine how much he will save by the end of the fourth year.

Calculate the future value of an annuity (LO3)

BEC–10 Calculate the future value of the following annuities, assuming each annuity payment is made at the end of each compounding period.

Calculate the future value of an annuity (LO3)

	Annuity Payment	Annual Rate	Interest Compounded	Period Invested
1.	$3,000	7%	Annually	6 years
2.	6,000	8	Semiannually	9 years
3.	5,000	12	Quarterly	5 years

BEC–11 Tatsuo has just been awarded a four-year scholarship to attend the university of his choice. The scholarship will pay $8,000 each year for the next four years to reimburse normal school-related expenditures. Each $8,000 payment will be made at the end of the year, contingent on Tatsuo maintaining good grades in his classes for that year. Assuming an annual interest rate of 6%, determine the value today of receiving this scholarship if Tatsuo maintains good grades.

Calculate the present value of an annuity (LO3)

BEC–12 Monroe Corporation is considering the purchase of new equipment. The equipment will cost $35,000 today. However, due to its greater operating capacity, Monroe expects the new equipment to earn additional revenues of $5,000 by the end of each year for the next 10 years. Assuming a discount rate of 10% compounded annually, determine whether Monroe should make the purchase.

Calculate the present value of an annuity (LO3)

BEC–13 Calculate the present value of the following annuities, assuming each annuity payment is made at the end of each compounding period.

Calculate the present value of an annuity (LO3)

	Annuity Payment	Annual Rate	Interest Compounded	Period Invested
1.	$4,000	7%	Annually	5 years
2.	9,000	8	Semiannually	3 years
3.	3,000	8	Quarterly	2 years

EXERCISES

EC–1 The four people below have the following investments.

Calculate the future value of a single amount (LO2)

	Invested Amount	Interest Rate	Compounding
Jerry	$12,000	12%	Quarterly
Elaine	15,000	8	Semiannually
George	22,000	7	Annually
Kramer	18,000	9	Annually

Required:

Determine which of the four people will have the greatest investment accumulation in five years.

Calculate the future value of a single amount (LO2)

EC–2 You want to save for retirement. Assuming you are now 20 years old and you want to retire at age 60, you have 40 years to watch your investment grow. You decide to invest in the stock market, which has earned about 12% per year over the past 80 years and is expected to continue at this rate. You decide to invest $1,000 today.

Required:

How much do you expect to have in 40 years?

Calculate the present value of a single amount (LO2)

EC–3 The four actors below have just signed a contract to star in a dramatic movie about relationships among hospital doctors. Each person signs independent contracts with the following terms:

	Contract Terms	
	Contract Amount	Payment Date
Derek	$500,000	2 years
Isabel	540,000	3 years
Meredith	450,000	Today
George	400,000	1 year

Required:

Assuming an annual discount rate of 10%, which of the four actors is actually being paid the most?

Calculate the present value of a single amount (LO2)

EC–4 Ray and Rachel are considering the purchase of two deluxe kitchen ovens. The first store offers the two ovens for $2,500 with payment due today. The second store offers the two ovens for $2,700 due in one year.

Required:

Assuming an annual discount rate of 10%, from which store should Ray and Rachel buy their ovens?

Calculate the present value of a single amount (LO2)

EC–5 Lights, Camera, and More sells filmmaking equipment. The company offers three purchase options: (1) pay full cash today, (2) pay one-half down and the remaining one-half plus 10% in one year, or (3) pay nothing down and the full amount plus 15% in one year. George is considering buying equipment from Lights, Camera, and More for $100,000 and therefore has the following payment options:

	Payment Today	Payment in One Year	Total Payment
Option 1	$100,000	$ 0	$100,000
Option 2	50,000	55,000	105,000
Option 3	0	115,000	115,000

Required:

Assuming an annual discount rate of 12%, calculate which option has the lowest total cost in present value terms.

Calculate the future value of an annuity (LO3)

EC–6 GMG Studios plans to invest $50,000 at the end of each year for the next four years. There are three investment options available.

	Annual Rate	Interest Compounded	Period Invested
Option 1	6%	Annually	4 years
Option 2	8	Annually	4 years
Option 3	12	Annually	4 years

Required:

Determine the accumulated investment amount by the end of the fourth year for each of the options.

Calculate the future value of an annuity (LO3)

EC–7 You would like to start saving for retirement. Assuming you are now 20 years old and you want to retire at age 60, you have 40 years to watch your investment grow. You

decide to invest in the stock market, which has earned about 12% per year over the past 80 years and is expected to continue at this rate. You decide to invest $1,000 at the end of each year for the next 40 years.

Required:
Calculate how much your accumulated investment is expected to be in 40 years.

EC–8 Denzel needs a new car. At the dealership, he finds the car that he likes. The dealership gives him two payment options:

1. Pay $30,000 for the car today.
2. Pay $3,000 at the end of each quarter for three years.

Calculate the present value of an annuity (LO3)

Required:
Assuming Denzel uses a discount rate of 12% (or 3% quarterly), determine which option gives him the lower cost.

*For additional exercises, visit **www.mhhe.com/succeed** for Exercises: Set B.*

PROBLEMS: SET A

PC–1A Alec, Daniel, William, and Stephen decide today to save for retirement. Each person wants to retire by age 65 and puts $10,000 into an account earning 9% compounded annually.

Calculate the future value of a single amount (LO2)

Person	Age	Initial Investment	Accumulated Investment by Retirement (age 65)
Alec	50	$10,000	$_____
Daniel	40	10,000	$_____
William	30	10,000	$_____
Stephen	25	10,000	$_____

Required:
Calculate how much each person will have accumulated by the age of 65.

PC–2A Bruce is considering the purchase of a restaurant named Hard Rock Hollywood. The restaurant is listed for sale at $1,100,000. With the help of his accountant, Bruce projects the net cash flows (cash inflows less cash outflows) from the restaurant to be the following amounts over the next 10 years:

Consider present value (LO2, 3)

Years	Amount
1–6	$ 90,000 (each year)
7	100,000
8	110,000
9	120,000
10	130,000

Bruce expects to sell the restaurant after 10 years for an estimated $1,200,000.

Required:
If Bruce wants to make at least 12% annually on his investment, should he purchase the restaurant? (Assume all cash flows occur at the end of each year.)

PC–3A Hollywood Tabloid needs a new state-of-the-art camera to produce its monthly magazine. The company is looking at two cameras that are both capable of doing the job and has determined the following:

Determine present value alternatives (LO2, 3)

Camera 1 costs $5,000. It should last for eight years and have annual maintenance cost of $200 per year. After eight years, the magazine can sell the camera for $400.

Camera 2 costs $4,500. It will also last for eight years and have maintenance costs of $800 in year three, $900 in year five, and $1,000 in year seven. After eight years, the camera will have no resale value.

Required:

Determine which camera Hollywood Tabloid should purchase. Assume that an interest rate of 9% properly reflects the discount rate in this situation and that maintenance costs are paid at the end of each year.

PROBLEMS: SET B

Calculate the future value of an annuity (LO3)

PC–1B Mary Kate, Ashley, Dakota, and Elle each want to buy a new home. Each needs to save enough to make a 20% down payment. For example, to buy a $100,000 home, a person would need to save $20,000. At the end of each year for five years, the women make the following investments:

Person	Annuity Payment	Type of Account	Expected Annual Return	Five-Year Accumulated Investment	Maximum Home Purchase
Mary Kate	$3,000	Savings	2%	$_____	$_____
Ashley	4,000	CDs	4	$_____	$_____
Dakota	5,000	Bonds	6	$_____	$_____
Elle	5,000	Stocks	12	$_____	$_____

Required:

1. Calculate how much each woman is expected to accumulate in the investment account by the end of the fifth year.
2. What is the maximum amount each woman can spend on a home, assuming she uses her accumulated investment account to make a 20% down payment?

Consider the present value of investments (LO2, 3)

PC–2B Woody Lightyear is considering the purchase of a toy store from Andy Enterprises. Woody expects the store will generate net cash flows (cash inflows less cash outflows) of $50,000 per year for 15 years. At the end of the 15 years, he intends to sell the store for $500,000. To finance the purchase, Woody will borrow using a 15-year note that requires 8% interest.

Required:

What is the maximum amount Woody should offer Andy for the toy store? (Assume all cash flows occur at the end of each year.)

Determine present value alternatives (LO2, 3)

PC–3B Star Studios is looking to purchase a new building for its upcoming film productions. The company finds a suitable location that has a list price of $1,500,000. The seller gives Star Studios the following purchase options:

1. Pay $1,500,000 immediately.
2. Pay $500,000 immediately and then pay $140,000 each year over the next 10 years, with the first payment due in one year.
3. Make 10 annual installments of $200,000, with the first payment due in one year.
4. Make a single payment of $2,200,000 at the end of five years.

Required:

Determine the lowest-cost alternative for Star Studios, assuming that the company can borrow funds to finance the purchase at 7%.

For additional problems, visit www.mhhe.com/succeed for Problems: Set C.

Answers to the Self-Study Questions
1. b   2. c   3. a   4. b

Learning Objectives

AFTER STUDYING THIS APPENDIX, YOU SHOULD BE ABLE TO:

■ **LO1** Explain why companies invest in other companies.

■ **LO2** Account for investments in equity securities when the investor has *insignificant* influence.

■ **LO3** Account for investments in equity securities when the investor has *significant* influence.

■ **LO4** Account for investments in equity securities when the investor has *controlling* influence.

■ **LO5** Account for investments in debt securities.

Why Companies Invest in Other Companies

To finance growing operations, a company raises additional funds either by issuing *equity securities,* such as the common and preferred stock we discussed in Chapter 10, or by issuing *debt securities,* such as the bonds we discussed in Chapter 9. These equity and debt securities are purchased by individual investors, by mutual funds, and also by other companies. In this appendix, we focus on investments by companies in equity and debt securities issued by other companies. Companies invest in other companies for a variety of reasons, primarily those indicated in Illustration D–1.

■ **LO1**
Explain why companies invest in other companies.

ILLUSTRATION D–1
Why Companies Invest in Other Companies

1. To receive dividends, earn interest, and gain from the increase in the value of their investment.

2. To temporarily invest excess cash created by operating in seasonal industries.

3. To build strategic alliances, increase market share, or enter new industries.

Companies purchase *equity securities* for dividend income and for appreciation in the value of the stock. Many companies pay a stable dividend stream to their investors. Historically, **General Electric** has been one of the most reliable, highest-dividend-paying stocks on the New York Stock Exchange. However, even GE cut its quarterly dividend payout in 2009, for the first time since 1938, to help free up cash during a severe down cycle in the economy. In contrast, some companies pay little or no dividends. Companies with large expansion plans, called *growth companies,* prefer to reinvest earnings in the growth of the company rather than distribute earnings to investors in the form of cash dividends. For example, **Starbucks**, founded in 1987, did not pay a cash dividend until March 2010. Even without receiving dividends, investors still benefit when companies reinvest earnings, leading to even more profits in the future and eventually higher stock prices.

Companies purchase *debt securities* primarily for the interest revenue they provide, although investment returns also are affected when the values of debt securities change over time. As we discussed in Chapter 9, the value of a debt security with fixed interest payments changes in the opposite direction of interest rates. For example, when general market interest rates decrease, the market value of a bond with fixed interest payments goes up because the fixed interest payments are now more attractive to investors.

The seasonal nature of some companies' operations also influences their investment balances. *Seasonal* refers to the revenue activities of a company varying based on the time (or season) of the year. For instance, agricultural and construction companies enjoy more revenues in the summer, and ski resorts earn most of their revenues in the winter. Most retail companies see their sales revenues increase dramatically during the holiday season. As a result of having seasonal operations, companies save excess cash generated during the busy part of the year to maintain operations during the slower time of the year. With this excess cash, companies tend to purchase low-risk investments such as money market funds (savings accounts), government bonds, or highly rated corporate bonds. These low-risk investments enable companies to earn some interest, while ensuring the funds will be available when needed during the slow season. Investing excess cash in stocks is more risky because the value of stocks varies more than the value of bonds. Stocks typically have greater upside potential, providing a higher average return to their investors than do bonds over the long run. However, stocks can lose value in the short run, making them a better choice for investments that are more long-term in nature.

Companies also can make sizeable long-run stock investments in other companies for strategic purposes. For instance, **AT&T** acquired **Cingular Wireless** to gain a stronger presence in the market for cell phones. **Coca-Cola** acquired **Minute Maid**, and **PepsiCo** purchased **Tropicana**, in order to diversify beyond soft drinks. Sometimes, a company will remove competition and increase market share by purchasing a controlling interest (more than 50% of its voting stock) in a competing company. Companies also might purchase a controlling interest in an established company in a *different* industry to expand into that industry and avoid many of the start-up costs associated with beginning a new business from scratch.

 KEY POINT

Companies invest in other companies primarily to receive dividends, earn interest, and gain from the increase in the value of their investment. Companies in seasonal industries often invest excess funds generated during the busy season and draw on these funds in the slow season. Many companies also make investments for strategic purposes to develop closer business ties, increase market share, or expand into new industries.

PART A

EQUITY INVESTMENTS

Equity investments are the "flip side" of issuing stock. One company issues stock, and another company invests by purchasing that stock. We discussed the issuance of stock in Chapter 10. Here, we discuss how companies that purchase stock account for their investment.

The way we account for equity investments is determined by the *degree of influence* an investor has over the company in which it invests. **A guideline for determining the degree of influence is the percentage of stock held by the investor.** Illustration D–2 summarizes the reporting methods for equity investments.

ILLUSTRATION D–2   Accounting for Equity Investments

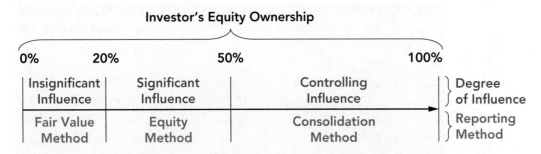

When one company (investor) purchases more than 50% of the voting stock of another company (investee), the investor has *controlling influence;* by voting those shares, the investor actually can *control* the investee's operations. Companies account for their controlling investments using the **consolidation method**. Under this method, both companies continue to operate as separate legal entities, but the investing company uses *consolidated* financial statements to report operations, as if the two companies were operating as a single combined company. We'll discuss consolidated statements in more detail later in this appendix.

When ownership is below 50% of the voting shares, the investor still might be able to exercise *significant influence* over the investee. This would be the case if the investor owns a large percentage of the outstanding shares *relative to other share- holders.* By voting all those shares with a single intent, the purchasing company can sway decisions in the direction it desires. When significant influence exists, we account for the investment using the **equity method**. In the absence of evidence to the contrary, an investor exercises significant influence when it owns between 20% and 50% of the voting shares.

In the most common investment scenario, a corporate investor has *insignificant* influence, often indicated by ownership of less than 20% of the voting shares. In this case, we use the *fair value method.* **Fair value** is the amount an investment could be bought or sold for in a current transaction between willing parties. For example, when you purchased your car, you and the car dealership (or whomever you bought the car from) came to an agreement on the purchase price, or fair value, of the car. What could you sell that car for today? That's the car's current fair value. When an investor has insignificant influence, we report the investment at fair value. We discuss accounting for equity securities with insignificant influence in more detail next.

Equity Investments with Insignificant Influence

As mentioned above, when the purchasing company has insignificant influence, we use the fair value method. Under the **fair value method**, equity investments are classified as either trading securities or available-for-sale securities. **Trading securities** are securities that the investor expects to sell (trade) in the near future. **Available-for-sale securities** are securities held for reasons other than attempting to profit from trading in the near future.

We first discuss some basic investment transactions, including the purchase of an investment, the receipt of cash dividends, and the sale of an investment. We then address how companies actually adjust their investments to fair value; that adjust- ment will depend on whether the investment is classified as trading securities or available-for-sale securities.

■ **LO2**
Account for investments in equity securities when the investor has *insignificant* influence.

PURCHASE EQUITY INVESTMENTS

To see how a company accounts for the purchase of an equity investment, let's assume Nathan's Sportswear purchases 100 shares of Canadian Falcon common stock for $30 per share on December 6, 2012. Nathan's Sportswear records the investment as follows:

A	=	L	+	SE		December 6, 2012	Debit	Credit
+3,000						**Investments**	3,000	
−3,000						**Cash**		3,000
						(Purchase common stock)		
						($3,000 = 100 shares × $30)		

RECEIVE CASH DIVIDENDS

If Canadian Falcon pays cash dividends of $0.50 per share on December 15, 2012, Nathan's Sportswear records the cash receipt on its 100 shares of stock as follows:

A	=	L	+	SE		December 15, 2012	Debit	Credit
+50						**Cash**	50	
				+50 Rev↑		**Dividend Revenue**		50
						(Receive cash dividends)		
						($50 = 100 shares × $0.50)		

SELL EQUITY INVESTMENTS

Now let's assume that Nathan's Sportswear wants to sell its shares of Canadian Falcon. We record the sale of equity investments similar to the sale of many other assets, such as land (discussed in Chapter 7). If the investment sells for *more* than its recorded amount, we record a *gain* on the sale of investments. If the investment sells for *less* than its recorded amount, we record a *loss* on the sale of investments. Gains and losses on the sale of investments are reported in the income statement, with gains being reported as part of other revenues and losses as part of other expenses.

If Nathan's Sportswear sells 10 shares for $36 per share on December 18, 2012, we record the following:

A	=	L	+	SE		December 18, 2012	Debit	Credit
+360						**Cash** *(10 shares × $36)*	360	
−300						**Investments** *(10 shares × $30)*		300
				+60 Rev↑		**Gain** *(difference)*		60
						(Sell investments above recorded amount)		

The difference between the selling price of $36 per share and the currently recorded amount of $30 per share represents a $6 gain on each of the 10 shares. If Nathan's Sportswear then decides on December 26, 2012, to sell another 10 shares for only $28 per share, we record the following:

A	=	L	+	SE		December 26, 2012	Debit	Credit
+280						**Cash** *(10 shares × $28)*	280	
				−20 Exp↑		**Loss** *(difference)*	20	
−300						**Investments** *(10 shares × $30)*		300
						(Sell investments below recorded amount)		

ADJUST TO FAIR VALUE: TRADING SECURITIES

At the end of each period, we adjust equity investments to fair value. For example, after selling 20 shares, Nathan's Sportswear still owns 80 shares of Canadian Falcon, originally purchased for $30 per share. If Canadian Falcon's stock at the end of 2012 has a current price of $32, then Nathan's Sportswear needs to adjust the recorded amount of the investment ($30) to its current fair value ($32). This requires a $2 upward adjustment to the Investments account.[1]

December 31, 2012	Debit	Credit
Investments	160	
Unrealized Holding Gain—Net Income		160
(*Increase investments to fair value*)		
(*$160 = 80 shares × $2*)		

Recording the adjustment to fair value involves an account we've not yet discussed, called *Unrealized Holding Gain—Net Income*. The term *unrealized* means the gain has not been realized (has not been obtained) in the form of actual cash (or the right to receive cash). The gain is *realized* when the investment has been sold and the gain is "locked in." **Because Nathan's Sportswear classifies this investment as a trading security, it reports the unrealized holding gain in the current year's income statement when calculating net income.** Even though the gain is unrealized, reporting it as part of current net income is appropriate because trading securities are actively managed for the purpose of profiting from short-term market price changes. Thus, gains and losses that result from holding trading securities represent measures of success or lack of success in managing investments, and these gains and losses are properly included as part of net income.

ADJUST TO FAIR VALUE: AVAILABLE-FOR-SALE SECURITIES

Unlike trading securities, available-for-sale securities are *not* acquired for the purpose of profiting from short-term price changes. Thus, unrealized gains and losses from holding available-for-sale securities are not considered current measures of performance to be included in net income. Instead, unrealized gains and losses from changes in the fair value of available-for-sale securities are reported as *other comprehensive income*, which we discuss below.

Referring to our previous example, if Nathan's Sportswear accounts for its investment in Canadian Falcon as available-for-sale securities, it will report the $2 increase in fair value at the end of the year as part of other comprehensive income rather than as part of net income:

December 31, 2012	Debit	Credit
Investments	160	
Unrealized Holding Gain—Other Comprehensive Income		160
(*Increase investments to fair value*)		
(*$160 = 80 shares × $2*)		

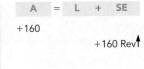

Most revenues, expenses, gains, and losses are included in net income that is reported in the typical income statement. Comprehensive income is a broader measure of income in which we report all changes in stockholders' equity other than investment by stockholders and payment of dividends. Comprehensive

---

[1]Many companies increase the investment *indirectly* with a debit to a Fair Value Adjustment allowance rather than to the Investments account itself. We record the fair value adjustment directly to the Investments account, as this is simpler and reinforces the concept that the adjustment to fair value directly affects the Investments account.

income includes all of the typical income statement items plus other comprehensive income items, such as unrealized holding gains and losses on available-for-sale securities:

Comprehensive income = Net income + Other comprehensive income

Illustration D–3 shows an example of the statement of comprehensive income for Nathan's Sportswear for 2012. The statement includes:

- revenues earned from receiving dividends on December 15.
- realized gain on the sale of 10 shares of stock on December 18.
- realized loss on the sale of 10 shares on December 26.
- and unrealized holding gain resulting from the upward fair value adjustment on December 31, the end of the year.

To complete the statement of comprehensive income, we assume sales revenue totals $2,000 and operating expenses are $1,500.

ILLUSTRATION D–3

Statement of Comprehensive Income

NATHAN'S SPORTSWEAR
Statement of Comprehensive Income (condensed)
For the year ended 2012

Sales revenue	$2,000
Operating expenses	1,500
Operating income	500
Dividend revenue	50
Gain on sale of investments	60
Loss on sale of investments	(20)
Net income	590
Unrealized holding gain	160
Comprehensive income	$ 750

Income Statement

Statement of Comprehensive Income

 KEY POINT

We report investments at fair value when a company has an insignificant influence over another company in which it invests, often indicated by an ownership interest of less than 20%. For investments classified as trading securities, unrealized holding gains and losses are included in net income. For investments classified as available-for-sale securities, unrealized holding gains and losses are included as other comprehensive income.

Let's Review

Flip Side

This problem is the flip side of a Let's Review problem presented in Chapter 10, on page 474. Sheer Designs, a custom clothing designer, has heard great things about Slacks 5th Avenue and has decided to make a small investment (insignificant influence) in the corporation's common stock. Sheer Designs has the following transactions relating to its investment in Slacks 5th Avenue.

January	1	Purchase 500 shares of common stock for $20 per share.
June	30	Receive a cash dividend of $1 per share.
October	1	Sell 100 shares of common stock for $25 per share.
December 31		The fair value of Slacks 5th Avenue's stock equals $23 per share.

Required:

1. Record each of these transactions, including the fair value adjustment on December 31. Assume the investment is classified as available-for-sale securities.
2. Calculate the balance in the Investments account on December 31.

Solution:

1. Record transactions:

	Debit	Credit
January 1		
Investments	10,000	
Cash		10,000
(Purchase common stock)		
($10,000 = 500 shares × $20)		
June 30		
Cash	500	
Dividend Revenue		500
(Receive cash dividends)		
($500 = 500 shares × $1)		
October 1		
Cash *(100 shares × $25)*...	2,500	
Investments *(100 shares × $20)*		2,000
Gain *(difference)*		500
(Sell investments above recorded amount)		
December 31		
Investments	1,200	
Unrealized Holding Gain—Other Comprehensive Income		1,200
(Adjust investments to fair value)		
($1,200 = 400 shares × $3)		

2. The balance in the Investments account on December 31 is $9,200, which equals the 400 remaining shares times $23 per share fair value. The balance in the Investments account can be verified by posting all transactions to a T-account, as follows.

Investments	
10,000	
	2,000
1,200	
Bal. 9,200	

Suggested Homework:
BED-3, BED-4;
ED-2, ED-3;
PD-1A&B

INTERNATIONAL FINANCIAL REPORTING STANDARDS (IFRS)

International accounting standards differ from U.S. accounting standards in the classification of investments. Under IFRS, the default classification for investments in equity securities is called FVTPL (Fair Value through Profit and Loss). Accounting for FVTPL is similar to that for trading securities under U.S. GAAP. Investments in equity securities classified as FVTOCI (Fair Value through Other Comprehensive Income) are treated similar to available-for-sale securities under U.S. GAAP. Investments in the FVTOCI category have *unrealized* gains and losses included in other comprehensive income.

Equity Investments with Significant Influence

■ LO3
Account for investments in equity securities when the investor has *significant* influence.

When a company owns between 20% and 50% of the common stock in another company, it is presumed that the investing company exercises significant influence over the investee. Share ownership provides voting rights, and by voting these shares, the investing company can sway decisions in the direction it desires, such as the selection of members of the board of directors. This significant influence changes the accounting for the investment. When a company has significant influence over an investee, the company is required to use the equity method. Under this method, the investor records the investment as if the investee is a part of the company. Let's discuss some specific transactions using the equity method.

PURCHASE EQUITY INVESTMENTS

Assume that, on December 6, 2012, Nathan's Sportswear purchases 25% of Canadian Falcon's common stock for $25,000. By holding 25% of the stock, Nathan's Sportswear can now exert significant influence over the operations of Canadian Falcon. Nathan's Sportswear records this equity investment as:

A = L + SE
+25,000
−25,000

December 6, 2012	Debit	Credit
Investments	25,000	
Cash		25,000
(Purchase common stock)		

RECOGNIZE EQUITY INCOME

Under the equity method, the investor (Nathan's Sportswear) includes in net income its portion of the investee's (Canadian Falcon's) net income. Assume that on December 31, 2012, Canadian Falcon reports net income of $30,000 for the year. Nathan's Sportswear records $7,500 of equity income, which represents its 25% share of Canadian Falcon's net income of $30,000.

A = L + SE
+7,500

+7,500 Rev↑

December 31, 2012	Debit	Credit
Investments	7,500	
Equity Income		7,500
(Earn equity income)		
($7,500 = $30,000 × 25%)		

Equity Income is a revenue account included in the "other revenue" portion of the income statement. The reason Nathan's Sportswear can record a portion of Canadian Falcon's net income as its own is that significant ownership essentially eliminates the independent operations of the two companies. Nathan's Sportswear can significantly influence the operations of Canadian Falcon. **Therefore, the success (or failure) of Canadian Falcon's operations should partially be assigned to Nathan's Sportswear and recognized as income (or loss) in its income statement, based on its portion of ownership.**

RECEIVE CASH DIVIDENDS

Because we record equity income when the investee reports net income (as in the transaction above), it would be inappropriate to record equity income again when the investee distributes that same net income as dividends to the investor. To do so would be to double-count equity income. Instead, the investor records dividend payments received from the investee as a *reduction* in the Investments account. Assuming Canadian Falcon pays total dividends of $500 to all shareholders,

Nathan's Sportswear receives its share of $125 (= $500 × 25%) and records the following:

	Debit	Credit
Cash	125	
Investments		125
(Receive cash dividends)		
($125 = $500 × 25%)		

A   =   L   +   SE

+125

−125

The rationale for this accounting is that the investee is distributing cash in the form of dividends. This distribution of assets by the investee reduces company value. Therefore, the value of the investment goes down based on its portion of ownership. The investor records this decrease in investment value by decreasing the Investments account.

We can see the balances in the Investments and Equity Income accounts for Nathan's Sportswear after posting the three transactions above.

Investments

Initial investment	25,000		
25% of net income	7,500	125	25% of dividends
Bal. 32,375			

Equity Income

		7,500	25% of net income
		Bal. 7,500	

The Investments account increases by the initial investment and the investor's share of the investee's net income, and it decreases by the investor's share of the investee's dividends. The Equity Income account reflects the investor's share of net income rather than its share of dividends.

KEY POINT

We initially record equity investments at cost. Under the equity method, the balance of the Investments account increases for the investor's share of the investee's net income and decreases for the investor's share of the investee's cash dividends. Equity Income reflects the investor's share of the investee's net income.

The equity method can differ significantly from recording investments under the fair value method. Under the fair value method, the investment by Nathan's Sportswear would be recorded at the purchase price of $25,000 and then be adjusted to fair value at the end of each period. Under the equity method, no adjustment is made to fair value.[2] In addition, Nathan's Sportswear would record only $125 of dividend revenue under the fair value method, rather than the $7,500 of equity income recorded using the equity method.

Let's Review

Sheer Designs, a custom clothing designer, has heard great things about Slacks 5th Avenue and has decided to make a 40% investment (significant influence) in the corporation's common stock. Sheer Designs has the following transactions relating to its investment in Slacks 5th Avenue.

[2]Adjustment to fair value is an allowable alternative under the equity method but is not common in practice.

January	1	Purchases 500 shares of common stock for $20 per share.
June	30	Receives a cash dividend of $500 (or $1 per share), representing its 40% share of Slacks 5th Avenue's total dividend distribution of $1,250.
December 31		Slacks 5th Avenue reports total net income of $5,000 for the year.
December 31		The fair value of Slacks 5th Avenue's stock equals $23 per share.

Required:

1. Record each of these transactions.
2. Calculate the balance of the Investments account on December 31.

Solution:

1. Record transactions:

January 1	Debit	Credit
Investments	10,000	
Cash		10,000
(Purchase common stock)		
June 30		
Cash	500	
Investments		500
(Receive cash dividends)		
($500 = 500 shares × $1)		
December 31		
Investments	2,000	
Equity Income		2,000
(Earn equity income)		
($2,000 = $5,000 × 40%)		

December 31

No adjustments are recorded for fair value changes when using the equity method.

2. The balance of the Investments account on December 31 is $11,500. The balance of the Investments account can be verified by posting all transactions to a T-account.

Investments	
10,000	
	500
2,000	
Bal. 11,500	

Suggested Homework:
BED-7, BED-8;
ED-6, ED-7;
PD-2A&B

 INTERNATIONAL FINANCIAL REPORTING STANDARDS

Like U.S. GAAP, international accounting standards require the equity method when the investor exerts significant influence over investees (which they call "associates"). A difference, though, is that IFRS requires that the accounting policies of investees be adjusted to correspond to those of the investor when applying the equity method. U.S. GAAP has no such requirement.

Equity Investments with Controlling Influence

If a company purchases more than 50% of the voting stock of another company, it's said to have a *controlling influence.* By voting these shares, the investor actually can control the acquired company. The investor is referred to as the *parent;* the investee is the *subsidiary.* Investments involving the purchase of more than 50% of the voting stock are accounted for by the parent using the consolidation method.

Under the consolidation method, the parent company prepares consolidated financial statements. These statements combine the parent's and subsidiary's operating activities as if the two companies were a *single* reporting company, even though both companies continue to operate as separate legal entities. Illustration D–4 demonstrates the concept of consolidation.

■ **LO4**
Account for investments in equity securities when the investor has *controlling* influence.

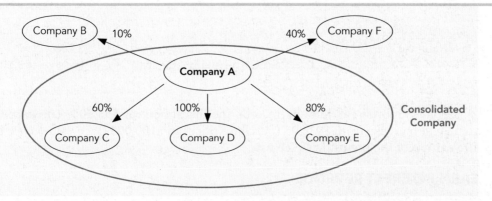

ILLUSTRATION D–4
Consolidation Method

Suppose Company A owns at least part of the common stock of five other companies. When preparing financial statements, Company A combines its financial statement results with those of all companies in which it has greater than 50% ownership (in this instance, Companies C, D, and E). For example, if Company A has $10 million cash and Companies C, D, and E have $2 million, $4 million, and $6 million, respectively, the consolidated balance sheet would report cash of $22 million.[3] The cash balances for Companies B and F are not included in the consolidated financial statements of Company A. The 10% ownership (insignificant influence) in Company B is accounted for using the fair value method, while the 40% ownership (significant influence) in Company E is accounted for using the equity method.

 KEY POINT

We account for investments involving the purchase of more than 50% of the voting stock of another company using the consolidation method. Under the consolidation method, the parent company prepares consolidated financial statements, in which the companies are combined as if they were a single company.

---

[3]Any transactions between Companies A, C, D, and E are eliminated from consolidated reporting because these transactions are not with external parties. This avoids "double-counting" those amounts in the consolidated statements. For example, we report amounts owed by Company C to Company D as accounts payable in Company C's balance sheet and as accounts receivable in Company D's balance sheet. However, these amounts are not included in the consolidated balance sheet because a company can't owe money to itself, and the consolidated company is treated as a single company for financial reporting purposes.

PART B

■ **LO5**
Account for investments in debt securities.

Flip Side

DEBT INVESTMENTS

Debt investments are the "flip side" of long-term debt: One party *borrows* by issuing a debt instrument, while another party *lends* by investing in the debt instrument. In Chapter 9, we discussed how to record the issuance of bonds (a specific type of debt instrument). Here, we discuss how to record an investment in bonds.

PURCHASE DEBT INVESTMENTS

Assume that on January 1, 2012, Nathan's Sportswear purchases $100,000 of 7%, 10-year bonds issued by RC Enterprises, with interest receivable semiannually on June 30 and December 31 each year. If the market rate of interest is 8%, Nathan's Sportswear will purchase the bonds at a discount, paying only $93,205 for the bonds.[4] Because the bonds pay only 7% compared to the prevailing market rate of 8%, we know that Nathan's Sportswear will buy them at less than the face amount of $100,000. Nathan's Sportswear records this bond investment as:

A = L + SE	January 1, 2012	Debit	Credit
+93,205	**Investments**	93,205	
−93,205	Cash		93,205
	(*Purchase bonds*)		

Nathan's Sportswear initially records the investment at $93,205. The carrying value will increase from $93,205 (purchase price) to $100,000 (face value) over the 10-year life of the bonds. Let's see why.

EARN INTEREST REVENUE

Interest revenue is the carrying value ($93,205 to start) times the market rate (8% annually, or 4% semiannually). The cash received is the face value ($100,000) times the stated rate (7% annually, or 3.5% semiannually). On June 30, 2012, six months after the initial bond investment, Nathan's Sportswear records interest revenue and cash received as follows:

A = L + SE	June 30, 2012	Debit	Credit
+3,500	**Cash** (= $100,000 × 7% × ½)......................................	3,500	
+228	**Investments** (difference)	228	
+3,728 Rev↑	Interest Revenue (= $93,205 × 8% × ½)		3,728
	(*Receive semiannual interest revenue*)		

The investment earned interest revenue of $3,728, but the investor received cash of only $3,500. Therefore, Nathan's Sportswear is entitled to receive the remaining $228 when the bond matures. That's why the investment's carrying value increases by that amount. Because the carrying value of bonds increases over time, interest revenue will also increase each semiannual interest period because it's calculated as a constant rate (8% × ½ in this example) times that increasing carrying value. On December 31, 2012, Nathan's Sportswear records cash received and interest revenue for the second six-month period as:

A = L + SE	December 31, 2012	Debit	Credit
+3,500	**Cash** (= $100,000 × 7% × ½)......................................	3,500	
+237	**Investments** (difference)	237	
+3,737 Rev↑	Interest Revenue (= [$93,205 + 228] × 8% × ½)		3,737
	(*Receive semiannual interest revenue*)		

[4]The bond price of $93,205 is calculated in Illustration 9–5.

The amortization schedule in Illustration D–5 demonstrates how the carrying amount of the bond investment would increase until it reaches maturity. Notice that the amounts in the amortization schedule are identical to those in the schedule we used for *bonds payable* in Chapter 9, Illustration 9–13.

Flip Side

(1) Date	(2) Cash Received	(3) Interest Revenue	(4) Increase in Carrying Value	(5) Carrying Value
	Face Amount × Stated Rate	Carrying Value × Market Rate	(3) − (2)	Prior Carrying Value + (4)
1/1/12				$ 93,205
6/30/12	$3,500	$3,728	$228	93,433
12/31/12	3,500	3,737	237	93,670
*	*	*	*	*
*	*	*	*	99,057
6/30/21	3,500	3,962	462	99,519
12/31/21	3,500	3,981	481	$100,000

ILLUSTRATION D–5

Amortization Schedule for Bonds Issued at a Discount

SELL DEBT INVESTMENTS

Let's assume that market interest rates have dropped from 8% to 6% during 2012. Nathan's Sportswear decides to sell the bonds on December 31, 2012, when their carrying value is $93,670 (see amortization schedule in Illustration D–5). When interest rates go down, the investment value of bonds goes up. If the market rate drops to 6%, the value of the bonds will increase to $106,877.[5] The bonds have a carrying value on December 31, 2012, of only $93,670, but Nathan's Sportswear sells them for $106,877 and records a gain for the difference.

December 31, 2012	Debit	Credit
Cash	106,877	
Investments		93,670
Gain (difference)		13,207
(Sell bonds before maturity)		

A	=	L	+	SE
+106,877				
−93,670				
				+13,207 Rev↑

The gain on the sale of bonds is reported in the income statement as an increase to net income. Of course, if the bond was sold for a loss, net income would decrease.

ADJUST TO FAIR VALUE

We classify debt investments as either (1) held-to-maturity securities, (2) trading securities, or (3) available-for-sale securities. **Held-to-maturity securities** are debt securities that the company expects to hold until they *mature*, which means until they become payable.[6] Since we do not expect to sell these securities until they mature, companies are not required to adjust held-to-maturity securities to fair value.[7]

The accounting for debt investments classified as trading securities or available-for-sale securities is nearly identical to that already discussed for equity securities. Recall that *trading securities* are securities that the investor expects to sell (trade)

---

[5]The $106,877 is based on the following inputs: future value, $100,000; interest payment each semiannual period, $3,500; market interest rate each semiannual period, 3% (6% ÷ 2 semiannual periods); and periods to maturity, 18 (9 years left × 2 semiannual periods each year).

[6]Equity securities do not have a held-to-maturity classification because equity securities do not have a maturity date.

[7]However, U.S. GAAP does allow companies to elect a fair value option. Under this option, companies may report held-to-maturity securities at fair value, with unrealized gains and losses recognized in income in the period in which they occur—the same approach we use to account for trading securities.

in the near future. These investments are adjusted to fair value with the unrealized gain or loss included in net income. *Available-for-sale securities* are investments that do not fit the other two categories; they are not expected to be sold in the near future, yet they are not expected to be held to maturity either. These investments are adjusted to fair value with the unrealized gain or loss included in comprehensive income.

 KEY POINT

Bond investments are the "flip side" of bonds payable. Bond investments are long-term assets that earn interest revenue, while bonds payable are long-term liabilities that incur interest expense.

Let's Review

Assume that on January 1, 2012, Wally World issues $200,000 of 9% bonds, due in 10 years, with interest payable semiannually on June 30 and December 31 each year. American Life Insurance Company (ALICO) purchases all of the bonds.

Required:

1. If the market rate is 9%, the bonds will sell for $200,000. Record the investment in bonds by ALICO on January 1, 2012, and receipt of the first semiannual interest payment on June 30, 2012.
2. If the market rate is 10%, the bonds will sell for $187,538. Record the investment in bonds by ALICO on January 1, 2012, and receipt of the first semiannual interest payment on June 30, 2012.
3. If the market rate is 8%, the bonds will sell at $213,590. Record the investment in bonds by ALICO on January 1, 2012, and receipt of the first semiannual interest payment on June 30, 2012.

Solution:

1. Market rate of 9%:

January 1, 2012	Debit	Credit
Investments	200,000	
Cash		200,000
(Purchase bonds)		
June 30, 2012		
Cash	9,000	
Interest Revenue		9,000
(Receive semiannual interest revenue)		
$(= \$9,000 = \$200,000 \times 9\% \times \frac{1}{2})$		

2. Market rate of 10%:

January 1, 2012	Debit	Credit
Investments	187,538	
Cash		187,538
(Purchase bonds)		
June 30, 2012		
Cash $(= \$200,000 \times 9\% \times \frac{1}{2})$	9,000	
Investments (difference)	377	
Interest Revenue $(= \$187,538 \times 10\% \times \frac{1}{2})$		9,377
(Receive semiannual interest revenue)		

3. Market rate of 8%:

January 1, 2012	Debit	Credit
Investments	213,590	
Cash		213,590
(*Purchase bonds*)		
June 30, 2012		
Cash (= $200,000 \times 9\% \times \frac{1}{2}$).......................................	9,000	
Investments (difference)		456
Interest Revenue (= $213,590 \times 8\% \times \frac{1}{2}$)		8,544
(*Receive semiannual interest revenue*)		

Suggested Homework:
**BED-11, BED-12;
ED-10, ED-11;
PD-4A&B**

KEY POINTS BY LEARNING OBJECTIVE

LO1 Explain why companies invest in other companies.

Companies invest in other companies primarily to receive dividends, earn interest, and gain from the increase in the value of their investment. Companies in seasonal industries often invest excess funds generated during the busy season and draw on these funds in the slow season. Many companies also make investments for strategic purposes to develop closer business ties, increase market share, or expand into new industries.

LO2 Account for investments in equity securities when the investor has *insignificant* influence.

We report investments at fair value when a corporation has an insignificant influence over another company in which it invests, often indicated by an ownership interest of less than 20%. For investments classified as trading securities, unrealized holding gains and losses are included in net income. For investments classified as available-for-sale securities, unrealized holding gains and losses are included as other comprehensive income.

LO3 Account for investments in equity securities when the investor has *significant* influence.

We initially record equity investments at cost. Under the equity method, the balance of the Investments account increases for the investor's share of the investee's net income and decreases for the investor's share of the investee's dividend payment. Equity income reflects the investor's share of the investee's net income.

LO4 Account for investments in equity securities when the investor has *controlling* influence.

We account for investments involving the purchase of more than 50% of the voting stock of another company using the consolidation method. Under the consolidation method, the parent company prepares consolidated financial statements, in which the companies are combined as if they were a single company.

LO5 Account for investments in debt securities.

Bond investments are the "flip side" of bonds payable. Bond investments are long-term assets that earn interest revenue, while bonds payable are long-term liabilities that incur interest expense.

GLOSSARY

Available-for-sale securities: Securities held for reasons other than attempting to profit from trading in the near future. **p. D–3.**

Comprehensive income: A broad measure of income that reports all changes in stockholders' equity other than investment by stockholders and payment of dividends. **p. D–5.**

Consolidated financial statements: Combination of the separate financial statements of the parent (purchasing company) and the subsidiary (acquired company) into a single set of financial statements. **p. D–11.**

Consolidation method: Method of recording equity investments when one company owns more than 50% of the voting stock of another company. Under this method, the investing company uses *consolidated* financial statements to report operations, as if the two companies were operating as a single combined company. **pp. D–3, D–11.**

Debt investments: Investments made in the debt issued by another party. **p. D–12.**

Equity investments: Investments made in the equity (or stock) issued by another party. **p. D–2.**

Equity method: Method of recording equity investments when an investor has significant influence over, yet does not control, the operations of the investee, often indicated by ownership of between 20% and 50% of the voting shares. Under this method, the investor company records the investment as if the investee is a part of the company. **pp. D–3, D–8.**

Fair value: The amount for which the investment could be bought or sold in a current transaction between willing parties. **p. D–3.**

Fair value method: Method of recording equity investments when an investor has insignificant influence, often indicated by ownership of less than 20% of the voting shares. Under this method, we classify equity investments as either trading securities or available-for-sale securities and report investments at their fair value. **p. D–3.**

Held-to-maturity securities: Debt securities that are expected to be held until they *mature*, which means until they become payable. **p. D–13.**

Trading securities: Securities that the investor expects to sell in the near future. **p. D–3.**

SELF-STUDY QUESTIONS

■ LO1

1. One of the primary reasons for investing in equity securities includes:
   a. Receiving dividend payments.
   b. Acquiring debt of competing companies.
   c. Earning interest revenue.
   d. Deducting dividend payments for tax purposes.

■ LO1

2. One of the primary reasons for investing in debt securities includes:
   a. Deducting interest payments for tax purposes.
   b. Receiving dividend payments.
   c. Earning interest revenue.
   d. Acquiring ownership control in other companies.

■ LO2

3. On November 17, 2012, Tasty Foods purchased 1,000 shares (10%) of Eco-Safe Packaging's voting stock for $12 per share. Because Tasty Foods' intent in making the investment is to make a quick profit by trading in the near term, the investment is classified as a trading security. By the end of 2012, Eco-Safe Packaging's stock price has dropped to $10 per share. How would the drop in stock price affect Tasty Foods' net income in 2012?
   a. Decrease net income by $12,000.
   b. Decrease net income by $10,000.
   c. Decrease net income by $2,000.
   d. No effect.

■ LO2

4. On November 17, 2012, Tasty Foods purchased 1,000 shares (10%) of Eco-Safe Packaging's voting stock for $12 per share. Because Tasty Foods has no immediate plans to sell the stock, the investment is classified as an available-for-sale security. By the end of 2012, Eco-Safe Packaging's stock price has dropped to $10 per share. How would the drop in stock price affect Tasty Foods' net income in 2012?
   a. Decrease net income by $12,000.
   b. Decrease net income by $10,000.
   c. Decrease net income by $2,000.
   d. No effect.

■ LO3

5. On January 1, 2012, Tasty Foods purchased 3,000 shares (30%) of Eco-Safe Packaging's voting stock for $12 per share. On December 31, 2012, Eco-Safe Packaging reports net income $10,000 and a total dividend payment of $2,000, and the stock price has dropped to $10 per share. For how much would Tasty Foods report its investment in Eco-Safe Packaging at the end of 2012?

    a. $30,000.

    b. $38,400.

    c. $36,000.

    d. $39,000.

6. On January 1, 2012, Tasty Foods purchased 10,000 shares (100%) of Eco-Safe Packaging's ■ **LO4** voting stock for $12 per share. Throughout the year, both companies continue to operate as separate legal entities. By December 31, 2012, Eco-Safe Packaging's cash balance is $2,000, and Tasty Foods' cash balance is $5,000. In preparing its year-end financial statements, for how much would Tasty Foods report its cash balance?

    a. $7,000.

    b. $5,000.

    c. $3,000.

    d. $2,000.

7. On January 1, 2012, Eco-Safe Packaging issues $100,000 of 8%, 5-year bonds with ■ **LO5** interest payable semiannually on June 30 and December 31. The market interest rate for bonds of similar risk and maturity is 6%. Tasty Foods purchases all of the bonds for $108,530. Which of the following would correctly record Tasty Foods' investment in bonds on January 1?

a. Cash	108,530	
Investments		108,530
b. Investments	108,530	
Cash		108,530
c. Cash	100,000	
Investments		100,000
d. Investments	100,000	
Cash		100,000

8. Refer to question 7. How much interest revenue would Tasty Foods record at the ■ **LO5** time it receives the first semiannual payment on June 30?

    a. $4,341.

    b. $8,000.

    c. $6,512.

    d. $3,256.

Note: For answers, see the last page of the appendix.

REVIEW QUESTIONS

1. Explain why a company might invest in another company. ■ **LO1**

2. How can an investor benefit from an equity investment that does not pay dividends? ■ **LO1**

3. How might the investing activity for a company that operates a ski resort vary throughout the year? ■ **LO1**

4. Provide an example of an equity investment in another company undertaken for strategic purposes. ■ **LO1**

5. What is the "flip side" of an investment in equity securities? ■ **LO1**

6. How does a company determine whether to account for an equity investment using the fair value method, equity method, or consolidation method? ■ **LO1**

7. Investments in *equity* securities for which the investor has insignificant influence over the investee are classified for reporting purposes under the fair value method in one of two categories. What are these two categories? ■ **LO2**

■ **LO2**   8. Explain how we report dividends received from an investment under the fair value method.

■ **LO2**   9. Discuss the difference between an unrealized holding gain and a realized gain.

■ **LO2**   10. When using the fair value method, we adjust the reported amount of the investment for changes in fair value after its acquisition. If the security is classified as trading, how do we report unrealized holding gains and losses?

■ **LO2**   11. When using the fair value method, we adjust the reported amount of the investment for changes in fair value after its acquisition. If the security is classified as available-for-sale, how do we report unrealized holding gains and losses?

■ **LO3**   12. Under what circumstances do we use the equity method to account for an investment in stock?

■ **LO3**   13. Explain how we report dividends received from an investment under the equity method.

■ **LO4**   14. Discuss the meaning of consolidated financial statements.

■ **LO4**   15. When is it appropriate to consolidate financial statements of two companies? Discuss your answer in terms of the relation between the parent and the subsidiary.

■ **LO5**   16. What is the "flip side" of an investment in debt securities?

■ **LO5**   17. If bonds are purchased at a *discount*, what will happen to the carrying value of the investment in bonds and the amount recorded for interest revenue over time?

■ **LO5**   18. If bonds are purchased at a *premium*, what will happen to the carrying value of the investment in bonds and the amount recorded for interest revenue over time?

■ **LO5**   19. When interest rates go down, what happens to the value of an investment in bonds that pay a fixed interest rate?

■ **LO5**   20. Investments in *debt* securities are classified for reporting purposes in one of three categories. Explain each of these three categories.

BRIEF EXERCISES

Identify reasons why companies invest **(LO1)**

BED–1 Indicate with an "X" which of the following represents a common reason why companies invest in other companies.

_____ 1. To invest excess cash created by operating in seasonal industries.

_____ 2. To increase employees' morale.

_____ 3. To build strategic alliances.

_____ 4. To reduce government regulation.

_____ 5. To receive interest and dividends.

Record equity investments with insignificant influence **(LO2)**

(Flip Side of BE10-3)

BED–2 On September 1, Leather Suppliers, Inc., purchases 100 shares of Western Wear Clothing for $12 per share. On November 1, Leather Suppliers sells the investment for $15 per share. Record the transactions made by Leather Suppliers for the purchase and sale of the investment in Western Wear Clothing.

Record trading securities **(LO2)**

BED–3 Fickle Financial buys and sells securities, expecting to earn profits on short-term differences in price. On December 28, Fickle purchased **Microsoft** common shares for $474,000. On December 31, the shares had a fair value of $473,000. Record the initial investment by Fickle and, if appropriate, an adjustment to record the investment at fair value.

BED–4 Fickle Financial buys and sells securities that it classifies as available-for-sale. On December 28, Fickle purchased **Microsoft** common shares for $474,000. On December 31, the shares had a fair value of $473,000. Record the initial investment by Fickle and, if appropriate, an adjustment to record the investment at fair value.

Record available-for-sale securities **(LO2)**

BED–5 On December 29, Adams Apples purchased 1,000 shares of **General Electric** common stock for $19,000 and placed the investment in an active trading account for immediate resale. On December 31, 2012, the market value of the stock is $20 per share. What is the appropriate reporting category for this investment, and at what amount will Adams Apples report it in the 2012 balance sheet?

Determine the appropriate classification and reporting for an equity investment **(LO2)**

BED–6 Adams Apples holds 1,000 shares of **General Electric** common stock. The stock was initially purchased in July 2011. On December 31, 2011, and December 31, 2012, the market value of the stock is $18 and $20 per share, respectively. What is the appropriate reporting category for this investment, and at what amount will Adams Apples report it in the 2012 balance sheet?

Determine the appropriate classification and reporting for an equity investment **(LO2)**

BED–7 Wendy Day Kite Company owns 40% of the outstanding stock of Strong String Company. During the current year, Strong String reported net income of $20 million. What effect does Strong String's reported net income have on Wendy Day's financial statements? Explain the reasoning for this effect.

Explain the effect of net income by the investee in an equity method investment **(LO3)**

BED–8 Wendy Day Kite Company owns 40% of the outstanding stock of Strong String Company. During the current year, Strong String paid a $10 million cash dividend on its common shares. What effect does Strong String's dividend have on Wendy Day's financial statements? Explain the reasoning for this effect.

Explain the effect of dividends by the investee in an equity method investment **(LO3)**

BED–9 Wendy Day Kite Company owns 100% of the outstanding stock of Strong String Company. At the end of the year, Wendy Day has total inventory of $14,000 and Strong String has total inventory of $8,000. Determine the amount of inventory that would be reported in Wendy Day's consolidated financial statements (assuming no transactions involving inventory occurred between the two companies).

Calculate consolidated amounts **(LO4)**

BED–10 Salt Foods purchases twenty $1,000, 6%, 10-year bonds issued by Pretzelmania, Inc., for $20,000 on January 1, 2012. The market interest rate for bonds of similar risk and maturity is 6%. Salt Foods receives interest semiannually on June 30 and December 31.
1. Record the investment in bonds.
2. Record receipt of the first interest payment on June 30, 2012.

Record investment in bonds **(LO5)**

(Flip Side of BE9–5)

BED–11 Salt Foods purchases twenty $1,000, 6%, 10-year bonds issued by Pretzelmania, Inc., for $18,579 on January 1, 2012. The market interest rate for bonds of similar risk and maturity is 7%. Salt Foods receives interest semiannually on June 30 and December 31.
1. Record the investment in bonds.
2. Record receipt of the first interest payment on June 30, 2012.

Record investment in bonds **(LO5)**

(Flip Side of BE9–6)

BED–12 Salt Foods purchases twenty $1,000, 6%, 10-year bonds issued by Pretzelmania, Inc., for $21,559 on January 1, 2012. The market interest rate for bonds of similar risk and maturity is 5%. Salt Foods receives interest semiannually on June 30 and December 31.
1. Record the investment in bonds.
2. Record receipt of the first interest payment on June 30, 2012.

Record investment in bonds **(LO5)**

(Flip Side of BE9–7)

EXERCISES

ED–1 Consider the following statements.

_____ 1. A reason companies invest in other companies is to build strategic alliances.
_____ 2. All companies are required to pay dividends to their investors.
_____ 3. When market interest rates increase, the market value of a bond increases as well.

Identify reasons why companies invest **(LO1)**

_____ 4. One way for a company to expand operations into a new industry is to acquire the majority of common stock in another company that already operates in that industry.

_____ 5. Stocks typically have greater upside potential, providing a higher average return to their investors over the long run than do bonds.

_____ 6. Companies purchase debt securities primarily for the dividend revenue they provide.

Required:

Indicate whether each statement is true (T) or false (F).

Record trading securities (LO2)

ED–2 Ralph's Bank buys and sells securities, expecting to earn profits on short-term differences in price. The company's fiscal year ends on December 31. The following selected transactions relating to Ralph's trading account occurred during December 2012.

December 20	Purchases 200,000 shares in Classic Computers common stock for $800,000.
December 28	Receives cash dividends of $5,000 from the Classic Computers shares.
December 31	The fair value of Classic Computers' stock is $3.80 per share.

Required:

1. Record each of these transactions, including an adjustment on December 31 for the investment's fair value, if appropriate.
2. Calculate the balance of the Investments account on December 31.

Record available-for-sale investments (LO2)

(Flip Side of E10–5)

ED–3 Mr. T's Fashions, once a direct competitor to Italian Stallion's clothing line, has formed a friendship in recent years leading to a small investment (less than 5%) by Mr. T in the common stock of Italian Stallion. Mr. T's engages in the following transactions relating to its investment.

February	1	Purchases 100 shares of Italian Stallion common stock for $15 per share.
June	15	Sells 40 shares of Italian Stallion stock for $12 per share.
October	31	Receives a cash dividend of $0.75 per share.
December	31	The fair value of Italian Stallion's stock is $10 per share.

Required:

1. Record each of these transactions, including an adjustment on December 31 for the investment's fair value, if appropriate.
2. Calculate the balance of the Investments account on December 31.

Record available-for-sale investments (LO2)

(Flip Side of E10–9)

ED–4 Gator Shoes, Inc., manufactures a line of stylish waterproof footwear. The following transactions relate to investments in common stock.

March	1	Purchases 2,000 shares of Power Drive Corporation's common stock for $52 per share.
July	1	Receives a cash dividend of $1.50 per share.
October	1	Sells 500 shares of Power Drive Corporation's common stock for $60 per share.
December	31	The fair value of Power Drive Corporation's common stock is $65 per share.

Required:

1. Record each of these transactions, including an adjustment on December 31 for the investment's fair value, if appropriate.
2. Calculate the balance of the Investments account on December 31.

Prepare a statement of comprehensive income (LO2)

ED–5 Lefty's Piranha Farm generates sales revenue of $250,000 and incurs operating expenses of $130,000. The company incurs a gain of $12,000 from selling securities classified as available-for-sale and records an unrealized holding loss of $18,000 from adjusting securities available-for-sale to fair value at the end of the year.

Required:

1. What is the meaning of comprehensive income?
2. Prepare a statement of comprehensive income for Lefty's Piranha Farm.

ED–6 On January 1, Lifestyle Pools purchased 30% of Marshall Fence's common stock for $600,000 cash. By the end of the year, Marshall Fence reported net income of $150,000 and paid dividends of $50,000 to all shareholders.

Record transactions under the equity method (LO3)

Required:
For Lifestyle Pools, record the initial purchase and its share of Marshall Fence's net income and dividends for the year.

ED–7 On January 1, Marcum's Landscape purchased 10,000 shares (40%) of the common stock of Atlantic Irrigation for $500,000. Below are amounts reported by both companies for the year.

Record transactions under the equity method (LO3)

	Marcum's Landscape	Atlantic Irrigation
Stock price on January 1	$75	$50
Net income for the year	$400,000	$120,000
Dividends paid for the year	$ 50,000	$ 30,000
Stock price on December 31	$84	$58

Required:
For Marcum's Landscape, record the initial purchase, its share of Atlantic's net income and dividends, and the adjustment for Atlantic's fair value at the end of the year, if appropriate.

ED–8 As a long-term investment, Fair Company purchased 20% of Midlin Company's 200,000 shares for $240,000 at the beginning of the reporting year of both companies. During the year, Midlin earned net income of $125,000 and distributed cash dividends of $0.30 per share. At year-end, the fair value of the shares is $250,000.

Compare available-for-sale securities and equity method investments (LO2, 3)

Required:
1. Assume no significant influence was acquired. Record the transactions from the purchase through the end of the year, including any adjustment for the investment's fair value, if appropriate.
2. Assume significant influence was acquired. Record the transactions from the purchase through the end of the year, including any adjustment for the investment's fair value, if appropriate.

ED–9 Alpha has made the following investments.

Determine which companies to consolidate (LO4)

_____ 1. 10% of the common stock of Beta.
_____ 2. 40% of the bonds of Gamma.
_____ 3. 75% of the common stock of Delta.
_____ 4. 15% of the bonds of Epsilon.
_____ 5. 25% of the common stock of Zeta.
_____ 6. 60% of the bonds of Eta.
_____ 7. 100% of the common stock of Theta.

Required:
Indicate with an "X" which of the companies above would be accounted for using the consolidation method.

ED–10 On January 1, 2012, Dora purchases 100 of the $1,000, 8%, 15-year bonds issued by Splash City, with interest receivable semiannually on June 30 and December 31 each year.

Record investment in bonds at a discount (LO5)

(Flip Side of E9–6)

Required:
Assuming the market interest rate on the issue date is 9%, Dora will purchase the bonds for $91,856.
1. Complete the first three rows of an amortization table for Dora.
2. Record the purchase of the bonds by Dora on January 1, 2012, and the receipt of the first two semiannual interest payments on June 30, 2012, and December 31, 2012.

Record investment in bonds at a premium **(LO5)**

(Flip Side of E9–7)

ED–11 On January 1, 2012, Splash City issues $400,000 of 8% bonds, due in 15 years, with interest payable semiannually on June 30 and December 31 each year. T. Bone Investment Company (TBIC) purchases all of the bonds in a private placement.

Required:

Assuming the market interest rate on the issue date is 7%, TBIC will purchase the bonds for $436,784.

1. Complete the first three rows of an amortization table for TBIC.
2. Record the purchase of the bonds by TBIC on January 1, 2012, and the receipt of the first two semiannual interest payments on June 30, 2012, and December 31, 2012.

PROBLEMS: SET A

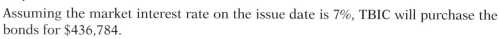 

Account for investments using the fair value method **(LO2)**

(Flip Side of P10–6A)

PD–1A Barry, Hank, and Babe form a company named Long Ball Investments, hoping to find that elusive home run stock. A new clothing company by the name of Major League Apparel has caught their eye. Major League Apparel has two classes of stock authorized: 5%, $10 par preferred and $1 par value common. Long Ball Investments has the following transactions during 2012. None of the investments are large enough to exert a significant influence.

January	2	Purchase 1,000 shares of Major League common stock for $60 per share.
February	14	Purchase 500 shares of Major League preferred stock for $11 per share.
May	15	Sell 200 shares of Major League's common stock for $52 per share.
December	30	Receive a cash dividend on Major League's common stock of $0.40 per share and preferred stock of $0.50 per share.
December	31	The fair values of the common and preferred shares are $62 and $12, respectively.

Required:

1. Record each of these investment transactions. (*Hint:* Preferred stock transactions are recorded like common stock transactions, but preferred stock has no voting rights and therefore ownership provides no influence.)
2. Calculate the balance in the Investments account as of December 31, 2012.

Account for investments using the equity method **(LO3)**

PD–2A As a long-term investment at the beginning of the year, Willie Winn Track Shoes purchased 30% of Betty Will Company's 24 million shares outstanding for $168 million. During the year, Betty Will earned net income of $120 million and distributed cash dividends of $1.25 per share.

Required:

Record for Willie Winn Track Shoes the purchase of the investment and its share of Betty Will's net income and dividends using the equity method.

Account for investments in debt securities **(LO5)**

(Flip Side of P9–2A)

PD–3A On January 1, 2012, Twister Enterprises issues $500,000 of 7% bonds, due in 20 years, with interest payable semiannually on June 30 and December 31 each year. The market interest rate on the issue date is 8%. National Hydraulics, a supplier of mechanical parts to Twister Enterprises, purchases 20% of the bond issue ($100,000 face amount) at a discount for $90,104.

Required:

1. Complete the first three rows of an amortization table for National Hydraulics.
2. Record the purchase of the bonds by National Hydraulics and the receipt of the first two semiannual interest payments on June 30 and December 31.
3. Record the sale of the bonds by National Hydraulics on December 31, 2012, for $105,000.
4. What happened to market interest rates between the beginning and end of the year?

PD–4A Justin Investor, Inc., purchases $160,000 of 8% bonds from M.R. Bonds Company, on January 1. Management intends to hold the debt securities to maturity. For bonds of similar risk and maturity, the market yield is 10%. Justin paid $132,000 for the bonds. It receives interest semiannually on June 30 and December 31. Due to changing market conditions, the fair value of the bonds at December 31 is $140,000.

Account for investments in debt securities **(LO5)**

Required:

1. Record Justin Investor's investment on January 1.
2. Record the interest revenue earned by Justin Investor for the first six months ended June 30.
3. Record the interest revenue earned by Justin Investor for the next six months ended December 31.
4. At what amount will Justin Investor report its investment in the December 31 balance sheet? Why?

PROBLEMS: SET B

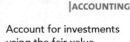
|ACCOUNTING

PD–1B Emmitt, Walter, and Barry form a company named Long Run Investments, with the intention of investing in stocks with great long-run potential. A clothing company named National League Gear looks like a great investment prospect. National League Gear has two classes of stock authorized: 6%, $20 par preferred and $5 par value common. Long Run Investments has the following transactions during 2012. None of the investments are large enough to exert a significant influence.

Account for investments using the fair value method **(LO2)**

(Flip Side of P10–6B)

February	2	Purchases 1,000 shares of National League Gear's common stock for $25 per share.
February	4	Purchases 500 shares of National League Gear's preferred stock for $22 per share.
July	15	Sells 300 shares of National League Gear's common stock for $30 per share.
November 30		Receives a cash dividend on National League Gear's common stock of $1 per share and preferred stock of $1.20 per share.
December 31		The fair value of the common and preferred shares equal $21 and $20, respectively.

Required:

1. Record each of these investment transactions. (*Hint:* Preferred stock transactions are recorded like common stock transactions, but preferred stock has no voting rights and therefore ownership provides no influence.)
2. Calculate the balance in the Investments account as of December 31, 2012.

PD–2B As a long-term investment at the beginning of the year, Acquisitions, Inc., purchased 2.5 million shares (25%) of Takeover Target's 10 million shares outstanding for $42 million. During the year, Takeover Target earned net income of $8 million and distributed cash dividends of $0.40 per share.

Account for investments using the equity method **(LO3)**

Required:

Record for Acquisitions, Inc., the purchase of the investment and its share of Takeover Target's net income and dividends using the equity method.

PD–3B Viking Voyager specializes in the design and production of replica Viking boats. On January 1, 2012, the company issues $2,000,000 of 8% bonds, due in 10 years, with interest payable semiannually on June 30 and December 31 each year. The market interest rate on the issue date is 9%. Antique Boat World, one of Viking Voyager's best customers, purchases 10% of the bond issue ($200,000 face amount) at a discount for $186,992.

Account for investments in debt securities **(LO5)**

Flip Side of P9–2B

Required:

1. Complete the first three rows of an amortization table for Antique Boat World.
2. Record the purchase of the bonds by Antique Boat World and the receipt of the first two semiannual interest payments on June 30 and December 31.
3. Record the sale of the bonds by Antique Boat World on December 31, 2012, for $182,000.
4. What happened to market interest rates between the beginning and end of the year?

Account for investments
in debt securities **(LO5)**

PD–4B Tsunami Sushi purchases $100,000 of 5-year, 6% bonds from Deep Sea Explorers, on January 1. Management intends to hold the debt securities to maturity. For bonds of similar risk and maturity, the market rate is 7%. Tsunami paid $95,842 for the bonds. It receives interest semiannually on June 30 and December 31. Due to changing market conditions, the fair value of the bonds at December 31 is $94,000.

Required:

1. Record Tsunami Sushi's investment on January 1.
2. Record the interest revenue earned by Tsunami Sushi for the first six months ended June 30.
3. Record the interest revenue earned by Tsunami Sushi for the next six months ended December 31.
4. At what amount will Tsunami Sushi report its investment in the December 31 balance sheet? Why?

Answers to the Self-Study Questions
1. a   2. c   3. c   4. d   5. b   6. a   7. b   8. d

International Financial Reporting Standards

Learning Objectives

AFTER STUDYING THIS APPENDIX, YOU SHOULD BE ABLE TO:

■ **LO1** Explain the reasons for differences in accounting practices across countries and the need for convergence.

■ **LO2** Understand the role of the International Accounting Standards Board (IASB) in the development of International Financial Reporting Standards (IFRS).

■ **LO3** Recognize the major differences between U.S. GAAP and IFRS.

The Globalization of Accounting Standards

On November 15, 2007, the U.S. Securities and Exchange Commission voted unanimously to accept from "foreign private issuers" financial statements that are prepared using International Financial Reporting Standards (IFRS) without reconciliation to U.S. generally accepted accounting principles. There is no doubt that the United States, followed by most of the rest of the world, is moving toward converging U.S. GAAP with IFRS. **Convergence** refers to the process by which U.S. GAAP and IFRS will eventually merge to become a single set of accounting standards.

But convergence of standards hasn't happened yet, and much misunderstanding exists about the status and timing of the convergence process. Why are these changes taking place? Who are the key players? What critical differences between U.S. and international GAAP exist currently? How can you keep up-to-date with this changing landscape of converging accounting standards? This appendix is designed to answer these questions.

We first explore the reasons for differences in accounting practices across countries. These differences created the need for convergence to a single set of international financial reporting standards. Then, we discuss a brief history and background regarding the development of international financial reporting standards. Finally, we review key differences between U.S. GAAP and IFRS for each chapter of the text. Given the fast pace of change in this area, this appendix will be updated periodically on our website to make sure you are up-to-date with the convergence process.

Differences in Accounting Practices

Most countries have organizations responsible for determining accounting and reporting standards. In some countries, the United Kingdom for instance, the organization responsible for standard setting is a private standard setter similar to the FASB in the United States. In other countries, like France, the organization responsible for standard setting is part of the government.

Financial accounting standards and practices differ from country to country for many reasons, including different legal systems, the influence of tax laws, sources of financing, inflation, culture, political influence of other countries, and the level of economic development. Illustration E–1 (next page) provides a summary and further explanation of the reasons why accounting practices differ across countries.

■ **LO1**
Explain the reasons for differences in accounting practices across countries and the need for convergence.

ILLUSTRATION E–1

Reasons Why
Accounting Practices
Differ across Countries

Reason	Further Explanation
1. Legal system	Common-law countries (the United States, the United Kingdom, and Canada) place greater emphasis on public information, while code-law countries (Germany and France) rely more heavily on private information.
2. Tax laws	For countries whose tax standards are closely tied to financial reporting standards (continental Europe and Japan), accounting earnings tend to be lower so companies can minimize tax payments.
3. Sources of financing	In countries where debt financing is more common (Germany and Japan) than equity financing, there is greater emphasis on reporting the ability of the company to repay debt than on its ability to earn profits for its investors.
4. Inflation	Historically high inflation in some countries (Argentina and Brazil) has created a need to account for the effect of inflation on assets and liabilities.
5. Culture	Some countries (Brazil and Switzerland) are more secretive, leading to fewer financial disclosures.
6. Political and economic ties	Countries that share strong political and/or economic ties (British colonies) often have similar accounting practices.
7. Economic development	More economically developed economies (the United States and the United Kingdom) have a need for more complex accounting standards.

Note that overlap exists in the reasons described. Accounting research has extensively focused on the legal system (common law vs. code law) as a way to describe overall differences in accounting practices between countries. *Common law* derives from English case law, in which rules are established over time primarily through private-sector professional organizations. *Code law* derives from Roman law, in which rules are an all-embracing set of requirements and procedures. Common-law countries such as the United States, the United Kingdom, Australia, and Canada share many similarities. For instance, these countries have separate rules for financial accounting and tax accounting, rely more on equity financing, and have political and economic ties with Britain. Code-law countries such as those in Central Europe and Japan also are influenced by the same factors, but in contrasting ways. Code-law countries have similar rules for financial accounting and tax accounting and rely more on debt financing. Many code-law countries have political and economic ties that began with Germany in World War II.

 KEY POINT

Differences in legal systems, tax laws, sources of financing, inflation, culture, political and economic ties, and economic development influence accounting practices across countries.

As you might imagine, differences in accounting practices can cause problems for investors who must struggle to compare companies whose financial statements are prepared under different methods. Investors unfamiliar with the accounting practices of a particular country are less likely to invest in firms from that country because of this uncertainty. Many believe that convergence of accounting practices among countries will increase the flow of resources across borders, making it easier for companies to raise international capital.

Divergent accounting rules also can cause problems for multinational corporations. A company doing business in more than one country may find it difficult and costly to comply with more than one set of accounting standards.

KEY POINT

Differences in accounting practices make it more difficult for investors to compare companies from different countries. Variations in accounting standards also make it more difficult for multinational corporations to comply with multiple accounting standards. Convergence of accounting practices is expected to increase the flow of investment across borders.

International Financial Reporting Standards

INTERNATIONAL ACCOUNTING STANDARDS BOARD

In response to differences in accounting standards and practices across countries, the **International Accounting Standards Committee (IASC)** was formed in 1973 to develop a single set of global accounting standards. The IASC reorganized itself in 2001 and created a new standard-setting body called the International Accounting Standards Board (IASB). The IASB has two objectives: (1) to develop a single set of high-quality, understandable, and enforceable global accounting standards that lead to transparent and comparable information in general purpose financial statements, and (2) to cooperate with national accounting standard-setters to achieve convergence in accounting standards around the world.

The IASC issued 41 International Accounting Standards (IAS), which the IASB endorsed at its formation. Since then, the IASB has revised many of the previous standards and has issued standards of its own, called International Financial Reporting Standards (IFRS), sometimes pronounced "eye-furs." Compliance with these standards is voluntary, since the IASB has no enforcement authority. However, many countries now base their national accounting standards on international accounting standards. The International Organization of Securities Commissions (IOSCO) approved a resolution permitting its members to use these standards to prepare their financial statements for cross-border offerings and listings. Over 100 jurisdictions, including China, Australia, and all of the countries in the European Union (EU), either require or permit the use of IFRS or a local variant of IFRS.[1]

■ **LO2**
Understand the role of the International Accounting Standards Board (IASB) in the development of International Financial Reporting Standards (IFRS).

PRINCIPLES- VS. RULES-BASED STANDARDS

Many Europeans, in comparing IFRS with U.S. GAAP, claim that IFRS is more principles-based and U.S. GAAP is more rules-based. *Principles-based accounting standards* emphasize broad principles of accounting with relatively less emphasis on detailed implementation rules. In comparison, *rules-based accounting standards* provide additional detailed guidance to help users implement the standards. An advantage of principles-based standards is that they are more concise, allowing preparers and users of accounting information to exercise judgment in focusing on the key issues. An advantage of rules-based standards is that they are more precise, providing additional guidance to preparers and users on an issue.

In reality, both U.S. GAAP and IFRS have standards that are more principles-based and standards that are more rules-based. However, both standard setters (the FASB and IASB) recognize that in order to achieve convergence and reduce the

[1]See *http://www.iasplus.com/useias.htm*.

volume of accounting rules internationally, future international accounting standards will need to be more principles-based.

NORWALK AGREEMENT

The FASB and IASB signed the *Norwalk Agreement* in 2002, formalizing their commitment to the convergence of U.S. GAAP and IFRS. Under this agreement, the two boards pledged to remove existing differences between their standards and to coordinate their future standard-setting agendas so that major issues are worked on together. Robert Herz, chairman of the FASB, testified before Congress: "We believe now is the appropriate time to develop a plan for moving all U.S. public companies to an improved version of IFRS and to consider any actions needed to strengthen the IASB as the global accounting standard setter." In fact, in that testimony he advocated working to develop a blueprint for moving U.S. public companies from U.S. standards to an improved version of IFRS. Herz emphasized that this move would need to be accompanied by consistent, high-quality enforcement, auditing, and education of participants in the capital markets.

Arguments against convergence to IFRS.   Not everyone agrees, though, with the idea of convergence set forth in the Norwalk Agreement. Although many argue that a single set of global standards will improve comparability of financial reporting and facilitate access to capital, others argue that U.S. standards should remain customized to fit the stringent legal and regulatory requirements of the U.S. business environment. There also is concern that differences in implementation and enforcement from country to country will make accounting appear more uniform than actually is the case. Another argument for maintaining the two sets of standards is that competition between alternative standard-setting regimes is healthy and can lead to improved standards.

Where convergence currently stands.   The Norwalk Agreement did not specify a timetable for convergence, but active efforts have been ongoing since 2002. U.S. standards and IFRS have not fully converged, but beginning in 2007 the SEC eliminated the costly requirements for foreign companies that issue stock in the United States to include in their financial statements a reconciliation of IFRS to U.S. GAAP. There also is serious discussion of allowing U.S. companies to choose whether to prepare their financial statements according to U.S. GAAP or IFRS.

 KEY POINT

The IASB seeks (1) to develop a single set of high-quality, understandable, and enforceable global accounting standards that lead to transparent and comparable information in general purpose financial statements, and (2) to cooperate with national accounting standard setters to achieve convergence in accounting standards around the world.

Differences between U.S. GAAP and IFRS

■ LO3
Recognize the major differences between U.S. GAAP and IFRS.

Conceptual framework

In this section, we provide chapter-by-chapter descriptions of the important differences that remain between U.S. GAAP and IFRS. Many of these differences are highlighted in IFRS boxes throughout the text.

Chapter 1: Accounting Information and Decision Making   In the United States, the FASB's conceptual framework serves primarily to guide standard setters, while internationally the IASB's conceptual framework also serves to indicate GAAP when

more specific standards are not available. The FASB and the IASB are working together to develop a common conceptual framework that would underlie a uniform set of standards internationally. This framework will build upon the existing IASB and FASB frameworks and will consider developments since the original frameworks were issued.

Chapter 2: The Accounting Information System U.S. GAAP and IFRS provide similar general guidance concerning the timing and measurement of revenue recognition. However, U.S. GAAP includes many additional rules and other guidance promulgated by the FASB, the SEC, and others. Some of those rules are designed to specify appropriate accounting for particular industries; others are designed to discourage aggressive revenue recognition.

It is unclear currently how the additional rules that are included in U.S. GAAP will be handled in the convergence process. Also, the FASB and IASB have undertaken a major project that is reconsidering the definition of revenue and when it should be recognized. Depending on the outcome of that project, revenue recognition practices could change dramatically.

Chapter 3: The Financial Reporting Process The FASB and IASB are working on a project to establish a common standard for presenting information in financial statements, including the classification and display of line items and the aggregation of line items into subtotals and totals. This standard will have a dramatic impact on the presentation of financial statements.

An important part of the current proposal involves organizing all of the basic financial statements using a common format—operating, investing, and financing activities. These three classifications would be used in the income statement, statement of stockholders' equity, balance sheet, and statement of cash flows.

Chapter 4: Cash and Internal Controls Accounting for cash under both U.S. GAAP and IFRS is essentially the same. No major convergence efforts are anticipated.

In the United States, *Section 404* of the Sarbanes-Oxley Act (SOX) requires management to document and assess the effectiveness of all internal control processes that could affect financial reporting. Many U.S. corporate executives complain about the high cost of compliance with Section 404. In other countries, the burden of documenting effective internal controls is much less, or even nonexistent. In fact, many feel that the increased burden of compliance with Section 404 has caused many foreign companies to be reluctant to list their shares on U.S. stock exchanges. Bob Greifeld, president and CEO of the NASDAQ stock exchange, stated: "In my travels to countries like China, India, and Israel, I meet with the new generation of international entrepreneurs who are building businesses and dreaming of the day they can take their companies public. . . . 90% of international small companies intending to go public are choosing to list abroad because of SOX costs and concerns."

Chapter 5: Receivables and Sales Accounting for receivables, including the allowance for uncollectible accounts, is essentially the same under both U.S. GAAP and IFRS. No major convergence efforts are anticipated.

CAREER CORNER

Many students believe that if they plan to develop their careers in the United States, they do not need to be familiar with international accounting standards. This most certainly is not true. We are in a global economy. It's likely that the companies you work for during your career will have relationships with companies in other countries. Even if that's not the case, it is likely that U.S. companies soon will be permitted to, or required to, use International Financial Reporting Standards.

Revenue recognition

Common format for financial statements

Cash

Assessing internal control

Receivables

Chapter 6: Inventory and Cost of Goods Sold

Inventory cost flow assumptions.   The LIFO inventory method is not allowed under IFRS, which likely will be a major convergence challenge. The *LIFO conformity rule,* which requires U.S. companies that use LIFO for tax purposes to also use LIFO for financial reporting, means that the elimination of LIFO for financial reporting also would require the elimination of its use for tax purposes. As discussed in Chapter 6, an advantage of using LIFO when inventory costs are rising is that it results in a lower tax burden. Resolving this issue would require agreement not only by the FASB and IASB, but also by the U.S. Congress, as it is responsible for setting tax laws in the United States.

Because of the LIFO restriction, many U.S. multinational companies use LIFO only for their domestic inventories and use FIFO or average cost for their foreign subsidiaries. **General Mills** provides an example (see Illustration E–2) with a disclosure note included in a recent annual report.

ILLUSTRATION E–2
Disclosure Note about Inventories

> **GENERAL MILLS**
> **Notes to the Financial Statements (excerpt)**
>
> **Inventories**
>
> All inventories in the United States other than grain are valued at the lower of cost, using the last-in, first-out (LIFO) method, or market. Inventories outside of the United States are valued at the lower of cost, using the first-in, first-out (FIFO) method, or market.

Market value in lower-of-cost-or-market

Lower-of-cost-or-market.   Under both U.S. GAAP and IFRS, inventory is reported at the lower-of-cost-or-market. In the United States, market value is defined as *replacement cost,* which is the cost to replace the item in its identical form. However, the designated market value according to IFRS is *net realizable value,* which is the selling price of inventory less any selling costs.

Cadbury Schweppes plc, a U.K. company, prepares its financial statements according to IFRS. The disclosure note in Illustration E–3 shows the designation of market as net realizable value.

ILLUSTRATION E–3
Disclosure Note about Net Realizable Value

> **CADBURY SCHWEPPES plc**
> **Notes to the Financial Statements (excerpt)**
>
> **Inventories**
>
> Inventories are recorded at the lower of average cost and estimated net realizable value.

Reversal of inventory write-downs

When market value falls below cost, companies are required to write down inventory from cost to market value, causing total assets to decrease and total expenses to increase. If in a future period the market value of this inventory increases, reversal of the inventory write-down is *required* for most types of inventory under IFRS, but *not allowed* under U.S. GAAP. This means that U.S. GAAP is more conservative by not allowing the asset reduction and expense recognition to be reversed when circumstances indicate that they should.

Chapter 7: Long-Term Assets

Valuation of property, plant, and equipment.   Under U.S. GAAP, companies are not allowed to revalue property, plant, and equipment (PP&E) to fair value for financial reporting purposes. IFRS allows, but does not require, revaluation of PP&E to fair value. *IAS No. 16* allows a company to value PP&E subsequent to initial valuation at (1) cost less accumulated depreciation or (2) fair value (revaluation). If revaluation is chosen, all assets within a class of PP&E must be revalued on a regular basis.

Fair values for PP&E

British Airways plc, a U.K. company, prepares its financial statements according to IFRS. The disclosure note in Illustration E–4 describes the company's choice to value PP&E at cost.

BRITISH AIRWAYS plc
Notes to the Financial Statements (excerpt)

Property, plant, and equipment

Property, plant, and equipment is held at cost. The Group has a policy of not revaluing tangible fixed assets.

ILLUSTRATION E–4
Disclosure Note about Valuation of Property, Plant, and Equipment

---

Valuation of intangible assets.   U.S. GAAP also prohibits revaluation of intangible assets to fair value. *IAS No. 38* allows a company to value an intangible asset subsequent to initial valuation at (1) cost less accumulated amortization or (2) fair value if fair value can be determined by reference to an active market. If revaluation is chosen, all assets within that class of intangibles must be revalued on a regular basis.

Fair values for intangibles

 COMMON MISTAKE

Many students have been taught that financial statements are based on historical cost. This is no longer the case. The only historical cost amounts in financial statements are those for cash and land in the domestic currency. All other amounts reflect changes in time, events, or circumstances since the transaction date. For instance, companies record an allowance on accounts receivable, write down inventory for impairment, depreciate or amortize long-term assets and write them down to fair value when impaired, recognize most investments at fair value, and amortize the discount or premium on long-term debt.

Research and development expenditures.   U.S. GAAP requires all research and development expenditures to be expensed in the period incurred. IFRS, though, draws a distinction between research activities and development activities. Research expenditures are expensed in the period incurred. However, development expenditures that meet specified criteria are capitalized as an intangible asset.

R&D expensed vs. capitalized

Heineken, a company based in Amsterdam, prepares its financial statements according to IFRS. The disclosure note in Illustration E–5 (next page) describes the criteria used for capitalizing development expenditures.

Chapter 8: Current Liabilities

Definition of liabilities.   As we discussed earlier, the FASB and the IASB presently are working together to develop a common conceptual framework that might eventually underlie a uniform set of standards internationally. One aspect of the project is examining the definition of liabilities, a change which could affect the way some current liabilities are reported.

Liabilities definition

ILLUSTRATION E–5

Disclosure Note about Capitalization of Development Expenditures

> ### HEINEKEN
> #### Notes to the Financial Statements (excerpt)
>
> **Software, research and development, and other intangible assets**
>
> Expenditures on research activities, undertaken with the prospect of gaining new technical knowledge and understanding, are recognized in the income statement when incurred. Development activities involve a plan or design for the production of new or substantially improved products and processes. Development expenditures are capitalized only if development costs can be measured reliably, the product or process is technically and commercially feasible, future economic benefits are probable, and Heineken intends to and has sufficient resources to complete development and to use or sell the asset.

Threshold for contingent liabilities

Contingencies. Accounting for contingencies is part of a broader international standard, *IAS No. 37*, "Provisions, Contingent Liabilities, and Contingent Assets." U.S. GAAP has no equivalent general standards on "provisions," but does provide specific guidance on contingencies. A difference in accounting relates to determining the existence of a contingent liability. We accrue a contingent liability under U.S. GAAP if it's both probable and can be reasonably estimated. IFRS rules are similar, but the threshold is "more likely than not," representing a lower threshold than "probable."

Valuation of long-term contingencies

Another difference is whether to report a long-term contingency at its face amount or its present value. Under IFRS, the present value of the estimated cash flows is reported when the effect of *time value of money is material.* According to U.S. GAAP, though, discounting of cash flows is allowed when the *timing of cash flows is certain.* Illustration E–6 shows a portion of a footnote from the financial statements of **Electrolux**, which reports under IFRS.

ILLUSTRATION E–6

Disclosure Note about Recognition of Contingencies

> ### ELECTROLUX
> #### Notes to the Financial Statements (excerpt)
>
> **Note 29: U.S. GAAP information**
>
> *Discounted provisions*
> Under IFRS and U.S. GAAP, provisions are recognized when the Group has a present obligation as a result of a past event, and it is probable that an outflow of resources will be required to settle the obligation, and a reliable estimate can be made of the amount of the obligation. Under IFRS, where the effect of time value of money is material, the amount recognized is the present value of the estimated expenditures. *IAS 37* states that long-term provisions shall be discounted if the time value is material. According to U.S. GAAP, discounting of provisions is allowed when the timing of cash flow is certain.

Chapter 9: Long-Term Liabilities The joint project of the FASB and the IASB to develop a common conceptual framework includes examining the definition of liabilities, potentially affecting the way we account for long-term liabilities. More specifically, the two boards are collaborating on projects related to "hybrid" securities that likely will eliminate differences in how we account for convertible debt. Longer term, the two boards are cooperating on a project that addresses the distinction between liabilities and equity, which likely will eliminate many existing differences.

Distinction between liabilities and equity

Treatment of convertible debt

Convertible bonds. Under IFRS, convertible debt is divided into its liability (bonds) and equity (conversion option) elements. Under U.S. GAAP, the entire issue price is recorded as a liability.

Chapter 10: Stockholders' Equity The joint "financial statement presentation" project, referred to earlier under the heading for Chapter 3, will dramatically change the format and display of all financial statements, including the balance sheet—referred to in the project as the *statement of financial position*. The proposed organization of all of the basic financial statements using the same format—operating, investing, and financing activities—will significantly affect the presentation of stockholders' equity items. Current differences between U.S. GAAP and IFRS include the following:

Use of the term "reserves." Stockholders' equity is classified under IFRS into two categories: common stock and "reserves." The term *reserves* is considered misleading and thus is discouraged under U.S. GAAP.

Stockholders' equity "reserves"

Distinction between debt and equity for preferred stock. Under IFRS, most preferred stock ("preference shares") is reported as debt, with the dividends reported in the income statement as interest expense. Under U.S. GAAP, most preferred stock is included in stockholders' equity, with the dividends reported as a reduction in retained earnings. Under U.S. GAAP, only "mandatorily redeemable" preferred stock is reported as debt. **Unilever** describes such a difference in a disclosure note, shown in Illustration E–7.

Classification of preferred stock

ILLUSTRATION E–7
Disclosure Note about Preferred Stock

UNILEVER
Notes to the Financial Statements (excerpt)

Additional information for U.S. investors

Preference shares
Under *IAS 32*, Unilever recognizes preference shares that provide a fixed preference dividend as borrowings with preference dividends recognized in the income statement. Under U.S. GAAP such preference shares are classified in shareholders' equity with dividends treated as a deduction to shareholders' equity.

Reacquired shares. IFRS does not permit the "retirement" of shares. All buybacks are treated as treasury stock.

Retirement of shares

Chapter 11: Statement of Cash Flows Like U.S. GAAP, international standards also require a statement of cash flows. Consistent with U.S. GAAP, cash flows are classified as operating, investing, or financing. However, U.S. GAAP designates cash outflows for interest payments and cash inflows from interest and dividends received as operating cash flows. IFRS allows companies to report cash outflows from interest payments as either operating *or* financing cash flows and cash inflows from interest and dividends as either operating *or* investing cash flows. U.S. GAAP classifies dividends paid to shareholders as financing cash flows. The international standard allows companies to report dividends paid as either financing *or* operating cash flows.

Classification of cash flows

In the proposed organization of the basic financial statements, the classification currently used in the statement of cash flows—operating, investing, and financing activities—will remain. The FASB is leaning toward requiring the direct method of reporting operating activities; the IASB is leaning toward permitting *either* the direct or indirect method.

Direct or indirect method

U.S. GAAP requires that significant noncash activities be reported either on the face of the statement of cash flows or in a disclosure note. IFRS requires reporting in a disclosure note, disallowing presentation on the face of the statement.

Disclosure of noncash activities

Chapter 12: Financial Statement Analysis

Definition of
discontinued operations

Discontinued operations. U.S. GAAP considers a discontinued operation to be a component of an entity whose operations and cash flows can be clearly distinguished from the rest of the entity that has either been disposed of or classified as held for sale. IFRS also defines a discontinued operation as a component of an entity that has been disposed of or is classified as held for sale. What constitutes a component of an entity, however, differs considerably between U.S. GAAP and IFRS. IFRS considers a component to be primarily either a major line of business or geographical area of operations. The U.S. definition is much broader than its international counterpart.

To better understand the effects of the different definitions on financial reporting, consider the case of **Gottschalks, Inc.**, a department and specialty store chain operating in the western United States. During the fiscal year ended February 3, 2007, the company reported a discontinued operation in its income statement and disclosed the following in a note, shown in Illustration E–8.

ILLUSTRATION E–8

Disclosure Note
about Discontinued
Operations

GOTTSCHALKS, INC.
Notes to the Financial Statements (excerpt)

Discontinued operations

The Company closed one underperforming store in the Seattle metro-area during the third quarter of fiscal 2006 and one underperforming store in the Seattle/Tacoma market during the first quarter of fiscal 2006. During fiscal 2005, the Company closed two underperforming stores in the Seattle/Tacoma market. These stores . . . are considered discontinued operations.

Because these closures qualified as discontinued operations under U.S. GAAP, Gottschalks reported the discontinued operations as a separate item in the income statement. However, because Gottschalks continued to operate eight stores in the state of Washington, the company's closing of a few stores does not constitute the discontinuance of either a major line of business or geographical area, so this would not be treated as a discontinued operation under IFRS. Instead, the income effects of operating the stores during the year and their sale would have been reported in various locations throughout the income statement.

Definition of
extraordinary items

Extraordinary items. U.S. GAAP provides for the separate reporting, as an extraordinary item, of a material gain or loss that is unusual in nature and infrequent in occurrence. In 2003, the IASB revised *IAS No. 1*, "Presentation of Financial Statements." The revision states that neither the income statement nor any notes may contain any items called "extraordinary."

KEY POINT

U.S. GAAP and IFRS are converging, but many differences still exist.

KEY POINTS BY LEARNING OBJECTIVE

LO1 Explain the reasons for differences in accounting practices across countries and the need for convergence.

Differences in legal systems, tax laws, sources of financing, inflation, culture, political and economic ties, and economic development influence accounting practices across countries.

Differences in accounting practices make it more difficult for investors to compare companies from different countries. Variations in accounting standards also make it more difficult for multinational corporations to comply with multiple accounting standards. Convergence of accounting practices is expected to increase the flow of investment across borders.

LO2 Understand the role of the International Accounting Standards Board (IASB) in the development of International Financial Reporting Standards (IFRS).

The IASB seeks (1) to develop a single set of high-quality, understandable, and enforceable global accounting standards that lead to transparent and comparable information in general purpose financial statements, and (2) to cooperate with national accounting standard setters to achieve convergence in accounting standards around the world.

LO3 Recognize the major differences between U.S. GAAP and IFRS.

U.S. GAAP and IFRS are converging, but many differences still exist.

GLOSSARY

Convergence: The process by which U.S. GAAP and IFRS will eventually merge to become a single set of accounting standards. **p. E–1**

International Accounting Standards Board (IASB): The body primarily responsible for creating a single set of global accounting standards. **p. E–3**

International Financial Reporting Standards (IFRS): Pronounced "eye-furs," these are the accounting rules previously set by the International Accounting Standards Committee (IASC) and currently set by the International Accounting Standards Board (IASB). **p. E–3**

SELF-STUDY QUESTIONS

1. Which of the following reason(s) help explain why accounting practices may differ across countries?   ■ **LO1**
   a. Legal system.
   b. Culture.
   c. Political and economic ties.
   d. All of the above.

2. The body primarily responsible for creating a single set of global accounting standards is the: ■ **LO2**
   a. International Federation of Accountants.
   b. International Accounting Standards Board.
   c. Financial Accounting Standards Board.
   d. International Organization of Securities Commissions.

3. For which of the following topics is accounting under both U.S. GAAP and IFRS essentially the same?   ■ **LO3**
   a. Receivables.
   b. Long-term assets.
   c. Stockholders' equity.
   d. Statement of cash flows.

4. Which inventory cost flow assumption does IFRS not allow?   ■ **LO3**
   a. Specific identification.
   b. FIFO.
   c. LIFO.
   d. Average cost.

5. Which of the following statements is true regarding revaluation of property, plant, and equipment to fair value?   ■ **LO3**
   a. Both U.S. GAAP and IFRS allow revaluation of property, plant, and equipment to fair value.
   b. Neither U.S. GAAP nor IFRS allows revaluation of property, plant, and equipment to fair value.

      c. U.S. GAAP allows, but IFRS does not allow, revaluation of property, plant, and equipment to fair value.

      d. U.S. GAAP does not allow, but IFRS allows, revaluation of property, plant, and equipment to fair value.

Note: Answers appear at the end of the appendix.

REVIEW QUESTIONS

■ LO1   1. How is the organization responsible for standard setting in the United Kingdom different from that in France? Which is closer to the organization responsible for standard setting in the United States (the FASB)?

■ LO1   2. Describe at least five reasons why accounting practices differ across countries.

■ LO1   3. Which factor explaining why accounting practices differ across countries do you think is most important? Explain why.

■ LO1   4. What difficulties do differences in accounting standards create for investors?

■ LO1   5. What difficulties do differences in accounting standards create for multinational corporations in preparing their financial statements?

■ LO2   6. What are the two primary objectives of the International Accounting Standards Board (the IASB)?

■ LO2   7. Provide at least one argument against the trend toward convergence between U.S. GAAP and IFRS.

■ LO2   8. Describe the Norwalk Agreement. What is the significance of this agreement?

■ LO3   9. What is meant by a conceptual framework in accounting? Why is it important that the FASB and the IASB develop a common conceptual framework?

■ LO3   10. Explain how an income statement might be organized along the same categories currently used in the statement of cash flows—operating, investing, and financing activities.

■ LO3   11. Which inventory cost flow assumption is allowed under U.S. GAAP but not under IFRS? Explain why some U.S. companies will lobby strongly to keep this method as an allowable alternative.

■ LO3   12. When using the lower-of-cost-or-market inventory method, how is market value defined under U.S. GAAP and under IFRS?

■ LO3   13. What effect does writing down inventory have on total assets and net income in that reporting period? The reversal of an inventory write-down in a future period, which is required under IFRS but not allowed under U.S. GAAP, has what effect on total assets and net income?

■ LO3   14. What does it mean to revalue a long-term asset? How do U.S. GAAP and IFRS differ regarding revaluation of long-term assets?

■ LO3   15. How do IFRS rules differ in the reporting of research and development costs? Which is more conservative in the reporting of research and development costs, U.S. GAAP or IFRS?

■ LO3   16. Would a company be more likely to report a contingent liability under U.S. GAAP or IFRS? Which is more conservative in the reporting of loss contingencies, U.S. GAAP or IFRS?

■ LO3   17. How is preferred stock reported differently under U.S. GAAP and IFRS? Do you think preferred stock is a liability or an equity item? Why?

■ LO3   18. How does the reporting of extraordinary items differ under U.S. GAAP and IFRS?

EXERCISES

EE–1 Match each reason with its description.

Identify reasons for differences in accounting practices across countries (LO1)

Reason	Description
1. Legal system	a. More-developed economies have more-complex business transactions.
2. Tax laws	b. The extent of public disclosure depends on the secretiveness of society.
3. Sources of financing	c. Common-law countries rely more heavily on public information.
4. Inflation	d. Countries share business activities and have political connections.
5. Culture	e. Alignment between financial reporting and tax reporting rules.
6. Political and economic ties	f. In some countries, asset values increase rapidly because of the general price level changes.
7. Economic development	g. Some countries rely more heavily on debt capital than on equity capital to fund operations.

EE–2 Below are seven reasons for differences in accounting practices among countries. For each reason, at least two options are provided.

Classify differences in accounting practices across countries (LO1)

Reason	Options
1. _____ Legal system	(a) Common-law (b) Code-law
2. _____ Tax laws	(a) Different tax and financial accounting rules (b) Similar tax and financial accounting rules
3. _____ Sources of financing	(a) More equity financing (b) More debt financing
4. _____ Inflation	(a) Low inflation (b) High inflation
5. _____ Culture	(a) Transparent (b) Secretive
6. _____ Political and economic ties	(a) British ties (b) German ties (c) Spanish ties
7. _____ Economic development	(a) Developed economy (b) Developing economy (c) Underdeveloped economy

Required:
For each of the countries listed below, select the seven options that best describe that country. For instance, the United States can be described as common-law, different tax and financial reporting, more equity financing, low inflation, transparent, British ties, and a developed economy. You may wish to search the Internet to learn more about each country.

1. Austria
2. Australia

EE–3 International Financial Reporting Standards are gaining support around the globe. In 2007, the SEC eliminated the requirement for foreign companies that issue stock in the United States to include in their financial statements a reconciliation of IFRS to U.S. GAAP. There also is serious discussion of allowing U.S. companies to choose whether to prepare their financial statements according to U.S. GAAP or IFRS.

Provide arguments for and against allowing U.S. companies to use IFRS (LO2)

Required:

Do you think U.S. companies should be allowed the choice of reporting under either U.S. GAAP or IFRS? Provide arguments both for and against this idea.

EE–4 Many Europeans claim that a problem with U.S. GAAP is that there are too many rules. Europeans argue for principles-based accounting standards in which the broad principles of accounting are emphasized and less emphasis is placed on detailed implementation rules. Americans counter that IFRS may lack quality and rigor. Additional rules are necessary to provide adequate guidance to users. Revenue recognition rules provide a good example. U.S. GAAP has a large volume of literature relating to proper revenue recognition. IFRS, on the other hand, provides broader, less-detailed guidance on revenue recognition.

Required:

1. Explain the difference between principles-based and rules-based accounting standards.
2. What are the advantages of principles-based standards?
3. What are the advantages of rules-based standards?
4. Do you think that future international accounting standards will need to be more principles-based or more rules-based?

EE–5 The format of financial statements varies from country to country. The FASB and IASB propose that financial statements in the future be organized using the same format currently used in the statement of cash flows—operating, investing, and financing activities. This would greatly change the current format used to prepare the income statement and the balance sheet.

Required:

1. Explain the differences among operating, investing, and financing activities. You might want to refer back to the first section in Chapter 11 on the statement of cash flows.
2. Provide at least one example of an account reported in the income statement that would be classified as (a) an operating activity, (b) an investing activity, and (c) a financing activity.
3. Provide at least one example of an account reported in the balance sheet that would be classified as (a) an operating activity, (b) an investing activity, and (c) a financing activity.

EE–6 During 2012, Noval Company sells 250 units of inventory for $100 each. The company has the following inventory purchase transactions for 2012.

Date	Transaction	Number of Units	Unit Cost	Total Cost
Jan. 1	Beginning inventory	60	$73	$ 4,380
Apr. 7	Purchase	180	75	13,500
Oct. 9	Purchase	80	77	6,160
		320		$24,040

Required:

1. Calculate ending inventory, cost of goods sold, and gross profit for 2012, assuming the company uses LIFO with a periodic inventory system.
2. To comply with IFRS, the company decides to instead account for inventory using FIFO. Calculate ending inventory, cost of goods sold, and gross profit for 2012.
3. Explain the effects in the company's income statement and balance sheet of using FIFO instead of LIFO to account for inventory.

EE–7 During 2012, Fueltronics spends $200,000 on several different research projects to gain new knowledge about the use of alternative fuels to operate motorized vehicles. Because one of the projects shows very high promise, the company spends an additional $50,000 near the end of the year to develop this product for future use. This project is considered to have a high probability of success, and management intends to continue to develop it for future consumer use.

Account for research and development **(LO3)**

Required:

1. Explain how the research cost of $200,000 and the development cost of $50,000 would be reported under U.S. GAAP.
2. Explain how the research cost of $200,000 and the development cost of $50,000 would be reported under IFRS.
3. Explain the effects in the company's income statement and balance sheet of using IFRS versus U.S. GAAP to account for these research and development costs.

EE–8 Most preferred stock is reported under IFRS as debt, with the dividends reported in the income statement as interest expense. Under U.S. GAAP, most preferred stock is reported as equity, with the dividends excluded from income and reported as a direct reduction to retained earnings.

Report preferred stock **(LO3)**

Required:

1. What is the definition of a liability? What is the definition of stockholders' equity? You may wish to refer back to Chapter 1.
2. Defend the IFRS position that preferred stock is a liability.
3. Defend the U.S. GAAP position that preferred stock is part of stockholders' equity.
4. Based on the above, where do you recommend preferred stock be reported?

Answers to the Self-Study Questions
1. d   2. b   3. a   4. c   5. d

Photo Credits

Subject Index

Note: Page numbers followed by *n* indicate material in footnotes.

Company Index

Present and Future Value Tables

This table shows the future value of $1 at various interest rates (i) and time periods (n). It is used to calculate the future value of any single amount.

TABLE 1 Future Value of $1

$$FV = \$1 \, (1 + i)^n$$

n/i	1.0%	1.5%	2.0%	2.5%	3.0%	3.5%	4.0%	4.5%	5.0%	5.5%	6.0%	7.0%	8.0%	9.0%	10.0%	11.0%	12.0%	20.0%
1	1.01000	1.01500	1.02000	1.02500	1.03000	1.03500	1.04000	1.04500	1.05000	1.05500	1.06000	1.07000	1.08000	1.09000	1.10000	1.11000	1.12000	1.20000
2	1.02010	1.03022	1.04040	1.05063	1.06090	1.07123	1.08160	1.09203	1.10250	1.11303	1.12360	1.14490	1.16640	1.18810	1.21000	1.23210	1.25440	1.44000
3	1.03030	1.04568	1.06121	1.07689	1.09273	1.10872	1.12486	1.14117	1.15763	1.17424	1.19102	1.22504	1.25971	1.29503	1.33100	1.36763	1.40493	1.72800
4	1.04060	1.06136	1.08243	1.10381	1.12551	1.14752	1.16986	1.19252	1.21551	1.23882	1.26248	1.31080	1.36049	1.41158	1.46410	1.51807	1.57352	2.07360
5	1.05101	1.07728	1.10408	1.13141	1.15927	1.18769	1.21665	1.24618	1.27628	1.30696	1.33823	1.40255	1.46933	1.53862	1.61051	1.68506	1.76234	2.48832
6	1.06152	1.09344	1.12616	1.15969	1.19405	1.22926	1.26532	1.30226	1.34010	1.37884	1.41852	1.50073	1.58687	1.67710	1.77156	1.87041	1.97382	2.98598
7	1.07214	1.10984	1.14869	1.18869	1.22987	1.27228	1.31593	1.36086	1.40710	1.45468	1.50363	1.60578	1.71382	1.82804	1.94872	2.07616	2.21068	3.58318
8	1.08286	1.12649	1.17166	1.21840	1.26677	1.31681	1.36857	1.42210	1.47746	1.53469	1.59385	1.71819	1.85093	1.99256	2.14359	2.30454	2.47596	4.29982
9	1.09369	1.14339	1.19509	1.24886	1.30477	1.36290	1.42331	1.48610	1.55133	1.61909	1.68948	1.83846	1.99900	2.17189	2.35795	2.55804	2.77308	5.15978
10	1.10462	1.16054	1.21899	1.28008	1.34392	1.41060	1.48024	1.55297	1.62889	1.70814	1.79085	1.96715	2.15892	2.36736	2.59374	2.83942	3.10585	6.19174
11	1.11567	1.17795	1.24337	1.31209	1.38423	1.45997	1.53945	1.62285	1.71034	1.80209	1.89830	2.10485	2.33164	2.58043	2.85312	3.15176	3.47855	7.43008
12	1.12683	1.19562	1.26824	1.34489	1.42576	1.51107	1.60103	1.69588	1.79586	1.90121	2.01220	2.25219	2.51817	2.81266	3.13843	3.49845	3.89598	8.91610
13	1.13809	1.21355	1.29361	1.37851	1.46853	1.56396	1.66507	1.77220	1.88565	2.00577	2.13293	2.40985	2.71962	3.06580	3.45227	3.88328	4.36349	10.69932
14	1.14947	1.23176	1.31948	1.41297	1.51259	1.61869	1.73168	1.85194	1.97993	2.11600	2.26090	2.57853	2.93719	3.34173	3.79750	4.31044	4.88711	12.83918
15	1.16097	1.25023	1.34587	1.44830	1.55797	1.67535	1.80094	1.93528	2.07893	2.23248	2.39656	2.75903	3.17217	3.64248	4.17725	4.78459	5.47357	15.40702
16	1.17258	1.26899	1.37279	1.48451	1.60471	1.73399	1.87298	2.02237	2.18287	2.35526	2.54035	2.95216	3.42594	3.97031	4.59497	5.31089	6.13039	18.48843
17	1.18430	1.28802	1.40024	1.52162	1.65285	1.79468	1.94790	2.11338	2.29202	2.48480	2.69277	3.15882	3.70002	4.32763	5.05447	5.89509	6.86604	22.18611
18	1.19615	1.30734	1.42825	1.55966	1.70243	1.85749	2.02582	2.20848	2.40662	2.62147	2.85434	3.37993	3.99602	4.71712	5.55992	6.54355	7.68997	26.62333
19	1.20811	1.32695	1.45681	1.59865	1.75351	1.92250	2.10685	2.30786	2.52695	2.76565	3.02560	3.61653	4.31570	5.14166	6.11591	7.26334	8.61276	31.94800
20	1.22019	1.34686	1.48595	1.63862	1.80611	1.98979	2.19112	2.41171	2.65330	2.91776	3.20714	3.86968	4.66096	5.60441	6.72750	8.06231	9.64629	38.33760
21	1.23239	1.36706	1.51567	1.67958	1.86029	2.05943	2.27877	2.52024	2.78596	3.07823	3.39956	4.14056	5.03383	6.10881	7.40025	8.94917	10.80385	46.00512
25	1.28243	1.45095	1.64061	1.85394	2.09378	2.36324	2.66584	3.00543	3.38635	3.81339	4.29187	5.42743	6.84848	8.62308	10.83471	13.58546	17.00006	95.39622
30	1.34785	1.56308	1.81136	2.09757	2.42726	2.80679	3.24340	3.74532	4.32194	4.98395	5.74349	7.61226	10.06266	13.26768	17.44940	22.89230	29.95992	237.37631
40	1.48886	1.81402	2.20804	2.68506	3.26204	3.95926	4.80102	5.81636	7.03999	8.51331	10.28572	14.97446	21.72452	31.40942	45.25926	65.00087	93.05097	1469.77160

This table shows the present value of $1 at various interest rates (i) and time periods (n).
It is used to calculate the present value of any single amount.

TABLE 2 Present Value of $1

$$PV = \frac{\$1}{(1+i)^n}$$

n/i	1.0%	1.5%	2.0%	2.5%	3.0%	3.5%	4.0%	4.5%	5.0%	5.5%	6.0%	7.0%	8.0%	9.0%	10.0%	11.0%	12.0%	20.0%
1	0.99010	0.98522	0.98039	0.97561	0.97087	0.96618	0.96154	0.95694	0.95238	0.94787	0.94340	0.93458	0.92593	0.91743	0.90909	0.90090	0.89286	0.83333
2	0.98030	0.97066	0.96117	0.95181	0.94260	0.93351	0.92456	0.91573	0.90703	0.89845	0.89000	0.87344	0.85734	0.84168	0.82645	0.81162	0.79719	0.69444
3	0.97059	0.95632	0.94232	0.92860	0.91514	0.90194	0.88900	0.87630	0.86384	0.85161	0.83962	0.81630	0.79383	0.77218	0.75131	0.73119	0.71178	0.57870
4	0.96098	0.94218	0.92385	0.90595	0.88849	0.87144	0.85480	0.83856	0.82270	0.80722	0.79209	0.76290	0.73503	0.70843	0.68301	0.65873	0.63552	0.48225
5	0.95147	0.92826	0.90573	0.88385	0.86261	0.84197	0.82193	0.80245	0.78353	0.76513	0.74726	0.71299	0.68058	0.64993	0.62092	0.59345	0.56743	0.40188
6	0.94205	0.91454	0.88797	0.86230	0.83748	0.81350	0.79031	0.76790	0.74622	0.72525	0.70496	0.66634	0.63017	0.59627	0.56447	0.53464	0.50663	0.33490
7	0.93272	0.90103	0.87056	0.84127	0.81309	0.78599	0.75992	0.73483	0.71068	0.68744	0.66506	0.62275	0.58349	0.54703	0.51316	0.48166	0.45235	0.27908
8	0.92348	0.88771	0.85349	0.82075	0.78941	0.75941	0.73069	0.70319	0.67684	0.65160	0.62741	0.58201	0.54027	0.50187	0.46651	0.43393	0.40388	0.23257
9	0.91434	0.87459	0.83676	0.80073	0.76642	0.73373	0.70259	0.67290	0.64461	0.61763	0.59190	0.54393	0.50025	0.46043	0.42410	0.39092	0.36061	0.19381
10	0.90529	0.86167	0.82035	0.78120	0.74409	0.70892	0.67556	0.64393	0.61391	0.58543	0.55839	0.50835	0.46319	0.42241	0.38554	0.35218	0.32197	0.16151
11	0.89632	0.84893	0.80426	0.76214	0.72242	0.68495	0.64958	0.61620	0.58468	0.55491	0.52679	0.47509	0.42888	0.38753	0.35049	0.31728	0.28748	0.13459
12	0.88745	0.83639	0.78849	0.74356	0.70138	0.66178	0.62460	0.58966	0.55684	0.52598	0.49697	0.44401	0.39711	0.35553	0.31863	0.28584	0.25668	0.11216
13	0.87866	0.82403	0.77303	0.72542	0.68095	0.63940	0.60057	0.56427	0.53032	0.49856	0.46884	0.41496	0.36770	0.32618	0.28966	0.25751	0.22917	0.09346
14	0.86996	0.81185	0.75788	0.70773	0.66112	0.61778	0.57748	0.53997	0.50507	0.47257	0.44230	0.38782	0.34046	0.29925	0.26333	0.23199	0.20462	0.07789
15	0.86135	0.79985	0.74301	0.69047	0.64186	0.59689	0.55526	0.51672	0.48102	0.44793	0.41727	0.36245	0.31524	0.27454	0.23939	0.20900	0.18270	0.06491
16	0.85282	0.78803	0.72845	0.67362	0.62317	0.57671	0.53391	0.49447	0.45811	0.42458	0.39365	0.33873	0.29189	0.25187	0.21763	0.18829	0.16312	0.05409
17	0.84438	0.77639	0.71416	0.65720	0.60502	0.55720	0.51337	0.47318	0.43630	0.40245	0.37136	0.31657	0.27027	0.23107	0.19784	0.16963	0.14564	0.04507
18	0.83602	0.76491	0.70016	0.64117	0.58739	0.53836	0.49363	0.45280	0.41552	0.38147	0.35034	0.29586	0.25025	0.21199	0.17986	0.15282	0.13004	0.03756
19	0.82774	0.75361	0.68643	0.62553	0.57029	0.52016	0.47464	0.43330	0.39573	0.36158	0.33051	0.27651	0.23171	0.19449	0.16351	0.13768	0.11611	0.03130
20	0.81954	0.74247	0.67297	0.61027	0.55368	0.50257	0.45639	0.41464	0.37689	0.34273	0.31180	0.25842	0.21455	0.17843	0.14864	0.12403	0.10367	0.02608
21	0.81143	0.73150	0.65978	0.59539	0.53755	0.48557	0.43883	0.39679	0.35894	0.32486	0.29416	0.24151	0.19866	0.16370	0.13513	0.11174	0.09256	0.02174
24	0.78757	0.69954	0.62172	0.55288	0.49193	0.43796	0.39012	0.34770	0.31007	0.27666	0.24698	0.19715	0.15770	0.12640	0.10153	0.08170	0.06588	0.01258
25	0.77977	0.68921	0.60953	0.53939	0.47761	0.42315	0.37512	0.33273	0.29530	0.26223	0.23300	0.18425	0.14602	0.11597	0.09230	0.07361	0.05882	0.01048
28	0.75684	0.65910	0.57437	0.50088	0.43708	0.38165	0.33348	0.29157	0.25509	0.22332	0.19563	0.15040	0.11591	0.08955	0.06934	0.05382	0.04187	0.00607
29	0.74934	0.64936	0.56311	0.48866	0.42435	0.36875	0.32065	0.27902	0.24295	0.21168	0.18456	0.14056	0.10733	0.08215	0.06304	0.04849	0.03738	0.00506
30	0.74192	0.63976	0.55207	0.47674	0.41199	0.35628	0.30832	0.26700	0.23138	0.20064	0.17411	0.13137	0.09938	0.07537	0.05731	0.04368	0.03338	0.00421
31	0.73458	0.63031	0.54125	0.46511	0.39999	0.34423	0.29646	0.25550	0.22036	0.19018	0.16425	0.12277	0.09202	0.06915	0.05210	0.03935	0.02980	0.00351
40	0.67165	0.55126	0.45289	0.37243	0.30656	0.25257	0.20829	0.17193	0.14205	0.11746	0.09722	0.06678	0.04603	0.03184	0.02209	0.01538	0.01075	0.00068

This table shows the future value of an ordinary annuity of $1 at various interest rates (i) and time periods (n). It is used to calculate the future value of any series of equal payments made at the *end* of each compounding period.

TABLE 3 Future Value of an Ordinary Annuity of $1

$$FVA = \frac{(1+i)^n - 1}{i}$$

n/i	1.0%	1.5%	2.0%	2.5%	3.0%	3.5%	4.0%	4.5%	5.0%	5.5%	6.0%	7.0%	8.0%	9.0%	10.0%	11.0%	12.0%	20.0%
1	1.0000	1.0000	1.0000	1.0000	1.0000	1.0000	1.0000	1.0000	1.0000	1.0000	1.0000	1.0000	1.0000	1.0000	1.0000	1.0000	1.0000	1.0000
2	2.0100	2.0150	2.0200	2.0250	2.0300	2.0350	2.0400	2.0450	2.0500	2.0550	2.0600	2.0700	2.0800	2.0900	2.1000	2.1100	2.1200	2.2000
3	3.0301	3.0452	3.0604	3.0756	3.0909	3.1062	3.1216	3.1370	3.1525	3.1680	3.1836	3.2149	3.2464	3.2781	3.3100	3.3421	3.3744	3.6400
4	4.0604	4.0909	4.1216	4.1525	4.1836	4.2149	4.2465	4.2782	4.3101	4.3423	4.3746	4.4399	4.5061	4.5731	4.6410	4.7097	4.7793	5.3680
5	5.1010	5.1523	5.2040	5.2563	5.3091	5.3625	5.4163	5.4707	5.5256	5.5811	5.6371	5.7507	5.8666	5.9847	6.1051	6.2278	6.3528	7.4416
6	6.1520	6.2296	6.3081	6.3877	6.4684	6.5502	6.6330	6.7169	6.8019	6.8881	6.9753	7.1533	7.3359	7.5233	7.7156	7.9129	8.1152	9.9299
7	7.2135	7.3230	7.4343	7.5474	7.6625	7.7794	7.8983	8.0192	8.1420	8.2669	8.3938	8.6540	8.9228	9.2004	9.4872	9.7833	10.0890	12.9159
8	8.2857	8.4328	8.5830	8.7361	8.8923	9.0517	9.2142	9.3800	9.5491	9.7216	9.8975	10.2598	10.6366	11.0285	11.4359	11.8594	12.2997	16.4991
9	9.3685	9.5593	9.7546	9.9545	10.1591	10.3685	10.5828	10.8021	11.0266	11.2563	11.4913	11.9780	12.4876	13.0210	13.5795	14.1640	14.7757	20.7989
10	10.4622	10.7027	10.9497	11.2034	11.4639	11.7314	12.0061	12.2882	12.5779	12.8754	13.1808	13.8164	14.4866	15.1929	15.9374	16.7220	17.5487	25.9587
11	11.5668	11.8633	12.1687	12.4835	12.8078	13.1420	13.4864	13.8412	14.2068	14.5835	14.9716	15.7836	16.6455	17.5603	18.5312	19.5614	20.6546	32.1504
12	12.6825	13.0412	13.4121	13.7956	14.1920	14.6020	15.0258	15.4640	15.9171	16.3856	16.8699	17.8885	18.9771	20.1407	21.3843	22.7132	24.1331	39.5805
13	13.8093	14.2368	14.6803	15.1404	15.6178	16.1130	16.6268	17.1599	17.7130	18.2868	18.8821	20.1406	21.4953	22.9534	24.5227	26.2116	28.0291	48.4966
14	14.9474	15.4504	15.9739	16.5190	17.0863	17.6770	18.2919	18.9321	19.5986	20.2926	21.0151	22.5505	24.2149	26.0192	27.9750	30.0949	32.3926	59.1959
15	16.0969	16.6821	17.2934	17.9319	18.5989	19.2957	20.0236	20.7841	21.5786	22.4087	23.2760	25.1290	27.1521	29.3609	31.7725	34.4054	37.2797	72.0351
16	17.2579	17.9324	18.6393	19.3802	20.1569	20.9710	21.8245	22.7193	23.6575	24.6411	25.6725	27.8881	30.3243	33.0034	35.9497	39.1899	42.7533	87.4421
17	18.4304	19.2014	20.0121	20.8647	21.7616	22.7050	23.6975	24.7417	25.8404	26.9964	28.2129	30.8402	33.7502	36.9737	40.5447	44.5008	48.8837	105.9306
18	19.6147	20.4894	21.4123	22.3863	23.4144	24.4997	25.6454	26.8551	28.1324	29.4812	30.9057	33.9990	37.4502	41.3013	45.5992	50.3959	55.7497	128.1167
19	20.8109	21.7967	22.8406	23.9460	25.1169	26.3572	27.6712	29.0636	30.5390	32.1027	33.7600	37.3790	41.4463	46.0185	51.1591	56.9395	63.4397	154.7400
20	22.0190	23.1237	24.2974	25.5447	26.8704	28.2797	29.7781	31.3714	33.0660	34.8683	36.7856	40.9955	45.7620	51.1601	57.2750	64.2028	72.0524	186.6880
21	23.2392	24.4705	25.7833	27.1833	28.6765	30.2695	31.9692	33.7831	35.7193	37.7861	39.9927	44.8652	50.4229	56.7645	64.0025	72.2651	81.6987	225.0256
30	34.7849	37.5387	40.5681	43.9027	47.5754	51.6227	56.0849	61.0071	66.4388	72.4355	79.0582	94.4608	113.2832	136.3075	164.4940	199.0209	241.3327	1181.8816
40	48.8864	54.2679	60.4020	67.4026	75.4013	84.5503	95.0255	107.0303	120.7998	136.6056	154.7620	199.6351	259.0565	337.8824	442.5926	581.8261	767.0914	7343.8578

This table shows the present value of an ordinary annuity of $1 at various interest rates (i) and time periods (n). It is used to calculate the present value of any series of equal payments made at the *end* of each compounding period.

TABLE 4 Present Value of an Ordinary Annuity of $1

$$PVA = \frac{1 - \frac{1}{(1+i)^n}}{i}$$

n/i	1.0%	1.5%	2.0%	2.5%	3.0%	3.5%	4.0%	4.5%	5.0%	5.5%	6.0%	7.0%	8.0%	9.0%	10.0%	11.0%	12.0%	20.0%
1	0.99010	0.98522	0.98039	0.97561	0.97087	0.96618	0.96154	0.95694	0.95238	0.94787	0.94340	0.93458	0.92593	0.91743	0.90909	0.90090	0.89286	0.83333
2	1.97040	1.95588	1.94156	1.92742	1.91347	1.89969	1.88609	1.87267	1.85941	1.84632	1.83339	1.80802	1.78326	1.75911	1.73554	1.71252	1.69005	1.52778
3	2.94099	2.91220	2.88388	2.85602	2.82861	2.80164	2.77509	2.74896	2.72325	2.69793	2.67301	2.62432	2.57710	2.53129	2.48685	2.44371	2.40183	2.10648
4	3.90197	3.85438	3.80773	3.76197	3.71710	3.67308	3.62990	3.58753	3.54595	3.50515	3.46511	3.38721	3.31213	3.23972	3.16987	3.10245	3.03735	2.58873
5	4.85343	4.78264	4.71346	4.64583	4.57971	4.51505	4.45182	4.38998	4.32948	4.27028	4.21236	4.10020	3.99271	3.88965	3.79079	3.69590	3.60478	2.99061
6	5.79548	5.69719	5.60143	5.50813	5.41719	5.32855	5.24214	5.15787	5.07569	4.99553	4.91732	4.76654	4.62288	4.48592	4.35526	4.23054	4.11141	3.32551
7	6.72819	6.59821	6.47199	6.34939	6.23028	6.11454	6.00205	5.89270	5.78637	5.68297	5.58238	5.38929	5.20637	5.03295	4.86842	4.71220	4.56376	3.60459
8	7.65168	7.48593	7.32548	7.17014	7.01969	6.87396	6.73274	6.59589	6.46321	6.33457	6.20979	5.97130	5.74664	5.53482	5.33493	5.14612	4.96764	3.83716
9	8.56602	8.36052	8.16224	7.97087	7.78611	7.60769	7.43533	7.26879	7.10782	6.95220	6.80169	6.51523	6.24689	5.99525	5.75902	5.53705	5.32825	4.03097
10	9.47130	9.22218	8.98259	8.75206	8.53020	8.31661	8.11090	7.91272	7.72173	7.53763	7.36009	7.02358	6.71008	6.41766	6.14457	5.88923	5.65022	4.19247
11	10.36763	10.07112	9.78685	9.51421	9.25262	9.00155	8.76048	8.52892	8.30641	8.09254	7.88687	7.49867	7.13896	6.80519	6.49506	6.20652	5.93770	4.32706
12	11.25508	10.90751	10.57534	10.25776	9.95400	9.66333	9.38507	9.11858	8.86325	8.61852	8.38384	7.94269	7.53608	7.16073	6.81369	6.49236	6.19437	4.43922
13	12.13374	11.73153	11.34837	10.98319	10.63496	10.30274	9.98565	9.68285	9.39357	9.11708	8.85268	8.35765	7.90378	7.48690	7.10336	6.74987	6.42355	4.53268
14	13.00370	12.54338	12.10625	11.69091	11.29607	10.92052	10.56312	10.22283	9.89864	9.58965	9.29498	8.74547	8.24424	7.78615	7.36669	6.98187	6.62817	4.61057
15	13.86505	13.34323	12.84926	12.38138	11.93794	11.51741	11.11839	10.73955	10.37966	10.03758	9.71225	9.10791	8.55948	8.06069	7.60608	7.19087	6.81086	4.67547
16	14.71787	14.13126	13.57771	13.05500	12.56110	12.09412	11.65230	11.23402	10.83777	10.46216	10.10590	9.44665	8.85137	8.31256	7.82371	7.37916	6.97399	4.72956
17	15.56225	14.90765	14.29187	13.71220	13.16612	12.65132	12.16567	11.70719	11.27407	10.86461	10.47726	9.76322	9.12164	8.54363	8.02155	7.54879	7.11963	4.77463
18	16.39827	15.67256	14.99203	14.35336	13.75351	13.18968	12.65930	12.15999	11.68959	11.24607	10.82760	10.05909	9.37189	8.75563	8.20141	7.70162	7.24967	4.81219
19	17.22601	16.42617	15.67846	14.97889	14.32380	13.70984	13.13394	12.59329	12.08532	11.60765	11.15812	10.33560	9.60360	8.95011	8.36492	7.83929	7.36578	4.84350
20	18.04555	17.16864	16.35143	15.58916	14.87747	14.21240	13.59033	13.00794	12.46221	11.95038	11.46992	10.59401	9.81815	9.12855	8.51356	7.96333	7.46944	4.86958
21	18.85698	17.90014	17.01121	16.18455	15.41502	14.69797	14.02916	13.40472	12.82115	12.27524	11.76408	10.83553	10.01680	9.29224	8.64869	8.07507	7.56200	4.89132
25	22.02316	20.71961	19.52346	18.42438	17.41315	16.48151	15.62208	14.82821	14.09394	13.41393	12.78336	11.65358	10.67478	9.82258	9.07704	8.42174	7.84314	4.94759
30	25.80771	24.01584	22.39646	20.93029	19.60044	18.39205	17.29203	16.28889	15.37245	14.53375	13.76483	12.40904	11.25778	10.27365	9.42691	8.69379	8.05518	4.97894
40	32.83469	29.91585	27.35548	25.10278	23.11477	21.35507	19.79277	18.40158	17.15909	16.04612	15.04630	13.33171	11.92461	10.75736	9.77905	8.95105	8.24378	4.99660

This table shows the future value of an annuity due of $1 at various interest rates (i) and time periods (n). It is used to calculate the future value of any series of equal payments made at the *beginning* of each compounding period.

TABLE 5 Future Value of an Annuity Due of $1

$$FVAD = \left[\frac{(1+i)^n - 1}{i}\right] \times (1+i)$$

n/i	1.0%	1.5%	2.0%	2.5%	3.0%	3.5%	4.0%	4.5%	5.0%	5.5%	6.0%	7.0%	8.0%	9.0%	10.0%	11.0%	12.0%	20.0%
1	1.0100	1.0150	1.0200	1.0250	1.0300	1.0350	1.0400	1.0450	1.0500	1.0550	1.0600	1.0700	1.0800	1.0900	1.1000	1.1100	1.1200	1.2000
2	2.0301	2.0452	2.0604	2.0756	2.0909	2.1062	2.1216	2.1370	2.1525	2.1680	2.1836	2.2149	2.2464	2.2781	2.3100	2.3421	2.3744	2.6400
3	3.0604	3.0909	3.1216	3.1525	3.1836	3.2149	3.2465	3.2782	3.3101	3.3423	3.3746	3.4399	3.5061	3.5731	3.6410	3.7097	3.7793	4.3680
4	4.1010	4.1523	4.2040	4.2563	4.3091	4.3625	4.4163	4.4707	4.5256	4.5811	4.6371	4.7507	4.8666	4.9847	5.1051	5.2278	5.3528	6.4416
5	5.1520	5.2296	5.3081	5.3877	5.4684	5.5502	5.6330	5.7169	5.8019	5.8881	5.9753	6.1533	6.3359	6.5233	6.7156	6.9129	7.1152	8.9299
6	6.2135	6.3230	6.4343	6.5474	6.6625	6.7794	6.8983	7.0192	7.1420	7.2669	7.3938	7.6540	7.9228	8.2004	8.4872	8.7833	9.0890	11.9159
7	7.2857	7.4328	7.5830	7.7361	7.8923	8.0517	8.2142	8.3800	8.5491	8.7216	8.8975	9.2598	9.6366	10.0285	10.4359	10.8594	11.2997	15.4991
8	8.3685	8.5593	8.7546	8.9545	9.1591	9.3685	9.5828	9.8021	10.0266	10.2563	10.4913	10.9780	11.4876	12.0210	12.5795	13.1640	13.7757	19.7989
9	9.4622	9.7027	9.9497	10.2034	10.4639	10.7314	11.0061	11.2882	11.5779	11.8754	12.1808	12.8164	13.4866	14.1929	14.9374	15.7220	16.5487	24.9587
10	10.5668	10.8633	11.1687	11.4835	11.8078	12.1420	12.4864	12.8412	13.2068	13.5835	13.9716	14.7836	15.6455	16.5603	17.5312	18.5614	19.6546	31.1504
11	11.6825	12.0412	12.4121	12.7956	13.1920	13.6020	14.0258	14.4640	14.9171	15.3856	15.8699	16.8885	17.9771	19.1407	20.3843	21.7132	23.1331	38.5805
12	12.8093	13.2368	13.6803	14.1404	14.6178	15.1130	15.6268	16.1599	16.7130	17.2868	17.8821	19.1406	20.4953	21.9534	23.5227	25.2116	27.0291	47.4966
13	13.9474	14.4504	14.9739	15.5190	16.0863	16.6770	17.2919	17.9321	18.5986	19.2926	20.0151	21.5505	23.2149	25.0192	26.9750	29.0949	31.3926	58.1959
14	15.0969	15.6821	16.2934	16.9319	17.5989	18.2957	19.0236	19.7841	20.5786	21.4087	22.2760	24.1290	26.1521	28.3609	30.7725	33.4054	36.2797	71.0351
15	16.2579	16.9324	17.6393	18.3802	19.1569	19.9710	20.8245	21.7193	22.6575	23.6411	24.6725	26.8881	29.3243	32.0034	34.9497	38.1899	41.7533	86.4421
16	17.4304	18.2014	19.0121	19.8647	20.7616	21.7050	22.6975	23.7417	24.8404	25.9964	27.2129	29.8402	32.7502	35.9737	39.5447	43.5008	47.8837	104.9306
17	18.6147	19.4894	20.4123	21.3863	22.4144	23.4997	24.6454	25.8551	27.1324	28.4812	29.9057	32.9990	36.4502	40.3013	44.5992	49.3959	54.7497	127.1167
18	19.8109	20.7967	21.8406	22.9460	24.1169	25.3572	26.6712	28.0636	29.5390	31.1027	32.7600	36.3790	40.4463	45.0185	50.1591	55.9395	62.4397	153.7400
19	21.0190	22.1237	23.2974	24.5447	25.8704	27.2797	28.7781	30.3714	32.0660	33.8683	35.7856	39.9955	44.7620	50.1601	56.2750	63.2028	71.0524	185.6880
20	22.2392	23.4705	24.7833	26.1833	27.6765	29.2695	30.9692	32.7831	34.7193	36.7861	38.9927	43.8652	49.4229	55.7645	63.0025	71.2651	80.6987	224.0256
21	23.4716	24.8376	26.2990	27.8629	29.5368	31.3289	33.2480	35.3034	37.5052	39.8643	42.3923	48.0057	54.4568	61.8733	70.4027	80.2143	91.5026	270.0307
25	28.5256	30.5140	32.6709	35.0117	37.5530	40.3131	43.3117	46.5706	50.1135	53.9660	58.1564	67.6765	78.9544	92.3240	108.1818	126.9988	149.3339	566.3773
30	35.1327	38.1018	41.3794	45.0003	49.0027	53.4295	58.3283	63.7524	69.7608	76.4194	83.8017	101.0730	122.3459	148.5752	180.9434	220.9132	270.2926	1418.2579
40	49.3752	55.0819	61.6100	69.0876	77.6633	87.5095	98.8265	111.8467	126.8398	144.1189	164.0477	213.6096	279.7810	368.2919	486.8518	645.8269	859.1424	8812.6294

This table shows the present value of an annuity due of $1 at various interest rates (i) and time periods (n). It is used to calculate the present value of any series of equal payments made at the *beginning* of each compounding period.

TABLE 6 Present Value of an Annuity Due of $1

$$PVAD = \left[\frac{1 - \frac{1}{(1+i)^n}}{i} \right] \times (1+i)$$

n/i	1.0%	1.5%	2.0%	2.5%	3.0%	3.5%	4.0%	4.5%	5.0%	5.5%	6.0%	7.0%	8.0%	9.0%	10.0%	11.0%	12.0%	20.0%
1	1.00000	1.00000	1.00000	1.00000	1.00000	1.00000	1.00000	1.00000	1.00000	1.00000	1.00000	1.00000	1.00000	1.00000	1.00000	1.00000	1.00000	1.00000
2	1.99010	1.98522	1.98039	1.97561	1.97087	1.96618	1.96154	1.95694	1.95238	1.94787	1.94340	1.93458	1.92593	1.91743	1.90909	1.90090	1.89286	1.83333
3	2.97040	2.95588	2.94156	2.92742	2.91347	2.89969	2.88609	2.87267	2.85941	2.84632	2.83339	2.80802	2.78326	2.75911	2.73554	2.71252	2.69005	2.52778
4	3.94099	3.91220	3.88388	3.85602	3.82861	3.80164	3.77509	3.74896	3.72325	3.69793	3.67301	3.62432	3.57710	3.53129	3.48685	3.44371	3.40183	3.10648
5	4.90197	4.85438	4.80773	4.76197	4.71710	4.67308	4.62990	4.58753	4.54595	4.50515	4.46511	4.38721	4.31213	4.23972	4.16987	4.10245	4.03735	3.58873
6	5.85343	5.78264	5.71346	5.64583	5.57971	5.51505	5.45182	5.38998	5.32948	5.27028	5.21236	5.10020	4.99271	4.88965	4.79079	4.69590	4.60478	3.99061
7	6.79548	6.69719	6.60143	6.50813	6.41719	6.32855	6.24214	6.15787	6.07569	5.99553	5.91732	5.76654	5.62288	5.48592	5.35526	5.23054	5.11141	4.32551
8	7.72819	7.59821	7.47199	7.34939	7.23028	7.11454	7.00205	6.89270	6.78637	6.68297	6.58238	6.38929	6.20637	6.03295	5.86842	5.71220	5.56376	4.60459
9	8.65168	8.48593	8.32548	8.17014	8.01969	7.87396	7.73274	7.59589	7.46321	7.33457	7.20979	6.97130	6.74664	6.53482	6.33493	6.14612	5.96764	4.83716
10	9.56602	9.36052	9.16224	8.97087	8.78611	8.60769	8.43533	8.26879	8.10782	7.95220	7.80169	7.51523	7.24689	6.99525	6.75902	6.53705	6.32825	5.03097
11	10.47130	10.22218	9.98259	9.75206	9.53020	9.31661	9.11090	8.91272	8.72173	8.53763	8.36009	8.02358	7.71008	7.41766	7.14457	6.88923	6.65022	5.19247
12	11.36763	11.07112	10.78685	10.51421	10.25262	10.00155	9.76048	9.52892	9.30641	9.09254	8.88687	8.49867	8.13896	7.80519	7.49506	7.20652	6.93770	5.32706
13	12.25508	11.90751	11.57534	11.25776	10.95400	10.66333	10.38507	10.11858	9.86325	9.61852	9.38384	8.94269	8.53608	8.16073	7.81369	7.49236	7.19437	5.43922
14	13.13374	12.73153	12.34837	11.98318	11.63496	11.30274	10.98565	10.68285	10.39357	10.11708	9.85268	9.35765	8.90378	8.48690	8.10336	7.74987	7.42355	5.53268
15	14.00370	13.54338	13.10625	12.69091	12.29607	11.92052	11.56312	11.22283	10.89864	10.58965	10.29498	9.74547	9.24424	8.78615	8.36669	7.98187	7.62817	5.61057
16	14.86505	14.34323	13.84926	13.38138	12.93794	12.51741	12.11839	11.73955	11.37966	11.03758	10.71225	10.10791	9.55948	9.06069	8.60608	8.19087	7.81086	5.67547
17	15.71787	15.13126	14.57771	14.05500	13.56110	13.09412	12.65230	12.23402	11.83777	11.46216	11.10590	10.44665	9.85137	9.31256	8.82371	8.37916	7.97399	5.72956
18	16.56225	15.90765	15.29187	14.71220	14.16612	13.65132	13.16567	12.70719	12.27407	11.86461	11.47726	10.76322	10.12164	9.54363	9.02155	8.54879	8.11963	5.77463
19	17.39827	16.67256	15.99203	15.35336	14.75351	14.18968	13.65930	13.15999	12.68959	12.24607	11.82760	11.05909	10.37189	9.75563	9.20141	8.70162	8.24967	5.81219
20	18.22601	17.42617	16.67846	15.97889	15.32380	14.70984	14.13394	13.59329	13.08532	12.60765	12.15812	11.33560	10.60360	9.95011	9.36492	8.83929	8.36578	5.84350
21	19.04555	18.16864	17.35143	16.58916	15.87747	15.21240	14.59033	14.00794	13.46221	12.95038	12.46992	11.59401	10.81815	10.12855	9.51356	8.96333	8.46944	5.86958
25	22.24339	21.03041	19.91393	18.88499	17.93554	17.05837	16.24696	15.49548	14.79864	14.15170	13.55036	12.46933	11.52876	10.70661	9.98474	9.34814	8.78432	5.93710
30	26.06579	24.37608	22.84438	21.45355	20.18845	19.03577	17.98371	17.02189	16.14107	15.33310	14.59072	13.27767	12.15841	11.19828	10.36961	9.65011	9.02181	5.97472
40	33.16303	30.36458	27.90259	25.73034	23.80822	22.10250	20.58448	19.22966	18.01704	16.92866	15.94907	14.26493	12.87858	11.72552	10.75696	9.93567	9.23303	5.99592

Summary of Ratios Used in This Book

	Chapter	Calculations
RISK RATIOS		
Liquidity		
Receivables turnover ratio	5	$\dfrac{\text{Net credit sales}}{\text{Average accounts receivables}}$
Average collection period	5	$\dfrac{365 \text{ days}}{\text{Receivables turnover ratio}}$
Inventory turnover ratio	6	$\dfrac{\text{Cost of goods sold}}{\text{Average inventory}}$
Average days in inventory	6	$\dfrac{365 \text{ days}}{\text{Inventory turnover ratio}}$
Current ratio	8	$\dfrac{\text{Current assets}}{\text{Current liabilities}}$
Acid-test ratio	8	$\dfrac{\text{Cash} + \text{Current investments} + \text{Accounts receivable}}{\text{Current liabilities}}$
Solvency		
Debt to equity ratio	9	$\dfrac{\text{Total liabilities}}{\text{Stockholders' equity}}$
Times interest earned ratio	9	$\dfrac{\text{Net income} + \text{Interest expense} + \text{Tax expense}}{\text{Interest expense}}$
PROFITABILITY RATIOS		
Gross profit ratio	6	$\dfrac{\text{Gross profit}}{\text{Net sales}}$
Return on assets	7	$\dfrac{\text{Net income}}{\text{Average total assets}}$
Profit margin	7	$\dfrac{\text{Net income}}{\text{Net sales}}$
Asset turnover	7	$\dfrac{\text{Net sales}}{\text{Average total assets}}$
Return on equity	10	$\dfrac{\text{Net income}}{\text{Average stockholders' equity}}$
Return on the market value of equity	10	$\dfrac{\text{Net income}}{\text{Stock price} \times \text{Number of shares outstanding}}$
Earnings per share	10	$\dfrac{\text{Net income} - \text{Preferred stock dividends}}{\text{Average shares of common stock outstanding}}$
Price-earnings ratio	10	$\dfrac{\text{Stock price}}{\text{Earnings per share}}$

Framework for Financial Accounting

Two primary functions of financial accounting are to *measure* activities of a company and *communicate* those measurements to investors and other people for making decisions. The measurement process involves recording transactions into accounts. The balances of these accounts are used to communicate information in the four primary financial statements, which are linked. For more detailed illustrations of financial statements, see the corresponding page in parentheses. A comprehensive list of accounts used to measure activities in this textbook is provided on the next page.

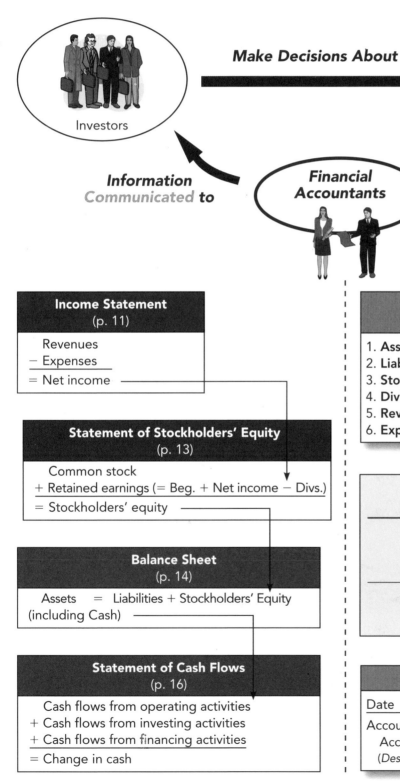

Income Statement
(p. 11)

Revenues
− Expenses
= Net income

Statement of Stockholders' Equity
(p. 13)

Common stock
+ Retained earnings (= Beg. + Net income − Divs.)
= Stockholders' equity

Balance Sheet
(p. 14)

Assets = Liabilities + Stockholders' Equity
(including Cash)

Statement of Cash Flows
(p. 16)

Cash flows from operating activities
+ Cash flows from investing activities
+ Cash flows from financing activities
= Change in cash

Accounts Used to Measure Activities

1. **Assets** – Resources owned
2. **Liabilities** – Amounts owed
3. **Stockholders' Equity** – Owners' claims
4. **Dividends** – Distributions to owners
5. **Revenues** – Sales of products or services
6. **Expenses** – Costs of earning revenues

Effect of Debit and Credit on Account Balances

Assets Dividends Expenses	Liabilities Stockholders' Equity Revenues
Debit = ↑	Debit = ↓
Credit = ↓	Credit = ↑

Recording Business Transactions

Date	Debit	Credit
Account Title	Amount	
Account Title		Amount
(Description of transaction)		

This is simply an outstanding textbook. It combines an interesting, engaging, and highly readable writing style with excellent, comprehensive, up-to-date, and conceptually rich discussions.—Marianne James, *California State University–Los Angeles*

I read the book in two weekends and was so delighted in the quality of content and the presentation style.—Steven Ault, *Montana State University*

You have created a text that is likely to become **the gold standard of Intro texts.**—Christian Wurst, *Temple University*

This is an excellent book and I love the writing style. I would describe the text as well-written with excellent examples that truly describes how accounting information is used to make better business decisions.—Mark Judd, *University of San Diego*

If you like Spiceland's intermediate text, you will be thrilled with the financial accounting principles text. It is written in the same conversational style, addresses topics directly and clearly, and the illustrations are terrific too.—Nancy L. Snow, *University of Toledo*

Have you experienced those moments in your course when students became fully engaged? When the "Aha!" revelations are bursting like fireworks? David Spiceland, Wayne Thomas, and Don Herrmann have developed a unique textbook based on over 50 collective years of experience in the classroom. They've brought together best practices like highlighting Common Mistakes, offering frequent Let's Review exercises, integrating the course with a running Continuing Problem, demonstrating the relevance of the course to nonmajors with a Career Corner, and communicating it all in a student-friendly conversational writing style. After the proven success of the first edition of *Financial Accounting*, we're confident that the new and improved second edition will not only motivate, engage, and challenge students—it will illuminate the financial accounting course like never before.

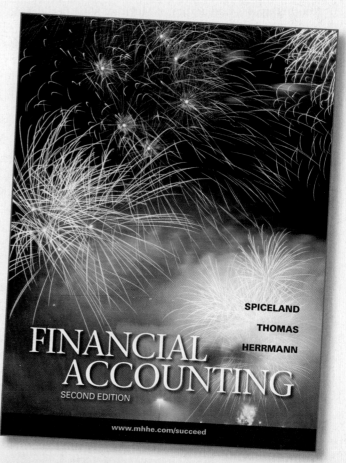

SPICELAND
THOMAS
HERRMANN

FINANCIAL ACCOUNTING
SECOND EDITION

www.mhhe.com/succeed

About the Authors

DAVID SPICELAND

David Spiceland is professor of accounting at the University of Memphis, where he teaches intermediate accounting and other financial accounting courses at the undergraduate and master's levels. He received his BS degree in finance from the University of Tennessee, his MBA from Southern Illinois University, and his PhD in accounting from the University of Arkansas.

Professor Spiceland's primary research interests are in earnings management and educational research. He has published articles in a variety of journals including *The Accounting Review, Accounting and Business Research, Journal of Financial Research,* and *Journal of Accounting Education.* David has received university and college awards and recognition for his teaching, research, and technological innovations in the classroom. David is lead author of McGraw-Hill's best-selling *Intermediate Accounting* text.

David is the Memphis Tigers' No. 1 basketball fan. He enjoys playing basketball, is a former all-state linebacker, and an avid fisherman. Cooking is a passion for David, who served as sous chef for Paula Deen at a Mid-South Fair cooking demonstration.

WAYNE THOMAS

Wayne Thomas is the John T. Steed Chair in Accounting at the University of Oklahoma, where he teaches introductory financial accounting to nearly 600 students per year. He received his bachelor's degree in accounting from Southwestern Oklahoma State University, and his master's and PhD in accounting from Oklahoma State University.

Professor Thomas's primary research interests are in markets-based accounting research, financial disclosures, financial statement analysis, and international accounting issues. He currently serves as an editor of *The Accounting Review* and has published articles in a variety of journals including *The Accounting Review, Journal of Accounting and Economics, Journal of Accounting Research, Review of Accounting Studies,* and *Contemporary Accounting Research.* He has won several research awards, including the American Accounting Association's Competitive Manuscript Award. Professor Thomas has won teaching awards at the university, college, and departmental levels, and has received the Outstanding Educator Award from the Oklahoma Society of CPAs.

Wayne enjoys playing sports (basketball, tennis, golf, and ping pong), solving crossword puzzles, and coaching little league sports. He has participated in several adventure races, like you'll read about in the Great Adventures continuing problem at the end of each chapter.

DON HERRMANN

Don Herrmann is the Chair of the Accounting Department at Oklahoma State University, where he teaches financial accounting, intermediate accounting, and a doctoral-level course in financial accounting research. He received his bachelor's degree in business from John Brown University, his master's degree in accounting from Kansas State University, and his PhD in accounting from Oklahoma State University.

Professor Herrmann's research interests are in earnings forecasts, segment reporting, financial statement analysis, and international accounting issues. He is past president of the American Accounting Association International Section and has served on the editorial and review board of the top research journal in the field of accounting, *The Accounting Review.* He has published articles in a variety of journals including *The Accounting Review, Journal of Accounting Research, Accounting Horizons, Journal of Business, Finance, and Accounting,* and the *Journal of Accounting and Public Policy.* Don Herrmann and Wayne Thomas often work together, having co-authored over 15 research articles. Professor Herrmann has received many teaching awards at the department, college, and university levels, including Professor of the Year in the University Greek System.

Don, like his co-authors, is a big sports fan. He played tennis on scholarship in college and enjoys playing soccer, basketball, running, biking, and swimming. He also coaches soccer, basketball, and little league baseball in his home town.